Europe, 1789

Gulf of Bothnia

Tornedälven

FINLAND
(Sweden)

Lake Onega

Lake Ladoga

Åbo

Helsingfors

Vyborg

St. Petersburg

ockholm

Saaremaa

Gotland

Volkhov

Dvina

Moscow

RUSSIAN
EMPIRE

Volga

Baltic Sea

Neman

Danzig (Poland)

A

Vistula

Minsk

Warsaw

POLAND

Bug

Kiev

Don

Donets

Vistula

Galicia

Dnieper

Volga

Carpathian Mts.

Southern Bug

HABSBURG
OSSESSIONS

Dniester

Pest

Tisza

ungary

Maros (Mures)

Siret

Prut

Moldavia

Transylvania

Kuban'

Caspian Sea

Belgrade

Morava

Wallachia

Bucharest

Danube

Black Sea

C A U C A S U S   M T S.

Balkan Mts.

Alps

MONTENEGRO

Maritsa

Vardar

O T T O M A N   E M P I R E

Constantinople

Sea of Marmara

A S I A

Aegean Sea

Athens

N

Crete
(Ottoman Empire)

Cyprus

U R A L   M T S.

ian
ea

nian
ea

40°E

| 0 | | 200 | | 400 mi. |
| 0 | 200 | | 400 km | |

EUROPE
1789 TO 1914

ENCYCLOPEDIA OF THE
AGE OF INDUSTRY AND EMPIRE

EDITORIAL BOARD

SCRIBNER LIBRARY OF MODERN EUROPE

EUROPE
1789 TO 1914

ENCYCLOPEDIA OF THE
AGE OF INDUSTRY AND EMPIRE

Volume 1

Abdul-Hamid II to Colonialism

John Merriman and Jay Winter

EDITORS IN CHIEF

CHARLES SCRIBNER'S SONS

An imprint of Thomson Gale, a part of The Thomson Corporation

Detroit • New York • San Francisco • San Diego • New Haven, Conn. • Waterville, Maine • London • Munich

THOMSON
GALE

Europe 1789 to 1914: Encyclopedia of the Age of Industry and Empire

John Merriman
Jay Winter
Editors in Chief

LIBRARY OF CONGRESS CATALOGING-IN-PUBLICATION DATA

Europe 1789 to 1914 : encyclopedia of the age of industry and empire / edited by John Merriman and Jay Winter.
      p. cm. — (Scribner library of modern Europe)
   Includes bibliographical references and index.
   ISBN 0-684-31359-6 (set : alk. paper) — ISBN 0-684-31360-X (v. 1 : alk. paper) — ISBN 0-684-31361-8 (v. 2 : alk. paper) — ISBN 0-684-31362-6 (v. 3 : alk. paper) — ISBN 0-684-31363-4 (v. 4 : alk. paper) — ISBN 0-684-31364-2 (v. 5 : alk. paper) — ISBN 0-684-31496-7 (ebook)
   1. Europe–History–1789-1900–Encyclopedias. 2. Europe–History–1871-1918–Encyclopedias. 3. Europe–Civilization–19th century–Encyclopedias. 4. Europe–Civilization–20th century–Encyclopedias. I. Merriman, John M. II. Winter, J. M.
   D299.E735 2006
   940.2'8–dc22   2006007335

This title is also available as an e-book and as a ten-volume set with
Europe since 1914: Encyclopedia of the Age of War and Reconstruction.
E-book ISBN 0-684-31496-7
Ten-volume set ISBN 0-684-31530-0
Contact your Gale sales representative for ordering information.

Printed in the United States of America
10 9 8 7 6 5 4 3 2 1

EDITORIAL AND PRODUCTION STAFF

Project Editors
Thomas Carson, Jennifer Wisinski

Art Editor
Joann Cerrito

Associate Editors
Andrew Claps, Pamela A. Dear

Editorial Support
Deirdre Blanchfield, Alja Collar, Angela Doolin, Carol Schwartz

Manuscript Editors
Jonathan G. Aretakis, John Barclay, Susan Barnett, Sylvia J. Cannizzaro,
Joanna Dinsmore, Ellen Hawley, Christine Kelley, John Krol, Mary Russell,
David E. Salamie, Linda Sanders

Proofreaders
Carol Holmes, Laura Specht Patchkofsky

Indexer
Cynthia Crippen, AEIOU, Inc.

Text Design
Pamela A. E. Galbreath

Cover Design
Jennifer Wahi

Imaging
Randy Bassett, Lezlie Light, Dan Newell,
Christine O'Bryan, Kelly Quin

Permissions
Andrew Specht

Cartographer
XNR Productions (Madison, Wisconsin)

Manager, Composition
Mary Beth Trimper

Assistant Manager, Composition
Evi Seoud

Manufacturing
Wendy Blurton

Senior Developmental Editor
Nathalie Duval

Editorial Director
John Fitzpatrick

Publisher
Jay Flynn

CONTENTS

C

VOLUME 5

INTRODUCTION

Europe 1789–1914: Encyclopedia of the Age of Industry and Empire covers what is known as "the long nineteenth century." The French Revolution that began in 1789 brought momentous changes not only in France but in much of Europe as the Revolution was carried across French borders. By 1790, references were already being made to the *ancien régime*. Many of the dramatic political struggles of the nineteenth century were waged in reaction to or in support of changes brought or accentuated by the Revolution. It represented the first successful challenge to monarchical absolutism on behalf of popular sovereignty. Republican ideals, nationalism, the espousal of the rights of the individual, the idea of "the nation at arms," the sanctity of economic freedom and of property, and the respective roles of the state and of religion in society people all influenced the subsequent evolution of European societies and spread their influence into much of the world. Similarly, ending the long nineteenth century in 1914 also makes good sense. World War I swept four empires away, changing the face of Europe. It took the lives of millions of Europeans and helped unleash many of the demons of the twentieth century, including fascism and communism, in "the Europe of Extremes." Like 1789, 1914 is a date that really matters, an undeniable turning point.

The editorial board has been careful to include attention to Russia, of course (including the expansion of the Russian Empire to include considerable chunks of Asia), but also the Balkans and the Ottoman Empire, which, after all, included a good part, however diminishing in size, of that region. We have also insisted on sufficient attention to economic, social, political, intellectual, and cultural history, presenting many articles organized along thematic lines, with cross-references back and forth between such articles and entries on individuals whose lives influenced in important ways the European experience.

We are proud of the remarkable illustrations that we think are worthy of attention in their own right, and of helpful maps, particularly useful in following, for example, the wars of the French Revolution and of the Napoleonic era, the unification of Germany and Italy, the expansion of European domination and influence in the age of imperialism, and much more.

Statemaking and nationalism were two of the dynamics of change that most affected the lives of ordinary people. The French Revolution struck a lasting blow against the absolute rule of monarchs in Europe, although Russian tsars and German emperors still retained such authority in 1914. There were two essential, related aspects to statemaking, whether that of autocracies or that of republics. States added to their bureaucracies, thus increasing the reach of state power on their subjects and citizens (taxes, military conscription, and more). And, at the same time, nationalism emerged as a political force in European states. More and more people, arguably most people—but not all—began to think of themselves as members of a national state. By 1789, British and French nationalism already existed. In the case of France, the experience of the Revolution and Napoleonic periods certainly accentuated the appeal of nationalism in France, but also generated nationalist reaction and resistance in Spain and in the German states. Yet even in France, a country in which only about half of the population spoke French as their first language in 1789, nationalism would be a long and necessarily incomplete process.

Nationalism came later in central and eastern Europe. Following the Revolutions of 1848, a group of Czech nationalists met in Prague and noted that if the roof of the hall in which they were meeting should somehow collapse, that would be the end of Czech nationalism. By 1914, this was no longer the case, and in the Balkans, where Serb, Croatian, and other nationalisms had existed only among a handful of intellectuals at midcentury, although pushed along by the Revolutions of 1848 in central Europe, competing nationalisms would help bring about the catastrophe of the Great War.

In about 1500, there were about that many independent territorial units or states in Europe, ranging in size from tiny bishoprics in Germany not much bigger than a sizeable cathedral garden to important monarchies like Spain, France, and England. In 1871, there were less than forty European states. This was the result of the consolidation of state power. The political unification of Germany, completed in January 1871, brought into a single nation a good many German states that had previously been independent. That of Italy during the same period had the same effect on the Italian peninsula (although the Austrian statesman Metternich's wry comment early in the century that Italy was but "a geographical expression" remained at least partially true). Increased schooling and teachers given the responsibility of teaching the dominate language or way of speaking in a state helped bring about increased allegiance to the nation (often undercutting, for example, dominant religious identities). Nationalism and statemaking thus went hand in hand.

The Industrial Revolution began, to be sure, in England, which benefited from the location of natural resources, such as coal, near waterways, flexible boundaries between nobles and elite commoners (who shared the quest for land and social exclusiveness, but also a willingness to invest in commerce and industry), an agricultural revolution that rapidly increased productivity, permitting a surplus that could be invested in manufacture, and a precocious banking system. But large-scale industrial production, whether concentrated increasingly in factories, or scattered in the countryside, where entire families, and particularly women, worked in "cottage industry," spread rapidly during the course of the century. Despite increased mechanized production and large factories, the Industrial Revolution was at first an intensification of forms of manufacturing that already existed. Here, too, continuities, then, were arguably as important as changes. The "Satanic mills" of Manchester and the mines of northern France—immortalized in Émile Zola's naturalistic *Germinal*—where men, but also women and child laborers were chewed up by dauntingly hard work and long hours, symbolized some aspects of the Industrial Revolution, but so did the single woman sewing in a Parisian garret, part of the "putting out of work" system in the garment industry. Large-scale industrialization spread west to east. Northern Italy, northern France, Barcelona and Zurich and their hinterlands, the German Rhineland, as well as northern England, became centers of manufacturing. Historians have long underestimated the rapid economic development of Imperial Russia, located in Moscow and St. Petersburg, as well as in the Ural Mountains. Industrial work gradually transformed the way people lived, although important continuities remained, for example in the work done by women. The "Second Industrial Revolution" that began in the 1860s was characterized by the use of steel, recently invented, the advent of electricity almost two decades later, and such inventions as the fountain pen and typewriter, serving an expanding army of clerks and sales people. By 1900, automobiles began to appear here and there, inching their way along dusty roads, and the first airplanes took off on short flights, while military planners dreamed of wartime uses for them.

The importance of the middle classes increased in what has been called "the Bourgeois Century." Over the long run, the French Revolution had eliminated much of noble domination, although aristocrats remained extremely powerful in Russia, Germany, Spain, and, within the Habsburg Empire, Hungary and Croatia. Economic change and increased industrialization accentuated the influence of manufacturers and bankers. There were more lawyers, doctors, and notaries than ever before, and lower middle-class professions such as teachers, policemen, and clerks developed rapidly in western Europe. Bourgeois culture, largely urban and increasingly urbane, took hold, increasingly privileged education and achievement. Elegant concert-halls, coffee-houses, and cafés attracted middle-class clients. However, to be sure, the middle class remained extremely small in Russia and the Balkans.

Europeans were divided socially in ways historians have understood in terms of social classes, the very terminology of which emerged during the nineteenth century. The plural of the word *class* is important, in that it suggests the complexity of social groupings of people who earned a living in similar and different ways. There was no one working class in nineteenth-century Europe, but many working classes, each different from each other to a degree, but each even further removed from people whose living came out of the fact that they owned property or land.

Similarly, there was no one middle class, although these middle classes—some whose wealth was based in land, others from banking and commerce, and others still from manufacture—intermarried and formed the domestic and dynastic alliances celebrated in the great novels of the nineteenth century, from Jane Austen to Gustave Flaubert to Theodor Fontane. Indeed this literature discloses one of the key features of nineteenth-century Europe. Far from being a period of untrammeled individualism, the nineteenth century was the heyday of the family. A stroll through Paris's Père Lachaise cemetery will show how this was so: sculptures of the dearly beloved were paeans of praise to the surviving family members.

Even within these families, women were almost always trapped in a subordinate position. The right of married women to hold property in their own right was not at all the rule in the nineteenth century, though major steps toward equality of property rights were made. Women were less well educated, paid lower wages, and excluded from political life throughout the century. Feminism was not born in the nineteenth century; it existed before the French Revolution, but it became a social movement growing in strength.

The growth of the middle class accompanied the rapid urbanization of much of Europe. Not only did major cities, indeed elegant capital cities such as London, Paris, Berlin, and Vienna, grow dramatically in size, but industrial cities such as Manchester, England, and Saint-Étienne, France, which were barely dots on eighteenth-century maps, increased even more rapidly in size. Middle-sized market and administrative centers, and small towns, as well, grew markedly. Suburbs, in Europe more often than not the domain of the poor and transient, people and activities unwanted in the center, stretched out beyond city walls in places as varied as Cologne, Milan, and Barcelona. Moreover, the percentage of the European population living in cities and towns increased rapidly. Mass immigration from the countryside, not natural population increase (as cities remained notoriously unhealthy, with more people dying than being born in cities), accounted for Europe's urbanization. Yet, to be sure, urbanization characterized western Europe more than eastern Europe, Russia, and the Balkans. Immigration from the countryside had another result, as well: cities like Budapest, Prague, and Talinn, among others, became increasingly peopled by ethnic Hungarians, Czechs, and Estonians, respectively—in each the proportion of Germans fell.

In Berlin, Paris, Milan, and Vienna, among other places, cafés began to line wide boulevards, such as those that Baron Georges Haussmann ploughed through Parisian neighborhoods in the 1850s and 1860s. These boulevards and their cafés, theaters, department stores, and kiosks became identified with the "Belle Époque"—the good old years—that period of remarkable cultural innovation and good times that would be particularly remembered with nostalgia after the Great War. In western, central, and southern European the middle classes pushed for political rights commensurate with their greater economic, social, and cultural status. Liberalism was a philosophy and politics that suited the middle classes. In Britain, the Reform acts recognized middle-class achievement, as did the establishment of universal manhood suffrage. By the 1880s, much of Europe entered the age of mass politics. Political parties, particularly socialist parties, competed for votes, using newspapers and brightly colored newspapers to make their appeals. Reform socialists demanded that states enact laws that would protect and improve the conditions of working people. Revolutionary socialists worked for a proletarian workers' revolution that they believed would inevitably sweep them into power. Anarchists, principally in Spain, Italy, France, and Russia, also wanted a revolution, but one that would sweep away the state, as well as capitalism. The last decades of the period were a great turning point in the evolution of modern politics and political contention.

Cultural life was still dominated by the very rich, but during the nineteenth century the institutions of popular culture grew into the world mass entertainment we know today. Photography, the cinema, the Olympic Games, football, rugby, the mass circulation press, all existed by the end of the century. Different social groups had their own entertainments, but for the mass of the working population, there was a world of leisure made possible both by increasing living standards and by the shortening of the work-week to enable people to take half of Saturday (as well as Sunday) off for their own pleasure.

The long nineteenth century has also been dubbed "the Rebellious Century." The French Revolution started it all off, to be sure. In Napoleon's large wake following his final defeat in 1815, the Great Powers formed the Concert of Europe, supporting the restoration in monarchy in France, in the hope of stifling liberal movements wherever they developed. Yet an insurrection began in Greece in 1821 that led to Greek independence from the Ottoman Empire in 1832, and this with British and French support. A liberal revolution in Spain failed in the early 1820s, with the help of French intervention. The Revolution of 1830 sent the Bourbon monarchy packing and an insurrection against Dutch rule in Belgium led to Belgian independence. In 1848, revolutions occurred in France, the German States, Austria, and in some of the Italian states, the "springtime of the peoples." Russian troops brutally crushed uprisings in Poland in 1831 and 1861. Subsequent major insurrections included the Paris Commune of 1871, and the Russian Revolution of 1905. These revolutions helped accentuate consciousness of national identity, as well as serving, at least in France, to expand the electoral franchise so that more people of means could vote in elections. They also brought unmitigated reaction. The Revolutions of 1848 brought successful conservative reaction virtually everywhere. In 1871, conservative forces slaughtered during "Bloody Week" in May about twenty-five thousand "Communards" who had participated in or at least supported the insurrection in Paris, or simply had been unable to leave the capital. The Russian Revolution of 1905 brought only short-lived concessions from the tsarist autocracy. Demonstrations and popular protest (for example, against the high price of grain, upon which most ordinary people depended) characterized much of the century.

Throughout the century, ordinary people acquired more rights, although the story varied considerably from place to place. Tsar Alexander II freed the serfs in Russia in 1861, leaving most of them free to remain miserably poor. Reform acts in 1832, 1867, and 1884 enfranchised at first more and then all men in Britain. Universal manhood suffrage came to France, the Netherlands, Germany, Italy, and many other smaller countries. Women, however, remained at a considerable disadvantage virtually everywhere. Yet women's literacy increased with that of men, and greater educational opportunity and new occupations opened up to them, notably teaching.

The long nineteenth century was also a time when Europe broke the link between numbers and the living standards of the population. While early commentators like Thomas Malthus spoke of limits to self-sustained economic growth, at the very same time those limits were breached. Europe's teeming population grew more rapidly than ever before. By the 1870s, the upward thrust of population growth was evident throughout the continent. But thereafter, a remarkable change took place, generalizing a trend evident as early as the eighteenth century in France. That trend was toward family limitation, first through a later age at marriage and then through a range of contraceptive practices, made safe and relatively reliable only in the 1960s. For those women who faced unwanted pregnancies, abortion was an option that was adopted throughout Europe at a high level; how high, no one knows. Yet overall aggregate population totals still rose, reflecting the high number of young people already at childbearing ages. There were far more Europeans in 1914 than ever before.

The nineteenth century also brought a dramatic increase in European emigration and thus immigration. A considerable percentage of the Irish population left their island during the deadly potato famine during the late 1840s for England, but above all for the United States. Hard times (as well as the Revolutions of 1848) sent refugees from Germany in great numbers to the United States, as well as smaller numbers (but proportionally even more relative to their populations) of Norwegians, Swedes, and other peoples. The last decades of the century brought a great exodus of Italians, particularly from the north, to the United States, as well. But hundreds of thousands of Europeans who left home for good moved to other countries on the Continent, above all, Jews fleeing hardship and indeed pogroms in the Russian Empire for the relative safety of Germany, France, and Great Britain. The nineteenth century was indeed a period of considerable geographic mobility, infusing western states in Europe and the United States with diverse immigrants bringing with them many languages and cultural background.

Changes and continuities also characterized the role of organized religion in Europe during the long nineteenth century. The French Revolution greatly eroded the public role of the Catholic Church in France, and challenged the church in countries over which the Revolution had swept. Yet the Catholic Church and other "established" churches—Protestant and Orthodox—maintained their influence in countries such as Spain, Italy, Russia, and in the Balkans. However, the erosion of religious practice (often referred to as "dechristianization") occurred in some places, notably some regions of France, and probably in Great Britain, as well. Yet the cult of miracles and the tradition of pilgrimages remained strong in Catholic countries. But the growing strength of states and the impact of growing national identities contributed to secularization of states in western Europe, particularly.

Intellectual currents influenced by scientific speculation and discoveries—notably Darwinism and Darwin's theory of evolution—also challenged organized religion. Traditional religious themes largely disappeared from painting, particularly as naturalist and realist currents, and then impressionism, postimpressionism, and cubism, followed Romanticism in the evolution of modern painting. Such currents joined subjectivist and symbolist themes in literature and poetry during the Belle Époque, centered in Vienna and Paris.

The nineteenth century was for the most part of the period devoid of major wars within Europe, which is ironic, given how the period had begun, with the wars of the French revolutionary and Napoleonic époques, and how it ended, with the cataclysm of 1914. A rough balance of power contributed to this. There were, to be sure, some wars, including the Crimean War of 1853–1856, pitting Britain, France, and the Ottoman Empire against Russia, the wars that indirectly led to German unification, including those of Prussia against Denmark (1864), Austria (1866) and France (1870–1871). But, over all, the nineteenth century was a period of relative peace.

During the long nineteenth century, the European powers took possession of most of the globe. The nineteenth century was the century of unbridled imperial expansion by the Great Powers. Although Britain, France, Spain, and the Netherlands were colonial powers well before 1789, the long nineteenth century was a period of globalization, on a scale which contradicts the claims of today's leaders that they live in an unprecedented time. Russia extended its empire to the east, an expansion that brought great tensions with Britain, which held India and Afghanistan, and in the first years of the twentieth century with Japan, the rising Asian power. Movements of capital, goods, and people across and out of Europe were on a scale perhaps equal to today's movements. The economic hegemon was Britain, not the United States, and its vast network of power was held together less by military might than by economic leverage. British imperialists did not try to control the globe by an iron fist; a velvet glove did just as well, and in many ways, much better.

The 1880s brought the "new imperialism," as the Great Powers, first Britain and France, and then Germany and Italy, began to compete aggressively for colonies, continuing their expansion in Southeast Asia. Africa, in particular, became the target for imperialism. The powers had by 1900 divided up virtually the entire continent. The New Imperialism reflected, above all, international competition (complete with the New Darwinian sense of the struggle and the chilling phrase "the survival of the fittest"), as well as the quest for sources of raw materials and new markets for manufactured goods. The goal of bringing western religions to Africa, Asia, and other places played only a very minor role in the New Imperialism, which basically was about great-power international politics. In 1500, the European powers held only about 7 percent of the land surface of the globe; by 1800, they held 35 percent. By 1914, the powers had divided up 84 percent of the lands of the globe. Expanded empires provided more opportunities for international tension and strife, helping pave the way for World War I which began in 1914.

The rivalries of the Great Powers, accentuated by economic competition and, above all, imperial struggles and accompanying "entangling alliances" that divided the European powers into essentially two armed camps, help explain the coming of the Great War in 1914. Because of these alliances, Europe was something of a deck of cards that would collapse with the great crisis of the summer of that momentous year.

Many of the articles in *Europe 1789–1914: Encyclopedia of the Age of Empire and Industry* reflect the impact of almost two decades of work by social historians, beginning in the mid-1960s. Studies by historians such as E. P. Thompson, Eric Hobsbawm, George Rudé, and Charles Tilly had tremendous influence on the subsequent period, focusing the attention of historians on the dynamics of change on ordinary people during the long nineteenth century, particularly statemaking, large-scale industrialization, and urbanization. Within this context, ordinary people made their own history during the French Revolution, the Revolutions of 1848, the Paris Commune, and the emergence of mass politics in the last decades of the nineteenth century.

We see *Europe 1789–1914: Encyclopedia of the Age of Empire and Industry* and *Europe since 1914: Encyclopedia of the Age of War and Reconstruction* as two parts of one set of encyclopedias, covering the experience of Europe from the French Revolution to the first years of the twenty-first century. World War I was without question a real turning point of such importance. It left a ravaged continent with millions of dead and revenge-minded states determined to reverse what they believed were awful decisions dictated by the Treaty of Versailles and the subsequent related treaties following the end of the war. The war helped lead almost inevitably, it might be argued, to what has been called "the Europe of

Extremes," as parties of the extreme right—not the least of whom were the Fascists in Italy and the Nazis in Germany—battled Communists inspired by the Russian Revolution of 1917. Yet salient continuities, too, between the two periods must be recognized. To take but one important example, the anti-Semitism that characterized all movements of the extreme right in the 1920s and 1930s did not just emerge out of a war- and economically ravaged Europe, but had significant antecedents in the prewar period. Thus, we view these two encyclopedias as two parts of the same trajectory.

Inevitably, there were some major figures whose lives and influence may clearly be seen in both the pre–World War I period and the post-1914 period. Sigmund Freud, Vladimir Lenin, and Tsar Nicholas II of Russia have entries in both, because their importance is clear both before and after the beginning of the Great War. Leon Trotsky's impact was overwhelmingly in the second period, and his entry is to be found in the second set. In general, in the interest of space, we have chosen to place a number of cultural figures, as well as important personages who have made significant contributions in other domains to the European experiences, in one set or another. Thus the operatic composer Giacomo Puccini is found in *Europe 1789–1914*, because his greatest works were written before 1914. Winston Churchill's greatest contributions to Great Britain without question were in the post–World War I period, and thus the article on him is found in *Europe since 1914*.

Above all, our aim has been to bring the best of recent scholarship to a wide population of people interested in finding out more about how Europe became what it is today in the early twenty-first century. This task has been a collective one, involving historians on four continents. This introduction is a guideline, and many scholars whose work we present here have their own views almost certainly at variance with those of the editors. That is right and proper and shows well how lively and creative is the field of European history today.

BIBLIOGRAPHY

Baumgart, Winfried. *Imperialism: The Idea and Reality of British and French Colonial Expansion, 1880–1914.* New York, 1982.

Berg, Maxime. *The Age of Manufacture, 1700–1820: Industry, Innovation, and Work.* New York, 1994.

Blackbourn, David, and Geoff Eley, *The Pecularities of German History: Bourgeois Society and Politics in Nineteenth-Century German History.* New York, 1984.

Blanning, T. C. W. *French Revolutionary Wars, 1792–1802.* New York, 1996.

Briggs, Asa. *Victorian Cities.* London, 1977.

Cobb, Richard. *The Police and the People: French Popular Protest, 1789–1820.* New York, 1972.

Englund, Steven. *Napoleon: A Political Life.* New York, 2004.

Forrest, Alan. *Conscripts and Deserters: The Army and French Society during the Revolution and Empire.* New York, 1989.

Gay, Peter. *Freud: A Life for Our Time.* New York, 1988.

Herbert, Robert. *Impressionism: Art, Leisure, and Parisian Society.* New Haven, Conn., 1988.

Hobsbawm, E. J. *The Age of Capital, 1848–1875.* New York, 1976.

Joll, James. *The Origins of the First World War.* New York, 1984.

Jones, Gareth Stedman. *Languages in Class: Studies in English Working-Class History, 1832–1982.* New York, 1983.

Jordan, David P. *Transforming Paris: The Life and Labors of Baron Haussmann.*

Landes, David. *The Unbound Prometheus: Technological Change and Industrial Development in Europe from 1750 to the Present.* New York, 1969.

McPhee, Peter. *The French Revolution, 1789–1799.* New York, 2002.

Merriman, John. *The Margins of City Life.* New York, 1991.

———. *A History of Modern Europe.* Vol. 2. 2nd ed. New York, 2004.

Moch, Leslie. *Moving Europeans: Migration in European History since 1650.* Bloomington, Ind., 1992.

Perkin, Harold. *The Origins of Modern English Society 1780–1880.* London, 1972.

Pilbeam, Pamela. *The Middle Classes in Europe 1789–1914: France, Germany, Italy, and Russia.* Houndmills, U.K., 1990.

Porter, Bernard. *The Lion's Share: A Short History of British Imperialism, 1850–2004.* New York, 2004.

Said, Edward. *Orientalism.* New York, 1979.

Schorske, Carl E. *Fin-de-Siècle Vienna: Politics and Culture.* New York, 1981.

Sheehan, James J. *German History, 1770–1866.* New York, 1989.

Silverman, Debra L. *Art Nouveau in Fin-de-Siècle France: Politics, Psychology, and Style.* Berkeley, Calif., 1989.

Sperber, Jonathan. *European Revolutions, 1848–51.* New York, 1994.

Thompson, E. P. *Making of the English Working Class.* New York, 1963.

Woloch, Isser. *New Regime: Transformations of the French Civic Order, 1879–1820s.* New York, 1994.

Woloch, Isser, ed. *Revolution and the Meanings of Freedom in the Nineteenth Century.* Stanford, Calif., 1996.

JOHN MERRIMAN, JAY WINTER

MAPS OF EUROPE, 1789 TO 1914

The maps on the following pages show the changes in European national boundaries from 1789 to 1914, including the unification of Italy and of Germany.

Europe, 1789
— International border
• City

0   100   200 mi.

0 100 200 km

Norwegian Sea

SWEDEN

Gulf of Bothnia

FINLAND (Sweden)

Helsingfors • • St. Petersburg

Gulf of Finland

NORWAY (Denmark)

Christiania •

Stockholm •

• Moscow

Faroe Islands

Shetland Islands

Orkney Islands

Scotland

Edinburgh •

North Sea

Ireland
GREAT BRITAIN
Dublin •

DENMARK Copenhagen •

Baltic Sea

RUSSIA

• Königsberg

PRUSSIA

POLAND

Wales **England**
Amsterdam •
NETH.
London •

Hanover
Hanover •
• Berlin

Warsaw •

HOLY ROMAN EMPIRE

Brussels •
Austrian Netherlands

Saxony

Bohemia

Moravia

GALICIA

HABSBURG POSSESSIONS

ATLANTIC OCEAN

Paris •

Bavaria

Austria
Vienna •

Buda • • Pest

Moldavia

TRANSYLVANIA

FRANCE

SWISS CONFED.

Tyrol

Munich •

HUNGARY

Wallachia

Black Sea

Bay of Biscay

Milan • **VENICE**
Venice •

PIEDMONT

Genoa •

Florence •

TUSCANY

PAPAL STATES

VENICE

RAGUSA

MONTENEGRO

Adriatic Sea

Constantinople •

ANDORRA

Corsica (France)

Rome •

NAPLES

Naples •

OTTOMAN EMPIRE

PORTUGAL

Madrid •

SPAIN

Minorca (Great Britain)

SARDINIA

Tyrrhenian Sea

Athens •

Lisbon •

Majorca (Spain)

Iviza (Spain)

Sicily

Ionian Sea

Algiers •

Tunis •

Malta

OTTOMAN EMPIRE

Crete (Ottoman Empire)

Mediterranean Sea

France in 1789

— International border
• City

GREAT BRITAIN

English Channel

AUSTRIAN NETHERLANDS

Flanders

Lille

GERMAN STATES

Rouen

Île de France

Normandy

Seine River

Paris

Nancy

Lorraine

Alsace

Rhine River

Brittany

Loire River

Nantes

FRANCE

Franche Comté

NEUCHÂTEL

SWISS CONFEDERATION

ATLANTIC OCEAN

Poitou

La Rochelle

Burgundy

Geneva

Lyon

KINGDOM OF SARDINIA

Bay of Biscay

Bordeaux

Garonne River

Rhône River

AVIGNON

NICE

REPUBLIC OF GENOA

Guyenne and Gascony

Toulouse

Languedoc

Provence

Marseille

0   50   100 mi.
0   50   100 km

ANDORRA

Corsica

SPAIN

Mediterranean Sea

KINGDOM OF NORWAY AND SWEDEN

FINLAND (to Russia)

•St. Petersburg

•Stockholm

North Sea

Baltic Sea

•Moscow

RUSSIAN EMPIRE

GREAT BRITAIN

DENMARK

N

NETHERLANDS

HANOVER

•Berlin

KINGDOM OF PRUSSIA

POLAND (to Russia)

BELGIUM

•Amsterdam

•London

•Frankfurt

Carlsbad•

Prague•

Vienna•

HUNGARY

Pest•

ATLANTIC OCEAN

•Paris

FRANCE SWITZER-LAND

Buda•

AUSTRIAN EMPIRE

Black Sea

•Milan

PIEDMONT

PARMA

Venice•

TUSCANY

Adriatic Sea

OTTOMAN

MODENA

CORSICA (France)

PAPAL STATES

PORTUGAL

•Madrid

SPAIN

KINGDOM OF SARDINIA

•Rome

•Constantinople

EMPIRE

SARDINIA

•Naples

•Gibraltar

KINGDOM OF THE TWO SICILIES

GREECE

•Athens

AFRICA

Mediterranean Sea

Europe, 1815

—— Boundary of the German Confederation, 1815

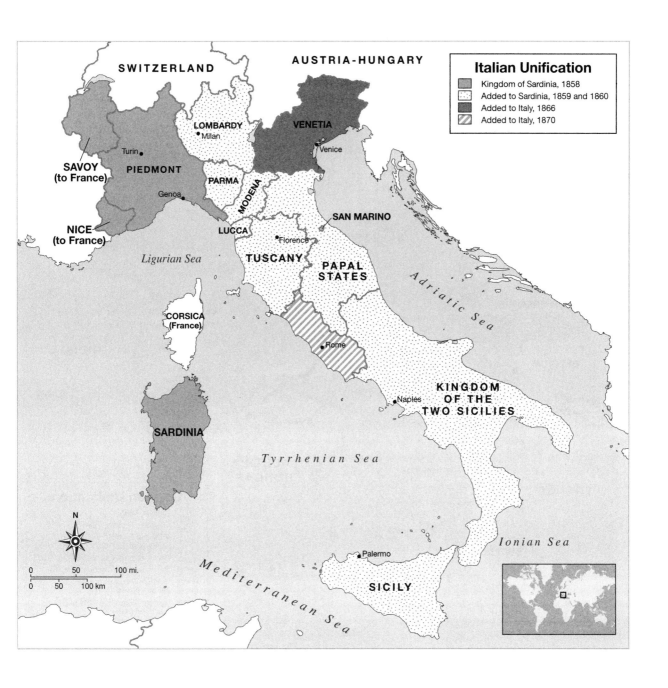

Italian Unification

- Kingdom of Sardinia, 1858
- Added to Sardinia, 1859 and 1860
- Added to Italy, 1866
- Added to Italy, 1870

SWITZERLAND

AUSTRIA-HUNGARY

SAVOY (to France)

NICE (to France)

PIEDMONT

Turin

LOMBARDY

Milan

VENETIA

Venice

PARMA

MODENA

Genoa

LUCCA

SAN MARINO

Ligurian Sea

TUSCANY

Florence

PAPAL STATES

Adriatic Sea

CORSICA (France)

Rome

KINGDOM OF THE TWO SICILIES

Naples

SARDINIA

Tyrrhenian Sea

Ionian Sea

Palermo

N

0   50   100 mi.

0   50   100 km

SICILY

Mediterranean Sea

German Unification

Prussia, 1865

Added to Prussia, 1866

Added to form North German Confederation, 1867

Added to form German empire, 1871

Boundary of German empire, 1871

Route of Prussian armies in Austro-Prussian War

Route of German armies in Franco-Prussian War

Battle sites

0   50   100 mi.

0   50   100 km

Europe, 1914
— International border

N

ICELAND

ATLANTIC OCEAN

NORWAY

SWEDEN

North Sea

Baltic Sea

DENMARK

UNITED KINGDOM

RUSSIA

NETH.

GERMANY

BELG.

LUX.

FRANCE

SWITZ.

AUSTRIA-HUNGARY

Caspian Sea

ITALY

ROMANIA

SERBIA

MONT.

BULGARIA

Black Sea

ANDORRA

ALBANIA

PORTUGAL

SPAIN

GREECE

OTTOMAN EMPIRE

PERSIA

Spanish Morocco

Tunisia (Fr.)

Mediterranean Sea

Morocco (Fr.)

Algeria (Fr.)

Libya (It.)

Egypt (Br.)

0   250   500 mi.
0   250   500 km

CHRONOLOGY

The chronology is arranged by year from 1789 to 1914 and is organized under seven major headings that cover the encyclopedia's scope both thematically and over time. Most items listed below are discussed in the encyclopedia's articles and can be found by referring to the table of contents and the index. Because the section headings are not always mutually exclusive, certain events may be listed under more than one heading.

DATE	POLITICS AND DIPLOMACY	SCIENCE AND TECHNOLOGY	ECONOMY AND SOCIETY
1789	France: Estates-Général opened; National Assembly declared; Bastille stormed; "Declaration of the Rights of Man and Citizen"; October Days; Selim III (Ottoman Empire), 1789–1807	Antoine Lavoisier, *Traité élémentaire de chimie*	Jeremy Bentham, *Introduction to the Principles of Morals and Legislation*
1790	Joseph II (Holy Roman Empire) dies; Leopold II (Holy Roman Empire), 1790–1792	William Cullen dies; French scientists develop metric system	Adam Smith dies
1791	3 May Constitution in Poland promoted by King Stanislaw; Louis XVI captured at Varennes; adoption of constitutional monarchy in France	Luigi Galvani, *De Viribus Electricitatis in Motu Musculari Commentarius*	Olympe de Gouges, *Rights of Women*; Chaplier Law
1792	Poland: Conservative Confederation of Targowica; Francis II (Holy Roman Empire), 1792–1806 (emperor of Austria, 1804–1835); French Republic declared		Mary Wollstonecraft, *Vindication of the Rights of Woman*
1793	Reign of Terror, 1793–1794; Louis XVI and Marie-Antoinette guillotined; Second Partition of Poland		France: Maximum prices set

LITERATURE AND THE ARTS	INTELLECTUAL LIFE AND RELIGION	WAR AND ARMED CONFLICT	EUROPE AND THE WORLD	DATE
Jacques-Louis David, *Lictors Bringing to Brutus the Bodies of His Sons*; William Blake, *Songs of Innocence*	Baron d'Holbach dies			*1789*
Wolfgang Amadeus Mozart, *Così fan tutte*	Immanuel Kant, *Kritik der Urteilskraft*; Edmund Burke, *Reflections on the Revolution in France*; Civil Constitution of the Clergy			*1790*
Franz Joseph Haydn's first visit to England; Wolfgang Amadeus Mozart, *Die Zauberflöte*; Wolfgang Amadeus Mozart dies; Marquis de Sade, *Justine*	James Boswell, *Life of Samuel Johnson*; John Wesley dies; Johann Herder, *Ideen zur Philosophie der Geschichte der Menschheit* completed, 1784–1791; citizenship granted to French Jews		St. Domingue slave revolt	*1791*
		France declares war on Austria; Battle of Valmy		*1792*
Jacques-Louis David, *À Marat*	France: Cult of Reason declared; Marie-Jean Caritat, marquis de Condorcet, *Esquisse d'un tableau historique des progrès de l'esprit humaine*	First Coalition against France, 1793–1797; *Levée en masse* in France	Macartney embassy in China	*1793*

DATE	POLITICS AND DIPLOMACY	SCIENCE AND TECHNOLOGY	ECONOMY AND SOCIETY
1794	Thermidor in France	Antoine Lavoisier dies	Prussian Civil Code
1795	Third Partition of Poland; French annexation of Belgium; Directory in France, 1795–1799; Treaty of Basel; Batavian Republic, 1795–1801	Nicolas Appert develops canned food	
1796	Catherine II "the Great" (Russia) dies; Paul I (Russia), 1796–1801		France: Babeuf conspiracy
1797	Treaty of Campoformio; Frederick William II (Prussia) dies; Frederick William III (Prussia), 1797–1840; John Wilkes dies		
1798	Roman Republic, 1798–1799; Helvetic Republic, 1798–1803	Pierre Simon de Laplace postulates theory of black holes	Thomas Malthus, *First Essay on Population*
1799	Coup of 18 Brumaire in France; Napoleon becomes First Consul, 1799–1804		
1800		Water chlorination developed	

LITERATURE AND THE ARTS	INTELLECTUAL LIFE AND RELIGION	WAR AND ARMED CONFLICT	EUROPE AND THE WORLD	DATE
William Blake, *Songs of Experience*	France: Cult of Supreme Being declared; Cesare Beccaria dies; Marie-Jean Caritat, marquis de Condorcet dies; Camille Desmoulins dies; Edward Gibbon dies	Poland: Kosciuszko uprising	Emancipation of slaves of St. Domingue	*1794*
William Blake, *Newton*; Josiah Wedgwood dies	James Boswell dies; Friedrich von Schiller, *Briefe über die ästhetische Erziehung des Menschen*		British take Cape of Good Hope from Dutch	*1795*
Robert Burns dies		France invades Italy		*1796*
				1797
Samuel Taylor Coleridge and William Wordsworth, *Lyrical Ballads*		Irish uprising; Second Coalition against France, 1798–1801	Napoleon's expedition to Egypt	*1798*
	Friedrich Schleiermacher, *Über die Religion: Reden an die Gebilden unter ihren Verächtern*; Novalis, *Die Christenheit oder Europa*; Rosetta Stone discovered			*1799*
Novalis, *Hymnen an die Nacht*; Friedrich von Schiller, *Wallenstein* trilogy, 1800–1801				*1800*

DATE	POLITICS AND DIPLOMACY	SCIENCE AND TECHNOLOGY	ECONOMY AND SOCIETY
1801	Act of Union creates United Kingdom of Great Britain and Ireland; Alexander I (Russia), 1801–1825; Treaty of Lunéville		
1802	Treaty of Amiens		Germaine Necker, Mme. de Staël, *Delphine*
1803			Jean-Baptiste Say, *Treatise of Political Economy*
1804	Napoleon crowned emperor, 1804–1814, 1815		Napoleonic Code
1805		Alexander von Humboldt, *Essai sur la géographie des plantes*	
1806	Francis II abdicates; Holy Roman Empire abolished		Continental System established
1807	Treaty of Tilsit; Mustafa IV (Ottoman Empire), 1807–1808		Prussia: Serfs declared emancipated
1808	Mahmud II (Ottoman Empire), 1808–1839	Étienne-Louis Malus discovers light polarization	Charles Fourier, *Théorie des quatre mouvements et des destinées générales*

LITERATURE AND THE ARTS	INTELLECTUAL LIFE AND RELIGION	WAR AND ARMED CONFLICT	EUROPE AND THE WORLD	DATE
	Concordat			*1801*
	François René de Chateaubriand, *Genius of Christianity*; William Paley, *Natural Theology*			*1802*
			Napoleon sells Louisiana Territory to United States	*1803*
Jean-Auguste-Dominique Ingres, *Napoleon on his Imperial Throne*; Friedrich von Schiller, *Wilhelm Tell*		Serbian revolt against Ottoman Empire, 1804–1813	Haiti gains independence from France	*1804*
Philipp Otto Runge, *The Hülsenbeck Children*		Third Coalition against France; Battle of Trafalgar; Battle of Austerlitz		*1805*
		Polish uprising against Russia; Battle of Jena		*1806*
	G. W. F. Hegel, *Phänomenologie des Geistes*		Britain abolishes slave trade	*1807*
Johann Wolfgang von Goethe, *Faust* Part I; Caspar David Friedrich, *Cross in the Mountains*		Peninsular War, 1808–1814		*1808*

DATE	POLITICS AND DIPLOMACY	SCIENCE AND TECHNOLOGY	ECONOMY AND SOCIETY
1809		Jean-Baptiste Lamarck describes first scientific theory of evolution	
1810			
1811	George III (UK) declared insane; George IV (UK), regent 1811–1820, king 1820–1830		
1812		German-Russian Gottlieb Kirchhoff discovers glucose	
1813			Robert Owen reorganizes New Lanark community
1814	Napoleon exiled; Louis XVIII (France), 1814–1824; Congress of Vienna, 1814–1815; Treaty of Kiel, Norway becomes independent of Denmark, union of Norway and Sweden; Kingdom of the Netherlands established		
1815	Hundred Days of Napoleon's return; Holy Alliance formed; Quadruple Alliance renewed; Peace of Paris; Kingdom of Poland established within Russian Empire		

LITERATURE AND THE ARTS	INTELLECTUAL LIFE AND RELIGION	WAR AND ARMED CONFLICT	EUROPE AND THE WORLD	DATE
	Friedrich Wilhelm University founded in Berlin; J. C. L. Simonde de Sismondi, *Histoire des républiques italiennes du moyen âge*, 1809–1818			*1809*
				1810
Jane Austen, *Sense and Sensibility*				*1811*
J. M. W. Turner, *Snow Storm: Hannibal and Army Crossing the Alps*; Jakob Grimm and Wilhelm Grimm, *Kinder- und Hausmärchen*		France invades Russia; Battle of Borodino		*1812*
		Battle of Leipzig		*1813*
Jean-Auguste-Dominique Ingres, *Grande Odalisque*; Francisco de Goya, *Third of May 1808*		Napoleon defeated	Cape Colony founded	*1814*
		Napoleon definitively defeated at Waterloo; Serbian revolt against Ottoman Empire, 1815–1817		*1815*

DATE	POLITICS AND DIPLOMACY	SCIENCE AND TECHNOLOGY	ECONOMY AND SOCIETY
1816			
1817			David Ricardo, *Principles of Political Economy and Taxation*
1818			Prussia: Simplified tariffs introduced
1819	UK: Peterloo massacre and Six Acts; German Carlsbad Decrees	First transatlantic steamboat voyage ends in Liverpool	
1820			
1821	Napoleon dies	Briton Michael Faraday describes electromagnetism as a force field	
1822			
1823		Briton William Sturgeon invents eletromagnet	
1824	Charles X (France), 1824–1830	Nicolas-Léonard-Sadi Carnot, *Reflections on the Motive Power of Fire*	

LITERATURE AND THE ARTS	INTELLECTUAL LIFE AND RELIGION	WAR AND ARMED CONFLICT	EUROPE AND THE WORLD	DATE
Benjamin Constant, *Adolphe*			United Provinces of La Plata (Argentina) gains independence from Spain; Dutch regain control of Java	*1816*
John Keats, *Poems*				*1817*
Théodore Géricault, *Raft of the Medusa, 1818–1819*; Caspar David Friedrich, *Wanderer above a Sea of Fog*; Mary Shelley, *Frankenstein*			Chile gains independence from Spain	*1818*
Lord Byron, *Don Juan*; Sir Walter Scott, *Ivanhoe*	Arthur Schopenhauer, *Die Welt als Wille une Vorsteullung*			*1819*
		Liberal revolts in Spain, Portugal		*1820*
	Joseph de Maistre, *Les Soirées de Saint-Petersbourg*	Greek revolution begins	Peru, Mexico, Venezuela gain independence from Spain	*1821*
	Roman Catholic Church lifts ban on Copernicus, Galileo, Kepler; Frenchman Jean-François Champollion deciphers Egyptian hieroglyphics		Brazil gains independence from Portugal	*1822*
				1823
Lord Byron dies; Ludwig van Beethoven, *Ninth Symphony*	Leopold von Ranke, *Towards a Critique of Modern Historiography*		Battle of Ayacucho	*1824*

DATE	POLITICS AND DIPLOMACY	SCIENCE AND TECHNOLOGY	ECONOMY AND SOCIETY
1825	Nicholas I (Russia), 1825–1855	UK: First railroad	Count Claude Henri de Saint-Simon dies; Robert Owen's New Harmony community founded
1826		Cholera pandemic begins, 1826–1837	
1827			
1828			Police forces created in London, Paris
1829	UK: Catholic Emancipation Act		
1830	Louis-Philippe (France), 1830–1848; Belgium becomes independent of Netherlands; Greece becomes independent of Ottoman Empire; Serbia becomes autonomous of Ottoman Empire; William IV (UK), 1830–1837	UK: First passenger railroad opens; Charles Lyell, *Principles of Geology*	
1831		Voyage of *The Beagle* with Charles Darwin begins	
1832	UK: Great Reform Bill	British Medical Association founded	

LITERATURE AND THE ARTS	INTELLECTUAL LIFE AND RELIGION	WAR AND ARMED CONFLICT	EUROPE AND THE WORLD	DATE
Alexander Pushkin, *Eugene Onegin*	France: Sacrilege Law	Russia: Decembrist Revolt		*1825*
				1826
Eugène Delacroix, *Death of Sardanapalus*; Heinrich Heine, *Buch der Lieder*				*1827*
Franz Schubert dies		Russo-Turkish War, 1828–1829		*1828*
Gioacchino Rossini, *Guillaume Tell*				*1829*
Hector Berlioz, *Symphonie Fantastique*		French revolution; Belgian revolution; Polish uprising against Russia	France aquires Algeria	*1830*
John Constable, *Salisbury Cathedral, from the Meadows*; Stendhal, *Le Rouge et le Noir*; Victor Hugo, *Notre-Dame de Paris*; Eugène Delacroix, *Liberty Leading the People*; Alexander Pushkin, *Boris Godunov*		Italian rebellions		*1831*
Johann Wolfgang von Goethe, *Faust* Part II; George Sand, *Indiana*				*1832*

DATE	POLITICS AND DIPLOMACY	SCIENCE AND TECHNOLOGY	ECONOMY AND SOCIETY
1833			UK: Factory Act
1834	UK: Peel's first government	Louis Braille develops Braille	Zollverein (Customs Union) founded
1835	Ferdinand I (Austria), 1835–1848	c.1835 Charles Babbage designs "analytical machine," the first computer	
1836			
1837	Victoria (UK), 1837–1901	Auguste Comte, *System of Positive Philosophy*	
1838			
1839	UK: Chartist petition rejected; Abdülmecid I (Ottoman Empire), 1839–1861; Tanzimat Era opens	Daguerrotype invented; Kirkpatrick MacMillan develops first bicycle	Louis Blanc, *The Organization of Labor*
1840	Frederick William IV (Prussia), 1840–1861		Pierre-Joseph Prouhon, *What is Property?*; Étienne Cabet, *Voyage to Icaria*
1841			
1842	UK: Chartist petition rejected second time		Sir Edwin Chadwick, *Report on the Sanitary Condition of the Labouring Population*
1843		Frenchman Marie-Jean-Pierre Flourens disproves phrenology assumptions	

LITERATURE AND THE ARTS	INTELLECTUAL LIFE AND RELIGION	WAR AND ARMED CONFLICT	EUROPE AND THE WORLD	DATE
	Thomas Carlyle, *Sartor Resartus*, 1833–1834; Jules Michelet, *Histoire de France*, 1833–1867	Carlist War, 1833–1839	Britain abolishes slavery	*1833*
Honoré de Balzac, *Le Père Goriot*				*1834*
	David Friedrich Strauss, *Das Leben Jesu kritisch bearbeitet*; Alexis de Tocqueville, *De la démocratie en Amérique*, 1835–1840			*1835*
				1836
				1837
				1838
Daguerrotype invented				*1839*
			Opium War, 1840–1842	*1840*
	Ludwig Feuerbach, *Das Wesen des Christentums*			*1841*
Nikolai Gogol, *Dead Souls*, Part I			Treaty of Nanking	*1842*
John Ruskin, *Modern Painters*, 1843–1860	Thomas Carlyle, *Past and Present*; Søren Kierkegaard, *Fear and Trembling*			*1843*

DATE	POLITICS AND DIPLOMACY	SCIENCE AND TECHNOLOGY	ECONOMY AND SOCIETY
1844		Robert Chambers, *Vestiges of the Natural History of Creation*	
1845			Irish famine begins; Friedrich Engels, *The Condition of the Working Class in England* (in German)
1846	UK: Repeal of Corn Laws		
1847		German Hermann von Helmholtz develops first law of thermodynamics; Matthias Jakob Schleiden and Theodo Schwann, *Beiträge zur Phytogenesis*; Ignaz P. Semmelweis discovers link between childbed fever and handwashing	UK: Ten Hour Act
1848	French Second Republic declared; Frankfurt Parliament, 1848–1849; Pan-Slavic Congress; Francis Joseph (Austria), 1848–1916; Swiss constitution; Louis-Napoleon Bonaparte elected French president	William Thomson, Lord Kelvin develops theory of absolute zero	Karl Marx and Friedrich Engels, *The Communist Manifesto*; workshops briefly created in France; Austria fully emancipates serfs; UK: Public Health Act
1849	Roman Republic declared; Prussian Frederick William IV declines German imperial crown		
1850	Prussian constitution decreed	German Rudolf Clausius develops second law of thermodynamics	
1851	France: Louis-Napoleon's coup		Great Exhibition in London; Karl Marx, *Eighteenth Brumaire of Louis Napoleon*

LITERATURE AND THE ARTS	INTELLECTUAL LIFE AND RELIGION	WAR AND ARMED CONFLICT	EUROPE AND THE WORLD	DATE
Alexandre Dumas, *père*, *Les Trois Mousquetaires*				*1844*
				1845
	George Grote, *History of Greece*, 1846–1856	Polish uprising against Russia		*1846*
Vuk Stefanović Karadzić translates New Testament into Serbian; Petar Petrović Njegoš' *The Mountain Wreath*; Felix Mendelssohn dies	Jules Michelet, *Histoire de la revolution française*, 1847–1853			*1847*
		Revolutions in France, Habsburg Empire, German states, Italian states; Polish uprising against Russia; French June Days	France abolishes slavery	*1848*
Juliusz Slowacki dies; Frédéric Chopin dies; Gustave Courbet, *Burial at Ornans and Stonebreakers*	Thomas Babington Macaulay, *The History of England from the Accession of James II*, 1849–1861	Hungary declares independence from Austria; revolutionaries crushed in Livorno, Rome, Prussia, Hungary		*1849*
				1850
Giuseppe Verdi, *Rigoletto*				*1851*

DATE	POLITICS AND DIPLOMACY	SCIENCE AND TECHNOLOGY	ECONOMY AND SOCIETY
1852	Louis-Napoleon declared Emperor Napoleon III, 1852–1870	Chloroform used in Queen Victoria's childbirth	
1853			Haussmannization begins; Count Arthur de Gobineau, *Essay on the Inequality of the Human Races*
1854			
1855	UK: Palmerston's first government; Alexander I (Russia), 1855–1881	Scot James Clerk Maxwell describes lines of force mathematically	
1856	Treaty of Paris	Neanderthal fossils discovered near Düsseldorf; Briton Henry Bessemer develops steelmaking process	
1857			Zollverein economic crash
1858	William I (Prussia), regent 1858–1861, king 1861–1871, emperor 1871–1888	First transatlantic cable message sent; Alfred Russel Wallace essay describing natural selection; Rudolf Virchow, *Die Cellularpathologie*; Henry Gray, *Gray's Anatomy*	
1859	Wallachia and Moldavia elect same ruling prince, creating Romanian state	Charles Darwin, *On the Origin of the Species by the Means of Natural Selection*	John Stuart Mill, *On Liberty*
1860			Cobden-Chevalier Treaty; Samuel Smiles, *Self-Help*

LITERATURE AND THE ARTS	INTELLECTUAL LIFE AND RELIGION	WAR AND ARMED CONFLICT	EUROPE AND THE WORLD	DATE
				1852
Giuseppe Verdi, *La Traviata*		Crimean War, 1853–1856		*1853*
Nadar's first photographs; Charles Dickens, *Hard Times*	Pius IX, *Ineffabilis Deus,* doctrine of the Immaculate Conception		British recognizes Boer republics	*1854*
Adam Mickiewicz dies				*1855*
	Alexis de Tocqueville, *L'Ancien Régime et la révolution*			*1856*
Jean-François Millet, *The Gleaners*; Gustave Flaubert, *Madame Bovary*; Charles Baudelaire, *Les Fleurs du mal*			Indian (Sepoy) Mutiny	*1857*
	Marian apparitions at Lourdes		Queen Victoria crowned empress of India	*1858*
Zygmunt Krasinski dies		Franco-Piedmontese alliance against Austria		*1859*
Charles Dickens, *Great Expectations,* 1860–1861	Jakob Burckhardt, *Die Kultur der Renaissance in Italien*	Giuseppe Garibaldi lands at Marsala and marches up Italian peninsula		*1860*

DATE	POLITICS AND DIPLOMACY	SCIENCE AND TECHNOLOGY	ECONOMY AND SOCIETY
1861	Kingdom of Italy declared under Victor Emmanuel II, 1861–1878; Abdülaziz (Ottoman Empire), 1861–1876		Russia emancipates serfs
1862	Prussia: Bismarck becomes prime minister		
1863		London Underground opens; Louis Pasteur develops pasteurization	
1864	First International founded	Herbert Spencer coins phrase "survival of the fittest"	
1865		Englishman Joseph Lister uses antiseptic; German August Ferdinand Möbius invents Möbius strip	
1866	Italy acquires Venetia	Alfred Nobel develops dynamite; Gregor Mendel develops laws of inheritance	Michael Bakunin, *Revolutionary Catechism*
1867	Austrians share rule with Magyar minority, forming dual-monarchy Austro-Hungarian Empire; UK: Second Reform Act; North German Confederation founded		Karl Marx, *Das Kapital*

LITERATURE AND THE ARTS	INTELLECTUAL LIFE AND RELIGION	WAR AND ARMED CONFLICT	EUROPE AND THE WORLD	DATE
Design firm Morris, Marshall, Faulkner				1861
Honoré Daumier, *Third-Class Carriage*; Victor Hugo, *Les Misérables*; Ivan Turgenev, *Fathers and Sons*				1862
Salon des Refusés; Édouard Manet, *Olympia and Déjeuner sur l'Herbe*	Ernest Renan, *La Vie de Jésus*	Polish uprising against Russia; International Committee of the Red Cross founded		1863
Camille Corot, *Souvenir de Mortefontaine*	Pope Pius IX, *Syllabus of Errors*	Danish War; Geneva Convention signed	Habsburg Maximilian made emperor of Mexico	1864
Leo Tolstoy, *War and Peace*, 1865–1869; Lewis Carroll, *Alice's Adventures in Wonderland*				1865
Fyodor Dostoyevsky, *Crime and Punishment*		Austro-Prussian War		1866
			Canada gains independence from UK; Maximilian executed in Mexico; British annex Republic of Transvaal	1867

DATE	POLITICS AND DIPLOMACY	SCIENCE AND TECHNOLOGY	ECONOMY AND SOCIETY
1868	UK: Disraeli and Gladstone's first governments		
1869		Dmitri Mendeleev develops period law and periodic table of the elements	Suez Canal opens; John Stuart Mill and Harriet Taylor, *The Subjection of Women*
1870	French Third Republic declared; Italy acquires Papal States		English Education Act
1871	German Empire declared under Emperor William I; Treaty of Frankfurt	Charles Darwin, *Descent of Man*	
1872			
1873	Three Emperors' League formed (Germany, Austria-Hungary, Russia); Spanish Republic declared	Cell mitosis recognized; Charles Hermite describes number e (= 2.718 . . .)	Worldwide depression
1874		London School of Medicine for Women founded	
1875			English Public Health Act; German Social Democratic Party founded

LITERATURE AND THE ARTS	INTELLECTUAL LIFE AND RELIGION	WAR AND ARMED CONFLICT	EUROPE AND THE WORLD	DATE
Wilkie Collins, *The Moonstone*		Spanish revolution	Cuban revolt against Spain, 1868–1878; Meiji Restoration	*1868*
Modest Mussorgsky, *Boris Godunov*; Jules Verne, *Vingt mille lieues sous les mers,* 1869–1870	First Vatican Council, 1869–1870			*1869*
Edgar Degas, *Orchestra at the Opéra*	Papal infallibility declared	Franco-Prussian War, 1870–1871		*1870*
George Eliot, *Middlemarch,* 1871–1872	Law of Guarantees concerning papal power; Kulturkampf in Germany; Oxford and Cambridge abolish religious tests	Paris Commune		*1871*
	Friedrich Nietzsche, *Die Geburt der Tragödie aus dem Geiste der Musik*			*1872*
Claude Monet, *Impression: Sunrise*; Jules Verne, *Le Tour du monde en quatre-vingts jours*; Arthur Rimbaud, *Une Saison en enfer*	John Henry Newman, *The Idea of a University Defined*; Matthew Arnold, *Literature and Dogma*; Heinrich Schliemann discovers Troy			*1873*
Bedřich Smetana, *Ma vlast* (My country), 1874–1879; first impressionist exhibit		Brussels peace conference		*1874*
Leo Tolstoy, *Anna Karenina,* 1875–1877			British control Suez Canal	*1875*

DATE	POLITICS AND DIPLOMACY	SCIENCE AND TECHNOLOGY	ECONOMY AND SOCIETY
1876	Murad V (Ottoman Empire), 1876; Abdul-Hamid II (Ottoman Empire), 1876–1909; first Ottoman constitution	Telephone invented; Cesare Lombroso, *The Criminal Man*; UK: women allowed to take qualifying medical exams	
1877	France: 16 May crisis	Ivan Pavlov begins conditioned response experiments	
1878	Treaty of San Stefano; Berlin Congress; Romania, Bulgaria, Montenegro recognized independent of Ottoman Empire; Austro-Hungarian occupation of Bosnia-Herzegovina		
1879	Dual Alliance formed (Germany, Austria-Hungary)	German Wilhelm Wundt establishes first psychology lab	
1880		Alphonse Laveran describes malaria parasite	
1881	Alexander II (Russia) assassinated; Alexander III (Russia), 1881–1894; first Italian socialist party founded	UK: First public power plant opens	France: First Ferry Law on education
1882	Triple Alliance Formed (Germany, Austria-Hungary, Italy); first Polish Socialist party founded, Proletariat; Italian suffrage expanded		

LITERATURE AND THE ARTS	INTELLECTUAL LIFE AND RELIGION	WAR AND ARMED CONFLICT	EUROPE AND THE WORLD	DATE
Pierre-Auguste Renoir, *Le Moulin de la Galette*; Bayreuth opera house founded; Richard Wagner's *Ring* cycle completed				*1876*
Peter Tchaikovsky, *Swan Lake*		Russo-Turkish War, 1877–1878		*1877*
W. S. Gilbert and Arthur Sullivan, *HMS Pinafore*				*1878*
Henrik Ibsen, *A Doll's House*; Berthe Morisot, *Summer's Day*; Fyodor Dostoyevsky, *Brothers Karamazov*, 1879–1880				*1879*
Émile Zola, *Nana*				*1880*
Pierre Puvis de Chavannes, *The Poor Fisherman*; Edgar Degas, *Little Fourteen-Year-Old Dancer*			France occupies Tunisia	*1881*
				1882

DATE	POLITICS AND DIPLOMACY	SCIENCE AND TECHNOLOGY	ECONOMY AND SOCIETY
1883			Germany: Sickness Insurance Law
1884	UK: Third Reform Act; UK: Fabian Society founded		
1885		Sir Francis Galton develops fingerprinting; Louis Pasteur tests rabies vaccination; Galileo Ferraris and Nikola Tesla both develop the rotating magnetic field; German Carl Friedrich Benz invents gasoline internal combustion engine	Germany raises tariffs
1886	UK: Liberal Party split over Irish Home Rule		UK: Contagious Diseases Act repealed
1887	Italy: Crispi's first government	Gottlieb Daimler invents automobile	Germany and Italy raise tariffs
1888	Frederick III (Germany), 1888; William II (Germany), 1888–1918		UK: Jack the Ripper murders
1889	France: Height of Boulanger crisis	Eiffel Tower constructed	
1890	Bismarck dismissed; Germany: Social Democrats plurality; Wilhelmina (Netherlands), 1890–1948		

LITERATURE AND THE ARTS	INTELLECTUAL LIFE AND RELIGION	WAR AND ARMED CONFLICT	EUROPE AND THE WORLD	DATE
Serbian Stevan Stojanvoic Mokranjac begins *Fifteen Songs*	Friedrich Nietzsche, *Also sprach Zarathustra*; Wilhelm Dilthey, *Einleitung in die Geisteswissenschaften*, vol. 1		French protectorate of Annam founded	*1883*
Georges Seurat, *Sunday Afternoon on the Island of La Grade Jatte*, 1884–1886; Belgian art nouveau group Les XX founded			Congo placed under Belgian king Leopold; the Mahdi besiege General Charles Gordon at Khartoum, 1884–1885	*1884*
Émile Zola, *Germinal*			Italy takes Red Sea port of Massawa; German protectorates in East Africa, the Cameroons, Togoland, Southwest Africa; Indian National Congress founded	*1885*
Franz Liszt dies; *neoimpressionism* coined				*1886*
Arthur Conan Doyle, *A Study in Scarlet*			French Union of Indochina founded; India: Muslim League founded	*1887*
	Mrs. Humphry Ward, *Robert Elsmere*			*1888*
Vincent van Gogh, *Starry Night*				*1889*
Claude Monet, *Haystacks* series, 1890–1891		The Hague peace conference		*1890*

DATE	POLITICS AND DIPLOMACY	SCIENCE AND TECHNOLOGY	ECONOMY AND SOCIETY
1891			French strikers killed at Fourmies
1892	Polish Socialist Party founded, soon led by Józef Piłsudski		Peter Kropotkin, *Conquest of Bread*
1893			
1894	Franco-Russian defensive alliance; Nicholas II (Russia), 1894–1917; French president Sadi Carnot assassinated	German Rudolf Diesel invents diesel engine	Italian strikes crushed
1895		Moving pictures invented; Gustave Le Bon, *Psychology of Crowds*; German Wilhelm Röntgen discovers x-rays	
1896		Radioactivity discovered; Nobel Prizes established	Theodor Herzl, *The Jewish State*; first modern Olympic Games
1897	Karl Lueger confirmed mayor of Vienna	Émile Durkheim, *Suicide*	

LITERATURE AND THE ARTS	INTELLECTUAL LIFE AND RELIGION	WAR AND ARMED CONFLICT	EUROPE AND THE WORLD	DATE
Henri de Toulouse-Lautrec, *Moulin Rouge, La Goulue*; Paul Gauguin's first visit to Tahiti; Thomas Hardy, *Tess of the d'Urbervilles*	Leo XIII, *Rerum Novarum*			*1891*
Claude Debussy, *Prelude à L'Après-midi d'un faune*, 1892–1894				*1892*
George Bernard Shaw, *Mrs. Warren's Profession*; Giuseppe Verdi, *Falstaff*; Mary Cassatt, *The Bath*				*1893*
				1894
Auguste Rodin, *Burghers of Calais*; Oscar Wilde, *The Importance of Being Earnest*			UK claims Sudan	*1895*
Giacomo Puccini, *La Bohème*; Alfred Jarry, *Ubu Roi*			Abyssinia defeats Italy	*1896*
Gustav Mahler directs Vienna Court Opera, 1897–1907; Johannes Brahms dies; Vienna Secession founded; Anton Chekhov, *Uncle Vanya*			German *Weltpolitik* policy launched	*1897*

DATE	POLITICS AND DIPLOMACY	SCIENCE AND TECHNOLOGY	ECONOMY AND SOCIETY
1898	France: Height of Dreyfus Affair, 1898–1899; anarchist assassination of Austrian consort Elizabeth	Marie Curie and Pierre Curie discover radium and polonium	Italian bread riots; Russian Social Democratic Party founded
1899	France: First socialist joins a European cabinet		H. S. Chamberlain, *Foundations of the Nineteenth Century*
1900	Anarchist assassination of Italian king Umberto I	Max Planck develops quantum theory; Sigmund Freud, *The Interpretation of Dreams*; Trans-Siberian Railway opens	
1901	British Labour Party founded in 1900 as Labour Representation Committee; Edward VII (UK), 1901–1910; Catalan Regionalist League founded	Italian Guglielmo Marconi transmits radio waves	
1902			Vladimir Lenin, *What Is to Be Done?*
1903	Italy: Giolitti's first government; Bolshevik-Menshevik split	Marie and Pierre Curie share Nobel Prize	
1904	Franco-British Entente (agreements) signed		
1905	Russian Revolution; Bloody Sunday; Nicholas II issues October Manifesto; Norway and Sweden separate	Albert Einstein develops special theory of relativity; Frenchman Alfred Binet develops IQ tests	Russian pogroms intensify

LITERATURE AND THE ARTS	INTELLECTUAL LIFE AND RELIGION	WAR AND ARMED CONFLICT	EUROPE AND THE WORLD	DATE
Camille Pissarro, *La Place du Théâtre Français, Paris*; Henry James, *The Turn of the Screw*			Fashoda Crisis; Spanish-American War	*1898*
Johann Strauss dies; Joseph Conrad, *Heart of Darkness* and *Lord Jim*	Kazimierz Twardowski, *On the Content and Object of Presentations*		Anglo-Boer War, 1899–1902	*1899*
Beatrix Potter, *The Tale of Peter Rabbit*; Maurice Denis, *Homage to Cézanne*; Arthur Schnitzler, *Leutnant Gustl*	Sir Arthur Evans begins to excavate Crete		Boxer Rebellion	*1900*
Thomas Mann, *Buddenbrooks*			Australia gains independence from UK	*1901*
Rudyard Kipling, *Just So Stories*; André Gide, *L'Immoraliste*				*1902*
Edvard Munch, *The Scream*; George Bernard Shaw, *Man and Superman*				*1903*
Paul Cézanne, *Mont Sainte-Victoire*; Antonín Dvořák dies			Russo-Japanese War, 1904–1905	*1904*
Die Brücke founded	France: Separation of church and state; Max Weber, *The Protestant Ethic and the Spirit of Capitalism*	Russian revolution	First Moroccan Crisis	*1905*

DATE	POLITICS AND DIPLOMACY	SCIENCE AND TECHNOLOGY	ECONOMY AND SOCIETY
1906	Russian Duma meets	German Walther H. Nernst develops third law of thermodynamics	Russian serfdom redemption payments cancelled
1907	Russo-British agreements signed		Norway: Women vote in national elections
1908	Young Turk Revolution; Austro-Hungarian annexation of Bosnia-Herzegovina; UK: Asquith's government		Britain: Robert Baden-Powell founds Boy Scouts
1909	Mehmed V (Ottoman Empire), 1909–1918; Spain: Tragic Week	Dutchman Wilhelm L. Johannsen coins the term *genes*; German Paul Ehrlich develops treatment for syphilis; Leo Hendrik Baekeland develops plastic; Robert. E. Peary reaches the North Pole	
1910	George V (UK), 1910–1936; First Republic of Portugal		Radicalization of British women's suffrage movement
1911		Marie Curie awarded Nobel Prize; Briton Ernest Rutherford develops model of atom	
1912			

LITERATURE AND THE ARTS	INTELLECTUAL LIFE AND RELIGION	WAR AND ARMED CONFLICT	EUROPE AND THE WORLD	DATE
Claude Monet, *Water Lilies* series, 1906–1926			German extermination of the Hereros in Southern Africa	*1906*
Henri Rousseau, *Snake-Charmer*; Pablo Picasso, *Demoiselles d'Avignon*	Edmund Gosse, *Father and Son*	The Hague peace conference	New Zealand gains independence from UK	*1907*
Gustav Klimt, *The Kiss*	Georges Sorel, *Reflections on Violence*			*1908*
Arnold Schoenberg, *Five Orchestral Pieces*; Filippo Marinetti, *Futurist Manifesto*; Henri Matisse, *Danse II*, 1909–1910; Blaue Reiter founded				*1909*
Georges Braque, *Violon et Palette*	Pope Pius X's antimodernist oath		Union of South Africa gains independence from UK	*1910*
Richard Strauss, *Der Rosenkavalier*; Franz Kafka, *Metamorphosis*			Second Moroccan Crisis; Italy conquers Libya	*1911*
Marc Chagall, *Self-Portrait with Seven Fingers*, 1912–1913; Marcel Duchamp, *Nude Descending a Staircase No. 2*		First Balkan War, 1912–1913	Spanish protectorate established in Morocco	*1912*

DATE	POLITICS AND DIPLOMACY	SCIENCE AND TECHNOLOGY	ECONOMY AND SOCIETY
1913	Albania gains independence from Ottoman Empire	Dane Niels Bohr describes atom; Swiss Carl Gustav Jung breaks with Sigmund Freud	
1914	Assassination of Austrian archduke Francis Ferdinand in Sarajevo; Austrian ultimatum to Serbia; alliances, aggression lead to war between Allies and Central Powers		

LITERATURE AND THE ARTS	INTELLECTUAL LIFE AND RELIGION	WAR AND ARMED CONFLICT	EUROPE AND THE WORLD	DATE
Igor Stravinsky, *Rite of Spring*; Wassily Kandinsky, *Improvisation No. 30*; Marcel Proust, *À la recherche du temps perdu, 1913–1927*; *Guillaume Apollinaire, Calligrammes,* 1913–1916; Ernst Ludwig Kirchner, *Street, Berlin*; Kandinsky and Franz Marc edit *Die Blaue Reiter*		Second Balkan War		*1913*
James Joyce, *Portrait of the Artist as a Young Man*; Henri Matisse, *Interior with Goldfish*; *Wyndham Lewis founds Vorticist movement; Charles Péguy dies*		Great War begins; Schlieffen Plan; Plan XVII; Battle of the Marne; German victory at Tannenberg; Austria's first invasion of Serbia		*1914*

A

ABDUL-HAMID II (1842–1918), sultan of the Ottoman Empire from 1876 to 1909.

Abdul-Hamid II's reign as sultan was marked by the attempted promulgation of a constitution in 1876, his subsequent suppression of the constitution, and, in 1908, the Young Turk Revolution that forced its reinstatement. Paradoxically, while in the early years of his reign Abdul-Hamid II was criticized for his liberal principles and his aggressive approach to reform, he was ultimately deposed in 1909 in the midst of a reformist movement that viewed him as an obstacle to reform. Repeatedly in the course of his rule he resisted undertaking reforms, despite the intense pressure of the Great Powers of Europe. In addition to the question of reform, internal economic crisis that led to European intervention and the proliferation of various nationalist/revolutionary movements that eroded Ottoman territorial control were two major recurring themes over the course of his rule.

In 1876, an international conference met in Istanbul. There a proposed constitution, written by the reformer Midhat Pasa (1822–1883), was unveiled. Despite the conference's demands, Abdul-Hamid II ultimately refused to accept the constitution and sent its author into exile. While he at first ratified the constitution, purely to stifle western complaints, he suspended it as soon as external pressure abated. Abdul-Hamid II's position annoyed both the Great Powers and an increasing number of his subjects. A group of reformers soon emerged, galvanized in large part by their opposition to the sultan's disregard for the notion of reform. The result was the formation of the constitutionalist reform group Committee of Union and Progress (CUP; in Turkish, the *Ittihad ve Terakki Cemiyeti*). Angered by the Ottoman loss of much of the Balkans, growing European intervention in the region, and the long-standing Ottoman political elite, the CUP established a base in the city of Salonica in the early twentieth century and began planning a revolution. In 1908, the Salonican CUP successfully forced the restoration of the 1876 constitution. Abdul-Hamid II was forced from power and exiled—ironically, to Salonica. As CUP troops threatened to march on Istanbul, Abdul-Hamid II capitulated immediately and agreed to step down. His brother Reshid Effendi, who was proclaimed Sultan Mehmet V (1844–1918) on April 27, 1909, succeeded him.

Economically, the Ottoman Empire was in crisis during portions of Abdul-Hamid II's reign. In the late 1870s, the empire became increasingly unable to manage its foreign debt burden. Ultimately an international finance control commission was formed to handle the empire's foreign debt, which passed an 1881 decree by which imperial revenues were passed on directly to the Public Debt Administration. This was a major blow to Abdul-Hamid II's attempts to rebuff the interventions of foreign powers and it angered many in the Ottoman Empire.

Externally, too, Abdul-Hamid II's reign was marked by major turbulence. While the Young Turks and other advocates of reform created internal

Abdul-Hamid II, Sultan of Turkey. Undated photograph.
©BETTMANN/CORBIS

control by coopting them, creating a special Kurdish cavalry—the Hamidiye cavalry—in 1891. The Kurds, who had traditionally enjoyed near autonomy, were now an armed autonomous element that the Ottomans had to struggle to suppress. At the same time, they had to contend with the growing Armenian nationalist movement, which by the 1880s was organized under the leadership of various revolutionary parties. In Egypt, Abdul-Hamid II failed satisfactorily to reassert Ottoman control, and it came increasingly under British domination.

Abdul-Hamid II's reign coincided with the development of an array of nationalist movements: the Internal Macedonian Revolutionary Organization (IMRO), the Greek "Great Idea," Pan-Slavism, and movements for a "Greater Bulgaria" and a "Greater Serbia." The guerrilla warfare of the multiple groups and contingents connected to these movements led to vicious internecine strife in outlying Ottoman territories and laid the ground for the series of bloody interethnic conflicts and mass population movements that characterized the early decades of the twentieth century. Notable among them is the Armenian genocide, the first wave of which (1915–1916) took place late in Abdul-Hamid II's reign. By its end in 1924, well over one million Armenians had been killed.

See also **Armenia; Balkan Wars; Eastern Question; Ottoman Empire; Russo-Turkish War; Young Turks.**

BIBLIOGRAPHY

Haslip, Joan. *The Sultan: The Life of Abdul Hamid II.* London, 1958.

Karpat, Kemal H. *The Politicization of Islam: Reconstructing Identity, State, Faith, and Community in the Late Ottoman Empire.* New York, 2001.

McCarthy, Justin. *The Ottoman Peoples and the End of Empire.* London, 2001.

Quataert, Donald. *The Ottoman Empire, 1700–1922.* New York, 2000.

K. FLEMING

difficulties, nationalist expansionist movements in the Balkans had a devastating impact as well. During the course of Abdul-Hamid II's reign, there was a major insurrection in Bosnia and Herzegovina, the Russo-Turkish War, a war with Serbia and Montenegro, and the Greco-Turkish War. Just years after his deposition came the Balkan Wars (which pitted a Bulgarian, Greek, and Serbian coalition against the Ottomans and ultimately gave Greece possession of Macedonia). Greece virtually doubled in size between the 1880s and the close of World War I, gaining Thessaly in 1881 and Epirus, Macedonia, and Crete in 1913. All of these territorial gains came at the expense of the Ottoman Empire. Abdul-Hamid II was resented by his subjects for his inability to stem the rapid successive loss of so much Ottoman territory.

Loss of Ottoman territorial control was not an issue only in the westernmost provinces. After the 1877–1878 Russo-Turkish War, Abdul-Hamid II attempted to bring Kurdish tribes under his

ABSINTHE. The characteristic alcoholic beverage of French city dwellers during the famous fin-de-siècle era, absinthe is forever associated with the world of belle epoque cafés and the Parisian artistic avant-garde. Following the end of the political repression of cafés under Napoleon III, emperor of France during the 1850s and 1860s, and the extensive rebuilding of the capital city under the direction of Georges-Eugène Haussmann, prefect of the Seine, Parisian café culture flourished. At the same time, an epidemic of phylloxera, an aphid-like insect, wiped out large portions of the French national wine crop. As a result, Parisians turned increasingly to liqueurs and aperitifs, and by around 1890 absinthe had emerged as the drink of choice.

Absinthe liqueur is distilled from the soaked leaves of wormwood, a course, shrublike plant. As served in the late nineteenth century, the drink was typically 140 to 160 percent proof, which explains the term's alleged origins in the Greek words for "impossible to drink." A key active ingredient is the toxic chemical thujone. The drink's color is a distinctive emerald green, hence its nickname *la fée verte* (the green fairy). *L'heure verte* (the green hour) likewise became slang for happy hour. The method of preparation was distinctive: consumers poured a shot (or two) of pure absinthe along with a carafe of water through a lump of sugar resting on a slotted silver spoon into an empty cone-shaped glass. (The elegantly shaped spoons are now collectors' items.) The taste of absinthe is thick and licorice-like.

The drink was associated with fashionable middle- and upper-class persons who frequented the stylish cafés, café-concerts, and brasseries that populated the French capital. Cheaper derivations were marketed to the lower classes. The late nineteenth century was also the golden age of the French poster, scores of which depicted the drink as glamorous and desirable. Its erotic associations were manifest; many paintings and posters represented the drink as a seductress that is simultaneously alluring and destructive. The drink's reputation was further enhanced by the idea that it heightened artistic creativity, reminiscent on this score of opium and hashish during the Romantic era.

Although absinthe is mentioned in many earlier works, including Egyptian papyri, the Bible, and ancient Syrian texts, it was French writers and painters of this period who lavished their attention on absinthe: Édouard Manet's early work *Le buveur d'absinthe* (1859; The absinthe drinker) takes the libation as the central subject of a paint-

In a Café, or The Absinthe, painting by Edgar Degas, c. 1875–1876. ERICH LESSING/ART RESOURCE, NY

ing, whereas the green glass figures as a background object in canvases by Vincent van Gogh and Henri de Toulouse-Lautrec, among many other painters. Provocatively, Edgar Degas in *L'absinthe* (1876) and Pablo Picasso in *Woman Drinking Absinthe* (1901) depict besotted female drinkers. French poets from Charles Baudelaire to Paul Verlaine and beyond imbibed notoriously. In his *Dictionnaire des idées reçues* (posthumously published in 1913; Dictionary of received ideas), Gustave Flaubert wrote "Absinthe: Extra violent poison. One drink, and you're a dead man" (1976 translation, p. 293). Its intoxicating, if not toxic, powers were legendary. Laboratory experiments reputedly caused animals to lapse into epileptic seizures, and van Gogh's well-known convulsions have been interpreted as absinthe-induced.

By around 1910, French men and women were drinking 36,000,000 liters (9,510,000 gallons) of absinthe yearly, which accounted for 90 percent of all aperitifs consumed in the country. By this time, the national craze was increasingly perceived as a medical and social problem. Contrasting with the colorful marketing images of the drink as fun and pleasurable were a growing number of public health posters, which visually linked the drink with dipsomania, self-destruction, and death. Indicatively, in both positive and negative representations, absinthe was invariably incarnated as a female figure. The pathological concept and category of alcoholism (as opposed to the popular notion of drunkenness) were comparatively new at the time. French temperance societies crusaded against the drink, but it took World War I to force a change in governmental policy toward a product around which a thriving industry had grown up. Fearing chronic absinthism in the army, the wartime government outlawed the beverage in March 1915. Since then, its sale has remained illegal in France. Nevertheless, it can still be purchased in Spain, Portugal, and the Czech Republic, although in much lower alcoholic concentrations and under regulation by the European Union. Critics have mischievously pointed out that the outlawing of absinthe coincides in time with a decline in creativity within the French cultural arts.

Both within and outside France, the lore and legend of absinthe remain powerful; cafés, restaurants, foods, rock bands, and all manner of popular-cultural paraphernalia continue to sport the name.

See also **Alcohol and Temperance; Avant-Garde; Drugs; Fin de Siècle; Paris; Tobacco.**

BIBLIOGRAPHY

Adams, Jad. *Hideous Absinthe: A History of the Devil in a Bottle.* Madison, Wis., 2004.

Baker, Phil. *The Book of Absinthe: A Cultural History.* New York, 2001.

Barnaby, Conrad, III. *Absinthe: History in a Bottle.* San Francisco, 1988.

Barrows, Susanna. "After the Commune: Alcoholism, Temperance, and Literature in the Early Third Republic." In *Consciousness and Class Experience in Nineteenth-Century Europe,* edited by John M. Merriman, 205–218. New York, 1979.

Delahaye, Marie-Claude. *L'absinthe: Son histoire.* Auvers-sur-Oise, France, 2001.

———. *L'absinthe: Les affiches.* Auvers-sur-Oise, France, 2002.

Flaubert, Gustave, et al. *The Dictionary of Received Ideas.* Translated with an introduction by A. J. Krailsheimer. London, 1976.

Marrus, Michael R. "Social Drinking in the Belle Epoque." *Journal of Social History* 7 (1974): 115–141.

Prestwich, Patricia E. *Drink and the Politics of Social Reform: Antialcoholism in France since 1987.* Palo Alto, Calif., 1988.

Taggart, Chuck. "What Is Absinthe?" Available at http://www.gumbopages.com/food/beverages/absinthe.html.

Mark S. Micale

ACTION FRANÇAISE. Action Française was responsible for the revivification of the moribund royalist movement in the years before World War I. In its combination of extreme hostility to the Left with the conviction that national regeneration required the violent overthrow of the existing political order, Action Française prefigured fascism. Insofar as it sought to reestablish the authority of monarchy, state, army, aristocracy, and the church, it owed more to authoritarian conservatism.

Maurice Pujo and Henri Vaugeois—neither of whom was a monarchist—founded the Comité d'Action Française in the spring of 1898. It was then a minor component of the nationalist anti-Semitic movement that campaigned against revision of the verdict condemning the Jewish staff officer, Alfred Dreyfus, to imprisonment for revealing military secrets to the German intelligence services. In 1899 Vaugeois met Charles Maurras, a young journalist from Provence. Maurras soon established his ascendancy in Action Française, persuading the organization to embrace royalism.

Action Française's monarchism differed from that of Henri, duc d'Orléans, the pretender or claimant to the throne, and his counselors. The latter, heirs of the Orleanist branch of the French royal family, were liberal and parliamentarian. They pursued a moderate policy in the hope that when the Republic "inevitably" collapsed, republican conservatives would turn to the king as guarantor of liberty in order. Action Française embraced royalism at a time when this strategy seemed fruitless to many royalists. Some, marked by Bonapartism and Boulangism, hankered after a royal dictator, able to speak for the "real country" against the parliamentarians who had allegedly perverted the sentiments of the people. Some dabbled with radical right movements, such as the Ligue Antisémitique. Meanwhile, the Jeunesse Royaliste demanded a more active pursuit of the cause. The Jeunesse Royaliste included many legitimists—partisans of the elder, Catholic, and antiliberal branch of the French royal family.

Maurras's neoroyalism chimed with the views of both liberals and their opponents. To the former, he spoke the language of science. A positivist, Maurras held that empirical observation permitted the identification of traditions governing national life, and that effective government must take account of these. Maurras comforted legitimists and Catholics with the belief that monarchy and church were essential French traditions. He also reached out to the new nationalist Right, identifying republicanism with Jews, Freemasons, and Protestants. He promised the destruction of the Republic, if necessary through violence.

In 1905, with the creation of the Ligue de l'Action Française, the movement began to reach a wider audience. In 1908 the Camelots du Roi were born. They sold the party press and demonstrated against cultural productions and university lecturers they did not like. In the same year, the daily newspaper *Action française* was launched. On the eve of war, the league claimed around three hundred sections. These were mostly in Catholic areas, although some such regions were inhospitable to the movement. In 1914 *Action française* had around eleven thousand subscribers and a circulation somewhat higher.

The tendentious wit of Action Française journalists conquered an audience in intellectual circles, including some of the brightest stars of right-wing letters, notably, the novelist Paul Bourget, the historian Jacques Bainville, and the polemicist and risqué novelist Daudet. In 1906 the Institut de l'Action Française was created—a sort of national-monarchist counteruniversity.

Despite Maurras's atheism and his merely pragmatic defense of the church, courtship of Catholics was decisive in the success of Action Française. In 1906 the League was widely believed to have been

the church's best champion in the struggle against the anticlerical government's taking of "inventories" of church property (a measure consequent upon the separation of the church and state, enacted in 1905). Neomonarchists were further encouraged by the papacy's abandonment of its instruction for Catholics to defend the church within the Republic. Many Catholics joined the league. Some bishops sympathized with the movement. The faithful prayed for Maurras's conversion.

Action Française was less successful in wooing the working class. Nevertheless, efforts to do so through support for revolutionary syndicalism alarmed liberal royalists, as did Action Française's turbulent street demonstrations. In 1909–1911, Action Française battled with liberal monarchists for the ear of the pretender. The eventual compromise favored Action Française. Liberals were forced out of the king's entourage.

In the last years before peace, Action Française participated in the so-called nationalist revival, the extent of which is still debated. It joined a center and right-wing coalition advocating lengthening of military service from two to three years. Action Française looked favorably on the new president of the Republic, Raymond Poincaré, elected in 1913, because of his support for three-year military service. Poincaré may have reciprocated. These affinities were as much a sign of "corruption" of republicanism by Action Française as of the debt owed by Action Française to the scientist outlook of republicans. Indeed, the readiness of so many Catholics to entrust their fate to a movement led by atheists worried some Catholics, particularly Christian democrats. In January 1914 a number of Maurras's works were placed on the Index Librorum Prohibitorum (Index of Prohibited Books), but the tenderness of Pope Pius X (r. 1903–1914) toward Maurras ensured that the decree was not published. During World War I, Action Française's status as a nationalist champion rendered it immune to criticism from Catholics. Only in 1926 did the papacy condemn Maurrassian doctrine, thus beginning the decline of Action Française and its displacement by a "republican" extreme right, as well as a fascist one.

See also **Anticlericalism; Anti-Semitism; Dreyfus Affair; France; Maurras, Charles; Poincaré, Raymond.**

BIBLIOGRAPHY

Goyet, Bruno. *Charles Maurras*. Paris, 2000.

Maurras, Charles. *L'enquête sur la monarchie* (1900). Paris, 1910.

Nguyen, Victor. *Aux origines de l'Action française: Intelligence et politique vers 1900*. Paris, 1991.

Prévotat, Jacques. *Les catholiques et l'Action française: Histoire d'une condamnation: 1899–1939*. Paris, 2001.

Sutton, Michael. *Nationalism, Catholicism, Positivism: The Politics of Charles Maurras and French Catholics, 1890–1914*. Cambridge, U.K., 1982.

Weber, Eugen. *The Nationalist Revival in France, 1905–1914*. Berkeley and Los Angeles, 1959.

———. *Action Française: Royalism and Reaction in Twentieth-Century France*. Stanford, Calif., 1962.

KEVIN PASSMORE

ACTON, JOHN (1834–1902), British historian.

Lord Acton (John Edward Emmerich Dalberg Acton), a Catholic, a Liberal, and a historian, was the heir of English and European nobility prominent in national and continental politics and diplomacy. Educated in France, England, and Germany and fluent in three languages, he belonged to the intellectual, political, and Catholic establishments of the second half of the nineteenth century. In addition to his wide-ranging scholarship, the greatest personal influences upon him were contemporary German thinkers. Acton went to Munich as a boy of sixteen to study with Johann Josef Ignaz von Döllinger (1799–1890), the priest-scholar who became his closest friend and intellectual father until Acton repudiated him over a theological dispute. In 1865 Acton married a cousin, Marie Arco, who had little in common with him intellectually or emotionally. They had four surviving children. Acton loved the Arco family and especially Marie's mother, the Italian Countess von Arco-Valley, whom he often referred to as his "dear mamma" but for whom he may have had stronger feelings.

Assiduously collecting what was probably the largest library of his day, Acton wanted to spend his life studying human nature and history through books. Instead, he passionately fought three public battles. First, he wanted his church to respect historical truth and objective inquiry as part of a Catholic spiritual life. To achieve that end, from 1858 to 1864, he edited the Catholic periodical, *The Rambler,* which later became *The Home and Foreign Review,* and he attempted to influence Catholic policies through extensive personal contacts—his uncle was a cardinal—within and around the papacy. In 1859, to please his English family, he reluctantly entered Parliament as a Liberal Party representative for the Irish constituency of Carlow, but made little impression in the House of Commons during his seven years there. Second, through his friendship with William Ewart Gladstone (1809–1898), the Liberal prime minister of Great Britain from 1868 to 1874, 1880–1885, 1886, and 1892–1894, he attempted to shape Liberal politics as an armchair advisor. Then, finally, for the happiest last seven years of his life, as Regius Professor of Modern History at Cambridge University, he tried to repudiate the narrow nationalism and positivism that characterized the writing and teaching of history in England. All three efforts failed.

Although Acton opposed the Syllabus of Errors in 1863 and the doctrine of papal infallibility in 1870, he submitted to the church's authority. Unhappily, he recognized that his political influence was circumscribed by his status as an outsider who was more European than English. Unlike his English colleagues, Acton insisted upon the role of moral judgment in history and believed dogmatically that history revealed moral ideas that transcended national boundaries to inform individual conscience, religion, and developments toward liberty. Acton could not persuade historians to accept his beliefs or to challenge the prevailing understanding of the past. He is remembered most for the dictum: "Power tends to corrupt and absolute power tends to corrupt absolutely," written in an 1887 letter to the Anglican Bishop Mandell Creighton (1843–1901).

Acton was recognized by his peers as a man of immense learning, even brilliance. His greatest ambition was to achieve a *Kulturgeschichte,* a unified history of human thought and morality, which recognized human evil and studied every aspect of experience, including science and religion. While he did undertake the editorship of the Cambridge Modern History in 1896, to realize his lifelong dream of demonstrating the broad role of ideas in the unity of history, he wrote nothing for it and died before the appearance of the first volume in 1902. All twelve volumes would have disappointed him by the narrowness of their approach.

Aside from some book reviews, the only historical work ever published in his lifetime was his inaugural address as Regius Professor of Modern History in Cambridge in 1895. In the early twenty-first century all that remains of his great projects are a diffuse collection of copious notes on slips of paper in the Cambridge University Library. No one has been able to explain satisfactorily why he never transformed those fragmentary scraps of thought into coherent and sustained written work. Those who knew him and subsequent commentators have suggested that, as a perfectionist, he never felt that he knew enough. Others have argued that he lacked the intellectual discipline to impose order upon his omnivorous reading. After his death, his students John Neville Figgis and Reginald Vere Laurence, although they were not his disciples, collected and published his Cambridge lectures. The only consistent evidence of the quality of Acton's mind appears in his letters to Mary Gladstone, the prime minister's daughter, and in other collections of letters, essays, and correspondence, all published posthumously. It is not clear whether the burden of his erudition left him unwilling, unable, or simply undone.

See also **Burckhardt, Jacob; Catholicism; Gladstone, William; Ranke, Leopold von.**

BIBLIOGRAPHY

Primary Sources

Acton, John. *Lectures on Modern History*. Edited by John Neville Figgis and Reginald Vere Laurence. London, 1906.

———. *Historical Essays and Studies*. Edited by John Neville Figgis and Reginald Vere Laurence. London, 1907.

———. *The History of Freedom and Other Essays*. Edited by John Neville Figgis and Reginald Vere Laurence. London, 1907.

———. *Lectures on the French Revolution*. Edited by John Neville Figgis and Reginald Vere Laurence. London, 1910.

———. *Letters of Lord Acton to Mary, Daughter of the Right Hon. W. E. Gladstone*. Edited by Herbert Paul. 2nd rev. ed. London, 1913.

———. *Essays on Freedom and Power*. Edited by Gertrude Himmelfarb. Boston, 1948.

———. *Essays on Church and State*. Edited by Douglas Woodruff. London, 1952.

———. *Essays in the Liberal Interpretation of History*. Edited by William H. McNeill. Chicago, 1967.

———. *The Correspondence of Lord Acton and Richard Simpson*. Edited by Josef L. Altholz, Damian McElrath, and James C. Holland. 3 vols. Cambridge, U.K., 1971–1975.

Secondary Sources

Chadwick, Owen. *Acton and History*. Cambridge, U.K., 1998. A perceptive series of essays reflecting a lifetime's grappling with Acton and his ideas.

Hill, Rowland. *Lord Acton*. New Haven, Conn., 2000. The most comprehensive and best study of Acton's life and times.

REBA N. SOFFER

ADDIS ABABA, TREATY OF. Concluded on 26 October 1896, the Treaty of Addis Ababa ended the First Italo-Abyssinian War of 1895–1896, confirmed the independence of Abyssinia, and ratified the decisive defeat its armies inflicted on an Italian expeditionary force at the Battle of Adwa six months earlier. The origins of the conflict can be traced to the previous decade. Italy, ambitious to assert its great-power status by establishing an empire in Africa, was sufficiently late on the scene that its greatest initial success was occupying the decrepit Red Sea port of Massawa in 1885. Italy continued to penetrate inland into Eritrea, whose mutually antagonistic tribes were increasingly coerced or compelled to accept Italian suzerainty.

An Abyssinian government regarding Eritrea as its territory encouraged local resistance and committed its own forces with fair amounts of success. Then in 1889, a coup brought Menelik II (r. 1889–1913) to Ethiopia's throne. For the sake of consolidating his power in a strongly feudal system, he negotiated the Treaty of Ucciali (or Wuchale) in 1889. Italy recognized him as emperor in return for his conceding their position in Eritrea, which was established as an Italian colony in 1890. The treaty, however, had two texts. The Amarhic version allowed Menelik to use Italian good offices in corresponding with other powers. The Italian version specified that Abyssinia's foreign relations must go through Rome.

The exact balance of conscious duplicity and linguistic confusion in the document remains debatable. What is certain is that Italy used the Treaty of Ucciali to proclaim a protectorate over Ethiopia. Menelik protested, and took advantage of the protracted negotiations to mobilize domestic support and import modern weapons from Turkey, Russia, and especially France, Italy's principal direct rival in the Mediterranean. He financed the imports in good part by the results of trading and raiding expeditions to Abyssinia's perimeters and occasionally across its borders. Gold and ivory, animal hides, coffee, and slaves were exchanged for rifles and ammunition. In September 1893, Menelik denounced the Treaty of Ucciali. In June 1894, the feudal lords of Ethiopia proclaimed him "King of Kings."

Italy responded by pushing its local forces across the Eritrean-Abyssinian frontier. For a year the adversaries jockeyed for military and diplomatic advantage. The Italian government and army were confident that a limited commitment, even by the standards of colonial conflicts, would be enough to finish Abyssinia, and began fortifying several towns in northern Abyssinia as a preliminary to further operations. Menelik in September 1894 summoned a *levée en masse* amounting to about 200,000 men to his capital of Addis Ababa. He took the best half north, destroyed a force of 1,300 *askari* (local troops under Italian command), and besieged the garrison at Makalie for a month and a half before allowing it to withdraw under safe conduct.

That and other gestures of conciliation failed in the face of the Italian government's increasing determination to make its protectorate of Abyssinia a political reality. In February 1895, Prime Minister Francesco Crispi (1818–1901) informed his field commander General Oreste Baratieri (1841–1901) that Italy was ready for every sacrifice, accused him of lacking a plan of campaign, and spoke of needing to save the honor of the army. The effect was like a backhand slap to the face. Baratieri took the field and advanced on the Abyssinian camp at Adwa with about 18,000 men, two-thirds Italian and the rest *askari*. On 1 March, he attacked in four uncoordinated columns and was overwhelmingly defeated.

It was the most spectacular disaster suffered by a Western army during the entire conquest of Africa. Italian losses amounted to 11,000 dead, wounded, and prisoners. Menelik counted around 17,000 casualties, but his force was much the larger. He withdrew to Addis Ababa, where he received a discomfited Italian government's overtures for peace.

Menelik set two conditions: nullification of the Treaty of Ucciali and recognition of Abyssinia's independence. With over 3,000 of its soldiers captives, Italy had no leverage. The Treaty of Addis Ababa confirmed Abyssinia's status as a full member of the world community of nations. In the next few years, other European nations established diplomatic and commercial relations with the last independent African government. Menelik proved a shrewd and flexible negotiator, taking advantage of his European connections to suppress the last remnants of resistance to central authority. In 1900 he even established a more or less firm boundary with Italian Eritrea. Abyssinia became, and to a degree remains, a symbol and a source of pride for people of African descent everywhere in the world.

See also **Crispi, Francesco; Imperialism; Italy.**

BIBLIOGRAPHY

Ahmad, A. H., and R. Pankhurst, eds. *Adwa Victory Centenary Conference.* Addis Ababa, 1998.

Rubenson, Sven. *The Survival of Ethiopian Independence.* London, 1976.

Vandervort, Bruce. *Wars of Imperial Conquest in Africa, 1830–1914.* London, 1998.

DENNIS SHOWALTER

ADLER, ALFRED (1870–1937), Austrian psychologist.

Alfred Adler was the founder of individual psychology, which, along with Sigmund Freud's psychoanalysis and Carl Jung's analytic psychology, form the three classical schools of depth psychology. From 1902 he was one of the first four members of Freud's "Wednesday Group," where he was among the most important and most stimulating participants. Adler's growing rift with Freud (after 1908) finally led to Adler's separation from Freud in 1911. Adler then founded the Association for Free Psychoanalysis, which became the Association for Individual Psychology in 1913. In contrast to Freud, Adler focused on the person as a whole. He viewed the individual as a unified, goal-oriented, and social being. By 1912, Adler had developed the two central pillars of individual psychology: "inferiority feelings" and their "compensation." After World War I, Adler modified his theories, introducing the concept of "community feelings." Adler was influenced by the philosophy of Friedrich Nietzsche, Immanuel Kant, Hans Vaihinger, Wilhelm Dilthey, and others. One can also find many similarities with other German philosophers and personality psychologists in the holistic tradition.

Adler was born on 7 February 1870, the second of six children. His father was a Jewish grain merchant in the Rudolfsheim suburb of Vienna. Adler studied medicine in Vienna from 1888 to 1895 and was a member of the Socialist Students Association. His wife, Raissa Timofejewena (1873–1962), a student from Russia, was also a member of a socialist organization. They had four children. In 1899, Adler set up as a medical practitioner in a popular section of town, not far from the Prater amusement park. From 1911 until his emigration in 1935, he lived and worked as a neurologist in a middle-class area of Vienna. In the aftermath of World War I, Adler identified strongly with the republican governments of Germany and Austria. He became involved in the problems of social reform, especially education reform and adult education in "Socialist Vienna." Adler gave a series of lectures and demonstrations in counseling in Vienna and across Germany and Europe. After 1926, Adler worked and lectured primarily in the United States, where he held a visiting professorship at the Long Island Physicians College in New York. In 1935 he and his family became permanent residents of the United States. He died two years later of a heart attack on 28 May 1937, in Aberdeen, Scotland.

In his first major work, *Studie über Minderwertigkeit von Organen* (1907; *Study of Organ Inferiority*, 1917), Adler held the view that illnesses and neuroses are caused by the unsuccessful compensation of an inferior organ, and that, in turn, high achievement can be the result of successful compensation. Between 1909 and 1911 Adler elaborated on his theory of personality and neurosis, which he presented comprehensively in his magnum opus, *Über den nervösen Charakter* (1912; *The Neurotic Constitution*, 1917). He contended that feelings of inferiority can be compensated for by feelings of superiority, which can help protect the individual against humiliation. Feelings of inferiority exist in a milder form in everyone and are a determining factor in the development of neuroses. These feelings can be traced back to such factors as organ inferiority, a cold or overprotective upbringing, as well as to social discrimination, as illustrated by the prevailing attitudes toward women. Feelings of inferiority lead to attitudes of passive avoidance, as expressed in traits such as timidity, insecurity, anxiety, submissive obedience. The compensatory striving for superiority leads to an exaggerated need for acknowledgement and power, the ambition to be better than others, more attractive, stronger, bigger, and more intelligent. One form of striving for superiority is the so-called masculine protest, that is, the wish to be a man or to not be a woman, because in the cultural judgment, victory is conceived as masculine, defeat as feminine. Both feelings are not based on realities but are fictions of the imagination, developed within the individual, as he sees himself in comparison to others. They form the basis of the "life style" of the individual, developing in early childhood.

Adler regarded the development of community feelings as a means for overcoming the compensatory needs for power needs in the individual, or at least for channelling these needs in socially useful directions. Community feeling or social feeling such as compassion, altruism, selflessness, or a unifying bond of mutual trust is a genuine psychological virtue and an index of man's inborn sociability. This community feeling was Adler's therapeutic goal and educational precept, to induce the individual to accept the desirability and the inevitability of social ties. It was Adler's personal mission to give people educational guidelines in mental health and the prevention of neurosis. His recommendation was to encourage the strengths of the individual in order to support his self-confidence.

In "Red Vienna" during the 1920s Adler was a teacher, reformer, popular orator, and political activist. He felt supported and stimulated by the increasing number of his associates who identified chiefly with social democratic policies. In this atmosphere, individual psychology flourished as a branch of applied clinical psychology and became a leading psychological movement. Adler's chief contribution was the establishment of educational counseling centers in cooperation with schools and other educational organizations. In addition, individual psychologists worked in progressive classes and, after 1931, in a progressive school, kindergartens, residential treatment centers, day-care centers, clinics for the disabled, and in a therapeutic outpatient center. Adler himself gave a series of lectures about education and group psychotherapy to students, schoolteachers, and to the public at large. He wrote a number of books in German and English. His most important publication during this period was his book *Menschenkenntnis* (1927; *Understanding Human Nature*).

At the beginning of the 1930s, Adler focused increasingly on the metaphysical and philosophical aspects of his work. This change in perspective is apparent in his book *Der Sinn des Lebens* (1933; *Social Interest: A Challenge to Mankind*).

See also **Freud, Sigmund; Jung, Carl Gustav.**

BIBLIOGRAPHY

Bruder-Bezzel, Almuth. *Alfred Adler. Die Entstehungsgeschichte einer Theorie im historischen Milieu Wiens.* Göttingen, Netherlands, 1983.

———. *Die Geschichte der Individualpsychologie.* Göttingen, Netherlands, 1999.

Ellenberger, Henri. *The Discovery of the Unconscious: The History and Evolution of Dynamic Psychiatry.* New York, 1970.

Hoffman, Edward. *The Drive for Self: Alfred Adler and the Founding of Individual Psychology.* Austin, Tex., 1994.

Stepansky, Paul. *In Freud's Shadow: Adler in Context.* Hillsdale, N.J., 1983.

ALMUTH BRUDER-BEZZEL

ADLER, VICTOR (1852–1918), Austrian socialist.

Victor Adler was born in Prague on 24 June 1852 and died in Vienna on 11 November 1918. He brought about the uniting of the socialist factions in Austria in the 1880s, and led the united movement from 1889. Adler was also foreign minister of the provisional government of German Austria in the last days of the Habsburg Monarchy, and hence a founding father of the First Austrian Republic.

Adler was the son of a Jewish merchant, Salomon Adler. As a believer in emancipation, Salomon supported the revolution of 1848, but he accepted the victory of the counterrevolutionary, neo-absolutist regime of Francis Joseph and, after escaping financial ruin by moving to Vienna in 1855, became a successful land speculator. Victor Adler attended the socially prestigious Schottengymnasium. Here he became a leading member of a circle of intellectually precocious and politically radical pupils, including Engelbert Pernerstorfer and Heinrich Friedjung, and later such figures as Siegfried Lipiner and Gustav Mahler, who became attracted to the irrationalist thought and culture of Richard Wagner and the young Friedrich Nietzsche.

This thought was linked to a radical, left-liberal critique of the accommodation of mainstream, "rationalistic" liberalism to both the Habsburg regime and laissez-faire economics. In Austria this critique, with its holistic stress on community, took on a strongly German nationalist, pan-German tinge. As a medical student at Vienna University Adler became a very active member of the radical, *völkisch* (populist), German nationalist student movement. Sigmund Freud and Theodor Herzl were also involved, to some extent. A major problem for such Jewish German nationalist sympathizers, however, was that anti-Semitism had been a major factor in the movement since almost its inception; and as early as 1875 a seminal speech by a prominent professor, Theodor Billroth, had set the "Jewish Problem" in bluntly racial terms.

Adler had great difficulty reconciling his Jewish descent with the movement's anti-Semitism (Adler's ambivalence about his Jewishness was to continue also in his socialist years). In 1878 he converted to Protestantism (shortly after having married Emma Braun in a Jewish ceremony), and in 1882 he was still a central figure in the creation of the Linz Program, which was a key ideological statement of Austrian German Nationalism. However, the stridency and increasingly vehement anti-Semitism of the movement, personified in its leader, Georg von Schönerer, eventually led in the 1880s to the alienation and exclusion of its erstwhile Jewish members, including Adler.

Adler had all along been more interested in social justice than national unity. Working after his student years as a physician in private practice, he came to see the crushing poverty in Vienna as due to an immense social injustice in the capitalist system. Alienated from the German nationalist movement, he turned, with the help of his brother-in-law, Heinrich Braun, and his acquaintance, Karl Kautsky, to another, more clearly antibourgeois form of political radicalism, Marxist socialism.

In 1886, the year of Austria's Anti-Socialist Law, Adler, with his own, inherited funds, set up a socialist journal, *Gleichheit* (Equality). This weekly reported on the deprivations visited on the Austrian working classes. A campaign on behalf of tramworkers in early 1889 led to the Habsburg authorities prohibiting the weekly and imprisoning Adler for four months. Adler's response was to use up much of his remaining wealth to start a new weekly, the *Arbeiter Zeitung* (Worker's paper), in July 1889. The "AZ" became a daily in 1895 and the main Austrian socialist mouthpiece.

Adler was central to the reuniting of the radical and moderate elements in Austrian socialism at the Hainburg Party Conference of 30 December 1888–1 January 1889. While Adler was initially mistrusted as a (Jewish) "bourgeois," his persecution by the authorities (Adler was to serve eighteen months in prison over his lifetime) greatly helped his acceptance by the working-class base as "one of us." Adler became the leader of the Austrian party, and remained such until his death in 1918.

The Austrian Social Democratic Party prospered under Adler. The Anti-Socialist Law lapsed in 1891, and the socialists soon became a major political force. Austria's restricted franchise kept them from gaining much representation, but the creation of a "fifth curia" in 1896 for the Reichsrat (Austria's parliament) enabled them to begin to show their potential electoral power. Unsurprisingly, one of Adler's major campaigns as party leader, and as a Reichsrat deputy from 1905, was for universal manhood suffrage. This was achieved for the Reichsrat in early 1907 (in an unlikely alliance with Emperor Francis Joseph). The Social Democrats emerged in the 1907 Reichsrat election as one of the two largest parties (along with their bitter rivals, the Catholic, populist, and anti-Semitic Christian Socials). The elections of 1911 saw further socialist gains, but this was tempered by the splitting off of the Czech Social Democrats in 1910 over

national issues. Adler's residual German national bias has been seen as a factor in this split.

Adler helped formulate the famous Brünn Program of 1899. Yet he was not that interested in theory, leaving that to other "Austromarxists" such as Otto Bauer, Karl Renner, and Max Adler. Victor Adler's major contribution was as a strategist and an organizer. Under Adler the Austrian Social Democrats set up an impressive infrastructure of educational and social support that offered party members a "counter-culture" of their own, in some ways a socialist version of the Wagnerian *Gesamtkunstwerk* with which Adler's boyhood circle had started.

Adler participated in the attempts of the Second International to secure peace before 1914, but when war came Adler backed the Austro-Hungarian war effort, seeing it as a defensive war against the aggression of the oppressive tsarist regime in Russia. His son, Friedrich, vehemently opposed the war, and in 1916 assassinated the Austrian prime minister, Count Karl Stürgkh, much to the horror of his father.

In 1918, with the collapse of the Habsburg Monarchy, Victor Adler played a major role in forming the new state of "German Austria" and, as foreign secretary in Karl Renner's provisional government, was a strong advocate of *Anschluss* with the new German Republic. He died on 11 November 1918, the eve of the founding of the First Austrian Republic.

See also **Austria-Hungary; Francis Joseph; Freud, Sigmund; Herzl, Theodor; Jews and Judaism; Marx, Karl; Nietzsche, Friedrich; Vienna; Wagner, Richard.**

BIBLIOGRAPHY

Ardelt, Rudolf G. *Friedrich Adler: Probleme einer Persönlichkeitsentwicklung um die Jahrhundertwende*. Vienna, 1984.

Braunthal, Julius. *Victor und Friedrich Adler: zwei Generationen Arbeiterbewegung*. Vienna, 1965.

Jacobs, Jack. *On Socialists and "the Jewish Question" after Marx*. New York and London, 1992.

McGrath, William J. *Dionysian Art and Populist Politics in Austria*. New Haven, Conn., and London, 1974.

STEVEN BELLER

ADRIANOPLE. The historian John Keegan noted that Adrianople has the "curious distinction as the most frequently contested spot on the globe" (p. 70). In fact, the city (known as Edirne by the Ottomans and Turks) has been the site of a major battle at least sixteen times since 300 C.E. Keegan also pointed out that it was the city's geography, lying on the invasion route to the Bosphorus and Constantinople, rather than its wealth or population, that made it a strategic epicenter. The city fell to the Turks in 1361 and was the capital of the Ottoman Empire until 1453. Under the Ottoman Turks, Adrianople became a significant cultural and religious center as well as home to many of the sultan's famous Janissary regiments.

In the Russo-Turkish War of 1828–1829, an unstoppable Russian offensive swept south out of Romania, aiming at the conquest of Thrace. By midsummer 1829, three Russian army corps of more than forty thousand men pushed a battered Ottoman army of fifteen thousand men into Adrianople. Threatened with encirclement, the Ottomans abandoned the city, which fell on 20 August 1829. The subsequent Treaty of Adrianople, however, ended the fighting and restored the city to the Ottoman Empire. During the Russo-Turkish War of 1877–1878, after an unexpectedly successful offensive in early 1878, the Russians again took the almost undefended city and swept toward the Ottoman capital. On 3 March 1878 Russia forced the Ottoman government to sign the humiliating Treaty of San Stefano, which ceded the city as well as most of Thrace to Russia's Bulgarian ally. This treaty, unilaterally forced on the Ottoman Empire by the Russians, so upset the balance of power in Europe that German Chancellor Otto von Bismarck convened the Congress of Berlin in June 1878 to restore the harmonious relationships among the Great Powers. At the conference, Bismarck succeeded in gaining the abrogation of the Treaty of San Stefano, which ended the possibility of a Russian-sponsored "Greater Bulgaria" dominating the Balkans and returned Adrianople to the Ottomans. Unfortunately, the Russians felt cheated of their hard-won gains, and the congress ended the delicate web of diplomatic relationships that had created security in Europe since 1815.

After 1878 the Ottoman Empire's new western border with Bulgaria lay just twenty kilometers (twelve miles) west of Adrianople, making the city acutely vulnerable to attack. Having lost the city twice, the Ottoman army decided to heavily fortify Adrianople and began to build concentric defenses with German assistance and modern Krupp cannons. In 1910 they began a second series of modern fortifications that included machine guns, telephones, and rapid-fire artillery. By 1912, the Ottoman army's fortress complex was substantially completed. Deploying 247 guns, accommodating sixty thousand soldiers, and blocking any Bulgarian advance on Constantinople, Adrianople was considered one of the strongest positions in Europe.

The First Balkan War broke out in October 1912, and the Bulgarians rapidly attacked and decisively defeated the Ottoman army at Kirk Kilise. The retreat of the Ottoman army left Adrianople isolated, and the Bulgarians, with Serbian assistance, besieged the city in early November 1912. Inside the city, General Mehmet Şükrü Paşa's fortress command (reinforced by the army's IV Corps) conducted a vigorous defense and occasionally sallied outside to attack the enemy. All Ottoman attempts to relieve the city failed. An armistice in January 1913 temporarily brought the combatants to the peace table, but fighting began again the next month. On 8 February the Ottoman X Corps staged an amphibious landing at Şarkoy to break the enemy's hold on the city, but withdrew as Bulgarian reserves sealed off the beachhead. The starving and exhausted defenders of Adrianople held out until 26 March 1913 when a dynamic Bulgarian offensive took the city. The battle was seen at the time as a victory for the artillery arm, but in fact, Bulgarian infantry broke into the defensive strong points of the fortress with aggressive night assaults.

The victorious Bulgarians fixed the new border on the Enez-Midye line, which left Adrianople fifty kilometers (thirty-one miles) inside Bulgaria. The Turks, however, incensed at their humiliation, took advantage of the war-weary Bulgarians (then engaged in the internecine Second Balkan War with Greece, Romania, and Serbia) and retook the city on 22 July 1913.

From 1829 until 1914, Adrianople acted as a magnet for both the Russians and the Bulgarians as it had for previous conquerors. The strategic instability caused by its loss in 1878 accelerated the process of disintegration that afflicted the Ottoman Empire and destroyed the Concert of Europe. Moreover, Adrianople's fate in the Balkan Wars highlighted the continuing military weakness of the Ottoman Empire. That the gateway city to Constantinople could be taken so easily, and could be held only with the consent of the Great Powers, confirmed the end of the Ottoman Empire's status as a European power.

See also **Balkan Wars; Congress of Berlin; Ottoman Empire; Russo-Turkish War; San Stefano, Treaty of.**

BIBLIOGRAPHY

Erickson, Edward J. *Defeat in Detail: The Ottoman Army in the Balkans, 1912–1913.* Westport, Conn., 2003.

Keegan, John. *A History of Warfare.* New York, 1993.

EDWARD J. ERICKSON

AFRICA. In 1789 the Atlantic slave trade was at its height. During the final quarter of the eighteenth century nearly two million captured Africans were carried across the Atlantic to lives of servitude in the European colonies of the New World. The major slave-trading nations during this period were Britain, which carried 39 percent of the slaves, Portugal (33 percent), and France (22 percent), while the Netherlands, Spain, Denmark, the United States, and the British Caribbean remained minor participants. The African regions most affected by the Atlantic slave trade were Congo-Angola, which provided 42 percent of the slaves, Biafra (19 percent), the Bight of Benin (14 percent), and the Gold Coast (13 percent).

Throughout the eighteenth century, the sources of African captives had moved steadily inland from the coastal regions. By 1789 the majority of the captives shipped from the Senegal and Gambia rivers came from Segu and Kaarta along the middle Niger Valley, some five hundred to eight hundred miles from the coast. Similarly, most of the slaves coming out of Angola had been captured during the wars of the expanding Lunda Empire, more than seven hundred miles from the coast. At the mouth of the Congo River, slaves were coming from as far away as the lower Ubangi, nearly seven hundred miles away. Along the Gold Coast and the Bight of Benin, the captives sold by the Asante Empire at the end of the eighteenth century came mostly from northern Ghana and southern Burkina Faso, and captives sold by the kingdom of Dahomey came from as far away as the Hausa states of northern Nigeria.

Enslavement was devastating to its millions of victims, and the warfare that accompanied it resulted in countless plundered villages and burned fields. At the same time, the ruling and merchant classes in African slave-trading societies accumulated large amounts of wealth in the form of luxury goods such as imported cloth, spirits, and bodily adornments that increased the differences in social status between those who had access to them and those who did not. The muskets, cannons, and gunpowder that poured into Africa at this time strengthened the military establishments in kingdoms such as Dahomey, Asante, Kayor, and Bawol, and led to the rise of warlord states in Angola. There is no evidence that the European and Asian goods that entered Africa by the shipload led to significant increases in productivity or to structural changes that put African economies on a path toward capitalist development. African trading states were exporting labor in exchange for luxury goods and military equipment, creating a bubble of prosperity for the ruling and merchant classes that was threatened when the Atlantic slave trade ended.

Between 1802 and 1818, the governments of Denmark, England, the United States, France, and Holland outlawed the transportation of slaves across the Atlantic, even though slavery itself remained legal throughout the New World. The British sent out naval squadrons to cruise the West African coast and occasionally to blockade major slaving ports. In 1808 they established the colony of Freetown on the Sierra Leone peninsula, which they used as a naval base for antislavery squadrons and as a resettlement colony for Africans who had been liberated from slave ships. But these measures had limited effect because both European traders and African merchants became adept at slave smuggling.

One of the most notorious slave smugglers was Felix De Sousa, the governor of the slaving port of

Whydah in the kingdom of Dahomey. Born in Brazil of mixed parentage, De Souza came to Dahomey to work in the Portuguese fort, but soon established himself as an independent trader. He used his friendship with the Dahomian King Gezo to gain an appointment as the governor of Whydah. He controlled commerce of the port from 1820 until his death in 1849 and gained a reputation as a master at slave smuggling. The British captured thirty of the slave ships that he loaded, but a quarter of a million slaves left Whydah and neighboring ports during De Souza's administration. In a similar fashion, the maze of creeks and waterways that made up the Niger River delta provided ideal cover for slave smugglers. Bonny and Kalabari, the leading slave ports of the Niger delta, continued to export slaves until 1837, when the British navy began concentrating its squadrons at the major delta ports. The town of Nembe, hidden deep in the mangrove swamps, thrived on the slave trade until the Brazilian slave markets closed in the 1850s.

The main impediment to the British antislavery efforts was the fact that Portugal did not agree to outlaw the Atlantic slave trade until 1830, and even then did not make any attempt to implement the agreement until the 1850s. During the second quarter of the nineteenth century, the Portuguese slave trade from the Congo-Angola area remained at eighteenth-century levels, while illegal traders from the major European slave trading nations frequented the coast of southwest Africa to purchase slaves far from the reach of the British squadrons. Nearly half of all slaves taken from Africa during this period came from Congo-Angola, while another 15 percent came from southwest Africa.

With British squadrons and high slave prices along the West African coasts, some slave traders turned to the Indian Ocean coast of southern Africa. The Portuguese port at Mozambique Island, where slaves were cheap, became a major slaving port in the first half of the nineteenth century, when nearly four hundred thousand slaves from southeast Africa were sent to Brazil, San Domingo, and Martinique.

LEGITIMATE TRADE

By the 1830s it was clear to most West African rulers and merchants that the Atlantic slave trade was winding down, and they began to search for

A Kenyan warrior. Photograph c. 1900. © HULTON-DEUTSCH COLLECTION/CORBIS

new ways to maintain the flow of European and Asian imports. At this time, England and other European countries were entering the early stages of industrialization and were seeking new sources of tropical oils for industry and exotic luxury items for the middle classes. During the era of the slave trade, Europeans had always purchased hides, ivory, gold, gum copal, and other African products along with slaves, but they were focusing on finding new products to meet the demands of changing European economies.

One African product that attracted a great deal of European attention was palm oil, which was used in making soap and candles. Oil palms grew abundantly in the Niger River delta and its hinterland, and British purchases of palm oil grew from five thousand tons per year in 1827 to thirty thousand tons in 1853. By 1869 five British steamships per month were visiting the Niger delta to buy palm oil. African merchants who had formerly traded in slaves scrambled to develop inland territories where they could monopolize the palm oil trade. They purchased large numbers of slave laborers to load and unload the casks of palm oil for transportation in dugout canoes along the delta waterways. African palm oil merchants at the former slave trading port of Old Calabar developed palm plantations worked by slave laborers. Slaves thus continued to flow into the delta ports long after the Atlantic slave trade ended.

A similar economic transformation occurred in the kingdom of Dahomey, where slave smuggling proceeded simultaneously with the buildup of palm oil plantations. By the 1840s there were many palm oil plantations around the port cities of Whydah and Porto Novo and the capital city of Abomey. These plantations were worked by slaves, who tended the trees and engaged in the laborious processes of extracting the oil from the fruit and transporting it to the ports. In 1851 Abomey was home to ten thousand slaves out of a total population of thirty thousand, and in 1855 there was a revolt of Yoruba slaves on the Abomey plateau. The transition from the slave trade to what the British called "legitimate trade" thus had the ironic effect of increasing the use of slave labor within Africa.

During the era of the slave trade, the kingdoms in the West African region bounded by the Senegal and Gambia rivers had developed a class of professional horse-mounted soldiers known as Cheddo. When the Atlantic slave trade ended, the Cheddo lost a valuable source of income, and they began to pillage agricultural villages in search of booty and captives, whom they sold into trans-Saharan slave trade to North Africa.

In 1840 the French discovered that peanut oil could be mixed with palm oil to make good soap, and they began to buy peanuts from the African peasants, who increased their production and often used the proceeds to buy guns to defend themselves from the Cheddo. As peanut exports rose from five thousand tons in 1854 to eighty thousand tons in 1882, gun battles between Muslim peasants and bands of marauding Cheddo warriors became more frequent. Cheddo war bands would even go into the village fields and uproot peanut plants in a vain attempt to halt the peanut trade.

In the Congo-Angola region, there were no agricultural products in great demand by the Europeans, but the rising middle class in Europe was creating a new demand for ivory that would be carved into piano keys, billiard balls, combs, fans, and other fineries. Whereas ivory from West African elephants was hard and suitable mainly for knife handles, equatorial African ivory was softer and could be carved into ornate objects and exquisite designs. The price of ivory at Luanda shot up 300 percent after the Portuguese government abolished its monopoly in 1836, and ivory exports rose from one and a half tons in 1832 to more than eighty tons in 1859.

The transition to the ivory trade provoked serious political upheavals in the hinterland of Angola that reached as far as the Lunda Empire in the heart of central Africa. The Lunda king had sold slaves captured in the course of his many wars in exchange for guns that he used for his army and European goods that he distributed as political patronage to loyal officials. With the closing of the Brazilian slave ports in the 1850s, the price of a male slave along the coast of Angola fell from seventy dollars to ten dollars, putting the Lunda Empire's delicate patronage system in jeopardy. By 1875 political unrest was growing both at the Lunda capital and in the provinces.

The highly mobile bands of Chokwe hunters living in the hinterland of Angola were in a position to profit from the new economic conditions by selling wax and ivory to the Portuguese in exchange for firearms and other trade goods that they used to purchase slave women. In response to the growing political unrest and fierce succession struggles in the Lunda Empire in the 1870s, contenders for political power in the western Lunda provinces invited Chokwe war bands to settle on their lands and aid them in their struggle against the imperial capital. Fighting their way eastward, the Chokwe mercenaries broke faith with their employers and sacked the capital in 1886, thus destroying the Lunda Empire.

With the decline of the slave trade, African traders in the equatorial rainforest refocused their efforts on the ivory trade. The Bobangi canoemen, who had controlled the slave trade along the middle Congo River and the lower Ubangi, continued to carry slaves for the internal African market but depended on the ivory trade to purchase cloth, guns, and other imported products. The ivory was carried down the Congo River in canoes to Malebo Pool, where a two hundred mile series of rapids blocked further advancement. The ivory was then transferred to caravans of porters, who carried it to the coast for sale to Europeans. By the 1880s ivory was coming from as far inland as Wagenia Falls, more than a thousand miles from the mouth of the Congo River. Investing the wealth they gained from their ivory sales mainly in purchasing slaves, the Bobangi developed a society that reproduced itself mainly through slave purchases. Bobangi trading towns along the middle Congo became populated overwhelmingly by persons of slave origin and their descendants and fostered a system of social mobility whereby slaves could become wealthy traders or even chiefs.

EAST AFRICA

East Africa was largely spared the ravages of the Atlantic slave trade, although there was a long-standing trade in slaves from the East African coast to the Middle East. In the nineteenth century the tiny island of Zanzibar, located just twenty-two miles off the East African coast, became the focal point for East African interactions with Europe. In the 1780s merchants from India began to visit Zanzibar in order to purchase ivory that had been brought there by boat from the mainland. The Indians believed that East African ivory was the best in the world. At the same time, French merchants began coming to Zanzibar in search of slaves for the sugar plantations being developed on the Indian Ocean islands of Reunion and Mauritius. This rise in commerce had little effect at first; in 1800 Zanzibar Town contained a few houses, but mostly huts of straw mat.

Things began to change when the sultan of Oman, which had claimed a loose hegemony over Zanzibar in the eighteenth century, made a voyage to the island in 1828. Four years later he transferred the capital of the Omani Empire from Muscat, in the Persian Gulf, to Zanzibar. One reason for the change was that the sultan had seen the two clove plantations established by an Omani merchant. Cloves, which had formerly been produced only in the Molucca Islands of southeast Asia, seemed to do especially well in Zanzibar. The sultan confiscated the clove plantations and took over land for new plantations. By the 1840s people all over the island were cutting down fruit trees in order to plant clove trees, and many Omani Arabs followed their sultan to Zanzibar in order to start clove plantations. The clove boom attracted the attention of Europeans. The United States established a consulate on Zanzibar in 1837, followed by the British in 1841 and the French in 1846.

The clove plantations were worked by slave laborers purchased from the East African mainland. By 1870 Zanzibar had between sixty thousand and one hundred thousand slaves working on the plantations, and it was importing ten thousand slaves per year to replenish the labor force. Zanzibar-based trading caravans financed by Indian merchants went farther and farther into the interior in search of slaves for the plantations or for shipment to the Middle East.

The trade routes had been pioneered in the early nineteenth century by the inland Nyamwezi, who brought ivory and slaves to the coast from their homeland in eastern Tanzania. Swahili and Arab traders from the coast began using the routes after 1825. The caravan trade greatly expanded with the development of clove plantations in Zanzibar and the surge in European demand for East African ivory. British imports of ivory rose from 125 tons per year in 1820 to 800 tons in 1875, causing prices in East Africa to rise 400 percent between 1823 and 1873.

With twenty-four thousand tusks exported annually from Zanzibar during the 1860s, the elephant herds in Tanzania were virtually extinct by 1872. Arab and Swahili traders began to cross Lake Tanganyika in the 1860s and search for ivory in the forested regions of eastern Congo. Hamed bin Muhammed, known as Tippu Tip, established permanent bases in the towns of Kassongo and Nyangwe along the upper Congo River. From there, his hired Nyamwezi soldiers would attack villages, seize stockpiles of ivory, and take captives, who could be ransomed with ivory or sold in Zanzibar. By the 1880s Tippu Tip's raiding state had congealed into a merchant-led confederation whose territory extended more than five hundred miles from north to south. Despite its state-like

Officials of the British East India Company present a treaty to a group of Kikuyu men, 1897. The British controlled the Kikuyu homelands in eastern Africa, in what later bacame Kenya, from 1886 through 1963. Their treaties with indigenous peoples almost invariably expropriated resources and exploited workers. MARY EVANS PICTURE LIBRARY

structure, it served mainly to funnel slaves and ivory to Zanzibar.

SOUTHERN AFRICA

In 1795 the British seized the Dutch East India Company's colony at the Cape of Good Hope and took definitive control of the Cape Colony in 1806. As the British began to solidify their control over the Huguenot and Dutch settlers, known as *Afrikaners* or *Boers*, political changes were taking place in the interior that would have ramifications throughout southern Africa.

In 1818, a minor chief named Shaka conquered the Nguni chiefdoms between the Tugela and Pongola rivers and established a powerful, centralized Zulu kingdom with a standing army of forty thousand men organized in closely drilled and highly disciplined age regiments. During the next decade, Shaka expanded his kingdom into

the Drakensberg foothills and sent soldiers to seize cattle and collect tribute south of the Tugela River, where they devastated hundreds of square miles, sending thousands of refugees fleeing to the inaccessible mountains and forests. Young men and women from newly conquered chiefdoms were incorporated into Zulu regiments.

In the Cape Colony, many Boer settlers were unhappy with the changes being introduced by the British colonial government, especially the 1828 ordinance that gave indigenous workers on Boer farms the right to move about and seek employment and the 1833 Emancipation Act, which promised to free slave workers by 1838. Between 1835 and 1841, about six thousand Boers left the Cape Colony, moving into areas that had recently been depopulated by the Zulu wars and extending white settlement far into the interior. They eventually created two Boer states, the Orange Free

State and the South African Republic. In 1843 the British annexed the region of Natal to keep it from falling into rival European hands.

European interest in Southern Africa was heightened when diamonds were discovered in the Orange Free State in 1867 and gold was discovered in the South African Republic in 1886. The discovery of precious minerals brought a flood of new investors, entrepreneurs, and miners, and by 1877 the diamond town of Kimberley was the second largest city in southern Africa. In 1878 the British government annexed the diamond mining area from the Orange Free State and incorporated it into the Cape Colony. At that time there were about ten thousand white diggers and thirty thousand black workers in the diamond fields. Soon the freewheeling private enterprise that had characterized the early diamond digging was replaced by a more consolidated and coercive system. In 1886 De Beers Consolidated Mines introduced closed compounds for its African workers, and by 1899 De Beers had established a virtual monopoly on worldwide diamond sales.

The gold mining city of Johannesburg quickly became the largest city in sub-Saharan Africa, attracting mining engineers and skilled miners from Europe and the United States. African migrant laborers from all over southern Africa were recruited to work in the mines, and by the turn of the century almost two-thirds of the labor came from Mozambique. African workers lived in compounds built by the mines for better control of the labor force. After 1896, all Africans in mining areas were required by law to have passes issued by their employers. Failure to produce a pass on demand could result in three weeks of hard labor for the first offense. By 1899 there were a million black workers and twelve thousand white workers working in the gold mines.

NORTH AFRICA

With the exception of Morocco, coastal North Africa was under the nominal control of the Ottoman Empire in 1789. Napoleon's army invaded Egypt in 1798 and defeated the forces of the archaic Mamluk oligarchy, but a British naval blockade of the Nile Delta ports persuaded the French to withdraw in 1801. In 1830 the French invaded Algeria and managed to overcome fierce resistance with an occupation army

of more than one hundred thousand men. White settlers from France and Spain moved into the agriculturally productive coastal strip, taking over the olive plantations, vineyards, and wheat farms. By the end of the century there were nearly a million European settlers in Algeria.

In the aftermath of the French withdrawal from Egypt, the Ottoman sultan appointed Mehmet Ali, an Albanian officer in the Ottoman army, as the viceroy of Egypt. Mehmet Ali created a modern state with a salaried civil service and a professional army based on European models. In 1811 he organized the massacre of several hundred Mamluk nobles who had previously controlled the military recruiting and tax farming system. In 1820 his army invaded Sudan and established the city of Khartoum as an administrative center at the confluence of the Blue and the White Nile. Many European military and administrative advisers were brought to Egypt, and French and British merchants were allowed to operate freely after 1838.

European interest in Egypt increased as the British developed a route to India through the Mediterranean and the Red Sea that used Egypt as the transshipment point. In the 1850s the British built railroads connecting the Red Sea port of Suez to Cairo and the Mediterranean port of Alexandria. In the 1860s the French began work on the Suez Canal, which opened in 1869. Encouraged by high prices for Egyptian cotton during the American Civil War, the ruler of Egypt, Khedive Ismail, undertook further expansion and modernization of his army and extended the railway up the Nile toward Sudan. The end of the cotton boom and the disappointing financial results of the Suez Canal forced Khedive Ismail to declare bankruptcy in 1876, and three years later the British and French took over dual control of Egypt's finances. Following a coup by Egyptian army officers that threatened to recapture Egyptian financial control, the British army occupied Egypt in 1882 and began ruling the country through an appointed pasha.

Resentment of Egyptian rule in Sudan was crystallized by a Muslim reformer named Muhammed Ahmed, who called himself The Mahdi, the "guided one." His call for a jihad against the foreigners met with an enthusiastic response. In 1885 his forces took Khartoum, and they eventually gained control of two-thirds of modern Sudan. The Mahdist state

Marketplace in Socco square, Tangiers, Morocco, c. 1870–1890. © MICHAEL MASLAN HISTORIC PHOTOGRAPH/CORBIS

was finally destroyed in 1898 by a combined Anglo-Egyptian army. After that, Sudan was ruled by an Anglo-Egyptian condominium.

THE SCRAMBLE FOR AFRICA

Until 1870 Europeans controlled only a few coastal enclaves in Africa aside from the British-controlled Cape Colony and Natal, and the colony of Sierra Leone, where they resettled African captives liberated from slave ships. The French had four enclaves in Senegal, the British had a small colony at Lagos, and the Portuguese controlled enclaves at Luanda and Benguela in Angola and at Mozambique Island and Quelmane in Mozambique. In the 1870s the British gained a trading monopoly over the Gold Coast by buying out the Dutch and Danish forts, and in 1874 they proclaimed the coastal Fante Confederation to be a crown colony in order to protect their trade.

Although the African trade amounted to less than 6 percent of Britain's overseas trade in the 1870s and even less for other European powers, there were persistent rumors of vast resources to be discovered in the interior of Africa. With the British involved in Egypt and South Africa, they were content to maintain informal spheres of influence in other parts of the continent. In response to a threat to their Gold Coast trade from the Asante Empire, the British army sacked the Asante capital in 1874 and then quickly withdrew in order to avoid the expense of formal occupation.

By the 1880s the colonization of Africa was becoming more feasible because of developments in technology. In the 1840s Europeans had discovered that quinine could be used to prevent malaria, a major killer of Europeans in Africa, and the British had developed advanced techniques of malaria prevention by 1874. Europeans were also developing new railroad and steamboat technology that incited dreams of creating vast transportation networks for the cheap transport of African products from the interior to the coast. European military technology was also advancing with the adoption of repeating rifles and a portable machine gun, the Maxim gun. Its impact was aptly summed up by the British ditty, "Whatever happens we have got / the Maxim gun and they have not."

The spark that may have set off the European "scramble for Africa" was the decision by the French in 1879 to build a railroad to transport peanuts between their coastal enclaves in Dakar and St. Louis in Senegal, even though the rail line ran through the African kingdom of Kayor. Over the next three years they moved inland, establishing new forts and surveying for a rail line to connect Dakar with the upper Niger River. The French exercise in formal empire in Senegal was quickly followed by other European actions on the continent. In 1882 the British occupied Egypt, and the French proclaimed protectorates over Porto Novo in Dahomey and over the north bank of the lower Congo. The Germans quickly followed by proclaiming protectorates over Togo, Cameroon, and South West Africa in 1884.

Intense international rivalries were causing England, France, Germany, and Portugal to lay claim to whatever territory they could before a rival power took it. At the Berlin West Africa conference in 1884–1885 the ground rules for the partition of Africa were laid out and the Congo River basin was declared a "free trade zone" under the authority of Belgian King Leopold II's International African Association. The actual boundaries of the colonies were worked out in a series of treaties between the colonizing powers between 1885 and 1891.

With the "paper partition" of Africa over, the European colonizers began a series of long and bloody campaigns to establish effective occupation of their colonies, as required by the Berlin Conference. The conquest of the territories was often aided as much by conflicts and rivalries among African states as by European military might. In southern Africa, conflicts between British mining interests and the Boer republics led to the Boer War of 1899–1902 in which the British conquered

the Boer republics, leading to the creation of a unified South Africa in 1910. By 1902 virtually the whole of Africa was the colony of one European power or another.

The main political problem facing the colonizers was how to make the transition from military conquest to orderly administration. The French in West Africa dismantled the empires of the Tukolor and Samori, as well as kingdoms such as Dahomey and Fuuta Jalon, replacing them with a chain of command that ran from the Ministry of Colonies in Paris all the way down to the French *commandant du cercle*. Local African chiefs remained in power as subordinate auxiliaries of the *commandant* and could be replaced at his pleasure. The authoritarian administrative structure was accompanied by an assimilation policy by which Africans who met certain education and professional requirements could become French citizens, but the requirements were so rigorous that very few Africans achieved this status.

British administrative policies were far less uniform because individual colonial governors were allowed considerably more flexibility to adapt to local circumstances. The most important influence on early British policy was Sir Frederick Lugard, who ruled northern Nigeria after defeating the army of the Sokoto Caliphate in 1906. In order to administer a territory three times the size of Britain with a handful of British officials, he devised a system of indirect rule by which the area would continue to be ruled by the traditional emirs, who would operate within a framework of British law and tax policy. By the 1920s indirect rule was the reigning doctrine for administering Britain's African colonies.

Having invested considerable resources in the conquest and administration of their African colonies, European colonizers were eager to get a payoff. In the Congo, Leopold II quickly abandoned his promise to provide a free trade zone and parceled out the land to European concession companies who used private armies to force Africans to bring in wild rubber, which was in high demand for industrial uses. Those Africans who failed to meet their rubber quotas were imprisoned, whipped, or killed. A similar situation reigned in neighboring French Equatorial Africa, where 70 percent of the territory was

African workers construct a railroad in Kenya as overseers watch. Late-nineteenth-century photograph.
©HULTON-DEUTSCH COLLECTION/CORBIS

allocated to private concession companies. After reports of colonial atrocities in the Congo were confirmed by an official commission of enquiry in 1905, the Belgian government took the Congo away from King Leopold and made it a Belgian colony in 1908.

Other colonies sought to bring in European settlers who would grow cash crops on land seized from Africans using cheap African labor. The British used this strategy in the highlands of Kenya and in Southern Rhodesia, which had climates amenable to European settlement, and the Portuguese encouraged settler plantations in Angola and Mozambique. Africans were pressured to work for the white settlers in order to get money to pay their taxes or were simply required to work a certain

number of days per year on a European farm or plantation.

The majority of the colonies lacked readily exploitable natural resources and European settlers. In such cases the colonial governments relied on tax levies to encourage cash crop production among the rural African populations and used conscripted African labor to build railroads to transport the crops to coastal ports. The British and French profited from the peanut production that was already widespread in Gambia and Senegal, as well as the palm oil production that was already in place in Nigeria and Dahomey. The British introduced cotton into Uganda in 1903, and production increased rapidly, although mandatory cotton production met with popular resistance in many other parts of Africa. In the Gold Coast and Nigeria, the British encouraged cocoa production, and by 1914 the Gold Coast had become the world's largest producer.

By the beginning of World War I, the earliest phase of colonial rule in Africa was coming to an end. After the war, the fledgling colonial administrations would become more systematic, and new tax and labor policies would be introduced. But the continent of Africa was already radically changed. The political and economic relations that predominated in 1914 bore little resemblance to those of 1789.

See also **Boer War; Colonialism; Colonies; Imperialism; Jingoism; Leopold II; Slavery; Suez Canal.**

BIBLIOGRAPHY

Alpers, Edward. *Ivory and Slaves in East Central Africa: Changing Patterns of International Trade to the Later Nineteenth Century.* Berkeley, Calif., 1975.

Brunschwig, Henri. *French Colonialism 1871–1914: Myths and Realities.* Translated by William Granville Brown. New York, 1966.

Dike, Kenneth Onwuka. *Trade and Politics in the Niger Delta, 1830–1885; an Introduction to the Economic and Political History of Nigeria.* Oxford, U.K., 1956.

Gifford, Prosser, and William Roger Louis, eds. *France and Britain in Africa: Imperial Rivalry and Colonial Rule.* New Haven, Conn., 1971.

Hammond, Richard James. *Portugal and Africa, 1815–1910: A Study in Uneconomic Imperialism.* Stanford, Calif., 1966.

Harms, Robert W. *River of Wealth, River of Sorrow: The Central Zaire Basin in the Era of the Slave and Ivory Trade.* New Haven, Conn., 1981.

Hargreaves, John D. *Prelude to the Partition of West Africa.* London, 1963.

———. *West Africa Partitioned.* 2 vols. Madison, Wis., 1985.

Headrick, Daniel. *The Tools of Empire: Technology and European Imperialism in the Nineteenth Century.* New York, 1981.

Hochschild, Adam. *King Leopold's Ghost: A Story of Greed, Terror, and Heroism in Colonial Africa.* Boston, 1998.

Lovejoy, Paul E. *Transformations in Slavery: A History of Slavery in Africa.* 2nd ed. Cambridge, U.K., 2000.

Packinham, Thomas. *The Scramble for Africa, 1876–1912.* New York, 1991.

———. *The Boer War.* New York, 1994.

Robinson, Ronald, and John Gallagher, with Alice Denny. *Africa and the Victorians: The Official Mind of Imperialism.* 2nd ed. London, 1981.

Sheriff, Abdul. *Slaves, Spices, and Ivory in Zanzibar: Integration of an East African Commercial Empire into the World Economy, 1770–1873.* Athens, Ohio, 1987.

Thompson, Leonard. *A History of South Africa.* 3rd ed. New Haven, Conn., 2001.

UNESCO International Scientific Committee for the Drafting of a General History of Africa. *General History of Africa.* Vols. 6–7. London, 1985–1989.

ROBERT HARMS

AGASSIZ, LOUIS (1807–1873), American geologist, zoologist, and institution-builder.

Born a Swiss Protestant on 28 May 1807, Jean Louis Rodolphe Agassiz studied at the universities of Zurich, Heidelberg, and Munich, earning an MD and two PhDs. His career began in 1829 with his description of the fish collected in Brazil by Johann Baptiste von Spix (1781–1826). After examining fossil fish in several museums across Europe, in December 1831 he went to Paris, where Georges Cuvier (1769–1832) and Alexander von Humboldt (1769–1859) became mentors. Cuvier's death in May 1832 cut short their relationship, but Agassiz always considered himself a pupil of the great Cuvier.

In September 1832 Agassiz moved to Neuchâtel, Switzerland, where he created a "scientific factory": working under his direction were clerks, colleagues, apprentice scientists, and artists. In 1837 he announced a new geological theory he called the Ice Age. The idea that alpine glaciers were formerly much larger was not original to Agassiz, but his observations, especially on the Unteraar Glacier where he set up a summer camp, taught geologists to recognize the effects of glaciers: moraines, erratic boulders, and polished, grooved bedrock. His Ice Age idea was much more radical: that most of Europe had been covered by a vast, thick mass of ice. Geologists resisted but eventually he was proven right. His own printing press turned out ten volumes on glaciers, fossil fish, and echinoderms between 1833 and 1844, but in 1845 Agassiz's wife left him and he was near bankruptcy. The solution was a year abroad.

"The divisions of animals according to branch, class, order, family, genus, and species, by which we express the results of our investigations into the relations of the animal kingdom, and which constitute the primary question respecting any system of Zoology seem to me to deserve the consideration of all thoughtful minds. Are these divisions artificial or natural? Are they the devices of the human mind to classify and arrange our knowledge in such a manner as to bring it more readily within our grasp and facilitate further investigations, or have they been instituted by the Divine Intelligence as the categories of his mode of thinking?"

Source: Louis Agassiz, *Essay on Classification*, London, 1859. Reprint edited by Edward Lurie, p. 8. Cambridge, Mass., 1952.

Arriving in Boston in 1846, he charmed everyone with his enthusiasm, and he found evidence of glacial action in North America. Wealthy admirers funded a professorship for him at Harvard in 1847 and a new institution, the Museum of Comparative Zoology, which opened in 1859. After the death of his wife, he brought his children to Cambridge and married Elizabeth Cabot Cary (1822–1907). She eased his entry into Boston society. His son Alexander helped run the museum and later rescued the museum's finances when mining made Alexander a millionaire.

Agassiz's lectures and writings advocated a fact-based science, in contrast to the speculative, poetic *Naturphilosophie* popular in his student days. Yet he also insisted that both geology and zoology point to divine causation, which endeared him to general audiences. His Ice Age had killed off all life, disproving the notion advanced by Jean-Baptiste Lamarck (1744–1829) that modern species were the changed descendants of fossil ones. He saw evidence of a thinking planner in the patterns of deep similarity between adult anatomy, embryological development, and fossil history: the so-called "threefold parallelism." Agassiz envisioned a comparative zoology that would be more scientific than

simple description, and he hoped to add a fourth dimension, geographical distribution. The sumptuous *Contributions to the Natural History of the United States*, with its illustrations of microscopic study of the embryology of turtles and jellyfish, displayed his contradictory ambitions, for he needed the support of nonscientists, but his aim was to make zoology more professional. Its first volume, published in 1857, contained an "Essay on Classification," in which Agassiz proposed that when biologists grouped species into genera, families, orders, and classes, these categories were real; the reason they are perceived by the human intellect was that they had first been conceived in the mind of the Creator. This was not the old "argument from design" based on the fit of form to function, but a new sort of natural theology reminiscent of neoplatonism. The twentieth-century biologist Ernst Mayr (1904–2005) argued that Agassiz's "typological thinking" or essentialism made evolution logically impossible, and Mayr was right to expand the understanding of this issue beyond religion. Agassiz's stubborn opposition to evolution probably had more to do with his psychology than with philosophy. Agassiz dug in his heels when Charles Darwin (1809–1892) published another theory of evolution in 1859. In debates in the scientific societies of Boston, botanist Asa Gray (1810–1888) and geologist William Barton Rogers (1804–1882) exposed the weakness of Agassiz's position, after which, Agassiz, without altering his views, focused his attention on the growth of his museum. It is misleading to take Agassiz as typical of his day, for his novel interpretation did not impress his scientific peers, and before long his own students accepted evolution.

Startled by the slaves he encountered in the American South, Agassiz decided they could not belong to his own biological species, a view that pleased some slaveowners and now disgraces his reputation. In 1863 he helped found the National Academy of Sciences. In 1864 and 1865 he led a group of students up the Amazon, collecting evidence for his three beleaguered ideas: the Ice Age, the fixity of species, and the several species of humans. His style of teaching became legendary, for he sometimes left a student for a week with a single fish, to teach the value of close observation. His message "Study nature, not books!" was the motto of the schoolteachers who attended his summer school on Penikese Island off

Cape Cod in 1873, a forerunner of later marine laboratories. He died in December 1873.

See also **Cuvier, Georges; Darwin, Charles; Evolution; Humboldt, Alexander and Wilhelm von; Science and Technology.**

BIBLIOGRAPHY

Lurie, Edward. *Louis Agassiz: A Life in Science.* Chicago, 1960. Thorough biography.

Mayr, Ernst. "Agassiz, Darwin, and Evolution." In *Evolution and the Diversity of Life*, 251–276. Cambridge, Mass., 1976. Introduces idea of Agassiz's "typological thinking" or essentialism.

Winsor, Mary P. "Louis Agassiz and the Species Question." *Studies in History of Biology* 4 (1979): 89–117. Contests Mayr's claim that philosophy made Agassiz blind to variation.

———. *Reading the Shape of Nature: Comparative Zoology at the Agassiz Museum.* Chicago, 1991. Agassiz's science and his teaching.

———. "Agassiz's Notions of a Museum: the Vision and the Myth." In *Cultures and Institutions of Natural History*, edited by Michael T. Ghiselin and Alan E. Leviton, 249–271. Los Angeles, 2000. Contests idea that Agassiz invented the separation within museums of exhibits and research collections.

MARY PICKARD WINSOR

AGRICULTURAL REVOLUTION.

Violent breaks with existing political and social structures are called revolutions: the French Revolution of 1789 and the Russian Revolution of 1917 being the standard examples. The notion of revolutionary change—so central to nineteenth- and twentieth-century social theory—was extended to other radical breaks with the past. The best known is the Industrial Revolution: that huge increase in productive capacities that occurred from 1780 to 1850 with the invention of steam-powered machinery, the concentration of labor in factories, vast improvements in mining, and the introduction of railways and steamships. Unlike political revolution, the effects of which were swift and brutal, the Industrial Revolution was more drawn out (and some argue equally pernicious), although it, too, could be ascribed a beginning: the mechanization of spinning and weaving in the late eighteenth century being the favorite candidate.

This concept of radical break with the past was then applied to the agrarian sector because it was thought that only major social transformations could account for the spectacular rise in population and sizable increases in productivity witnessed in England (and in other parts of western Europe) between 1750 and 1850, breaking all previous ceilings. England, as the "cradle of the Industrial Revolution" was taken to be the site of this Agricultural Revolution. European historians presumed until quite recently that the blockages that the English had managed to overcome continued to stifle productivity on the Continent. The only other contender, the Netherlands with its advanced economy, had doubled its population between 1500 and 1650 but then stabilized at around 2 million, without industrializing. By 1650 England had regained its medieval peak of 5.5 million inhabitants (from 2.5 million in 1500), and then reached 8.6 million in 1800 and 16.6 million in 1850. France displayed similar patterns with its population rising from 21 million in 1700 to 28.5 million in 1800 and 36 million in 1850. Population booms had in the past been accompanied by rising food prices and growing dearth, ending in severe crises that decimated the population. By the turn of the nineteenth century such growth had become sustainable. Because increased imports could not account for this change, crop yields and labor productivity must have increased. The percentage of those employed in agriculture declined in England from 80 percent in 1500 to 40 percent in 1800 (a level reached in the Netherlands by the 1670s) and 24 percent by 1850, whereas in 1870, 50 percent still worked the land in France and Germany, 60 percent in Italy, and 65 percent in Sweden. Given the overall rise in population, the absolute number employed in agriculture actually grew, but their proportion dropped: it took far fewer hands to feed more people. The rate of urbanization is another good indicator because the countryside must produce surpluses to supply the towns. In 1600, 8.3 percent of the English lived in towns of more than five thousand inhabitants, 27.5 percent in 1800, and 40 percent by 1850. These are the changes that scholars have striven to explain. They have done this, for the most part, without census data or agricultural statistics (which were first gathered systematically in the nineteenth century), piecing together indirect evidence from parish

The Winnowers, 1855, painting by Gustave Courbet. Courbet depicts the tedious task of separating grain from chaff by hand, imbuing his subjects with beauty and dignity. The works of Courbet and other European realist and naturalist artists drew attention to the hardships of labor in the nineteenth century. MUSÉE DES BEAUX-ARTS, NANTES/BRIDGEMAN ART LIBRARY/GIRAUDON

records, tax records, farm leases, estate accounts, probate records, tithes, tolls, market price lists, and agronomic literature. This accounts for their different assessments of and debates about the pace, breadth, and cause of change.

AGRICULTURAL IMPROVEMENTS

For despite attempts to link the Agricultural Revolution to technological innovations (such as Jethro Tull's seed drill of circa 1701 or Andrew Meikle's horse-drawn threshing machine of 1784) it soon became clear that neither new technology nor new sources of power could account for dramatic increases in the food supply. Revolutionary innovations such as mechanical threshers and reapers appeared only in the 1840s and 1850s (tractors would await the early 1900s) and would spread widely only in the late nineteenth or even mid-twentieth centuries. Chemical fertilizers were invented by the German chemist Justus von Liebig in 1845. This is not to say that there were no technological improvements at all, but that they were of a much simpler sort, such as using scythes rather than sickles to harvest cereals (scythes cut three times as fast but could be wielded only by men), increasing horsepower, improving drainage, improving iron plows, and sowing higher quality seeds. Altogether new crops were introduced such as maize and potatoes (which became especially popular on small landholdings), but the most significant additions to the early modern catalog were turnips and clovers because they restored nutrients to the ground. Farmers had known since the seventeenth century (from Dutch and Flemish examples) that turnips and clovers benefited the soil (without understanding their "nitrogen-fixing" properties), and they discovered that, in proper rotation, they allowed crops to grow continuously—a system known in England as the Norfolk four-course rotation (wheat-turnips-barley-clover). By 1700, only 20 percent of the arable land in England remained under fallow, a figure that fell to 4 percent by 1871. The introduction of turnips in the sixteenth century and then clover in the seventeenth seemed to offer another starting date for the Agricultural Revolution except that there is little evidence that they were commonly planted until the eighteenth century.

Growing crops year after year on the same soil exhausts its fertility. The late medieval solution, adopted throughout much of western Europe and England, was to divide a village's arable land into three large sections of open fields (with nothing more than a stone indicating where one peasant's plot ended and another's started) and to sow these fields, in rotation, with a winter cereal followed by a spring cereal followed by a third year of lying fallow so that the field could rest, renew its nutritional reserves, and rid itself of pests. Peasants scattered their holdings over the three parts of the arable (although they maintained vegetable gardens by their houses) to lessen risk, but this scattering became frowned upon in the eighteenth century as a waste of energy. Animals were herded on the fallow for their manure (and on the other two sections after the harvest). Livestock could also be kept in stalls and given fodder or fed on meadows, but the combination of open-field farming and pasturing was the most common. Because the fields were open, the entire village community had to sow and harvest the same crops at the same time. For a long time scholars believed that one of the blockages to innovation was the open-field system and that increases in productivity and yields could have come about only with the creation of fenced (or enclosed) individual farms and the institution of private property. Meadows, separate from the open fields, were usually fenced in or protected from trespass, and the enclosures that took place in

fifteenth- and sixteenth-century England were mainly of that sort. Arable land was taken over and turned into enclosed meadows as sheep's wool became more profitable than cereals, and fewer workers were needed to tend sheep than to grow crops—leading to Thomas More's famous condemnation in *Utopia* (1516) of "sheep eating men." The enclosures associated with the Agricultural Revolution took place later and were more likely to reverse the process, turning pastures into arable, as a new demand for cereals made this profitable and the more complex rotations described above provided sufficient fodder. The second wave of enclosures did not necessarily involve savings on labor. The redistribution of open fields and their division into compact enclosed farms could be done either with the consent of 80 percent of local landowners (or sometimes of the village population) or by petition to Parliament. The majority of enclosures, historians now conclude, took place in the seventeenth century when 24 percent of English farmland was enclosed, as opposed to 2 percent in the sixteenth century, 13 percent in the eighteenth, and 11 percent in the nineteenth. These enclosures were accompanied by a parallel, though separate, phenomenon of increasing farm size. By 1800 the average English farm was 60 hectares (150 acres) in southern England and 40 hectares (100 acres) in the north, as opposed to an average of 26 hectares (65 acres) in the early eighteenth century. Such engrossments also took place on the Continent following the demographic crises of the sixteenth and seventeenth centuries. Landlords reconstituted their demesnes (having earlier sold or leased a large proportion in perpetuity to their peasants) and then leased them in single units to farmers, while, alongside, small peasant landholdings continued to splinter through inheritance. There was much variation here as well with sizable family farms more common in Germany and multifamily sharecropping in northern Italy.

Eighteenth-century agronomists held it as self-evident that large enclosed farms produced more efficiently because they responded better to market conditions and encouraged investments and improvements while lowering costs (including wages), hence raising yields, rents, and profits. The relationship between demand and prices was a complicated one: higher prices stimulated

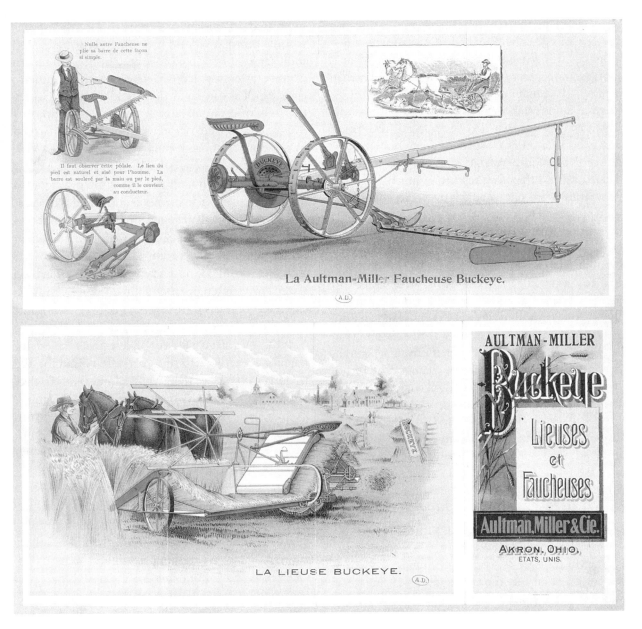

Advertisement for Aultman-Miller Buckeye Binders and Reapers, late nineteenth century. By the end of the nineteenth century, mechanical reapers and binders were being utilized in a few agricutural regions with the requisite wealth and topography. BIBLIOTHÈQUE DES ARTS DÉCORATIFS, PARIS, FRANCE/BRIDGEMAN ART LIBRARY

greater cereal production at first, and an ever-increasing demand did so thereafter. Enclosure clearly raised rents—and this was its major appeal to landlords. Like their forebears, historians bolstered by modernization theories presumed that, technological innovations lacking, it was economies of scale and liberty of production that stimulated production in the eighteenth century (though some dated it back to the seventeenth). A new market economy was replacing traditional communal self-sufficiency.

All these suppositions have been overturned. Regional studies have demonstrated that agricultural improvements were perfectly compatible with the open-field system and took place as much on small as on large farms, even if, on the whole, large, consolidated holdings facilitated and encouraged innovations. Moreover, rather than presuming that the Agricultural Revolution had to precede the Industrial Revolution, be it by a decade or a century, evidence showed that it (or much of it) occurred alongside the Industrial Revolution with a real takeoff in the second half of the eighteenth century or even the first half of the nineteenth—although this remains a contentious issue. What is more, some regions of England advanced faster than others, discouraging sweeping generalizations. Despite disagreements over timing, English historians now concede that the Agricultural Revolution consisted of a series of small, incremental changes rather than sudden revolutionary transformations. Their England therefore resembles much more the "backward" Europe studied by their colleagues, long presumed to lag far behind. What is more, parts of Europe have been shown to experience similar rates of growth as advanced British regions. For example, large, consolidated farms in northern France, especially around Paris, responded to increased demand, improving techniques, reducing the fallow, introducing new crops—and raising yields. Similar improvements have been observed on the open fields and on small farms, although, here as in England, the pace of change varied from region to region. But highly commercialized English farms could no longer be contrasted to self-sufficient European villages. If piecemeal improvements explained population and productivity increases in England, the same could be shown for other areas, such as France, which managed to sustain growth of 30 percent over the eighteenth century.

POLITICAL AND CULTURAL FRAMEWORK

Thus far, economic factors have taken front stage. Market forces were at work that stimulated a search for profit resulting in improvements (and some innovations) in husbandry and changes in landholding patterns (consolidation of farms, engrossment, and leaseholds). For a long time it was presumed that peasant communities steeped intraditional values and averse to innovations resisted these forces. Individualism and capitalism could therefore have invaded the countryside only from the outside. Dispelling these myths and showing that peasants objected neither to profit nor to the market did not explain what had stimulated improvements during the seventeenth century and in the eighteenth century in particular. For this explanation one must examine the "temper of the times." Improvements were in the air, novelties became exciting, experiments were granted respectability by the establishment of academies of science throughout Europe. And governments became

interested in agricultural growth. In the seventeenth century, states had privileged trade and industry as the source of wealth. In the eighteenth century attention focused once more on agriculture, especially in countries (such as France) where the bulk of taxation came from the land. Stimulating agricultural investments, it was argued, would increase production, profits, rents, and taxes. Agricultural societies were established to encourage new methods, and, although they were often misguided and ineffectual (their members dismissed by practitioners as "armchair agronomists"), they represented one facet of a broad-based Enlightenment infatuation with the countryside. The philosopher Voltaire remarked on the "agromania" that had seized his contemporaries in the 1750s, with an explosion of learned treatises by political economists and plays, paintings, and poems celebrating the delights of village life. As philosophers called for happiness and liberty, demands were voiced for free trade as the panacea that would allow cereals to flow from regions of plenty to areas of dearth. Free trade in grains was briefly enacted in France in the 1760s and again in the 1770s, while other countries stuck to protectionist legislation. Political will was not enough, however. Markets had to be better integrated and communications much improved before such measures could be contemplated. There too there were visible advances. In England, especially, new canals and improved roads made food transport faster and cheaper, and similar ventures were undertaken in France—but its territory was far bigger and harder to connect. Governments encouraged drainage and land clearance with tax subsidies where private initiative failed. In England, enclosures were supported by Parliament but not in other countries. The Agricultural Revolution is thus best understood within the context of the state and the ambient culture. But let the last words be those of one prominent scholar:

> Private property was not essential for innovation or agricultural improvement but it certainly assisted it. Innovation took place on both large and small farms, although the heavy capital investment involved in land reclamation and enclosure required farmers or landlords of substance to carry it out. The key to the relationship between institutional change and farming practice lay more with commercialization and the market than with the social relations of production. The inte-

Fat Cattle. Hand-colored etching by James Gillray, 1802. This caricature depicts Francis Russell, 5th Duke of Bedford, a prominent English politician who took an active interest in improving agricultural techniques. COURTESY OF THE WARDEN AND SCHOLARS NEW COLLEGE, OXFORD/BRIDGEMAN ART LIBRARY

Clark, Gregory. "The Economics of Exhaustion, the Postan Thesis, and the Agricultural Revolution." *Journal of Economic History* 52, no. 1 (1992): 61–84.

de Vries, Jan, and Ad van der Woude. *The First Modern Economy: Success, Failure, and Perseverance of the Dutch Economy, 1500–1815.* Cambridge, U.K., 1997.

Hoffman, Philip T. *Growth in a Traditional Society: The French Countryside, 1450–1815.* Princeton, N.J., 1996.

Milward, Alan S., and S. B. Saul. *The Economic Development of Continental Europe, 1780–1870.* London, 1973.

Moriceau, Jean-Marc. *Terres mouvantes: Les campagnes françaises du féodalisme à la mondialisation, 1150–1850.* Paris, 2002.

Ogilvie, Sheilagh, ed. *Germany: A New Social and Economic History.* Vol. 2: *1630–1800.* London, 1996.

Overton, Mark. *Agricultural Revolution in England: The Transformation of the Agrarian Economy, 1500–1850.* Cambridge, U.K., 1996.

Scott, Tom, ed. *The Peasantries of Europe from the Fourteenth to the Eighteenth Centuries.* London, 1998.

Turner, Michael. "English Open Fields and Enclosures: Retardation or Productivity Improvements." *Journal of Economic History* 46, no. 3 (1986): 669–692.

Vardi, Liana. *The Land and the Loom: Peasants and Profit in Northern France, 1680–1800.* Durham, N.C., 1993.

Wrigley, E. A. *Poverty, Progress, and Population.* Cambridge, U.K., 2004.

LIANA VARDI

gration of local markets and a new willingness of farmers to exploit commercial opportunities provided the impetus for innovation and enterprise which led to the agricultural revolution. (Overton, p. 207)

See also **Industrial Revolution, First; Industrial Revolution, Second; Landed Elites; Peasants.**

BIBLIOGRAPHY

Allen, Robert C. "Agriculture during the Industrial Revolution, 1700–1850." In *The Cambridge Economic History of Modern Britain.* Vol. 1: *Industrialisation, 1700–1860,* edited by Roderick Floud and Paul Johnson, 96–116. Cambridge, U.K., 2004.

Chorley, G. P. H. "The Agricultural Revolution in Northern Europe, 1750–1880: Nitrogen, Legumes, and Crop Productivity." *Economic History Review,* 2nd series, 34, no. 1 (1981): 71–93.

AGRICULTURE. *See* Agricultural Revolution; Peasants.

AIRPLANES. The emergence of the airplane, an aircraft capable of powered, controlled flight, marked one of the most revolutionary advances in human civilization. Dreams of true flight abound throughout history, ranging from the story of Daedalus and Icarus, through the notions of Leonardo da Vinci (1452–1519), to the literary fantasies of Jules Verne in the nineteenth century, but it was not until the Wright brothers actually achieved and then demonstrated controlled, powered flight in 1903 that it became a reality. Since then airplanes have radically changed the world, hugely curtailing continental and global traveling times, altering the speed of cultural interaction, and revolutionizing the face of warfare.

Flight in balloons had been a reality since the time of the Montgolfier brothers (Joseph-Michel and Jacques-Étienne) in the late eighteenth century, but balloons were too often at the mercy of the vagaries of the weather. Gas-filled airships, directionally powered by engines, offered a partial solution and for a few decades (1890s to 1930s) rivaled the airplane for mastery of the skies. Indeed, the earliest airships predated the airplane, but ultimately they proved to be too costly, cumbersome, and dangerous to provide a long-term challenge. Certainly in military terms, once the vulnerability of the inflammable hydrogen-filled airship had been demonstrated, the faster and nimbler airplane became dominant. Nevertheless, the airship remained viable until airplanes became large enough to carry heavy payloads.

Thoughtful and scientific approaches to the conquest of the air date back well into the nineteenth century, when a series of intrepid innovators, adventurers, and scientists began the first efforts to develop powered and controlled flight. The British air enthusiast Sir George Cayley (1773–1857) pioneered fixed-wing gliders in the early-to-mid nineteenth century but could not overcome the problem of how to power his flights. Steam power, the marvel of the Victorian age, seemed to offer a line of development, and some short flights of a few dozen yards were managed in the final quarter of the century. However, the necessary weight of steam-powered engines precluded their effective employment in aircraft.

By the 1890s the new petrol-fired internal combustion engine appeared to be a more likely source of adding power to the growing body of glider-based knowledge provided by the work of Otto Lilienthal (1848–1896); he conducted over two thousand glider flights before being killed in 1896. His work was picked up in Britain by Percy Pilcher (1866–1899), who patented a design for a glider powered by a petrol engine in the same year. Pilcher may have been on the point of success, but was killed in a glider accident in 1899. The way was now open for the Wright brothers.

POWERED, CONTROLLED FLIGHT
In Dayton, Ohio, Orville and Wilbur Wright had been following the work of Lilienthal and integrating it with their own experiments and ideas. On 17 December 1903 in the Kill Devil Hills, near Kitty Hawk, North Carolina, Orville piloted the Wright Flyer for the first powered, controlled, and sustained flight, in the first instance for a period of twelve seconds, in front of witnesses. There was no immediate acclamation or media furor; in fact, the event was first reported in the journal *Gleanings in Bee Culture*. The first attempts by the Wrights to sell their idea to the military for $200,000 faltered due to skepticism; the U.S. military had invested $50,000 in Samuel Langley's (1834–1906) plans for a viable aircraft and this had come to nothing. Foreign governments also lacked enthusiasm, and the Wrights retreated to Ohio to fine-tune their ideas, not flying between October 1905 and May 1908.

In Europe, French experiments led the way with powered gliding and development of the most powerful lightweight aero-engine yet in 1905. By 1908 Henri Farman had managed to stay aloft for thirty minutes, but all was put into perspective when Wilbur Wright appeared in Europe in August 1908 and promptly demonstrated how far behind the Europeans were. The Wrights had made considerable technical progress, and flights of over three hours across eighty miles were now possible. The era of the airplane had arrived.

Interest in flight, airplanes, and airships grew enormously, fueled by the growth in "air mindedness," itself driven by air shows, literature (most obviously that of the novelist H. G. Wells [1866–1946]), and the development of air leagues. Air power and the emergence of flight as a reality was one of the wonders of the age, and its impact on strategy and war was obvious. Indeed, Lord Northcliffe (Alfred Charles William Harmsworth), the newspaper baron, proclaimed that Britain was no longer an island after Louis Blériot flew across the English Channel in 1909.

MILITARY IMPLICATIONS
The military implications of powered, controlled flight were apparent, though it should be remembered that this was still an emerging science and technology, and many military leaders were rightly skeptical about what airplanes could realistically achieve in the short term. Nevertheless, they were open minded enough to begin investigating how airplanes might be integrated in military affairs.

Hélène Dutrieu, pioneering aviator. She made her first solo flight in France in 1909 and went on to set many altitude and distance records. ©BETTMANN/CORBIS

Despite the lead offered to the United States by the Wrights, it was in Europe, especially France, that the leading air powers developed in the years before the outbreak of World War I. Governments across Europe quickly established air elements in their armed forces, usually seeing reconnaissance and observation as the likely roles for airplanes in future conflicts. Aircraft, however, were used for combat and not just for observation during Italy's campaigns against the Turks in Libya in 1911 and 1912. Airplanes dropped explosives on enemy positions, presaging the mass destruction from the air that was to follow, most obviously in World War II.

Nevertheless, there were severe limitations on the capabilities of airplanes in the years leading up to World War I. They were flimsy, unreliable, and dangerous and were unable to carry heavy offensive weaponry or payloads; even for reconnaissance they were of limited value, as there were no suitable air-to-ground communications devices available in 1914. Airplanes had nonetheless indicated their potential and, powered by the demands of World War I, by 1918 many of the key roles and capabilities now associated with air power had been established.

See also **Science and Technology.**

BIBLIOGRAPHY

Buckley, John. *Air Power in the Age of Total War.* London, 1999.

Crouch, Tom. *A Dream of Wings: Americans and the Airplane, 1875–1905.* Washington, D.C., 1981.

Jakab, Peter L. *Visions of a Flying Machine: The Wright Brothers and the Process of Invention.* Washington, D.C., 1997.

Morrow, John Howard. *The Great War in the Air: Military Aviation from 1909 to 1921.* Washington, D.C., 1993.

JOHN BUCKLEY

ALBANIA. Albania was the last nation-state to emerge from the Ottoman Empire in the years before World War I. As with the other states, however, its emergence would not have been possible without the interference of the Great Powers.

The Albanians were late in the nationalist process for two reasons. The first was that the nation was divided. There were two main linguistic groups, the Ghegs in the north and the Tosks in the south; and there were three main religious communities, with 70 percent of the population being Muslim, 20 percent Orthodox Christian, and 10 percent, mostly in the north, Roman Catholic. In addition to these divisions there were intense clan or tribal loyalties, especially in the north, which impeded the emergence of any unified national movement. The second reason was that the Ottoman administration allowed the Albanians a number of privileges, particularly the right to carry arms and to be exempt from conscription and from many taxes. In return, the small Albanian intelligentsia remained loyal to the sultan for most of the nineteenth century.

When nationalist quickening came it was caused not by the Ottoman government but by its enemies. In the great Eastern Crisis of 1875–1881, the Slav states of Serbia and Montenegro both received additional territory. Both states had aspirations on areas inhabited by Albanians, and worried Albanian intellectuals met in Prizrend in 1878 to state Albanian claims to nationhood. This first statement of Albanian national pretensions had little immediate impact. Although it encouraged education in Albanian, there was, for example, no agreement on a standard Albanian literary language.

The next and decisive assertion of Albanian national feelings came after the Young Turk revolution and the Austro-Hungarian annexation of Bosnia-Herzegovina in 1908. The consequences of the first angered the Albanians, and the second transformed the European diplomatic situation and eventually brought the Albanian question to the center of the international political arena. The Young Turks wished to centralize and modernize their extensive domains. This meant an end to Albanian privileges, and the imposition of greater central authority involved conscription, taxation, and restrictions on the right to carry arms. The Albanians objected. In the summer of 1909 in the mountainous areas of the north, there were outbreaks of violence directed against agents of the central government; twenty thousand Ottoman troops were brought in to contain the discontent. Their ruthlessness ensured that the outbursts were repeated with more force in 1910. The situation was even more tense in 1911 because this time the Albanian intelligentsia joined the northern clansmen and gave the rising a political agenda. This demanded recognition of the Albanians as a separate nation, and virtual self-government for Albania, which, for the first time, was given a territorial definition; it covered the Ottoman *vilayets* (provinces) of Scutari (Shkoder), Yanina, Monastir (Bitola), and Kosovo.

By 1911 changes in the international situation brought about by the Austro-Hungarian annexation of Bosnia had an impact on Albania. From 1897 to 1908 Russia and Austria-Hungary had agreed to cooperate to contain crises in the Balkans. In 1908 the Russians believed they had not been consulted about the annexation and were frightened that the Habsburgs intended to expand into the Balkans and toward Salonika. There was no such intention, but Russia, given its enfeebled state after the Russo-Japanese war and the Revolution of 1905, was in no position to assert itself. It therefore welcomed signs that Bulgaria and Serbia appeared willing to bury their many hatchets and conclude an alliance. In the first half of 1912, this alliance was expanded into the Balkan League of Bulgaria, Greece, Montenegro, and Serbia. The Russians convinced themselves that the League was an anti-Austrian defensive alliance. In fact, it was an aggressive combination that intended to partition the Ottoman Empire in Europe.

This was the Albanians' worst nightmare. They had revolted against Ottoman centralism, but par-

Albanian refugees. A 1912 photograph shows Albanians who have fled to Montenegro to escape Turkish forces during the Balkan Wars. ©BETTMANN/CORBIS

tition of the Albanian lands between Serbia, Montenegro, and Greece would end any hope of saving Albanian autonomy or securing independence. Austria too was concerned by the new diplomatic alignment in the Balkans.

Matters came to a head in the summer of 1912. Yet again the Albanians revolted and this time they drove the Ottoman administration out of the center of the Balkans. Vienna intervened with a diplomatic initiative aimed at forcing the Ottomans to reform their empire. Reform of the empire with the backing of the Great Powers was the last thing the Balkan states wanted; it would end their chances of partitioning the Ottoman lands. In October, before Austria's initiative could come to fruition, the Balkan League went to war with the empire. The war was spectacularly successful and by the end of the year the Ottomans

had been driven out of almost all their European territories.

The Great Powers now intervened. A conference of belligerents was convened in London. The Balkan states and the Ottomans were told that they could regulate the peace subject to a number of conditions. One of them was that an independent Albania must emerge from the settlement.

Albanian political leaders had declared independence on 28 November 1912. The boundaries of the state, together with its basic political structure, were to be defined by the ambassadors of the Great Powers in London. Austria-Hungary was the main defender of the new state, aiming to make it as extensive as possible so as to limit Serbian expansion. Russia backed the Serbs. The discussions were conducted against a background of renewed fighting in the Balkans, part of which involved

Montenegrin forces besieging Scutari, which fell when its Ottoman commander, an ethnic Albanian, sold it to the Montenegrins in April 1913. Further problems arose through Serbian intrigues in the new state and through Greek attempts to secure a slice of southern Albania. International commissions finally delimited the frontiers. The ambassadors decided that Albania should become a hereditary principality and elected Prince Wilhelm zu Wied (r. 1914) as its first head of state. However, he failed to establish any central authority and fled soon after the outbreak of World War I.

See also **Balkan Wars; Eastern Question; Greece; Montenegro; Ottoman Empire; Serbia; Young Turks.**

BIBLIOGRAPHY

Durham, Edith. *High Albania.* Boston, 1985. Originally published in 1909 and a classic portrait of northern Albania.

Malcolm, Noel. *Kosovo: A Short History.* New York, 1998.

Skendi, Stavro. *The Albanian National Awakening, 1878–1912.* Princeton, N.J., 1967. Essential.

Swire, Joseph. *Albania: The Rise of a Kingdom.* London, 1929. Contains a great deal of carefully researched detail.

RICHARD CRAMPTON

ALCOHOL AND TEMPERANCE.

Between 1789 and 1914, alcohol production and consumption became one of the most controversial questions throughout Europe and was deeply intertwined with economic, social, and political life. Alcohol was one of the first mass-produced consumer commodities, and drinking establishments became a favored site of leisure and recreation in the dawning age of urban industrial society. The dynamics of the "drink question," as it came to be known, varied widely across Europe due to such variables as class, gender, nation, region, and climate. By the start of World War I in 1914 consumption rates had peaked, temperance movements had waned, and government regulation had increased. By the 1920s, the advent of new forms of mass leisure—movie theaters especially, but also home entertainment (radios and phonographs) and the growing use of the car for recreation—steadily diminished the

importance of the public drinking establishment. In short, the years between the French Revolution of 1789 and World War I formed a coherent period: a golden age of public drinking and sociability or a dark era of intemperance and debauchery, depending on one's perspective.

The traditional image of Europe divided into the northern immoderate imbiber of spirits and the southern moderate wine drinker was largely sustained but nevertheless underwent some important modifications. The "traditional" image had become especially prevalent during the eighteenth century, when various forms of distilled spirits such as gin (created in Holland but particularly popular in the United Kingdom), aquavit (in Sweden), schnapps (in Germany), and vodka (in Russia) became pervasive across northern Europe. Southern Europe, in contrast, aside from homemade wine distillers—known in France as *boulleurs de cru*—never saw its wine cultures challenged by distilled spirits. Before unification in 1871, the various regions that would become Germany had distinctively different drinking cultures that overlapped these northern and southern distinctions. Southern and western Germany were primarily areas of wine and beer consumption, while the north and the east, especially Prussia, preferred spirits.

In general, these northern nations experienced first a rise in heavy drinking between the 1720s and the 1750s, then a decline into the early nineteenth century, followed by a steady rise across the rest of the century, in both spirit and beer consumption. Britain led the world in beer production for most of the century, to be surpassed in the 1880s by Germany, which in turn would be superseded by the United States on the eve of World War I. Some of the most dramatic changes in production and consumption patterns occurred in France and the Austrian (later Austro-Hungarian) Empire. The long tradition of moderate wine drinking in these states was shaken, especially in the case of France, first by a dramatic rise in wine consumption and then, after the 1870s (when diseases and bacteria devastated its harvests), in spirit consumption, especially the highly potent absinthe. In the case of Austria-Hungary, spirit and beer consumption challenged wine but did not cause major problems or controversies compared to the rest of northern Europe. While Russia saw the apex of its per capita

The Housekeeper, from Silhouettes **by Honoré Daumier, c. 1870.** Daumier's caricature shows a wily housekeeper surreptitiously sampling her employers' wine. ©CHRIS HELLIER/ CORBIS

alcohol consumption in the 1860s, consumption peaked in England and Germany in the 1870s and 1880s, respectively, and France reached its zenith early in the twentieth century. In the first decade of the twentieth century Denmark led all European nations in consumption, followed by France, Germany, Sweden, the United Kingdom, Norway and Russia. Overall per capita alcohol consumption in Europe doubled between the French Revolution and World War I.

Government regulation of all facets of the drink industry steadily grew across the century. Although rural production of wine and spirits in France and Russia remained obscure, government regulation and taxation steadily became more refined and accurate. A wide variety of regulatory systems emerged. Naturally, governments continued to use increases or decreases in taxation as a means of inhibiting or encouraging the consumption of various drinks. As guild restrictions declined and the doctrine of freedom of commerce gained steam,

regulations on drinking establishments lessened in the early nineteenth century. To stem a renewed gin binge, the United Kingdom deregulated beer retail licensing in the 1830s, and the number of beer shops soared and gin consumption declined. Until the 1850s and then after the 1870s, France also had an unregulated system of drink retailing. Both these nations saw dramatic increases in the number of drinking establishments. In the United Kingdom, the total number of drink retailers jumped from 49,000 in 1809 to 120,000 in 1869, while in France the number climbed, though periodically interrupted by political revolutions and repressions, from around one hundred thousand on the eve of the French Revolution to around five hundred thousand prior to World War I. Not surprisingly, in both countries as temperance movements developed so did associations to defend the wholesale and retail trade in drink. The French alcohol industry had the easier task, because the temperance movement in this wine-producing nation developed later and more slowly than in other nations in part because of the status of wine as a national icon. Indeed, in France wine was considered a "hygienic drink."

One of the most notable alternatives to laissez-faire developed in Sweden during the 1860s. In 1865 the seaport and factory town of Göteborg (Gothenburg), created a system of "disinterested" alcohol sales. This "Gothenburg system" allowed managers and/or owners of restaurants and retail stores to realize only 5 percent profit, with any additional profit going to the local or national government. In addition, on-premise alcohol consumption was allowed only with the sale of meals. The system's advocates in Sweden and around the world, especially in England, argued that it was an attractive alternative to either outright prohibition or a liberal licensing policy that encouraged a drink proprietor to increase consumption to increase profits. Russia instituted a somewhat similar system after the 1894 implementation of the vodka monopoly that limited sales to government-run shops. Although agitation for temperance had developed early in the United Kingdom and also in Germany at the end of the century, prohibition would first be enacted by Iceland (1915), Norway (1916), and Finland (1919).

Temperance movements developed out of a complex set of interacting motives: social control, social mobility, reform, revolution, and feminism.

The modern impetus for temperance dates from the Protestant Reformation in Germany. Although Swedish Lutheran clergy first began temperance organization in 1818, the movement had its heart in the British Isles among Evangelicals and dissenters. The great antislavery crusader William Wilberforce and the influential moralist of domestic life Hannah Moore, in the early London suburb of Clapham, were important precursors to the teetotal movement. The term *teetotal* dates from an 1833 anti-drink rally at which Richard Turner, a worker and reformed drunkard, coined the term to denote his repudiation of all drink (not just spirits, as had been the case with most earlier temperance advocates). The first nationwide teetotal organization was the British Association for the Promotion of Temperance (1835). In later decades this group modified its name and cooperated with the most influential prohibitionist organization, the United Kingdom Alliance (UKA), to form the National Temperance Federation (1883). Alongside, and competing with, the UKA was the Church of England Temperance Society (1873), one of the largest private associations in late nineteenth-century Britain. Its strategy of licensing restriction would eventually triumph, in the early twentieth century, over prohibition. British women were influential at all stages and in all facets of the movement, from encouraging sailors to abstain to creating the Salvation Army, the British Women's Temperance Association, and, ultimately, the YWCA. The sheer diversity of the British teetotal effort, as compared to the most unified efforts in the Scandinavian nations, best explains the geography of prohibitionist success. One of the most dramatic (though short-lived) temperance campaigns was that of Father Theobald Matthew, whose abstinence crusade in Ireland during the early 1840s persuaded upward of half of the population to take a total abstinence pledge.

The labor and socialist movements had an ambivalent relationship with both drink sellers and the temperance movement. In Britain, the Chartist movement of the 1830s and 1840s, in its attempt to democratize the British political system, walked a fine line between temperance and drink cultures. Although Chartists advocated temperance, they let local chapters organize and socialize in beer halls and pubs. In France, a tradition of militant grassroots politics developed in working

Hungarian anti-alcohol placard, c. 1900–1914. This poster, created by the Hungarian Worker's Union, warns that the "poison of alcohol brings dullness and poverty." CHRISTEL GERSTENBERG/CORBIS

class cafés, reaching its apogee during and immediately after the 1848 revolution. The ruling classes, fearing cafes as sites of sedition, closed roughly sixty thousand shops between 1849 and 1853, with the total number falling from 350,000 to 290,000 during that period. Repression, though not on the same overt scale, occurred in the new German Empire between 1878 and 1890, when Bismarck attempted to ban the Social Democratic Party. By the 1890s, when the German socialist movement, like similar movements across Europe, had gained full civil and political rights, a lively debate emerged as to whether the movement should continue to secretly use drinking establishments for their meetings. In short, could temperance and sociability be combined? Most socialist and working class movements before World War I were able to combine these contrasting temperance and sociable elements without much trouble.

By end of the century, temperance took on a more international and scientific scope. Many of these organizations were founded or inspired by American temperance groups. For example, the Good Templars (founded in 1851) came to the United Kingdom in the early 1870s and to Sweden later. The Blue Ribbon movement, which awarded these symbols to its followers as a proof of abstinence, crossed the Atlantic in the late 1870s. Finally, the Woman's Christian Temperance Union, based in Evanston, Illinois, helped organize the World's Woman's Christian Temperance Union in 1884. In the following year, the first in a series of international temperance congresses was held at Antwerp; fourteen more would be held by the start of World War I. Doctors became prominent at these congresses and helped diffuse and develop the disease concept of alcoholism, which was first enunciated by the Swedish doctor Magnus Huss in the 1850s and developed into theories of alcoholic degeneration in the succeeding decades by research scientists such as Benedict Morel in France and August Forel in Switzerland. The Berlin Congress in 1885 in essence divided the African continent between European powers and also raised the question of alcohol's role in the slave trade in Africa. Two years later in England a new voluntary association emerged: the United Committee for the Prevention of the Demoralization of the Native Races by the Liquor Traffic. This group, supported by the British government, launched subsequent attempts at conventions in Brussels between 1890 and 1912 to prohibit the importation or production of alcohol in European colonies in Africa. Finally, by 1909 a World Prohibition Federation had emerged, inspired by the prohibitionist Scandinavian efforts. The onset of World War I brought reduced alcohol production in all nations. In the most immediate and dramatic fashion the French banned absinthe and the Russians vodka.

See also **Absinthe; Phylloxera; Public Health; Wine.**

BIBLIOGRAPHY

Barrows, Susanna, and Robin Room, eds. *Drinking: Behavior and Beliefs in Modern History.* Berkeley, Calif., 1991.

Brennan, Thomas. "Drinking and Drugs." In *Encyclopedia of European Social History from 1350 to 2000*, vol. 5, edited by Peter N. Stearns, 89–101. New York, 2001.

Gutzke, David W. *Protecting the Pub: Brewers and Publicans against Temperance.* Woodbridge, Suffolk, U.K., 1989.

Haine, W. Scott. *The World of the Paris Café: Sociability among the French Working Class, 1789–1914.* Baltimore, Md., 1996.

Harrison, Brian. *Drink and the Victorians: The Temperance Question in England, 1815–1872.* London, 1971.

Snow, George. "Alcohol and Temperance." In *Encyclopedia of European Social History from 1350 to 2000*, vol. 3, edited by Peter N. Stearns, 483–496. New York, 2001.

Tyrell, Ian. *Woman's World/Woman's Empire: The Woman's Christian Temperance Union in International Perspective, 1880–1930.* Chapel Hill, N.C., 1991.

SCOTT HAINE

ALEXANDER I (1777–1825; ruled 1801–1825), emperor of Russia.

At his birth on 23 December (12 December, old style) 1777, Alexander was removed from his parents—the future emperor Paul I (r. 1796–1801) and the Grand Duchess Maria Fyodorovna—by his grandmother, the reigning empress Catherine II (r. 1762–1796). He was an impressionable youth and eagerly absorbed the writings chosen for him by his tutor, Frédéric-César de la Harpe, a Swiss republican. At the same time, the young Alexander was influenced by his visits to the military maneuvers organized by Paul at his establishment at Gatchina. It has been claimed that this is when Alexander learned the art of dissimulation as he had to please both his grandmother and father. Alexander certainly suffered from moments of self-doubt during his reign, but this does not mean that he was either weak or fundamentally inconsistent in his aims and principles. He came to the throne in March 1801, following the assassination of his father, an event that haunted him the rest of his life.

Alexander's foreign policy underwent various shifts, but he was consistent in his belief that Russia had a key role to play in Europe. This led him to propose an ambitious scheme to Britain in 1804 that the two countries should together determine a settlement for Europe. When this was rejected, Alexander became a major player in the formation of the Third Coalition against Napoleon I. Alexander took part in the battle, and defeat, of Austerlitz in 1805, and was fortunate to escape capture. He had to come to terms with Napoleon at the Treaties of Tilsit in 1807. The invasion of Russia by Napoleonic forces in 1812 presented Alexander with the greatest test of his reign, during which he underwent a spiritual experience. Alexander remained steadfast in his refusal to negotiate with Napoleon after the occupation of Moscow in 1812. The Russian invasion was the turning point in the Napoleonic Wars. Russia played a leading role in the victorious Fourth Coalition against France, and Alexander led the triumphant Russian troops into Paris in March 1814. The subsequent Congress of Vienna (1814–1815) was dominated by Russian ambitions and reflected Russia's newfound strength. Not only did Russia acquire new territory (the Congress Kingdom of Poland was formally joined to Russia through the person of the tsar), but Alexander was also able to force almost all other major European powers to adhere to his vision of Europe as expressed in the Holy Alliance, a union of rulers who would maintain order and peace through the application of Christian principles. Alexander continued to play a significant role in European congresses between 1818 and 1822.

Alexander expressed interest in social and political reform throughout his reign. He had a personal abhorrence for serfdom and praised the merits of constitutionalism (to Thomas Jefferson, among others). In the early years of his reign, he encouraged discussion of social and political reform by a group of radical young friends, known as the "Unofficial Committee." He later commissioned plans for constitutional reform by Mikhail Speransky and then Nikolai Novosiltsev. Proposals for the introduction of representative institutions became linked with the question of the rights of serfs, but Alexander also commissioned separate plans for the abolition of serfdom. Alexander introduced a constitution into the Congress Kingdom of Poland and abolished serfdom in the Baltic provinces. But Alexander was always protective of his own power and reluctant to allow any other institution to limit his freedom of action. He could not risk alienating the Russian nobility by abolishing serfdom against their wishes. Alexander was also conscious of the backwardness of Russia compared with other central and western European countries, and with western and non-Russian areas of the empire, and

came to the conclusion that Russia was insufficiently mature for constitutional experiments. Revolts in the Italian and Iberian Peninsulas after 1820, and what he perceived as the obstructiveness of the Polish diet, also made him less certain that constitutions ensured the peaceful and orderly rule that he had sought for both Russia and other European countries.

The Napoleonic Wars transformed Russia's great-power status and established her as the dominant military power in continental Europe. Domestically, however, Alexander did not implement any major social or political reforms. It was the contrast between Russia's newfound international status and the perceived stagnation domestically at a time of fundamental changes elsewhere that was at the root of the rising discontent among young, educated, radical Russians and that led to the formation of secret societies in the last years of Alexander's reign, and then an abortive attempt at an uprising (known as the Decembrist revolt) following his death on 1 December (19 November, old style) 1825.

See also **Austerlitz; Congress of Vienna; French Revolutionary Wars and Napoleonic Wars; Russia; Speransky, Mikhail.**

BIBLIOGRAPHY

Hartley, Janet M. *Alexander I.* London, 1994.

McConnell, Allen. *Tsar Alexander I: Paternalistic Reformer.* New York, 1970.

Palmer, Alan. *Alexander I: Tsar of War and Peace.* London, 1974.

JANET HARTLEY

ALEXANDER II (1818–1881; ruled 1855–1881), emperor of Russia.

Alexander II came to the Russian throne on the death of his father, Nicholas I (r. 1825–1855), in the middle of the Crimean War (1853–1856). Born on 29 April (17 April, old style) 1818, he was the oldest of seven children and had been brought up in the military tradition that was central to the life of both his father and grandfather, Paul I (r. 1796–1801). The immediate problem that faced the new emperor was Russia's poor performance in the Crimean War: British and French forces were inflicting a heavy defeat on Russia, made all the more humiliating because the war was taking place on Russian territory. The peace terms in the Treaty of Paris of 1856 represented a significant setback for Russia, but were not as harsh as they could have been. The new emperor's success in ending the war provided Alexander II with the springboard to introduce the most far-reaching set of reforms that Russia had experienced since Peter the Great's reign 150 years earlier.

Alexander II and his advisers were very aware of the symbolic impact of military defeat on Russia as a whole. During Nicholas I's reign, Russia had been seen as the preeminent European military power, and the outcome of the Crimean War forced a reevaluation of the foundations upon which Russian power had been built. Between 1861 and 1874, Alexander II implemented a set of reforms that reshaped Russian society. The most important reform was the emancipation of the serfs in 1861, which changed the legal status of the majority of the Russian population. The abolition of serfdom had important implications for other areas of policy as it established the freed peasantry as full members of Russian society. Local government was fundamentally reformed by the introduction in 1864 of zemstvos, elected local councils in the countryside, and this was followed in 1870 by the establishment of elected urban councils. The legal system underwent a fundamental overhaul in 1864 with the introduction of trial by jury, the establishment of an independent judiciary, and the creation of a court system with clear lines of appeal. Education also underwent reform: the secondary school curriculum was broadened to allow greater study of scientific subjects, and greater autonomy was given to universities. In 1874 a major military reform introduced a system of conscription aimed at creating a more professional army, and this was accompanied by improvements to military education.

The emperor personally supported these reforms, but Alexander II's enthusiasm for reform waned during the second half of his reign. An assassination attempt in 1866 shook him, and he began to have doubts about the wisdom of making reform because it appeared to have provoked opposition to the tsarist regime, rather than ensuring universal support for the emperor and his govern-

ment. The number of revolutionaries that emerged during Alexander II's reign was small, but they had a disproportionate influence. Opposition was intensified by the government's treatment of non-Russian nationalities in the growing empire. During Alexander II's reign, Russia expanded its empire in central Asia, bringing significant numbers of Muslims into the Russian state. In 1863 a rebellion in the Polish provinces of the empire was put down with great force by the Russian regime, and in Ukraine action was taken to stem the growth of separatist tendencies. In Europe, Russia recovered its confidence in the aftermath of the Crimean War, and the waning power of the Ottoman Empire encouraged Alexander II to test Russia's strength in the Balkans. After claims of Turkish ill-treatment of the Serbs and Bulgars, Russia declared war on Turkey in 1877, setting off the last of the Russo-Turkish Wars. Russia was victorious and at San Stefano imposed a peace treaty on Turkey that was extremely favorable to Russia. The other European powers objected strongly to this growth in Russian power, and at the 1878 Congress of Berlin subjected Russia to a diplomatic humiliation by putting a check on Russia's expansionist plans.

Alexander II's last years were a time of turmoil. His wife, the empress Maria, died in 1880; six weeks later the emperor married his long-time companion, Catherine Dolgorukova. The international reversals after the Russo-Turkish War were matched by renewed discontent at home and a series of assassination attempts on the emperor's life. Alexander II was persuaded that further reform was the best way to stem opposition and to restore social cohesion to the empire. Count Mikhail Loris-Melikov, the minister of the interior, persuaded Alexander that he should introduce a consultative national assembly to advise the emperor on legislation. On 13 March (1 March, O.S.) 1881, the very day that the emperor was to sign this decree into law, he was driving through St. Petersburg when a terrorist threw a bomb at his carriage. Alexander II was critically injured and died a few hours later in the Winter Palace with his family around him.

See also **Alexander III; Crimean War; Great Reforms (Russia); Russia; Russo-Turkish War; Serfs, Emancipation of.**

BIBLIOGRAPHY

Eklof, Ben, John Bushnell, and Larissa Zakharova, eds. *Russia's Great Reforms, 1855–1881.* Bloomington, Ind., 1994.

Zakharova, Larissa G. "Emperor Alexander II, 1855–1881." In *The Emperors and Empresses of Russia,* edited by Donald J. Raleigh, 294–333. Armonk, N.Y., 1996.

PETER WALDRON

ALEXANDER III (1845–1894; ruled 1881–1894), emperor of Russia.

Alexander III reigned as Russian tsar at a time of great change for the country. He ascended to the throne in 1881 after terrorists assassinated his father, Tsar Alexander II, and died before the age of fifty, leaving the country to his son, Nicholas II, the last Russian tsar, in 1894. The thirteen years of Alexander III's reign were characterized by political reaction, in particular an almost complete crushing of the Russian revolutionary movement. Alexander also pursued policies of "Russification," that is, enhancing the role of Russian culture and the Russian central government throughout the diverse multinational Russian Empire. At the same time, it was during his reign that Russia began to industrialize rapidly, a process that would continue after his death. Alexander's reign was thus one of contradictions, of reactionary policies and the growth of the Russian economy, of a major famine in 1891 and the growth of Russian cities.

Born in 1845, the second son of Alexander II, Alexander never expected to become tsar. Physically he was a bear of a man, big, square-built, with an impressive beard. Despite his aristocratic bloodlines, Alexander preferred family life to court ceremonies, simple fare to fancy dishes, and Russian vodka to French wines. While no intellectual, the future tsar held firm beliefs in family, religion, and Russia. Alexander feared that the reforms of his father's reign had gone too far—and when radicals succeeded in killing his father, his conservative views were only strengthened.

Profoundly shocked by his father's assassination, Alexander III rapidly changed political course away from his father's semiliberal concessions. His was a policy of strict and consistent conservatism, aiming to limit the role of the public in governance, and striking hard at any sign of political radicalism. His father's assassins were hunted down and executed, including one young woman. The reforms in local government introduced by his father in cities and rural areas were scaled back, limiting participation to more well-to-do elements and favoring the nobility.

Alexander III's reign is remembered as a dark one for non-Russians. During the spring and summer of 1881, anti-Jewish attacks or pogroms broke out in the southwest (Ukrainian) provinces of the empire. While scholarship since the 1970s has shown that the government did not sponsor or encourage these pogroms, Alexander's open anti-Semitism did not reassure Russia's Jewish community. Alexander once famously remarked, "When they beat the Jews, one's heart rejoices." He then added, "It cannot, however, be allowed." During Alexander's reign, a massive immigration wave of Jews from the Russian Empire began, especially to the United States and Britain.

Alexander felt no more affection for Poles or Germans than for Jews. In Russia's Polish provinces (including the city of Warsaw), government policy restricted the teaching of Polish and required bilingual (Polish and Russian) signs for shops and restaurants. In the empire's Baltic provinces, Alexander abolished many of the privileges of the German nobility, who had long ruled over Estonian and Latvian peasants. The German-language University of Dorpat (now Tartu, Estonia) was transformed into the Russian University of Yurev in 1893. Ironically, Alexander III's policies to weaken the German upper class in the Baltic area helped to strengthen Estonian and Latvian national movements there, though this was certainly not his intention.

Alexander III's reign also saw a major upswing in Russian industrialization. In the late 1880s and early 1890s Russia began to industrialize rapidly, with large industrial plants rising up in and around St. Petersburg, Moscow, Warsaw, and other areas. Under Alexander's gruff but brilliant minister of finance, Sergei Witte, Russia managed to secure foreign loans that propelled industrialization forward. Witte's policies also enabled Russia to go on the gold standard in 1897, enabling further economic growth.

In foreign policy, too, Alexander III's reign saw a major shift. For all his conservatism, Alexander hated militarism, particularly its German variety, perhaps in part because of the influence of his Danish-born wife. The growth of Germany's industrial and military might was of great concern for Russia. In 1893 Alexander signed a military convention with France, astonishing his contemporaries. The most conservative state in Europe thereby became a military ally of the liberal French Republic. The reason was clear: both France and Russia feared Germany and hoped that by banding together they would reduce the chance of German military aggression. This fateful alliance would be one of the many factors that brought all of Europe into war in August 1914.

See also **Alexander II; Nicholas II; Russia; Witte, Sergei.**

BIBLIOGRAPHY

Byrnes, Robert F. *Pobedonostsev: His Life and Thought.* Bloomington, Ind., 1968.

Kennan, George F. *The Fateful Alliance: France, Russia, and the Coming of the First World War.* New York, 1984.

Naimark, Norman M. *Terrorists and Social Democrats: The Russian Revolutionary Movement under Alexander III.* Cambridge, Mass., 1983.

Rogger, Hans. *Jewish Policies and Right-Wing Politics in Imperial Russia.* Berkeley and Los Angeles, 1986.

Von Laue, Theodore H. *Sergei Witte and the Industrialization of Russia.* New York, 1963.

THEODORE R. WEEKS

ALEXANDRA (1872–1918), empress of Russia.

Empress Alexandra Fyodorovna, wife of the last Romanov emperor of Russia, Nicholas II (r. 1894–1917), lived in revolutionary times fatally dangerous to a ruler with so little instinct for political self-preservation. Born in 1872 to Grand Duke Louis IV of the German principality of Hesse-Darmstadt and Princess Alice of England, she was left motherless at the age of six and grew up in Hesse-Darmstadt with close attention from her grandmother, Queen Victoria of England. Several prestigious matches were proposed to her in her youth, including one with the heir to the British throne. But she had met the young heir to the Russian throne at the age of fourteen and risked spinsterhood rather than give up her attachment to him, though his parents were initially no more enthusiastic about the match than was Queen Victoria. Acceptance of the match by their elders and an ardent proposal from Nicholas led at first to new reservations, as Alexandra would be obliged to give up her Lutheran faith for Russian Orthodoxy; but ultimately she opened the way for their marriage by converting wholeheartedly. They were married in 1894 and entered into a marriage and family life of emotional intimacy and warmth.

Yet Alexandra found it difficult to adapt to Romanov clan and court life, and was quickly overwhelmed by its complex partisan networks. She watched as her husband, newly anointed emperor yet ill-trained for leadership, struggled against the domination of other powerful Romanovs. Nicholas II's mother, Maria Fyodorovna, tended to compete with Alexandra rather than to mentor her in learning the duties of a Russian empress. As serious about Orthodoxy as she had once been about her Lutheran faith, Alexandra alienated many in the Russian court through her condemnation of some of its members as frivolous and immoral. These difficulties contributed to Alexandra's and Nicholas's growing isolation from clan, court, and high society as they retreated into private life. Other contributing factors were the births of four daughters, each a disappointment, because a male child was necessary to ensure the Romanov succession. A son, Alexis, was finally born in 1904; but the discovery that he had hemophilia, inherited through his mother from his grandmother Queen Victoria, led the royal family to withdraw even more as its members joined forces to preserve his health and to keep his illness secret from all but domestic intimates.

Alexandra allowed only a few outsiders into the family circle; noteworthy among these was the charismatic peasant Orthodox monk Grigory Rasputin. In the royal presence, Rasputin offered a spiritual counterpoint to what Alexandra experienced as the artificiality and corruption of Russia's capital, St. Petersburg. Despite his raucous and lascivious conduct elsewhere, he had a hypnotic calming effect on members of the royal family; this was invaluable to the young Alexis, whose hemophiliac bleeding episodes may have been worsened by anxiety and who made several striking recoveries after Rasputin's interventions. Rasputin also fed Alexandra's spiritual identity as the *Matyushka*, or mother of the Russian peasantry. She believed that the peasants were the true Russians, and that they loved her as she loved them, unlike the "false" Russians of St. Petersburg court and high society among whom she was unpopular.

The influence of Rasputin over Alexandra and the royal family circle might have had little historical impact but for two events: the Revolution of 1905 and the outbreak of World War I in 1914. The Revolution of 1905 brought into existence a system of elected Dumas, or parliaments, to which Nicholas and Alexandra, believing themselves chosen by God to rule Russia, found it impossible to fully reconcile themselves. World War I placed severe pressures on the Russian military, economy, and society, and Nicholas's leadership was widely questioned. In 1915 Nicholas chose to demonstrate his military commitment as emperor by ousting his powerful Romanov cousin Grand Duke Nicholas as head of the Russian army, and by departing St. Petersburg for military headquarters in the field. He left leadership of the country to Alexandra.

Alexandra was eager to exert power but oblivious to the political importance of the Duma as well as to the significance of the growing dissatisfaction and disorder across the empire. She enlisted Rasputin's aid in an attempt to bring the Duma under her control; together they created a highly unstable political environment by hiring and firing a series of cabinet ministers as they sought unquestioning personal loyalty. Their efforts led to a national uproar. Alexandra was believed to have excessive influence over the tsar and his policies. The involvement of Rasputin, by now notorious for his sexual proclivities, stained the reputation of the royal family; Alexandra herself was reputed to engage in sexual relations with him. She and Rasputin were also accused of conspiring in the interest of Russia's enemy, Germany. There is no evidence to support the former accusation, and little to support the latter.

As the events of the Russian Revolution of 1917 began to unfold, Alexandra and her family found themselves isolated, abandoned even by their own relatives. Nicholas's cousin Grand Duke Kirill withdrew the military battalion protecting them and joined the revolution, then declared himself head of the Romanov family, while another cousin, King George V of England, refused to accept them in Great Britain as refugees. Following Nicholas's abdication on 15 March 1917, the royal family was held at Tsarskoye Selo (now Pushkin) for several months, then transferred under guard first to Tobolsk, and finally to Yekaterinburg. Alexandra, Nicholas, and their five children were killed by members of the Bolshevik secret police in Yekaterinburg on the night of 16–17 July 1918.

See also **Nicholas II.**

BIBLIOGRAPHY

Primary Sources

Alexandra, Empress. *Letters of the Tsaritsa to the Tsar, 1914–1916.* Introduction by Bernard Pares. London, 1923. Reprint, Westport, Conn., 1979.

Kozlov, Vladimir A., and Vladimir M. Khrustalev, eds. *The Last Diary of Tsaritsa Alexandra.* New Haven, Conn., 1997.

Steinberg, Mark D., and Vladimir M. eds. *The Fall of the Romanovs: Political Dreams and Personal Struggles in a Time of Revolution.* Russian documents translated by Elizabeth Tucker. New Haven, Conn., 1995.

Secondary Sources

Erickson, Carolly. *Alexandra: The Last Tsarina.* New York, 2001.

Ferro, Marc. *Nicholas II: Last of the Tsars.* Translated by Brian Pearce. New York, 1993.

Massie, Robert K. *Nicholas and Alexandra.* New York, 1967.

Radzinsky, Edvard. *The Last Tsar: The Life and Death of Nicholas II.* Translated by Marian Schwartz. New York, 1992.

BARBARA WALKER

ALGERIA. In 1800 what is now northern Algeria was an Ottoman province—known as the Regency of Algiers—one of three regencies created after the Ottoman conquest of the area in the fifteenth century. The regencies were initially administered by an Ottoman pasha (provincial governor), but Ottoman power weakened over the ensuing three centuries creating economic and political changes. Simultaneous to the decline in political power was a decline in the profitability of Algerian privateering, once an important source of income for both the Algerian regency and the government of the empire. These two processes undermined Ottoman institutions, and in Algiers the Ottoman pasha was replaced by an Algerian dignitary, the dey. At first the dey was elected by a council, or divan, the majority of whose members were Janissaries (elite Turkish soldiers). By 1800, however, the divan was no longer an Ottoman bastion but comprised an oligarchy whose interests lay in supporting the dey. Although Algeria was still an Ottoman province as the nineteenth century began, Ottoman authority there was weak. The European powers, in particular France and Britain, had started their encroachment into the area. Economic ties between France and the regency had developed during the eighteenth century, and by the end of the century Algiers was supplying grain to the south of France and to the Napoleonic armies in Italy.

Relations with the European powers may have developed differently had the first three decades of the nineteenth century not been characterized by economic and political upheavals that greatly undermined the regency's strength. The area had always been subject to sporadic revolts, particularly by the mountain-dwelling Kabyles, but the major rebellion that broke out in the rural areas at the beginning of the nineteenth century, led by the tribal elites and religious brotherhoods, destabilized the central government. To the political turmoil was added the misery of disease and economic hardship. Bubonic plague ravaged the countryside from 1793 to 1799 and again in 1815. Cholera and smallpox also took their toll. Harvest failures and locusts jeopardized grain exports, caused economic uncertainty, and created shortages in the countryside. Hungry peasants either joined the revolts or moved into urban areas in search of improved economic conditions. The influx of rural dwellers into urban areas created added economic and political tensions.

In the early nineteenth century the population of Algeria, which was estimated to total approximately three million, was made up of many different ethnic and religious groups, the largest of which were the Arabs and the Berbers, most of whom were pastoralists or agriculturalists. The Berbers comprised four subdivisions, whose socioeconomic singularities were shaped by geographic location and occupational differences; the most numerous were the Kabyles. Less important in number but still politically influential were the Turks, all of whom lived in or around urban centers where the population was largely non-Algerian. Other urbanites included the Koulouglis, men of mixed Algerian and Turkish origin who had significant urban economic interests, and the Moors, descendants of Andalusian refugees who dominated the cultural and commercial life in Algiers and other towns. Finally, there were Jewish communities in towns throughout Algeria. The most influential of these were the *juifs francs*, Jews of Italian and French origin, who acted as the regency's commercial middlemen. They kept their distance from the older Jewish communities of Spanish origin, establishing strongholds in Algiers, Bône (now Annaba), and Constantine. Added to the existing economic and political instability, the social diversity of the regency, with its potential for fractiousness, created a setting that was propitious to European interference.

The Napoleonic invasion of Ottoman Egypt put a temporary stop to the grain trade between France and Algeria, and the two houses of Bushnaq and Bakri that handled the trade were not paid. Although negotiations to clear the account were carried on throughout the three decades leading up to French conquest, the debt was never settled. In 1827 when the French consul, Pierre Deval, was paying his respects to the dey, the question of repayment was brought up. In the ensuing altercation the dey tapped the consul with a fly whisk. Three years later the French prime minister, Jules de Polignac, wanting to divert attention from French domestic problems, used this breach of etiquette as an excuse for a punitive expedition to Algiers.

FRENCH CONQUEST

On 14 June 1830, having assembled the largest naval force since the Napoleonic wars, the French landed west of Algiers at Sidi-Ferruch. Three weeks later Algiers was in French hands, and the dey and his family went into exile. The arbitrary imprisonments and killings and the pillaging, destruction, and expropriations of property were a mark of the brutality that was to characterize the whole colonial period.

The conquest of Algeria took twenty-seven years; seventeen of these were taken up in subduing the coastal regions and areas bordering the coast inhabited by nomadic pastoralists, mainly Arabs. A further ten years were necessary to subdue the mountainous region of the Djurdjura, which the French had dubbed Kabylia after the Kabyles who inhabited it. Initially the French sought to secure only the towns along the coast, which would provide the French strategically important outposts on the southern Mediterranean shore. Any British activity in the area could thus be countered from both sides of the sea. The French moved eastward from Algiers to Philippeville (present-day Skikda), but conquest was not easy. They encountered fierce resistance on the part of the Arabs, who combined forces under the leadership of the charismatic Abdelkader. Furthermore, cholera, malaria, and other ailments took a heavy toll, demoralizing the troops. In France indecision about the merits of colonizing the area meant that there was no coherent colonial policy.

The arrival in February 1841 of General (later Field Marshal) Thomas Bugeaud as military commander of Algeria (and governor-general as of 1845) transformed the situation for the French and eliminated existing uncertainties about whether or not to colonize. Bugeaud's innovative military strategies and brutal tactics gave the French the upper hand, and his theory of colonization, by the plough and the sword, encouraged the idea of military occupation and administration. By 1847 Abdelkader had been vanquished. A year later the area under French domination was divided into three departments and thus incorporated administratively into the French mainland. The same year Marshal Randon began the conquest of Kabylia. By 1858 the military deemed the pacification of Algeria to be complete.

MILITARY ADMINISTRATION

It was during Bugeaud's tenure that the Bureaux Arabes (Arab bureaus), military administrative units established as liaisons between the French central government and the local chiefs, acquired their definitive form. A bureau comprised one or more French officers, depending on the size of the *cercle,* or unit,

administered; a "native" adjunct; and if necessary an interpreter and a French medical officer. A number of *cercles* were grouped together into subdivisions, which were in turn grouped into divisions, each commanded by an officer of appropriate rank. During the period of military rule, tribal administration was left to the officers of the Bureaux Arabes. Policies were not formulated in Paris but were developed by the officers, evolving out of past experience in the *cercles.* "Indigenous" policy thus bore the imprint of the officers of the Bureaux Arabes.

As Bugeaud's conquests progressed, a scientific commission was established to reconnoiter the area under French control. In the tradition of the Napoleonic scholars who compiled the *Description of Egypt* (1809–1828), the commission's members covered every conceivable aspect of research that could be of use in understanding, administering, and colonizing the area, producing thirty-nine volumes published between 1844 and 1867. Although the period from 1830 to 1870 was one of military rule, civilian activity in the colony increased steadily. Periods of crisis in France led to an influx of new settlers. For example, following the coup d'état of 2 December 1851, which completed the destruction of the Second French Republic, the "mixed commissions" set up by Louis-Napoleon Bonaparte (later Napoleon III) shipped thousands of men to Algeria, many of whom were sent there because they had risen up in defense of the republic or because they had been prominent Montagnards (leftists). Land expropriation, first in the urban centers and then in the rural areas, started the social dislocation that was to pauperize much of the local population. In the early days of conquest the French paid little attention to the moral or legal aspects of such expropriation. With time, however, they justified their actions by a series of legal measures designed to clarify land tenure procedures and allow the local population to present their case for retaining their property. A notable example was the Senatus-Consulte of 1863. Local landowners, who were not versed in French law, were at a distinct disadvantage in legal transactions, and unscrupulous settlers used this to their benefit.

Throughout the 1860s, the last decade of military administration, dubbed the *royaume arabe* (Arab kingdom) because of the pro-Arab policies of

Biskra, Nomad Camp (Smalah de Cheik-El-Arab), c. 1857–1859. Waxed-paper negative photograph by Gustave de Beaucorps. Réunion des Musées Nationaux/Art Resource, NY

Napoleon III, marked tensions developed between the military and the civilians. The strident civilian accusations of military Arabophilia were the manifestation of a power struggle to control the way in which colonization was to take shape. Military efforts to influence its progress, by stopping what the officers deemed to be civilian abuses, were unsuccessful. Paradoxically many of the policies instigated during the military administration to protect the local population from undue exploitation, such as the 1863 Senatus-Consulte, did more harm than good.

DISTURBANCES AND REVOLTS

Arab and Berber discontent manifested itself in sporadic revolts, the setting of forest fires, and passive resistance to French impositions, all of which fueled anti-"indigenous," and by extension antimilitary, sentiments among much of the civilian population. The collapse of the Second Empire in 1870 discre-

dited the French army and provided an opportunity for the civilians to take over the administration of the colony. Furthermore, the 1870 events in France and the demise of the military regime in Algeria prompted the Kabyles to revolt. The Great Kabyle Rebellion of 1870–1871 nearly succeeded in expelling the French. In the wake of their near-defeat, French reprisals were draconian. Land expropriations, from which the military had largely sheltered the Kabyles until then, created long-term economic hardship and prompted the Kabyles to migrate in search of a livelihood first to urban centers and eventually to France. In the aftermath of the rebellion the settler lobby in Paris persuaded the National Assembly to enact a series of laws, applicable only to the Muslims of the colony, transgression of which would lead to imprisonment or fines. The numerous offenses included being disrespectful to a French official, traveling without a permit, defaming the

Laghouat, Algerian Sahara, 1879. Painting by Gustave Guillaumet. French painter Guillaumet visted Algeria numerous times between 1862 and his death in 1887 and is renowned for his realistic depictions of life in that region. ERICH LESSING/ART RESOURCE, NY

French Republic, refusing to fight forest fires, and so forth. Designed as a temporary measure to control resistance in the aftermath of the 1871 rebellion, the Code de l'Indigénat lasted until World War II and was a humiliating reminder to the Muslims that they were mere subjects, and second-class ones at that.

CIVILIAN RULE

The early years of civilian rule developed in tandem with the establishment of the Third Republic in France. Citizenship, education, and economic development were central concerns of the colonial regime. In 1870 the Crémieux decrees granted French citizenship to Algerian Jews. The Muslims, on the other hand, could not obtain French citizenship unless they renounced their personal status as set down in Muslim customary law, an act that amounted to apostasy for the devout. Settler society in Algeria was made up largely of nationals from southern Europe: Italians, Spanish, Portuguese, Maltese, and Greeks. The French, always reluctant to emigrate, were the minority. Fears that the demographic imbalance between the French and their subjects would lead to serious sociopolitical problems prompted the colonial authorities to pass a law in 1889 granting French citizenship to all children of European origin born in Algeria. By the 1890s, therefore, all but the Muslims had obtained French citizenship. Citizenship, however, was not the ticket to social equality. Those of southern Mediterranean origin were considered to be *neo-français* by the "true" French. Frenchness became the yardstick by which one's social standing was measured, creating a hierarchy with ethnocultural markers that were easily transformed into racist configurations. The Arabs and Berbers who, with few exceptions, were neither citizens nor sufficiently acculturated to be considered "French" were inevitably at the bottom.

From 1870 to 1914 settler society took root in Algeria. Diseases, such as cholera and malaria, which had taken such a heavy toll in the early years, were kept in check so that the expansion of the European population in the colony was no longer just a question of immigration. The mosquito-infested swamplands of the Mitidja were cleared and cultivated. The phylloxera epidemic in France prompted the development of the Algerian wine industry, which became one of the colony's leading sources of wealth. The economy was gradually transformed from an indigenously controlled subsistence economy to a settler controlled capitalist one. Land sequestration provided the land for these developments, while the ensuing pauperization of the local population meant that there was a constant supply of cheap labor for the labor-intensive capitalism that the settlers were developing.

In the face of such aggressive colonization and systematic settler opposition to any reforms, there was little the Algerians could do but retrench and bide their time. French education, the pathway to economic and political empowerment in the colony, was largely inaccessible and would remain so until after World War I. Islam became the refuge from which to counter French influences. It was only during the interwar period that opposition to French rule achieved the necessary organizational structure that eventually led to independence in 1962.

See also **France; Imperialism.**

BIBLIOGRAPHY

Ageron, Charles Robert. *Les algériens musulmans et la France (1871–1919)*. 2 vols. Paris, 1968.

———. *Histoire de l'Algérie contemporaine*. Vol. 2: *De l'insurrection de 1871 au déclenchement de la guerre de libération (1954)*. Paris, 1979.

Bennoune, Mahfoud. *The Making of Contemporary Algeria, 1830–1987*. Cambridge, U.K., 1988.

Clancy-Smith, Julia A. *Rebel and Saint: Muslim Notables, Populist Protest, Colonial Encounters (Algeria and Tunisia, 1800–1904)*. Berkeley, Calif., 1994.

Djebari, Youcef. *La France en Algérie: Bilans et controversies*. 3 vols. Algiers, Algeria, 1995.

Exploration scientifique de l'Algérie pendant les années 1840, 1841, 1842 publiée par ordre du gouvernement et avec le concours d'une commission académique. 40 vols. Paris, 1844–1881.

Julien, Charles-André. *Histoire de l'Algérie contemporaine*. Vol. 1: *La conquête et les débuts de la colonisation (1827–1871)*. Paris, 1964.

Lorcin, Patricia M. E. *Imperial Identities, Stereotyping, Prejudice, and Race in Colonial Algeria*. London, 1995.

Perkins, Kenneth J. *Qaids, Captains, and Colons: French Military Administration in the Colonial Maghrib, 1844–1934*. New York, 1981.

Prochaska, David. *Making Algeria French: Colonialism in Bône, 1870–1920*. Cambridge, U.K., 1990.

Rey-Goldzeiguer, Annie. *Le royaume arabe: La politique algérienne de Napoléon III, 1861–1870*. Algiers, Algeria, 1977.

Ruedy, John. *Modern Algeria*. Bloomington, Ind., 1992.

Valensi, Lucette. *On the Eve of Colonialism: North Africa before the French Conquest*. Translated by Kenneth J. Perkins. New York, 1977.

Yacono, Xavier. *Les Bureaux Arabes et l'évolution des genres de vie indigènes dans l'ouest du Tell algérois*. Paris, 1953.

PATRICIA M. E. LORCIN

ALLIANCE SYSTEM.

The European alliance system that was in place prior to World War I is often seen as one of the long-term causes for the outbreak of war in 1914. On the eve of war, Europe was divided into two opposing camps, with Germany, Austria-Hungary, and Italy on one side and France, Russia, and Britain on the other. The roots of this division reached back over thirty years and its origins can be traced to Bismarck's foreign policy from the 1870s to 1890 and can only be explained with reference to Bismarck's complicated system of alliances.

BISMARCK'S ALLIANCE SYSTEM

Bismarck's alliance system laid the foundations for the alliances of 1914 and had its origins in the so-called German wars of unification (1864 against Denmark, 1866 against Austria, and 1870–1871 against France). Following the German defeat of France in 1871 and the annexation of the French provinces of Alsace and Lorraine, the German Empire was founded, with a kaiser, William I, at its helm. Germany was one of the strongest military powers in Europe and was fast becoming the leading industrial power on the continent, and this newly powerful country at the heart of Europe, having emerged from a decade of success in war, seemed a tangible threat to the other great European powers, whatever its policies. Imperial Germany's first Chancellor, Otto von Bismarck, was concerned to avoid further conflict and to consolidate the gains the country had made in its three successful wars and its subsequent unification. His foreign policy eventually resulted in a complicated alliance system designed to ensure that what he considered a "nightmare of coalitions" against Germany would not threaten the new status quo. Bismarck declared that Germany was "satiated" following her recent unification and that it sought no further conflict with its neighbors. Historians now believe that his foreign policy was not always driven by the desire to establish a system of alliances, but that it amounted initially to a "system of stop-gaps." Underlying this policy, however, was Bismarck's desire to keep Germany allied to at least two other major powers and to prevent alliances from being forged against Germany. His particular concern was to keep France isolated and prevent it from forming closer ties with any of the other great powers.

During Bismarck's time in office, the alliance system that resulted from his policy successfully preserved the peace between the major European powers and prevented Germany's neighbors from drawing up alliances against it. Germany was allied to Austria-Hungary in the Dual Alliance of 1879 (Bismarck forced the aging Kaiser William I to agree to the alliance despite the latter's opposition to a treaty with Germany's former enemy), which became in practice the Triple Alliance when Italy joined in 1882. In 1883, Serbia and Romania established separate links with the Triple Alliance. In 1879, Germany had effectively abandoned its previously close ties with Russia in favor of Austria-Hungary. However, Bismarck had been able to balance his alliance with Austria-Hungary with friendly relations with Russia, primarily through the Three Emperors League between Germany, Russia, and Austria-Hungary, which William I signed in October 1873 and which was renewed twice in 1881 and 1884. A few years later, in 1887, Bismarck encouraged the formation of a Mediterranean entente among Britain, Austria-Hungary, and Italy, and in the same year Germany concluded the secret Reinsurance Treaty with Russia, in which Germany promised to support Russia's Balkan interests (contradicting its Dual Alliance agreement with Austria-Hungary).

Britain and France remained, for the most part, diplomatically isolated during this time, the former by choice, pursuing a policy of "splendid isolation" and reaping the benefits of being the world's largest imperial power. Britain had turned down Bismarck's offer of a defensive alliance in 1889 and there seemed to be little chance that either of them would settle their colonial differences. With Kaiser William II's 1888 accession to the throne in Germany, however (and particularly following Bismarck's dismissal in 1890), this carefully constructed system of alliances began to be dismantled. Bismarck's successors were less concerned to preserve the status quo in Europe and envisaged a more powerful role for the new German Empire, both on the continent and worldwide. As a result, German foreign policy under William II became more erratic and began to threaten the balance of power that had kept Europe relatively peaceful since 1871. Even without this radical policy change, however, it is unlikely that Bismarck's system of stop-gaps could have lasted indefinitely; he believed that alliances could be reneged on as easily as they had been concluded, and he did not feel bound by the agreements that Germany had signed. It would probably have been only a matter of time before the other great powers united against Germany. However, Berlin's policy change certainly sped up this process.

RIVAL ALLIANCE SYSTEMS
Under William II's leadership and in pursuit of the goal of becoming a *Weltmacht* (world power), the powerful new Germany soon began to challenge its neighbors, who were quick to react by forming defensive alliances. When Germany allowed the secret Reinsurance Treaty with Russia to lapse in 1890, the consequences were especially grave. Somewhat unexpectedly, republican France (which still begrudged Germany the annexation of Alsace-Lorraine) and autocratic Russia overcame their substantial differences and united in a defensive alliance against Germany and Austria-Hungary. Their initial vague agreement of 1891 was expanded by a military convention in 1892 and culminated in a military alliance that was ratified in 1894. The conclusion of this military alliance gave rise to a feeling of encirclement in Germany. Given its geographic position, Germany, although allied still to

Austria-Hungary and Italy, now faced potential enemies both in the west and the east and felt encircled by envious and potentially dangerous neighbors who were forming alliances against her.

Britain only joined the alliance game late when it gave up its "splendid isolation" and allied itself to Japan in 1902. Its main rivals at the time were France and Russia, rather than Germany. Between 1898 and 1901, further half-hearted attempts had been made to conclude an Anglo-German alliance, but the two countries' interests were too divergent to make this a viable proposition. Threatened by France in Africa and Russia in the Far East, Britain met its need for diplomatic support in Asia by concluding an alliance with Japan in January 1902.

Worse still for Germany, which continued to fear diplomatic isolation, France and Britain overcame their substantial differences concerning the territories of Morocco and Egypt, and France (which Bismarck had tried so hard to keep isolated) secured an Entente Cordiale with Britain in 1904. Although the Entente was not a formal alliance, it was a potentially threatening development for Germany, whose political leaders tried in vain to break up the new Entente during the first Moroccan crisis (1904–1905). Their actions only served to strengthen the emerging Anglo-French accord, however, and the Entente Cordiale remained in existence until the outbreak of war and was one of the reasons Britain joined France in its fight against Germany.

Germany's Kaiser William II also attempted to extend existing Russo-German trade agreements into an alliance, but the defensive treaty he negotiated personally with the Russian Tsar Nicholas II was vetoed by the Russian foreign minister and as a result the Treaty of Björkö of July 1905 never came into effect and Germany was unable to forge closer links with Russia at this crucial time.

Instead, Britain further abandoned its isolation when it entered into negotiations with Russia in 1906. Such an accord had been coveted by some British ministers since the late 1890s, but only following its defeat in the Russo-Japanese War (1904–1905) was Russia willing to negotiate the areas of mutual interest and potential conflict: Persia, Tibet, and Afghanistan. Agreement was reached in August 1907 with the conclusion of the Anglo-Russian con-

vention. This led, in effect, to a Triple Entente among France, Russia, and Great Britain, competing with the Triple Alliance of Germany, Austria-Hungary, and Italy. However, Britain was not formally allied to either France or Russia and its commitment to the other powers was limited. This gave Germany's decision makers hope, until the last days of July 1914, that Britain might decide to stay neutral in the coming war.

Germany's political leadership feared the threat of political isolation once its primary potential enemies—France, Russia, and Britain—had joined forces. The origins of German fears of encirclement can be traced to this time. With only one reliable ally (Austria-Hungary), Germany's politicians were even forced to turn their previously defensive agreement into an offensive one during the Bosnian annexation crisis, when Germany pledged unconditional support to Austria-Hungary. In the following years, Germany tried to escape its diplomatic isolation not only by attempting to reach agreements with Britain as part of Chancellor Theobold von Bethmann Hollweg's foreign policy, but also by testing, once again, the Entente's stability, this time during the second Moroccan crisis, known as the Agadir Crisis, in 1911. As a result of its posturing, Germany only forced Britain firmly onto the side of its Entente partner, France, thus demonstrating the strength of the Franco-British agreement. Further German attempts at reaching a détente with Britain failed (for example, in February 1912 during the Haldane Mission), although when the two great powers came to amicable agreements over the future of the Portuguese colonies in August 1913 and the future of the Baghdad Railway in June 1914, some hope for friendlier relations remained. Ironically, on the eve of World War I, Anglo-German relations were better than they had been for years.

THE ALLIANCE SYSTEM AND THE OUTBREAK OF WAR

When the Austro-Hungarian heir to the throne, Archduke Francis Ferdinand, was assassinated by a Serbian terrorist on 28 June 1914 and the leadership in Vienna used this event to unleash a war against Serbia, the full effect of the alliance system became evident. Germany, Austria-Hungary's alliance partner, was if anything even more bent on war against its main potential enemies, France and Russia, than was Austria-Hungary and promised to support Vienna in any action it might undertake. At the same time, France and Russia pledged to make good on their agreement for mutual military action in case one of them was attacked by Germany or Austria-Hungary. Thus, a war in the Balkans ended up embroiling the major powers of the two opposing alliances, and soon involved the other powers that were more or less loosely allied to one side or the other. Although it is often maintained that the alliance system contributed to the outbreak of World War I, the alliances of the prewar years were largely defensive and their members regarded them as arrangements that could be (and frequently were) canceled if necessary. A good example of this is Italy, which remained neutral in 1914 and eventually even joined the fighting on the side of the Entente even though it had been allied to Germany and Austria-Hungary. Bismarck himself also believed that national interests should, if necessary, supersede international treaty obligations, and British statesmen felt the same way when the question of Belgian neutrality arose. In 1914, however, when faced with a war on the continent in which one of Britain's greatest potential rivals, Russia or Germany, was likely to be victorious, abandoning its Entente partners was not an option for Britain. The Triple Entente powers went to war against the Dual Alliance partners and it seemed to contemporaries that one of the root causes for the catastrophe that followed was the system of secret alliances. Little wonder that "secret diplomacy" was condemned by commentators after the war and that many people hoped the League of Nations (established in 1920) would prevent such secrecy and alliance systems in the future.

See also **Bismarck, Otto von; Metternich, Clemens von; Moroccan Crises; Naval Rivalry (Anglo-German).**

BIBLIOGRAPHY

Bell, P. M. H. *France and Britain, 1900–1940: Entente and Estrangement*. London, 1996.

Canis, Konrad. *Von Bismarck zur Weltpolitik: Deutsche Aussenpolitik, 1890 bis 1902*. Berlin, 1997.

Hildebrand, Klaus. *German Foreign Policy from Bismarck to Adenauer: The Limits of Statecraft*. Translated by Louise Willmot. Boston, 1989.

Imanuel, Geiss. *German Foreign Policy, 1871–1914*. Boston, 1976.

Joll, James. *The Origins of the First World War*. New York, 2006.

Lerman, Katharine A. *Bismarck*. New York, 2004.

Rich, Norman. *Great Power Diplomacy, 1814–1914*. New York, 1992.

Seligmann, Matthew S., and Roderick R. McLean. *Germany from Reich to Republic, 1871–1918: Politics, Hierarchy, and Elites*. New York, 2000.

ANNIKA MOMBAUER

ALSACE-LORRAINE. The Franco-Prussian War of 1870–1871 placed the borderland provinces of Alsace and Lorraine at the center of the European historical stage, where they remained until the collapse of Nazism in 1945. The Treaty of Frankfurt (10 May 1871) officially gave the victorious and newly unified German Empire control of Alsace and part of Lorraine, provinces that had progressively come under French rule between the mid-sixteenth and the mid-eighteenth century. The hyphenated term *Alsace-Lorraine* (*Elsass-Lothringen*), popular on both sides of the Rhine, dates from this period of German rule (1871–1918) and refers to the imperial territory (*Reichsland*) established by the Germans. Before that date, Alsace and Lorraine were not thought of in tandem; in the late nineteenth century, however, their fate became irrevocably linked in the French and German national imaginations.

THE FRENCH REVOLUTION

The French Revolution firmly anchored Alsace and Lorraine to the French nation and imbued both regions with a lasting sense of patriotism. The Revolution's republican civic culture—more popular in Alsace than in Lorraine—also tied the region to France. By transforming subjects into citizens and creating a vibrant political life, the Revolution gave the French state legitimacy and helped German speakers in the region identify themselves as French citizens. An often-cited sign that greeted visitors crossing the Rhine to Strasbourg in 1790 read, "Here begins the country of Liberty." The outbreak of the revolutionary wars in 1792 resulted in the occupation of parts of Lorraine and Alsace by Austrian and Prussian troops and solidified patriotic sentiment—just when support for the Revolution was waning. The Revolution simplified the complex geographical and administrative structures of both provinces. The abolition of feudalism, the centralization of power in the hands of prefects, and the adoption of common laws mitigated legal and administrative particularisms. In 1790 the revolutionaries divided the region into six departments and established customs barriers along the Rhine River; in 1798 they welcomed the free city of Mulhouse, long allied to Switzerland, into the French nation.

Early-nineteenth-century Alsace and Lorraine constituted two provinces that differed religiously and linguistically. Alsace was an overwhelmingly German-speaking region; one-fourth of the population was Protestant (predominantly Lutheran), and the region was home to a significant Jewish population, both urban and rural. Lorraine, on the other hand, was largely Catholic and divided between a francophone region in the west and a smaller germanophone strip in the east. In Alsace, Protestants proved more supportive of the Revolution than Catholics, and in both provinces Catholics resisted dechristianization. The Revolution's campaign against local customs and the use of the German language during the Terror met with failure. Napoleon I continued on the path the revolutionaries had set out: his centralization of power and his military campaigns reinforced the integration of Alsace and Lorraine into France. Unlike the revolutionaries, Napoleon I was little concerned with the linguistic issue, and he was often quoted as saying, "Little matter that they speak German, as long as they wield the saber in French." While agriculture remained the central economic activity throughout the nineteenth century, industrial growth was impressive, especially under German rule after 1870. Mulhouse developed into the center of France's textile industry in the early years of the century, and metallurgical industries settled in the region around Strasbourg. Important coal and iron-ore deposits fueled Lorraine's heavy industry.

THE FRANCO-GERMAN CONFLICT

The war of 1870 transformed Alsace-Lorraine into the key site of a Franco-German conflict that endured until after World War II—a period during which the province changed hands on four separate occasions. Alsace-Lorraine became a symbol of national and ethnic conflict in late-nineteenth-century Europe, and claims to its ownership gave rise to crucial debates about nationalism. As early as

the summer of 1870, the French historians Numa-Denis Fustel de Coulanges and Ernest Renan and their German counterparts Theodor Mommsen and David Friedrich Strauss engaged in a charged exchange over national belonging in Alsace-Lorraine. Was Alsace-Lorraine French or was it German, and why? To Mommsen's and Strauss's claim that language and ethnicity made the region German and justified the annexation, Fustel de Coulanges and Renan replied that neither race nor language constituted the basis of nationality. On the contrary, a community of ideas, interests, and historical experiences bound Alsace-Lorraine to the French nation. Its inhabitants were French by choice. The debates of 1870 later inspired Renan to write *What Is a Nation?* (1882), in which he famously argues that the nation is a "daily plebiscite"; to this day, his text remains one of the most influential analyses of the subject. The "Alsace-Lorraine question" was thus a burning subject for writers and publicists of all stripes well beyond 1914 and further cemented two contrasting understandings of citizenship and nationhood: for the Germans, citizenship was based on ethnicity and culture; for the French, it was rooted in a voluntary adhesion to the values of the national community.

The 1871 peace settlement altered the geographical boundaries of both provinces: France retained control of only the small southwestern tip of Alsace, renamed the Territoire de Belfort, while Germany acquired one-third of Lorraine—the German-speaking regions and a French-language area that included the city of Metz. The Franco-German border now stood on the crest of the Vosges Mountains, and not along the Rhine River. Within Alsace-Lorraine, a significant proportion of the population remained hostile to the German annexation. In France, Alsace and Lorraine became known as the "lost provinces," and the nation, it was claimed, could not be whole without them. On French school maps the region was shrouded in black as a sign of mourning. The female allegories of Alsace and Lorraine, known as the "twin sisters" (*les sœurs jumelles*), figured prominently in state propaganda, the press, and advertising and the myth of Alsace-Lorraine was perpetuated by writers, artists, and songwriters. Thus, in the French imagination, between 1871 and 1914 this German-speaking region—87 percent of the population considered German or a German dialect to be its native language in 1900—was transformed into a sentimental homeland of French nationalism. However, the pervasive talk of revenge (*la revanche*) in the wake of the 1870 defeat did not translate into policy, save for the brief nationalist Boulangist episode (1886–1887). France was not prepared for a military conflict with Germany. The Alsace-Lorraine question remained the fundamental barrier to Franco-German reconciliation.

German rule transformed the political, social, and economic structure of Alsace-Lorraine. The province's demographic makeup underwent profound changes. The Treaty of Frankfurt allowed inhabitants of both provinces to opt for French citizenship and move to France, and over 125,000 Alsatians and Lorrainers (out of a population of 1.5 million) had done so by the October 1872 deadline. More emigrated after that date. The young, the educated bourgeoisie (often francophone cadres and notables), and workers and artisans figured prominently among those who departed. Alsatian Jews also departed in significant numbers. German immigration compensated for these demographic losses but also provoked enduring tensions with native inhabitants. Politically, Alsace-Lorraine never achieved equality with German states. Ruled directly as an imperial territory by Berlin, the region was, as of 1879, governed by an administrator (*Statthalter*) who was responsible to the emperor; high level German bureaucrats managed the region at the local level. Alsatians and Lorrainers, however, moved from initial protest against German rule in the 1870s and 1880s to demands for autonomy in the 1890s and beyond. By the turn of the century the young generations had been schooled entirely in German and the links with France proved to be increasingly distant. German social legislation (more advanced than its French counterpart), substantial economic development, and urban renewal projects (notably in Strasbourg) all helped to anchor Alsace-Lorraine to the Reich. The Constitution of 1911 gave Alsace-Lorraine increased political rights and autonomy without awarding the province equal status with German states.

Both the French and the Germans attempted (with mixed success) to forge national allegiances through linguistic and educational policies. Under the Second Empire (1852–1870), French authorities, increasingly convinced that one needed to speak French in order to be French, changed the language of instruction in primary schools to French

and limited the teaching of German. Schoolteachers, however, did not always master French sufficiently to apply this policy effectively. The Germans, too, focused on primary schools as a key tool to transmit German language, culture, history, and identity to a lukewarm population. They applied a policy of Germanification to German-speaking areas (eventually banning French instruction from primary schools altogether) and sought to increase the teaching of German in French-language regions. After 1918 the French would pursue similar policies in a much more draconian fashion, just as they would undertake extensive purges of civil society and expel all the "old German" immigrants. The nineteenth century Franco-German clash over Alsace-Lorraine was thus a harbinger of far more violent ethnic and national conflicts that would divide Europe in the twentieth century.

See also **France; Franco-Prussian War; Germany; Nationalism.**

BIBLIOGRAPHY

Primary Sources

Renan, Ernest. "What Is a Nation?" Translated and edited by Martin Thom. In *Nation and Narration,* edited by Homi K. Bhabha, 8–22. London, 1990.

Secondary Sources

Caron, Vicki. *Between France and Germany: The Jews of Alsace-Lorraine, 1871–1918.* Stanford, Calif., 1988.

Harp, Stephen L. *Learning to Be Loyal: Primary Schooling as Nation Building in Alsace and Lorraine, 1850–1940.* DeKalb, Ill., 1998.

Harvey, David Allen. *Constructing Class and Nationality in Alsace, 1830–1945.* DeKalb, Ill., 2001.

Silverman, Dan P. *Reluctant Union: Alsace-Lorraine and Imperial Germany, 1871–1918.* University Park, Pa., 1972.

Wahl, Alfred, and Jean-Claude Richez. *La vie quotidienne en Alsace entre France et Allemagne, 1850–1950.* Paris, 1993.

LAIRD BOSWELL

AMSTERDAM. Unlike Europe's three largest cities—London, Paris, and Naples—Amsterdam, with its 217,000 inhabitants in 1800, owed its somewhat more modest ranking not to the presence of court, church, or government but to its past economic glories. After Napoleon's defeat, the Netherlands became a kingdom that inherited the centralist state from the French occupation. Once insignificant, the Hague became the dominant political and administrative center. Although Amsterdam was seen as the capital, it lacked the consuming power of the court, ministries, parliament, and foreign diplomats of the Hague.

Amsterdam's revival was thwarted by the loss of its staple market to London. When Great Britain returned the East Indies to the Dutch, the colony recovered, but did so under strict state control, preventing Amsterdam's entrepreneurs from benefiting from its many resources. Despite the construction of a new shipping lane in 1824, the city's poor maritime accessibility remained an obstacle. Amsterdam's population loss was matched by the deplorable state of its townscape. Landlords facing vacancies decided to tear their houses down to avoid paying property taxes.

The Dutch economy recovered in the 1850s as laissez-faire liberalism came to dominate the political arena. In 1870 most restrictions on private investments in the East Indies were abolished. Few cities benefited from this policy as much as Amsterdam. After the construction of the Suez Canal in 1869, which sharply reduced traveling time to the colony, Amsterdam invested in the North Sea Channel. It opened in 1876, transforming the city's sleepy port into a booming hub that recalled the Golden Age of Amsterdam in the seventeenth century.

THE "SECOND GOLDEN AGE"

From the 1870s until the outbreak of World War I, Amsterdam enjoyed a period of sustained economic growth, led by its commercial and financial sector. The stock exchange grew into the Continent's leading market for U.S. railroad bonds and was the gateway for investment in the Dutch East Indies and one of Europe's leading markets for foreign loans, particularly from Russia. Amsterdam banks increasingly controlled the national financial market. Though never considered a leading sector, manufacturing became the city's main employer, specializing in consumer industries and shipbuilding.

Face-to-face communication dictated a tight clustering of offices in the city center, where staff

TABLE 1

Population of Amsterdam, 1795–1910		
Year	Population	Relative change
1795	217,000	107
1815	180,000	89
1830	202,000	100
1850	225,000	110
1860	243,000	120
1870	265,000	131
1880	317,000	157
1890	408,000	202
1900	511,000	252
1910	566,000	280
1914	609,000	301

and errand boys were within walking distance of the stock exchange and the Bank of the Netherlands, the national clearing house. Proximity to the modernized Post and Telegraph office was mandatory, as it provided the only rapid international communication facilities of the time. The opening of the new Central Railway Station in 1889 added further to the attraction of the area. Department stores, hotels, and leisure and entertainment outlets also fought for a place in the core area.

Few deplored the fact that the legacy of the seventeenth century fell prey to the new building frenzy; it was the toll to be paid so that Amsterdam could escape the fate of "dead cities" such as Venice. But linking the city center with new residential quarters posed substantial problems. In the seventeenth century the city had been planned as a perfect machine for water carriage, the most cost-efficient form of pre-industrial transport. Roads were seen as a necessary evil, which explained their minimal size and poor consistency. Initially, private developers came up with grandiose plans for new boulevards to run through the historic city center, clearly inspired by Baron Georges Haussmann's *Grands Travaux* in Paris. Eventually, these private plans failed due to a lack of funding. The huge costs of redoing the transportation network necessitated the intervention—however reluctant—of the city.

IN SEARCH OF A MONUMENTAL CAPITAL

By filling in some of the canals the municipality sought the cheapest solution to traffic problems. But a major cut linking the new western quarters with the inner city was unavoidable. It took ten years before the new *Raadhuisstraat* was open to the public, a delay mainly due to the time-consuming process of compulsory land purchase.

Although the new artery proved effective in reducing congestion, as a new boulevard it could not withstand the comparison with Haussmann's creations. The facades facing the new artery were a far cry from the strict neoclassical monumentality that made New Paris so impressive. Amsterdam lacked both the funds and the legal tools to realize such embellishment.

That the dominant politics of laissez-faire were incompatible with grandiose urban design was a lesson learned in 1867 during discussions of an extension plan drawn by the city's architect, J. G. Van Niftrik. Fearing chaos in the urban periphery where uncontrolled speculative building had led the way, the local council had ordered Van Niftrik's plan. But critical politicians soon realized that despite the design's aesthetic qualities and strict social segregation, the city lacked the means to impose the plan onto private landowners. Van Niftrik suggested massive expropriation of the land that his plan proposed to use. The alderman for public works refused this initiative, rightly suspecting that neither the government nor parliament would be convinced by the request for compulsory purchase "for the common interest." Each expropriation required a separate Act of Parliament, as well as compensation costs paid at market value of the land. This procedure was ruled out by Amsterdam's financial situation.

Yet the need for some planning remained, as even the staunchest liberals conceded. Thus, in 1878 they accepted a plan proposed by the Director of Public Works, J. Kalff. The new plan was "realistic," not once mentioning expropriation. Kalff had accepted the main property lines, such as roads and ditches, as the skeleton for his design. Although legally forbidden to impose a street plan, Kalff convinced developers to permit major radial arteries to run over their property.

Although aesthetically and technically impaired, this plan triggered an unprecedented building boom. Thus Amsterdam received its nineteenth-century belt. Speculative builders constructed flimsy three- to four-story houses, often subdivided into back-to-back single room apartments, along narrow, straight streets. The new quarters were mainly the domain of the lower middle classes, although all had their "golden fringes." Developers built higher quality, more spacious, and luxurious housing along parks, waterways, and broad streets. These houses were often richly decorated with Dutch neo-Renaissance ornaments, referring to the dominant vernacular of the Golden Age and testifying to their tenants' wealth.

PRIDE AND EMBARRASSMENT

Although Amsterdam failed to produce a modern, monumental townscape, civic pride compensated for the lack of state-funded institutions that elsewhere on the Continent were seen as the prerogative of a capital city. In 1876 Amsterdam finally got its own university, after years of lobbying parliament. The city had to pay for this prestigious institution out of its own pocket, but the burden was gladly accepted. From its start, Amsterdam University funded studies that were seen as essential for a merchant city. The university's geography department—the first in the Netherlands—explored the unmapped areas of the Dutch East Indies, where entrepreneurs rightly expected to find great investment opportunities. The city also donated resources to modern laboratories of the university. The rewards came in 1902 and 1910, when two of the university's professors became Nobel laureates in physics.

The bourgeoisie demonstrated its loyalty to the city that had enabled them to amass their fortunes by funding a zoo, several museums, a new park, and the Concertgebouw, a concert hall that within a few years became one of Europe's leading temples of music, where contemporary composers such as Gustav Mahler and Richard Strauss conducted their own works. Without a cent of state funding or royal patronage, the city successfully established itself as the cultural heart of the Netherlands.

All this was hardly relevant for the working class. Increasing immigrant labor led to serious overcrowding of inner city slums, which were within walking distance of the port and major industries. This congestion, combined with rough labor conditions, led to social unrest, including regular and sometimes violent confrontations with police forces. In 1903 unions and the young Socialist Party achieved a major victory when a local strike by dockers and railway men turned into a national confrontation with the right-wing government. Although not a classical factory town, Amsterdam became the epicenter of the Dutch labor movement. The "Red Capital" would continue its role well into the twentieth century.

TURNING POINT: 1900

Amsterdam opinion leaders led the way to Amsterdam's turning point with their criticism of capitalism. In addition to exposing the conditions of the working class, they, like their British counterparts of the Arts and Crafts movement, focused on the poor aesthetic performance of industrial society. Blind laissez-faire, they claimed, had produced a depressing urban landscape. Speculative development had transformed the historic core into a free market townscape, with a cacophony of styles, each building trying to shout down its neighbors, and pockmarked with slums. In 1896, when Amsterdam's expansion reached city limits, the city was granted a major annexation. Critics convinced the local council that therein lay the chance for a truly impressive town plan. In 1901 parliament passed a reformist housing act. It enabled cities with an approved expansion plan to expropriate the area on which it was projected, though compensation was still to be paid at market prices.

Amsterdam seized this opportunity and commissioned Hendrik Petrus Berlage, one of the nation's leading architects, to design an expansion plan. It was accepted in 1905, and after major alterations, was executed after 1918.

Few urban designs in the Netherlands were as monumental. Broad boulevards offered wide vistas for public buildings. Building densities were considerably lower than in any other part of the city, offering residents green squares and intimate parks. Here, many felt, Amsterdam finally offered an urban landscape worthy of a capital city.

See also **Cities and Towns; Netherlands.**

BIBLIOGRAPHY

Bank, Jan. *Stads mecenaat en lokale overheid: Honderd jaar private en publieke kunstbevordering in Amsterdam 1899–1999.* Amsterdam, 1999.

Knotter, Ad. *Economische transformatie en stedelijke arbeidsmarkt, Amsterdam in de tweede helft van de negentiende eeuw.* Zwolle, Netherlands, 1991.

Pistor, Rob, et al., eds. *A City in Progress: Physical Planning in Amsterdam.* Translated by Harold Alexander. Amsterdam, 1994.

Stieber, Nancy. *Housing Design and Society in Amsterdam: Reconfiguring Urban Order and Identity, 1900–1920.* Chicago, 1998.

Tijn, Theo van. *Twintig jaren Amsterdam: De maatschappelijke ontwikkeling van de hoofdstad van de jaren '50 der vorige eeuw tot 1876.* Amsterdam, 1965.

Wagenaar, Michiel. "Amsterdam 1876–1914: Economisch herstel, ruimtelijke expansie en de veranderende ordening van het stedelijk grondgebruik." Ph.D. diss., Historisch Seminarium Universiteit van Amsterdam, 1990.

———. "Conquest of the Center or Flight to the Suburbs? Divergent Metropolitan Strategies in Europe, 1850–1914." *Journal of Urban History* 19, no. 1 (1992): 60–83.

———. "Amsterdam as a Financial Centre, 1876–1914." In *Cities of Finance,* edited by Herman Diederiks and David Reeder, 265–279. Amsterdam, 1996.

———. "Capital without Capitol: Amsterdam's Quest for a Convincing Urban Image, 1870–1940." In *Capital Cities: Images and Realities in the Historical Development of European Capital Cities,* edited by Lars Nilsson, 10–27. Stockholm, 2000.

———. "Between Civic Pride and Mass Society: Amsterdam in Retrospect." In *Amsterdam Human Capital,* edited by Sako Musterd and Willem Salet, 49–67. Amsterdam, 2003.

MICHIEL WAGENAAR

ANARCHISM. The belief that justice requires the abolition of states and other authoritarian institutions not based on some form of cooperative agreement between autonomous individuals—often referred to as anarchism—can be traced back to the ancient Greek philosopher Zeno of Citium (c. 335–c. 263 B.C.E.) and followed through utopian and millenarian religious movements like the Brethren of the Free Spirit of the thirteenth century and the Anabaptists of the sixteenth century. Modern anarchism, however, is rooted in the reorientation of sociopolitical thought that took place in Europe following the outbreak of the French Revolution. Stimulated by revolutionary hopes for fundamental moral and sociopolitical regeneration, anarchists argued that human beings possessed sufficient moral and rational capacities to hold societies together without traditional political institutions like the state and without political practices like elections.

This does not mean that anarchists rejected all organizations that coordinated collective action or that they denied the significance of all interactions that one would consider "political." They were antipolitical in their rejection of traditional political institutions, but they remained political in their concern to foster human communities dedicated to justice. Characteristically, they looked for ways to bring individuals together in voluntary associations in order to coordinate production and to provide social solidarity for specific purposes. In the words of Jean Grave (1854–1939), the most prominent French anarchist journalist of the late nineteenth century, anarchists wished to demonstrate "that individuality cannot develop except in the community; that the latter cannot exist unless the former evolves freely; and that they mutually complement each other." States, however, were unacceptable associations in their eyes because they were coercive, punitive, exploitative, and destructive. And because state action was identified with politics, hopes for progress were predicated on the absorption of this political realm into the moral and economic realms.

Though champions of liberty vis-à-vis the state, anarchists were not advocates of an absolute ideal of liberty that implied the absence of impediments to whatever the individual wished to do. Though advocates of "negative liberty," to use the English philosopher Isaiah Berlin's (1909–1997) terminology, anarchists were also dedicated to an ideal of "positive liberty," which evaluated actions in accordance with conceptions of the true or essential self; that is, in terms of obedience to normative conceptions of reason and morality. The failure to recognize the moral dimension of anarchist thought has led some to assume that anarchists were dedicated to disorder. In fact, most anarchists disliked chaos and argued that anarchy was, in the words of the French anarchist geographer Jean-Jacques-Élisée Reclus (1830–1905), "the highest expression of order." Anarchists believed that stateless societies did not imply disorder because, in their eyes, humans could most successfully achieve rational and moral fulfillment in arenas of human interaction not identified with the state.

Different anarchist theorists looked to different institutions to stimulate cooperation and community. The Englishman William Godwin (1756–1836), the first modern writer to make a reputation condemning government, argued that close interpersonal discussion or conversation was the best means to foster the growth of reason that makes individuals independent and the expansion of sincerity that ties individuals together. The French theorist Pierre-Joseph Proudhon (1809–1865), who was the first to call himself an anarchist (in his 1840 book *What Is Property?*), favored the association of the workshop and, in his later, federalist phase, regional communities as the appropriate loci for stimulating respect and the altruistic concern for others. The famous Russian anarchist Mikhail Bakunin (1814–1876), and the other anarchists connected with the Jura Federation during the 1870s, like Reclus and Paul Brousse (1844–1912), also searched for social solidarity in the context of trade and industrial groupings (*corps de métier* or *la corporation*), organized federally and by contract. Brousse, however, distinguished himself by emphasizing that the Commune (1871) was the privileged agent for the achievement of a stateless society. During the 1890s, Peter Kropotkin (1842–1921), Reclus, and Grave translated anarchism into a language of solidarity and mutual aid, emphasizing extended neighborhoods that fostered benevolence and reciprocal support. After the mid-1890s, anarchist-syndicalists like Paul Delesalle (1870–1948) looked to working-class *syndicats* as the context for education and libertarian organization. Central to all anarchist visions was the conviction that the growth of solidarity, neighborhoods, free associations, *syndicats,* and so forth, would lead to the development of moral and rational individuality and would stimulate cooperation and community.

Where anarchists obviously differed from other sociopolitical thinkers was in their belief that the rational and moral capacities of individuals were vigorous enough—or could be improved sufficiently through education—to permit the elimination of the threat and use of force associated with states. There is an obvious assumption here that morality and rationality are not related to state politics; indeed, they are diametrically opposed. Anarchists viewed states as poisons that contaminated social relations with impersonality, distrust, and resentment. And they argued that it was the inherent nature of states that produced the evil, not a particular form of state control, as might be suggested by liberal or socialist theorists. "Under whatever form that the state exists and functions,"

Anthropometric portrait of Émile Henry, c. 1894. Henry was guillotined after exploding a bomb in a Paris café. This photograph was taken by the Paris police following his arrest. MUSÉE DE LA PREFECTURE DE POLICE, PARIS, FRANCE/BRIDGEMAN ART LIBRARY/ARCHIVES CHARMET

wrote Octave-Henri-Marie Mirbeau (1850–1917), "it is degrading and deadly to human activity: because it prevents the individual from developing his normal sense." Bakunin put it succinctly when he wrote that "despotism lies less in the *form* of the state or of power than in their very *principle*."

MOVING TOWARD A STATELESS SOCIETY

There was significant divergence among anarchists concerning how to move toward the goal of a stateless society. Many placed high hopes in education. Proudhon, for example, insisted on the importance of articulating the "worker idea." Reclus conceived in the 1870s a plan for a "scientific socialist education." Grave wrote of the need to disseminate "propaganda" to emancipate people from prejudice, ignorance, and the intellectual supports of the bourgeois

system. Beyond calls for education, anarchists proposed a wide variety of means. Early anarchists like Godwin and Proudhon disapproved of revolution, believing that rational discussion, education, and (for Proudhon) credit reform and productive cooperation based on contracts were the appropriate means for ushering in the stateless society of their dreams. Later anarchists like Bakunin, Brousse, Kropotkin, Reclus, and Grave believed that education, monetary reform, and workers' associations were insufficient and that, therefore, spontaneous popular revolt was necessary.

Some advocated "propaganda by the deed," a controversial concept that can be traced to anarchists in Italy and Switzerland during the 1870s, and that was formally adopted as a tactic at an international meeting of anarchists and social revolutionaries held in London in 1881. Whether propaganda by the deed sanctioned acts of terrorism, or whether it should be confined to periods of insurrection, was a much-debated issue. This became a central issue during the *l'ère des attentats* (1892–1894) when self-professed anarchists in France—like Ravachol, Auguste Vaillant, and Émile Henry—set off bombs in public places and in the homes of public figures. Anarchists assassinated six heads of state between 1881 and 1901, including the French president Sadi Carnot in 1894 and the U.S. president William McKinley in 1901. Many anarchist writers were embarrassed with the association and condemned these acts, even though they were reluctant to condemn the actors, whom they depicted as driven to action by circumstances. In 1891, Kropotkin wrote that "it is not by heroic acts that revolutions are made. . . . Revolution, above all, is a popular movement." And Jean Grave defensively stated that "we are not among those who preach acts of violence." But, it is equally clear that Kropotkin and Grave were disturbed only by violence directed at individuals; violent acts that destroyed institutions or that were part of a widespread revolution were entirely justified. "Once the struggle has begun," wrote Grave, "sentimentality will have no place, the multitude will distrust all phrase makers and unmercifully crush all who try to stand in the way." Many late-nineteenth-century anarchists believed in the necessity of violent insurrection, but most did not support individual acts of political terrorism.

Reclus and the majority of Italian anarchists refused to make these distinctions between

The Explosion of a Bomb on the Avenue de la République, Paris, by the Russian Anarchists and Nihilists.
Illustration from *Le Petit Journal,* February 1905. PRIVATE COLLECTION/BRIDGEMAN ART LIBRARY/ROGER-VIOLLET, PARIS

insurrection and terrorism. They advocated propaganda by the deed in the late 1870s; they defended anarchist thefts in the 1880s; they wrote admiringly of the terrorists in the 1890s. The popular image of the anarchist as a bomb-throwing extremist, not surprisingly, grew accordingly.

ANARCHIST MOVEMENTS

European anarchist movements were strongest in Italy and Spain. In the late 1860s, young Italian radicals became dissatisfied with Mazzini's conservative stance on social change, and they sided with Bakunin and the other "nonauthoritarians" against Karl Marx (1818–1883) within the International Workingmen's Association (IWA) when it split in 1872. The rapid growth of the IWA in Italy during the early 1870s was due to the activities of young militants like Carlo Cafiero (1846–1892), Andrea

Costa (1851–1910), and Errico Malatesta (1853–1932). These men were enchanted by Bakunin, and won over by his writings that extolled the virtues of labor, attacked capitalists, defended atheism, proposed social revolution, and denounced the state. In August 1874, Italian anarchists made plans for a coordinated series of uprisings in Bologna, Rome, Florence, and other cities, but lack of popular support and early detection by the authorities led to the easy suppression of the uprising and the quick arrest of most of the anarchist leaders. Three years later, in April 1877, there was a second attempt in the mountain villages of the Campagna; again it failed and led to a cycle of government repression.

Anarchism was vigorous on the Iberian peninsula during the same years. It was propagated by representatives of the nonauthoritarian wing of the IWA in the late 1860s, especially in the years following the September Revolution of 1868, which overthrew Queen Isabella II (r. 1833–1868). Until the Bourbon Restoration of 1875, there was intense social turmoil in Spain, which allowed radicals of various ideological colorations (including collectivist anarchists, who called for workers to receive the integral product of their labor, and communist anarchists, who called for a communal system of economic distribution) to bid for influence among disaffected rural and urban workers. The repression that accompanied the Restoration forced anarchist groups underground, giving proponents of insurrection and terrorism a stronger voice. With the establishment of the right of association in 1881, syndicalist forces within the anarchist movement became stronger. The most vocal and visible anarchists—writers like Fernando Tárrida del Mármol (1861–1915) and Ricardo Mella (1861–1925)—embraced an anarchism that appealed to the strong Spanish tradition of working-class associations, unions, *circulos, ateneos,* and similar organizations. Their so-called *anarquismo sin adjetivos* (anarchism without adjectives) converged with the ideal of the general strike to form the anarchosyndicalist ideology of the Confedercíon Nacional del Trabajo (CNT), founded in 1910.

In England, there was a split in 1884 between left-wing theorists who advocated political action and those who opposed parliamentarianism. In this year, William Morris (1834–1896) and others broke off from the Social Democratic Federation to form the Socialist League. For the next five years, Morris and his close associates advocated a radical change of the economy and society through education and revolution. In *Commonweal,* the paper of the Socialist League, workers were warned against compromising with contemptible politics and advised to put their faith in militant trade-unionism. The battles of "Bloody Sunday" between police and demonstrators at Trafalgar Square on 13 November 1887, and the success of the great Dock Strike of 1889 led some British militants to imagine that revolutionary change could be achieved through a universal strike.

Anarchism in France was usually associated with militant labor organizations (*syndicats*) that called for class war, the suppression of government, and the turning of workshops and factories over to the workers. This anarchosyndicalism, as it is sometimes called, was the orientation, for example, of Fernand Pelloutier (1867–1901), a young anarchist journalist who inspired and organized labor exchanges (Bourses du Travail) in the last years of the nineteenth century. In 1902, the Bourses merged with the Confédération Générale du Travail (General Confederation of Labor—CGT), and their doctrine, called revolutionary syndicalism, remained radical, violent, and directed against politicians and the state. The 1906 CGT congress at Amiens voted overwhelmingly for workers to shun politics and to prepare for the general strike for their "integral emancipation."

Like all nineteenth-century anarchists, French revolutionary syndicalists believed that states were immoral, coercive, bureaucratic machines responsible for the many oppressions and injustices of the modern age. For humans to achieve moral fulfillment and social justice, states must be replaced by interpersonal conversations, working-class associations, and local communities.

See also **Anarchosyndicalism; Bakunin, Mikhail; Kropotkin, Peter; Labor Movements; Proudhon, Pierre-Joseph; Ravachol (François Claudius Koenigstein-Ravachol); Socialism; Syndicalism.**

BIBLIOGRAPHY

Crowder, Georges. *Classical Anarchism: The Political Thought of Godwin, Proudhon, Bakunin, and Kropotkin.* New York, 1991.

Guérin, Daniel. *Anarchism: From Theory to Practice.* Translated by Mary Klopper. New York, 1970.

Joll, James. *The Anarchists.* 2nd ed. Cambridge, Mass., 1980.

Maitron, Jean. *Le mouvement anarchiste en France.* 2 vols. Paris, 1975.

Préposiet, Jean. *Histoire de l'anarchisme.* Paris, 1993.

Ritter, Alan. *Anarchism: A Theoretical Analysis.* Cambridge, U.K., and New York, 1980.

Sonn, Richard D. *Anarchism.* New York, 1992.

Woodcock, George. *Anarchism: A History of Libertarian Ideas and Movements.* Cleveland, Ohio, 1962.

K. STEVEN VINCENT

ANARCHOSYNDICALISM.

As its compound form suggests, anarchosyndicalism is best defined as an uneasy pairing of distinct but related theories or movements. Like each of its halves (anarchism and syndicalism), the whole is most easily understood by examining in turn its theoretical roots, its organization and practice, and some of its many national variants, as they evolved from its conceptual origins in the mid-nineteenth century through its heyday in the years before World War I. Its postwar legacy can be said to extend beyond the Bolshevik Revolution and through the popular fronts of the 1930s, and even into the "new social movements" of the 1960s and beyond.

THEORETICAL ROOTS

If purist anarchists pushed individual autonomy to the point of spurning all formal associations or movements, anarchosyndicalists embraced the trade union (*syndicat*) as a self-sufficient organ of revolution and as the embryo of future society. The term appears to have been coined in 1907 by the Russian anarchist Novomirsky (Daniil Kirilovsky, editor of *Novy Mir* [New world]), and it soon was used pejoratively by Marxists and Leninists, who scorned it as a pseudorevolutionary and petit bourgeois vestige of immature capitalism. The usage also allowed right-wing journalists and state authorities to evoke the specter of mindless bombings. The term later came to be used interchangeably with revolutionary syndicalism, a left-wing unionism most characteristic of pre–World War I France, where anarchism rose as a passing but potent rebuff of socialist orthodoxy. Yet true anarchosyndicalism retains more of its core libertarian, federalist, and antistatist precepts, while revolutionary syndicalism extols antiparliamentary direct action, social autonomy, and political neutrality from rival parties and movements, including anarchism itself.

Whereas anarchism has an older history and affirms the critical capacities and goals of all human individuals, anarchosyndicalism can be traced to the newer ideas of Pierre-Joseph Proudhon and Mikhail Bakunin, who privileged the workshop as the terrain for the economic struggle, and workers' status as producer and consumer as the basis for their central role in the revolutionary process. A subsequent wave of "propaganda by the deed"—a surge of assassination and terrorism, swelled by the invention of dynamite—distanced anarchists from workers and

crested in the years from 1892 to 1894. It was in retreat from this phase, and in contempt for the organizational hierarchies and ideological compromises of "bourgeois" socialism, that the hybrid anarchosyndicalism was born, heir to the "labor movement anarchism" of the First International. Even after renouncing "bombism," purist anarchists such as Peter Kropotkin and Errico Malatesta never accepted syndicalism as "sufficient unto itself" or the general strike as a proxy for insurrection. Yet once syndicalism had grown (for a time) more revolutionary and independent from political socialism, the International Anarchist Congress in Amsterdam (1907) approved it as a branch of "associationist federalism," as the parent doctrine was now defined.

ORGANIZATION AND PRACTICE

The syndicalist Charter of Amiens (1906) was the guiding manifesto of the General Confederation of Labor (CGT), founded in 1895 and later dubbed the "anarchist workers' party" of prewar France. The Charter affirmed the class struggle and proclaimed autonomy from all regimes and all "parties and sects," including anarchism; hence its support from both reformists and revolutionaries, free to engage in politics outside union doors. The CGT's hybrid structure, born of the merger (1902) of craft-based industrial federations with locally based *bourses du travail* (labor exchanges that also linked up a town's separate trade unions), gave the body its crucial tension between federalism or local autonomy and the growing centralism of nationally based occupational groups. Fernand Pelloutier, "father of revolutionary syndicalism" and leader of the labor exchange network, came to the movement from political socialism but called on anarchists to join in. He termed unions "free associations of free producers" that would school the worker in anarchist practice, social economy, and "the science of his unhappiness." Thus he prized action above theory, and union autonomy as not just method but goal.

Yet even those with roots in the anarchist movement, arguably surer of the masses' revolutionary instincts, likewise set out to rouse them from passivity. The French anarchist convert Émile Pouget, briefly exiled in London during the movement's terrorist phase, grew to admire British-style trade unions. But he still approved partial strikes as the "revolutionary gymnastics" that would train workers for the final, cataclysmic general strike. Further anarchosyndicalist tactics ranged from sabotage and antimilitarism (though not always antiwar fervor) to electoral abstention and other forms of "direct action" by "active minorities" whose power of will would compensate for their lack of numbers. Indeed, a main premise for direct action was that unions stood for the whole working class, not just their formal members: hence their disdain for dues payment as the mark of membership and their rule in the CGT (as in the old Estates-General) of one vote per union, regardless of size.

This denial of proportional representation, confirmed at the CGT's Congress of Bourges (1904), gave the smallest and most militant unions the greatest weight in leadership and decision-making. The larger unions (and most workers), however, preferred milder strategies. Revolutionary syndicalism was thus to some extent a movement whose reformist voice went unheard. Yet this critique overstates the gap between leaders and members and discounts the convergence between moderate and radical ends and means. Revolutionary syndicalism's propensity for violence may even have reflected the cultural "irrationalism" of the fin de siècle and could be considered a source of the fascism that surged after World War I. The alleged influence of Georges Sorel (in fact more an observer than a theorist of syndicalism) and his gravitation from Left to Right have encouraged such thinking, even though outside Italy the movement's right-wing ties were only marginal. Still, it is valid to see syndicalism as a lasting trait of political culture, not a technologically "determined" trace of capitalism in a stage of transition. This point emerges through comparing the varied national experiences of syndicalism in Europe before and after 1914.

NATIONAL VARIANTS

In France, syndicalism's quest for social autonomy stemmed from the early onset of universal manhood suffrage plus the late legalization of unions. Workers enjoyed full political representation, but their social marginalization led unions into voluntary secession, not just from party politics but from bourgeois society. This zeal for autonomy has endured in France as a sign that class lines remain culturally important despite growing affluence or alleged "embourgeoise-

ment." In Britain and Germany, where anarchosyndicalism was rare although not unknown, especially in localist craft unions, most workers instead were integrated socially and enjoyed social protection laws, but their delay in winning political rights left them more preoccupied with the vote than in France.

In Britain, machinist Tom Mann's industrial syndicalism grew both from a visit to France and from longer contacts with the Industrial Workers of the World (IWW) in Australia. James Connolly's and James "Big Jim" Larkin's Irish syndicalism likewise had roots in the IWW in the United States. Although resembling Continental syndicalism and guild socialism in their distrust for employer and state authority, these movements envisioned "one big union" that merged industrial and transport workers rather than a federalist network based in skilled crafts. These syndicalist currents surged in violent strikes on the eve of World War I, despite ebbing elsewhere, including in France by 1910. In prewar Germany, the small federalist Free Association of German Unions embraced local autonomy and the general strike and severed its ties to the Social Democratic Party. Yet most German unions prized the political struggle above labor radicalism, even after the rise of a syndicalist-tinged "council communism" in 1918.

Like France, "Latin" Italy and Spain are also renowned for their anarchist and syndicalist movements, with lasting echoes long after they quieted elsewhere. Both cases revealed the influence of Bakunin, whose delegates founded both national sections of the First International. Italy's network of *camere del lavoro* (chambers of labor) were modeled on France's *bourses du travail,* and its General Confederation of Labor (founded 1906) shared the hybrid structure of France's CGT. But it kept close ties with the Socialist Party and followed a mostly reformist path, while a growing minority formed the rival Italian Syndicalist Union in 1912, with anarchist support.

Although Italy's syndicalists embraced direct action and the general strike, sometimes in partnership with anarchists and left-wing socialists, they remained a largely intellectual force with few links to organized labor. Their critique of socialist reformism included a Sorelian rejection of Marxist positivism so as to highlight the power of violence and will. Syndicalists such as the journalist Arturo

Labriola also denounced anarchist individualism and wished to destroy the state but not all social authority. Indeed, hating the state for its weakness, not its strength, many syndicalists joined or helped create postwar Italian fascism, although Benito Mussolini's own roots lay in left-wing socialism.

In socioeconomic terms, Italian syndicalism won support in some northern industries and embarked on postwar strikes centered in Milan and Turin. While Malatesta remained skeptical, anarchists and syndicalists grouped together to occupy the factories, with "council communists" typically at the helm. Labriola, from Naples, also spoke for Italy's poorest southern peasants, who joined in postwar land seizures. Peasant populism underlay anarchist theory since the days of Proudhon and Bakunin, for whom "the people" stretched well beyond Karl Marx's factory proletariat. Although rural anarchism had scant yields among France's small peasant owners, it fed the syndicalist movements in both Spain and Russia before World War I.

Spain's National Confederation of Labor (CNT), founded on the French model in 1911, was at first a minority group based mainly in Catalonia. Yet it grew to surpass the older Socialist-led labor federation and became the world's largest syndicalist body, poised to take part in Spain's Popular Front government and the civil war that began in 1936. Banned shortly after its birth and again for a time after World War I, the CNT adopted flexible structures well suited to clandestinity, plus violent tactics akin to Russia's insurrectionalism. Critics have scorned its millenarianism as primitive and impotent, but others note its appeal to small producers, not just the desperately poor.

In Russia, where unions and strikes were illegal until after the Revolution of 1905, the anarchist and populist traditions yielded a more Leninist than syndicalist revision of Marxism. Yet locally organized *soviets* (workers' councils) rose to prominence in the revolutions of 1905 and 1917, events that enthralled syndicalists around the world. Despite ideological disparities, Western militants hailed the Bolshevik victory as a triumph for syndicalism and took Vladimir Lenin's word that the dictatorship of the proletariat was meant to wither away. The suppression of Russia's left-wing Workers' Opposition, plus the new Comintern's rules on party–union linkage, would lead most anarchosyndicalists to reconsider and form their own separate groups.

Over the long run, anarchosyndicalism has fostered modern notions of workers' control, self-managing socialism, and direct action campaigns for feminism, consumerism, decolonization, antinuclearism, and ecology. It no longer limits its purview to production or wage labor but avows broader aims of "the people" for whom Proudhon and Bakunin had always spoken. Given its zeal for direct action, anarchosyndicalism is sometimes better known as "direct action syndicalism," or a movement whose quest for autonomy outflanked its revolutionary mission. Direct action alone promised the emancipation that political revolution failed to win. Years before confirmation from Russia, French syndicalists had already decried the dictatorship of the proletariat and chosen the general strike as a revolutionary means to forestall a dictatorial outcome. By 1914, syndicalism may also have marked less an ideological battle between parties and unions than a generational (and gendered) shift within each branch, from an elite male vanguard to a younger and less-skilled mass corps. In retreat from class struggle, parties and unions alike seemed to settle for bombast in lieu of the real revolution they would not make. Beyond economic trends, it was also the course of class integration that led syndicalists to halt their withdrawal from bourgeois society. World War I marked a climax but not a final phase of this action; the endgame played out at different times in different places, if indeed at all.

See also **Anarchism; Class and Social Relations; Labor Movements; Second International; Socialism.**

BIBLIOGRAPHY

Amdur, Kathryn E. *Syndicalist Legacy: Trade Unions and Politics in Two French Cities in the Era of World War I.* Urbana and Chicago, 1986.

Esenwein, George Richard. *Anarchist Ideology and the Working-Class Movement in Spain, 1868–1898.* Berkeley and Los Angeles, 1989.

Geary, Dick, ed. *Labour and Socialist Movements in Europe before 1914.* Oxford, U.K., 1989.

Jennings, Jeremy. *Syndicalism in France: A Study of Ideas.* London, 1990.

Julliard, Jacques. *Autonomie ouvrière: Études sur le syndicalisme d'action directe.* Paris, 1988.

Launay, Michel. *Le syndicalisme en Europe.* Paris, 1990.

Mommsen, Wolfgang J., and Hans-Gerhard Husung, eds. *The Development of Trade Unionism in Great Britain and Germany, 1880–1914.* London, 1985.

Ridley, F. F. *Revolutionary Syndicalism in France: The Direct Action of Its Time.* Cambridge, U.K., 1970.

Robert, Jean-Louis, Friedhelm Boll, and Antoine Prost, eds. *L'Invention des syndicalismes: Le syndicalisme en Europe occidentale à la fin du XIXe siècle.* Paris, 1997.

Roberts, David D. *The Syndicalist Tradition and Italian Fascism.* Chapel Hill, N.C., 1979.

Rosanvallon, Pierre. *La question syndicale: Histoire et avenir d'une forme sociale.* Paris, 1988.

Rubel, Maximilien, and John Crump, eds. *Non-Market Socialism in the Nineteenth and Twentieth Centuries.* Basingstoke, U.K., 1987.

Sagnes, Jean, Bartolomé Bennassar, Catherine Collomp, et al. *Histoire du syndicalisme dans le monde: Des origines à nos jours.* Toulouse, France, 1994.

Schecter, Darrow. *Radical Theories: Paths Beyond Marxism and Social Democracy.* Manchester, U.K., 1994.

Skirda, Alexandre. *Facing the Enemy: A History of Anarchist Organization from Proudhon to May 1968.* Translated by Paul Sharkey. Oakland, Calif., 2002.

Van der Linden, Marcel, and Jürgen Rojahn, eds. *The Formation of Labour Movements, 1870–1914: An International Perspective.* 2 vols. Leiden, Netherlands, 1990.

Van der Linden, Marcel, and Wayne Thorpe, eds. *Revolutionary Syndicalism: An International Perspective.* Aldershot, U.K., 1990.

KATHRYN E. AMDUR

ANDREAS-SALOMÉ, LOU (1861–1937), German writer.

Perhaps the most brilliant woman of her generation in Europe was born Louise Salomé on 12 February 1861 in St. Petersburg, Russia. She was the fourth and last child, and only daughter, of an aging general turned high state official. Her family background and household language were mostly German.

YOUTH

By her later account of her introverted childhood, Salomé told tall tales night and day to a grandfatherly personal god who would swallow them one and all, thereby certifying them as true.

Exposed once by a cousin as the fantasist she was, she reacted by teaching herself to register facts with painstaking exactitude by way of earning the right to play free and loose with them. Her childhood ended when at length she pressed her god to appear in person; he vanished instead, leaving her to sustain her imaginings alone. All the while she resisted learning from a French governess, an English private school, and finally a German lyceum, where she was demoted to mere auditor for plagiarism on top of poor grades.

Her father's death when she turned seventeen brought on a nervous crisis during which she was smitten with a charismatic pulpit philosopher named Hendrik Gillot, who took the lonely underperformer in hand and exacted disciplined study from her in return for hearing out her fantasies. The blissful, fruitful spell broke when she discerned Gillot's intent to divorce his wife and marry her—or so she related late in her life, on her poetic license to re-edit her past. More prosaically she worked herself sick for Gillot, so that her mother took her to western Europe for treatment early in 1880. That autumn she began studying comparative religion as an auditor at the University of Zurich.

A year later, well schooled now, Salomé was chaperoned farther south for her worsening health. January 1882 found her in Rome under the wing of a patroness of high-minded youngsters, Malwida von Meysenbug (1816–1903). A young utilitarian moral philosopher and lovable yet self-hating Jew, Paul Rée (1849–1901), joined the party in March. Infatuated with Salomé, Rée summoned his senior partner in philosophical mischief, Friedrich Nietzsche (1844–1900), down from Genoa to meet this most promising prospective disciple who was all eagerness to set up a chaste ménage with the two of them. The itinerant reclusive genius sailed instead to Messina until, a full month later, the sirocco drove him to Rome to meet his fate at last in the person of a frail and bewitching twenty-one-year-old pious freethinker flushed with fervent fever for life and electrically responsive to his deepest thoughts and pithiest aphorisms. She craved an intellectual mentor, and he an intellectual heiress, each with a passion that neither recognized as erotic deep down.

Returning north with her party, Salomé met with Nietzsche and Rée along the way to map out

Lou Andreas-Salomé. MARY EVANS/SIGMUND FREUD COPYRIGHTS

their future course. To reassure Nietzsche, she insisted vociferously that marriage would not be necessary, appearances be damned. He arranged for a trial stay together in Tautenburg near Jena that August with his sister, Elisabeth, as duenna. But first Salomé went to the Rées' country manor in Tütz upon her mother's return to Russia, and then attended the premiere of *Parsifal* in Bayreuth, rooming with Elisabeth.

Rée, jealous, cautioned Salomé against Nietzsche's possible designs on her, and Elisabeth, jealous, warned Nietzsche against the Russian adventuress on the make. Thus the trial stay got off to a stormy start. The two nonetheless thrilled to each other's kindred thinking for a fortnight, above all on religious psychology. Nietzsche even wept over a poem by Salomé that he later set to music. No matter: reports from Bayreuth of her boasting about having the two philosophers in harness, as in a comic photograph she had engineered on the way

from Rome, were too much for the thin-skinned moral revolutionary Nietzsche. He opted out of the tense triangle after five weeks of it in Leipzig that autumn, then bombarded Salomé with wildly rancorous letters. So Salomé set up in Berlin chastely with Rée alone. While ostensibly shrugging Nietzsche off, she made several futile tries at reconciling, once even spending some weeks with Rée in Celerina, Switzerland, just below Nietzsche's summer retreat in Sils-Maria, and dispatching the sociologist Ferdinand Tönnies (1855–1936), then desperately wooing her, on that fool's errand. She novelized the whole triangular misadventure of 1882 in *Im Kampf um Gott* (Struggling for God) three years later. Nietzsche found it both lofty and girlish—rightly.

He reciprocated with the Christian "reversal of values" in *The Genealogy of Morals* (1887), whereby the Jews, notably Paul, incited the slaves against their masters, these being infected with slavish rancor in the process. After madness struck Nietzsche in 1889, Salomé published a sketch of his late philosophy interspersed with fond tributes to his person and prose in a series of ten articles that became *Friedrich Nietzsche in seinen Werken* (1894; Friedrich Nietzsche in his works). She drew on, besides their Tautenburg repartee, his letters to her with slyly suggestive elisions, and his old letters to Rée without due distinction, so as to come off as a long-standing intimate confidante turned wayward heiress. Nietzsche's sister called her bluff, and Salomé countered with a whispered refusal over the years to rebut her openly out of pretended discretion about a marriage proposal by Nietzsche. Against all the evidence, Nietzsche as Salomé's spurned suitor has held his own in the popular literature. This triumphant trickery notwithstanding, Salomé never settled her Nietzsche account: the shock she suffered from his raging rebuff, then from the collapse of his kindred mind, haunted her later life and works.

MATURITY

Rée exited his relationship with Salomé in 1886. He learned medicine, practiced charitably for some years in Tütz, but then returned to Alpine Celerina and fell to his death there in 1901. Rée gone, Salomé's collection of frustrated proposals culminated in a white marriage in 1887 to a prodigious exotic philologist surnamed Andreas: he took the forename Friedrich for the occasion. Married, Lou Andreas-Salomé (as she was now known) tormented her men and herself only the more. In 1894 the socialist radical Georg Ledebour (1850–1947) told her off for it and the avant-garde playwright Frank Wedekind (1864–1918) embarrassed her over it. One last sentimental casualty was the writer Richard Beer-Hofmann (1866–1945), and at the turn of 1896 Andreas-Salomé launched an "almost rhythmic turnover" (her own words) of junior lovers with an internist named Friedrich Pineles (1868–1936). She would blend her erotic escapades into frenetic rounds of socializing that alternated with long spells of writing at home in Berlin or, as of 1903, in Göttingen. Her calendars and correspondence richly chronicle German, and at one point also Russian, letters and theater of her time.

In 1897 Andreas-Salomé began reliving her failed romance with her master and taskmaster of 1882 as mistress and taskmistress to a budding poet of twenty-one, Rainer (or at first René) Maria Rilke (1875–1926). In early 1901, soon after a trip across Russia beside him through which she exultantly discovered her dormant Russian identity, she dispatched the "homunculus" (as she called him to Gerhart Hauptmann [1862–1946]) with a parting warning against his potential for madness. Relenting gradually as his fame grew, she let him resume writing her in 1903, then also seeing her ever so reticently beginning two years later, only to wind up memorializing their unbroken closeness after his death. Their amour was the time of her own greatest fame as a fictionist in a storybook vein far removed from the unique intellectual and lyrical intensity of the essays she wrote alongside. Of these, "Der Mensch als Weib" (1899; The human being as woman), "Gedanken über das Liebesproblem" (1900; Thoughts on the problem of love), and "Alter und Ewigkeit" (1901; Old age and eternity) stand with many an exquisite miniature in her journals among the finest specimens in any language.

Her golden age of letters well behind her, Andreas-Salomé struck out on an exhilarating new course after a psychiatrist lover took her to a psychoanalytic congress in September 1911. She lapped up the new science in the making first at home for a year, then in Vienna at Sigmund Freud's (1856–1939) elbow in 1912–1913, attending his university lectures, meeting with his

weekly working circle, and twice chatting lengthily about her childhood with him. The rest of her life she practiced psychoanalysis expertly and enthusiastically, charging very little as Freud would allow. Her clientele included referrals from Freud—among them his daughter, whom, however, she refused to pry loose from him as he urged. She contributed several classic theoretical studies—on femaleness, on anality, on narcissism—all marked by her impassioned penchant for primal, selfless, indiscriminate affectivity. Her devotion to Freud and his work was total from first to last; when once he poured scorn on a former lover of hers from his Vienna circle, Viktor Tausk, in reporting Tausk's suicide to her, she reworked the event into a short story, "Geschwister" (Siblings), which above all showed the new "father-face over my life" as replicating that of his great predecessor of 1882 in her emotional underworld.

Freud relished Andreas-Salomé's devotion, finding her the soul of authenticity. He called a grand open letter of 1931 by her to him for his seventy-fifth birthday "an unintentional proof of your superiority over us all as suits the heights from which you came down to us." In 1935 Freud excitedly sent her the first sketch of his Moses book just as in 1922 Rilke had ecstatically sent her the first tidings of his *Duino Elegies* delivered all at once full-blown after a decade's gestation and followed by his unexpected *Sonnets to Orpheus* a few days later. What surer demonstration could there be of the power of her personality at all ages? Alone after Andreas's death in 1930, Andreas-Salomé increasingly refashioned her past in pseudo-memoirs, purging and pruning her papers accordingly while grooming a literary heir with the aim to "remain preserved, laid out in state," after her death. She died on 5 February 1937, believing death to be a "homecoming."

See also **Freud, Sigmund; Nietzsche, Friedrich.**

BIBLIOGRAPHY

Primary Sources

Andreas-Salomé, Lou. *Im Kampf um Gott.* Leipzig, 1885.

———. *Friedrich Nietzsche in seinen Werken.* Vienna, 1894.

———. *Rainer Maria Rilke.* Leipzig, 1928.

———. *Mein Dank an Freud.* Vienna, 1931.

Secondary Sources

Binion, Rudolph. *Frau Lou: Nietzsche's Wayward Disciple.* Princeton, N.J., 1968.

RUDOLPH BINION

ANNEKE, MATHILDE-FRANZISKA.

(Mathilde-Franziska Giesler; 1817–1884), German writer, publisher, educator, and women's rights activist.

Born on 3 April 1817 in Ober-Leveringhausen near Blankenstein on the Ruhr River in Germany, Mathilde-Franziska Anneke was the eldest of the twelve children of the bourgeois family of Karl Giesler, a city councillor and tax assessor, and his wife, Elisabeth. Only one year after marrying Alfred von Tabouillot in 1836, and with an infant daughter, she asked for a divorce, having been abused by her husband. Through a long fight in court, she experienced the discrimination against women in the legal system. She became a writer and soon made a reputation as an advocate for women's rights. In her book *Das Weib im Konflikt mit den socialen Verhältnissen* (1847; Woman in conflict with social conditions) she defended Louise Aston, a divorced woman who had been expelled from Berlin for her advocacy of gender equality and for "unwomanly" behavior.

In 1846 she joined oppositional groups in Münster. There she met the former Prussian officer Fritz Anneke, who had been discharged from the army for his "democratic leanings." They married in June 1847 and moved to Cologne. Their home became a meeting place for liberal poets and writers such as Ferdinand Freiligrath, and the Annekes helped to found the revolutionary *Kölner Arbeiterverein* (Cologne Workers' Association). Fritz Anneke was unhappy about the political passivity of the association, but he did not openly oppose its leader, Andreas Gottschalk. When both men were arrested in early July 1848, a group led by Karl Marx took over and tried to bring the association more in line with Cologne's Democratic Society.

Her husband's arrest did not stop Mathilde Anneke's work on a newspaper project that had been her idea. The *Neue Kölnische Zeitung* "for the enlightenment of the working people" was first published on 10 September 1848 but was soon suppressed. Anneke continued it as the *Frauenzeitung* (Women's newspaper). It was not strictly a feminist paper, but this way Anneke hoped to circumvent censorship and at the same time introduce the question of women's rights into the democratic movement. The newspaper was published earlier than Louise Otto's *Frauen-Zeitung*, making it the first women's rights periodical in Germany. After only two issues the paper, which had advocated radical ideas such as the separation of school and church, was suppressed. In October 1848 the *Neue Kölnische Zeitung* was allowed to resume publication. Marx made it the successor to his *Neue Rheinische Zeitung* when the latter was prohibited in May 1849.

Fritz Anneke, who had been released in December 1848, joined the revolutionary forces in Baden and the Palatine in mid-May. The next month Mathilde Anneke left Cologne and served her husband as an unarmed orderly. In *Memoiren einer Frau aus dem badisch-pfälzischen Feldzuge* (A woman's memoirs of the Baden-Palatinate campaign), published in 1853, she explained why she as a woman had been on the battlefield. When the Rastatt fortress surrendered in July 1849, the Annekes fled Germany. Later that year they emigrated to the United States, where they were among the most prominent Forty-Eighters.

The Annekes settled in Milwaukee in March 1850 and soon became active in political and cultural affairs. She restarted the publication of her *Deutsche Frauenzeitung*, a "Central Organ of the Organizations for the Improvement of the Position of Women," in March 1852 and continued the publication after the family moved to Newark, New Jersey. It had up to two thousand subscribers. Anneke published translations of articles by the leading American suffragists and also reprinted parts of her own works. Poor health and family responsibilities forced her to stop its publication in 1855. Three years later the family moved back to Milwaukee. From 1860 to 1865 Mathilde Anneke lived in Switzerland, working for American and German newspapers, while her husband fought in the Civil War. She returned to Milwaukee with Cäcilie Kapp, the daughter of a prominent educator. Together they founded a boarding and day school especially for girls—the Töchter-Institut—which closed after Anneke's death on 25 November 1884.

Mathilde Anneke was an outspoken freethinker, opponent of slavery, and supporter of radical democratic movements. While living in New Jersey she joined the American suffrage movement, gave speeches in many cities in the Northeast and Midwest, and became friends with Susan B. Anthony, Elizabeth Cady Stanton, and other suffrage leaders. When the movement split in 1869, Anneke sided with Anthony, Stanton, and others who formed the National Woman Suffrage Association. Never being fluent in English somewhat limited her activities, but as vice-president for the Wisconsin Woman Suffrage Association she was an important adviser to the national leadership and became one of the best-known speakers of the movement.

Her feminism, based on the ideas of the German Enlightenment and on idealism, was radically democratic and antireligious; she fought both temperance and nativism. For her the liberation of women was part of a much larger struggle for democracy, equality, and social justice. In 1930 the League of Women Voters honored Mathilde-Franziska Anneke along with seventy other women—among them Anthony, Stanton, and Jane Addams—as a pioneer of women's rights activism in the United States.

See also **Feminism; Suffragism.**

BIBLIOGRAPHY

Brancaforte, Charlotte Lang. *Mathilde Franziska Anneke: An Essay on Her Life.* Milwaukee, 1998.

Bus, Annette. "Mathilde Anneke and the Suffrage Movement." In *The German Forty-Eighters in the United States,* edited by Charlotte L. Brancaforte, 79–92. New York, 1989.

Wagner, Maria. *Mathilde Franziska Anneke in Selbstzeugnissen und Dokumenten.* Frankfurt, 1980. Includes long excerpts of letters, articles, and other documents.

ANDREAS ETGES

ANTICLERICALISM. The word *anticlericalism* can first be found in the correspondence of French officials in the 1850s, and it became an important term in the religious and political vocabulary of Europeans in the last third of the nineteenth century. But resentment of the power of the clergy can be found in the Middle Ages, and was a central element in the Protestant Reformation and the Enlightenment. In the nineteenth century Protestant ministers sometimes had strained relations with the laity and political establishments, but anticlericalism most often refers to antipathy directed at the Roman Catholic clergy and, to a lesser extent, the clergy of the Anglican Church in Great Britain. Anticlericalism is a complex phenomenon, which varied significantly depending on time and place. For purposes of analysis we can look at anticlericalism in its social, political, and cultural manifestations. These different strains of anticlericalism came together at certain moments to produce culture wars that defined sharply different positions and in some cases violent conflict over the role of the clergy and the church in modern Europe.

Anticlericalism was particularly potent in France during the 1790s and throughout Europe in the early 1830s. In the last third of the nineteenth century anticlericalism was an important political and cultural force that produced major legislation on church-state relations and expressed anxieties about the loyalty of citizens and the solidarity of families.

SOCIAL RESENTMENT OF THE CLERGY

The Catholic clergy constituted a powerful elite in Catholic Europe as religious leaders charged with defining and defending the moral values of their communities. In carrying out this role they interacted with the laity in a number of ways that generated conflict and resentment. Clerical control of the sacraments was one important source of trouble, for many parishioners resented the efforts by priests to use these rituals as a way of imposing their will. French archives, for example, contain numerous complaints in which priests are accused of rejecting parental choices about godparents, of prohibiting children from receiving first communion, of deferring absolution in the confessional, and of refusing the last sacraments and religious burial to people as they faced death. Such selective prohibitions were aggravated by the fees clergy charged for the performance of their duties. Preaching directed against communal festive events was another source of tension, with dancing a particularly contentious issue. Throughout the first half of the nineteenth century the clergy fought a losing battle against the growing popularity of the waltz, which they saw as a source of moral corruption for the young. Conflicts over the costs of maintaining churches, presbyteries, and cemeteries could also threaten relations between clergy and laity. Many clergy managed to get along well with the people they served, but even in the best of circumstances some tension was inevitable, and when priests took an imperious manner and played favorites communities could dissolve into hostile factions. There is no solid evidence that clerical behavior became worse in the nineteenth century and some reason to believe that priests became more accommodating to those who came to church. But the political and cultural critics whose agenda included control of and in some cases elimination of the clergy could rely on a base of social resentment based on experience and memory.

POLITICAL ANTICLERICALISM

As monarchical states accumulated more and more power over their subjects in the seventeenth and eighteenth centuries they acted to control the wealth and influence of the clergy, who were feared as alternative sources of authority. In the late eighteenth century this policy led to a series of measures directed against the clergy, summarized as "Josephism," because they were most fully articulated by the Holy Roman Emperor Joseph II (r. 1765–1790). Joseph seized the property of monastic houses and interfered with the communications between the pope and the churches in the empire. Joseph's assault on religious congregations was part of a larger pattern, exemplified most dramatically in the suppression of the Jesuits by Pope Clement XIV (r. 1769–1774) in 1773, who acted under the pressure of several Catholic monarchs. Policies targeting the clergy, especially religious congregations, were adopted in some form by almost all the European states in the course of the nineteenth century.

Political anticlericalism was a central element in the revolutionary legislation enacted by the French National Assembly in 1789, which released monks and nuns from their vows, abolished monasteries and convents, and seized church property as a way of dealing with the national debt. The refusal of

about half of the clergy to swear an oath to the Civil Constitution of the Clergy (July 1790), which called for the lay election of curés and bishops, was a major source of political conflict in France, which lasted until the Napoleonic treaty with Pope Pius VII (r. 1800–1823) was signed in 1801. The Catholic clergy were among the most visible targets of the Reign of Terror (1793–1794), when hundreds of priests were murdered as defenders of the fallen monarchy, and as proponents of superstition who kept the people in ignorance as a way of maintaining their own power.

This association of the clergy with political reaction and the pursuit of ecclesiastical power remained a central theme in European political life, with the French Revolution setting a pattern for popular violence and legislation directed against the clergy that was repeated at several times and in several places throughout the nineteenth century. In the wake of the French Revolution of 1830 mission crosses raised by preachers during the Bourbon Restoration (1814–1830) were torn down, and the palace of the archbishop of Paris was sacked in February 1831. In England the bishop of Bristol's palace was sacked in October of 1831 by a crowd angered over his opposition to the Reform Act that was intended to expand the suffrage. In Spain anticlericalism was a particularly potent force linking liberal reformers and urban workers and producing periodic outbursts of legislative repression and crowd action. About one hundred members of religious orders were killed in Madrid and Barcelona in 1834 and 1835, where they were suspected of supporting the pretender Charles against Queen Isabella in the Carlist war over the succession to the Spanish throne. A liberal government in Spain abolished monasteries and seized their property in 1837.

A second major wave of anticlerical political activity occurred in the last third of the nineteenth century. The clergy were targeted by a number of radical leaders of the Paris Commune of 1871, such as Raoul Rigault, a disciple of the socialist and militant atheist Louis-Auguste Blanqui. Inspired by Blanquist ideals the police of the Commune took a number of clerical hostages, including the Archbishop Darboy, who was among the dozen or so priests executed in the chaotic last days of the Commune in May 1871. A more moderate version of anticlericalism was a basic element in the estab-

A Child Claimed by the Church, the State, and the Freemasons. Caricature by Charles Felix Gir from the satirical French journal *L'Assiette au Buerre*, 1907. A priest is depicted as one of three threats to the autonomy of a French worker's family. PRIVATE COLLECTION/BRIDGEMAN ART LIBRARY. © 2005 ADAGP, PARIS/ ARTISTS RIGHTS SOCIETY (ARS), NEW YORK.

lishment and development of the French Third Republic. In the 1880s the state began enforcing restrictions on religious congregations, and forced priests, brothers, and nuns out of the public school system. As a result of the Dreyfus affair, when the Assumptionist fathers took a leading role in attacking Captain Alfred Dreyfus (1859–1935), the government passed a Law of Associations (1901) that prohibited religious congregations and led to the exile of thirty thousand clergy. The separation of church and state, enacted in 1905, abolished the Concordat of 1801, and thereby eliminated the state salaries that had supported the clergy throughout the century. The program of *laïcité* defended by the Fifth Republic, which seeks to exclude religious expression from the public sphere, is a direct descendent of the policies put in place by the anticlericals of the Third French Republic.

Political anticlericalism was a potent force throughout Europe in the last years of the nineteenth century and the early twentieth century. A wave of anticlerical legislation followed the Spanish revolution of 1868, and in 1909 workers in Barcelona destroyed forty convents and twelve parochial churches in a series of riots known as "the tragic week." As a result of the repression that followed, including the execution of the anticlerical Francisco Ferrer, workers in Barcelona and elsewhere in Spain were even more convinced that social and political progress depended on eliminating the power of the clergy. The animosity of Spanish anticlericals and supporters of the clergy that developed in the nineteenth century set the stage for much of the violence that occurred during the Spanish Civil War (1936–1939).

In Italy and Germany political anticlericalism was a prominent force insofar as many politicians suspected the clergy of being more loyal to the church than to the nation. During the German Kulturkampf (culture war) in the 1870s Chancellor

Otto von Bismarck (r. 1871–1890) won approval for laws that established Prussian state control over clerical education (1873) and abolished religious orders and congregations (1875). Opposition resulted in at least some time in jail for five of the twelve German bishops and hundreds of prosecutions directed at the lower clergy. The Kulturkampf ended in 1887, in part because Bismarck sought Catholic support in his attack on the socialists, but the Protestant League formed that year became a powerful mass organization that saw Catholics, and particularly their clergy, as disloyal to the nation.

CULTURAL ANTICLERICALISM

Anticlericalism as a political force has sometimes been viewed as a maneuver by liberal politicians to draw in a working-class constituency without having to offer any fundamental social reforms. Anticlericalism did provide an agenda for cross-class alliances, an obvious benefit that was apparent to liberal politicians. In addition to such political motives anticlericalism became increasingly fueled by an intense hatred of the clergy, who were seen as destroying the emotional lives of families and ruthlessly seeking to defraud them in order to accumulate wealth. These attitudes were conveyed in a growing literature that included pamphlets and press reports highlighting clerical scandals, as well as novels by some of the leading literary figures of the late nineteenth century. Masonic lodges and societies of freethinkers were also conduits for attacks on the clergy, and were particularly important in France and Belgium in the last third of the century.

The French historian Jules Michelet gave powerful expression to some of the most important cultural complaints of anticlericals in *Le prêtre, la femme, et la famille* (1845; The priest, the woman, and the family), where he attacked priests for using the darkness and isolation of the confessional to form an intimate bond with wives and daughters of French families, alienating them from their husbands and fathers. For many anticlerical writers this intimacy led easily into the seduction of young women, a central element in the plots of Émile Zola's *La Faute de l'Abbé Mouret* (1875; The Sin of Father Mouret) and José Maria Eça de Queirós's *O crime do Padre Amaro* (1880; The Crime of Father

Amaro). Stories of such sexual misconduct were common in newspapers as well as in novels in the last third of the century, with nuns as well as priests being accused of immorality. The heavily sexualized content of much of the anticlerical writing suggests that the clergy were in part a useful screen on which people projected anxieties about the separate spheres that determined the lives of middle-class men and women, a social pattern that coexisted uneasily with a desire for domestic intimacy.

The Jesuits were the most widely loathed religious congregation among anticlericals, and the target of some of the most lurid literature. Eugène Sue's *Le Juif errant* (*The Wandering Jew*), which first appeared as a popular serial in the French newspaper *Le Constitutionnel* (1845), revolves around a Jesuit plot to seize the inheritance of the Rennepont family, part of their larger conspiracy to dominate the world through wealth and intrigue. This "Jesuit myth" resembles much of the anti-Semitic literature of the period, for both drew on simplistic and titillating scenarios that described villainous enemies conspiring to destroy the social order. In its moderate form anticlericalism pushed European states toward policies directed against religious congregations, clerical influence on education, and the exclusion of Catholicism from the public sphere. In its more radical form anticlericalism is part of a larger history of the demonization of political and cultural enemies, of the use of distorted and invented images that carry a religious charge, and which propose a Manichean view of history as the battle of good against evil.

See also **Catholicism; Catholicism, Political; French Revolution; Kulturkampf; Separation of Church and State (France, 1905).**

BIBLIOGRAPHY

Primary Sources

De Queirós, Eça. *The Crime of Father Amaro: Scenes from the Religious Life*. 1880. Translated from the Portugese and with an introduction by Margaret Jull Costa. New York, 2003.

Zola, Émile. *The Sin of Father Mouret*. 1875. Translated by Sandy Petrey. Lincoln, Nebr., 1983.

Secondary Sources

Aston, Nigel, and Matthew Cragoe, eds. *Anticlericalism in Britain, c. 1500–1914*. Phoenix Mill, U.K., 2000.

Callahan, William J. *Church, Politics, and Society in Spain, 1750–1874.* Cambridge, Mass., 1984.

Cubitt, Geoffrey. *The Jesuit Myth: Conspiracy Theory and Politics in Nineteenth-Century France.* Oxford, U.K., and New York, 1993.

Evans, Eric. "Some Reasons for the Growth of Anti-Clericalism in England." *Past and Present,* no. 66 (1975): 84–109.

Gross, Michael B. *The War against Catholicism: Liberalism and the Anti-Catholic Imagination in Nineteenth-Century Germany.* Ann Arbor, Mich., 2004.

Lalouette, Jacqueline. *La république anticléricale: XIXe–XXe siècles.* Paris, 2002.

Rémond, René. *L'anticléricalisme en France, de 1815 à nos jours.* Paris, 1976

Sánchez, José. *Anticlericalism: A Brief History.* Notre Dame, Ind., 1972.

Smith, Helmut Walser. *German Nationalism and Religious Conflict: Culture, Ideology, Politics, 1870–1914.* Princeton, N.J., 1995.

Ullman, Joan Connelly. *The Tragic Week: A Study of Anti-clericalism in Spain, 1875–1912.* Cambridge, Mass., 1968.

THOMAS KSELMAN

ANTI-SEMITISM.

The term *anti-Semitism* first appeared and gained currency in Europe in the early 1880s to describe, it was claimed, a modern and objective hostility to the Semitic race, in contrast to hatred derived from earlier religious fantasies about Jews. The distinction was a key point in a defining document of modern anti-Semitism, Wilhelm Marr's best-selling book *Der Sieg des Judentums über das Germanentum* (The Victory of Jewry over Germany), first published in 1879. Marr, a sixty-year-old journalist of middling talent, attempted to turn this publishing success in a political direction by establishing an anti-Semitic league, which was to take up the fight against the alleged Jewish victors. His political initiative is also considered by historians to have been a key development in hostility to Jews moving from a diffuse social prejudice intertwined with Christian belief to an organized political movement based on modern racist ideology and looking to legislation that would limit Jewish rights and curtail what was believed to be a rising Jewish power. In October 1880, the Anti-Semites' Petition gathered more than a quarter of a million signatures, and in the early 1880s the anti-Semitic Berlin Movement challenged the ruling and generally pro-Jewish leftist coalition in Berlin.

The distinction made by Marr between religious and racial hostility, however, was from the beginning not consistently observed. Within the diverse ranks of those who began to use the new term, its meaning remained imprecise, more or less synonymous with such earlier generic terms as Judeophobia or *Judenhass* (Jew-hatred) that had not made such explicit claims to racism as a science. Similarly, Marr was by no means the first to insist that Jews were a separate race with destructive proclivities. What made his pamphlet stand out was its focus on the growing dangers of the Jewish rise in the economic, political, and cultural realms—so much so that Jews had, he claimed, already effectively taken over Germany from behind the scenes. Marr's claim gained credence in part because of what was indeed a remarkable rise of Jews in nineteenth-century German-speaking areas, especially in Berlin. That Jewish culprits had been very prominent among those linked to financial scandals in the 1870s further enhanced the plausibility of Marr's charges.

The generic usage of the new term came to prevail not only in Germany but also in the rest of the Europe, gradually coming to be applied to any and all forms of antagonism to Jews, from simple irritation to murderous detestation. "Religious anti-Semitism" was a contradiction in terms, ignoring the very point made by Marr, but nonetheless religious hostility to Jews in the 1880s was also increasingly termed anti-Semitic. For example, Adolf Stoecker (1835–1909), the chaplain to the court of the German Kaiser, launched a series of notorious attacks on Jews in the 1880s that featured both religious and economic themes but that nonetheless was considered part of the general surge of anti-Semitism in those years. Stoecker occasionally used vaguely racist language and was particularly interested in the role of Jews in modern capitalism, but he accepted Jewish converts to Christianity—indeed, took pride in them—in a way that a doctrinaire racist could not have.

Similarly, the harsh criticisms of Jews by the popular professor and nationalist historian Heinrich von Treitschke (1834–1896), starting in the late 1870s, lacked a hard-core racist consistency, even though he too used the term anti-Semitism (*Antisemitismus*) and indeed had employed the notion of "Semitism" (*Semitentum*) in his writings as early as the 1860s. In a series of much-discussed articles in 1879–1880, Treitschke urged Germany's Jews to reform, to become Germans wholeheartedly, abandoning their lingering separatist identity, with its implications of superiority to non-Jews. However, whereas Marr's pamphlet described the "un-German" behavior of Jews in Germany as an expression of their fundamentally unchangeable racial essence, Treitschke believed that in fact many Jews had already accomplished the reform he asked for. He observed that there were Jews in Germany, "baptized and unbaptized … [who were] Germans in the best sense of the word" (Mendes-Flohr and Reinharz, pp. 280–283), but he was also deeply troubled by what he saw as a new arrogance and separatist spirit among Jews, especially those arriving from eastern Europe.

In short, the "anti-Semitism" of both Stoecker and Treitschke, while using vaguely racist vocabulary, lacked Marr's belief in rigid racial determinism. Similarly, their approach, unlike Marr's, remained largely hortatory, urging Jews to reform, religiously or cultural-nationalistically. Both men warned against the danger of violence against Jews and did not support stripping Jews in Germany of their recently granted civil equality. But they both also predicted that violence would be the result if the mounting impudence of so many Jews was not curbed.

Whatever the genuine intent of these two men, the emotional power of their language, linked to their respected position in German society, added much fuel to the flames of what was increasingly called the anti-Semitic movement. Treitschke's name became associated with the notorious slogan, "The Jews are our misfortune!" (*Die Juden sind unser Unglück*), which would be picked up by more extreme activists and, eventually, the Nazis. Stoecker, in his many public speeches, caustically dismissed Judaism as "dead at its very core"; Jews no longer honored the god of their fathers but instead worshiped Mammon—in their new temple, the stock exchange; and in the leading ranks of the new capitalist rulers of Europe.

THE SPREAD OF ANTI-SEMITISM IN THE 1880S AND 1890S

A rising hostility to Jews, often but not consistently using the new vocabulary of race, was in evidence elsewhere in Europe in the 1880s, although there were important and revealing variations from country to country and much inconsistency in what anti-Semitism seemed to mean. In the western regions of tsarist Russia, Jews were violently attacked in a series of riots, or pogroms (a Russian word for riot), killing scores and resulting in much property damage, following the assassination of Tsar Alexander II in 1881. Jews were special targets in part because revolutionaries of Jewish origin had previously participated in violent attacks on a number of tsarist officials and also numbered among the assassins of the tsar.

Those revolutionaries did not in fact claim to speak for the Jews, and the rampaging mobs made no mention of the Semitic race, a term that was not in their vocabulary or world view. The more fundamental origins of the pogroms were to be found in the serious economic and social tensions in Russia at the time and the incompetence of the tsarist authorities in dealing with them. The immediate catalyst of the pogroms was a rumor—mistaken but widely believed—that the new tsar, Alexander III, had given an order to punish the Jews for participating in the murder of his father. At any rate, the pogroms, although subsequently described as anti-Semitic, were not racist in Marr's sense, nor were they the product of modern political organization; instead, they resembled the episodic, disorganized uprisings of the Russian peasantry in the past.

To state that Russian mobs in 1881 and subsequent years were not motivated by racial hatred may seem to make a mere verbal distinction; Russians of all classes certainly recognized Jews as profoundly different, because most of Russia's large Jewish population looked different (in physical traits and dress), spoke a different language (Yiddish), followed a different religion (one that itself greatly emphasized the separate lineage and nature of Jews and non-Jews), engaged in different economic activities (typically as middlemen rather than as peasants tied to the land), and were ruled by separate laws (Jewish with tsarist oversight). In short, one might easily conclude that Jews in Russia constituted a race without the word. However, tsarist regulations defined Jews as a religious group, not as a race in Marr's sense, and those Jews who converted to Christianity were treated differently; in a few cases some even entered government service.

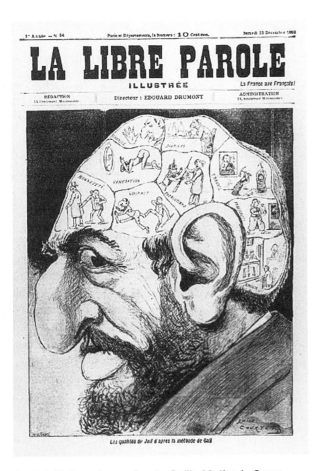

Jewish Virtues According to Gall's Method. Cover illustration by Emile Courtet for the 23 December 1893 edition of the French anti-Semitic newspaper *La Libre Parole*. "Gall's method" refers to the discipline of phrenology. PHOTOMECHANICAL PRINT, 38 × 28.5 CM. THE JEWISH MUSEUM, 1990-189. PHOTO ©THE JEWISH MUSEUM, NEW YORK. PHOTO BY JOHN PARNELL. THE JEWISH MUSEUM/ART RESOURCE.

In the west, there was also much variety. A racial-political movement against Jews was almost completely lacking in Italy, whether among the peasants or the rest of the population, but in Vienna, capital of the sprawling Austro-Hungarian Empire, Karl Lueger (1844–1910), was elected mayor in 1897 on an anti-Semitic program, after being disqualified in several previous elections by the emperor, Francis Joseph, who thoroughly disliked Lueger and feared the implications of race-based movements in his multinational empire. Lueger's Christian Social Party, which may be considered Europe's most successful anti-Semitic organization before 1914, was another example of a party that attacked Jews with racist language but that also resorted to religious imagery and,

indeed, relied upon support from the Catholic Church.

The Jewish population in most of western and central Europe by the 1880s was significantly unlike that in Russia; their status as a separate people—a "race" apart—was more subtle and ambiguous. By the late nineteenth century, they had been granted equality under the law, had prospered economically and risen socially, and in a number of areas had even served as high-ranking government officials, both appointed and elected. Their numbers were generally far smaller than in Russia (in Germany, around 1 percent of the population, and in most of the rest of western Europe, only a fraction of 1 percent). Most western Jews had adopted, or were adopting, the language, dress, and customs of the surrounding populations. It was widely assumed, especially by the liberal Left, that Jewish assimilation would continue as an aspect of the general progress of modern societies.

THE LATE EIGHTEENTH AND EARLY NINETEENTH CENTURIES

Hostility to Jews of course much predated the 1880s. By the late eighteenth century what was termed "the Jewish question" was widely discussed, at least by the intellectual elites, among whom there were often ill-tempered dissents about the assertion that Jews could be expected to assimilate into the nations of Europe. The issue of whether Jews could become citizens was passionately debated in the first years of the French Revolution; they were finally granted civil equality in the revolutionary constitution of 1791, but by a very narrow majority. As French revolutionary armies expanded into the rest of the Europe, civil equality was extended to the Jews in all the lands ruled by the French. Still, deep and recurring misgivings about the issue remained in both France and the rest of Europe in the early nineteenth century.

Most of these misgivings might, again, be termed anti-Semitic before the actual word existed, in that they assumed some sort of unchangeable essence in Jews, one that was dangerous to non-Jews. In the many efforts to formulate the nature of that essential difference, the term *race* came to play a growing role. Still, there were pervasive and lasting uncertainties associated with what race in general, and the Semitic race in particular, actually referred to. Usage of the word *race* evolved in the course of the nineteenth century, with different nuances in each language, from initially being more or less synonymous with "sort" or "kind" (as in the "human race") to becoming a more precise or scientific term designating inherent physical and psychological traits. Still, even by the end of the nineteenth century, there was no clear consensus among the many theorists of race, let alone in the general population, about what constituted a race, or how completely membership in a race determined an individual's nature and behavior.

THE MID-NINETEENTH CENTURY

The rise of nationalism in the middle years of the nineteenth century further complicated matters. Many who advocated granting equal protection under the law to Jewish residents nonetheless did not believe that Jews could possibly become authentic members of a European people or nation. And insofar as it was believed that nations were to be composed of a single race, or of closely kindred races, the problem was even larger, since even if Jews did learn non-Jewish languages and embrace non-Jewish customs, they could not become a different race. "Semites" remained a non-European people with no obvious homeland in Europe.

The issue had parallels in the much earlier and long-standing doubts by some Christians about whether Jewish converts to Christianity had genuinely abandoned their Jewishness. Such was the issue in Spain at the time of the Inquisition, when Jewish converts allegedly lacked *limpieza de sangre,* or purity of blood (often cited by modern historians as an early-modern proto-racist concept). Many observers in the nineteenth century, including many Jews, emphasized that Jews would always remain in some significant sense separate, never wholly blending into the people of the various European nations. At the same time, it should not be assumed that Marr, in his dogmatic assertion of the unchangeable and destructive essence of Jews, spoke for more than a minority, even in Germany. There is no question that Europeans in the nineteenth century became increasingly fascinated with the concept of racial determinism; many blended racist and nationalist language, but differences of opinion, inconsistency, and contradiction contin-

ued to characterize racist thought up to 1914 and beyond.

The case of Count Arthur de Gobineau (1816–1882), often described as the father of modern racism, is revealing in those regards. His very widely read *Essai sur l'inegalité des races humaines* (1853–1855; Essay on the inequality of the human races) offered the controversial theory that Europe's upper classes were racially different from and superior to its lower classes. Gobineau popularized another new term, *Aryan,* which he applied to the upper classes. Although he has often also been identified as an anti-Semite, Gobineau in his *Essai* placed the Jews among the superior "white" races. On the other hand, in his rankings the black or Negro race was at the bottom of the world's inferior races, and he described France's lower classes as having similar traits to blacks—especially low intelligence and a proclivity to outbursts of violence.

The qualities Gobineau attributed to blacks and other allegedly inferior races were rarely associated with Jews, even by anti-Semites. Marr had in fact written that the Semitic race was stronger and tougher than the German; he and most other anti-Semites also stressed the high intelligence of the Jews, made all the more dangerous because of their "un-German," slippery morality. Negative associations with the term *Semite* came from a wide range of other forms, seen perhaps most influentially in the extremely popular writings of the French scholar Ernest Renan (1823–1892). He introduced racial determinism as an important interpretive tool, although often in imprecise and paradoxical ways—and applied it in a negative way to other European races, not only the Semites. He wrote, for example, that France's courageous and combative "Frankish" race had been much weakened by its mixing over the centuries with the garrulous and effete "Celtic" racial strain, which helped explain France's defeat in the Franco-Prussian War of 1870–1871.

Renan's description of the role of the Semites in history contained both positive and negative elements—positive in their bringing monotheism to the world, but negative thereafter, because Jews gradually lost their creativity and became overly or destructively critical. However, he did not attribute those negative or destructive traits to his Jewish contemporaries in France, among whom he had many admirers and close friends. Indeed, as he observed the mean-spirited direction that political-racial anti-Semitism had taken toward the end of his life, he made efforts to disassociate himself from it. Marr, too, in his old age backed away from his earlier positions, apologizing to the Jews and quipping that the anti-Semites turned out to be worse than the Jews.

THE LATE NINETEENTH CENTURY

Renan's and Marr's second thoughts were not unusual; imagery about Jews as the nineteenth century progressed was characteristically shifting and paradoxical, not predominantly or uniformly negative. Sympathy for the sufferings of Jews and recognition of their virtues existed side-by-side with jealousy over Jewish successes and worries about growing Jewish power, especially that exercised behind the scenes. Jews were portrayed, on the one hand, as frail, physically unattractive, and even malformed, but also as more resistant to disease than non-Jews and as reproducing faster than they were. As the new racial terminology spread, Aryan-Semitic contrasts or dualities seemed to gain credence and currency, mostly pointing to the degenerate spiritual qualities of Jews: Aryan creativity versus Semitic destructiveness, Aryan tolerance and generosity versus Semitic intolerance and egotism, Aryan bravery and idealism versus Semitic cowardice and "realistic" materialism, Aryan honesty and simplicity versus Semitic cunning and deviousness, Aryan chastity and morality versus Semitic sensuality and licentiousness.

Nonetheless, with a few exceptions, anti-Semitic political movements did not gain broad popular support or achieve any notable legislative victories until 1914. Jews continued to prosper, to grow in numbers, and to move up socially, especially in western Europe; the Rothschilds and many other Jewish financiers and entrepreneurs became legendary millionaires. One of the nineteenth century's most celebrated politicians, Benjamin Disraeli (British prime minister, 1868, 1874–1880), not only was of Jewish origin but also was well known for his boasting about the racial superiority of Jews.

ANTI-SEMITISM IN THE GENERATION BEFORE 1914

It is revealing that none of the previously discussed anti-Semites or alleged anti-Semites described Jews as vermin, or as worthy of death. Even the most influential anti-Semitic theorist of the pre-1914 period, Houston Stewart Chamberlain (1855–1927), whose work is often cited as linking pre-1914 anti-Semitism with Nazism, did not call for violence against the Jews and in other ways was considered moderate. His best-selling and almost universally praised volume, *The Foundations of the Nineteenth Century* (first published in 1899 with many subsequent editions into the 1920s), emphasized, as had Renan's works, the role of racial determinants in history—and the negative role of the Semites—but his definition of race, too, was elastic and hardly doctrinaire. He wrote, for example, "A purely humanized Jew is no longer a Jew because, by renouncing the idea of Judaism, he *ipso facto* has left that nationality." There were certainly others, theorists and popular agitators in the generation before 1914, who did describe Jews as vermin, implicitly deserving death or destruction, but they remained on the fringes, with nothing like the readership or popular following of Chamberlain or the other previously mentioned figures.

The successes of anti-Semitism before 1914 were limited but also difficult to gauge confidently. Lueger was indeed a very popular mayor, but his success had to do with his personal charisma and his "municipal socialism" in Vienna; he in fact did very little in terms of putting anti-Semitic programs into action. Laws were passed in Russia against the Jews, but by tsarist decree, not legislation initiated by elected anti-Semitic politicians, and those laws were notably unsuccessful. Even the most notorious explosion of anti-Semitic hatred in nineteenth-century history, the Dreyfus affair, cannot finally be termed a success for anti-Semitism, because it ended in victory—legal, political, and in other regards—for the so-called Dreyfusards, those opposed to anti-Semitism.

Nonetheless, the Dreyfus affair, arising out of charges that Captain Alfred Dreyfus, a highly assimilated French Jew, had sold military secrets to the Germans, became much more than a trial; the extent of the hatred for Jews it unleashed shocked both Jews and non-Jews, especially because it occurred in a country where Jews had widely been considered better off than in any other. In the course of the affair's complex development, beginning in late 1896 and lasting into the

Pogrom victims. Photograph showing bodies of some of the nearly one thousand Jews killed during the 1905 pogrom in Russia. ©Hulton-Deutsch Collection/Corbis

early years of the next century, political alliances, personal friendships, and even families were torn apart. Crowds chanted "death to the Jews!" and the language used by some of the anti-Dreyfusard militants was rabidly hate filled.

Issues of racial anxiety and social-Darwinistic struggle were central to the Dreyfus affair, as they were in Marr's writings and in those of other anti-Semites. The French were haunted by the fear of further defeats at the hands of the Germans; that men of dubious racial fidelities seemed to have gained power in the government and in high-ranking military positions, pushed many to panic and irrational judgments. The evidence against Dreyfus was in fact weak, largely circumstantial, and some of the testimony against him would later be revealed as false, but anti-Semitic agitators succeeded in whipping up mass hysteria, often resorting to reckless charges and bald-faced lies.

Theodore Herzl (1860–1904), a Jewish journalist reporting on the trial of Dreyfus for a Viennese newspaper, recorded that observing the anti-Jewish

hatred in France at this time finally convinced him that Jews faced implacable hatred in the lands of non-Jews; the Jewish dream, his earlier dream, of becoming a respected part of European civilization was turning into a nightmare. Herzl, who would become known as the iconic founder of Zionism, concluded that Jews needed their own nation. A Jewish state and a Jewish homeland was the only realistic solution to the Jewish question.

In Russia, where Nicholas II considered himself to be at war with the Jews both inside and outside the country, violent pogroms again burst forth from 1903 to 1906, partly linked to Russia's disastrous war with Japan in 1904 and the ensuing revolution in 1905. The anti-Jewish violence this time was far worse than in 1881. That many of the most prominent leaders of the revolution were Jews, perhaps most famously, Leon Trotsky, reinforced an anti-Semitic theme—that Jews were both capitalist and socialist destroyers—that would become ever more powerful after 1917, central to Nazism.

THE IMPORTANCE OF ANTI-SEMITISM IN THE NINETEENTH CENTURY

Historians have disagreed about the precise role of anti-Semitism in the arrest and conviction of Dreyfus, and even about anti-Semitism's power and general appeal in the affair, in part because of how much the country seemed to settle down afterward; the efforts to use anti-Semitism for reactionary political purposes seemed deeply discredited. Whatever the validity of Herzl's conclusions, very few French Jews left the country or embraced Zionism. Moreover, they continued to prosper after the affair as they had before. Parallel questions have been posed about the power and significance of anti-Semitism in Vienna, since Jews also continued to move into the city at a great rate until 1914. Moreover, the period when Lueger was mayor corresponded to a golden age for Jews, a time of prosperity and unparalleled creativity. Again, whatever the meaning of the popularity of Chamberlain's volume, the German anti-Semitic political parties of the generation before 1914 also fizzled, with their leaders discouraged and discredited. In Russia, where anti-Semites enjoyed governmental support, the sensational "blood libel" trial of Mendel Beilis in 1913, often termed the Russian Dreyfus affair, ended in his acquittal—to the apparent jubilation of the general population and the dismay and discredit of those, including government officials, who tried to exploit it for reactionary purposes.

For such reasons, some historians have warned against exaggerating the importance of anti-Semitism in the nineteenth century, or of considering it narrowly through the filter of later Nazi victories and the Holocaust. Historians have similarly differed about the very nature of anti-Semitism: Was racial-political hatred to be defined as something new, or was it simply a modern variant of a much larger and more basic entity—a unique, endlessly baffling hatred, stretching back through the Christian period into the ancient world? Should anti-Semitism be conceptualized as a modern, secular problem, or is it closer to a religious belief, embedded so deeply and obscurely in the consciousness of European civilization that it is naive to believe in practical or "rational" solutions within any foreseeable future?

In related ways, some scholars have described hatred of Jews as a deep-seated and self-generating "diseased discourse" of Western civilization. This general approach maintains that Jewish activity or Jewish nature has had little or nothing to do with provoking anti-Semitism; the hatred has been, in the deepest sense, an expression of the psychic needs of non-Jews for a scapegoat. To suggest that Jews themselves played a significant role in provoking hatred has been dismissed as "blaming the victim." Opponents of the scapegoat theory have argued that conflict between Jews and non-Jews has usually involved significant elements of mutuality, having to do with "normal" competition and genuinely contrasting values (not only bigoted illusions or miscommunication); the tenets of Jewish religion, it has been argued, are inherently tension creating (strict monotheism entails intolerance; claims to being a divinely chosen people have engendered an offensive sense of Jewish superiority), just as characteristically Jewish occupations, such as money lending, tend to produce understandable resentments. Those emphasizing mutuality also describe typically Jewish occupations as being the result of conscious choice by Jews, emerging out of Jewish tradition, not only choices imposed by surrounding society. It is argued, at any rate, that the frictions between Jews and others are best conceptualized as comparable to what other merchants and money lenders, such as the Chinese or Indians, have faced in other civilizations, and not as utterly unique, irrational, or involving moral responsibility only on one side.

To some extent these contrasting interpretations parallel those familiar in other historical controversies, touching upon issues of agency and responsibility. Just as historians in the once-raging debates over guilt for World War I put primary emphasis on individuals, nations, or impersonal forces, so the controversies about anti-Semitism have often been about the relative importance or responsibility of individuals (Chamberlain, Nicholas II), nations (Germany, Russia), or impersonal forces (industrialism, nationalism). Signs of the kind of consensus that finally emerged from the war guilt controversies have begun to appear in regard to the origins and nature of anti-Semitism, but passionate disagreement also continues to characterize the field.

See also **Alexander III; Chamberlain, Houston Stewart; Dreyfus Affair; Jews and Judaism; Lueger, Karl;**

Nationalism; Nicholas II; Pogroms; Race and Racism; Renan, Joseph-Ernest.

BIBLIOGRAPHY

Bredin, Jean-Denis. *The Affair: The Case of Alfred Dreyfus.* New York, 1986.

Field, Geoffrey. *Evangelist of Race: The Germanic Vision of Houston Stewart Chamberlain.* New York, 1980.

Holmes, Colin. *Anti-Semitism in British Society: 1876–1939.* New York, 1979.

Katz, Jacob. *From Prejudice to Destruction: Anti-Semitism, 1700–1933.* Cambridge, Mass., 1980.

Levy, Richard S. *The Downfall of the Anti-Semitic Parties in Imperial Germany.* New Haven, Conn., 1975.

———. *Antisemitism in the Modern World: An Anthology of Texts.* Lexington, Mass., 1991.

Lindemann, Albert S. *Esau's Tears: Modern Anti-Semitism and the Rise of the Jews.* New York, 1997.

Marrus, Michael. *The Politics of Assimilation: The French Community at the Time of the Dreyfus Affair.* Oxford, U.K., 1971.

Mendes-Flohr, Paul, and Yehuda Reinharz, eds. *The Jew in the Modern World.* New York, 1980.

Poliakov, Léon. *The History of Anti-Semitism.* Vol. 3: *From Voltaire to Wagner;* vol. 4: *Suicidal Europe, 1870–1933.* New York, 1975; Philadelphia, 1977.

Pulzer, Peter. *The Rise of Political Anti-Semitism in Germany and Austria.* New York, 1964.

Rogger, Hans. *Jewish Politics and Right-Wing Politics in Imperial Russia.* Berkeley, Calif., 1986.

Slezkine, Yuri. *The Jewish Century.* Princeton, N.J., 2004.

Zimmermann, Moshe. *Wilhelm Marr: The Patriarch of Anti-Semitism.* New York, 1986.

ALBERT LINDEMANN

ARISTOCRACY. In 1914, at the end of the long nineteenth century, the European aristocracy was in a weaker position than had been the case on the eve of the French Revolution. In regard to political power, social status, and cultural influence, the traditional ruling and landowning class faced more powerful competition than had existed in the 1780s. Nevertheless, in most of Europe the aristocracy still remained a very powerful force in government, politics, and society. One hundred and twenty years after the French Revolution had challenged the old European order, what may in fact be most surprising was just how much power and status parts of the aristocracy had retained.

It is important to stress the word *parts*, however. While many of the greatest aristocratic families had become the core of an evolving plutocratic elite, the wealth of most of the traditional landowning class had declined sharply in comparison to non-landed fortunes in the half-century before 1914. Meanwhile in some European states the political power of the aristocracy had declined steeply, whereas in others the power of the traditional ruling class had remained very great or even in certain respects had grown between 1789 and 1914.

DEFINITION

Before going into these issues in more detail, it is useful to define briefly what *aristocracy* means in the nineteenth-century European context. In almost every European state in 1789 there existed a group called the nobility whose membership was defined in law and that enjoyed a range of privileges. The term *nobility* had vastly different meanings from one European society to another, however. In England, at one end of the European spectrum, it meant the peerage, a group numbered in the low hundreds. At the other end of the spectrum lay Poland and Hungary, where nobles constituted 5 percent of the population or more. Between lay France, where roughly 1.5 percent of the population enjoyed noble status in 1789. Clearly all European nobles were not aristocrats.

It was much more nearly the case that all titled nobles (from barons up to dukes and princes) were aristocrats, but even this was actually an illusion. Again England was the extreme case in which not only titles but all landed property were inherited exclusively by eldest sons. In almost all cases throughout the nineteenth century one could assume that an English (though not necessarily an Irish) peer was a wealthy man with high status in his society. Elsewhere in Europe, where titles and property were often inherited by all sons, the automatic English correlation of title, wealth, and status did not apply. Russia, where all children—both sons and daughters—inherited titles and only a minority of the greatest aristocratic families passed their main estates to eldest sons (save in the Baltic provinces where this custom was more widespread), provides the counterpoint to England. It was the case in

The Countess of Carpio (1757–1795), Marquesa de la Solana. Portrait by Francisco José Goya y Lucientes c. 1793.
Louvre, Paris, France/Bridgeman Art Library/Giraudon/Lauros

nineteenth-century Europe that the great majority of the richest and most prestigious aristocratic families were titled, but there were exceptions, even in Britain and in Russia. Throughout the period 1700 to 1914, for example, the Naryshkins were one of the richest, most powerful, and most respected aristocratic families in Russia and were indeed closely related to the Romanovs. They never, however, had titles. Nor in late-nineteenth-century Britain did the statesman Arthur Balfour, whose wealth, connections, and values made him an unequivocal aristocrat.

Aristocracy ultimately can be defined only in relatively loose sociological terms, rather than in more tight legal ones. Aristocrats were members of the traditional ruling class. They inherited wealth, status, and power from their ancestors. In the overwhelming majority of cases in 1789 the core of their wealth lay in land. The precise nature of their political power differed from one European country to another. In 1789 the English and Scottish aristocracy dominated Parliament, which itself wholly controlled government. The British aristocracy was a ruling class in the fullest meaning of the word. Matters were a little more equivocal in most of continental Europe where supposedly absolute monarchs ruled through various species of bureaucracy. Even in Russia, however, where monarchical absolutism was most extreme, the emperor could not rule without the landowning elite. Without the landowners' cooperation the tiny bureaucracy even in 1825 had no hope of governing (i.e., taxing and conscripting) the peasant masses, on whose fiscal and military exploitation the whole tsarist state rested. Moreover, the aristocracy totally dominated the court, the guards regiments, and the top ranks of government in St. Petersburg. Monarchs who alienated this aristocratic elite between 1725 and 1825 risked their lives.

The best definition of European aristocracy in 1789 therefore is "traditional ruling and landowning elite." It makes sense to reserve the term *aristocracy* proper for the top echelon of this elite, usually very wealthy, usually titled, and dominating the top positions in metropolitan government. The lesser, usually nontitled, landowners who dominated provincial society and who possessed the means to live the lives of leisured gentlemen are best defined as gentry. Herein, however, the word *aristocracy* is used to cover both groups, save where an attempt is being made to distinguish between them.

CHALLENGES CONFRONTING ARISTOCRACY

Two overall challenges confronted aristocracy in the long nineteenth century. The first were the egalitarian values and ideologies that sprang from the eighteenth-century radical Enlightenment and were embodied in the French Revolution. The second were a number of interrelated changes in society that can broadly be defined as modernization. These included industrialization and urbanization; mass literacy; the vast growth in industrial, commercial, and financial wealth; and the increasing complexity of both society and government, which gave birth to a vast swathe of professional and technical experts without whose skills a modern community could not flourish.

Enlightenment and French Revolution The radical Enlightenment and the French Revolution rejected corporate privilege and inherited inequality in the name of rationality, efficiency, and individual merit. They asserted that the individual rather than the family or the corporation was the building block of society, and they assumed a fundamental equality between individuals, at least in regard to the rights possessed by all of a community's citizens. These ideas had great appeal to many Europeans in the nineteenth century. The French Revolution turned these ideas into political reality and provided a model to which subsequent generations of European radicals looked with admiration.

The impact of the Revolution was equivocal, however. In the first place, though the French Revolution was hostile to legal inequality and inherited privilege, it was far less egalitarian in socioeconomic terms and did not reject private property. Indeed some of the reforms pushed through in Europe in the Napoleonic era actually strengthened private property by, for example, handing church and common land over to wealthy individuals. Though the aristocracy were not in most countries the major beneficiary of these changes, they were nevertheless very great property owners and could often turn to their own advantage the new era of absolute property rights. A striking example of this were the great profits that many nineteenth-century aristocrats made from their forests, whose use was previously very often shared with the peasantry, but which now became the unrestricted possession of noble landowners.

In a century in which wood prices grew enormously, this could be a crucial factor in the survival of large sections of the traditional rural elite.

Though the 1790s inflicted a very heavy blow to the French aristocracy from which the latter never fully recovered, the damage was not mortal. Napoleon I went out of his way to reconcile the aristocracy to his regime and to draw them back into court, civil, and military service. He was partly successful in this endeavor. To some extent one can see the evolution of the French aristocracy from 1789 to 1815 as a sudden and very brutal example of a change that overtook much of the European aristocracy in the nineteenth century. Losing part though not most of its land, the French aristocracy turned in the direction of becoming a government service elite. In this sense it moved closer to the pattern of the Russian, Prussian, and even lesser Austrian aristocracies of the late eighteenth century. Like them but in the face of much stiffer non-noble competition, it had to sustain its status by military and civil service to the growing bureaucratic state. Over the long nineteenth century one was to see a variant on this theme even in Britain. Financial pressures, changing aristocratic values, and the need to sustain aristocratic legitimacy by public service all pushed in this direction throughout Europe, albeit to differing degrees.

It is also important to remember that if the memory of the French Revolution attracted some Europeans, it appalled others—including very many nonaristocrats. If the French aristocracy as a group had been the single largest victim of the Terror, most of those who died under the guillotine were not aristocrats. What had seemed initially a movement for moderate and rational constitutional reform had spiraled quickly into a terrifying dictatorship that had consumed innocent bystanders and its own children alike. Particularly in Brittany, the civil war unleashed by the Revolution had been waged with near-genocidal frenzy by the republic. The army that had emerged from the Revolution as the dominant force in French politics had created a military despotism in France and subjected Europe to twenty-two years of warfare and conquest. Relative to its population, Europe suffered more casualties in the Revolutionary and Napoleonic wars than in World War I.

Not surprisingly, the lesson many Europeans drew from this was that even moderate reform could easily spiral out of control and that the traditional pillars of political order (monarchy, church, aristocracy) were crucial bulwarks against anarchy and terror. The history of the unicameral French National Assembly was used to justify conservative upper houses in much of nineteenth-century Europe. Most of the newly created upper houses gave many seats to aristocrats. This was just one reflection of a broader result of the French Revolution, namely the coming together of those old rivals monarchy, aristocracy, and church against the common revolutionary enemy.

This new unity was not total or immediate in the nineteenth century. The 1848 revolutions in Hungary and Italy had much of the old court versus country flavor. Because monarchical absolutism survived longest in Russia, so too did traditional aristocratic resentment of dynastic regimes that denied political representation or guaranteed civil rights even to aristocrats. The last fling of traditional European court versus country aristocratic liberalism was the Russian gentry's participation in the run-up to the Revolution of 1905. But the events of 1905 provided graphic evidence why in the modern age monarchs and aristocrats could no longer afford to fight. Having weakened the tsarist regime by its opposition in the decade before the revolution, the Russian nobles saw their estates overrun by peasant rioters in 1905 and then threatened with wholesale expropriation by the parliament that the regime had been forced to concede. As a result of this experience regime and aristocracy drew back together in the period from 1906 to 1914, not least in united support for policies that made private property in land secure. In so doing, the Russians conformed to a European conservative norm.

Modernization Radical ideologies were dangerous because they were underpinned by the social changes inherent in modernization. Industrialization, urbanization, and mass literacy had the potential to transform the consciousness of the masses and their capacity for political organization, while making them much less susceptible to control by the landowning elite. As democracy spread in the last quarter of the

Studies for the portraits of Lord Douglas, Lord Stradbroke, and Lord Eglinton. These sketches by English painter Richard Ansdell were done in preparation for his 1840 painting *The Waterloo Cup Coursing Meeting,* which depicts the most important event of the coursing, or hare-hunting, season and a favorite gathering for British aristocrats. YALE CENTER FOR BRITISH ART, PAUL MELLON COLLECTION, USA/BRIDGEMAN ART LIBRARY

nineteenth century the aristocracy usually lost control over the urban mass electorate, though this was not universally and immediately true. The English Conservatives had many working-class supporters in the late nineteenth century, not least in Lancashire, where the earls of Derby were able to tap not just local deference but also the Protestant mass electorate's dislike of Catholic Irish immigration. In Germany the Catholic Centre Party, in whose leadership aristocrats were still important in the early twentieth century, had mass electoral support even from many urban workers. Nevertheless in time it was the case that mass urban politics everywhere ultimately undermined the power of traditional rural elites.

A number of factors determined whether the aristocracy could effectively mobilize rural society as a conservative bulwark against urban radicalism. In England the Conservative Party succeeded in doing this to a great extent by the 1880s but by that time the degree of urbanization in England, added to rural radicalism in the Gaelic fringe of the United Kingdom, made this of limited use. In the two 1910 general elections, fought in large part over the role and power of Europe's most aristocratic and most powerful upper house, the Conservatives actually won by a narrow margin in England, only for that victory to be reversed by the votes of the Scots, Welsh, and Irish. More

successful was the German aristocracy, who provided the core leadership for the Bund der Landwirte, Europe's most formidable agrarian lobby group in the early twentieth century. Not merely, however, did this force the aristocratic leaders to accept the overriding logic of rural populist politics (e.g., the ruthless pursuit of agrarian sectional interests and a demagogic anti-Semitism that did not sit easily with the claim to provide responsible national leadership), it also was a weakening asset as Germany became Europe's increasingly urbanized industrial powerhouse.

Meanwhile in Europe's "second-world" western, eastern, and southern periphery—an arc that stretched from Ireland through Iberia and Italy to Hungary and Russia—where the population was still overwhelmingly rural, it was also usually radical and often very hostile to the aristocracy. In these countries mass politics by 1900 often entailed the risk of social revolution and the expropriation of aristocratic landholding. Huge differences in wealth and culture between rural elite and mass, combined with the masses' growing political consciousness and organization, made this a real threat in much of Europe's second-world periphery at the turn of the twentieth century. The threat might become reality through peasant revolution and jacqueries (peasant revolts) or, in those countries where democracy was spreading, through the ballot box. Because by 1905 even Russia had acquired a parliament elected by near universal (though not equal) male suffrage, the challenge of managing democracy was becoming a matter of life and death for much of the aristocracy of peripheral Europe.

Social revolution was somewhat less likely in rural societies where the Catholic Church was strongly rooted and where the aristocracy had powerful potential allies in a substantial peasant farmer class owning its own land and employing a handful of laborers, who might or might not be family members. The perfect example of such a conservative society was the Spanish province of Navarre, home of Carlism, a mass Catholic and royalist movement that opposed the eighteenth-century Enlightenment and all other aspects of modernity. But though equivalent areas did exist in other parts of rural and peripheral Europe in 1900 they were exceptional. At the other end of the spectrum, rural radicalism was enhanced if the local aristocracy was alien to the rural masses not just in wealth and culture but also in ethnicity and religion. Facing this reality in Ireland as the era of democratic politics dawned, the British government bought out the landed elite on generous terms, thereby disarming social (though not national) revolution. But this policy reflected not just British wisdom but also the unique wealth of Britain's state and society. Nowhere else in the European periphery was such a policy either politically or financially conceivable, and almost everywhere the landowners were the most vulnerable element within the property-owning and relatively wealthy minority.

In the wealthy "first-world" core of Europe where by 1900 a big middle class existed and property was much more secure, the aristocracy could find powerful allies in both urban and rural society against emerging working-class socialist parties, let alone social revolution. To somewhat varying degrees and with many local nuances the aristocracy increasingly allied itself politically with the representatives of commercial, industrial, and financial wealth. In many countries parts of the rapidly growing professional middle class might also be potential recruits for the conservative alliance, especially where professional elites were traditionally linked to the gentry (e.g., English lawyers) or in countries where the expanding state bureaucracy

was recruited very often from the sons (often younger sons) of aristocratic or more often gentry families. Hungary, after the creation in 1867 of the dual monarchy of Austria-Hungary, was probably the perfect example of the latter phenomenon, and its administrators for that reason retained an unusually clear gentry ethos and style. But in relatively unbureaucratic England the Indian and colonial services provided a similar outlet for the sons of the gentry, and the British public schools created common elite values and lifestyles that served to integrate the sons of aristocracy, gentry, high finance, big business, and the professions into a single expanded ruling class. Just as Britain's immense wealth, power, and prestige helped to legitimize this elite in the nineteenth century, so a similar process could be seen in Germany in the period between 1871 and 1914, though in the German case religious differences and very recent unification made this process more fraught.

Every European aristocracy came to its own compromise with newly emerging, modern business, financial, and professional elites. Some of these compromises were more successful than others, but each case inevitably embodied the specific national context to which an aristocracy brought its own values (e.g., militarist or civilian, authoritarian or parliamentary), as did the often very heterogeneous elements of the new "bourgeois" elite.

For example, the very wealthy British aristocracy with its old and close links to the London financial world found it relatively easy to embrace (very often literally via marriage) the enormous fortunes made by nineteenth-century financiers and to consolidate a united plutocratic ruling class by the Edwardian era (1901–1910). In Prussia/Germany, Europe's other financial-industrial superpower, the process was bound to be much more difficult. The traditional Prussian core elite was not a true aristocracy but the relatively poor and somewhat puritanical gentry of the eastern provinces. By tradition this group had minimal contact with the world of high finance and shared neither its wealth nor its values. Indeed most of the key families in the Prusso-German financial world originated not in old Prussia but in Frankfurt, which had been very unwillingly (on both sides) absorbed into the Hohenzollern state in 1815. The fact that so much of this new financial wealth by

1900 was Jewish greatly complicated the consolidation of a united Prusso-German plutocratic elite on British Edwardian lines. But the very different natures of the British and Prussian aristocratic and gentry elites goes a long way to explaining why the British aristocracy found it easier to live alongside the (also very often Jewish) vast wealth of the London financial elite in the early twentieth century.

Even the most successful aristocratic compromise with the new business, financial, and professional classes entailed some dilution of aristocratic power and some change in aristocratic values. Thus Otto von Bismarck, probably the most important aristocratic politician of the nineteenth century, succeeded brilliantly in legitimizing the Hohenzollern dynastic-aristocratic elite by annexing and controlling the energies of German nationalism. But as his conservative critics pointed out, he did so by twisting many of the traditional religious and political values of the Prussian aristocracy. The next generation of aristocratic politicians, ever deeper enmeshed in the logic of agrarian and nationalist populism, strayed even further from the Pietist and dynastic loyalties of their grandfathers. Equally the English plutocratic grandee of the Edwardian era was already halfway to being a member of a rentier, leisured elite rather than of a true ruling class in the sense of the English aristocracy of 1800.

Coming to terms with the industrial-era European economy was far easier for some sections of the European aristocracy than for others. For that reason, although gradations of wealth within the aristocracy were already considerable in 1800, they were far more extreme by 1914. A large gap had opened between a plutocratic-aristocratic elite that had made huge fortunes from the growth of the urban and industrial economy, and the bulk of the aristocracy and almost all the provincial gentry. Inevitably this was most true in the more advanced economies, but all European landowners were hit by the decline of agricultural prices in the last decades of the nineteenth century. No one whose core income depended on agriculture could hope to even remotely match the wealth of those who had a stake in the new urban and industrial economy, and the financial and commercial worlds that sustained it.

A minority of aristocrats did have a huge stake in this world. Unlike in previous centuries, few of these aristocrats were themselves industrialists in the sense of owning and running big industrial enterprises. By 1900 even most of the great Silesian landowners, the most successful aristocratic entrepreneurs of the nineteenth century, were retreating from this role. Running big enterprises required great effort, huge capital, and entrepreneurial talent. For rich men usually deeply conscious of their responsibility to pass on a family's wealth and status to their heirs, the risks of industrial entrepreneurship were often unacceptable. Even the duke of Devonshire was embarrassed by the sums he poured into the new town and shipbuilding industry he created at Barrow-in-Furness on one of his estates. The collapse in 1909 of the business interests of Prince Christian-Kraft von Hohenlohe-Ohringen, the Duke of Ujest, caused great scandal in Wilhelmine Germany.

By 1900, however, it was possible to tap the wealth of the Industrial Revolution through shareholding without taking the risks or bearing the burdens of unlimited liability, ownership, and management of industrial enterprises. By then many aristocrats had invested large sums in government, railway, and corporate bonds and shares. Though most great aristocrats in 1914 still owned big rural estates, almost everywhere they had diversified their assets and bought significant amounts of government and private paper. The Russian aristocracy and gentry are a case in point. After the emancipation of the serfs many estates in infertile, central Great Russia became uneconomical as agricultural enterprises, nor did the aristocracy have the capital to develop them. With the onset of the agricultural depression in the 1870s, matters worsened. Meanwhile relations with the local peasantry were often conflict-ridden, and rural life was less attractive than the cities. With the growth in population leading to ever-rising land prices, the logic for the individual aristocrat of selling out and becoming an urban rentier was often clear, even if this logic undermined the aristocracy's dominant position in rural society. Very similar though less pronounced shifts occurred in Piedmont: if the overall pressures were the same, noble–peasant relations were on the whole not as strained as in Russia and rural life was not so isolated.

For much of the gentry financial pressures might mean withdrawal from the countryside and absorption into the urban professional and rentier world. For wealthy aristocrats such stark choices were unnecessary, however. At the very top of the German aristocratic world, for example, Prince von Thurn und Taxis still owned 1.3 million hectares (3.2 million acres) in 1895, but the family had also received massive financial compensation from a number of German states for lost seignorial and other inherited rights in the nineteenth century. Even by the late 1850s when the process remained uncompleted, recorded compensation exceeded £800,000—a vast sum in the mid-nineteenth century and one that allowed large-scale and diverse investments in stocks, bonds, and shares.

Though all the great aristocratic families had far more chance than the gentry to diversify their assets and enrich themselves by tapping the urban and industrial economy, the greatest fortunes were usually made by families who owned urban property or coal mines. In 1914 probably the richest aristocrat in Europe was the duke of Westminster, with an income of roughly £1 million per year. Though the Grosvenors had never played a very prominent role in British political or military affairs, they were the happy beneficiaries of a seventeenth-century marriage that brought them a large slice of what later turned into London's fashionable West End. The other richest aristocrats in Britain at that time were also either great urban landlords or owners of extensive coal mines or both. In Germany the history of the Holy Roman Empire meant that very few aristocrats were big urban landlords, but Prussia's richest aristocrats in 1914 usually derived a huge slice of their incomes from Silesian or Ruhr mines. The vagaries of Italian history meant that some regional aristocracies were far likelier to own urban property than others. Meanwhile Russian aristocratic incomes from urban property and mines in 1914 were usually less enormous than British or German for the simple reason that the urban-industrial economy was less developed, but in a few cases they topped £200,000 per year. With urbanization and industrialization taking off in Russia before 1914 there was every reason to expect that the fortunate minority of aristocrats who owned extensive urban property or mines would in time match the very richest German and British plutocrats.

Portrait of Millicent, Duchess of Sutherland by John Singer Sargent, 1904. ©ART RESOURCE, NY

The most accurate generalization about aristocracy's fate in the long European nineteenth century would therefore emphasize the very powerful trans-Continental challenges to which all aristocrats were subject, the common fundamental strategies that they used to meet those challenges, but at the same time the way in which the aristocracies of some countries and regions, and above all certain sections of the aristocracy, were much better placed to cope with these challenges than others.

THE SPECIAL CASE OF THE BRITISH
Throughout the long nineteenth century the British aristocracy was the most admired and emulated in

Europe. To some extent this was but one aspect of widespread admiration and emulation of the world's richest, most powerful, but also in many ways most liberal, society and polity. There were also, however, very specific aristocratic reasons for admiring Britain. At a time when Continental aristocracy was coming under increasing challenge, there was comfort to be had from the fact that Britain was both Europe's most successful country and the one in which the aristocracy was uniquely powerful.

As already mentioned, of all European aristocracies in 1815 the British came closest to meeting every definition of a ruling class. In terms of power and wealth, the British monarch was at best primus inter pares (first among equals) with regard to the aristocratic elite. No absolute monarch could infringe the civil rights or deny the freedoms of the British aristocracy, nor indeed challenge their role as hereditary legislators or rulers of the polity. Nevertheless, Britain remained a monarchy down to 1914 and this was important for aristocrats in Britain as elsewhere in Europe. The monarch and his court accentuated, legitimized, and put a stamp of public approval on the social hierarchy.

Even in 1914 royal patronage and traditions still mattered a great deal in the core institutions of the old regime, meaning the armed forces and diplomacy. Despite the continuing role of French aristocrats in the army, diplomatic service, and (especially) navy of the Third Republic, there was a big difference in the overall origins and ethos of British and French top soldiers and diplomats.

It was not just the power, wealth, and freedom of British aristocracy that were envied and emulated by many of its European peers. So too was the English cool aristocratic hauteur, the public face of Victorian aristocratic respectability and service, and the gentlemanly lifestyle. If French remained the lingua franca of European high society in 1914, the English nanny was making a growing impact on upper-class European values and mentalities. British bloodstock, horse racing, and fox hunting were widely admired. As is always the case with high society's fashions there was much that was silly and superficial in this emulation of England. But there was also a more serious and political aspect to the admiration of English aristocratic public rectitude and political skill, not to mention English rural sports and county lifestyle. Faced with the challenge of the urban and industrial world an aristocracy needed to justify its position as a ruling class under the gaze of middle-class newspapers and public opinion.

It needed also to consolidate its leadership of rural society. It was a commonplace among nineteenth-century aristocratic publicists that the royalist counterrevolution in the Vendée and other areas of western France in the 1790s owed its strength in part to local loyalty to a resident and paternalist rural nobility. It was therefore seen as important for other European aristocrats to spend more time on their estates, providing patronage, example, and leadership to their rural neighbors. Because traditionally much of the European high aristocracy had devoted its life to royal courts, military service, or metropolitan society and politics, this required a considerable change in lifestyles and mentalities. What better model than the English aristocrat, whose manic pursuit of foxes kept him deeply attached to county society, in whose life the aristocratic household remained a great source of patronage and leadership throughout the nineteenth century.

By 1914, however, the British aristocracy's political power was clearly slipping. The aristocracy no longer dominated the Liberal Party, a mass socialist party was emerging, and the House of Lords had been stripped of much of its power. The logic of democratic politics with a mass electorate had persuaded even the Conservative Party to buy out the Anglo-Irish landlords and reject agricultural protection. As a result the British gentry had suffered much more severely than its Prusso-German counterpart from the collapse of agricultural prices in the late nineteenth century. After three election defeats and facing the threat of Irish Home Rule, many Conservative British aristocrats were beginning to harbor very serious doubts about the virtues of democracy in 1914. Not at all surprisingly, in the rest of Europe, where democracy might prove far more dangerous to aristocracy than was the case in Britain, doubts about democracy went much deeper in aristocratic circles, and the British political model was losing some of its charm.

Nevertheless as the European aristocracy approached 1914, its political position was by no means everywhere weak. In Germany, the Austrian empire, and by 1905 Russia the monarchical regimes' creation of aristocratic upper houses and lower houses with restricted franchises had actually given the aristocracy much more freedom to articulate its interests, choose its own leaders, and block reforms than was the case in the heyday of absolutism. In that sense constitutionalist and semidemocratic politics had actually enhanced the leverage of a traditional social elite that had most to lose from democracy. Everywhere in Europe by 1914 aristocracy felt itself under increased challenge, but in 1914 most European aristocracies were by no means powerless or resigned to extinction.

See also **Bourgeoisie; Class and Social Relations; Landed Elites; Peasants; Popular and Elite Culture.**

BIBLIOGRAPHY

Becker, Seymour. *Nobility and Privilege in Late Imperial Russia.* DeKalb, Ill., 1985.

Berdahl, Robert M. *The Politics of the Prussian Nobility: The Development of a Conservative Ideology, 1770–1848.* Princeton, N.J., 1988.

Cannadine, David. *The Decline and Fall of the British Aristocracy.* New Haven, Conn., 1990.

Cardoza, Anthony L. *Aristocrats in Bourgeois Italy: The Piedmontese Nobility, 1861–1930.* Cambridge, U.K., 1997.

Gibson, Ralph, and Martin Blinkhorn, eds. *Landownership and Power in Modern Europe.* London, 1991.

Higgs, David. *Nobles in Nineteenth-Century France: The Practice of Inegalitarianism.* Baltimore, 1987.

Lieven, Dominic. *The Aristocracy in Europe, 1815–1914.* Houndmills, U.K., 1992.

Reden-Dohna, Armgard von, and Ralph Melville, eds. *Der Adel an der Schwelle des Bürgerlichen Zeitalters, 1780–1860.* Wiesbaden, Germany, 1988.

Reif, Heinz. *Westfälischer Adel, 1770–1860.* Göttingen, Germany, 1979.

D. LIEVEN

ARMENIA. The Armenians transformed during the nineteenth century from being members of widely dispersed ethno-religious communities speaking mutually unintelligible dialects to rediscovery of themselves as a people (*zhoghovurd*) with a shared history and culture and, for progressive intellectuals and political activists, as a nation (*azg*). Since the loss of their last kingdom in 1375, the Armenians had survived as subjects of multinational empires—primarily Turkic and Persian and, since the early nineteenth century, Russian. The historic homeland, bounded roughly by the Euphrates River and Anti-Taurus Mountains in the west, the Pontic Mountains in the north, the Taurus Mountains in the south, and the plain of Ararat and Karabagh highlands in the east, was divided unequally. In 1878, after several Russo-Persian and Russo-Turkish wars, about three-fourths of this plateau made up the eastern *vilayets* (provinces) of the Ottoman Empire (Van, Bitlis, Diarbekir, Kharpert, Sivas, Erzerum), known unofficially as Turkish or Western Armenia, while one-fourth (Erevan *guberniya*, or province, and adjacent districts in the provinces of Tiflis, Elizavetpol, and Kars) was incorporated into the Russian Caucasus region and called Russian or Eastern Armenia.

Although large numbers of Armenians continued to live on these traditional lands, they no longer constituted a majority in many areas because of the centuries of immigration and settlement of Turkish, Kurdish, and other Muslim elements. Beyond the plateau, on the other hand, major Armenian communities flourished everywhere from the Balkans and Constantinople (Istanbul) to Tiflis (Tbilisi) and Baku on the Caspian Sea and from Isfahan/New Julfa and Tabriz in Persia (Iran) to Armavir, Astrakhan, Nor Nakhichevan/Rostov, Feodosia, Moscow, and St. Petersburg in Russia. Of the approximately five million Armenians worldwide, half lived in the Ottoman Empire in mid-century, while in the Russian Empire their numbers grew steadily to more than two million by 1914 as the result of natural growth, inmigration, and Russian annexations of several Ottoman border districts. In the Russian Caucasus alone, the Armenian element climbed from 565,000 in mid-century to about 1,250,000 at its end and to nearly 1,800,000 by the time of the Russian revolutions in 1917. In addition, more than 200,000 Armenians lived in Persia, and there were sizable communities in the Balkan states and eastern Europe, as well as those evolving in western Europe and the United States. Older mercantile communities still prospered in places such as India, Burma, Singapore, and Java. In fact it was in Madras, India, that the first Armenian journal was published and where merchant-sponsored Armenian thinkers, influenced by English political philosophy and the example of the American Revolution, produced political tracts and even a draft constitution for an imagined future free Armenia.

With such broad geographic, linguistic, and socioeconomic variance, it was the Armenian Apostolic Church that served as the primary common denominator. In due course, however, a sense of collective history and national identity emerged among intellectuals, shaped first by the prolific scholarship and classicism of the Armenian Catholic Mekhitarist order in Venice and Vienna, then the romanticism inspired by the European revolutionary movements, and ultimately the romantic-realism of the late nineteenth century. The need for utilitarian, mission-oriented literature brought to the fore a bitter struggle between proponents of a new vernacular literary language (*Ashkharhabar*) and those who regarded such innovations as the vulgar defiling of the classical language (*Grabar*) used for centuries by the Church and educated elite. With the spread of newspapers and journals since mid-century in cities such as Constantinople, Smyrna (Izmir), Tiflis, and St. Petersburg and the rapid expansion of popular education, the literary vernacular eventually triumphed among both Western Armenian and Eastern Armenian intellectuals.

EASTERN (RUSSIAN) ARMENIANS

The establishment of Russian dominion in the Caucasus between 1801 and 1828 was welcomed by most Armenians and placed more than a third of their worldwide population into a common state. The merchant and emerging capitalist classes took advantage of the new opportunities to expand their role in regional and long-distance trade, textile production (represented foremost by the Lazarian family of St. Petersburg), tobacco processing, and subsequently in the booming oil industry around Baku, where M.I. Mirzoev (Mirzoyan) drilled the first well in 1871 and Armenians came to own a third of the petroleum companies. Armenian magnate Alexander Mantashev (1849–1911) merged his interests with several non-Armenian firms to form the industrial giant known as the Russian General Oil Corporation. In Tiflis, the historic capital of Georgia, Armenians constituted a majority or plurality throughout the century and dominated the municipal duma, which elected a succession of Armenian mayors, the last being Alexander Khatisian (1876–1945) who served from 1907 to 1917 and went on to become a prime minister of the postwar Armenian republic.

Although these educated, prosperous urban elites had little in common with the tradition-bound semi-servile peasantry in agrarian Erevan province and the rest of the great plateau, Armenian teachers, scholars, and activists labored tirelessly to foster a shared sense of nationality encompassing all the disparate social and economic classes and extending over Eastern Armenians, Western Armenians, and diasporan Armenians alike. Persistent calls for action and change resounded, as in the first Armenian vernacular novel, *Wounds of Armenia*, by Khachatur Abovian (1805–1848, published posthumously in 1858); the radical populist journalism of Mikayel Nalbandian (1829–1866); the sentimental patriotic poetry of Raphael Patkanian (1830–1892); the evocative novels of Raffi (1835–1888), who vividly depicted the oppression and groaning lifestyle of the Turkish Armenian peasantry; the short stories of Perj Proshian (1837–1907), who exposed the brutality of traditional social and gender relations among the Eastern Armenian populace; and the realist theater of Gabriel Sundukian (1825–1912), who focused on the ills of unbridled capitalism, the corruption of the Armenian middle classes and tsarist officials, and the harmful superstitions of the peasantry.

By and large, the Armenian experience under Russian rule was positive, as the Armenian element increased rapidly in numbers and economic activity. Many Armenians climbed the social ladder through military service. It was no coincidence that the most noted generals on the Caucasus front during the Russo-Turkish War of 1877–1878 were Armenian—A. A. Ter-Gukasov (1819–1881), I. D. Lazarev (1820–1879), and especially Count Mikhail Loris-Melikov (1825–1888), who went on to become the special adviser of Tsar Alexander II (r. 1855–1881) and the chief architect of a far-reaching political reform program. That project was shelved, however, with the assassination of Alexander II in 1881 and the accession of the reactionary Alexander III (r. 1881–1894), whose anti-minority policies included first the closure of Armenian schools and then, after they were allowed to reopen, the attempted Russification of their curricula.

The tsar's actions undermined previously favorable Armenian dispositions, propelling some youthful intellectuals into populist and revolutionary movements. This ferment was also fueled by the plight of the Turkish Armenians across the border and their failure to attain the basic security of life and possessions through various reforms promulgated by successive Ottoman sultans. The formation of Armenian clandestine political societies was largely the work of alienated Russian Armenian intellectuals who had lost faith in achieving change through legal means. The Marxist Hunchakian party, organized by exiles in Geneva in 1887, advocated the liberation of Turkish Armenia and the establishment of a socialist state within a world socialist order, whereas the Armenian Revolutionary Federation or Hai Heghapokhakan Dashnaktsutiun, formed in Tiflis in 1890, adhered to the populist tradition by emphasizing emancipation and uplifting of the peasantry and autonomous development in the Turkish Armenian homeland—the *erkir*. These immediate objectives, it was reasoned, necessitated postponement of active engagement against the tsarist autocracy.

Despite these high ideals and the silent sympathy of a significant segment of the agrarian population, most Armenians of all classes shied away from or feared involvement with the revolutionary societies. The urban elites preferred the enlightened liberalism and Westernization advocated by Grigor Artsruni (1845–1892), editor of the Tiflis newspaper *Mshak* (Tiller), which held out evolutionary change, not revolutionary violence, as the correct path for the Armenian people.

Such a measured approach was not rewarded by the tsarist bureaucrats and policymakers, however. At the turn of the century, the governor of the Caucasus, Prince Grigory Golitsyn, persuaded Tsar Nicholas II (r. 1894–1917) that the Armenian Church, as a hotbed of Armenian nationalism, had to be neutralized. In violation of the statutes regulating the Armenian Church

in the empire, the tsar in June 1903 decreed the confiscation of all Church-owned properties and placed the Church under direct state control, at the same time imposing strict censorship on the Armenian press. The popular Catholicos (Supreme Patriarch) Mkrtich Khrimian (1820–1906) refused to submit and aroused a pan-Armenian storm of protest, in which even the anticlerical political parties came to the Church's defense and, for the first time, engaged in acts of sabotage and violence against tsarist officials. The standoff continued until January 1905 when Nicholas rescinded his decree at a time when failure in the Russo-Japanese War had revitalized the Russian revolutionary movement and massive strikes were crippling the state.

The reactionary bureaucracy then tried to isolate the Caucasus from the ferment in central Russia by stoking already-existing ethnic, social, and religious antipathies in Baku, Karabagh, and other areas of mixed Armenian-Azerbaijani (then called "Tatar") habitation, including even Erevan itself. The "Armeno-Tatar War" was not halted until 1907, by which time Nicholas had weathered the first Russian revolution with promises of political reforms. Such pledges were soon reneged on and superseded by the "Stolypin reaction," when, along with thousands of others empire-wide, hundreds of suspected Armenian subversives and intellectuals were arrested and either imprisoned or exiled.

It was not until 1912, with the outbreak of the first Balkan War and the growing prospect of a much larger European conflagration, that the imperial government reversed its anti-Armenian policies by courting Catholicos Gevorg (George) V (1847–1930), releasing most political prisoners, and even showing itself to be the champion of the downtrodden Ottoman Armenian population by proposing a new program of reforms specifically for the Turkish Armenian provinces. The rapprochement with the tsar was sealed in the autumn of 1914 when Russian Armenian leaders agreed to organize volunteer battalions to assist the imperial armies in case of war with the Ottoman Empire.

WESTERN (TURKISH) ARMENIANS

The Armenian experience under Ottoman rule was also greatly varied. Most of the peasantry had lost their landholdings through usurpation, becoming sharecroppers of Muslim notables known as *begs* or *aghas*. The peasants lived in perennial debt and constant fear of kidnappings, raids, and forced conversion and were subject to heavy, often extra-legal, taxation and discrimination because of their Christian infidel (*giavur*), second-class status. The harshness of daily life was attenuated by the colorful celebrations of religious holidays and the ritualized observances of the cycle of life—forty-day birth rites, baptisms, betrothals and seven-day wedding festivities, and tradition-laden funerals and requiems.

The nineteenth century brought major changes as American and European missionaries established schools, churches, and hospitals. This spurred the Armenian Apostolic Church to meet the challenge, so that by the end of the century nearly every Armenian town and village had schools for boys and many had opened schools for girls as well. The gradual enlightenment of the Armenian agrarian population and relative prosperity of its merchants and craftsmen further aggravated the sharpening inter-ethnic and inter-religious antagonisms in the countryside.

In contrast with the harsh rural scene, urban Armenians living along the seacoasts and especially in Constantinople, the Ottoman capital, and Smyrna enjoyed relative security. Some used their knowledge of foreign languages and contacts with Armenians abroad to engage in international trade or to fill important civil posts. As it happened, the more than 200,000 Armenians living in Constantinople in the latter part of the nineteenth century formed the largest settlement of Armenians anywhere in the world. Their elite *amira* class included powerful bankers and money lenders. Some held quasi-hereditary positions in the sultan's administration, such as chief architect (Balian), director of the imperial mint (Duzian), and superintendent of gunpowder mills (Dadian). It was also this oligarchy that dominated the affairs of the Ottoman Armenian community (*millet*) through the Armenian Patriarchate of Constantinople.

During the Ottoman reform period known as the *Tanzimat* (1839–1876), the power of the *amiras* was curtailed by challenges from the *esnafs,* middle-class guildsmen who broadened but did not fully democratize the governing base of the patriarchate and *millet* through adoption and con-

firmation of the Armenian National Constitution (Statutes) between 1860 and 1863. Meanwhile, the position of the Armenian Church was undermined somewhat by the sultan's recognition of European- and American-supported Catholic and Evangelical *millets*, made up largely of Armenian converts.

While the Eastern Armenian intellectuals drew much of their inspiration from Russian and German sources, the Western Armenians were heavily influenced by French, Italian, and English literary and political currents. The indisputable success of the Western Armenian vernacular literary language based on the Constantinople dialect was evidenced, for example, in the contributions of young realist writers in the journal *Arevelk* (Orient), founded in 1884 by Arpiar Arpiarian (1852–1908). Of the scores of prominent Western Armenian authors, Bedros Turian (1852–1872) captured an indelible place during his brief lifespan with his romantic poetic themes of love, solitude, nature, and imminent death. Hagop Baronian (1841–1892) excelled as a master of social satire, especially of the classes represented by hypocritical church trustees and society dames who peppered their speech with ridiculous-sounding French expressions. Among the small circle of women writers, novelist Srpouhi Dussap (1842–1901) stirred up strong controversy with forthright advocacy of feminist rights and emancipation. Finally, Western Armenian poetry reached its apex at the turn of the twentieth century with the unparalleled use of imagery and the sensual language of pagan renewal by Daniel Varoujan (1884–1915) and the powerful epical verses of revolt and heroism by Siamanto (1878–1915), both destined to become victims of the Armenian Genocide.

THE ARMENIAN QUESTION

The unending stream of complaints from the interior provinces regarding extortion, double taxation, kidnappings, devastating raids, and land usurpation emboldened the Armenian patriarchate at the conclusion of the Russo-Turkish War in 1878 to petition supreme commander Grand Duke Nicholas (1856–1929) to include provisions for the safety and security of the Turkish Armenian population in the negotiations for peace. The preliminary Treaty

John Bull's Dilemma. An 1895 cartoon depicts English indecision over aid to Armenia at the beginning of the Turkish persecution. Still economically linked to the waning Ottoman Empire, Britain was nevertheless sympathetic to the plight of the Armenians and anxious to see the further decline of Ottoman influence in the region. ©BETTMANN/CORBIS

of San Stefano in February 1878, aside from granting independence or autonomy to several Balkan states, ceded to Russia five districts bordering the Caucasus and stipulated through Article 16 that Russian withdrawal from Erzerum and other parts of the Armenian plateau to be handed back to Sultan Abdul-Hamid II (r. 1876–1909) was contingent on the implementation of reforms to safeguard the Armenians from Kurdish and Circassian depreda-

tion. But the subsequent European-imposed Treaty of Berlin in July 1878 left only three districts (Kars, Ardahan, Batum) under Russian rule and, in an ironic reversal of numerals, by Article 61 required the immediate withdrawal of Loris-Melikov's army from Erzerum. The article also internationalized the Armenian Question by placing on the European Powers collectively the responsibility to oblige the sultan to effect the necessary reforms. But as it happened, "what is everybody's business is nobody's business." Although punitive raids against the Armenian villages did not cease, the Europeans soon lost interest as they became embroiled in the scramble for empire in Africa.

Failure to achieve legal reforms led some Armenian youth to form self-defense groups in Erzerum, Van, and other towns on the Armenian plateau. These ephemeral groups were succeeded between 1885 and 1890 by the Armenakan (at Van), Hunchakian, and Dashnaktsutiun political parties. The revolutionaries had limited resources in the face of the awesome power of the state, yet they attracted followers among ideologically-driven intellectuals and rural youth who cared little about ideology other than protecting their villages and striving as freedom fighters (*fedayis*) for Armenian emancipation.

In 1894, encouraged by Hunchakian field workers, the rugged mountaineers of the Sasun district refused to pay double taxation, leading to their siege and ultimate massacre by both the sultan's Kurdish (*Hamidiye*) detachments and regular army. The brutal killings of an estimated four thousand people who had laid down their arms in exchange for a promise of amnesty raised an international outcry that forced the European powers back to the Armenian Question. A resulting new package of reforms was negotiated with Abdul-Hamid II in 1895, but once again the Europeans turned away, while the sultan, playing on Muslim fears about loss of dominance, unleashed a series of massacres that began along the Black Sea at Trebizond in October and then spread to every *vilayet* on the Armenian plateau. The massacre of some 200,000 Armenians in 1895 and 1896 demonstrated that Armenian defense groups and revolutionaries were incapable of protecting their people. A desperate attempt to force European intervention by seizing the European-administered Ottoman Bank in the autumn of 1896 led to the further indiscriminate killing of several thousand Armenians in Constantinople itself, and a plot to assassinate Abdul-Hamid in 1905 came to naught.

There was still hope, however, as disaffection from the sultan had become widespread among other ethnic groups as well, including Turkish dissidents who believed that only drastic reforms and reorganization could save the Ottoman Empire from final collapse and dissolution. The Armenian parties, especially the Dashnaktsutiun, interacted with the so-called Young Turk intellectuals in Europe for several years before a near bloodless revolution in July 1908 forced Abdul-Hamid II to become a figurehead constitutional monarch. The Young Turk revolution was greeted with enthusiasm by nearly all Armenians, and improvements immediately followed. Armenian political parties and cultural associations were legalized, Armenian deputies were elected to parliament, and exiled intellectuals returned to participate in what was to become the final phase in a brilliant Western Armenian literary movement.

The revolution soon soured, however, in the face of setbacks in the Balkans and resentment domestically among conservative traditionalist forces. In an attempted countercoup by Abdul-Hamid's supporters in April 1909, Armenian blood flowed once again, this time in the region of Cilicia, where some thirty thousand Armenians perished and scores of city quarters, towns, and villages were pillaged and burned. Then in January 1913, in the wake of the first Balkan War, the extreme nationalist wing of the Young Turk party (Ittihad ve Terakki), led by Ismail Enver (1881–1922), Mehmed Talaat (1874–1921), and Ahmed Jemal (1872–1922), seized power and guided the Ottoman Empire down the road to World War I as an ally of imperial Germany. Ironically, Russia was then posing as a champion of the Turkish Armenians and with the support of the now-allied governments of France and Great Britain negotiated the final Armenian reform program by which Turkish Armenia was merged into two semi-autonomous super provinces with European inspectors general. But the reform project, signed in February 1914, would soon be repudiated and give the chauvinist Young Turk dictators one more excuse to implement the "final solution" of the Armenian Question in 1915, when under the convenient cover of a raging world war the Turkish Armenian provinces were combined.

See also **Abdul-Hamid II; Ottoman Empire; Russia; Russo-Turkish War; Young Turks.**

BIBLIOGRAPHY

Bournoutian, George A. *A Concise History of the Armenian People*. Costa Mesa, Calif., 2003.

Hovannisian, Richard G., ed. *The Armenian People from Ancient to Modern Times.* 2 vols. New York, 1996.

Lynch, H. F. B. *Armenia: Travels and Studies.* 2 vols. London, 1901. Reprint, New York, 1990.

Nalbandian, Louise. *The Armenian Revolutionary Movement.* Berkeley, Calif., 1963.

Peroomian, Rubina. *Literary Responses to Catastrophe.* Atlanta, 1993.

Suny, Ronald Grigor. *Looking toward Ararat.* Bloomington, Ind., 1993.

Walker, Christopher J. *Armenia: The Survival of a Nation.* Rev. 2nd ed. New York, 1980.

RICHARD G. HOVANNISIAN

ARMIES. Like their predecessors in the period of the *ancien régime,* armies in the period from 1789 to 1914 continued to serve as vital instruments of the state's will. That is, they continued to fight the wars decided upon by heads of state and to defend the state's borders from aggressive neighbors. Unlike their predecessors, however, European armies in this period also served increasingly as an expression of the nation's will. In other words, armies ceased to be the exclusive property of heads of states and governments. Instead, they became expressions of the nation more generally. Thus between 1789 and 1914 armies became a generally accepted, in many cases quite widely supported, facet of European life, as witnessed by the confidence placed in them in the years before World War I and the early years of the war itself.

Much of the credit for this transformation belongs to the French revolutionaries. They argued that the nation should be defended not by armed servants of the monarch, but by those people with the largest stakes in the goals and aspirations of the nation itself. By thus creating an important connection between soldiering and citizenship, they changed military service (and by extension armies themselves) from institutions largely apart from society and made them representative of not just political goals, but social goals as well. As the influential French philosophe Denis Diderot said, "The citizen must have two sets of clothes, one for his trade and one as a soldier." As the French revolutionaries put Diderot's words into actions, armies came to be used as schools through which young males were to learn the precepts of nationalism and the virtues of communal service to the state and to the nation more generally.

The cornerstones of the new French system were nationalist motivations for military service and promotion of men based on talent. The revolutionaries based their armed forces on the presumption that men would fight longest and hardest for causes in which they deeply believed. An educated, self-motivated soldiery, they concluded, would need none of the brutal discipline of the sort made notorious by most eighteenth-century armies. French soldiers would ideally fight for the hopes of what they might accomplish for their nation rather than out of fear of punishment from officers and sergeants. In practice this system often turned to harsh discipline, especially in the later years of the Revolutionary Wars, but virtually all observers admired the spirit and energy of highly motivated French soldiers.

Talent, not birth, formed the second cornerstone of French Revolutionary ideology. Because the French Revolutionary system marginalized or physically removed the aristocracy, it had perforce to create a new elite. This elite came from educated and talented middle-class men, who quickly assumed places of importance in the army. The Napoleonic system built on these changes, employing an officer corps that was younger, more energetic, and more motivated by personal and national ambition than those of the armies they faced. Napoleon's proclamation that every French soldier carried a marshal's baton in his haversack was largely hyperbole, but it captured the spirit of a system of upward mobility based on talent that was truly revolutionary.

These new armies led France to a series of dramatic battlefield victories such as those over the Russians and Austrians at Austerlitz in 1805 and over the Prussians at Jena in 1806. These victories allowed France to impose its will upon much of the Continent, a feat that even the proficient armies of King Louis XIV (r. 1643–1715) could never have achieved. Even Napoleon's eventual defeat in 1815 failed to dispel the aura of the French system and its accomplishments. In the decades immediately following Napoleon's exile to St. Helena, a series of military writers tried to dissect and explain his success. The two most famous, the Prussian Carl von Clausewitz and the Swiss banker-turned-officer Antoine-Henri Jomini, came to radically different conclusions about the keys to Napoleon's success, but both were influential in keeping Napoleon and the mystique of the French Revolutionary Army at the center of European military thinking.

Moreover, as the obvious benefits of the French system became manifest during the Napoleonic period, they inspired imitation across Europe with local variations in each nation. Conservative regimes in Germany and Russia changed their systems slowly, but even they were affected by the desire to imitate at least some of the features of the French system. To cite one example from later in the century, Russia's humiliation in the Crimean War (1853–1856) against France and Britain contributed greatly to the growing pressures for emancipation of the serfs. That decision, effected in the 1860s, came in large part from the hopes that emancipation might create in Russians the sort of nationalistic fervor that had proven so valuable to the cohesion of French armies of the 1790s.

The central role of the army in national affairs became almost inevitable given the intense competition between European nation-states. In Imperial Germany, seating at social and official functions was contingent upon an individual's military rank, leaving even the great Chancellor Otto von Bismarck to be introduced and seated after German colonels, given that Bismarck's highest army rank attained was major. The many roles that armies came to play in so many aspects of European life gave rise to the pejorative term *militarism,* first popularized by opponents of Napoleon III's regime (1852–1870) in France. The term came to mean the use and role of the army and military symbols far in excess of that needed to defend a nation's central interests.

As the popularization of that term indicates, not all Europeans looked favorably upon the growth of armies. To many peasants, especially in states with underdeveloped senses of nationalism such as Italy, Russia, and Austria-Hungary, the army represented conscription, time away from home, and a potential loss of opportunity in the civilian job market in the service of an oppressive and alien state. To many urban workers, the army

represented state oppression and strike breaking. As scandals such as France's Dreyfus affair of the late 1890s revealed, armies also became, in the minds of many Europeans, centers of authoritarianism, secret plots, and clericalism that were out of place in liberal society. Ethnic minorities also tended to see armies more as instruments of oppression and the enforcement of a nonrepresentative version of nationalism.

Throughout the nineteenth century, the new, more powerful militaries, most notably in France and Great Britain, played a critical role in the expansion of European empires in Africa and Asia. Although scholars correctly point to superior Western technology as a primary reason for the success of imperialism, the structure of European armies should not be ignored. Discipline, nationalism, and the development of a professional soldier's ethic also played key roles in the ability of European armies to control large territories with relatively few men.

STRUCTURE AND ORGANIZATION OF EUROPEAN ARMIES

Because European armies competed so often with one another, and because officers tended to move rather fluidly from army to army until the middle of the nineteenth century, European military structures shared many important features. These similarities are not surprising given the numerous shared political, social, and cultural assumptions of European nation-states. Most armies used the battalion as their main tactical unit. Normally commanded by a lieutenant colonel and containing five hundred to eight hundred infantrymen, the battalion was the largest unit that could be commanded effectively in the heat of battle. Two or more battalions made up a regiment, commanded by a colonel; the regiment formed the main social unit of an army. Indeed, regimental traditions and linkages could be so strong that many men felt themselves more loyal to the regiment than to the army as a whole.

Added to the infantry were two other principal arms, the cavalry and the artillery. The former comprised an elite arm that normally attracted a disproportionate number of aristocrats, in part because the social and martial expenses of life in the cavalry far exceeded an officer's salary. In the late eighteenth and nineteenth centuries, cavalry

GLEASON'S PICTORIAL DRAWING-ROOM COMPANION.

POINT IN QUARTE.   POINT IN TIERRE.   PRIME POINT.   THE BLOW DELIVERED.

Bayonet tactics of the French. Illustration of French foot soldiers, c. 1854. ©Corbis

performed scouting and reconnaissance roles and ideally administered a coup de grâce to a retreating army or one in disarray. In the years just before World War I, many officers had begun to recognize the vulnerabilities of cavalry on a modern battlefield dominated by rifle and machine gun fire. British General Ian Hamilton famously observed that the only role for the cavalry in the Russo-Japanese War (1904–1905) was to prepare rice for the infantry. Others, such as Hamilton's colleague Douglas Haig, retained a faith in cavalry as an arm of exploitation into the 1920s.

Artillery, requiring a high degree of technical expertise, attracted large numbers of middle-class men and lesser nobles, most famously Napoleon. Also an elite arm, the artillery possessed a power that led to a wide variety of euphemisms, such as "preparing" or "softening" the battlefield. In practice, these terms meant bombarding infantry and cavalry in order to open holes in the enemy's formations. A wide variety of light artillery weapons developed in this period, including light, mobile field artillery pieces and much heavier pieces designed to reduce enemy fortifications from long distances. The introduction of breech-loading rifled artillery in the middle of the century rapidly increased the rate and accuracy of fire.

Ideally, the artillery created panic and casualties in the opponent's main infantry formations that cavalry could then exploit. Celebrated charges, such as the British "Charge of the Light Brigade" at the Crimean War battle of Balaklava in 1854, immortalized by Alfred, Lord Tennyson, became part of national legend even when they failed. Cavalrymen, such as those in the Light Brigade, were expected to display gallantry and courage, especially in death. This charge, through which 113 members of the 673-man brigade were killed and another 134 wounded, was famously belittled by a French officer who observed, "It is magnificent, but it is not war." Still, the cavalry charge remained in the public imagination as one of the last remnants of an older, and presumably more honorable, age of chivalric warfare amid growing mechanization and modernization.

One of the most important organizational changes in European armies was the Napoleonic innovation of the *corps d'armée,* which combined infantry, artillery, and cavalry into one parent unit, under a single commander. A corps could therefore operate, move, and fight independently of other units, providing maximum flexibility and, if done properly, allow for several corps to converge on a given point at roughly the same time. By moving separate corps on different axes, moreover, the corps system greatly eased the problems of logistics and movement. Over time, corps also absorbed many of the necessary administrative functions of armies such as quartermaster (supply), medical, and topographic units. Two or more corps formed an army and, by 1914, two or more armies formed an army group.

In the middle of the nineteenth century, Prussia introduced the next important innovation, the general staff. Building upon ideas from the Napoleonic era, the Prussians created an organization dedicated to planning for war and for studying all of the associated contingencies and new technologies of both the military and civilian worlds. For Prussia, the most important of these new technologies was the railroad, which provided Prussia with the ability to concentrate forces across a broad state's interior lines of communications. This ability provided Prussia with a tremendous advantage over both Austria in 1866 and France in 1870, although critics of German war planning after 1870 assert that the Germans became too dependent on railroad timetables, creating the overly rigid war plan with which Germany went to war in 1914.

The man most commonly associated with the development of the general staff is Prussian General Helmuth von Moltke (1800–1891). By recruiting talented officers and placing them into a career-long system of education and training, Moltke nurtured a system that planned for wars by envisioning the future of strategy and by estimating the responses of potential enemies. The success of this system in planning wars against Denmark (1864), Austria (1866), and France (1870–1871) led to the institution of general staffs in all of the Great Powers by the time of the outbreak of World War I.

The needs of general staffs to plan for future wars led, in turn, to the need to identify potential allies and opponents. This military requirement drove the pursuit of alliances (usually defensive) in order to reduce the number of contingencies for which an army had to plan. The 1879 Dual Alliance between Germany and Austria bandaged many of the wounds left over from Prussia's defeat of Austria in 1866 and allowed each signatory to focus on other areas of concern. The Entente Cordiale signed between Britain and France in 1904 similarly allowed two traditional rivals to bury long-standing hatchets and, eventually, develop schemes for fighting a coordinated war with Germany.

LEADERSHIP AND SOLDIERING

The bifurcated system of dividing armies into officers and enlisted men (whom the British revealingly called the "other ranks") remained one of the most important hangovers inherited from the *ancien régime*. In theory, there is no necessary reason for armies to divide themselves in this manner, but all European armies did so. The reasons for the maintenance of this system were less functional than social and political. Not even the French republics were willing to abandon the notion that armies should be led by a small elite, whether determined by birth, talent, or a mixture of both. Although coups d'état have been rare in European history, the sheer disruptive potential of armies argued further for placing reliable men in positions of authority. Rather than challenge the authority of the state, armies have more commonly been used to destroy threats to the state's domestic authority, most famously in the series of revolts that rocked Europe between 1830 and 1848. Armies therefore served as reliable instruments for maintaining, through violence if necessary, regimes in power.

Officers therefore had to be politically and socially reliable, even at the cost of a certain level of military acumen. Officers attained their positions through a variety of means. As late as the mid-nineteenth century, many armies sold officers' commissions, ensuring that only wealthy men closely linked to the goals of the ruling regime could attain senior ranks. Promotion from the ranks to the officer corps remained a rare exception.

Educating and preparing men for their jobs as officers became more scientific in the course of the nineteenth century. Almost all major powers established and maintained schools for teaching officership in this period. Most had technical curriculums and limited their student bodies to men of privilege. France's two great military schools, the École polytechnique and Saint-Cyr, were formed in 1795 and 1802, respectively. Great Britain opened the Royal Military Academy at Woolwich in 1799 (later moved to Sandhurst), and Prussia opened its Kriegsakademie (War Academy) in 1810, demonstrating a shared approach to military leadership and the professionalism of the officer corps despite divergent political climates.

Enlisted men tended to come from much lower social strata than their officers. As the unifying logic of nationalism took general root in Europe, however, the use of foreign mercenaries became less common. Thus armies had to fill their ranks largely from those men unable to sustain themselves in the civilian economy. Most armies preferred peasants, believed to be sturdier, in better mental and physical health, and less prone to socialism. Despite occasional periods of rural overpopulation and cyclical poverty, farmers rarely volunteered for military service in sufficient numbers to fill the ranks. In practice, therefore, armies often had to rely on the masses of unemployed urban workers produced by the dislocations caused by industrialization.

The disadvantaged backgrounds of so many soldiers led to a general low status for enlisted men in European society. The Duke of Wellington once referred to the men who filled his army as the "scum of the earth," although the wide social and cultural chasms between Wellington and the average British soldier also account for his generalization. Over the course of the nineteenth century, the social acceptance of European soldiers improved as education improved and as armies themselves became more representative of their societies. Still, most men who could find a way to avoid military service did so, leaving the enlisted ranks largely to men with few other options, those who allowed a recruiting sergeant to buy them a few too many drinks, and men who had a pressing need to get out of town.

Enlisted men who stayed in the army beyond their required terms could aspire to the ranks of the noncommissioned officers (NCOs). These men, who carried the ranks of corporals and sergeants, were responsible for the training and disciplining of men in their units. They also served as middlemen between the officers and their soldiers. To the former they were an invaluable source of information on the unit, while to the latter they were the most important sources of immediate authority. To new recruits, NCOs were father figures who dispensed discipline and rewards to show their approval or disapproval. Most armies reserved NCO positions for volunteers, providing an incentive for men to join the army voluntarily before taking their chances with notoriously capricious systems of conscription. NCOs became the backbones of armies, taking the most direct roles in training and small-unit leadership on the battlefield.

Armies often recruited heavily among men from ethnic minorities, especially in heterogeneous states. The relatively larger degree of economic marginalization of many minority groups partially explains this pattern. Many of these groups had quite ambivalent feelings toward the very state that the army served, but they enlisted in large numbers anyway. In most cases, such men served without much friction, suggesting that ethnic tensions were not as divisive as is sometimes assumed. Thus the British army depended upon the accession of disproportionate numbers of Irish soldiers, most of whom loyally served the empire as long as they were not asked to suppress rebellions inside Ireland. Similarly Poles served, albeit often reluctantly, in the Russian, German, and Austro-Hungarian armies. This problem existed even in relatively homogenous states such as France and Italy, because many men identified themselves more in local terms than national ones. Indeed part of the logic of conscription came from the hope that shared military service might help men see themselves in national terms.

Relatively few men from minority groups became officers. Many states had official proscriptions against minorities achieving officer rank, such as the bans on Jewish service in Imperial Germany and Russia. Other armies found informal means to limit the upward advancement of minorities. Religion could also serve as a barrier to the upward advancement of officers. Republican France was theoretically open to men of talent, but found ways to discriminate against both Jews and devout Catholics, as men as different as Alfred Dreyfus and Ferdinand Foch both discovered to their dismay.

When volunteerism fell short, most Continental armies looked to access men via conscription, systematically introduced by the French in the 1790s. In determining how many men to conscript, states had to balance the army's need for soldiers with the costs of training and equipping them as well as the costs associated with removing large numbers of men from the civilian job market. The latter problem presented another reason to recruit and conscript soldiers from among the groups of men with the least economic potential. In many cases, most often in years of peace, states attempted to reduce the number of men they conscripted, creating controversies when the conscription laws disproportionately exempted certain

An English officer from the Bombay Lancers, mid-nineteenth century. The Bombay Lancers were part of the Indian army, wherein native Indian troops served under British officers. SEF/ART RESOURCE, NY

nineteenth century such subterfuges became less effective and therefore less common.

Of the large European powers, only Great Britain consistently resisted conscription. Protected by the Royal Navy and relying heavily on indigenous allies to maintain the empire, Britain managed to raise an army without compulsion. As a result, Britain consistently sought to find ways to keep men in service long-term, while simultaneously limiting the amount of money spent on them. This process resulted in a small but highly trained force that Britain committed to Continental wars only rarely. The small size of the British army and the unwillingness of British leadership to risk its destruction limited British ability to respond to Continental crises such as the Wars of German Unification.

Active-duty armies were backed by other formations, including the reserves and the militia. The former was composed mostly of men who had completed compulsory service but were still subject to periodic military training for periods as long as thirty years. In times of war they were subject to recall to the active forces, although they usually performed minor roles such as garrison duty and protection of lines of supply. Various militia schemes developed in Europe as well. They shared in common a joint local–national method of control that regular officers usually disdained, often with good reason. Nevertheless, the local traditions of such units as the German *Landwehr* and the British territorials remained strong, even in the face of a military modernization that made part-time soldiering less relevant to the rapidly changing conditions of the modern battlefield.

Not all Europeans disdained the militia model. Socialists such as France's charismatic Jean Jaurès (1859–1914) advocated militias as the best way for armies to protect the nation from outside aggression without threatening civil liberties. Locally based units formed from among the people they served, Jaurès argued, would be less likely to suppress strikes and also less likely to act as an armed servant of a tyrant. Being less technically proficient would also discourage their use as agents of imperialism or in offensive wars against neighboring states. Of course, because the rulers of many states envisioned using their armies in just such roles, the militia model never became dominant.

groups such as the middle class, or seminary students. To cite another pressure limiting the number of men recruited, in Prussia many conservatives wanted to set clear limits on the number of men conscripted because they also wanted to limit the number of non-nobles they needed to admit into an expanding officer corps.

Most conscription systems operated at the local level. Some towns drew lots, some attempted to send their criminals and malcontents, and others raised money to hire substitutes. In almost all cases, local chicanery and favoritism played key roles in determining who served and who stayed home. Most communities tried to send as few men to the army as possible because of the economic and social dislocations that military service could create. In at least one case, a French town avoided sending men to the army by listing all new births as girls. As the power of central authorities grew during the

TECHNOLOGY, TACTICS, AND PERFORMANCE IN BATTLE

Changing technology provided tremendous challenges for European armies. Industrialization led to a dizzying series of new weapons and dramatic improvements in old weapons. Muskets gave way to rifles, with attendant revolutionary improvements in range and accuracy. Whereas a Napoleonic smoothbore musket had an effective range of approximately 90 meters (100 yards), a rifle's range could exceed 900 meters (1,000 yards). The technology of rifling had been understood for decades and was quite simple, merely requiring a groove to be cut inside the barrel. European industrial and productive capacity allowed for rifles and custom-made ammunition to be manufactured in mass quantity to exacting specifications. By the 1840s rifles were commonplace in all European armies. Bolt actions, smokeless powder, and magazines further increased the lethality of rifles.

The impact of science and technology produced similar changes in artillery, making the artillery pieces of the 1870s appear quaint by the outbreak of World War I. New metal alloys and more powerful propellants led to rifled artillery pieces that could fire shells over distances of 4.8 kilometers (3 miles) or more. When the German army invaded Belgium in 1914, it employed 28-centimeter howitzers that fired shells weighing 748 pounds each and traveling at a speed of 1,133 feet per second, yielding a striking energy of more than 6,000 tons per shell. On the battlefield, artillery largely served as an anti-infantry weapon. Canister and grapeshot ammunition contained hundreds of pieces of metal fired out of a cannon to clear the field of enemy soldiers. British officer Henry Shrapnel invented an airburst antipersonnel weapon that still carries his name.

Largely owing to these changes in technology, armies in this period moved far away from the linear formations of the *ancien régime*. The introduction of rifles forced significant changes in the middle of the nineteenth century. Battalions learned to fight with more dispersed formations, leading to much larger battlefields. The introduction of machine guns further tilted the advantages on the battlefield toward the defense. The Russo-Japanese War seemed to demonstrate the overwhelming power of defensive technologies, although not all armies made corrections to their doctrines based on these experiences.

Armies also had to respond to a variety of political taskings and, therefore, needed to develop an adaptability to a wide variety of circumstances. Large armies such as the French had to prepare for deterrence against neighbors, limited offensive actions such as those in Italy in 1859, and colonial expeditions as far flung as Algeria, Madagascar, and Indochina. The rapid evolution of the Prussian/German army in this period owed much to its state's limited overseas colonial empire, thereby allowing it to focus almost exclusively on Continental taskings. The British army, by contrast, had to learn to fight in a number of divergent environments, greatly complicating the development of coherent doctrines and ideologies.

European armies took their new technologies and their sophisticated systems of organization and training with them around the world. In the main, native Africans and Asians had few military responses to European forces, but European armies were not always successful. In one of the most famous examples, a British column of 1,800 Europeans and 1,000 Africans was ambushed in 1879 by a mobile Zulu force of 10,000 highly disciplined warriors in the battle of Isandhlwana. The Zulus killed 1,745 of the Europeans and nearly all of the Africans. Nevertheless, even a victory as dramatic as Isandhlwana proved ephemeral. Before the year was out, British forces had won a series of victories that had put an end to the military power of the Zulus.

Another British foe, the Boers, combined the hit-and-run tactics of the Zulus with modern European weaponry. Descendants of Dutch settlers, the Boers unwittingly found themselves in possession of territory rich with diamonds and gold. Between 1899 and 1902 they decided to resist British incursions into their lands. Assisted by modern rifles and machine guns given to them by Germany, they forced Britain into a long and frustrating war that, although successful, led to considerable self-examination and hand-wringing.

Modern weapons made battles between European armies bloodier as the killing zone of a battlefield grew ever larger. Nevertheless, many officers, even many who personally witnessed the frustrations of the Boer War and the carnage of the Russo-Japanese War, continued to hold to a heroic,

British soldiers fighting in the Boer War, c. 1900. Soldiers of the Royal Munster Fusiliers are positioned behind barriers constructed of sandbags at Honey Kloof, South Africa, c. 1900. ©CORBIS

personal vision of war. French leaders such as Louis de Grandmaison and, in his younger years, Ferdinand Foch, taught a generation of French officers that offensive spirit and élan could overcome even the thickest and most deadly enemy fire. Many of the officers who learned their trade under this sys-

tem later led the bloody charges of 1914 and 1915. Grandmaison was dead before World War I began, but Foch underwent a dramatic transformation in which he rejected his old teachings as infantile. Still, the doctrine of the offensive that was prevalent in all armies in 1914 was a product of more than simplistic reactions to changes in war. It also served as an expression of nationalism and a rejection of the notion that machines, not men, determined the outcomes of battles.

INSTRUMENTS FOR DOOMSDAY

During the course of the nineteenth century, the armies of Europe evolved from being relatively small instruments of the limited political goals of heads of states to massive, conscript-based reflections of their societies more generally. This transformation had a dramatic effect on Europe in this period as armies became more closely linked to the goals and fears of Europeans than ever before. Where once Europeans had understood armies to belong to distant and unrepresentative states, by the 1890s armies had become a part of the larger process of individuals identifying with their states. As Eugen Weber succinctly described this process in France, the army stopped being "theirs" and began to be seen as "ours."

This change, of course, was based on a variety of larger changes in Europe, most of them not directly military in nature. The emergence of nationalism as the dominant European ideology placed national armies at the forefront of national identity, especially as conscription resulted in a much larger percentage of European males having direct contact with the army. To be sure, not all men recalled their years of service fondly, but the mere presence in the ranks of a more representative class of European males argued against the army being seen as an alien separate class. Over the course of the nineteenth century, moreover, the state itself became a less alien institution and more closely connected to positive involvement in daily lives, most notably in public education and social welfare.

Industrialization also played a key role in the development of armies, both by providing them with new weapons and by creating a perpetual underclass for whom military service always remained a last-ditch employment option. Industry and its attendant economic effects also fueled the already heated competition between European states on the Continent itself, in overseas empires, and on the high seas. This competition in turn led to high levels of parliamentary funding for armies, even from many nominally socialist deputies.

The combination of high funding, new technologies, extreme nationalism, and conscription combined to make armies, and the political and social systems that supported them, much more influential and powerful by 1914 than they had been in 1789. They had become doomsday machines, capable not only of deterrence and protection of borders but also of global power projection and mass killing on an unprecedented scale. The many cemeteries and monuments in Europe that memorialize the dead of World War I stand as stark testimony to this dramatic transformation of European armies.

See also **Aristocracy; Clausewitz, Carl von; Jaurès, Jean; Moltke, Helmuth von; Napoleon; Wellington, Duke of (Arthur Wellesley).**

BIBLIOGRAPHY

Bertaud, Jean-Paul. *The Army of the French Revolution: From Citizen-Soldiers to Instrument of Power.* Translated by R. R. Palmer. Princeton, N.J., 1988.

Black, Jeremy. *Western Warfare, 1775–1882.* Bloomington, Ind., 2001.

Bond, Brian. *The Victorian Army and the Staff College, 1854–1914.* London, 1972.

Bushnell, John. *Mutiny amid Repression: Russian Soldiers in the Revolution of 1905–1906.* Bloomington, Ind., 1985.

Chandler, David G. *The Campaigns of Napoleon.* New York, 1966.

Cobb, Richard. *The People's Armies: The Armées Révolutionnaires, Instrument of the Terror in the Departments, April 1793 to Floreal Year II.* Translated by Marianne Elliott. New Haven, Conn., 1987.

Elting, John R. *Swords around a Throne: Napoleon's Grande Armée.* New York, 1988.

Esdaile, Charles J. *The Wars of Napoleon.* London, 1995.

Forrest, Alan. *The Soldiers of the French Revolution.* Durham, N.C., 1990.

Howard, Michael. *The Franco-Prussian War.* New York, 1961.

Karsten, Peter. "Irish Soldiers in the British Army, 1792–1922: Suborned or Subordinate?" *Journal of Social History* 17, no. 1 (1983): 31–65.

Muir, Rory. *Tactics and the Experience of Battle in the Age of Napoleon.* New Haven, Conn., 1998.

Porch, Douglas. *The March to the Marne: The French Army, 1871–1914.* Cambridge, U.K., 1981.

Showalter, Dennis E. *Railroads and Rifles: Soldiers, Technology, and the Unification of Germany.* Hamden, Conn., 1975.

———. "From Deterrence to Doomsday Machine: The German Way of War, 1890–1914." *Journal of Military History* 64, no. 3 (2000): 679–710.

———. *The Wars of German Unification.* London, 2004.

Spiers, Edward M. *The Army and Society, 1815–1914.* London, 1980.

Strachan, Hew. *European Armies and the Conduct of War.* London, 1983.

———. *Wellington's Legacy: The Reform of the British Army, 1830–1854.* Manchester, U.K., 1984.

Wawro, Geoffrey. *Warfare and Society in Europe, 1792–1914.* London, 2000.

Weber, Eugen. *Peasants into Frenchmen: The Modernization of Rural France, 1870–1914.* Stanford, Calif., 1976.

MICHAEL S. NEIBERG

ARNOLD, MATTHEW (1822–1888),
English poet, critic, and polemical writer.

Matthew Arnold was born at Laleham, England, in 1822. His father, Dr. Thomas Arnold, was a teacher and clergyman who subsequently became famous as the reforming headmaster of Rugby School. Educated at Rugby and Balliol College, Oxford, Arnold became a fellow of Oriel College, Oxford, in 1845. This was a nonteaching post, which he combined, between 1847 and 1851, with a job as secretary to Lord Lansdowne (Henry Petty-Fitzmaurice), a senior cabinet minister in the Whig government of Lord John Russell. In 1851 he married and became an inspector of schools, rising to chief inspector in 1884 and retiring in 1886. He died in 1888.

POETRY
Arnold's early verse was published in two anonymous volumes, *The Strayed Reveller* (1849) and *Empedocles on Etna and Other Poems* (1852). This was a poetry of ideas, some of it written in a pioneering prototype of modernist "free verse," in which Arnold reflects on the dilemmas created by the decline of traditional religious authority. The "modern" condition was "the dialogue of the mind with itself." In poems such as "The Forsaken Merman" and "Resignation" he considers hedonist and stoic alternatives to the established Christian ethic. In "Empedocles on Etna" he uses a pre-Socratic Greek philosopher as a parallel for his own experience of living in an era of transition from religious faith to anxious doubt.

Despite its intellectual stress, Arnold came to feel that this poetry was overly Romantic in its subjectivity and lack of formal control. In 1853 he replaced *Empedocles on Etna* with a volume simply entitled *Poems*—no longer anonymous, and equipped with a preface that argued for a new, post-Romantic poetics. Literature, he suggested, should address not the inner life of the author but external "actions." Literary texts should display "Architectonicè" or coherent form. If Arnold's attempts to embody these ideas in the brief epics "Sohrab and Rustum" (1853) and "Balder Dead" (1855) were not entirely successful, his theoretical contribution to a shift of taste from the Romantic enthusiasm for spontaneous and fragmentary expression to the late-nineteenth-century cult of form was considerable.

In 1857 Arnold became professor of poetry at Oxford, a part-time post that he occupied for ten years. In his inaugural lecture, "On the Modern Element in Literature," he added another criterion to his poetic theory—"adequacy," or the demand that a satisfactory poetry should reflect the most advanced thought of its era. His 1867 volume, *New Poems*, contains several poems that endeavor to meet this demand—most notably "Dover Beach."

CRITICISM
In the 1860s Arnold began to publish his lectures and to contribute to the periodical press. In "The Function of Criticism at the Present Time" (printed in *Essays in Criticism*, 1865) he sets out his assumptions as a critic and suggests, by implication, how he wishes to reform English literary criticism. Previously criticism had been party political: the Whig *Edinburgh Review* dismissed the Tory William Wordsworth; the Tory *Quarterly* condemned John Keats for his association with the "Cockney School" of Whig and Radical writers. Inspired by the example of the French critic Charles-Augustin Sainte-Beuve (1804–1869), Arnold recommended instead the values of "disinterestedness" and objectivity, or the endeavor "to see the object as in itself it really is."

In the twentieth century Arnold's aspiration to objectivity was sometimes dismissed as an illusion, and an overtly political literary criticism (Marxist, feminist, green, queer, or postcolonialist) reasserted itself. Arnold would have seen this development as reactionary. In "The Study of Poetry" (1880) he identifies two obstacles to a "real estimate" of a text: the "historic" fallacy (or the scholarly tendency to overvalue texts because they are old) and the "personal" fallacy, which overestimates writers on grounds of national, social, political, or sexual affinity. What we should seek is "high seriousness," whether or not we sympathize with the views of the author. One way to test this is the application of "touchstones"—a constant comparison with passages acknowledged to be of the highest quality.

Arnold's criticism is not, however, narrowly literary. In 1860, in the lectures published in *On Translating Homer* (1861), he identified critical objectivity as a necessary endeavor in "all branches of knowledge,—theology, philosophy, history, art, science." Accordingly, he himself published essays on other topics.

The underlying problem for his social writing is the advent of democracy. If every man is to have a vote, then every man needs to be educated—and Arnold had been struggling, since the 1840s, with the obstacles that religious sectarianism placed in the way of a compulsory school system. *Culture and Anarchy* (1869) addresses this difficulty. Religion cannot, in the absence of a common faith, provide the core values for a universal elementary education. Instead, Arnold proposes the secular value of "culture." His polemical manner is witty and pugnacious. British society is divided into "Barbarians" (the aristocracy), "Philistines" (the middle classes), and "Populace." Moral earnestness is characterized as "Hebraism," to which a counterbalance is required in the form of "Hellenism" or the "free play of mind on every object." But beneath the playful surface there is a recommendation that has been widely adopted as a basis for education in multicultural or postreligious human societies.

The playfulness reaches its peak in *Friendship's Garland* (1871), a witty sequel to Voltaire's *Candide* (1759) and Thomas Carlyle's *Sartor Resartus* (1833–1834) that recommends German intellectual rigor to the unsystematic Anglo-Saxons. In *Litera-*

ture and Dogma (1873) Arnold turned, more seriously, to theology. His purpose was simultaneously to rescue religion from the Bible (that is, from the misreading of this poetic text as a series of falsifiably scientific statements) and to rescue the Bible from religion—stressing its literary value to retain it as part of the "culture" in an era of declining religious assent. Thomas Arnold had sought to invent a creed for a national church from which no citizen could feel excluded. Pushing this liberal theology to a controversial extreme, his son redefines religion as "morality touched with emotion" and God as "the something not ourselves which makes for righteousness."

Matthew Arnold has been attacked as a poet of limited range and a prose writer whose elegantly witty manner makes rigorous argument impossible. He is better understood as an author who works, distinctively, and in an ingenious combination of verse and prose, to unsettle assumptions and suggest new directions for literary and intellectual life.

See also **Carlyle, Thomas; Education; Great Britain; Liberalism.**

BIBLIOGRAPHY

Primary Sources

Allott, Kenneth, and Miriam Allott, eds. *The Poems of Matthew Arnold.* 2nd ed. London, 1979.

Super, R. H. ed. *The Complete Prose Works of Matthew Arnold.* 11 vols. Ann Arbor, Mich., 1960–1977.

Secondary Sources

Collini, Stefan. *Arnold.* Oxford, U.K., 1988.

Coulling, Sidney. *Matthew Arnold and His Critics: A Study of Arnold's Controversies.* Athens, Ga., 1974.

Culler, A. Dwight. *Imaginative Reason: The Poetry of Matthew Arnold,* New Haven, Conn., 1966.

Trilling, Lionel. *Matthew Arnold.* New York, 1939.

NICHOLAS SHRIMPTON

ARTISANS AND GUILDS. In most European countries artisans have played a decisive role in developing industrial production, propagating democratic and socialist ideas, and promoting new cultural values. In the past, historians had too often described them as victims of capitalist industrialization and followed in this the diagnostic of Karl Marx and Friedrich Engels's *Communist Manifesto* (1848), which predicted the agony of small enterprises as a result of capitalist accumulation. More recently, the different paths of development of artisan professions during the nineteenth century have been underlined, and historians have shown how in the second half of the century some artisan professions survived, others adapted to the new economic conditions, while in other cases the character of artisan production was transformed as new occupations entered the small enterprise sector. The originally high number of shoemakers, tailors, and carpenters often declined because of the development of new forms of production and commercialization that limited their independence or field of production, whereas other artisan groups, including plumbers, electricians, and mechanics, grew in number and expanded as part of a broad process of industrial development.

In the middle of the nineteenth century great European cities such as Paris and London were dominated by small workshops and artisan producers. By the beginning of the twentieth century professions with close links to the consumer market, such as butchers and bakers, increased in number and often also in wealth, while others connected to building, such as bricklayers, carpenters, and plumbers, also profited from urbanization. The reason for these different developments can be found in the very nature of capitalism, which not only is based on big capital and big enterprises but also developed links between small workshops and larger firms. The forms of dependence and of cooperation varied from one sector to another and over time. The French economic historian Maurice Lévy-Leboyer described the functions of small enterprises as the "soupape de sécurité" (safety valve) of industrial capitalism.

ARTISANS AND POLITICAL RADICALISM

From the French Revolution of 1789 onward, artisans have been linked with ideas of political radicalism. The sans-culottes movement with its stress on direct democracy, social equality, and nationalism initiated an evolution that was continued with different national variations throughout the nineteenth century. Radical artisans showed up again in the Revolution of 1848 in France, as well as in the Paris Commune (1871), and were a major force in

the French socialist movement at the end of the nineteenth century. But they can also be seen in the Fratellanza artigiana d'Italia (founded 1861; Fraternity of artisans of Italy) which attempted to create a national democratic movement in Italy. They were active in German social democracy—August Bebel, co-founder of the Social Democratic Party, was a wood turner—despite the fact that the party was more committed to representative democracy and centralism. The Chartist movement (1838–1848) in Britain should also be seen in this context. The world of small producers who owned their means of production not only formed the backbone of many radical organizations but also played an important part in influential social utopian projects in nineteenth-century Europe. Charles Fourier's phalanxes as well as Étienne Cabet's *Icarie* were based on the image of the artisan, while in Germany Friedrich Wilhelm Raiffeisen's agricultural cooperative banks and Hermann Schulze-Delitzsch's cooperatives were addressed primarily to the artisans and their interests.

The radicalization of the artisans did not contribute to the politics of the Left alone, and during the century artisans also moved to the Right. German artisans were well known for their defense of traditional guild structures, which, especially in urban centers, gave them control of production, an eminent role in the formation of apprentices, as well as important political rights in urban administration. During the 1850s and 1860s they adopted the ideas of self-help, but following the founding of the German Empire in 1871 their right-wing orientation predominated. They wanted to monopolize the right to have apprentices, to open a workshop, and to link the title of master to a successful *cursus honorum* (course of honors)—and they succeeded in obtaining most of these demands. By the end of the century membership in corporative organizations was obligatory if two-thirds of the masters of an occupation in a town agreed to make it so. This created important links with political parties because artisan organizations had become one of the most successful lobbies in the German Empire.

ARTISANS AS CULTURAL MEDIATORS

Artisans were also important cultural mediators. In direct and personal contact with their clients, they

The guildhalls in Brussels, Belgium, c. 1885. ©MICHAEL MASLAN HISTORIC PHOTOGRAPHS/CORBIS

exercised an undeniable cultural and political influence. Situated in the heart of towns or in bigger city's quarters, they formed the backbone of sociability and associations. All across Europe they took part in singing associations, in religious circles, or in gymnastic groups. While such groups were committed to national goals in central and eastern Europe, artisans played a major part in promoting not only nationalism but also regionalism and localism. In Italy, Austria, and Germany, from the medieval era on, they started to invent their own national traditions, collect specific idioms of former artisans, and develop collections and museums. The past was used to legitimize their demands, but also to mobilize images of social harmony, quality work, and public commitment. Artisans were especially effective in defending values that were closely linked to their activities, and their strong commitment to local affairs and conditions

made them suspicious of international capital. The need for capital to open a workshop made them defenders of private property, and the key value in this context was their independence in producing and selling their products. During the second half of the nineteenth century this independence came under pressure from state and capital interventions, and was sharply defended. Artisans presented images of social life that were antagonistic to the industrial mass society: personal links instead of isolation in the masses, quality work instead of mass production, family bonds instead of dissolution of social forms.

THE ROLE OF THE GUILDS

The development of artisan occupations in Europe was also linked to the survival of guilds. Historians have seen guilds as the typical organizations of the *ancien régime* because their function was to limit the production and regulation of each occupation. They also played an important role in urban politics and were associated with a specific morality and a code of honor. Seen as expressions of a corporate society based on legal privileges and on the power of professional and familiar traditions, they came under pressure in different European countries at the end of the eighteenth century and were abolished in France by the Law Le Chapelier (1791). It was Napoleon who promoted the freedom of commerce all around Europe and interdicted the corporations. Even if the contradiction between corporations and freedom of commerce existed more in theory than in practice—because the control of corporations was limited and important occupations ceased to be under their control—the abolition of the guilds was part of a liberal program. With the Restoration of 1815, however, the guilds came back and were restored in several countries.

In the United Kingdom the guilds had lost their importance during the seventeenth and eighteenth centuries, but they continued to play an important role after 1815 in most European countries. In the Netherlands, they continued to provide welfare services, while in the south of Germany they were seen as an integral part of "hometowns" based on birth control and limited mobility. In other German and Austrian towns they were defended as institutions that at very low cost imposed bargaining procedures on journeymen and prevented social conflicts from becoming dangerous. In the Italian states they survived also during the first half of the nineteenth century, as well as in the central and eastern European countries. It was only in France that the abolition of the guilds was definitive, and all attempts made by artisans to restore them during the Restoration period (1815–1830) failed.

COMPARISON OF GUILD SITUATION IN GERMANY AND FRANCE

The effect of the guilds on the development of artisan trades can be seen from a comparison between Germany and France. In France, guilds were seen as organizations that obstructed a direct connection between citizens and government and hence prevented the expression of the "general will." Not only liberals and republicans but also the royalist government of the restored monarchy were hostile to them. It is a paradox of the French

history of ideas that the republican sociologist Émile Durkheim should have promoted the idea of corporations as a means of social dialogue in order to overcome the anomic structures of industrial society. In Germany, by contrast, guilds were part of the conservative diagnostic of modern society and influenced the demands and programs of artisan organization after 1871. Beside this difference in ideas, the abolition of guilds in France had lasting effects. It thoroughly destroyed the organizational structure of the artisan occupations, which could survive only as *chambers syndicales* in which they had to cohabit either with bigger firms or with journeymen. It also abolished the traditions of apprenticeship, which in nineteenth-century France never acquired the importance that it continues to hold in Germany even in the early twenty-first century. The *cursus honorum* within the artisan occupations also collapsed, and the title of master lost its importance. Compared to the organizational structure and the bargaining power of German artisans, in France the opportunities for collective action and organization were heavily reduced. It was only during the 1920s and as a result of the influence of models of artisan organization that drew on the experience of Alsace-Lorraine (and the German system) that the artisan sector in France became structured and organized. Before 1914, the retailing traders were the main representatives of the French middle-class movement.

HISTORICAL IMPORTANCE OF ARTISANS

Artisans were far less numerous than workers or peasants during the nineteenth century, but historians have nonetheless frequently underlined their importance. For German historians, they have been cited to explain the success of the National Socialist German Workers' Party's nostalgia for the past and have been seen as a reason for the German Sonderweg, the belief that Germany's strong monarchy, military, and disciplined hierarchy destined Germany for world power status, along with a belief in spiritual over material values. Many have underlined the links between artisans and shopkeepers and right-wing politics, a tendency that was reinforced after the 1918/1919 revolution, so that it is not surprising that the lower middle class was overrepresented among those who voted for Adolf Hitler before 1933. According to the German sociologist Theodor Geiger, their vote was attributed to a "panic reaction in the middle classes." Artisans and shopkeepers have therefore been seen as part of the traditional, premodern classes and features of the German society that made National Socialism possible.

This thesis has, however, met with increasing criticism since the 1980s as historians have differentiated between artisans and shopkeepers, stressed the political variety of the occupations, and underlined the very varied ways in which they have participated in modern economic life. In relativizing the importance of membership in interest groups and in stressing studies that demonstrate the diversity of urban situations and commitment, it has become clear that the lower middle classes lived in the social, political, and cultural worlds of their worker and white-collar neighbors. The deconstruction of the term *middle class* has also proved helpful in this discussion. In the first half of the nineteenth century the term was used to describe the different bourgeois professions and occupations that asserted their distance from the aristocracy and from the working poor. In the second half of the century the term was used to describe artisans and shopkeepers and to legitimate their demands in the liberal tradition of the bourgeoisie. The notion was less used in Germany where the term *Mittelstand* was prominent and referred not to a class society but to a society of orders. This negation of class structures was seen as a German particularity. This "othering" of the German middle classes was questioned. Social historians could demonstrate that corporate traditions played a certain role in relation to German artisans and shopkeepers, but that artisans did not hinder economic growth, social and geographic mobility, and political diversity. Their self-definition was more complex than the reference to a society of orders suggests.

See also **Capitalism; Class and Social Relations; Economic Growth and Industrialism; Industrial Revolution, First; Industrial Revolution, Second.**

BIBLIOGRAPHY

Crossick, Geoffrey, and Heinz-Gerhard Haupt. *The Petite Bourgeoisie in Europe, 1780–1914: Enterprise, Family, and Independence.* London, 1995.

Crossick, Geoffrey, and Heinz-Gerhard Haupt, eds. *Shopkeepers and Master Artisans in Nineteenth-Century Europe.* London, 1984.

Johnson, Christopher H. *Utopian Communism in France: Cabet and the Icarians, 1839–1851.* Ithaca, N.Y., 1974.

Kaplan, Steven L., and Philippe Minard, eds. *La France, malade du corporatisme? XVIIIe–XXe siècles.* Paris, 2004.

Núñez, Clara Eugenia, ed. *Guilds, Economy, and Society: Proceedings of the Twelfth International Economic History Congress.* Seville, Spain, 1998.

Sewell, William H., Jr. *Work and Revolution in France: The Language of Labor from the Old Regime to 1848.* Cambridge, U.K., 1980.

HEINZ-GERHARD HAUPT

ART NOUVEAU. Art nouveau was a style in the visual arts that flourished in the major urban centers of Europe between 1890 and 1914. Originating in Great Britain, Belgium, and France, the style was quickly adopted by avant-garde artists and craftsmen throughout Europe, who adapted the genre by incorporating elements from their own national, historical, and ethnic heritages. Art nouveau, or "the new art," was a reaction to what its advocates regarded as an uninspired copying of past architectural styles referred to as historicism. In opposition to the neoclassicism that dominated architecture in the mid-nineteenth century, art nouveau designers replaced straight lines and symmetry with asymmetrical curves. They sought to integrate form and decoration, using motifs from the natural world, including plants (especially flowers and stems), animals (particularly sea creatures and insects), and the human body (especially women's faces). These elements were not copied directly from nature, however, but were highly stylized. The most common line used in art nouveau was a sinuous, asymmetrical curve that could resemble a tight whiplash or a slightly curved flower stem, giving rise to one label for Belgian art nouveau—the stem style. But certain art nouveau practitioners, notably Charles Rennie Mackintosh (1868–1928) in Scotland and Josef Hoffmann (1870–1956) in Austria, favored rectilinear forms that prefigured twentieth-century art and architecture.

Art nouveau theorists and practitioners sought to break down what they regarded as an artificial dichotomy between the arts and crafts or industrial arts. Many art nouveau artists learned crafts such as weaving, furniture making, ceramics, and metalwork, and elevated these crafts by infusing them with modern design elements. Art nouveau architects and designers sought to create what they termed *Gesamtkunstwerk*—a total work of art—in which all elements—exterior, interior, furniture, fixtures, lighting, wallpaper, floor coverings, stair railings, and even plates, door knobs and street numbers—were designed to make a harmonious and coherent stylistic statement.

An instantly recognizable style, art nouveau was nevertheless full of contradictions. While it was an international style, practitioners in various countries developed such distinctive styles that different terms arose to describe art nouveau manifestations in individual countries, for example, Secession in Austria and Germany, modernismo in Spain, Jugend (Youth) in Finland, Stile Floreale (Floral Style) in Italy, as well as the somewhat derisive "art métro" in France. While some art nouveau designers and entrepreneurs sought to bring soundly designed objects to working- and middle-class households, many art nouveau works were individual creations made of the highest quality materials by skilled craftsmen, and therefore available only to the very wealthy. While borrowing peasant motifs and craft techniques, art nouveau was an urban phenomenon catering to an urban clientele. Although art nouveau celebrated the female form and face, women were sometimes portrayed as sinister—Salomé and Medusa being frequent subjects of art nouveau imagery. And while art nouveau designers looked to their countries' artistic past to create works of art that reflected their regional and national heritage, art nouveau theorists and the public at large considered the style to be thoroughly modern.

Even in its heyday, the new art had its detractors. One critic referred to it as "ornamental hell," another as "chaos in design." Others saw it as reflective of the anxiety and nervousness of the era, condemning it as decadent, subversive, or merely kitsch.

EVOLUTION

As a modern style that broke with artistic tradition, art nouveau was initially proselytized by theorists in art journals. Henry van de Velde (1863–1957), a self-trained Belgian architect and designer, wrote a pamphlet entitled *Déblaiement d'art* (A clean sweep for art) in 1894, in which he called for crafts

to be put on an equal footing with fine art. Siegfried Bing, a German art collector and dealer, opened a gallery in Paris in 1895 called L'Art Nouveau, providing a name for the new style as well as an important distribution center for the new art.

Major international expositions served as important vehicles for the dissemination of art nouveau design. An estimated 170 million people visited the nine international expositions that featured art nouveau buildings, interiors, and objects between 1897 and 1908. The Brussels Exposition Universelle of 1897, the Exposition Universelle of 1900 in Paris, and the Prima Esposizione d'arte Decorativa in Turin in 1902, among other international expositions, brought art nouveau architectural styles, art works, and objets d'art to a curious public. Leading art nouveau architects, interior designers, furniture makers, glass and ceramic manufacturers, and textile designers created pavilions that expressed the *Gesamtkunstwerk* ethic as well as their own nation's variant of the new art. Companies displaying their goods at these expositions, such as Liberty of London and Gallé and Daum of France, produced, marketed, and sold art nouveau–inspired products to a mass market, and by 1900 art nouveau had become mainstream. In addition to sponsoring international exhibitions, some governments encouraged modern design through support of colleges of industrial design and the establishment of craft museums, which became important vehicles for the diffusion of national art nouveau styles.

But just as art nouveau became omnipresent, it became déclassé among the most avant-garde artists and art theorists, who now favored simple, functional design and eschewed what they considered to be the decorative excesses of the new style. The career paths of two Belgian architects are emblematic: after creating the first art nouveau building in 1893, Victor Horta (1861–1947) returned to a more geometric classical style in Belgium's Art Deco pavilion for the 1925 Exposition Internationale in Paris, while Henry Van de Velde went on to become an early exponent of the International Style, designing a streamlined steel and glass pavilion for the Exposition Universelle in Paris in 1937.

Many of art nouveau's noteworthy buildings and interiors were built for universal expositions, and so were by their nature temporary. In the twentieth century, many art nouveau buildings succumbed to the ravages of war or urban renewal (for example, the Maison du Peuple, designed by Horta, and most of the Paris métro entrances designed by Hector Guimard). But the style enjoyed renewed popularity at the turn of the next century, and many surviving art nouveau buildings have been restored and turned into showpieces, attracting thousands of visitors who marvel at the elegance, audacity, and individuality of art nouveau designers.

ANTECEDENTS

Art nouveau designers took inspiration from a variety of sources. The Japanese woodblock prints admired by the French impressionists also influenced art nouveau artists, who appreciated the Japanese emphasis on line, the predominance of flat, unshaded blocks of color, and the use of empty space. The Japanese treatment of nature, including minute renderings of animals and plants, as well as a penchant for asymmetrical composition, appealed to art nouveau designers. The whiplash curve, a hallmark of art nouveau, was a common feature of Japanese, as well as Islamic art, another source of inspiration. The arabesque, or teardrop curve, found repeatedly in Islamic art, was adopted and modified in art nouveau, as was the Moorish "horseshoe" arch.

European trends in art and literature, including spiritualism and symbolism, influenced many art nouveau designers. New discoveries in medicine, including theories about the subconscious and hypnotism, were also reflected in art nouveau works, especially in France.

BEGINNINGS

The English Arts and Crafts movement, which sought to eliminate the dichotomy between fine art and crafts, served as a philosophical point of departure for art nouveau designers. The socialist credo of improving the lives of common people through art was adapted by some, but not all, art nouveau adherents, some of whom preferred the aestheticism championed by James Whistler and Oscar Wilde, who advocated "art for art's sake." In 1893, the icon of English art nouveau, Aubrey Beardsley (1872–1898), created a sensation at the age of twenty-one with publication of his macabre, and at times sinister, drawings that illustrated editions of Oscar Wilde's play *Salomé* and Thomas Malory's *Morte d'Arthur*. Beardsley, who had tuberculosis and died at the age

of twenty-six, published his trademark black and white ink drawings widely in avant-garde English art journals. His work was ultimately viewed as decadent by English observers—one critic remarked on its "diabolic beauty"—but he continued to be lionized in art nouveau circles on the Continent.

BELGIAN ART NOUVEAU

In the same year Beardsley published his first drawings, Victor Horta, a Belgian architect, designed Tassel House, the first art nouveau building, which exhibited the sinuous whiplash curve in its mosaic floors, wall decoration, and iron railings. Horta went on to design many private homes and several department stores and shops in Brussels, using stained-glass skylights to provide soft natural light, as well as electric light fixtures shaped like exquisite flowers or starbursts. He sought to create housing for workers that was light and airy and designed the Maison du Peuple for the Union of Socialist Workers in which he used iron as the supporting structure for a wall of glass, prefiguring modern architecture's use of the curtain wall. The building was demolished in 1962.

Henry van de Velde, an art nouveau theorist and architect, was heavily influenced by William Morris and socialist art theory. He designed across the spectrum of the visual arts, including architecture, metalwork, textiles, posters, furniture, and clothing. He designed virtually every aspect of his own house in Brussels, including furniture, decorations, silverware, and his wife's clothing.

Philippe Wolfers (1858–1929), a metalworker and jeweler, worked extensively with ivory, encouraged by King Leopold II, who sought to promote trade with the Congo. Wolfers created a disturbing interpretation of nature in his silver, ivory, and onyx sculpture entitled *Civilization and Barbary*, which depicts a swan doing battle with a serpent.

FRENCH ART NOUVEAU

Art nouveau in France was spearheaded by Hector Guimard (1867–1942), a Parisian architect who designed apartment buildings and houses that combined the use of new materials and building techniques with archetypal art nouveau decoration for a middle-class clientele. Guimard designed furniture, dinner plates, garden fixtures, door hardware, and even street numbers with sinuous, organic lines. He also designed the entrances for

Dining room of Victor Horta's house, Brussels, 1898. ERICH LESSING/ART RESOURCE, NY

the Paris metro, pioneering the use of prefabricated components. The tall, overarching light fixtures of some metro stops resembled insect eyes, and covered entrances combined iron and glass to create for subway passengers the sensation of emerging from a starburst. Other French designers, including Georges DeFeure (1868–1928) and Émile Gallé (1846–1904), created furniture and interiors that reinterpreted the French rococo style of the eighteenth century, using gilded wood, floral motifs, and luxurious silks in designs with restrained and elegant curves.

Parisian jewelers combined new techniques with art nouveau subjects, including flowers and insects, to create startling works of art. René Lalique (1860–1945) developed new techniques of enameling metal and molding glass and used opals and ivory extensively. He reinterpreted natural forms, especially exotic flowers and insects, in audacious and elegant necklaces, brooches, and hair ornaments. His corsage ornament, consisting of a dragonfly metamorphosing into a woman, considered an icon of art nouveau, created a stir when it was exhibited at the Exposition Universelle in Paris in 1900.

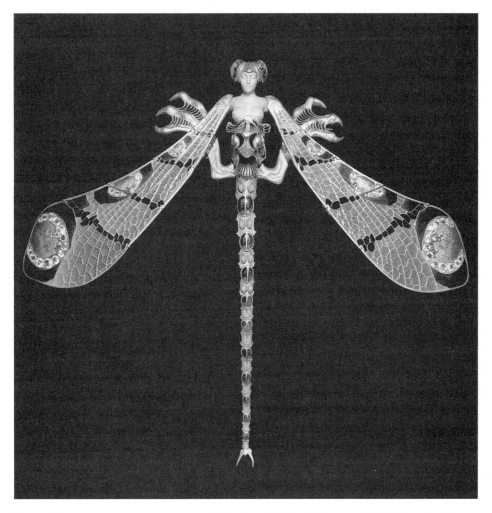

Dragonfly woman corsage ornament. Designed by René Lalique c. 1897. Made of gold, enamel, moonstones, and diamonds, the piece exemplifies the use of stylized animal forms in art nouveau design. CALOUSTE GULBENKIAN FOUNDATION, LISBON/©ARTISTS RIGHTS SOCIETY (ARS), NEW YORK/ ADAGP, PARIS

Art nouveau design also flourished in Nancy, in eastern France, where Louis Majorelle (1859–1926) and others created elegant inlaid wood furniture that featured vegetal decoration in the classic asymmetrical art nouveau curve. Nancy was also the center of a thriving art nouveau art glass industry. Gallé designed ceramic and glass vases that gained a worldwide reputation for elegance, uniqueness, and craftsmanship. He took many motifs from nature, including marine animals, insects, flowers, bats, and beetles, portraying them with Japanese overtones. The Daum brothers produced art glass with clear colors, utilizing many technical advances, including *pate-de-verre* (a technique using a paste of crushed colored glass to create dramatic effects).

In 1901, art nouveau artists and entrepreneurs created the École de Nancy, a society devoted to promoting the arts in industry, which encouraged the creation of high-quality, commercially viable art nouveau products over its twenty-year lifespan.

Several sources of support served to make art nouveau a semi-official style in France in the first decade of the twentieth century. Officials of the Third Republic viewed art nouveau's embrace of eighteenth-century rococo elements as the expression of a distinctly French national style. The government sponsored the Exposition Universelle of 1900 and financed construction of the Paris metro, both showpieces of art nouveau style, and supported the creation of a national museum to showcase French crafts.

SPANISH ART NOUVEAU

In Spain, art nouveau architecture was centered in Barcelona, a major industrial center with an active and forward-looking business class. Spanish art nouveau bifurcated into two opposing strains: modernismo, which combined expressive symbolism, local traditions and crafts, and modern technology, and the singular architecture of Antoni Gaudí (1852–1926). Modernismo's main practitioner was Lluís Domènech i Montaner (1849–1923), who designed the auditorium of the Palau de la Música Catalana and the Santa Creu Hospital.

Modernismo was overshadowed by Gaudí, who detested the new style and modern civilization in general. Although his early designs were eclectic, using elements from Moorish architecture and local traditions such as colorful ceramic tiles, his later work, especially the Sagrada Familia temple, reflected a modern treatment of Gothic design.

THE GLASGOW SCHOOL

Scottish art nouveau was created largely by two couples: Charles Rennie Mackintosh and his wife, Margaret Macdonald, and her sister, Frances Macdonald and her husband, Herbert McNair. Their art took inspiration from spiritualism and symbolism, and favored rectilinear lines over the asymmetrical curves of other art nouveau styles. Mackintosh and Macdonald designed many tearooms, such as Miss Cranston's, which featured white paneled walls, simple stained glass windows, and high-backed chairs. Their austere, white interiors have been interpreted as an escape from the intensely urban, gritty world of late nineteenth-century Glasgow. Macintosh also designed Hill House, an austere, fortress-like house, and the Glasgow School of Art, a brownstone edifice with metal detailing.

SECESSION STYLE

In Munich, young artists broke away from the established artists' association to form their own organization in 1892. They called their headquarters the Secession building, giving rise to the designation for their style of art nouveau. Also termed Jugendstil (Young Style), German art nouveau took its inspiration from symbolism and natural forms. Otto Eckmann (1865–1902), a printmaker and furniture and textile designer heavily influenced by Japanese prints, designed the "Five Swans" tapestry. Hermann Obrist (1862–1927) created vibrant embroidery designs, including the iconic "whiplash," evoking nature in an abstract fashion. August Endell (1871–1925) designed the Elvira Studio, with its extravagant seahorse-like motif. The facade was removed by the Nazis, who considered it decadent, and the building itself was destroyed in World War II.

In Vienna, young artists took a lead from their German counterparts, withdrawing from the established artists' organization to form their own society in 1897. Their headquarters, designed by Josef Maria Olbrich (1867–1908), featured a white rectilinear facade decorated with gold floral motifs. Gustav Klimt (1862–1918) exhibited his painting *Pallas Athene* at the opening of the Secession building. The dark portrayal of a Greek goddess suggests the power and threat of femininity, a common theme in Klimt's work. Josef Hoffmann designed furniture and houses with bold straight lines punctuated by void spaces. In his Palais Stoclet in Brussels, commissioned by a wealthy Belgian, every detail—wallpaper, carpets, silverware, furniture, and lighting—was designed to create a streamlined *Gesamtkunstwerk*. Hoffmann and Koloman Moser (1868–1919), an illustrator and textile designer, founded the Wiener Werkstätte (Vienna Workshops) in 1903 to elevate middle-class taste by producing soundly designed and luxurious hand-crafted furniture, wallpaper, textiles, jewelry, clothing, and tableware.

EASTERN EUROPE

In Hungary, art nouveau designers sought to create a distinct national style by incorporating elements from peasant art, especially weaving. The Gödöllő Workshops, a colony of artists and designers outside of Budapest, produced leather work, stained glass, furniture, and tapestries inspired by peasant designs. Ödön Lechner (1845–1919?) used brick faced with glazed tile and wrought ironwork in his design for the Museum of Applied Arts. The iron and glass canopy was meant to suggest the tents of semi-nomadic Magyar tribes, and the notched arches were derived from Mogul art. He also used motifs borrowed from the Hungarian countryside, including bees and tulips, the latter regarded as a symbol of Hungarian identity. Craftsmen at the Zsolnay ceramics factory created sophisticated ceramics using an iridescent metal glaze called Eozin that produced brilliant and variegated colors.

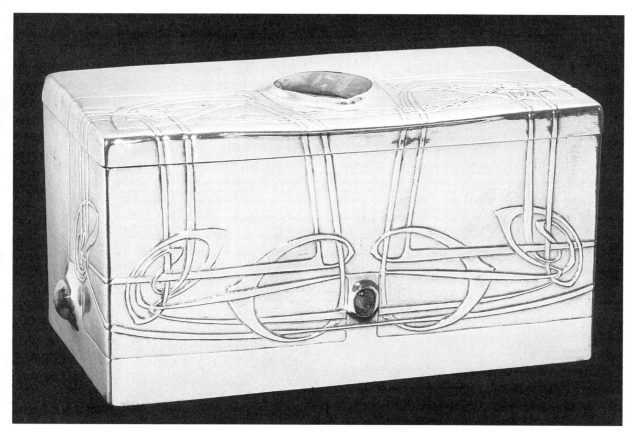

Cigarette box designed by Archibald Knox, 1903—1904. This opal-studded box reflects the sinuous elegance of art nouveau design. Knox, who worked in silver and pewter, developed the Celtic Revival style that became popular in Britain, Ireland, and Scandinavia. V & A IMAGES/VICTORIA AND ALBERT MUSEUM

In Prague, modern trends from abroad combined with influences from Czech peasant culture to create a varied and eclectic art nouveau style. The Municipal House, commissioned by Prague's city government, was intended to represent Czech identity, and included art works by leading Czech artists and craftsmen. Czech textile factories produced carpets designed by artists such as Alphonse Mucha (1860–1939) and Josef Maria Olbrich, and an artists' cooperative created glass, ceramics, furniture, jewelry, and textiles in art nouveau styles. After 1900, Czech designers moved away from French influences to adopt a more geometric style. Jan Kotěra (1871–1923), an influential art professor, advocated the primacy of function over decoration. He designed a strikingly simple crystal glass punch bowl and glasses for the St. Louis World's Fair of 1904. His later furniture and architecture emphasized cube-like forms and prefigured Art Deco and cubist styles.

NORTHERN EUROPE

In Finland, the Jugend style was spearheaded by Gottlieb Eliel Saarinen (1873–1950) and his associates Herman Gesellius (1874–1916) and Armas Lindgren (1874–1929), whose architecture firm was known as G. S. and L. The Finnish Pavilion they designed for the 1900 Paris Exposition Universelle resembled a Finnish country church, with rough stone, a large semi-circular entrance, a horizontal band of windows, a shingle roof, and a stocky tower crowned with folk-inspired motifs. The firm went on to win the competition to design the National Museum, a restrained granite and wood structure that housed Finnish archaeological, historical, and ethnographic collections. In 1900 Saarinen designed the Suur-Merijoki Farm. The home's interior, which featured vivid colors and abstract folk motifs, had built-in furniture, tiles, stained glass, tapestries, and *ryijy* rugs, all carefully designed to create a harmonious whole. The partners then designed Hvitträsk, a residential complex and studio that housed their three families until the partnership broke up in 1905.

In Moscow, stil modern (as art nouveau was known) artists sought to fuse international influences and native folk motifs. Fyodor Shekhtel (1859–1926), Russia's leading art nouveau architect, transformed the Moscow railway station, creating a hat-like roof above the entrance reminiscent of a northern Russian church. He later designed a house that successfully fused modern and traditional elements: the interior featured a dramatic staircase that resembled a cascading waterfall while the exterior presented more sedate rectangular lines, with a mosaic border of orchids below the roof line.

See also **Fin de Siècle; Furniture; Gaudí, Antonio; Painting; Paris.**

BIBLIOGRAPHY

Fahr-Becker, Gabriele. *Art Nouveau.* Cologne, 1997.

Greenhalgh, Paul, ed. *Art Nouveau: 1890-1914.* London and Washington, D.C., 2000.

Masini, Lara-Vinca. *Art Nouveau.* Translated by Linda Fairbairn. London, 1984.

Silverman, Debora. *Art Nouveau in Fin-de-Siècle France: Politics, Psychology, and Style.* Berkeley, Calif., 1989.

CAROL P. MERRIMAN

ASQUITH, HERBERT HENRY (1852–1928), British politician.

Herbert Henry Asquith was born 12 September 1852, in Morley, Yorkshire, the son of a minor textile owner. He demonstrated a formidable intellect early on at the City of London School, enough to win the first classical scholarship from that school to Balliol College. Asquith won a first in classics and after finishing went into the law. He was called to the bar in 1876, married Helen Melland, the unassuming daughter of a doctor, in 1877, and had his first son, Raymond, in 1878. His first step in politics came in 1886, when he won the seat for the Scottish borough of East Fife.

Asquith rose steadily in Parliament, becoming home secretary under William Ewart Gladstone in 1892. Asquith could not enjoy his achievement fully, for his office came shortly after the death of his wife from typhoid. He quickly remarried, this time to Margot Tennant, the daughter of a rich Scottish baronet, in 1894. She was everything Helen had not been: outgoing, ambitious, and often irreverent, for good and ill.

The Liberals were out of power from 1895 to 1905. But when they returned, Henry Campbell-Bannerman, the Liberal leader, offered Asquith the office of chancellor of the Exchequer. In the election that followed in 1906, the Liberals defeated the Unionists, ending up with a majority of 356, the largest in the House since 1832. The Liberal government seemed well positioned to put into place a substantially progressive program.

Campbell-Bannerman's health proved not up to premiership and he resigned in April 1908. Asquith replaced him. Asquith's achievements as prime minister have been dulled by the difficulties of World War I, and by the strange death of the party in the years after 1918, but it should not be forgotten that his government laid the foundations upon which Labour built the welfare state in the period from 1945 to 1951.

The first years were frustrating. The House of Lords refused to pass reformist legislation, and the Liberals had no effective way to overcome the veto, despite their immense majority. The breaking of that blockade started in 1909, with the introduction of the so-called People's Budget by David Lloyd George (1863–1945), the chancellor of the Exchequer. The budget loaded a number of reforms on the back of a finance bill, which the Lords traditionally did not touch. The Lords, however, summarily rejected the budget, provoking a constitutional crisis.

The election that resulted in January 1910, returned the Liberals to power, though with a reduced majority. Asquith pushed ahead with the confrontation and the Conservatives remained stubborn. The only way for the Liberals to break the impasse was to have the king flood the House of Lords by appointing hundreds of Liberal peers. This idea was unpopular, and Edward VII (r. 1901–1910) insisted on another election before he would contemplate it. The situation worsened when Edward died unexpectedly in May 1910 and was replaced by his son, George V

(r. 1910–1936). The new king was reluctant to make his first major act a constitutional hamstringing of the House of Lords. But here Asquith was firm, and after the second general election of 1910, in November, the Lords caved in under pressure and passed the Parliamentary Bill of 1911, which ended their veto. It was a massive shift of power, indisputably confirming the Commons as the dominant House.

Perhaps the most difficult period of Asquith's premiership followed this signal triumph. The issue of Irish Home Rule caused a continuing series of crises, including mutterings of unrest within the army. There was a substantial amount of industrial unrest, the most since the 1890s, and the prospect of a general strike loomed large. Finally, many women's suffrage groups turned to violence to press their case, violence that included attacks on ministers. Asquith did not handle these as well as he might have. Irish Home Rule was likely an impossible task, but he showed a tin ear in dealing with the women's groups and with labor. By 1914, none of the crises had really been resolved.

Despite that, Asquith's position was mostly secure. Liberal by-election losses had not been severe, and another general election was not due until late 1915. Within the party, the only real threat was Lloyd George, and the two of them had a friendly relationship. The issue of relations between the Liberals and the Labour Party loomed, but Labour was not strong enough to be an independent electoral threat. The Irish problem remained, but it had been that way for centuries. Asquith could not know that his sternest test lay ahead.

See also **Great Britain; Lloyd George, David.**

BIBLIOGRAPHY

Brock, Michael, and Eleanor Brock, eds. *H. H. Asquith: Letters to Venetia Stanley.* Oxford, U.K., 1982.

Hobhouse, Charles. *Inside Asquith's Cabinet: From the Diaries of Charles Hobhouse.* Edited by Edward David. New York, 1978.

James, Robert Rhodes. *The British Revolution: British Politics, 1880–1939.* Volume 1: *From Gladstone to Asquith, 1880–1914.* London, 1976.

Jenkins, Roy. *Asquith.* New York, 1964.

DAVID SILBEY

ASSOCIATIONS, VOLUNTARY.

In the mid-eighteenth century, a plethora of new forms of sociability—beyond the traditional bonds of family, state, court, and the established church—arose in the cities of the European-controlled world. In contrast to those older forms, voluntary entry was the most important criterion for the new clubs, Masonic lodges, and reading, charitable, and learning societies. Socially open in theory, the new associations gave themselves formal rules, rituals, and constitutions; assumed the equality of their members; and formulated common goals, in most cases in the realm of *moral improvement*. Members were to learn to govern themselves, their interests, and passions, and to shape, both morally and politically, all of society on their utopian model. Though many of the old elites belonged to these associations, the demand for self-organization and enlightenment implicitly called the political order of the old regime into question. In nineteenth-century Europe, voluntary associations became the most important organizing principle of civil society; they formed a dense and vibrant network of civic activism beyond church, state, and corporation, and were a vehicle for the most important political ideologies of the time: liberalism, nationalism, and socialism.

TOCQUEVILLE'S QUESTION

The United States is still seen today as the classic nation of joiners. One reason for this is that Alexis de Tocqueville's (1805–1859) *De la démocratie en Amérique* (*Democracy in America*), the most important text on the political theory of voluntary associations (appearing in two volumes in 1835 and 1840), is based on examples from his trip through North America. Tocqueville marveled at the way Americans—in contrast, he thought, to continental Europeans—participated in countless associations, thereby breathing life into their democracy. Instead of appealing to a state authority to solve their problems, Americans founded an association, taking their lives into their own hands and working for the common good. For these reasons, the freedom of association, more than even freedom of the press, was, for Tocqueville, one of the most important rights in a democracy.

But Tocqueville was interested in more than the associations' purely practical significance, for he saw feelings and habits of the heart as more important for the polity than rationally thought-out rights and interests. He was convinced that a polity was formed not only by its written constitution, but also by the inner constitution and virtue of its citizens. The deciding question for Tocqueville was how to avoid the spiritual impoverishment that threatens people in a democratic society and opens the door to despotism and terror. The Terror of the French Revolution was never far from his thoughts.

Tocqueville saw an answer to this problem in voluntary associations. According to Tocqueville, only in social interaction could people develop their ideas and enlarge their hearts. This interaction, which was subordinated to strict rules in corporate societies, had to be brought to life voluntarily in a democracy—a task only associations could perform. Associations for moral improvement, seemingly apolitical and above special interests, freed the individual from his selfishness and created new bonds in modern, egalitarian societies. "Among the laws that rule human societies," writes Tocqueville, "there is one that seems more precise and clearer than all others. In order that men remain civilized or become so, the art of associating must be developed and perfected among them in the same ratio as equality of conditions increases" (*Democracy in America*, p. 492). Conversely, he thought, if the bonds between individuals loosen, democracy's political foundation will erode. The less citizens practice the art of association, the greater the toll on their civility and the greater likelihood that equality will degenerate into despotism.

ENTANGLEMENTS AND VARIATIONS

Research in the 1990s has shown that nineteenth-century "practitioners of civil society" on both sides of the Atlantic believed in the political significance of sociability and civic virtue. The high (and widespread) esteem of voluntary associations was not just an American phenomenon, but rather part of an entangled history of the eighteenth- and nineteenth-century European and transatlantic world. Following the American historian Philip Nord, one can discern, after the initial growth of sociability in the Enlightenment (a period that came to an end in the French Revolution and will not be covered in what follows), three phases between the French Revolution and World War I in the transnational spread and entanglement of voluntary associations.

Refuge of the middle class Historians generally consider the three decades before the European revolutions of 1848–1849 as the heyday of voluntary associations. Simultaneously with the United States, where the years between 1825 and 1845 are known as the "era of associations," a *first* burst of civic activism formed a dense network of associations in English, French, and German cities. The voluntary associations, which at this time were socially exclusive and open, for the most part, only to educated and propertied men, were supposed to provide relief from conflicts in career, family, and politics. The associations, of course, also fulfilled immediate social or political goals: they blurred boundaries with respect to the nobility and differentiated themselves even more starkly from the lower classes. Nevertheless, it is also clear that one reason for the nineteenth-century passion for association lies in the political and moral understanding of the same problems inherent in a rapidly changing society that Tocqueville had described so forcefully.

Socially, an important difference between the growth of sociability in the Enlightenment and voluntary associations in early nineteenth-century England, France, or Germany is the participation of the middle classes—middle-class men, to be more precise, because the strict and obsessive exclusion of women was one of the hallmarks of nineteenth century associations. Social historians have described voluntary associations as a means by which western European middle classes attempted to exert cultural hegemony and overcome the deep social, political, and economic crises in the decades after 1800. Progress and improvement were key concepts for these associations that claimed moral leadership of society. Thus, even the first working men's clubs and gymnastics societies came under the auspices of the middle classes.

However, the idea and practice of civil society was not bound solely to the rising bourgeoisie as a social class. Several popular as well as aristocratic sociable traditions continued into the early nine-

Volunteer riflemen. Members of the Home Guard in England are shown at the meeting of the National Rifle Association, Wimbledon, c. 1867. The annual event, held in Wimbledon from 1860 to 1899, featured contests of marksmanship. ©HULTON-DEUTSCH COLLECTION/CORBIS

teenth century and merged with the associational ideal. Moreover, the associational ideal crossed social and national borders, emerging even in societies—like Austria-Hungary and Russia—without a strong middle class.

Eastern central Europe's own associational life, though delayed, began to emerge in the 1830s, particularly in reading societies, clubs, and charitable organizations. Hungarian nobles enthusiastic for reform brought liberal ideas back home from their trips to France, England, and Germany. Clubs founded in the period from 1825 to 1827 by the Hungarian liberal Count Istvan Széchenyi (1791–1860) after a trip through England promoted entertainment and social interaction, and especially education through reading the foreign press. This was the beginning of an association-based reform movement in Hungary, which in a few years had clubs and associations in all important provincial

towns, and by 1845 had an estimated 500 associations total. It is not without reason that Prince Clemens von Metternich (1773–1859), the conservative state chancellor of the Habsburg Empire, is said to have called associations a "German plague." Associations formed in Berlin spread from Prague to Vienna, and from there to Buda, Pest, and the provincial towns of Austria-Hungary. They spread to Russia in a similar fashion, particularly to St. Petersburg and Moscow.

The revolutions of 1848–1849 mark the high point and end of this first phase of civic activism. Many associations ceased to exist with the failure of the liberal movement in central Europe and the onset of government repression. But not for long.

Nations of joiners The passion for association in the first half of the century turned out to be only a prelude to the "club mania," as it was soon to be called, in the two decades after Tocqueville's death (1859). This *second* upsurge in civic activism occurred simultaneously in western and eastern Europe where industrialization and urbanization had given rise to similarly far-reaching social upheavals and had strengthened the will for liberal reform of society. Again, England, where developments in voluntary associations typical for the 1860s and 1870s had begun a half-century earlier, is the lone exception. The density of associations clearly fell off as one moved east. Surprisingly, however, similarities—in the types of associations, the motives for their founding, and the moment of their increase—abound in this second burst of activity.

In Russia's western provincial towns after the Crimean War and during the era of great reforms, particularly after the abolition of serfdom, the first signs of a local civil society emerged and began forming voluntary associations. They met alongside the *zemstvo*s, the local governing bodies created after 1864, and existing informal social groups like circles and salons. The social range of voluntary associations in the tsarist empire also widened, though relatively modestly. The thin layer of the educated and propertied middle class rapidly discovered these associations for themselves.

In continental Europe, the liberalization of states that became nations (or multinational in the case of Austria-Hungary) is likewise tied to an increase in voluntary associations. Historians have only recently realized how associational life exploded after 1860 in local urban society of the French and German provinces. It seemed that the liberal utopia was becoming a reality: a step-by-step reform of society under bourgeois-liberal auspices and without revolutionary violence. Contemporary statistics include only officially registered associations and therefore must be used with care. Nevertheless, one can still discern distinct trends. For example, in 1868 all of Cisleithania, the Austrian part of the empire, had around 5,200 associations, 8,000 already by 1870, and experienced almost a doubling in each of the next three decades: to 15,000 in 1880, over 30,000 in 1890, just short of 60,000 in 1900, and 103,000 in 1910.

The gymnastics movement illustrates the new problems that lay behind this sharp increase in associations. One of the century's most popular types of association, gymnastics clubs began form-

ing in the German states with the Napoleonic Wars, stagnated after the suppression of the revolutions of 1848–1849, and revived in central Europe at the beginning of the 1860s. Contemporary statistics from 1862 indicate 1,284 gymnastics clubs with 134,507 members in the German states; the overwhelming majority of these new associations came into being during the previous two and half years. By 1864 the number of gymnastics clubs had almost doubled. The number sank toward the end of the 1860s under the pressure of the wars of 1866 and 1870–1871, but a few years later again began to grow enormously—and not only in the German Kaiserreich but in France as well. Before World War I, the Deutsche Turnerschaft (German Gymnast Society) counted 1.4 million members, and the Union des Sociétés Francaises de Gymnastique had over 300,000.

In the last three decades of the nineteenth century, gymnastics became one of the most popular pastime activities for young men in both countries, with the clubs promoting physical and moral-political education and the militarization of social life. Similar to the German movement's rise out of German military defeat, French gymnastics clubs grew wildly after the military humiliation of the Franco-Prussian War. Both the German and French gymnastics clubs were markedly nationalistic, as were the Czech *Sokol* clubs founded throughout Habsburg Bohemia in the 1860s; they all stressed the importance of physical and moral fitness for the social improvement of the nation. This rise in civic activism was thus accompanied with increased militarism and nationalism.

Civic activism, connected histories This tendency to combine social participation with nationalism was even more pronounced in the third surge (from the 1890s to about 1910) in civic activism. At no other point did associations permeate social life in Europe as strongly as in these two decades. Hardly a segment of society was not touched by this transnational club mania. Even opponents of the club mania founded associations so as not to remain alone in their displeasure. In those countries that already had a developed associational life, the numbers exploded and reached rural society and the European colonies extensively for the first time.

Again, ideas and social practices moved across national borders. For example, in the mass emigrations beginning in the 1880s, approximately half a million predominantly rural "Slovaks," few of whom would have identified themselves as Slovaks, moved to the United States. There they founded, like almost all other immigrant groups, their own voluntary associations and began for the first time to see themselves as Slovaks in an ethnic sense. About a fourth to a third of them returned with this experience to their home country and founded associations. There was a true export of forms of voluntary association across national borders. Another example is the B'nai Brith order, which took the Masonic lodge as its model. The order was founded by German Jewish emigrants in New York in 1843 and spread to the European continent starting in the 1880s, partly as a reaction to the anti-Semitism that was particularly rampant in central Europe.

Victorian reform societies, like learning societies or the temperance movement, even spread their message of moral improvement and alcoholic abstinence to Russia. Often, as in the case of temperance societies, the impulse to reform fed on doubts about the legitimacy of Russia's autocratic regime. As in other associations for social reform (e.g., the fight against prostitution), middle-class women played an independent role. Prostitution and alcoholism were seen as problems that would not be solved by the state but by civil society. Charitable organizations, which also belong to this category, registered another dramatic increase at this time. More than half of the 2,200 charitable organizations counted by the Russian state in the early twentieth century were formed after 1890. The actual number of organizations was surely much higher, as many charitable organizations of national minorities, especially of Jews, were not counted in the government numbers. According to contemporary estimates, 4,800 new associations and societies were formed in Russia between 1906 and 1909 alone. Sociable life in Moscow and St. Petersburg was hardly different from that of Europe's other major cities, and the passion for association reached, though modestly, into the sleepy provincial towns.

CIVIL SOCIETY AND THE STATE

If, according to Tocqueville, voluntary associations are essential to the life of a democracy, how can one explain their significance for nineteenth-century European societies? In the end, with the exception of France after 1871, all of these societies were, at best,

constitutional monarchies, and none of them granted the unrestricted freedom of association in the nineteenth century. Rather, there was a successive loosening of the prohibition of association: in 1867 in Germany and Austria-Hungary; 1881 in France; and after the Revolution of 1905 in Russia. Clearly one must distinguish between the often-restrictive right to associate, that is, the state's official position on associations, and the actual extent of urban sociability tolerated by the state. Throughout nineteenth-century continental Europe, a society enthusiastic for associations confronted states that tended to be hostile to them. For a long time in the twentieth century, historians' views of civic activism in continental Europe were obstructed by a fixation on the state and an allegedly authoritarian tradition; in those countries, however, like Great Britain and the United States, which see themselves in an unbroken liberal tradition, historians attribute paramount importance to associations as evidence of this tradition.

Moreover, it is not clear that one can so easily draw such a stark distinction between the state and civil society. At times government elites expected societal reform to result from a loosening of the laws governing associations and were often, ironically enough, themselves members of associations that the state was watching. To be sure, after the revolutions of 1789 and 1848, the state tried to suppress the uncontrolled growth of associations. But in the long run, the demand for social and political participation could not be controlled. In the 1860s, Austria-Hungary's government gave in to the demand for a relaxing of the prohibition on association in order to remain on top of the situation. Political associations often remained prohibited while associations devoted to moral or sociable aims were tolerated. In practice, however, this distinction was difficult to maintain, since those associations that were allegedly dedicated to nonpolitical goals aimed, by their very nature, for a self-organized civil society beyond the state. By the 1890s, at the latest, the governments in Germany, Russia, and Austria-Hungary only seldom, or at most perfunctorily, made use of their right to monitor local sociability. That France (1901) and Germany (1908) enshrined the freedom of association without any restrictions in their law only relatively late is less a result of the allegedly authoritarian character of the state than the fear liberals had of their "uncivil" enemies such as the Catholics and socialists.

THE TEAM THAT REPRESENTED STOKE IN SEASON 1877-8.
Top Row: T. KINGSLAND. G. LOCKHART. R. SLEIGH. G. LAKE.
Second Row: { T. C. SLANEY, Captain. } W. BODDINGTON. J. MALLETT. H. ALLEN.
Bottom Row: R. McMILLAN. H. R. BROWN. E. JOHNSON

The Stoke City Football Club, 1877. MARY EVANS PICTURE LIBRARY

DEMOCRACY AND ITS DISCONTENTS

At their high point in terms of raw numbers, voluntary associations paradoxically lost, in the eyes of many contemporaries, the moral and political significance Tocqueville and others had once accorded them. Accompanying the wild spread of associational life throughout all levels of society over the course of the century was an increasing fear among liberal elites that they might lose their claim to moral leadership, a claim which they had, up to that point, exercised through their domination of the associations. The more associational culture spread and engaged previously excluded groups, the more shallow sounded the language of virtue and civility. "A Skat club is still a Skat club even if it calls itself 'Freedom Skat Club,'" wrote one observer contemptuously when he surveyed what he considered the philistinism of the countless worker associations supposedly devoted to political and moral improvement. This disintegration of the claim to virtue and moral improvement was, however, a result of social democratization, not its opposite. Across Europe, associational life became increasingly more democratic as, for example, workers, Catholics, and women began using and forming voluntary associations. This democratization was accompanied by a change in associations' goals and aims. At the turn of the twentieth century, these new goals broke apart into their own associations and grew into unions, parties, and federations that gradually did away with the social and moral inheritance of the associational ideal. They now served solely to represent special interests and mobilize their members politically.

Liberal and conservative elites interpreted the political plurality and social popularity of associational self-organization—a hallmark of democracy—as a sign of decline. Anti-Semites and philo-Semites, socialists and Catholics, veterans and pacifists, scientists and occultists, friends of sociability and its enemies—they all gathered in associations that promoted their own objectives. More than anything else, though, nationalism spurred innumerable associations in central Europe, which also bitterly fought each other. The spread of voluntary associations democratized society and gave the previously excluded a place and a voice—not necessarily, though, a deeper belief in the liberal idea of a civil society.

CONCLUSION

The history of nineteenth-century associations reveals three major trends: expansion, democratization, and politicization. Voluntary associations spread in waves, with each wave making the associational network denser and giving rise to new associational goals. This expansion can only be understood against the background of global migration, trade, and communication of ideas and practices. New voluntary associations that arose out of exclusive Enlightenment circles around 1800 set off a true passion for associations in North America and Europe in the 1830s and 1840s. The associations combined enlightened ideas and practices with the contemporary political currents of liberalism, republicanism, socialism, and nationalism, and continental European states tried, with varying degrees of success, to control their citizens' passion for associations. At the same time, the associations' causes multiplied: national, confessional, or social reform associations broadened the spectrum, often with new claims of social exclusivity and moral-political missions. In the 1860s and 1870s a new wave of associations arose, which both helped bring about and was the result of society's liberalization and nationalization. This trend intensified dramatically at the end of the century, when nearly

all aspects of urban society in the countries under consideration were organized around associations. The expansion and specialization of voluntary associations produced new forms of organized interests, politics, and modern mass culture that adopted, and went beyond, many of the older associations' goals and aims.

The expansion of voluntary associations led to more social participation and drew, at the same time, new political borders. The era between the French Revolution and World War I surely was not a democratic age, but rather the age of *democratization*. In a time when none of the states considered here had universal suffrage, nineteenth-century associations served as schools for democracy. Joiners experienced a constitution of statutes, the right to vote and to freedom of speech, and engagement for self-defined causes and goals; but also the often-related experience of everyday conflicts and frustrations that are part and parcel of democracy. In this sense, those associations dedicated to nonpolitical or trivial causes (measured by twenty-first-century standards) also had a democratizing effect. However, the secret ballot in voluntary associations could serve not only as practice in democracy, but also as a mechanism for excluding those who did not meet specific social or moral criteria. The desire to participate in social and political life and to have one's own social spaces and practices was, consequently, an important driving force behind the ever new waves of association formation in the long nineteenth century, in spite of—or, rather, because of—experiences of exclusion. The increasing competition between voluntary associations and their political and moral ideas, and the resulting conflicts within civil society, were not a sign of the decline of associational life but rather of its democratization. Voluntary associations no longer served to secure a small elites' political and moral claim to leadership and their vision of social harmony, but rather cleared the way for new forms and institutions that would shape political demands.

Democratization also brought with it a politicization of voluntary associations in all the societies under consideration. Enlightened sociability experienced an initial politicization before, during, and after the revolutions of the late eighteenth century when the states of continental Europe set off a wave of government repression against the free association of its citizens. Even more noteworthy is the readiness with which the "practitioners of civil society" formed associations in the early nineteenth century. On both sides of the Atlantic, associations served as supposedly nonpolitical, sociable spaces for social and moral improvement of their individual members and society. The related liberal ideas of social harmony and reform competed, beginning in the 1830s and 1840s, with new political-social movements that made use of the associations for shaping of an alternative culture. Not only did they adopt the ideas and practices of civil associations, but also developed their own political and moral ideas of the significance of sociability, thereby making the tension between liberalism and democracy more apparent. Simultaneously, the nationalization and "ethnization" of society, and therefore also of sociability, began, producing a new dynamic in the passion for associations in the 1860s and 1870s. At the end of the century, the passion for associations encompassed nearly all social, confessional, and political groups and aspects of society. However, the more voluntary associations at the turn of the twentieth century became places of self-organization for differentiated and often mutually exclusive social and political actors (and thus an expression of democratic plurality), the more they lost, in the eyes of many of their contemporaries, moral authority and the utopian promise to reform society. They were no longer perceived as a remedy for, but rather as a sign of, the loss of society's cohesion and moral compass—the loss, in other words, of precisely that civic virtue that theorists and practitioners of civil society in the eighteenth and nineteenth centuries had understood as vital for a polity. The expansion, democratization, and politicization of voluntary associations were consequently—and only seemingly paradoxically—causes of the crises of European liberalism and civil society before World War I.

See also **Bourgeoisie; Civil Society; Class and Social Relations; Cooperative Movements; Freemasons; Leisure; Working Class.**

BIBLIOGRAPHY

Agulhon, Maurice. *Le Cercle dans la France bourgeoisie: 1810–1848, Etude d'une mutation de sociabilité.* Paris, 1977. Classic study on the history of French sociability.

Bermeo, Nancy, and Philip Nord, eds. *Civil Society before Democracy: Lessons from Nineteenth-Century Europe.* Lanham, Md., 2000. A comparative collection of essays on the different fate of European civil societies in the nineteenth century with an excellent introduction to the subject by Philip Nord.

Bradley, Joseph. "Subjects into Citizens: Societies, Civil Society, and Autocracy in Tsarist Russia." *American Historical Review* 107 (2002): 1094–1123.

Davidoff, Leonore, and Catherine Hall. *Family Fortunes: Men and Women of the English Middle Class, 1750–1850.* London, 1987. Classic study of the gendered nature of middle class life and associational culture.

Eley, Geoff. "Nations, Publics, and Political Cultures: Placing Habermas in the Nineteenth Century." In *Habermas and the Public Sphere,* edited by Craig Calhoun, 289–339. Cambridge, Mass., 1992.

Goltermann, Svenja. *Körper der Nation: Habitusformierung und die Politik des Turnens 1860–1890.* Göttingen, 1998. Looks at the nationalism of the German Gymnastics Clubs.

Harrison, Carol Elizabeth. "Unsociable Frenchmen: Associations and Democracy in Historical Perspective," *Tocqueville Review* 17, no. 2 (1996): 37–56.

———. *The Bourgeois Citizen in Nineteenth-Century France: Gender, Sociability, and the Uses of Emulation.* Oxford, U.K., 1999.

Hoffmann, Stefan-Ludwig. "Democracy and Associations in the Long Nineteenth-Century: Toward a Transnational Perspective." *Journal of Modern History* 75 (2003): 269–299.

———. *Politics of Sociability: Freemasonry and German Civil Society 1840–1918.* Translated by Tom Lampert. Ann Arbor, Mich., 2006.

King, Jeremy. *Budweisers into Czechs and Germans: A Local History of Bohemian Politics, 1848–1948.* Princeton, N.J., 2002.

Lidtke, Vernon L. *The Alternative Culture: Socialist Labor in Imperial Germany.* New York, 1985. Classic study of the associational culture of German workers.

Lindenmeyr, Adele. *Poverty Is Not a Vice: Charity, Society, and the State in Imperial Russia.* Princeton, N.J., 1996.

Morris, R. J. "Clubs, Societies and Associations." In *The Cambridge Social History of Britain, 1750–1950,* edited by F. M. L. Thompson, 403–443. Cambridge, U.K., 1990.

Nemes, Robert. "Associations and Civil Society in Reform-Era Hungary." *Austrian History Yearbook* 32 (2001): 25–45.

Nipperdey, Thomas. "Verein als soziale Struktur in Deutschland im späten 18. und frühen 19. Jahrhundert." In *Gesellschaft, Kultur, Theorie,* 174–205. Göttingen, 1976. A comprehensive survey of associational life in Germany around 1800 that has had a lasting impact on German historiography of the subject.

Nolte, Claire E. *The Sokol in the Czech Lands to 1914: Training for the Nation.* Basingstoke, U.K., 2003.

Roberts, M. J. D. *Making English Morals: Voluntary Association and Moral Reform in Nineteenth Century England.* Cambridge, U.K., 2004.

Tocqueville, Alexis de. *Democracy in America.* Edited by Harvey C. Mansfield and Delba Winthrop. Chicago, 2000.

Trentmann, Frank, ed. *Paradoxes of Civil Society: New Perspectives on Modern German and British History.* Providence, R.I., 2000.

STEFAN-LUDWIG HOFFMANN

ATGET, EUGÈNE (1857–1927), French photographer.

Eugène Atget became a photographer after a relatively unsuccessful career as an artist, and this background strongly influenced his photography. Atget set out to become a servant of the arts and kept the inscription "documents pour artistes" (documents for artists) above the door of the photographic store that he opened in 1892. His clientele consisted mainly of painters, sculptors, and architects. The photos that he presented there—reproductions of pictures, landscapes, and monuments—were in themselves creative documents.

Architectural subjects were a natural choice for Atget. The abundance of endangered architectural constructions, which were inventoried by the Commission of Old Paris so that they could be documented, meant that he had an important source of images. From 1898 onward, he devoted himself to this work exclusively, producing 8,500 negatives that document Paris and the surrounding areas. These negatives required a rigorous filing system to be commercially viable, and Atget therefore numbered each of his negatives and established an archiving system that led, after several modifications, to a body of work that falls into six broad categories:

- *Paysage-documents divers* (landscapes-various documents)
- *Paris pittoresque* (picturesque Paris)—series that portrayed city life: *Les Petits Métiers* (1899–1901; Small trades), and two commis-

sions from the Bibliothèque Nationale, *Métiers, boutiques et étalages de Paris* (Trades, shops, and stalls of Paris) and *Zoniers: Vue et types de la zone militaire* (1910; Zoniers: View of the military zone and its inhabitants)
- *Le Vieux Paris* (Old Paris [1898–1900])—topographical views and architectural features
- *L'art dans Le Vieux Paris* (Art of Old Paris [from 1901])—photographs of architectural features (door knockers, moldings, staircases, wooden paneling, balconies, signs), which became the source of Atget's professional prestige
- *Environs de Paris* (Parisian suburbs [after 1901] and major suburbs)—Versailles, Saint Cloud, Sceaux, Rouen, Beauvais, Amiens
- *Topographie de Vieux Paris* (Topography of Old Paris)—commissioned and supervised by the Bibliothèque de la Ville de Paris (1906)

In general, aside from any commercial purpose it may have, photography breaks the bounds of genre. Although the concern with detail, the clarity of the image, and the mastery of light are essential characteristics of the documentary genre, Atget deployed them with a strong emotional intent. It is probably the American photographer Walker Evans who best expressed this quality of Atget's work, writing in 1931: "His general note is lyrical understanding of the street, trained observation of it, special feeling for patina, eye for revealing detail, over all of which is thrown a poetry which is not 'the poetry of the street,' or 'the poetry of Paris,' but the projection of Atget's person" (pp. 125–128).

The image in Atget's photography may show a casual stroller, but the photographer was a convinced socialist (Atget lectured in educational institutions for working-class adults and read the socialist press), which casts some doubt on the objectivity of the document produced. Everyday objects in the streets (brooms, carts) and the faces of café waiters reflected in the brasserie facades are details superimposed on the purely cadastral document while also evoking a city that belongs to those who live and work there.

This divergence between the intention of the image and the actual product, whether it springs from a conscious or unconscious intent or from an interpretation that no image ever escapes, means

Rue Brise-Miche, Paris. Photograph c. 1898 by Eugène Atget. GETTY IMAGES

that Atget is remembered more as a creator than as a simple producer of images. It was this disparity that interested the surrealists, leading then to publish some of Atget's later photographs in the June 1926 issue of *La Révolution surréaliste* and to adopt him as a surrealist artist. However, by stating that "these are simple documents that I am making," Atget firmly rejected any artistic status.

See also **Paris; Photography.**

BIBLIOGRAPHY

Badger, G. *Eugène Atget*. London, 2001.

Evans, Walker. "The Reappearance of Photography." *Hound and Horn* (October–December 1931): pp. 125–128.

Nesbit, Molly. *Atget's Seven Albums*. New Haven, Conn., 1992.

Nesbit, Molly, and F. Reynaud. *Intérieurs parisiens*. Paris, 1992.

Szarkowski, John, and Maria Morris Hambourg. *The Work of Atget*. 5 vols. New York, 1981–1985.

ALEXANDRA KOENIGUER

ATHENS. In 1789 Athens was neither the city that it was in antiquity nor the one it would become in modern times. Instead it was only a modest provincial town. Home to a mixed population of a few thousand souls consisting of Orthodox Greeks, Muslims, and a smattering of foreigners, it served as the capital of an Ottoman province and as a regional market for central Greece. Under the iron-fisted governorship of Hadji Ali Haseki (r. 1775–1795), the town grew in prominence and received an enceinte wall and a sizeable Ottoman garrison. The Acropolis was occupied exclusively by Muslims and the Parthenon served as a mosque. The lower town was divided into thirty-nine districts and its center was dominated by the market, the public baths, and the governor's residence. According to foreign observers in the early nineteenth century, Athens was a dirty, dusty, provincial backwater, noteworthy only for its antiquities.

During the Greek War of Independence (1821–1829), Athens was the scene of constant fighting as both sides vied for control of the Acropolis; at war's end, the town was a ruin. Its fortunes changed irrevocably when Greece's first monarch, Otto I (r. 1832–1862), decided that because of its antiquities and its ancient pedigree, Athens was the ideal site for the nation's capital. Even before the king relocated there in 1834, construction and in-migration had begun. During this growth phase, Athens expanded through the movement of wealthy Greeks from abroad, political office holders and functionaries, bureaucrats, and those members of the lower social orders needed to provide services to them. Athens became a small, bourgeois city replete with neoclassical public buildings and western-style townhouses, but with few other amenities.

A second, and far more profound, period of urban expansion began during the 1860s and then took off during the 1870s and 1880s. Between 1870 and 1890, Athens grew by 271 percent and manifested annual growth rates of an astonishingly high 5.17 percent. The flow of people into the city would continue, albeit at a slightly lower rate, until 1914. Unlike the earlier growth phase, the movement of peasants and workers fueled this second spurt. Land shortages and an overabundance of labor created such a tense rural situation that only a massive exodus could relieve it. Simultaneously, the Industrial Revolution slowly came to Greece and investors built factories in Athens and Piraeus. The latter developed as the port for the burgeoning conurbation. Jobs beckoned and rural migrants responded.

The result of this new movement was that alongside bourgeois Athens another city developed. This one was home to the lower classes. Housing shortages rose to crisis levels during the 1870s and 1880s as ten of thousands of people poured into Athens and Piraeus. Some migrants threw together shacks to house their families. Others built multiple dwelling houses with an eye to renting one or more of them to newcomers at very steep rates. The central core of bourgeois and "respectable" Athens became ringed with poorer neighborhoods and working-class slums.

As Athens and Piraeus grew in size and complexity, the usual social problems that accompanied nineteenth century urbanization developed. The crime rate, for example, soared. During the period of peak in-migration, the greater Athens area experienced a profound increase in homicides. During the years from 1888 to 1891, when the homicide rates in cities

A market street in the old quarter of Athens. Illustration by Andre Castaigne for *The Century* magazine, January 1897.
MARY EVANS PICTURE LIBRARY

such as London, Paris, Berlin, and Amsterdam were less than two killings for every hundred thousand people, Athens recorded the extraordinary rate of 107. The overwhelmingly young male migrants brought with them the propensity to violence inculcated during their rural upbringing, except that circumstances in the city brought their violent tendencies more frequently to the fore.

Along with violence, other public order issues emerged. Street crimes such as robbery and larceny became a constant problem in Athens. Beggary, infant abandonment, vagabondage, and prostitution also became issues of social and political importance, as did a variety of environmental issues such as the need to supply water, build sewers, provide streetlights and pavement, and regulate traffic. All of these issues required direct state intervention.

Spurred on by events such as the Olympics of 1896 and the "unofficial" Olympics of 1906, both of

which Athens hosted, the national government and private benefactors gave the city a face-lift. New public buildings were constructed, along with a public transportation system and new roads. The sewerage and water system was expanded to include some of the poorer neighborhoods. The initiative to transform Athens into a "western" city continued to the extent that by the eve of World War I it could be truly said that Athens had taken its place as a major European city.

See also **Cities and Towns; Greece.**

BIBLIOGRAPHY

Bastéa, Eleni. *The Creation of Modern Athens: Planning the Myth.* Cambridge, U.K., 1999.

Gallant, Thomas W. "Murder in a Mediterranean City: Homicide Trends in Athens, 1850–1936." *Journal of the Hellenic Diaspora* 24 (1998): 1–27.

Leontidou, Lila. *The Mediterranean City in Transition: Social Change and Urban Development.* Cambridge, U.K., 1989.

Llewellyn Smith, Michael. *Athens: A Cultural and Literary History.* Northampton, Mass., 2004.

THOMAS W. GALLANT

AUCLERT, HUBERTINE (1848–1914),
militant feminist and the leading founder of the women's suffrage movement in France.

Hubertine Auclert was born to a family of prosperous peasants in central France, local notables who provided mayors to two villages in Allier. She received a convent education and considered taking religious vows, but was rejected due to her adamant personality. The death of her father provided Auclert with an inheritance large enough to give her independence—she never needed to work or to marry.

The words of Victor Hugo, which Auclert read in an account of a women's rights banquet in 1872, drew her to Paris: "It is sad to say that there are still slaves in today's civilization … women. There are citizens, there are not citizenesses" (quoted in Hause, p. 19). The twenty-four-year-old Auclert was soon one of the most active members of the leading liberal-democratic women's rights organization in Paris, L'Avenir des femmes (Women's Future), led by Léon Richer and Maria Deraismes.

THE FOUNDING OF THE FRENCH WOMEN'S SUFFRAGE MOVEMENT
Auclert left L'Avenir des femmes in 1876 after concluding that Richer and Deraismes "went too slowly in their claims." With a small group of militants, Auclert founded (and financed) her own organization, le Droit des femmes (Women's Rights), bluntly dedicated to winning "the accession of women, married or not, to full civil and political rights, on the same legal conditions as apply to men" (quoted in Hause, p. 237). Although the rupture with Richer and Deraismes worsened in 1878 over the issue of women's suffrage, Auclert found new allies in the nascent socialist movement. In 1879 Auclert attended the Marseilles congress that founded the first socialist party in France, the Parti ouvrier français (French Workers' Party), and she persuaded the party to include women's suffrage on its agenda. Auclert remained nominally a socialist for much of the 1880s, but she grew disillusioned with all socialist parties for their inaction on women's rights.

Hubertine Auclert. BIBLIOTHÈQUE MARGUERITE DURAND, PARIS, FRANCE/BRIDGEMAN ART LIBRARY/ARCHIVES CHARMET

During the 1880s, Auclert conducted an energetic but lonely campaign for women's suffrage. She renamed her organization Suffrage des femmes (Women's Suffrage) to stress this emphasis, and she founded (and financed) a weekly newspaper, *La Citoyenne* (The Citizeness), to publicize the cause, as soon as the press law of 1881 allowed women to publish newspapers. Auclert's campaigns included an effort to register women to vote, a tax boycott, letters to the editor, petitions to parliament (twenty-two petitions between 1880 and 1887), court cases, protests at public ceremonies (including weddings), marches in the streets, a census boycott, and the organizing of women's candidacies. After an exhausting decade, Auclert had persuaded neither parliament nor the women's movement to adopt women's suffrage. Tired and lonely, Auclert abandoned her opposition to marriage (as unequally constituted in French law) and left Paris to marry one of her longtime supporters, Antonin Lévrier, who had accepted a judicial appointment in Algeria.

THE PROGRAM OF HUBERTINE AUCLERT'S *LE DROIT DES FEMMES*, APRIL 1877

Droit des femmes will seek, from the beginning and by all means in its power:

1. The accession of women, married or not, to full civil and political rights, on the same legal conditions as apply to men.

2. The reestablishment of divorce.

3. A single morality for men and for women; whatever is condemned for one cannot be excusable for the other.

4. The right for women to develop their intelligence through education, with no other limitation than their ability and their desire.

5. The right to knowledge being acquired, the free accession of women to all professions and all careers for which they are qualified at the same level as applies to men (and after the same examination).

6. The rigorous application, without distinction by sex, of the economic formula: Equal Pay for Equal Work.

Source: *Le Radical*, 3 April 1877. Translated by Steven C. Hause.

SECOND SUFFRAGE CAREER

Auclert enjoyed her married years in North Africa, and published a book on the situation of Arab women, but the early death of Lévrier led her to return to Paris in 1892, although her newspaper and her few followers had been lost. She rebuilt Suffrage des femmes, but it remained a small organization in the era when the French women's rights movement—now called a "feminist" movement (a term Auclert claimed to have coined)—began to grow into a mass movement. Auclert was never comfortable with reserved and respectable bourgeois women, such as the leaders of the National Council of French Women (which had one hundred thousand members by 1914), but she was hurt not to be invited to lead the French Union for Women's Suffrage, which became the first large-scale women's suffrage organization in France when a coalition of feminists founded it in 1909.

Between 1900 and her death in 1914, Auclert and a few followers conducted more vehement demonstrations. In addition to her old tactics, such as petitions (twenty-eight between 1900 and 1912), she was now more militant in the streets. For the centennial of the Napoleonic Code in 1904, Auclert publicly burned a copy of the code. In 1908 she seized the title of "the French suffragette" when she broke into a polling hall on election day, smashed a ballot box to the ground, and stomped on the ballots—the most violent demonstration that French suffragism ever produced. Auclert was convicted of a misdemeanor and paid a small fine, but the episode underscored her unacceptability for women of the respectable middle class. Auclert died in 1914, thirty years before the Comité français de la liberation adopted the ordinance allowing women to vote "on the same terms as men" in the departmental elections of February 1945 and the national elections for a Constituent Assembly in October 1945.

See also **Deraismes, Maria; Feminism; France; Napoleonic Code; Richer, Léon; Suffragism.**

BIBLIOGRAPHY

Primary Sources

Auclert, Hubertine. *Le vote des femmes.* Paris, 1908.

———. *Les femmes au gouvernail.* Paris, 1923.

———. *La Citoyenne: Articles de 1881 à 1891.* Edited by Edith Taïeb. Paris, 1982.

Secondary Sources

Hause, Steven C. *Hubertine Auclert: The French Suffragette.* New Haven, Conn., 1987.

Scott, Joan Wallach. "The Rights of the Social: Hubertine Auclert and the Politics of the Third Republic." In her *Only Paradoxes to Offer: French Feminists and the Rights of Man,* 99–124. Cambridge, Mass., 1996.

STEVEN C. HAUSE

AUGSPURG, ANITA

AUGSPURG, ANITA (1867–1943), legal scholar, writer, peace activist, and prominent member of the radical women's movement in Imperial and Weimar Germany.

Anita Augspurg was born on 22 September 1857, the youngest of five children, to a bourgeois family in Verden, Germany. As a young woman, she pursued various careers in order to push the boundaries constricting her choices as a "respectable" woman: in 1878 she moved to Berlin to work toward a certificate in teaching; later she studied acting and toured Germany and Europe with various companies before settling in Munich in 1886 to open a photo studio with her friend, the photographer Sophia Goudstikker. In Berlin and Munich, Augspurg came into contact with women's rights groups and started giving speeches on controversial topics, female education in particular. She quickly became an important figure in the growing bourgeois German women's movement. In 1893, Augspurg moved to Zurich to study law, because German universities did not enroll women. She viewed legal education as training for her activism and as the logical culmination of her commitment to improved educational opportunities for women. In 1895, Augspurg spent a semester in Berlin to audit courses and became involved in the fight against the proposed new German Civil Code (*Bürgerliches Gesetzbuch*). In 1896 she organized a series of protest rallies and published in the newly emerging feminist press her lectures condemning the restrictions on married women codified by the new laws. Her subsequent open letter calling for a boycott of bourgeois marriage revealed her increasing radicalization and her commitment to women's self-determination (politically, personally, professionally, and sexually).

After finishing her doctorate in 1897, Augspurg returned to Berlin, where her feminist activities became increasingly radical. In fact, Ausgpurg, Minna Cauer, and others broke with the moderate wing of the bourgeois women's movement in 1899 and formed a new radical organization, the Association of Progressive Women's Groups, which not only rejected the separation of bourgeois and working class women, but also made women's suffrage one of its main goals.

At an international women's congress in Berlin in 1896, Augspurg met Lida Gustava Heymann, a women's activist from Hamburg, and the two began a lifelong political cooperation and personal relationship. Although Augspurg had female partners throughout her life, she never spoke publicly about lesbianism. Heymann worked on women's issues in her hometown of Hamburg, where she

was particularly interested in combating regulated female prostitution. In 1899, Heymann founded the first German chapter of the International Abolitionist Federation in Hamburg, an organization founded by Josephine Butler in England that was dedicated to the abolition of regulated female prostitution. Although Augspurg was not officially a member, she visited the chapter frequently and gave public lectures on its behalf, focusing on the legal implications of the sexual dependency of women. In the wake of her own mistaken arrest in 1903, Augspurg became passionate about the injustices of sexual politics in Imperial Germany. Augspurg and Heymann saw women's suffrage as an important next step in the fight for women's rights. In 1902, they formed a women's suffrage association in Hamburg, which evolved into a national and international organization. Their goal was to achieve women's suffrage as soon as possible and to prepare women for political participation in the interim. In the following years, disagreements emerged within the women's movement about the overall goals of the movement, specifically the kinds of suffrage to be championed. In 1907, Augspurg and Heymann moved to Bavaria to run a farm. Their geographic remoteness was symbolic of their increasing isolation in the bourgeois women's movement as they took on more marginalized causes (animal rights, vegetarianism) and became alienated from some of the important radical leaders of the movement.

Augspurg interpreted the outbreak of war in 1914 as a culmination of male aggression and saw feminist pacifism as the only solution to the war. In 1915, she helped to organize and participated in the pacifist International Congress of Women in The Hague. Her pacifism and internationalism clashed with the strong resurgence of wartime nationalism in Germany. After the war, Augspurg and Heymann participated in the short-lived revolution in Munich, excited about the transformative potential of this new political beginning. Throughout the Weimar Republic, they continued their pacifist and feminist work.

Augspurg and Heymann were surprised by the advent of the Nazis to power in 1933 while on vacation in Mallorca, Spain. They decided not to return to Germany and remained in exile in

Switzerland. Augspurg died on 20 December 1943, just five months after her friend's death on July 31.

See also **Anneke, Mathilde-Franziska; Butler, Josephine; Dohm, Hedwig; Feminism; Otto, Louise; Suffragism.**

BIBLIOGRAPHY

Braker, Regina. "Betha von Suttner's Spiritual Daughters: The Feminist Pacifism of Anita Augspurg, Lida Gustava Heymann, and Helene Stöcker at the International Congress of Women at The Hague, 1915." *Women's Studies International Forum* 18(2) (1995): 103–111.

Dünnbier, Anna, and Ursula Scheu. *Die Rebellion ist eine Frau: Anita Augspurg und Lida G. Heymann—Das schillerndste Paar der Frauenbewegung.* Munich, 2002.

Evans, Richard J. *The Feminist Movement in Germany, 1893–1933.* London, 1976.

Gelblum, Amira. "Feminism and Pacifism: The Case of Anita Augspurg and Lida Gustava Heymann." *Tel-Aviver Jahrbuch für deutsche Geschichte* 21 (1992): 207–225.

Henke, Christiane. *Anita Augspurg.* Hamburg, 2000.

Heymann, Lida Gustava, in collaboration with Anita Augspurg. *Erlebtes Erschautes: Deutsche Frauen kämpfen für Freiheit, Recht, und Frieden,* edited by Margrit Twellmann. Meisenheim am Glan, 1972. New edition, Frankfurt am Main, 1992.

JULIA BRUGGEMANN

AUSTEN, JANE (1775–1817), English novelist.

Jane Austen is one of the most important English-language novelists and probably the earliest woman writer whose work is consistently considered part of the canon of great literature. She completed six novels: *Sense and Sensibility* (1811), *Pride and Prejudice* (1813), *Mansfield Park* (1814), *Emma* (1815), *Northanger Abbey* (1817), and *Persuasion* (1817). Her work was widely read during her lifetime and has been popularly and critically acclaimed since her death.

Her first four novels were published anonymously during her lifetime (though her identity was known to many), her last two posthumously.

Stylistically and thematically, her work anticipates that of later nineteenth-century authors, including realist novelists such as Charles Dickens (1812–1870) and popular writers such as Mary Elizabeth Braddon (1837–1915).

For many decades family members and biographers portrayed Austen as a reclusive spinster and an apolitical portraitist of village life, and praised her for her style and modest purview. However, since the 1970s critics have been more willing to study Austen in broadly historical rather than narrowly biographical context and to recognize the critiques of gender, class, and imperialism that are intrinsic to her works.

LIFE

Jane Austen was born on 16 December 1775, in the village of Steventon, in rural Hampshire, England, where her father was the rector, or head priest. As was typical of educated families at that time, five of her brothers were better schooled than Jane and her sister Cassandra (one brother, George, was disabled and an exception). The Austens were socially well connected—they traveled in what is called "polite" society, which consisted of locally elite families—but were of very modest means. Her father's death in 1805 left Jane Austen, her mother, and her sister in difficult financial circumstances (her brothers were by that time independent). As a single, middle-class woman, Austen had few options for earning her living; she made some money from her novels, but was never self-supporting. She spent most of her adult life without her own home or income, dependent on her brothers, and obliged to accept the living arrangements others imposed on her. As an adult she lived in various places, including the resort town of Bath, where some of her novels take place. She died on 18 July 1817 in Winchester at the age of forty-two, probably of Addison's disease.

SCOPE OF THE NOVELS

In an 1814 letter, Austen wrote that "3 or 4 families in a country village is the very thing to work on." All of her novels center on a few comfortable families in a provincial setting, and in all of them the protagonist is a young, single woman who marries at the end of the novel. In *Sense and Sensibility,* sensible Elinor Dashwood suffers heartsickness but ends happily married to Edward Ferrars, while her overly romantic sister Marianne,

Yes, novels; for I will not adopt that ungenerous and impolitic custom so common with novel-writers, of . . . joining with their greatest enemies in bestowing the harshest epithets on such works, and scarcely ever permitting them to be read by their own heroine, who, if she accidentally take up a novel, is sure to turn over its insipid pages with disgust. Alas! If the heroine of one novel be not patronized by the heroine of another, from whom can she expect protection and regard? . . . The person, be it gentleman or lady, who has not pleasure in a good novel, must be intolerably stupid.

Northanger Abbey, chapters five, fourteen.

"Did not you hear me ask him about the slave-trade last night?"

"I did—and was in hopes the question would be followed up by others. It would have pleased your uncle to be inquired of farther."

"And I longed to do it—but there was such a dead silence!"

Mansfield Park, chapter twenty-one.

subdued by illness, ends engaged to Colonel Brandon. In *Pride and Prejudice,* Elizabeth Bennet overcomes her prejudice, and the extremely wealthy Mr. Darcy his pride, and the two find love and marriage with one another. Such settings and plots seem in some ways limited, and Austen herself called her work a "little bit (two Inches wide) of Ivory on which I work with so fine a Brush, as produces little effect after much labour."

GENDER, CLASS, AND IMPERIALISM IN THE NOVELS

For many years critics tended to take Austen's self-effacing descriptions of her work at face value. Austen was praised as a brilliant stylist, but one whose work was divorced from the larger concerns of the day. In the late twentieth and early twenty-first centuries scholars have revised their opinions of her life and work. While Austen was single, she was hardly reclusive; on the contrary, she was involved in the lives of her nieces and nephews; was close to her sister, Cassandra; and was part of a supportive network of female friends. Her novels are shaped by her love of contemporary theater and her appreciation of regency society as fundamentally theatrical. They also reflect her readings of and critiques of contemporary novels and ideas about them; many characters in her novels are novel-readers, and *Northanger Abbey* is a satire of the gothic novels with which it competed in the marketplace.

Austen is also recognized as a critic of gender and class hierarchies. She was a harsh observer of the legal, economic, and cultural limitations placed on the women of the upper-middle classes who were her main characters. For instance, in *Pride and Prejudice,* Elizabeth Bennet and her sisters must marry because they cannot inherit their father's "entailed" estate—that privilege is reserved for a distant male relation. Women in polite circles could not earn a living without giving up their respectability; marriage was the only economic alternative—the only career—open to them. All of Austen's heroines marry happily and well, but not all marriages in the novels are successful; many minor characters have unhappy or loveless marriages. In *Pride and Prejudice,* Charlotte Lucas accepts Mr. Collins not because she loves him but because she knows that she needs a husband. Furthermore, many unmarried female characters suffer economic deprivation. In *Emma,* the widowed Mrs. Bates and her unmarried adult daughter Miss Bates are of Emma's social circle, but are forced by their small income to live in rented rooms. This brings them perilously close to lower-middle-class status, and subjects them to Emma's social derision.

Finally, much attention has been paid during the 1990s to the relationship between Austen and imperialism. The theorist of empire Edward Said maintains that *Mansfield Park,* in which Sir Thomas Bertram's wealth is derived from a plantation in Antigua maintained by slave labor, was a key part of an imperial culture that helped to make later expansion and oppression possible. The 1999 film version of *Mansfield Park* reinforces other critical readings of the novel that see slavery as the core of the moral satire of *Mansfield Park,* and the Bertram estate represented in it as morally blighted. Recent outpourings of Austen criticism and film interpretations of Austen's novels demonstrate the author's ongoing significance and relevance to contemporary culture.

See also **Dickens, Charles; Eliot, George; Great Britain.**

BIBLIOGRAPHY

Primary Sources

Austen, Jane. *Jane Austen's Letters.* Collected and edited by Deirdre Le Faye. Oxford, U.K., and New York, 1995.

Secondary Sources

Fraiman, Susan. "Jane Austen and Edward Said: Gender, Culture, and Imperialism." In *Janeites: Austen's Disciples and Devotees,* edited by Deidre Lynch, 206–223. Princeton, N.J., 2000.

Said, Edward W. *Culture and Imperialism.* New York, 1993.

Tomalin, Claire. *Jane Austen: A Life.* New York, 1997.

SUSIE L. STEINBACH

AUSTERLITZ. The Battle of Austerlitz was fought on 2 December 1805 between the armies of France, Austria, and Russia, commanded in person by Napoleon, Francis II, and Alexander I respectively. It was the culmination of a war that had begun in late August with the Austrian invasion of Bavaria and the Battle of Ulm, which destroyed the main Austrian army in Germany. By November, Napoleon had chased the Austrian remnants and General Mikhail Kutuzov's auxiliary Russian corps into Moravia, where they joined with reinforcements coming from Russia at Olmütz (modern-day Olomouc). Napoleon feared that a hostile Prussia might intervene against him and that Austrian reinforcements commanded by Archduke Charles might arrive in his rear. He launched diplomatic feelers toward Alexander to explore the possibilities for a negotiated peace, and simultaneously prepared for a climactic battle he hoped would end the war.

Alexander, exhilarated by his first appearance at the head of an army and encouraged by the size of the force at his command, rudely rejected Napoleon's peace overtures. The tsar and his advisors believed that they might be able to isolate

Napoleon's main body, concentrated at Brünn (modern-day Brno), from reinforcements near Vienna by enveloping the French from the south. The difficulties of supplying the Allied army in the poor lands of Moravia contributed to this decision. The Allied army accordingly marched southwest from Olmütz in the last days of November, and by 1 December had taken up position near the village of Austerlitz (modern-day Slavkov u Brna).

The Allied battle plan came from the Austrian chief of staff, Colonel Franz von Weyrother, and was approved by Tsar Alexander over the objections of the nominal commander in chief, General Kutuzov. Alexander was eager to attack; Kutuzov feared to fight with the patchwork Allied force he commanded. The tsar supported Weyrother's plan because it promised the action he wanted, and Kutuzov, unable to derail the unwise decision, remained silent about the plan's obvious flaws.

Napoleon had initially occupied a formidable defensive position anchored on the Pratzen Heights to the west of Austerlitz. He feared, however, that the Allies would not attack so strong a position, and so withdrew from it, leaving the high ground to the Allies. On 2 December the Allies attacked in accord with Weyrother's plan. The bulk of the Allied army streamed to the southwest from the Pratzen Heights in four columns, while a separate corps commanded by Prince Peter Bagration held the army's northern flank. The Allies aimed to turn Napoleon's right flank and envelop and then destroy his army from two directions.

Napoleon had prepared for precisely just such a maneuver, which the nature of the terrain strongly encouraged. He waited until most of the Allied troops had left the Pratzen Heights and then struck with his main forces against the Allied center. The fight for control of the Pratzen was fierce, and Napoleon's commanders nearly gave in at a critical moment. But the French had the great advantage of knowing what they were doing, while the Allies tried desperately to react to the total collapse of their own plans and preconceptions. The determination of the French generals contrasted with the confusion that swept the Allied upper echelons at this critical moment, and allowed the French finally to drive the defenders away from the Pratzen and retake the heights they had abandoned a few days before. Napoleon was aided in this effort by the timely arrival of Marshal Louis-Nicolas Davout with reinforcements from Vienna after a three-day, 145-kilometer (90-mile) forced march.

The French command of the Pratzen Heights allowed Napoleon to turn the Allies' retreat into a rout by stationing artillery on the dominating hills at the southern end of the range beyond which the Russians tried to withdraw. Even so, the Allied army lost only about a third of its strength in the battle, and the remnant still outnumbered Napoleon's disposable forces when the fighting stopped. Archduke Charles continued his northward march with reinforcements, and Prussia continued its preparations to enter the fight on the Allies' side.

Napoleon now brought his diplomatic skill to bear to turn a solid victory into a decisive one. He began at once to negotiate with both the Austrians and the Prussians and succeeded in driving the Prussian emissary, Count Christian von Haugwitz, to a treaty on 15 December (the Treaty of Schönbrunn). Tsar Alexander had been devastated by the loss of his first battle and had withdrawn in haste as soon as he had collected his army. The beleaguered and abandoned Austrians were forced to accept the disastrous Treaty of Pressburg on 26 December, yielding Napoleon substantial Austrian territory, including the Tyrol, Venice, and Dalmatia.

The opposing armies at Austerlitz were evenly matched in tactical skill. Russian, Austrian, and French soldiers all fought using roughly similar techniques and equal determination. The outcome of the battle resulted from political complexities within the Allied command structure that led to a premature and ill-considered attack, and from Napoleon's skill in setting the terms of the battle very much in his favor from the outset. At that, had Alexander kept his nerve or Napoleon not been as skillful a diplomat as he was a warrior, the battle would not have ended the war. It might, in fact, have been simply the prelude to the early destruction of the French army and Napoleon's rule.

See also **Alexander I; Clausewitz, Carl von; French Revolutionary Wars and Napoleonic Wars; Napoleon; Napoleonic Empire; Ulm, Battle of.**

BIBLIOGRAPHY

Duffy, Christopher. *Austerlitz, 1805.* London, 1977.

FREDERICK W. KAGAN

AUSTRALIA. The history of Australia from the close of the eighteenth century to World War I is a chapter in the eclipse of indigenous peoples, the rise of the British Empire, mass emigration from Europe, the spread of democracy, and the growth of a world economy.

FALL OF ABORIGINAL AUSTRALIA

The establishment of a tiny enclave of British convicts and soldiers at Sydney in 1788 was accompanied by a formal British claim to all of New South Wales, as the eastern half of Australia was dubbed after its coast was charted by the navigator James Cook. The British claim was later (1828) extended to Australia's western half. Yet Australia was already occupied, if thinly, by perhaps four hundred thousand Aborigines. They lived in small clans of hunter-gatherers, without knowledge of kings or constitutions, metalwork or money, writing or the wheel. Their ties to each other and to the land were difficult for outsiders to discern. Ironically it was their one obvious impact on the landscape, that of clearing undergrowth by fire, that helped lure the British to settle the continent they merely claimed. No other European power was lured, though. The French might have lodged in the west of the continent and the Dutch in the north, but the French revolutionary and Napoleonic wars left Britain the undisputed maritime and colonizing power of the age.

The British enclave expanded significantly when the wars were over. Peace permitted British attention to shift from Europe to its colonies. It also brought recession, retrenchment, and reform agitation, flooding British courts with offenders. The result was an acceleration of convict transportation to Australia, which ended only in 1868. By that date more than 160,000 convicts, mostly male English thieves, had served long sentences of forced labor in Australia. Some had erected public buildings, roads, wharves, and bridges. Others had worked for free immigrants. Few returned home when their sentence expired. The passage was expensive, but in any case they found living conditions and wages better in Australia than back home.

Inland Australia seemed dry and infertile to British explorers who entered it looking for a second Mississippi and great plains. Yet sheep could live on the grasslands that, thanks to the Aborigines, covered

AUSTRALIA

When the English socialist Beatrice Webb visited Australia in 1898 she detected the same "bad manners, ugly clothes, vigour and shrewdness" she knew from England, but something else too. "On the other hand," Webb wrote, "there is more enjoyment of life, a greater measure of high spirits among the young people of all classes. Australians are obviously and even blatantly a young race proud of their youth."

Source: *The Webbs' Australian Diary,* edited by A. G. Austin, 107–108. Melbourne, 1965.

much of southeast Australia, and Britain's looms needed more fine wool than Europe could supply. Raising and shearing sheep to feed those looms thus became the bedrock of Australia's economy for more than a century, and the rich yield immediately encouraged free immigration. By the 1830s, convict arrivals were outpaced by immigrants, nearly all from Britain's working and lower-middle classes. Convicts opened up the island of Tasmania off the continent's south (from 1803), but immigrants founded the colonies of Western Australia (1829), which soon received convict labor, and South Australia (1836), which spurned it. Pastoralists looking for grazing land sparked the creation of two more colonies: Victoria (which separated from New South Wales in 1851) and Queensland (which separated in 1859).

Wool and the immigrants it encouraged doomed Aboriginal Australia. News of the pale invaders had been unsettling enough. Worse harbingers were European diseases like smallpox and syphilis. When significant numbers of colonists finally arrived they insisted the land was theirs, cut down or dug up its natural features, proclaimed what seemed a simplistic religion, imposed what seemed confusing laws, and met any resistance with firmness or even violence. Perhaps twenty thousand Aborigines were killed in the process; twenty-first-century historians argue over the number. What is clear is that few Aborigines died from soldiers' bullets. Sustained,

bloody military campaigns like those that cleared other nineteenth-century frontiers for white settlers were never needed in Australia; the Aborigines were generally stripped of everything by civilians and police. By 1900 they were reduced to perhaps ninety thousand. Only those in the tropics and the remote inland still lived lives that were partly traditional. By then, many white Australians had never seen an Aborigine. They believed their predecessors had settled an empty continent, and that their society was unique for not having known war.

RISE OF COLONIAL AUSTRALIA

Australia was represented at London's great exhibition of 1851 by animal skins, whale teeth, and bird feathers. Had the exhibition been held a year or two later these exhibits would have given way to gold nuggets. Inspired by the Californian gold rush, prospectors found gold across New South Wales and Victoria. An Australian gold rush began in 1851, joined by miners from Canton to California. Over the next forty years new finds prompted new rushes in Western Australia and the tropical north. Australia's gold fields were never as riotous as America's. Yet tension between miners and the authorities yielded a bloody skirmish at Victoria's Eureka Field (3 December 1854), while anti-Chinese riots erupted at Lambing Flat in New South Wales (July 1861).

The gold seekers were the vanguard of 1.4 million immigrants who came to Australia from 1851 to 1890, trebling the colonial population in the 1850s and nearly trebling it again during the subsequent two decades. As before, the vast majority of immigrants were from Britain's working and lower-middle classes. The earliest sought gold, the rest a brighter future in a land being made prosperous by gold and wool and by their own need for food, housing, transport, and manufactures. Sheep flocks expanded fivefold from the 1850s to the 1880s, and wool began to attract European and Asian buyers as well as British ones. British investors began to back Australian ventures, especially the railways that were tethering the sheep runs to the sea ports. Towns grew, and grew further as most settlers decided against making a living from the hard land. Melbourne's population approached five hundred thousand and, along with slightly smaller Sydney, ranked among the chief cities of the British Empire. Australia became an even more urbanized white frontier than North America.

Gold and the wave of immigration it launched hastened the coming of self-government for the Australian colonies, and ensured that it took democratic form. Before the gold rushes, prosperous pastoralists hoped to form a governing class. Most immigrants and former convicts wanted the fraternal democracy of male voters for which England's Chartists were campaigning. The British government handed the decision to the colonists, and numbers proved decisive. By 1860 all the colonies except Western Australia (which followed in 1890) were self-governing polities within the British Empire, enjoying something like English municipal government on a grand scale. Almost every male colonist was eligible to vote by secret ballot for lower houses of parliament, which controlled and dispensed his colony's lands and revenues, lightly restrained by a rural bias to electoral boundaries and by more cautious upper houses of parliament whose members were sometimes nominated.

Effectively confined until the 1900s to English-speaking adult males, the colonial political class was small and homogeneous. There was no aristocracy in Australia, no peasantry, and few truly wealthy families. Social mobility and the absence of an established church eased the divide between the Irish Catholic–descended minority and the Protestant English, Scottish, and Irish majority. There was confidence in the future, and much agreement about the present. The main political concerns were to manage the infrastructure needed to sustain prosperity (governments, not private companies, managed the railways), and to distribute a little of that prosperity. One form of distribution, adopted by Victoria and South Australia, was to tax imports to encourage local industry and increase employment. Another form adopted in Victoria and New South Wales, generally unsuccessfully, was to settle families on small blocks of rural land. A third means emerged outside the parliaments in the 1880s with the growth of trade unions. The unions wanted better wages and compulsory union membership, not an end to capitalism. But their growth brought a real divide among the colonial political class.

DEPRESSION AND FEDERATION

The promise of the golden 1850s was never quite realized. The lion's share of British investment went to America. No great fortunes were made in Australia like those made in the United States.

Pastoralists and farmers always battled drought and distance. There were pockets of distressing poverty in Sydney and Melbourne. Employment was uncertain for some colonists, and prices were high for everyone. Away from the settled southeast, colonization seemed to have stalled. Skin color quickly veered toward tan, brown, or black there. In the tropical north, labor was often performed almost free by indentured Chinese or Melanesian men. Most white colonists wanted these men out of Australia, and colonial governments did what they could to turn Asian immigrants away.

In the 1890s the colonial economy faltered. The need for new railways and dwellings was exhausted, overseas prices for wool had plunged, and the Baring crisis of 1890 panicked British investors. Spending, prices, and employment slumped across Australia, and immigration slowed to a trickle. Trade unions, which had hoped to exploit the prosperity of the 1880s, now fought employers over a shrinking cake. They lost a series of strikes (1890–1894), and the defeat hastened the formation of union-based Labor parties that most electors would support by 1914.

Recovery from economic depression was delayed in the second half of the 1890s by a long drought and obscured by a rise in national and imperial sentiment. Native-born colonists had outnumbered immigrants for a generation, and colonial art and literature had become increasingly Australian in subject matter. Now the colonies resolved to follow Canada and federate as a way of pooling their economic and military resources and standing against Asian immigration or—an even deeper fear—an Asian invasion. At the same time, there was increasing affection for Queen Victoria and growing pride in membership in the world's largest empire. Twenty thousand soldiers from Australia helped make the empire even larger when they enlisted for the South African War (1899–1902) and helped crush the Boer republics.

The colonies federated during the war (1 January 1901) to form the Commonwealth of Australia. The new federal parliament legislated to bar Asian immigrants and deport Melanesian workers (1901) and raise tariff walls around the continent to encourage manufacturing and urban employment (1908). After Japan's naval victory in 1905 at Tsushima and

Female emigrants waiting to depart for Australia. This illustration appeared in the 12 March 1853 edition of the *Illustrated London News.* ©CORBIS

the dreadnought crisis of 1909, it made militia service compulsory and approved the construction of an Australian navy. The parliament also set up an arbitration court to settle strikes (1904). Encouraged by progressive politicians, the court came to set widely heeded wage levels. The court's *Harvester* judgment (1907) based those levels on the needs of a male worker and his family, not an employer's ability to pay.

That a male worker was taken to be the typical breadwinner reflected the notably masculine tenor of Australian society. Men outnumbered women; there were eleven males to every ten females in Australia in 1901. Strength and sporting prowess were highly praised. The distinctive Australian was said to be the bushman, as the white male inhabitant of the inland was called. But Australia was not entirely a man's country and hardly at all compared with more traditional societies. Women had the same legal protections as their female cousins in Britain, and political rights in advance of them. They could vote in South Australian elections from 1894, in Western Australian ones from 1899, in federal elections from 1902, and in all elections by 1914.

Prosperity returned to Australia by the second decade of the twentieth century. Some said a new nation with a great future was being born. Whatever its future, Australia seemed likely to remain a transplanted, improved Britain. "When the Australian uses the word 'home,'" visiting journalist John Foster Fraser observed in 1910, "he does not mean his home. He means England." No wonder, then, that when the bugles of England sounded in August 1914, Australians responded eagerly.

See also **Canada; Colonies; Emigration; Great Britain; New Zealand.**

BIBLIOGRAPHY

Adams, David, ed. *The Letters of Rachel Henning*. Sydney, 1952. Australian colonial life as experienced by a middle-class English migrant.

Blainey, Geoffrey. *A Shorter History of Australia*. Port Melbourne, 1994.

"Emigrant Mechanic." *Settlers and Convicts; or, Recollections of Sixteen Years' Labour in the Australian Backwoods*. Melbourne, 1953. Reprint of a blend of memoir and fiction by an English settler of the 1830s.

Kingston, Beverley. *The Oxford History of Australia*. Vol. 3: *1860–1900: Glad, Confident Morning*. Melbourne, 1988. A dissection of colonial Australian beliefs, culture, and activities.

Reynolds, Henry. *The Other Side of the Frontier: Aboriginal Resistance to the European Invasion of Australia*. Ringwood, Australia, 1981.

Sinclair, William Angus. *The Process of Economic Development in Australia*. Melbourne, 1976. Contains a clear account of the economic history of colonial Australia.

Smith, Bernard, ed. *Documents on Art and Taste in Australia: The Colonial Period, 1770–1914*. Melbourne, 1975.

Souter, Gavin. *Lion and Kangaroo: The Initiation of Australia, 1901–1919*. Sydney, 1976.

CRAIG WILCOX

AUSTRIA-HUNGARY.

In 1789 the Habsburg Monarchy covered an area that today lies within the borders of Austria, Hungary, Poland, the Czech Republic, Slovakia, Slovenia, Croatia, Romania, Serbia, Ukraine, Belgium, and Italy. By 1914 the Monarchy was geographically more consolidated, having lost its outlying territories in today's Belgium and most of those on the Italian peninsula, and having gained Bosnia-Herzegovina at the expense of its Ottoman neighbor to the south. In the west, the Habsburg dynasty's holdings included Bohemia and Moravia, territories originally acquired by marriage and election in 1526, and later claimed through hereditary rule. The family's traditional hereditary lands included the provinces of Lower and Upper Austria, Carinthia, Carniola, Styria, Salzburg, and Tirol— essentially today's Austria and Slovenia. To the east, the Habsburgs ruled as elective, and later hereditary, kings of Hungary, a kingdom that in 1789 included the semiautonomous regions of Transylvania and Croatia. Although the dynasty had acquired Hungary in 1526, it had fought the Ottoman Empire for control over that kingdom in a series of wars that had ended only at the beginning of the eighteenth century and that had prevented the Habsburgs from consolidating administrative control over Hungary. More recently the dynasty had augmented its holdings in the northeast with the first partition of Poland, gaining the newly invented Kingdom of Galicia and Lodomeria in 1772 and, in 1775, a slice of neighboring territory farther to the east that was christened the Duchy of Bukovina.

As in the case of many other European states around 1800, the Habsburg Monarchy included diverse regions that had experienced very different degrees of economic development and urbanization, and whose people had access to different types of education and social mobility. Particularly in the west, Bohemia, Moravia, Lower Austria, Styria, and Lombardy had developed strong interregional markets and boasted levels of industrial production as sophisticated as any in continental Europe. Here urban merchants, artisans, elements of the aristocracy, and immigrants from western Europe with access to capital had founded textile, mining, and agriculturally based industries. The spread of large-scale commercial firms had begun to challenge the prevailing legal and customary concepts of property ownership, banking and commercial practices, labor organization, and technological development. To the east and south, however, economies remained relatively isolated from interregional trade, overwhelmingly agricultural in nature, and far less productive. At the start of the eighteenth century all these territories had sported very different administrative structures and legal relations to the regime in Vienna, and in some cases, little or no relationship to each other. The central government in Vienna had in turn exercised its power differently over most of these territories. Local elites expressed their provincial interests in traditional noble-dominated diets that generally met irregularly and that struggled increasingly during the eighteenth century to enforce traditional privilege against their Habsburg rulers' administrative encroachments.

AN AGE OF REFORM

The year 1789 found the Habsburg Monarchy in considerable political turmoil due to the imposition of a series of particularly radical reforms authored by Emperor Joseph II (r. 1780–1790) and enforced against the wishes of most interests represented in the regional diets. During the eighteenth century the Monarchy had experienced an inexorable progression of reform initiatives from Vienna that sought to forge a centralized state and to create an economically more productive society out of the diverse collection of territories that owed allegiance to the Habsburg ruler. A series of agreements in the seventeenth and early eighteenth centuries had already transformed the dynasty's rule from elective to hereditary in character, and the acceptance of the Pragmatic Sanction (1713) had ensured the succession through the female branch of the family as well. Maria Theresa (r. 1740–1780) sought not only to consolidate her political power vis-à-vis the diets, but also to transform, rationalize, and improve all aspects of society. She, her sons, and her ministers intended to reinvigorate a stagnating empire, to stimulate greater economic growth, to ensure generalized prosperity, and to raise the moral and educational level of their poorest subjects. By 1789 the Habsburgs' centralizing efforts had largely succeeded in wearing down the most stubborn cases of institutional and administrative diversity. In their place, the contours of a centralized state had emerged, one administered by a professional bureaucracy loyal to Vienna.

The main obstacles to royal reform, however, remained the crushing social and economic weight of local noble privilege, the often-landless and unproductive peasantry enserfed by that nobility, the monopolistic power exerted over production by local guilds, and the lack of an educated citizenry. Maria Theresa took steps to remedy each obstacle with the aid of a greatly expanded state civil service that gradually assumed the local and regional powers of administration from local nobles and the noble-dominated diets. Members of this growing civil service, in turn, whether themselves of noble or middle-class origin, identified their interests increasingly with those of the reforming state from which they derived their mandate to interfere in local society. In the 1770s Maria Theresa even instituted a mandatory system of schools in her Austrian, Bohemian, and Hungarian lands as a means not only to improve knowledge and morality among her peasant subjects, but also to produce a cadre of educated commoners for the expanding civil service.

With the accession of Joseph II in 1780, the pace of imperial reform moved swiftly to more radical conclusions. Joseph was a tireless worker who traveled frequently across his vast realms with the object of observing local conditions, cataloging and measuring economic resources, and developing effective policies for their rational exploitation. In 1781 Joseph abolished the physical rights nobles exercised over serfs in Austria and Bohemia, giving peasants the right to move, marry, and gain an education without their lord's permission (although the manorial system continued to remain in effect). In 1785 he extended this abolition of physical control over peasants to Hungary as well. Edicts promulgated in 1784 and 1786 further relaxed local guild powers of economic regulation, and in 1785 Joseph undertook a land survey of the entire Monarchy as the prelude to developing a unified system of land taxation.

In cultural matters Joseph also proceeded rapidly, issuing an Edict of Toleration in 1781 that legalized the practice of Protestant, Orthodox, and Uniate (Greek Catholic) religions, placing their adherents on an equal legal footing with Catholics and removing many forms of discrimination against Jews. Jews were now eligible for military service, a transformation that called into question remaining limits on their freedom as citizens. Joseph's intentions regarding the Catholic Church were not to subvert its predominant position in Austrian society so much as to bring it and the other constituted religions under the control of the state. He established seminaries for Catholic and Uniate (Greek Catholic) priests in Galicia, as well as a university in L'viv/Lwów/Lemberg, for example, thus raising the level of required education for priests, but also exerting state control over its content. Joseph also relaxed censorship laws and encouraged the expansion of public and private education at all levels. Radical new civil and criminal codes followed in 1786 that applied equally to noble and non-noble offenders.

What later nationalists considered the most execrable or praiseworthy of Joseph's many acts, depending on their political outlook, was the privileged legal status he assigned to the German language in the civil service and much of the school system. Joseph himself would not have understood the controversy because to him and his successors, these measures had nothing to do with a German nationalist impulse, a desire somehow to "Germanize" the Monarchy's linguistically diverse peoples. Rather, Joseph believed that using the German language would enhance the institutional unity of the state and facilitate interregional commerce and administration. Latin, which had previously been the language of much official communication (serving, for example, as the language of the Hungarian Diet), was considered by Joseph to be inadequate in an age of technical innovation. The language law provoked angry reactions, however, particularly in Hungary where, in 1785, administrators were given just one year and judicial officials three years in which to learn German as a replacement for Latin. Proof that Joseph did not envision a Germanization of his peoples may be found in his policies to promote use of vernacular languages other than German in some provinces as well. While its implementation as the new lingua franca for the Monarchy required the greater promotion of German language study in secondary schools and universities, the regime continued to recognize the importance of communication with the population in other locally used languages. The dynasty did not intend German to replace customary usage in regions where the vernacular differed from it. In Bohemia, for example, the government continued its traditional custom of proclaiming new laws in both the Czech and German languages.

In 1789 Joseph announced a tax law based on his new land survey that would have diminished the money paid by peasants to their lords and increased the amounts owed by those lords to the state. This measure would have completed the abolition of serfdom and in some parts of the Monarchy would have cut noble agricultural income by more than half. As Joseph's reign came to a tumultuous close, the dynasty faced growing revolts in the Netherlands, in Hungary, and among nobles throughout the Monarchy. Joseph's temperamentally more moderate brother and successor, Leopold II (r. 1790–1792), hoped to calm the uprisings by moderating the reforms, without backing down from their original intent, and in 1791 he reached a compromise with the Hungarian Diet. But by this time the reformers faced an entirely different set of challengers who forced nobles, bureaucrats, and emperor together in a common alliance to protect the social order at home and to combat military aggression from abroad.

REACTION

The outbreak of the French Revolution in 1789, its subsequent radicalization and military challenge to aristocratic Europe, forced the dynasty to reconsi-

Women in traditional dress of the Mehadia region.
Illustration from the book *Costumes de Hongrie,* 1810, by J. H. Bikkesy. Mehadia is an ancient market town in the Cerna River valley, now part of Romania. BIBLIOTHÈQUE NATIONALE, PARIS, FRANCE/BRIDGEMAN ART LIBRARY/ARCHIVES CHARMET

der the measures it had taken to weaken the powers of the nobility and church, two potentially conservative and stabilizing elements in Habsburg society. Threatened by the specter of revolutionary social unrest, Leopold's son Francis II/I (r. 1792–1835) made peace with the nobility. He did not, however, renounce the centralist achievements of his predecessors. Instead, he used their formidable bureaucratic machinery for more socially conservative ends. During the next fifty years the Austrian bureaucracy assumed the unfamiliar and often uncomfortable role of preserving a socially conservative status quo, often by intruding on and censoring the activities and writings of an emerging middle-class civil society. Prince Clemens von Metternich, foreign minister from 1809 to 1848, epitomized this harsh domestic Habsburg policy that sought to suppress any signs of revolution, both at home and abroad.

During the Napoleonic Wars (1803–1815) the Monarchy survived countless defeats and considerable territorial losses. The Holy Roman Empire, of which the Habsburgs were nominal emperors, collapsed in the face of Napoleonic alliances and armies. In 1804 Emperor Francis II of the Holy Roman Empire declared that the Habsburg realms constituted an "empire" of their own and that he would henceforth be known as "Emperor Francis I of Austria." The final defeat of Napoleon in 1815 made the Habsburg state victorious in Europe, but victory came at the price of near bankruptcy. Financial crisis combined with Metternich's ambition to police the rest of Europe led Emperor Francis to try to squeeze greater funds and soldiers from his territories. During the Napoleonic Wars the nobility had provided increased revenues for the military, while the Habsburgs had provided the nobility with protection against popular sedition. Nobles in some regions had prospered thanks to their exploitation of wartime economic needs. But by the 1820s they were doing much worse economically, and when, for example, the Hungarian nobles finally refused to pay up any longer, they also demanded the convocation of a Hungarian national diet in 1825.

Already during the eighteenth century, protesting nobles had couched their political opposition to Maria Theresa's and Joseph II's reforms in a language that invoked the concepts of "states' rights" and "national liberties." The Hungarian Diet of 1825 (as well as those that followed in the next decade) was understood by the nobles to speak for the so-called Hungarian nation. At this point in history, however, the term *Hungarian nation* (or in Latin, *natio Hungarica*) referred only to those groups with the right to representation in the diet: the nobility, the Catholic clergy, and a few enfranchised burghers of the free royal town. The vast majority of the country's population, those who paid the taxes, served in the military, and bowed to the whims of the nobility, were commoners with no public role or voice, and no part in the political "nation." This traditional understanding of the term *nation* applied equally well, for example, to the Polish nation, which is how nobles in Galicia referred to themselves. Nowhere in this region did the term *nation* share the more socially universal definition it had gained under the French Revolutionary and Napoleonic regimes. Furthermore, while language use and religious practice later came to define national identity, at this point the number of self-styled nationalist nobles who could even speak the Magyar or Czech languages was quite small. While some historians believe that Joseph II's centralizing policies had inadvertently "awakened" the slumbering consciousness of nations in the Monarchy, this formulation presumes there was something there to be awakened in the first place. Noble opponents of royal centralization framed their opposition to absolutism increasingly in terms of their so-called national liberties, but the collective body they invoked referred to their own narrow social class interests. It did not refer to some imagined mass of people who consciously shared some vital (if nebulously defined) characteristics such as language use, a common "culture," or religion. The nobility spoke for the rights of their ancient states (Hungary, Bohemia, and Poland) against the encroachments of their imperial rulers.

Some critical observers such as Count István Széchenyi (1791–1860) in Hungary blamed Hungary's political weakness and economic poverty precisely on a shortsighted nobility that gave little thought to the economic welfare of the larger society and fought only to maintain its class privilege. Nobles in Galicia learned the hard way that if a Polish nation did in fact exist, its membership was limited to the uppermost classes, who were often hated by the rest of society. In another sign of the limited extent of national self-identification in these regions, peasants often mythologized their Habsburg rulers for having attempted to intervene on their behalf over the years against their noble masters. Such peasants did not see themselves as part of an imagined Hungarian or Polish nation. When in 1846 Polish nobles in Galicia rebelled against the Habsburgs, Polish- and Ukrainian-speaking peasants famously turned on their rebellious landlords in large numbers and massacred them, claiming to oppose the oppressive Polish nation in whose name the nobles had rebelled.

Nobles invoking national myths were not the only emerging opponents of the regime under the harsh rule of Francis and his mentally incompetent successor, Ferdinand I (r. 1835–1848). During the 1830s and 1840s an emerging urban civil society in cities throughout the monarchy (Vienna, Pest, Pressburg/Pozsony, Prague, Graz, Ljubljana/Laibach, L'viv) created social and economic institutions that posited alternate models of rule to Habsburg despotism or noble privilege. Early industrialist associations lobbied for more industry-friendly policies from a government that seemed intent on holding the potentially political ills of industrialization at bay. Noble and middle-class educational, scientific, professional, gymnastics, choral, and charity societies all attempted to effect some kind of social change through collective activity. Historians developed nationalist histories in vernacular languages serving the interests of incipient Czech, Hungarian, and Polish nationalist movements. The noble-dominated diets remained the locus of whatever forms of political protest were possible, but the discourses their members invoked and the policies they promoted began to follow more middle-class and less purely aristocratic formulations of interest. When strikes in the textile industry threatened social order in Moravia in 1844 or hunger threatened disorder in Vienna in 1847, middle-class journalists and reform-minded noble nationalists alike blamed both the incompetence and the arrogance of the oppressive central government.

1848

In 1848, when a series of revolutions broke out across Europe, Pest, Vienna, and Prague were among the cities at the forefront of experiments with political reform. In Hungary, under the leadership of Lajos Kossuth (1802–1894), the diet rapidly proclaimed a new constitutional regime in April (the April Laws). This arrangement confirmed Hungary's existence independent of other Habsburg territories, promised liberal rights of citizenship and enfranchisement to many more inhabitants (although not to Jews or to small property owners), and maintained full enfranchisement for any noble, no matter how poor. The Hungarian reformers postponed any significant transformation of the manorial system, a tack that pleased the broad gentry class and nobility but did little to satisfy the peasantry. Furthermore, the April Laws imposed the Magyar language on state and society, and this tended to diminish revolutionary unity, provoking opposition among leaders in Croatia and Transylvania who rejected Magyar predominance and insisted on using Latin in their communications with the government. In fact the question of defining the nation and the privileged role of the

Magyar language helped to alienate many who spoke other languages and who might otherwise have sympathized with the new liberal constitutional regime. Later in 1848 and 1849 the Habsburg military carefully exploited this alienation as the dynasty struggled to reimpose control over Hungary. The dynasty's strategy of divide and conquer ultimately provoked the Hungarian revolutionaries in turn to depose the Habsburgs and to declare full independence in April 1849.

In Vienna the government collapsed in March 1848, Metternich fled, and the emperor's advisors promised a constitutional regime with liberal franchise laws, civil rights, the abolition of censorship, and, eventually, an end to the remaining vestiges of serfdom and the manorial system (which in Galicia were considerable). Occasional outbursts of popular violence in Vienna throughout the spring continued to drive the revolution further to the left, until the court found it expedient to remove itself to the safer, more conservative city of Innsbruck. In July an Austrian parliament elected by means of an extremely generous suffrage set about writing a constitution, and it too was eventually removed to the sleepy town of Kremsier/Kroměříž in Moravia in order to avoid the political pressures exerted by the radical crowd in the streets of Vienna. At the same time, the issue of political nationalism came to the fore in several different and often contradictory contexts. Austria sent a large delegation to the Frankfurt National Assembly, which struggled in 1848 and 1849 to forge a new united Germany. Liberal Austrians who sat in the Frankfurt National Assembly tended to share an idealistic vision of a future united Germany that would include the non-German-speaking Habsburg territories. The inhabitants of these territories, it was imagined, would receive linguistic rights where necessary from the fraternal German people, and they would reap considerable benefits from their participation in the high cultural and economic development of the German nation. In fact, using a universal language of inclusion, many Austro-German liberals imagined their nation to be defined by its very commitment to the values of liberal humanism, values available to any struggling people in east-central Europe.

At the same time, and in reaction to the events at Frankfurt, Czech national liberal leaders proclaimed their own adherence to an Austria separate from Germany and defined by Slav interests. The (bilingual) Bohemian historian František Palacký (1798–1876), who had been invited to participate in the planning process for the Frankfurt National Assembly, used the occasion of his reply to articulate this Austro-Slav position most effectively. Calling for an Austria organized around a principle of Slav solidarity, since this would protect the so-called smaller nations of central Europe from German and Russian hegemony, Palacký argued that had Austria not existed, it would have had to be invented for this very purpose. In June an informal Slav Congress even met in Prague, although its activities tended to demonstrate the difficulties of forging a common program that would unite the political interests of Czech, Polish, Ukrainian, Slovak, Serbian, and Slovene speakers across the Monarchy.

Many historians have since judged nationalism rather than liberalism to have been the major source of discontent in 1848. Such a judgment accepts the nationalist rhetoric of 1848 at face value, and views it in the context of modern nationalist sensibilities, rather than in terms of the specific and limited meanings that attached to such language over 150 years ago. The fact that Austro-Slav declarations by Czech nationalist leaders caught their German-speaking counterparts in Bohemia by surprise should alert the observer to the relative novelty and insignificance of the national issue to most Austrians in 1848. Nationalist discourse became a critical vehicle for conveying regional demands that year, but the nations it invoked were largely figments of the nationalists' own imagination. More often than not, regional and class loyalties far outweighed their nationalist counterparts. German and Czech-identified deputies to the Austrian parliament from Bohemia (many of whom were bilingual) agreed more often with each other, for example, than they did with German-speaking delegates from Lower Austria or Styria. And unlike their Polish noble counterparts, Polish-speaking peasant deputies to the parliament sought an immediate end to all forms of manorialism. Many historians of 1848 have also argued that the work of the constitutional committee at the parliament in Kremsier constituted the last possibility for a friendly constitutional understanding among the various "nations" of Austria. Indeed the work of the committee provided a notable

model for later Austrian constitutions, but the compromises achieved by the committee emerged from its members' powerful conviction that their common liberal sympathies far outweighed nationalist differences. Whether they held centralist or federalist views, German national or Slav national orientations, the men at Kremsier largely put aside their differences over the latter issues to produce a bill of rights and state structure that would have transformed dynastic Austria into a genuinely constitutional regime.

Their efforts, however, would not pay off for another twenty years. Already in the summer of 1848 the regime had begun to reassert its dominance against the revolution, even against its more moderate proponents. In June, Field Marshal Prince Alfred Windischgrätz successfully laid siege to Prague, ending both the Slav Congress and a radical student uprising there. In October the military besieged revolutionary Vienna, long since abandoned by the court and most moderates. In early December the regime replaced the faltering Emperor Ferdinand with the eighteen-year-old Francis Joseph I (r. 1848–1916), and in the spring of 1849 the new emperor and his prime minister, Felix Schwarzenberg, sent the Austrian parliament home, imposing a constitution of their own devising on Austria. Later in 1849, with the help of the Russian military, the Austrians finally managed to defeat the armies of the Hungarian rebels, and in 1851 the emperor decided to rule openly as an absolute monarch by abrogating the constitution he had issued a year before.

FAILED ABSOLUTISM AND LIBERAL REFORM

The absolutist system of the 1850s did not, however, represent a return to the Metternich years. After a brief period of harsh retribution following the revolutionary denouement, the regime focused on promoting industrial development, economic modernization, educational reform, and political quiescence. The regime invested close to 20 percent of its annual expenditures during the 1850s in railway construction, for example, an unheard of amount second only to its expenditure on the military. Starting in 1850 the state also sponsored the creation of chambers of commerce to promote local business interests in cities and towns throughout the monarchy. Several revolutionary reforms,

The Hungarian Revolution of 1848: Austrian Troops Assault the Buda Castle on 21 May 1849. Watercolor on paper, Hungarian School, nineteenth century. Private collection/Bridgeman Art Library/Archives Charmet

including the abolition of serfdom (confirmed in 1849 in Austria and 1853 in Hungary), and the beginnings of municipal autonomy remained in force. Censorship returned, but in far less draconian form than its pre-1848 versions. Liberalism as a set of progressive and modern attitudes toward the transformation of society grew ever more popular throughout Austrian and Hungarian society, but was now shorn of its radical democratic implications.

Two severe and related weaknesses undermined the potential success of this new absolutist system, and eventually provoked liberal political reform, an international reorientation of Austria's foreign goals, and a radical structural transformation of the monarchy. The first of these weaknesses was financial. Economic growth was substantial during the 1850s, but so was investment. Economic consolidation at home demanded a less activist policy abroad. Yet Francis Joseph and his ministers were determined during the 1850s to maintain both Austria's great-

power status and its political hegemony in the German Confederation. Both of these policies demanded significant investment in the military. In 1858 already 40 percent of the government's expenditures went to service the state debt. An expensive mobilization during the Crimean War (1853–1856) and a disastrous campaign against Piedmont-Sardinia in 1859 brought the state to the verge of bankruptcy. The threat of fiscal insolvency and the demands of his creditors for an open and credible budgetary process forced the unwilling Francis Joseph to authorize political reform. The second and related weakness in the 1850s was the government's inability to rule Hungary successfully. Widespread passive resistance in the form of withholding taxes in Hungary did not help the fiscal situation either. In the face of attempts to reintroduce German as the language of administration and to restructure and centralize local administration, the regime faced determined hostility and a resurgence in Magyar nationalism among the political classes.

For these reasons, the regime was forced to offer significant political reform both to the liberals and to the Hungarians, eventually creating the Dual Monarchy, Austria-Hungary, from the ruins of the unitary absolutist Austrian state. Military defeat at the hands of Prussia in 1866 also reoriented Austria's foreign policy decisively by removing it from the German question. What is often forgotten is that domestic reform in 1861 and 1867 established firmly constitutional, if structurally very different regimes in both halves of the Dual Monarchy. The dynasty managed to retain its supremacy in foreign policy and military affairs, but liberal reform ended the unquestioned dominance of the Catholic Church in domestic affairs and established an independent judiciary as well as public school systems. Even Francis Joseph's powers in foreign and military affairs were restricted by constitutional budget procedures. The compromise agreement, or Ausgleich, that created Austria-Hungary in 1867 gave each of the two new states complete independence from the other in its internal affairs, and required only that representatives from the two parliaments renegotiate common tariffs, debt policy, and joint finances every ten years. The emperor/king appointed three joint ministers for foreign affairs, defense, and joint finances. In his capacities as emperor of Austria and king of Hungary, Francis Joseph I appointed the prime ministers of each state and presided over both sets of cabinet meetings as well as the meetings of the joint cabinet (usually the three common ministers plus the two prime ministers). Finally it is important for subsequent developments to note that each state maintained the capability to block any significant constitutional change proposed by the other.

HUNGARY AFTER 1867

In Hungary the new regime immediately orchestrated a compromise of its own with Croatia, the *nagodba* of 1868, which offered broad administrative autonomy and a smaller degree of legislative autonomy to Croatia within the Kingdom of Hungary. The governor or *ban* of Croatia, however, was appointed from Budapest, and this arrangement eventually created considerable unrest among Croatian nationalists after 1900. The Hungarian regime formulated a comparatively generous nationality law, designed to facilitate the voluntary assimilation over time of several language groups

who together accounted for over half of Hungary's population. In the 1870s, however, this law was augmented by increasingly draconian policies of forced Magyarization that reduced the rights of linguistic minorities (except for the Croatians) to organize their own education and voluntary cultural associations. Additionally, the restrictive suffrage laws in Hungary privileged the gentry and aristocracy and ensured that political parties representing linguistic minorities never elected more than a 5 to 6 percent share of the deputies to the parliament. In this sense, Hungary constituted a nation-state (or nationalizing state) similar to many of the successor states of the Habsburg Monarchy in the interwar period. But a critical difference between the liberal Kingdom of Hungary and those later interwar states was the relative openness and tolerance the country's leading classes maintained toward those who chose to assimilate, most notably the Jews. An individual who adopted the Magyar language and adhered to its cultural norms gained national rights, whatever religion the person practiced, a situation that was rarely the case in the region after 1918. According to census statistics, these policies had a powerful transforming effect on Hungarian society. Whereas in the 1840s and 1850s only 40 to 42 percent of the population had spoken Magyar, by 1910 that figure had reached 55 percent with the figure for the urban population standing closer to 75 percent.

Hungarian national economic policy produced intensive investment both by the state and private banks in industry and particularly in railroad construction. Although Hungary remained an important agricultural exporter to the Austrian half of the Dual Monarchy, it also experienced significant industrial and per capita income growth during the sixty years after the Ausgleich. Nationalist concerns tended to dominate politics in Hungary, and both social antagonisms and political opposition to the ruling elite liberal party were frequently expressed using a nationalist discourse. At the turn of the century nationalist radicals frequently demanded a revision of the links between Austria and Hungary to loosen the relationship to a merely personal union, and to create a separate Hungarian military with Magyar as its language of command. Francis Joseph parried these challenges by threatening to impose universal manhood suffrage on elections to parliament, a reform that would undoubtedly have weakened the Hungarian political class to the benefit both of linguistic minorities and a disaffected peasantry, landless peasants making up a quarter of the total population in 1900.

AUSTRIA AFTER 1867

Politics in the Austrian or Cisleithanian half of the Monarchy too were dominated by questions of nationalism, but for the opposite reason as in Hungary. Austria was neither a national nor a nationalizing state. The Austrian constitution provided for full equality of language use in the schools and in the civil administration. These guarantees created a significant political space in which nationalist activists might agitate for full implementation and then extension of this promised equality into ever-increasing areas of public life. Although Czech nationalists may have failed to achieve their own compromise that would have given the Kingdom of Bohemia an independent status similar to that enjoyed by Hungary, their activism in the parliament and diets and in the courts helped transform the school system, the internal civil service, and the judiciary by institutionalizing the official use of the Czech language in Bohemia, Moravia, and Silesia. Slovene nationalists gained the same rights for their language in Ljubljana and Carniola as did Italian nationalists in Trieste. Galicia, meanwhile, gained a significant degree of autonomy that gave Polish nationalist politicians broad powers of self-government and replaced the German language with Polish in the administration of the province. This arrangement helped Polish nationalists maintain a harsh political, social, and cultural hegemony over the largely peasant Ruthene or Ukrainian-speaking population that constituted a majority in eastern Galicia. As Ruthene nationalism gained adherents and momentum under the guidance largely of Uniate priests in eastern Galicia, however, Polish rulers were eventually forced to accede to some compromise in their nationalist rule.

As a result, nationalist parties appeared to dominate legislative bodies and popular political discourse throughout the Austrian half of the Monarchy. Most historians have seen this development as injurious to the unity and broader interests of the Monarchy. As suffrage reform mobilized growing numbers of people into public life, political conflict around national issues became increasingly polarized. Activists used strategies of boycott, filibuster, and occasionally street violence to gain their political ends, or to prevent their opponents from gaining theirs. Historians and contemporary observers, however, often misread the significance of much of this radicalism in three distinct ways. First, the radicalizing dynamic was far more the product of conflict *within* the nationalist communities than between them. As a political tool, nationalism tended to produce greater radicalism, as one faction tried to defeat the other by comparing its own virtuous intransigence to its opponent's alleged willingness to compromise. This tactic characterized both the Czech and German nationalist parties in Bohemia, which directed their ire as much against rivals within their national communities as against their national opponents. Second, with some marginal exceptions such as pan-German Georg von Schönerer, nationalist politicians before 1914 never conceived of secession from the Monarchy as their aim. They worked within the system and did not seek its destruction, only its reform. Third, nationalists frequently strengthened dynastic loyalty by counterposing their own loyalty to the crown to the questionable loyalty of their opponents. This last point can be applied to the case of religious diversity in the Monarchy as well. Catholic emperor-king Francis Joseph became the unquestioned and beloved patron of many of the Monarchy's varied religious communities, often seen by them as a beneficent protector in the face of local intolerance from practitioners of other religions.

Taken together these points suggest that traditional interpretations that questioned the state's ability to maintain the loyalty of its peoples, and therefore the very viability of the Austrian half of the Monarchy before 1914, should be treated with caution. If one adds to the equation the significant economic transformation of Austrian society in the two decades before 1914—the growth of a social democratic movement largely loyal to the idea of the multinational state, the success of local self-government institutions, the advent of universal manhood suffrage in 1907, and the national compromises in Moravia, Bukovina, and Galicia—the image of a society on the verge of destruction seems difficult to justify.

FOREIGN POLICY IN THE FINAL DECADES

If anything, Austria-Hungary's foreign policy ambitions and not its domestic political situations suggested far more reasons for concern about its long-term ability to survive. In 1873 Austria-Hungary had joined in a conservative alliance with the Russian and German Empires, the so-called Three Emperors' League. The alliance with Germany outlasted that with Russia, however, as Austria-Hungary clashed continuously with the latter for hegemony in the Balkans. At the Congress of Berlin of 1878, referred to by one historian as "the Monarchy's last unqualified foreign political success" (Okey, p. 370), Austria-Hungary's intervention served the interests of the British and French by helping to check Russian expansion in the region. The Monarchy's subsequent occupation of Bosnia-Herzegovina was controversial at home for its budgetary implications, and among its neighbors because it effectively prevented Serbia from gaining a desired outlet to the Adriatic. The Three Emperors' League was renewed in 1881 at the insistence of Otto von Bismarck, the German chancellor, but it collapsed later in the decade during the Bulgarian crisis when Austria-Hungarian and Russian rivalry over influence in Bulgaria brought the two powers close to war. In 1897 Russian preoccupation with events in the Far East helped make an implicit agreement possible between the two states that informally divided their spheres of influence between the west and east Balkans. Following Russia's defeat at the hands of Japan, however, the Balkan agreement collapsed when Austria-Hungary suddenly annexed Bosnia-Herzegovina in 1908. The annexation was meant to counter Young Turk designs to give Bosnians representation in the new Ottoman parliament, as well as to give Austria-Hungary a foreign policy success. Instead, the annexation permanently frustrated Serb ambitions and severely damaged relations with Russia. The subsequent Balkan Wars of 1912 and 1913 effectively removed the Ottoman Empire from Europe and also saw the considerable territorial expansion of Serbia and the creation of Albania, once again to frustrate Serb hopes for an outlet to the Adriatic. Bosnia-Herzegovina, meanwhile, did not join either half of the Monarchy, but was given special status outside the dual system with its own elected diet.

In 1914 Austria-Hungary certainly had enemies in Serbia and Russia and among Romanian irredentists. Nevertheless, both the Ottoman Empire and Bulgaria were anxious to ally themselves with the Central Powers (the Monarchy, Germany, and Italy), and it could be argued that these developments pointed toward a new balance of power in the Balkans. As in the case of domestic politics, it is difficult to maintain a balanced view of the Monarchy's foreign policy that does not depend in some way for its coherence on the particular outcome of World War I.

See also **Adler, Victor; Bohemia, Moravia, and Silesia; Ferdinand I; Francis I; Francis Joseph; Kossuth, Lajos; Lueger, Karl; Metternich, Clemens von; Palacký, František; Prague Slav Congress; Revolutions of 1848.**

BIBLIOGRAPHY

Berend, Iván T., and György Ránki. *Economic Development in East Central Europe in the Nineteenth and Twentieth Centuries.* New York, 1974.

Boyer, John W. *Political Radicalism in Late Imperial Vienna: The Origins of the Christian Social Movement, 1848–1897.* Chicago, 1981.

———. *Culture and Political Crisis in Vienna: Christian Socialism in Power, 1897–1918.* Chicago, 1995.

Bucur, Maria, and Nancy M. Wingfield, eds. *Staging the Past: The Politics of Commemoration in Habsburg Central Europe, 1848 to the Present.* West Lafayette, Ind., 2001.

Cohen, Gary B. *The Politics of Ethnic Survival: Germans in Prague, 1861–1914.* Princeton, N.J., 1981.

———. *Education and Middle-Class Society in Imperial Austria, 1848–1918.* West Lafayette, Ind., 1996.

Deák, István. *The Lawful Revolution: Louis Kossuth and the Hungarians, 1848–1849.* New York, 1979.

———. *Beyond Nationalism: A Social and Political History of the Habsburg Officer Corps, 1848–1918.* New York, 1990.

Garver, Bruce M. *The Young Czech Party, 1874–1901, and the Emergence of a Multi-party System.* New Haven, Conn., 1978.

Good, David F. *The Economic Rise of the Habsburg Empire, 1750–1914.* Berkeley and Los Angeles, 1984

Himka, John-Paul. *Galician Villagers and the Ukrainian National Movement in the Nineteenth Century.* Edmonton, Alta., 1988.

Janos, Andrew C. *The Politics of Backwardness in Hungary, 1825–1945.* Princeton, N.J., 1982.

Jászi, Oscar. *The Dissolution of the Habsburg Monarchy.* Chicago, 1929.

Judson, Pieter M. *Exclusive Revolutionaries: Liberal Politics, Social Experience, and National Identity in the Austrian Empire, 1848–1914.* Ann Arbor, Mich., 1996.

Kann, Robert A. *A History of the Habsburg Empire, 1526–1918.* Berkeley, Calif., 1974.

King, Jeremy. *Budweisers into Czechs and Germans: A Local History of Bohemian Politics, 1848–1948.* Princeton, N.J., 2002.

Macartney, C. A. *The Habsburg Empire, 1790–1918.* London, 1968.

Nemes, Robert. *The Once and Future Budapest.* Dekalb, Ill., 2005.

Okey, Robin. *The Habsburg Monarchy, c. 1765–1918: From Enlightenment to Eclipse.* New York, 2002.

Sked, Alan. *The Decline and Fall of the Habsburg Empire, 1815–1918.* 2nd ed. New York, 2001.

Stauter-Halsted, Keely. *The Nation in the Village: The Genesis of Peasant National Identity in Austrian Poland, 1848–1914.* Ithaca, N.Y., 2001.

Stourzh, Gerald. "Ethnic Attribution in Late Imperial Austria: Good Intentions, Evil Consequences." In *The Habsburg Legacy: National Identity in Historical Perspective*, edited by Ritchie Robertson and Edward Timms, 67–83. Edinburgh, 1994.

Wandruszka, Adam, and Peter Urbanitsch, eds. *Die Habsburgermonarchie, 1848–1918.* 7 vols. Vienna, 1973–2000.

PIETER M. JUDSON

AUSTRO-PRUSSIAN WAR.

The Austro-Prussian War of 1866, also known as the Seven Weeks' War, was the culmination of a century's tension between the two major German powers. Both Prussia and Austria had vested interests in a status quo that acknowledged Austria's primacy of honor in the German lands while accepting Prussia's status in a "special relationship" acknowledging its de facto influence over its smaller immediate neighbors. Neither state, however, fully trusted the other's long-term goodwill—an underlying tension exacerbated after the revolutions of 1848 on one hand by Prussia's growing economic power and on the other by Austria's declining influence in a Europe increasingly shaped by liberalism and nationalism.

It was in that context in August 1864 that Otto von Bismarck, the Prussian minister-president (prime minister), made an offer it seemed Vienna could not refuse. Prussia and Austria had cooperated to prevent Danish absorption of the "German" duchies of Schleswig and Holstein earlier in the year. Now Bismarck proposed their annexation to Prussia in return for a guarantee of Prussian military support against France in Germany and Italy. Was this meant sincerely, or as a ploy to begin levering Austria out of Germany altogether? Vienna was no more scrupulous and no less ambitious than Berlin. Had it become time to draw a line against the whole pack of Junker militarists? Or was it possible to do business even with a profound cynic like Bismarck?

For almost two years the diplomats jockeyed for position in a pas de deux that saw Bismarck increasingly taking the lead. His goal was to force Austria out of Germany and replace the loose German Confederation by a more structured federal system, centered on Berlin and dominated by Prussia. In addition to challenging directly Austria's position in Schleswig-Holstein, he secured French neutrality through discussions of compensation, and Italian cooperation, using as a lure the Austrian-controlled province of Venetia. In February 1866 Austria responded by beginning a mobilization that was intended to deter further Prussian pressure.

While war was not Bismarck's preferred solution, he was ready to accept it as an ultimate alternative. Prussia's King William I was unwilling to embark on what he regarded as a civil war without indisputable evidence of its necessity. That evidence was provided by Helmuth von Moltke, the chief of the general staff, who as the weeks passed made an increasingly compelling case that Prussia could counter Austria's initiative only by prompt, total mobilization based on the state's comprehensive railway network. Nevertheless it was not until May, and then only in a series of limited orders, that William authorized the mobilization and concentration of Prussia's army. Not until mid-June, a week after Austria had called for the German Confederation's mobilization against Prussia, did the king approve an offensive into Bohemia, where the main Austrian army stood waiting.

That inaction was the taproot of Austrian defeat. The army had no prepared plans for war with

Prussia. Ludwig von Benedek, commanding the North Army, was unwilling to move in any direction as the Prussians mobilized, concentrated, and finally penetrated Bohemia. Moltke had made a strategic virtue of the technical necessity for initially deploying his forces in an arc determined by the major railway junctions. He proposed to march three armies into Bohemia on separate axes, enmeshing his opponent in a retiarius's net and combining only for battle. Insofar as Benedek possessed a strategy, it was that of a secutor: to turn on and eviscerate Moltke's forces in detail as they came within range.

Benedek's options were further reduced when on 24 June the Austrian South Army won a hard-fought victory over the Italians at Custoza—but paid a price that prohibited the immediate dispatch of reinforcements north of the Alps. The Austrians were nevertheless confident in their ability to defeat the Prussians in pitched battle through the use of shock tactics: massed columns of infantry delivering bayonet charges supported by the fire of a rifled artillery significantly superior to its Prussian counterpart. Instead, once the Prussians came through the Bohemian mountains, the Austrians confronted flexible, small-unit fire tactics based on the needle gun, a breech-loading single-shot rifle that despite its technical shortcomings dominated the battlefields of 1866. In a series of preliminary encounters Austrian losses were so high that, as his battered units reeled back, Benedek abandoned thoughts of an operational offensive. Withdrawing to the Elbe River near the old fortress of Königgrätz, he proposed instead to make the Prussians come to him.

With the Elbe behind him, his position was not optimal. In offering compact high ground it nevertheless resembled the developed Union line at Gettysburg, and the Prussians played an even more obliging role on 3 July 1866 than Robert E. Lee's Confederates had done three years earlier. Their First Army pinned itself down in an abortive frontal attack against entrenchments supported by artillery. The Elbe Army, seeking to envelop the Austrian left flank, made slow and uncertain progress. But Benedek had no grip on the battle, and his subordinates in turn became enmeshed in a futile effort to turn the Prussian left. The North Army was off balance and facing the wrong direction when the Prussian Second Army came in from the northwest,

striking the Austrians like a thunderbolt. Only a series of suicidally sacrificial counterattacks enabled Benedek's battered remnants to withdraw across the Elbe.

The "crowning mercy" of Königgrätz deterred any French thoughts of intervention. It convinced the Austrian government to request an armistice on 22 July. William and his generals wanted a victors' peace. Bismarck brokered a compromise that replaced the German Confederation with a North German Confederation firmly under Prussian auspices, but avoided inflicting on Austria the kinds of humiliation that generate long-running antagonism. The Austro-Prussian War was the last of Europe's cabinet wars: a limited conflict for limited objectives. Yet at the same time it established a modern paradigm of deciding wars by single, decisive victories that continues to shape the policy goals of states in the twenty-first century.

See also **Armies; Austria-Hungary; Bismarck, Otto von; Military Tactics; Moltke, Helmuth von.**

BIBLIOGRAPHY

Bucholz, Arden. *Moltke and the German Wars, 1864–1871.* Basingstoke, U.K., 2001.

Craig, Gordon A. *The Battle of Königgrätz: Prussia's Victory over Austria, 1866.* Philadelphia, 1964. Reprint, Philadelphia, 2003. Still the best introduction.

Showalter, Dennis. *The Wars of German Unification.* London, 2004.

Wawro, Geoffrey. *The Austro-Prussian War: Austria's War with Prussia and Italy in 1866.* Cambridge, U.K., 1996. The most detailed account, presented from an Austrian perspective.

DENNIS SHOWALTER

AUTOMOBILE. Germans Carl Friedrich Benz (1844–1929) and Gottlieb Wilhelm Daimler (1834–1900), working separately in the 1880s, both invented small and sufficiently efficient internal combustion engines for a variety of uses. Showing potential applications, each mounted his engine on a chassis. Soon French metalworking firms, most notably Panhard et Levassor and Peugeot, but including a host of other companies, began using the new technology to produce small, gasoline-powered cars. When Édouard Michelin

GENDERING THE AUTOMOBILE

In the late nineteenth century, automobiles were often compared with women, suggesting that both automobiles and women were male possessions. In advertisements, half-naked women were draped over automobiles, implying that the male buyer of the automobile either got the woman as part of the package, or that he would become so irresistible in his new car that any woman would happily undress for him.

The Michelin tire company similarly made the comparison between women and automobiles. But unlike most advertisers, which used mere images and little text, Michelin published weekly newspaper articles, designed to be humorous. In 1914, in the mass-circulation *Le Journal,* the "Michelin Man" declared the ways that an automobile resembled a woman:

> Woman, says the Arab proverb, shares our pains, doubles our joys, and triples our expenses. One can

say the same thing about the automobile. ... The automobile, like woman, makes us see the country. ... To steer her one needs softness, a certain touch, and one recognizes this experience among those who have gotten around. You will tell me that the automobile has the superiority of silence. Would you be quiet! A pretty woman and a car, what could be better for expanding one's circle of acquaintances? The owner of a pretty car and the husband of a pretty woman never risk having too few friends ... and which costs the most, whether you are talking about a woman or a car? Maintenance ... I can't pursue this comparison. It could go on into infinity. ("Le Lundi de Michelin," *Le Journal,* 6 April 1914, p. 5)

Automobiles were clearly gendered, and they were gendered in a way that tended to reinforce existing stereotypes, not to mention male dominance.

(1856–1940) placed the new contraption on pneumatic tires, the automobile became more efficient, more comfortable, and more marketable. The internal combustion engine riding on pneumatic tires became the dominant way to power an automobile.

Until the first decade of the twentieth century, automobiles were the domain of inventors and very wealthy sportsmen. Although the French were widely reputed to have the best roads in Europe—a fact attributed to the elite Corps des Ponts et Chaussées, Napoleonic road building, and better maintenance—even there conditions were hazardous. Across Europe, driving was an adventure, requiring neither drivers' licenses nor car inspections. Early road races, in which circuits were established on preexisting country roads, were feats of survival given uneven surfaces, curves, hills, lack of safety features on cars, mechanical breakdowns, and frequent tire blowouts.

At the turn of the century, wealthy Europeans began to buy automobiles for touring and not just sport, pressuring governments for better roads and creating a veritable tourist infrastructure. Automobile and touring clubs began to publish road maps

and directories of mechanics, hotels at which to stay, and businesses selling tires and gasoline. Tire companies followed suit, as they wanted to encourage tourists to travel more, using more tires: Michelin set the pace with the first *Red Guide* to France in 1900, then Continental and Dunlop copied the effort. Touring clubs and manufacturers both placed road signs designed for automobiles and lobbied governments to take on the responsibility and substantial cost.

With engines invented in Germany, cycling technology perfected in Britain, and a series of French innovations, the automobile was at root European. Within Europe and the world, France quickly became the center of the prewar automobile industry. Until 1904–1905, when cheap Oldsmobiles and Fords emerged in the United States, France produced more automobiles than any country in the world. In 1914, France still exported more automobiles than any other country, including the United States. Within Europe, there were more cars produced in France, and more driven in France, than in any other country. Within France and in Europe generally, the automobile was an *article de luxe,* a luxury item much like the fine silks

Gottlieb Daimler. The pioneering German automobile manufacturer is shown (left) riding in one of his automobiles in this 1886 photograph. LIBRARY OF CONGRESS

and wines that French manufacturers sold to the European bourgeoisie.

SOCIAL DISTINCTIONS

Without much practical use in Europeans' daily lives before 1914, automobiles offered the kind of social distinction money could buy. Neither the working class nor the lower middle class could afford automobiles, let alone the very steep maintenance costs: in 1901, a single tire, unlikely to last more than a couple of thousand kilometers, cost the equivalent of thirty-three days of work by an adult male laborer in the French provinces. The well-heeled upper middle class constituted the primary market before World War I, and advertisements implied that they could be aristocratic if they bought automobiles and their accessories. Advertisements reminded potential buyers that King Edward VII (r. 1901–1910) of the United Kingdom was an auto enthusiast. Automobile and tire makers

named which heads of state and which famed aristocrats drove their products or rode on their tires. The message was clear: by buying a certain kind of automobile, a bourgeois man could have the next best thing to royal or aristocratic lineage.

Early distribution reinforced the image of automobiles as a luxury good. In the annual automobile salons, manufacturers set up exhibits, showing off their products. Potential buyers walked through the salon and ordered a chassis, a motor, any accessories, and then waited for their automobile to be built. The assembly line was not introduced until the eve of World War I and was not widespread in Europe until the interwar years; automobiles before 1914 were essentially custom-made, much as a bourgeois man would go to a tailor, choose a fabric, be measured, and have his suit made. Advertising posters also focused on automobiles as a luxury, a means of setting oneself off from others.

LIMITS OF NINETEENTH-CENTURY AUTOMOBILISM

The environmental challenges posed by the automobile were not obvious in 1914, as most people still traveled by foot, horse, and train, when they traveled at all. And despite the dreams of automobile manufacturers, it was not obvious that the automobile would eventually become a practical conveyance for many, let alone most, Europeans. It was, after all, World War I that first illustrated just how practical automobiles might be: in September 1914, prewar Renault taxis from Paris helped to halt the German advance at the battle of the Marne; in 1917, truck traffic on the *voie sacrée* to Verdun moved men and supplies to the fortress. Only in the interwar years did the lower middle class begin to buy automobiles, and the mass market for automobiles in Europe developed only after World War II.

See also **Airplanes; Railroads; Tourism; Transportation and Communications.**

BIBLIOGRAPHY

Bardou, Jean-Pierre, et al. *The Automobile Revolution: The Impact of an Industry.* Translated by James M. Laux. Chapel Hill, N.C., 1982.

Bertho Lavenir, Catherine. *La roue et le stylo: Comment nous sommes devenus touristes.* Paris, 1997.

Fridenson, Patrick. *Histoire des usines Renault.* Vol. 1: *Naissance de la grande entreprise, 1898–1939.* Paris, 1972.

Harp, Stephen L. *Marketing Michelin: Advertising and Cultural Identity in Twentieth-Century France.* Baltimore, Md., 2001.

Haubner, Barbara. *Nervenkitzel und Freizeitvergnügen: Automobilismus in Deutschland, 1886–1914.* Göttingen, 1998.

Laux, James M. *In First Gear: The French Automobile Industry to 1914.* Liverpool, U.K., 1976.

O'Connell, Sean. *The Car and British Society: Class, Gender, and Motoring, 1896–1939.* Manchester, U.K., 1998.

STEPHEN L. HARP

AVANT-GARDE. Artists as the spiritual leaders of a coming society were first called the avant-garde in a dialogue written in 1825 by the French mathematician and early socialist Olinde Rodrigues (1794–1851), a close friend of the socialist count Henri de Saint-Simon (1760–1825). This first mention of vanguard artists having a key role in shaping the consciousness of the citizens of a coming, utopian society exalts the artists, but restricts their role to transmitting the ideas of the future political leaders. The concept of the avant-garde broke free from this original idea, and has come to refer to a future-bound attitude in the arts associated with radical social progress.

DEFINING CHARACTERISTICS

The military term *avant-garde* (meaning vanguard, or advanced guard) started to be widely used as a metaphor for cultural attitudes in the late nineteenth century, but it never entirely lost its militant overtones. It was applied to literary and artistic currents that blended political dissent with artistic modernity. Artists whose new and unusual work was controversial tended to adopt the strategy of forming groups, thus engendering movements, in the frames of which they would collectively show their work, explain their ideas to the public in writing (which often took the form of manifestos), and thus validate each other's activity. Group presence was more protective and efficient than an individual claim to new concepts and aesthetics. The artists could hold their collectively accepted ideas and works as a shield between themselves and the rest of the society. Avant-garde always refers to a group, or a representative of it, not just an innovative individual.

Avant-garde has become an umbrella term for art pervaded by political, social, and aesthetic radicalism and critique. Socialist, anarchist, communist, or even protofascist ideologies were as frequent among avant-garde artists as apolitical attitudes, but a sense of elitism, an awareness of superiority with regard to traditional art and thinking, characterized the avant-garde movements.

Some of the avant-garde groups did not articulate any program that would transcend their artistic production. Nevertheless, even such groups as the fauves are considered avant-garde by consensus because of their artistic radicalism.

One of the great paradoxes of the various groups and generations of the avant-garde was that they saw themselves as potential leaders of a spiritual and social rebirth while they claimed full independence from any political establishment. Another contradiction lies between the elitism of their aesthetics and their politically egalitarian views.

The avant-gardes came to being amid the religious, philosophical, and cultural crises around the end of the nineteenth century, which followed a time of increasing secularization in Western culture. This culture was not able to provide answers to those basic questions that the French postimpressionist painter Paul Gauguin (1848–1903) asked in the title of one of his last paintings: *Where Do We Come From? What Are We? Where Are We Going?* (1897–1898).

The revolt of the avant-gardes manifested itself in their detachment from the tradition of mimetic representation and the illusion of three-dimensionality. Dissatisfied with Western culture, many avant-garde artists sought truthful and authentic artistic expression in faraway cultures—of Africa, Asia, Oceania, and other tribal cultures—or in the uncorrupted artistic output of children and the mentally ill.

The previously unparalleled development of the sciences and new technologies had a great impact on the visual artists of the avant-garde. In the face of these developments, the avant-garde artists could not be contented with copying the surface of nature. They explored underlying structures, tectonic and/or psychological. The home of the avant-garde was the modern metropolis, where fast-paced life and the synchronicity of parallel events were palpable. The avant-garde was an eminently urban phenomenon unfolding in the print media: the daily press, the little journals, regular art criticism, as well as ongoing debates in cafés, theater lobbies, and just all over town.

Romanticism in the early and mid-nineteenth century, mid-nineteenth-century realism and naturalism, the shocking appearance of impressionism in the 1870s, and the great personalities of postimpressionism, all featured some of the characteristics of the avant-garde either in their innovative aesthetics or subversive ideas, but were not full-fledged movements with political or radical aesthetical agendas. The Arts and Crafts movement in late-nineteenth-century England, with protagonists William Morris (1834–1896), Charles Robert Ashbee (1863–1942), and William Richard Lethaby (1857–1931), was an important precursor of later twentieth-century, socially committed design initiatives, but did not go beyond the needs of the upper middle classes in England.

ART NOUVEAU

Art nouveau was not a subversive movement either, but it reached out to several social classes and brought about profound changes in their lifestyles. This fin-de-siècle new style was an apparently smooth revolt against the disciplined eclecticism and academic rigor of middle-class taste. Its sensuous, curvilinear, or whiplash lines and floral motives conveyed suppressed eroticism and responded to a new desire for decorative ornaments in architecture, design, painting, and sculpture. While the new style was very popular and vigorously promoted modern interior design and product design, it also conveyed the melodramatic, soul-searching, decadent aestheticism of much of the pre–World War I middle-class youth.

The Belgian architects Victor Horta (1861–1947) and Henry van de Velde (1863–1957), the latter also active in design, tapestry, and painting, introduced the new style, which rapidly spread on both sides of the Atlantic. Called Jugendstil in Germany (named after the magazine *Jugend* [Youth], launched in Munich in 1896), art nouveau in France, and Liberty Style in Italy (for the brand name of a textile product with typical art nouveau design), it was in Vienna where the new style became the face of an antiacademic and antitraditional movement called Sezession, in reference to a group of young artists and architects who seceded from the mainstream art world. They built their own exhibition hall, the Vienna Sezession Gallery in 1898 and 1899, the work of the German architect Joseph Maria Olbrich (1867–1908). The central artist of the new wave was the painter Gustav Klimt (1862–1918), a prodigy who had been expected to be the next authority of the Vienna Academy of Fine Arts. Instead Klimt took the liberty to live and paint in the new style. Living unmarried with his girlfriend Emilie Flöge, usually wearing a long blue, self-designed gown, and speaking up against the academy, he indulged in lush, often golden finishes in his pictures, and lavish ornamental details. A favorite of highly erudite upper-class ladies, whom he portrayed, he conveyed the new sense of early-twentieth-century nervousness and anxiety, also found in the Austrian literature of those years. The other successful, but more controversial Viennese painters were the boldly erotic Egon Schiele (1890–1918), the visionary Oskar Kokoschka (1886–1980), and the composer Arnold Schoenberg (1874–1951) who were expressionists rather than representatives of art nouveau.

The architects of the Vienna Sezession included Josef Hoffmann (1870–1956) and Otto Wagner (1841–1918). The designer Kolomann Moser (1868–1918), together with Hoffmann, founded the Wiener Werkstätte, or the Vienna Workshops for Handicrafts, in 1903, a direct offshoot of the Sezession movement. Also based on the concept of the Arts and Crafts movement in England, they turned out a great number of household accessories in the new, fashionable style.

THE FAUVES

The fauves (French for "wild beasts") were the first subversive group of painters in Paris, although the fabric of traditional artistic expression was loosened up in every field and genre. The so-called fauve scandal broke out at the 1905 Paris Salon d'automne, an exhibition venue established for the more radical artists in 1903. Its vice president, Georges Desvallières (1861–1950), who was also in charge of hanging the pictures, hung already controversial works by Henri Matisse (1869–1954)—considered controversial because they were viewed as brutal and unfinished—in the same room with the equally highly colored works of his friends Maurice de Vlaminck (1876–1958), André Derain (1880–1954), Georges Rouault (1871–1958), Albert Marquet (1875–1947), Charles Camoin (1879–1965), and Henri Manguin (1874–1949), so that the new-style paintings appeared as a collective statement on boldly intense, pure colors and deliberate stylization. According to legend, the art critic Louis Vauxcelles spontaneously coined the name *fauves* upon entering this exhibition room. The original group was soon joined by the painters Édouard Vuillard (1868–1940), Raoul Dufy (1877–1953), and Othon Friesz (1879–1949), the Dutch artist Kees van Dongen (1877–1968), and the young Georges Braque (1882–1963).

The fauves had an intense desire for novelty and the direct expression of their emotions by using splashes of raw, strong color. Instead of using color to describe objects, they explored its expressive potential. Matisse's 1905 paintings *Green Stripe (Madame Matisse)*, *Open Window,* and *Woman with the Hat* explode with color. Putting color first—as the visceral element in painting—appeals to the unconscious, and it entails a revolt against the traditional concept of balanced artistic composition. "What I seek above all is expression," Matisse said in the 25 December 1908 issue of *La grande revue,* "Composition is the art of arranging in a decorative manner the various elements which express the painter's feelings and ideas . . . Composition should aim at expression."

According to H. H. Arnason, "The Fauve revolt was the first violent explosion of twentieth century art" (Arnason, p. 104), but it did not last longer than two or three years. After 1908 the fauve painters adopted different idioms.

PRE–WORLD WAR I THEATER AND BALLET IN PARIS

Vibrant theater life was an intense component of the pre–World War I Paris art scene. It was indeed on stage that bourgeois comformism was most violently challenged. The first rogue author was Alfred Jarry (1873–1907), who wrote the scandalous *Ubu roi* (King Ubu) at the age of fifteen, originally as a parody of his math teacher. *Ubu roi,* an absurd piece inspired by William Shakespeare's *Macbeth,* is about the cowardly Ubu whose ambitious wife urges him to murder the king of Poland and become king himself, terrorizing the country until being defeated by the Russian tsar. It was first performed at the Théâtre de l'Oeuvre in 1896. Its harsh language and bold statements on the nature of power—as well as the frequent use of the word *merde* (shit) for bourgeois culture—outraged the audience, but left an indelible memory. Jarry, who wrote two sequels to *Ubu roi, Ubu enchaîné* (1900; Ubu enchained) and *Ubu sur la butte* (1901; Ubu cuckolded), is considered the forerunner of Dada and surrealism.

Cover illustration for Alfred Jarry's play *Ubu Roi*, woodcut by the author, 1896. Jarry, whose works inspired the Theater of the Absurd as well as the Dada and surrealist movements, wrote his most influential work at the age of 15 and died at 34. MARY EVANS PICTURE LIBRARY

Innovative changes in classical ballet were introduced by Sergei Diaghilev (1872–1929), the founder of the Russian Ballet, who moved to Paris in 1906 after a career in St. Petersburg that included artistic and art collecting/exhibition activities. Diaghilev's performances were based on the modern music of Claude Debussy, Maurice Ravel, Sergei Prokofiev, and Igor Stravinsky, among others, which inspired spectacular stage design and modernized choreography, which, in turn, attracted much wider audiences than the aristocratic style of classical ballet. But even this modern version of ballet was challenged by the widely popular American dancer Isadora Duncan (1877–1927) who moved to Paris in 1900 to champion *danse moderne* (modern dance) and made the radical statement that classical ballet was "ugly and against nature." Her bold art and extravagant lifestyle inspired many artists, among them Maurice Denis and Antoine Bourdelle who portrayed her

in the reliefs and murals of the Théâtre des Champs-Élysées, which opened in 1913.

PRE-1914 EXPRESSIONISM IN GERMANY

The fauves had a great impact on German expressionism, and the reasons why these tendencies are categorized separately are historical rather than aesthetic. All these artists were influenced by the expressive art of Vincent van Gogh (1853–1890) and, to a lesser extent, Gauguin.

In 1905 four German students of architecture—Ernst Ludwig Kirchner (1880–1938), Erich Heckel (1883–1970), Karl Schmidt-Rottluff (1884–1976), and Fritz Bleyl (1880–1966)—formed a group in Dresden that they called Die Brücke (The Bridge), following their favorite philosopher Friedrich Nietzsche's line about man being "a bridge between the animal and the superman." In 1906 Kirchner carved their program in wood: "With faith in development, in a new generation whether creative contributors or recipients, we call together all youth who hold to the future. We want to gain elbow room and freedom of life against the well-established older forces. Everyone who with directness and authenticity conveys that which drives them to create—belongs to us."

The group adopted a highly stylized and colorful painterly idiom. Sensitive to the social inequalities in Germany, they expressed the suffering of the deprived in dramatic woodcuts, the rough-hewn texture of which was an adequate vehicle for their emotions. Several German expressionist sculptors, including Käthe Kollwitz (1867–1945), Ernst Barlach (1870–1938), Wilhelm Lehmbruck (1881–1919), and Gerhard Marcks (1889–1981), were also printmakers. In 1906 the leaders of Die Brücke invited the already established painter Emil Nolde (1867–1956) and Max Pechstein (1881–1955) to join the group. In 1910, when the works of Otto Mueller (1874–1930) were rejected by the Berlin Sezession, they quitted it and joined Die Brücke. In 1911 the Czech painter Bohumil Kubista (1884–1918) joined. Bold unmixed colors, posterlike stylization, representations of children, African masks, and artifacts in their paintings indicated their opposition to traditional artistic standards.

In 1911 the group moved to Berlin, where Kirchner painted street scenes, urban landscapes, and sinister cabaret scenes, and Nolde's paintings of similar subject matters also conveyed an anticipation of danger and catastrophe. In Berlin, however, Die Brücke failed to secure subscribers to its planned graphic portfolios, and the group soon dissolved.

The epicenter of expressionist art in Berlin was Der Sturm Gallery, opened in March 1912 by the musician and writer Herwarth Walden (1878–1941). Der Sturm Gallery carried the latest of the avant-garde art from Der Blaue Reiter (The Blue Rider) to the futurists, showed an international array of works from Italy, France, Holland, Russia, and the Czech lands, and invited leading personalities of the avant-garde to give talks. Walden had already been publishing since 1910 a provocative avant-garde weekly, *Der Sturm* (The storm), as a forum for expressionist literature.

Modeled on the Paris Salon d'automne, the Erste Deutsche Herbstsalon (First German Autumn Salon), which Walden organized in Berlin in 1913, was the most important survey show of contemporary avant-garde art in Europe. It included a rich selection of French artists from postimpressionists to cubists and orphists, Italian futurists, Czechs, Russians, and most groups of German expressionists.

In Munich, the capital city of the southern German state of Bavaria, another group of expressionist artists, the Neue Künstlervereinigung (New Artists' Association), was organized in 1909 by the Russian painter Vasily Kandinsky (1866–1944), who moved to Munich in 1896 and became the student of Franz von Stuck (1863–1928). The group first met at tea parties hosted by the Russian émigré baroness and painter Marianne Werefkin (1860–1938). The original members included the German painters Gabriele Münter (1877–1962), Erma Bossi, and Paul Baum (1859–1932), and the Russian artists Alexei Jawlensky (1864–1941), Vladimir Bechtejeff (1878–1971), and Moissei Kogan (1879–1943). In 1910 the French artists Pierre Girieud (1876–1948) and Henri Le Fauconnier (1881–1946) joined. Paul Klee (1879–1940), who first met Kandinsky at Stuck's classes, also exhibited with the group. Typically for the avant-garde, both Kandinsky and Klee were involved with the Munich Artists' Theater (founded in 1908), which aimed at a total aesthetic experience by returning to the mystical-religious origins of the theater as a celebration of life.

The artistic concepts of the group were theorized by Kandinsky, later published in his book *Über das Geistige in der Kunst* (1912; Concerning the spiritual in art): artists have to listen only to their inner inspiration, and not pay attention to the visual appearance of things, which would reduce them to being mere "recording machines" like the impressionists. Kandinsky painted his first abstract painting in 1911. Abstraction divided the group: the German painter Franz Marc (1880–1916), another member of the association, agreed with Kandinsky that dematerialization and spiritualization were the most important pursuits of a painter, but the more conservative elements of the group, led by Alexander Kanoldt (1881–1939) and Adolph Erbsloh (1881–1947), insisted on mimetic representation. The group split in 1911, when the more radical members led by Kandinsky and Marc, and also joined by August Macke (1887–1914), founded the new group Der Blaue Reiter (The Blue Rider), taking the name from the title of the almanac Kandinsky and Marc were working on (published in 1912). Der Blaue Reiter stood for the autonomy of the artist and his work. Nature was no longer reproduced, but *expressed* through autonomous combinations of colors and forms in a certain rhythm. The inner vision of the artist was accepted as the real truth, which proved to be a subversive idea in German culture. This idea had already been championed by the German art historian Wilhelm Worringer, considered the first theorist of expressionism, in his book *Abstraktion und Einfühlung* (1908; *Abstraction and Empathy*, 1953), where he proposed that the work of art is as autonomous an organism as any natural one.

The *Blaue Reiter* almanac demonstrated the equal importance of all creative fields—poetry, prose, music, dance, painting, sculpture, and printmaking by an international selection of artists. The "First Exhibition of the Editors of the Blue Rider" opened on 18 December 1911 and then toured Germany. It was the opening exhibition of the Sturm Gallery. Marc wrote in the almanac: "In this time of the great struggle for a new art we fight like disorganized 'savages' against an old, established power. The battle seems to be unequal, but spiritual matters [are decided] ... only by the power of ideas.... New ideas kill better than steel and destroy what was thought to be indestructible" (Marc, p. 28).

German expressionism did not come to an end in 1914, but during and after World War I it was becoming intensely political, oppositional, and even revolutionary. At the same time, a religious-mystical version of expressionism gained new meaning in the postwar context.

CUBISM

Cubism was created in Paris by the Spanish painter Pablo Picasso (1881–1973) and the French painter Georges Braque (1882–1963) around 1907, under the influence of Paul Cézanne (1839–1906) and, indirectly, the changes in the worldview due to new scientific discoveries. The term *cubism* was coined by the same Louis Vauxcelles who coined the term *fauves,* inspired by Braque's 1908 painting *Houses at L'Estaque,* featuring a crowd of cubic forms. Early cubism was also influenced by African art, which Picasso studied during his many visits to Paris's ethnographic museum, the Musée Trocadéro. Picasso's *Les demoiselles d'Avignon* (1907) was declared the "first twentieth-century painting" by Alfred H. Barr Jr., founder and first director of New York's Museum of Modern Art. The first cubists were joined by further artists including Juan Gris (1887–1927), Jean Metzinger (1883–1956), and Albert Gleizes (1881–1953).

The early cubist paintings, made between 1908 and 1914, are labeled "analytic cubism" for the breaking up—"analysis"—of the objects into small, geometric, intersecting facets, which remained allusive of the original motive (as opposed to post–World War I "synthetic cubism," the synthesizing of originally abstract elements into an evocative composition). The cubists eliminated one-point perspective, interweaving the foreground, middle ground, and background of the painting and compressing a multitude of picture planes into one flat surface.

Around 1912, Picasso started to make his first collages out of fragments of images, textured papers, letters, and numbers. Cubism also influenced twentieth-century sculptors, including

Alexander Archipenko (1887–1964), Raymond Duchamp-Villon (1876–1918), and Jacques Lipchitz (1891–1973).

ORPHISM

Orphism was a version of cubism, the term having been coined in 1912 by the French poet Guillaume Apollinaire for the paintings of Robert Delaunay (1885–1941), which he related to Orpheus, the poet who also played music in Greek mythology. Delaunay, who was originally a cubist, painted colorful pictures that appear as if seen though a prism, which breaks down colors. His wife, Sonia Delaunay-Terk (1885–1979), and the Czech painter František Kupka (1871–1957) were also referred to as Orphist, or Orphic cubist, artists. This short-lived movement briefly included the Duchamp brothers—Marcel Duchamp (1887–1968), his brother Raymond Duchamp-Villon, and their half-brother, Jacques Villon (1875–1963)—and Roger de la Fresnaye (1885–1925). The Orphists' lyrical use of color aiming at color harmonies influenced Der Blaue Reiter as well as the American synchromists.

FUTURISM

Caroline Tisdall and Angelo Bozzolla have argued that "Italian Futurism was the first cultural movement of the twentieth century to aim directly and deliberately at a mass audience" (Tisdall and Bozzolla, p. 7). The movement was single-handedly inaugurated by the poet and editor Filippo Tommaso Marinetti (1876–1944), who published "The Founding and Manifesto of Futurism" in the conservative Paris daily *Le Figaro* on 20 February 1909. He republished it in Italian in the same year in his own Milan-based journal *Poesia* (Poetry). The manifesto was a sweeping wake-up call to fellow Italian artists via the French print media to put their country and culture onto the fast track of history, practicing and celebrating the use of new, speedy vehicles, and new technologies. He calls for the destruction of the monuments of the past, such as museums, libraries, and academies, that he claims are standing in the way of progress; glorifies war as "the hygiene of mankind"; and expresses scorn for women. With "a sort of science fiction prescience" (Perloff, p. 3), Marinetti understood the way the media works, and to what extent the media is the message. He put through his message bluntly, ultimately aiming at changing the world rather than just the arts. He published a number of manifestos and pamphlets, including "Let's Murder the Moonshine" (1909), "Futurist Speech to the English" (1910), and "Futurist Synthesis of the War" (1914). Led by Marinetti, "the caffeine of Europe," futurism was the most radical attempt at destroying the religious and secular authorities and the fake ideals of European cultural tradition. His later fascination with Italian Fascism, however, puts him and his movement apart from the mostly left-leaning currents of the avant-garde.

Marinetti pretended to speak in the name of a group that was nonexistent at the time of the writing of his pamphlet, but that came to being immediately after its publication, when he was joined by the painter and sculptor Umberto Boccioni (1882–1916) and the painters Giacomo Balla (1871–1958), Carlo Carrà (1881–1966), Gino Severini (1883–1966), and Luigi Russolo (1885–1947). The futurists hardly share a painterly style, but they were all fascinated by capturing moving objects within the static picture frame. The futurist architect Antonio Sant'Elia (1888–1916) designed utopian, multilevel metropolises, visions of the future with a never-ending flow of trains, cars, ships, and airplanes.

RAYONISM

Since the late nineteenth century, Russian art was increasingly interconnected with the art of western Europe, and some of the most radical avant-garde originated from Russia. Inspired by the revolutionary times following the Revolution of 1905, the Russian painters Mikhail Larionov (1881–1964) and Natalia Goncharova (1881–1962) launched the Blue Rose group in Moscow in December 1906. Between 1906 and 1909 they began published the avant-garde periodical *Golden Fleece*, the forum of the group, in which they wrote, "We intend to propagate Russian art beyond the country of its birth…in the very process of its development." They were strongly influenced by the primitivist currents of German expressionism, cubism, and futurism—resulting in a cubo-futurist painterly language in Russia, a language they adopted.

In 1911 they launched a new movement, rayonism, which was aesthetically based on the representation of fractured light and light reflec-

tions instead of the light-reflecting objects themselves. Painting the rays of light resulted in abstract paintings, but the rayonists also had a political and sociological agenda. Clearly inspired by Marinetti's manifesto, they emphasized the superiority of everyday technology over artistic achievements: "We declare; the genius of our days to be: trousers, jackets, shoes, tramways, buses, airplanes, railways, magnificent ships—what an enchantment—what a great epoch unrivaled in world history!" they wrote in their own manifesto. They also "translated" Marinetti's nationalism into the Russian context, shunning the West, which, they claimed, is "vulgarizing our Oriental forms." In 1913 Larionov, together with the futurist writer Ilya Zdanevich (1894–1975), also wrote "Why We Paint Ourselves: A Futurist Manifesto," a text quite similar to some of the Italian futurist manifestos.

Larionov and Goncharova worked for Diaghilev's Russian Ballet as set designers and happened to be staying in France at the outbreak of World War I. They never returned to Russia, so rayonism came to an end in 1914.

RUSSIAN FUTURISM AND SUPREMATISM

Russian futurism, like its Italian counterpart, was as much a literary as an artistic movement. The short-lived ego-futurist group (1911–1913) was followed by the hylaens, who were interested in a synthesis of Italian futurism and French cubism. The graphic artist David Burliuk (1882–1967) organized the group, the members of which included the poets Velimir Khlebnikov (1885–1922), Alexei Kruchenykh (1886–1970), and Vladimir Mayakovsky (1893–1930). They closely cooperated with artists who designed their book covers and illustrated their volumes of poetry. The group's manifesto, *A Slap in the Face of Public Taste*, was published in Moscow in 1912.

Suprematism was the initiative of the Russian painter (of Polish and Ukrainian background) Kazimir Malevich (1878–1935). In 1913 Malevich, previously a postimpressionist, worked together with his futurist friends Kruchenykh, Khlebnikov, and the musician, artist, and theorist Mikhail Matyushin (1861–1934) on the theatrical performance of a futurist opera, *Victory over the Sun*. Malevich designed the stage settings and the geometric costumes for the play, which was set "in the tenth house of the future." Out of the black backdrop that he had designed for Act II, he developed a painting by 1915 titled *Black Square on a White Ground*. Out of this abstract picture he developed a body of abstract geometric work with a new sense of bottomless space—a cosmic void rather than the rationalized and illusory space of one-point perspective. He coined the term *suprematism* in reference to "the supremacy of pure sensation" claiming that these images belong to the future, and only the superior sensitivity of the artist can sense and transmit them into the present. He first showed these paintings in an exhibition in Petrograd called "0.10: The Last Futurist Exhibition" in December 1915, where he placed one of several versions of the *Black Square,* which he dubbed "The Zero Point of Painting," or a "Royal Infant," in an upper corner of the room, which is traditionally the shrine for religious icons in Russian Orthodox houses.

See also **Art Nouveau; Cubism; Diaghilev, Sergei; Fauvism; Futurism; Jarry, Alfred; Kandinsky, Vasily; Klimt, Gustav; Matisse, Henri; Picasso, Pablo.**

BIBLIOGRAPHY

Altshuler, Bruce. *The Avant-Garde in Exhibition: New Art in the 20th Century.* New York, 1994.

Arnason, H. H. *A History of Modern Art.* Rev. ed. London, 1977.

Bowlt, John E., ed. and trans. *Russian Art of the Avant-Garde: Theory and Criticism, 1902–1934.* Rev. ed. London, 1988.

Calinescu, Matei. *Five Faces of Modernity: Modernism, Avant-Garde, Decadence, Kitsch, Postmodernism.* Durham, N.C., 1987.

Dube, Wolf-Dieter. *The Expressionists.* Translated by Mary Whittall. London, 1972. Reprint, 1991.

Foster, Hal, Rosalind Krauss, Yve-Alain Bois, and Benjamin H. D. Buchloh. *Art since 1900: Modernism, Antimodernism, Postmodernism.* London, 2004.

Fry, Edward F. *Cubism.* London, 1966.

Kandinsky, Wassily. *Concerning the Spiritual in Art.* Translated by M. T. H. Sadler. New York, 1977. Reprint of *The Art of Spiritual Harmony.* London, 1914.

Lawton, Anna, ed. *Russian Futurism through Its Manifestoes, 1912–1928.* Ithaca, N.Y., 1988.

Marc, Franz. "Die 'Wilden' Deutschlands." In *Der blaue Reiter,* edited by Wassily Kandinsky and Franz Marc. 1912. Reprint, Munich, 1965.

Marinetti, Filippo Tommaso. *Let's Murder the Moonshine: Selected Writings.* Edited by R. W. Flint. Los Angeles, 1972.

Perloff, Marjorie. Preface to *Let's Murder the Moonshine: Selected Writings,* by Filippo Tommaso Marinetti. Edited by R. W. Flint. Los Angeles, 1972.

Tisdall, Caroline, and Angelo Bozzolla. *Futurism.* London, 1977.

Whitfield, Sarah. *Fauvism.* London, 1991.

EVA FORGACS

B

BADEN-POWELL, ROBERT (1857–1941), British army officer and founder of the Boy Scout and Girl Guide movements.

Born in London on 22 February 1857, Robert Stephenson Smyth Baden-Powell was the sixth son of the polymath theologian, the Reverend Baden Powell (1796–1860). After failing the entrance examination for Oxford University, Baden-Powell successfully negotiated the army's tests and was posted as a lieutenant to a cavalry regiment in India in 1876. Following an uncertain start, his career began to flourish and he rose to the rank of lieutenant-colonel in 1897, after seeing service in India, Africa, Ireland, and the Mediterranean. He supplemented his army salary through writing, penning reports for national newspapers, and publishing a number of texts, including a handbook on *Pig-Sticking or Hog Hunting* (1889), a popular pastime among officers in India. Success at pig-sticking, he wrote, proved "our claim to superiority as a dominant race."

Baden-Powell won international fame during the second South African War (1899–1902) between British colonists and South African Boer farmers of Dutch origin. Appointed Commander-in-Chief of North-West forces in South Africa in July 1899, Baden-Powell withdrew his small contingent of troops to the frontier town of Mafeking (now Mafikeng). A large Boer force besieged the town for 217 days between October 1899 and May 1900. The announcement of the relief of Mafeking on 18 May proved one of the high points of popular imperialism in Britain before World War I, igniting frenzied celebrations in London and throughout the country. Baden-Powell won acclaim for his ingenious leadership during the siege, drawing on his passion for theatrical performance by laying false minefields and organizing entertainments to maintain morale. Some scholars, however, have criticized his record, highlighting a disastrous assault on a Boer outpost at the end of 1899 and the suffering of the town's black African population.

The conflict generated intense anxieties about national efficiency, imperial decline, and racial degeneration in Britain. On his return, Baden-Powell was appointed Inspector General of Cavalry and learned that Christian youth groups had been using the handbook of reconnaissance tips that he had completed just before the war, *Aids to Scouting* (1899). Baden-Powell took on the vice-presidency of the Boys' Brigade in 1903, and, inspired by the ideas of Ernest Thompson Seton (1860–1946), founder of the Woodcraft Indians in the United States, began to formulate his own plans to rejuvenate the nation's youth, countering the enervating effects of urban life with strenuous outdoor activity. Encouraged by newspaper magnate Sir Cyril Arthur Pearson (1866–1922), Baden-Powell held an experimental camp for twenty-two boys on Brownsea Island off the south coast of England in July 1907 and composed a new training manual, *Scouting for Boys,* which initially appeared in fortnightly installments in January 1908 before the publication of a single volume in May. *Scouting for Boys* was an eclectic collection of scout rules,

Almost every race, every kind of man, black, white, or yellow, in the world furnishes subjects of King Edward VII.

This vast empire did not grow of itself out of nothing; it was made by your forefathers by dint of hard work and hard fighting, at the sacrifice of their lives—that is, by their hearty patriotism.

Robert Baden-Powell, *Scouting for Boys* (2004 [1908]), p. 26.

stories, games, and practical advice. The book expressed a range of historical and literary influences, from the myth of King Arthur to the writings of Rudyard Kipling (1865–1936), mixing the public school games ethic, Victorian ideas of self-help, an ecumenical Christianity, and imperial patriotism.

The combination of tips on scoutcraft, from tracking horses to tying knots, with uniforms, songs, and rituals, proved highly attractive. Scout troops sprang up throughout the country and in 1908 Baden-Powell was forced, somewhat reluctantly, to establish his own organization, the Boy Scouts. By 1910, when Baden-Powell retired from the army, there were already estimated to be over 100,000 scouts in Britain. Demand led to the publication of a handbook for girls in 1912, the year in which Baden-Powell married Olave St. Clair Soames (1889–1977), who would play an increasingly prominent role in the Girl Guides Association founded in 1915. The movements grew rapidly and Baden-Powell was proclaimed "chief scout of the world" at the first international "jamboree" in London in 1920. The ethos he had sketched out proved adaptable, shifting away from military training after the war, to a more pacific emphasis on good citizenship.

By 1939, membership of the scout and guide movements had reached five million, while *Scouting for Boys* was estimated to have sold more copies than any other book published in English between the wars except the Bible. Baden-Powell died peacefully at his Kenyan bungalow on 8 January 1941, survived by his wife, two daughters, and

one son. Sensational accusations of imperial cruelty and repressed homosexuality have kept Baden-Powell in the public eye in the late twentieth and early twenty-first centuries. Historians continue to debate the balance between militaristic indoctrination and benign self-improvement within the early scouting movement, reflecting tensions and ambiguities in Baden-Powell's own writings.

See also **Childhood and Children; Citizenship; Imperialism.**

BIBLIOGRAPHY

Baden-Powell, Robert. *Scouting for Boys: A Handbook for Instruction in Good Citizenship.* London, 1908. Reprint, Oxford, U.K., 2004.

Jeal, Timothy. *Baden-Powell.* New Haven, Conn., 2001.

MAX JONES

BAGEHOT, WALTER (1826–1877), British writer.

Born in 1826 at Langport, Somerset, the son of the banker Thomas Watson Bagehot and Edith Stuckey, Walter Bagehot was educated at Bristol College, and then at University College, London, where he excelled in classics and philosophy. After completing his MA in 1848, he flirted with a legal career, before following his father into banking. It was, however, a visit to Paris in 1851, coinciding with Louis Napoleon's coup on 2 December, that prompted his first significant literary excursion: a series of letters, published in the Unitarian periodical *The Inquirer*, defending the usurper. Throughout the second half of the 1850s, he combined responsibility for part of the family business with his role as cofounder and coeditor, with his friend R. H. Hutton, of the *National Review*. In 1857, Bagehot commenced his long involvement with *The Economist*, publishing a series of articles on banking. The following year he married Eliza Wilson, the daughter of *The Economist*'s owner, James Wilson. Bagehot soon succeeded Hutton into the editorial chair in 1861, where he remained until his death in 1877. Bagehot maintained an involvement in banking, but it was literary affairs that henceforth dominated his time.

Bagehot's posthumous fame rests primarily upon *The English Constitution*, published in serial form between May 1865 and January 1867. Bagehot presented his essay as a necessary corrective to the notion that the constitution was characterized by the separation of powers and the division of sovereignty. He argued that legislative and executive functions were combined in the cabinet, which governed through the House of Commons. In the first two-thirds of the twentieth century, Bagehot was usually credited with the discovery of the cabinet and the demolition of myths about the mixed constitution. Subsequent research has revealed the extent to which Bagehot—no stranger to an arresting literary device—exaggerated his own novelty. The constitutional preeminence of the Commons, and the role of the cabinet, were both recognized well before the publication of *The English Constitution*. Indeed, Bagehot built upon the foundations of skeptical whigs like the politician Earl Grey, who analyzed the relationship between social structure and the machinery of government. Bagehot has received considerable credit for his claim that "deference" lay at the root of loyalty to the constitution. He distinguished between "dignified" and "efficient" features of the constitution, arguing that it was the glittering appeal of the former—best embodied in the monarchy—that secured the uncomprehending allegiance of the bulk of the populace. The essentially Burkean notion of "deference" has exercised a persistent influence over historical understanding of English politics in the period between the First and the Second Reform Act. Since the 1980s greater emphasis has been laid upon negotiation and contestation in accounts of the relationships between political elite and nation in this period.

There has been much debate over the influence of Bagehot's famous book. Some suggest that the advent of a broader suffrage in 1867 brought the era of Bagehotian parliamentary government to an end, and thus that *The English Constitution* achieved almost instant obsolescence; while others contend that its analysis of the relation between social forces and political traditions offers lasting insights into the development of the British political system. Dispute has been most acute over Bagehot's legacy. Bagehot has been hailed for the perspicuity of his insights into the operation of power, but also chastised for reinforcing a consequentialist focus on political outcomes that neglects questions of justice and entitlement.

In his own time, Bagehot was as renowned for his other works as for *The English Constitution*. His evolutionary and psychological study of *Physics and Politics* (1872) reveals the analytical underpinnings of his work on nineteenth-century Britain. It was much translated in the nineteenth century and influenced the crowd psychologists of the 1890s. His study of *Lombard Street* (1873) provided a much-cited description of the banking system, and an authoritative account of the duty of the Bank of England as the lender of last resort. His studies in political economy were characterized more by practical expertise than by systematic rigor. The former was evident in his invention in 1876 of the treasury bill. His fascination with the psychology of business is apparent in *Postulates of Political Economy* (1876) and *Economic Studies* (1880). In both the variety and the extent of his writing, Bagehot was representative of a particular type and time: the prolific mid-Victorian polymath. Where he excelled, however, was in the brio and verve with which he pursued this role.

See also **Burke, Edmund; Conservatism; Great Britain.**

BIBLIOGRAPHY

Primary Sources

Bagehot, Walter. *The Collected Works of Walter Bagehot.* Edited by Norman St. John-Stevas. 15 vols. London, 1965–1986.

Secondary Sources

Buchan, Alastair. *The Spare Chancellor: The Life of Walter Bagehot.* London, 1959.

Vile, M. J. C. *Constitutionalism and the Separation of Powers.* Oxford, U.K., 1967.

JAMES THOMPSON

BAKUNIN, MIKHAIL (1814–1876), Russian anarchist.

Born a Russian nobleman, Mikhail Alexandrovich Bakunin became a revolutionary and died one of his century's most charismatic and controversial men. He is most famous for leading the anarchist opposition to Karl Marx within the International Workingmen's Association. Their rivalry caused a split within the International and hastened its demise. Bakunin's anarchist criticism of modern life also stimulated theories of "creative destruction" across a range of disciplines, from art to economics. His hairy, bearded image remains a radical icon.

Bakunin lived an adventure-filled life. He was born on his family's serf estate in the province of Tver on 30 May (18 May, old style) 1814; completed the Imperial Artillery School and served briefly as a lieutenant; and then spent the years from 1835 to 1840 studying German idealism and preparing to become a scholar. After traveling to Germany in 1840, however, he abandoned his hopes for a university career and declared himself done with all philosophizing. In 1842 he published a blistering critique of contemporary society titled "The Reaction in Germany: A Fragment by a Frenchman." The essay ended with Bakunin's most famous pronouncement: "The urge to destroy is also a creative urge."

Living in Paris in the 1840s, Bakunin met other radicals, such as Pierre-Joseph Proudhon, George Sand, Louis Blanc, and Marx. During the revolutions of 1848, Bakunin sought to upend the Habsburg and Russian Empires by sparking a pan-Slavic revolutionary movement—but the spark failed to catch. Arrested in Saxony in 1849, Bakunin spent much of the next decade in Austrian and Russian prisons, before being exiled to Siberia by the tsar. Escaping his exile, Bakunin crossed the Pacific and Atlantic Oceans and returned to London, where he was taken in by his fellow Russian émigré, Alexander Herzen.

This began the final and most active phase of Bakunin's life as a revolutionary. First, in 1863, he sought to rally Russian support for the Polish Uprising (a stance that alienated many of his countrymen). Then, in 1869, Bakunin led a group of his Geneva supporters into the International (Marx later accused Bakunin of planning a conspiratorial takeover of the organization). Bakunin's popularity among radicals in Spain, France, and Italy soared, as the Paris Commune made his vision of immediate revolution seem feasible. His ideas also found enthusiastic reception in his native Russia, where university students went out "to the people" inspired by Bakunin's vision of "revolution from below." The Commune's defeat, however, and Bakunin's collaboration with a particularly blood-

thirsty revolutionary named Sergei Nechayev gave Marx an excuse to exclude his rival from the International (1872). Bakunin's health declined thereafter, and he died in Bern, Switzerland, on 1 July (19 June, old style) 1876.

Historians agree that the rivalry between Marx and Bakunin was in part caused by their outsized egos and temperaments. But their antipathy also reflected profound philosophical differences over the nature of revolution, and revolutionary tactics. Marx held that the revolution would be made by the most advanced elements of the working class, who would organize to seize political power. Bakunin, by contrast, believed that Europe's most exploited individuals—its unskilled laborers and peasants—were its most radical revolutionary force. Having no stake in contemporary society, Bakunin argued, the dispossessed masses were also the least corrupted by it. Bakunin also believed that the goal of revolution must be to smash the state, rather than seize it. He held that humanity's future was to live in free federations of small, egalitarian communities. While Marx derided Bakunin as hopelessly naive, Bakunin declared that Marx's vanguard, having seized the state, would inevitably become despotic.

Marx and Bakunin also differed on tactics. While Marx believed the working class must organize politically, Bakunin argued that the role of the revolutionary was merely to strike the spark that unleashed "revolution from below." Attempting to organize or control the revolution would only dampen its progressive energy, he felt, and corrupt radical democracy with the seeds of new political oppression.

Bakunin has passionate critics as well as supporters. His critics see him as an oddly abstract and domineering personality, unwilling and perhaps incapable of imagining the human consequences of his ideas. For his admirers, Bakunin remains an acute critic of modern politics, and an uncompromising symbol of revolution. A gifted polemicist and orator, Bakunin never had the patience for sustained theoretical activity. Most of his effort went into personal letters, journalism, and a few, unfinished longer projects.

See also **Anarchism; Blanc, Louis; First International; Herzen, Alexander; Marx, Karl; Nechayev,**

Sergei; Proudhon, Pierre-Joseph; Revolutions of 1848; Socialism.

BIBLIOGRAPHY

Carr, E. H. *Michael Bakunin.* London, 1937. Reprint, London, 1975.

Crowder, George. *Classical Anarchism: The Political Thought of Godwin, Proudhon, Bakunin, and Kropotkin.* Oxford, U.K., 1991.

International Institute of Social History. *Bakounine: Oeuvres complètes.* CD-ROM. Amsterdam, 2000.

Kelly, Aileen. *Mikhail Bakunin: A Study in the Psychology and Politics of Utopianism.* Oxford, U.K., 1982.

JOHN W. RANDOLPH JR.

BALKAN WARS. The Balkan Wars of 1912–1913 initiated a period of conflict in Europe that would last until 1918 and would endure in one form or another until 1999. These Balkan wars originated in the aspirations of the small nationalist states of southeastern Europe, already having achieved independence from the Ottoman Empire during the nineteenth century, to incorporate members of their nationalities remaining under Ottoman rule and thus achieve their maximum nationalist claims. In this way, the states of Bulgaria, Greece, Montenegro, and Serbia sought to emulate the nineteenth-century nationalist successes of Germany and Italy.

Competing claims to Ottoman-held territories, especially Macedonia, had long prevented the Balkan states from cooperating against the Ottomans. When the Young Turks threatened to reinvigorate the Ottoman Empire after their 1908 coup, the leaders of the Balkan states began to seek ways to overcome their rivalries. Russian diplomacy facilitated their efforts. The Russians wanted to compensate for their setback in the Bosnian Crisis of 1908–1909 by establishing a pro-Russian Balkan alliance intended to impede any further Austro-Hungarian advances in the region. In March 1912, the Bulgarians and Serbs concluded an alliance under the aegis of Russia. Contained within this alliance agreement was a plan for the settlement of the Macedonian problem, including a provision for Russian mediation. The Bulgarians and Serbs then made individual agreements with the Greeks and Montenegrins, who themselves reached an agreement. By September 1912 this loose confederation, the Balkan League, was ready to achieve its goals.

THE FIRST BALKAN WAR

Montenegro began the First Balkan War on 8 October 1912 by declaring war on the Ottoman Empire. Before the other allies could join in, the Ottomans declared war on 17 October on the Balkan League. The Ottomans were confident that their army, recently upgraded with the help of German advisers, would quickly prevail against their Balkan adversaries.

The main theater of the ensuing conflict was Thrace. While one Bulgarian army besieged the major Ottoman fortress at Adrianople (Edirne), two others achieved major victories against the Ottomans at Kirk Kilisse and at Buni Hisar/Lule Burgas. The latter was the largest battle in Europe between the Franco-Prussian War of 1870–1871 and World War I. The Ottomans rallied at the Chataldzha, the last lines of defense before Constantinople. An attack by the exhausted and epidemic-ridden Bulgarians on 17 November against the Ottoman positions failed. Both sides then settled into trench warfare at Chataldzha.

Elsewhere the Serbian army broke the western Ottoman army at Kumanovo on 23 October. The Serbs then advanced against diminishing resistance into Macedonia, Kosovo, and on into Albania, reaching the Adriatic coast in December. The Greek navy prevented the Ottomans from shipping reinforcements from Anatolia to the Balkans. The Greek army advanced in two directions, entering Salonika on 8 November, and further west, bringing the town of Janina under siege. Montenegrin forces advanced into the Sanjak of Novi Pazar and besieged Scutari.

The Ottomans signed an armistice with Bulgaria, Montenegro, and Serbia on 3 December. Greek military operations continued. By this time, Ottoman Europe was limited to the three besieged towns of Adrianople, Janina, and Scutari; the Gallipoli peninsula; and eastern Thrace behind the Chataldzha lines. As a result of the Ottoman collapse, a group of Albanian notables, supported by Austria and Italy, declared Albanian independence on 28 November 1912. While delegations from the

Italian forces invade Albania during the Balkan War of 1912. ©Bettmann/Corbis

Balkan allies attempted to negotiate a final peace with the Ottomans in London, a conference of Great Power ambassadors met also in London to ensure that the interests of the Powers would prevail in any Balkan settlement.

A coup on 23 January 1913 brought a Young Turk government to power in Constantinople. This government was determined to continue the war, mainly in order to retain Adrianople. They denounced the armistice on 30 January. Hostilities recommenced, to the detriment of the Ottomans. Janina fell to the Greeks on 6 March and Adrianople to the Bulgarians on 26 March.

The siege of Scutari, however, incurred international complications. The Austrians demanded that this largely Albanian inhabited town become a part of the new Albanian state. Because of this demand, Serbian forces aiding the Montenegrin

siege withdrew. The Montenegrins persisted in the siege, however, and succeeded in taking the town on 22 April. A Great Power flotilla off the Adriatic coast forced the Montenegrins to withdraw less than two weeks later, on 5 May.

Meanwhile in London, peace negotiations resulted in the preliminary Treaty of London, signed on 30 May 1913 between the Balkan allies and the Ottoman Empire. By this treaty, the Ottoman Empire in Europe consisted of only a narrow band of territory in eastern Thrace defined by a straight line drawn from the Aegean port of Enos to the Black Sea port of Midya.

SECOND BALKAN OR INTERALLIED WAR
During the First Balkan War, while the Bulgarians contended with the major portion of the Ottoman army in Thrace, the Serbs had occupied most of

THESSALONIKI   SURVIVORS

Four young survivors of the Balkan Wars wait on a ship off the coast of Thessaloniki, Greece, c. 1912. ©CORBIS

Macedonia. Austrian prohibitions had prevented the Serbs from realizing their ambitions to an Adriatic port in northern Albania. The Serbs then sought to strengthen their hold on Macedonia in compensation for the loss of an Albanian port. The Greeks had never agreed to any settlement over Macedonia, and also indicated that they would retain the Macedonian areas they had occupied. The Bulgarians had fought the Ottomans for Macedonia. They remained determined to obtain this area. Hostilities among the allies over the Macedonian question escalated throughout the spring of 1913 from exchanges of notes to actual shooting. Russian attempts at mediation between Bulgaria and Serbia were feeble and fruitless.

On the night of 29–30 June 1913, Bulgarian soldiers began local attacks against Serbian positions in Macedonia. These attacks became the signal for the outbreak of general war. The initial Greek and Serb counterattacks pushed the Bulgarians back past their old frontiers. Just

as the Bulgarian army began to stabilize the situation, Romanian and Ottoman soldiers invaded the country. The Romanians sought to obtain southern Dobrudzha to broaden their Black Sea coast and to balance Bulgarian gains elsewhere in the Balkans. The Ottomans wanted to retake Adrianople. The Bulgarian army, already heavily engaged against the Greeks and Serbs, was unable to resist the Romanians and Ottomans. Under these circumstances, Bulgaria had to sue for peace. By the resulting Treaty of Bucharest signed on 10 August, Bulgaria lost most of Macedonia to Greece and Serbia, and southern Dobrudzha to Romania. The Treaty of Constantinople, signed on 30 September 1913, ended Bulgaria's brief control of Adrianople.

CONSEQUENCES

The Balkan Wars resulted in huge military casualties. The Bulgarians lost around 65,000 men, the Greeks 9,500, the Montenegrins 3,000, and the

Serbs at least 36,000. The Ottomans lost as many as 125,000. In addition, tens of thousands of civilians died, from disease and other causes. Deliberate atrocities occurred throughout every theater of war, especially in Kosovo.

The consequences of the Balkan Wars inflamed the nationalist appetites of all participants. The Greeks sought additional gains in Asia Minor, the Serbs in Bosnia, and the Bulgarians seethed with a desire, still unrealized, for Macedonia. The Ottomans also wanted to regain power lost in the Balkan Wars by participating in World War I. These pursuits led to catastrophes for all during or after World War I.

The Great Powers struggled to manage the Balkan Wars. The ambitions of the Serbs to northern Albania and the Adriatic coast and of the Montenegrins to Scutari caused some tensions among them, particularly between Austria-Hungary supporting Albania and Russia supporting Montenegro and Serbia. The Powers themselves coped with these tensions at the London Ambassadors Conference. They even cooperated to eject the Montenegrins from Scutari.

One important consequence of the Balkan Wars was the alienation of Bulgaria from Russia. Up until 1913, Bulgaria had been Russia's most important connection in the Balkan region. Bulgaria's proximity to Constantinople, especially after the gains of the First Balkan War, afforded Russia with a valuable base from which to bring pressure upon this vital area. The failure of Russian diplomacy to mediate the Bulgaro-Serbian dispute over the disposition of Macedonia led to Bulgaria's catastrophic defeat in the Second Balkan War and Bulgaria's turn to the Triple Alliance for redress. This left Serbia as Russia's only ally in the Balkans. When Austro-Hungarian chastisement threatened Serbia in July 1914, the Russians had to act to protect Serbia or else lose the Balkans completely.

The ambitions of the Montenegrins and Serbs in Albania greatly increased Austro-Hungarian antipathy toward these two south Slavic states. The Viennese government became determined that the Serb power should not increase in the Balkans. On three separate occasions, in December 1912, in April 1913, and again after the Balkan Wars in October 1913, the Austro-Hungarians came into conflict with the Serbs and Montenegrins over Alba-

nian issues. Even though war resulted in the summer of 1914 from an event in Bosnia, the conflicts over Albania facilitated the Austrians' decision to fight the Serbs. World War I was not the Third Balkan War, rather the Balkan Wars were the beginning of World War I. Nationalist conflicts persisted in the region from 1912 to 1918. Problems of nationalism, especially in Kosovo and Macedonia, endured over the rest of the twentieth century.

See also **Albania; Bulgaria; Greece; Montenegro; Ottoman Empire; Serbia.**

BIBLIOGRAPHY

Erickson, Edward J. *Defeat in Detail: The Ottoman Army in the Balkans, 1912–1913.* Westport, Conn., 2003.

Hall, Richard C. *The Balkan Wars 1912–1913: Prelude of the First World War.* London, 2000.

Hellenic Army General Staff. *A Concise History of the Balkan Wars, 1912–1913.* Athens, 1998.

Helmreich, E. C. *The Diplomacy of the Balkan Wars, 1912–13.* New York, 1969.

RICHARD C. HALL

BALTIC PROVINCES. *See* **Finland and the Baltic Provinces.**

BALZAC, HONORÉ DE (1799–1850), French novelist best known for his *La Comédie humaine.*

Basically dishonest in love and business, Honoré de Balzac often carried on several affairs at once, even while courting Madame Evelina Hanska, the love of his life, and he viewed debt and contracts as little more than inconveniences until backed against a wall and threatened with prison. Nonetheless, despite his personal flaws, few would disagree that he was one of the great artists of the Western world, a master craftsman who invented devices that became commonplace in the subsequent novel. Proust took the basic idea for the organization of *A la recherché du temps perdu* from Balzac, and virtually all major writers that followed helped themselves to the devices he devised for making his characters come vibrantly alive. He wrote some ninety novels, thirty short stories, five plays, and numerous articles, essays, and letters. None of his fictive works are failures; all can still be read with pleasure. At least a dozen continue to strike readers with the admiration normally reserved for masterpieces. In the course of producing several thousand characters for *La Comédie humaine*, he helped bring the European novel to maturity.

Though a thoroughly mediocre student, young Balzac managed to finish his coursework and in 1816 passed his baccalaureate in law. In the midst of the rejoicing, however, Balzac announced that the law was not for him; he would be a famous author. The family finally promised to support him for two years in a garret while he tried writing, but by 1821 he had still not published anything. He turned to potboilers. Although it is traditional for scholars to find evidence of Balzac's genius in these appalling novels, it takes a considerable amount of good will to do so. Balzac himself termed *L'Héritière de Birague* (1822) "veritable literary pig swill." But he was writing and learning the craft.

At least as important as his writing was the relationship he established with Madame Laure de Berny, a neighbor in Tours. She was born in 1777 and raised at Versailles under the monarchy. Not only had she retained the courtly graciousness of her youth, she had many amusing stories about the court. Balzac found her irresistible. Much of Balzac's vaunted insight into women was due to Mme de Berny's frankness. Mme de Berny did not occupy all of Balzac's time, however. He made another middle-aged conquest in an impoverished Napoleonic duchess, Mme d'Abrantès. While continuing to write, he was encouraged by some small critical success with *Wann-Chlore* (1826). Still, financial success eluded him.

Encouraged by his family, several friends, and his mistresses, he decided to become a businessman. The endeavor set a pattern that would be repeated with few variations through the course of his life. After becoming enthusiastic about some possibility, he invested what funds he had, borrowed more from family, friends, and mistresses, and, then, by one means or another, lost it all. Though the experiences always provided fodder for his creative works, they were otherwise disastrous.

Honoré Balzac. Sculpture by Auguste Rodin, 1897.
©Philadelphia Museum of Art/Corbis

Many of the elements of what would later become *La Comédie humaine* are apparent in *Les Chouans*, the novel Balzac published in 1829 and the first he signed with his own name (to which he added the aristocratic "de"). Although the work is held together by a melodramatic love affair that catered to the public's taste, the novelist rises above the popular elements with an artistic portrayal of his society. From 1829 until 1846, Balzac was to work at a fever pitch, often publishing five or six works a year, with as many others at various stages of completion.

Literary success arrived in 1831. With the acclaim of his novels, financial independence should have followed, but the bills for his tailor, for wine, bookbinding, gloves, entertaining, and finally for a tilbury carriage with a fashionable "tiger" to hold the whip were staggering. Since neither thrift nor moderation were a part of his character, he was forced to develop extraordinarily clever stratagems to avoid his creditors. Most important, he wrote furiously. The year 1831 brought another masterwork, *La Peau de chagrin*. Here, Balzac opens with an impoverished young man, Raphaël de Valentin, living in a garret and struggling to complete a seminal work on the human will. At the moment when Raphaël has been driven by poverty and failure to consider suicide, he is given a magic skin that permits him to do as he wishes by focusing his will. As he wills and receives his wish, however, the skin shrinks, thus reducing the span of his life.

The young novelist was receiving letters from female fans who recognized themselves in his characters. No one knows how many adventures they occasioned, but there were certainly several and at least one child. The most important letter arrived in 1832, signed *L'Etrangère* (the Foreigner or Stranger). A fabulously wealthy Polish countess, married to a man twenty-two years her senior, Evelina Hanska began an affair that was to last, more or less, until Balzac's death.

Eugénie Grandet, one of Balzac's most widely acclaimed masterpieces, appeared in 1833. In spite of being surrounded by gross materialism, the heroine establishes and pursues the spiritual values central to her love of Charles and of the Church. *La Recherche de l'absolu* (1834) considers another kind of spiritualism. Balthazar Claës, an insane scientist who suffers from the monomania that marks so many of Balzac's characters, focuses not on money but on the attempt to find the hypostasis or essential force underlying reality.

Scholars cite *Le Père Goriot* (1834–1835) as the work in which Balzac first made use of the device of systematically reappearing characters. For the novel, he took half a dozen characters from previous novels and short stories. He also mixed in the names of historic personages and added a number of new creations. *Goriot's* dual plots of a dying father and of a young man determined to use any means to rise in society are subordinated to the vision of a degraded world in the early years of the Industrial Revolution, where familial love has no more value than it will bring in cold cash.

In the midst of all this, Balzac was also writing articles, essays, and stories for various reviews and newspapers. Because of modern printing methods and machinery, high-volume, low-cost periodicals became possible. The addictive phrase "continued in the next installment" provided a faithful readership, and "art" became the business of serialized novels. Editors and publishers solicited Balzac's work. Reading rooms waited impatiently for the next installments. *Illusions perdues* (1837–1843) describes the revolutionary changes taking place in printing and publication and, as well, the process of speculation, credit, debt, and bankruptcy.

No one could maintain Balzac's pace, and, in the midst of long hours with pen, manuscripts, and proofs, he had a stroke. It did not slow him for long, however. Soon he began an affair with the Countess Guidoboni-Visconti, continued his abundant correspondence with Mme Hanska claiming undying fidelity, and of course wrote more novels and short stories, including "La messe de l'athée" (1836), "Facino Cane" (1836), *Gambara* (1837), *Les Employés* (1837), and *Massimilla Donni* (1839). Another novel, *Histoire de la grandeur et de la décadence de César Birotteau* (1837), tells the story of one of the thousands who came to Paris to make their fortunes. Unlike many, César does very well, until his notary Roguin embezzles his money and flees. The novel continues the writer's investigation of the world of the small shopkeeper and the demon of speculation. In *Béatrix* (1839–1845), he told the thinly veiled story of Franz Liszt (1811–1886) and Marie-Catherine-Sophie d'Agoult (1805–1876), if not of George Sand (Amandine Dudevant, 1804–1876) and Jules Sandeau (1811–1883).

Eighteen forty-two was an important year for the novelist. Most significant was the publication of the first volume of his monumental cycle, *La Comédie humaine*. The collective title was shrewd. Not only did *Comédie* suggest the personal dramas that would satisfy the hungers of a nineteenth-century audience, it promised something with the significance and beauty of Dante's *Divine Comedy*. In the Avant-propos, Balzac announced that he was a naturalist who would study the various varieties of human beings—whether soldiers, shopkeepers, or criminals—in the same way that scientists investigate plants and animals. The size of Balzac's project and the ultimate shape were outlined several times. He explained that his cycle would be broken into three parts or études. The *Études de mœurs* (Studies of manners) would consider particular social "effects," with a view to universals and types. The subsequent *Études philosophiques* (Philosophical studies) would portray the causes: life struggling with desire. And in the terminal *Études analytiques* (Analytical studies), he would deal with the overriding principles that governed the preceding sections.

It was also in 1842 that Balzac learned that Mme Hanska's husband had passed away. Unfortunately, her ardor had cooled, and his staggering debts chained him to his desk. Even his now impoverished mother was beginning to press for repayment. In his late forties, as he approached the end of his life, he had no peace. Bailiffs beat on the doors of both his hideaways; his tilbury was seized; his investments in the Northern Railways had soured; Louise de Brugnol had stolen Mme Hanska's letters and was blackmailing him; the French Academy preferred mediocrities to him; jealous journalists pilloried him; and worst of all, his lifetime dream of marriage into aristocracy and wealth was crumbling around him. He fell into depression, unable to work.

Fortunately, his fire was reignited when Mme Hanska suddenly announced a visit to Paris. He found the energy to complete *La Dernière Incarnation de Vautrin* (1847, part four of *Splendeurs et misères de courtisanes*), and more important, since they represent two stars in his crown, he finished *La Cousine Bette* (1846) and *Le Cousin Pons* (1847). The terrible account of cousin Bette uses an everyday story of jealousy and weakness to demonstrate how France can be destroyed by its own demons, by the self-indulgence of the idle "haves" that was feeding the envious hatred of the "have-nots." Both of *Les Parents pauvres* paint a France where family, church, and state are so weakened that the depredations of self-centered greed and lust can be controlled only by an evil genius like Vautrin, who was named chief of police.

Balzac's health had definitely turned. His eyes were not functioning properly, he frequently had trouble getting his breath, and his heart was acting up. He wanted nothing so much as to flee Paris and marry his dream. Once he arrived at Mme Hanska's estates in Ukraine, he had another heart attack. Nonetheless, when Mme Hanska finally received the tsar's permission for the marriage, the dying Balzac and gout-suffering Mme Hanska made the long trip to the church in Berdichev and were married on 14 March 1850. Though he perked up on returning to Paris, Balzac was soon bedridden and would die just a few months later on 18 August. "La peau de chagrin," the magic skin, had shrunk to nothing.

Though Balzac's personal life was distressing, he was a genius, and he bestowed the work of a genius on the world. *La Comédie humaine* includes sufficiently numerous masterpieces to have made half a dozen writers famous. It stands comfortably with the great opuses of the Western world, and was to have enormous impact on the novel of France, Italy, Germany, Spain, Russia, England, and, as well, of the Americas. Looking at the matter more than a hundred years later, though Charles Baudelaire's aesthetic importance has been more profound, perhaps only François Rabelais (c. 1494–c. 1553) and Marcel Proust (1871–1922) rival Balzac in impact and only Jean-Jacques Rousseau (1712–1778), Voltaire (1694–1778), and Victor Hugo (1802–1885) have had more impressive international influence. Truly, Balzac was a giant.

See also **Baudelaire, Charles; France; Hugo, Victor; Paris; Zola, Émile.**

BIBLIOGRAPHY

Auerbach, Erich. "In the Hôtel de la Mole." In *Mimesis*, translated by W. R. Trask, 468–82. Princeton, N.J., 1953.

Barbéris, Pierre. *Balzac et le mal du siècle*. 2 volumes. Paris, 1970.

Bardèche, Maurice. *Balzac, romancier*. Paris, 1940.

Citron, Pierre. *Dans Balzac*. Paris, 1986.

Hemmings, F. W. J. *Balzac: An Interpretation of* La Comédie humaine. New York, 1967.

Larthomas, Pierre. "Sur le style de Balzac." *L'Année balzacienne* (1987): 311–327.

Maurois, André. *Prometheus: The Life of Balzac*. Translated by Norman Denny. London, 1965.

Pasco Allan H. *Balzacian Montage: Configuring* La Comédie humaine. Toronto, 1991.

Prendergast, Christopher. *Balzac: Fiction and Melodrama*. London, 1978.

Pugh, Anthony R. *Balzac's Recurring Characters*. Toronto, 1974.

Robb, Graham. *Balzac: A Biography*. London, 1994.

ALLAN H. PASCO

BANKS AND BANKING.

The formalized provision of specialist banking services was beginning to develop in Europe at the opening of the nineteenth century, largely spurred by the growing financial demands of industrialization. Although historians since the 1970s have increasingly considered Europe's modern economic growth to have been a gradual rather than a revolutionary process, they have continued to apply the term *financial revolution* to England at the end of seventeenth century, and to the Continent as a whole during the mid-nineteenth century. The phrase *English financial revolution* relates to the state's increasing use of long-term, funded borrowing for prosecuting war, with the Bank of England's chartering in 1694 being one part of this significant development. The phrase *nineteenth-century European financial revolution* has been used by historians attempting to encapsulate the emergence of large commercial corporate banks starting in the 1850s, in particular, of institutions pursuing both credit and investment banking—"mixed" banking—as undertaken by the ultimately ill-fated French Société Générale de Crédit Mobilier.

These introductory sentences require some immediate qualification and for at least two reasons. Industrialization was a process of regional, if not local, economic change that was more intense in northwestern Europe. As a result, the Continent had a "gradient" of economic transformation throughout the nineteenth century, with the forces of industrialization and their related demands for formalized banking services being progressively weaker toward the Continent's eastern and southern margins. Second, banking was not a new activity, emerging as a response to the Continent's structural economic changes. In particular, merchant bankers had long been present, primarily financing trade—local, regional, and international—with some, such as Hope & Co. in Amsterdam, also becoming increasingly engaged starting in the 1750s in raising loans for European states. Merchant bankers remained a very important group of financial intermediaries, especially in London and Paris, where the most prestigious houses were called collectively *la haute banque*. They continued to facilitate international trade, which expanded rapidly from the 1830s with Europe's industrialization to become global by the 1880s. As before 1800, the major firms, all private partnerships, constituting "high finance" also issued long-term loans, and their security issues enabled infrastructure projects, such as railway building, to be undertaken in Europe starting in the 1830s and around the world in the 1850s.

Although banking's modernization over the nineteenth century was primarily a private, market response to the gamut of industrialization's financial demands, the state played a significant role, as in England at the close of the seventeenth century. Positively, the state chartered a select number of banks, initially called "public banks" and, later, "national banks of issue," some evolving over subsequent decades to be the central banks of the twentieth century. The motives for founding these sizable and powerful—by contemporary standards—institutions were varied, and consequently they fulfilled a wide range of functions for some considerable time. The Austrian National Bank was established in 1815 to assist the Habsburg Monarchy's government in resolving the financial problems caused by the French Revolutionary and Napoleonic Wars (1792–1815). The Bank of France was formed by Napoleon in 1800 to finance his expanding empire. It undertook the state's business and issued notes but also, like merchant bankers, provided credits by discounting bills of exchange. The bank was reorganized in 1805–1806 and again in 1814–1815, when its governor made an unsuccessful attempt to free it from government influence so that it could be a "simple commercial bank." The Bank of France did not become a national bank of issue until the political and economic crises of 1848 resulted in it gaining a monopoly of issuing banknotes.

The foundation of "national banks" beginning in the nineteenth century's early decades was related to the emergence of nation-states. This was particularly the case in Greece where, following the revolt against Ottoman rule (1821–1829), establishing a bank was regarded as a key ingredient of consolidating the new liberated state. Efforts were made starting as early as 1827 but were not successful until 1841 when the National Bank of Greece commenced business. It not only acted as the government's bank and a bank of issue but also was a commercial bank providing mortgage loans as well as discounting bills. Political liberation and unification, however, did not always result in one "national bank of issue." When Italy was created in 1861, it inherited the banks of issue of the former kingdoms and states, and the establishment of a single note issuer was thereafter opposed in parliament and by public opinion. Furthermore, resolving the consequences of the 1866 financial crisis led to a forced solution maintaining a plural note issue. Finally, a compromise 1874 law restricted the number of banks of issue to six. These continued in operation until the severe financial crisis of 1893 resulted in the Bank of Italy's establishment, formed by merging three banks of issue. Nevertheless, the Italian note issue was not to be fully unified and in the hands of the central bank until 1926.

German monetary union preceded political unification. Its germ lay in Prussia's need to have a common coinage in its eastern and western provinces following the kingdom's territorial enlargement at the peace settlement of the Napoleonic Wars. This was achieved by the Coinage Law of 1821, which introduced a common silver standard, the taler—silver currency being common then in Europe. The formation of the Prussian-led Zollverein (customs union) in 1834 and its subsequent extension provided the context for, and made necessary, greater monetary union among its growing number of member states. This was brought about by the Munich Coinage Treaty of 1837 and the Dresden Coinage Convention of 1838. The next step forward came with the Vienna Coinage Treaty of 1857 between Austria and the Zollverein that confirmed the taler's now dominant role and required German state banks of issue to circulate only notes convertible into bullion. In 1867 responsibility for monetary policy was transferred from the Zollverein to the North German Confederation. The creation of the German Reich in 1871, following the Franco-Prussian War (1870–1871), quickly led to the introduction of a new common currency for the German Empire—the gold-based mark—by the coinage laws of December 1871 and July 1873. Soon thereafter, in 1876, the Reichsbank was established, modeled on the Bank of Prussia, which had previously accounted for 66 percent of the total note issue in the German states. The terms of the Reichsbank's charter were deliberately framed to prompt the existing thirty-three note-issuing banks to surrender their circulation rights, while the Reichsbank's own rapid establishment of a considerable branch network together with its inception of giro payments also brought about this desired outcome.

The development of extensive branch networks by some national banks of issue, as in Austria-Hungary, France, and Germany, had the effect of sustaining small, local banks and quasi banks. The Bank of France had 94 provincial branches in 1890, rising to 143 by 1913. These provided a wide range of services that included rediscounting the bills of exchange by which local private houses provided credit to their own customers. In 1891 there were still at least 404 private banks of some size in the French provinces, and a further "census" of French financial institutions in 1908 also enumerated a further 1,200 discount houses and 100 "counting houses" that also provided some banking services, including current accounts.

The ability of these small banks to continue in business until the early twentieth century stemmed from many factors, including local particularism, but one factor that had been significant until the last quarter of the nineteenth century in many European countries was the state's hostility to the establishment of joint-stock banks. This derived from the view that such banks in particular, together with joint-stock companies in general, generated destabilizing speculation. It chimed with individual enterprise being regarded as superior as well as the proper moral basis for conducting business through bankers and other businessmen fully responsible for meeting the debts they incurred. This mind-set among not only legislators but also business communities was especially directed against the free incorporation of joint-stock companies whose shareholders enjoyed limited liability. The result was to delay the substantial development of commercial joint-stock banking until either the impact of financial crisis forced governments to reconsider or the growing demand for credit and other financial facilities led governments, first, to be more readily prepared to charter individual banking institutions and, then, to introduce company law codes permitting free incorporation.

In very broad terms, two forms of commercial joint-stock banking developed across Europe. In England, the emphasis was on these banks taking deposits from the public whereas in Germany and other countries it was their assets that were stressed, *Kreditinstitut* becoming a synonym for the word *bank*. A range of factors was responsible for the long persistence of these differing views of the prime function that a bank performed, but a number have particular importance. England was the first industrialized country with a middle class that was fully developed earlier than in other countries and needed a safe place of deposit for their funds, socioeconomic factors that, in turn, resulted in a very much greater use of checks for making payments than elsewhere in Europe, even in 1914. As a country experiencing the full onset of industrialization somewhat later, the key financial demand in Germany was for credit to facilitate expanding trade and manufacturing.

Commercial joint-stock banking had begun in Scotland during the eighteenth century, undertaken by three chartered banks and subsequently also by provincial banking companies, with Scottish law, exceptionally, not being hostile to banks having large numbers of partners. The "Scottish system" pioneered precociously not only the joint-stock organization of banks but also the granting of overdraft facilities in the form of "cash credits" and the establishment of branch networks. Scottish joint-stock banks accepted deposits, but the initial prime reason for their branches and agency offices was to give each the widest distribution of its notes, put in circulation through discounting. Elements of the Scottish system were subsequently emulated in Ireland, England, and Wales as well as other European countries, including Sweden.

Developing commercial joint-stock banking within Ireland and, then, England and Wales, required overturning the corporate monopolies of both the Bank of Ireland and the Bank of England. The severity of banking crises experienced in Ireland in 1820 and in England in 1825 and 1826 caused the state to intervene. The resultant legislation of 1821, 1824, 1825, and 1826 substantially circumscribed the privileges of, first, the Bank of Ireland and, then, the Bank of England, enabling the ready formation of commercial joint-stock banks in the provinces beyond Dublin and London. The state accepted the argument that the country private banks, which had become numerous since the 1780s, had failed in 1820 and 1825

to 1826 because they lacked equity capital by being restricted by their charters to having no more than six partners. This contention was persuasive because Scotland, with its joint-stock institutions, had not been plagued by bank failure for many years. Nonetheless, shareholders in the new joint-stock banks were not given limited liability by the crisis-induced legislation, whereas the great majority of those subsequently formed in England and Wales did not become branching institutions, but rather remained rooted in their localities for the ensuing half century. Furthermore, until the 1840s managements of the joint-stock banks regarded note issuing as the basis of their businesses.

Joint-stock deposit banking on a substantial scale was developed in London starting in 1833, when its inception was permitted by legislation that confined even further the Bank of England's corporate privileges. From 1834, beginning with the London & Westminster Bank, a growing number of major joint-stock banks of deposit were established in the English metropolis. By mid-1851, their deposits amounted to £14.13 million. A concentration on deposit banking was not an entirely new departure because London private banks, many of which had their origins in goldsmith shops of the late seventeenth century, had developed it over the preceding century. But while London private bankers had supplied, and continued to supply, their services to select clienteles—the aristocracy and major merchants—the new joint-stock banks turned to cultivate their customer bases among the metropolis's growing middle classes, in particular, by the innovation of paying interest on current (or drawing) accounts. In this, there was a further diffusion of Scottish banking practice, the London & Westminster being established by Scotsmen, whereas, with London and the southeast being the English economy's wealthiest region, there was a ready consumer market to penetrate and develop. Undertaking banking through mobilizing deposits liable to be withdrawn on demand or at seven days notice meant that these banks' assets were to comprise primarily short-term bills or overdrafts. These needed to match, in terms of maturities, their liabilities—deposits—so they required an emphasis on maintaining liquidity. This in turn, called for their managements to concentrate principally upon extending short-term credit, for

The Bank of England's weighing room about 1845. ©CORBIS

which discounting the self-liquidating, three-month bill of exchange arising from trade—domestic or international—was an ideal instrument.

It has been argued that countries that industrialized somewhat later than England—"follower countries"—encountered financial problems of different order, which were reflected in the patterns of business pursued by the joint-stock banks that came to be established. In these countries, industrialists sought capital, as well as credit, to exploit the new centralized techniques of production that had been developed in England beginning in the mid-eighteenth century. Furthermore, the supply of capital to manufacturers for building and equipping factories was constrained because investors were risk averse and, consequently, primarily subscribed for government bonds that had stipulated returns rather than the more speculative shares of industrial companies. This particular constellation of financial demand and supply led to the formation of corporate investment

banks—active development institutions—of which the French Société Générale de Crédit Mobilier, established in 1852, is regarded as the prototype.

Although the Crédit Mobilier was emulated in many European countries, leading to the term *mobilier banking*, its underlying conception was not new. The possible need for such a financial institution had been considered in Austria in the late eighteenth century whereas the first corporate investment bank was established in the Low Countries. The Algemeene Nederlandsche Maatschappij ter begunstiging van de Volksvlijt (subsequently the Société Générale de Belgique) was founded by William I on 23 December 1822 to aid the economic development of his new kingdom's southern provinces. Despite this intention, its management did not embark upon investment banking until the late 1820s and then only to a limited degree. A full involvement in mobilier banking commenced in 1835, when the bank issued the shares of two colliery companies and the bank's directors joined the boards of these mines to assist the management of their respective affairs. This innovative step was taken when the bank was beginning to encounter competition from a newly formed, imitative rival, the Banque de Belgique. Over the next four years, the two banks floated fifty-five joint-stock companies, but, as Belgian investors were hesitant over acquiring their shares, they were forced to form holding, or trust, companies, such as the Société Nationale pour Entreprises Industrielles et Commerciales (1835), to take up and retain the securities that the public would not buy. A financial crisis in 1838 was followed by a decade of agricultural depression and a slump in the linen industry that brought the Belgian banks' precocious experiment in investment banking almost to an end.

The banner of investment banking was firmly taken up, almost brazenly so, by the Crédit Mobilier, chartered in 1852 by the regime of Louis-Napoleon Bonaparte (subsequently Napoleon III), whose coup d'état had received little backing from either the Bank of France or among the Parisian *haute banques*. Its management pursued the approach to banking that had been initiated in Belgium over the second quarter of the nineteenth century, albeit concentrating primarily on financing railway building and public works. These interests led the Crédit Mobilier to establish comparable, affiliated banks elsewhere in Europe, such as in Spain and Italy, but a growing involvement in the urban development of Paris and other French cities from the early 1860s led to its crash in 1867.

France's enduring corporate banks were established from 1859, beginning with the chartering of the Crédit Industriel et Commercial. Initially, the founders intended to introduce English deposit banking and the use of the check into France, but over its first years the bank's management largely developed a pattern of business comparable to that of the Crédit Mobilier. With the liberalization of French company law in 1863 and 1867 that allowed free incorporation, further joint-stock banks were formed, of which the most important proved to be the Crédit Lyonnais and the Société Générale pour Favoriser le Développement du Commerce et de l'Industrie en France (to be generally known as Société Générale). Both their managements undertook some investment banking, but its importance

declined with the depression encountered by the French economy during the 1870s. This led the two banks to become more like their English counterparts through being institutions that accepted deposits and discounted bills. Furthermore, they, together with the Comptoir d'Escompte (formed by the government in 1848 to overcome the year's financial and economic crisis, but which had become a chartered commercial bank in 1854), began to set up extensive branch networks, including overseas offices. This move into branching, a decade or more before it was developed on any extensive scale by English joint-stock banks, led to France having a "hybrid" banking structure. By the 1890s, branches of the Comptoir d'Escompte, Crédit Lyonnais, and Société Générale could be found on the principal streets of every French city and town, whereas the numerous local and regional joint-stock banks together with their private counterparts had their offices on side roads or backstreets.

Investment banking had a somewhat different development path in the German states, being initially pursued by private bankers, the heirs of the previous century's court bankers. These banks were located in the principal German cities and continued to be the main agents for financing state governments, undertaken by further developing funding and issuing techniques that their partners were later to employ in assisting private enterprise. This was carried out through mobilizing the houses' equity capital—their clients' deposits—and extending acceptance credits. When their short-term credits were continually renewed, it allowed industrial clients to utilize them for financing capital outlays. This primarily occurred in the Rhineland, bequeathed a liberal economic regime by its Napoleonic occupation, and resulted, for instance, in the overhaul of Gutehoffnungshütte, an integrated iron-making and engineering works, being financed during the 1830s by two private banks: A. Schaaffhausen and von der Heydt-Kersten und Söhne. Rhenish private bankers turned to railway finance and forming insurance companies during the 1830s, and subsequently founded joint-stock banks, with in nearly every case retaining a managing interest in their corporate progenies' affairs. Following the lead that the private banks in the Rhineland took in this form of banking, which involved a close, direct connection with the businesses of major customers, were their counterparts in Berlin, Saxony, and Silesia. During the mid-1850s private bankers in both Rhenish Westphalia and Silesia and, then, Berlin also promoted a number of joint-stock industrial companies.

The baton of investment banking in the German states began to be passed to corporate banks—the *Kreditbanken*—after 1848, when the private bank of A. Schaaffhausen was rescued from collapse, caused by the year's political revolution, by its conversion into a joint-stock company. It resumed business in Cologne as Schaaffhausen'schen Bankverein. The first entirely new institution was the Disconto-Gesellschaft, Berlin, established in 1851 on the model of the French Comptoir d'Escompte, and that, following its reconstitution in 1856, began to develop banking in the mode of the Crédit Mobilier. The problems of financing fixed capital were soon experienced by the Bank für Handel und Industrie zu Darmstadt (generally known as the Darmstädter), set up in 1853. It supported enterprises in the southern German states but, ultimately, to its cost, which, together with the negative effects of the 1857 crisis, led to its management subsequently pursuing more conservative policies. The suite of Germany's foremost corporate banks was filled out by the formations of the Berliner Handelsgesellschaft in 1856, the Deutsche Bank in 1870, and the Dresdner Bank in 1872.

When highlighting the economic development role of corporate investment banks, or "mixed banks" as they became in Germany starting in the 1870s, emphasis is frequently given to their promotion of joint-stock companies, especially industrial undertakings, and their directors becoming board members of these incorporated enterprises, thereby constituting lasting personal interlocks between banking and manufacturing. However, and comparable to the business of private bankers, these corporate banks' importance lay more in their supply of credit, often continually renewed, so that they became, in effect, providers of medium-term finance. Furthermore, as in Germany starting in the 1880s, the managements of investment or mixed banks tended to concentrate on large-scale firms, such collieries or iron and steel works, because they perceived these to involve less risk. Consequently, it has been argued that the patterns of business

followed by the mixed banks of the German Empire had the effect of distorting the economy's structure through supporting heavy industry while neglecting the financial requirements of small and medium-sized firms—the *Mittelstand* of manufacturing industry.

Drawing a dividing line between deposit banking and investment banking can be taken too far because the differences between the businesses pursued by joint-stock banks in England and on the European continent, at least until the 1890s, were more a matter of degree than arising from totally different approaches to meeting customers' requests. Although English joint-stock bankers did not undertake company promotion, their clients had ongoing overdraft facilities that were equivalent to rolled-over, or repeatedly renewed, lines of credit. Furthermore, English bankers "nursed" their manufacturing customers when they experienced major financial problems, if only because bankers had as much interest in ultimately having their loans repaid as industrialists had in rebuilding their businesses. Finally, when an industrial client required capital financing, English bankers would assist by providing advice and indications of where those funds might be obtained.

In 1914 London and Paris were Europe's two major centers of banking. London was the location of 141 bank head offices, and these various banks had in total 6,173 branches. Among them were some of the biggest joint-stock banks in the world—London, City & Midland; Lloyds; London, County & Westminster; and National Provincial Bank of England. They had grown in stature with the onset of the amalgamation movement within English domestic banking during the 1880s, a process that greatly accelerated from the beginning of the twentieth century. Alongside them were British multinational banks, whose fields of operations lay in Africa, Australasia, the Orient, and South America, financially reflecting the British economy's global reach. These institutions were the British expression of the European financial revolution of the mid-nineteenth century, their numbers having substantially increased starting in the late 1850s, following the reform of company law that allowed free incorporation. Uniquely, London also had a money market in which the principals were the discount houses whose operations intermeshed the various businesses undertaken by all of the City's financial undertakings, domestic, colonial, and foreign. This structure, in turn, had arisen from a banking and financial system characterized by each of its component parts increasingly pursuing a specialized function.

Financially, Paris was less than half the size of London, with 57 bank head offices and being the node of branch networks that totaled 1,875 offices. Nevertheless, some of its principal institutions—Crédit Lyonnais, Société Générale, and Comptoir d'Escompte—were equal in size to those of London. Although primarily joint-stock deposit banks, their managements undertook "mixed" banking through developing overseas branch networks, although primarily within the Mediterranean world, and with an increasing turn to investment banking starting in the 1890s.

While Deutsche Bank was the biggest bank in the world in 1914, and Dresdner, Disconto-Gesellschaft, and the Darmstädter featured among the twenty-five largest, Berlin ranked third after London and Paris. This position was particularly pointed up by Berlin-based banks having limited branch networks, the total number of their various constituent offices amounting to only 152. One factor in play was Germany's still developing economic and financial unification. For instance, while Deutsche Bank had formally only fourteen branches in 1914, this was extended through pooling arrangements (*Interessengemeinschaft*) by which it took interests in key provincial banks, although outwardly these linked institutions retained their independence as a gesture to local particularism. Nonetheless, some German provincial banks sustained their autonomy and grew in size, resulting in Bayerische Hypotheken- und Wechsel-Bank, Bayerische Veriensbank, and Schaaffhausen'schen Bankverein being among Europe's largest in 1914. Another shaping characteristic had been the major banks substantial concentration on meeting the demands of the domestic market. Although Deutsche Bank had initially been conceived as an institution for supporting German overseas trade, this strategy began to be successfully executed only in the mid-1880s, when it established an affiliate, Deutsche Uebersee-Bank, and subsequently took an interest in Deutsche-Asiatische Bank.

Starting in the 1880s Europe entered an age of great banks, preeminently those of Britain, France, and Germany, whose "reign" was to continue until the Great Depression of the 1930s. Their size provoked debates at the beginning of the twentieth century over "finance capitalism"—the extent of the power that these great banks wielded over the economies and politics of the nations of Europe. These banks had developed with industrialization and had played some role, which historians continue to debate, in furthering the Continent's economic development. Their growth had also depended upon the state's attitude—whether to permit the establishment, let alone the free formation, of joint-stock banks—and the state's need, as a borrower, for financial resources. In the European rivalry that developed beginning in the 1880s, banks also came to be seen as valuable buttresses of foreign policy through aiding overseas colonial expansion, and by supplying resources to an ally in the alliances that were developing, being most especially the case with the French banks' support of tsarist Russia starting in the 1890s. Furthermore, at the beginning of the twentieth century a persisting question arose regarding the extent to which the state should regulate the activities of banks.

See also **Economic Growth and Industrialism; Monetary Unions; Zollverein.**

BIBLIOGRAPHY

Cameron, Rondo. *Banking in the Early Stages of Industrialization.* New York, 1967.

Cameron, Rondo, ed. *Banking and Economic Development.* New York, 1972.

Cameron, Rondo, and V. I. Bovykin, eds. *International Banking, 1870–1914.* New York, 1991.

Kindleberger, Charles P. *A Financial History of Western Europe.* 2nd ed. New York, 1993.

Pohl, Manfred, and Sabine Freitag, eds. *Handbook on the History of European Banks.* Aldershot, U.K., 1994.

Sylla, Richard, Richard Tilly, and Gabriel Tortella, eds. *The State, the Financial System, and Economic Modernization.* Cambridge, U.K., 1999.

PHILIP COTTRELL

BARBIZON PAINTERS. Although often termed an artistic *school* of Romantic-era France, the Barbizon painters were only sometimes united by place: the village of Barbizon on the edge of the

Fontainebleau forest. Only thirty miles southwest of Paris yet not quite the suburbs, Barbizon was home to an artists' colony from the 1820s that thrived into the 1870s. The old-growth forest (preserved originally as hunting grounds for the king) provided a range of pictorial motifs from ancient oaks and massive boulders to sandy wastelands. Jean-Baptiste-Camille Corot (1796–1875) and some of his followers worked there first in the early 1820s; after the hospitable and economical Auberge Ganne inn opened its doors in 1824, the seasonal bohemian community trooped down from Paris each year in greater numbers. However, few artists associated with Barbizon stayed there for very long; many passed through for just part of a season. When the train line from Paris was extended to Fontainebleau in 1849, the artists' colony became so open to city visitors that artists complained it had become almost a suburb of Paris. By the mid-1850s, painters and the tourists that followed them had become such a large component of the local economy that Barbizon's saint's day festival was changed from winter to late spring to become a large-scale spectacle.

As early as the 1850s, the artistic community at Barbizon had the reputation of being an alternative to the Italianate tradition taught in the École des beaux arts; as such, it attracted an international contingent of artists such as the American painters William Babcock (1826–1899) and William Morris Hunt (1824–1879), who encouraged the purchase of Barbizon paintings by American collectors. In the 1860s, the young painters Jean-Fréderic Bazille (1841–1870) and Claude Monet (1840–1926) (who later would be prominent impressionists) spent summers away from their academic instruction, painting in the forest of Fontainebleau. Artists' colonies sprung up in many nearby towns such as Marlotte, home to playwright Henri Murger (1822–1861) after 1850. The novelist brothers Edmond de Goncourt (1822–1896) and Jules de Goncourt (1830–1870) visited both Marlotte and Barbizon in the 1860s while doing research for their novel of the bohemian artists' life, *Manette Solomon*. After 1870, Barbizon had become a chic vacation spot and spa town.

THE PAINTINGS

Barbizon painters used a traditionally dark palette but left broad brushstrokes visible in the finished

Jean-Baptiste-Camille Corot. Photograph by Nadar, 1854. GETTY IMAGES

work. Dutch seventeenth-century landscapes and the rustic, painterly works of British artist John Constable (1776–1837) were very influential. Due to innovations in artists' materials, namely the recent invention of the portable easel and the marketing of oil paint in metal tubes, the artist could work from nature with more ease than ever before. Typically, Barbizon landscape paintings convey an effect of unfiltered visual sensation before nature; such unmediated freshness was the consequence of painting out of doors and on the spot. This new plein air approach implied a reversal of values in which a personal, subjective response to nature was given priority over the ideal landscape then promoted by the classically minded École de beaux arts in its prize for historical landscape painting (*paysage historique*). Although Barbizon painting was radical in that sketchy, painterly responses to nature were exhibited as finished works, working from direct observation of landscape had roots in seventeenth-century landscape practices. What was new was a shift of assumptions: what had previously been merely a practice of collecting natural views with the goal of recombination and idealization in the studio became an end in itself. Nature, formerly an artistic backdrop for human activity, moved to center stage. And it was the French landscape, close to Paris and neither sublime like the Alps nor conventionally beautiful like the outskirts of Rome, that was now the focus. The forest interior was a staple of Barbizon artists; unlike the classical landscape format that depicts natural forms as defined entities, the certainty of a vista is sacrificed to immerse the viewer's senses in nature. Barbizon painting set an important example for the impressionist style that emerged in the late 1860s; it encouraged young artists to work freely and quickly out of doors, from the visual sensation of the French landscape rather than from an idealized notion of art.

CRITICISM AND RECEPTION

Critics noted that landscape paintings without traditional narrative subjects were increasingly being shown in the Paris Salons of the 1830s. Sometimes indistinguishable one from another, these painters of forest interiors, marshy clearings, and humble peasant scenes were grouped together as the "School of 1830." By midcentury, each critic proposed a different leading figure of this landscape-based school and each labored to define his divergent terms. There were, however, some intersections among the so-called Barbizonnières: most of these men had youthful memories of the July Revolution of 1830 and had experienced the Revolution of 1848 as adults. They had their feet in both the Romantic and realist movements and only cohered as a group by their dedication to the French landscape and their opposition to the classical grip that the Academy still had on the Salons.

Industrialists and other newly monied bourgeoisie, ironically, bought Barbizon paintings with enthusiasm. Unlike large-scale history painting, these typically small paintings were affordable, enjoyable, and thus suitable for the décor of an urban apartment. Art dealers successfully marketed Barbizon painting as a democratic art form that was easy to understand without a privileged education. Its somewhat nostalgic view of nature and the French peasantry was constructed with an urban viewer in mind who appreciated the artists' immersion in nature.

THE ARTISTS

Among the acclaimed Barbizon painters who arrived in the 1830s was Narcisse-Virgile Diaz de La Peña (1808–1876), a charismatic painter of horizonless forest interiors, gypsies, and orientalist fantasies. Also arriving in the 1830s were Jules Dupré (1811–1889) and Théodore Rousseau (1812–1867), who like Diaz found their landscape motifs among the ancient oaks and great boulders of the forest of Fontainebleau. Constant Troyon (1810–1865) was also among this early group in the forest and he later became a specialist in animal genre painting, as did the year-round resident and breeder of pedigree chickens Charles-Émile Jacque (1813–1894). The painting style of Charles-François Daubigny (1817–1878) is closely associated with this group, although he preferred to paint views along the banks of the river Oise and he settled in the town of Auvers-sur-Oise. Unlike the later impressionists, this was not an urbane group that frequented cafés or showed their work apart from the official Salon. Some painted side by side, and many of these somewhat reclusive artists developed strong friendships.

The most acclaimed artists of Barbizon were its few year-round painters. Rousseau spent many summers and the last decade of his life there; Jean-François Millet (1814–1875) arrived in 1849 fleeing the cholera that ravaged Paris on the heels of the Revolution of 1848. Rousseau came to be known as "the great refused one" because his dark, painterly landscapes were so consistently excluded by the classically oriented Salon juries from 1836 to 1841. His unfortunate technique of multiple layers of pigments and varnish has caused many of his landscapes to permanently darken. After the Revolution of 1848, the defiant stance taken by the Barbizon painters against the conservative ideals of the Academy had broad appeal as a Republican, anti-authoritarian aesthetic. In the short-lived Second Republic (1848–1852), Rousseau received his first official commission and won medals of honor, but con-

The Haymakers, painting by Jean-François Millet, 1850. ERICH LESSING/ART RESOURCE, NY

tinued to struggle with the classical prejudices of the Academy until his death in 1867. Rousseau's ecological sentiments were ahead of his time: from the 1840s onward, the artist lobbied for the preservation of the forest.

Millet's memories of his childhood in coastal Normandy informed his many rural images, such as *The Sower* (1850). Popular biography of the later nineteenth century celebrated him as the one "true peasant" of Barbizon with the most authentic contact with rural life. Primarily a painter of the figure, after relocating from Paris to Barbizon in 1849 Millet focused on the French peasant. Although the poverty and piety of his youth was greatly exaggerated by late-nineteenth-century

biographers, Millet had a sustained and informed interest in depicting the rituals of seasonal rural labor. Millet rarely worked from models or in the landscape, preferring to refine his drawings until he had achieved the essence of a bodily gesture. Many critics have pointed to the classicism underlying his compositions. As seen in *The Gleaners* (1857), his attitude seemed to have been sometimes nostalgic, sometimes ambivalent to the changes that the peasantry were undergoing due to rural depopulation and increasingly mechanized agricultural practices. Millet denied politicized interpretations of his paintings yet continued to produce works that inspired readings of socialist sympathy for the plight of the impoverished peasant. In the case of

Man with a Hoe (1862), Millet proclaimed a fatalistic view of the peasants' bond to the soil. Like Rousseau, Millet was supported by leftist art critics like Théophile Thoré (1807–1869), who found their realist "savagery" crucial to the revitalization of art in France. Millet's death in 1875 and his ensuing deification as peasant painter encouraged many young artists to make pilgrimages to Barbizon and seek out rural subject matter in other artists' colonies that were being founded across Europe.

See also **Corot, Jean-Baptiste-Camille; Impressionism; Millet, Jean-François; Painting; Realism and Naturalism.**

BIBLIOGRAPHY

Adams, Steven. *The Barbizon School and the Origins of Impressionism.* London, 1994.

Brown, Marilyn. "Barbizon and Myths of Bohemianism." In *Barbizon: Malerei der Natur, Natur der Malerei,* edited by Andreas Burmester, Christoph Heilmann, and Michael Zimmerman. Munich, 1999.

Green, Nicholas. *The Spectacle of Nature: Landscape and Bourgeois Culture in Nineteenth-Century France.* Manchester, N.Y., 1990.

Herbert, Robert L. *Barbizon Revisited.* New York, 1962.

Jacobs, Michael. *The Good and Simple Life: Artist Colonies in Europe and America.* Oxford, U.K., 1985.

Lübbren, Nina. *Rural Artists' Colonies in Europe, 1870–1910.* New Brunswick, N.J., 2001.

McWilliam, Neil. "Mythologizing Millet." In *Barbizon: Malerei der Natur, Natur der Malerei,* edited by Andreas Burmester, Christoph Heilmann, and Michael Zimmerman. Munich, 1999.

Thomas, Greg M. *Art and Ecology in Nineteenth-Century France: The Landscapes of Théodore Rousseau.* Princeton, N.J., 2000.

MAURA COUGHLIN

BARCELONA. Until the end of the eighteenth century Barcelona had a long tradition in the production and overseas trade of textiles. Textile and wine production represented the two most important sectors of the Catalan economy. In the textile industry, the effects of early industrialization were evident in signs of workers' unrest. Peasants and workers from factories outside the Barcelona wall kept migrating to the city looking for jobs in the mills. Unemployment, taxes, and high corn prices caused the food riots of March 1789. In this year 130,000 people lived in cramped conditions inside the city walls.

Barcelona began the nineteenth century with an economic disaster. Spain had sided with the French during the Napoleonic Wars, which brought about a British blockade of Spanish trade with America. The corresponding slowdown in textile and wine production caused widespread unemployment. Exports to the American colonies declined drastically, from 20 million pesetas in 1804 to fifty thousand in 1807. When Napoleon's army occupied the peninsula from 1804 to 1814, Catalonia refused to acknowledge the French monarch who seized the throne. Like the rest of the cities in the peninsula, Barcelona was occupied, but resistance in the countryside continued. The French presence made Catalans reconsider the future course of their state. In 1810 a national parliament met in Cadiz and laid the basis for a new liberal bourgeois state. However, when King Ferdinand VII (r. March–May 1808, 1814–1833) returned in 1814, he effectively allied with the church, the nobility, and other conservative groups to block liberal reform.

CITY CHANGES AND CONVENT BURNING
The changes to Old Barcelona during the nineteenth century were the result of the French occupation, of the continuous attacks on the symbols of royal authority and the church, and of town planning by liberal politicians. During the French occupation, convents and monasteries were emptied and used as barracks, stores, and stables. The fourteenth-century convent of Jonqueres became a military hospital. The Cementiri de l'Est (Eastern Cemetery) was inaugurated on a plot of land on the outskirts of the city. Although initially opposed by many, by the end of the century it became accepted as one of Barcelona's landmarks. In 1820, during a brief period of liberalism, a project to improve the status of the Barri Gotic (Gothic Quarter) began. The squares of Plaça Reial, the Plaça Sant Jaume, and the Carrer de Ferran marked the first stage of the project. The project of the Plaça Sant Jaume required the demolition of one of the finest Romanesque churches in Barcelona, the Church

of Sant Jaume. In 1821 a paved street, a continuation of the line of the Ramblas, was designed to link the Ramblas with the village of Gracia, thus emerging as the Paseo de Gracia. This area became popular among the upper middle classes when a park called the Camps Elisis was built in 1853 next to the Paseo de Gracia. This new site replaced the Jardi del General, which was located in the port area, as the most attractive place for Barcelonese social life. The Camps Elisis offered extensive promenades among fountains, inns, dance halls, and an open theater. As the botanical gardens were moved out of the walls in 1834, a breach was opened for the first time in the city walls to connect the gardens with the Paseo de Gracia.

When Ferdinand VII died, a conflict over the legitimacy of the Bourbon succession broke out in 1833. In the summer of 1835 revolutionary mobs who opposed absolutism burned many convents; among them the great Cistercian abbey of Poblet, the Benedictine monastery of Sant Cugat del Valles, and the Carthusian convents of Scala Dei and Montalegre. In Barcelona, angry crowds destroyed the interior of the church and convent of the Carme. Infuriated workers attacked the first steam factory of Spain, the Bonaplata works, burning it down.

In 1837 the liberal government declared that all church land inside the city walls could be sold by auction. The entrepreneurship of the bourgeoisie who had acquired this land brought about the destruction of important buildings: the Royal Chapel of Saint Agatha, the sixteenth-century Convent of Saint Joseph and the fourteenth-century Convent of Saint Mary of Jerusalem. Only then did the city have space for the emergence of new buildings that would enhance Barcelona's cultural life. The Theater del Liceu was originally built in 1847 on the site of an old convent. Although the Liceu was destroyed by a fire in 1861, the construction of a new edifice within a year indicates the importance that the city's elites placed on opera. The Palau de la Música Catalana was built on the site of the Church of Saint Vincent de Paul to house a musical organization called Orfeó Català. The Plaça Reial was designed by Francesc-Daniel Molina i Casamajo, modeled after residential squares of France. The shine of the Plaça Reial darkened after 1880, when the bourgeoisie who had occupied its luxurious apartments moved to the Eixample, the new urban development of the city. The municipality established a committee in 1848 to control the building of highways. Between 1840 and 1860 the railway expanded, and a modern port opened to allow for the growth of trade.

SOCIAL UNREST AND ANARCHISM

In 1843 the Barcelonese revolted against the liberal government. The insurrection became known as the Pastry Cooks' revolt because it began as a small merchant and artisan protest influenced by socialists, and later became an integral part of Catalan politics from the 1840s onward.

Barcelona's population rose to 189,000 in 1850. The living and working conditions for workers in Barcelona worsened; wages decreased 11 percent between 1849 and 1862. In 1854, after a cholera epidemic, many enraged unemployed industrial workers took part in the demolition of the city walls, which were seen as a symbol of oppression. Malnutrition, sickness, and appalling living conditions were the norm among the working class. By the end of the century anarchist ideas had permeated the workers in Barcelona. Throughout the 1890s Barcelona saw a continuous chain of bomb explosions. The targets of these attacks were the authorities and the rich. One bomb exploded during an opera at the Liceu, killing fourteen people. Another spectacular episode occurred when a bomb was thrown at a religious procession on the feast of Corpus Christi in 1896. The authorities responded with a general roundup of anarchists and anticlericals, some of whom who were tortured in Montjuic. Some of them were convicted and executed, while others were sent into exile.

TRAGIC WEEK

The 1898 loss of Cuba to the United States was one of the biggest humiliations in Spanish history. This event had important repercussions for Catalan industry; without colonial markets, the economic growth of Barcelona slowed. Several sectors of Catalan society demanded drastic government reforms. By 1900 class warfare was the biggest threat to Barcelona's economic and political progress. A violent episode of mass revolts known as the "Tragic Week" occurred in Barcelona on July

1909. Eighty buildings were set on fire, most of them convents and parish churches. Although it is clear that the power and influence of the church in secular matters was challenged, Catalan regionalism also played an important role.

CATALANISM

In the 1860s several intellectuals, inspired by the idea that Catalan culture was under attack from foreign influence, began a campaign to revive interest in folk culture—literature, language, and music—where, according to them, the roots of Catalanism laid. This idealization of the Catalan past was the origin of a cultural movement called the Renaixença (the Renaissance or rebirth). Anselm Clere, a musician with political interests, contributed to the emergence of a new appreciation for popular songs. In poetry, Antoni de Bofarull i de Brocà promoted the work of poets in Catalan. In 1859 the Salo de Cent de Barcelona hosted a literary showcase called the Jocs Florals, whose origin dated from the Middle Ages. During the first ten years of the Restoration, Catalanism was transformed from a cultural movement into a political one. The first Catalan-language newspaper was founded in Barcelona in 1879. Three years later, a political party called Centre Català was founded and became the unifying organization for Catalanist aspirations.

GOLD FEVER

Between 1876 and 1883 there was a surge in economic growth; production in the cotton industry tripled and sixteen new banks were created. During this period, known as the Febre d'Or, or "gold fever," massive amounts of credit were used to finance railroads, mines, and urbanization. The largest urban-planning project of the century was commissioned to Ildefons Cerdà, a civil engineer who firmly believed that the embrace of technological innovations—gas, steam, and electricity—could improve peoples' living conditions. Unlike other European cities, Barcelona's old city did not need to be altered because there was open space between the city and the adjacent towns that surrounded the city. Modern Barcelona has been the result of a process of conurbation—the city growing outward, and the hinterland towns growing to meet it. The Eixample, as the new part of the city is called, was a grid with no relation to the old city. A modular city with no center, it could be expanded without apparent limits. Cerdà's contemporary critics found his project vulgar and monotonous. On 4 October 1860 Queen Isabella II (r. 1833–1868) laid the first stone of the Eixample. By 1872 there were around one thousand residential buildings housing forty thousand people. The buildings were not equipped with proper drainage and water supply; as a result, by 1890 the Eixample was regularly hit by epidemics of cholera and typhoid. Cerdà had planned for structures 57 feet high, but already by 1891 new building codes allowed 65-foot constructions.

In 1870 two public markets were built: the Mercat del Born and the Mercat de Sant Antoni. In the Eixample, the new University of Barcelona was built in 1868 under the design of architect Elias Rogent i Amat. This building was an amalgam of architectural styles, but its Catalan Romanesque reflected national sensibilities emphasized by intellectuals of the Renaixenca. La Ciutadella (The Citadel) had survived the destruction of the Bourbon walls early in the century. During the Revolution of 1868 La Ciutadella was destroyed, and a public park and private housing was built on its site.

THE UNIVERSAL EXPOSITION

By 1883 the Catalan economic boom came to an end. A plague that had destroyed French vineyards reached Catalonia, where it destroyed the industry almost in its totality. The situation worsened when a crisis at the Paris stock exchange drove the Catalan economy into a recession. Migration to Barcelona was a consequence of fewer opportunities in the region. While in 1887 one of seven Catalans lived in the city, by 1900 one in four Catalans lived in Barcelona. By 1834 the population was 135,000, and by 1900 it had risen to 500,000. The Exposition of 1888 was organized with the hope of bringing fast relief to the stagnant economy. The most important symbol of Barcelona was the statue of Christopher Columbus built in the Place del Portal de la Pau. Nineteenth-century Catalans believed that Columbus was Catalan. It is significant that the statue is pointing to the sea with its back to Castile, a gesture of the tension that existed between the central government in Madrid and Catalonia. Several avenues were urbanized to prepare the city for the major event. In

Casa Battló, Barcelona. This house is one of the many important structures created in a radical art nouveau style by architect Antonio Gaudi during the early decades of the twentieth century. ©OWEN FRANKEN/CORBIS

1882 the Passeig de Colom was the first street in the city to have electric light. Given the lack of first-class lodgings, the Gran Hotel International was a much-needed structure for the occasion. It was built in fifty-three days and was not able to satisfy the demand for lodging. The Exposition remained opened for nine months and attracted around six thousand people a day.

MODERNISM

The last decade of the nineteenth century brought a sense of confidence in the economic prospects for the future. Nevertheless, labor strikes and anarchist attacks darkened the optimism of the middle classes. The *colonias industrials* were built in response to workers' demands. In these communal factory towns, the bosses would provide food,

education, housing, and medical assistance. Eusebi Güell, one of the richest entrepreneurs in Catalonia, commissioned Antoni Gaudi for the construction of the church in the mill town that Güell was building to improve living and working conditions. In the 1890s a group of very talented and imaginative architects gave the city some of the most important buildings of the century. Catalan modernism was a combination of styles—mainly Gothic and Arabic—that found its inspiration in the past. The most remarkable landmark of early Modernista architecture is the Café-Restaurant by architect Lluis Domenech i Montaner. In this building, he defied architectural standards by using mostly brick, a material considered unattractive. Domenech was commissioned to design several private residences: the Editorial Montaner i Simon, the Casa Tomas, and the Casa Iuster. His biggest project was the Hospital de la Santa Creu i Sant Pau, or Hospital of the Holy Cross and Saint Paul. This project was welcomed by the Barcelonese, who until 1900 did not have an acceptable general hospital. Domenech wanted to create an original and appealing building in order to break with the similarities between hospitals and prisons.

The next great architect of Barcelona was Josep Puig i Cadafalch. He was mostly interested in High Gothic style. His most remarkable works are also private residences: the Casa de les Punxes, or the House of Points, built in 1903–1905, and the Casa Amatller in 1898. Antoni Gaudi is still considered by many the most grandiose architect of Catalan origin since the Middle Ages. The Guell park was commissioned to Gaudi when he was fifty years old. This project was originally designed to become a high-income housing enterprise. With the construction materials and designs used in the park, Gaudi made a statement on Catalan nationalism. Gaudi saw Catalans as inherently different from all other Spaniards in all respects. Gaudi remodeled La Casa Batllo for the textile tycoon Josep Batllo. After this project, he began the Casa Milà, known as La Pedrera, or "The Stone Quarry." His project of crowning the building with a gigantic sculpture of the Virgin Mary was canceled in response to the events of the Tragic Week. In 1884 Gaudi started working on the Sagrada Familia (Holy Family), a project that had been started by another architect. According to Catholic conservatives, the Sagrada

Familia was meant to be a place of prayer and contrition for the sins of modernism that were displacing the traditional world. It was never finished for lack of funds. Gaudi begged from door to door for money to complete the project. Japanese foundations and Spanish Catholics still contribute to its construction with important sums, but it remains incomplete.

See also **Cities and Towns; Spain.**

BIBLIOGRAPHY

Connelly Ullman, Joan. *The Tragic Week: A Study of Anticlericalism in Spain, 1875–1912.* Cambridge, Mass., 1968.

Ealham, Chris. *Class, Culture, and Conflict in Barcelona, 1898–1937.* London, 2005.

Fernandez-Armesto, Felipe. *Barcelona: A Thousand Years of the City's Past.* London, 1991.

Hughes, Robert. *Barcelona.* New York, 1992.

Thomson, J. K. J. *A Distinctive Industrialization: Cotton in Barcelona, 1728–1832.* New York, 1992.

Wray McDonogh, Gary. *Good Families of Barcelona: A Social History of Power in the Industrial Era.* Princeton: N.J., 1986.

ELOINA M. VILLEGAS TENORIO

BARRÈS, MAURICE (1862–1923), French writer and political figure.

Regarded as a leading writer of his day, Maurice Barrès is now seen as a second-rate novelist, at best. However, while his contemporaries considered him a fairly minor political presence, Barrès has become, in the hands of historians, an important, indeed an emblematic, personnage of late-nineteenth- and early-twentieth-century French society. He remains one of those characters with whom the historian of Third Republic France is all too familiar, if never comfortable: an ambiguous, difficult-to-slot, controversial figure—of a certain notoreity and very uncertain fame in two different realms, the political and the literary-cultural.

The coddled son of Lorraine bourgeoisie, Barrès came to Paris in his late teens, ostensibly to study law, but in fact intent on making a name in letters. Before he was thirty, Barrès had produced reams of tendentious journalism and numerous books and novels (mostly romans à clef), including *L'Ennemis des lois* (1893; The enemy of law) and *Le culte du moi* (The cult of myself), comprising *Sous l'oeil des barbares* (1888; Under the eye of the barbarians), *Un homme libre* (1889; A free man), and *Le jardin de Bérénice* (1891; The garden of Berenice). Elegantly crafted, stingingly ironic toward received values and hierarchies, and, throughout, unfailingly and remorselessly self-absorbed, Barrès's works earned him the sobriquet "Prince of [Today's] Youth."

The works are quite apolitical and sophisticated in outlook. In a famous piece (published in 1892 in *Le Figaro*, the leading conservative newspaper of the day) on the ongoing literary "quarrel between the nationalists and the cosmopolitans" Barrès sided squarely with the latter. The young Barrès exercised a huge influence over the minds and sensibilities of many French literary giants, from Marcel Proust (1871–1922) and André-Paul-Guillaume Gide (1869–1951), to Henry-Marie-Joseph Montherlant (1896–1972), Jean Cocteau (1889–1963), and François Mauriac (1885–1970), all superior to him in talent. If many of them would criticize the later Barrès; none would gainsay his inspiration to them.

In the midst of a sky-rocketing literary career, while all of twenty-five years old, Barrès became embroiled in one of the most seductive and complex affairs of modern French political history: the movement led by a renegade general, Georges-Ernest-Jean-Marie Boulanger (1837–1891), aimed against the constituted government of the Third Republic. The renowned aesthete, dilletante, narcissist, and cosmopolitan Barrès committed himself to a panoply of conservative political views, ranging from irredentism (*revanchisme*; a policy directed toward recovering the lost territories of Alsace and Lorraine, taken by Germany in 1871) and jingoist xenophobia, to antiliberalism and a species of anti-Semitic populist socialism that can be considered a precursor of French fascism of the 1930s. Barrès furthermore became an expert on Napoleon Bonaparte (Napoleon I; r. 1804–1814/15) and other such "professors of energy," as he famously dubs dubious military heroes.

The political masts to which Barrès henceforward lashed himself thus included the most rebarbative movements in pre–World War I French history—

Boulangism, anti-Dreyfusism, and anti-Semitism. He served them in a number of ways, standing in many elections and being returned to the Chamber of Deputies for Nancy, and later for Neuilly, a fashionable suburb of Paris. He edited a newspaper (*La cocarde*) that became a kind of factory of "radical" rightwing political thought, and, above all, he published novels—huge romans à clef, like *Le roman de l'énergie nationale* (1897–1902; The novel of national energy; in three volumes), *Colette Baudoche* (1909), *La colline inspirée* (1913; The inspired hill), and so forth—that recast French history since 1870 in passionate patriotic terms and that promoted the nationalist goals in which he believed.

Barrès insisted he was only "defending my native land and my dead," and "serving France," and that his cause was therefore "national" and not political. He accused his opponents (and sometimes his allies) of being "men who put their systems ahead of France," but what he never grasped was that there could be no "serving France" without (sooner or later) producing a "system."

Barrès has been seen by some as a leading precursor of the French version of fascism. Most French historians and biographers, on the other hand, do not agree. Yet, in all, politicians and others reading Barrès, even some on the left, supported authoritarian policies that worked against the classical Enlightenment tradition in France. Barrès left the high ground of his original thoughtful ambiguity for the low and treacherous marshes of instinctual and irrational politics.

See also **Boulanger Affair; Dreyfus Affair; France; Maurras, Charles; Nationalism; Sorel, Georges.**

BIBLIOGRAPHY

Primary Sources

Barrés, Maurice. *Scènes et doctrines du nationalisme.* Paris, 1902.

Secondary Sources

Bécarud, Jean. *Maurice Barrès et le Parlement de la Belle Époque (1906–1914).* Paris, 1987.

Broche, François. *Maurice Barrès.* Paris, 1987.

Chiron, Yves. *Maurice Barrès: Le prince de la jeunesse.* Paris, 1986.

Curtis, Michael. *Three against the Third Republic: Sorel, Barrès, and Maurras.* Princeton, N.J., 1976.

Doty, Charles Stewart. *From Cultural Rebellion to Counterrevolution: The Politics of Maurice Barrès.* Athens, Ohio, 1976.

Soucy, Robert. *Fascism in France: The Case of Maurice Barrès.* Berkeley, Calif., 1972.

Sternhell, Zeev. *Maurice Barrès et le nationalisme français.* Paris, 2000. Orig. pub. 1972.

Vajda, Sarah. *Maurice Barrès.* Paris, 2000.

Vartier, Jean. *Barrès et le chasseur de papillons.* Paris, 1989.

STEVEN ENGLUND

BARRY, CHARLES (1795–1860), British architect.

Charles Barry is best known for his design of the Houses of Parliament in London and the introduction of the Renaissance Revival style in the design of commercial buildings. The son of a wealthy London shopkeeper, Barry was apprenticed to Middleton and Bailey, a firm of London surveyors, between 1810 and 1817. After completing his apprenticeship he undertook an architectural tour of Europe and the Middle East. His study of Renaissance buildings in Italy was to become an important influence in his subsequent career. Barry's abilities as a draftsman were soon evident, and he partly funded his trip by the sale of his sketches for publication. The ability to produce attractive and clear drawings was to be a crucial factor in Barry's career. Many of his commissions were to be the result of winning design competitions, and his ability to present a project visually (through plans, elevations, and perspective drawings) was a key element in this success.

Barry returned to London in 1820 and set up an architectural practice. His first projects were churches in London, Manchester, and Brighton, followed by the Royal Institute of Fine Arts in Manchester (1824–1835). These early works showed that Barry was not restricted to a particular style, for the London churches were Gothic and the Manchester Institute was in Greek Revival style. In 1829 Barry won the competition for the Travellers Club in London. Built between 1830 and 1832 on a prestigious site in Pall Mall, the building was neither Greek nor Gothic in style, but took its inspiration from the great city palaces of the Italian Renaissance, particularly those of sixteenth-century Rome. It was an early example of the style that became known as Renaissance Revival.

Barry followed the Travellers with two more clubs in Renaissance Revival style, the Athenaeum in Manchester (1837–1839) and the Reform Club (1838–1840), next door to the Travellers Club. Regarded by some as his best work, the Reform Club was inspired by the Farnese Palace in Rome, with a plain astylar (without columns) facade enlivened by rich moldings around the windows and a deep cornice. The simple elegance of the design relied on symmetry, careful proportions, and the regular placing of windows. Equally important was the clarity and simplicity of Barry's internal planning. As with Renaissance palaces, the Reform Club is designed around a central courtyard. But Barry took advantage of recent technical advances and covered his courtyard with a glazed roof and installed the latest methods of heating and ventilation, creating an elegant and usable central circulation space that was much admired by contemporaries.

Barry's mastery of internal planning was evident in his best-known work, the Houses of Parliament (1840–1870). On 16 October 1834 a fire destroyed much of the ancient Palace of Westminster, which had housed the English parliament since 1547. Given the political and historical associations of the palace and a desire to integrate the surviving fragments, Parliament organized an architectural competition for a new building, requiring the design to be in the "Gothic or Elizabethan" style. Barry's entry was chosen and building began in 1840. His design was a masterpiece of logical planning, with four axes radiating from an octagonal central hall, providing both ceremonial routes and easy circulation through a vast building containing over a thousand rooms. Although on plan the building has an almost classical symmetry, the exterior appearance is given a more picturesque outline through the use of three asymmetrically placed towers. The decorative details are largely the work of Barry's collaborator, A. W. N. Pugin, whose designs are adaptations of the Perpendicular Gothic style of the fifteenth century. The building was unfinished at the time of Barry's death and was completed by his son, Edward Middleton Barry.

While working on the Houses of Parliament Barry found time for numerous other commissions. He further developed the Renaissance Revival style at the British Embassy, Istanbul (1842–1848), Bridge-water House, London (1847–1857), Halifax Town Hall (1860–1862; his last work), and in several country houses: Trentham Park, Staffordshire (1834–1849), and Cliveden House, Buckinghamshire (1850–1851). He also produced works in the Elizabethan style—Highclere Castle, Hampshire (1839–1842)—and the Scottish baronial style—Dunrobin Castle, Scotland (1845–1848).

As the chief designer of one of Britain's most recognizable and symbolic buildings, Barry's historical position is assured. Although his willingness to work in any number of styles was frowned upon by some commentators, a greater appreciation of his versatility and mastery of planning has emerged.

See also **London; Nash, John.**

BIBLIOGRAPHY

Barry, Alfred. *The Life and Works of Sir Charles Barry.* London, 1867. Reprint, New York, 1976.

Fell, Bryan H., and K. R. Mackenzie. *The Houses of Parliament.* Revised by D. L. Natzler. 15th ed. London, 1994.

Summerson, John. *Georgian London.* Edited by Howard Colvin. New Haven, Conn., 2003.

MARK FOLEY

BAUDELAIRE, CHARLES (1821–1867), French poet.

Charles Baudelaire's short life spanned only the middle decades of the nineteenth century. Born in Paris on 9 April 1821, he was five years old when his father died and not yet seven when his mother was remarried to Jacques Aupick, a military officer who eventually became a general, an ambassador, and a senator. Having envisioned a diplomatic career for his stepson, Aupick opposed Baudelaire's vocation for literature and put a stop to his bohemian student years by sending him on a voyage to India in 1841. But Baudelaire so resented this exile from Paris that he interrupted the trip at the island of Reunion and returned home several months earlier than planned. Upon inheriting his father's fortune in 1842, Baudelaire plunged into an extravagant life as a dandy among artists and writers until his mother, appalled to find nearly half his inheritance spent in just two

Charles Baudelaire. Portrait by Emile Deroy, 1844. RÉUNION DES MUSÉES NATIONAUX/ART RESOURCE, NY

years, appointed a legal guardian to manage his affairs. Baudelaire remained under this humiliating guardianship for the rest of his life, perennially unable to live within his means and given to begging frequent loans from his mother. His health progressively deteriorated, undermined throughout the 1850s by the syphilis he had contracted in 1839 as well as by his use of alcohol and laudanum. In 1864, Baudelaire went to Belgium in an unsuccessful attempt to earn an income from public lectures and to find a publisher for his collected works. He was still living in Brussels when, in the spring of 1866, he suffered a stroke that resulted in aphasia and partial paralysis. His mother brought him back to Paris, where he died on 31 August 1867.

Although Baudelaire was known within French literary circles, he did not achieve widespread celebrity during his lifetime. His posthumous fame grew steadily, however. Both a reasonably complete edition of his works and a fairly reliable biography appeared within a few years of his death; among others, symbolist authors of the 1880s and surrealist writers of the 1920s recognized him as a major

precursor. Paul Valéry emphasized in 1924 that Baudelaire was one of very few French poets to attain genuinely international stature, and his reputation has never diminished.

POET

Baudelaire is principally admired today for *Les fleurs du mal* (The flowers of evil), the sole volume of poetry that he authored. Although he began writing poems for it in the early 1840s, the collection was not published until June 1857. Within two weeks, it was first attacked in the press for its alleged immorality, then denounced by government censors as an affront to public decency. When the case was tried a month later, the court condemned Baudelaire to pay a fine and suppress six of the poems. In 1861, he published a second edition of *Les fleurs du mal*; originally composed of one hundred poems grouped into five sections, it now included 126 poems divided into six sections ("Spleen and Ideal," "Parisian Scenes," "Wine," "Flowers of Evil," "Revolt," "Death"). Following Baudelaire's claim during the trial that the book's meaning and moral implications were implicit in its structure as a whole rather than explicit in individual poems or sections, various scholars have debated the possibility of discovering what Jules Barbey d'Aurevilly posited in 1857 as its "secret architecture."

From the mid-1850s on, Baudelaire also composed and published short texts that he described as poetry in prose, a genre he did much to found. A group of twenty prose poems appeared in 1862 in *La Presse*, together with a preface dedicating them to his friend Arsène Houssaye, the journal's literary director, and linking them to the complex rhythms of modernity in "enormous cities." Baudelaire intended eventually to prepare a larger collection of prose poems as a counterpart to *Les fleurs du mal*, but this project remained unfinished at his death. The fifty poems in prose now collected under the title *Le Spleen de Paris* (Paris spleen) were first published together among Baudelaire's posthumous complete works in 1869.

TRANSLATOR

By far the most immediately lucrative of Baudelaire's literary endeavors—and those most appreciated by his contemporaries—were his translations of works by Edgar Allan Poe, whose reputation

Baudelaire established in France. He discovered "The Black Cat" in 1847 and started translating Poe's short stories, poems, and essays for literary reviews the following year. His collected translations later appeared in five volumes: *Histoires extraordinaires* (Extraordinary stories) in 1856, with five more editions issued by 1870; *Nouvelles histoires extraordinaires* (New extraordinary stories) in 1857, with three more editions by 1865; *Les Aventures d'Arthur Gordon Pym* (The adventures of Arthur Gordon Pym) in 1858; *Eurêka* in 1863; and *Histoires grotesques et sérieuses* (Grotesque and solemn stories) in 1865. In addition to his work on Poe, Baudelaire made a free, elaborately glossed translation of Thomas De Quincey's *Confessions of a English Opium Eater*, publishing this as part of the book *Les paradis artificiels* (Artificial paradises) in 1860.

CRITIC, ESSAYIST, AND AUTOBIOGRAPHER
Although he began composing poems early in his life, Baudelaire actually launched his career in letters as an art critic; his first substantial publications were reviews of the Salons of 1845 and 1846, both of which—like his subsequent reviews of the 1855 Exposition Universelle and the 1859 Salon—were notable for their eloquent praise of Eugène Delacroix. His art criticism culminated with a groundbreaking exploration of the esthetics of modernism in "Le peintre de la vie moderne" (The painter of modern life, 1863). Baudelaire showed equal acumen for scrutinizing other contemporary figures, and his critical corpus includes important essays on Victor Hugo, Théophile Gautier, Edgar Allan Poe, and Richard Wagner. His impulsion toward self-scrutiny first appeared in *La Fanfarlo* (Fanfarlo), the 1847 novella whose main character resembles the young Baudelaire, and critical introspection also provided part of the impetus for the extensive reflections on substance use and abuse (wine, hashish, and opium) that he published between 1851 and 1860. Beginning in 1859, Baudelaire made notes toward a series of autobiographical projects entitled "Fusées" (Rockets), "Mon Cœur mis à nu" (My heart laid bare), and "Pauvre Belgique!" (Poor Belgium!), but he was unable to complete any of them before his death.

Baudelaire's works have been widely read, taught, glossed, and translated since the late nineteenth century. They continue to stimulate much interest, particularly in their reflections on urban life, their inquiry into the dynamics of memory, and their stringent questioning of the ties between ethics and esthetics in modern art.

See also **Avant-Garde; Flâneur; Paris; Symbolism.**

BIBLIOGRAPHY

Primary Sources

Baudelaire, Charles. *Œuvres complètes.* Edited by Claude Pichois. 2 vols. Paris, 1983–1985.

Baudelaire, Charles. *Correspondance.* Edited by Claude Pichois and Jean Ziegler. 2 vols. Paris, 1973.

Secondary Sources

Benjamin, Walter. *Charles Baudelaire: A Lyric Poet in the Era of High Capitalism.* Translated by Harry Zohn. London, 1997. Translation of *Charles Baudelaire: Ein Lyriker im Zeitalter des Hochkapitalismus* (1955). Celebrated study of relations between Baudelaire's work and social conditions in nineteenth-century Paris.

Lloyd, Rosemary. *Baudelaire's World.* Ithaca, N.Y., 2002. A thoughtful, highly readable discussion of the main themes running through Baudelaire's writing, together with helpful reflections on reading Baudelaire's poetry in translation.

Pichois, Claude. *Baudelaire.* Additional research by Jean Ziegler. Translated by Graham Robb. London, 1989. Translation of *Baudelaire* (1987). An excellent biography, comprehensive and scrupulously researched.

Valéry, Paul. "Situation de Baudelaire." In *Oeuvres* by Paul Valéry, edited by Jean Hytier. Vol. 1, pp. 598–613. Paris, 1957. Presented as a lecture in 1924, this essay was the first to analyze Baudelaire's rise to the status of a canonical author.

MARGARET MINER

BÄUMER, GERTRUD (1873–1954), prominent leader in the German women's movement.

Gertrud Bäumer was born in 1873 in Hohenlimburg, in Germany. When her father, a pastor and school inspector, died in 1883, Bäumer's mother was forced by financial necessity to return with her three children to her parents' house in Halle. Bäumer, who was determined to gain financial independence, trained as a teacher and taught in a girls' elementary school. After rising to a leadership position in the German Female Teachers'

Association (Allgemeiner deutscher Lehrerinnen-verein), she moved to Berlin, where she obtained a doctoral degree in German literature from the Friedrich Wilhelm University in 1905. In Berlin she met Helene Lange, a prominent figure in the German women's movement with whom she lived and worked until Lange's death in 1930.

Under Lange's tutelage, Bäumer soon gained visibility as an advocate of women's rights. Along with Lange, she edited the feminist journal *Die Frau* (Woman) and published several books as a single author and as a coauthor with Lange. Among her most important works of the prewar era was *Die Frau in der Kulturbewegung der Gegenwart* (Women in contemporary culture), published in 1904.

In this book and in her other writings, Bäumer argued that women deserved the full rights of citizenship. She based that claim not on women's similarity to men, but on their distinctive traits, which she called the *weibliche Eigenart* (female char-acter). Because of women's sensitivity to personal relationships—a trait that she attributed to their socialization as mothers—she claimed that they were equipped to restore balance to a culture that was distorted by the one-sided predominance of men. Bäumer called on women to counteract men's characteristic competitive and aggressive spirit by emphasizing compassion, altruism, and care for dis-advantaged and vulnerable members of society. This was a powerful argument for women's access to education and to the caring professions, includ-ing teaching, social work, medicine, and nursing. Bäumer's ideology was accepted by the majority of those in the German women's movement—a group that called itself "moderate," and distinguished itself from the "radical" faction that advocated a more militant struggle for gender equality.

Until 1908, German women were not allowed to belong to political parties. After this prohibition was lifted, Bäumer joined the *Fortschrittliche Volks-partei* (Progressive People's Party)—a liberal group that was strongly committed to social reform. In 1910 she was elected to head the *Bund Deutscher Frauenvereine* (League of German Women's Associa-tions, or BDF), the organization that led the struggle for women's rights in Germany.

When World War I broke out in 1914, Bäumer rallied German women to their country's war effort. She became the head of the *Nationaler Frauendienst* (National Women's Service)—an organization that coordinated women's wartime work. An ardent patriot, Bäumer rejected the paci-fist program of the International Committee of Women for a Permanent Peace—a women's group that met at the Hague in 1915 and called on women of all nations to oppose the war. But Bäumer opposed some wartime policies, especially those that put women under pressure to bear children. Motherhood, she insisted, was not just a means of producing cannon-fodder.

At the war's end, when German women won the right to vote and to run for public office, Bäumer joined the liberal politician Friedrich Nau-mann (1860–1919) in founding the *Deutsche Demokratische Partei* (German Democratic Party, or DDP), and became one of the party's leaders. She served as a DDP delegate to the Reichstag (national parliament) from 1919 until 1932. From 1920 until 1933, she also held a government post in the ministry of the interior, where she made policy on education and child welfare. Although a strong supporter of democratic government, she had many reservations about the Weimar political system, which she claimed was too politically frag-mented to offer inspiring leadership.

When the Nazis (*Nationalsozialistische deutsche Arbeiterpartei,* or National Socialist Workers' Party) came to power in 1933 under the leadership of Adolf Hitler (1889–1945), the BDF chose to disband rather than to accept the Nazis' demand for complete conformity to governmental policies. Bäumer was dismissed from her post at the ministry of interior because of her liberal and feminist con-nections. However, she continued to edit *Die Frau* until 1944. While in general conforming to the limits set by the totalitarian government, she some-times engaged in cautious dissent. She also wrote historical novels and an autobiography. After the war's end in 1945, she was among the founders of a new political party, the *Christlich-Soziale Union* (CSU) but soon shifted her allegiance to another party, the *Christlich-Demokratische Union* (CDU). Bäumer died in 1954 in the Bethel Hos-pital, near Bielefeld. More than any other indivi-dual, except perhaps her partner Helene Lange, Bäumer defined the German women's movement during the first half of the twentieth century. Her legacy is controversial. As a courageous campaigner and brilliant publicist, she did much to advance the status of women in many areas. But many feminists of later generations regard her view of the "female character" as a confining stereotype that prevents women from reaching their full potential.

See also **Feminism; Fin de Siècle; Germany.**

BIBLIOGRAPHY

Primary Sources

Bäumer, Gertrud. *Die Frau in der Kulturbewegung der Gegenwart.* Wiesbaden, Germany, 1904.

———. *Die Frau in Volkswirtschaft und Staatsleben der Gegenwart.* Stuttgart and Berlin, 1914.

———. *Lebensweg durch eine Zeitenwende.* Tübingen, Germany, 1933.

Secondary Sources

Allen, Ann Taylor. *Feminism and Motherhood in Germany, 1800–1914.* New Brunswick, N.J., 1991.

Greven-Aschoff, Barbara. *Die bürgerliche Frauenbewegung in Deutschland, 1894–1933.* Göttingen, Germany, 1981.

Repp, Kevin. *Reformers, Critics, and the Paths of German Modernity: Anti-Politics and the Search for Alternatives, 1890–1914.* Cambridge, Mass., 2000.

Schaser, Angelika. *Helene Lange und Gertrud Bäumer: Eine politische Lebensgemeinschaft.* Cologne, Weimar, and Vienna, 2000.

ANN TAYLOR ALLEN

BEARDS. The beard's absence or presence is fundamental to the male appearance, a prominent feature of the most visible part of the body—the face. Since deliberate action is required to remove this natural growth, a decision is necessary about whether to shave or not. Thus, all men must choose on this matter of taste, even if only to ignore its growth. This makes the beard most significant in the evolution of male visual identity. But its aesthetic impact should be viewed in conjunction with the other elements of the male image, such as dress, hairstyles, jewelry, footwear, and other personal accessories. The whole thus forms an aggregate of evolving designs, an interweaving of elements that constitutes the cultural history of male visual identity.

Beards have long been associated with maturity, masculinity, strength, wisdom, and virility. In ancient Egypt, the beard was so important as a royal symbol of authority that women ascending the throne were depicted wearing false beards made of spun gold. In the Middle Ages, to cut off a man's beard was often considered a worse offense than wounding him. But throughout their history, writers have vehemently defended or attacked beards as being either essential to—or destructive of—physical and mental health and even morality and decency.

Beards declined in fashion in Europe from the mid-seventeenth century. By 1789 smooth shaving was the norm among European elites, fashionable gentlemen, and commoners as well, especially in western and southern Europe. The daily trip to the barbershop—a center for conversation—was considered as much a social visit as a grooming obligation, though many aristocrats were shaved by servants. At the turn of the eighteenth century, to help westernize the appearance of his people, the Russian tsar Peter the Great (r. 1682–1725) even discouraged beards by ordering that they be taxed. But some men did wear beards, including Jews, southeastern European Muslims, a few artists (including English poet William Blake [1757–1827]), eccentrics, hermits, eastern and northern European peasants, and peasants elsewhere too, especially in remote mountainous or forested regions. Beards were then worn in armies (usually by regulation) almost exclusively by ax-wielding "pioneers," who preceded armies to clear away thick underbrush, an image evoking the woodsman.

During the eighteenth and early nineteenth centuries, researchers who sought to understand the differences between the various human races asserted that the thickness of beard growth differentiated "superior" and "inferior" races. White Europeans' beards indicated their superiority, while less heavily bearded Africans, East Asians, and Native Americans were deemed inferior, although heavy-bearded Arabs and Turks were apparently ignored. Some medical writers linked beards to virility, asserting that male facial hair (and sweat) was semen that had been reabsorbed by the body.

Beards first revived in the late 1790s among nonconformist French artists called the "Barbus" (bearded ones), and some fancy Continental cavalry officers soon followed this trend with small, neatly trimmed beards. But beards only significantly increased in popularity around 1840, a reaction in part against the artificiality of the clean-shaven, self-indulgent, decadent, and arrogantly self-important image of the elitist "dandy" fashion look. The middle classes had gained substantially in economic power, due to the Industrial Revolution and expanded trade. Thus a more respectable outward appearance became socially required, as cities grew and business was thus increasingly conducted between strangers—an absolutely fundamental shift from the past. So the importance of a respectable public image became all-important. Because Christianity was then intrinsic to an appearance of respectability, beards gained in popularity in part because they were associated with the bearded Biblical patriarchs, and it was not uncommon for men by the 1840s and later to wear them without moustaches.

But in the long-term ebb and flow of fashion, the younger generation of this early Victorian era increasingly felt that a new look had become appropriate and desirable, symbolically rejecting the older generation's visual identity, with this emblem of their own. As usual, this was at first condemned, often for being "revolutionary"—an association that continues to the present—by those who felt disturbed by this deviation from the status quo. The "imperial," a small, stylish, pointed goatee-like beard, was popularized by French Emperor Napoleon III (r. 1851–1870), but more men wore the plainer, full beard, and its greatest popularity occurred from the 1860s to the early 1890s.

Afterward, the beard declined and became increasingly associated with older men, especially those viewed as being out of step with the changing times. Razors for self-shaving had appeared by the mid-nineteenth century, and more men shaved themselves, but as with other aspects of fashion, "the look" was what really mattered, and the usual arguments about convenience, health, and so on, were primarily rationalizations to legitimize taste. By 1914 the beard was again largely unfashionable.

See also **Body; Bourgeoisie; Class and Social Relations; Clothing, Dress, and Fashion.**

BIBLIOGRAPHY

Cooper, Wendy. *Hair: Sex, Society, Symbolism.* New York, 1971.

Corson, Richard. *Fashions in Hair: The First Five Thousand Years.* New York, 1965.

Leach, E. R. "Magical Hair." *The Journal of the Royal Anthropological Institute of Great Britain and Ireland* 88 (July–December 1958): 147–164.

Peterkin, Allan. *One Thousand Beards: A Cultural History of Facial Hair.* Vancouver, 2001. Popular illustrated history.

Reynolds, Reginald. *Beards: Their Social Standing, Religious Involvements, Decorative Possibilities, and Value in Offence and Defense Through the Ages.* Garden City, N.Y., 1949.

Schiebinger, Londa. *Nature's Body: Gender in the Making of Modern Science.* Boston, 1993. Good brief overview of cultural development of the beard.

SCOTT HUGHES MYERLY

BEARDSLEY, AUBREY (1872–1898), British literary visual artist of the 1890s avant-garde.

Born in Brighton, England, Aubrey Vincent Beardsley attended Brighton Grammar School, where he won popularity with amusing sketches for friends and teachers. By the conclusion of his formal education in 1888, three of his poems had been published in the Brighton newspaper and some drawings had appeared in school publications. Moving to London with his family, he developed his passionate love of the theater by attending plays starring the great actors and expanded his already considerable musical knowledge to encompass the operas of Richard Wagner (1813–1883). That he became a critical viewer and auditor is apparent in his drawings.

In 1891 Beardsley met Sir Edward Coley Burne-Jones (1833–1898), the Pre-Raphaelite painter who became his mentor and recommended that he attend art school, which Beardsley did for about eighteen months. During this time, Beardsley began evolving his personal style. He studied the work of his contemporaries, particularly James Abbott McNeill Whistler (1834–1903), Burne-Jones, Walter Richard Sickert (1860–1942), Walter Crane (1845–1915), and

Pierre Puvis de Chavannes (1824–1898), as well as prints by Japanese woodblock artists, whose layouts and techniques he would adapt. Frederick H. Evans (1853–1943), a bookshop owner and noted photographer, introduced Beardsley to the publisher J. M. Dent (1849–1926) who commissioned Beardsley to illustrate *Le Morte Darthur*, permitting him to draw full time and polish his style. His best work, such as for the 1894 play *Salome* by Oscar Wilde (1854–1900), invokes a rich vocabulary of style. Strong curvilinear compositions, they feature an economical and elegant use of line that shapes massed blacks and whites. The drawings comment on the texts for which he made them. Consequently, Beardsley's chiseled designs, with their links to symbolist art, were starkly different from the *horror vacui* (fear of empty space) and literal illustrations pervading contemporary art. His drawings anticipate, among others, Pablo Picasso (1881–1973), who saw the English artist's work in 1900, before he left Barcelona; Wassily Kandinsky (1866–1944), who knew Beardsley's work before he left Russia in 1896; Frank Lloyd Wright (1867–1959), whose spare architectural planes were enhanced by Beardsley's designs no less than by his collection of Japanese prints; and Scottish architect Charles Rennie Mackintosh (1868–1928), who acknowledged Beardsley's influence by autumn 1893.

Unfortunately, Beardsley had tuberculosis and knew he would die young; getting his work published and disseminated consumed him. In order to ensure the spread of his reputation, he calculatedly shocked middle-class London viewers by including in drawings erotic elements that were witty rather than pornographic, but critics were scandalized that he refused to follow formulaic presentation. From the first, therefore, Beardsley's work was praised for his handling of line but deplored for his treatment of content. Cementing that reputation was the jealousy of some less creative artists, and a scandal. After *Salome* was published, Beardsley and Wilde were irretrievably linked in the public mind; shortly after Wilde's arrest in 1895, Beardsley was unceremoniously sacked from *The Yellow Book*, the avant-garde periodical he cofounded and served as art editor.

Beardsley's importance as an artist did not, however, arise from scandal. In the 1890s, his drawings—in books he illustrated, posters he designed, and periodicals he planned and art-edited (the second was *The Savoy*)—compelled immediate international attention because he exploited the line block, a new method of photomechanical reproduction which permitted his drawings to be accurately, economically, and speedily disseminated. His posthumous reputation rests on his revolution in both style and composition of book illustration and his assistance in transforming the field of graphic art into a major medium of visual expression. His contribution to the developing field of commercial art paved the way for the public acceptance of advertising. His 1894 essay on the poster, a fledgling field in 1890s England, articulates his conviction that commercial design should be at once practical and beautiful—one reason his 1894 Avenue Theatre poster had a revolutionary effect on both sides of the Atlantic. His drawings reflect a coherent philosophy built on the dual ambitions of his work, literary and visual. He examined gender relations and the motifs of the grotesque and the voyeur, which comment on two visual preoccupations of western culture. He undercut each (potential) interpretation with its opposite; therefore, the meanings of many drawings cannot ultimately be "read."

A force in the creation of art nouveau, Beardsley is recognized as one of the few British artists in the forefront of the modernist movement that swept Europe, America, and Russia. Beardsley influenced, as the painter and graphic artist George Grosz (1893–1959) noted in 1946, "practically every modern designer after 1900," leaving few media in Europe and North America untouched: In addition to painting and architecture, his book illustrations and posters influenced the stage sets of Léon Bakst (1866–1924) for the Ballets Russes, the decorative art of Erté (Romain de Tirtoff; 1892–1990), Jean Cocteau's (1889–1963) designs for Rosenthal porcelain, the costumes of Sir Cecil Walter Hardy Beaton (1904–1980), Peter Max's (b. 1937) graphics for *The Yellow Submarine*, and the early work of the American contemporary artist Masami Teraoka (b. 1936). Through this varied and profound influence, Beardsley altered "perception" in visual art.

See also **Art Nouveau; Avant-Garde; Wilde, Oscar.**

The Peacock Skirt. Illustration by Aubrey Beardsley for an 1894 edition of Oscar Wilde's play *Salome*. Fogg Art Museum, Harvard University Art Museums, USA/Bridgeman Art Library/Bequest of Grenville L. Winthrop

BIBLIOGRAPHY

Kooistra, Lorraine. "Beardsley's Reading of Malory's *Morte Darthur*: Images of a Decadent World." *Mosaic* 23, no. 1 (1990): 55–72. First article to interpret the content of his drawings for Malory.

Maas, Henry, J. L. Duncan, and W. G. Good, eds. *The Letters of Aubrey Beardsley*. London, 1970. Most of the artist's letters are included.

Reade, Brian. *Aubrey Beardsley*. London, 1966. First book to present almost half of Beardsley's drawings in the order they were made and to append scholarly notes.

Snodgrass, Chris. "Beardsley's Oscillating Spaces: Play, Paradox, and the Grotesque." In *Reconsidering Aubrey Beardsley*, edited by Robert Langenfeld, 19–52. Ann Arbor, Mich., 1989. Theory about interpreting Beardsley's drawings.

Sturgis, Matthew. *Aubrey Beardsley: A Biography*. London, 1998. Presents new information.

Wilson, Simon. *Beardsley*. Oxford, U.K., 1983. Thorough and convincing discussion of some of the major drawings.

Zatlin, Linda Gertner. *Beardsley, Japonisme, and the Perversion of the Victorian Ideal*. Cambridge, U.K., 1997. First thorough study of Beardsley's technical and conceptual adaptation of Japanese art.

———. *Aubrey Beardsley: A Catalogue Raisonné*. New Haven, Conn., 2007. First to trace the literary, ownership, and exhibition history and document the criticism of each of Beardsley's 1,097 drawings plus almost fifty others in books and letters.

LINDA GERTNER ZATLIN

BEBEL, AUGUST (1840–1913), German socialist.

August Bebel was cofounder (with Wilhelm Liebknecht [1826–1900]) and longtime leader of the German socialist movement in the years before 1914. Given his origins in a Saxon working-class family, he was unusual among prominent figures in the German movement, who were mostly from middle-class families. In 1863, Bebel and Liebknecht founded one of the groups that eventually merged to form the German Social Democratic Party (*Sozialdemokratische Partei Deutschland* [SPD], the name adopted in 1891), the world's first mass-based political party. Under his able leadership, the party not only survived a twelve-year assault by Otto von Bismarck (1815–1898) during the so-called Outlaw Period (1878–1890), but also managed to grow significantly. The party finally outlasted the Iron Chancellor, who left office in 1890, the same year the Socialists became the most popular party in Germany. Bebel led the party from its founding until his death in 1913.

Bebel was also important as a leader of the opposition to the Prussian-dominated Bismarckian Reich. He was the only person elected to every term of the German Reichstag from its establishment in 1871 through the last election before World War I in 1912. In the Reichstag, in addition to defending the rights of the working class, Bebel fought, mostly unsuccessfully, to loosen the stranglehold the Prussian Junkers (members of the landholding aristocracy) had on the German state.

However, Bebel's major single achievement was to mold the diverse and fractious elements of the SPD into a unified party. He used theoreticians like Karl Johann Kautsky (1854–1938) to shore up his own stands on major party issues and emerge time and again as the architect of policies that kept German socialism united. He was respected and even revered by nearly all other elements of a party notable for its diversity. This respect allowed him to attract to his side the able people who made up the party leadership at the national, state, and local levels. Bebel delicately balanced party policies and actions between the extremes of the compromisers of the right and the radical revolutionaries of the left to oversee the growth of the SPD into the largest party in Europe prior to 1914. His masterful handling of party sentiment with regard to the mass-strike tactic at the 1906 Mannheim party congress is an example of his skill at balancing the right and left wings of the movement.

Although primarily important as an orator, organizer, and party leader, Bebel made one significant contribution to the literature of European socialism in 1879 when he published *Die Frau und der Sozialismus* (published in English as *Woman: Past, Present, and Future*). In this book, which went through dozens of editions in several languages, Bebel argued that the status of women was a key measure of the advancement of any society (echoing Karl Marx [1818–1883] on this matter). He contended that capitalist society—and earlier feudal society also—depended to a great extent on the political, economic, social, and sexual oppression of women. Only socialism, he held, could truly liberate women from this oppression and afford them their rightful place as productive contributors to modern society. For its time, this was a bold and radical assertion; this widely read book won Bebel considerable respect among both male and female activists in the movement.

Bebel was the dominant figure of German social democracy for nearly forty years. As a speaker he had few peers in the party, as a leader, none. His ability to identify the mood of the membership and then form it into official policy was remarkable. Although now often remembered as a somewhat benign figure, he was a fiery, aggressive leader who frequently assaulted party opponents sharply, but he could also be generous in his praise for the achievements of others. While he was often closely allied with the Marxist factions of the party, his commitment to Marxism was not a central element of his political activities; he was a pragmatic politician with a special concern for and sense of obligation to the needs of the workers, not an ideologue. Bebel's death in August 1913 created a leadership void that none of his successors could fill entirely.

Considering Bebel's central importance for the history of the SPD, there is surprisingly little debate about his contribution to the movement. Although he was the most important source of the SPD's centrist position with regard to the right-wing reformists and the left-wing revolutionists, Bebel is much less often criticized for his stances than are the party theoreticians. This is testimony to his exalted position in the eyes of most SPD members and scholars and commentators who came after him.

See also **Engels, Friedrich; Germany; Jaurès, Jean; Kautsky, Karl; Marx, Karl; Second International; Socialism.**

BIBLIOGRAPHY

Primary Sources

Bebel, August. *My Life, by August Bebel.* London, 1912. Although this account ends in the early 1880s, it is a very useful source.

Secondary Sources

Carsten, Francis L. *August Bebel und die Organisation der Massen.* Berlin, 1991.

Maehl, William Harvey. *August Bebel: Shadow Emperor of the German Workers.* Philadelphia, 1980.

Schorske, Carl E. *German Social Democracy, 1905–1917: The Development of the Great Schism.* Cambridge, Mass., 1955.

Steenson, Gary P. *"Not One Man! Not One Penny!" German Social Democracy, 1863–1914.* Pittsburgh, Pa., 1981.

GARY P. STEENSON

BEETHOVEN, LUDWIG VAN (1770–1827), German-Austrian composer.

Ludwig van Beethoven was born into a family of musicians serving at the electoral and archiepiscopal court at Bonn. His grandfather, of the same name, was *kapellmeister*, or director of music, at the court when Beethoven was a small child, and his father was a singer there. The boy Beethoven was trained to be a court musician as well; he played viola in the orchestra and organ in the chapel; for opera performances he accompanied rehearsals and coached singers. In 1787 he traveled to Vienna, presumably to study with Wolfgang Amadeus Mozart (1756–1791), but was called back almost immediately by the illness of his mother; owing to her death soon thereafter and his father's alcoholism he became responsible at the age of seventeen for the care of two younger brothers. The young Beethoven's budding career as a composer, though apparently little supported by the Bonn court, got off to a fairly promising start: by the age of twenty-one he had produced two cantatas, three piano sonatas, three piano quartets (piano and strings), an early version of what became the Second Piano Concerto, and many shorter compositions.

EARLY LIFE

In November 1792, as the armies of Napoleon were threatening the town and court, Beethoven left Bonn again for Vienna, there to remain for the rest of his life. His previous position in Bonn served him well there too, for the court establishment at Bonn was closely related by blood lines and marriage with the court of the Holy Roman Empire at Vienna, and his early supporters in the imperial city, such as the Lichnowskys and the Lobkowitz and von Fries families, were among the most exalted of the nobility. But Beethoven, like Mozart before him, never officially entered the employ of any person or institution there. In Vienna he made an early reputation as a pianist, gave piano and composition lessons, conducted and performed his music at private and public concerts, and sold his compositions to publishers in Vienna and Germany, later in England and Paris as well. He often composed on commission, an arrangement whereby the granter of the commission typically received the dedication of the composition together with exclusive rights to its performance for a fixed period of time, after which Beethoven was free to publish it.

Especially during his earlier years as a composer in Vienna, Beethoven specialized in music for his own instrument, the piano, an instrument only recently ascended to a position of dominance in European music, one which continued to undergo technical change throughout his life. The sonata for solo piano, previously associated largely with amateur performance, became in Beethoven's hands a vehicle for far-reaching innovation in musical expression: in harmonic language, form, sonority, texture, and in referential and associative richness. His thirty-two sonatas (plus juvenilia), distributed rather evenly across all but his final half-dozen years, are the single genre that provides a reasonably full glimpse of the majestic course of Beethoven's musical thought, from the youthful pathos and exaggerated Haydnesque wit of op. 2 and 10 (1795–1797) to the contemplation, violence, and exaltation of opp. 109, 110, and 111 (1820–1822).

The five concertos for piano, intended for public concerts, fall in the earlier part of Beethoven's career; following in the steps of Mozart, he wrote these concertos (with the exception of the last concerto, the "Emperor" of 1809) for his own performances. Thus they show all the brilliance requisite for virtuoso performance. But in addition they share in the expressive strength and imagination of Beethoven's maturing style. A marvelous example is the Fourth Concerto, op. 58, which combines military themes with ones of near-pastoral serenity, while the middle movement plays out a dialogue of fierce opposition ending in something like reconciliation and tranquility.

Ludwig van Beethoven. Portrait engraving with Beethoven's signature. SNARK/ART RESOURCE, NY

In Beethoven's day the kind of music that enjoyed the greatest social prestige was still opera. Though he considered possible opera libretti for composition nearly all his life, Beethoven composed only one, *Fidelio,* an adaptation of a French "rescue opera" libretto in which the heroic Leonore saves her husband Florestan from death at the hands of a villainous tyrant. The premiere of the opera, in November 1805, unfortunately coincided with Napoleon's invasion of Vienna, and closed after only three performances. Revised versions created with new librettists were mounted in 1806 and 1814, this last being the version seen in modern performances. In these subsequent incarnations the opera shifts emphasis dramatically from the saving of a single person to the liberation of all humankind from the bonds of tyranny, Florestan's fellow prisoners having been implicitly transformed into the suffering masses at large. Many have seen this change as indicative of Beethoven's own political sympathies, of liberal and humanitarian impulses that again come strongly to the fore in the Ninth Symphony (1824).

SYMPHONIES

The genre most indelibly associated with Beethoven's name is the symphony. From the First (1800) to the Ninth a quarter of a century later, his symphonies are a study in diversity. The Third Symphony, the "Eroica" (1804), decisively broke with the traditions Beethoven inherited. Its intended dedication to Napoleon, later changed to "the memory of a hero"; its monumental funeral march implicitly commemorating that hero; the unprecedented scope and expressive extremes of individual movements all seemed to mark this as a symphony that transcended its genre to become the larger-than-life embodiment of an idea. The Sixth Symphony, the "Pastoral" (1808), again laden with extramusical reference, but of a nearly opposite significance, makes elaborate use of accepted musical signifiers of the pastoral, of a celebration of nature, of the imagined virtue and simplicity of country life. And in the Ninth Symphony (1824), Beethoven famously rejected the basic presuppositions of the genre by adding text (Schiller's "Ode to Joy") and voices that sounded a ringing proclamation of human goodness and the triumph of universal brotherhood.

Beethoven contributed to all the standard musical genres of his time: there are two masses, including the monumental *Missa solemnis* (1823), concert arias, songs for voice and piano, programmatic overtures, music for wind ensemble, and character pieces and variations for piano. His music has long formed the centerpiece of the instrumental chamber music repertoire, with ten sonatas for piano and violin, five for piano cello, and six piano trios (piano, violin, and cello). But most central of all have been the sixteen string quartets (plus the separate *Grosse fuge*), composed from around 1800 until his death. Of these the final five, commonly known as the "late" quartets, were finished within the space of about a year and a half at the end of his life. Their expressive world ranges from near-crude good humor to a kind of serene, timeless otherworldly musing that Beethoven's contemporaries were at a loss to fathom, but which has since come to be be seen as the apex of his art.

Early in his career the critical response to Beethoven's music was often negative or grudging: his works were often seen as obscure, bizarre, eccentric, and excessively long (at the first public

performance of the "Eroica," it is reported, someone shouted "I'll give another Kreutzer if the thing will but stop!"). But in about 1805 a rather different strain of Beethoven criticism began to make an appearance, especially in Germany. Newly serious and technically competent reviews attempted to penetrate the obscurities and difficulties to find aesthetic justification for them. This new criticism reached a high point in the expansive reviews of E. T. A. Hoffmann in the years 1810 to 1813. And as Beethoven's late works, especially the late quartets, diverged ever more from contemporary practice, they inspired in his listeners a curious blend of puzzlement and awe. They seemed to illustrate the paradox of the genuine masterpiece: art that is in important ways unique, quite unlike other works of its kind, and at the same time exemplary, comprising a lasting standard of achievement and a model for others to follow.

By mid-career Beethoven had become the most famous musician in the world. His compositions routinely commanded high prices from both aristocratic patrons and publishers in several countries; as he produced them his symphonies quickly became standard fare at concerts all over Europe. Artists and intellectuals gathered in impressive numbers to visit him on his deathbed, and at the funeral of this reclusive man the crowd in attendance was estimated at ten to twenty thousand.

Until the end of the nineteenth century and beyond, his achievement cast its shadow over European music. Musicians felt he held proprietary rights over vast areas of composition—the symphony, the sonata, the string quartet, the piano concerto—and to compose in these genres meant meeting Beethoven on his own territory. Franz Schubert, Hector Berlioz, Felix Mendelssohn, Johannes Brahms, and at the end of the century, Gustav Mahler, all felt his example as both an imperative of sorts and an inhibiting factor, a standard that seemed at once to demand and discourage emulation.

INTELLECTUAL AND SOCIAL LIFE

By comparison with the exaltation of his aspiration and achievement, the course of Beethoven's life in Vienna seems prosaic. The central personal drama in this life was his advancing deafness. As early as in the so-called Heiligenstadt Testament of 1802, the

The manuscript of Beethoven's *Third Symphony*, also known as *Eroica*, photographed with his hearing trumpet. ERICH LESSING/ART RESOURCE, NY

composer declared himself on the verge of suicide over his affliction, but overcame his despair with a Promethean resolve to carry on in fulfillment of the artist's responsibility to society. Succeeding generations have seen in this pattern of dire crisis and its resolution through the exercise of indomitable will a psychological paradigm for the expressive arc of Beethoven's compositions, particularly in the larger symphonic movements. For some years the composer made efforts to conceal his condition, fearful that its being known would injure his status as a musician. But beginning about 1816 necessity led him to use an ear trumpet, and two years later he resorted to "conversation books," in which his interlocutors entered their side of any exchange. Beethoven tended to save his documents compulsively; the survival of many conversation books has provided extraordinary material for biographers.

Strongly attracted to women from his adolescence, Beethoven, despite great apparent effort, was never able to attain a satisfactory relationship with any one of them. In Vienna he typically pursued

women of a higher social standing than himself, some of them already attached, and some piano students of his who tended to be a good deal younger as well. In 1812 he wrote in several installments (but apparently never sent) a rhetorical *cri du coeur* to an unnamed "immortal beloved" expressing both his love for her and his resignation to their inevitable separation. This document has unleashed a torrent of speculation as to the identity of the addressee; by far the most likely candidate, recently identified by Maynard Solomon, is one Antonie Brentano, a native of Vienna married to Franz Brentano, a wealthy Frankfurt merchant. There have been various explanations for the melancholy story of Beethoven's relations with women. But there were two constant factors, probably related, in virtually all his encounters: a pursuit of the unattainable and an avoidance of commitment.

Beethoven's contemporaries saw him as a participant in that multifaceted, perplexing artistic and intellectual movement of his time, Romanticism. E. T. A. Hoffmann, surely a central figure in that movement, declared of Beethoven, "He is a completely Romantic composer." Subsequent generations have sought to distance the composer from such associations. Viennese scholars of the early twentieth century, alarmed at the radical modernism of Arnold Schoenberg and his group, extolled an earlier "classical" period consisting nearly exclusively of Haydn, Mozart, and Beethoven. And modernists of various stripes ever since, eager to dissociate Beethoven from a despised Romanticism, have cemented his position in such a classical school. Charles Rosen's *The Classical Style: Haydn, Mozart, and Beethoven,* first published in 1971 and since become a staple in every university music department in the English-speaking world, has carried on the tradition. Beginning in the late 1990s there has been some reassessment of this position by James Webster, who has questioned the validity of a "classical period" in music altogether, and Maynard Solomon, who has made a renewed exploration of Beethoven's ties with Romanticism.

Various schools of interpretation in the twentieth century have found Beethoven an inviting subject. Editha and Richard Sterba's *Beethoven and his Nephew* (English translation 1954) advanced a neo-Freudian and largely disapproving view of the composer's personality, particularly of his troubled relationship with his nephew Karl whose guardianship he assumed, after bitter legal wrangling with Karl's mother, in 1818. Among others who have applied concepts of psychoanalysis to the study of Beethoven's life, the most influential has been Maynard Solomon in his *Beethoven* (1977). Feminist scholarship has generally been critical of Beethoven, seeing the forcefulness of his music as a celebration of male hegemony. An analysis of Beethoven's career by the sociologist Tia DeNora (*Beethoven and the Construction of Genius*, 1995) sees the composer's towering reputation as a social construction, the result of a conscious effort of Beethoven's highly placed supporters to advance him as the embodiment of a new cult of "serious" music. A 2004 book by Stephen Rumph, *Beethoven after Napoleon*, construes the late works as a reflection of the conservative political and social ideals of the Metternich period. A perceptive and balanced account of the composer's life and work is Lewis Lockwood, *Beethoven: The Music and the Life* (2003).

See also **Berlioz, Hector; Brahms, Johannes; Mahler, Gustav; Romanticism; Schubert, Franz; Vienna.**

BIBLIOGRAPHY

Burnham, Scott. *Beethoven Hero.* Princeton, N.J., 1995.

DeNora, Tia. *Beethoven and the Construction of Genius: Musical Politics in Vienna, 1792–1803.* Berkeley, Calif., 1995.

Lockwood, Lewis. *Beethoven: The Music and the Life.* New York, 2003.

Plantinga, Leon. *Beethoven's Concertos.* New York, 1999

Rumph, Stephen. *Beethoven after Napoleon: Political Romanticism in the Late Works.* Berkeley, Calif., 2004.

Solomon, Maynard. *Beethoven.* 2nd rev. ed. New York, 1998.

Thayer, Alexander Wheelock. *Thayers Life of Beethoven.* Revised and edited by Elliot Forbes. 2 vols. Princeton, N.J., 1964.

LEON PLANTINGA

BELGIUM. A small, densely populated country in northwestern continental Europe, Belgium exemplified many of the classic trends of nineteenth-century Europe. The second country to industrialize after England, Belgium boasted a strong liberal movement in the mid-nineteenth century. By 1900, it was home to a large socialist party. Belgium was created in 1831 as a neutral country, whose borders were guaranteed by all the great powers. Violation of this neutrality by Imperial Germany in 1914 began World War I and ended nineteenth-century Europe.

Belgium owed its existence as a nation to two accidents of history. The Belgian provinces were the southern region of the Low Countries that the Spanish reconquered in the sixteenth century after the northern, largely Protestant provinces successfully broke away. The provinces in the northern Low Countries became the independent Netherlands ruled by Dutch Protestants. Under the Spanish in the seventeenth century, the southern Low Countries became one of the most Catholic regions of Europe. Under both Spanish rule in the seventeenth century and Austrian rule in the eighteenth century, the southern provinces deepened their strong tradition of local autonomy. After passing under French rule during the Revolution and Napoleonic period, the Belgian provinces were again joined with the Netherlands to the north after Napoleon's defeat in 1815. The goal of the victorious Allies who defeated Napoleon—Britain, Austria, Prussia, and Russia—was to create a larger country to the north of France that could more easily check French military expansion. The new "United Kingdom of the Netherlands" lasted only fifteen years. In 1830, the kingdom of Belgium emerged from a revolution against the Dutch in the north. The new state survived, however, only because the great powers agreed to prevent its annexation by France or its reconquest by the recently ousted Dutch.

The southern Netherlands provinces that became the modern nation of Belgium consisted of a group of semiautonomous provinces that had little historic or cultural unity. The northern part was Dutch-speaking. Gradually, this area came to be known as Flanders, even though the medieval county of Flanders only partially overlapped this area. The southern part of the provinces was French-speaking. This area was sometimes referred to as "Walloon" or Wallonia, after the Walloon dialect of French. In the period of Spanish rule until 1715, and continuing under the Austrians from 1715 to 1792, French slowly became the language of education, government, business, and the Catholic Church all over the region, including Dutch-speaking Flanders. The occupation and annexation of the region by the French Revolutionary and Napoleonic governments from 1794 to 1815 only accelerated the use of French. By the early nineteenth century, Dutch, or rather local dialects of Dutch sometimes called Flemish, was the everyday language only of farmers, workers, and sections of the middle class in Flanders.

THE BELGIAN REVOLUTION

The Belgian revolution of 1830 was launched because King William I of the Netherlands disregarded the Belgian provinces' long tradition of local autonomy and Catholic piety. Remarkably for post-1815 Europe, both anticlerical liberals angered by the king's political heavy-handedness and conservative Catholic bishops afraid of Protestantism united against Dutch rule. This "Unionism" of liberals and Catholics kept the infant nation together while the Great Powers debated its fate and the Dutch threatened to invade. The revolution permanently divided Dutch-speaking Flanders in what became Belgium from the Dutch-speaking northern Netherlands. There was only limited affinity for the Netherlands among the Flemish. Textile industrialists in the Flemish city of Ghent, most of whom were more likely to speak French than Dutch, worried that they would lose the Dutch colonial empire as an export market. Workers in cities such as Ghent and Antwerp resented the dominance of French-speaking elites in Brussels that separation from the Netherlands would bring. But these groups of "Orangists" were not united among themselves. (The Dutch royal family came from the House of Orange.) The alliance of the French-speaking south with the largely French-speaking church and upper and middle class in Flanders meant that separation from the Netherlands had wide support.

The new nation might easily have disappeared. The Dutch reinvaded in 1831, but Dutch rule was clearly opposed by the mass of the middle and upper class. Militarily, Belgium was protected from the Dutch only by the intervention of the French army, supported by the British navy. For many observers, the most likely solution for Belgium was union with France. The Great Powers, particularly Britain, Prussia, and Austria, preferred independence for Belgium to strengthening France, and the newly installed French king Louis-Philippe did not push the proposal. Belgium was provided with a king, Leopold I, of Saxe-Coburg, the uncle of Queen Victoria of Britain, who conveniently married the daughter of Louis-Philippe.

THE EARLY BELGIAN STATE

For its time, the new Belgian state had a progressive constitution. Leopold I, like all subsequent Belgian kings, ruled as a constitutional monarch with very limited powers. Parliament effectively controlled decisions through cabinet governments. Approximately 10 percent of the adult males voted, about the same as in France under the July monarchy and more than was the case in most German states. Freedoms of press, assembly, and religion were guaranteed. The new Unionist regime balanced the interests of liberals with those of practicing Catholics. In vain, the Vatican denounced the constitution for not establishing Catholicism as the state religion. The Belgian bishops decided that, given the predominance of Catholics in the population, they could utilize religious freedom to create a strong position for the church. They chose wisely. The church in Belgium soon controlled much of education and social welfare. Local governments, although not the central government, gave Catholic-controlled institutions subsidies. Under the constitution, any religious organization had a right to financial support from the state. Because the country was 99 percent Catholic, in practice, Catholicism had almost as much support as if it were the state church.

The Unionist compromise broke down in the 1860s and 1870s when the Liberals tried to undo the powerful Catholic hold on education and social welfare. Many Liberals were practicing Catholics, but they opposed the church's privileged position and wanted education, in particular, to be secular and state-controlled. In 1879, Liberals took control of parliament, cut state subsidies to schools controlled by the church, and expanded the secular school system. The Catholics responded by a massive campaign to support church-supported schools and to win the 1884 elections. From 1884 until 1914, the Catholic party controlled all governments.

Ships approaching the port of Ostend, Belgium. Illustration c. 1815. ©HULTON-DEUTSCH COLLECTION/CORBIS

Catholics and Liberals, both upper-middle-class parties, differed little in supporting economic development and free markets. Already under the French and Dutch, Belgian entrepreneurs, some-time with British capital and technical help, had built the first mechanized cotton, woolen, and linen mills and set up the first coal mining and iron smelting complexes on the Continent. Governments aided this process by removing almost all internal tariff barriers, keeping external tariffs very low, and building the densest railroad network in the world across the small country. On canals, railroads, and harbor traffic, Belgium carried a great deal of the transit trade linking western Germany, northern France, and Switzerland with the rest of the world.

The economy of the newly independent state suffered several severe setbacks in the middle of the nineteenth century, but continued to be more industrialized than most of the rest of Europe. The textile industries had to find new markets in Latin America and Asia after losing the Dutch colonies. Belgian industrialists competed on price, not quality. They relied more on lower paid women and children as workers than did British firms.

Belgian workers also worked one or two hours longer than their British counterparts. Flemish rural textile workers and farmers suffered horribly in the potato famine of the 1840s. The Flemish countryside remained a depressed area until the early twentieth century. Thousands of Flemings emigrated to cities such as Brussels or Ghent, to the southern French-speaking areas in Wallonia to work in the coal and metallurgical industries, or to northern France. Belgians were the largest immigrant group in France throughout the nineteenth century. Cities such as Roubaix near Lille in northern France were over 50 percent Belgian for several decades. Very few Belgians emigrated to the New World. The textile industries in Ghent and other Flemish cities always struggled, but managed to compete at the lower end of the market with cheaper, lower quality cloths and by holding down labor costs. In 1870, women made up 36 percent of the workforce in Belgium, 30 percent in Britain. Belgium did better in metallurgy. With little iron ore and with coal deposits that were narrower and less easily worked than those in Britain and Germany, the Walloon industries nonetheless did remarkably well until World War I. As late as 1860, Belgium produced sixty-nine kilograms of pig iron per capita, while France produced only twenty-six and Germany thirteen.

Labor costs could be kept lower both because people were numerous and lacked skills. Although Belgium's population grew only slowly during the nineteenth century, it began the Industrial Revolution with one of the highest population densities in the world. The intensive cultivation of agriculture in Flanders and the widespread network of rural industry supported a large, though frequently impoverished, population. Even in 1913, Belgium, with a population of seven and a half million, had perhaps the highest density in the world at 259 people per square kilometer. Britain, considered very densely populated, had only 238 in 1911. Battles over education kept the school system inadequate. As late as 1914, 10 percent of the population was illiterate, the highest rate in Western Europe north of the Pyrenees.

LANGUAGE

The new Belgian nation created in 1831 used French as its national language. Approximately 55 to 60 percent of the population in fact spoke Dutch, or more accurately, versions of Dutch dialects as their first language, and 40 to 45 percent French, or dialects of French. Because Flanders had been cut off for centuries from the Dutch-speaking northern Netherlands, a standardized written and spoken Dutch language had never emerged. The government, law, education, the church, and middle-class business in Flanders used French, even though many French speakers also spoke a Dutch dialect at home or with lower-class people. Until 1898, the official text of laws was always the French version. The dominance of French in public life conferred a great advantage on French-speakers. Workers, farmers, or middle-class people in Flanders often tried to learn French or have their children educated in French as a means of social mobility. As a union newspaper complained, "In front of the bosses, you always have to use French."

Throughout the nineteenth century, there was a strong association of French with progress and wealth and Dutch or Flemish dialects with backwardness and poverty. Flanders was poor and agricultural, except for Ghent and the harbor city of Antwerp. The French-speaking southern provinces of Hainaut and Liége were the industrialized heartland of Belgium. The effects of this can be seen most powerfully in the capital and largest city of the country, Brussels. In the medieval period, Brussels was a Flemish city like Bruges, Ghent, or Antwerp. Like them, it acquired a Francophone upper class by the time of the French Revolution. Unlike them, after 1830, Brussels eventually became a bilingual city. Workers were still usually Dutch speakers, but the middle class and the better paid workers gradually began using French more and more. Immigrants to the city from French-speaking areas rarely learned Dutch. Those from Flanders often learned French. Upper-class people, and increasingly even middle-class individuals, used only French. By the end of the century, Dutch became a language of a small minority, while the bilingual population also shrank and the numbers of French speakers rose.

It was to prevent this fate from befalling the rest of Flanders that there arose a small Flemish-rights movement. These middle-class *Flamingants* promoted Dutch-language theater and literature, called on the government to allow more use of Dutch in legal proceedings, and protested the exclusive use of French in public life. They made almost no attempt to reach out to workers or the rural poor. The elite-dominated Liberal and Catholic political parties, as Francophone in Flanders as they were in Wallonia and Brussels, largely ignored them. Flamingants, too, split into rival Liberal and Catholic cultural organizations, the Willemfonds and Davidsfonds, respectively. Flamingants did not see the language issue in regional terms. They wanted to have Dutch as an accepted standard language in Flanders. Thus, their biggest opponents were upper-class Flemings who insisted on using French as their normal spoken and written language even though they lived in Flanders. Even local governments followed the lead of the Flemish elite. In 1885, a bilingual official in Brussels reported that it was pointless to use Dutch with local officials in Flanders. When he wrote them letters in Dutch, they responded in French. This was the situation Flamingants wanted changed. They had few issues with French-speaking Walloons, except that the latter were indifferent to the Flemish cause. The Flemish question, in other words, was not one of Belgian identity or unity. It was a battle within Flanders.

LABOR AND POLITICAL PROTEST

Belgium, Karl Marx once said, was "the paradise of the capitalist, landlord, and the priest." Britain may have invented laissez-faire economics, but Belgium epitomized it. Workers had almost no protections in labor law. Only in 1866 were labor unions legalized, and they still suffered many legal handicaps. Liberals and Catholics, for all the virulence of their battles over education and social welfare, differed little in their support for unfettered free markets. Unlike Liberals in Britain or Radicals in France, the Belgian Liberals did almost nothing to reach out to workers. There was a small wing of so-called progressives within the Liberal party in the 1870s to 1890s, but they lacked any influence on the national party. Catholic charities such as the Society of St. Vincent de Paul organized workers' clubs, distributed welfare, and provided relief. Until the 1890s, "Social Catholics" created "guilds" of workers supposedly modeled on those of the Middle Ages. These were usually run by upper-class individuals and did nothing to help workers to express their grievances. Small unions of skilled artisans in the capital city of Brussels and textile factory workers in Ghent briefly joined the First International of Workingmen's Association between 1866 and 1874. Once the First International fell apart, however, these groups of unions lost any connection between them. The artisanal unions in Brussels, mostly printers, glovers, and bronze workers, were much less radical than the textile workers in Ghent whose leaders began to adopt socialism as a result of ties with Dutch and German workers.

Opposition to the restricted electoral system eventually mobilized workers. The suffrage or right to vote that was progressive for its time in the 1830s was still unchanged in the 1880s. Whereas only 10 percent of males could vote in elections in Belgium, France and Germany had both adopted universal male suffrage in 1871, and Britain, by the Second Reform Bill of 1867, had granted approximately two-thirds of males the right to vote. Conservative Catholics opposed a wider suffrage because of their fears of more democratic rule. Liberals feared that a wider suffrage would enfranchise the Catholic countryside. In 1884, Edmond Van Beveren and Edward Anseele, the leaders of the Ghent Socialists, persuaded a number of Brussels artisanal unions to collaborate in forming the Belgian Labor Party, Belgische Werkliedenpartij/Parti Ouvrier Belge. The platform of the tiny party called for universal suffrage, that is, in practice, universal male suffrage. The party had only a few knots of supporters in the coalfields and ironworks in Wallonia, in southern Belgium, where most workers lived, but its pamphlets calling for universal suffrage were distributed widely.

The watershed event in Belgium's history in the nineteenth century occurred in March 1886. In the midst of the worst economic depression since the 1840s, coal miners and metallurgists in southern Belgium organized demonstrations, went on strike, and engaged in acts of violence in reaction to the government's use of police and the army. Small groups of anarchists helped spark the demonstrations, but the strikes were a genuine economic protest in which anarchists often had no role. At least thirty-two people died, all, it appears, killed by the police or army. At its peak, the wave of protests may have brought almost 200,000 workers out on strike, out of a total industrial workforce of perhaps 800,000. It was arguably the first general strike in the world.

SUFFRAGE AND POLITICAL CHANGE

The Socialists in the new Labor Party had not organized the strike wave, nor were they able to control it. In its wake, however, they fanned out across the industrial regions trying to organize consumer cooperatives, mutual insurance societies, labor unions, and political clubs. Many of these eventually faded away. Enough survived to be a network supporting the Labor Party as a fledgling national movement. It was still largely led by artisans and middle-class intellectuals—journalists, teachers, and lawyers—in Brussels and labor union leaders in Ghent. For the first time, however, it had intermittent support from the mass of miners and metallurgists in the industrial provinces of Hainaut and Liége in southern Belgium. The party's newspapers and propagandists preached a simple message: universal suffrage. In principle, the party had a socialist platform in calling for the nationalization of private property, but the party's leaders never displayed a commitment to Marxism. Universal suffrage would, they believe, allow workers to vote the Labor Party into power in parliament, where it would be able to bring about reforms. The party's leaders were all close to the Liberals in their anticlericalism. They called for complete separation of church and state by ending subsidies to church-related institutions.

The ripple effects of 1886 overturned the elite-dominated political and social system. The Catholic government introduced a few cautious reforms. Labor inspection laws, laws against garnishing wages, and elected consultative councils for workers and employers all were introduced. More importantly, 1886 forced both Liberals and Catholics at last to consider extending the suffrage. Few supported universal male suffrage. Liberals wanted to enfranchise the middle class that they hoped would vote for them. Catholics feared that workers would vote Liberal or Socialist. Like Disraeli and Bismarck, they also calculated that farmers and the lower middle class might vote more conservatively than the middle class or workers. The stalemate strengthened the attractiveness of the simple Socialist call for universal suffrage. In 1893, the Socialists organized a massive general strike of some 250,000 workers. The government responded with repression and confusion, and finally agreed to consider reform. Universal male suffrage was introduced the next year, although wealthier or more educated voters had up to two additional votes. The number of voters went from 136,000 to 1,370,000. The Catholics' calculations proved correct. They won 103 seats, the Socialists 28, Liberals only 20. The Liberals actually outpolled the Socialists, but were thinly spread across the country. Under the winner-take-all system, the Socialists' concentration in industrial areas in Wallonia was a major advantage.

The political system might have continued to change, except that the Catholics, Liberals, and Socialists all made strategic choices that put a new stalemate into place. Under the winner-take-all system in which only one party captured all the seats in a district, the Liberals and Socialists were shut out unless they allied against the Catholics. Meanwhile, within the Catholic party, democratic elements among workers, farmers, and the lower middle class for the first time could pressure the old elite. When Socialists, Liberals, and democratic Catholics in 1899 all called for proportional representation, the conservative Catholic government gave in. The number of seats held by the Catholics, Liberals, and Socialists went from 112, 12, and 28, respectively, to 86, 33, and 32. The Catholics'

majority was reduced, but they succeeded in keeping their opponents from uniting. Replacing the Socialists as the major opposition party, the Liberals never definitely committed to an alliance to turn the Catholics out of power or get rid of plural votes. The Socialists, meanwhile, never firmly allied with democratic Catholics on economic issues, but clung to anticlericalism. As Emile Vandervelde, the Socialist leader put it in a May Day speech, "Christian holidays are those of a world that is dying." Only gradually, Socialists, the increasingly larger democratic Catholic camp, and a few progressives among the Liberals combined to put through social reforms in parliament on a piecemeal basis. In elections until World War I, Socialists and Liberals campaigned against the Catholics on separate anticlerical platforms and lost.

The Socialists were the primary beneficiaries of universal male suffrage, but in the long run the sea change of 1886 to 1894 had as great an effect on the Catholics and Flemish activists. In anticipation of the struggle under universal suffrage, in 1891, democratic Catholic leaders created the Belgian Democratic League (Belgische Volksbond/Ligue Democratique Belge), an association of middle-class, farmer, and workers groups to broaden the Catholic party. They also created the Boerenbond (Farmers' League) to help Flemish small farmers switch from unprofitable grain production to dairying and truck farming. A large Catholic labor union movement also arose. After 1894, the Catholic elite could only win elections by taking account of these groups' grievances and letting more of their leaders into decision-making. In Flanders, both Christian Democrats, as these groups came to be known, and Socialists had to use Dutch to reach lower-class voters. This, in turn, transformed Flemish activism. By 1900, there was a group of Catholic, Socialist, and Liberal deputies in parliament successfully demanding that Dutch be more widely used in schools, courts, and the military. This paved the way for a transformation whereby the Francophone elite in Flanders was forced to change and the region became a genuinely Dutch-speaking area.

Despite Belgium's small size and neutral status, the country played a role in world affairs. The second Belgian king, Leopold II, who ruled from 1865 to 1909, chafed at the limits imposed on his power by the constitution. He skillfully convinced the European Great Powers to turn over most of the huge Congo River basin in central Africa to him as the Congo Free State, which he personally ruled. The king's subcontractors exacted huge profits for him from sales of ivory, rubber, and other products supplied by the Congolese at a horrible cost in human life. Finally, as a result of perhaps the first international human rights campaign, led by British journalists and activists Roger Casement and E. D. Morel, the Belgian government was shamed into taking over the rule of the Congo as a Belgian colony in 1908. More wisely, Leopold II had advocated stronger defenses for Belgium against German attack and an increased army. Antimilitarism ran deep among both Catholics and Socialists, however. Combined with tight-fisted economic policies, this meant that only in the years right before 1914 did Belgium begin to build up its forts. As a neutral country where commerce among Britain, France, and Germany flowed freely, Belgium was a strong supporter of international organizations. *La vie internationale*, the journal that documented the explosion of international organizations in the pre-1914 era, was published in Brussels. Belgium produced several Nobel Peace Prize winners before 1914, among them Charles Beernaert, Catholic prime minister and international negotiator. The Socialist Second International (1889–1914), the federation of Socialist parties worldwide, was headquartered in Brussels, and its secretary was the Flemish Socialist Camille Huysmans. In the last days of July 1914, the Belgian Socialists gathered French and German Socialists together for a meeting to help head off an impending war. No resolution came from the meeting. Within a few days, German troops poured over the lightly defended Belgian border. The end of Belgian neutrality marked the end, too, of nineteenth-century Europe.

See also **Leopold I; Leopold II; Netherlands.**

BIBLIOGRAPHY

Primary Sources

Hermans, Theo, ed. *The Flemish Movement: A Documentary History, 1780–1990.* London and Atlantic Highlands, N.J., 1992.

Reed, Thomas H. *The Government and Politics of Belgium.* Yonkers-on-Hudson, N.Y., 1924.

Rowntree, B. Seebohm. *Land & Labour: Lessons from Belgium.* London, 1910.

Secondary Sources

Ascherson, Neal. *The King Incorporated: Leopold II in the Age of Trusts.* New York, 1984.

Goddard, Stephen H., ed. *Les XX and the Belgian-Avant Garde: Prints, Drawings, and Books ca. 1890.* Lawrence, Kansas, 1993.

Kossmann, E. H. *The Low Countries, 1780–1940.* Oxford, U.K., and New York, 1978.

Lesthaeghe, Ron. J. *The Decline of Belgian Fertility, 1800–1970.* Princeton, N.J., 1977.

Lijphart, Arend, ed. *Conflict and Coexistence in Belgium: The Dynamics of a Culturally Divided Society.* Berkeley, Calif., 1981.

Mallinson, Vernon. *Power 1961.* London, 1963.

McRae, Kenneth. *Conflict and Compromise in Multilingual Societies.* Vol. 2: *Belgium.* Waterloo, Ont., Canada, 1986.

Mokyr, Joel. *Industrialization in the Low Countries, 1790–1850.* New Haven, Conn., 1976.

Polasky, Janet. *The Democratic Socialism of Emile Vandervelde: Between Reform and Revolution.* Oxford, U.K., 1995.

Scholliers, Peter. *Wages, Manufacturers, and Workers in the Nineteenth-Century Factory: The Voortman Cotton Mill in Ghent.* Oxford, U.K., and New York, 1996

Strikwerda, Carl. *A House Divided: Catholics, Socialists, and Flemish Nationalists in Nineteenth-Century Belgium.* Lanham, Md., 1997.

Witte, Els, Jan Craeybeckx, and Alain Meynen. *Political History of Belgium from 1830s Onwards.* Antwerp and Brussels, 2000.

Zolberg, Aristide. "Belgium." In *Political Development in Western Europe and the United States,* edited by Raymond Grew. Princeton, N.J., 1979.

——. "The Making of Flemings and Walloons: Belgium, 1830–1914." *Journal of Interdisciplinary History* 5 (1974): 179–235

CARL J. STRIKWERDA

BELGRADE. Geography and national and international politics determined the history of the city of Belgrade. Placed at the confluence of two major rivers—the Danube and the Sava, which connected central and southeastern Europe with the eastern Mediterranean—the city played a significant role in the wars waged by European powers against the Ottomans for the heritage of their empire.

From the end of the seventeenth century, when the Ottomans were defeated at the siege of Vienna by the Christian coalition in 1683 until the end of the eighteenth century, Serbia was a constant battleground. The country was devastated and depopulated; the few travelers visiting the area described it as a desert, invaded by warring armies, outlaws, and brigands. During four wars (1683–1699, 1716–1718, 1737–1739, and 1788–1791), Belgrade changed hands between both Ottoman and Austrian masters and was besieged and bombarded by both sides. The captured Serbian population was enslaved and sold in the slave market in Istanbul. Finally after the peace treaty of 1791 signed in Svishtov between the Austrians and the Turks, Belgrade became a border city in the hands of the Ottomans. The frontier nature of Belgrade had a dual effect on the role that the city was to play in history. Externally it introduced Serbia into European diplomacy and the Eastern Question. Domestically it offered a political and economic leader to the nation, the role of administrative and cultural center of the nascent Serbian statehood, first a principality, later a kingdom, the autonomy of which was granted in 1830 by the sultan's hatti-sherif (decree). After a brawl between Serbs and Turks, and the bombardment of the city, the Turkish garrison had to withdraw from the Belgrade fortress and all Serbian cities (1867). Independence was granted to Serbia by the European Great Powers at the Berlin Conference in 1878. The price to accomplish this was high: war after war, conflict and strife, as well as two Serbian uprisings in 1804 and 1815.

The Serbian Orthodox Church, seated in Belgrade, became independent from the Greek patriarch in 1879. A concordat with the Vatican, concluded in 1914, confirmed the rights of Catholics in Serbia.

All European powers played an important role in Serbian politics. The most influential was Russia, until the turn of the twentieth century, when France and western Europe took the lead. Of the two rival Serbian dynasties, the Obrenovićes were Austrophiles, the Karadjordjevićes Russophiles.

The public in Belgrade considered Russia a protector of its Slavic brother, while Austria-Hungary was suspected as an opponent of the Slavic cause. The first Russo-Serbian Convention of military and political alliance was concluded in 1807, and the Russian diplomatic representative arrived in Belgrade. The Austrian consulate in Belgrade was opened in 1836, the British in 1837, and the French in 1839. When studying abroad, Belgrade's young intelligentsia chose France for law and the political sciences, Germany for economy and finance, and Russia for military studies.

During the nineteenth century, Belgrade went through significant demographic changes. The number of Serbs rose and the number of Turks steadily declined. According to censuses made annually by Serbian authorities, the population of Belgrade rose from 4,500 in 1810 to 89,876 in 1910. Belgrade and Serbia became attractive to immigrants from surrounding regions settled by Serbs, as well as South Slavs in Balkan areas. According to statistics, in 1900 there were 21,105 Belgrade citizens who were born abroad. Among them were educated professionals from Vojvodina (then in Hungary). Most became teachers, civil servants, army officers, and policemen.

Belgrade entered the Industrial Age rather late, having relied on cattle breeding, pig farming, and the export of these livestock for its main source of revenue. The construction of railroads after the Berlin Congress (1878) encouraged the investment of foreign and domestic capital in industry. However, at the end of the nineteenth century, there were only twenty industrial establishments in the city. The Austrian sanctions imposed on Serbia during their Custom War of 1906–1911 removed Austrian industrial competition and facilitated the development of Serbian industry, especially food processing, flour milling, and breweries.

Improved economy, traffic, and communication required a new urban plan for the city. The narrow, winding, little streets in the center of the city were replaced by tree-lined, large, straight avenues. The urban architecture of new Belgrade showed a strong French influence. The city boasted imposing buildings: the new palace, the Serbian National Bank, the National Theatre, the Grand Hotel, and many others. These were designed by young domestic architects trained abroad. Street squares were ornamented with monuments of distinguished Serbs made by domestic sculptors. City traffic was regulated and facilitated. The first telephone was installed in Belgrade in 1882; electricity in the streets was introduced in 1892. The first streetcars, pulled by horses, were replaced by electric versions. In 1884, Belgrade was connected by railways with central Europe and other Balkan cities.

Receptive to western European culture, Belgrade also preserved and further developed Serbian national culture. The Royal Serbian Academy of Sciences, founded in 1887, replaced the former Serbian Learned Society and the previous Great School (Velika Skola) was transformed in 1905 into the University of Belgrade. Among cultural institutions were the National Library, the National Museum, the Ethnographic Museum (1901), the National Theatre (1868), the School of Music, and the Clerical College. Together, they produced internationally and nationally recognized scholars.

Parliamentarism and democracy were introduced in Serbia under King Peter I after the 1903 regicide in Belgrade. During the decade preceding World War I, Belgrade was at the helm of the Serbian and Yugoslav national movement for liberation and unification. It also caused a conflict with Austria-Hungary during and after its 1908 annexation of Bosnia and Herzegovina. The government in Belgrade was one of the main architects of the Balkan Alliance in 1912, which enabled the victory in the Balkan Wars of 1912, but clashed with its Bulgarian ally in 1913. On the eve of World War I the Belgrade government was accused of involvement in the assassination of Austrian archduke Francis Ferdinand in Sarajevo, which triggered the started of World War I.

See also **Balkan Wars; Bosnia-Herzegovina; Cities and Towns; Nationalism; Serbia.**

BIBLIOGRAPHY

Glumac, Slobodan. *Belgrade.* Translated by Karin Radovanovic. Belgrade, 1989.

Istorija Beograda. 3 vols. Belgrade, 1974.

Pavlowitch, Stevan K. *Serbia: The History of an Idea.* New York, 2002.

Petrovich, Michael Boro. *A History of Modern Serbia, 1804–1918.* 2 vols. New York, 1976.

DIMITRIJE DJORDJEVIĆ

BELINSKY, VISSARION (1811–1848), Russian literary critic.

Vissarion Grigorievich Belinsky achieved renown and influence both as Russia's first literary critic and as a founding member of the Russian intelligentsia. He became known as "Furious Vissarion" (*neistovyi Vissarion*) for his strongly held convictions and passion in expressing them, a reputation that in the Soviet period under Joseph Stalin, whose patronymic Vissarionovich reflected Belinsky's forename, was used to justify some of the more rigid orthodoxies of socialist realism. He was labeled a revolutionary democrat and treated as a socialist cultural icon. More recently, serious attempts have been made to free his reputation of these adulterations and to give a more positive assessment of his place in Russia's cultural history.

Born on 11 June (30 May, old style) 1811 into an unprivileged background as the son of a provincial doctor in Penza, Belinsky succeeded in achieving his ambition of gaining entrance to Moscow University. Incipient tuberculosis, poverty, and uninspired teaching left him largely self-taught, although he hoped to alleviate his poverty by composing a wordy, melodramatic play, *Dmitry Kalinin,* which had the aim of exposing the evil of serfdom. It was immediately rejected by the authorities, and he was expelled from the university. This setback made him all the more determined to oppose serfdom and the semifeudal system that promoted it.

At the heart of all his endeavors, however, was Russian literature. In 1834, within a couple of years of his expulsion from Moscow University, Belinsky published a highly personal but influential review ("Literaturnye mechtaniya" [Literary reveries]) that made exalted claims for the role of literature in terms of German Romantic idealism, particularly Friedrich Wilhelm Joseph von Schelling, but could not as yet identify a specifically Russian literature. Throughout the 1830s, partly under the influence of Mikhail Bakunin, he looked to Johann Gottlieb Fichte and Georg Wilhelm Friedrich Hegel for a guiding philosophical ideal that he could apply to Russian literature. In fact, this led to a period of so-called reconciliation with reality when he praised the Russian autocracy and the political status quo and seriously misinterpreted Alexander Griboyedov's satirical play *Woe from Wit* (1822–1824).

On moving from Moscow to St. Petersburg in 1839 to work for the leading "fat journal" (a term used to denote an authoritative, encyclopedic style of journal), *Otechestvennye zapiski* (Notes of the fatherland), Belinsky abandoned his former ideals and adopted a philanthropic socialism, based to some extent on French Utopian Socialism. If the conditions of censorship under which he always worked prevented him from overt commitment, he used many of his critical articles and annual reviews both to emphasize the historical perspective of Russian literature, beginning with the Westernization of Russian culture under Peter the Great (r. 1682–1725), whom he always admired, and to make literature more realistic (though he never used the term *realism*) and more critical of the injustices in Russian society. His review, for example, of Mikhail Lermontov's famous novel *A Hero of Our Time* (1840) offered a sympathetic and sensitive analysis of the "superfluous," psychologically complex hero, Pechorin. More acutely, if only obliquely, he indicated the social implication of Nikolai Gogol's masterpiece *Dead Souls* (1842) as an exposure of serfdom. Belinsky's only extended piece of critical writing (1843–1846) was a survey of pre-Pushkinian poetry as well as the first detailed treatment of Alexander Pushkin's work, culminating in a famous assessment of *Yevgeny Onegin* (1833). He also "discovered" Fyodor Dostoyevsky, was friendly with Ivan Turgenev, and was an admirer of Ivan Goncharov.

His love letters to his future wife, a remarkable cache, reveal him as all too human. Meanwhile, in 1846 and 1847, as leading contributor to the newly reconstituted journal *Sovremennik* (The contemporary), he wrote some of his most influential articles, but his health was failing. After a lengthy visit to southern Russia in an effort to improve it, he went abroad in 1847 to find a cure. Shortly before, Gogol, then Russia's leading writer, had published an eccentrically reactionary work *Selected Passages from Correspondence with Friends*. While in Salzbrunn, Silesia, freed of censorship, Belinsky wrote his famous *Letter to Gogol* in which he attacked the writer's reactionary views, his religiosity, and his betrayal of the high standards demanded of a writer; advocated the abolition of serfdom; and delivered the furious denunciation: "Proponent of the knout, apostle of ignorance, upholder of obscurantism and the black arts, panegyrist of Tartar morals, what are you doing?"

This was Belinsky's final legacy, composed within a year of his death. It became Turgenev's lifelong credo, the pretext for Dostoevsky's ten-year exile after he read it aloud, and a fundamental text of the Russian intelligentsia. Though often prolix in expressing his ideas, Belinsky usually demonstrated an acute critical sense related more to generalities than specifics. His deliberate refusal to serve in any official sense enhanced his moral authority and ensured his influence for generations. He died in St. Petersburg on 7 June (26 May, old style) 1848.

See also **Dostoyevsky, Fyodor; Gogol, Nikolai; Intelligentsia; Pushkin, Alexander; Turgenev, Ivan.**

BIBLIOGRAPHY

Primary Sources

Belinskii, V. G. *Polnoe sobranie sochinenii*. 13 vols. Moscow, 1953–1959. Collected works.

Matlaw, Ralph E., ed. *Belinsky, Chernyshevsky, and Dobrolyubov: Selected Criticism*. New York, 1962. Translations of "Thoughts and Notes on Russian Literature," "A Survey of Russian Literature in 1847: Part Two," and "Letter to Gogol."

Secondary Sources

Bowman, Herbert E. *Vissarion Belinski, 1811–1848: A Study in the Origins of Social Criticism in Russia*. Cambridge, Mass., 1954.

Freeborn, Richard. *Furious Vissarion: Belinskii's Struggle for Literature, Love, and Ideas*. London, 2003.

Nechaeva, V. S. *V. G. Belinsky*. 4 vols. Leningrad, 1949–1967. Standard biography.

Terras, Victor. *Belinskij and Russian Literary Criticism: The Heritage of Organic Aesthetics*. Madison, Wisc., 1974.

RICHARD FREEBORN

BELY, ANDREI (1880–1934), Russian poet and novelist.

A writer of great versatility and prodigious talent, Andrei Bely excelled in highly original poetry, experimental prose, and innovative studies of literature; he also was a major theorist of the

Peterburg is a quintessentially modernist narrative about one's mind and its self-doubts. The action takes place in the northern capital of the Russian Empire at the time of the failed Revolution of 1905. The central character is an old senator and acting minister in the imperial government—Apollon Apollonovich Ableukhov—the embodiment of Western determination and will, who dreams of preserving the geometric design of the city (his first name and patronymic meaning Apollo, son of Apollo; his last name is of obviously Asian origin). Other characters include Ableukhov's son, Nikolai, who is affiliated with the revolutionaries and is desperately in love with his friend's wife. As the only way out of his inner emotional turmoil, Nikolai accepts an assignment to plant a bomb in a government official's study, only to find that the doomed official is his own father. The bomb explodes but kills no one, and Nikolai, a personification of Eastern introspection, dedicates the rest of his life to studying religious philosophy and mystical contemplation.

Russian symbolist school. As a public intellectual, Bely championed a "spiritual revolution" in Russia, thus introducing a different dimension into the debate about his country's identity.

Bely was born Boris Nikolayevich Bugayev on 26 October (14 October, old style) 1880 in Moscow, into the family of a prominent mathematician, Nikolai Vasilyevich Bugayev (1837–1903). After contemplating a career as a composer and thinking about taking monastic vows, he turned his back on both and dedicated himself entirely to literature. At the same time, he yielded to his father's pressure, and in 1903 he earned a master's degree from the respectable Natural Sciences Department of the Moscow Imperial University.

Bely's first published book was the experimental narrative *Simfoniya, 2-ya, dramaticheskaya* (1902; Second symphony, the dramatic). Three more so-called symphonies appeared in print between 1904 and 1908. These works deliberately blurred the distinction between poetry and prose, the subjective and the objective, and were modeled

on four symphonies by the German composer Robert Schumann. The explosive effect of Bely's second "symphony" in particular was its ability to combine a vivid caricature of the educated society of the day; innovative narrative structure; a highly elevated, at times mystical, tone; and an apocalyptic vision of the future. Bely's second book, a collection of poems called *Zoloto v lazuri* (1904; Gold in azure), further solidified his reputation as a literary revolutionary, and introduced a wide thematic range, unusual rhyming patterns, deliberately shocking imagery, and engaging color symbolism into his poetry.

In 1905 Bely fell in love with the wife of a fellow symbolist, St. Petersburg poet Alexander Blok. This event coincided with the failed Russian revolution of the same year, thus tempting Bely to symbolically reinterpret his own confused feelings and those of the Bloks as an echo of the general crisis of the Russian national psyche. Bely's most powerful collection of poems, *Pepel* (1909; Ashes), which the author himself called "a book of self-immolation and death," and his groundbreaking novel *Peterburg* (published serially 1913–1914), were the direct result of this reinterpretation.

A powerful statement on the psychology of political terror, which Bely interpreted as the ritual destruction of paternal authority, *Peterburg* also exposed growing conflicts inside European modernity and questioned Russia's cultural identity. Bely maintained that the country was neither fully European nor Asian, thus becoming one of the forerunners of the Eurasianist ideology.

Not surprisingly, Bely's idiosyncratic mix of revolutionarism, spiritualism, and strict moralism earned him criticism and praise from both the Left and the Right. When the revolution finally got its way in Russia during 1917 and 1918, Bely very easily felt out of favor with the new ruling elite, and from 1921 to 1923 he went into temporary exile in Germany. This was not his first extensive stay outside Russia; from 1910 to 1916 Bely had traveled abroad with his companion, Asya Turgeneva (the couple were married in 1914, but divorced in 1923). From the 1910s through the early 1920s, Bely became actively involved in the work of the Anthroposophical Society.

In the 1920s and 1930s Bely worked on voluminous memoirs and dedicated considerable time to rigorous studies of literature, which resulted in two major books—one (published in 1929) on the fluctuations of meter in Alexander Pushkin's apocalyptic poem "The Bronze Horseman," the other (published in 1934) on the literary craftsmanship of Nikolai Gogol In this period Bely experienced difficulty in publishing some of his work in the Soviet Union. He died in Moscow on 8 January 1934.

Bely's work strived to transcend ideas of a limited creative "self" and of literature defined solely by its historical or social significance. For him, everything written was only a point of departure in a quest for a final liberation from false authorities—a way to restore the unity of humanity. In accordance with his belief in the essential oneness of different artistic and intellectual discourses, Bely maintained that poetry was a true "philosophy of practical reason."

See also Blok, Alexander; Eurasianism; Modernism; St. Petersburg; Symbolism.

BIBLIOGRAPHY

Primary Sources

Bely, Andrei. Petersburg. Translated by Robert A. Maguire and John E. Malmstad. Bloomington, Ind., 1978. Translation of Peterburg, 3rd ed. (1922).

———. The First Encounter. Translated by Gerald Janecek. Princeton, N.J., 1979. Translation of Pervoe svidanie (1921).

———. Selected Essays of Andrey Bely. Edited and translated by Steven Cassedy. Berkeley, Calif., 1985.

———. The Dramatic Symphony. Translated by Roger and Angela Keys. And The Forms of Art. Translated by John Elsworth. Edinburgh, 1986.

Secondary Sources

Alexandrov, Vladimir E. Andrei Bely: The Major Symbolist Fiction. Cambridge, Mass., 1985.

Janecek, Gerald, ed. Andrey Bely: A Critical Review. Lexington, Ky., 1978.

Keys, Roger. The Reluctant Modernist: Andrei Belyi and the Development of Russian Fiction, 1902–1914. Oxford, U.K., 1996.

Malmstad, John E., ed. Andrey Bely: Spirit of Symbolism. Ithaca, N.Y., 1987.

IGOR VISHNEVETSKY

BENTHAM, JEREMY (1748–1832), English philosopher and political theorist, founder of utilitarianism.

The son of a wealthy lawyer and Tory, Jeremy Bentham was born in London on 15 February 1748. A child prodigy—studying historical tomes at age three and Latin at age six—he entered Oxford at twelve and at fifteen was admitted to Lincoln's Inn, one of the four English Inns of the Court where undergraduates studied law in preparation for being called to the Bar as barristers. Awkward in public, he did not practice the law he had studied under the legal scholar William Blackstone (1723–1780), who wrote the first definitive compilation of English law, Commentaries on the Laws of England (volumes published between 1765–1769). In 1776 Bentham gained notoriety for printing Fragment on Government, a critique of Blackstone and the legal system's reliance on fictions, common law, obscure language, and convoluted reasoning, among other things. Thereafter, his writing provided groundwork for continuing analysis of English jurisprudence. Establishing the school of utilitarianism (otherwise known as Benthamism or philosophical radicalism), he worked to codify regulations for every societal institution to produce the best citizenry and form of government for the greatest number of people. He had avid disciples in Britain and Continental Europe. Indeed, later in life, he provided utilitarian blueprints of constitutional principles (which featured the legislature as dominant over the executive) for Greece and Portugal.

Bentham based his utilitarian ideas on the writings of David Hume (1711–1776), Claude-Adrien Helvétius (1715–1771), David Hartley (1705–1757), and Joseph Priestley (1733–1804), from whom he took the phrase most associated with utilitarian thought: "the greatest happiness of the greatest number." Laying out the foundations and taxonomies of utilitarianism in his major work, Introduction to the Principles of Morals and Legislation (1789), Bentham asserted that humans are motivated by self-interest and that they will always seek pleasure and avoid pain. The term utilitarianism referred to the notion that everything has an effect that can be measured and that one could decide what laws to invoke based on their usefulness in fulfilling the greatest happiness. Grounded in Enlightenment reason, Bentham created the "felicific calculus," a mathematical method of discovering the greatest quantity of happiness by numerically calculating the intensity, purity, and degree of pleasure and pain caused by specific actions.

To Bentham the group ("the greatest number") was as important as "the greatest pleasure" as he attempted to solve the problem of how to make self-interested governmental and individual entities choose actions that are responsive to the needs of the whole community. Intensely aware of the ideals and failures of the French Revolution, he believed that with the guidance of utilitarian philosophers and the extension of citizenship to the masses, the more responsible British government could be about seeking the happiness of the greatest number. Likewise, citizens could be trained through utilitarian principles and punishments to achieve self-interest precisely by seeking the happiness of the majority. Not surprisingly, contemporary and current critics charge that utilitarianism's assumptions are questionable and unquantifiable, and that they discount quality of pleasure, human altruism, and the needs of the minority. Nevertheless, John Troyer notes that Bentham's greatest happiness model "dominates" modern economics by seeing "rational action as an attempt to maximize net utility" (p. vii).

A prolific, often disorganized and idiosyncratic writer, Bentham relied on his followers—including James Mill (1773–1836) and his son John Stuart Mill (1806–1873)—to edit and collate his massive stockpile of manuscripts. Though some current scholars question the degree of Bentham's influence, it has been traditional to view his ideas as helping to spawn political reforms that transformed British government, founding it on the science of governing. During the Victorian period (1830s–1901), utilitarians are commonly seen as an important force in bringing about the New Poor Laws, the 1832 Reform Bill, the civil service, the secret ballot, Catholic Emancipation, universal suffrage, the end of aristocratic sinecures, and the abolition of slavery, as well as laws establishing education reforms.

Particularly interested in prison reform, for twenty years Bentham worked on a blueprint for a "Panopticon," a prison that featured a semicircular penitentiary with a central observation tower that constantly had a view into the surrounding cells. He argued that making prisoners perpetually subject to the guard's observation would cause them to internalize self-discipline and thus learn behavior that was in the self-interest of society. In *Discipline and Punish: The Birth of the Prison* (1977), the philosopher Michel Foucault (1926–1984) famously uses the Panopticon as a metaphor for what he sees as the oppressive, omniscient modern state that engenders and depends on self-monitoring individuals. Many critics have incorporated this influential concept into their work, while others argue that Foucault's use of Bentham's complex ideas is simplistic, monolithic, and lacking in appreciation for Bentham's democratic impulses.

See also **Mill, James; Mill, John Stuart; Utilitarianism.**

BIBLIOGRAPHY

Cosgrove, Richard A. *Scholars of the Law: English Jurisprudence from Blackstone to Hart.* New York, 1996.

Harrison, Ross. *Bentham.* London, 1983.

Kelly, Paul J. *Utilitarianism and Distributive Justice: Jeremy Bentham and the Civil Law.* Oxford, U.K., 1990.

Mack, Mary Peter. *Jeremy Bentham: An Odyssey of Ideas.* New York, 1963.

Troyer, John. "Introduction." In *Classical Utilitarians: Bentham and Mill,* edited by John Troyer, vii–xxviii. Indianapolis, Ind., 2003.

GAIL TURLEY HOUSTON

BERDYAYEV, NIKOLAI (1874–1948), Russian philosopher.

Nikolai Alexandrovich Berdyayev was born into an aristocratic family on 18 March (6 March, old style) 1874, near Kiev. Rather than follow the family tradition of military service, he entered Kiev University in 1894. His formal education ended in 1898, when he was arrested and expelled for socialist activity. Two years later he was sentenced to a three-year exile in Vologda, a town in the northern part of European Russia. Soon after returning to Kiev, he met and married Lydia Trushova. They had no children.

Berdyayev was a prominent figure in the intellectual debates of his time. In 1894 he helped launch a "back to Kant" movement intended to supplement Marxism with an autonomous ethic, among other goals. In 1902 he rejected Marxist materialism, but not socialism. That year, he participated in the pathbreaking symposium, *Problems of Idealism,* which challenged the positivism, rationalism, and materialism championed by the intelligentsia. In 1909 he participated in the symposium *Landmarks,* a harsh critique of the revolutionary intelligentsia. Between 1900 and 1916, Berdyayev published seven books and over seventy articles on literature, philosophy, religion, and contemporary issues. Throughout, he emphasized the supreme value of the person and extolled freedom, opposing it to "natural necessity" and Isaac Newton's "mechanical universe."

In "The Ethical Problem of the Light of Philosophical Idealism" (his contribution to *Problems of Idealism*), Berdyayev linked ethics, metaphysics, religion, and politics. Arguing that Kant's idea of the autonomous value of every individual provides the philosophic basis for ethical individualism, and emphasizing Immanuel Kant's distinction between "is" and "ought," Berdyayev advocated a metaphysical liberalism based on personhood (a concept that encompasses body, soul, and spirit), and urged Russians to struggle for personal freedom, legal equality, self-realization, and moral self-perfection. In the same essay, he praised Friedrich Nietzsche for overcoming Kant's "middle-class morality" and preparing the free morality of the future, the morality of strong human individuality. According to Berdyayev, "Man [*Chelovek*] has not only the right but the duty to become a Superman, because the Superman is the path from man to God."

Around this time, Berdyayev became interested in the "new religious consciousness" being propagated by Dmitri S. Merezhkovsky, cofounder of the Religious-Philosophical Society of St. Petersburg (1901–1903, 1906–1917) and of the journal *Novy put* (New path). In 1904 Berdyayev moved to St. Petersburg to become coeditor of this journal. He was profoundly influenced by Merezhkovsky's contentions that people need religious faith, that Christianity must be reinterpreted to address the problems of modern life, and that the Second Coming of Christ is imminent.

When *Novy put* folded, Berdyayev became coeditor of its successor journal *Voprosy zhizni* (1905; Problems of life). He was instrumental in reviving the Religious-Philosophical Society in 1906. In 1908 Berdyayev moved to Moscow and became active in the Vladimir Soloviev Religious-Philosophical Society (1906–1917).

During the Revolution of 1905, Berdyayev at times expressed a millennial enthusiasm and praised anarchism, but at other times he criticized the intelligentsia's extremism and advocated a "neutral socialism," one guaranteeing everyone the necessities of life, as distinct from "socialism as religion," a dogmatic, obscurantist creed that would lead to despotism. Berdyayev's social ideal was a personalistic socialism similar to the Slavophiles' conception of *sobornost,* a free society united by love and common ideals in which the members retain their individuality (understood as self-expression). He supported the Constitutional Democrats (the Kadets), but reluctantly, because he considered them too rational, too lacking in religious passion, to appeal to the masses.

In "Philosophical Truth and the Moral Truth of the Intelligentsia" (his contribution to *Landmarks*), Berdyayev contended that the intelligentsia's utilitarian approach to truth as justice and law (*pravda*) has rendered it indifferent to philosophical truth (*istina*), and that the regeneration of Russia requires a new consciousness in which truth as justice (*pravda*) and philosophical truth (*istina*) are organically united. Such a consciousness can be achieved only on the basis of positive religion. *Landmarks* went through five printings in one year and provoked over two hundred newspaper and journal articles in praise or denunciation of its assault on the intelligentsia.

In *The Meaning of Creativity: An Attempt at the Justification of Man* (1916), which Berdyayev considered his most significant work, he maintained that creativity is not permitted or justified by religion; creativity is itself religion and is man's vocation. He believed that humankind was on the verge of an eschatological leap from the realm of necessity to the realm of freedom. The Third Testament (Merezhkovsky's term) will be the work of man.

By "man" Berdyayev meant men. He considered "woman" generative but not creative.

Berdyayev hailed the February Revolution of 1917, but not the October Revolution, which he considered a purely negative phenomenon. He remained active in Russian intellectual and cultural life until the government expelled him from Russia at the end of 1922. He settled in Clamart, near Paris, in 1924 and died there on 23 March 1948.

See also **Intelligentsia; Nietzsche, Friedrich; Russia; Slavophiles; Soloviev, Vladimir.**

BIBLIOGRAPHY

Primary Sources

Berdyayev, Nikolai. *The Meaning of the Creative Act.* Translated by Donald A. Lowrie. New York, 1955. Translation of *Smysl tvorchestva: Opyt opravdanie cheloveka* (1916).

———. *Dream and Reality: An Essay in Autobiography.* Translated by Katharine Lampert. New York, 1962. Translation of *Samopoznanie* (1949).

———. "Philosophical Truth and the Moral Truth of the Intelligentsia." In *Landmarks,* edited by Boris Shragin and Albert Todd, 3–22. Translated by Marian Schwartz. New York, 1977. Second English translation, as "Philosophical Verity and Intelligentsia Truth." In *Landmarks,* translated and edited by Marshall S. Shatz and Judith E. Zimmerman, 1–16. Armonk, N.Y., 1994. Translations of *Vekhi* (1909).

———. "Socialism as Religion." In *A Revolution of the Spirit: Crisis of Value in Russia, 1890–1924,* edited by Bernice Glatzer Rosenthal and Martha Bohachevsky-Chomiak, 107–133. Translated by Marian Schwartz. New York, 1990. Translation of "Sotsializm kak religiia" (1906).

———. "The Ethical Problem of the Light of Philosophical Idealism." In *Problems of Idealism,* translated and edited by Randall A. Poole, 161–197. New Haven, Conn., 2003. Translation of *Problemy idealizma* (1902).

Secondary Sources

Ermichev, A. A., ed. *N. A. Berdiaev: Pro et contra.* St. Petersburg, 1994.

Lowrie, Donald A. *Rebellious Prophet: A Life of Nicolai Berdyaev.* New York, 1960. Reprint, Westport, Conn., 1974.

Rosenthal, Bernice Glatzer. "Philosophers." Chap. 2 in *New Myth, New World: From Nietzsche to Stalinism,* 51–67. University Park, Pa., 2002.

Zenkovsky, V. V. "The Religio-Philosophic Renaissance in Early Twentieth Century Russia." Chap. 26 of vol. 2 of *A History of Russian Philosophy,* 754–791. Translated by George L. Kline. New York, 1953.

BERNICE GLATZER ROSENTHAL

BERGSON, HENRI (1859–1941), French philosopher.

The French philosopher Henri Bergson became an international celebrity following the 1907 publication of *Creative Evolution;* elected to the French Academy in 1914, he received a Nobel prize in literature in 1927. His major books include *Time and Free Will* (1889), which described the temporal dimension of human consciousness as synonymous with creative freedom, and *Matter and Memory* (1896), a philosophical analysis of the relation of mind to body. In addition he published more specialized studies, the most notable being *Duration and Simultaneity* (1922) and *The Two Sources of Morality and Religion* (1932); his complete writings and additional correspondence were later collected in his *Oeuvres* (1959) and *Mélanges* (1972).

Born in Paris on 18 October 1859, Bergson came from a Jewish background: his father, an accomplished musician, was Polish, while his mother hailed from northern England. After attending the École Normale Supérieure from 1878 to 1881, Bergson was appointed professor of philosophy, eventually gaining a post at the Lycée Clermont-Ferrand in 1883. In 1888 he moved back to Paris where he taught at the Lycée Henri IV (1890–1897) before being appointed senior lecturer at the École Normale Supérieure (1897–1900). In 1891 he married Louise Neuberger, and in 1893 they had a daughter, Jeanne, who would later become a painter. In 1900 Bergson was named professor of philosophy at the Collège de France, where he remained until his resignation in 1921 because of poor health. Before 1914 Bergson disseminated his ideas through public lectures at the Collège de France and speaking tours that took him to Italy (1911), England (1911), and the United States (1913). Aside from attracting such period luminaries as the writer Charles Péguy, the Catholic Thomist Jacques Maritain, and the anarchosyndicalist Georges Sorel, Bergson's weekly lectures drew an educated public, which further consolidated his international fame. By 1914 all his major works had been translated into English, German, Polish, and Russian.

Bergson's influence before 1914 was pervasive, in part because of the relation his philosophy had to the widespread "revolt against positivism" that typified the era. Central to Bergson's philosophy was an instrumental conception of the intellect and an attempt to define intuition as a mode of cognition able to grasp the creative essence of *durée* (duration), Bergson's term for time. The intellect reduced all temporal phenomena—the very essence of life—into quantative and deterministic schemas designed to suit the intellect's utilitarian ends. Intuition by contrast allow humans to enter into living things to grasp their unique character and creative potential. As a result intuition revealed the qualitative, rhythmic, and organic properties of the natural world. Bergson labeled all forms of life material manifestations of a vital impulse (*élan vital*) resulting in the rhythmic unfolding of temporality into extensity, Bergson's term for spatial form. Concrete extensity, argued Bergson, is composed of nothing more than changes in tension or energy, in short, qualitative movement. Bergson compared this movement to a melody and argued that all that distinguished the durational melody of matter from that of human consciousness is the faster rhythm of the latter when compared to the former. In Bergson's cosmology, matter itself possessed a latent consciousness, taking its place as the slowest rhythm on the scale of being whose degrees of rhythmic tension are a function of the degree of freedom inherent in their activity. Human beings, by virtue of their unique ability to intuit duration, are at the apex of the cosmological chain of being, and within the human species itself, artists, mystics, scientists, and metaphysicians are singled out as having developed their intuitive capacities to the utmost. Thus artists took up an exalted position in Bergson's metaphysics, which accounts for his widespread appeal among avant-garde artists of his generation.

Historians have charted the impact his concept of psychological *durée* had on the development of Anglo-American literature: authors as diverse as Willa Cather, T. S. Eliot, James Joyce, Dorothy Richardson, Gertrude Stein, and Wallace Stevens all registered his influence. In France Bergson gained a widespread following among French symbolists and a younger generation that included Péguy, the novelist Marcel Proust, and the poet and essayist Paul Valéry. In Russia the pattern repeated itself, with symbolists such as Andrei Bely and postsymbolists such as Osip Mandelstam and the futurist Velimir Khlebnikov all falling under the sway of Bergsonism. Bergson's impact was just as central to European avant-gardists associated with the visual arts. The fauvist Henri Matisse, the French cubists Albert Gleizes and Jean Metzinger, the Italian futurists Umberto Boccioni and Gino Severini, the English vorticist Wyndham Lewis, and the Russians Mikhail Larionov and Kazimir Malevich were among those profoundly influenced by the philosopher.

Among contemporary scientists and philosophers, Pierre Teilhard de Chardin, William James, Nishida Kitaro, Henri Poincaré, and Alfred North Whitehead all benefited from exposure to Bergson. Bergson's claim in *Creative Evolution* that *durée* found expression not only in art but also in an *élan vital* (vital impulse) was welcomed by occultists as support for their spiritualist critique of scientific and biological determinism. Bergson also influenced proponents of Catholic modernism, including Édouard Le Roy, and Alfred Firmin Loisy, who critiqued the rationalist assumptions underlying the thought of Thomas Aquinas. The rise of modernism provoked a backlash within the Catholic Church, which culminated in the placing of Bergson's book on the papal index of prohibited books in 1914. Bergson was caught up in other "culture wars": members of Charles Maurras's monarchist organization, Action Française, attacked Bergson in the name of French rationalism; Sorel conjured with Bergson's philosophy in formulating a voluntarist theory of revolution; and the writers Henri Massis and Alfred de Tarde pitted Bergson against Émile Durkheim in their well-publicized attack on pedagogy at the Sorbonne. Prominent intellectuals even switched sides in the battle over Bergson: thus the former Bergsonian Jacques Maritain wrote a neo-Thomist diatribe against him in 1913, while the British critic T. E. Hulme rejected Bergson following his exposure to Action Française in 1911. The "Bergsonian controversy" came to an abrupt end, however, when the European intelligentsia was swept up in World War I, and Bergson temporarily suspended his philosophical pursuits while playing a diplomatic role in the French war effort.

See also **Avant-Garde; Fin de Siècle; France; Modernism.**

BIBLIOGRAPHY

Primary Sources

Bergson, Henri. *Time and Free Will: An Essay on the Immediate Data of Consciousness.* Translated by F. L. Pogson. London, 1910. Translation of *Essai sur les données immédiates de la conscience* (1889).

———. *Creative Evolution.* Translated by Arthur Mitchell. New York, 1911. Reprint, Lanham, Md., 1984. Translation of *L'Évolution créatrice* (1907).

———. *Matter and Memory.* Translated by Nancy Margaret Paul and W. Scott Palmer. London, 1911. Reprint, Mineola, N.Y., 2001. Translation of *Matière et mémoire: Essai sur la relation du corps à l'esprit* (1896).

———. *Oeuvres.* Edited by André Robinet. Paris, 1959.

———. *Mélanges.* Edited by André Robinet. Paris, 1972.

Secondary Sources

Antliff, Mark. *Inventing Bergson: Cultural Politics and the Parisian Avant-Garde.* Princeton, N.J., 1993.

Burwick, Frederick, and Paul Douglass, eds. *The Crisis in Modernism: Bergson and the Vitalist Controversy.* Cambridge, U.K., 1992.

Fink, Hilary L. *Bergson and Russian Modernism, 1900–1930.* Evanston, Ill., 1999.

Gillies, Mary Ann. *Henri Bergson and British Modernism.* Montreal, 1996.

Grogin, R. C. *The Bergsonian Controversy in France, 1900–1914.* Calgary, Alta., 1988.

Mullarkey, John, ed. *The New Bergson.* Manchester, U.K., 1999.

Pilkington, A. E. *Bergson and His Influence: A Reassessment.* Cambridge, U.K., 1976.

Quirk, Tom. *Bergson and American Culture: The Worlds of Willa Cather and Wallace Stevens.* Chapel Hill, N.C., 1990.

MARK ANTLIFF

BERLIN. Berlin, with its unprepossessing location on the north German plain, rose to prominence first as a garrison town and then as the capital of a major military power, Prussia.

PRUSSIAN CAPITAL

By the time Frederick I (Frederick the Great, r. 1740–1786) died in 1786, not only Berlin's size but also its intellectual and cultural vitality made it a nascent rival to Vienna, the major city of central Europe. Frederick was a great devotee of the French Enlightenment, but his main contribution to intellectual life in his capital was the relaxation of censorship. After 1780, the city emerged as a center of publishing and of interaction across class and gender lines in literary salons, the most notable of which were hosted by Jewish women, Henriette Herz (1764–1847) and Rahel Levin (later Rahel Levin-Varnhagen; 1771–1833). The salons nurtured the writers who cultivated the new literary sensibility that came to be known as Romanticism. Although revolutionary ideas from France were much discussed in the salons, the distant rumblings left Berlin largely untouched until the army of Napoleon I (r. 1804–1814/15) defeated Prussia's army and occupied Berlin from 1806 to 1808. The anti-French feelings that had already emerged in Romantic theories of nationalism took their most pointed form in the 1808 lectures of the philosopher Johann Gottlieb Fichte (1762–1814) and a cult of bodily fitness promoted by the schoolteacher Ludwig Jahn (1778–1852). After the French defeats of 1813–1814, however, political repression and censorship quieted nationalists and other reformers.

The Prussian reforms that followed the 1806 defeat gave Berlin an elected city council—with a limited franchise and limited powers—as well as a university, intended by its founder Wilhelm von Humboldt (1767–1835) as the embodiment of humanistic education. It quickly emerged as a major center of theology and philosophy (most notably with Georg Wilhelm Friedrich Hegel [1770–1831]) and later became one of Europe's leading centers of scientific research, even attracting Albert Einstein (1879–1955) to its faculty in 1914. Humboldt's efforts to stake a claim for art in the capital also helped promote the work of the royal architect Karl Friedrich Schinkel (1781–1841), whose state theater and museum were the most prominent of the buildings that reshaped the vicinity of the royal palace in the early decades of the nineteenth century.

After rumbles of dissent and occasional violence from 1830 on, the political explosion in

Schauspielhaus, Berlin. Designed by Karl-Friedrich Schinkel with sculptural decoration by Friedrich Tieck and Christian Rauch, this Berlin concert hall opened in May of 1821 with performances of works by Gluck, Goethe, and Mecklenburg. ©ANDREA JEMOLO/CORBIS

March 1848 resembled that of many other cities. News from Paris and Vienna provoked a demonstration to demand reforms from Frederick William IV (r. 1840–1861). Attempts to disperse the 10,000 demonstrators on 18 March turned bloody, prompting the king to pull his troops out of the city. He bowed to the demands of the demonstrators both substantively and symbolically, paying his respects to the 200 dead and naming a new government. A newly elected Prussian national assembly convened in Berlin in May. The freedom of the press established in March also permitted a national workers' congress to meet there in August. Continuing demonstrations and riots strengthened the hand of the king's conservative advisors, however, leading to the forcible adjournment of the

national assembly in November, followed by arrests and a reimposition of censorship.

INDUSTRY AND GROWTH

Berlin was a rare national capital that also became a major center of large-scale, cutting-edge industry. The city's eighteenth-century economy had been shaped by two royal policies: the growth of the army, and the religious toleration that made the city a home to persecuted Protestant and Jewish refugees with artisanal and entrepreneurial skills. Berlin's population and industry continued to grow rapidly in the early nineteenth century, but the more fundamental transformation came at mid-century, as Germany's new joint-stock banks clustered in Berlin and helped to finance the

EUROPE AND THE WORLD

Sultan Mahmud II in Procession. Watercolor, Greek school, 1809. Mahmud II became the ruler of the Ottoman Empire in 1808, at a time when the empire was facing dissolution. The breakup of the Ottoman Empire and the fate of its component states became a source of great concern for European powers during the nineteenth century. VICTORIA & ALBERT MUSEUM, LONDON/ART RESOURCE, NY

LEFT: *An Arab by a Doorway.* Mid-nineteenth-century painting by Giuseppe de Nittis. CHRISTIE'S IMAGES, LONDON, UK /BRIDGEMAN ART LIBRARY

BELOW: *Algerian Women in Their Apartment.* Painting by Eugène Delacroix, 1834. In 1832, the renowned French painter accompanied diplomat Charles de Mornay on a trip to meet with the Sultan of Morocco. Greatly impressed with the visual richness of the region, Delacroix subsequently created a number of paintings based on his observations there. His depictions served as a first glimpse of North Africa for many of his compatriots in France. RÉUNION DES MUSÉES NATIONAUX/ART RESOURCE, NY

LEFT: An Englishman shooting a tiger from an elephant. Miniature by a Kalighat artist, c. 1830. Kalighat painters, so called because they worked in the neighborhood of the Kalighat temple in Calcutta, often depicted the changes being introduced into Indian society by the British colonists. VICTORIA & ALBERT MUSEUM, LONDON, UK/BRIDGEMAN ART LIBRARY

BELOW: *Heke Fells the Flagstaff at Kororareka.* Lithograph by Arthur David McCormick from the book *New Zealand* by Reginald Horsley, 1908. Hone Heke Pokai, a Maori chieftain, and his followers rebelled against British colonization in a series of attacks in 1844–1845, now known as Hone Heke's War. Although Heke did successfully repel British troops sent to reestablish control of the area, he was later defeated by a rival chieftain. MARY EVANS PICTURE LIBRARY

TOP: *Transept from the grand entrance to the Great Exhibition.* Lithograph, c. 1851. Titled the "Great Exhibition of the Works of Industry of All Nations," the first world's fair, held in London in 1851, was intended to prove the superiority of British goods by placing them in competition with goods from other nations. In doing so, it offered visitors an unprecedented, though distorted, view of non-European nations and cultures. © HISTORICAL PICTURE ARCHIVE/CORBIS

MIDDLE: *Series of Entertainments of Foreigners.* Print by Utagawa Yoshitora, 1861. The presence of Europeans in the newly opened port of Yokohama led to the creation of what are now known as Yokohama prints, depicting the lives of the settlers about whom the Japanese were exceedingly curious. It has been suggested that Utagawa had never in fact seen a European and based his prints instead on images from Western art. RÉUNION DES MUSÉES NATIONAUX/ART RESOURCE, NY

BOTTOM: *Allegory of the British Empire Strangling the World.* Cartoon from an Italian edition of the French journal *Le Perroquet,* 1878. A French artist laments the results of British colonial policies, particularly in the Middle East, India, and Australia. BIBLIOTHÈQUE NATIONALE, PARIS, FRANCE/BRIDGEMAN ART LIBRARY/ARCHIVES CHARMET

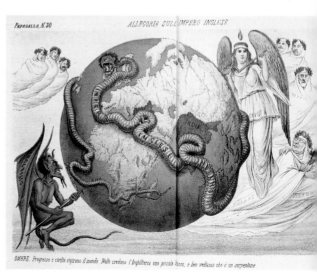

The Day of the God. Painting by Paul Gauguin, 1894. Perhaps no other European artist of the nineteenth century was more influenced by contact with non-European culture than Paul Gauguin. His trip to Tahiti in 1891 led to a number of paintings considered revolutionary for their simplified forms and use of color for expressive effect. Gauguin's innovations were adopted by many of his contemporaries and became a major element in the subsequent development of modernism in painting. HARRY N. ABRAMS, INC.

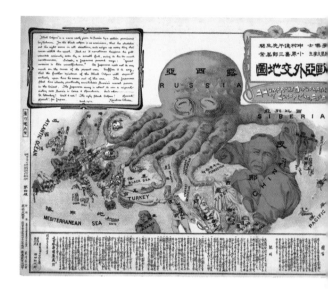

RIGHT: Ohara map, 1904. Fred Rose's 1877 vision of Russia as a voracious octopus was adapted in this 1904 Japanese version by Kisaburo Ohara. The accompanying text celebrates Japanese victories in the Russo-Japanese War. REPRODUCED COURTESY OF MAP COLLECTION, YALE UNIVERSITY LIBRARY

BELOW: *Angling in Troubled Waters.* Map based on the designs of Fred Rose, 1899. Rose updated his political caricature map of Europe at the end of the nineteenth century, once again focusing on the Asian territorial aims of Russia. REPRODUCED COURTESY OF MAP COLLECTION, YALE UNIVERSITY LIBRARY

THE PRIZE

. XII. [New Series.]   DECEMBER, 1901.   [One Penny.

A SCRIPTURE LESSON.

THE MODERN CIVILIZATION OF EUROPE
FRANCE IN MOROCCO & ENGLAND IN EGYPT

دكرى دنشواى او مدرية اوربا الحديثة
انجلترا في مصر وفرنسا في مراكش

TOP LEFT: Illustration from *The Prize,* December 1901. This illustration from a British children's magazine reflects the European concept of the moral inferiority of Asian peoples. MARY EVANS PICTURE LIBRARY

BOTTOM LEFT: *The Modern Civilization of Europe.* Lithograph by A. H. Zaki, c. 1914. An Arab artist presents his view of the nature of European colonial policy in a lithograph clearly designed for European, notably English, audiences. © CORBIS

BELOW: *Honor to the Heroes of Colonial Expansion.* Cover of a supplement to the French newspaper *Le Petit Journal,* 6 March 1910. The sacrifices of French soldiers and their African colleagues in establishing French control in North Africa are celebrated. MARY EVANS PICTURE LIBRARY

HONNEUR AUX HEROS DE L'EXPANSION COLONIALE !

large factories that accompanied the arrival of the railroads (the locomotive manufacturer Borsig being Berlin's first industrial behemoth) and telegraphy (to which the Berlin firm Siemens made major contributions). In 1859, two decades after he had been a student there, Karl Marx (1818–1883) wrote, "If you saw Berlin ten years ago, you would not recognize it now. From a stiff place of parade it has been transformed into the bustling center of German machine-building." Berlin became a major producer of both machinery and electrical goods. The large factories first clustered at the northern gates and later scattered to many suburbs, while the Luisenstadt district in the southeast attracted hundreds of small courtyard workshops, especially in the clothing industry. The army's contribution to this industrial revolution is difficult to measure, but just as the demand for uniforms helped make eighteenth-century Berlin a major center of textile manufacturing, it is notable that the Prussian army took an early interest in the military uses of the telegraph and railroad, refining their use to devastating effect in the wars of 1866 and 1870.

These victorious wars made Berlin the capital of a unified Germany. The federal nature of the new state meant that its presence in Berlin remained much smaller than that of the growing Prussian bureaucracy. Wilhelmstrasse, with its row of ministries in converted palaces, became synonymous with government and especially with the diplomacy of Otto von Bismarck (1815–1898), who presided over both the chancellery and foreign ministry and served as host of the Congress of Berlin in 1878. A few blocks away, the Reichstag building was completed in 1894 to house the imperial parliament created in 1871. The national government was just one catalyst for the creation of a far more dominant metropolis than decentralized Germany had ever had, as Berlin drew political, economic, and cultural elites from the provinces and also became a target for anti-urban passions.

After midcentury, Berlin grew outward rapidly. Although its eighteenth-century customs wall remained in place until 1868, in 1841 and 1861 the city annexed large chunks of territory beyond it, growing from 1,330 to a still-compact 5,923 hectares. The city's population of 150,000 in 1786 was some seven times as large as a century before, but nearly a quarter of the residents were garrison soldiers and their dependents. By 1877 another sevenfold increase brought the total over a million, with a second million added by 1905. By then, growth had long since spilled over into the suburbs: bourgeois Charlottenburg grew from 20,000 residents in 1871 to 306,000 in 1910, proletarian Rixdorf (later called Neukölln) from 8,000 to 237,000. When Berlin annexed its suburbs in 1920, it doubled its population to about four million. The heart of the Prussian capital had been the royal palace and the stately boulevard Unter den Linden, with commerce centered on adjacent Friedrichstrasse. Around 1900 the city's commercial center pushed southwest into grand new buildings on Leipziger Strasse and Potsdamer Platz, and a rival center was emerging along the fashionable new boulevard Kurfürstendamm, west of the Tiergarten park. Six major rail terminals ringed the city by 1882, when a new east-west rail line, built by the state railway, opened the city center to rail commuters. The first privately built subway line was completed in 1902, but most workers still commuted on foot or by streetcar.

Berlin had been a Protestant city since the Reformation, and most migrants were Protestant as well, although ever fewer attended church. Late in the century, many Roman Catholics came from eastern and western Prussian provinces, including many Poles. By the early 1900s, 11 percent of Berliners were Catholic. Jews never exceeded 5 percent of the population, but they attracted attention—much of it unwanted—as Jews and Gentiles alike came to acknowledge a prominent Jewish role in the city's economy and culture. Some assimilated German Jews advanced to modest prosperity, a few to great wealth. Most had little to do with the poor, Yiddish-speaking new arrivals from the east who clustered in Berlin's most notorious slum, the so-called shed quarter near Alexanderplatz, which was mostly leveled after 1906 in Berlin's only major slum clearance project before World War II.

Berlin faced the typical public health problems of a burgeoning city, and responded fairly well to them, although it was widely regarded as a laggard by the impressive standards of German municipal government. The Prussian state's infringement on what were elsewhere regarded as municipal prerogatives sometimes imposed vital reforms, but it also

The Friedrichstrasse, a major shopping area in Berlin, photographed in 1894. © MICHAEL MASLAN HISTORIC PHOTOGRAPHS/ CORBIS

hampered the formation of a civic-minded local elite. Past the middle of the century, Berliners were entirely at the mercy of wells, cesspools, open gutters, and the meager flow of the filthy Spree River. The Prussian government licensed the city's first waterworks in 1852, and a sewer system was built in the 1870s. In 1872, the English sanitary reformer Sir Edwin Chadwick (1800–1890) urged approval of the latter by telling Berliners that visitors arriving elsewhere from their city could be recognized by the foul odor of their clothes. In the following decades, cholera vanished and typhoid became much less common, but tuberculosis persisted as a killer.

Well into the twentieth century, critics blamed the city's miserable housing conditions on the 1862 city extension plan drawn up by the engineer James

Hobrecht (1825–1902), although it is difficult to imagine how a better plan could have overcome the problems of poverty and overcrowding in most neighborhoods. Hobrecht's plan was little more than a sketch of broad streets and deep blocks covering the vast area that would be developed in the following decades. Apart from a few old sections, Berlin became a city of wide streets, as Hobrecht intended, but also of warrens of courtyard dwellings, something he did not foresee. Most streets were lined with enormous five-story apartment buildings with ornate facades concealing tiny flats, luxurious apartments, or, typically, both, with the larger flats facing the street. In western and southwestern suburbs such as Charlottenburg, Schöneberg, and Wilmersdorf, upscale apartments predominated, and beyond them, villa districts such as Grunewald and Wannsee stretched as far as the old royal town of Potsdam in an expanse of suburbs unmatched on the Continent. In most other directions, working-class tenements were interspersed with factories. Berlin's speculative real estate market produced these solidly constructed and spacious buildings at an astonishing rate, but they acquired a dreadful reputation. Most rooms faced gloomy courtyards and most flats were badly overcrowded; a typical building had a hundred or more residents. They were short on toilets and baths, and the upper classes feared them as breeders not only of disease but also of loose morals and subversive ideas. Certainly they did not fulfill a middle-class ideal of privacy, as working-class families typically could afford their own flats only by taking in single male lodgers. Reformers decried the tenements but effected little change.

CLASS AND CULTURE

The tenements bred a vigorous working-class subculture in which courtyard peddlers and corner pubs played a role, as did the Social Democratic Party and the labor unions it sponsored. Berlin's factories proved fruitful ground for socialist and union organizing, and the city became known as a Red stronghold. Although the unequal Prussian franchise kept the municipal government in the hands of middle-class liberals, by 1912 the Social Democratic Party received 75 percent of Berlin's vote in the Reichstag election. Berlin's teeming streets and other public spaces became places of convivial sociability but also of frequent tension between the police and the restive majority. The early 1900s saw increasingly large and frequent street protests, some occasioned by strikes, others by Social Democratic marches and rallies for democratic reforms. Compromises and tensions marked the relationship between the crowds and the police, which had to adjust to recently established legal rights of assembly and to ever larger but usually orderly demonstrations. A rare outbreak of large-scale disorder, sparked by a strike, lasted for several days in 1910 in the district of Moabit, which, like neighboring Wedding, was an area of large factories and tenements with a more exclusively proletarian population than most other parts of the city. Along with strikes and demonstrations, crowds also assembled to cheer the emperor on festive occasions, and to show their support for him and the nation in the summer of 1914.

Berlin's loyalty to Prussian traditions, especially military ones, was often exaggerated, but foreign visitors were inclined to see Berliners as servile, a reputation cemented by a notorious incident in 1906 when a drifter acquired a used army captain's uniform and proceeded to commandeer a passing squad of soldiers, seize a suburban town hall, arrest the mayor, and abscond with the treasury, all without resistance. Countervailing images emphasized bourgeois strivers (often stereotyped as Jewish) and cheeky proletarians. Ordinary Berliners were renowned for their irreverent sense of humor, a spirit captured in the drawings and engravings of the popular artist Heinrich Zille (1858–1929). Visitors like Mark Twain (1835–1910) in 1892 remarked on the newness of "the German Chicago" and the dynamism as well as the rawness of its society.

Although the wealthier classes were largely united in their antipathy to Social Democracy, the cultured bourgeoisie sometimes chafed under the yoke of the court, nobility, and army. One bourgeois institution that quickly rose to international prominence was the Berlin Philharmonic Orchestra, founded in 1882. There was more discord at the royal opera, where Emperor William II (r. 1888–1918) objected to the tastes of the composer Richard Strauss (1864–1949), its conductor from 1898 to 1918. That was only one example of a growing conflict between the official culture and the growing oppositional one. Prussian wealth, power, and cultural ambition enabled Berlin to amass great museum collections of European art and classical antiquities, including the Hellenistic altar from Pergamon and the treasures Heinrich Schliemann (1822–1890) unearthed at Troy, but the museum director Hugo von Tschudi (1851–1911) was forced out in 1909 because William II abhorred his acquisitions of modern art. The emperor's taste for grand neoclassical painting and sculpture was apparent in Berlin's museums and public squares, but during his reign, modern writers and artists flocked to Berlin from across central Europe, drawn by like-minded publishers and gallerists as well as the palpable excitement they felt in the demimonde of seamy Friedrichstrasse, the crowds and lights of Potsdamer Platz, and the glittering entertainment district emerging on Kurfürstendamm.

Street, Berlin, 1913. Painting by Ernst Ludwig Kirchner. Kirchner's expressionist style captures the elegance and excitement of early-twentieth-century Berlin. DIGITAL IMAGE © THE MUSEUM OF MODERN ART/LICENSED BY SCALA/ART RESOURCE, NY; © BY INGEBORG AND DR. WOLFGANG HENZE-KETTERER, WICHTRACH/BERN

In the 1880s Berlin became the center of German literary naturalism, with a circle of writers attentive to the miseries of the urban working class. This new literature attracted most attention on the stage as Berlin became the center of the central European theatrical world, with new theaters playing the shocking works of foreign playwrights such as Henrik Johann Ibsen (1828–1906) as well as those of local writers, notably Gerhart Hauptmann (1862–1946). Some theaters also broke new ground in their attempts to reach a working-class audience. Much of the formal innovation and daring subject matter that made Berlin theater and cabaret world-famous in the 1920s was developed before 1914. Another example of Berlin's drawing power is the group of expressionist painters known as Die Brücke, all of whom moved from Dresden to Berlin around 1910. Ernst Ludwig Kirchner (1880–1938) in particular became famous for his lurid paintings of Berlin street life. During the same years,

the brief flowering of literary expressionism was also largely a Berlin phenomenon, and attention to the urban crowd by the Berliners Georg Simmel (1858–1918) and Max Weber (1864–1920) helped create the discipline of sociology. Evidence that the new urban dynamism was felt beyond intellectual circles can be found in the city's many mass-circulation newspapers spreading their tales of crime and vice through the streetcars and cafés.

See also **Cities and Towns; Demography; Germany.**

BIBLIOGRAPHY

Bergdoll, Barry. *Karl Friedrich Schinkel: An Architecture for Prussia.* New York, 1994.

Fritzsche, Peter. *Reading Berlin 1900.* Cambridge, Mass., 1996.

Gay, Peter. *Freud, Jews, and Other Germans: Masters and Victims in Modernist Culture.* New York, 1978.

Hertz, Deborah. *Jewish High Society in Old Regime Berlin.* New Haven, Conn., 1988.

Hett, Benjamin Carter. *Death in the Tiergarten: Murder and Criminal Justice in the Kaiser's Berlin.* Cambridge, Mass., 2004.

Jelavich, Peter. *Berlin Cabaret.* Cambridge, Mass., 1993.

Large, David Clay. *Berlin: A Modern History.* New York, 2000.

Lindenberger, Thomas. *Strassenpolitik: Zur Sozialgeschichte der öffentlichen Ordnung in Berlin 1900 bis 1914.* Bonn, 1995.

Paret, Peter. *The Berlin Secession: Modernism and Its Enemies in Imperial Germany.* Cambridge, Mass., 1980.

Ribbe, Wolfgang, ed. *Geschichte Berlins.* 2 vols. Munich, 1988.

Taylor, Ronald. *Berlin and Its Culture: A Historical Portrait.* New Haven, Conn., 1997.

Townsend, Mary Lee. *Forbidden Laughter: Popular Humor and the Limits of Repression in Nineteenth-Century Prussia.* Ann Arbor, Mich., 1992.

BRIAN LADD

BERLIN CONFERENCE. The "Scramble for Africa" had commenced in earnest by the latter half of the nineteenth century, intensifying competition between European states and commercial interests intent on staking their claims to Africa.

The Berlin Conference of 1884–1885 was organized by the chancellor Otto von Bismarck of Germany to address a number of diplomatic and political problems arising from this European expansion into Africa. The broad purpose of the conference was to create a free-trade region in the Congo basin and neighboring areas, in the belief that such a regime would reduce disputes among European states. Fifteen states participated in the conference, which extended from November 1884 to February 1885; it included all the Great Powers of Europe at the time—Germany itself, France, Great Britain, and Portugal. Also present at the conference were a number of secondary European powers, such as Denmark, Spain, and Italy, as well as the United States and the Ottoman Empire. While the Berlin Conference had an enduring and profound impact on the peoples of Africa, no African societies were represented at the conference.

THE GENERAL ACT

The General Act signed on 26 February 1885 indicates the main preoccupation of the conference. The first article of the act stipulated that freedom of commerce was to prevail in a defined area centering on the Congo basin. The provisions were far-reaching, protecting all traders, regardless of nationality, from all taxes except those necessary to maintain the conditions in which commerce could take place. Monopolies were prohibited, and all nationalities were to enjoy free access to the specified territory and waters. Freedom of navigation of the Congo and Niger Rivers was guaranteed, although different regimes were applicable to each river, this a consequence of the fact that Britain and France had already made claims to sovereignty to the waters of the Niger.

Commerce, however, was not the only preoccupation of the act, which makes it clear from the outset that trade and humanitarianism were intrinsically linked. The act was designed, in the words of the preamble, to further the development of "commerce and of civilization in certain regions of Africa," and it was by this means that "the moral and material well being of the indigenous populations" was to be improved. The signatories undertook to "watch over the conservation of the indigenous populations and the amelioration of their moral and material conditions." Toward this end,

they were required to protect those missionary societies and philanthropic institutions that were created to "instruct the natives and to make them understand and appreciate the advantages of civilization." Freedom of worship and conscience were guaranteed. More particularly, the act sought to eliminate the slave trade by prohibiting the use of the specified territory as "a market or way of transit for the trade in slaves." Finally, the act articulated the concept of "effective occupation" as a mode of acquiring sovereignty over African territories, and set out a procedure by which signatory states asserting such sovereignty were required to notify other states of these claims. The act might be seen as an attempt to establish a set of principles that would regulate what had previously been a disorderly, haphazard, and unseemly grab for African land.

The act's emphasis on doctrines and mechanisms of international law is further reflected by the articles that sought to create an international commission charged with the basic task of ensuring that the provisions relating to the navigation of the Congo were complied with. The broad goals of the act—the promotion of free trade and the bringing of civilization to the benighted peoples of the dark continent that had been so vividly presented to the west through the explorations of David Livingstone (1813–1873) and Henry Morton Stanley (1841–1904)—won widespread support in Europe and North America.

DUAL CHARACTER OF THE GENERAL ACT

Unsurprisingly, the official proceedings and the General Act offer only a partial idea of the issues at stake at the conference. While publicly proclaiming the virtues of peaceful competition through free trade, Bismarck was also intent on asserting Germany's international prominence and ambitions and on combining with various other European powers to negate the strength of Great Britain, which had only a few years previously won significant control over Egypt. Britain, equally, was intent on protecting its various interests in Africa and on ensuring that the broad principles articulated at the conference were applicable only to limited areas in Africa. The British feared that their interests would be seriously compromised, for instance, by the application of the principle of "effective occupation" to all their colonial claims. The official multilateral proceedings that resulted in the General Act took place in parallel with convoluted bilateral negotiations between the powers gathered in Berlin. The idea was that multilateral negotiations would establish "general principles" and that this would be followed by various territorial settlements that would be subject to those principles. A complex relationship exists between the multilateral and bilateral negotiations, and it is this dual character of the conference that has given rise to ongoing debates about its results. Although justified as giving effect to the broad principles outlined in the General Act, these bilateral negotiations more frequently undermined, if not defeated, the purposes of the conference. Consequently, while the General Act itself makes no mention of partitioning Africa among imperial powers, this is what occurred. Thus, for example, Britain, seeking German support for various British claims to Egypt as against the French, conceded certain German claims to Togoland and Cameroons in return for control over the Niger. Partitions also took place in more geographically distant regions: following Berlin, the British and the Germans divided up the Pacific into spheres of influence.

The dual character of the Berlin Conference is further suggested by the fact that the General Act makes no explicit reference to the International Association of the Congo, which became the principal beneficiary of the proceedings. The association was a cover for King Leopold II of Belgium (r. 1865–1909), who harbored his own imperial ambitions. Leopold pursued these by employing Henry Morton Stanley, famed for finding Livingstone, to explore the region of the Congo. Stanley was noted for his ambition and brutality, and he entered into hundreds of treaties with the African chiefs he encountered. Leopold claimed that, by these treaties, the chiefs had granted the International Association a trade monopoly over their territories. Many of the treaties—which could hardly be regarded as comprehensible to the chiefs who supposedly signed them—went even further and ostensibly transferred sovereignty to the International Association. Armed with these treaties, Leopold, who was not present at the conference, made powerful claims to the Congo. Stanley attended the conference as adviser to the United States delegation. Leopold presented the International Association as a humanitarian and philanthropic organization intent on spreading the virtues of free trade and missionary activity. According to Adam Hochschild, the name itself was chosen to confuse the public into thinking that it was the same organization as a previous philanthropic organization, the International African Association (p. 65). Even while making these proclamations, Leopold made a number of private promises to various powers in Europe. These machinations finally resulted in the "Congo Free State" being recognized by several European states, giving Leopold control over this massive territory.

Given all the tensions and complexities involved in the proceedings, it is hardly surprising that the conference was careful to elide various problematic issues while appearing to resolve them. The question of how European states could claim sovereignty over African territories had been a vexed one to which international lawyers could give no coherent response. International lawyers had asserted that African states, being uncivilized, lacked legal personality. Simultaneously, the argument that private actors, the International Association of the Congo, could assert sovereignty over African peoples was acquiring widespread acceptance. Despite denying African sovereignty, European states entered into treaties with African leaders, and later proclaimed that these treaties gave them rights over African territories. In an attempt to resolve this issue, and the dangerous uncertainties that resulted from European states making extravagant claims about their "spheres of influence" with respect to vast African territories, the General Act outlined the concept of "effective occupation" with respect to the "the coasts of the African continent." The relevant article required signatory states that took possession of African territory to notify all the other signatories to the act, this in order to enable them to lodge protests. The concept of effectiveness implied that only if a signatory power could exercise real authority over a territory—as evidenced by its ability to discharge a number of responsibilities with regard to that territory, that is, to protect acquired rights and to ensure liberty of commerce—could it make a claim to effectively occupy it. As a consequence of this principle, European states that had assumed that their claims to various African territories were recognized as valid by their European rivals, felt threatened and compelled to establish clear title to what they believed to be their sphere of influence. Inchoate title had to be translated into "effective possession." As a result, the Berlin Conference, which was intended to manage the colonial scramble, instead accelerated and intensified it.

IMPLICATIONS

Although scholarly debate continues as to whether the conference itself partitioned Africa, it appears evident that at the very least it led to the further partition of the continent. The "failure" of the conference could be explained at a number of different levels. Too many difficult questions were evaded in the deliberations, and the idea of creating a free trade area in the Congo contradicted the economics of imperialism. European powers that invested heavily in acquiring colonies and managing them were hardly likely to then allow free trade within them. Leopold exploited the situation by suggesting that a disinterested, non-state entity, the International Association of the Congo, would adopt a different set of policies in administering African territory, and it was partly for this reason that he succeeded in winning recognition for his claims over the Congo.

Further, in many ways, the official conference became simply the arena in which states could acquire bargaining power for the more intricate bilateral negotiations. Virtually all the participating states understood the conference to be simply a front for the real deals that were being struck elsewhere. Equally importantly, of course, the realities of Africa could hardly be resolved by the meeting of statesmen in Berlin. None of the diplomats had any first-hand knowledge of Africa. And the notion that a group of statesmen gathered in Berlin could manage complex African societies with their own forms of authority and governance soon proved to be absurd.

None of the major purposes of the conference was achieved. The principle of free trade was entirely defeated, as the Congo, placed under Leopold's authority, became a monopoly. The humanitarian sentiment of the Final Act was made a mockery by Leopold, whose attempts to exploit the riches of the Congo led to the deaths of millions of Africans. The practice of amputating limbs, which is a tragically commonplace characteristic of contemporary ethnic conflicts in Africa was one of the punishments inflicted on natives in Leopold's Congo. It is estimated that more than twenty million Africans were killed in the Congo under Leopold.

The significance of the Berlin Conference diminished quickly in European history. Bismarck himself, the architect of Berlin, moved on to more pressing issues in his efforts to expand German power. The proceedings at Berlin were the subject of much scholarly commentary by international lawyers at the time, but the attempts to ensure that European expansion into Africa occurred in an orderly manner as provided for by international law, proved to be a failure. The international commission contemplated in the General Act was never established, and the principal of effective occupation did not resolve ongoing disputes as to how sovereignty over African territories was to be asserted. But these failures created a legacy in the form of a project that has preoccupied international lawyers and institutions ever since: that of devising an effective system of international governance of conquered territories and apparently dependent peoples.

For Africa, however—and the Third World more generally—the conference is important not only for what occurred there, but also because it symbolizes and embodies the realities of imperialism. Humanitarian sentiment became the guise for massive exploitation. And while European states carved up Africa between themselves both before and after the treaty, the glitter and publicity surrounding the conference made particularly vivid the enormous hubris and injustice embodied in the very idea, taken entirely for granted by the participants at the conference, that a group of European statesmen could gather together to divide up among themselves an enormous territory with no regard for the wishes of the inhabitants. The African press at the time—the newspapers in what is now Nigeria, for instance—had no illusion about the hypocrisy and arrogance suffusing the grand proceedings in Berlin.

CONSEQUENCES

A close study of the conference suggests it was doomed to fail. But this is far from saying that it had no consequences. The consequences were felt most tragically by the peoples of Africa, for the partitions that followed it established many African boundaries. These were the products of negotiations between European states rather than a result of any understanding of the peoples to be governed, who found themselves, consequently, living together in these artificially created states. These boundaries have contributed to ethnic tensions that continue to be a common problem in Africa, and which have led some scholars to call for a redrawing of the map of Africa. Somewhat ironically, African states themselves have asserted that these colonial boundaries must be respected, this because of the understandable fear that any prospect of renegotiating boundaries would intensify instability in an already vulnerable continent. It is in this way that the contradictions and problems that the diplomats in Berlin failed to resolve continue to haunt the peoples of Africa. The Berlin Conference is remembered in sharply contrasting terms: in Europe it is seen as a failed enterprise and largely a matter of historical interest, in Africa, the consequences of the conference have an enduring and tragic significance that has been the subject of ongoing debate and scholarship.

See also **Africa; Colonialism; Colonies; Imperialism; International Law; Leopold II.**

BIBLIOGRAPHY

Primary Sources

General Act of the Berlin Conference on West Africa, Feb. 26 1885, translated in Official Documents. *American Journal of International Law* 3 (1909): 7.

Secondary Sources

Anghie, Antony. *Imperialism, Sovereignty and the Making of International Law.* Cambridge, U.K., 2005.

Conrad, Joseph. *The Heart of Darkness.* Edinburgh, 1902.

Crowe, Sybil Eyre. *The Berlin West African Conference, 1884–1885.* Westport, Conn., 1942; reprinted 1970.

Förster, Stig, Wolfgang J. Mommsen, and Ronald Robinson, eds. *Bismarck, Europe, and Africa: The Berlin Conference, 1884–1885, and the Onset of Partition.* Oxford, U.K., 1988.

Hochschild, Adam. *King Leopold's Ghost: A Story of Greed, Terror, and Heroism in Colonial Africa.* Boston, 1998.

Koskenniemi, Martti. *The Gentle Civilizer of Nations: The Rise and Fall of International Law, 1870–1960.* Cambridge, U.K., 2002.

Mutua, Makau. "Why Redraw the Map of Africa: A Legal and Moral Inquiry." *Michigan Journal of International Law* 16 (1995): 1113–1176.

ANTONY ANGHIE

BERLIOZ, HECTOR (1803–1869), French composer and writer.

Louis-Hector Berlioz was born at La Côte-St.-André in the *département* of Isère in southeast France, the first of six children born to Louis-Joseph (a physician) and Marie-Antoinette (née Marmion) Berlioz.

Berlioz was a dashing and intriguing personality, an imaginative and innovative composer, and an erudite and perceptive music critic and journalist. Much of his reputation rests on his innovative handling of the many colors of the orchestra, and his treatise on orchestration remains an important text in the field. To many, he remains the quintessential representative of the Romantic era, for his music reflects the basic themes of Romanticism— the classics, Shakespeare's plays, love, nature, and the supernatural. His music—highly original in concept, structure, and variety of musical process—was unlike any in his time, and was not always understood or appreciated, even by some contemporary composers and musicians.

His father took charge of his early education, including studies in French and Latin literature, both of which were to significantly influence his compositions and prose writings. His musical training was quite unlike that of earlier composers; he taught himself basic music theory and his father gave him musical instruction on the flute and guitar, but he had virtually no training or competence on the customary instruments, such as the piano.

After receiving a bachelor's degree in 1821, he was sent (against his wishes) to the École de Médecine in Paris, where he eventually completed the *baccalauréat de sciences physiques* (1824). However, his passion for music soon led to his enrollment in the Conservatoire de Musique, to the dismay of his family, who hoped he would follow his father's path in medicine. He had, by then, published several musical works and some writings on music, but his rebellious nature left him continually at odds with the musical conservatism of the faculty.

After several unsuccessful attempts, Berlioz finally won the coveted Prix de Rome, which resulted in the completion of his *Symphonie fantas-*

tique: Episode de la vie d'un artiste (1830; *Fantastic Symphony: Episode in the Life of an Artist*). The symphony is autobiographical, based on his own passionate infatuation with the actress Harriet Smithson, with whom he fell in love at first sight while attending a play she was appearing in. It describes the many moods of a young artist who, in a fit of despondence over his passion for a woman, takes an overdose of opium to end his life. The drug induces many emotions and delusions, which are conveyed brilliantly through innovative orchestration and harmonic effects. The work's five movements also incorporate a musical theme (the *idée fixe* or obsessive idea) that undergoes many rhythmic manipulations, illustrating the young man's wildly conflicting emotional states about the beloved. Berlioz distributed a *programme* (a written description of the story) to the audience; to this day, the term *program music* denotes music that deals with extramusical historic or narrative events.

Berlioz's romantic nature is illustrated by his many intense and agonizing love interests, as early as his teenage years. Shortly after his first encounters with Harriet Smithson, he had a year-long affair with a beautiful (and apparently "accessible") young pianist, Camille Moke. He proposed marriage, but this came to naught, and she chose instead to wed the famous piano maker Pleyel. Berlioz's eventual marriage to Harriet (1834) produced a son, but proved disastrous, partly due to his affair with the singer Marie Recio; his later marriage to her (1854) was also unsuccessful.

Much of his mature life was spent conducting concerts of his and other composers' music throughout Europe and was widely recognized in these foreign lands. But, to his frustration, he was less successful in achieving the respect he deserved in his native country. During his many concert tours, he met and was befriended by some of the most important composers of the time—Robert Schumann, Franz Liszt, Felix Mendelssohn, Richard Wagner—and the famous violin virtuoso Niccolò Paganini.

Berlioz had been plagued for some time by a neurological condition, and in 1864 his physical and emotional health began to deteriorate. A few years after completing and revising his *Mémoires*

(published posthumously in 1870; *Memoirs*), he died in Paris and was buried in the cemetery at Montmartre. His grave site was improved during the 1969 centennial of his death, and his family home in La Côte-St.-André is now the site of the Musée Berlioz.

His major vocal compositions include: several operas, *Benvenuto Cellini* (1838), *Les Troyens* (1858; *The Trojans*), and *Béatrice et Bénédict* (1862; *Beatrice and Benedict*); a requiem mass (1837); a Christmas oratorio, *L'Enfance du Christ* (1856; *The Childhood of Christ*); a song cycle, *Les nuits d'Été* (1852; *Summer Nights*); a *Te Deum* (1849); and a "Dramatic Legend," *La damnation de Faust* (1846; *Damnation of Faust*).

His principal orchestral works include: *Fantastic Symphony* (1830); *Romeo and Juliet* (1839); *Harold en Italie* (1834; *Harold in Italy*); *Symphonie funebre et triomphale* (1840; *Grand Funeral and Triumphal Symphony*); and several concert overtures, the most important of which are *Waverley* (1828), *Le roi Lear* (1831; *King Lear*), *Rob Roy* (1831), and *Le carnival romain* (1843; *Roman Carnival*).

Equally important are his many prose writings, which include concert critiques and commentaries about the musical scene in his day, many of which ring true even today. He championed those composers who he felt espoused the best musical values and ideals, and railed mercilessly about such topics as government "intrusion" into the arts, the many idiosyncrasies of performers and managers, and the gullibility and fickleness of audiences of his day. His criticisms and observations are often biting and sarcastic, but well informed and erudite, and are enriched by frequent references to French and classical literature.

The most important of the published writings are: *Voyage musical en Allemagne et en Italie* (1844; *Musical Voyages in Germany and Italy*); *Les soirées de l'orchestra* (1852; *Evenings with the Orchestra*); his *Memoirs* (published posthumously in 1870), and, of course, his *Grand traité d'instrumentation et d'orchestration modernes* (1843; 2nd ed., 1855; *Treatise on Instrumentation and Modern Orchestration*).

See also **Liszt, Franz; Music; Paganini, Niccolò; Romanticism; Wagner, Richard.**

BIBLIOGRAPHY

Primary Sources

Berlioz, Hector. *Evenings with the Orchestra.* Translated and edited with an introduction and notes by Jacques Barzun. New York, 1969. 2nd ed., Chicago, 1999.

———. *Memoirs of Hector Berlioz, 1803–1865.* Translated by Rachel (Scott Russell) Holmes and Eleanor Holmes. Revised and annotated by Ernest New Newman. New York, 1932.

———. *Selected Letters.* Edited by Hugh Macdonald. Translated by Roger Nichols. New York, 1995.

Secondary Sources

Barzun, Jacques. *Berlioz and the Romantic Century.* 3rd ed. 2 vols. New York and London, 1969. The first extensive biography, it remains an essential source, despite some factual errors, and contains valuable information on nineteenth-century culture.

Bennett, Joseph. *Hector Berlioz.* London, 1884.

Bloom, Peter. *The Life of Berlioz.* Cambridge, U.K., and New York, 1998.

Cairns, David. *Berlioz: The Making of an Artist.* London, 1989.

Holoman, D. Kern. *Berlioz.* Cambridge, Mass., 1989. An important source with a very complete biographical account of Berlioz's life and his musical and social activity, with many illustrations and musical examples, as well as an annotated appendix of the composer's works.

Langford, Jeffrey, and Jane D. Graves. *Hector Berlioz: A Guide to Research.* New York, 1989.

Macdonald, Hugh. *Berlioz.* London, 1982.

———. "Berlioz," in *The New Grove Dictionary of Music and Musicians,* edited by Stanley Sadie, 579–610. Vol. 2. London, 1980.

Rose, Michael. *Berlioz Remembered.* London, 2001. Contains interesting observations and impressions of the composer by his contemporaries.

WILLIAM E. MELIN

BERNADOTTE, JEAN-BAPTISTE

(1763–1844; ruled 1818–1844), known as Charles XIV John (in Swedish, Karl XIV Johan), king of Sweden and Norway.

Jean-Baptiste Bernadotte was born in 1763 in Pau, France, the son of a provincial attorney. In 1780 he enlisted in the army as a common soldier. The French Revolution opened up new opportunities for men in the ranks, and Bernadotte was commissioned as a lieutenant in 1790. By 1794 he was already a general. He served briefly during 1798 as French ambassador in Vienna, then as minister of war the following year. In 1798 he became related by marriage to Napoleon Bonaparte. When Napoleon proclaimed himself emperor in 1804, Bernadotte was made a marshal of France, and in 1806 prince of Ponte Corvo. He served with distinction in Napoleon's campaigns, but his relations with the emperor were never cordial, and by 1810 Bernadotte was in Paris without assignment.

Opportunity now came from an unexpected quarter. After Napoleon and Tsar Alexander I concluded both peace and an alliance at Tilsit, Prussia (now Sovetsk, Russia), in 1807, the Russians conquered Finland from Sweden in 1808–1809, proclaiming it an autonomous grand duchy under the tsar. King Gustav IV Adolf (Gustavus IV Adolphus) of Sweden was deposed by a palace revolution in 1809. The Swedish Riksdag (parliament) excluded his heirs from the succession; elected his elderly, childless uncle as King Charles (Karl) XIII; and drafted a new constitution. Anticipating the breakdown of the Tilsit Alliance, influential Swedes in 1810 persuaded Bernadotte to stand as a candidate for the Swedish succession. As a capable and experienced French field marshal, it was expected that he would reconquer Finland from Russia in alliance with Napoleon.

Bernadotte was elected successor by the Riksdag in August 1810, converted to the Lutheran faith, was adopted by Charles XIII as Crown Prince Charles John (Karl Johan), and almost immediately became the real ruler of Sweden. He felt none of the Swedes' emotional attachment to Finland, which for centuries had been part of the realm, and saw that with its long border with Russia it would always be a strategic liability. But if Sweden acquired Norway from France's ally, Denmark, this would assure the security of the entire Scandinavian Peninsula. He was by now convinced that Napoleon's empire would not last. In 1812 he allied himself with Russia and Britain before the French invaded Russia. He thereby renounced any future claim to Finland in return for Russian military and British diplomatic support to obtain Norway in compensation.

In 1813 Charles John and his Swedish forces entered the war against Napoleon in Germany. He commanded the coalition's Army of the North and is credited with the overall strategic plan leading to the French retreat from Germany. Charles John thereupon detached his Swedish and Russian force to attack Denmark, compelling it in the Treaty of Kiel in January 1814 to cede Norway to the king of Sweden.

Charles John hesitated to attack his old homeland on its own soil in the vain hope, encouraged by Madame de Staël and Benjamin Constant, of being elected king of France following Napoleon's defeat. This delayed him in making good Sweden's claim to Norway. The Norwegians refused to accept a change in sovereignty in which they had played no part. In May 1814 they convened a Storting (parliament) that drafted a liberal constitution and elected the Danish Prince Christian Frederik as their king.

Charles John invaded Norway in late July, outmaneuvering the outnumbered Norwegian forces. But he quickly, on 14 August, concluded the Convention of Moss, recognizing Norway as a separate kingdom, and accepted its new constitution. In return, Christian Frederik abdicated and the Storting concluded a dynastic union with Sweden.

The crown prince became King Charles XIV John of Sweden and Norway in 1818. In Sweden the old Jacobin pursued from the start a rigidly conservative policy, leading already by 1815 to the beginnings of liberal opposition. From 1821 on, he made determined efforts to amend the Norwegian constitution to increase his powers, efforts that were effectively blocked by the Storting until he gave up the attempt by 1836. In Sweden during the 1830s and the early 1840s, there were repeated confrontations with the Riksdag, with the liberal and radical press, and in the streets of Stockholm. Charles XIV John's opponents, however, overreached themselves in their vituperate attacks, and during his last years the aging monarch enjoyed growing popularity in both his kingdoms. He died in 1844, claiming on his deathbed that no one had ever had a career such as his. Norway would become fully sovereign in 1905, but to this day the Bernadotte dynasty reigns in Sweden.

See also **French Revolutionary Wars and Napoleonic Wars; Napoleonic Empire; Norway and Sweden.**

BIBLIOGRAPHY

Barton, H. Arnold. *Scandinavia in the Revolutionary Era, 1760–1815.* Minneapolis, Minn., 1986.

Höjer, Torvald. *Carl XIV Johan.* 3 vols. Stockholm, 1939–1960. The definitive Swedish biography. Abridgment in French: *Bernadotte: Maréchal de France, roi de Suède.* 2 vols. Paris, 1971.

Palmer, Alan. *Bernadotte: Napoleon's Marshal, Sweden's King.* London, 1990.

Scott, Franklin D. *Bernadotte and the Fall of Napoleon.* Cambridge, Mass., 1935.

H. Arnold Barton

BERNARD, CLAUDE (1813–1878), French scientist.

Since his death in the last quarter of the nineteenth century, very few French scientists have become as famous as Claude Bernard. This fame, which triggered much interest among historians, had declined in the early twentieth century, but works by historians of science such as Mirko Drazen Grmek and Frederick Lawrence Holmes renewed the interest in and interpretation of Bernard's achievements.

Claude Bernard was born on 12 July 1813 in the small village of Saint-Julien, near Lyon, France. The son of a wine grower, he was educated at a Jesuit college and then moved to Lyon, where he studied medicine. At that time he also had some literary ambition. He wrote a play that met some success, but a meeting with the famous Parisian critic Saint-Marc Girardin persuaded him to carry on with his medical studies. By 1839 he was an intern and worked with François Magendie, a professor of physiology at the Collège de France. Soon after he became his assistant (*préparateur*). Although Bernard failed to pass the *agrégation* (the highest competitive examination for teachers in France) and thus was deprived of the prestigious status of *agrégé*, or professor, his position allowed him to conduct extensive research. He studied the pancreas and then discovered the glycogenic function of the liver (1848). In 1847 he was appointed supply or substitute teacher of Magendie, whom he succeeded as professor of medicine at the Collège de France (*Leçons de physiologie expérimentale appliquée à la médecine, faites au Collège de France*) in 1855–1856. During that time, he conducted research on the nervous system, the effects of toxic and medicinal substances, and animal heat regulation (*Leçons sur la physiologie et la pathologie du système nerveux,* 1858). He also studied the internal organization of the body and he coined the expression *milieu intérieur* (1857; interior milieu), which remained one of his major achievements. From the 1860s on, Bernard led a successful career despite fragile health. The emperor Napoleon III (r. 1852–1871) supported his work and provided his protégé with two fully equipped laboratories—the best possible conditions for the pursuit of research. The emperor was also interested in making science more visible, and thus made Bernard senator in 1869. Bernard had previously been elected to the Academy of Science (1854) and to the Academy of Medicine (1861).

Bernard was the most influential French scientist of his day when he compiled his *Rapport sur les progrès et la marche de la physiologie générale en France* (1867; Report on the state and progress of physiology in France). In 1868 he was appointed professor of general physiology at the Natural History Museum and subsequently was elected to the *Académie française.* His predecessor was the monogenist and anti-Darwinian Marie-Jean-Pierre Flourens (1794–1867), and his successor was Joseph-Ernest Renan (1823–1892). His inaugural lecture to Academicians was moderate, published under the title *La science expérimentale* (1789; The experimental science). In it, he sought to reduce the oppositions between materialism and spiritualism. It is to be noted that in the years preceding his death Bernard showed a growing interest in religion. The fact that he had been the emperor's protégé did not alter his celebrity, and when he died in 1878, the then young Third Republic organized a national funeral that included a church service.

Bernard is perhaps best known for his *Introduction à l'étude de la médecine expérimentale* (1865; *Introduction to the Study of Experimental Medicine*). His claims about experimental physiology have been largely endorsed by successive generations of medical students. The reason for this success lies in the fact that he did not limit himself to technical explanations or descriptions of his work. Once experiments had been carried out and repeated successfully, Bernard sought general prin-

ciples both of the methodology of experimentation and of physiology itself and its place in the interpretation and understanding of life. Thus, his papers on experimentation and lab discoveries are coupled with other writings more typical of the philosophy of medicine and general biological considerations. Bernard's reflections also cover his own discipline and the methods of scientific investigation as well as experimentation itself. This eventually paved the way for considerations of ethics, a crucial point in current clinical research.

D. G. Charlton's classic book, *Positivist Thought in France during the Second Empire, 1852–1870* (1959), considered Claude Bernard as a true friend of positivism. Later works propose a much more nuanced interpretation: Bernard is seen as part of the positivist culture of his time but should be sharply distinguished from the legacy of Auguste Comte (1789–1857). For instance, Bernard's classification of sciences has very little to do with Comte's own. In addition, Bernard regarded philosophers, including Comte, with quiet disdain. He was highly suspicious of "making a specialty of generalizations" (*Introduction à l'étude de la médecine expérimentale*) and there is some evidence that Comte is implicitly designated as one of those responsible for that attitude. Finally, Bernard's interpretation of science appears much more modest than that of Comte, who developed a kind of metaphysics of scientific process.

Bernard's interpretation of human life—as the experience of the body submitted to physical and chemical laws—raised criticism because of the fundamental determinism it implied. His attacks against vitalism opened cracks in the model of interpretation of life that remained dominant well beyond the first half of the nineteenth century. Thus, Bernard's theories were at the center of many debates, some of which have not yet ended. This is why Bernard continues to be a subject of interest in the early twenty-first century; not so much because he is a representative of science and its success but because the critical analysis of his writings contributes to the understanding of epistemology past and present.

See also **Comte, Auguste; Positivism; Public Health; Renan, Joseph-Ernest; Science and Technology.**

BIBLIOGRAPHY

Grmek, Mirko Drazen. *Le legs de Claude Bernard*. Paris, 1997.

Olmsted, James Montrose Duncan, and E. Harris Olmsted. *Claude Bernard and the Experimental Method in Medicine*. New York, 1952.

Petit, Annie. "Claude Bernard and the History of Science." *Isis* 78, no. 2 (1987): 201–219.

Robin, Eugene Debs, ed. *Claude Bernard and the Internal Environment: A Memorial Symposium*. New York, 1979.

JEAN-CHRISTOPHE COFFIN

BERNHARDT, SARAH (1844–1923), French stage actor.

The most famous woman in the world at the height of her popularity around 1900, Sarah Bernhardt (originally Henriette Rosine Bernard) was the most widely acclaimed stage actor who ever lived. Although many details of her life remain sketchy, she was almost certainly born in Paris in October 1844 to an unmarried Jewish woman from Amsterdam; her father may have been a French naval officer from Le Havre. Bernhardt's childhood was difficult; her mother, a courtesan, was an intermittent presence in her life. Baptized at the age of twelve, Sarah was educated in a convent school and considered becoming a nun; in 1860, with the help of a family friend, she entered France's great drama school, the Paris Conservatoire.

Bernhardt's career was slow to take off. Her 1862 debut at the Comédie Française, France's most prestigious theatrical troupe, went largely unnoticed, and the following year Bernhardt, known for her temper and moodiness, left the company because of a dispute with a more established actress. After the birth in 1864 of her only son, Maurice, probably fathered by a Belgian aristocrat, in 1866 Bernhardt joined the Odéon Theater, where she had her first great successes in Dumas's *Kean* (1868) and especially François Coppée's *Le Passant* (1869). But it was not until after the Franco-Prussian War (1870–1871), during which she ran a clinic for wounded soldiers, that Bernhardt became a sensation, playing the Queen of Spain in the 1872 revival of Victor Hugo's *Ruy Blas.*

That same year Bernhardt was invited to rejoin the Comédie Française, where she received her first acclaim for classical roles, playing the title characters of the great French tragedian Racine's *Andromaque* (1873) and *Phèdre* (1874). After the triumphant 1877 revival of Hugo's *Hernani,* she became increasingly restless, and in 1879 she signed a contract with the American theatrical agent Edward Jarrett, who booked private engagements for her during a Comédie Française tour in London, where Bernhardt became the toast of the town. Upon returning to Paris she again resigned from the Comédie Française and in 1880 embarked upon a long series of foreign tours. Her travels in Europe, the Americas, and Australia, which continued intermittently until she was in her late seventies, earned unimaginable sums of money and raised her fame to unprecedented heights.

Back in Paris Bernhardt founded and directed several theatrical troupes, including L'Ambigu (1882), Porte Saint-Martin (1883), and Renaissance (1893). In 1898 she opened the Théâtre Sarah-Bernhardt, henceforth her sole theatrical venue in Paris until her death in 1923. In 1915 her right leg was amputated because of chronic knee pain, but she continued to perform using a special chair. Among the roles associated with Bernhardt are Marguerite Gautier in Dumas's *La Dame aux camélias,* Joan in Paul Jules Barbier's *Jeanne d'Arc,* and several masculine roles, including Lorenzo de' Medici in Alfred de Musset's *Lorenzaccio* and Shakespeare's *Hamlet.*

Known as "the Golden Voice" for her extraordinary ability to deliver lines, Bernhardt also mesmerized audiences with her unsettling beauty and graceful movements. Legendary for her unfashionable thinness, she took on ingenue roles even as an elderly woman, and at sixty-five played teenager Joan of Arc. Afflicted with a strange combination of sickliness—she may have suffered from tuberculosis—and hyperactivity, Bernhardt was also a sculptor and painter; she was also, arguably, the world's first media star, cultivating her image as a charismatic, unpredictable trendsetter. Fans were eager to hear about every aspect of her personal and professional life, including her numerous (often famous) lovers, her extravagant taste in clothing and furniture, and her countless idiosyncrasies. From an early age she sometimes slept in

Sarah Bernhardt. Photograph by Nadar. ©STEFANO BIANCHETTI/CORBIS

the silk-lined coffin in which she was ultimately buried, and she had herself photographed in it; she wrote a book about a balloon ride she took; and her menagerie of exotic pets included a monkey named Darwin.

Since the late twentieth century Bernhardt's career has been revisited especially by feminists. Some see her as a throwback figure of the seductress profiting from her feminine charms, while others consider her an example of the fin-de-siècle New Woman, the independent, self-supporting female. In 1882 Bernhardt did marry, but her husband, a Greek man named Jacques Damala, was a drug addict who died several years later, and in spite of the many men—and, probably, women—in her life, Bernhardt always retained her independence. A skillful self-promoter and master of publicity and "spin," Bernhardt earned—and spent—immense sums throughout her life. She is an early example of not only the marriage of entertainment and high capitalism, but also the commodification

of a fabricated and carefully managed personal image.

See also **Fin de Siècle; Popular and Elite Culture.**

BIBLIOGRAPHY

Bernhardt, Sarah. *My Double Life: The Memoirs of Sarah Bernhardt.* Translated by Victoria Tietze Larson. Albany, N.Y., 1999.

Brandon, Ruth. *Being Divine: A Biography of Sarah Bernhardt.* London, 1991.

Gold, Arthur, and Robert Fizdale. *The Divine Sarah: A Life of Sarah Bernhardt.* New York, 1991.

Roberts, Mary Louise. "The Fantastic Sarah Bernhardt." In her *Disruptive Acts: The New Woman in Fin-de-Siècle France,* 165–219. Chicago, 2002.

RICHARD E. GOODKIN

BERNSTEIN, EDUARD (1850–1932), German politician and theorist.

Eduard Bernstein was a leading German social-democratic politician and theorist. His life is a microcosmic reflection of the first century of the German Social Democratic Party (SPD). Like the German labor movement itself, Bernstein started out as a socialist eclectic, then he "converted" to Marxist orthodoxy only to return to an eclectic position which, enriched by Marxist theory, nonetheless espoused a nonrevolutionary, democratic socialism that recognized Marxism only as one among several important theoretical sources.

Born in Berlin on 6 January 1850, Eduard Bernstein grew up in modest circumstances. After a short career as a bank clerk in Berlin, he joined the SPD as a campaign speaker and pamphleteer. Expelled from Germany in 1878 as a result of the German chancellor Otto von Bismarck's repressive "Anti-Socialist Laws," Bernstein settled in Zürich, Switzerland, from where he edited *Der Sozialdemokrat,* the rallying point of the underground SPD press. When Bismarck secured his expulsion from Switzerland, Bernstein continued publication of the periodical from London, where he cultivated close contacts to Friedrich Engels (1820–1895) and the leaders of the British socialist Fabian Society. When Engels died in 1895, Bernstein served as his literary executor and was widely regarded as one of the leading Marxist voices in Europe.

Thus, it came as a shock to his party comrades when Bernstein launched a series of tough criticisms against Marxist theory. In a number of articles and books that appeared between 1896 and 1900, the former Marxist stalwart rejected the central Marxist dogma of the inevitable collapse of capitalist society and the ensuing revolutionary seizure of power by the working class. In his view, Karl Marx (1818–1883) and Engels had painted an unrealistic picture of a utopian "final goal." As he put the matter famously, "I must confess that I have very little interest in what is usually referred to as the 'final goal of socialism.' This goal, whatever it may be, is nothing to me, while the movement is everything. By 'the movement' I mean the progressive social change and its political and economic organization by working people" (quoted in Tudor and Tudor, pp. 168–169).

Suggesting that capitalism was getting better at containing its weaknesses, Bernstein advocated an "evolutionary" road to socialism through peaceful, parliamentary means centered on success at the ballot box and gradual democratic reforms. Stressing the tight connection between means and ends, he insisted that the extension of democracy required democratic methods. Moreover, he argued that the SPD ought to broaden its narrow working-class base and appeal to the middle class as well, thus turning itself into a genuine "people's party." Finally, rejecting the Marxist view that liberalism and socialism constituted diametrically opposed worldviews, Bernstein urged socialists to consider themselves "the legitimate heirs of liberalism" and embrace the Enlightenment language of citizenship, human rights, rule of law, and universal ethics.

Although Bernstein's views became the widely accepted cornerstones of modern European social democracy after World War II, they were severely condemned at three successive SPD congresses at the turn of the century. Various European Marxists, such as V. I. Lenin (1870–1924) in Russia and Rosa Luxemburg (1870–1919) and Karl Johann Kautsky (1854–1938) in Germany, wrote vitriolic pamphlets against Bernstein, calling him a "muddle-headed revisionist" betraying the cause of the working class. Unlike these leading Marxist theorists, however, Bernstein proved himself to be a skillful orator and organizer who recognized the importance of practical politics. Allowed to return to Berlin in 1901 after twenty-three years of political exile, he was elected to the Reichstag, the German parliament, and served from 1902 to 1906, 1912 to 1918, and 1920 to 1928.

At the outbreak of World War I in 1914, Bernstein first voted with the entire SPD leadership in favor of the war, but reversed his opinion a year later, arguing that the German imperial government had been the aggressor. Three years later, when the Bolsheviks successfully seized power in Russia, Bernstein emerged as one of their earliest and fiercest critics, warning that Lenin's brand of Soviet communism was based on the "erroneous belief in the omnipotence of brute force." He predicted, correctly as it turned out, that the Soviet regime represented an "odd repetition of the old despotism of the Czars" that would lead Russia into a "social and economic abyss." In the short-lived German Weimar Republic (1918–1933), the aging Bernstein held high political posts, including the cabinet position of undersecretary of the treasury. During his parliamentary tenure from 1920 to 1928, he concentrated on matters of taxation and foreign affairs while maintaining his busy journalistic schedule. Eduard Bernstein died on 18 December 1932, only six weeks before Adolf Hitler took power in Germany.

See also **Engels, Friedrich; Kautsky, Karl; Lenin, Vladimir; Marx, Karl; Second International; Socialism.**

BIBLIOGRAPHY

Primary Sources

Bernstein, Eduard. *The Preconditions of Socialism.* Edited and translated by Henry Tudor. Cambridge, U.K., and New York, 1993.

———. *Selected Writings of Eduard Bernstein, 1900–1921.* Edited and translated by Manfred B. Steger. Atlantic Highlands, N.J., 1996.

Secondary Sources

Gay, Peter. *The Dilemma of Democratic Socialism: Eduard Bernstein's Challenge to Marx.* New York, 1952.

Steger, Manfred B. *The Quest for Evolutionary Socialism: Eduard Bernstein and Social Democracy.* Cambridge, U.K., and New York, 1997.

Tudor, Henry, and J. M. Tudor. *Marxism and Social Democracy: The Revisionist Debate of 1896–98.* Cambridge, U.K., 1988.

MANFRED B. STEGER

BETHMANN HOLLWEG, THEOBALD VON (1856–1921), German statesman, served as imperial chancellor, 1909–1917.

Often called the "Hamlet" of German politics, Theobald von Bethmann Hollweg combined a legalistic and bureaucratic mind with inner doubt and misgiving. He was appointed Prussian minister of the interior in 1905 and German state secretary of the interior two years later. In 1909 he replaced the unctuous Bernhard Heinrich Martin Karl von Bülow (1849–1929) as German chancellor. Bethmann Hollweg's peacetime accomplishments were modest: in 1911 he promulgated a more liberal constitution for Alsace-Lorraine, but in December 1912 he suffered the first-ever vote of no-confidence in the German parliament over his inept handling of a civil-military confrontation at Zabern, Alsace. In January 1914 the Prussian Upper House censured him for failing to uphold conservative principles; most critically, he was unable to master the Reich's chaotic fiscal situation caused by Admiral Alfred von Tirpitz's (1849–1930) fleet building against Britain.

Bethmann Hollweg came to the Chancery with no diplomatic experience, yet his career would be defined by four diplomatic-military crises. In July 1914 it fell to him to manage the crisis evinced by the assassination of Archduke Francis Ferdinand (1863–1914) at Sarajevo. His mindset was pessimistic and fatalistic. He feared the growing power of Russia; he saw the coming war as a racial contest between Slavs and Teutons; and yet he orchestrated what he called "a leap into the dark." For Bethmann Hollweg had developed the rationale of a calculated risk: he would escalate the July Crisis up to the point of breaking the "iron ring" of the Anglo-French-Russian entente either by diplomacy or war—and then fall back on the last-minute mediation of a more disinterested power, Britain. When that failed to eventuate on 29–30 July, he took Germany into war.

Bethmann Hollweg's second major diplomatic step came on 9 September 1914, when he drafted the September Program, a war-aims program designed to make Germany master of Central Europe "for all imaginable time." France was to be permanently reduced to the rank of a secondary power. Russia was to be thrust back as far as possible from Europe and its domination over non-Russians ended.

Luxembourg was to become a federal German state, Belgium a German vassal state. The Netherlands were to be forced into closer relationship with the German Empire, and Central Europe tied economically to Germany. Finally, a continuous Central African colonial empire was to be carved from the holdings of other European colonial powers.

The collapse of the Schlieffen plan east of Paris and the resulting bloodbath in Flanders prompted the chief of the German General Staff, Erich Georg Anton Sebastian von Falkenhayn (1861–1922), on 18–19 November 1914 to inform Bethmann Hollweg that victory was no longer attainable, and recommended that a separate peace be negotiated first with Russia ("war indemnities but no major territorial concessions") and then, he hoped, with France. The chancellor refused this advice. A return to the status quo of before the war after his September Program would constitute a major political defeat. Germany's "incredible sacrifice" (700,000 casualties) demanded rewards in the form of vast territorial annexations. Bethmann Hollweg was prepared to fight to the bitter end.

Bethmann Hollweg's fourth great diplomatic act was to endorse unrestricted submarine warfare as a military necessity at a critical meeting of Germany's political and military elite at Pless on 9 January 1917. The submarine campaign, he stated, was Germany's last card in pursuing a victorious peace. He deemed its prospects to be very favorable. Promising to try to keep America out of the war, the chancellor cast the decisive vote by assuring Kaiser William II (1859–1941) that if the military deemed this step necessary, "I am not in a position to speak against it." The United States declared war on Germany on 6 April 1916. The military forced Bethmann Hollweg from office in July 1917. He died a broken man in January 1921.

See also **Alsace-Lorraine; Germany; Military Tactics.**

BIBLIOGRAPHY

Fischer, Fritz. *Germany's Aims in the First World War.* London, 1967. The classic statement of Bethmann Hollweg's prewar and wartime role, and especially of his war-aims program.

Herwig, Holger H. "Germany." In *The Origins of World War I,* edited by Richard F. Hamilton and Holger H. Herwig, 150–187. Cambridge, U.K., 2003. A reassessment of Bethmann Hollweg's role in the July Crisis of 1914.

Jarausch, Konrad H. *The Enigmatic Chancellor: Bethmann Hollweg and the Hubris of Imperial Germany.* New Haven, Conn., 1972. A spirited defense of Bethmann Hollweg as a "moderate" war leader.

HOLGER H. HERWIG

BIRTH CONTROL. *See* Population, Control of.

BISMARCK, OTTO VON (1815–1898), German statesman.

Otto von Bismarck was perhaps the most significant European statesman in the second half of the nineteenth century. As minister-president of the north German state of Prussia from 1862, his policies resulted in the creation of a politically unified German national state in central Europe. As Reich chancellor of the new German Empire (or Reich) from 1871, he determined Germany's political course for a further nineteen years until he was forced to resign by Kaiser William II (r. 1888–1918), the new emperor, in 1890.

EARLY LIFE

Otto Eduard Leopold von Bismarck was born on 1 April 1815 at his father's estate of Schönhausen, about sixty miles west of Berlin. His father, Ferdinand von Bismarck, was a typical representative of the Prussian land-owning nobility or Junker class, while his mother, Wilhelmine Louise Mencken, was the daughter of an influential state bureaucrat with close connections to the Prussian court. Bismarck's mother was the dominant partner in the marriage and sent Otto and his older brother, Bernhard, away from home at an early age to attend school in Berlin. In later life Bismarck expressed resentment of his mother's intellectual and social ambitions, which he blamed for his banishment from his idealized rural home, and he had a lifelong contempt for the influence of "petticoats" in marriage and in public life. Bismarck was never close to either of his parents, both of whom died before he achieved high office. He also

had a much younger sister, Malwine (born in 1827), with whom he developed an affectionate relationship.

Bismarck attended the Plamann Institute and then two grammar schools (*Gymnasia*) before studying law at the universities of Göttingen and Berlin. He never exploited the intellectual and academic opportunities offered by these institutions. As a student, despite evidence of a strong intellect, he preferred riding, gambling, womanizing, and dueling to studying, and he gained notoriety on account of his wild lifestyle and striking appearance. He resisted parental pressure to embark on a military career (although he completed his obligatory military service) and instead opted in 1836 to join the Prussian civil service, which constituted the main avenue to political influence in the bureaucratic-absolutist Prussian monarchy. But he found the degree of subordination required of him in state service intolerable. He passed his exams but bitterly resented the loss of his personal autonomy. After accumulating serious debts and going absent without leave in pursuit of a love interest, he finally abandoned the service in 1838.

Bismarck subsequently spent eight years living the life of a country Junker, farming the paternal estate of Kniephof in Pomerania (which he inherited, along with Schönhausen, on his father's death in 1845). But although he had a deep emotional attachment to the land and he successfully alleviated the family's debts in the adverse economic conditions of the 1840s, he eventually grew bored with rural life. He made a further, brief, and unsuccessful foray into state service in 1844; he traveled in England, France, and Switzerland; and he found intellectual and spiritual sustenance among an influential circle of Pomeranian pietists, who also provided him with new political and social contacts. In 1846 he moved to Schönhausen, where he could exploit the opportunities for political patronage offered by Ludwig von Gerlach, the president of the court of appeals in Magdeburg and brother of the king Frederick William IV's (r. 1840–1861) adjutant-general, Leopold von Gerlach. He also assumed his first public office as a dyke-reeve responsible for overseeing flood defenses on a stretch of the river Elbe.

In 1847 Bismarck anchored his private life by marrying Johanna von Puttkamer, a pious and compliant woman from his own social background who remained his lifelong partner until her death in 1894. They had three children, Marie (1848–1926), Herbert (1849–1904), and Wilhelm, known as Bill (1851–1901). Herbert was the most talented and he became an indispensable political support for his father, eventually becoming state secretary of the German Foreign Office (1886–1890).

EARLY POLITICAL CAREER

Bismarck launched his political career during the revolutions of 1848 and he became closely identified with the uncompromising ideological conservatism of his political patrons, the Gerlach brothers. His first direct experience of Berlin politics was in the spring of 1847, when he sat as an ultraconservative member of the Prussian province of Saxony in the short-lived United Diet summoned by Frederick William IV to give approval for a railway loan (which it rejected). When the European revolutionary contagion reached the Prussian capital in March 1848, Bismarck immediately offered his services to the cause of counterrevolution. He told military commanders in Potsdam that he was ready to march his Schönhausen peasants to Berlin to defend the king. He also headed a misconceived Junker deputation to Princess Augusta, the wife of the king's brother who later became Kaiser William I (r. 1861–1888). He incurred the lasting enmity of the future empress by suggesting that her husband or son might head a reactionary coup to oust the reigning monarch.

Bismarck's initial response to the revolution was hot-headed, but he nevertheless thrived in the new conditions it created and benefited from the introduction of constitutional government in Prussia. During the revolutionary upheavals he worked indefatigably to mobilize popular support for the conservative cause. He played a role in the establishment of a new conservative newspaper, the *Neue Preußische Zeitung* (or *Kreuzzeitung,* as it came to be known). In the new climate created by the explosive growth of political associations, he excelled as an energetic organizer and campaigner. And in elected assemblies he proved highly effective as a cool, rational, and caustic speaker. In 1850 he sat in the parliament convened at Erfurt to discuss

Prussian plans for a *kleindeutsch* (small German) union, a scheme that he categorically rejected for its failure to take account of international realities and its implications for the conservative basis of the Prussian state.

Bismarck's energetic defense of conservative interests and his aggressive and combative style won him friends on the right, even if his conservatism was never as inflexible and intransigent as his identification with the Gerlachs and their "court party" suggested. His reward for his services to the monarchy at a time of acute political crisis was his appointment as Prussian minister to the newly restored German Confederation at Frankfurt in 1851. He lacked the usual qualifications and diplomatic experience for such a position, but his advocacy of conservative solidarity and Austro-German friendship, as well as the gratitude of the king, catapulted him over these obstacles.

BISMARCK AS DIPLOMAT

Bismarck served his diplomatic apprenticeship at Frankfurt (1851–1859) and subsequently as Prussian minister in St. Petersburg (1859–1862) and briefly in Paris (1862). He developed his views about foreign policy and how best to secure Prussia's position in Germany and Europe during a period that witnessed the establishment of Napoleon III's (r. 1852–1871) Second Empire in France, the Crimean War (1853–1856), and the wars of Italian unification. Bismarck became convinced that the German Confederation was merely an instrument for Austrian domination of Germany, that there was no room for both Austria and Prussia in German affairs, and that their dualism had to be resolved in Prussia's favor. But, unlike more traditional and ideological conservatives, he was flexible and pragmatic in his choice of means to achieve this goal, provided that those means signified no liberalization of Prussia's social and political system. He was willing, for example, to consider an alliance with Bonapartist France as a means of pressuring Austria, even if this meant sacrificing the principle of conservative solidarity in Europe against the forces of revolution. Similarly, he argued during the Italian war of 1859–1860 that Prussia should seize control of northern Germany, march south, and proclaim Prussia as the kingdom of Germany, a recommendation that was deemed irresponsibly reckless by his political masters in Berlin.

Bismarck's political views turned him into something of a maverick and counted against him by the late 1850s. Despite his obvious political ambitions, he was unable to capitalize on his exceptional promotion in 1851. When Frederick William IV suffered a stroke in 1858 and was succeeded by his brother as prince regent (William became king in 1861), Bismarck had few political supporters in Berlin and was effectively sidelined. He was out of tune with the more liberal and anglophile conservatives who formed William's "New Era" government and was sent to St. Petersburg, where he enjoyed better relations with the Russian government than with his own. His health was also poor during this period, and his chances of political advancement seemed remote. Once again he owed his eventual promotion to exceptional and unforeseen circumstances and the elimination of all political alternatives.

BISMARCK AS PRUSSIAN MINISTER-PRESIDENT

Bismarck was appointed Prussian minister-president in September 1862 as the result of another major crisis affecting the Prussian monarchy, namely the deepening constitutional crisis over the issue of army reform from 1860. When the liberal majority in the Prussian parliament rejected the king's plans to reform the Prussian army, William I refused to heed his government's advice and compromise. Instead, he considered abdication. However, his war minister, Albrecht von Roon, persuaded him to grant Bismarck an interview. Bismarck, who had been recalled from St. Petersburg in April 1862 and sent provisionally as envoy to Paris, hastened back to Berlin and met the monarch at the royal residence at Babelsberg on 22 September 1862. Sensing his opportunity, he was prepared to pledge fealty to his lord in order to gain William's trust. He committed himself to defy the Prussian parliament in the constitutional struggle, rule without a legal budget, and secure the army reform unmodified. But he avoided any further discussion of policy. Bismarck was appointed Prussian minister-president on 23 September. Despite William's continuing misgivings about the kind of foreign policy he

advocated, Bismarck on 8 October also became Prussian foreign minister, a position he considered vital if he were to secure Prussia's power in Germany and Europe.

Bismarck achieved his major diplomatic triumphs in the 1860s as Prussian minister-president and foreign minister, positions he held continuously (apart from a brief interlude when he ceased to be minister-president in 1872–1873) until 1890. Under his leadership Prussia fought three victorious wars against Denmark, Austria, and France, the most significant consequence of which was the proclamation of the German Empire from Versailles in January 1871. He also resolved the Prussian constitutional crisis in a way that safeguarded the prerogatives of the Prussian monarchy and he determined the constitutional and political structures of the emerging new Germany. As Prussian minister-president, however, Bismarck was formally only first among equals in the Prussian ministry of state, a body that had an executive and consultative role in the monarchical state but was not comparable with a modern cabinet presided over by a prime minister in a parliamentary system. Bismarck's political successes brought him immense power and prestige but he remained a servant of the crown.

GERMAN UNIFICATION

Bismarck's first great success in foreign policy was his handling of the complicated Schleswig-Holstein crisis, which resurfaced as an international problem in 1863. Bismarck refused to support the view, popular among national liberals and in the lesser German states, that the two duchies should sever their ties with the Danish crown and become an independent German state under a German prince within the German Confederation. Rather than place Prussia at the head of the national movement, Bismarck insisted that the future of the two duchies was a European problem, subject to an international treaty of 1852. Prussia, like Austria, its main rival in Germany, was first and foremost a European great power, and its policy should be conducted in accordance with its own interests (*Realpolitik*). Bismarck undermined the German Confederation and Austria's credibility within it by cooperating with Austria bilaterally over the Schleswig-Holstein issue. The two powers

French caricature of Otto von Bismarck. In this Franco-Prussian War–era cartoon, Bismarck is shown prodding reluctant German soldiers to attack the French. The legend has Bismarck saying: "Let's go! Go or Die! Faster than that or the French will eat your sauerkraut." ©GIANNI DAGLI/CORBIS

eventually went to war and defeated Denmark in 1864, establishing a condominium over the duchies. Such an arrangement could only be temporary given the strategic location of the duchies in the north of Germany and Bismarck's willingness to sanction policies aimed at their eventual annexation by Prussia.

The Austro-Prussian War of 1866 grew out of tensions over the future of the duchies, Austria's plans to reform the German Confederation, and the wider issue of Austro-Prussian dualism in Germany. Bismarck took a supreme gamble in risking war against Austria and its German allies in the Confederation in June 1866. Austria was the more established military power, and the conflict had the character of an unpopular German civil war, provoked by the upstart Prussian state and its belligerent minister-president. The international constellation was favorable in the wake of the Crimean War, since France, Russia, and Britain were initially not inclined to intervene, but Italy was Prussia's only ally. Nevertheless Prussia defeated Austria in seven weeks and imposed a lenient peace, thus forestalling foreign intervention. The German Confederation was destroyed, and Austria renounced the ties it had enjoyed for centuries with the non-Habsburg German lands. Prussia annexed territories in northern Germany, including Schleswig-Holstein, and established a new Prussian-dominated North German Confederation, north of the river Main. Bismarck clearly hoped that the new federal constitution, which included the very radical innovation of a national parliament or Reichstag elected by universal male suffrage, would facilitate the eventual political unification of Germany. The south German states of Bavaria, Württemberg, and Baden retained their independence but were already tied to Prussia economically through the Prussian-led customs union or Zollverein and were now forced additionally to conclude military alliances with their powerful neighbor.

Bismarck's hopes after 1866 that German unity would progress through evolutionary means or through mere friction with France were frustrated. The south German states resisted their incorporation into the new Confederation. It took the outbreak of the Franco-Prussian War in 1870, precipitated as much by France's inept diplomacy as by Bismarck's guile, to activate the southern states' military alliances with Prussia and inflame German nationalism. The brutal "people's war" against the traditional enemy and the French defeat led to the foundation of the new German Empire. Although some special privileges were granted to the southern states, the constitution of the new empire was not significantly changed from that of the North German Confederation. Bismarck ensured that Prussia would dominate the new entity and that its king would now additionally be the German kaiser.

Bismarck was at the pinnacle of his power in 1871 as the "founder of the Reich," yet he had never planned to unify Germany nor anticipated the path that the wars of German unification eventually took. He was always flexible and pragmatic in his diplomacy, conscious of what he wanted to avoid but often willing to devise imaginative alternative strategies. Bismarck never ruled out peaceful solutions if these edged him closer to his goals and even in 1866 he was pursuing negotiations with Bavaria that might have led to different political arrangements in "Germany." Seen in context rather than with the benefit of hindsight, his actions might have led to different outcomes.

Some historians have argued that, rather than unifying Germany, Bismarck divided or dismembered the German nation in 1866 by casting aside the Austrian Germans. Bismarck is often seen as placing Prussian interests over and above German interests; his first priority was always to secure Prussia's position in northern Germany and ensure Prussian parity with Austria. But he used German nationalism to legitimize Prussian expansion and, although he can be seen as an archproponent of an amoral and unprincipled form of power politics, he effectively committed himself from 1866 to work toward the completion of German political unification by integrating the southern states.

Bismarck has also been called a "white revolutionary" who used revolutionary means, unleashing the forces of nationalism and democracy, to achieve essentially conservative goals, the expansion of Prussia and the consolidation of its military monarchy. He has been likened to the "sorcerer's apprentice" who conjured up new political forces he could not possibly control. Bismarck, however, did not determine the course of German unification single-handedly. It was no accident that German and Italian unification occurred at much the same time, and there were many autonomous forces pushing for a resolution of the German problem. Bismarck's ability to manipulate and control events has often been exaggerated by both his supporters and his detractors.

THE DOMESTIC CONTEXT

Bismarck conducted his foreign policy between 1862 and 1866 against a background of domestic strife. The bitter constitutional struggle over the army reform intensified under Bismarck's leadership and reinforced contemporary perceptions that he was an archreactionary and unrepentant "conflict minister" who would stop at nothing to achieve his aims. Bismarck initially underestimated the liberal opposition in the Prussian parliament. In his famous "blood and iron" speech in September 1862, he sought to rally the liberals behind his foreign policy by suggesting that the goal of national unification might be better served by the army reform than by "speeches and majority verdicts." He himself, however, was more ready to compromise over the reform than the king, but, until he could deliver tangible successes, his position depended on the continuation of the crisis.

Bismarck's government implemented the army reform and collected the necessary taxation without parliamentary consent. As legal justification it argued that there was a "gap" in the constitution, hence when the executive monarch and the legislature could not agree, power returned to the former. Bismarck persistently endeavored to divide, undermine, or win over part of the liberal opposition between 1862 and 1866, but most of his efforts between 1862 and 1866 only served to forge a more cohesive and hostile parliamentary bloc. The Schleswig-Holstein crisis revealed a potential line of fissure within the liberal opposition, since the more nationalist liberal deputies could not fail to be enthused by the Prussian victory over Denmark and its consequences. But the liberal opposition condemned Bismarck's illiberal policies at home. They also castigated his apparent cynicism in proposing to reform the German Confederation by introducing a national, elected parliament when he rode roughshod over the will of the Prussian parliament. On the eve of the Austro-Prussian War, the Prussian liberals remained solidly opposed to Bismarck and appeared to head a national opposition.

The Austro-Prussian War of 1866, however, proved a watershed in Prussian domestic politics as well as in German affairs. Elections to the Prussian parliament were held on the same day as the Battle of Königgrätz (3 July), and in a wave of patriotic support the conservatives made substantial gains, and the liberal majority was significantly reduced. Moreover, the effect of the Prussian victory was to produce cleavages in all major political groupings. Many national liberals admired what Bismarck had achieved for the cause of German unification and they were now willing to reach an accommodation with him. Bismarck conciliated them by supporting the introduction of an indemnity bill in the Prussian parliament, admitting that the government had acted unconstitutionally, if in return the parliament retrospectively approved the budget. The constitutional struggle was thus laid to rest, for only the most principled liberals remained immune to the intoxication of war and conquest. Many ideological conservatives, however, also never forgave Bismarck for the war against Austria, the deposition of legitimate German princes, and his adoption of a revolutionary, democratic franchise for the new Reichstag.

Some historians have asserted the primacy of domestic politics in interpreting Bismarck's policies in the 1860s. They have suggested that Bismarck's foreign policy was primarily an instrument to divide the parliamentary opposition at home and win the constitutional struggle. The domestic settlement in 1866 left the conservative pillars of the Prussian monarchy untouched and was thus highly significant for the future political and constitutional development of the German Empire, which was dominated by an unreformed Prussia up to 1918. The liberals' compromise with Bismarck in 1866 has consequently been seen as a fateful capitulation. But Bismarck also made concessions to the liberals, and the future development of Germany was not predetermined from 1866. He never believed he could defeat liberalism. Rather, he hoped to ally moderate liberals, who represented the most articulate and dynamic sections of the population, with the monarchy's traditional supporters. Moreover, Bismarck was never motivated primarily by domestic considerations and he pursued his foreign policy in the 1860s regardless of the domestic opposition.

BISMARCK AS CHANCELLOR

Historians' views of Bismarck would have been very different if he had left office in 1871 or shortly afterward. But he wielded power for a further nineteen years, during which time his efforts to safeguard his new creation became increasingly repressive and authoritarian, and this perspective obviously colors assessments of his legacy. As Reich chancellor, the single, legally responsible German minister, Bismarck played a key role in the development of the new empire's political institutions, the domestic policies of Prussia and the empire, and Germany's relations with foreign powers. His role in foreign policy is often judged more positively than his role

in domestic policy, especially in the light of Germany's disastrous diplomacy after his dismissal in 1890. But Bismarck's reputation for diplomatic prowess has also been challenged, and historians no longer accept uncritically claims that he was intent on preserving the peace of Europe after 1871.

Bismarck devoted his energy to consolidating the new empire after 1871, but both his temperament and his policies often appeared unsuitable for this task. In the early 1870s he was willing to delegate some of the responsibility for imperial domestic policy to his deputy, Rudolf Delbrück, who headed the Reich Chancellor's Office. He also collaborated closely with the National Liberal Party in the German Reichstag to promote the legal and economic unification of Germany. But in Prussia, with liberal support, he launched the Kulturkampf or "struggle for civilization," an unequal war waged against the Catholic Church and its political representative, the newly formed Catholic Center Party. Bismarck mistrusted political Catholicism because of its Austrian and *großdeutsch* (greater German) sympathies and he saw the Kulturkampf in many ways as a continuation of the struggle to achieve a national state. But his policies alienated German Catholics and contributed to the growth of the Center Party, which, skillfully led by Ludwig Windthorst, developed into a militant opposition to Bismarck.

Bismarck was never a consensual politician. He disliked being dependent on a particular parliamentary majority or constrained by a collective form of government. By nature he gravitated toward authoritarian solutions to problems. From the late 1870s he ensured that it was the Reich chancellor alone who was responsible for the domestic policy of the empire. Bismarck instituted what some have seen as a "chancellor dictatorship," even though he was never happy with the balance of institutions in the empire and often experimented in diverse ways with its political arrangements.

In 1878–1879 he deliberately sought to end his dependence on national liberalism by adopting policies that split the National Liberal Party. After two failed assassination attempts on the life of William I, Bismarck supported the introduction of repressive antisocialist legislation, which aimed to stifle the infant socialist movement in Germany. He also abandoned free trade and, with the support of conservatives and part of the Center Party, adopted protectionist economic policies. Some historians claim that he "refounded" the empire on a conservative basis by engineering a marriage of "iron and rye," an alliance between the political representatives of heavy industry and large-scale agriculture whose economic interests converged. But in the first half of the 1880s Bismarck was forced to govern "above the parties" on the basis of shifting parliamentary majorities and he suffered a series of legislative defeats.

From 1880 Bismarck promoted social welfare legislation, providing for sickness, accident and invalidity insurance, and old-age pensions, in an attempt to woo the working class away from social democracy and win its loyalty. The legislation served as a model for other countries to follow, but Bismarck had little contact with Germany's rapidly growing urban population and few remedies for the problems of an industrial society. By the late 1880s he no longer saw political Catholicism as a major threat to the empire and he began to dismantle some of the Kulturkampf laws. But his continuing efforts to consolidate the national state now included coercive policies against the empire's Polish and Danish minorities. He supported sweeping Germanization measures against the Polish population of Prussia's eastern provinces, seeking to reinforce German ethnicity through a land settlement program as well as by imposing cultural and linguistic uniformity.

Bismarck's domestic policies have been seen as conservative, illiberal, and anachronistic at a time of rapid social and economic change. They were not necessarily devoid of progressive potential but, even when promoting radical initiatives such as the introduction of the democratic franchise or the social insurance scheme, he was primarily motivated by the desire to increase the power of the authoritarian state. He knew that political unification did not signify national unity and he always feared that his new edifice, forged through militarism and war, might collapse in ruins around him. Hence it has been claimed that he sought to consolidate his creation by artificial means, fostering a sense of nationhood through campaigns against "internal enemies" or the fabrication of war scares. His efforts may have

helped to shape a new German national identity, albeit one that was predominantly Prussian and Protestant, but they also exacerbated religious, ethnic, and social divisions.

FOREIGN POLICY

From 1871 Bismarck's primary goal in foreign policy was to preserve his new Reich and prevent any attempt by the powers of Europe to undo his work of unification. Much has been written about his famous "alliance system" by which he isolated France and ensured that no hostile coalition formed against Germany. But it was not until the later 1870s that Bismarck fully appreciated the significance of placing Berlin at the center of a stable international system, and his commitment to European peace after 1871 can also be qualified. In 1875 he precipitated the so-called War in Sight Crisis, raising the specter of another war between France and Germany. Britain, Russia, and Austria made clear their intention to contain German aggression since they could not tolerate another French defeat like that of 1871. Bismarck subsequently formulated his Kissingen Dictate in 1877, in which he argued that Germany should always seek to be one of three among the five Great Powers of Europe and that it was important to ensure that all the Great Powers, apart from France, needed German friendship and support. He came to realize that war no longer served Germany's interests after 1871. Germany was now a "satiated state," and provoking another war would be akin to committing suicide for fear of death. Bismarck, however, had no attachment to European peace as an ideal. He saw utility in sowing dissension between the Great Powers and exploiting conflicts on the periphery of Europe and overseas.

Bismarck's diplomacy in the 1870s and 1880s benefited from tensions in the Balkans and the Near East, notably between Austria and Russia, as well as from imperialist rivalries between the European Great Powers. Bismarck posed as the "honest broker" at the Congress of Berlin in 1878, and his prestige was such in 1879 that he was able to force Kaiser William I into agreeing to conclude a Dual Alliance with Austria (which became the Triple Alliance when the Italians joined it in 1882). Bismarck also entered into a series of

Otto von Bismarck (right) with Kaiser William II. PRIVATE
COLLECTION/BRIDGEMAN ART LIBRARY/KEN WELSH

In 1884–1885 he displayed a sudden interest in colonial acquisitions, leading to the establishment of German protectorates in East Africa, South West Africa, and the Pacific. This episode has been seen by some historians as a form of "social imperialism," attempting to divert public attention from problems at home. Others suggest that Bismarck was motivated by international considerations or the desire to secure his position at a time when the accession of the liberal and anglophile crown prince to the throne appeared imminent. Bismarck rapidly lost interest in colonies once he saw how costly they were, and by the late 1880s he was forced to devote his full attention to Germany's deteriorating position in Europe.

Bismarck's diplomacy was criticized by contemporaries for being tortuous and unnecessarily complex, as well as for conciliating Russia at a time when Russia was perceived as a growing threat. Most historians, however, have expressed admiration for his diplomatic skill, which was markedly superior to that of his successors, who failed to renew the Reinsurance Treaty in March 1890, encouraged Germany's diplomatic isolation, and finally precipitated World War I. Some scholars have seen Bismarck's diplomacy, for all its cleverness, as an improvised form of crisis management that could not have been sustained over the longer term. By the late 1880s the international situation no longer favored Germany. The latent hegemony Germany had enjoyed since 1871, reinforced by its dramatic economic and demographic growth and its military power, could only be preserved if it acted with restraint.

DISMISSAL

Bismarck's long tenure of power depended on the support of the Prussian king and German kaiser who had appointed him. In March 1888 the ninety-year-old William I died and was succeeded by his son, Frederick III, who was already terminally ill with cancer of the throat. On his death three months later, his son, William II, succeeded to the throne at the age of twenty-nine.

The new kaiser had no wish to be eclipsed by the "Iron Chancellor," nor was the seventy-three-year-old Bismarck inclined to subordinate himself to his new master. There thus followed a protracted power struggle between kaiser and

treaties with other European powers, the most important of which was the secret Reinsurance Treaty of 1887 with Russia. The clash of interests between Austria and Russia in the Bulgarian crisis from 1885 meant that it was no longer possible to preserve a conservative understanding between the three monarchical empires. Hence Bismarck officially remained loyal to Austria, while maintaining "the wire to St. Petersburg" by means of a duplicitous treaty with Russia that promised support of its interests in the region.

Bismarck always professed German disinterest in the Balkans, but he deliberately used the prospect of acquiring formerly Ottoman territory as bait to divert all the Great Powers from Germany and to make anti-German coalitions impossible.

chancellor, in which personal antagonisms, the generational divide, and political differences all played a role. William II wanted to be "his own chancellor" but he lacked sufficient prestige to dismiss Bismarck immediately and hoped Bismarck might relinquish power gradually. But Bismarck refused to be eased out of office and instead sought to tighten his grip over the government. He also supported controversial new legislation, notably a more draconian antisocialist law and revised military estimates, which were unacceptable to the parliamentary majority and apparently designed to provoke a conflict with the Reichstag. While William II was keen to start his reign as a "social kaiser" who conciliated the working class, Bismarck appeared intent on precipitating another constitutional crisis that would make his removal from office impossible. After a violent confrontation between the two men on 15 March 1890, Bismarck was effectively forced to write his letter of resignation three days later.

Bismarck never forgave William II for forcing him out of office. After 1890 he became an important focus of opposition to the kaiser and his new government. He thus contributed to the protracted period of political instability after his dismissal. Bismarck retired to his estate at Friedrichsruh near Hamburg, where he wrote his memoirs and nurtured his growing reputation as a national hero. He died on 30 July 1898.

Bismarck's political career was always controversial. Once deified as the architect of German unification, he has also been demonized for setting Germany on a peculiar path of modernization that eventually led to two world wars and the collapse of the Third Reich in 1945. At the height of his powers he was an exceptionally creative statesman who was capable of utilizing the forces of his day and devising imaginative and flexible solutions to the problems he faced. But he also promoted political authoritarianism, intolerant nationalism, militarism, and the glorification of war. His long tenure of power stifled the evolution of the empire's political institutions and impeded political progress. He ultimately served the interests of the Prussian military monarchy. In augmenting its power, he eventually destroyed his political career.

See also **Alliance System; Austro-Prussian War; Bebel, August; Franco-Prussian War; Frederick William III; Frederick William IV; Germany; Kulturkampf; Revolutions of 1848; William I; William II; Windthorst, Ludwig.**

BIBLIOGRAPHY

Primary Sources

Bismarck, Otto von. *Bismarck: The Man and the Statesman: Being the Reflections and Reminiscences of Otto Prince von Bismarck.* 2 vols. Translated by A. J. Butler. London: 1898.

Secondary Sources

Blackbourn, David. *History of Germany, 1780–1918: The Long Nineteenth Century.* 2nd ed. London, 2003.

Blanke, Richard. *Prussian Poland in the German Empire, 1871–1900.* Chicago, 1980.

Carr, William. *The Origins of the Wars of German Unification.* London, 1991.

Eyck, Erich. *Bismarck and the German Empire.* London, 1950.

Feuchtwanger, Edgar. *Bismarck.* London, 2002.

Gall, Lothar. *Bismarck: The White Revolutionary.* 2 vols. Translated by J. A. Underwood. London, 1986. Translation of *Bismarck: Der Weiße Revolutionär* (1980).

Langewiesche, Dieter. *Liberalism in Germany.* Translated by Christiane Banerji. London, 1999. Translation of *Liberalismus in Deutschland* (1988).

Lerman, Katharine Anne. *Bismarck.* Harlow, U.K., 2004.

Mommsen, Wolfgang J. *Imperial Germany, 1867–1918: Politics, Culture, and Society in an Authoritarian State.* Translated by Richard Deveson. London, 1995. Translation of *Der Autoritäre Nationalstaat* (1990).

Nipperdey, Thomas. *Germany from Napoleon to Bismarck, 1800–1866.* Translated by Daniel Nolan. Princeton, N.J., 1996. Translation of *Deutsche Geschichte, 1800–1866* (1983).

Pflanze, Otto. *Bismarck and the Development of Germany.* 3 vols. Princeton, N.J., 1990.

Röhl, John C. G. *Young Wilhelm: The Kaiser's Early Life, 1859–1888.* Translated by Jeremy Gaines and Rebecca Wallach. Cambridge, U.K., 1998. Translation of *Wilhelm II.: Die Jugend des Kaisers, 1859–1888* (1993).

———. *Wilhelm II: The Kaiser's Personal Monarchy, 1888–1900.* Translated by Sheila de Bellaigue. Cambridge, U.K., 2004. Translation of *Wilhelm II. Der Aufbau der Persönlichen Monarchie, 1888–1900* (2001).

Ross, Ronald J. *The Failure of Bismarck's Kulturkampf.* Washington, D.C., 1998.

Schöllgen, Gregor, ed. *Escape into War?: The Foreign Policy of Imperial Germany.* Oxford, U.K., 1990.

Schulze, Hagen. *The Course of German Nationalism: From Frederick the Great to Bismarck, 1763–1867.* Translated by Sarah Hanbury-Tenison. Cambridge, U.K., 1991. Translation of *Der Weg zum Nationalstaat: Die Deutsche Nationalbewegung vom 18 Jahrhundert bis zur Reichsgründung* (1990).

Sheehan, James J. *German History, 1770–1866.* Oxford, U.K., 1989.

Simms, Brendan. *The Struggle for Mastery in Germany, 1779–1850.* London, 1998.

Urbach, Karina. "Between Saviour and Villain: 100 Years of Bismarck Biographies." *The Historical Journal* 41 (1998): 1141–1160.

Wehler, Hans-Ulrich. *The German Empire, 1871–1918.* Translated from the German by Kim Traynor. Leamington Spa, U.K., 1985. Translation of *Das Deutsche Kaiserreich, 1871–1918* (1980).

KATHARINE ANNE LERMAN

BLACK HAND. The Black Hand, an underground nationalist organization whose official name was Union or Death, was founded in 1911 in Belgrade by a group of Serbian officers and civilians. The officers, who formed the nucleus of the organization, had become increasingly impatient with the Serbian government's cautious approach to the Serbian national question. They were especially dissatisfied with the government's acceptance of Austria-Hungary's annexation of Bosnia and Herzegovina (1908), after which it curbed its nationalist activities in the province by reducing its military presence, hindering the formation of irregular military groups, and restraining the activities of subversive nationalist organizations. The idea of forming a secret organization to carry out the struggle for national liberation and unification more vigorously had existed among Serbian officers since 1909. However, not until Colonel Dragutin Dimitrijević-Apis joined their ranks was it realized. The group was prodded by the increasing power enjoyed by the Serbian military since playing a central role in dethroning the Obrenović dynasty in 1903, which cleared the way for the current government, led by Prime Minister Nikola Pašić, to come to power.

The organization was headed by a central committee of eleven members. Its primary aims, as articulated in its constitution, involved fighting for the national liberation of all Serbs living under the Ottoman and Austro-Hungarian empires and their unification into a single Serbian kingdom. They identified as Serbian provinces Bosnia and Herzegovina, Montenegro, Old Serbia, Macedonia, Croatia, Slavonia, Vojvodina, and Primorje. While uniting Serbs into a single state was a goal that Serbian civilian and military leaders shared, the military was willing to risk war to realize its goals, whereas the civilian government was more cautious. Members of the Black Hand vowed to fight outside Serbian borders with all means necessary against all enemies. They proclaimed themselves opposed to both the government and the opposition. The organization was militaristic, symbolized by a hand holding a black flag with a skull and crossbones in front of which stood a knife, a bomb, and poisonous berries. The activities of the organization were highly secretive. All members received numbers as aliases and had to communicate orally. The Black Hand organized an underground revolutionary network, sometimes infiltrating older organizations, to carry out acts of agitation, including propaganda and the formation of armed bands. As Chief of Intelligence of the Serbian General Staff, Dimitrijević also relied on his own network of agents within the army.

The Black Hand is most famous for its role in the assassination of Archduke Francis Ferdinand on 28 June 1914 in Sarajevo, which sparked a series of events that led to the outbreak of the First World War. Six young Bosnian men, of whom Gavrilo Princip is best known, carried out the assassination in an effort to eliminate what they deemed to be a major obstacle to the union of Bosnia-Herzegovina to Serbia. Extensive debate has surrounded the establishment of responsibility for the assassination. The Austro-Hungarian government was convinced that the young students had acted under direct orders from Black Hand officers, who in turn had received orders from the Serbian government. The limited existing evidence suggests that it was Princip and his collaborators who sought out Dimitrijević's help. After meeting in Belgrade in May 1914, Dimitrijević provided them with pistols and bombs from an official army arsenal and made arrangements to smuggle the youths back to Bosnia. Dimitrijević acted without the consent of the organization's central committee, which ordered him to halt the plan when it learned of his actions. More poignant has been the question of Prime Minister Pašić's involvement in the plot. While evidence suggests that he knew of some unspecified action and that Serbian officials had helped students cross the border, it does not support a direct link between him and the assassins. In fact, he attempted to warn the Austro-Hungarian government through his representative in Vienna, but to no avail.

The Black Hand dissolved in 1917 when Dimitrijević was executed after having been found guilty of treason in the Salonica trial. Premier Pašić and Prince Regent Alexander used these proceedings to eliminate this long-standing military source of dissension by fabricating charges that Dimitrijević and a group of co-conspirators were plotting a mutiny in the army and the assassination of the Prince Regent. The Prince Regent tried to give the impression that Dimitrijević was executed principally because of his involvement in the assassination of Archduke Francis Ferdinand. Some scholars have postulated that his motive was to reach a separate peace with Austria-Hungary. However, this has never been proven.

See also **Austria-Hungary; Bosnia-Herzegovina; Francis Ferdinand; Nationalism; Serbia.**

BIBLIOGRAPHY

Dedijer, Vladimir. *The Road to Sarajevo*. New York, 1966.

Gavrilovic, Stojan. "New Evidence on the Sarajevo Assassination (in Documents)." *The Journal of Modern History* 27, no. 4 (December 1955): 410–413.

Jelavich, Charles, and Jelavich, Barbara. *The Establishment of the Balkan National States, 1804–1920*. Seattle, Wash., 1993.

Lampe, John. *Yugoslavia as History: Twice There Was a Country*. New York, 1996.

Stavrianos, L. S. *The Balkans since 1453*. New York, 2000.

JOVANA L. KNEŽEVIĆ

BLACK SEA. The Black Sea, into which flow the Danube, Dnieper, Dniester, and Don Rivers, is connected to the Aegean Sea and eventually the Mediterranean Sea by the Bosphorus, the Sea of Marmara, and the Dardanelles. To the east of the Crimean Peninsula, which extends from the north into the Black Sea, the Kerch Strait leads to the considerably smaller Sea of Azov. Having facilitated trade for centuries, the Black Sea was virtually an Ottoman lake in the sixteenth and seventeenth centuries. Its history for much of the eighteenth and all of the nineteenth century was the struggle for supremacy of the two major powers on its shores: the Ottoman Empire and Russia. In the course of this struggle by the mid-nineteenth century, Russia emerged as the clear winner, but it was a long process that ended with the major debacle of the Crimean War.

Ever since the reign of Catherine the Great (r. 1762–1796) the Russian Empire had been expanding at the expense of the Ottomans. Catherine's dream (which turned out to be utopian) was the final conquest of Istanbul and the resurrection of the Byzantine Empire under Russian protection. With the Treaty of Küçük Kaynarca (1774), the annexation of the Crimea (1783), and the Treaty of Adrianople (1829) Russian power increased. Russian victory in the War of the Dnepr Estuary (1788–1789) resulted in the fall of the last Ottoman fortresses and the emergence of Sevastopol as the major Russian naval base in the Black Sea. Crimea became the "New Russia," *Novorossiya*, the symbol of the expanding Russian frontier. Commerce also thrived as a result of the development of the ports of Kherson and Odessa. Particularly Odessa became the new hub of commerce and the symbol of the New Russia. From 1790 onward, with Ottoman agreement for the free passage of foreign-flag merchant ships through the Straits (Bosphorus and the Dardanelles), Russia became a major exporter of grain and salt to the Mediterranean and western Europe. Developed by a series of able governors, Odessa was a city numbering some seventy-eight thousand inhabitants by 1845; with a mainly Greek, Tatar, Armenian, and Jewish population. Odessa was declared a tax-free zone, and improvements to its harbor meant that the Black Sea was integrated into European commerce as it had never been before.

The Crimean War (October 1853–February 1856) was the only time that the Black Sea would dominate the world limelight in the nineteenth century. Ostensibly a war between the Ottoman Empire and Russia, its origins lay in the growing rivalry between Great Britain and Russia in the course of what came to be called the "Great Game"; struggle for supremacy in the Near East, Central Asia, and India. Although the Straits Convention of 1841 had determined that in times of peace the Black Sea would be closed to the warships of all powers, Britain and France continued to fear that Russia would make a dash across the Black Sea to seize Istanbul. The Crimean War ostensibly broke out over the demand of the Russian tsar, Alexander II (r. 1855–1881) to protect the privileges of the Orthodox Church in Jerusalem against the Catholics, who were backed by the French. Russian forces crossed the Ottoman frontier on the Danube in October 1853 and officially started what came to be known as the Crimean War. The war was so named largely because its major theater was to be the Crimean Peninsula. After the destruction of the Ottoman fleet at Sinop on the north Anatolian littoral on 30 November, it appeared as though the Ottoman Empire was defenseless. In March 1854 Britain, France, Austria, and the Kingdom of Sardinia joined the Ottoman Empire. The key to the Allied campaign was the siege of Sevastopol. Much of the Russian navy was scuttled to block the entrance to the harbor, and after the landings at Balaklava, the battle for Sevastopol became an eleven-month siege in which more soldiers on both sides died of disease than in actual combat.

Western history books glorified the war, and romantic imagery such as Alfred, Lord Tennyson's (1809–1892) poem "The Charge of the Light Brigade" (1854), created the impression that the "Turks," whose war it actually was, were virtually absent. In fact the Ottoman forces, commanded by a very able general, Omar Pasha (a Croat convert to Islam), provided the main "cannon fodder" and Istanbul became the center for logistical support. It was there, outside Sevastopol, that Florence Nightingale (1820–1910), the "lady with the lamp," set up what would become the most legendary war hospital of pre–World War I Europe. On 11 September 1855 the Russians evacuated Sevastopol and scuttled what remained of their Black Sea fleet.

For most of the second half of the nineteenth century, the Black Sea would actually be dominated by the Ottoman fleet. The Ottomans, chastened by their experience during the Crimean War, built up a fleet of dreadnoughts that became the third-largest battle fleet in the world. The Russians, forbidden by the Treaty of Paris of 1856 from building a fleet, were virtually erased as a naval presence in the Black Sea up to World War I.

See also **Crimean War; Nightingale, Florence; Ottoman Empire; Russia.**

BIBLIOGRAPHY

Anderson, Matthew. *The Eastern Question, 1774–1923: A Study in International Relations.* London, Melbourne, and New York, 1966.

King, Charles. *The Black Sea: A History.* Oxford, U.K., and New York, 2004.

Ortaylı, İlber. *İmparatorluğun En Uzun Yüzyılı.* Istanbul, 1983.

SELIM DERINGIL

BLAKE, WILLIAM (1757–1827), English poet and visual artist.

William Blake, now regarded as a major poet and visual artist, was born and lived all of his life in London with the exception of three years that he spent in the hamlet of Felpham on the southern coast. He was self-educated, having been sent to drawing school at an early age and then apprenticed to an engraver. A painter and professional engraver himself, he published his own works by an original process called "relief etching." These hand-colored works included designs, were produced in small numbers, and are now highly prized. The best known are the collections of short poems *Songs of Innocence* and *Songs of Experience*, brought together in 1794. His early longer poems *America* (1793), *Europe* (1794), and *Visions of the Daughters of Albion* (1794) had been preceded by the conventionally printed *The French Revolution* (1791), one book being set in type but never distributed and the others lost or perhaps never written. Blake knew many of the political radicals of his day: Thomas Paine (1737–1809), Mary Wollstonecraft (1759–1797), William Godwin (1756–1836), Horne Tooke (1736–1812), Thomas Holcroft (1745–1809), and others; and to his death he called himself a "liberty boy." However,

***Jacob's Ladder,* by William Blake.** Pen and watercolor on paper, c. 1800. Blake's illustrations of passages from the Old Testament are mystical and visionary. Bʀɪᴛɪsʜ Mᴜsᴇᴜᴍ, Lᴏɴᴅᴏɴ, UK/Bʀɪᴅɢᴇᴍᴀɴ Aʀᴛ Lɪʙʀᴀʀʏ

his later long works are less overtly political than those mentioned above. Perhaps his most intellectually important work was *The Marriage of Heaven and Hell* (1792), which is partly a satirical treatment of the Swedish mystic Emanuel Swedenborg (1688–1772) and an expression of a theory of "contraries" derived from but also at odds with that writer's notions. For Blake, "without contraries is no progression"; the human world proceeds by the prolific clash of opposite but necessary forces.

Beginning around 1795, Blake worked on an enormous manuscript poem first called *Vala* and later *The Four Zoas*. He never completed it, and the poem was unknown to readers and scholars until Edwin John Ellis (1848–1916) and William Butler Yeats (1865–1939) published an inaccurate transcription in 1893. Though chaotic, it is the fullest presentation of the mythology Blake created. It tells of a fall into division of the archetypal giant Albion, representing England, the strife between his parts, and his eventual restoration to unity. Without knowing the story eccentrically told here, readers find Blake's two great later poems *Milton* and *Jerusalem* quite obscure. There is some political allegory in all of these poems, but Blake's eccentric, humanistic, radically Protestant religious views had become more important.

Blake's political interests were deeply affected by two events. The first was the anti-Catholic Gordon riots of 1780, in which he was physically caught up. His hatred of violence was fueled by this experience. The second was an accusation made against him in 1803. Blake and his wife were living in Felpham at the time, when a drunken soldier entered his garden and refused to leave. Blake forced him up the road toward his barracks. The soldier accused Blake of seditious remarks about the king, a serious charge given the war with France. Since Blake had written critically of George III in *Europe*, though not actually naming him, it is not implausible that in his anger he may have uttered something quite uncomplimentary. In 1804, Blake stood trial for high treason and was acquitted.

Blake was deeply influenced by the Bible and by the work of John Milton (1608–1674). His *Milton* (1804–c. 1811) tells of Milton's return from heaven into the spirit of Blake in order to correct the errors of his life and work, one of which in *Paradise Lost* was the giving of more life and energy to the devil than to God and Jesus. In *Jerusalem* (completed 1820), Blake tells in one hundred elaborately designed pages of the alienation of Albion from his creations, particularly his daughter Jerusalem, and their eventual reconciliation.

Blake's late years were spent in severe poverty, but in continued artistic activity. In these years he executed some of his greatest designs: the illustrations to the Book of Job, the illustrations to Dante's *Commedia*, and the splendid woodcuts for Robert John Thornton's 1821 edition of the pastorals of Virgil. In these years, a group of young artists, including George Richmond (1809–1896), Edward Calvert (1799–1883), John Linnell (1792–1882), and Samuel Palmer (1805–1881), gathered about him. Blake influenced these painters and those of the Pre-Raphaelite Brotherhood. There was a biography in 1863, and Algernon Charles Swinburne (1837–1909) wrote a study of Blake's poetry in 1868, but his reputation was really rescued from relative obscurity by poets and critics in the early twentieth century.

See also **Godwin, William; Great Britain; Paine, Thomas; Wollstonecraft, Mary.**

BIBLIOGRAPHY

Bentley, Gerald E., Jr. *Stranger from Paradise.* New Haven, Conn., 2001.

Bindman, David. *Blake as an Artist.* Oxford, U.K., 1977.

Blake, William. *The Complete Poetry and Prose of William Blake.* Edited by David V. Erdman. Berkeley, Calif., 1982.

Erdman, David V. *Blake: Prophet Against Empire.* Princeton, N.J., 1954.

Essick, Robert N. *William Blake and the Language of Adam.* Oxford, U.K., 1989.

Frye, Northrop. *Fearful Symmetry: A Study of William Blake.* Princeton, N.J., 1947.

Mitchell, W. J. T. *Blake's Composite Art: A Study of the Illuminated Poetry.* Princeton, N.J., 1978.

Viscomi, Joseph. *Blake and the Idea of the Book.* Princeton, N.J., 1993.

HAZARD ADAMS

BLANC, LOUIS (1811–1882), French socialist.

Louis Blanc was the first socialist in any country to hold a government post. The son of a legitimist official dispossessed of his pension by the 1830 revolution, Blanc was a scholarship student at the *collège* in Rodez. His direct, simple style and useful connections (he started life as tutor to the children of Frédéric Desgeorges, a liberal notable and newspaper editor in the Pas-de-Calais) quickly made him a leading radical journalist. Writing first in 1834 for the *Bon Sens,* a weekly paper directed at workers, in 1839 he helped found *La Revue du Progrès politique, social et littéraire.* In 1840 a selection of his articles became *L'Organisation du Travail.* Within two weeks, three thousand copies had been sold and the next printing disappeared equally fast, probably helped by a government confiscation order. Quoting statistical evidence of poverty published by Ange Guépin, L. R. Villermé, and E. Buret, Blanc argued that free competition, much vaunted by liberal economists, was enslaving workers—especially women—and would ultimately leave the economy in the hands of a tiny minority of the most ruthless employers. His solution was a blend of worker cooperatives, not unlike those set up by Philippe Buchez (1796–1865) and Pierre Leroux (1797–1871), but financed, in a somewhat Fourierist style, by the state as the "banker of the poor." Such worker associations would be kick-started with repayable government loans, after which they would be autonomous. By 1848, Blanc's first book had gone through five editions, each growing fatter as he refuted his critics, who pointed out that social workshops would compete with each other and might also become oppressive to workmen.

By 1848 Blanc had also helped launch the powerful radical daily *La Réforme,* which promoted both social and suffrage reform. He had written a five-volume influential critique of the Orleanist regime, *Histoire de dix ans* (1841–1844), and published two of his fifteen volumes of the history of the 1789 revolution in which he revealed considerable sympathy for the ideas of Maximilien Robespierre (1758–1794). Unlike Etienne Cabet (1788–1856) and the Fourierists, he did not attempt to create a socialist movement around himself, nor did he try to set up worker associations as did Leroux and Buchez. Up to this stage, Blanc's contribution was essentially that of a popularizer and synthesizer.

The February revolution of 1848 seemed to offer an opportunity to radicals and socialists to find solutions to the social question. Blanc joined the republican provisional government along with other journalists from *La Réforme* and *Le National.* As secretary of the Workers' and Employers' Luxembourg Commission, appointed by the government to advise on the economic crisis, Blanc persistently but vainly urged the ministers to adopt his notion of social workshops. They preferred traditional national workshops, which provided little more than a tiny dole. Blanc's commission managed to arbitrate industrial disputes in the capital and organize a couple of workshops, one of which made the embroidery for national guard uniforms, but his radicalism worried his fellow republican ministers.

Like other radicals, Blanc was alarmed at the lack of a republican majority in the new Constituent Assembly, despite its being elected by direct universal male suffrage for the first time ever. Blanc participated in the workers' march against the Assembly on 15 May 1848, with the ostensible motive of encouraging government support for revolutions abroad, notably in Poland. The big issue, however, was the fate of the government's workshops, which by May had more than a hundred thousand members and seemed both a physical threat as well as a financial burden to the Assembly. After some delay, the conservative majority in the Assembly decreed their closure. The resulting worker rebellion in June was somewhat unjustifiably blamed on Blanc, who had fled to London after the May fiasco. The divisions among radicals about the form of the new republic, plus the lack of majority support for a republic among voters, contributed to the election of Napoleon I's nephew as president and the subsequent reinvention of an empire. Although Blanc had fused a number of socialist strands into his own pet projects, his intransigence and self-conceit in the spring of 1848 helped to isolate him and divide radical reformers.

In enforced residence in London until 1870, Blanc might have been a uniting focus, but he spent his time constantly reiterating his own solutions and arguing with fellow socialists and republicans. Although more of his writing was translated into English than that of other French socialists, he does not seem to have established as much contact with English radicals and Owenites as did the Fourierists. He opposed the Commune of 1871 and was elected to the new National Assembly where he sat as an elder statesman. He was regarded as an inspiration for the radical socialist movement that emerged at the turn of the century. Probably the best-known socialist in his day, he has been the least-remembered in recent years.

See also **France; Socialism.**

BIBLIOGRAPHY

Loubère, Leo A. *Louis Blanc: His Life and His Contribution to the Rise of French Jacobin-Socialism.* Evanston, Ill., 1961.

Pilbeam, Pamela M. *French Socialists before Marx: Workers, Women, and the Social Question in France.* Teddington, U.K., 2000.

Sewell, William. "Beyond 1793: Babeuf, Louis Blanc and the Genealogy of 'Social Revolution.'" In *The French Revolution and the Creation of Modern Political Culture.* Vol. 3: *The Transformation of Political Culture, 1789–1848.* Edited by François Furet and Mona Ozouf. Oxford, U.K., 1989.

PAMELA PILBEAM

BLANQUI, AUGUSTE (1805–1881), French republican political activist.

Louis-Auguste Blanqui is among the most romantic figures in the nineteenth-century European revolutionary tradition. As a conspirator in secret societies, a journalist for ephemeral newspapers, and a popular club orator, he aspired to foment popular insurrections against the authoritarian regimes of mid-nineteenth-century France—from the Bourbon Restoration to the Second Napoleonic Empire. Frequently imprisoned, he acquired a legendary reputation as an idealistic pariah willing to suffer for the cause of social justice.

Blanqui was born on 8 February 1805 in Puget-Théniers (Alpes-Maritimes), where his father was a sub-prefect during the First Napoleonic Empire. Intellectually precocious, the young Blanqui studied law and medicine in Paris, though he never earned a degree. Instead, he drifted into the political underground of secret societies and left-wing journalism during the Bourbon Restoration. He manned the barricades during the popular insurrection in Paris in July 1830, through which the Bourbon monarchy was toppled. Unhappy with its Orleanist successor, he again went underground, organizing two secret societies during the following decade. He played a supporting role in a spectacular but failed coup d'état against the regime in 1839. Periodically, he was arrested, tried, and sentenced to lengthening prison terms (in total forty-three years). Free at the outset of the revolution of 1848, he returned to Paris to become a ubiquitous club orator and an agitator rousing the crowds that menaced the National Assembly. In the midst of this campaign, his reputation was irreparably damaged by the highly publicized charge that he had betrayed his comrades-in-arms to the police in the abortive coup of 1839. During the early years of the Second Empire, he was sent to remote prisons, and his legend, now tarnished, began to fade.

The aging Blanqui was rediscovered by a younger generation of would-be republican revolutionaries in the early 1860s (appropriately in a political prison), and he became their mentor, educator, and guide in the tactics of insurrection. With his oversight, they organized a secret society and carried out street demonstrations against the imperial regime. Blanqui remained hidden on the margins, but emerged publicly once more as journalist, club orator, and national guard commander while Paris was under siege during the Franco-Prussian War in the fall of 1870. Arrested after the armistice by a moderate provisional government that had grown tired of his strident opposition, he was again imprisoned and so never participated in the Paris Commune of 1871, though several of his disciples played major roles therein. He was freed in the amnesty of 1879 and died two years later on 1 January 1881, by then revered among the left generally as the grand old man of the revolutionary tradition.

Though he traveled in a left-wing milieu increasingly drawn to socialist ideas as the century progressed, Blanqui can be characterized as a socialist only in loose terms. He was dismissive of the ideas of both Pierre-Joseph Proudhon (1809–1865) and Karl Marx (1818–1883) and was suspicious of rival factions on the left, notably the First Workingmen's International

Association. His credo, insofar as he articulated one, might be characterized as a religious atheism. He argued for facing the trials of life courageously, free of sentimental illusions about otherworldly human destiny. He preached uncompromising activism in the face of political oppression, with faith in its existential value if not much hope for its efficacy in fashioning a different kind of human future. His atheist materialism assumed metaphysical proportions in his *L'Eternité par les astres* (1871), a philosophical meditation on the idea of the eternal return of the cycles of the material forces of the cosmos. His ideas had more influence on the Free Thought movement than on the socialist cause. Committed to a conception of revolution modeled on the popular uprisings of the French Revolution, his political method had become obsolete in the emerging democratic politics of mass political parties of the late nineteenth century in western Europe. The most direct parallel of his politics is with Vladimir Lenin's (1870–1924) leadership of the Russian Bolshevik party in the early twentieth century.

Until the mid-twentieth century, Blanqui was portrayed sympathetically by his left-wing biographers for his combative politics and by some literary critics for his purity of heart in his devotion to his cause. Late-twentieth-century scholarship, however, reveals a man of complex motives, self-doubt, political irresolution, and narcissistic selfishness behind his mask of selfless resolve.

See also **France; Republicanism.**

BIBLIOGRAPHY

Primary Sources

Blanqui, Louis Auguste. *Lettres familières d'Auguste Blanqui et du Docteur Louis Watteau.* Edited by Maurice Paz. Marseille, 1976.

————. *Un Révolutionnaire professionnel, Auguste Blanqui.* Paris, 1984.

Secondary Sources

Bernstein, Samuel. *Blanqui.* Paris, 1970.

Dommanget, Maurice. *Auguste Blanqui: Des origines à la révolution de 1848.* Paris, 1969. See also his other works on Blanqui.

Howorth, Jolyon. *Edouard Vaillant: La création de l'unité socialiste en France.* Paris, 1982.

Hutton, Patrick H. *The Cult of the Revolutionary Tradition: The Blanquists in French Politics, 1864–1893.* Berkeley, Calif., 1981.

Spitzer, Alan B. *The Revolutionary Theories of Louis-Auguste Blanqui.* New York, 1957.

PATRICK H. HUTTON

BLOK, ALEXANDER (1880–1921), Russian poet.

One of the major European poets and dramatists of the twentieth century, Alexander Alexandrovich Blok emerged as a symbolist at the beginning of his career but quickly transcended the confines of that movement. Born in St. Petersburg on 28 November (16 November, old style) 1880 to a family of the intelligentsia, Blok was raised by his mother and her family after his parents' divorce.

Whereas the so-called first generation of Russian symbolists acknowledged French symbolism as a formative influence, Blok turned to the poetry of his mother tongue, the romances and love poetry of Vasily Zhukovsky, Alexander Pushkin, Yakov Polonsky, and Afanasy Fet. The most telling influence, however, was that of Vladimir Soloviev, whose poetry, drama, and complex persona provided models for Blok throughout his career. In particular, Soloviev's conception of the Sophia, the divine feminine who would redeem and reconcile humanity, inspired Blok as he created his early poems, collected in *Verses about the Beautiful Lady* (1904). The most overtly symbolist of Blok's work, this cycle constitutes a diary in verse that recounts the poet's anticipation of and encounters with the Beautiful Lady, who mediates between the mundane world that surrounds the poet and the divine that he intuits beyond his senses. The cycle becomes ever more dramatic as the poet grapples with doubt and foreboding, which endow the entire work with an eschatological character. Blok resurrects and renews the key concerns of European love poetry, and *Verses* stands apart as a twentieth-century exemplar of a tradition that goes back to the troubadours, Petrarch, Dante, and beyond.

The doubt and foreboding that lent *Verses* its drama intensified after the Revolution of 1905. Thanks in part to the impact of the poet Valery Bryusov's volume *Urbi et Orbi* (1903; To the city and the world), Blok turned increasingly to urban themes. As an unforeseen consequence, the Beautiful Lady underwent a metamorphosis, arising as an Unknown Woman who is as much angel as whore. The work of Blok's so-called second period provoked a firestorm of recrimination, abuse, and charges of apostasy. The poet and novelist Andrei Bely went so far as to challenge Blok to a duel. Although the duel never took place, the crisis demonstrates how far Blok had strayed from his erstwhile friends and colleagues.

Blok's persona continued to evolve. He transformed it in the poems collected in such collections as *Joy Unhoped-for* and *The Snow Mask* (1907) through romantic irony and overt self-parody. This process was inherently dramatic, and it is telling that Blok turned to drama at this time. His first play, *A Puppet Show* (1906), is a complex parody of both his own work and of theatrical tradition. It so moved the great director Vsevolod Meyerhold that he staged it twice: The first production, at the Vera Kommissarzhevskaya Theater, turned into a seminal event in modern Russian culture as the play elicited a near riot. The second production, a double bill with Blok's third play, *An Unknown Woman*, proved more tranquil, yet still historic as it was here that Meyerhold began to work out the basic tenets of his constructivist phase.

While irony and self-parody leavened his earlier solemnity, Blok remained dissatisfied and sought positive meaning in his work. His seeking came to fruition as gradually the divinity of the Beautiful Lady melded with the earthliness of the Unknown Woman and became reified in Russia, whose image was at once concretely feminine and historically ordained. Much of Blok's best poetry, the collection *Homeland* (1907–1916) and the cycle *On Kulikovo Field* (1908), for example, issued from his historical vision of Russia. Blok's increasing preoccupation with history, Russia, and its mission informs not only his essays and lyric poetry but also his narrative poetry, which includes the unfinished *Retribution* (1910–1921) and culminates in *The Twelve* and *The Scythians* (both 1918). Even such seemingly independent works as *The Rose and the Cross* (1913), one of the finest plays of the era, and the literary folktale "Nightingale Garden" betray a debt to a vision that is at once mythic and historical. Blok died in Petrograd on 7 August 1921.

No poet after Blok has escaped his shadow. Poets as diverse as Anna Akhmatova and Marina Tsvetaeva acknowledged the impact of Blok's work on their own, but even poets who repudiated symbolism, such as Vladimir Mayakovsky, drew on his technique. As the poet Osip Mandelstam put it, Blok was a "canonizer of uncanonized forms," who introduced and popularized nontraditional rhymes and accentual verse meters, such as *dolniki*, that had rarely appeared before in high literature. Just as influential is Blok's persona. In surrendering himself to the historical elements of the revolution, Blok shaped the image of what a poet should be for a generation and beyond.

See also **Bely, Andrei; Pushkin, Alexander; Silver Age; Soloviev, Vladimir; Symbolism.**

BIBLIOGRAPHY

Primary Sources

Blok, Aleksandr. *Selected Poems.* Translated by Jon Stallworthy and Peter France. Manchester, U.K., 2000. Originally published as *The Twelve, and Other Poems.* London, 1970.

———. *Aleksandr Blok's Trilogy of Lyric Dramas.* Translated by Timothy C. Westphalen. London, 2003. Contains *A Puppet Show, The King on the Square,* and *The Unknown Woman.*

Secondary Sources

Berberova, Nina. *Aleksandr Blok: A Life.* Translated by Robyn Marsack. Manchester, U.K., 1996.

Chukovsky, Kornei. *Alexander Blok as Man and Poet.* Translated and edited by Diana Burgin and Katherine O'Connor. Ann Arbor, Mich., 1982.

Mochulsky, Konstantin. *Aleksandr Blok.* Translated by Doris V. Johnson. Detroit, Mich., 1983.

Orlov, Vladimir. *Hamayun: The Life of Alexander Blok.* Translated by Olga Shartse. Moscow, 1980.

Pyman, Avril. *The Life of Aleksandr Blok.* Vol. 1: *The Distant Thunder, 1880–1908.* Oxford, U.K., 1979.

———. *The Life of Aleksandr Blok.* Vol. 2: *The Release of Harmony, 1908–1921.* Oxford, U.K., 1980.

Sloane, David A. *Aleksandr Blok and the Dynamics of the Lyric Cycle.* Columbus, Ohio, 1988.

Vogel, Lucy, ed. and trans. *Blok: An Anthology of Essays and Memoirs.* Ann Arbor, Mich., 1982.

Westphalen, Timothy C. *Lyric Incarnate: The Dramas of Aleksandr Blok.* London, 1998.

TIMOTHY C. WESTPHALEN

BODY. Ever since the early twentieth century, when the Annales school of historical scholarship issued the call for a total human history, the body has figured prominently in the writing of the social history of Europe. The vision for a total history comprised two objectives. It aimed at extending the study of past lives beyond the traditional focus on monarchs, religious leaders, and social elites. And it sought to shift the examination of human activity away from events and toward the everyday experiences of ordinary people.

Attention to the body promised to realize this agenda in a number of ways. Historians recognized the body as a universal aspect of human experience, and so its examination would offer the possibility of a more inclusive consideration of human actors in the past. The body intersects with social organization in numerous and various ways, including birth, sex, reproduction, work, disease, and death, and so historians saw in it an ideal vantage point for expanding the scope of social life worth studying.

Historians also appreciated the special relationship between science and the body in the modern age. They recognized the limited relevance of traditional historical sources—political pamphlets, treatises, memoirs, works of art and literature—for the task of studying everyday life. By contrast, demography held the potential to transform individual births and deaths into meaningful series illuminating the influence of anonymous social and economic structures while medicine might cut through the arcane morbid classifications of the past, reveal the true nature of the diseases people suffered, and identify the conditions that produced them. But historians' interest in the relationship between scientific endeavor and the body was as much substantive as it was instrumental. The modern scientific disciplines of anatomy, physiology, and medicine defined the traits of the body, distinguished the body from its environment, and pursued an understanding of the relationship between them. In doing so they fostered a seamless identity between body and person, making it possible to appreciate the characteristics that human beings held in common as well as the conditions that accounted for their diversity. These accomplishments, at once material and ideological, fit well with the humanistic tenor of the social history enterprise.

The marriage of social history, science, and the body yielded impressive results. Demographic evidence of high birth and death rates (organized in series) revealed the prevalence of famine and nutrition-related diseases that characterized premodern subsistence economies. The efforts of women to combine childbirth with other forms of (agricultural) labor illuminated the multiple and difficult tasks associated with family life in premodern Europe. In the modern era, the study of epidemic diseases like cholera and typhoid fever contributed to a more nuanced portrait of the squalid living conditions and harsh work environment endured by an industrializing and urbanizing workforce. The bourgeois male's patronage of prostitution as an outlet for the expression of sexual desire, and the abusive syphilis examinations imposed on the prostitute in police-sponsored dispensaries, exposed the fragile and hypocritical foundations of the much-vaunted family in modern social life. The slow but inexorable introduction of water supplies and toilets in urban areas, and the growing popularity of practices such as bodily washing and the wearing of undergarments bore witness to the beginnings of an influential role for social reform in urban and industrial areas. Surprised by their discovery of the alarming incidence of "old-world" afflictions like malaria, typhus, and birth deformities in the nineteenth- and early-twentieth-century European countryside, historians concluded that modern economic and social transformation was uneven at best.

These few examples only hint at the vast amount of information resulting from social history's focus on the body. They also suggest the problems that have been involved in using the body as a source of historical evidence. In a project that claimed to value the diverse and complex contours of a universal human experience and that approached the myriad manifestations of the body as a crucial aspect of that experience, the focus on the body instead resulted in normative judgments of past forms of social life. Evidence of the body—its diseases, deformities, and shape; the specific kinds of practices lavished upon it and the forms of knowledge employed to understand and give it meaning—ended up revealing and measuring the distance separating past societies from modernity. This normative tendency of social historical

Woman Combing Her Hair. Pastel by Edgar Degas, 1885. The impressionist approach to the nude, demonstrated here, was both more naturalistic and more intimate than that of earlier painters. ©ALEXANDER BURKATOVSKI/CORBIS

interpretation betrayed a clear, if sometimes unarticulated, assumption about the body. Even if the past reveals bodies characterized by various shapes and functions, there exists a specific and identifiable body. Its realization, and the ability to perceive it, is the product of the interrelated modern accomplishments of industrial capitalism, urbanization, civil society, scientific understanding, and the affective family unit, and it has in turn fostered the possibility of individuality. This confidence in the stability of the body has served to legitimize the social historian's evaluation of the present in terms of the past and has made historical writing central to the recognition of modernity's unique stature among societies.

CULTURE AND THE BODY

Since the 1980s a new generation of historians, loosely organized around an enterprise referred to as cultural history, has developed new historical approaches for understanding of the body. These approaches differ in important ways. But for the most part they address the tension, evident in social history, between the assumption of an individual/body identity that informs the historian's interest in the past and the normative conclusions about social life that often characterize subsequent interpretations. One approach, especially popular among historians of distant epochs, has been to search out and affirm radically different conceptions and practices of the body as examples of the manifold variety of individual experience. For example, classical and medieval historians have considered the early Christian practices of sexual renunciation and somatic piety (such as fasting among women) outside of a modern framework. While a reliance on such a framework in the past had led more often than not to the fashioning of interpretations emphasizing religious repression or psychosomatic illness, these historians instead found practices expressive of deeply felt human impulses, even if they do not conform to modern notions of personhood. In the modern period historians have taken seriously the study of spinsters, single mothers, the varieties of sexual practices, and bizarre conceptions of the body (lascivious queens, women reproducing rabbits, and men giving birth to children) deployed in the heat of political argument and contention. While historians do not claim that such bodily concepts and practices are representative of modern social life, they accept them as expressions of the affective, psychological, social, and political life of individuals and thus as deserving of historical recognition. What all of these historical endeavors leave unanswered is the question of whether or how a body "really" exists apart from the individual's conception and experience of it, and how the historian should approach the relationship between individual experiences of the body and its normative formulations.

A very different approach has guided other historical investigations of the body in the modern age. In this second approach, cultural historians focus on the body's normative status as the basis for a critical revaluation of the modern notion of the individual. According to the lines of this interpretation, the body prescribes the social roles and social relations necessary for the exercise of individual liberty. Such a perspective affirms the body's normative status as a product of science. In contrast to social historians who insist on the independence of science from politics and affirm that independence as the source of a definitive understanding of the body, these cultural historians regard scientific knowledge of the body as discursive. It is the product of a specific historical context characterized by the interrelation of quasi-autonomous disciplines of inquiry and political events.

That context concerns the problematic relationship of the individual to society in the modern era. The problem manifested itself in numerous ways in nineteenth- and twentieth-century Europe: the violent expressions of the general will during the French Revolution, the debate over the correct interpretation of rights that animated labor conflict in early nineteenth-century industrial and urban centers, national rivalries pursued through war and imperial conquest. All of these crises brought into focus, in one way or another, tensions between liberty and sociability (or morality) and introduced the question of how (or whether) free individuals could realize meaningful and productive relations with others and with society (and societies) at large.

Even as these challenges to the foundations of European liberal social order unfolded, new ways of thinking about the possibilities of social organization involving the body appeared. A new appreciation of women's reproductive capacities emphasized their moral nature, fostering a role for the family as an antidote to the competitive and contentious relations of free individuals in the political and economic realms. Scientists and social reformers joined forces to rethink labor not as a question of rights but as a physical capacity requiring the analysis and management of the physiological processes that produced the energy for work. Public health officials visited working-class dwellings in urban neighborhoods where cholera spread and emphasized the importance of properly constituted family relations for the prevention of epidemic disease. Hygienic practices—the washing of the body and privatization of toilets, to name just two—became an important component of bourgeois identity and facilitated the sublimation of class conflict through new criteria for social distinctions based upon cleanliness.

Many of these examples figure prominently in social historical writing. Some social historians have viewed them as signs of progress while others have situated them in relation to class conflict and the ideological operations of hegemony. Whatever position they take, the principle guiding their interpretations is the (potential) identity between body and individual. For cultural historians employing a discursive analysis, however, these examples serve as evidence of the significant transformation in the possibilities of individualism wrought by modernity's focus on the social capacities of the body. If such a transformation is easily overlooked, it is due to the

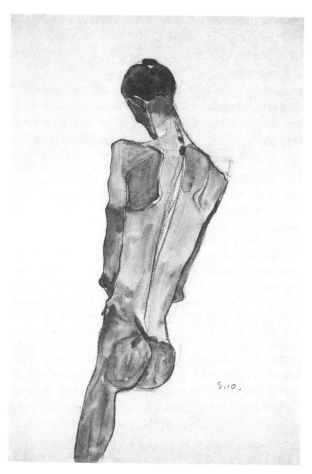

Male Nude, Back View. Painting by Egon Schiele, 1910. Austrian expressionist Schiele focused in particular on the human body, subverting classical notions of perfection while emphasizing sexuality to the degree that he was briefly imprisoned for obscenity in 1912. ©GEOFFREY CLEMENTS/CORBIS

ambiguous relationship of the body to the individual in scientific discourse. Even as scientists searched for human social capacities in the body and accepted them as characteristic of individuals, they carefully avoided any connection between them and subjective states such as will or reason. They presented these capacities as immanent in the body, a precondition of individuality rather than its expression. These bodily capacities were neither dependent upon nor signs of agency and autonomy but often necessitated government and experts for their realization. The prominent roles accorded to public health, psychiatry, and family assistance in the understanding and regulation of bodily capacities is telling in this regard.

Taken together, these examples testify to the elaboration of a moral and social framework out-

side the contentious play of individual subjectivity. That framework was both strategic and effective; it is also paradoxical. The crux of the paradox can be understood by (again) considering the body's ambiguous relationship to the individual. In their attempts to identify individual social capacities in bodily characteristics without any recourse to reason, will, or desire, scientists rejected the unity of subjectivity, sociability, and morality that informed the Enlightenment's vision of the individual. In doing so, the modern scientific conception of the body at once confirmed and undermined the value of the individual and the expression of individuality. In this sense the body did not provide a horizon for the individual but a barrier to it. The manifestations of this paradox of the body in the social life of modern Europe are (again) important and varied. The reproductive organs that rendered women the source of morality in a free social world also prevented them from the exercise of reason and participation in the spheres of politics and economics. In other contexts the body figured negatively, as a destructive social force to be reckoned with. Such was the case in the preoccupation with degeneration after 1850. Discussions about degeneration that focused on the interconnected phenomena of criminality, vice, and racial predisposition merely illuminated the limitations of individualism in the task of producing a progressive, productive, and harmonious social framework. Whether considered as the source of social prescription or as the symptom of a crisis in the terms of liberal social representation, the body often failed to provide an adequate or coherent understanding of the relationship of the individual to social order. In the analysis of social phenomena, the influence of physical (bodily) predispositions became confused with environmental influences, and pathological states (like specific diseases) become mixed up with social ones (such as criminality). In the final analysis, the social characteristics and implications of individuality defied analysis. What remained was the shocking, provocative, but ultimately inexplicable evidence of the incestuous relations of the urban poor, the hungry and hollowed-out faces of Irish peasants, and the sexual perversions of the prostitute.

For those Europeans whose bodies have excluded them from the privilege of individuality, the paradox of the body has not simply been experienced as an inescapable limitation. They have embraced it as a productive source of change. Women dressing *"en homme"* have sought to expose and overturn the biological determinants of their supposedly social destiny. In his poignant yet humorous and upbeat memoirs, the French writer Hervé Guibert approached the social ostracism encountered by him and other gay men "living with AIDS" as an opportunity to fashion an alternative subjectivity to the heterosexist norms informing modern conceptions of individuality. None of these attempts produced a definitive solution to the normative functioning of the body in modern European society, nor were they intended as such. Rather, they posed the indeterminacy of bodies and individuality and insisted on the importance of specific social contexts in fashioning the meaning of their relationship. In doing so they have restored the utopian potential to the modern vision of personhood.

See also **Degeneration; Demography; Disease; Gender; Phrenology; Public Health; Sexuality.**

BIBLIOGRAPHY

Aisenberg, Andrew. *Contagion: Disease, Government, and the Social Question in Nineteenth-Century France.* Stanford, Calif., 1999.

Brown, Peter. *The Body and Society: Men, Women, and Sexual Renunciation in Early Christianity.* New York, 1988.

Bynum, Caroline Walker. *Holy Feast and Holy Fast: The Religious Significance of Food to Medieval Women.* Berkeley, Calif., 1987.

———. *The Resurrection of the Body in Western Christianity, 200–1336.* New York, 1995.

Caron, David. *AIDS in French Culture: Social Ills, Literary Cures.* Madison, Wis., 2001.

Cartwright, Lisa. *Screening the Body: Tracing Medicine's Visual Culture.* Minneapolis, Minn., 1995.

Cody, Lisa Forman. *Birthing the Nation: Sex, Science, and the Conception of Eighteenth-Century Britons.* Oxford, U.K., 2005.

Corbin, Alain. *The Foul and the Fragrant: Odor and the French Social Imagination.* Translated by Miriam L. Kochan, with Dr. Roy Porter and Christopher Prendergast. Cambridge, Mass., 1986.

———. *Women for Hire: Prostitution and Sexuality in France after 1850.* Translated by Alan Sheridan. Cambridge, Mass., 1990.

Duden, Barbara. *The Woman beneath the Skin: A Doctor's Patients in Eighteenth-Century Germany.* Translated by Thomas Dunlap. Cambridge, Mass., 1991.

Engelstein, Laura. *The Keys to Happiness: Sex and the Search for Modernity in Fin-de-Siècle Russia.* Ithaca, N.Y., 1992.

Foucault, Michel. *Discipline and Punish: The Birth of the Prison.* Translated by Alan Sheridan. New York, 1979.

———. *The History of Sexuality.* Vol. 1: *An Introduction.* Translated by Robert Hurley. New York, 1980.

Hunt, Lynn. *The Family Romance of the French Revolution.* Berkeley, Calif., 1992.

Laqueur, Thomas. *Making Sex: Body and Gender from the Greeks to Freud.* Cambridge, Mass., 1990.

———. *Solitary Sex: A Cultural History of Masturbation.* New York, 2003.

Mandrou, Robert. *Introduction to Modern France, 1550–1640: An Essay in Historical Psychology.* Translated by R. E. Hallmark. London, 1975.

Nye, Robert A. *Crime, Madness, & Politics in Modern France: The Medical Concept of National Decline.* Princeton, N.J., 1984.

Pick, Daniel. *Faces of Degeneration: A European Disorder, c. 1848–c. 1918.* Cambridge, U.K., 1989.

Porter, Roy. "History of the Body." In *New Perspectives on Historical Writing,* edited by Peter Burke. University Park, Pa., 1991.

Rabinbach, Anson. *The Human Motor: Energy, Fatigue, and the Origins of Modernity.* New York, 1990.

Revel, Jacques, and Jean-Pierre Peter. "Le corps: l'homme malade et son histoire." In *Faire de l'histoire,* vol. 3: *Nouveaux objets,* edited by Jacques Le Goff and Pierre Nora. Paris, 1983.

Shorter, Edward. *The Making of the Modern Family.* New York, 1977.

Vigarello, Georges. *Concepts of Cleanliness: Changing Attitudes in France since the Middle Ages.* Translated by Jean Birrell. Cambridge, U.K., 1988.

Vila, Anne C. *Enlightenment and Pathology: Sensibility in the Literature and Medicine of Eighteenth-Century France.* Baltimore, Md., 1998.

Weber, Eugen. *Peasants into Frenchmen: The Modernization of Rural France, 1870–1914.* Stanford, Calif., 1976.

ANDREW AISENBERG

BOER WAR.

The origins of the Boer War (1899–1902), also known as the Anglo-Boer War or South African War, lay in British empire-building in the African subcontinent toward the end of the nineteenth century. Comfortably in control of the coastal colonies of the Cape and Natal by midcentury, imperial authorities adopted a mostly complacent view of their regional hegemony. Boer republicans who wanted freedom from crown authority were allowed to migrate to the northern interior and establish independent settler states (the Transvaal and Orange Free State) through conquest. Thereafter, except for a brief period of failed British federation pressure in the 1870s, these skinny agrarian republics were left largely to their own devices.

But the discovery of colossal gold deposits in the South African Republic (Transvaal) in 1886 soon transformed this picture. Within little more than a decade, the Witwatersrand mines had become the world's largest single source of gold, and the economic hub of South Africa had moved from British territory to a free Boer republic. Meanwhile, London was also growing increasingly uneasy about Germany currying diplomatic and commercial favor with the Republic government of Paul Kruger (1825–1904). Previously, British coastal supremacy had meant control of the whole of South Africa. This was all changed by the rise of a wealthy Transvaal with continental European friends. Anxious British politicians now saw the threat of a possible loss of strategic Cape naval facilities to a European great-power rival in league with an expansionist and upstart Boer ally.

Concerns about the challenge to British regional hegemony posed by the robust development of the Republic were accompanied by a no less pressing worry. With London the financial core of world trade, and the supremacy of British sterling backed by gold, City financial markets had an interest in ensuring not only that Transvaal bullion went to London rather than Berlin or Paris, but also that mining conditions were as favorable as possible. On this latter front, British mining magnates (or Randlords) were disgruntled.

ANGLO-BOER CRISIS AND THE ONSET OF WAR

Through the 1890s there were allegations that the Kruger state was too lethargic in its response to the needs of the mining industry, was incapable of grasping the modernity of capitalist industrialization, and was too deeply in the pocket of agrarian

Cartoon depicting Lord Kitchener announcing the annexation of the Transvaal. From the French satirical journal *Assiette au Beurre*, 28 September 1901. CENTRAL SAINT MARTINS COLLEGE OF ART AND DESIGN, LONDON, UK/BRIDGEMAN ART LIBRARY

Boer notables. Some mine owners argued that tilting the balance of power in the Republic in favor of the primary needs of long-term gold production required the toppling of its government. British policy did not require actual control of the Transvaal mines, as informal capitalist influence could assure London's position. But it did require the upholding of British supremacy in South Africa, and that could be held to include a decisive say in the strategic needs of its vital mineral production. Within the capitalist and imperialist political elite a loose common purpose emerged to bring the republicans to heel.

The 1895 Jameson Raid, a botched coup against the Transvaal, fanned anti-imperialist Boer sentiment and alerted Kruger to the imperative of war preparedness. Meanwhile, tactical British demands for Republican citizenship reform to ease access to the franchise for mainly English *uitlanders* (foreigners) on the Witwatersrand grew increasingly menacing. Pushed to the end of its tether, the South African Republic, in a military alliance with its sister republic of the Orange Free State, declared war on Britain in October 1899. It was a desperate first-strike gamble by Boer republicanism to preserve its independence against intensifying imperial aggression.

In the ensuing colonial conflict, Britain anticipated a short war and an easy victory. Instead, it experienced a shock. Before badly organized and indifferently led imperial forces could be reinforced, well-armed and skillfully deployed Boer *burgher* (citizen) armies lunged deep into British colonial territory, inflicting several major defeats in set-piece battles at the end of 1899. Knocked back on their heels, the British were expected to make terms, especially given popular pro-Boer pressure from European capitals. But the Boers were wrong. For a determined London, there could be no loss of face anywhere in the empire. With British forces reorganized, stiffened by massive reinforcements, and strengthened by more competent general command, the tide began to turn early in 1900. Slowly breaking the regular Boer armies through sheer weight of numbers, increasingly adept use of ground, and improved mobility, the British pushed north inexorably. By June 1900, the republican capitals of Bloemfontein and Pretoria had been pocketed, Kruger had decamped to exile in the Netherlands, and Boer armies were disintegrating. With the Republics conquered, the British commander-in-chief, Frederick Sleigh Roberts (1832–1914), declared the war at an end.

TRANSITION TO GUERRILLA WARFARE

Now it was the turn of the British to be wrong. Down, but by no means out, younger and more agile Boer generals like Christiaan Rudolf de Wet (1854–1922) and Jacobus Hercules ("Koos") De la Rey (1847–1914) rallied the remaining fighting rump of their forces, made a tactical switch to highly dispersed guerrilla warfare, and for nearly two more years sustained an effective irregular campaign against an occupying imperial army. Living off the countryside, mounted Boer commando bands delivered destructive glancing blows, raiding British garrison posts, cutting communication lines, sabotaging enemy supply depots, swooping on convoys,

and riding deep into the Cape Colony to conquer vulnerable outlying districts. As the whole axis of the war swung toward guerrilla struggle, die-hard republican patriots kept the British bleeding in the hope of forcing a peace that would not entail the political ignominy of unconditional surrender.

Imperial generals responded by waging a fierce campaign of attrition. To deprive roving commandos of the lifeline of food supply, intelligence, and moral sustenance provided by rural homesteads, Roberts's successor, Horatio Herbert Kitchener (1850–1916), expanded a punitive scorched earth policy, destroying livestock, incinerating crops, and looting and burning thousands of farms in the Boer states. Displaced Boer women and children, as well as African farm tenants and laborers were penned into a network of unhygienic concentration camps, where thousands died mainly from epidemic diseases. For Kitchener, the camps served the purpose of keeping civilian enemy families hostage: only by surrendering would commandos ever again be reunited with their kin. Thousands of Boer republican prisoners-of-war were shipped off to internment in other imperial territories, including India and Ceylon, and the property of prominent war leaders was either confiscated or destroyed. By 1902, roughly half the small white settler population of the Boer states were either incarcerated in camps or being held as war prisoners. For the Boer republicans, the experience of 1899–1902 was close to that of total war.

FORCING BOER SURRENDER

The British also laced the countryside with thousands of blockhouses around which their forces, mustered into flying columns, mounted sweeping drives against commandos, systematically squeezing resisting guerrillas into pockets of the countryside that could be cordoned off. As their belligerent capacity was throttled, Boer war unity evaporated. Numerous desperate, poorer republicans lost faith in their struggle, and either scrambled to surrender or turned against their former compatriots, serving in the imperial forces as armed National Scouts.

Britain's implacable resolve to grind its enemy into surrender, sliding republican morale in the field, deepening economic misery, and the suffering of women and children eventually eroded the

British soldiers with a machine gun, Krantz Kloof, South Africa, c. 1900. ©Bettmann/Corbis

will and capacity of remaining Boer resistance. By 1902, shrewd commanders like Jan Christian Smuts (1870–1950) and Louis Botha (1862–1919) were coming to terms with the futility of their position. It was one that was also being made increasingly perilous because of African and Colored involvement in what was supposed to have been a "white man's war," either through collaboration with British forces, partisan resistance to Boer authority, or hostile intervention to reclaim lost agricultural land. Facing the disintegration of society as they had known it, and responsive to British willingness to strike a negotiated peace settlement, republican military leaders accepted what became known as the Peace of Vereeniging on 31 May 1902. Although its terms required the Republics to sign away their independence, Britain footed the bill for the Boers' war debt, and made available massive reconstruction resources. Having drawn the teeth of its republicanism, Britain now

needed to conciliate Boer society as its power in South Africa rested on the collaboration of white settlers. Where their supremacy over the black majority had been eroded by Anglo-Boer hostilities, the postwar effort was to restore authority.

COSTS AND OUTCOME

By the end, the British had put almost 450,000 imperial troops into the field, the Boers at most around 80,000 combatants. In the largest and most costly war fought by Britain between 1815 and 1914, it had taken the world's greatest empire nearly three years to defeat two of the colonial world's smallest agrarian states, with a combined settler population of under 250,000 inhabitants. About 28,000 refugees, or over 10 percent of the Boer population, died in camps, as well as some 20,000 displaced Africans. Although officially depicted as a war between European powers by both sides, the republicans conscripted around

10,000 trusted black retainers as fighting auxiliaries, while the black labor contribution to the British war effort topped 100,000 men, as many as 30,000 of whom bore arms.

With Boer society fractured between die-hard republican patriots and those who had thrown in their lot with the British, and with hundreds of thousands of the region's black majority entangled in its campaigns, the war was never a straightforward Anglo-Boer confrontation. It also took on the character of a civil war between segments of South African society. Peace brought to an end not merely bloodletting, but also the social and political crisis spawned by this bitter colonial conflict.

See also **Africa; Colonies; Great Britain; Imperialism; Jingoism.**

BIBLIOGRAPHY

Gooch, John, ed. *The Boer War: Direction, Experience, and Image.* London, 2000.

Judd, Denis, and Keith Surridge. *The Boer War.* London, 2002.

Lowry, Donal, ed. *The South African War Reappraised.* Manchester, N.Y., 2000.

Nasson, Bill. *The South African War 1899–1902.* London, 1999.

Omissi, David, and Andrew S. Thompson, eds. *The Impact of the South African War.* London, 2002.

WILLIAM NASSON

BOHEMIA, MORAVIA, AND SILESIA.

The Kingdom of Bohemia (Čechy in Czech; Böhmen in German), the Margraviate of Moravia (Morava; Mähren), and Duchy of Silesia (Slezko; Schlesien; Śląsk in Polish) comprise the historical Bohemian Lands, approximately the twenty-first century's Czech Republic, which came under the rule of the Habsburg crown in 1526. The three provinces retained some formal independence within Austria even after the Habsburg-led counter-reforming forces defeated the Bohemian Protestant nobility at the Battle of White Mountain in 1620. Eventually their unity and independence were undermined and the Bohemian Lands were subjected to direct rule from Vienna, the imperial capital, until the dissolution of the Monarchy in 1918. Bohemia, the westernmost of the three provinces, was the largest at 51,947 square kilometers, while Moravia to its east comprised 22,222 square kilometers, and Silesia, 5,147 square kilometers. Their provincial capitals were Prague (Prag/Praha), one of the largest cities in the Monarchy; Brünn (Brno); and Troppau (Opava), respectively.

Beginning in 1880, the Habsburg Monarchy produced a decennial census in which citizens declared their language of daily usage, which became the basis for identification by ethnic group. Both Bohemia and Moravia had majority Czech populations, large and influential German minorities, and smaller Jewish minorities. According to the last census of the Monarchy in 1910, the population of the Bohemian lands constituted 36 percent of the population of the Austrian half of the Monarchy. Bohemia had a population of 6,712,960, while Moravia had a population of 2,622,271. Bohemia's population was 64 percent Czech and 36 percent German, while Moravia's was 72 percent Czech and 27 percent German. The composition of Silesia, with 756,949 residents the least populous of the three provinces, was significantly different than Bohemia and Moravia. It had a German plurality of 44 percent, followed by a smaller population of Poles of 34 percent, and a still smaller population of Czechs of 26 percent. Roman Catholicism was the major religion in all three provinces.

The emancipation of the Jews of the Bohemian Lands had begun in 1782 with the Edicts of Toleration issued by enlightened-absolutist Habsburg Emperor Joseph II (r. 1765–1790). They achieved complete emancipation in 1859. Religion rather than language defined Jews, and although many were bilingual, most Jews counted German as their language of daily use in the late nineteenth and early twentieth centuries. They had long identified themselves with—and were identified with—the Germans of the Bohemian Lands, although more had begun to claim the Czech language by the twentieth century.

INDUSTRIALIZATION AND MODERNIZATION

The German-populated mountainous border regions of the Bohemian Lands had long been the site of proto-industrial activity, including glass,

A late-nineteenth-century allegorical photograph representing Czech nationalism. Girls dressed in traditional costumes of Czech groups from Bohemia, Moravia, and Silesia pay homage to a figure (at center) representing a Czech homeland. ©SCHEUFLER COLLECTION/CORBIS

spinning, and mining. The modernizing and centralizing bureaucratic, economic, and educational reforms undertaken by Empress Maria Theresa and her son Emperor Joseph II in the second half of the eighteenth century provided the impetus for the rapid industrialization of the Bohemian Lands, which soon became the most economically advanced provinces in the Monarchy. Among the social characteristics aiding this development were a free peasantry, a high literacy rate, and the increasing availability of technical training in the form of three polytechnics. Although rich in natural resources, the production of finished goods was the main source of income in the Bohemian Lands. Textile production provided the first engine of industrialization after 1800, but was replaced by heavy industry at mid-century. The Ostrau-Karwina (Ostrava-Karviná) coalmines, together with the nearby iron works at Witkowitz (Vítkovice) on the Moravian-Silesian border, would become one of the leading industrial regions of the Monarchy. Mechanized production slowly superceded handwork in most industries by the late nineteenth century. Advanced agricultural industries developed, including sugar beet and beer production, in the predominantly Czech interior. Sugar beet production became the most advanced industry in the Bohemian Lands, as well as a leading export. In addition to Ostrau-Karwina and Prague, the latter surrounded by textile and machine-producing industrial suburbs, Brünn—known as the Manchester of Moravia for its textile factories—was an important industrial center. The southwestern Bohemian city of Pilsen (Plzeň) had long been a busy trade center, linking the Bohemian Lands with the German cities of Regensburg and Nuremberg. It was the home of Škoda works, founded in 1859 and by the twentieth century the largest armaments producer in the Monarchy.

The rapid growth of railroads in the Bohemian Lands both encouraged and reflected their rapid industrial development. The first railroad in the monarchy opened between Linz in Lower Austria and Buweis (Budějovice) in southern Bohemia in 1832. Some of the earliest and best-traveled lines were between Vienna and Moravia-Silesia and Vienna and Bohemia: the first part of the line connecting Brno with Vienna opened in 1839. A Vienna-Prague line followed soon afterward. All three provinces benefited from a state railroad-building program at mid-century.

These industrial cities, together with others including Karlsbad (Karlovy Vary) and Marienbad (Mariánské Lázně), spa towns near the thermal springs in western Bohemia, had large increases in population during the nineteenth century, in part due to expansion of the railroad system after 1870. Reflecting some of the vast changes in the social structure that accompanied modernization, Karlsbad saw a shift in its guests from the aristocracy and the European cultural elite during the late eighteenth and early nineteenth centuries, when it was the site of diplomatic and political negotiations, to the wealthy bourgeoisie a century later.

Industrialization brought with it the physical and material impoverishment of the workers, including child labor, tuberculosis, high rates of alcoholism, and infant mortality. The situation of the working class remained critical, despite the growing social democratic organization of the workers, in part because continued Czech migration into the predominantly German industrial regions insured an inexpensive labor supply.

In the course of modernization, the center of Karlsbad was almost completely rebuilt beginning in the last third of the nineteenth century. Like other expanding cities in the Bohemian Lands, it began to construct the necessary infrastructure to incorporate numbers of people migrating from the countryside to urban areas. Much of the development took place under auspices of the Imperial Municipal Law of 5 March 1862, which laid out the obligations under the jurisdiction of the municipalities. These included maintenance of streets, squares, and bridges, together with building and fire control. Particularly under Czech or German political liberal leadership from the 1860s through the 1880s, cities and towns built public libraries and schools, as well as railroad stations and theaters.

THE DEVELOPMENT OF TWO NATIONAL COMMUNITIES

The so-called Czech national revival (*národní obrození*) in the late eighteenth and early nineteenth century was initially a linguistic-cultural movement that affected mainly the nascent Czech intellectual elite. The reform of secondary schools in the 1770s and the establishment of a Czech-language chair at the university in Prague in 1791 helped strengthen the Czech language. In 1818 adherents of the national revival founded the Museum of the Bohemian Kingdom as a center for Czech scholarship in Prague. Among the early achievements of the revival were scholarly volumes on Czech history, language, and literature, as well as dictionaries and grammars under the auspices of the Matice Česka, a group of Czech intellectuals devoted to scholarly and popular publications. The national revival was part of a slow process of popular national differentiation in the Bohemian Lands that led to increased Czech-German conflict, especially after the historian František Palacký (1798–1876), a leader of the revival, chose not to participate as Bohemia's representative in the Frankfurt Parliament during the revolutions of 1848. Beginning in the 1830s, Czechs had agitated for language rights in schools and public administration. From the 1860s, many Czech claims were couched in terms of the principle of Bohemian state rights, which demanded the historical integrity of Bohemian territory. German opposition to these demands—and others—for parity with the Germans would be a source of national conflict for the duration of the Monarchy. Czech and German society continued to develop in opposition to one another during the second half of the nineteenth century.

National differentiation manifested itself in the second half of the century in the growing numbers of nationally based civic and occupational groups into which Czechs and Germans increasingly organized their social lives. They included bands, choirs, and volunteer firefighting groups, together with fraternal and gymnastics organizations. Reflecting the division of public life in the Bohemian Lands by nationality, Czechs and Germans constructed their own cultural centers, the *Beseda* or *Besední dům* and the *Deutsches Haus*. Numerous secular monuments, often representing Czech or German national heroes, were also unveiled. Another manifestation of national differentiation was the development of nationally based celebrations and commemorations. The nominally Roman Catholic Czechs chose the Bohemian priest Jan Hus, whom the Church executed for heresy in 1415, as the primary symbol of their national identity. The anniversary of his death at the stake in Constance on 6 July became the most popular Czech national celebration in the second half of the nineteenth century.

"National defense" organizations were formed, including the Deutscher Schulverein, to establish and maintain German-language schools along the "linguistic frontiers," and its Czech analogue, the Matice školská, both founded in 1880. The Czech defense organizations sought to protect members of the Czech minority who had moved to the predominantly German industrial regions to work, while the German organizations sought to protect and maintain German cultural heritage and property in the face of Czech migration into what they considered German regions. By the 1890s, the Bohemian Lands were increasingly the site of battles between Czechs and Germans for political supremacy. Sometimes this competition manifested itself in Czech calls for national economic boycotts of the Germans and Jews ("*Svůj k svému*," or "each to his own"), to which the Germans responded, in less organized fashion, with their own calls for national boycotts. In the conflation of Germans and Jews, national conflict helped feed a persistent anti-Semitism.

NATIONAL POLITICS IN THE BOHEMIAN LANDS

The French defeat of Austria in 1859 forced Emperor Francis Joseph I (r. 1846–1916) to abandon the neo-absolutist policies he had followed in the decade since the defeat of the revolutions of 1848. The February Patent of 1861 standardized the structure and rights of all the lands of the Monarchy, and representatives to unicameral Diets were elected based on three curiae. The unequal franchise of the Diets, the highest provincial bodies in the Bohemian Lands, remained limited to the best-educated, wealthiest men even as the Imperial Parliament moved toward universal franchise after the turn of the century. The Moravian Diet passed a power-sharing agreement known as the Moravian Compromise in 1905. It fixed percentages of Czech and German representatives, but retained an unequal franchise so that recently formed mass parties in Moravia, like those in Bohemia and Silesia, remained disadvantaged at the communal and provincial level. Particularly the Bohemian Diet in Prague was the site of boycotts and obstruction by Czech and German deputies staking their positions in the national conflict.

The Seven Weeks' War (also called the Austro-Prussian War) of 1866 was primarily fought in the Bohemian Lands. Following the Prussians' victory at the Battle of Königgrätz (Sadowa) in eastern Bohemia on 3 July 1866, Austria sued for armistice. Austria then left the German Confederation (Deutscher Bund), which had been founded at the Congress of Vienna in 1815 to replace the defunct Holy Roman Empire. Austrian departure paved the way for the *kleindeutsch* state Otto von Bismarck (1815–1898) founded in 1871. Another important outcome of this war was the *Ausgleich*, or Compromise, of 1867 that created Austria-Hungary. It provided Hungarians control of their internal affairs in return for a centralized foreign policy and the continued union of the Austrian and Hungarian crowns in the Habsburg ruler. Czech political leaders sought—and failed—to gain a similar agreement.

There was periodic Czech-German violence at the local, provincial, and imperial level during the last decades of the monarchy. The most destructive national conflict took place throughout the provinces in 1897, 1905, and 1908. In April 1897, the Imperial Minister-President, Polish Count Kasimir Felix Badeni (1846–1909), proposed language ordinances calling for the equality of Czech and German in official usage among civil servants of Bohemia and Moravia, who would be required to demonstrate proficiency in both languages by June 1901. The language ordinances threatened the livelihood of German-speaking civil servants, most of whom could not speak Czech. The Germans staged violent demonstrations, reflecting their fear that recognition of the indivisibility of province, as implied in the ordinances, both conceded the Czechs' demand for Bohemian state rights and signified loss of the privileged position of the German language. Badeni's resignation on November 28 precipitated furious clashes in Prague, where

Moravian villagers pose for a photograph c. 1890–1910. ©Scheufler Collection/Corbis

members of the Czech majority attacked German and Jewish property, resulting in the declaration of martial law. The anti-German, anti-Semitic protests in Prague were echoed in Pilsen and other predominantly Czech towns in Bohemia.

One ancillary effect of the 1897 protests was the unleashing of the Austrian-wide political anti-Catholic and anti-Habsburg Los von Rom (Away from Rome) movement under the leadership of the anti-Semitic Pan German politician Georg von Schönerer (1842–1921), who sought to strengthen the German character of Austria. It called upon Germans to leave the Roman Catholic Church and become Protestants in preparation for the unification of Austria with the German Reich. The movement found support among some of the radical nationalist Germans in Bohemian Lands.

The Bohemian Lands were twice more the scene of violence after the turn of the twentieth century. In autumn 1905, Brno was rocked by a series of demonstrations, beginning with several days of Czech-German violence over the former's call for a Czech-language university in Moravia (there were five German-language universities in Austria and only one Czech-language university). Czech and German worker protests throughout Moravia occurred shortly thereafter against the unequal franchise foreseen in the negotiations of the Moravian Compromise. They were followed by the social-democratic-led demonstrations for universal franchise that shook all of Cisleithania. Ongoing national tensions again erupted into violence throughout the Bohemian Lands at the beginning of December 1908 in connection with the year-long Emperor's Diamond Jubilee, resulting in the declaration of martial law in Prague.

Despite calls for Bohemian state rights, Czech politicians worked within the framework of the Austrian state for increased autonomy until World

War I. Conflict among the European Great Powers spelled the end to this approach. On 6 July 1915, the five-hundredth anniversary of Hus's death, philosopher-politician Tomáš Garrigue Masaryk (1850–1937), who had left Austria shortly after the outbreak of hostilities, called for complete Czech independence. The reconvening of the Imperial Parliament, which had been suspended at the war's outbreak until March 1917, and a general amnesty the following summer, including several important Czech politicians, increased Czech émigré political activity, and gained support for Masaryk's program. By autumn 1918, all of the important political forces in Czech society supported Masaryk. Bohemian state rights constituted only one of several claims—economic, geographic, strategic, and ethnic—on which the postwar independent Czechoslovak Republic, proclaimed in Prague on 28 October 1918, was based.

See also **Austria-Hungary; Austro-Prussian War; Masaryk, Tomáš Garrigue; Nationalism; Palacký, František; Prague; Young Czechs and Old Czechs.**

BIBLIOGRAPHY

Agnew, Hugh LeCaine. *The Czechs and the Lands of the Bohemian Crown.* Stanford, Calif., 2004. A comprehensive introduction to the major themes—cultural, intellectual, political, and social—of Czech history.

Kieval, Hillel J. *Languages of Community: The Jewish Experience in the Czech Lands.* Berkeley, Calif., 2000. This exhaustive study traces two hundred years of Jewish history, beginning with the enlightened-absolutist era of reforming Habsburg Emperor Joseph II in Bohemia and Moravia.

King, Jeremy. *Budweisers into Czechs and Germans: A Local History of Bohemian Politics, 1848–1948.* Princeton, N.J., 2002. An innovative history of nation building at the local level from the revolutions of 1848 to the communist seizure of power in Czechoslovakia.

Seibt, Ferdinand, ed. *Die Chance der Verständigung: Absichten und Ansätze zu übernationaler Zusammenarbeit in den böhmischen Ländern, 1848–1918.* Munich, 1987. A collection of essays by international scholars that examine the possibilities for cooperation between Czechs and Germans in the Bohemian Lands in an era of increasing nationalism after the Revolutions of 1848.

Teich, Mikuláš, ed. *Bohemia in History.* Cambridge, U.K., 1998. A collection of essays addressing aspects of Bohemian history from the ninth century to 1989.

Urban, Otto. *Česká společnost, 1848–1918.* Prague, 1982. A comprehensive social and political history of Czech-German relations in the last years of the monarchy.

Nancy M. Wingfield

BOLSHEVIKS. The Bolsheviks represented one wing of the Marxist Russian Social Democratic Labor Party that had emerged in tsarist Russia at the end of the nineteenth century. Closely identified with its leader and founder, Vladimir Lenin (Vladimir Ilyich Ulyanov; 1870–1924), the Bolsheviks sought to take political and intellectual leadership of a revolutionary movement that would use the mass organization of workers to overthrow the autocratic government of the Romanov dynasty.

EARLY DEVELOPMENT OF MARXISM IN RUSSIA

Marxism first attracted radical Russian intellectuals in the 1880s, when a few disillusioned populists saw in the emerging urban proletariat the key to transforming Russia's repressive political and social system. The movement gathered momentum in the 1890s with the acceleration of Russian industrialization. Inspired by the analysis of the early converts to Marxism, Georgy Plekhanov, Pavel Axelrod, and Vera Zasulich, and by the rise of labor unrest in Russian cities, a new generation of radical intellectuals took the lead to organize workers' circles and to channel their energy into a revolutionary political movement. From the start, Marxist activists disagreed on whether to concentrate on the political task of overthrowing the autocracy or on more immediate goals of organizing workers around economic grievances. In the late 1890s, an activist of the younger generation, Lenin, joined with Plekhanov and Axelrod in opposing the approach of working only for economic gains. Meanwhile, an independent Marxist movement representing impoverished Jewish workers in Russia's western Pale of Settlement, the Bund, also began to recruit members and to advocate revolutionary change. In 1898, nine representatives of these scattered Marxist groups and circles came together in Minsk to found the Russian Social Democratic Labor Party. This founding congress sought to emphasize

"We demand that the tactics that have prevailed in recent years be changed; we declare that 'before we can unite, and in order that we may unite, we must first of all firmly and definitely draw the lines of demarcation between the various groups.'" (Vladimir Lenin, *What Is to Be Done*, 1902)

unified organization over theory, but as labor unrest continued to mount, groups of Social Democrats began to disagree on theory and tactics, using political newspapers published outside Russia to articulate their points of view and to rally supporters.

Lenin argued that such a newspaper should serve as the organizing center for underground committees inside Russia. Together with Yuli Martov, who had once favored the tactics of economic agitation, Lenin founded the newspaper *Iskra* (The spark) in late 1900 to articulate their position: for the priority of the political struggle to overthrow tsarism. Inside Russia, followers of the *Iskra* line began to agitate within the underground committees to win activists over to the goal of revolution. Lenin further elaborated his ideas on revolutionary tactics in his pamphlet *What Is to Be Done?* (1902), which emphasized the need for a centralized and conspiratorial revolutionary party.

BOLSHEVIK–MENSHEVIK SPLIT

To consolidate its leadership over the Social Democratic movement, the *Iskra* group of Lenin, Martov, Plekhanov, Axelrod, Zasulich, and Alexander Potresov called for a party congress to ratify their position. The second congress of the Russian Social Democratic Labor Party met first in Brussels in July 1903 and later reconvened in London after being harassed by the Belgian police. By this time, however, serious divisions had emerged within the party and even within the *Iskra* group over the structure and tactics of the party. The Bund wanted the exclusive right to organize all Jewish workers; others in the party objected. Lenin insisted on the primacy of the central newspaper, published abroad, as the organizing center of the movement; a central committee inside Russia would merely supervise local activities. Most contentiously, Lenin

advocated a very narrow definition of party membership: he insisted that Russia's repressive political conditions demanded that only committed professional revolutionaries should be considered as members. His opponents argued that this would exclude many workers and that anyone who embraced the principles of social democracy should be allowed to join the party. In a carefully arranged series of votes, Lenin first defeated the Bund's position, provoking that group to leave the congress. Next he won a vote making *Iskra* the central party organ, spurring another walkout. Finally, with a majority of one, he pushed through his remaining organizational points, with his supporters taking the majority of positions on the central committee and *Iskra* editorial board. Lenin triumphantly named his group the Bolsheviks (majorityites), and his opponents, which now included his former ally Martov, the Mensheviks (minorityites).

The Mensheviks fought back, and after winning Plekhanov over to their side, regained *Iskra* for their faction: Lenin's majority had been short-lived. Efforts to reunite the factions would continue into 1917, but the Bolshevik–Menshevik split would never fully heal. The two factions remained close on many points, but the Bolsheviks continued to place primacy on the political revolution, and a centralized and secretive party, whereas the Mensheviks emphasized that the revolution must come from workers, not just professional revolutionaries, and they directed their efforts toward organizing the labor movement.

REVOLUTION OF 1905 AND ITS AFTERMATH

The Russian Revolution of 1905, which began with worker unrest in January 1905, revealed the isolation of the Social Democratic movement. Neither faction played much of a leadership role. Independently, workers' groups mounted strikes and organized trade unions: local Social Democratic organizations arose in the excitement of the revolutionary moment and increasingly called for the central leaders to forget their differences and come together as one Social Democratic party. The creation of an elected parliament, the Duma, in the aftermath of 1905 gave the Social Democratic parties new incentives for unity, and the Menshevik–Bolshevik split ended officially at the fourth (Unification) congress in Stockholm in the spring of

The St. Petersburg League of Struggle for the Emancipation of the Working Class, photographed in 1895. From left to right: standing, A. L. Malachenko, P. K. Zaporozhets, A. A. Vaneyev; sitting, V. V. Starkov, G. M. Krzhizhanovsky, V. I. Ulyanov (Lenin), and Y. O. Martov. Lenin later founded the Bolshevik Party, while Martov became an important Menshevik leader. ©BETTMANN/CORBIS

1906. Many Mensheviks had moved closer to the Bolsheviks on the necessity of centralized party leadership, and they held sway in the new central committee, which consisted of seven Mensheviks and three Bolsheviks, later augmented by five more members from the Polish and Latvian Social Democratic parties and from the Bund, which had rejoined the movement.

The Social Democrats remained ambivalent about whether they should participate in the elections to the Duma or to boycott them. Formally united, Mensheviks and Bolsheviks still disagreed on major points of doctrine: the Mensheviks believed that the Duma represented the necessary bourgeois stage of Russian development and that they should cooperate with Duma liberals in opposing tsarist policy. Organizing a mass movement of workers remained a key goal. The Bolsheviks preferred to work to undermine the Duma as well as the autocracy, and while professing unity, adopted more violent tactics of armed robbery in order to support their faction's activities. As the government rebounded from the shock of the 1905 revolution, however, it became less tolerant of the Duma and of revolutionary political parties, driving the Bolsheviks further underground and making labor organization very difficult for Mensheviks. A radical wing of the Bolshevik fraction, based inside Russia, responded to the deteriorating political climate by demanding that the Social Democrats withdraw altogether from the Duma. Left Bolshevik intellectuals, including

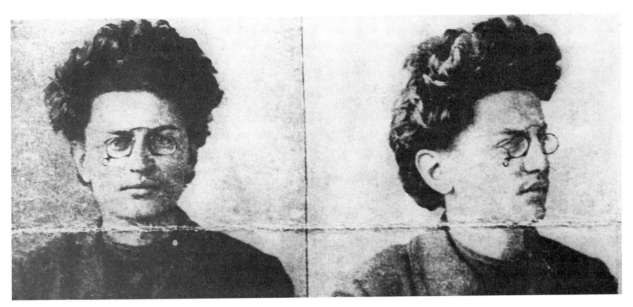

Photographs of Leon Trotsky that appeared on his arrest warrant, 1895. ©HULTON-DEUTSCH COLLECTION/CORBIS

Alexander Bogdanov and Anatoly Lunacharsky, also challenged Lenin on theoretical grounds. Lenin's hold on the Bolshevik movement had become very tenuous by 1910, as even his former supporters Plekhanov and Leon Trotsky now attacked him for his excessive sectarianism. Meanwhile, rank-and-file Social Democrats still agitated for a resolution of these sectarian differences, while party leaders abroad continued to disagree.

LEAD UP TO 1917

Inside Russia, and once again largely independent of Social Democratic leadership, a growing labor force became increasingly militant as Russia's economy began to revive after 1910. When government troops fired upon striking miners in the Lena goldfields in Siberia in April 1912, new waves of unrest spread across the empire. The slow and steady trade union organizing of the Mensheviks now seemed too tame for increasingly militant skilled workers. The Bolsheviks had earlier disdained trade union agitation, but at the party's conference in Prague in January 1912, they now called on the trade unions to become the mass instrument of insurrection. This Prague conference also sealed a new break with the Mensheviks, because Lenin had called it unilaterally to the exclusion of the Menshevik faction.

The Bolsheviks' more militant approach to the trade union movement gained significant support during the years from 1912 to 1914. Emphasizing how the repressive autocratic regime impeded workers' efforts to organize and improve their working conditions, the Bolsheviks appealed to the labor movement to become the instrument of the overthrow of tsarism as well as of capitalism. Increasingly, proletarian Bolsheviks emerged as the radical leaders of the network of trade unions and strike committees, winning additional converts through the proletarian physiognomy of the party and by the appeal of its task-oriented tactics. The Mensheviks, by contrast, stuck to their belief that trade unions must work to raise the long-term cultural, political, and economic levels of Russia's workers. Only a mass movement, fully mobilized and conscious of its goals, could make a legitimate socialist revolution. For the Mensheviks, that revolution required Social Democratic unity. The Bolsheviks, however, following Lenin's lead, were willing to split the socialist movement and go the revolutionary path alone.

See also **Bund, Jewish; Lenin, Vladimir; Martov, L.; Mensheviks; Plekhanov, Georgy; Revolution of 1905 (Russia); Zasulich, Vera.**

BIBLIOGRAPHY

Bonnell, Victoria E. *Roots of Rebellion: Workers' Politics and Organizations in St. Petersburg and Moscow, 1900–1914.* Berkeley, Calif., 1983. Thorough sociological study of the self-organization of Russian urban workers and their interactions with the Bolshevik and Menshevik parties.

Haimson, Leopold H. *The Russian Marxists and the Origins of Bolshevism.* Cambridge, Mass., 1955. Classic study of the intellectual origins of the Menshevik–Bolshevik split, taking the story up to 1905.

Lane, David. *The Roots of Russian Communism: A Social and Historical Study of Russian Social-Democracy, 1898–1907.* Assen, Netherlands, 1969. Analysis of the structure, social composition, and activities of Social-Democratic Party organizations nationally and in seven regions, including St. Petersburg, Moscow, the Caucasus, and Siberia.

Schapiro, Leonard. *The Communist Party of the Soviet Union.* 2nd ed. New York, 1971. Massive and detailed history of the Communist Party from its origins to the end of the Khrushchev era.

Service, Robert. *Lenin: A Political Life.* 3 vols. Bloomington, Ind., 1985–1995. Thorough biography focusing on Lenin's political writings and party organization.

Ulam, Adam B. *The Bolsheviks.* New York, 1965.

Wildman, Allan K. *The Making of a Workers' Revolution: Russian Social Democracy, 1891–1903.* Chicago, 1967. Pioneering study of the relationship between Marxist intellectuals and activist workers in the Russian revolutionary movement.

Williams, Robert C. *The Other Bolsheviks: Lenin and His Critics, 1904–1914.* Bloomington, Ind., 1986.

DIANE P. KOENKER

BONALD, LOUIS DE (1754–1840),
French counterrevolutionary theorist.

Most of the major European political ideologies of the nineteenth century can be traced to the French Revolution, whose apparent overthrow of the old order, or alleged failure to achieve that end, could each give warrant to conservatives' and socialists' shared ambition of reestablishing communal bonds such as they imagined the Enlightenment and the Revolution together had undermined. An appreciation of the socially consolidating role of religion often characterized both reactionary and radical commentaries of the early nineteenth century, and particularly in France it inclined some pre-Marxist socialists to judge Christianity's merits in terms similar to those of counterrevolutionary monarchists like the vicomte Louis-Gabriel-Ambroise de Bonald, scion of a long-established family of the provincial aristocracy.

Born in 1754 in Le Monna near Millau in the south of France and educated mainly at the Oratorian Collège de Juilly near Paris, Bonald soon acquired a taste for mathematics and the physical sciences, which he never found incompatible with his Christian pietism and which would come to distinguish his own theological conservatism from the doctrines of other counterrevolutionary figures of his day. Briefly enlisted with the king's musketeers, he returned to his estate until the late 1780s and from there campaigned to liberate French municipal and provincial government from central control, in 1790 becoming Millau's mayor. After the outbreak of the Revolution, and especially in the light of France's abolition of the vestiges of feudalism in August 1789, he began to shift the focus of his critique of despotism from the monarchy to the National Assembly itself, whose compulsory enforcement of the Civil Constitution of the Clergy prompted his flight to Germany, where he joined other émigré opponents of the Revolution. From Heidelberg in 1796 he supervised the publication of his *Théorie du pouvoir politique et religieux*, whose first volume sets out his principles of an integrative science of society that expressed a divine presence as well as a collective power, which he deemed necessary to combat the fractious tendencies of human egoism.

Returning to France under the Directory in 1797, Bonald at first campaigned in newspapers for the royalist cause in that summer's elections, but its success in gaining popular support provoked the Directory's wrath. In isolation in Paris he now drafted his second major contribution to political thought, the *Essai analytique sur les lois naturelles de l'ordre social* (1800), resurfacing in public life after Napoleon Bonaparte's (1769–1821) coup d'état of the Eighteenth Brumaire in November 1799. Publication of the *Essai*, followed in 1802 by the appearance of his *Législation primitive*, his longest work and the most illustrative of his conception of language as a system of signs of ultimately divine origin, established Bonald's credentials as one of France's most authoritative secular advocates of religious traditionalism. Around 1804 he drafted a study of the life of Jesus, unpublished until 1843, in which he portrayed Christ's self-sacrifice as designed to promote mankind's spiritual regeneration along lines that appeared to culminate in Napoleonic Europe. But soon disheartened by what he took to be Napoleon's purely personal ambitions, he once again abandoned political journalism and only resumed that career in 1815, following the monarchy's restoration, when he came to champion not just the ultraroyalist cause and ideals of a Gallican church independent of papal control but also the interests of the old aristocracy. Adopting those features of the physiocratic science of society that suited him, he depicted the agricultural system that had prevailed in France for centuries before the Revolution as more organically durable than the commercial system generated by the growth of towns, and, now more than ever before, he decried the institutions of popular government when compared to the rule of theologically sanctioned natural law. Already hostile to the parliamentary monarchies of Louis XVIII (r. 1814–1815, 1815–1824) and Charles X (r. 1824–1830), he was even more contemptuous of the bourgeois character of Louis Philippe's (r. 1830–1848) July Monarchy launched by the Revolution of 1830, and thereafter retired to Millau, where he died at his château ten years later at the age of eighty-six.

Together with Joseph-Marie de Maistre (1753–1821) and François-René Chateaubriand, Bonald was one of counterrevolutionary France's principal luminaries of the early nineteenth century, whose religious, linguistic, and evolutionary conceptions of societal development were to have some influence on Hughes-Félicité-Robert de Lamennais (1782–1854), a profoundly conservative theologian of the next generation who was at the same time politically liberal. For much of his life, however, Bonald took issue with both de Maistre and Chateaubriand and was in turn challenged by them, above all because he was in many respects an admirer of eighteenth-century scientific doctrines they despised and was never drawn to their conceptions of either religious irrationalism or religious aestheticism as an antidote to the Enlightenment's alleged abuse of reason. Although not the inventor of the term, he was perhaps the chief interpreter of *bureaucracy*—which he defined as a form of government distinct from both aristocracy and democracy—among political commentators before Max Weber (1864–1920).

See also **Burke, Edmund; Chateaubriand, François-René; Conservatism; France; Maistre, Joseph de.**

BIBLIOGRAPHY

Primary Sources

Oeuvres complètes de M. de Bonald. 3 vols. Paris, 1864.

Secondary Sources

Klinck, David. *The French Counterrevolutionary Theorist Louis de Bonald (1754–1840).* New York, 1996.

McMahon, Darrin. *Enemies of the Enlightenment: The French Counter-Enlightenment and the Making of Modernity.* Oxford, U.K., and New York, 2001.

ROBERT WOKLER

BONAPARTISM. Napoleon Bonaparte (1769–1821), the most successful general in the French Revolutionary Wars (1792–1815), First Consul (1799–1804), then Emperor of France (1804–1814/15), left a potent but ambiguous legacy that his nephew, Louis-Napoleon Bonaparte (Napoleon III, 1808–1873) used to construct and destroy a Second Empire (1851–1870). The death of his son, the Prince Imperial, in 1879, signaled the end of Bonapartism, although some of the sentiments that had fuelled it fed into Boulangism and later into support for Philippe Pétain (1856–1951) and Charles-Andre-Marie-Joseph de Gaulle (1890–1970).

What Bonapartism signified depended to some extent on time and the observer. In 1814 at the emperor's first defeat, it spoke of national glory, strong authoritarian rule, and bureaucratic centralism. Drawn from a Corsican minor noble family, Napoleon I, charismatic general and superb publicist, helped to create the most extensive French empire since the days of Charlemagne, lost it all, but was rarely blamed. Drawn into the fraught arena of revolutionary politics, he finished unpicking the vestiges of liberal aspects of the French Revolution of 1789, while efficiently completing the centralized governmental, administrative, judicial, and legal structures launched by the revolutionaries. Despite his defeat at Waterloo, his deposition, and second exile in 1815, Napoleon was revered by his former soldiers and those officers and officials who had not defaulted to the restored Bourbons. His centralized state framework was never contested, was inherited by his Bourbon successors, and much of it remains in the early twenty-first century.

The Hundred Days reconfigured Napoleon as the man who secured the gains of 1789. Benjamin Constant de Rebecque (1767–1830), the most respected liberal thinker and former opponent, drafted the Additional Acts to the Constitution of the Empire that softened the military dictatorship with an elected assembly, similar to that in the 1814 constitution of Louis XVIII (r. 1814–1824). Even some of those Jacobins and liberal republicans who had been suspicious of Napoleon joined the volunteer federations in the Hundred Days to defend the emperor because they detested the monarchism and clericalism of the First Restoration (1814–1815) even more than they disliked Napoleon. Ultra-royalists subsequently unconsciously helped cement this alliance of Bonapartism with aspects of the Revolution when they lumped together all their opponents as "Jacobins" irrespective of what they really were.

Former Napoleonic soldiers and officers retired on half-pay along with defeated imperial officials took a lead in the romantic celebration of Bonapartism in the 1820s, sitting in cafés recalling the war. Napoleon was remembered in songs, especially those of Pierre-Jean de Béranger (1780–1857), flags, medals, the popular woodcut *images d'Epinal,* and countless other illustrations. Frédéric Hartmann (1816–1874), liberal leader in the Bas-Rhin, had his new house built as a replica of Napoleon's on St. Helena.

Napoleon's memoir, *Le Mémorial de Sainte-Hélène,* dictated to Emmanuel-Augustin-Dieudonne-Joseph de Las Cases (1766–1842) before his death in 1821, helped shape Bonapartism. Between 1823 and 1842 it went through six editions and was one of the bestsellers of the century. Napoleon presented himself as a national hero and powerful ruler, but he also stressed that he bridged the gap between the old regime and the Revolution. Above all he claimed to be a man of the people, essentially liberal in his intentions. Even more amazing, he claimed he had been forced into repeated war by the aggression of other states. From the 1820s, numerous histories of the Revolution elaborated aspects of this legend. Adolphe Thiers (1797–1877), then a young liberal journalist, first in his history of the Revolution and later in his twenty-five-volume *History of the Consulate and Empire* (1845–1862), which sold a million copies, although critical of his dictatorial ways of ruling, defended Napoleon's reputation as the hero who secured the gains of the Revolution.

By 1830, Bonapartism had absorbed some of the conflicting republican memories of the first revolution. When revolution came again in 1830, many of the leading liberals, in the provinces as well as in Paris, shared Bonapartist and republican sympathies. However, Napoleon's young son, often referred to as the "little eagle," was not considered as a replacement for Charles X (r. 1824–1830), being a sickly child (he died in 1832) and effectively a foreigner, living in Austrian Italian lands with his mother, Marie-Louise (1791–1847), Archduchess of Parma. Instead the majority liberal deputies gave the throne to the king's cousin, Louis-Philippe (r. 1830–1848), duc d'Orléans.

Aware of the extent of Bonapartist feeling and hoping to gain reflected glory for himself, and encouraged by Thiers—now a government minister—the new king refashioned the royal palace at Versailles, and Paris itself, to Napoleon's memory. The Arc de Triomphe, which honored Napoleon's victories, was completed between 1833 and 1836. In 1833 a new statue of Napoleon was placed on top of the Vendôme column, built to commemorate the 1830 revolution. Louis-Philippe transformed Versailles into a Napoleon museum (1837–1843), commissioning numerous massive portraits of the emperor's battles. Victor Hugo (1802–1885), Alfred de Musset (1810–1857), Honoré de Balzac (1799–1850), and numerous playwrights celebrated his glories. In 1840 Napoleon's ashes were brought back to France and installed in Les Invalides by the king's eldest son, the duc d'Orléans, with immense ceremony.

At this time France was fairly prosperous, and Bonapartism an increasingly sentimental memory from which most republicans, now committed to democracy, were divorced. The emperor's nephew, Louis-Napoleon, tried to imitate his uncle's "Flight of the Eagle" in abortive risings in the military garrisons of Strasbourg (1836) and Boulogne (1840). The first time he was deported, the second he was imprisoned in the fortress of Ham. No one, especially the Bonaparte clan, thought of him as the obvious Bonapartist heir. He had toyed with being part of the Carbonari, the Italian nationalist conspiratorial sect, and wrote *Des Idées Napoléoniennes* (1839), in which he developed the Bonapartist myths that his uncle had first floated in his memoirs. In 1844, while in prison, he also wrote *L'Extinction du paupérisme,* which attracted socialists by proposing worker associations as the solution to poverty. In 1846 he escaped from Ham and made his way to London. Rather contradictorily, he also briefly joined a volunteer battalion fighting against the Chartists in London.

A totally unknown quantity, universal male suffrage, helped turn a virtual comic opera character into the major political player. After the February revolution in 1848, Louis-Napoleon was elected to the Constituent Assembly by four constituencies in the June by-election, but the government would not allow him into France to take his seat. In by-elections in September he was elected by five constituencies. He was elected on his uncle's name, reinforced by a Bonapartist propaganda campaign in the press and by mass circulation of small Bonapartist memorabilia such as matchboxes and ribbons. Louis-Napoleon was presented as a republican, a democrat, and, like his uncle, a man of the people. When he made his maiden speech in the Assembly, members were reassured that he posed no threat to the republic. He spoke French diffidently with a thick German accent. The deputies were sufficiently confident that Louis-Napoleon would never command mass support that they decided that the new president of France should be elected by universal male suffrage.

Louis-Napoleon was elected president with 5.5 million votes out of 9 million. Nightmares of the violent conflicts of the June Days (1848) and Louis-Napoleon's assurance that he was the only candidate who could unite all factions, but above all Bonapartist sentiments, secured him the votes, including those of a large proportion of the peasants and workers. Thiers, confident that Louis-Napoleon was an insignificant donkey who would be led by elite politicians, organized his Party of Order behind Louis-Napoleon, which gained him useful press backing.

Within three years, Louis-Napoleon had fought against republicans and dismantled the parliamentary republic in a military coup (2 December 1851). However, he was careful to surround his revived empire a year later with democratic illusions, manhood suffrage, and plebiscites. Aware that he had totally alienated republicans and that Bonapartism was a dream ticket rather than a concrete political reality, he constructed his regime on a combination of social reforms intended to appeal to workers, the cultivation of traditional elites, and populist military adventures in Italy, the Crimea, Mexico, and finally and disastrously against Prussia in 1870. Bonapartist sentiment, plus fear of socialism, gained him the presidency, but he never ruled in association with a Bonapartist party, merely an uneasy coalition of members of traditional elites driven by negatives.

Napoleon I's own success had been firmly grounded in military victory and excellent publicity. His nephew was a civilian, whose attractions were his name and his promise to provide a secure alternative to social conflicts. While he was content to pursue economic modernization and the gradual transformation of his autocratic empire into a parliamentary model, he was secure. The "democratic" Bonapartist myth was achievable, and this was confirmed in successive plebiscites. Louis-Napoleon's mistake was to pursue the military glory legend. The French army was no longer either Bonapartist or in a position to dominate Europe. Louis-Napoleon was destroyed in 1870 by a disastrous war that he could have avoided. His defeat eliminated both his empire and Bonapartism. The dynasty was finished when his son died in 1879 fighting for the British army in South Africa. Authoritarian populism was not dead and resurfaced with Georges-Ernest-Jean-Marie Boulanger (1837–1891), Philippe Pétain (1856–1951) and Charles de Gaulle (1890–1970).

See also **France; Hundred Days; Napoleon; Napoleon III; Revolutions of 1830; Revolutions of 1848.**

BIBLIOGRAPHY

Alexander, R. S. *Bonapartism and Revolutionary Tradition in France: The Fédérés of 1815.* Cambridge, U.K., 1991.

Furet, François. *Revolutionary France, 1770–1870.* Oxford, U.K., 1992. A good introduction.

Hazareesingh, Sudhir. *The Legend of Napoleon.* London, 2004.

——. *The Saint-Napoleon: Celebrations of Sovereignty in Nineteenth-Century France.* Cambridge, Mass., 2004.

Pilbeam, Pamela M. *Republicanism in Nineteenth-Century France.* Basingstoke, U.K., 1995.

PAMELA PILBEAM

BORODINO. Fought on 7 September 1812, Borodino was the climactic battle of Napoleon I's Russian campaign of 1812. The Treaties of Tilsit, which ended the last Franco-Russian war in 1807, had committed Russia to Napoleon's Continental System—a complete embargo on trade with Great Britain. By 1810 Tsar Alexander I of Russia had decided that this embargo was hurting Russia too badly and that Napoleon was too unreliable an ally. He abandoned the system, therefore, and tensions between St. Petersburg and Paris rapidly rose. By mid-June 1812, Napoleon had assembled a vast army of well over a half-million men on the Russian frontier, drawn from all of the nations of conquered Europe. Alexander had mustered an army that was large for Russia, but still much smaller than Napoleon's.

Alexander stationed his forces in four main armies arrayed along his frontier from the Baltic to the Black Sea. The forces directly opposite the French were divided into two armies. The First Army, under the command of Mikhail Barclay de Tolly, was to withdraw at the beginning of hostilities to a fortified camp at Drissa on the Western Dvina River, while the Second, commanded by Prince Peter Bagration, was to sweep into the rear of the French army that the Russians expected would follow Barclay.

Napoleon had invaded Russia hoping to force a battle near the frontier. He drove the bulk of his army between Barclay's and Bagration's forces, aiming to keep them separated and to defeat them in detail. The outnumbered Russian armies retreated rather than fighting, however, and Napoleon pursued them. Barclay and Bagration managed to join forces at Smolensk, and Napoleon tried to force them to fight there. He attempted to envelop the Smolensk position to facilitate the destruction of the Russian army, but Barclay learned of his aims and withdrew without fighting. His efforts to force a decision at Smolensk having failed, Napoleon decided to advance toward Moscow hoping to compel the Russian army, now under the command of General Mikhail Kutuzov, to stand and fight. Pressed hard by Tsar Alexander to do so, Kutuzov selected the field near the small village of Borodino, some 110 kilometers (70 miles) west of Moscow, for the battle. He concentrated his force, still nominally divided into two armies under Bagration and Barclay, and constructed field fortifications in preparation for the fight.

Napoleon eagerly seized upon Kutuzov's decision and prepared for battle. Napoleon's normal practice would have been to try to turn one of the flanks of the Russian army, which Kutuzov had fortified. Mindful of the Russians' retreat from Smolensk when he had tried a similar maneuver, however, Napoleon rejected this approach in favor of a frontal assault. The extremely bloody battle that ensued centered around French attempts to seize and hold Kutuzov's field fortifications, especially the Raevsky Redoubt. Both sides fought skillfully and with determination. By this point in the Napoleonic Wars, the Russians were organized under and trained to virtually the same structure and doctrine as the French. Most of the Russian commanders and soldiers were now veterans of several wars. The Grande Armée of Napoleon, on the other hand, included a large number of troops drawn from more or less unwilling satellite states. The odds in battle between Napoleon and his enemies were now sufficiently even that he had little hope of success in a straightforward frontal assault. Napoleon's initial advantages in manpower had evaporated, moreover, as the long march, Russian scorched-earth tactics, and the need to garrison his lines of communications had left the French emperor with only slightly more troops than his enemy had on the battlefield. The battle was thus a stalemate militarily, although Kutuzov decided to abandon the field during the night, continuing his retreat to Moscow.

Borodino was effectively a victory for the Russians and a turning point in the campaign.

Napoleon sought to destroy the Russian army on the battlefield and failed. Kutuzov had aimed only to preserve his army as an effective fighting force, and he succeeded. Napoleon's subsequent seizure of Moscow turned out to be insufficient to overcome the devastating attrition his army had suffered. Russia's losses were, nevertheless, very high, and included Bagration, wounded on the field, who died from an infection two weeks later.

See also **Alexander I; Continental System; French Revolutionary Wars and Napoleonic Wars; Napoleon.**

BIBLIOGRAPHY

Duffy, Christopher. *Borodino and the War of 1812.* New York, 1973.

FREDERICK W. KAGAN

BOSNIA-HERZEGOVINA.

For most of the nineteenth century, Bosnia and Herzegovina were Balkan frontier provinces of the Ottoman Empire, bordering the Habsburg Empire to the north, and Serbia and Montenegro to the east and south, respectively. The provinces were administered by a provincial governor appointed directly by the sultan. Nominally he exercised supreme power over Bosnia, but in actuality his power was limited by the local elite. According to the Ottoman millet system, local peoples were organized into religious communities, where they enjoyed significant religious and cultural freedom, as well as administrative and fiscal autonomy, under their own ecclesiastical leaders.

SOCIAL AND POLITICAL STRUCTURE

Bosnia's population was about 33 percent Muslim, 43 percent Orthodox, and 20 percent Catholic. The Muslims enjoyed a privileged status even though they did not represent a majority. This ruling class, which was predominantly Slavic in origin and language, was composed of the old Bosnian nobility and peasants, who had converted to Islam on a large scale during the eighteenth century. Other Muslims in Bosnia had come from outside the province, as military men, government officials, or refugees. During the seventeenth and eighteenth centuries, large numbers of the sultan's elite military infantry (Janissaries) settled in the provincial capital of Sarajevo, where they became merchants and craftsmen. Captains comprised another important military group whose chief duty was to guard the frontier with the Habsburg Empire and Venetian Dalmatia, in exchange for which they received hereditary fiefs. In addition, many cavalrymen (*sipahis*) had settled in Bosnia, where according to the Ottoman feudal system they received land-estates (*timar*) for military service, although these were not hereditary. These various Muslim elites often warred among themselves for political power, thus weakening the provincial administration.

By the nineteenth century the Ottoman feudal system in Bosnia had changed, with most *timar* lands being converted into private estates. Both Christian and Muslim peasants, who constituted 90 percent of the population, worked these lands and paid a tithe in kind, some smaller dues, an annual land tax, and a poll tax to the sultan, in addition to performing obligatory labor. Local Muslim elites maintained economic and political power in the province by holding this land. This situation differed significantly from that in the fifteenth century, when both estate-holders and peasants could be either Muslim or Christian. Two forms of estates existed in nineteenth-century Bosnia, *begliks* and *agaliks*. *Begliks* were owned by the upper nobility, *begs* or *beys*, who numbered a few hundred. *Agaliks* were controlled by the lower nobility, the *agas*, comprising small landholders, *sipahis*, and Janissaries. The conditions for peasants were less favorable on the *begliks*, as they did not have rights to the land and had to pay a large percentage of the harvest to the *beg*. On the *agaliks*, peasants had certain rights regarding both land use and required payments.

The condition of peasants in general was dire because of high state taxes and abuses of tax farming by the local elite. As the feudal system decayed because of the abuses of local landholders, the plight of the peasants worsened. Their dissatisfaction led to constant rebellions against the local Muslim landholders at the beginning of the nineteenth century. The central Ottoman authority, or Porte, tried to subdue the unrest by instituting agricultural and land reforms. However, the efforts of the central authorities met with limited success, as they encountered difficulties in controlling the *begs* and *agas*.

German postcard showing young Muslim women in Bosnia, 1904. PRIVATE COLLECTION/BRIDGEMAN ART LIBRARY/ARCHIVES CHARMET

The conflict among local elites, between peasants and local elites, and between local elites and the Porte made Bosnia a place of great unrest throughout the nineteenth century. The Porte attempted to regain control of the province, reassert its authority, and quell peasant rebellion by introducing modernizing, westernizing reforms. Collectively known as the *Tanzimat*, they aimed at centralizing authority, and involved measures of both military and land reform. The Bosnian Muslim elites, who wanted greater power and autonomy from the Porte, resisted and rebelled against these attempts that threatened to undermine their privileged status in the provinces.

The opposition of the local elite to these reforms led to a number of uprisings in the early decades of the nineteenth century. In 1831, a captain named Hussein led a revolt against Ottoman authorities, demanding administrative autonomy and an end to reforms. He also demanded both a promise that the vizier of Bosnia always be a member of the local elite (a Bosnian *beg* or captain) and his immediate appointment to the position. Employing a common tactic of provoking rivalries among Bosnian *begs* to suppress rebellions, the Ottomans used the captains of Herzegovina to suppress Husejn, rewarding them by making Herzegovina a separate territory under

their rule. In 1835, the Ottomans abolished the system of captains entirely, revoking their hereditary posts and command of their forces, and replaced them with officials appointed by the governor. Surprisingly this measure did not meet with a great deal of resistance, and the Ottomans succeeded in suppressing all successive revolts until the governor tried again to institute military reforms in 1849.

A DELICATE BALANCE

The sultan sent a succession of governors to the province, until finally Omer Pasha Latas succeeded in establishing peace and order in the province in the 1850s. He put down the rebellion and decisively broke the political power of the old land-owning class, sending *begs* and *agas* into exile. After establishing full military control of Bosnia and Herzegovina, Latas could finally attempt to introduce *Tanzimat* reforms. Latas, who possessed knowledge of western languages and military and political affairs, was one of Bosnia's most capable governors. Among the most significant changes he instituted was the 1859 reform, which regulated the landholder-peasant relationship on *agalik* estates.

Latas was succeeded by Topal Osman-Pasha, who administered Bosnia in the 1860s, which came

A Bosnian family photographed c. 1880. ©HULTON-DEUTSCH COLLECTION/CORBIS

to be known as its golden decade. The governor reorganized Bosnia and Herzegovina administratively, in addition to founding a joint Muslim-Christian court of appeal and a consultative assembly that met yearly to advise him on economic and financial matters. He also created a small executive council composed of three Muslims, two Christians, and one Jew, who met weekly under his supervision. Osman-Paša also made efforts to improve the infrastructure of the province by constructing roads and a stretch of railroad. He also built new Muslim schools and allowed the Christian community to build its own schools.

As the Porte depended on Muslims for support, the governors had to be cautious not to alienate the Muslim leaders with reforms that ameliorated conditions for Christians. The Muslim attitude toward Christianity had become more hostile during the first half of the nineteenth century,

as local Muslim elites increasingly feared the ties that the Catholic and Orthodox populations had with their coreligionists in the adjacent Habsburg lands and Serbia, especially since the leaders of the national movements in these countries increasingly looked to Christians in Bosnia as natural allies, and even as potential conationals. Nevertheless, it must be emphasized that the unrest in nineteenth-century Ottoman Bosnia was predominantly of political, economic, and social nature, rather than a national and religious one.

In 1875 an agrarian rebellion broke out in Herzegovina that had far-reaching consequences for the status of Bosnia in the Ottoman Empire. It began when tax-collectors resorted to harsh measures in order to compensate for a crop failure the previous year. The uprising precipitated an international crisis when Serbia and Montenegro, with ambitions to divide Bosnia and Herzegovina between themselves, declared war on the Ottoman Empire. The following year, Russia also declared war on the Ottomans, quickly defeating the empire in the Russo-Turkish War and forcing the Treaty of San Stefano, which gave it significant territorial gains in the Balkans at the Porte's expense. The treaty was revised in 1878 at the Congress of Berlin by the Great Powers, which felt that Russia's influence in the Balkans had become too great. At Berlin, Austria-Hungary received authority to occupy Bosnia and Herzegovina, although the province nominally remained Ottoman.

OCCUPATION BY AUSTRIA-HUNGARY

Many Hungarians opposed the occupation of the province, as they feared that the addition of more Slavs would threaten their position in the empire. Ultimately, however, it was better that Bosnian Slavs be under their control than that of Serbia, which threatened to acquire the province as part of its Greater Serbian foreign policy. In a compromise between Austrian and Hungarian officials over who would administer the newly acquired territory, it was placed under the direct authority of the joint Ministry of Finance, led by Minister Benjamin von Kállay until 1903. Kállay was succeeded by Baron Stephan von Burián von Rajecz, who then ruled until 1912. Austria-Hungary was under the false impression that it would be welcomed in the province, especially by the Christian subjects, only to learn that it was regarded by the people as merely another imperial power. The Habsburg military had to overcome significant resistance to secure the territory. Once they did, a significant number of Muslims emigrated from the province. However, parallel trends elsewhere in the region indicated that most migration resulted from economic factors, rather than Austro-Hungarian rule per se.

Austria-Hungary pursued a policy of "continuity and gradualism" (Malcolm, p. 138), maintaining the Ottoman administrative organization of the province and Ottoman land reforms. However, they also instituted many new reforms in an attempt to develop the economy, treating the province as a permanent possession. First, the Habsburg government created one administrative unit, Bosnia-Herzegovina, from the two separate provinces. They built roads, railroads, and bridges. They also developed coal-mining and forestry and introduced modern techniques into agriculture. In order to further develop agriculture, they successfully established agrarian colonies, but did not pursue a policy of mass colonization. The Austro-Hungarian government also made strides in education, building hundreds of primary schools, as well as high schools and a technical school, and introducing compulsory education in 1909. As a result of these measures, Bosnia-Herzegovina made substantial progress under Austro-Hungarian rule, leading some scholars to describe this period as the golden age in Bosnian history.

Austria-Hungary had to handle religious issues in the province delicately. It pursued an even-handed policy aimed at gaining the cooperation of all religious communities. Nonetheless, the Catholic population grew most significantly in both number and activity, and the government encountered problems with conversions, especially of Muslim girls to Catholicism by their future husbands. Kállay's primary aim was to protect the province from the annexation tendencies of neighboring Croats and Serbs, by developing a separate Bosnian nationhood that would unify people of all denominations living in Bosnia-Herzegovina. He promoted this Bosnian identity to counteract the development of modern national identity, which had begun around the mid-nineteenth century in Bosnia under the influence of Serbian and Croatian national movements in neighboring countries. He considered that Muslims would be the first to assume this identity as they had no sponsor nation. Ultimately, Austro-Hungarian policies served to strengthen national identities and replace the religious identities that had prevailed under Ottoman rule.

In 1908, Austria-Hungary annexed Bosnia, mainly to prevent the neighboring Balkan countries from taking over the province. Austria-Hungary's action was virulently opposed by the other Great Powers and brought Europe to the brink of war. During the annexation, internal political life flourished. In 1910, a Bosnian parliament was elected, in which the Muslim National Organization, Serbian National Organization, and the Croatian National Society, which had been formed in recent years, began to function as political parties. Their representation in the Parliament was roughly proportional to their population, meaning that a majority could be formed only if one of the Christian groups allied with the Muslim. The Catholics met with

Sarajevo, photographed in the late nineteenth century. In the foreground is a Muslim cemetery. © ALINARI ARCHIVES/CORBIS

greater success in winning Muslim cooperation, both politically and culturally. Nonetheless, these alignments were motivated by political opportunism and were thus always fluid. During this period, the Muslims became established as a separate political entity and acquired a distinct identity. Serbian national resistance to Austro-Hungarian rule in the province continued and culminated in the assassination of the heir apparent to the Habsburg throne, Archduke Francis Ferdinand, by a young member of the Black Hand in the Bosnian capital of Sarajevo on 28 June 1914, leading to the outbreak of World War I.

See also **Austria-Hungary; Balkan Wars; Montenegro; Ottoman Empire; Serbia.**

BIBLIOGRAPHY

Donia, Robert. *Islam under the Double Eagle: The Muslims of Bosnia and Hercegovina, 1878–1914.* New York, 1981.

Donia, Robert, and John V. A. Fine. *Bosnia and Hercegovina: A Tradition Betrayed.* New York, 1994.

Jelavich, Barbara. *History of the Balkans.* New York, 1983.

Jelavich, Barbara, and Charles Jelavich. *The Establishment of the Balkan National States, 1804–1920.* Seattle, Wash., 1977.

Malcolm, Noel. *Bosnia: A Short History.* New York, 1994.

Sugar, Peter F. *Industrialization of Bosnia-Hercegovina, 1878–1918.* Seattle, 1963.

JOVANA L. KNEŽEVIĆ

BOSPHORUS. The Bosphorus is one of the most coveted sea routes in the world, possibly rivaled in importance only by the Panama and Suez Canals. Unlike the latter two, the Bosphorus is an entirely natural waterway, linking the Black Sea to the Sea of Marmara and thence via the Dardanelles to the Mediterranean. It was the site of Byzantine Constantinople and, after 1453, Ottoman Istanbul. The Bosphorus divides Istanbul into European and Asian sections, making Istanbul the only city in the world to straddle two continents.

Ever since the expansion of Russian power starting in had the reign of Peter the Great (r. 1682–1725), the Russian Empire had sought control of the Black Sea straits, the Bosphorus and the Dardanelles. As the Russian Empire became the dominant power in the Black Sea, Russia's rulers became obsessed with control of the straits in order to give the Russian fleet access to the warm waters of the Mediterranean. This was the root of the so-called Eastern Question, which so dominated international diplomacy in the nineteenth century. The basic assumption in the Eastern Question, which turned out to be false, was that the Ottoman Empire could collapse at any moment and that it was vital for Britain and France to deny Russia control of the Bosphorus. In a sense the Bosphorus was the eye of the storm in the high politics of the belle epoque.

Nor was Russia alone in coveting the Bosphorus. The ultimate aim of Napoleon Bonaparte's Egyptian expedition was to march through Asiatic Turkey, conquer Istanbul, and set it up as the capital of his "Empire in the Orient," thus controlling the Bosphorus and denying it to Russia.

As the economy of the Russian Empire became more and more intertwined with that of Europe, exports of Russian foodstuffs, particularly wheat, became a major factor in the fate of the Bosphorus. With the advent of steam and railways the importance of this strategic seaway increased as regular steamship services started up between major Black Sea ports, such as Odessa and Varna, and Europe. Accordingly, control of the Bosphorus became the number one foreign policy goal of the Russian Empire. In 1833, in return for backing against the sultan's rebellious vassal Muhammad Ali of Egypt, the Russians secured the Treaty of Unkiar Skelessi, which granted the Russians extensive rights on the Bosphorus, tantamount to joint control with the Ottoman Empire. For the first and only time, a Russian army and navy were invited into Ottoman territory by Sultan Mahmud II (r. 1808–1839). The Russian navy sailed into the Bosphorus, and Russian troops encamped on its hills. The treaty was abrogated in 1841 by the Straits Convention, which again greatly curtailed Russian influence and basically enabled the Ottomans to close down the straits at times of war. The principle of international law that in times of peace the Bosphorus would be closed to all ships of war was first established in the Treaty of the Dardanelles (1809) between Britain and the Ottoman Empire.

The Crimean War (1853–1856) was fought largely as a war for the control of the Bosphorus. For the first time in modern warfare the Ottomans fought alongside two great-power allies, Britain and France. Florence Nightingale, the mother of modern nursing, became world famous for her care of the war wounded in her hospital barracks, the Selimiye, overlooking the Bosphorus and the Golden Horn. Mark Twain wrote extensively and pejoratively on what he saw of the city and the Bosphorus in *The Innocents Abroad* (1869), becoming the first American journalist to write extensively on the city.

The Bosphorus was salient in the run-up to World War I in the Balkans. After the Young Turk takeover of power in 1908, the Ottoman Empire moved closer to Germany as the war approached. Defense of the straits became a priority issue for the Ottoman state. The Germans supplied extensive weaponry, such as powerful shore batteries, that proved decisive in World War I, particularly during the Gallipoli campaign. On 11 August 1914 the Ottoman Empire allowed safe passage through the straits to two German battle cruisers, the *Goeben* and the *Breslau*, which were handed over to the Ottoman Empire in a fictitious sale. On 30 October the two ships, flying Ottoman flags but manned by German crews, exited the Bosphorus and bombarded Russian ports, in effect bringing the Ottoman Empire into World War I.

See also **Balkan Wars; Black Sea; Eastern Question; Ottoman Empire.**

BIBLIOGRAPHY

Anderson, M. S. *The Eastern Question, 1774–1923: A Study in International Relations.* London, 1966.

Kent, Marian, ed. *The Great Powers and the End of the Ottoman Empire.* 2nd ed. London, 1996.

King, Charles. *The Black Sea: A History.* Oxford, U.K., 2004.

Shaw, Stanford J., and Ezel Kural Shaw. *History of the Ottoman Empire and Modern Turkey.* 2 vols. Cambridge, U.K., 1976–1977.

SELIM DERINGIL

BOULANGER AFFAIR.

Between 1886 and 1887, General Georges-Ernst-Jean-Marie Boulanger (1837–1891) was at the center of French political life. A dashingly handsome man, given to parading around Paris on his black horse Tunis, he also professed advanced republican views then relatively rare among senior members of the French officer corps. For many in a nation still traumatized by France's crushing military defeat and territorial losses in the Franco-Prussian War of 1870–1871, Boulanger became the symbol of the hoped-for revenge, the origin of his nickname, "Le général revanche." All of this brought him to the attention of left-wing republicans known as the Radicals upon whom the more moderate republicans depended in order to sustain a majority in a parliament, where fully a third of the deputies were royalists or Bonapartists (who usually called themselves conservatives). Inclusion of Boulanger as minister of war in the government of Charles de Freycinet (1828–1923) in January of 1886 and that of his successor René Goblet (1828–1905) in December of the same year was the price of Radical support.

Boulanger certainly did not disappoint his Radical supporters. As minister of war he sponsored a bill ending the exemption of seminarians from military service, expelled members of the royal family from the military, and expressed sympathy for striking workers. His deportment as minister of war sufficiently irritated the German Empire to prompt a brief war scare in the spring of 1877. All of this enhanced his popularity with political figures on the extreme left, who soon came to be known as Boulangists. Moderate republicans, much like their royalist opponents, were unnerved by Boulanger since both, mindful of the still-fresh experience of the Paris Commune, feared the prospect of war with its attendant revolutionary consequences. As a result, in May 1877, Maurice Rouvier (1842–1911), with the tacit support of conservatives, formed a government without Boulanger. His exclusion from government prompted mass protests from the popular classes of Paris, chanting the innumerable popular songs celebrating the virtues of the dashing general.

Life in the barracks was unappealing to Boulanger, who was soon conspiring with politicians of every hue to renew his political career. His political activities, technically illegal for a serving officer, were by the spring of 1888 sufficiently overt that the government dismissed him from the army. Boulanger promptly began running for office in a series of by-elections. He campaigned on a platform of constitutional "revision." Although vague, this platform suggested that he, like Radicals in general, sought a more democratic republic with a democratically elected president and Senate. No sooner elected (and often with substantial majorities), he would resign his seat to run elsewhere. In August 1888 he was simultaneously elected in three departments and was transparently conducting a series of plebiscites on his very name. In January 1889, he was triumphantly elected in Paris. The significance of a military man conducting a plebiscitary campaign did not escape contemporaries; it was uncomfortably reminiscent of the two previous Bonapartes. By early 1889 many were openly predicting a Boulangist dictatorship. But Boulanger was no Bonaparte. When in March 1889 the government, in what was almost certainly a bluff, leaked word of Boulanger's imminent arrest, the general panicked and fled to Brussels where he would commit suicide in 1891.

THE AGENT OF ROYALIST RESTORATION

Boulanger's phenomenal electoral successes owed something to his dynamic image and to the energetic campaigning of his supporters. But they owed rather more to the covert support coming from an unlikely source: French royalists. As a result of a series of secret agreements struck with the royalist leadership between November 1887 and April 1888, the man who still posed as a left-wing republican became the agent of a proposed royalist restoration. Boulanger, now thoroughly disaffected by the republican regime, abandoned his advanced republican views (which were in any case of relatively recent date) and promised to help restore the monarchy in exchange for royalist support for his ministerial ambitions. Of necessity the accord remained secret since any revelation of a deal with royalists would instantly alienate Boulanger's left-wing supporters. The arrangement posed even greater difficulties for the royalist rank and file, who had for the previous two years subjected Boulanger to principled venomous attacks. But by 1888 the royalists had little choice. Their electoral success in 1885, when they obtained nearly a third of the seats in parliament, proved ephemeral and in subsequent years their appeal to most Frenchmen had significantly diminished. As they were only too aware, the royalist pretender, Louis-Philippe Albert d'Orléans (1838–1894), the Comte de Paris, although both intelligent and dignified, was hardly charismatic and, worse, had been in exile in Great Britain since 1886. The local royalist leadership was elitist and singularly out of tune with the demands of modern electoral campaigns; consequently its electoral organization was often rudimentary. Although royalists harped incessantly on the demonstrable flaws of the republican regime, ever fewer Frenchmen were finding their proposed monarchist alternative attractive. Only by harnessing the dynamism of Boulanger and his allies could they hope to supplant the republic with a monarchy. In order to render this partnership more palatable to their respective followers, Boulanger and the royalists disguised it as a "parallel march" for constitutional revision. Discreetly left unsaid was the fact that whereas most of Boulanger's followers believed that revision would yield a more democratic constitution, the royalists intended it to produce a monarchist one.

Royalist support for Boulanger was secret but tangible. With the exception of Paris, Boulanger invariably ran in conservative departments, replacing a conservative deputy. Never did he face a conservative rival. In all cases, save Paris, the great majority of Boulanger's votes came from people who ordinarily voted for royalists or Bonapartists. When Boulanger resigned a seat, he was invariably replaced by a conservative deputy who enjoyed the support of local Boulangists. That this should be the case was an explicit condition of conservative support. Boulanger's campaign managers always worked closely with the local conservative electoral agents and with the local conservative press. And the very expensive

Boulangist campaigns were funded exclusively from royalist coffers, initially from the ample funds of the rich but parsimonious pretender, later from equally rich but more generous royalist supporters like the Duchesse d'Uzès (Marie-Clémentine de Rochechouart-Mortemart; 1847–1933), and the Barons Alphonse de Rothschild (1827–1905) and Maurice de Hirsch (1831–1896). For royalists the central lesson of Boulanger's plebiscitary campaign was that while, Paris excepted, most of his votes came from conservative voters, a critical percentage came from republican voters who would never knowingly vote for the royalist party. By their calculations, attracting those critical swing voters was the key to mobilizing an electoral majority that might revise the republic out of existence.

Boulanger's abrupt departure on 1 April 1889 disillusioned some of his followers. By contrast, the royalists were neither surprised (they knew their man) nor troubled. Boulanger might have been out of France, but there were plenty of Boulangists left behind. Moreover, royalists thought they knew just how to use them for the national legislative elections scheduled for September 1889. In about one constituency in six, a royalist running on a purely monarchist platform might stand a good chance of election. But there were many more constituencies in which royalists could hope for election only if they could count on a critical percentage of erstwhile republican voters that only the Boulangists could mobilize. Boulangists would be moved to do so in exchange for the assurance of royalist support in other constituencies where royalists had even less chance of electoral success. To make any of this work, royalists running with Boulangist support would have to play down their adhesion to the monarchy and Boulangists hoping for royalist support would have to be somewhat ambiguous about their true political valence. This was an inherently difficult challenge and required long and bitter negotiations. But it was not impossible either. No small number of royalist and Bonapartist candidates were prepared to disguise their dynastic allegiances with ambiguous electoral labels. Even more Boulangists were prepared to be comparably disingenuous. Careful royalist calculations suggested that there was a serious chance of electing enough "revisionist" candidates for the subsequent legislature to have a majority in favor of revising the constitution from a republican one to a monarchist one. True, there was the real danger that Boulangist candidates would rediscover their republicanism once elected. But royalists took pains to minimize this risk. At their insistence, many of the Boulangist candidates were thinly disguised conservatives. Many of those who were not were entirely dependent on royalist financing, and since the royalists took elaborate steps to document this financing (insisting upon explicit receipts in many instances), their postelection tractability seemed likely.

THE FAILURE OF BOULANGISM

In the end, the gambit failed. Royalists and Boulangists faced a tenacious republican administration that used all of the considerable resources at its disposal to ensure local republican victories. Many of the Boulangist candidates were accommodating to the royalists precisely because they were rogues and scoundrels of one kind or another and not therefore electorally appealing. The combined total of elected royalist and Boulangist deputies did not, in the end, improve on the results of 1885.

In the wake of the electoral defeat of 1889 the royalist party gradually disappeared, many of its most prominent leaders rallying reluctantly to the republic. The Boulangist movement was dead before its namesake was but would survive in the Third Republic, albeit under different guises and labels. Most Boulangists gradually drifted into the "new Right" of the turn of the century; their descendants could be found in the antiparliamentary leagues of the 1930s.

See also **Bonapartism; Boulangism; France; Franco-Prussian War.**

BIBLIOGRAPHY

Harding, James. *The Astonishing Adventure of General Boulanger.* New York, 1971.

Irvine, William D. *The Boulanger Affair Reconsidered.* New York, 1989.

Levillain, Phlippe. *Boulanger, fossoyeur de la monarchie.* Paris, 1982.

Seager, Frederick H. *The Boulanger Affair.* Ithaca, N.Y., 1968.

WILLIAM D. IRVINE

BOULANGISM. Boulangism was the movement that failed to put in power the charismatic but empty-headed French general Georges-Ernest-Jean-Marie Boulanger (1837–1891). The Boulanger affair operated a major political realignment, leading indirectly to the creation of twentieth-century democratic socialism and directly to the constitution of a new right, beginning to free itself from the hopeless cause of restoring the monarchy.

BOULANGER AND THE REPUBLICANS, 1885–1887

The republicans in power in France during the 1880s were on the lookout for a republican army officer to be minister of war and reorganize the army. Boulangism began when they found General Boulanger. He was popular with his troops and cut a dashing figure on horseback, thanks to his full red beard. While most army officers were clerical and indeed monarchist in their sympathies—the army's traditional association with the nobility and its hierarchical character made it, like the church, a refuge for monarchists—Boulanger was known not to attend Mass; as a result he passed for a republican. In January 1886 he was named minister of war, thanks to the leading young "radical" republican, Georges Clemenceau (1841–1929). Boulanger, however, was not a republican; he was simply an ambitious general with a commanding physical presence who was ready to exploit popular prejudices, republican or monarchist, to gain power. As minister of war, he improved draftees' food and authorized the use of the new Lebel rifle, but he proved a poor administrator, and his continual gaffes embarrassed the government. Beginning with Clemenceau, republicans began to distance themselves from Boulanger.

Boulanger, however, developed a following among a public eager for "Revanche" (revenge) against Germany, since France had ceded Alsace and much of Lorraine to the newly constituted German Empire by the treaty ending the Franco-Prussian War (1870–1871). In January 1887, trying to scare the Reichstag into voting increased credits for the army, the German chancellor Otto von Bismarck mentioned Boulanger as an indication that France was becoming dangerous again. This increased Boulanger's popularity in France: if

Bismarck were scared of him, he must be a new Napoleon. But while this made Boulanger a hero to the masses, it made him a national danger: the politicians knew that the army was no better prepared for war than it had been in 1870. In May 1887 they used a cabinet reshuffle to ease Boulanger out of his position as minister of war. On 8 July 1887 he was sent to a provincial post. Crowds prevented his train from leaving, but, still obedient as a soldier, he agreed to be smuggled out in a switch engine.

To Boulanger's appeal as a nationalist was added appeal in the face of disillusionment with the Republic installed on 4 September 1870 and gradually solidified during the 1870s, the Third Republic (1870–1940). To most republicans, especially since 1848, the Republic had meant "the social and democratic Republic," but the Republic now in power seemed to foster big business and industry. The severe recession of 1882, which hit farmers and increased unemployment, particularly in construction and textiles, increased resentment against the Republic among workers, artisans, and small-businesspeople. This resentment was further increased by a corruption scandal that broke in October 1887. President Jules Grèvy's son-in-law, Daniel Wilson, who lived in the presidential residence, was selling his influence on the president: payment to Wilson was a sure way to get the Legion of Honor. The president was forced to resign at the end of 1887.

Boulanger's appeal grew, but Boulanger had no aim except to be minister of war again. Shunned now by republicans, he sought other backers, beginning negotiations with monarchist groups in November 1887 and profiting from Bonapartist support in February 1888 by-elections. On 26 March 1888, he was dismissed from the army for his political activity. The day after, the president's son-in-law got his imprisonment quashed. It seemed that brave generals were punished while corrupt politicians were spared.

BOULANGER, THE NEW RIGHT, AND THE NEW NATIONALISM, 1887–1889

During the remainder of 1888, Boulanger won by-elections with resounding majorities, thanks to five hundred thousand francs from the royalist pretender, three million francs from the royalist duchesse d'Uzès, and the slogan "Dissolution, Constituent, Revision": Dissolution of the Chamber of Deputies (the lower house of parliament), Constituent Assembly to revise the Constitution, Revision of the Constitution.

Agitation for Boulanger reached a climax in January 1889, when he won a Paris by-election. His supporters expected him to stage a coup d'état and take power. Instead he lost his nerve and disappeared, some said to the bed of his mistress. Republicans won massively in the legislative elections of 1889, benefiting from the development of republicanism in the country, where Boulangism had never caught on to the same extent as in the city. Republicans also made effective propaganda use of the Paris Universal Exposition celebrating the centenary of 1789. Boulangism disintegrated. Boulanger fled to Brussels in 1891 and shot himself on the grave of his mistress, who had died of tuberculosis two months earlier.

Understanding of Boulangism has been confused by cultural analyses of fascism, which see "leftist" origins of fascism in Boulanger's initial support among early socialists (see particularly Sternhell; for an interpretation of French fascism based on social history, see Soucy). But the Boulanger affair is best understood as a crisis that helped transform the archaic politics of the post-Revolutionary era. The affair led socialists to recommit to the Republic despite disappointment with its social and economic policies; henceforth socialism would be perceived as the fulfillment of the Republic, not as an alternative obtained by overthrowing the Republic. The Boulanger affair thus led indirectly to twentieth-century democratic socialism, of which Jean Jaurès (1859–1914) soon became the charismatic leader.

The affair led directly to a new right. Until Boulangism, nationalism had been linked to the Revolutionary tradition of the *levée en masse* (the nation at arms) and royalists had disdained it. Now nationalists began to envisage authoritarian methods. In the mid-1880s, under a journalist named Paul Déroulède (1846–1914), *La ligue des patriotes* (the Patriots' League) developed a new vision: the way to rebuild the nation was to inculcate obedience among the people and authority among their leaders. Monarchists and other conservatives who had initially disdained Boulanger soon saw the value of this kind of nationalism through Boulanger's ability to draw popular support. If they could not restore the monarchy, they could use this nationalism to aim at an authoritarian regime based on values of nationalism, deference, and hierarchy. And conservatives learned about mass politics. The Dreyfus affair would further hasten their learning process.

See also **Clemenceau, Georges; France; Nationalism.**

BIBLIOGRAPHY

Burns, Michael. *Rural Society and French Politics: Boulangism and the Dreyfus Affair, 1886–1900.* Princeton, N.J., 1984.

Irvine, William D. *The Boulanger Affair Reconsidered: Royalism, Boulangism, and the Origins of the Radical Right in France.* New York, 1989.

Seager, Frederic H. *The Boulanger Affair: Political Crossroad of France, 1886–1889.* Ithaca, N.Y., 1969.

Soucy, Robert. *French Fascism: The First Wave, 1924–1933.* New Haven, Conn., 1986.

———. *French Fascism: The Second Wave, 1933–1939.* New Haven, Conn., 1995.

Sternhell, Zeev. *Neither Right Nor Left: Fascist Ideology in France.* Translated by David Maisel. Berkeley, Calif., 1986.

Tombs, Robert, ed. *Nationhood and Nationalism in France: From Boulangism to the Great War, 1889–1918.* 2nd ed. London, 2001.

CHARLES SOWERWINE

BOURBON RESTORATION. *See* **Restoration.**

BOURGEOISIE.

In 1800 the traditional division of society into "orders" or "estates" was rapidly giving way to concepts of class. The bourgeoisie straddled this change. The term *bourgeoisie,* no longer used to describe part of an order, became interchangeable with *middle classes* to embrace all economically secure groups between the nobility and urban and rural workers. Writers also divided the "bourgeoisie" or "middle classes" into upper, middle, and lower segments. The language of class described socioeconomic status, political convictions and hostilities, and educational and cultural attitudes, including the self-conscious awareness of belonging to a particular strata in society. The term soon became one of abuse in the nineteenth century, much used by socialist critics such as Karl Marx (1818–1883).

By the early nineteenth century the bourgeoisie was expanding both in scope and scale. It included professionals, notably lawyers, doctors, and engineers; civil servants; and landowners; as well as businessmen, bankers, and industrialists. The size and growth of the bourgeoisie, never recorded with any precision, depended on the extent of economic modernization, the development of the professions, and above all the bureaucratization of the state. By the end of the century the category had become much broader, embracing nearly all nonmanual workers, including clerks in local government and in large manufacturing units.

In 1800, France—the richest, most industrialized, most centralized country—probably had the largest bourgeoisie in continental Europe. About one million of the twenty-nine million counted as well-off bourgeois, while another nine million who belonged to artisan and shopkeeper families, would be thought of as lower middle class. By 1900, 50 percent of the population of Paris would have considered itself bourgeois, if office workers are included with all the other groups.

Because Italy was slow to industrialize, the entrepreneurial bourgeoisie there remained tiny and was limited to northern cities such as Milan, where in 1838 the manufacturing and commercial elite of the city numbered in excess of 1,000, plus dominant professionals, including 500 engineers and 170 lawyers. Russia had a small and fragmented bourgeoisie, partly due to the survival of serfdom until 1861, the slowness of industrialization, and the dominance of foreign money in capitalist development. Around 1800 roughly 2 percent of Russians were judged to be middle class, by 1900, 10 percent.

The French Revolution of 1789 helped define the bourgeoisie as a social and political class, particularly the abolition of the privileges of clergy and nobility (the First and Second Estates) on the night of 4 August 1789 and the Declaration of the Rights of Man and of the Citizen later that month. The traditional professional, official, and landowning bourgeoisie gained most from the Revolution in land and politics and in the state bureaucracy. The Revolutionary and Napoleonic Wars (1792–1814/15) ensured that similar social changes occurred in the huge amounts of Europe that France conquered. As in France, the bourgeoisie bought confiscated church land and acquired jobs in the state bureaucracy.

ECONOMIC MODERNIZATION

Economic modernization also increased both the size and political power of the bourgeoisie. In Russia the extravagant lifestyle of the nobility and their decreasing willingness to engage in trade and industry led to the rapid decline of some families. Long before the emancipation of the 1860s, ambitious serfs began to gain their freedom and establish themselves in the cotton industry, banking, and trade. Families such as the Morozovs, transformed from serf ribbon sellers into a commercial and industrial bourgeoisie, dominated the government of St. Petersburg and Moscow in the second half of the nineteenth century.

Elsewhere the high profile of cotton and railway kings encouraged the view that a capitalist bourgeoisie was taking power. In Britain, publicists like Samuel Smiles (1812–1904) eagerly created the idea that entrepreneurial growth liberated society from old bonds, offering new opportunities for the "self-made" man. In the mid-eighteenth century the brewer, Whitbread, bought big estates and a seat in Parliament. In 1830 and 1831 successively, two bankers, Jacques Laffitte and Casimir-Pierre Périer, were (briefly) chief ministers in France. Marx assumed that their elevation showed that the 1830 Revolution had replaced the nobility with a financial aristocracy, but entrepreneurs were never dominant in politics.

Economic "modernization" did not produce the social and political change some commentators feared and others welcomed. The revolutionaries in France in the 1790s raged first about "aristos," then about the bourgeoisie. Heads of families, many of them noble, who emigrated during the Revolution lost some land, but the proportion of noble-owned land fell by only 5 percent to 20 percent. The nobility was still the richest group in France well into the second half of the nineteenth century. The revolutionaries abolished nobility in the 1790s, but Napoleon created new titles, and in 1814 a hereditary Chamber of Peers shared legislative power with an elected Chamber. From 1831 no new hereditary titles were created in France, but families continued to luxuriate in the social snobbery of the plethora that survived, and to invent new ones. Both before and after 1789 French nobles and bourgeois shared political and economic power. In Prussia nobles retained control of the top jobs in the state and army throughout the century, alongside some newer bourgeois families whose fortunes had been made in banking, trade, and industry. In Russia tsars continued to appoint nobles as provincial governors, senior bureaucrats, and army officers. In addition, much of the investment for railway construction and rapid industrial growth in Russia at the end of the nineteenth century came from French, British, and German banks and did not stimulate the growth of the native middle class. Thus in 1914 the Russian middle class was tiny, fragmented, and in no position to claim a substantial role in government.

In Britain the power and wealth of the aristocracy actually increased in the nineteenth century. Land was the basis of their wealth, then there were the considerable rewards of patronage; government office; and industrial, business, and other financial investments. Although the middle class grew in size and influence, Britain was supremely dominated by aristocratic, rather than bourgeois entrepreneurial groups, to an extent unmatched elsewhere in Europe.

MIDDLE-CLASS PROFESSIONALS

Elsewhere it was the landed and professional middle classes, already established in state service, whose numbers and influence increased most rapidly in the century. The real bourgeois revolution was not so much a consequence of industrialization, as of the increase in the power of the state and the consequent vast growth in the number of official appointments at all levels from menial to managerial. This growth was achieved at a cost. In the eighteenth century those who ran the judiciary in France, Prussia, and elsewhere had a degree of autonomy. Faced with defeat by successful French armies in the 1800s, European rulers accelerated their efforts to centralize and modernize the apparatus of the state, bringing previously semiautonomous professional bodies under their control.

Professionals responded by asserting that they were a service elite imbued with social duty and honor. The size and character of existing professions altered, and new jobs jostled for recognition as professions. The need for definition became acute as traditional fee-earning professionals were joined by salaried sectors, the first being the expanding army of bureaucrats. They led the way by defining a new professional ideal in which public esteem rather than independence was the prime feature.

The professions began to demand specific educational prerequisites for acolytes and standardized training under their corporate control. A profession became an increasingly closed corporation, limiting membership to protect "standards," but also to defend the income of existing members and to ensure that access to the professions was restricted to the wealthy. In France in the 1860s, 80 percent of law students were upper middle class. It was common for sons to follow fathers as lawyers or doctors.

Ironically, protecting their professions allowed states' power to increase. The newly required certificates of secondary education were taught and examined in state-run institutions. In Prussia, degree courses were officially validated, and no one could practice as a lawyer without a state appointment. In the early nineteenth century changes in the Prussian legal system made it the norm that after ten to twelve years of expensive legal training, a man had to spend nearly as long again working unpaid within the courts before he could hope to secure an official post. Even then his prospects for promotion were less than they had been a generation earlier. In France although lawyers could practice without an official post, they complained that the rationalization, standardization, and centralization involved in creating a single legal system for France in the 1790s reduced their autonomy.

Leading professionals remained critics of the state in the years up to 1848, and not entirely for selfish reasons. In Prussia and other German states members of the judiciary were prominent in demands for written constitutions on the model of the French constitution of 1814. Such individuals took the lead in the 1848 revolution. But partly because they were alarmed at the scale of popular unrest their protest engendered, lawyers

Alfred Dedreux as a Child with His Sister Elise.
Portrait by Theodore Gericault. The son of an architect, Dedreux later formatted his name with the aristocratic particle (as de Dreux) and became a well-known painter of equestrian scenes. PRIVATE COLLECTION/BRIDGEMAN ART LIBRARY

were subsequently mostly transformed into faithful and obedient servants of autocracy. Their reward was employment; job opportunities in the German bureaucracy increased and from the early 1880s the growth was astronomical as lawyers were allowed to practice privately.

Bourgeois doctors had key roles in movements for social reform and in the 1848 republic in France. Their politicization was ethical and altruistic. A generation of European doctors was appalled at the social effects of industrial and urban change. In England in 1830 Dr. James Phillips Kay (later Kay-Shuttleworth) drew attention to the plight of women and children cotton operatives. In France Drs. Louis-René Villermé and Eugène Buret wrote influential commentaries, the first detailing conditions among workers, especially women and children, in all of the textile industries, the second comparing their circumstances in England and France. Villermé, although sympathetic to capitalism, drew up the first French legislation restricting child labor. Republican socialist doctors like Ange Guépin in Nantes and Tissot Raspail in Paris set up free clinics to help the poor. However, doctors were drawn into an expanding state bureaucracy, vaccinating children against smallpox, taking part in state health insurance schemes, and so on.

EDUCATION AND THE BOURGEOISIE

Education was crucial to the growth, definition, and development of middle-class groups. The huge expansion of education during the century was the product of middle-class initiative and was mainly for their benefit. Secondary and tertiary education were formalized by the introduction of state-administered secondary leaving certificates as well as certificates for specialized tertiary colleges. Revolutionary France led the way. Much criticized church-run secondary establishments were replaced by lycées providing a secular, state education. In 1808 the baccalaureate, or secondary leaving examination, was introduced. The failings of existing universities were compensated for by the creation of high-level colleges for aspiring state engineers, civil servants, and army officers. Other states imitated the French example.

Such secondary and tertiary education was strictly limited to the elite by cost and content: high fees and obligatory Latin. There were some scholarships to the Napoleonic lycées in France, but they were available mainly to sons of officials and army officers. Secondary school-leaving certificates, such as the new baccalaureate in France and the *abitur* in Germany, were rarely completed by pupils from poorer families. They became prerequisites for professional training and access to higher education.

Secondary education was enjoyed by a tiny bourgeois minority. In France roughly 60 percent of candidates, constituting 0.5 percent of the age cohort, successfully passed the baccalaureate. From 1812 secondary education in the German states consisted of annual examinations that had to be repeated if the student failed, culminating in the *abitur*. In 1820, one thousand boys passed the *abitur*. By 1830 this number had doubled, but was to fall subsequently due to a panic that there was a glut of qualified men, who were likely to be disaffected. Only in 1860 did the figure rise again to two thousand. In Germany in 1870 only 0.8

percent of nineteen-year-olds had the *abitur*; in 1911, 1.2 percent. As in France and elsewhere, many pupils left without the *abitur*, or attended other schools teaching the far less prestigious modern-scientific *abitur*.

The secondary syllabus, whether in a British public school, a French lycée, or a gymnasium in Germany, Italy, or Russia, was almost 50 percent Latin and Greek. In a Prussian gymnasium typically 46 percent of the time was spent on Latin and Greek, 17.5 percent on math, physics, and philosophy, and 4 percent was devoted to French. Until well into the second half of the nineteenth century only the classical secondary schools were allowed to prepare pupils for the leaving certificate. Middle-class families often preferred classical secondary education that would have no direct career significance, even when more modern scientific and technical alternatives emerged later in the century. There was a common assumption that unmitigated scientific learning bred socially discontented citizens, even revolutionaries. Classical learning conferred status. In some countries, Russia for instance, it gave automatic exemption from military service and a position in the Table of Ranks, the elite system developed by Peter the Great in the early eighteenth century that led, through state service, to noble rank. In 1879 German civil engineers objected when graduates of nonclassical secondary schools qualified for their branch of state service, not because the engineers needed Latin, but because they claimed the classics built character and added status. The upper layers of the middle class tried to use education to define themselves and create an impermeable barrier to social advance from below.

Education was a tool manipulated by the middle classes to control others. Primary schools trained the lower-middle class and urban and rural workers to accept their station in life. Pupils could not transfer from a primary to a secondary school. Primary schooling provided basic learning in the preferred national language and taught obedience to the state. Technical schools provided the chance to "advance" to foreman status; teacher-training colleges allowed sons and daughters of the lower classes to become primary-school teachers. Education was defined by gender as well as class. Until almost the end of the century girls were confined to primary education, often delivered by nuns.

BOURGEOIS WIVES AND FAMILIES

The family was honored as the basic social unit. Monogamous, lifelong marriage was the norm. Families were essentially patriarchal. In France the authority of the father was enhanced by the Civil Code (1804). A wife lost control over the dowry she brought to a marriage; if she worked, her income was paid to her husband; she could not hold a bank account without her husband's consent; her husband could dictate where she lived. In 1816 the law permitting divorce, in place since 1792, was abolished and not restored until 1884.

A wife had less status than her children, and even by the end of the century reforms were modest. French inheritance laws were more favorable than elsewhere, sharing property among all surviving offspring, regardless of sex. In reality wealthy bourgeois families, like the aristocracy, practiced male primogeniture. Middle-class women only had a chance of independence if they were widowed. However the wife was the queen bee, managing home and servants and developing social contacts, vital to reinforce the social standing and marriageability of the family. Women were often idealized as the spiritual and moral force within the family. The Roman Catholic cult of the Virgin Mary served to intensify this notion, vital because women were the main churchgoers. Women organized religious charities and crèches (day nurseries), giving them a busy public existence. In the artisan economy, when workshops adjoined the home, wives helped run the business. As larger units, department stores, and factories developed, pressures of scale introduced professional managers, excluding wives, and sometimes husbands, from the day-to-day running of the business.

Bourgeois sexual morality was gender and class specific. An active sex drive, exercised with servants or prostitutes long before marriage, was held to be an essential feature of masculinity. Unmarried bourgeois women were supposed to be uninterested in sex. The French Civil Code imposed penal sanctions on an adulterous wife, but tolerated her spouse's mistresses. The poor were reckoned to be without morality, although whether prostitutes were supposed to be driven solely by financial need, or were thought to have sexual appetites because they were nearer to the animal kingdom, was never clear.

BOURGEOIS CULTURE

Culture was another area where the middle classes imposed their values. Art galleries, museums, theaters, concert halls, and libraries were built by governments, local authorities, and sometimes by private associations of wealthy citizens. The first public art gallery was opened in Vienna in 1781, in Paris the Louvre opened in 1793. The National Gallery in London was launched in 1823, when the Austrians repaid their war loan. Soon municipal pride demanded that every substantial town have its own gallery/museum. Such "rational recreation" was the preserve of the bourgeoisie; the poor were excluded, either by price or by a variety of strategies. The British Museum, which opened in 1759, demanded a letter requesting admission.

Royal and noble private collectors of art were joined by the most wealthy bourgeois, who bought at annual salons, or by direct commission. Industrialists and businessmen in northern England amassed impressive collections of art. A prosperous dry-salter in Manchester, William Hardman, owned paintings by Titian, Canaletto, Veronese, Ruisdael, Rembrandt, Wilson, Wright, and Fuseli. A family of Manchester cotton manufacturers, the Ashtons, owned a collection that included Constable, Turner, Collins, Holman Hunt, Egg, and Leighton. Thomas Holloway, a manufacturer of patent medicines not only collected Constable, Turner, Holman Hunt, and other fashionable artists but also endowed a women's college that became part of the University of London, as well as a sanatorium. Similar examples can be cited throughout Europe. In Moscow a small number of former serfs who had become millionaires amassed art collections. The present outstanding collection of impressionist art in the Tretyakov Gallery is the result of such enterprise. Savva Morozov helped to found the Moscow Art Theater.

The middle classes busied themselves running academies and literary societies such as the Literary and Philosophical Society (Manchester, 1781; Leeds, 1819). Mechanics' Institutes and Schools of Design were popular. They organized art exhibitions and concerts. In Manchester there were Gentlemen's Concerts, and Hermann Leo, a calico printer, intitiated Charles Hallé's long-lasting orchestral association with the city in 1848. In Leeds the musical association organized recitals in members' homes.

Middle-class observers poured scorn on the preferred leisure activities of workers—music halls, prizefights, and public hangings. Middle-class pressure groups made the second and third of these illegal in Britain in 1868, and music halls were subject to constant criticism because they combined food and entertainment with, worst of all, strong drink. In Britain bourgeois temperance and Sunday Observance societies bustled around to ensure that the working classes did not enjoy their very limited leisure. During the nineteenth century municipalities and private charities run by the middle classes began to try to "civilize" working people by creating public reading rooms and libraries and providing housing, hospitals, and clinics.

LEISURE

For those with money, leisure was a way of life. Until the improvement of roads and especially the construction of railways that made even distant places easily accessible, the European bourgeois family would spend the summer in spa towns such as Bath. Town centers were developed with luxury housing and public gardens where the wealthy could "promenade" safely for hours, discussing marriages (and more informal liaisons) and maybe business. Elegant and commodious assembly rooms were built with space to show off fashionable clothes, to see, and even more important, to be seen. Leisure activities, theater companies, exhibitions, and even waxworks adapted by touring to capture this temporarily static captive market. Madame Tussaud, who brought her collection of wax royals and revolutionary deaths' heads from Paris in 1802 spent the next thirty-three years touring Britain and Ireland with a fleet of touring caravans displaying the Tussaud's logo in gold letters. As soon as there was a dip in profits in Brighton she would move on with her growing collection of coronation displays and executed villains.

The railway revolutionized leisure and entertainment. It put Brighton a mere two hours from London. Although the cost was still substantial—in 1862 the price of a ticket was only one-third less than a coach ticket in 1820—far more people made the trip. On Easter Monday 1862, 132,000 people took the

Brighton train. The "season" was dead. The middle classes went to Brighton for a day, indeed it became so crowded that the very rich abandoned the place. Theater companies and others began to travel far less. The railway meant that customers rather than the entertainment did the traveling. At first most of this traveling was limited to the comfortably off, although special excursion trains allowed workers to go on day trips to the sea. Third-class carriages were not introduced until the 1870s.

As travel became less a mark of prosperity, the rich began to tour farther. Queen Victoria set the trend when she decamped from the royal pavilion in Brighton, but she set her sights modestly on the Isle of Wight. Others mimicked the aristocratic "grand tour" of earlier times by venturing abroad. Normandy became popular with the British, but the Mediterranean was soon more chic. The tourist population of Nice rose from 575 in the winter of 1815 to 5,000 by 1861. There were fifty hotels in the city, twenty more than in 1847.

The concept that leisure should be built into the working life of the less wealthy middle classes developed. Annual seaside holidays within Britain became the norm. Thomas Cook led the way. The first Cook excursions were to the Great Exhibition of 1851. Also, government legislation gradually limited the working day. In Britain a ten-hour working day for women and children became the law in 1847, France followed for workers in mechanized factories in 1848, and for women in 1904. Some firms introduced half-day work for Saturdays. In 1870 a Bank Holiday Act was passed in Britain, and paid holidays were gradually introduced. Gradually, leisure ceased to be the preserve of the bourgeoisie.

BOURGEOIS CONSUMERS

In recent years historians have suggested that the bourgeoisie were united less as a producing than as a consuming class. With increasing prosperity bourgeois women became the spearhead of a consumer society. The epicenter was the department store that provided for, or invented, all domestic needs. For the first time one store could provide clothes, shoes, hats, and underwear for the entire family, plus bedding, towels, furniture, jewelry, cosmetics, and even food. The first department stores opened in the 1860s. In Paris, the capital of culture at the time, the most famous, the Bon Marché was the first,

Luxembourg Gardens at Twilight. Painting by John Singer Sargent, 1879. The growth of the bourgeoisie exerted a direct influence on the urban landscape as the number of parks, the preferred site for leisure activities, grew. MINNEAPOLIS INSTITUTE OF ARTS, MN, USA/BRIDGEMAN ART LIBRARY

opened by Aristide Boucicaut and his wife in 1869. It served as Émile Zola's model for *Au Bonheur des Dames* (1883), in which he tried "to create the poetry of modern activity."

Department stores revolutionized mere shopping, creating a new culture of consumption. The main customers were bourgeois ladies, attracted by the safety, respectability, comfort, cleanliness, and elegance of the buildings, which were well lit and fitted. Stores stressed that ladies could visit their stores knowing that nothing would jar their feminine sensibility and moral uprightness. The department store was a freely available public space, but the female customers were reassured that it was a home-away-from-home that they could visit alone,

unlike a theater or concert hall, where it was assumed ladies would have a male escort.

The stores did far more than satisfy the needs of their customers, they also taught them what they ought to buy. In the later years of the century the catalogs of these "palaces of purchasing" shaped the standards of the middle-class home. They taught those who aspired to be more middle class the ground rules of the game. The stores and their catalogs cultivated a fantasy of culture, decorating the departments to turn them into an enchanting fairyland of design, color, and light. The shopper was invited to move from her own mundane domestic existence to a dream world of exciting drapery, mirrors, entrancing perfumes, and endlessly courteous staff. Department stores presented themselves as the peak of modernity. Technical advances facilitated this process, whether it was plate-glass windows to replace earlier tiny panes of glass, or gas and later electric lighting. This was still luxury consumption for a small elite, but with the appealing illusion of democratic availability.

POLITICS AND THE BOURGEOISIE

The middle classes organized themselves into, and excluded the poor from, a vast range of associations, from cultural and sporting to political. The most successful associations from which workers and also women were excluded were representative assemblies. The liberal bourgeoisie tried to manage their rulers and contain the potential subversive poor by asserting the principle of the sovereignty of the nation in elections. The French revolutionaries experimented unsuccessfully with representative institutions in the 1790s but soon acquired a dictatorial emperor instead. After the Napoleonic Wars, British radicals demanded reform of the House of Commons, and the French argued over voting rights within a constitution modeled to some degree on that of Britain. Campaigns for suffrage reform were mainly the initiative of middle-class reformers. In Britain the Chartist movement of the 1830s and 1840s, backed by some members of the lower-middle classes, artisans, and better-off factory workers, pressed for a democratic electorate as did societies like the mainly middle-class Friends of the People in France. The French enfranchised all adult males after the 1848 revolution, and in 1867 all male householders got the vote in Britain. Elected assemblies at all levels, municipal to national, gradually became the norm in all countries. Until 1919 none rivaled the French by enfranchising all adult males. Few worried that the 50 percent of adults who happened to be female had no vote.

The extension of the right to vote tended to perpetuate traditional elites. In Britain the Reform Act of 1832 had no impact on the composition of Parliament. In 1840, 80 percent of members still represented the landed interest and the proportion of bourgeois entrepreneurs—97 members out of 658, or about 14 percent—was the same as at the end of the eighteenth century. Perhaps this was unsurprising, given the limited nature of the legis-

lation. However, the same was true in France, even after the introduction of universal male suffrage in 1848. In 1861 the new united Italy adopted a 40-lira tax qualification for voters, which produced an electorate comparable to that of France before 1848. The Italian ruling elite was not only wealthy, it was also almost exclusively northern. Universal male suffrage had to wait until 1919. Frederick William IV of Prussia (r. 1840–1861) established in 1849 a graded suffrage for the elected Landtag, which allowed the richest 18 percent of taxpayers to elect two-thirds of the new legislative assembly he created. This system was retained for the assemblies of some of the individual states after unification. The Reichstag, the representative assembly for the whole German Empire created in 1871, was elected by all adult males, but it exercised little power. When elected local councils, zemstvos, were set up in Russia in the 1860s and an imperial parliament or Duma after the 1905 revolution, an even narrower hierarchical voting system was inaugurated. Elected assemblies only began to make a role for themselves in Russia during World War I. Unsurprisingly, in an age of unpaid MPs, assemblies tended to be staffed by, as well as represent the interests of, wealthy bourgeois elites. However, by 1914 the socialists were the largest single group in both the German Reichstag and the French assembly, and a growing, though a very divided, number in Italy. In the German Reichstag a majority of both socialist voters and a substantial number of assembly members were workers, a situation aided by a modest salary from the Social Democratic Party (SPD), thirty years before Reichstag members were paid by the state. However in excess of half of the SPD members in the Reichstag (122 out of 215) were journalists. In France and Italy the proportion of lower-middle-class voters was much higher, and the assembly members were predominantly middle class, with leaders often from the legal profession.

Throughout the century middle-class groups were concerned that radicals and socialists would exploit the very evident social and economic inequalities that increased as a result of modern industrialization. Marx preached inevitable bourgeois, then proletarian revolution as the ultimate consequence of capitalist development. However although the century was punctuated with revolutions in 1830, 1848, and in 1871 in Paris, tensions were defused by social insurance schemes, private and state-run, by the legalization of trade unions, and by the provision of state-organized education. The development of parliamentary institutions created the illusion of consultation and democratic control, and the promotion of nationalist and imperialistic sentiments stimulated the illusion of all social groups sharing common goals. The Socialist International's demand for international proletarian solidarity in 1914 went unheard.

The gap between rich and poor widened. This was most visible at the top. In Britain in 1803 the top 2 percent owned 20 percent of the wealth of the country; by 1867 they owned 40 percent. Wealth had always corresponded closely to power. The elites of the nineteenth century institutionalized the equation by demanding tax qualifications for voters, while pretending to eliminate privilege. Hierarchically structured education systems, professions, and assemblies of all sorts plus improved policing, military control, and the monitoring and managing of public opinion allowed a narrow section of society to dominate. One should take care, however, not to assume that this was a "bourgeois" century. In most states aristocratic families maintained their economic, social, and political control.

To what extent did shared attitudes to education and social values give the bourgeoisie common political ideas? Liberalism is often spoken of as the creed of the middle classes. In reality, although many members of the middle classes may have favored somewhat elitist, rather than democratic, political systems, the middle classes ranged among all political formations and attitudes, from right wing to socialists, from nationalist to internationalist, and from laissez-faire to more protectionist economic ideas.

This dissection of "the bourgeoisie" has revealed the diversity and huge range of occupations, income, and attitudes within the bourgeoisie. Middle-class groups came nearest to unity in ideas on education, on the family, on the role of women, and on culture. They were farthest apart on politics. If bourgeois liberalism had been a reality instead of a myth and a convenient shorthand, the liberals in the Prussian Landtag would have

united to secure liberal constitutional as well as economic objectives in return for their concurrence with the chancellor Otto von Bismarck's cynical manipulation of nationalist sentiments; the constitutional monarchy would have triumphed over fascism in Italy; and the Russian Revolution would have been avoided. Class did not correspond to political interest and identity.

See also **Aristocracy; Capitalism; Cities and Towns; Class and Social Relations; Education; Housing; Marriage and Family; Peasants; Professions; Working Class.**

BIBLIOGRAPHY

Blackbourn, David, and Richard J. Evans, eds. *The German Bourgeoisie: Essays on the Social History of the German Middle Class from the Late Eighteenth Century to the Early Twentieth Century.* London, 1991.

Crossick, Geoffrey, and Heinz-Gerhard Haupt, eds. *Shopkeepers and Master-Artisans in Nineteenth-Century Europe.* London and New York, 1984.

Davis, John A. *Italy in the Nineteenth Century, 1796–1900.* Oxford, U.K., 2000.

Evans, Eric J. *The Forging of the Modern State: Early Industrial Britain, 1783–1870.* London, 1983.

Harrison, Carol E. *The Bourgeois Citizen in Nineteenth-Century France: Gender, Sociability, and the Uses of Emulation.* Oxford, U.K., 1999.

Marsden, Gordon, ed. *Victorian Values: Personalities and Perspectives in Nineteenth-Century Society.* New York, 1990.

Maza, Sarah. *The Myth of the French Bourgeoisie : An Essay on the Social Imaginary, 1750–1850.* Cambridge, Mass., 2003.

Miller, Michael. *The Bon Marché: Bourgeois Culture and the Department Store, 1869–1920.* London, 1981.

Pilbeam, Pamela. *The Middle Classes in Europe, 1789–1914: France, Germany, Italy, and Russia.* Basingstoke, U.K., 1990.

———. "From Orders to Classes: European Society in the Nineteenth Century." In *The Oxford Illustrated History of Modern Europe,* edited by T. C. W. Blanning. Oxford, U.K., 1996.

———. *Madame Tussaud and the History of Waxworks.* London, 2003.

Raeff, Marc. *Understanding Imperial Russia: State and Society in the Ancien Regime.* Translated by Arthur Goldhammer. New York, 1984.

Rieber, Alfred J. *Merchants and Entrepreneurs in Imperial Russia.* Chapel Hill, N.C., 1982.

Schwartz, Vanessa. *Spectacular Realities: Early Mass Culture in Fin-de-Siècle Paris.* Berkeley, Calif., 1998.

Wahrman, Dror. *Imagining the Middle Class: The Political Representation of Class in Britain, c.1780–1840.* Cambridge, U.K., 1995.

Williams, Rosalind H. *Dream Worlds: Mass Consumption in Late Nineteenth-Century France.* Berkeley, Calif., 1982.

PAMELA PILBEAM

BOXER REBELLION.

The term *Boxers* (a shortened form of Boxers United in Righteousness [*Yihequan*]) first appeared in official records in 1898. The rebellion that took their name originated in spring 1898 in Shandong Province, the birthplace of the two founding figures of Confucianism: Confucius and Mencius. The principal causes of the Boxer Rebellion were economic issues and the disputes between the Chinese and foreign missionaries in the wake of the Opium Wars (1839–1842 and 1856–1860). After the legalization of the propagation of Christianity in China around 1860, foreign missionaries were very active in Shandong. But none were more disruptive than the German Society of the Divine Word led by Johann Baptist von Anzer. This missionary order entered Shandong in the 1880s and was aggressive in its intervention in secular disputes and arrogant toward the Chinese. But it attracted converts by virtue of its power to offer protection and support, and the friction between the Christians and the local communities escalated quickly in many areas of Shandong and other parts of China, especially the north, leading to the Boxer Rebellion.

RISE OF THE BOXERS AND THE QING COURT'S WAR ON THE GREAT POWERS

The proximate cause of the uprising was the murder of two German missionaries of the Society of the Divine Word, Richard Henle and Francis Xavier Nies, in Shandong in November 1897 by local villagers. The German government wanted to expand German influence and in particular to acquire Jiaozhou Bay in Shandong. It had been looking for a pretext to gain Jiaozhou prior to the murders, and when Kaiser William II heard of the murders he saw that a "splendid opportunity" had at last arrived and immediately dispatched

"You must know, my men, that you are about to meet a crafty, well-armed foe! Meet him and beat him! Give no quarter! Take no prisoners! Kill him when he falls into your hands! Even as, a thousand years ago, the Huns under their King Attila made such a name for themselves as still resounds in terror through legend and fable, so may the name of Germany resound through Chinese history … that never again will a Chinese dare to so much as look askance at a German."

Kaiser William II, in a speech on 27 July 1900 at Bremerhaven on the occasion of the departure of the first contingent of German troops to China to suppress the Boxer Rebellion. In Preston, p. 209.

Germany's East Asian naval squadron to occupy Jiaozhou Bay. He built the port city of Qingdao and quickly turned a large part of Shandong into a German sphere of influence. The Germans forced the Chinese to accept other demands too: the extensive punishment of all local and provincial officials for their alleged antipathy to foreign activities and the building of a cathedral in the village where the missionaries had been killed. The Germans in Shandong became more aggressive and peremptory after they turned Shandong into their sphere of influence, which triggered a new round in the Great Powers' "scramble for concessions" in China. In the months following the Germans taking Jiaozhou, Russia seized Dalian and Port Arthur on the Liaodong Peninsula, Britain claimed Weihaiwei in Shandong as well as a ninety-nine-year lease of the New Territories opposite Hong Kong, and France made southwest China its sphere of influence.

The escalation of foreign aggression after the murders of the German missionaries intensified the anger and hostility felt by many non-Christian Chinese toward the local Christian people and their foreign supporters and drove Chinese xenophobia to even higher levels. It was in this context that the Boxers in Shandong turned against the Christians in 1898. Although female Boxers (called Red Lanterns) later joined the movement, the Boxers were mainly young male

French soldiers at a barricade in Tianjin during the Boxer Rebellion, c. 1900.
©UNDERWOOD & UNDERWOOD/CORBIS

farmers who practiced a combination of spirit possession and martial arts. Their targets were Chinese Christians and foreign Christians and missionaries, but to prevent the Qing state from militarily suppressing them the Boxers adopted the slogan "Support the Qing, destroy the foreign" (*Fuqing mieyang*), in which *foreign* meant the foreign religion (Christianity) and its Chinese converts as much as the foreigners themselves. The Boxer movement gradually spread through northern China in 1899 and then reached Beijing where the Qing court was located and that was home to a substantial number of foreigners. By June 1900 the Boxers were moving into Beijing by the thousands. There, they blocked the foreign relief expeditionary forces, besieged the foreign legations, and eventually provoked a war with the Great Powers.

The Qing state was already substantially weakened by the Sino-Japanese War of 1894 to 1895 and now feared that the organized Boxer groups might turn into an anti-Qing movement. In the meantime the Qing court came under extremely hostile pressure from the Great Powers to suppress the Boxers. The Qing court faced a very difficult situation, and it now tried to suppress the Boxers and had several military confrontations with them. But when the Great Powers, especially Germany and Great Britain, took military action against China, the Empress Dowager Cixi decided that it was wiser to work with the Boxers against the foreigners. On 21 June 1900 the Qing government declared war on the Great Powers, and the Boxers were officially addressed as *yimin* (righteous people) and were enlisted in militia under the overall command of a royal prince in the capital.

THE COMING OF INTERNATIONAL MILITARY FORCES IN BEIJING AND THE BOXER PROTOCOL

In the meantime, the Great Powers had sent international military expeditionary forces to China to fight against the Boxers and the Qing and to protect their people. Germany took the lead role in sending troops to China. In June 1900 the German minister to Beijing, Baron Clemens von Ketteler, had been shot dead by a Chinese soldier while on his way to a meeting at the Zongli Yamen (foreign ministry), and the kaiser used this development to argue that a German general should command the international troops. The kaiser's nomination was Field Marshal Count Alfred von Waldersee, who eventually was chosen as supreme commander of the international military expedition. The poorly equipped Chinese military and Boxers were no match for the modern troops of the Great Powers. The powerful governors in southeastern China declared neutrality, and in the summer of 1900 the international military forces marched to Beijing with minimal resistance. The soldiers and missionaries of the "civilized nations" wreaked terrible revenge against the Chinese. They burned historical buildings, robbed China of its national treasures and many private properties, killed many Chinese, and raped Chinese women. Although everyone joined in the looting, the Europeans were the worst perpetrators. Cixi and the court fled from Beijing in humiliation. In September 1901 the Great Powers forced the Qing state to accept the Boxer Protocol, which involved eleven foreign signatories, most of them European countries. The terms were mainly punitive: ten high officials were executed and one hundred others punished; the civil service examinations were suspended in forty-five cities; foreign troops were to be stationed in Beijing permanently and to be positioned at strategically important points between Beijing and the coast; Chinese official missions were to be sent to Germany and Japan to convey regret for the deaths of von Ketteler and a Japanese diplomat; and a monument was to be erected in Beijing on the spot where the German minister had been killed. The indemnity imposed on the Chinese was 450 million taels (about US$625 million)—one tael for each Chinese—to be paid in thirty-nine annual installments with an interest rate of 4 percent. The total was more than four times the annual revenue of the Qing state, and the annual payments represented about one-fifth of the national budget.

The Boxer Rebellion was a pivotal episode in China's fractured relationship with the West and left a lasting impact on Chinese politics and China's foreign relations. The rebellion reinforced negative European perceptions of China and its people, and the defeat and humiliation suffered at the hands of international expeditionary forces soon led to the final fall of the Qing dynasty in 1912.

See also **China; Imperialism; Opium Wars.**

BIBLIOGRAPHY

Cohen, Paul A. *History in Three Keys: The Boxers as Event, Experience, and Myth.* New York, 1997.

Elliot, Jane E. *Some Did It for Civilization, Some Did It for Their Country: A Revised View of the Boxer War.* Hong Kong, 2002.

Esherick, Joseph W. *The Origins of the Boxer Uprising.* Berkeley, Calif., 1987.

Preston, Diana. *The Boxer Rebellion: The Dramatic Story of China's War on Foreigners That Shook the World in the Summer of 1900.* New York, 2000.

Xiang, Lanxin. *The Origins of the Boxer War: A Multinational Study.* London, 2003.

XU GUOQI

BRAHMS, JOHANNES (1833–1897), one of the most important Austro-Germanic composers of the second half of the nineteenth century.

Johannes Brahms was born in Hamburg, but from 1862 spent the majority of his adult life in Vienna. Active in all the major genres of the period apart from opera and program music, he was also a virtuoso concert pianist, a conductor, and an editor of older music. His mature compositional style presents a remarkable synthesis—of sixteenth- and seventeenth-century choral music, Baroque music (especially Johann Sebastian Bach [1685–1750]), the Viennese Classics, Beethovenian rhetoric and technical procedures, Schubertian lyricism, and folk and popular idioms.

Brahms's work was informed by a number of ideological positions, including historicism, Romanticism, later nineteenth-century political liberalism, proto-modernist strains, and aspects of the age's materialism. Such breadth of reference bespeaks an almost democratic artistic open-mindedness, and the latent political ramifications of this were sometimes overtly manifested. For example, the composer's *Ein deutsches Requiem* (A German requiem) op. 45 (completed in its final form in 1868), which established Brahms as a major European composer, aspires toward a universal message (Brahms referred to it as a "human" requiem) rather than a specifically Christian one. Democratic artistic tendencies also placed Brahms at a tangent to the predominant artistic cult of originality, and the increasingly chauvinistic political atmosphere of his times—although it should be noted that Brahms himself could be deeply jingoistic.

Brahms achieved this flexibly synthetic style through self-conscious, almost scholarly contemplation and self-criticism, activities that were further to distinguish Brahms from his era, which often valorized the creative act in radically Romantic terms, as an unmediated overflow of expression. This self-consciousness also placed an intimate stamp on his music that led the music critic Paul Bekker (1882–1937) to describe Brahms in 1918 as an essentially bourgeois composer of chamber music; on the other hand, later writers (including Theodor Adorno [1903–1969] and Carl Dahlhaus [1929–1989]) saw it as a sign of progressiveness. Brahms, however, started out strongly within the orbit of Romanticism and the musical avant-garde: as a young man he read the Romantic literature of E.T.A. Hoffmann (1776–1822) and Jean Paul (1763–1825). His compositional style, while already eclectic in its sources (though not fully fused), could be oriented toward turbulent Romantic expression and formal fantasy, and also the up-to-date musical techniques of thematic transformation with which the composer Franz Liszt (1811–1886), whom Brahms met in Weimar in 1853, was then presently working. The composer Robert Schumann (1810–1856) famously wrote in 1853, the year he met Brahms, that each of Brahms's works was then "so different from the others that it seemed to stream from its own individual source."

Brahms transformed these creative sources into one synthesized compositional identity during the 1850s, leading in the first half of the 1860s to what the English music critic Sir Donald Francis Tovey (1875–1940) referred to as Brahms's "first maturity": a group of works (including the remarkably integrated Piano Quintet in F Minor, op. 34) that set the basic agenda for Brahms's compositional style for the rest of his life. The 1850s were also marked by intense interest in the music of the past (including a course of study in counterpoint)—a historicist tendency that remained with Brahms, and which is most famously expressed later by his dramatic use of the Baroque passacaglia form for the last movement of his Symphony no. 4, op. 98 (1885). Finally, the decade saw Brahms briefly withdraw from the arena of German musical life, resulting in compositional silence toward the end of the 1850s, and the formulation of a critical distance to the so-called New German School of composition and its claims to stand for the "music of the future." This latter move led, to Brahms's embarrassment, to his name appearing at the head of manifesto in 1860 asserting that the programmatic aspirations of Liszt and others were contrary to the "inner spirit of music." The repercussions were that Brahms became associated with the music critic Eduard Hanslick (1825–1904) and the idea of absolute music, and also scripted as an antipode to Richard Wagner (1813–1883)—misleadingly, since Brahms held Wagner, whom he met in 1862, and his music in high esteem. Such associations were only strengthened, particularly in 1876, by the milestone first performance of Brahms's First Symphony, which brought to an end the mid-century domination of orchestral symphonic music by the programmatic agendas of Liszt and his followers.

Scholarship around the turn of the twenty-first century has emphasized extra-musical elements and influences, but the association of Brahms with absolute music and musical formalism remains important. However surprising, lyrical, or Romantic its expressive appearance, Brahms's music is frequently grounded in the more purely musical parameters of what the composer Arnold Schoenberg (1874–1951) famously was to call "developing variation": a seamless and highly economical musical logic, where each moment in the score can be justified in terms of its motivic derivation from the preceding material. For Schoenberg, this marked Brahms as a protomodernist; and indeed, the increasingly material concentration of Brahms's music (culminating in such late examples as the *Vier ernste Gesange* [Four serious songs], op. 121) whereby entire musical structures are unified by webs of thematic and motivic cross-references and derivations, is remarkably prophetic. But such unifying techniques, which ground Brahms's music in quantifiable musical relations, also like Brahms strongly to the materialist predilections of European thought at that time, which rejected the metaphysical and idealist strains of early-nineteenth-century Romanticism for having contributed to the failure of the Revolutions of 1848 and thus sought a theoretical outlook, both within the arts (for example, in realism and naturalism) and the sciences (with positivism), orientated more toward the empirically verifiable constituents of existing reality. Ironically, though, Brahms's materialist credentials helped to distinguish him from the predominant musical culture of the second half of the nineteenth century, which was driven by a metaphysics of music inspired by the early-nineteenth-century philosopher Schopenhauer, and thus continued to align itself with the transcendental tendencies of Romanticism, if in a somewhat overdetermined form.

In the final analysis, Brahms is a slippery combination of seemingly contradictory positions (simultaneously modernist, retrospective, and contemporaneous) unique in the later nineteenth century. As a result, the man and his music have been open to appropriation by a number of divergent polemics, thus making him a fascinating subject for reception history in our own pluralistic postmodern world.

See also **Liszt, Franz; Modernism; Music; Romanticism; Schoenberg, Arnold; Schopenhauer, Arthur; Wagner, Richard.**

BIBLIOGRAPHY

Frisch, Walter. *Brahms and the Principle of Developing Variation.* Berkeley, Calif., 1984.

Frisch, Walter, ed. *Brahms and His World.* Princeton, N.J., 1990.

Musgrave, Michael. *The Cambridge Companion to Brahms.* Cambridge, U.K., 1999.

————. *The Music of Brahms.* London, 1985.

Schoenberg, Arnold. "Brahms the Progressive." In *Style and Idea: Selected Writings of Arnold Schoenberg,* edited by Leonard Stein, translated by Leo Black. London, 1975.

JAMES CURRIE

BRAILLE, LOUIS (1809–1852), French teacher who devised the Braille system of raised-point reading and writing for the blind.

Louis Braille, the youngest of four children, was born in Coupvray (Seine-et-Marne), a small village near Paris. His father, Simon-René Braille, was a saddler by trade. When he was three years old Louis, trying to mimic his father, injured his left eye with a cutting tool. The eye became infected, the infection spread to the right eye, and the boy was eventually left completely blind. His parents nevertheless sent him to the village school at a very early age, while at home his father gave him small tasks to perform that helped develop his manual skills. When he was ten the family succeeded in having him admitted to the Institution Royale des Jeunes Aveugles (Royal Institution for Young Blind People), located at that time in the old buildings of the former Saint-Firmin seminary in rue Saint-Victor, in one of the poorest neighborhoods of Paris. Louis entered the institution on 15 February 1819.

According to Alexandre-René Pignier, the institution's director from 1821 to 1840, who left a biographical report on Louis Braille, the boy soon showed great aptitude not only for literary and scientific studies but also for manual work and for music. Braille was twelve years old when Pignier had the institution adopt a nonalphabetical writing system for the blind, based on raised dots or points, which had been invented by a sighted person, Charles Barbier de La Serre. The boy tried out this new system and sought to suggest "several improvements" to its inventor. Barbier paid no attention to the young man, but Braille carried on with his thinking and experimentation, relying on his own insights and the critical suggestions of his peers. Pignier says that by 1825 the adolescent had already conceived the broad outlines of his system, the first published version of which appeared in relief in 1829. Pignier was well aware of the importance of Braille's method and encouraged its use within the institution, where it would eventually replace the Barbier system.

Upon its first formal presentation, however, the method was not yet perfect. Some of its signs used smooth dashes as well as raised points, and they were too hard to distinguish by means of touch from two points occupying the same position. As Braille continued to improve his method, however, the signs with dashes were soon jettisoned. He was appointed to a teaching position at the Institution Royale in 1828, and beginning in 1830 his system, as taught by himself, was used by his students for taking notes and writing homework. In 1837 Braille produced a second, revised account of his system under the title "Procedure for Writing Words, Music and Plainsong by Means of Points, for the Use of, and Arranged for the Blind." Like his writing system, the equipment used by Braille was built on that developed by Charles Barbier for his "sonography": a grooved writing tablet; a metal guide punched with three oblong holes corresponding to three lines (rather than six, as in the Barbier model, which relied on twelve-point combinations as opposed to Braille's six-point ones); a wooden frame enclosing the guide and attached to the writing tablet by hinges; and a blunt awl as the writing tool.

By 1837 Braille had already for several years been experiencing symptoms of the tuberculosis that was to cut his life short fifteen years later. This did not prevent him from continuing to work on writing systems or from addressing the problem of how the blind and the sighted might correspond with one another. He was thus able to perfect a device that could punch out patterns resembling ordinary letters and figures, so that the output was readable by blind and sighted alike. He described this solution in 1839, in a small work titled "A New Method for Representing by Points the Very Forms of Letters, Geographical Maps, Geometrical Figures, Musical Notations, etc., for the Use of the Blind." A former institution student named Pierre Foucault, who had a mechanical bent, immediately saw how well this invention would serve the blind, and his collaboration with Braille led to the first typewriter allowing the blind to communicate directly with the sighted.

Braille globe. This bronze globe with place names in Braille was created for the Institute for Young Blind People in France in 1833. Musée Valentin Hauy, Paris, France/Bridgeman Art Library/Archives Charmet

The incalculable benefits bestowed on the blind by Louis Braille's inventions aroused great enthusiasm among educated blind people and admiration among many sighted teachers. The use of writing systems based on raised points was nevertheless somewhat eclipsed at the Institution Royale after Pignier went into retirement in 1840. His successor, Pierre-Armand Dufau, tried for a time to return to the earlier methods of reading and writing for the blind based on ordinary letters; students were still permitted to use the point-based system for taking notes, but very few books were now printed in this way. But Dufau eventually recognized the superiority of the Braille method, and it was definitively adopted by the institution in 1854.

Sadly, Louis Braille had died in the institution's infirmary on 6 January 1852, overwhelmed by the illness that had been besetting him for more than twenty years. All those he left behind remembered him as a modest, gentle man and a faithful friend, his sharp mind and great sensitivity often concealed by a perhaps excessive reserve. Braille was also a tireless worker, a talented musician, and an excellent teacher.

The austere and seemingly unremarkable existence of Louis Braille, marked by handicap and illness, might easily have remained sterile; instead, thanks to an enlightened intelligence, great courage, an unwavering scientific curiosity, and a desire to help his peers, it was extraordinarily fruitful. At the end of his life, short as it was, Louis Braille bequeathed to the blind of the entire world the means to gain full access at last to written culture, be it literary, scientific, or musical. It was not, however, until the Universal Congress for the Amelioration of the Condition of the Blind and Deaf-Mute, held in Paris in the context of the Universal Exposition of 1878, that the general espousal of the Braille system was approved by a large majority. Among European-language-speaking countries, only the United States waited until the twentieth century to adopt Braille (1918). Later in that century, the use of the system would be extended to African and Asian languages under the aegis of UNESCO.

See also **Education; Literacy.**

BIBLIOGRAPHY

Bicknel, Lennard. *Triumph over Darkness: The Life of Louis Braille.* London, 1988.

Henri, Pierre. *La vie et l'œuvre de Louis Braille: Inventeur de l'alphabet des aveugles 1809–1852.* Paris, 1952.

Pignier, Alexandre-René. "Notice sur Louis Braille. Professeur et ancien élève de l'Institution des jeunes aveugles de Paris." In *Notices biographiques sur trois professeurs anciens élèves de l'Institution des jeunes aveugles de Paris.* Paris, 1859.

Weygand, Zina. *Vivre sans voir: Les aveugles dans la société française du Moyen Age au siècle de Louis Braille.* Preface by Alain Corbin. Paris, 2003.

ZINA WEYGAND

BRENTANO, FRANZ (1838–1917),

German-Austrian philosopher.

A revolutionary figure in empiricist European philosophy at the turn of the century, Franz Clemens Honoratus Hermann Brentano is most famously associated with his distinction between psychological and physical phenomena on the basis of the "aboutness" or intentionality of thought. Brentano championed an Aristotelian approach to philosophy and psychology. He developed ethics and value theory by means of the concepts of correct pro- and anti-emotions or love and hate attitudes, and he made important contributions to syllogistic logic (unpublished during his lifetime), epistemology or theory of knowledge, metaphysics, and philosophy of religion. His teaching prepared the way for rigorous approaches to philosophy of science and theory of meaning in the later work of the so-called Vienna Circle of Logical Positivists, as well as on Gestalt and other branches of experimental psychology, the theory of objects (*Gegenstandstheorie*), and descriptive philosophical psychology or phenomenology. Lecturing first in Würzburg, Germany, and later in Vienna, Austria, Brentano's ideas touched many important thinkers who self-consciously considered themselves as constituting a Brentano School. The philosophers and psychologists of note who were part of the Brentano orbit included such leading lights of the Austro-Hungarian Empire as Alexius Meinong, Ernst Mally, Alois Höfler, Carl Stumpf, Anton Marty, Frans Weber, Kazimierz Twardowski, Christian von Ehrenfels, Edmund Husserl, and Sigmund Freud.

Between 1859 and 1860, Brentano attended the Academy in Münster, reading intensively in the medieval Aristotelians, and receiving in 1862 the doctorate in philosophy in absentia from the University of Tübingen. He was ordained a Catholic priest in 1864 and was later involved in a controversy over the doctrine of papal infallibility, eventually leaving the church in 1873. He taught first as *Privatdozent* in the Philosophical Faculty of the University of Würzburg from 1866 to 1874, and then accepted a professorship at the University of Vienna, which he held until 1880. After the death of his wife in 1893, Brentano left Vienna in 1895 and retired to Italy, spending summers in the Austrian Danube valley, and finally relocating to Zurich, Switzerland, shortly before Italy entered World War I. Here he remained active both in philosophy and psychology, despite his increasing blindness. He continued writing philosophy, and maintained an extensive philosophical-literary correspondence until his death from complications following the relapse of an appendicitis attack.

In *Psychologie vom empirischen Standpunkt* (1874; *Psychology from an Empirical Standpoint*), Brentano argues that intentionality is the mark of the mental, that every psychological experience has contained immanently within it an intended object that the thought is about or toward which the thought is directed. To consider just one of Brentano's examples, *in* desire something is desired. According to the immanent intentionality thesis, this means that the desired object is literally contained within the psychological experience of desire. Brentano holds that this is uniquely true of mental as opposed to physical or nonpsychological phenomena, so that the intentionality of the psychological distinguishes mental from physical states. The immanent intentionality thesis provides a framework in which Brentano identifies three categories of psychological phenomena: presentations (*Vorstellungen*), judgments (*Urteilen*), and emotions (*Gefühle*).

In the period from 1905 through 1911, with the publication in the latter year of *Von der Klassifikation der psychischen Phänomene* (On the classification of psychical phenomena), Brentano abandoned the immanent intentionality thesis according to which intended objects are contained within the thoughts that intend them in favor of his later philosophy of reism, according to which only individuals exist, excluding putative nonexistent *irrealia*, such as lacks, absences, and mere possibilities. In the meantime, his students Twardowski, Meinong, and Husserl, reacting negatively to the psychologism and related philosophical problems apparent in the early immanent intentionality thesis, developed alternative nonimmanence approaches to intentionality, leading in the case of Twardowski and Meinong and his students in the Graz school of phenomenological psychology to the construction of a theory of (transcendent existent and nonexistent intended) objects, and to Husserl's transcendental phenomenology. The intentionality of the mental in Brentano's revival of this medieval Aristotelian doctrine is one of his most important contributions to contemporary nonmechanistic theories of mind, meaning, and expression. Brentano's doctrine of immanent intentionality was rejected by philosophers who otherwise agreed with his underlying claim that thought is essentially object-directed, and who used Brentano's thesis as a springboard to further philosophical investigations that have influenced the subsequent history of Continental and intentionalist analytic philosophy. Through his impact on Freud, Brentano additionally exerted a profound effect on psychology, psychoanalytic theory and practice, and consequently on the scientific, literary, and artistic traditions that followed in its wake. Through the more widely read works of Husserl and above all Freud, Brentano indirectly influenced the course of modernist literature, exemplified among many others by the writings of Henry James, Virginia Woolf, James Joyce, Franz Kafka, Gertrude Stein, Robert Musil, and John Dos Passos. Brentano continues in this sense to contribute to the uniquely introspective outlook that has shaped all of contemporary culture.

See also **Freud, Sigmund; Husserl, Edmund; Modernism; Vienna.**

BIBLIOGRAPHY

Primary Sources

Brentano, Franz. *On the Several Senses of Being in Aristotle.* Edited and translated by Rolf George. Berkeley, Calif., 1975. Translation of *Von der mannifgachen Bedeutung des Seienden nach Aristoteles* (1862).

———. *Psychology from an Empirical Standpoint.* Translated by Antos C. Rancurello, D. B. Terrell, and Linda L. McAlister. Introduction by Peter Simons. 2nd ed. London, 1973. Translation of *Psychologie vom empirischen Standpunkt* (1874); 2nd ed. 1924.

Secondary Sources

Albertazzi, Lilian, Massimo Libardi, and Roberto Poli, eds. *The School of Franz Brentano.* Dordrecht, Boston, and London, 1996. Essays on Brentano's work and that of his students influenced by his contributions to philosophy and psychology.

Chisholm, Roderick M. *Brentano and Meinong Studies.* Atlantic Highlands, N.J., 1982. Anthology of papers on Brentano's epistemology and value theory and of Brentano's student Alexius Meinong from one of the premier Brentano scholars of the twentieth century.

Jacquette, Dale. "*Fin de Siècle* Austrian Thought and the Rise of Scientific Philosophy." *History of European Ideas* 27 (2001): 307–315. Exploration of Brentano's role in supplanting neo-post-Kantian transcendentalism by scientific Aristotelian empiricism in turn of the twentieth century Austrian philosophy.

———. "Brentano's Scientific Revolution in Philosophy." *Southern Journal of Philosophy*, Spindel Conference Supplement, 40 (2002): 193–221. Spindel Conference 2001, *Origins: The Common Sources of Analytic and Phenomenological Traditions*. Critical evaluation of Brentano's descriptive psychology and the methodological problems encountered by his efforts to ground a new science of phenomenology in first-person inner perception.

Jacquette, Dale, ed. *The Cambridge Companion to Brentano*. Cambridge, U.K., and New York, 2004. Historical and philosophical essays on Brentano's philosophy, with special emphasis on his intentionality thesis, descriptive psychology, metaphysics, theory of knowledge, value theory, and philosophical theology.

Johnston, William M. *The Austrian Mind: An Intellectual and Social History, 1848–1938*. Berkeley, Calif., 1972. Insightful introduction to the scientific and philosophical background of intellectual traditions associated with the Austrian Habsburg empire.

McAlister, Linda L., ed. *The Philosophy of Brentano*. London, 1976. Collection of recollections, biographical sketches and critical essays on Brentano's philosophy from his students, contemporaries, and later thinkers.

Poli, Roberto, ed. *The Brentano Puzzle*. Aldershot, U.K., and Brookfield, Vt., 1998. Conference proceedings on Brentano's philosophy; the "puzzle" refers to Brentano's importance to subsequent philosophy and at the same time his near invisibility when compared with other more frequently discussed philosophers of the period.

Smith, Barry. *Austrian Philosophy: The Legacy of Franz Brentano*. Chicago, 1994. Detailed discussion of Brentano's intentionality thesis and metaphysics, with separate chapters on principal members of the Brentano school.

Srzednicki, Jan. *Franz Brentano's Analysis of Truth*. The Hague, 1965. Detailed analysis of Brentano's concept of truth in the context of his empiricist psychology and epistemology.

DALE JACQUETTE

BRONTË, CHARLOTTE AND EMILY.

Few literary biographies have inspired as much interest and myth as those of poet-novelists Charlotte (1816–1855) and Emily Jane Brontë (1818–1848). This fascination is provoked both by the genuine peculiarity of their background and the strong influence of the feelings and scenes of that background upon their writing.

Their father, Patrick Brunty, the child of Irish laborers, gained admission to Cambridge University, changed his name to "Brontë," was ordained and, in 1820, became perpetual curate of Haworth in the West Riding of Yorkshire. In spite of his name-change, Patrick was never thoroughly at home in middle-class society, and he himself linked the idiosyncrasy of his daughters' literary productions with his own social marginality. His Cornish wife, Maria Brontë, died in 1821, leaving five daughters and a son.

In 1824 the girls were sent to a subsidized school for the daughters of impoverished clergymen at Cowan Bridge, near Gretta Bridge, the setting for the hellish Dotheboys Hall of Charles Dickens's *Nicholas Nickleby* (1838–1839). Although, according to Juliet Barker, there is little hard evidence to substantiate the fact, Charlotte's fictionalization of the school as the Lowood of *Jane Eyre* (1847) suggests that it shared the poor living conditions of the notorious "Yorkshire schools" that so incensed Dickens. Charlotte attributed the deaths in 1825 of her elder sisters Maria and Elizabeth to their stay there.

For a period after this scarring experience the children were all educated at home, where they collectively constructed the imaginary worlds of Angria and Gondal, the setting for their highly colored juvenilia, and a source of ongoing fascination into their adult lives. Their writing, from the beginning, was fueled by a passionate reading of Romantic poetry, as well as of Shakespeare, Milton, the Arabian Nights, and other works of fantasy, but they were also deeply immersed in the more worldly literary atmosphere of the periodicals, in particular *Blackwood's Magazine*. They shared with their father a keen interest in politics, and a preoccupation with those two political giants of the early nineteenth century, Napoleon and the Duke of Wellington, whose attributes seem recognizable in the powerful and violent heroes of the sisters' fiction.

From 1831 to 1832 Charlotte was at school at Roe Head. A classmate recalled her eccentric appearance and strong Irish accent. She made two very different friends, who brought out a tension in her personality, later very prominent in her fiction. Mary Taylor, from a family immersed in radical politics, shared Charlotte's intellectual and

Charlotte Brontë. ©CORBIS

rebellious proclivities. Ellen Nussey was pious and conventional. After a period in her early twenties back at Roe Head as a teacher, Charlotte became a governess.

Emily spent a few very brief periods away at school and as a governess, but she found herself overwhelmed by an acute physical homesickness whenever removed from the moorlands of home. Both sisters spent a period in Brussels studying languages under M. Heger, with whom Charlotte fell unrequitedly in love. Her experiences there are reworked in *Villette* (1853).

Finding teaching unbearable, the sisters struggled instead toward authorship. In 1846 they published, with their sister Anne, a volume of poetry, *Poems by Currer, Ellis and Acton Bell* (pseudonyms of Charlotte, Emily, and Anne, respectively), which received little critical regard. Emily is now regarded as the strongest poet of the three. Such is the originality and raw feeling of her apparently simple lyrics that they are sufficient on their own to guarantee her literary reputation.

The Brontës are best known, however, for the fiction they wrote in 1847. *Jane Eyre* was published in that year and, despite a number of hostile reviews targeting its unseemly realism, "hunger, rebellion and rage" (to quote Matthew Arnold's review) proved very popular. Like all Charlotte's fiction, it is in some respects a defiantly "realist" novel. Its plain governess heroine advances through experiences of cruelty and poverty, registered in scenes drawn from life and meticulously described, to the attainment, finally, of a prosaic domestic contentment. On the other hand, the novel has strong gothic elements, and its heightened emotionalism and Byronic hero, Rochester, strongly recall the spirit of the Romantic movement in its more fantastic aspect. Charlotte was much more deeply immersed in the poetry of her century than in its fiction—she had never read Jane Austen, for instance, until recommended to do so by G. H. Lewes after the publication of *Jane Eyre,* and even then was distinctly unimpressed.

Charlotte Brontë completed only three other novels: *The Professor* (1857), *Shirley* (1849), and *Villette.* All manifest a tension between, on the one hand, a vivid engagement with matters that *Shirley,* a novel which explores social issues such as the Luddite riots and the Woman Question, dubs "as unromantic as Monday morning" and, on the other, a use of supernatural motifs, heightened allegorical imagery, and a psychological and emotional intensity recalling gothic and religious writing, that together seem the very antithesis of realism.

Emily's *Wuthering Heights,* published in 1848, makes use of a number of partially reliable narrators, a convoluted time-scheme, and a bleak though vital and vividly realized moorland setting. It portrays a shockingly violent and amoral universe on which no final judgment is ever passed, and in which the destructive forces of nature and civilization come into irreconcilable conflict. An exceptionally poised and sophisticated novel, pervaded by a biting, worldly irony, it places in mutually complicating juxtaposition the Wordsworthian view of a benevolent Nature, the cult of the Byronic hero, and the conventions of domestic realist fiction. The result is explosive.

Charlotte alone of the sisters, however, experienced literary celebrity during her lifetime. She met many of the most prominent literary figures of the time in London, but her enjoyment of fame was prevented by the illness and deaths, in 1848 and 1849, of her brother Branwell and of her sisters Emily and Anne.

Right up to the time of her early death, Emily had no close friends, and very little is known about her inward life beyond the little that can be inferred from *Wuthering Heights*, that most enigmatic of novels. More light is thrown on Charlotte by a biography (1857) by Elizabeth Gaskell, who became a friend in her later years. In 1854, after much hesitation, Charlotte married her father's curate, A. B. Nichols, but died a few months later, probably from complications relating to pregnancy.

It is not particularly easy to place the Brontës' fiction within a wider literary tradition, though post-1970s criticism has tried to resist F. R. Leavis's resigned identification of *Wuthering Heights* as a freakish, if awe-inspiring, literary sport. Terry Eagleton made one of the first and most influential critical efforts to resist this dehistoricizing, reading the Brontë novels as expressions of a wider Victorian ideological conflict over the establishment of bourgeois ideological hegemony, but his reading has difficulty accommodating the genuine idiosyncrasy of the sisters' background and output. Andrea Henderson's reading of Emily as a female Romantic is rather more successful—the novels of both sisters do feel more akin to the poetry of the previous generation than to the fiction of their own. Heather Glen's study of Charlotte's fiction combines a thoughtful placing of it in relation to the society in which it was produced, with an acknowledgement of the "singularity" that has continued to strike readers of the Brontës for a century and a half.

See also **Austen, Jane; Dickens, Charles; Gaskell, Elizabeth; Romanticism.**

BIBLIOGRAPHY

Allott, Miriam, ed. *The Brontës: The Critical Heritage*. London and Boston, 1974. Reprint, 1997.

Barker, Juliet. *The Brontës*. London, 1994.

Barker, Juliet, ed. *The Brontës: A Life in Letters*. London, 1997.

Eagleton, Terry. *Myths of Power: A Marxist Study of the Brontës*. London, 1975. Reprint. New York, 2005.

Gaskell, Elizabeth. *The Life of Charlotte Brontë* (1857). Harmondsworth, U.K., 1975.

Glen, Heather. *Charlotte Brontë: The Imagination in History* Oxford, U.K., and New York, 2002.

Henderson, Andrea K. *Romantic Identities: Varieties of Subjectivity, 1774–1830*. Cambridge, U.K., and New York: Cambridge University Press, 1996.

Leavis, F. R. *The Great Tradition: George Eliot, Henry James, Joseph Conrad* (1948). London, 1993.

BRIGID LOWE

BROUGHAM, HENRY (1st Baron Brougham and Vaux; 1778–1868), British politician and reformer.

Born in Edinburgh on 19 September 1778, and educated at the University of Edinburgh, Henry Brougham displayed a remarkable talent for learning in a city steeped in the cosmopolitanism of the Scottish Enlightenment. Yet his ambition required a wider scope. He made his way to London, where he began a long career as a Whig politician and reformer. Trained as a lawyer and called to both the Scottish and English bars, Brougham made a name, as well as a substantial income, in this profession. The legal victory for which he acquired the most recognition was his 1820 defense of Queen Caroline in the House of Lords. Brougham had served as her legal advisor since 1812 and became her attorney general when George IV (r. 1820–1830) insisted on a divorce soon after inheriting the throne. After Brougham delivered a speech that lasted for two days, the bill to dissolve the royal marriage passed the Lords with only a handful of votes, which convinced the government to drop the matter and avoid what promised to be a crushing defeat in the Commons. As the public demonstrations celebrating the queen's victory demonstrated, popular opinion was firmly with the queen, and thus also with Brougham.

Commentators at the time recognized that Brougham's rhetorical skills far surpassed his understanding of complex legal issues. His particular talents were perfectly suited for politics. He began his political career in journalism, when in 1802 he helped Sydney Smith, Francis Horner, and Francis Jeffrey establish *The Edinburgh Review*, a quarterly periodical with a strong Whig bias that soon became a leading platform for political debate. Brougham frequently contributed articles, which in the first eight years of the *Review*'s run numbered over one hundred. Brougham entered Parliament for the first time in 1810 as MP for Camelford. Though he lost and regained seats in Parliament over the years, he nevertheless managed to attain high political office by serving as lord chancellor from 1830 to 1834 in the administrations of the prime ministers Charles Grey (1830–1834) and Lord Melbourne (William Lamb; 1834).

Brougham was routinely associated with the radical wing of the Whig Party, since his positions reflected those of many nineteenth-century reform movements. He was an early supporter of the abolitionists and promoted their efforts to end the slave trade with two pamphlets, *An Inquiry into the Colonial Policy of European Powers* (1803) and *A Concise Statement of the Question Regarding the Abolition of the Slave Trade* (c. 1804). In 1812 he received much applause for leading a successful parliamentary fight against the Orders in Council (1807), which many merchants condemned for the blockade it established in response to Napoleon's attempt, through the continental system to close all European ports to ships from Britain and its colonies. Brougham encouraged one of the most significant political shifts of the century by making parliamentary reform a main tenet of his election campaign in Yorkshire in 1830 and then by helping to secure passage of the 1832 Reform Act in the House of Lords. His interest in educational policy took him in several directions. First, in 1820 he proposed a bill promoting publicly funded education; the bill failed, but Brougham remained committed to the cause. Second, in 1826 he founded the Society for the Diffusion of Useful Knowledge, which published cheaply priced works aimed at the working classes. And third, he was among the active supporters of England's first nonsectarian university, the University of London (later renamed University College), which opened in 1828.

Brougham became Parliament's most consistent champion of law reform, in part because in 1828 he delivered a brilliant six-hour speech that turned law reform into a popular cause. His position as lord chancellor also enabled him to follow through on important initiatives. He established the judicial committee of the Privy Council, a central criminal court, and bankruptcy courts, and he also laid the foundation for a county court system. Brougham made the Court of Chancery, a court of equity where rulings could conflict with the common law, another target of reform by eliminating abuses and reducing its backlog. He continued to push for legal reform when his term as lord chancellor ended by supporting, for example, the 1857 Matrimonial Causes Act, which permitted divorce cases in the courts and granted women certain property rights.

Brougham had an interest in science as well as politics. He was a fellow of the Royal Society and was credited with designing the brougham, a four-wheeled carriage. He died and was buried at Cannes, where his frequent residence during the last three decades of his life helped make the French Mediterreanean town a destination for British tourists.

See also **George IV; Whigs.**

BIBLIOGRAPHY

Huch, Ronald K. *Henry, Lord Brougham: The Later Years, 1830–1868.* Lewiston, N.Y., 1993.

Lobban, Michael. "Henry Brougham and Law Reform." *English Historical Review* 115 (2000): 1184–1215. Also authored an extensive article in the *Oxford Dictionary of National Biography*, Oxford, U.K., 2004.

Stewart, Robert. *Henry Brougham, 1778–1868: His Public Career.* London, 1986.

ELISA R. MILKES

BRUNEL, ISAMBARD KINGDOM
(1806–1859), English engineer.

Isambard Kingdom Brunel has come to be regarded as one of the heroic engineers of the British Industrial Revolution, a reputation that stems from his visionary roles in building the Great Western Railway (GWR) and constructing large steamships. He was the only son of Sir Marc Isambard Brunel (1769–1849), a civil engineer. From an early age, Isambard Kingdom shared his father's professional interests, and these were fostered by parental guidance in draftsmanship and the proper application of tools. He received a formal education in first England and then France, when his French-born father enabled him to spend a period with Louis Breguet (1747–1823), one of the foremost clockmakers. Isambard Kingdom completed his introduction to engineering through assisting his father's project for a tunnel under the River Thames. Despite an innovative tunneling process involving a shield, the scheme was ill-fated, and Isambard Kingdom nearly lost his life when the workings were flooded on 12 January 1828. The tunnel finally opened to pedestrians in March 1843, and in 1869 a railway was laid within it—to ultimately form a north–south link in London's underground system.

Following the Thames tunnel's collapse in 1828, Isambard Kingdom convalesced at Bristol, circumstances that led to his design for the Clifton suspension bridge. His second essay was accepted but Isambard Kingdom never saw his bridge. The erection of its two towers exhausted construction funds, and the elegant bridge was only completed in 1864, undertaken by the Institution of Civil Engineers as a memorial to him. The connections that Isambard Kingdom developed within Bristol business circles also resulted in his acting as a consultant for improvement of the city's docks and being appointed in March 1833 the engineer to the GWR. Over the next fifteen years, he designed a complete railway, including locomotives, for a line initially between London and Bristol (fully opened in 1841), but which was ultimately extended to Penzance in the southwest, to Milford Haven in southwest Wales, to Birmingham in the midlands, and to Birkenhead in the northwest.

Isambard Kingdom took a unique approach to railway building, eschewing methods that stemmed from early northeastern colliery lines and were pursued by his rivals George Stephenson (1781–1848) and Robert Stephenson (1803–1859). He introduced broad gauge—seven feet between the rails—and laid the track on longitudinal sleepers to provide a stable permanent way on which trains could be run safely at speed. This objective was also obtained by detailed surveying that resulted in a very carefully graded routeway. Care with establishing the line went along with fine designs for its bridges, tunnels, and viaducts. However, not all of his innovations were successful, as with the South Devon

Isambard Kingdom Brunel posing before the launching chains of the *Great Eastern*, 1858. Victoria & Albert Museum, London/Art Resource, NY

"atmospheric" (pneumatic) railway, and broad gauge soon lost its competitive advantage, forcing the GWR to abandon it, first for its extensions to the midlands and the northwest and, ultimately, for its initial lines in southern England and Wales. Furthermore, although he was an outstanding civil engineer, Isambard Kingdom's locomotives performed poorly and GWR's timetable performance only came about following the introduction of haulage designed by Daniel Gooch (1816–1889).

As the GWR was being conceived, Bristol was being rapidly overtaken in the Atlantic trades by Liverpool and Glasgow. This may have led to Isambard Kingdom suggesting in spring 1833 that the projected railway should go to New York, undertaken by an associated shipping company. As its engineer he designed the *Great Western*, a very large wooden paddle steamer of 2,300 tons, which gave it the capacity to carry its fuel. Although the Cunard line operating from Liverpool won the North Atlantic mail contract, Isambard Kingdom designed a further vessel, *Great Britain,* which was even larger, over 3000 tons. The *Great Britain,* which was constructed of iron, was screw-propelled. Too big to use Bristol as a homeport, the *Great Britain* sailed principally from Liverpool until its stranding in 1846 forced the liquidation of the GWR's associated steamship enterprise.

Isambard Kingdom undertook his design work from a London office, and it included docks at Sunderland and an Italian railway. The growth of trade with the Orient led him to design and financially sponsor an enormous iron steamship, *Great Eastern,* of 32,000 tons, propelled by paddles and a screw. For its construction he formed a partnership with John Scott Russell (1808–1882), who had a yard on the Thames at the Isle of Dogs. The project was marked by quarrels between its engineer and its shipbuilder as well as technical difficulties. Isambard Kingdom was dying when the *Great Eastern* made its maiden voyage in September 1859, surviving just long enough to learn that it had suffered an explosion in the boiler room when in the English Channel. However, the strength of the ship's structure enabled the *Great Eastern* to continue to sail until 1888, although never at a profit. Its construction almost financially ruined Brunel, who died on 15 September 1859.

See also **Engineers; Railroads; Transportation and Communications.**

BIBLIOGRAPHY

Primary Sources

Brunel, Isambard. *The Life of Isambard Kingdom Brunel, Civil Engineer.* 1870. Introduction by L. T. C. Rolt. Newton Abbot, U.K., 1971.

Gibbs, George Henry. *The Birth of the Great Western Railway: Extracts from the Diary and Correspondence of George Henry Gibbs.* Edited by Jack Simmons. Bath, U.K., 1971.

Secondary Sources

Brunel Noble, Celia. *The Brunels, Father and Son.* London, 1938.

Buchanan, R. Angus. *Brunel: The Life and Times of Isambard Kingdom Brunel.* London, 2002.

Rolt, L. T. C. *Isambard Kingdom Brunel.* London, 1957.

PHILIP COTTRELL

BRUSSELS. Located at the crossroads of Europe and the center of Belgium, the Belgian capital of Brussels lies in a valley of the Senne River. The name probably derives from *Bruocsella,* or "village of the marsh." The village, documented as early as 966, prospered as a river crossing on the trade route between Cologne and Ghent. The town received its first charter in 1312. Walls surrounding Brussels were raised between 1357 and 1387 and strengthened in the sixteenth century. It was first designated as the government seat of the Netherlands in 1531 and has continued to serve as a capital to the present day. Article 126 of the Belgian Constitution of 1830 made Brussels the capital of Belgium and the seat of its government. The commercial, industrial, administrative, financial, and political institutions of Belgium were concentrated in Brussels.

Brussels has traditionally been known for the production of luxury goods. In the mid-nineteenth century, the majority of Brussels workers were employed in the production of clothing, leather, and paper; as printers; and in metal- and woodworking, and construction. Through the 1890s, Brussels remained the principal center of production in the country, employing 101,948 industrial workers out of a national total of 1,130,000. Linked by rail—the first continental railway ran from Brussels to Mechelen—as well as by canal to points throughout Belgium and Europe, Brussels served as an important commercial center for Belgium and Europe as a whole.

At the beginning of the nineteenth century, the city of Brussels occupied only 416 hectares. The central pentagon was separated from neighboring rural villages by walls and taxes. Napoleon I (r. 1804–1814/15) ordered the destruction of the ramparts surrounding Brussels, work that continued for two decades. A ring of boulevards, inaugurated in 1871, replaced the fortifications. That allowed development to spread outward, especially to the north with the creation of the Botanical Gardens and the extension of the Rue Royale and to the east through the gates of Louvain and Namur with the Quartier Léopold. The bourgeoisie and the aristocracy abandoned the flood-ridden lower plains of the city and moved to higher ground in the Upper Town and beyond the former walls in

La Grande Place, Brussels. Photograph c. 1890–1910. At left is the Maison du Roi, formerly a palace, restored in the neo-gothic style during the 1860s and used as a museum after 1887. At right is the Maison des Ducs de Brabant, which is actually a single façade covering six dwellings, designed by Palladio in 1698. THE LIBRARY OF CONGRESS

the Quartier Léopold. Brussels workers remained behind, occupying two- to four-roomed houses of one to two stories on dead-end alleyways or *impasses*. By 1878, the central pentagon was completely encircled by the suburbs (or faubourgs).

The city of Brussels experienced its most significant growth in the first half of the nineteenth century, with the population rising from 66,000 in 1801 to 150,244 in 1856. By the end of the century, residents began flowing outward to the suburbs. The population of the Brussels agglomeration increased from 288,400 residents in 1866 to 458,700 in 1890.

Jules Anspach, mayor of Brussels from 1863 to 1879, inspired by the Parisian schemes of the Baron Georges-Eugène Haussmann (1809–1891), canalized and built over the Senne and replaced the

warren of narrow streets in the Lower Town with wide, straight boulevards. The monumental Palace of Justice, designed by Joseph Poelaert (1816–1879), was built between 1866 and 1883 on a plateau overlooking the city, also requiring the clearance of extensive areas of worker housing. Charles Buls, who served as mayor from 1886 to 1889, championed municipal activism in urban planning. Linked to the question of public health was national pride—the capital symbolized the kingdom—and Belgian king Leopold II (r. 1865–1909) called upon the Brussels officials to "embellish the center of government to increase its air of elegance and pleasure." Planners drew up plans beginning in 1895, at the initiative of Leopold II, for the Mont des Arts that would be connected to a central railway station and join the upper and lower quarters of the city.

The nineteen Brussels communes, Anderlecht, Auderghem, Berchem-Ste-Agathe, Brussels Etterbeek, Evere, Forest, Ganshoren, Ixelles, Jette, Koekelberg, Molenbeek-St-Jean, Saint-Gilles, Saint-Josse-ten-Noode, Schaerbeek, Uccle, Watermael-Boitsfort, Woluwe-St-Lambert, and Woluwe St. Pierre, remained administratively separate throughout the nineteenth century. They issued their own proclamations regarding public works, police, building, and so on, and joined together only informally through sporadic meetings of the mayors at the City Hall in the center of Brussels. Unable to cooperate officially with the surrounding communes, Brussels pursued a deliberate policy of annexation, expanding its territorial limits ten times between 1851 and 1913.

The Communal Council of Brussels was directly elected every six years, meeting in the City Hall whenever required by communal business, usually every other Monday in the nineteenth century. The mayor, named by the king, presided over the Council. The Council elected nine *échevins* to manage finances, education, public works, and other business of the city. At the end of the eighteenth century, the upper bourgeoisie and the aristocracy with roles in the government tended to speak French, while the workers and the artisans spoke Flemish or Dutch. By the end of the Napoleonic regime, the civil service was completely French-speaking. The exclusive use of French in the institutions of independent Belgium precipitated a reaction, first among intellectuals and later politicians who claimed rights for Flemish speakers in the Belgian capital. Brussels was a bastion of the Liberal Party throughout the nineteenth century. Increasingly, the left wing of the Liberal Party in Brussels coalesced with moderate socialists in municipal and national politics; they were both vehemently anticlerical.

The architecture of Baron Victor Horta (1861–1947), employing glass and steel, made Brussels the center of art nouveau. Horta completed the Maison du Peuple, with its facade of metal and greenery, in 1899. The painter and sculptor Constantin Meunier (1831–1905), together with other avant-garde artists, founded the Société Libre des Beaux-Arts in Brussels in 1868. His visits to glassworks and mines in the Borinage in Southern Belgium in the 1870s inspired his heroic depictions of the working class. Baron James Sydney Ensor (1860–1949), who

Hotel Solvay, Brussels, 1903. Designed by the noted architect Victor Horta and built at the end of the nineteenth century, this town house is considered a landmark of art nouveau style. FOTO MARBURG/ART RESOURCE, NY

painted *The Entrance of Christ into Brussels,* was born in Ostend, but was tied to Brussels by his studies at the Academy of Fine Arts as well as his relations with Les XX, an association of artists that promoted individualism and freedom of artistic expression.

The Université Libre de Bruxelles was founded in 1834. The Royal Conservatory of Music was opened in Brussels in 1876; the violinist Eugène-Auguste Ysaye (1858–1931) was named a professor of music there in 1886.

See also **Amsterdam; Belgium; Cities and Towns.**

BIBLIOGRAPHY

Archives d'Architecture Moderne. *Art nouveau in Brussels.* Translated by Brigid Grauman. Brussels, 1988.

Goddard, Stephen H., ed. *Les XX and the Belgian Avant-garde.* Lawrence, Kan., 1992.

Henne, Alexandre. *Histoire de la ville de Bruxelles.* 3 vols. Brussels, 1845.

Smolar-Meynart, A., and J. Stengers, eds. *La région de Bruxelles: des villages d'autrefois à la ville d'aujourd'hui.* Brussels, 1989.

Stengers, J. ed. *Bruxelles: Croissance d'une capitale.* Antwerp, 1979.

JANET L. POLASKY

BRUSSELS DECLARATION. The abolition of the slave trade was one of the great diplomatic themes over which the Great Powers both cooperated and clashed in the nineteenth century. For over two centuries, Britain had been the main European nation engaged in slave trading, its monopoly to bring Africans as slaves to the Spanish territories in the New World having been confirmed as late as the Peace of Utrecht in 1713. Between 1680 and 1780 over 2.1 million Africans were brought into slavery in the British Antilles alone. By the late eighteenth century, however, the abolition movement was well under way, especially in Britain. Its ideological background lay in part in humanitarian philosophy, as reflected in the liberal individualism of the French Revolution, in part in English Puritanism, especially the Quaker movement. The importation of slaves to its colonies was first prohibited by Denmark in 1792. Britain followed in 1807 and the U.S. Congress outlawed the slave trade one year later. The question was included at British Foreign Secretary Castlereagh's initiative on the agenda of the 1815 Vienna Conference. A declaration was passed in which the Great Powers proclaimed slave trade as "repugnant to the principles of humanity and of universal morality" and recognized "the obligation and necessity of abolishing it."

Nevertheless, while most European states enacted domestic legislation to prohibit and punish slave trade, no agreement was attained on concerted international action. Nor did Britain's efforts to agree on a universal system at London (1817–1818), Aix-la-Chapelle (1818), or Verona (1822) bear fruit. The declaration of principles was repeated without agreement on how to apply it in practice. Britain suggested the assimilation of slave trade with piracy with the attendant right of visit on foreign warships on vessels suspected of engaging in illegal trade. This was vigorously opposed by other powers, especially by France and the United States who saw the proposal as an illegitimate attempt to designate the British navy as the police of the seas.

In the absence of a general settlement, Britain concluded bilateral treaties providing for reciprocal rights of visit in strictly defined geographical locations and with regard to particular types of ships. Only military ships could carry out the visit, whose purpose was strictly confined to checking whether the suspected vessel was carrying slaves. A general convention associating slave trade with piracy was finally signed between Britain, France, Prussia, Austria, and Russia in 1841, again with both limitations as to location and manner of carrying out the visits. However, France refused to ratify the convention and concluded a bilateral treaty in 1845 that provided, instead of a right of visit, the right to verify the flag of suspected ships, with the assumption that any enforcement would be taken by the flag state. Also the United States remained initially outside the general convention that it saw as serving predominantly British interests. The need to take more efficient measures, however, induced the United States to sign a treaty on reciprocal visits with Britain in 1861.

The virtual cessation of slave trade on Africa's western coast prompted Britain to conclude treaties also with Egypt, Turkey, and Italy in the 1870s and 1880s in order to implement the prohibition of trading in the Indian Ocean. A provision (Article IX) was also included in the Berlin Act of 1885 in which the Great Powers declared that their territories in the Congo basin would not be used "as market or means of transit for the trade in slaves."

At the initiative of the Pope and of Lord Salisbury, King Leopold II of the Belgians invited the signatories of the Berlin Act, as well as Luxembourg, Persia, and Zanzibar, to a conference in Brussels to take further measures against slavery and slave trade not only at sea—after all, slaving dhows could easily escape formal navies—but at the source in Africa. Despite the shared humanitarian hyperbole, the Brussels Conference dragged on from November 1889 until a deal was struck early the following summer that authorized King Leopold to deviate from the free trade provisions of the 1885 Berlin Act ostensibly to finance the antislavery measures in his Independent State of the Congo.

The General Act of the Brussels Conference Relative to the African Slave Trade was adopted on 2 July 1890. It provided for far-reaching economic, military, and legal measures, in over one hundred articles, to combat slave trade. Measures to be taken in Africa included the strengthening of the local administrations, establishment of observation posts, construction of roads and railways, and communication mechanisms to substitute for the practice of human porters that had contributed to slavery. Such "good government" measures also included increased security on the roads and the prohibition of the importation of firearms and munitions into territories where slave trading was practiced. An international office was set up in Zanzibar to give instructions and assistance on the repression of the slave trade in countries of destination; national laws and regulations were to be communicated to the office which would then circulate that information to other powers.

On the right of visit, the conference agreed on a compromise that restricted this right to the verification of the flag of the suspected vessel. Detailed instructions were provided concerning the ship's papers and the use of the flag. Only vessels with a tonnage below five hundred tons could be inspected (most slave trading in the Indian Ocean took place by small vessels to enable unmarked landings). Enforcement jurisdiction would as the main rule remain with the flag state. However, the capturing vessel was authorized to bring suspected ships to the closest harbor and follow through the enquiry conducted by the flag state's national officials. A vessel condemned of illegal traffic would become the property of the captor. Liberated slaves were to be accorded protection by national authorities.

Most states ratified the act within one year. As the French National Assembly continued to object, the government nevertheless remained bound by its earlier bilateral agreements.

The Brussels Act was abrogated by the Peace of Saint-Germain-en-Laye in 1919. In the twenty-first century, the prohibition of slavery and the slave trade are contained in the 1926 Slavery Convention and the Supplementary Convention of 1956. Analogous practices such as traffic in persons, prostitution, and debt bondage—more important in the early twenty-first century than chattel-like slavery—are the object of increasing regulation by the United Nations and international organizations.

See also **Africa; Colonialism; Imperialism; International Law; Leopold II; Slavery.**

BIBLIOGRAPHY

Fischer, G. "Esclavage et le droit international." *Revue générale de droit international public* 61 (1957): 71–101.

Fisher, H. "The Suppression of the Slave Trade." *International Law Quarterly* 1 (1950): 28–51, 503–522.

Kern, Holger Lutz. "Strategies of Legal Change: Great Britain, International Law and the Abolition of the Transatlantic Slave Trade." *Journal of the History of International Law* 6 (2004): 233–258.

Thomas, Hugh. *The Slave Trade. The Story of the Atlantic Slave Trade, 1440–1870.* New York, 1997.

MARTTI KOSKENNIEMI

BUDAPEST. Budapest, the capital of Hungary, was also one of the two capitals, along with Vienna, of the Dual Monarchy after the 1867 Ausgleich (compromise). Its current name is the outcome of the 1873 administrative unification of three adjacent towns on the Danube River: Buda and Pest, and the smaller Óbuda (Old Buda). This act was the culmination of a steady urban development that took off in the eighteenth century. Budapest, however, came into its own in the long nineteenth century—a period of almost uninterrupted expansion. At the beginning of the nineteenth century the combined populations of Pest, Buda, and Old Buda was smaller than that of Vienna, but by the early 1870s Pest was the second-largest city in the Monarchy—and the sixteenth-largest in Europe—and by 1910 Budapest ranked eighth among European cities. By the closing of the nineteenth century Budapest was a formidable metropolis and a real capital city. But it had to be made into one; earlier Hungary had had no real capital.

THE SHARED CAPITAL

In 1784 Joseph II made Buda the political and administrative center of the country, and the university was moved to Pest. The twin cites divided the tasks of a capital: Buda was the administrative center of Hungary, Pest the economic and cultural center. Although the diet met in Pozsony (Bratislava) until 1848 and the palatine's seat remained in Buda, the center of politics shifted gradually to Pest during the "reform era" (1825–1848)—a move that culminated in the 1848 revolution, the first urban revolution to start and spread from the cafés and streets of the city. By the first half of the nineteenth century Pest was a significant regional commercial hub, trading mostly in agricultural produce and livestock. The economic center of the city shifted from the walled historical downtown to the north, followed by an eastward expansion to the suburbs. Accelerated by the 1838 flood and the ensuing building regulations, multistoried Pest sprang up in the form of neoclassical palaces, apartment buildings, and new genres of notable public buildings, such as the National Museum, the Redoute, the Board of Trade, and the German, later the Hungarian, Theater of Pest. The long-debated proposal for a permanent bridge between Buda and Pest was implemented in this period, reinforcing the ideal of physical, administrative, and—by levying a universal toll regardless of social class—social unification of the twin cities. The bridge was inaugurated only in 1849, following the revolution. The years of political oppression did not put the growth of the twin cities back; in fact, an economic boom preceded unification. Commercial capital started to move into the food processing and manufacturing industry, and by the end of the century commerce lost its dominance to industry and finance. Pest became a mill town on a world scale with significant sugar and machinery production and distilleries. Neoabsolutism did not add much to the cityscape other than reconstructing the royal palace and erecting the Citadel—the Hungarian Bastille—a jerry-built symbol of oppression whose arms were aimed at rebellious Pest.

THE NATIONAL CAPITAL

The metropolitan outlook of the city is the result of the construction boom that picked up after the Ausgleich of 1867 and, following the London example, the establishment in 1870 of the Metropolitan Council of Public Works, which imposed comprehensive planning principles and building codes on the twin cities even before they became unified in 1873. The almost complete home rule that the compromise granted to Hungary and the territorial enlargement that followed from unification threw Budapest into a frenzy of "catching up." The task of constructing both a European metropolis and a national capital gave rise to the most spectacular growth in the history of the city, and, except for Berlin, the fastest in Europe. The population of Budapest rose from 270,000 in 1869 to 880,000 in 1910, or, including the suburbs, to 1.1 million. The twin processes of industrialization and urbanization transformed the social landscape accordingly. The proportion of agricultural laborers declined, and by the end of the nineteenth century the majority of the population consisted of proletarians, with the two most dynamically growing groups being industrial workers and maids. The continued mass influx of labor from the countryside to the capital shifted the ethnic composition of the city in favor of the Hungarian-speaking population, which, combined with the invigoration of assimilation, made multiethnic Budapest a Hungarian city. The 1880 linguistic census recorded 55 percent of the total population as native Hungarian speakers, one-third German, and 6 percent Slovak—a marked difference from the previous German dominance, especially in Buda. From the 1860s onward Hungarian was the exclusive language of public education.

Between 1873 and 1896 the number of buildings almost doubled under the guidance of the Metropolitan Council of Public Works. The infrastructure of a modern metropolis was established. The achievements of the period were duly acknowledged and displayed during the Millennium Exhibition in 1896—a Universal Exposition of sorts with an acute historical consciousness—commemorating a thousand years of settled Hungarian history. The city commissioned a new town hall (completed in 1875), a customs house (1874), and a municipal slaughterhouse (1872), constructed a new water plant, opened the Central Market Hall (1897), engaged in large-scale hospital building from the 1880s, and organized the public health system. The number of students enrolled in primary and secondary schools rose by 110 percent in the period. With the construction of the Parliament (completed in 1904) and the neighboring ministries, a central government district emerged on the Pest side as a counterpoint to the Royal Palace in

Parliament building, Budapest. Designed by architect Imre Steindl in the neo-gothic style and constructed between 1884 and 1902, the immense building intended to house the legislature of the Transleithania states of the Austro-Hungarian empire provided a compelling vision of state power. ©ADAM WOOLFITT/CORBIS

Buda. The first grand achievement of coordinated town planning was the Avenue (later Andrássy Avenue)—the Champs-Elysées of Budapest—a major thoroughfare and symbol of embourgeoisement lined with elegant apartment buildings, villas, historical monuments, and representative public buildings including the Opera House (1884) and several art museums. The construction of a second bridge (1876), Western Station (1877), and Central Station (1884); the rationalization of traffic by the cutting of the Grand Boulevard; and the electrification of mass transit and the opening of the Millennium underground—the first on the Continent—led to a new integration and compression of urban space.

The Millennium closed the first and most impressive—and also the least controversial—period of development in the history of Budapest. Following the turn of the century economic and population growth began to lose momentum, and a still vigorous but more controversial development was rife with social and political tension. The municipal authorities pursued an active policy in order to alleviate the problems that followed from population growth and the lack of adequate infrastructure. This was a period of a dynamic expansion and differentiation of municipal services, the municipalization of public utility companies, and the institutionalization of social policy, which ultimately made an increase in urban consumption possible. It was in the early twentieth century that the city saw the first mass mobilization of industrial workers who by then not only outnumbered any other social group but also showed a strong territorial concentration. By the eve of World War I, politics and culture had become radicalized, social criticism had taken a new turn, and political change loomed large—but the explosion came only after the war.

See also **Austria-Hungary; Cities and Towns; Vienna.**

BIBLIOGRAPHY

Bender, Thomas, and Carl E. Schorske, eds. *Budapest and New York: Studies in Metropolitan Transformation, 1870–1930.* New York, 1994.

Frojimovics, Kinga, Géza Komoróczy, Viktória Pusztai, and Andrea Strbik. *Jewish Budapest: Monuments, Rites, History.* Edited by Géza Komoróczy. Translated by Vera Szabó. Budapest and New York, 1999.

Gerő, András, and János Poór, eds. *Budapest: A History from Its Beginnings to 1998.* Translated by Judit Zinner, Cecil D. Eby, and Nóra Arató. Boulder, Colo., 1997.

Gyáni, Gábor. *Identity and Urban Experience: Fin-de-Siècle Budapest.* Translated by Thomas J. DeKornfeld. Boulder, Colo., and Wayne, N.J., 2004.

Hanák, Péter. *The Garden and the Workshop: Essays on the Cultural History of Vienna and Budapest.* Princeton, N.J., 1998.

Lukacs, John. *Budapest 1900: A Historical Portrait of a City and Its Culture.* New York, 1988.

Melinz, Gerhard, and Susan Zimmermann, eds. *Wien, Prag, Budapest: Blütezeit der Habsburgermetropolen; Urbanisierung, Kommunalpolitik, gesellshaftliche Konflikte, 1867–1918.* Vienna, 1996.

JUDIT BODNAR

BULGARIA. The so-called national awakening of Bulgaria is often traced to the appearance in 1762 of *Slavic-Bulgarian History* (1762), written by Father Paisii Hilendarski (1722–c. 1773). Bulgarian cultural nationalism focusing on language and ecclesiastical issues developed throughout the nineteenth century. Bulgarians, however, lagged behind other Balkan peoples, such as the Serbs and Romanians, in the application of a political context to national self-awareness. Only in the second half of the nineteenth century did Bulgarians begin to develop active opposition to Ottoman rule. This culminated in the April Uprising of 1876. Russian sympathies for the Bulgarian cause, inflamed by reports of Ottoman massacres of Bulgarian civilians, led to the Russo-Turkish War of 1877–1878.

The Treaty of San Stefano, signed on 3 March (19 February, old style) 1878 outside of Constantinople after a series of Russian victories, ended the Russo-Turkish War. It also restored a Bulgarian state, after a period of almost five hundred years of Ottoman Turkish domination. Bulgaria's new borders included Bulgaria proper, Macedonia, and Thrace, and satisfied the demands of most Bulgarian nationalists. Austro-Hungarian and British objections to the establishment of a Russian client so close to Constantinople and the Straits forced a revision of the treaty. The Congress of Berlin, meeting at the behest of German Chancellor Otto von Bismarck, considerably revised the parameters of Bulgaria. As a result of the Treaty of Berlin, signed on 13 July (1 July, old style) 1878, the Great Powers divided San Stefano Bulgaria into three parts, a Bulgarian principality under the nominal sovereignty of the Ottoman sultan; a southern Bulgarian province, Eastern Rumelia, under a Christian governor but remaining under Ottoman rule; and Macedonia and Thrace, which returned to direct Ottoman control. Subsequently the Bulgarian government directed much of its energy during the period of 1878 to 1914 to the establishment of a Bulgaria with at least the San Stefano frontiers.

A Grand National Assembly met in the medieval capital of Turnovo in 1879 to determine the political basis for Bulgaria. The assembly adopted the so-called Turnovo Constitution, which established Bulgaria as a constitutional monarchy with a unicameral assembly. The assembly also elected Prince Alexander of Battenberg (1857–1893) as the first prince of Bulgaria. Alexander, a German prince related to the Russian royal family, was a veteran of the Russo-Turkish War. He soon chaffed under the limitations of the Turnovo Constitution, and at the same time alienated his Russian cousin, Tsar Alexander III, by his disinclination to follow Russian directives. Prince Alexander attempted to improve his position by supporting the union of Eastern Rumelia with Bulgaria in 1885 and leading the Bulgarian army in the subsequent Serbo-Bulgarian War (1885–1886). An enlarged Bulgarian principality emerged victorious in the war, but Prince Alexander's position was no longer viable because of Russian opposition. Under pressure, he abdicated his throne and left Bulgaria in 1886.

A leading politician, Stefan Stambolov (1854–1895), engineered the election of the Austro-German Prince Ferdinand of Saxe-Coburg-Gotha (1861–1948) as Bulgaria's next prince in 1887. Ferdinand

and Stambolov soon clashed over authority issues. In 1894 Stambolov resigned as prime minister, and the next year he fell victim to assassins. Ferdinand then restored good relations with Russia, in part through the baptism into the Bulgarian Orthodox Church of his son and heir, Boris (1894–1943).

Land reform after the emigration of most Ottoman landlords after 1878 left Bulgaria a largely egalitarian peasant society. Few large landholdings existed. Major crops included wheat, tobacco, and fruit. What little industry existed involved agricultural product processing. Trade was largely with western Europe and with the traditional markets of the Ottoman Empire. After the end of Ottoman rule, the country made significant strides in education. By 1900, 36 percent of Bulgarian males and 11 percent of Bulgarian females were literate. These percentages were the highest in southeastern Europe. Even after 1878 Bulgaria retained a significant Turkish minority, especially in the southern and northeastern parts of the country. Jewish, Armenian, Greek, and Roma minorities also resided in Bulgaria.

The chief foreign policy objective of Bulgaria remained unification with Macedonia and Thrace. To this end the Bulgarian state devoted much of its energies and revenues toward establishing a capable diplomacy and a strong army. The diplomatic turmoil caused by the Young Turk coup of 1908 afforded Prince Ferdinand an opportunity to abandon all ties to the Ottoman Empire, and to adopt the title *tsar*, held by Bulgaria's medieval rulers. The threat of the revitalization of the Ottoman Empire posed by the Young Turks also provided impetus for Bulgaria to combine with its Balkan neighbors to realize nationalist claims and to expel the Ottomans from Europe. The result in 1912 was a loose Balkan League supported by Russia. The Balkan League went to war against the Ottoman Empire in October 1912 in the first of the two Balkan Wars. The Bulgarians and their Balkan allies achieved outstanding successes against the Ottomans. By November 1912, Ottoman forces had suffered defeat throughout the Balkan Peninsula. A preliminary peace signed in London on 30 May 1913 ended the fighting between the Balkan allies and the Ottomans. The next month fighting began among the allies over the disposition of the Ottoman spoils, especially Macedonia. The resulting

Second Balkan War proved disastrous for Bulgaria. Bulgaria's erstwhile allies Greece and Serbia, joined by the Ottomans and the Romanians, soon overwhelmed the Bulgarian army. Macedonia and much of Thrace were again lost. The Treaties of Bucharest, with Greece, Romania, and Serbia in August 1913 and Constantinople with the Ottoman Empire in September confirmed these and other losses. The loss of the national goal, as well as the sacrifice of 176,000 casualties, devastated Bulgaria. The Russian cause in Bulgaria suffered a severe setback because of Russia's failure to support Bulgarian claims against the Balkan allies. In the aftermath of the catastrophe of the Second Balkan War, anti-Russian politicians assumed control of the National Assembly and the government. Together with Tsar Ferdinand, they led Bulgaria into World War I on the side of the Central Powers in 1915.

See also **Balkan Wars; Congress of Berlin; Ottoman Empire; Russo-Turkish War; San Stefano, Treaty of; Young Turks.**

BIBLIOGRAPHY

Constant, Stephan. *Foxy Ferdinand, Tsar of Bulgaria.* New York, 1980.

Crampton, Richard J. *Bulgaria, 1878–1918: A History.* Boulder, Colo., 1983.

Hall, Richard C. *Bulgaria's Road to the First World War.* Boulder, Colo., 1996.

Perry, Duncan M. *Stefan Stambolov and the Emergence of Modern Bulgaria, 1870–1895.* Durham, N.C., 1993.

RICHARD C. HALL

BUND, JEWISH. Founded in Vilnius, Lithuania, in October 1897 by Jewish revolutionaries, the General Jewish Workers' Union in Lithuania, Poland, and Russia, popularly known as the Bund, was the first Marxist party in the Russian Empire with a mass following. A constituent member of the Russian Social Democratic Labor Party (RSDLP, established in 1898), the Bund boasted a membership of some thirty thousand members by 1914 and rivaled the Zionist movement for the loyalty of Russian Jewry. It also played a critical role in the development of both Russian Social Democracy and a revolutionary

The following material illustrates the evolution of the Bund's embrace of national, cultural, and linguistic autonomy for Jews.

"The Convention deems that the term 'nationality' applies to the Jewish people" (Fourth Party Convention, May 1901)

" (2) The right, guaranteed by law, for the Jews to use their own language in all legal and governmental institutions. (3) National-cultural autonomy (on an extra-territorial basis): the removal of all functions connected with cultural matters (e.g., popular education) from the administrative responsibility of the state and local government and the transference of these functions to the Jewish nation." (Sixth Party Convention, October 1905)

"(5) All limitations on the use of one's mother tongue in public life, assemblies, the press, business institutions, schools, *et cetera* must be abolished." (Eighth Party Conference, October 1910)

Source: Mendes-Flohr, Paul, and Jehuda Reinharz, eds. *The Jew in the Modern World: A Documentary History,* 2nd ed., 419–421. New York, 1995.

Jewish labor movement predicated on Marxism and Jewish nationalism. The Bund best exemplified efforts to unite revolutionary socialism and Jewish nationalism in one political party.

ORIGINS

The Bund emerged from the efforts of young, radical Jewish activists to organize Jewish workers in the northwest region of the Pale of Settlement, the border region of imperial Russia in which Jews were allowed to live. Beginning in the 1880s Russified Jewish revolutionaries established small circles of Jews among workers primarily engaged in handicraft production. The organizers hoped to prepare the circle member workers for socialism by gradually raising their political consciousness through propaganda, education, and exposure to the classics of the socialist tradition. By the mid-1890s these circles had evolved into fledgling trade unions devoted to the economic improvement of the workers' lives. The revolutionaries then sought to foment labor militancy and unrest by agitating among as many Jewish workers as possible. Because the vast majority of Jewish workers in the Russian

Empire spoke Yiddish, not Russian, the Jewish activists recognized the need to reach out to workers in their native language. At the same time the Jewish revolutionaries realized the need to spearhead the struggle to end official anti-Jewish discrimination.

PLATFORM

Subsequent to its founding, the Bund gradually developed a platform calling for the official recognition of Jewish national and cultural rights. In 1901 the Bund declared Jews living in the Russian Empire a nationality. Historians point to the inspiration of the writings of the Austrian social democrats Otto Bauer (1881–1938) and Karl Kautsky (1854–1938), who combined Marxism and Diaspora nationalism; the challenges posed by the Polish Socialist Party; and the growing influence of Bundists who embraced the notion of Jewish nationalism as the chief reasons for the Bund's decision. Despite its illegal status in autocratic Russia, the Bund over the course of the next decade expanded its role as defender of civil and political rights for Jews. The Bund demanded recognition of the Jewish people as a nationality with Yiddish acknowledged as the native language of the Jewish proletariat regardless of whether or not such workers were russified. In addition, the Bund promoted a secular, Marxist Jewish culture rooted in Yiddish by demanding the establishment of state-sponsored Yiddish schools and the right of Jews to use Yiddish in all dealings with the tsarist government. In a synthesis of socialism and nationalism, the Bund claimed that Russian Jewry was entitled to national and cultural autonomy regardless of where they lived in the Russian Empire, a principle known as extraterritorialism.

The Bund's endorsement of a Jewish national identity not predicated on the end of the Jews' existence in the Diaspora distinguished the movement from political Zionism, which insisted that Jews establish a modern nation-state in the land of Israel. Moreover, the Bund also strengthened the conviction among many Jews that the negative aspects of life in the Diaspora could be overcome by remaining dispersed among the other nations of the world. The Bund believed that the solution to the Jews' problems could be found by applying the principles of Marxism to the conditions of life in early twentieth-century Europe.

The Bund's insistence to speak on behalf of Jewish workers wherever they lived in the Russian Empire led to a confrontation with its Marxist allies in the RSDLP and resulted in the Bund's decision in 1903, at the party's second congress, to withdraw from the party it helped create. Vladimir Lenin (1870–1924) and other leaders of the RSDLP vehemently opposed the Bund's insistence on extraterritorial representation of Jews as a threat to the centralized nature and ideological unity of Russian Marxism. By walking out of the congress, the Bund's delegates enabled Lenin and his supporters to win the critical vote on party membership, thereby leading to the rift between the Leninist (Bolshevik) and non-Leninist (Menshevik) factions.

The Bund played a significant role in the revolutionary events that swept the Russian Empire between 1903 and 1906. Not only did Bundists help organize Jewish self-defense units in the aftermath of the devastating Kishinev pogrom in 1903, but they also played a role in mobilizing Jewish workers and radical students, stockpiling weapons, and organizing antigovernment demonstrations during the revolutionary events of 1905. In 1912 the Bund sided with the Mensheviks when the latter's dispute with Lenin and the Bolsheviks over the nature of party membership and structure led at last to a formal organizational split between these two factions of the RSDLP. During the tumultuous year of 1917 the Bund's political fortunes grew, as membership in several hundred branches reached approximately forty thousand. But the establishment of a communist government under the control of the Bolsheviks spelled the end for the Bund in the Russian Empire. The Bolsheviks made it difficult for the Bund and other left wing political parties to continue their activities and eventually hounded them out of existence in the early 1920s.

However, the Bund in those regions of the Russian Empire situated in independent Poland after World War I continued to thrive. Along with Zionist organizations, the Bund in Poland in the interwar years played a major role in Jewish society and politics until Poland once again lost its independence when the Soviet Union and Germany partitioned the country at the end of the 1930s. The enduring legacy of the Bund is evident in other twentieth-century political movements that called for the national and cultural autonomy of minorities without linking such rights to a specific territory. The conditions that gave rise to the Bund in the Russian Empire no longer exist, but the appeal of extraterritorial national and cultural rights for minorities has been evident in European politics since the Bund's founding more than a century ago.

See also **Jews and Judaism; Lenin, Vladimir; Mensheviks; Pogroms.**

BIBLIOGRAPHY

Frankel, Jonathan. *Prophecy and Politics: Socialism, Nationalism, and the Russian Jews, 1862–1917.* Cambridge, U.K., 1981.

Jacobs, Jack, ed. *Jewish Politics in Eastern Europe: The Bund at 100.* New York, 2001.

Levin, Nora. *While Messiah Tarried: Jewish Socialist Movements, 1871–1917.* New York, 1977.

Mendelsohn, Ezra. *Class Struggle in the Pale: The Formative Years of the Jewish Workers' Movement in Tsarist Russia.* Cambridge, U.K., 1970.

Peled, Yoav. *Class and Ethnicity in the Pale: The Political Economy of Jewish Workers' Nationalism in Late Imperial Russia.* New York, 1989.

Tobias, Henry J. *The Jewish Bund in Russia: From Its Origins to 1905.* Stanford, Calif., 1972.

Zimmerman, Joshua D. *Poles, Jews, and the Politics of Nationality: The Bund and the Polish Socialist Party in Late Tsarist Russia, 1892–1914.* Madison, Wisc., 2004.

ROBERT WEINBERG

BURCKHARDT, JACOB (1818–1897), Swiss historian.

Jacob Christoph Burckhardt occupies a distinctive place among the great historians of the nineteenth century. He did not subscribe to the then widely held belief in historical progress, took a decidedly skeptical view of both liberalism and nationalism, and focused his attention on the history of cultures and the history of art rather than on political history and the history of nations.

Burckhardt was born on 25 May 1818 into a professional branch of a politically prominent merchant family in Basel, then an independent city-state within the Swiss Confederation—which, until 1848, was little more than a defensive alliance of small, independent polities, some rural, some urban, some democratic, some aristocratic, some, like Basel, dominated by their artisan guilds and commercial elites. His father was the city-state's *Antistes*, or chief pastor.

EDUCATION

Burckhardt attended the local Gymnasium and the University of Basel. His teachers included refugees from the reactionary Germany of the Carlsbad Decrees, some of whom transmitted to their students the liberal spirit of Humboldtian neohumanism, with its ideal of individual freedom and personal development, while others introduced them to a form of textual criticism that undermined the historicity of many Biblical narratives. Burckhardt's Christian faith was shaken by this education and in 1839 he abandoned the theological studies he had been pursuing in deference to his father's wishes and switched to history. At the same time he transferred from the ancient but much diminished university of his homeland to the recently founded but already world-class University of Berlin. It was a natural move. Academic history at the time was often a secular narrative of redemption and Berlin was one of its centers.

Burckhardt's teachers there included Leopold von Ranke (1795–1886) and the young Johann Gustav Droysen (1808–1884) in European and ancient history, August Böckh (1785–1867) in classical studies or *Altertumswissenschaft*, and Franz Kugler (1808–1858) in the new field of art history. From Ranke, for whose seminar he prepared his earliest published scholarly work—on topics of medieval history—and who thought well enough of him to propose him later, in 1854, for a Chair of History at Munich, he learned the importance for the practice of history not only of critical method and archival research but also of literary style, even though his own style, brusque and laconic, was quite different from Ranke's. From Droysen and Böckh he learned to question important aspects of the Winckelmannian, neohumanist vision of classical Greece that he had grown up with and to take an unbiased view of periods that, in comparison with Periclean Athens, had come to be labeled

"decadent," such as the post-Alexandrian Hellenistic age and the age of Constantine—though his fresh approach to these periods was not inspired, as Droysen's was, by the conviction that theodicy is the highest goal of historical scholarship and that it is therefore the historian's task to discover the value of even the seemingly most unpromising times. To Kugler, who encouraged his interest in art, introduced him to the lively Berlin cultural scene, and invited him to take charge of a revised edition of his own *Handbuch der Geschichte der Malerei seit Constantin dem Grossen* of 1837 (*Handbook of the History of Painting from Constantine the Great to the Present*, 1862), he remained devoted all his life. Teacher and student dedicated works to each other, and Burckhardt modeled his first art history course at the University of Basel in 1851 on Kugler's 1839–1840 course in Berlin. In 1841 he spent a semester in Bonn where he formed a close friendship with Gottfried Kinkel (1815–1882), the future socialist and revolutionary hero, then a student of theology with a lively interest in the arts, and was drawn into Kinkel's circle of poetic and liberal-minded friends, the so-called *Maikäfer*. Through Kinkel's wife, Johanna Matthieux, he gained entrance to the fabled Berlin salon of Bettina von Arnim (1785–1859), where he pleased the hostess by his singing of lieder and may have encountered the young Karl Marx (1818–1883).

Burckhardt was multitalented. Like Droysen, he composed music and wrote poetry, and he sketched the buildings and paintings he saw on his travels with flair. Though he soon recognized that his true bent did not lie in music, poetry, or art, his intimate familiarity with all three was an invaluable asset to him as his focus shifted from political to cultural history.

POLITICS

For the first thirty years of his life Burckhardt was a political liberal in the sense that term had in early nineteenth-century Germany. That is, he identified with a common German fatherland, even though he was a citizen of an independent Swiss city-republic, and advocated a union of all the German-speaking lands on a liberal, constitutional basis. The fellow students to whom he became attached during the years at Berlin and Bonn were all restless, rebellious, idealist spirits. As for Basel, he complained constantly of the narrowness of its "purse-proud merchants" and of the "odious sympathy" of the ruling clique "for absolutism of every sort." His liberalism, however, was Humboldtian rather than Lockean. Its emphasis was less on the political freedom of the abstract individual subject than on the freedom of the concrete historical individual to develop his or her personality to the fullest extent possible without interference or obstruction from any external power. He was not an egalitarian and he was not a democrat.

Moreover, Burckhardt's sympathy with political liberalism declined drastically in the years 1844 and 1845 when *Freischaren* (volunteer brigades) from the Protestant Swiss cantons marched threateningly on the Catholic canton of Lucerne, which had abrogated legal restrictions on the Jesuits and invited them back to run its schools. Burckhardt was appalled and frightened by this demonstration of popular revolutionary force. He warned his romantic radical friends in Bonn that they were "political innocents" with no idea of the slavery they could expect "under the loudmouthed masses called 'the people'."

"Freedom and respect for law are indissolubly linked," he wrote in the *Basler Zeitung,* of which he had been appointed editor in 1843. The Swiss Civil War (between the mostly liberal, commercial, Protestant cantons favorable to an expansion of federal authority and the weaker, predominantly Catholic rural cantons fearful for their autonomy) aggravated Burckhardt's disillusionment with liberal politics. He had "quietly but completely fallen out" with "this wretched age," he told a friend, and "was escaping from it to the beautiful South, which has dropped out of history." History pursued him, however, for it was in the Eternal City that the Revolution of 1848 caught up with him. Burckhardt was convinced, like Alexis de Tocqueville (1805–1859), that he was living in an Age of Revolutions, but unlike Tocqueville, he had come to believe that liberal policies were encouraging exorbitant popular demands that could be met in the end only by tyrannies of the Left or of the Right. The inevitable conflict between modern socialism and modern industrial capitalism, both of which promote uniformity and discourage independent thought, would destroy, he claimed, "the old culture of Europe." The moderate optimism of the years in Berlin and Bonn was lost for good.

CAREER AND WORK

The change in the political climate in the late 1840s and the change in Burckhardt's political views affected both his career decisions and his understanding of what history-writing was about.

In 1843 he had returned, somewhat unwillingly, to Basel, but had difficulty establishing himself in his homeland, where he was too familiar a figure not to be taken for granted. He got to teach occasional courses at the university, but failed to obtain a permanent position; he lectured on art to the general public; for a few years he served as editor of the *Basler Zeitung;* and he spent as much time as he could away from Basel, in Italy. Along with *Die Kunstwerke der belgischen Städte* (1862; Art works of the cities of Belgium), in which he first expressed his lifelong enthusiasm for Peter Paul Rubens (1577–1640), he added more publications: in 1847, a thoroughly revised edition of Kugler's 1837 *Handbuch der Geschichte der Malerei*, and a year later an augmented edition of Kugler's *Handbuch der Kunstgeschichte* (Handbook of the history of art); in 1853, *Die Zeit Constantins des Grossen* (*The Age of Constantine the Great*, 1949), originally conceived as the first of a series of books on cultural rather than political history; and in 1855 *Der Cicerone. Eine Anleitung zum Genuss der Kunstwerke Italiens* (*The Cicerone, or Art Guide to Painting in Italy*, 1873). In addition, he contributed hundreds of entries on art, among them several substantial short articles (for instance, those on Karl Friedrich Schinkel [1781–1841] and Johann Friedrich Overbeck [1789–1869]), to the ninth edition of the Brockhaus *Conversations-Lexikon* (1843–1848).

In 1855 Burckhardt was at last offered a permanent academic appointment—that of professor of art history at the newly founded Federal Polytechnic in Zurich, where his colleagues included Theodor Mommsen (1817–1903), Gottfried Semper (1803–1879), and Francesco De Sanctis (1817–1883). Burckhardt's move to Zurich caused the Basel authorities finally to bestir themselves, and after three successful years at the Federal Polytechnic, the errant native son was brought back to his homeland to fill the Chair of History at the University of Basel. He occupied it until his retirement in 1886, and never again left Basel, except for trips to Italy or to museums in France,

Germany, and England. He received offers from several far larger, more prestigious (and better paying) universities in Germany and in 1872 was sounded out about succeeding his old teacher Ranke in the Chair of History at Berlin. He turned everything down. "My business is simple," he declared. "It is to stay at my post."

After the appearance in 1860 of the work for which he is best known—*Die Cultur der Renaissance in Italien: Ein Versuch* (*The Civilization of the Renaissance in Italy*, 1878)—Burckhardt also stopped writing for publication, devoting himself entirely to his university teaching and to the public lectures he gave regularly to the citizens of Basel. With the exception of *Geschichte der neueren Baukunst: Die Renaissance in Italien* (*The Architecture of the Italian Renaissance*, 1985), which he allowed to be published in 1867 out of respect for his former teacher Kugler (it had been planned as volume four of Kugler's five-volume *Geschichte der Baukunst* [History of architecture]), all his other major works were put together from his lecture notes and published posthumously. These include *Griechische Kulturgeschichte* (1898–1902; *The Greeks and Greek Civilization*, 1998), *Weltgeschichtliche Betrachtungen* (1905; *Reflections on History*, 1943), the late essays "Das Altarbild" ("The Altarpiece in Renaissance Italy," 1988) "Das Porträt" (The portrait), and "Der Sammler" (The collector) in 1898, and his great tribute to Rubens, *Erinnerungen aus Rubens* (1898), the first two much edited, in the interest of readability, by his nephew Jacob Oeri. New works based on Burckhardt's lecture notes have continued to appear: in 1918 the well-attended public lectures he gave at Basel; in 1929, *Historische Fragmente* (*Judgments on History and Historians*, 1958), in 1974, *Über die Geschichte des Revolutionszeitalters* (On the history of the age of revolutions); and *Aesthetic der bildenden Kunst* (Aesthetics of the fine arts) in 1992. The year 2005 saw the publication, in English translation, of a manuscript as yet unpublished in German, *Italian Renaissance Painting according to Genres*. A complete edition of his works in fourteen volumes, with valuable introductions by a team of outstanding scholars, was published in Basel and Stuttgart from 1929 to 1934. Even so, philologically authentic texts of the lectures edited by Oeri are being issued in the

early twenty-first century as part of a new edition of the *Complete Works*, the aim of which is to make Burckhardt's own voice more audible than in Oeri's smoothed out versions and to reveal the historian's thinking and writing processes.

Burckhardt's withdrawal to Basel and his decision to give up writing and publishing in favor of his teaching and public lecturing—that is to say, in favor of preserving authentic humanist culture, as he understood it, in at least one small but venerable European city—reflect not only his political disillusionment and a decidedly critical stance toward the modern world of mass communication, academic careerism, and institutionalized scholarship, but a well-considered and, at the time, original view of what the study of history is or should be about.

VIEW OF HISTORY AND HISTORIOGRAPHY

The lessons Burckhardt learned from the events of 1844–1845 in Switzerland and the 1848 Revolutions throughout Europe did not turn him into a radical pessimist. He no longer believed, as Droysen and Georg Wilhelm Friedrich Hegel (1770–1831) in their different ways both did, in a single movement of history toward freedom. He had simply ceased to believe in any underlying direction of history at all. If there was one, only the Divinity knew what it was. From a human perspective, history was constant change: it was by no means impossible, for instance, that the age of mass culture and mass politics would be followed by a new aristocratic age. The task of the individual was not therefore to try to second-guess a putative divine plan of history and then work to promote it. It was, first, by internalizing the literature, art, and experience of past humanity, to cultivate his own humanity and thus preserve in himself what had already been achieved; and second, to protect the cultural achievement of humanity as vigorously as possible, whatever the historical circumstances and the apparent "movement of history"—against these, in fact, if necessary—so that what had been achieved would not be squandered or destroyed but would continue to be available to succeeding generations. Each individual had to write his own historical role, in other words, in accordance with his or her moral and cultural values, not to fit a supposedly prescribed role. Similarly, both past and present actions and societies were to be judged in accordance with those same values, not measured and justified according to their contribution to some alleged "progress" of history.

Burckhardt's understanding and practice of historiography corresponds to this view of history. The aim of the historian, as he understood it, was not to promote ephemeral political ends, or to make his auditors—in his own case, the students and citizens of Basel—"shrewder (for next time)" but to make them "wiser (for all time)." The goal he set himself as a scholar-teacher was *Bildung* (which means the process of educating or forming a human being as well as the humane content with which that human being is informed), not *Wissenschaft* (positive or "objective" knowledge of external events and phenomena). Thus he turned away from the current practice of historiography as the establishing of facts and the narrating of events. Instead he devoted all his attention either to cultural history—the history of the ways in which human beings have organized their lives and made sense of their experiences—or to the history of art, one of the chief media, along with myth and literature, through which men and women have expressed their views of the world.

Through his teaching and writing on the history of art and on the history of culture (he taught art history at Basel in addition to his regular teaching of history, and in 1886 became the first occupant of a newly founded Chair of Art History at the university, a position he retained after he retired from the Chair of History and did not relinquish until 1893, four years before his death), Burckhardt hoped to develop in his audiences both the capacity for contemplative delight in the individual manifestations of human creativity and the habit of reflecting critically on the changing spectacle of human cultures, of weighing up the good and the bad, the losses and the gains, and of attending to the processes by which one culture is transformed into another, as during those periods of crisis or major transition that he especially liked to teach and write about (the Hellenistic age, the age of Constantine, the Renaissance). Contemplative delight (*Anschauung, Genuss*) was not, for him, a matter of pleasurable consumption. As well as a consolation in hard times, it was an essential transforming and humanizing activity. Similarly,

coming to an understanding of historical processes was not a means of acquiring practical political skills for the here and now; on the contrary, it provided a degree of independence from history, an "Archimedean point"—similar to the city-state of Basel itself—from which the great pageant could be observed *sine ira et studio* (without bitterness or bias).

Burckhardt's position has been criticized—understandably—as an aestheticizing of history. But he was by no means indifferent to politics. He was keenly aware that political conditions, like religious beliefs, might be more or less favorable to that development of human culture that was the highest value he knew; he was also convinced that the goals of the three *Potenzen* (powers, energies) he had identified as the primary moving forces in history—the State, Religion, and Culture—were not by any means always in harmony. Though culture, for instance, which was material as well as mental and included economic activity as well as the arts, was dependent on the security provided by the state, its development might in certain cases undermine the state and thus the very condition of its own existence; equally, however, the state could develop in such a way that it undermined the culture that it was ideally its proper function to protect. Burckhardt's classic *Civilization of the Renaissance in Italy* and many of his other major works are in fact explorations of the relations between the three *Potenzen*. Living, as he believed he was, in a time of cultural change comparable to the Hellenistic age or the age of Constantine, it was inevitable that he would follow developments in contemporary European politics and society with great, even anxious, attention.

INFLUENCE
Burckhardt is the father of modern cultural history, even though his interest was generally directed more toward intellectual and artistic culture than toward the material culture that engages contemporary cultural historians, with the result that his sources were chiefly literary and artistic rather than archival or archaeological. While his histories are not without significant narrative elements, they resemble modern narratives more than those of the nineteenth century. Instead of a sequence of events laid out with assurance by an omniscient narrator, they are full of uncertainties and aporias and are composed of synchronic

tableaux that have a considerable degree of independence of each other. His *Civilization of the Renaissance in Italy,* though much contested in the light of new ideas and new knowledge, is still the point of departure of all reflection on that period. His vision of Greek culture as agonal rather than harmonious has influenced all later scholars, albeit chiefly through its expression in the work of Friedrich Wilhelm Nietzsche (1844–1900), who was his colleague and disciple at Basel and who sat in on his courses on Greek cultural history. His contribution to the history and aesthetics of art is only now being properly evaluated, but many of his ideas and methods were disseminated through the widely read works of his student Heinrich Wölfflin (1864–1945). As an analyst of modern society and politics, a critic of modern state power, and a prophet of totalitarian regimes to come, the Burckhardt revealed to the English-speaking public only with the belated translation and publication, during World War II, of *Reflections on History* touched many of the leading minds of the twentieth century, from Jose Ortega y Gasset (1883–1955) to Ernst Cassirer (1874–1945), Karl Löwith (1897–1973), and Leo Strauss (1899–1973). Burckhardt's influence as a political thinker was especially strong during the Cold War.

See also **History; Painting; Ranke, Leopold von.**

BIBLIOGRAPHY

Bauer, Stefan. *Polisbild und Demokratieveständnis in Jacob Burckhardts "Griechischer Kulturgeschichte."* Basel, 2001.

Dürr, Emil. *Jacob Burckhardt als politischer Publizist mit seinen Zeitungsberichten aus den Jahren 1844/45.* Zurich, 1937.

Gossman, Lionel. *Basel in the Age of Burckhardt: A Study in Unseasonable Ideas.* Chicago, 2000.

Hardtwig, Wolfgang. *Geschichtsschreibung zwischen Alteuropa und moderner Welt: Jacob Buckhardt in seiner Zeit.* Göttingen, 1974.

Hinde, John R. *Jacob Burckhardt and the Crisis of Modernity.* Montreal, 2000.

Kaegi, Werner. *Jacob Burckhardt: Eine Biographie.* 7 vols. Basel, 1947–1982.

Löwith, Karl. *Jacob Burckhardt: Der Mensch inmitten der Geschichte.* Berlin, 1936.

Martin, Alfred von. *Nietzsche und Burckhardt.* Munich, 1941.

Maurer, Emil. *Jacob Burckhardt und Rubens.* Basel, 1951.

Meier, Nikolaus. *Stiften und Sammeln für die Öffentliche Kunstsammlung Basel.* Basel, 1997.

Salomon, Albert. "Jacob Burckhardt: Transcending History." *Philosophy and Phenomenological Research* 6 (1945–1946): 225–269.

Sigurdson, Richard. *Jacob Burckhardt's Social and Political Thought.* Toronto, 2004.

Trevor-Roper, Hugh. "Jacob Burckhardt." *Proceedings of the British Academy* 70 (1984): 359–378.

Wenzel, Johannes. *Jacob Burckhardt in der Krise seiner Zeit.* Berlin, 1967.

LIONEL GOSSMAN

BUREAUCRACY. The term *bureaucracy* was first used in France in 1802. Pierre-Joseph Proudhon (1809–1865) offered a definition of bureaucracy in his *Idée générale de la révolution* in 1851 that covers almost all the reasons why citizens detested and still resent bureaucracy. Proudhon said

> To be governed is to be kept in sight, inspected, spied upon, directed, law-driven, numbered, enrolled, indoctrinated, preached at, controlled, estimated, valued, censured, commanded by creatures who have neither the right, nor the wisdom, nor the virtue to do it.

Bureaucratic structures developed everywhere in nineteenth-century Europe, even in Britain, where dominant Liberal thinking decried state interference.

During the eighteenth century the costs and setbacks of war meant rulers had to find new ways to tax subjects. The massive development of state power in the guise of bureaucratic institutions in the nineteenth century was also closely linked to the demographic explosion, rapid urbanization, consequent public health crises, economic growth, and the transportation revolution. It was also tied in with the declining influence of other agencies. In Roman Catholic countries the church had, albeit often very scantily, provided some education and a little social welfare. The sale of church lands, spurred on by the French Revolution, mostly eliminated the social role. Private charities, mutual aid societies, trade unions, and sometimes, as in Britain, parish committees, addressed a variety of social issues. The first national insurance schemes for sick pay and pensions were introduced by the chancellor Otto von Bismarck (1871–1890) in Germany in the 1880s.

Religious schools played a major role in education in France and in Britain until the 1870s. Around this date governments began to accept responsibility for education, driven by widening suffrage and, in Roman Catholic countries, anticlerical concerns. Repeated popular unrest meant that law and order could no longer be left to the local community, while the continuing scale of foreign war necessitated the conscription and training of mass armies. Civil servants were needed as tax collectors and much more. Just as Proudhon said, they inspected, checked, and—because it had become essential to run regular population censuses—they above all counted. The sharpest bureaucratic tools were official statistics and inquiries, well publicized in increasingly numerous newspapers.

The most vital features that distinguish modern bureaucracies from earlier administrative structures are size, scope of activity, and the imposition of a centralized, uniform, rational, and legal framework. Rulers needed senior officials who would both command the respect of local notables and have a good knowledge of the area they ran but accept direction from the center, qualities fraught with contradictory tensions. In the nineteenth century, European bureaucracies emerged as extremely hierarchical bodies run by a tiny, sometimes noble, increasingly isolated elite and a burgeoning mass of lower civil servants. The fastest growth took place in the second half of the nineteenth century, as vast armies of junior officials were needed as clerks, teachers, postal and rail workers, and so forth.

BUREAUCRACY IN FRANCE

In prerevolutionary France private companies bought the right to perform key administrative functions, including tax collection. Others bought the privilege not to pay tax. Many argued that privatization and privilege explained France's near bankruptcy in 1789. Standardized systems run by the state and applicable to all seemed to be the answer if one was at the top looking down. The

1789 revolution set up administrative structures that were imitated elsewhere and that are essentially still in place in France. Within five years there were a quarter of a million civil servants, five times as many as in 1789. Lower and higher ranks were totally separate. Most of the middle and senior ranking were bourgeois, 8 percent had some higher education. A degree in law or science in one of the new higher education colleges became a prerequisite for appointment into the lower reaches of the council of state, the start of a senior career. Old privileged families soon muscled in and formed part of a family tradition of state service.

Despite entrance exams and law degrees, from the start it was obvious that the French model for rational, centralized, bureaucratic structures was highly politicized. The separation of powers never seemed to apply to bureaucracy. All officials were appointed, and dismissed, from Paris, which meant that a career bureaucrat had to be politically sensitive. After Napoleon I's (r. 1804–1814/15) defeats in 1814 and in 1815, the newly restored Bourbon king, Louis XVIII (r. 1814–1815, 1815–1824) struggled to square the ambitions of former exiled royalists with the need for trained officials. Even after Waterloo (1815) only one of the new Bourbon prefects had not served the empire. But Napoleon's emphasis on professional training was forgotten. By 1816 more than 75 percent of prefects were nobles. However by 1830 it was clear that a title and royalist sympathies were not enough for a modern prefect whose prime task in his department was to win elections, which Restoration prefects visibly failed to do.

The 1830 revolution led to the biggest upheaval in any nineteenth-century bureaucracy. Only seven of the old prefects survived, and all of the generals commanding the nineteen military districts were replaced, as were four hundred senior magistrates. Middle-class officials triumphed over noble, but the distinguishing feature of the changes, which was to mark the character of modern bureaucracy, was political compatibility. The modern state imposed an oath of allegiance. Many of those eager to take the oath to the new Orléanist king were former Napoleonic officials, out of work since 1815.

France settled down with successive generations of professionally trained bureaucratic families, eager to adapt to changes of regime. Politicians and officials were indistinguishable. Forty percent of the chamber of deputies in the 1840s held official posts. Notable families dominated. Only three (1 percent) of the Second Empire prefects came from modest backgrounds. Eighty-eight (40 percent) were nobles.

For other than the most senior jobs in the localities—prefect, military commander, and so forth—centralization meant local patronage. Local notables elected to parliament expected to have a major influence on appointments from subprefects to postmasters. For subprefects the prestige of their family in the locality was conclusive.

Nonetheless the French bureaucracy was becoming more professional. Sons of officials filled the new *lycées,* or high schools, and won the bulk of the six thousand high school scholarships endowed by Napoleon I. Higher education became the norm. Over half (130) of Louis-Napoleon's (Napoleon III; r. 1852–1871) prefects studied at the Paris law faculty, a further thirty-six at provincial faculties. A glance at letters of recommendation however confirms that the writers of these letters stressed the applicants' genealogy and that an essential prerequisite was family money. Official posts brought prestige, but by 1900 other careers paid far better. A fairly senior official earned fifteen hundred francs per year, compared with twenty-five thousand francs for a senior salesman in one of the Parisian department stores.

ITALIAN BUREAUCRACY

Under Napoleon I the French conquered an empire larger than any since the time of Charlemagne (742–814) and, driven by the need to collect revenue for war, imposed new institutions on it. New administrative elites in areas such as Italy, already emerging in the eighteenth century under Enlightened rulers such as the Holy Roman Emperors Joseph II (r. 1765–1790) and Leopold II (r. 1790–1792), were strengthened. In northern districts new elite families such as the Cavours and the Pignatellis acquired land, investments, and bureaucratic posts.

With Napoleon's defeat, much of Italy fell under Habsburg rule. Italian bureaucrats were replaced by Austrian, the Italians having to be satisfied with more junior posts. In Naples, supporters of the restored king asserted their right to displace French-appointed officials. Centralized systems were replaced with a traditional blurring of the public and the private as all manner of public services, from taxation to social welfare, were sold to private individuals. The dispossessed Napoleonic bourgeoisie, like the old nobility, invested in the private companies. The French bureaucratic model did not disappear totally. After the 1848 revolution the Piedmontese restored a French-style prefectoral system and codes of law, which were applied to the whole country after unification in the 1860s. Unification meant the virtual colonization of south by north. Piedmontese officials dominated the new centralized state and the acquired southern provinces.

Most Italian bureaucrats were trained lawyers, although this was not a requirement. There were no formal structures for promotion, salary increases, rules for dismissal, or pensions. Patronage was the norm. Each ministry recruited its own officials, who were poorly paid. Local notables and politicians each had jobs to bestow. Unification brought a 50 percent increase in administrative jobs. There were the same number of magistrates as in France, although there were only half the courts. The colonial ministry employed twice as many officials as its British counterpart. Between 1882 and 1912 the size of Italy's bureaucracy mushroomed from 98,000 to 260,000. To some extent this was genuine growth; many of the new jobs were in rail and telephone services. Most were very poorly paid; primary school teachers received less than agricultural laborers. As alternative ways of earning a living were lacking, low pay was better than nothing.

RUSSIAN BUREAUCRACY

Throughout the nineteenth century the enormous Russian empire was held together by military governors, who were mini-tsars in their provinces. Military, civil, and judicial functions were indistinguishable and Russia did not begin to develop a recognizably modern civil service until after the emancipation of the serfs in 1861.

In the early eighteenth century Peter the Great (r. 1682–1725) created a system that lasted virtually intact until the 1917 revolution. Using

France and Sweden as models, he set up an administrative senate and five "colleges" or government departments and inspectors were appointed to monitor officials. Peter the Great also set up a table of fourteen ranks that would reward worthy commoners with nobility. Hereditary noble status was conferred upon any nonnoble who reached the eighth civil rank or the fourteenth military rank. However, throughout the nineteenth century nobles successfully froze aspiring middle-class applicants out of jobs, ironically asserting their superior rights as "service" nobles. Nobles also manipulated the system so that a nonnoble had to reach not the eighth, but the fifth rank before he gained nobility. By the middle of the nineteenth century, between two-thirds and three-quarters of senior officials were still nobles, but the service was becoming less the preserve of a land-owning elite. By 1900 most bureaucratic posts were held by low-ranking nobles or bourgeois. Only slowly did the service take on the characteristics of a modern bureaucracy, demanding educational prerequisites and not merely an army record for its applicants.

Alexander I (r. 1801–1825) tried to modernize his civil service by setting an examination for entry to the eighth rank and beyond, but his successor Nicholas I (r. 1825–1855) was pressured by nobles to abandon it. In 1828 graduates of district schools gained preferential entry, gymnasium graduates even more so, while a knowledge of Greek guaranteed instant appointment in the fourteenth rank. Fast-track entry for high fliers was restricted to the noble establishments of Tsarskoe Selo *lycée* or the School of Jurisprudence. On the other hand, in the years 1894 and 1895 over half of the more than four thousand new men lacked even secondary education. When technical or engineering experts were needed, a vital and respected part of the French and German systems, Russia had to import them from abroad.

The Russian bureaucracy grew from 38,000 in 1800 to 113,990 in 1856. By the end of the century it had quadrupled, servicing new areas in railways, postal services, and so forth. It was still tiny compared with the size and scale of populations of other major states; 62 for every 1,000 inhabitants in European Russia (40 in the whole empire), compared with 176 in France and 126 in Germany.

Russian bureaucrats were poorly paid. Although ambassadors received fifty thousand rubles per year, senior officials netted a mere fifteen hundred. Only about 20 percent earned more than one thousand rubles, barely enough to maintain a middle-class lifestyle. The deficit was covered by ubiquitous corruption. Promotion depended solely on seniority, but there was no security of tenure. Furthermore, whereas in Germany bureaucrats were respected, in Russia they were treated with social and intellectual condescension.

Nor did the Russian bureaucracy possess a corporate identity. The gulf between central and local officials was huge. There were very few senior posts in the provinces; only 1 to 2 percent at rank five or higher, whereas in St. Petersburg 15 percent were at this rank. Provincial offices were staffed by poorly paid and educated local men, with no prospects of promotion. Their seniors were imported from the army or St. Petersburg.

BUREAUCRACY IN PRUSSIA AND THE GERMAN EMPIRE

An effective bureaucracy was needed in Prussia because the territories owned by the ruler were so physically scattered. Following defeat by Napoleon I, the reforming minister, Heinrich Friedrich Karl vom und zum Stein (1757–1831), shaped a bureaucracy increasingly dominated by a service, rather than a landed nobility. This service elite was not a closed caste. The absence of formal entry requirements or rules for promotion allowed some clever sons of peasants and artisans to compete for posts. In the 1830s nearly 30 percent of those recruited into the bureaucracy from the universities were sons of minor officials, peasants, or artisans. More than half of the rest came from existing bureaucratic or professional families. Only 9 percent were sons of big landowners.

However in the decades after 1815 the job market slumped as a result of Stein's reduction of senior bureaucratic posts by 50 percent. People began to worry that there was a dangerous excess of educated men. More rigorous standards were imposed. In the 1830s German universities began to demand a pass in the *abitur* or school-leaving certificate as a precondition for university study. The proportion of university students from poorer families fell as a direct consequence. Meanwhile more senior bureaucratic posts were restricted to university graduates, while only those students who had been members of student societies, including military groups, could apply. Such societies refused to admit sons of poorer families.

In the years up to and including the revolutions of 1848, bureaucrats whose careers suffered played a leading role in promoting liberal and constitutional reforms. Forty-two percent of those elected to the Prussian National Assembly were officials, 26 percent members of the judiciary, and 16 percent civil administrators. Fifty percent of the Berlin city council elected in the wake of the 1848 revolution were bureaucrats. The prospective of a revolutionary bureaucracy seemed imminent. However in May 1849 the number of conservative bureaucrats in the new Prussian assembly rose from 40 to 113. By 1855 the vast majority of bureaucrat MPs were progovernment, including 55 percent of the magistrates elected to the assembly. An increasingly conservative bureaucracy effectively triumphed over liberal parliamentarianism.

The reasons were complex. Some 1848 liberals were alarmed at the scale of popular unrest and radicalism, others were disappointed that the constitutional movement was emasculated in May 1849 by the introduction of a hierarchical three-class franchise. Others came to accept that their own interests were best served by obedience to centralized authority. Frederick William IV (r. 1840–1861) cleverly introduced salary increases and extensive judicial reform on the French model, which led to a 75 percent increase in the size of the bureaucracy in the second half of the century. In France, Italy, and Britain, officials elected to parliament gained promotion; in Prussia they did not.

The Prussian bureaucracy was gradually transformed from a privileged, almost self-recruiting corporation into part of a new, more consolidated, upper class. Up to 1850, more than half of the law students destined for the bureaucracy were sons of senior officials; by 1870 the figure had fallen to 36 percent. Careers in business or industry, previously thought inferior, were beginning to appeal. By 1900 a military career was the first choice for a bureaucrat's son. Meanwhile a bureaucratic career was increasingly appealing to sons of landed nobles whose family estates had become less profitable. By 1916, 50 percent of senior officials came from landed families. Over the century the social composition of the German bureaucracy had undergone a major transformation. At the outset they regarded themselves as a platonic guardian class, recruited from all social groups and thus representing the whole of society. Gradually they came to represent, and reflect the interests of, a tiny upper-class elite, increasingly fraught with social ignorance and fear. Whereas in Russia major landowning noble families lost interest in running the bureaucracy, in Germany the opposite occurred.

The consequences for policy making were considerable. Whereas before unification south German bureaucrats tended to follow liberal policies, unification left an increasingly conservative bureaucracy in control. German bureaucrats could point to triumphs, especially the first national system of education. However the conservative bureaucratic elites later in the century were accused of being ignorant of the need to encourage entrepreneurial growth and of petty and negative meddling.

GREAT BRITAIN AND BUREAUCRACY

In 1780 in Britain there were only about sixteen hundred government employees, mostly customs and excise men appointed through patronage. By 1870 there were fifty-four thousand; these served as regulators and coordinators of the Poor Law and prisons, ran Royal Commissions of Enquiry and a regular ten-year census of the population, and served as inspectors of factories and in a whole range of economic activities. Patronage was gradually replaced by competitive examination, which became open in 1870. Some of the leading civil servants were professionals, lawyers, doctors, or engineers. Government gradually took over prisons between 1835 and 1877. No one wanted state-run railways in Britain, but the board of trade acquired some obligations to inspect on safety grounds after a number of spectacular accidents.

Whereas the states already discussed gradually assembled centralized bureaucracies, in Britain many of the functions were managed by parishes and financed by local rates. Poverty and public health were major issues. The problem of how to help the poor cheaply without encouraging them into idleness, traditionally the responsibility of the church in Catholic countries in earlier times, became acute, particularly in the cyclical economic depressions of the nineteenth century. Poverty was dealt with by ad hoc combinations of private, municipal, and state charity and only after revolutionary upheaval. Britain avoided revolution, but more by luck than by generosity or farsightedness. After much debate a new Poor Law (1834) gave central government the power to order local landowners and other notables to create boards of guardians. They tried to replace traditional parish outdoor relief with parish-run and parish-financed workhouses. The tragedy of the potato famine in Ireland (1845–1846) led to government commissions overseeing Poor Law inspections and massive land sales, although it is hard to imagine that the poor benefited when they swapped Catholic for Protestant landlords.

Concern over public health was a major factor in breaking Liberal resistance to official intervention. Cholera was a catalyst because it affected rich and poor. With the second epidemic, Sir Edwin Chadwick, commissioner of the board of health from 1848 to 1854, managed to gain acceptance for the Public Health Act in 1848 and for the General Board of Health, but after ten years the board was abolished. The investigations of a nonpartisan professional, Sir John Simon, medical officer in the Privy Council (1855–1876), helped to produce the Local Government and Public Health Acts, 1871–1872. Worries over the spread of venereal disease led to legislation in the 1860s that ordered health checks on known prostitutes.

The state had no role in running schools in Britain until 1870. Until then charity school and competing religious schools held the day. The 1870 legislation encouraged ratepayers to elect school boards to set up and run elementary schools where they were needed. The state provided inspectors. This did not produce a uniform or total solution. In 1895 state schools served only 20 percent of children, but the new state system already needed a substantial body of teachers and inspectors.

Proudhon's stirring definition of the objectives of bureaucracy may not be entirely proved by the examples given here, but many will feel deep sympathy with him when they tackle their tax returns

or parking fines. A country is generally described as bureaucratic when extensive aspects of the state machinery are centralized and run by unelected officials. There is an assumption that these officials should be trained to blind obedience and in return be guaranteed a secure career structure. Bureaucrats were directly answerable to single rulers, while their status in countries with parliaments was more complex. It was common for large numbers of officials to sit in parliaments and local assemblies and voters in France and Italy, and probably elsewhere, saw the resulting patronage as opportunities for their families and their area. In Britain, on the contrary, there used to be a myth that secure career structures in the civil service ensured that the senior figures could offer independent advice to government, an aspect of the separation of powers that used to be understood in Britain but was not recognized in other countries, including the United States.

See also **Education; Professions.**

BIBLIOGRAPHY

Beck, Hermann. "The Social Policies of Prussian Officials: The Bureaucracy in a New Light." *Journal of Modern History* 64 (1992): 263–298.

Davies, John Anthony. *Conflict and Control: Law and Order in Nineteenth-Century Italy.* Basingstoke, U.K., 1988.

Fulbrook, Mary, ed. *German History since 1800.* London, 1997.

Lee, W. R. "Economic Development and the State in Nineteenth-Century Germany." *Economic History Review* 41 (1988): 346–367.

Pilbeam, Pamela. *The Middle Classes in Europe, 1789–1914: France, Germany, Italy, and Russia.* New York, 1990.

Pintner, Walter McKenzie, and Don Karl Rowney. *Russian Officialdom: The Bureaucratization of Russian Society from the Seventeenth to the Twentieth Century.* London, 1980.

Saunders, David. *Russia in the Age of Reaction and Reform, 1801–1881.* Harlow, U.K., 1992.

Simms, Brendan. *The Struggle for Mastery in Germany, 1779–1850.* Basingstoke, U.K., 1998.

Strauss, E. *The Ruling Servant: Bureaucracy in France, Russia, and Britain.* London, 1961.

PAMELA PILBEAM

BURKE, EDMUND (1729–1797), British statesman and writer.

One of Western civilization's masters of the art of rhetoric and in British history among the finest writers ever to have served in Parliament, Edmund Burke has come to be best remembered as the principal spokesman of English conservatism in the late eighteenth century. Yet he was neither a native Englishman nor politically conservative with regard to any of the causes he championed, until his sixties when the outbreak of the French Revolution prompted him to assess its sources and threats in terms that thereafter would come to lie at the heart of the conservative reaction to the excesses, both philosophical and political, of the age of Enlightenment. Thanks to Burke and his followers the perfect union of true knowledge with actual government that in the ancient world had been advocated by Plato, and in the eighteenth century came to be termed "enlightened despotism," would thereafter be associated less with philosophical kingship than with doctrines of revolutionary change, the creation of a new world in the light of first principles, and the leveling of an old order's traditional bonds of community. No one who denied that political life should be steered by abstract ideas has exercised a greater influence on modern conservatism's mistrust of political theory as a guide to the practice of politics. Interpreters of communism have often portrayed its social upheavals as analogous to the achievements of the French revolutionaries decried by Burke, and postmodernist critics of Enlightenment philosophy, seldom conservatives themselves, frequently object in similar terms to its pretensions and the political hazards of implementing its ideals.

EARLY LIFE AND WRITINGS

Born in 1729 in Dublin, the son of a Protestant father and Catholic mother, and educated first at a Quaker boarding school and then at Trinity College Dublin, Burke arrived in London in 1750 to study law and prepare for a career at the bar, a profession to which he soon felt scant attraction and many of whose most prominent practitioners he would later condemn for their dogmatic zeal and personal ambition. That England had no written constitution but instead a collection of inherited practices and conventions lent political stability to its civic institutions, he thought, in ways that the late eighteenth century's new republics in America and France could not hope to acquire at a stroke through constitutional blueprints couched in purist and specious language that tied the legitimacy of a government to a people's express consent. After abandoning the study of law, he turned his attention, in his chief publications of the late 1750s, to other subjects that had become fashionable in the eighteenth century through the influence of John Locke, George Berkeley, Francis Hutcheson, and David Hume. In his *Vindication of Natural Society,* published anonymously in 1756, he presented what he later portrayed as a satire of the rationalist critique of revealed religions offered by the first Viscount Bolingbroke, although some modern commentators have suggested that the work should instead be read as a libertarian tract against the manufactured powers of the state. In his *Philosophical Enquiry into the Origin of Our Ideas of the Sublime and Beautiful* (1757), he developed an epistemology of aesthetic wonder, horror, and delight that sought to explain such passions with reference to the diverse objects that excited them.

Both texts display a grasp of the complexities of the human mind and of the social situations in which persons find themselves, as well as a subtle appreciation of religious sentiment, that were to distinguish Burke's later writings from the doctrines of many of his more theologically skeptical contemporaries. These themes can be traced in some measure to his background as an Irishman destined to lead his life abroad and to his Anglican schooling in a predominantly Catholic world, with mixed religious roots but also anxieties about the political influence of clerics and the papacy. "Man is by his constitution a religious animal," he would come to claim in his commentary on the French Revolution. His perception of France's Civil Constitution of the Clergy and of the destruction of monasteries and confiscation of church lands in 1789 were to underpin his charge against what he took to be the French revolutionaries' atheism, which had proceeded hand in hand with their relish of equality. But by contrast with the views of other thinkers of his age who judged all religions to be superstitious idolatry, there was nothing sectarian about Burke's sense of the social cohesion afforded by Christianity.

POLITICAL CAREER

By the late 1750s he had formed friendships with Samuel Johnson, Oliver Goldsmith, David Garrick, and other luminaries of London society, introduced to such circles in part by his physician's daughter, Jane Nugent, whom he married in 1757. In the following year he began to edit the *Annual Register*, chronicling the most notable cultural achievements of Britain's capital. In 1759 he became the assistant of William Gerard Hamilton, who was two years later appointed to chief secretary of Ireland. This political apprenticeship prepared Burke well for similar service in 1765 to the Marquess of Rockingham, when he became prime minister. Elected to Parliament himself in December 1765, Burke was for the next two decades much concerned with Britain's need to free its governments of royal patronage and, abroad, with the American colonists' mounting opposition to British rule. One of the most eloquent of the Rockingham Whigs, the Liberal Party's progenitors, he was throughout this period an advocate of liberal ideals, proclaiming in his *Thoughts on the Cause of the Present Discontents* (1770) the need for party governments to be formed from shared convictions rather than at the behest of the king, and in his "Conciliation with the Colonies" (1775) the duty of the crown to respect the civil rights and privileges of British subjects in America. The latter, a speech delivered in Parliament, may be regarded as a manifesto of the associated rights and obligations of a free people subject to the rule of law, while his "Speech to the Electors of Bristol" of the previous year is perhaps the foremost statement of a political representative's obligation to his constituents to form independent judgments. Having in 1773 lost his original seat, in Wendover, Burke won the election in Bristol in 1774 but was subsequently defeated when he stood again in 1780. Thereafter he continued his political career, until 1794, as the designated member of Parliament (MP) for the pocket borough of Malton.

One of the reasons for Burke's unpopularity in England in this period was his advocacy of the interests of the Catholic population of Ireland, a cause that in the early 1760s had prompted the composition of his *Tracts on the Popery Laws* and for which he continued to campaign at least until 1783, when penal restrictions against Catholics were eased by Ireland's temporarily independent parliament established by Henry Grattan (1746–1820). Throughout the 1770s and 1780s he was vexed even more by the affairs of the East India Company and the abuse of the rights of that subcontinent's inhabitants under the administration of Warren Hastings, India's first governor-general. In 1788 Burke orchestrated the ultimately failed impeachment of Hastings by the House of Commons. It was because Burke had so enthusiastically embraced such principles that his readers could not initially comprehend his hostility to the events that informed his *Reflections on the Revolution in France*, which he drafted in the winter and spring of 1790. How could an admirer of England's Glorious Revolution and its Declaration of Right of the previous century fail to welcome the French people's subjection of their own king to the rule of law, likewise hallowed and sanctioned by their Declaration of the Rights of Man?

THE FRENCH REVOLUTION

Burke set himself the task of distinguishing the French Revolution, "the most astonishing that has hitherto happened in the world," he contended, not only from its alleged English precedent but also from all the other movements he had championed. The revolutionists of France did not seek the restoration of their traditional rights such as had been regained by Englishmen, he claimed, through both the monarchy's and Parliament's reaffirmation of a Protestant succession. They sought instead to realize the whole of mankind's abstract rights in general in defiance of the particular customs of their nation. Those metaphysical rights, invented, he believed, by Jean-Jacques Rousseau, Voltaire, and other philosophers of the age of Enlightenment, and implemented not by French statesmen or bishops but by the republic of letters' hack journalists, petty lawyers, dissident priests, and an associated "monied interest," had brought down rather than reformed the French state. Their authors and promoters had attempted to create a new order by destroying all that should have been nurtured and preserved. They had failed to recognize that a society's true contract is an entailed inheritance that binds the living to the dead and the yet to be born. Instead of valuing the real wealth of France's soil they had placed their faith in paper currency, as specious as their arguments. Their speculations of ideas and in the stock market had together bankrupted the nation. They had not grasped that populations are held together by deep convictions, prejudice, and "untaught feelings" rather than by philosophical abstractions. Following the advent of the Jacobin Terror in the autumn of 1793 many commentators came to agree with Burke's assessment, which by then struck them as all the more powerful for having apparently predicted the French Revolution's trajectory. After pursuing themes similar to those of his *Reflections* in his *Letter to a Member of the National Assembly* (1791), he completed the last of his *Letters on a Regicide Peace* in 1797 and died soon afterward, on 9 July of that year, in Beaconsfield, bequeathing his lament for an age of chivalry whose "decent drapery of life" had been rudely stripped away to post–French Revolutionary Europe and modern conservatism.

See also **Conservatism; French Revolution.**

BIBLIOGRAPHY

Primary Sources

Burke, Edmund. *The Writings and Speeches of Edmund Burke.* Edited by Paul Langford et al. 9 vols. Oxford, U.K., 1981–2000.

Secondary Sources

Freeman, Michael. *Edmund Burke and the Critique of Political Radicalism.* Oxford, U.K., 1980.

Kramnick, Isaac. *The Rage of Edmund Burke: Portrait of an Ambivalent Conservative.* New York, 1977.

O'Brien, Conor Cruise. *The Great Melody: A Thematic Portrait and Commented Anthology of Edmund Burke.* Chicago, 1992.

ROBERT WOKLER

BUSINESS FIRMS AND ECONOMIC GROWTH.

The business firm was the basic building block of the Western world's economic growth during the First and Second Industrial Revolutions. Its evolution has been often disregarded, and historians have generally emphasized issues related to technology and/or to the social transformation introduced by the industrialization process. Historians have also been more inclined to examine the macroeconomic effects on general indicators (demographic or economic, for instance, the gross national product [GNP] growth rate) of the revolutions in production and trade that occurred from the early nineteenth century than the transformations that occurred at a micro-organizational level.

From the beginning of the First Industrial Revolution to World War I, almost everywhere in the West the business enterprise was radically transformed, both in its internal structures and processes and in its relationships with the external environment. The sources of these changes were both technological and related to changes in the size and dynamism of the market. To achieve its goals the firm had to become innovative at the production and organizational level. In this process entrepreneurs played a central role.

THE FIRST INDUSTRIAL REVOLUTION

The mechanized factory in which hundreds of salaried workers were concentrated started to be diffused during the First Industrial Revolution (which occurred in Britain roughly from the last decade of the eighteenth century to the 1850s), replacing (although not completely) the old system of production based on craftwork and putting out. The "rise of the factory" as the dominant organizational form is one of the most intriguing issues in business and economic history. The main explanations emphasize (1) the requirements of the new technologies of production (economies of scale and division of labor); (2) the inadequacy of the previous organizational forms to cope with an increased dynamism in market demand (transaction and information costs); (3) a more efficient exploitation of the workers by the entrepreneurs; and (4) the radical change in the nature of knowledge, which had to be transmitted through new processes that called for a centralization of training. In legal terms the transformation was much slower: for a long period, from the beginning of the Industrial Revolution to the second half of the nineteenth century, in fact, the individual firm and the partnership (very often based on kinship ties) remained the rule, while the diffusion of the joint-stock company was limited all over Europe because of legal obstacles. The persistence of simple legal arrangements, based mainly on the family, points to the limited capital needs and governance structure of the business firm during the First

Industrial Revolution, as well as the need to cope with a high degree of uncertainty in business activity. At this stage the mechanization of several parts of the production process in textiles and fundamental innovations in mining, metalworking, and mechanics did not require increases in investment; a single wealthy individual, sometimes in partnership with an inventor, could typically afford the required capital. Individual or family patrimonies accumulated from commerce or land were enough to sustain the needs of investments in fixed and working capital, other sources of finance such as regional banks being active mostly locally. The scarce integration of the production process (merchants, for instance, were still distributing manufactured goods to the final customer) made it possible for the owner-entrepreneur and his partners to manage directly all the aspects of the activity with just the help of foremen. The result was to create an organizational structure characterized by elementary information flows, reflected in double-entry book-keeping accounting methods.

Another feature of the low degree of integration of the production process was the tendency of business firms to cluster geographically to minimize transportation and communication costs and to link external economies, for instance, in terms of human capital availability, knowledge circulation, and transport facilities. European industrialization was more a regional than a national process. "Industrial districts" and specialized production areas were present, sometimes crossing borders all over the Continent, from the British Midlands (metalworking) to Alsace (metalworking, textiles, and mechanics), from Lyon (silk production) to the pre-Alpine region in northern Italy (silk, cotton, and wool production, metalworking, furniture). This resulted in an industrialization pattern committed more to product differentiation than to standardization. This orientation toward specialization would remain a permanent feature of European industrialization well into the twentieth century in industries such as engineering that elsewhere were undergoing processes of integration and standardization. This was particularly evident in Italy and France where the roles of small specialized firms and the industrial district remained prominent throughout the twentieth century.

RELATIONSHIP TO ECONOMIC GROWTH

The relationship between the diffusion of the business firm and economic growth is evident when national economies are taken into consideration, even if there were significant differences in the timing of the takeoff and in the degree of development introduced by the industrialization process. Around 1860, the production of raw cotton in kilograms per capita was 15.1 in the United Kingdom, 2.7 in France, 1.4 in Germany, and only 0.2 in Italy. More striking are the figures for iron production: 54 kilograms per capita in the United Kingdom, 25 in France, and 14 in Germany. Other general estimates of the degree of industrialization put Britain first, with a level of industrialization more than three times that of Germany, four times that of France, and around ten times that of Italy. Not surprisingly, in the latecomer countries these differences soon called for the intervention of the state to fill the gap. This was the case in Italy and Russia, and partially in Germany, countries in which the state contributed heavily to the industrialization process, through tariffs, contract subsidies, and other kinds of support. The relationship between the nature and structure of the business firm and the process of economic growth was revolutionized by a radical transformation in production, communication, and transport technologies, which had an effect on strategies and hence on the organizational structures adopted by the business firm itself.

THE SECOND INDUSTRIAL REVOLUTION

The impact of the transport and communication revolution on the business firm was also notable in Europe. The new technologies of production typical of the Second Industrial Revolution (starting in the United States and diffusing among the industrialized countries during the last quarter of the nineteenth century) were adopted in many industries, such as steel, chemicals, and food processing, while the spread of the railway network at a national and transnational level fostered the formation of a wide system of distribution that made it necessary for large corporations to adopt economies of scale, as was happening in the United States. Europe adopted the new technologies and strategies of the Second Industrial Revolution in capital-intensive industries, but with radical modifications. There were marked national differences in the degree of diffusion of large firms in Europe for a number of reasons, including the dynamism and dimensions of the national market, the dominant business cultures of each nation, and the type of national industrial specialization. Germany quickly took a leading role in this process, while other nations that had led the way during the First Industrial Revolution, such as Britain, as well as latecomers such as Italy, experienced many difficulties in the new environment, and instead of adopting the large, integrated enterprise, they maintained an industrial system oriented toward small and medium-sized firms and specialization of the production process. But large firms in modern, concentrated industries were nevertheless needed to stay among the most industrialized nations. Almost everywhere in Europe this meant a further involvement of the state through various economic policies designed to increase the competitiveness of the industrial system, ranging from financing to direct intervention through the creation of state-owned enterprises.

From the beginning, the European route to the Second Industrial Revolution was slightly different from the American one, giving rise to a particular version of capitalism now commonly known as Rhineland capitalism to stress its Continental origins. The first difference was in the governance system; the European corporation has generally been characterized by the persistence of family leadership, very often accompanied by collaborative relations with the trade unions, and normally by close links with a powerful financial institution providing the owner-entrepreneur some of the resources necessary for the firm's growth and integration. As happened in the United States, the legal structure of the large firm also changed from the individual firm and partnership to the joint-stock corporation, which came into general use in Europe in the late nineteenth century.

Until the eve of World War I, the market for corporate control remained generally reduced almost everywhere, and the separation between ownership and control remained as well, resulting in the diffusion of the large family firm as a Continental model of management associated with companies that were in general smaller than their American counterparts. For instance, in 1912 the median market capitalization of the

largest U.S. corporation, U.S. Steel, was $757 million, more than twice that of the largest British corporation, J & P Coats, and five times that of the German steel company Krupp. In the same year, the top hundred firms accounted for 22 percent of the net manufacturing output in Germany, whereas the same figure was 16 percent in Britain and only 12 percent in France. Another feature of the European capitalism of the Second Industrial Revolution was the diffusion (sometimes on an international scale) of cartels and other cooperative agreements, aimed at regulating the competition among the large firms to reduce uncertainty.

BIG BUSINESS AND THE WEALTH OF NATIONS

The advent of the large business firm typical of the Second Industrial Revolution meant a further change in the equilibrium among the most industrialized nations of the Western world. Germany's capacity for meeting the requirements typical of the new technologies of production (high and constant throughput, a wide distribution network, and backward/forward integration policies) made that country the European leader of the Second Industrial Revolution, surpassing Britain in terms of economic growth and dynamism. Notwithstanding the relevant contribution of the small firms and of the specialized industrial districts, on the eve of World War I the correlation between the presence of large firms in capital-intensive industries and a country's economic welfare was indisputable. By 1913 the rankings among the leading nations had been transformed, with Germany now close to Britain (the industrialization index standing at 115 in Britain and 85 in Germany) and the others lagging far behind (the same index showing 59 for France, 36 for Italy, and only 20 for Russia). Germany by 1910 had overtaken the United Kingdom not only in steel production but also in the share of world industrial output (in 1870 the British share of the latter amounted to 32 percent, the German 13 percent; by 1913 the percentages were 14 and 16, respectively). More interesting, however, are the indicators of aggregate economic growth during the period from 1870 to 1913, which show the close relationship between the presence of big business and the wealth and welfare of a nation. Throughout this entire period, the average annual American growth rate was 2 percent, the German 1.6 percent, the French 1.5 percent, and the British only 1 percent, reflecting a relative decline of the country that had led the First Industrial Revolution, as well as the rise of the European champion of the Second Industrial Revolution, Germany.

See also **Economic Growth and Industrialism; Industrial Revolution, First; Industrial Revolution, Second.**

BIBLIOGRAPHY

Boyce, Gordon, and Simon Ville. *The Development of Modern Business.* London, 2002.

Chandler, Alfred D., Jr., Franco Amatori, and Takashi Hikino, eds. *Big Business and the Wealth of Nations.* Cambridge, U.K., 1997.

McCraw, Thomas K., ed. *Creating Modern Capitalism: How Entrepreneurs, Companies, and Countries Triumphed in Three Industrial Revolutions.* Cambridge, Mass., 1997.

Micklethwait, John, and Adrian Wooldridge. *The Company: A Short History of a Revolutionary Idea.* New York, 2003.

Pollard, Sidney. *The Genesis of Modern Management: A Study of the Industrial Revolution in Great Britain.* London, 1965.

Rosenberg, Nathan, and L. E. Birdzell, Jr. *How the West Grew Rich: The Economic Transformation of the Industrial World.* New York, 1986.

Schmitz, Christopher J. *The Growth of Big Business in the United States and Western Europe, 1850–1939.* Basingstoke, U.K., 1993.

ANDREA COLLI

BUTLER, JOSEPHINE (1828–1906), British feminist activist.

Josephine Butler was born on 13 April 1828 at Milfield Hill, Glendale, Northumberland, the fourth daughter and seventh of ten children of John Grey (1785–1868), an enlightened agricultural expert, and his wife Hannah Eliza (née Annett; 1794–1860). The Greys were a prominent but progressive family, connected to the Whig aristocracy of Georgian England. John embraced antislavery, the repeal of the Corn Laws, and philanthropic reforms and encouraged his children to take a lively interest in current affairs. The Greys nominally attended St. Andrew's Anglican Church, Corbridge, but family prayers and bible readings, influenced by Hannah's Moravian roots, were much more important.

In January 1852, Josephine married George Butler (1819–1890), a classicist at Durham University. They moved to Oxford, where George was appointed public examiner. The son of the dean of Peterborough, George shared his new wife's deep faith, and was ordained into the Anglican ministry in 1854 although he continued his academic career. Butler's first child, George, was born in October 1882, and the young family lived an enjoyable if financially restrained life, although Butler found some aspects of Oxford life repressive, particularly the lack of female companionship. In reaction to the misogyny she perceived around her, she took her first "rescue" case, offering a position to a young woman incarcerated in Newgate Gaol for infanticide.

In 1857, respiratory illness forced Butler to leave the damp Oxford air. George had failed to secure a university appointment, so he accepted the vice principalship of Cheltenham College and moved his wife and two sons there. Another son and a daughter Evangeline Mary (Eva) were born in Cheltenham, but the family's time there ended in tragedy when Eva died in a fall as she rushed to greet her parents on their return home. Devastated, George sought a new location for his wife and sons. The family moved to Liverpool in 1866, when George became headmaster of Liverpool College.

Butler, still deeply depressed, lost herself in the work of seeking "other hearts which ached night and day, and with more reason than mine" (1892, p. 182). Encouraged by a local radical Baptist minister Charles Birrell, she began visiting the city's notorious Brownlow Hill workhouse and talking and praying with the women who worked in its oakum sheds. She welcomed some of the more disadvantaged inmates into her home, which did little to endear the new headmaster's wife to many of the college's parents. Undaunted, Butler involved herself in a series of feminist campaigns alongside prominent northern radicals. At the invitation of Anne Clough (1820–1892), later the founder and first principal of Newnham College, she joined the North of England Council for the Higher Education of Women, becoming its president. Through the council, Butler met Elizabeth

Wolstoneholme and joined with her and Lydia Ernestine Becker (1827–1890) to work in Manchester for the Married Women's Property Committee as well as the National Society for Women's Suffrage. Along with campaigning, Butler began to publish. *The Education and Employment of Women* appeared in 1868 followed by an edited collection, *Woman's Work and Woman's Culture,* in 1869.

The same year, Butler began the work for which she is best known, leading the Ladies National Association for the Repeal of the Contagious Diseases Acts (LNA). The acts of 1864, 1866, and 1869 outraged feminists. Aimed at curtailing venereal disease in the British armed forces, they applied only to women and permitted punitive measures against prostitutes. The campaign against the acts ended in victory in 1886 but at great personal cost to Butler, who had been virulently ridiculed and even physically attacked during her speaking tours.

Butler extended her concerns to child prostitution and toured Europe speaking and gathering information. Helped by W. T. Stead (1849–1912) of the *Pall Mall Gazette,* which ran a series of shocking articles on the procuration of young girls, she raised public awareness to the extent that the British Parliament raised the age of consent from thirteen to sixteen. The indelicate nature of much of her work shocked certain sections of Victorian society and attracted heavy criticism to her husband. When George resigned in 1882 the couple faced an uncertain financial future, and were helped by an annuity fund established by friends who realized the sacrifices both the Butlers had made for Josephine's work.

George was appointed canon of Winchester, and Josephine spent much of the next decade nursing him through increasing ill health. After his death in 1890 she took on some public work and edited the paper *The Storm Bell* for the LNA. She died in 1906.

See also **Feminism.**

BIBLIOGRAPHY

Primary Sources

Butler, Josephine. *Recollections of George Butler.* Bristol, U.K., 1892.

———. *Personal Reminiscences of a Great Crusade.* London, 1896.

Secondary Sources

Caine, Barbara. *Victorian Feminists.* Oxford, U.K., 1992.

Jordan, Jane. *Josephine Butler.* London, 2001.

KRISTA COWMAN

BYRON, GEORGE GORDON (1788–1824), English poet.

George Gordon, sixth baron Byron entered Harrow School in 1801 and Trinity College, Cambridge, in 1805. He took his seat in the House of Lords in 1809. The final stage of Byron's education was the grand tour of Europe, which he undertook from 1809 to 1811. The Napoleonic Wars (1803–1815) prevented the usual culmination of the tour in Italy, and Byron traveled instead through Portugal, Spain, Gibraltar, and Malta to the more exotic regions of Albania, the Greek provinces of the Ottoman Empire, and Asia Minor.

His first volume of poetry was *Fugitive Pieces* (1806), which he destroyed; his subsequent *Hours of Idleness* (1807) received a sharply critical notice in the *Edinburgh Review* (January 1808), which provoked Byron to a satiric riposte, *English Bards and Scotch Reviewers* (1809). Byron's first major success was achieved with the publication of the poetic journal of his grand tour, the first two cantos of *Childe Harold's Pilgrimage* (1812). As he commented, he "awoke and found himself famous." His travels continued to provide him with exotic coloring for a series of oriental romances: *The Giaour* (1813), *The Bride of Abydos* (1813), *The Corsair* (1814), *Lara* (1814), and *The Siege of Corinth* (1816). The sensational success of these poems can be attributed to his creation of the Byronic hero, a powerful and misanthropic outlaw figure who is also a man of feeling. The public identified the poet with his creation and saw him as sexually attractive. Numerous sexual scandals were followed by a hasty marriage, in 1815, to an heiress, Anne Isabella Milbanke, who separated from him in 1816 in a cloud of vague allegations that included homosexuality and incest with his half sister, Augusta Leigh.

Lord Byron. Undated portrait by Theodore Gericault. MUSÉE FABRE, MONTPELLIER, FRANCE/BRIDGEMAN ART LIBRARY/GIRAUDON

Byron retired abroad and never returned to England. He lived for a while on Lake Geneva with Percy Bysshe and Mary Wollstonecraft Shelley. From Switzerland he moved to Venice and he remained in Italy, in various locations, until his departure to Greece (1823) to join the insurgents in the Greek War of Independence. His best known sexual liaison at the time involved Teresa Guiccioli (wife of Count Gamba). Politically, he committed himself to an Italian nationalist secret society, the Carbonari. His death in Greece (19 April 1824) gave him the status of a martyr for national freedom. As both a person and a poet, Byron became an inspiration for nationalist movements in Europe throughout the nineteenth century.

The immediate poetic products of his life abroad were two further cantos of *Childe Harold* (1816–1818), which lamented the condition of post-Napoleonic Europe, which he conflated with his individual predicament, and the Faustian drama *Manfred* (1817), which has often been interpreted as a confession of love for his half sister. A number of his other works reflect the personal and political frustrations of the time, notably *The Prisoner of Chillon* (1816) and two Venetian political dramas about failed aristocratic revolt, *Marino Faliero* and *The Two Foscari* (both 1821). The metaphysical drama *Cain* (1821) was condemned by many as a satanic attack on Christianity.

In 1818 Byron's writing took an unexpected direction with *Beppo,* a comic tale in ottava rima, in which a cuckolded Venetian husband happily settles for an open marriage. The verbal felicity and satiric potential of the new style led Byron to begin the first canto of what became his uncompleted epic, *Don Juan* (1819–1824). This retelling of the Don Juan story subverted the usual moralistic treatment of the legend by making Juan the innocent victim of women. Juan's adventures took him from Spain to Turkey, Russia, and England and provided an opportunity for Byron to comment on current history and the uncertainty of all philosophical explanations of the human condition. The poem was uncompleted when Byron died, leaving Juan on the verge of joining the French Revolution as Anarchasis Cloots, the spokesman for all humankind, who would be guillotined by his own side.

The other major poem of Byron's last years is *The Vision of Judgment* (1822), which was published as a riposte to the English poet laureate Robert Southey's elegy on the death of George III. Southey had attacked Byron as a member of a "Satanic School" of poetry. Byron parodied Southey's poem, turning it into an attack on the king and ridiculing Southey as a prostitute sycophant.

Nineteenth-century criticism of Byron admired his early sentimental verse. Recent criticism has preferred his later satires for their liberalism, their commitment to freedom (both political and personal), and their postmodern sense of irony. The poet's sympathetic portrayal of women (despite his promiscuity) has attracted feminist critics and his (recently revealed) homosexuality has made him a gay icon. His most admiring audience, however, remains the Greeks.

See also **Greece; Romanticism; Shelley, Mary; Shelley, Percy Bysshe.**

BIBLIOGRAPHY

Primary Sources

Marchand, Leslie A., ed. *Byron's Letters and Journals: The Complete and Unexpurgated Text of All Letters Available in Manuscript and the Full Printed Version of All Others.* 13 vols. London, 1973–1994.

McGann, Jerome J., ed., *Lord Byron: The Complete Poetical Works.* 7 vols. Oxford, U.K., 1980–1993.

Nicholson, Andrew, ed., *Lord Byron: The Complete Miscellaneous Prose.* Oxford, U.K., 1991.

Secondary Sources

Marchand, Leslie Alexis. *Byron: A Biography.* 3 vols. New York, 1957.

MALCOLM KELSALL

CABARETS. The word *cabaret* has been applied to venues ranging from upscale nightclubs to sleazy striptease joints, but the historically most interesting form has been the French *cabaret artistique* and its imitators. Such locales were notable not only for their witty satires of politics and social and sexual mores, but also for their encouragement of experimentation in the performing and visual arts.

The French word *cabaret* originally meant, quite simply, tavern, but it acquired its modern meaning in 1881, with the founding of the Chat Noir (Black Cat) in Montmartre. Having entertained themselves with evenings of improvised singing and recitation, Rodolphe Salis (1851–1897) and a number of other young writers, artists, and composers decided that they could earn some much-needed income by opening their revelries to a paying public. Salis presided over a wide range of entertainment, which largely consisted of satirical songs by composers like Jules Jouy and Maurice Mac-Nab. But the Chat Noir also had much to offer the eye: the graphics of Theophile-Alexandre Steinlen and Adolphe Willette adorned posters and sheet music, and the innovative shadow plays of Henri Rivière soon became the major attraction. When the Chat Noir moved to larger premises in 1885, the original venue was taken over by one of its singers, Aristide Bruant. An imposing and flamboyant figure, so memorably captured in a number of posters by Henri de Toulouse-Lautrec (1864–1901), Bruant named his venture the Mirliton (the "Reed Pipe," but also, by implication, "Doggerel"). A consummate provocateur, Bruant regularly insulted bourgeois members of his audience, and he expressed sympathy for the downtrodden classes in his biting songs, replete with vulgar expressions and lower-class argot.

Bruant left the Mirliton in 1895, and two years later the Chat Noir closed after the death of Salis, but the commercial and artistic success of these ventures inspired a host of imitators. In Paris itself, most of them were little better than tourist traps, though the Lapin Agile (Agile Rabbit) was a rendezvous for outstanding young writers and artists, most notably Guillaume Apollinaire (1880–1918). It was in other European cities that avant-garde cabaret flourished. One direct offshoot of the Parisian ventures was Els Quatre Gats (The Four Cats) in Barcelona, cofounded in 1897 by Miquel Utrillo (the father of the painter Maurice Utrillo [1883–1955]), who had participated in the Chat Noir. The Barcelona venture became a center of the Catalan cultural revival, and it was especially known for its puppet shows and its exhibitions of young artists, above all Pablo Picasso (1881–1973).

After the turn of the century, the cities of central and eastern Europe were especially receptive to cabaret. The first German cabaret, founded in January 1901 in Berlin, was Ernst von Wolzogen's Buntes Theater (Motley Theater), also known as the Überbrettl (Super-Stage). Performing in a regular theater, rather than a café setting, Wolzogen's troupe addressed an upscale audience and was only mildly critical of Wilhelmine society. A much more aggressive tone was set by Schall und Rauch (Sound and Smoke), another Berlin venture, which

La chanteuse. Pastel by Edgar Degas, c. 1878. Degas attempted to convey the great energy of cabaret performances in this depiction. FOGG ART MUSEUM, HARVARD UNIVERSITY ART MUSEUMS, USA/BRIDGEMAN ART LIBRARY/BEQUEST FROM THE COLLECTION OF MAURICE WERTHEIM, CLASS 1906

grew out of the convivial gatherings of a group of young actors, including Max Reinhardt (1873–1943). They began by staging send-ups of the serious dramas in which they performed, but their repertoire turned political when they added the character Serenissimus. Ostensibly a fictitious potentate of a small German state, who sat in the proscenium loge and provided a very benighted running commentary on the performance, the character was clearly a takeoff on Kaiser William II (r. 1888–1918). After little more than a year, Schall und Rauch turned from cabaret to staging one-act plays and later evening-long works, and thus launched Reinhardt's career as Germany's outstanding theatrical director of modern times. His roots in cabaret were significant, though, since it was there that he experimented with the nonverbal performing arts—song, dance, pantomime—that so enlivened his later productions of classical and modern drama.

Not Berlin but Munich was the home of Germany's most innovative cabaret, the Elf Scharfrichter (Eleven Executioners), which opened in April 1901. It was explicitly political from the start, since it was founded in part as an offshoot of an anticensorship movement; that issue was especially acute in Munich, the center of the Germany's sensual Jugendstil (art nouveau) movement, as well as the home of illustrated satirical weeklies like *Jugend* and *Simplicissimus*. Many members of the troupe were associated with those journals, most notably Frank Wedekind (1864–1918), who had made a name for himself as an avant-garde playwright and satirical poet. His songs, performed by himself or by the venture's chanteuse, Marya Delvard, pilloried the sexual hypocrisy of the Wilhelmine era. Founded in response to censorship, the Elf Scharfrichter fell victim to it by the end of 1903, as more and more numbers were cut from their repertoire.

Delvard and Marc Henry, a fellow Frenchman who had managed the Munich cabaret, eventually moved to Vienna, where they founded first the Nachtlicht (Nightlight) in 1906, and the Fledermaus (Bat) a year later. Housed in a small theater whose auditorium, café, program books, and promotional posters and postcards were designed by Josef Hoffmann (1870–1956) and other members of the Wiener Werkstätte, the Fledermaus was a showcase of the most advanced Viennese design. By staging the premieres of short plays by Oskar Kokoschka (1886–1980), it also put itself at the forefront of the theatrical avant-garde. Unlike other cabarets, which focused on songs, the repertoire of the Fledermaus was best known for witty monologues and dialogues by some of Vienna's best-known essayists, such as Egon Friedell, Alfred Polgar, Roda Roda, and Peter Altenberg.

Cabaret rapidly spread farther east, and important ventures were founded in Budapest (the Modern Stage) and Kraków (the Green Balloon), which became important centers of Hungarian and Polish modernism. Cabaret reached Russia in 1908, with the founding of the Letuchaya Mysh (Bat) in Moscow. Like Schall und Rauch, it was launched by actors who at first specialized in parodies of drama. But soon it became visually innovative, as it featured sets and costumes by Leon Bakst (1866–1924). The Letuchaya Mysh became best known for its "living dolls," brightly colored figures who acted out Russian fairy tales. Prewar cabaret attained its epitome in St. Petersburg, where the Brodyachaya Sobaka (Stray Dog) opened in 1911. It provided a forum for recitations by the greatest poets of Russian modernism, Anna Akhmatova (1889–1966) and Vladimir Mayakovsky (1893–1930).

Cabaret was to have a distinguished future after 1914, but already in its first thirty years it was a haven for social and political critics and it served as a laboratory for experimentation in literature and the visual and performing arts.

See also **Berlin; Modernism; Paris; Picasso, Pablo; St. Petersburg; Toulouse-Lautrec, Henri.**

BIBLIOGRAPHY

Appignanesi, Lisa. *The Cabaret.* London, 1975.

Jelavich, Peter. *Berlin Cabaret.* Cambridge, Mass., 1993.

Segel, Harold B. *Turn-of-the-Century Cabaret.* New York, 1987.

PETER JELAVICH

CABET, ÉTIENNE (1788–1856), French left-wing political leader and writer.

The son of a Dijon cooper and one of the few left-wing political leaders of the era with roots in the working classes, Cabet's long career spanned the entire "age of revolution" as well as two continents. Although his place in the history of the Left was established rather pejoratively by the Marxist mainstream as the author of one of the archetypical texts of "utopian" socialism, *Voyage en Icarie* (1840), and the founder of a "little Icaria" in America, Cabet was in fact the creator, during the 1840s, of the largest "proletarian party" in Europe, a man whose name, as Karl Marx (1818–1883) remarked, was synonymous with communism.

Raised as a Jacobin, Cabet became a lawyer after a stellar school career, pleading cases during the early Restoration on behalf of the politically oppressed. Arriving in Paris in 1820, he was embraced in liberal circles, joined the anti-Bourbon Charbonnerie conspiracy, and became a protégé of the moderate republican leader Jacques-Charles Dupont de l'Eure (1767–1855). He dedicated himself to Republican politics thereafter, largely as a journalist and pamphleteer. As the Revolution of 1830 rapidly turned reactionary, Cabet resigned a judicial post in Corsica and won fame for his book on the "betrayal" of the recent revolution, as an indefatigable organizer of opposition associations, and then as editor of *Le Populaire,* which gained the largest circulation of any weekly in France before it was suppressed in 1834. As its editor, Cabet was convicted of lèse-majesté (crime against a sovereign power) and chose exile in London over prison in France.

To that point, Cabet's republicanism was of the moderate sort, with few hints of socialism. London (where his common-law wife and daughter joined him) proved transformative. Mixing with other Continental exiles while learning English and living by teaching French, Cabet read widely in both languages. In French, it was the history of the Revolution of 1789 and the texts of its leaders. He fell under the spell of Philippe Buonarotti's (1761–1837) notion that social and economic equality was the "last consequence" of Maxmilien Robespierre's (1758–1794) vision of the Republic and proceeded to write his own version of the Revolution to confirm it. At the same time he read Robert Owen (1771–1858) and Thomas More's (1478–1535) *Utopia.* Hence the *Voyage en Icarie.* Cabet's novel portrays a nation born in revolution led by a benevolent dictator (Icar) who speaks for the people during a fifty-year transition to a perfectly egalitarian society based on an idealized version of the extended family where everyone seems related—a gigantic *cousinage.* (It should be recalled that this was an age of frequent cousin marriage and deep sibling bonds, both romanticized in fiction.) Everyone worked, but their jobs were "pleasant and easy" and their workdays short, made that way by the triumph of modern technology. Leisure time would be the creative heart of existence. Administrative decisions were taken by consensus in a context where politics had effectively disappeared.

The format and the message proved enormously appealing to ordinary working people whose livelihoods were now increasingly threatened by uncontrolled capitalism. Returning to Paris in 1839, "Father" Cabet, as his followers soon called him, flew into action, publishing his two books, explaining his ideas in brochures aimed at specific audiences, including women, re-creating *Le Populaire,* and sending its salesmen to every nook and cranny of France. Local groups, forming around subscribers, met in cafés and homes to discuss *La Communauté,* Cabet's term for his communist society. Cabet combated not only the "heartless" system of economic and political "egotism" but also rival socialist "schools," sparing only fellow Jacobins like Louis Blanc (1811–1882). But in general, his vituperative pen and demand for ideological conformity seemed to pay off: by 1846 his following across France (and elsewhere) numbered perhaps one hundred thousand men and women. Cabet was particularly solicitous of the latter (though silent on their right to vote), stressing their dual oppression as domestic captives under the Napoleonic Code and as the most exploited of the exploited in the world of work, paid and unpaid. How different things would be in Icaria! Finally, he also sought the support of the upper classes, who should understand that their current status was becoming increasingly precarious, based as it was on the extreme degradation of "the people," whose patience would soon run out.

In 1847, believing that violent revolution was imminent, but unable to advocate it, Cabet combined a new line—that "communism was Christianity in its primitive purity"—with the notion that his people must now establish a New Jerusalem across the waters. Such escapism caused a wholesale turnover within his following, as Christian millenarians moved in and republican revolutionaries moved out. As Cabet prepared to establish the "promised land" in Texas, the actual Revolution of 1848 occurred, leaving him in a strange position. But he rallied, ignored the "avant garde" that had left for America two weeks before, and suddenly found himself the main scapegoat of the Revolution, as the Right accused the entire Left of being communists, a tactic that made Marx's "specter" seem all the more real. In the end, Cabet, though he continued to work with Louis Blanc and Alexandre-Auguste Ledru-Rollin (1807–1874) to build a stable neo-Jacobin Left in the Republic, revitalized the "emigration" to the "Icarian colony," which, after the disastrous collapse of the Texas venture, came to be established at Nauvoo, Illinois, recently abandoned by Brigham Young (1801–1877) and his persecuted Latter-Day Saints.

Cabet joined his "pioneers" permanently in 1849, being no longer welcome in France, and established Icar's dictatorship of the people. His idealistic "citizens" (few of whom came from the distraught poor Cabet had lamented in *Le Populaire,* given the 600-franc entry fee—a year's wages—required of recruits) cheerfully submitted but rapidly lost their zeal, as has been beautifully documented by Jacques Rancière and Robert Sutton. Principal among them were the women who, lo and behold, not only were denied the vote but also cooked the meals and did the laundry. Diana Garno argues that the egregious failure of the Nauvoo experiment, which ended with Cabet's expulsion, was largely due to the growing disenchantment of women, whose idealism had been no less vibrant than the men's. Cabet died of apoplexy in Saint Louis. Icarian communities struggled on in various rural areas of the United States, but Cabet's main legacy remained in France, where he contributed mightily to the vision among working people of a society where they counted.

See also **Blanc, Louis; Jacobins; Ledru-Rollin, Alexandre-Auguste; Owen, Robert; Revolutions of 1848; Utopian Socialism; Working Class.**

BIBLIOGRAPHY

Garno, Diana. *Citoyennes and Icaria.* Lanham, Md., 2005.

Johnson, Christopher H. *Utopian Communism in France: Cabet and the Icarians, 1839–1851.* Ithaca, N.Y., 1974.

Rancière, Jacques. *The Nights of Labor: The Workers' Dream in Nineteenth-Century France.* Translated from the French by John Drury; with an introduction by Donald Reid. Philadelphia, 1989.

Sutton, Robert. *Les Icariens: The Utopian Dream in Europe and America.* Urbana, Ill., 1994.

CHRISTOPHER H. JOHNSON

CAILLAUX, JOSEPH (1863–1944), French politician.

Joseph Caillaux was one of the most paradoxical leaders of the French Third Republic (1870–1940). Despite his origins as a *grand bourgeois,* Caillaux championed fiscal reforms accused of soaking the rich. Against the native nationalism of his conservative milieu, he advocated compromise and conciliation with the "hereditary enemy" across the Rhine. And in a political culture that expected outward observance of strict moral codes, Caillaux flaunted his mistresses and did not shy away from divorce, which was legalized only in 1884.

As a young man, Joseph Caillaux studied law and economics at the elite École libre des sciences politiques, becoming a specialist in government finance. He was elected to the National Assembly in 1898 and, the following year, at the tender age of thirty-six, named minister of finance. Caillaux's cautious republicanism together with his economic expertise recommended him to the prime minister, René Waldeck-Rousseau, who sought conservative ballast for his left-leaning "government of national defense," formed in the wake of the Dreyfus affair.

During this early period, Caillaux's political views remained relatively conventional; it was his style and demeanor that stood out. At a time when male politicians and business leaders dressed in basic black, Caillaux looked like a "dandy straight out of Balzac" (Vergnet, p. 1) As for his personality, commentators found him so unique that "Even the genius of a Shakespeare could never have captured him" (Vergnet, p. 3). His imperious, manic behavior aroused hostility, and when he moved to the left after 1905, his parliamentary opponents were all the more determined to silence him. But Caillaux's political skills were such that he managed to steer a highly controversial income tax bill though both the Assembly and the Senate. Republican politicians had been working to enact such a tax since 1848.

On becoming prime minister in 1911, Caillaux antagonized his opponents still more by compromising with Germany over opposing colonial claims. Rather than risk war over Morocco, Caillaux agreed to give the Kaiser a portion of the French Congo in exchange for a German withdrawal from the port of Agadir. Outraged nationalists toppled Caillaux's government after only three months in office.

Elected president of the center-left Radical Party in 1913, Caillaux was the logical choice for a new term as prime minister in December of that year. But President Raymond Poincaré preferred a more pliable politician, and Caillaux had to settle once again for the ministry of finance. He nonetheless dominated the new government, and opponents feared he would abrogate a new law requiring three years of military service rather than two. Though Caillaux's sometime allies on the socialist left wanted to scale back military service, there is no evidence the finance minister shared this position. No matter, the editor of *Le Figaro,* Gaston Calmette, undertook a ferocious press campaign designed to oust Caillaux from office. The editor accused the former prime minister of treasonous machinations with Germany, stock market manipulation, and illegal judicial interventions. *Le Figaro*'s attacks culminated with the publication on 13 March 1914 of a personal letter the finance minister had written thirteen years earlier. The letter revealed some political double-dealing on Caillaux's part and included an affectionate closing that suggested he and the married Berthe Gueydan, later his first wife, were having an intimate affair. In publishing a personal letter, Calmette had violated a journalistic taboo, shocking Caillaux's current wife, Henriette. The latter became convinced, or so she later claimed, that *Le Figaro* would now reveal embarrassing letters Joseph had written her.

On 16 March 1914, Henriette Caillaux entered Calmette's office and shot him six times at point-blank range. The editor's horrified colleagues handed her to the police, smoking gun in hand. Her husband resigned from the cabinet, and four months later she stood trial for murder. Joseph Caillaux dominated these proceedings as he had the French parliament, but it was Henriette Caillaux's testimony that swayed the jury. No feminist femme fatale, she claimed to be a weak-willed woman governed by passions beyond her conscious control. Just three days before the outbreak of World War I, Madame Caillaux was acquitted of all charges.

Despite the favorable outcome, the "pro-German" and morally compromised Joseph Caillaux was excluded from the wartime cabinet, his once-brilliant career in shambles. Caillaux's fortunes sank so low that France's wartime premier, Georges Clemenceau (1841–1929), had him arrested for treason. But Caillaux returned briefly to the finance ministry in the mid-1920s and was elected to the Senate, where he served continuously until the fall of France in June 1940. He died at home in Mamers (Sarthe) shortly after the liberation of Paris in 1944.

See also **Anticlericalism; Clemenceau, Georges; France; Radicalism.**

BIBLIOGRAPHY

Allain, Jean-Claude. *Joseph Caillaux.* 2 vols. Paris, 1978.

Berenson, Edward. *The Trial of Madame Caillaux.* Berkeley and Los Angeles, 1992.

Caillaux, Joseph. *Mes mémoires.* 3 vols. Paris, 1947.

Vergnet, Paul. *Joseph Caillaux.* Paris, 1918.

EDWARD BERENSON

CAJAL, SANTIAGO RAMÓN Y (1852–1934), Spanish biologist.

The reputation of Santiago Ramón y Cajal (1852–1934) as the greatest of the nineteenth-century pioneers of twentieth-century neuroscience seems secure. In 1889, when he showed his most important discovery, the neuron, to the Congress of Anatomists in Berlin, the field of neuroscience had yet to be named. Not long after he died, the neuron doctrine and his other four hypotheses about brain-cell structure and development were the central doctrines of the new field.

Cajal made his mark in the area he called "histology," or the study of tissue structure, a field first laid out by Marie-François-Xavier Bichat (1771–1802) in the early years of the nineteenth century. Histology used the nineteenth century's preeminent tool, the optical microscope, to find and describe the cell structure of tissue like heart muscle, not only to discover how it worked and how it might go wrong but also to essentially classify it, that is, to offer a taxonomy of the different tissues and the cells within those tissues. It was a strongly materialist pursuit, and Cajal was a strong materialist. This was unusual at the time in Spain, a country that was both popularly idealist and officially Catholic.

Cajal had a very tenacious character. His autobiography, *Recuerdos de mi Vida* (Recollections of my life), recounts a patient pursuit of mastery, starting in childhood, of everything from body-building to championship chess. His earliest ambition was to become a painter. Discouraged by his parents, who he says thought painting "a sinful amusement," and the monastics who were his teachers, Cajal nevertheless mastered drawing skills that were indispensable to histological illustration before microphotography.

The ruling hypothesis of nineteenth-century biology, the 1839 "cell theory" of Matthia Jakob Schleiden (1804–1881) and Theodor Ambrose Hubert Schwann (1810–1882), reduced all living things to separate parts, but most of the central nervous system looked like a partless mass to nineteenth-century scientists. The central nervous system in *Homo sapiens*, which is now known to contain something on the order of ten billion separate cells with perhaps a trillion connections, appeared to leading investigators like Rudolf Albert von Kölliker (1817–1905) to be a tangle of fibers, interrupted only occasionally by recognizable cells. Massed fibers were dubbed "gray matter" and "white matter," the fibers usually thinning down beyond the resolving power of optical microscopes, even those with oil-immersion lenses. Microdissecting the fibers seemed beyond human skill. Otto Deiters (1834–1863) died young after years of teasing apart the neural net under a microscope using threadlike needles, but he did leave notes about axons (extended, single fibers) that did not branch and tiny "protoplasmic processes" (now called "dendrites") that branched out from them. Some histologists fixed on the chemical dyes and stains that might make nerves stand out against their cloudy background by coloring only one or two at a time, but the dyes proved unpredictable and unreliable. If they worked once they might not work again. In the spirit of trying everything, in 1872 Joseph von Gerlach (1820–1896), the inventor of the carmine dye, tried gold.

In the end, however, it was not gold that did the trick, but silver: silver nitrate, in fact, the chemical that made photography possible at the beginning of the century. The Italian histologist Camillo Golgi (1843 or 1844–1926) was the first scientist to use it productively, publishing his first papers "on the structure of the gray matter" in summer 1873. He used a soak of potassium bichromate, to which he added a dilute solution of silver nitrate. The bichromate already in the cells reduced the silver nitrate to metallic silver, which precipitated and stained the inside of the entire cell black, magnificently distinct against the yellow left by the chromates. Somehow it could stain cells in the middle of a three-dimensional cube of tissue, one cell at a time, all the way out to their ends, so that they stood out clearly. The stain was very temperamental. Golgi never stopped working on it. His most comprehensive work, published in 1886, would lead to a Nobel prize in medicine in 1906.

Working as an assistant in the Zaragoza Medical Faculty in 1880, Cajal used gold-chloride staining in his first published paper and suggested ammoniacal silver nitrate in his second. As a professor of histology at the University of Valencia in 1883, he had no colleague who knew Golgi and his stain. Cajal saw the Golgi technique only in 1887 when he paid a visit to Madrid before joining the faculty at Barcelona and saw examples of silver-bichromate staining in the house and lab of Luís Simarro Lacabra (1851–1921), who had just returned from France. He immediately gave up all other methods and improved on this one in 1888 by making two separate soaks out of what had been a continuous procedure. Cajal found his method just in time. The extraordinary hypothesis that the entire mass of the central nervous system was composed of the extensions of separate and distinct cells had already been advanced in October 1886 by Wilhelm His (1831–1904) of Leipzig, in January 1887; by Auguste Henri Forel (1848–1931), the Director of the Burghölzli Asylum in Zurich; and four months later in Oslo, Norway, by Fridtjof Nansen (1861–1930) in his Ph.D. thesis, just before he set off for Greenland. Their proof was unsatisfactory, however, and in 1887 the old hypothesis that all the nerve fibers of the gray matter were mutually connected in a single network, the so-called reticular hypothesis (from Latin *reticulum*, network), was still being vigorously promoted by von Gerlach, the pioneer of carmine and later of gold chloride, and subscribed to by most histologists, including the budding neuroanatomist Sigmund Freud (1856–1939) and his mentor Theodor Meynert (1833–1898) in Vienna. Its great champion was in fact none other than the discoverer of silver-chromate dye, Camillo Golgi himself. "Ruled by

the theory," Cajal remembered, "we who were active in histology then saw networks everywhere." It was a beautiful theory and, he wrote, "as always, reason is silent before beauty" (*Recollections,* p. 303).

In 1888 Cajal set up a laboratory in the back room of his house in Barcelona and made one more change in the method, using unhatched chick brains to study the central nervous system, which in vertebrate embryos is incomplete at birth. Some nerves have grown dendrites and axons, but not all are fully extended; and the "glial" cells have hardly begun covering the nerve extensions with myelin. Even the Golgi stain works better in embryos. Cajal was able to see very long unmyelinated axons whose tips came up close enough to another cell to touch it but never actually penetrated, or even touched, its cell wall. His conclusion: the famous central network, "that sort of unfathomable physiological sea, into which, on the one hand, were supposed to pour the streams arising from the sense organs, and from which, on the other hand, the motor or centrifugal conductors were supposed to spring like rivers originating in mountain lakes" (*Recollections,* p. 336) did not exist at all. The right metaphor was not hydraulic but electronic, something like a contemporary telephone exchange.

In 1889 Cajal brought his new idea, together with the indispensable hard-won proof, to the anatomists' conference in Berlin. The patriarch of the society, Rudolf Albert von Kölliker (1817–1905), swept Cajal into his carriage, took him to his hotel, and gave him a dinner, promising to have everything Cajal wrote published in Germany. In 1891 the formidable Berlin expert Heinrich Wilhelm G. von Waldeyer-Hartz (1836–1921) published a series of six long articles in the *German Medical Weekly* in which he attributed the new gray-matter-discontinuity hypothesis to Cajal and gave it the name *neurone doctrine*. The publication secured Cajal's scientific reputation for the rest of his life. News of his discovery passed beyond the small world of histology and became an example of "science," ever progressing in the nineteenth-century manner. In 1894 the British Royal Society offered him its most prestigious award in biology, the Croonian Lectureship, at the behest of England's leading neuroanatomist, Charles Scott Sherrington (1857–1952). In 1899 Cajal was among the presenters at Clark University's anniversary international conference in Worcester, Massachusetts, ten years before Freud received the same honor.

In the 1890s Cajal advanced and provided evidence for four additional hypotheses about the nervous system. The first of these, which has acquired the name of the *Law of Dynamic Polarization,* asserts that the axons of nerve cells are always outputs for nerve impulses and that dendrites are always inputs. The second hypothesis is the idea that neurons grow from the ends of the axons at a point analogous to the root hair of a plant. Cajal found this in chick embryos in 1890 and called it the "cone of growth." The third of these ideas Cajal advanced in 1892 and eventually called the "Chemotactic Hypothesis," that the growth cones of axons find their way along one trajectory instead of another by following trails of chemicals already laid down among the other nerves. These three hypotheses are now conventional wisdom so taken for granted that Cajal's name has become completely detached from them and they are taught as if anatomists had always known them. Not that Cajal himself ever found a proof for them, or indeed had anything in his experimental repertoire that could have provided one. Cajal's fourth hypothesis, however, remained very much in the center of debate in the last decade of the twentieth century—the Decade of the Brain. This is the view that the phenomenon we call memory is a product of particular states of the entire central nervous system. Memory, thought Cajal, was not the effect of some chemical or of changes in one or a few nerve cells. It was, he thought, a global property of the brain as a whole. The mind may not govern, as the nineteenth-century thought. It may simply "emerge," an undetermined consequence of the simple interactions of more than ten billion cells making a trillion connections.

In 1906 Cajal's disciple Sherrington coined the word *synapse* to describe the gap at the junction between one nerve cell and another. In the same year Cajal was awarded half of the sixth Nobel prize in medicine. The other half went to Camillo Golgi, who met Cajal for the first time at the ceremony. The next day Golgi gave his Nobel acceptance lecture and the day after that, Cajal gave his (both in French). Golgi's lecture, "The Neuron Doctrine, Theory and Facts," was a sustained attack on the independence of the neuron. Cajal's address,

"The Structure and Connexions of Neurons," was a sustained defense of the same idea.

The neuron doctrine is a twentieth-century idea that emerged in a nineteenth-century context. Separate and atomized units, interacting without an overall plan, give rise to minds as well as molecules, neither entirely predictable.

See also **Science and Technology.**

BIBLIOGRAPHY

Primary Sources

Cajal, Santiago Ramón y. *Histologie du système nerveux de l'homme et les vertebres.* 1909. Translated by L. Azoulay. 2 vols. Paris, 1911. Cajal's definitive textbook on neuroanatomy.

———. *Recollections of My Life.* Translated by E. Horne Craigie. 1937. Cambridge, Mass., 1989.

———. *Cajal on the Cerebral Cortex: An Annotated Translation of the Complete Writings.* Edited by Javier DeFelipe and Edward G. Jones. New York, 1988.

———. *New Ideas on the Structure of the Nervous System in Man and Vertebrates.* Cambridge, Mass., 1990.

Secondary Sources

Cannon, Dorothy F. *Explorer of the Human Brain: The Life of Santiago Ramón y Cajal (1852–1934).* New York, 1949.

Everdell, William R. "Santiago Ramón y Cajal: The Atoms of Brain, 1889." In *The First Moderns: Profiles in the Origins of Twentieth-Century Thought, 1872–1913.* Chicago, 1997. Reprinted in Jennifer Blaise, ed., *Twentieth-Century Literary Criticism,* new edition. Detroit, 2000.

Grisolía, Santiago, et al., eds. *Ramón y Cajal's Contribution to the Neurosciences.* New York, 1988.

Hydén, H., ed. *The Neuron.* Amsterdam, 1967.

Marijuán, Pedro C., ed. *Cajal and Consciousness: Scientific Approaches to Consciousness on the Centennial of Ramón y Cajal's Textura. Proceedings of a November–December, 2000 Conference.* New York, 2001.

Shepherd, Gordon M. *Foundations of the Neuron Doctrine.* New York, 1991.

WILLIAM R. EVERDELL

CANADA. Early-twentieth-century Canada was the product of two distinct periods of European expansion into the Americas. During the first period from the sixteenth century until the end of the

Napoleonic Wars the number of European migrants crossing the Atlantic to the northern part of North America was small and the French colonies attracted fewer settlers than any of the major overseas European colonies. At most 35,000 migrants went to New France and close to 70 percent were transients who did not stay for long. Acadia attracted a few hundred more. Acadia became the British colony of Nova Scotia in 1713 but the population remained overwhelmingly French until the expulsion of the Acadians after 1755 and the resettlement of the colony by New Englanders following the Seven Years' War. By the Treaty of Paris of 1763 New France also became a British colony and was renamed Quebec. But neither Nova Scotia nor Quebec attracted many migrants from Europe, although a substantial number of American loyalists moved north after the American Revolution, doubling the population of Nova Scotia and increasing significantly the size of the English-speaking minority in Quebec.

In response to Loyalist demands, the British government created the province of New Brunswick out of Nova Scotia in 1784 and divided Quebec into Upper and Lower Canada in 1791. Upper Canada and to a lesser degree Lower Canada continued to attract American immigrants after 1783 and all of the British North American colonies received a trickle of migrants from the British Isles, especially from the Scottish Highlands. But until the 1820s British North America had a French-speaking majority concentrated overwhelmingly in Lower Canada. The French-Canadian population of Lower Canada (or Quebec as it became again in 1867) grew almost entirely by natural increase, they were almost all Catholics, and there was very little intermarriage between French Canadians and later migrants from other sources. The British minority in Quebec did grow substantially in the nineteenth century, peaking at around 25 percent in the 1830s and shrinking to around 20 percent by the end of the century, but it was overwhelmingly concentrated by 1914 in the city of Montreal. Quebec was (and still is) a unique place on the North American continent, because nearly 80 percent of its population was directly descended from the few thousand French migrants who settled in New France prior to 1763. No other place in the Americas had such a substantial and homogeneous majority directly descended from the first wave of European migration to the Americas. Because it was cut off from its European roots after 1763, Quebec developed a distinctive French-Canadian culture that had little in common with postrevolutionary France. Unlike France, Quebec remained a very Catholic and deeply conservative society. Indeed, it became more so after the abortive rebellions against British rule in 1837–1838 forced many French-Canadian liberals into exile and greatly strengthened the power of the hierarchy of the Catholic Church. Until well after World War I most French Canadians in Quebec lived in rural communities and worked at agriculture or in resource industries. The political elite was small, drawn from the professional classes, who had been educated in Catholic schools and who had limited sympathy for either "Godless" France or republican America. Their primary concern was to ensure the survival of a distinctively French Canadian and Catholic culture in Quebec and they were prepared to cooperate with the elites in the rest of Canada on that basis.

CANADIAN IDENTITY

The identity of the other provinces of Canada (and of the English-speaking minority in Quebec) was formed during the second and much larger wave of European migration to the Americas that began slowly after 1815, but was largest in the century from 1830 to 1930, peaking in the period from 1880 to 1914. Canada received only a small proportion of this enormous wave of European migrants and the vast majority of the immigrants to Canada before 1914 came from the British Isles. Indeed, Canada was the only major country in the Americas that remained the colony of a European power and drew most of its immigrants from its mother country. During most years in the nineteenth century (except briefly during the early 1830s and again after 1900) the majority of British migrants went to the United States but there they formed only one immigrant group among many and were fairly easily absorbed into American culture. But in British North America the British immigrants overwhelmed the existing population (outside of Quebec) and reshaped the culture, making it less American and more British. In 1815 the population of British North America was just over 500,000; 335,000 of them lived in Lower Canada, 90 percent of whom were French speaking. Over the next fifty years about one million migrants entered Canada and about half became permanent residents. Except for a small influx of Germans, who formed the only significant non-British, non-French minority, almost all of British North America's migrants were drawn from the British Isles. By 1867 the population of the newly created Dominion of Canada was about 3.5 million and every province except Quebec had a majority composed of the British-born and their offspring.

Fewer than 10 percent of the British migrants were assisted migrants and the vast majority paid their own way across the Atlantic. Since none came as indentured servants and slavery was effectively abandoned even before formally abolished in 1833, British North America was developed almost entirely by free labor. Male migrants outnumbered women, but the majority of British migrants came as part of a family migration. Most migrants, even those from urban areas, sought to acquire land of their own and most ended up occupying family farms, though a significant and growing minority became wage laborers in the urban centers of British North America. The huge influx of British immigrants transformed the landscape. In 1815, except in Lower Canada, British North America consisted of a series of thinly populated colonies. Most settlers were engaged in subsistence agriculture, although the fisheries were critical in Newfoundland and important in the Maritimes and in Quebec and the timber trade was becoming increasingly significant in the colonies along the Atlantic seaboard. There were few large urban concentrations and limited contact between the tiny provincial capitals and the rural communities in which most of the people lived. After 1815, the population soared, villages sprang up across the countryside and were linked by roads and by the 1850s in the more densely populated regions by canals and railroads. The frontier experience of most immigrants was short lived. The majority of British immigrants came after 1830 and by the 1860s virtually all of the productive agricultural land (and much of the not-so-productive) had been granted to settlers. Eastern British North America had been transformed into a series of comparatively densely populated communities within a single generation. The native peoples were too few in number to resist the British invasion. Decimated by the ravages of European diseases and by the prolonged conflicts of an earlier period, they were dispossessed of their land without any serious confrontations. The earlier immigrants from the thirteen colonies and, later, the United States, who formed a majority outside of Quebec before 1815, were overwhelmed by the British influx. Lower Canada continued to have a substantial French Canadian majority but even the French Canadians were compelled to make substantial changes in their institutions in order to survive within a Canada in which the British immigrants and their descendants formed a majority of the population.

THE BRITISH CONNECTION

The commercial system was based on a chain of credit that stretched back to Britain and the British market continued to absorb the bulk of British North America's exports, especially its wheat and timber, even after the protective duties on those items were removed and Britain adopted free trade in the 1840s. Most of British North America's imports also came from Britain, as did the capital that financed the railways that linked Canada from the Atlantic to the Pacific coast by the mid-1880s. Not everyone benefited from immigrating. There was upward mobility in British North America but the earliest settlers benefited most from the inflation in land prices that followed large-scale migration. Those migrants with even small amounts of capital were usually able to acquire good agricultural land; those without capital were more likely to end up on land suitable only for subsistence agriculture and were forced to supplement their incomes by off-farm labor. The other real beneficiaries of rapid economic growth were the colonial merchants, lawyers, and administrators. Inevitably they were drawn largely from among the British immigrants and quite naturally were the most enthusiastic supporters of the imperial connection.

The British North American colonies not only imported British goods and capital but also British engineers and British technology, British troops to defend them during the boundary disputes with the United States, British lawyers and judges to shape and run the legal system, doctors from

Canadian Parliament Houses, Ottawa, photographed sometime before their destruction by fire in 1916.
©Hulton-Deutsch Collection/Corbis

British medical schools to establish standards for the medical system, British university graduates to teach in their schools and colleges, and British architects to design their public buildings. Few countries in the nineteenth century were more influenced by British imperial culture than Canada. Indeed, during the nineteenth century the distance between Britain and its North American colonies shrank as the passage across the Atlantic became easier and quicker and cheaper. Canadian newspapers carried regular reports of events in Britain and the members of the British North American elites frequently crossed the Atlantic to lobby the imperial government, to strengthen commercial alliances, and to arrange for loans from British banks, or simply to visit friends and relatives at "home." Not everyone welcomed this growing integration.

The rebellion of 1837–1838 in Lower Canada reflected the fears of many French Canadians that they would be absorbed by the rapidly growing British population and in Upper Canada a much smaller rebellion reflected the concerns of the pre-1815 American migrants and their descendants that they would be marginalized in a colony dominated by the British-born. In the aftermath of the rebellions the British government united the two Canadas into a single colony but the experiment was not a success and in 1867 at the time of confederation Quebec and Ontario were reconstituted as separate provinces in the Dominion of Canada. The decision of the British North American colonies to unite into a confederation was taken by the British North Americans themselves and reflected their worries over the growing power and expansionist ambitions of the United States. It also reflected their desire to remain British subjects and part of the British Empire.

CONFEDERATION AND POPULATION GROWTH

One objective of confederation was to open to European settlement the areas in the West still under the jurisdiction of the Hudson's Bay Company. In 1689 this vast territory was purchased by the government of Canada, and British Columbia, created as a British colony in 1866, was persuaded to enter confederation by the promise of a railway that would link the eastern provinces with the Pacific coast. But Canada grew slowly from the 1870s to the 1890s, steadily losing population to the United States. The decision to introduce a Canadian protective tariff in 1879 did encourage industrial development and slow the pace of out-migration but hundreds of thousands of Canadians continued to seek a better future in the United States and the Canadian West could not compete with the American West for settlers. British migrants continued to pour into Canada but the vast majority of the 673,000 who entered Canada between 1871 and 1901 joined the native-born Canadians heading south. Approximately 176,000 British migrants did make their home in Canada, a substantial proportion of them British women recruited as domestic servants or British children brought to Canada by charitable organizations such as Barnardos. Unlike the British migrants before confederation, the British migrants of the late nineteenth century were drawn heavily from Britain's overcrowded cities, a large proportion were single, and most became industrial laborers in Canada.

By 1901 English Canada was as homogeneously British as it would ever be. The majority of the English-speaking population could trace their roots to the British Isles and they defined themselves as British. At the same time, English Canadians also had a very strong sense of their own identity within the empire. Canada already had home rule and controlled all areas of domestic policy formation. Given Canada's small size and its vulnerable position on the North American continent, it is hardly surprising that most Canadians (even most French Canadians) were prepared

to accept British leadership in foreign policy. But English Canadians saw themselves as partners in the running of the British Empire. They were proud of their British institutions, proud to live under the Union Jack, and proud to have the British monarch as their head of state.

Between 1901 and 1921 the population of Canada increased dramatically as well over one million Europeans (and many Americans) settled in Canada, mainly between 1901 and 1913. The Canadian population grew from just over 5.3 million in 1901, to 7.2 million in 1911 and 8.7 million in 1921. By far the major source of migrants was the United Kingdom. Indeed, in 1911 the total number of British-born in Canada (around 11.6 percent of the population) exceeded the total number of migrants born in all other European countries combined (about 10.4 percent of the population). In the first half of the nineteenth century the Irish (the majority of them Protestants) and the Scots were disproportionately represented among the British immigrant cohort but in the late nineteenth and early twentieth centuries the English predominated and English-speaking Canada became much more English and even more Protestant in its culture. There was a very large influx of non-British migrants, particularly after 1900, drawn increasingly from eastern and central Europe. The non-British immigrants were predominantly agriculturalists who headed for the three Prairie Provinces in the Canadian West. But even in these provinces the British-born and the Canadian-born of British origin formed a clear majority of the population. Some of the non-British immigrants refused to assimilate into the dominant British culture—particularly those who formed distinct religious communities like the Mennonites and the Doukhobors—but many were prepared to pay the price of acceptance and to abandon those features of their ancestral culture that the Anglo-Canadian majority found offensive. Certainly most were prepared to become loyal British subjects and to embrace the Union Jack, the British royal family, and the British Empire.

As World War I would reveal, most English-speaking Canadians, particularly but not exclusively those of British descent, continued to view Canada as part of a Greater Britain. In 1914 Canada was automatically at war, but Canada itself determined the scale of the contribution it would make to the war effort. Hundreds of thousands of English-speaking Canadians volunteered to fight, not just for Britain, but for their king and their empire. In 1914, alone among the nations formed out of the major European colonies in the Americas, Canada continued to perceive itself as essentially a European—or more accurately a British—rather than a New World society.

See also **Australia; Colonies; France; New Zealand.**

BIBLIOGRAPHY

Berger, Carl. *The Sense of Power: Studies in the Ideas of Canadian Imperialism, 1867–1914*. Toronto, 1970.

Bridge, Carl, and Kent Fedorowich, eds. *The British World: Diaspora, Culture and Identity*. London and Portland, Oreg., 2004.

Buckner, Phillip. "Whatever Happened to the British Empire?" *Journal of the Canadian Historical Association* 4 (1993): 1–31.

————. "Making British North America British." In *Kith and Kin: Canada, Britain and the United States from the Revolution to the Cold War*, edited by C. C. Eldridge. Cardiff, 1997.

Buckner, Phillip, and R. Douglas Francis, eds., *Rediscovering the British World*. Calgary, 2005.

Bumsted, J. M. "The Cultural Landscape of Early Canada." In *Strangers within the Realm: Cultural Margins of the First British Empire*, edited by Bernard Bailyn and Philip D. Morgan. Chapel Hill, N.C., 1991.

Cowan, Helen I. *British Emigration to British North America: The First Hundred Years*. Reprint. Toronto, 1961.

Francis, R. Douglas, Richard Jones, and Donald B. Smith. *Origins: Canadian History to Confederation* and *Destinies: Canadian History since Confederation*. 5th ed. Scarborough, 2004.

Greer, Allan. *The People of New France*. Toronto, 1997.

Young, Brian, and John A. Dickinson. *A Short History of Quebec: A Socio-economic Perspective*. 3rd ed. Toronto, 2003.

PHILLIP BUCKNER

CANOVA, ANTONIO (1757–1822),
Italian sculptor, painter, draftsman, and architect.

Antonio Canova was the most accomplished and best-known sculptor associated with the revival of classicism at the end of the eighteenth and beginning of the nineteenth century. Easily the most celebrated artist of his time, Canova developed an idealized, purified style of sculpture based on classical antiquity that many came to esteem more highly than even his classical models.

Canova was born to a stonecutter in Possagno, Italy. He apprenticed with Giuseppe Bernardi, a minor sculptor, with whom he moved to Venice. He achieved modest success producing sculptures of classical figures, whose naturalism and technical finesse impressed his contemporaries and gained him admission in 1779 to the Venetian Accademia.

In 1789 Canova moved to Rome, where he lived for a period as the guest of Girolamo Zulian, the ambassador of the Venetian Republic, and joined a circle of artists, connoisseurs, scholars, archaeologists, and theorists engaged in the exploration and revival of classical antiquity. He had received no formal education, but now immersed himself in the study of ancient Greece and Rome. The following year he began his *Theseus and the Minotaur* (1781–1783), which quickly became seen as the embodiment of the noble simplicity and calm grandeur that Johann Joachim Winkelmann had considered the hallmark of the greatest classical sculpture. Canova's reputation soared, and he began to receive some of the most important sculptural commissions in Europe: funerary monuments for Clement XIV (1783–1787) and Clement XIII (1783–1792) and the tomb of Maria Christina of Austria (1798–1805). All of these monuments distinguished themselves by moving away from the turbulence, pomp, and triumphalism of the baroque to far more simplified, somber forms.

Collectors vied for Canova's work as they did for that of no other artist. Monarchs and nobility from across Europe came to him with commissions; even the fledgling and financially strapped state of North Carolina turned to him for a statue of George Washington. His clientele was international, and the market for his work extended from the wealthiest patrons of his day to those who could only afford one of the many prints made after it. More biographies of Canova appeared in his lifetime than did for any other artist prior to him.

Canova fashioned an unusually autonomous artistic practice. He vigilantly preserved his inde-

Venus Italica. Marble sculpture by Antonio Canova c. 1815–1822. SCALA/ART RESOURCE, NY

pendence, declining positions at court, refusing numerous projects that did not interest him, and even turning down honors and awards. His fame allowed him to work outside the confines of any one of the established institutional frameworks for art, such as courts, academies, or local markets and exhibition systems. Unlike most sculptors of the time, Canova often suggested subjects to his patrons or guided their ideas to suit his. He was able to do an unusually large amount of work on speculation, creating small-scale models that he would transform into finished marble sculptures when a buyer came forth.

Canova's independence allowed him to indulge his predilection for free-standing sculptures of one or a few idealized figures drawn from classical mythology. Unlike most monumental sculpture of the period, which was built to suit a preexisting architectural surround, his sculptures were self-contained art objects, and collectors often built environments in which to display them. Works that came directly from the artist's hand, as opposed to copies made under his supervision, were especially valued because of the way he subtly modulated and textured their surface to achieve refined, sensual effects and exquisite details. The independence of his sculptures from the demands of specific patrons and contexts made them eminently collectible, as they could pass from collection to collection without losing any essential aspect of their appeal.

Canova's overall output was enormous. Many of the sculptor's mythological works, such as his *Cupid and Psyche* (1783–1793), were in a graceful, sensuous manner, but by the mid-1790s he wished to distinguish himself in a more heroic and virile mode. Thus he created works such as the *Hercules and Lichas* (1795–1815), in which the terrible rage of the Greek god flinging a boy into the sea is paradoxically contained within a single plane and sharply defining outline. In addition to his free-standing works on mythological themes, he did a great many reliefs, stele, idealized heads, and especially portraits, and was sought after in this last regard by all the ruling houses of Revolutionary and Napoleonic Europe.

Canova produced many paintings and drawings, but he used these media primarily to explore ideas for sculpture. His other activities included working as a tireless advocate for the arts and for archaeology. He was devastated by Napoleon's looting of Italy and worked to recover the nation's artistic riches after Napoleon's fall.

Though immensely influential and unrivaled in fame during his own lifetime, Canova's work fell out of favor with the Romantic generation and never recovered its widespread appeal. Within art history, however, he remains recognized as the presiding sculptural genius of the period and a precocious example of modern artists' obsessions with experimentation and autonomy.

See also **David, Jacques-Louis; Napoleon; Painting.**

BIBLIOGRAPHY

Primary Sources

Canova, Antonio. *I quaderni di viaggio: (1779–1780)*. Edited by Elena Bassi. Venice, 1959.

———. *Antonio Canova: Scritti*. Edited by Hugh Honour. Rome, 1994.

Secondary Sources

Johns, Christopher M. S. *Antonio Canova and the Politics of Patronage in Revolutionary and Napoleonic Europe*. Berkeley, Calif., 1998.

Licht, Fred, with photographs by David Finn. *Canova*. New York, 1983. The most comprehensive modern survey in English.

Pavanello, Giuseppe, and Giandomenico Romanelli, eds. *Antonio Canova*. Translated by David Bryant. New York, 1992. Thorough exhibition catalogue.

DAVID O'BRIEN

CAPITALISM. Disciples of Karl Marx generally define capitalism as a system of commodity production dependent on capitalists, accumulators of capital, and proletarians, laborers dependent on wages. Followers of Max Weber typically describe it is a system of economic organization reliant on markets and market structures. Everyone agrees that in Europe between 1789 and 1914 capitalism underwent an amazing metamorphosis both in regard to production and to exchange. After the end of the Napoleonic Wars an industrial revolution that first began in Britain in the late eighteenth century spread through western and central Europe. European society had hardly come to a rest before a second and even greater industrial revolution swept all before it between 1870 and 1914.

In the 1830s and 1840s, astute observers from the communist Marx to the laissez-faire champion John Bright initially believed that capitalist expansion would undermine state borders and that international markets and commercial entrepôts would replace states and their armies. But predictions of a pacific international capitalism undermining militaristic European monarchies proved tragically wrong.

A CENTURY OF ECONOMIC GROWTH

Toward the later part of the eighteenth century, a wave of technological innovation, the expansion of British commerce into Caribbean and American markets during the wars of the French Revolution, and the large numbers of wage laborers in agriculture enabled Great Britain to be the first large state to operate on capitalist economic principles both in international trade and in industrial production. By 1840 more British workers were employed in manufacturing, mining, and construction than in agriculture. England was already more devoted to industry than the rest of Europe, and it continued to lead the industrial world throughout the nineteenth century. In England and Wales in 1891, 10 percent of the labor force was employed in agriculture and 44 percent in industry (manufacturing, mining, and construction); in Germany in 1895 comparable figures were 37.5 percent in agriculture and 36.4 percent in industry; while France in 1891 still had 40.3 percent of its labor force in agriculture and only 27.9 percent employed in industry.

A distinctive feature of European growth during this period was increased population growth combined with even faster economic growth. In 1700 the population of western and central Europe was more than 81 million; in 1820 it had grown to 133 million; in 1870, 188 million; and in 1913, 261 million. But over these time spans economic growth exceeded population growth. The contrast between levels of per capita gross domestic product (GDP) in Europe and Asia is remarkable (see Table 1). Although population growth was substantial between 1789 and 1914, it did not drown out economic growth.

TABLE 1

Contrasting Levels of Per Capita GDP in Europe and Asia, 1700 to 1913			
	1700	1820	1913
Britain	1,404	2,121	5,150
France	986	1,230	3,485
China	600	600	552
India	550	553	673

THE FIRST INDUSTRIAL REVOLUTION, 1770–1870

In 1851 amazed continental Europeans traveled to the London Great Exhibition to marvel at the new technologies based on steam, iron, and cotton mills, technologies that were already spreading from their British epicenter to western and central Europe. Between 1820 and 1870, the years in which the First Industrial Revolution spread through the Continent, western and central Europe witnessed a growth in per capita GDP of 0.95 percent per year; this was relatively modest judged by the standards of the golden years between 1950 and 1974, but it was six times faster than annual economic growth for the more than three centuries between 1500 and 1820.

Despite this record of economic growth, the Industrial Revolution inflicted real hardships on the British population, and the people who sacrificed were not those who benefited. In 1799, at the age of seven, the orphan Robert Blincoe was removed from the St. Pancras poorhouse in London and, along with other young boys and girls, sent by the municipal authorities to cotton mills in Nottingham in north central England. At five o'clock in the morning the young orphans were awakened and fed a breakfast of milk porridge and a scarcely digestible rye bread. By five thirty, the boys and girls were at work in the factory, where they stood without interruption until twelve noon and worked a total of fourteen hours per day, sometimes extended an additional hour or two. The manager told them to "do your work well and you'll not be beaten."

Did the living standards and social condition of most British workers decline during the First Industrial Revolution? The controversy over living standards has been one of the longest sustained scholarly debates, but new findings by anthropometric historians have renewed interest in the question. Anthropometric historians study the height of human populations. While height is influenced by inheritance, it is also strongly influenced by nutrition. Populations that are well fed and live in healthy environments grow taller than malnourished populations in disease-ridden or polluted areas. Anthropometric studies show that heights were increasing in the early years of the Industrial Revolution but began to fall after 1840 as larger and larger proportions of the working-class population urbanized. Heights did not reach 1840 levels again until the eve of World War I. These findings constitute a serious challenge to optimistic interpretations of the First Industrial Revolution.

Unemployment was an enduring problem created by the expansion of a working-class population dependent on wage labor. Sending homeless children such as Robert Blincoe to the mills relieved Poor Law guardians of part of the burden, but emigration was another and more comprehensive solution. In hard times, British municipal authorities subsidized the emigration of the unemployed and of workhouse orphans, and these joined British and Irish rural migrants already on their way to North America. During the Irish Potato Famine (1846–1851), landlords offered emigration as an alternative to ejection and the murderous Irish Poor Laws. After the famine, Irish migrants followed their friends and kin, mainly to the United States but also to Australia, Canada, and New Zealand. German peasants too fled an increasingly crowded countryside. Given the cost of the journey and its length and hazards, very few returned.

By increasing continental Europe's contacts with Britain, the fall of Napoleon I promoted the spread of the Industrial Revolution. The French Revolution and Napoleon may have retarded Continental economic growth, but they created a legal framework that would be crucial for the spread of capitalist industry on the Continent. The Napoleonic Code of 1804 legislated a new quasi-absolute conception of property rights. It undercut complex systems of property holding that gave peasants usage rights while retaining eminent domain for local nobles. It abolished *morte-main*, perpetual leases and rents, entailments, and primogeniture.

The code traveled with Napoleonic armies, but long after their retreat it remained in effect or served as a model for European legislators. At the same time, continental European states, struggling to catch up with Great Britain, played a much more active role in encouraging industrialization, underwriting the cost of railroad building and subsidizing heavy industry.

Still in the years before 1848 the progress of Industrial Revolution was relatively slow throughout continental Europe. Only Belgium, parts of France, a few areas in Germany, and a portion of Bohemia had really begun to adopt the new English industrial technologies. Large-scale coal production was confined to the Liège basin in Belgium and the Stéphanois basin in France. The Upper Silesian coalfields were in production in both Prussia and Bohemia, but transportation costs limited production to local purposes. Of all the technologies of the Industrial Revolution, only textiles had spread across the Continent from Barcelona to Lódz. Cotton textile towns such as Barmen, Elberfeld, Elbeuf, Ghent, Mulhouse, and Verviers more or less recapitulated the miserable living conditions of their English urban contemporaries.

While still in the process of assimilating the mills and furnaces of the First Industrial Revolution, Europe was soon shaken by a second and greater wave of industrial transformation: a second industrial revolution centered in western and central continental Europe, in Germany perhaps even more than in Britain.

THE SECOND INDUSTRIAL REVOLUTION, 1870–1914

The 1889 Exhibition Universelle in Paris was dominated by Gustave Eiffel's great tower marking the beginning of the age of steel. This Second Industrial Revolution was based on steel, electricity, chemicals, rubber, undersea cable, and great metal factories. Many of the important features of the economy of this age stemmed from its need for the enormous amount of fixed capital required for the integrated steel factories and the great metalworks and coal mines of the period. Often located near vital resources such as iron ore or coal, these new technologies were capable of producing large amounts of cheap steel, but their economies of scale required a large and steady mass market.

By 1914 industrialized Germany, endowed with abundant coal and access to ore, dominated the Continent, but everywhere wage labor was expanding rapidly as a proportion of the economically active population. In the era of the Second Industrial Revolution between 1870 and 1914, GDP per capita grew at an annual rate more than 30 percent faster than that of the era of the First Industrial Revolution. Whereas the mills of the First Industrial Revolution had increased the percentage of women and children such as Robert Blincoe working for wages, the factories of the Second Industrial Revolution sought adult males. While light metal factories sometimes employed young women as finishers, the great metal factory and the mining basin generally offered little employment for women. Both large employers and male workers saw the household as women's natural territory. Large employers preferred married males because they were considered more stable than single men. And at home women could feed and clothe male workers, tend to them when they were sick, and raise their children. Despite male convictions that women belonged in the home, the vagaries of employment and domestic need usually required even married women to work for wages at least for some portion of their lives.

Women had more opportunity in the growth of the white-collar workforce. Stereotypes of the workforce of the Second Industrial Revolution often focus on the male factory worker, the burly fellow with the muscular hand featured in the socialist posters of the time. But growing just as fast as the blue-collar factory workforce was a white-collar clerical workforce that often included women, although usually at the lower levels and for lesser pay. The spread of the department store, cooperatives, grocery chains, and mail-order houses and the expansion of branded, packaged consumer goods further increased the number of white-collar workers at the expense of the small shopkeepers and small producers who belonged to the lower middle class. After 1860 Félix Potin built a grocery empire of chain stores selling his own products made in his own factories and stored in his warehouses on the edge of Paris; in Great Britain, Thomas Lipton's sale of standardized quarter-pound tea packages was the

Idyll de mai. Caricature of capital as a fat bulldog and labor as a hungry wolf. Cover illustration by Gilbert-Martin for the French journal *Le Don Quichotte*, 3 May 1890. PRIVATE COLLECTION/BRIDGEMAN ART LIBRARY/ARCHIVES CHARMET

basis of his grocery empire. Many white-collar workers, both men and women, were teachers whose numbers grew as compulsory education spread throughout many areas of western Europe (it already existed in many German and Scandinavian states). At the same time the new diversified corporations of the period needed secretaries and typists; originally these were males, but by the second half of the nineteenth century the clerical profession feminized.

The rapid evolution and diversification of the European economy was made possible by its global expansion. Intercontinental regulatory organizations developed rapidly. In 1865 the International Telegraph Union was formed and in 1874 what was later called the Universal Postal Union; these international organizations established consistent standards and common practices for new technologies and new institutions. They would soon be joined by a host of similar organizations such as the International Bureau of Weights and Measures (1875), the International Union for the Protection of Industrial Property (1883), the International Railway Congress Association (1884), and the International Union for the Publication of Customs Tariffs (1890). Although none of these organizations possessed armies, the growing international economy of the second half of the century could not have developed if leading nations had not followed their rules.

No aspect of intercontinental expansion is more striking than the relatively unregulated international labor migration of Europeans to the Americas in the second half of the nineteenth century. Between 1850 and 1914 the steamship, the locomotive, and the marine cable produced classic transportation and communication revolutions. New inventions, the introduction of the screw propeller, and the construction of better designed, more fuel-efficient boilers increased the speed of travel while decreasing its cost. Over this period, technological innovation and fierce competition reduced the average time spent on the "Atlantic Ferry" from five to six weeks to ten to fourteen days. In 1869 the opening of the Suez Canal almost halved the trip between the United Kingdom and India. On land the railroad brought a similar revolution, and by 1914 the basic railway network had been constructed in India, the United States, and western and central Europe (but not Canada or Russia).

Between 1870 and 1914 roughly 14 million Europeans left the "Old Country" for good, mainly moving to the United States or Latin America or within the British and French empires to Algeria, Australasia, Canada, or South Africa. Combined with the movement of Indian and Chinese labor to Africa, the Caribbean, and Southeast Asia, no such transcontinental movements have been seen before or since. States' policies of leaving European migration relatively unregulated contrast strongly with their attitudes toward non-European migration; the United States, Canada, and Australasian states welcomed white Europeans while closing the doors to non-Caucasians. Reduced transportation costs and more powerful steamships that shortened the sailing time made return practical. In fact many Poles and Italians did return.

Mass migration affected the condition of unskilled labor throughout most of the greater Atlantic region. In the late nineteenth century, European living standards began to catch up with those in the Americas while the living standards of the Irish, Scandinavians, and Italians moved toward those of industrialized England and Germany. Inevitably calls for state restriction of emigration swelled among trade unionists and popular movements in receiving countries.

A communications revolution enabled Europeans to follow international events. From 1867 onward the development of cables made possible rapid communication across the Atlantic. By 1914 submarine cables linked all the continents. While news passed instantly across continents, it was transmitted to Europeans through daily mass newspapers printed in newly standardized national languages and often cast in the language of an increasingly strident nationalism.

The growing domination of world trade by the gold standard introduced still another important example of transnational economic regulation. In the 1870s major European countries and the United States joined the United Kingdom in fixing their national currencies in terms of a specific amount of gold. At its most ideal, a client ordering a commodity from a foreign producer could calculate the cost of the transaction knowing the price of the commodity and the exchange rates of the currencies in question for gold, largely avoiding the fluctuating currency exchange rates that introduce another element of uncertainty into trade. Through a combination of bank rates, foreign loans, and open market exchanges, the Bank of England enforced the gold standard, usually in coordination with French and German bankers.

Communication revolutions also facilitated foreign investment, and rates of foreign domestic investment attained remarkably high and sustained levels in the pre–World War I period. The years between 1870 and 1914 witnessed a massive outflow of British capital for overseas investment. The United Kingdom directed half of its saving abroad, and French, German, and Dutch investments were also substantial. By far the largest part of foreign investments was confined to Europe, North America, Australasia, and South Africa. Still the colonial world benefited from these investments. In part, the construction and expansion of great colonial empires by the British, Dutch, and French, imitated on a smaller scale by the Americans, Belgians, and Germans, encouraged investment in the colonial world. In theory the British Empire was committed to free trade, but the practice was sometimes more problematic. Indian administrators' decisions to opt for heavier and more expensive British railway engines instead of cheaper and lighter U.S. engines were probably influenced by considerations of imperial loyalty.

Despite the creation of an Atlantic labor market, the spread of technological and communicative revolutions binding continents, and the growth of transnational regulatory agencies, the internationalism of the epoch generally benefited states that provided regulatory control for capitalist markets and protection from the fluctuations of international trade. Consolidated states—bureaucratized, centralized states—created the legal foundations of the modern capitalist order. New business structures and financial relations were necessary to attract the enormous capital necessary for late-nineteenth-century heavy industry. At the beginning of the nineteenth century most partnerships were based on the principle of unlimited liability, making even inactive partners totally liable for debt in case of business failure. This seriously limited the ability to raise capital. In France the limited liability partnership had its roots in the late seventeenth century and the beginnings of the modern corporation dated to 1815, but the practical obstacles to their formation were formidable and had only slowly eroded by the 1860s. In the United Kingdom limited liability corporations made slow progress until a spate of acts between 1844 and 1856 made their formation relatively easy.

In the 1850s and 1860s many manufacturers and agriculturalists remained committed to free trade, which seemed to promise immediate economic benefits; even many French manufacturers who supported protectionism were in favor of free trade "in principle." Everything changed between 1877 and 1896 when even hitherto successful large-scale industrialists and most agriculturalists

At the Stock Exchange. Painting by Edgar Degas, c. 1878–1879. The figure at the center of the painting is financier Ernest May, a major patron of the impressionists, depicted here practicing his profession at the Paris stock exchange. MUSÉE D'ORSAY, PARIS, FRANCE/BRIDGEMAN ART LIBRARY

discovered their own vulnerability. The 1889 bankruptcy of the great Terrenoire steel plant, the largest Bessemer producer in France, revealed that even the most modernized plants were not secure. This economic crisis led many steel producers to realize that the high fixed costs of their great factories, required to achieve economies of scale, made these plants utterly dependent on steady markets. At the same time, European agriculture found itself under assault. New refrigerator ships that could travel from Australia and the Americas in only a few days drastically lowered the cost of meat, and shipping plus the extension of the railways put cheap wheat from the U.S. Midwest and Russian Ukraine on western and central European tables.

As a result of their experiences during the 1870s and 1880s some of the most powerful groups in European society, both large industrialists and agriculturalists, rallied to create a new protectionist political order. In 1892 French industrialists joined agriculturalists to support the protectionist Méline tariff. In 1902—in a sure indicator of changing attitudes—the Birmingham industrialist and former Liberal leader Joseph Chamberlain publicly called for protectionism. For many industrialists, however, protectionism was only part of the story. These large producers used protectionism to stabilize their position in the home market so as to better compete in foreign markets. States and diplomats were used to sell the products of heavy industry and to promote metropole industry in the colonies. One relatively stable home market was the military market, and many industrialists began to cater to the new need for cannons and battleships. By the end of the century, early dreams that international capitalism was a pacific force for free trade gave way to the realities of military–industrial alliances.

The protectionism structuring international economic relations was accompanied by the formation of national business cultures and by a statism shaping internal industrial relations. Structured by state laws, the giant corporation that developed in the years after 1870 became a permanent feature of the capitalist world and also created a national culture of capitalist relations. To make its costly new technologies pay, producers had to be proactive in the search for markets. They involved themselves in marketing and sales. To keep production and marketing in balance a new type of manager was required: a person not only proficient in the new technologies but also able to coordinate different corporate sectors and divisions. Germany and the United States, both younger capitalist nations, were more innovative and imaginative in employing corporate forms than Great Britain. British family firms had led the way, but their continued reliance on family ownership limited their ability to raise funds. Further, the heads of family firms often followed the founder in focusing on production, thereby failing to appreciate the importance of marketing and sales so essential to the success of U.S. and German corporations.

The example of Germany illustrates how capitalist corporations formed distinctively national cultures. German businessmen adopted corporate forms quickly, and early on they established relations with government-supported German universities, which were at that time world leaders in scientific research. Unlike in either the United States or the United Kingdom, a handful of large banks played a leading role in financing German industrialists and established close relations with corporate leaders, all starting in the 1870s. Bankers played a key role partly because of the difficulties of raising capital in Germany but also because their intimate involvement with company affairs, as shareholders and representatives of shareholders, provided a guarantee of corporate integrity. While providing venture capital, industrial banks minimized the risks of cutthroat competition, promoting cooperation among leading Germany companies.

The intimate relationship between banks and heavy industry in Germany was unique, but among industrial nations governmental action to promote growth produced substantial variation in the economic environment. Since the Revolution, the French state had focused on training highly qualified engineers with close ties to government. Although modest efforts were made to train skilled workers later in the century, most skilled workers were trained on the job, where they learned plant-specific information. By contrast, in the 1890s the German state invested substantially in creating a system of schools for white-collar engineers and technicians and a separate system for blue-collar skilled workers. In 1897 this dual system was made uniform throughout Germany and enabled German industry to rely on a standardized, qualified labor force. The presence of well-trained skilled workers in Germany and the importance of technical elites in the French system importantly influenced the evolution of industry in both countries.

Dependence on states for protectionism, for regulation, and for infrastructure encouraged capitalist nationalism, as did the growing state demand for armaments among European states embracing both colonialism and militarism simultaneously. As illustrated in the first Opium War (1839–1842) between Britain and China, advances in steamboat technologies enabled Western powers to extend their domination from the coast to the interior of Asian and African nations. The technologies of the Second Industrial Revolution produced powerful new weapons pioneered on European battlefields but soon adapted for colonial warfare. The invention of the breechloader enabled gunmakers to construct rifles that were fast, more accurate, tough, and impervious to the weather. French

The Belgian *bourse*, or stock exchange, in Brussels. ©MICHAEL MASLAN HISTORIC PHOTOGRAPHS/CORBIS

chemists developed smokeless gunpowder, and in the 1870s the repeater rifle spread. Within a few years, British troops were using the Maxim machine gun. This new weaponry combined with growing experience with tropical diseases and the means to forestall or overcome them made feasible military expansion into the interior of the Asian and African continents.

If capitalists increasingly identified themselves with their state so did many of their workers. The international socialist organizations were splendid ideological structures, but consolidated states loomed ever larger in working-class life. The growth of a large blue-collar working class that depended on wage work tied social stability to the boom-and-bust cycle of capitalism. Increasingly, political leaders in countries with large numbers of industrial workers began to take action, creating the foundations of modern welfare states. The

German Empire was the pioneer. Otto von Bismarck (1815–1898), the "Iron Chancellor" who had united the German state, created the framework for the first national welfare state. After prolonged resistance in the Reichstag, in 1883 Bismarck passed a compulsory sickness insurance bill; in 1884, compulsory accident insurance; and in 1889, compulsory old-age insurance. The targets of this legislation were mainly skilled male workers; it is worth underlining how closely the welfare state was linked to the proletarians of the Second Industrial Revolution. Only later were these programs extended to white-collar workers. After a sweeping Liberal victory in 1906, the United Kingdom passed its own legislation, most importantly the National Insurance Act of 1911, which included provisions for unemployment insurance targeted exclusively at skilled industrial workers. By 1914 all the major European countries except

Russia had compulsory accident insurance laws, and even Austria-Hungary had old-age pensions.

By 1914 capitalist industrialization had spread to every country in Europe, but it had not spread everywhere equally; it was concentrated in great industrial regions that sometimes straddled territorial borders. One such region stretched through northwestern Europe from Lille in northeastern France to Namur in southern Belgium to Dusseldorf in western Germany. The Ruhr in western Germany included the greatest agglomeration of mines and factories in the world, while textile plants proliferated in Barcelona and its hinterlands and in the Lódz basin in Russian-held Poland.

In regard to the dissemination of technology, the migration of labor, and participation in the gold standard, European capitalism in the years between 1789 and 1914 was thoroughly internationalist. The basic trends sweeping European economies were transnational, the same as those shaking the United States and beginning to sway Japan. Yet European capitalism ultimately reinforced and enhanced the power of European states. States supported capitalism but made themselves its gatekeepers. State regulation imparted a national character to European capital. The turn toward protectionism made states central to the new industrial economy, and the growing armament of the pre-1914 world made states important customers of capitalist industry. While European capitalism had powerful currents both nationalist and internationalist, in the end, in August 1914 statism triumphed over internationalism.

See also **Banks and Banking; Business Firms and Economic Growth; Class and Social Relations; Economic Growth and Industrialism; Emigration; Immigration and Internal Migration; Imperialism; Industrial Revolution, First; Industrial Revolution, Second; Labor Movements; Marx, Karl; Socialism.**

BIBLIOGRAPHY

Primary Sources

Brown, John. *A Memoir of Robert Blincoe*. Manchester, U.K., 1832.

Secondary Sources

Chandler, Alfred D., Jr. *Scale and Scope: The Dynamics of Industrial Capitalism*. Cambridge, Mass., 1990.

Fligstein, Neil. *The Architecture of Markets: An Economic Sociology of Twenty-first-Century Capitalist Societies*. Princeton, N.J., 2001.

Floud, Roderick, Kenneth Wachter, and Annabel Gregory. *Height, Health, and History: Nutritional Status in the United Kingdom, 1750–1980*. Cambridge, U.K., 1990.

Hall, Peter A., and David Soskice, eds. *Varieties of Capitalism: The Institutional Foundations of Comparative Advantage*. Oxford, U.K., 2001.

Harvey, David. *The Condition of Postmodernity*. Oxford, U.K., 1989.

Headrick, Daniel R. *The Tools of Empire: Technology and European Imperialism in the Nineteenth Century*. New York, 1981.

Hudson, Pat. *The Industrial Revolution*. London, 1992.

Landes, David. *The Unbound Prometheus: Technological Change and Industrial Development in Western Europe from 1750 to the Present*. 2nd ed. Cambridge, U.K., 2003.

Maddison, Angus. *The World Economy: A Millennial Perspective*. Paris, 2001.

Murphy, Craig N. *International Organization and Industrial Change: Global Governance since 1850*. New York, 1994.

O'Rourke, Kevin H., and Jeffrey G. Williamson. *Globalization and History: The Evolution of a Nineteenth-Century Atlantic Economy*. Cambridge, Mass., 1999.

Polanyi, Karl. *The Great Transformation: The Political and Economic Origins of Our Time*. 1944. Reprint, with a foreword by Joseph E. Stiglitz. Boston, 2001.

Pollard, Sidney. *Peaceful Conquest: The Industrialization of Europe, 1760–1970*. Oxford, U.K., 1981.

Strikwerda, Carl. "The Troubled Origins of European Economic Integration: International Iron and Steel and Labor Migration in the Era of World War I." *American Historical Review* 98, no. 4 (1993): 1106–1129.

MICHAEL HANAGAN

CAPTAIN SWING. "Captain Swing" was the mythical leader of the laboring rural poor who rose up to destroy threshing machines in England in 1830. The number of rural laborers in England had been swollen by the return of sailors and soldiers after the Battle of Waterloo (1815), as about 250,000 men were demobilized. This glutted the labor market, providing a permanent surplus of labor and reducing the wages of those who could find work to subsistence level.

CAUSE FOR UNREST

Parliamentary acts of enclosure, which had begun in Tudor times and accelerated during the French Revolution and Napoleonic Era, assisted the consolidation of productive land and the division of common land. An English cottager whom the English agriculturalist Arthur Young (1741–1820) encountered in 1804 told him, "Enclosing was worse than ten wars." The enclosures helped destroy many cottage holders and small farmers. It also compromised the existence of landless laborers, by taking away their access to common lands, which were enclosed and bought up by people of means. The big fish ate the little ones. Thus by 1830, in sharp contrast to the Continent, there were very few landowning peasants remaining in England. The countryside was definitively divided between landlords, tenant farmers, and hired laborers. As the number of agricultural proletarians swelled, their wages plummeted. Farmers paid them as little as possible, taking them on as hired hands for shorter periods of time. The gulf between them and the farmers who hired them widened—for example, rarely did they eat at the same table as the farmers who employed them.

Agricultural capitalism helped increase productivity but, increasingly, fewer of the returns went to the laborers. The Speenhamland System, which had been established in 1795, supplemented the wages of laborers with funds generated from property taxes in parishes. Doles were based on the price of bread and the number of dependents in each poor family. This further encouraged landowners to pay lower wages. All of this increased the "sullen hatred" of many poor people for the rich. Conversely, solidarity among the wealthy with the poor and hungry seemed to vanish. Crime, including poaching and even arson, increased following the skimpy harvest of 1828 and an even worse one in 1829.

RIOTS

The Swing riots began in the southeast of England in August 1830. Protestors at the first gatherings demanded higher wages. The first threshing machine was destroyed at Lower Hardres, near Canterbury in East Kent. The movement spread rapidly in Kent, and then to East Sussex and West Sussex, ultimately reaching at least sixteen other counties, most in southern England, including Hampshire, Berkshire, Wiltshire, Norfolk, Dorset, Worcester, Essex, Warwickshire, and Devon. These were hardly the first cases of the poor smashing machines. The Swing riots came not long after a certain Ned Ludd (fl. 1779)—who may or may not have actually existed—and his followers, mostly glove makers, had destroyed about a thousand stocking-frames in Nottingham in 1811 and 1812, machines undercutting their chances to find work and their wages. "Luddites" wanted a return to the economic order, to a so-called moral economy that they believed had existed before mechanization.

During the Swing riots, bands of laborers numbered between twenty-five and on one occasion as high as one thousand people. Letters warned farmers to destroy their threshing machines. One letter said, "We don't want to do any mischief, but we want that poor children when they go to bed should have a belly full of taties instead of crying with half a belly full." Another warned: "This is to acquaint you that if your threshing machines are not destroyed by you directly, we shall commence our labors. Signed on behalf of the whole. Swing." Scrawled warnings such as "Revenge for thee is on the wing, from thy determined Captain Swing" suggested an organization that was not really there. Captain Swing did not exist, but he came to represent the moral fury of the crowds of impoverished, determined laborers.

Attacks concentrated on prosperous farmers who could afford threshing machines, which were expensive and frequently broke down. Farmers with less land who could not afford the machines probably were not unhappy to see attacks on their wealthier neighbors. In some places, the smashing of threshing machines were just part of a movement that included arson threats (a potent arm of the poorest of the poor) aimed at increasing wages. The movement generated its own momentum and in some places paper mills were attacked also.

Local elites sometimes blamed political radicals, or occasionally even the French, as, following the July Revolution of 1830, tricolor flags appeared here and there. But in almost all cases, radicals had no link to the movement. Machine-breakers were most likely to find allies among craftsmen, particularly shoemakers. The participants were not necessarily the most miserable of the poor, and were most likely to be young or sometimes middle-aged men, with the average age being about twenty-seven to twenty-nine years. Unlike in grain riots in Britain and on the Continent, women played only occasional roles in the Swing riots. In some cases, the laborers elected their own leaders during meetings. The atmosphere of the movement was sometimes festival like, but accompanied by violence. In an atmosphere of fear, local gentry formed self-defense groups. Yet local magistrates assumed responsibility for the repression.

REPERCUSSIONS

In all, courts heard 1,976 cases and condemned 252 people to death, of whom 19 were executed (all but 3 for arson), 505 were to be transported to Australia or Tasmania (of whom 481 sailed), 644 were sent to jail, 7 received fines, and 1 was whipped; 800 were acquitted or bound over for trial on lesser crimes. The Swing riots would remain in the collective memory of the English poor and those who defended them. In the poet John Clare's "Remembrances," penned in 1832, poor folk "sweeing [swaying] to the wind" is probably an allusion to those condemned to the gallows during the Swing riots.

The Swing riots probably contributed indirectly to the passage of the Poor Law Amendment Act of 1834, which ended the Speenhamland System and led to the creation of workhouses, in which poor people without jobs would be incarcerated, splitting families apart. In 1841, some two hundred thousand people in Britain were inmates in workhouses. Even if in some areas the purchase of threshing machines fell off, in the end the Swing rioters lost.

In France at about the same time, a strikingly similar series of events reflected the fact that on the continent, too, the wealthy were easily able to get the law on their side to promote agricultural capitalism. During the period from 1829 to 1831, in the mountainous department of the Ariège in the Pyrenees mountains, peasants disguised as women chased charcoal-burners and forest guards from the forests, to which the former had always had access. The forest code of 1827, recognizing that the price of wood had risen because of metallurgical production, had deprived them of usage. Like "Captain Swing," scrawled warnings signed by "Jeanne, lieutenant of the Demoiselles," sug-

gested an organization that really did not exist. "The Demoiselles" represented a "moral economy" in which, like enclosures and threshing machines in England, if things were as they should be, everyone would have access to the forests to glean and pasture their animals, as they had always had. It was not to be. Moreover, by disguising themselves as women, in what amounted to an "enraged Carnival," they were standing reality on its head, as well as disguising themselves. When the Revolution of 1830 came along, "liberty" took on a new guise, and the peasants of the Ariège briefly became petitioners for liberty as they saw it. When the forest code remained intact and the guards and charcoal burners returned, the "Demoiselles" returned, but only for a couple of years, and then briefly in 1848, and in 1872 for the last time. Large numbers of the peasants of the region gave up the struggle to survive in the mountains and left for cities and towns in hope of a better life. In England, impoverished landless laborers remained even more part of rural life.

See also **Agricultural Revolution; Chartism; Luddism; Machine Breaking.**

BIBLIOGRAPHY

Hammond, John L., and Barbara Hammond. *The Village Labourer, 1760–1832: A Study in the Government of England before the Reform Bill.* 2 vols. New York, 1970.

Hobsbawm, Eric J., and George Rudé. *Captain Swing.* New York, 1968.

Merriman, John M. "The 'Demoiselles' of the Ariège, 1829–1831." In *1830 in France,* edited by John M. Merriman. New York, 1975.

Thompson, Edward P. *Customs in Common.* New York, 1993.

Thomson, Eric P. "The Moral Economy of the English Crowd in the Eighteenth Century." *Past and Present* 50 (1971): 76–136.

Tilly, Charles, Louise Tilly, and Richard Tilly. *The Rebellious Century, 1830–1930.* Cambridge, Mass., 1975.

JOHN MERRIMAN

CARBONARI. The Carbonari were one of the many secret societies that proliferated in the years after the French Revolution, and especially after the Bourbon Restoration. Indeed, the secret societies and the fears of secret conspiracies were skillfully exploited by legitimist governments after 1814 to justify often extreme measures of political repression and the curtailment of individual liberties.

ORIGINS

Since the numbers of the secret societies and the often impossible actions attributed to them were deliberately exaggerated as much by their supporters as by opponents, it is often still difficult to distinguish fact from fiction. But the secret societies existed, among them the Carbonari, which were prominent and especially prolific in southern Italy. Like nearly all the other secret societies, the Carbonarist lodges were modeled on the freemasonic lodges that had spread widely in Europe in the late eighteenth century and were officially promoted throughout Napoleon's empire (1804–1814/15). As opposition to French imperialism grew, however, the secret societies offered the emperor's opponents a less visible alternative to freemasonry.

The first references to the Carbonari in southern Italy came at precisely the moment when relations between Napoleon I and his brother-in-law Joachim Murat (1767–1815), were breaking down. Murat had ruled Napoleon's satellite Kingdom of Naples since 1808, but relations with Paris deteriorated to the point that in 1811 he nearly lost his throne. As Murat's position in the imperial enterprise weakened, he became more dependent on his Neapolitan supporters, who in turn pressed for a constitution.

This became the principal political platform of the Carbonarist lodges, whose name was adopted from the *Charbonnerie,* an informal secret association among the charcoal burners (*charbonniers*) of the Jura Mountains between France and Switzerland. The name seems to have been taken at random by a group of French officers, hostile to Napoleon, whose regiment took part in the conquest of southern Italy in 1806. One of the first Carbonarist lodges was founded in Calabria by Pierre-Joseph Briot, a senior French official who was also an unreconstructed Jacobin and a longtime opponent of Bonaparte's dictatorship.

The Carbonarists had adopted two alternative political projects. One was the constitution con-

ceded by the king of Spain to the Cortes (legislative assembly) of Cadiz in 1812, and the other was the very different constitution that the British had imposed on Sicily in the same year. Support for these demands spread quickly, and an insurrection in the Abruzzi in 1813 revealed strong support in the army as well. The government immediately banned the Carbonarist lodges, and in Milan, Napoleon's viceroy Eugène Beauharnais did the same. But when in 1814 Murat defected from the empire, on three separate occasions his generals demanded a constitution as the condition for their support.

RESTORATION

In southern Italy the Carbonarist lodges played an important role in the transition of power after the fall of Napoleon and Murat and the restoration of the Bourbon monarchy in 1815. Their great hope was that the Bourbons would extend the Sicilian constitution to the whole kingdom, but instead it was abolished. As a result, the lodges began to spread both on the mainland and now also in Sicily much to the alarm of the authorities.

Those fears were shared more widely as numerous new and old secret societies began to appear all over Europe. They had a bewildering panoply of names and projects: the Adelfi, the Decisi, the Perfect Sublime Masters, the Calderai, to name only a few. Some supported the legitimist restorations, others opposed them, and others had their own projects, like the Russian Decembrists, the Polish Patriotic Society, and the Greek Hetaira Philiké. A growing source of public alarm, the presence of these conspiracies, real or imagined, provided the authorities with pretexts for draconian public security measures, whereas for an inveterate conspirator like Filippo Michele Buonarroti (1761–1837), a conspirator in the 1796 "Conspiracy of Equals" in Paris and now in the safety of Geneva, these fears gave substance to a revolutionary threat that he knew did not exist but dearly wanted to create.

In southern Italy the Bourbon government was paralyzed by its fear of the Carbonari. The fears grew when an insurrection at Macerata in the Papal State in 1817 was attributed to the Carbonari, but in Naples the generals reported that the lodges were too many and too powerful for a frontal attack. When the Spanish revolution took place in January 1820, southern Italy at first seemed calm. But when a protest began in the cavalry barracks at Nola at the beginning of July, within days the protest spread to other regiments. Faced with a general mutiny the monarchy was forced to concede the Spanish constitution.

The revolutions in Naples and Sicily in 1820 succeeded because the constitutional program had overwhelming support in the army, but there is strong evidence to suggest that they were planned in the Carbonarist lodges, where the constitutional project was prepared and which during the nine months of constitutional government played an important role in maintaining order. But it was hardly surprising that the Carbonarist revolution in Naples and Sicily rang fresh alarms through Restoration Europe and many now claimed that the secret societies were the invisible hand that linked the revolutions in Spain, Naples, and Sicily to the Cato Street conspiracy in London, the murder of the duc de Berri in France and of the journalist August von Kotzebue in Germany in 1819, which was the immediate pretext for the draconian Carlsbad Decrees.

In November, Prince Clemens von Metternich (1773–1859) summoned the European rulers to meet at Troppau in October to coordinate action against the forces of revolution. During the meeting, when the tsar, Alexander I, was informed of a mutiny in one of the St. Petersburg regiments, he immediately detected the work of the secret societies. With the willing complicity of the king of Naples, an Austrian army was dispatched to southern Italy in March 1821, and the revolutions were crushed. The Carbonarist lodges were closed, and their members arrested or placed under police surveillance, dismissed from public office, and banned from the professions.

According to Metternich, the Carbonari were "prelates, priests and citizens of distinguished rank." In fact, they also included many artisans and lesser landowners, but overwhelmingly the Carbonarist lodges gave political voices for the first time to the provincial gentry, of which they were now deprived. However, the police records also show that their numbers were much smaller than the authorities liked to believe, and their suppression served primarily to justify political purges that extended to the entire army, public officials, and the clergy.

Despite the defeat of the revolutions in Naples and Sicily, elsewhere in Europe fear of the secret societies now reached a peak. In December 1821 the Carbonari were banned by the pope, but the discovery of plans by a French *Charbonnerie* to stage revolts in Belfort and Saumur in December 1821 caused new alarms that were exacerbated when four sergeants who were put on trial at La Rochelle for complicity refused to divulge any information.

DECLINE OF SECRET SOCIETIES

By 1824 the panic was subsiding, Europe was not in flames, and Metternich decided that the threat had been grossly exaggerated all along. By now the revolutionaries were also losing patience, and the failed insurrections that took place in the Papal State in 1831 were the last strike of the Carbonari. A year later Giuseppe Mazzini (1805–1872) founded Young Italy, the revolutionary society that explicitly rejected the tradition of secret conspiracy. Mazzini had begun his career as a member of the Carbonari in Genoa, but now he called on Italian revolutionaries to declare themselves openly and to proselytize the young to the national cause, accusing the Carbonari of adhering to the revolutionary strategies of the French Jacobins that he believed to be outdated and unworkable.

The Carbonari now disappeared as quickly as they had materialized. Under attack from the revolutionaries and under growing pressure from the police, the secret societies came to be seen as anachronistic. Former Carbonarists found new berths in a variety of political movements, some more some less militant, while others reverted to mainstream freemasonry. In France, for example, the *Charbonnerie* made a brief reappearance during the July Revolution in 1830 but were subsequently absorbed into the republican movement. However, while the political threat they posed was certainly exaggerated, the Carbonari and other secret societies enabled European governments to impose even tighter controls—over the press and public associations but also on army officers, public servants, the clergy, and the independent professions—that remained in force down to 1848, and in many cases well beyond.

See also Carlsbad Decrees; Jacobins; Kingdom of the Two Sicilies; Mazzini, Giuseppe; Metternich, Clemens von; Napoleon; Secret Societies.

BIBLIOGRAPHY

Davis, J. A. *Naples and Napoleon: Reform, Revolution, and Empire in Southern Italy, 1750–1820.* Oxford, U.K., forthcoming.

Roberts, John Morris. *The Mythology of the Secret Societies.* New York, 1972.

Spitzer, Alan B. *Old Hatreds and Young Hopes: The French Carbonari against the Bourbon Restoration.* Cambridge, Mass., 1971.

JOHN A. DAVIS

CARDUCCI, GIOSUÈ (1835–1907), Italy's most notable poet of the post-Risorgimento era and the first Italian to win the Nobel prize.

Giosuè Carducci's poems, essays, editorial activities, and an occasional excursion into political life expressed the bitter discontent of many intellectuals with the new Italy that had been created in 1860. Although he did not participate in the wars of national unification, Carducci was a supporter of the republican nationalist Giuseppe Mazzini, but in 1859 and 1860 he accepted the necessity of uniting behind the monarchy. The triumph of the house of Savoy over the popular forces of Mazzini and Giuseppe Garibaldi provided a harbinger of the compromises and political deal making of the new parliamentary political class that Carducci judged incapable of realizing the potential greatness of the new Italy. The age of poetry seemed to give way to the age of accountants' ledgers. During the 1860s Carducci returned to republicanism and to faith in a popular leader who could embody the aspirations of the people.

What particularly annoyed him were the efforts of the new Italy to find a modus vivendi with the Catholic Church. Carducci was a life-long anticlerical who held the church responsible for Italy's cultural and political backwardness, and he was incensed by the decision of the new government to bow to the wishes of the French emperor Louis Napoleon by blocking Giuseppe Garibaldi's attempts to seize Rome. In one of his first poems from the collection *Juvenilia* (1859–1860), Carducci wrote of independence and love of liberty that were "highly contemptuous of the Holy and Catholic Idea of a Church fixed on the firm foundation / of servile Europe's humiliation" (p. 3). His most notorious poem, *Hymn to Satan* (1865) identified Satan with nature, reason, and the spirit of rebellion against the combined forces of the church and the reactionary state. His collections *Levia gravia* (1868; Light and heavy) and *Giambi ed epodi* (1867–1869; Iambs and epodes) hammered away at the failure of the new state to respond to the currents of patriotic sentiment that had been unleashed by the Risorgimento, the movement for the political unification of Italy.

Despite his youthful reputation as a rebel, the new liberal monarchy appointed Carducci to the chair of rhetoric at the University of Bologna in 1860, a post he would hold until 1904. Although he never accepted the wheeling and dealing of parliamentary life, Carducci's republicanism became increasingly muted during the 1870s. He ran for Parliament in 1876 but failed to take his seat on a technicality. His poetry also became less overtly political and more personal and historical over time. In 1878, on the occasion of a visit by Italy's royal couple, Umberto I and Queen Margherita, Carducci was so taken by Margherita that he dedicated one of the poems in the collection *Odi barbari* (Barbarous odes) to her. The *Odi barbari*, published in various editions from 1877 to 1889, was Carducci's most significant work. The poems were marked by a rejection of Romanticism, which Carducci judged a foreign import, in favor of a renewed classicism. Carducci's productivity declined after a stroke in 1885, but by then his reputation in Italy was established.

During the 1880s and 1890s Carducci's politics became increasingly nationalistic. He was a firm supporter of the Sicilian statesman Francesco Crispi, who tried to combine a degree of social and economic reform with strong personal government and a dose of imperialism. The disastrous end to Crispi's government in 1896, when Italy was defeated by the Ethiopians at Adwa, failed to shake Carducci's loyalty to the Sicilian leader. For many post-Risorgimento intellectuals, of which Carducci was representative, an aggressive foreign policy and strong government were shortcuts to great-power status. They held that failure resulted not from bad planning or misguided policies but from the incapacity of parliamentary government to focus the national will. Thus Carducci's politics fed the growing antiparliamentary tradition that manifested itself after 1900 in organizations like the Italian Nationalist Association.

See also **Anticlericalism; Crispi, Francesco; Italy; Mazzini, Giuseppe; Nationalism.**

BIBLIOGRAPHY

Carducci, Giosuè. *Carducci: A Selection of His Poems with Verse Translations, Notes, and Three Introductory Essays.* Edited by G. L. Bickersteth. London, 1913.

Drake, Richard. *Byzantium for Rome: The Politics of Nostalgia in Umbertian Italy, 1878–1900.* Chapel Hill, N.C., 1980.

ALEXANDER DE GRAND

CARIBBEAN.

CARIBBEAN. Modern Europe, it might be said, was born in the Caribbean. From Christopher Columbus's landing in the region in 1492 through the nineteenth century, the economic productivity, political revolutions, and cultural dynamics generated by the Caribbean profoundly shaped the evolution of European empires, most notably those of Spain, Britain, and France. The Caribbean was the first zone of European colonization in the Americas, and it attracted the attention of successive waves of colonists and merchants whose actions decimated the indigenous populations and created a new population of enslaved individuals brought across the Atlantic from Africa. European economic systems, administrative models, philosophical ideas, music, and language had a profound influence in the Caribbean. But the imperial projects carried out there also led to a massive and unprecedented movement of population into the region that created economic, cultural, and political dynamics that indelibly shaped the colonizing nations who sought (often unsuccessfully) to control their colonies.

The Caribbean can be understood most fruitfully through the lens of what the Cuban anthropologist Fernando Ortiz called "transculturation," as a zone of both violent and productive encounter between a bewildering series of cultures: the indigenous civilizations who, though brutally decimated by Europeans, nevertheless survived in important numbers well into the eighteenth century in the eastern Caribbean; the Gascons, Scots, Provençals, Castilians, and members of other European tribes who nominally served various states but also often served themselves much more successfully; the East Indian and Chinese contract laborers who were brought to work in the region during the nineteenth century; the Middle Eastern merchants who came voluntarily to the region; and of course, most importantly, the multiple and diverse groups of Africans who were brought on slave ships from the early sixteenth century through the late nineteenth century and who, as laborers but also as survivors, revolutionaries, and eventually citizens have made the Caribbean what it is today.

The period from 1789 to 1914 was an era of profound transformation in the Caribbean. At the end of the eighteenth century, the region was booming, as was the slavery and the slave trade that made its plantations prosperous. By the early twentieth century there was no slavery anywhere in the Caribbean, though the inheritances of the institution remained quite powerful and shaped the economic and political crises that were to come in the ensuing decades. In addition to witnessing emancipation in the region, the period saw the emergence of three independent nations there: Haiti, the Dominican Republic, and Cuba. But they were surrounded by islands that remained under the control of France, Britain, Holland, and (though not for much longer) the Danes. If, in 1789, it was the French and British who dominated the colonies of the Caribbean, by the early twentieth century it was clear that its future would evolve under the shadow of another empire: that of the United States.

SPANISH, BRITISH, AND FRENCH COLONIZATION

The island of Española (known as Hispaniola in the Anglophone world) was colonized by the Spanish in the early fifteenth century, but after a brief boom in Santo Domingo that included the construction of sugar plantations on the island, the Spanish empire turned most of its energies to mainland Latin America. Cuba became the site of well-fortified stopping points for convoys of silver and other goods, and, like Santo Domingo, was populated mainly by small farmers, though both societies included slaves. During the sixteenth century, the British and French began colonizing the eastern Caribbean, an area neglected by the Spanish, founding colonies first (jointly) in Saint Christopher (Saint Kitts) and then (separately) in Barbados and Antigua and Martinique and Guadeloupe. Within a few decades new ventures were launched on the larger islands near Cuba. The British took Jamaica, which became their most important colony, and the French squatted and then gained official title to the west of Santo Domingo, which became the thriving colony of Saint Domingue.

THE SITUATION IN THE LATE EIGHTEENTH CENTURY

Despite the relatively small size of its territory, the Caribbean was at the center of the Atlantic economy in the eighteenth century because its climate was very well suited for the cultivation of sugar, which became a staple of European diets. Coffee, indigo, cotton, and cacao supplemented this important crop. The success of these commodities did not assure the success of planters in the Caribbean. Especially once the best land in the colonies had been settled, new arrivals there often ended up bankrupt. Yet many did make important fortunes from producing and selling sugar and other commodities. Some planter families grew extremely wealthy, and merchants in the metropole profited handsomely from importing and selling their goods. Whereas Britain consumed most of its colonial sugar domestically, France exported much of what its colonies produced to the rest of Europe, and those involved in this trade did very well. The port towns of Britain and France boomed thanks to the Caribbean colonies. Indeed, the economic and accompanying social changes that resulted from the Atlantic economy were one of the forces that helped set up, and then drive the twists and turns of, the French Revolution.

While in the early days of colonization the population included many European indentured laborers, who often worked alongside African slaves, as soon as the sugar boom hit in the various islands the population generally became heavily Africanized. By the late eighteenth century the populations of the major sugar islands were dominated by a vast majority of slaves. Resistance was constant, and some communities of enslaved individuals who escaped to the mountains (called Maroons) won their freedom from the British and Dutch in the 1730s. Then, in the 1790s, the most profitable colony in the region, and in the world—French Saint Domingue—exploded in a revolt that became a revolution.

REVOLUTION IN THE FRENCH CARIBBEAN

In August 1789, before news of the fall of the Bastille had reached the region from France, slaves in Martinique began to gather, stirred by an exciting rumor: the king of France had abolished slavery. Unfortunately, however, local leaders and planters were conspiring to repress the decision. It was therefore necessary to force them, with violence if necessary, to apply the abolition decree. The small revolt that began in Martinique in 1789 was quickly repressed, but the idea that emancipation was imminent helped drive a remarkable series of insurrections through the French Caribbean during the next years. The most important of these took place in August 1791 in the northern plain of Saint Domingue, where a coalition of plantation workers launched the only successful slave revolt in history. Transforming themselves into an unbeatable military force, they positioned themselves strategically in the volatile situation of revolution and imperial war, and in 1793 administrators in Saint Domingue decreed the abolition of slavery there as a way of avoiding the loss of the most valuable colony in the world to the British and Spanish. The National Convention in Paris ratified the decision in 1794, and so the French Empire ended an institution that had brought wealth pouring into its coffers for a century. It was a remarkable political triumph, the most radical of the Age of Revolution: from being chattel, the men and women of the French Caribbean had gained not only liberty but also citizenship and equality, in the process expanding the meaning and possibilities of republican universalism in dramatic ways.

Emancipation took root in the midst of war and embodied many contradictions. Administrators, the most famous of them Toussaint Louverture, remained committed to maintaining plantation production with liberty, developing a variety of coercive mechanisms for doing so. The ex-slaves, meanwhile, did what they could to secure autonomy, notably by seeking to gain control over land for themselves. It was a struggle that would be replayed in every other postemancipation context in the Americas, notably in the British Caribbean after the abolition of slavery there in 1833, and in Cuba in the 1870s. Despite the efforts of Toussaint to maintain and rebuild plantation production, however, the French government under Napoleon Bonaparte turned against him in late 1801. Attempting to regain direct control over the colony, and to reverse the transformations brought about by emancipation, they incited a large-scale war in the colony that culminated, in 1804, with a French defeat and the creation of a new nation called Haiti.

The Haitian Revolution had a profound impact on the Caribbean region. Refugees fanned out from the colony to neighboring islands, particularly Cuba. The vast opening in the sugar market was filled, in the early nineteenth century, by a plantation boom on Cuba, which experienced the rapid proliferation of sugar production and the massive importation of African slaves that Saint Domingue had in the eighteenth century. As Spain lost its mainland colonies in the first decades of the nineteenth century, Cuba, long a marginal zone in its American empire, became its center.

RESHAPING OF THE BRITISH CARIBBEAN
The British Caribbean was also reshaped in the wake of the Haitian Revolution. The precise impact of the dramatic revolution has been a subject of some controversy among historians. Some have argued that the abolitionist movement was actually stalled by the violent uprising in Haiti, because critics of slavery were saddled with the accusation that they had abetted the killing of white masters. Others have argued that the example of successful slave revolution in fact spurred on the abolitionist campaign in various ways. Whatever the case, by 1807 the abolitionists had succeeded in abolishing the British slave trade, a decision that had a profound impact on the Caribbean colonies. During the next decades a series of revolts took place in the British Caribbean, notably in 1816 in Barbados, often directly inspired by abolitionist advances.

Popular and parliamentary pressure for an abolition of slavery increased during the next decade, and in 1831 an uprising in Jamaica, called the "Baptist War" because of the large number of Baptist slaves involved, helped spur on the final push to end the institution.

Slavery was abolished in 1833 but replaced in all the British colonies—with the exception of Antigua—with a system of "apprenticeship" that kept the former slaves tied to plantation labor. Many former slaves intensely disliked the limited freedom granted to them by apprenticeship, and their resistance helped assure that it was ended earlier than planned. During the next decades former slaves struggled to establish some form of economic autonomy and independence, often by settling on available land in the interior of the colonies. Planters, meanwhile, struggled to maintain their power, finding ways to limit access to land and diminish the economic options of the former slaves. Tensions exploded in Jamaica with the Morant Bay uprising of 1865, to which the administration responded by dismantling many of the democratic reforms augured in with emancipation and by making the island a crown colony.

Slavery was abolished in Martinique and Guadeloupe in 1848, and there a similar dynamic took shape during the rest of the nineteenth century. Citizenship was granted to former slaves in 1848 and then retracted in 1851, and finally only firmly established with the advent of the Third Republic in 1870. The colonies elected representatives in the National Assembly, but their local administration was nevertheless controlled by governors appointed from Paris, and planters found many ways to protect their traditional power in the society.

CUBA
Cuba was the last Caribbean society in which slavery was abolished. As in Haiti, emancipation and independence were intertwined in Cuba. The end of slavery began in 1868 when Carlos Manuel de Céspedes began an uprising against Spanish rule by freeing his own slaves and calling on them to fight with him for both freedom and independence. The insurgent policy of freeing slaves who joined the uprising against Spain did not assure victory: after ten years, the uprising was effectively defeated. But the Spanish accepted the freedom of

those slaves who had fought in the insurrection. Soon afterward, in 1880, they passed a "Free Womb" law, which meant that all children of slaves would henceforth be free, and put in place a process of gradual emancipation similar to the apprenticeship system in the British Caribbean. Once again, this gradual process was accelerated by the resistance and sophisticated legal maneuverings of slaves, and by 1886 slavery was abolished outright in Cuba with many slaves having already secured their full freedom. Many former slaves would take part in the second war of independence in Cuba from 1895 to 1898, and some of the great leaders of this struggle, most famously Antonio Maceo, were men of African descent. Through their participation, they helped craft a political discourse of raceless citizenship that, for all its ambiguities, continues to shape Cuban culture. The end of Spanish empire in Cuba in 1898, however, was combined with the assertion of power over Cuba by the United States, which during the twentieth century ultimately replaced the European empires as the most significant external force shaping Caribbean political and economic realities.

See also **Colonialism; Colonies; Haiti; Toussaint Louverture.**

BIBLIOGRAPHY

Blackburn, Robin. *The Overthrow of Colonial Slavery, 1776–1848.* London, 1988.

Dubois, Laurent. *Avengers of the New World: The Story of the Haitian Revolution.* Cambridge, Mass., 2004.

Ferrer, Ada. *Insurgent Cuba: Race, Nation, and Revolution, 1868–1898.* Chapel Hill, N.C., 1999.

Holt, Thomas C. *The Problem of Freedom: Race, Labor, and Politics in Jamaica and Britain, 1832–1938.* Baltimore, Md., 1992.

Knight, Franklin W. *The Caribbean: The Genesis of a Fragmented Nationalism.* 2nd ed. New York, 1990.

Knight, Franklin W., ed. *General History of the Caribbean.* Vol. 3: *The Slave Societies of the Caribbean.* London, 1997.

Scott, Rebecca J. *Slave Emancipation in Cuba: The Transition to Free Labor, 1860–1899.* Princeton, N.J., 1985.

Sheller, Mimi. *Democracy after Slavery: Black Publics and Peasant Radicalism in Haiti and Jamaica.* Gainesville, Fla., 2000.

LAURENT DUBOIS

CARLISM.

Carlism is the name generally given to an ultratraditionalist movement in Spanish politics that emerged in the 1820s and remained in existence until the Spanish civil war of 1936–1939.

CONTEXT AND ORIGINS

Between 1814 and 1876, at least, the defining feature of Spanish politics may be said to have been the clash between liberalism and conservatism. Resulting in no fewer than five civil wars, this was eventually settled in favor of the former: under King Alfonso XII (r. 1874–1885) Spain settled down as a parliamentary monarchy and enjoyed a period of relative stability that lasted until the overthrow of the constitution by a military coup in September 1923. However, the ideology of nineteenth-century conservatism survived intact and in the Spanish Civil War of 1936–1939—a conflict in which it secured a terrible revenge—it re-emerged as the chief basis of the dictatorship of General Francisco Franco (1892–1975).

Conventionally, this great ideological divide is dated to the Peninsular War of 1808–1814 and, in particular, the Constitution of 1812. Based on the sovereignty of the people, the latter was accompanied by a series of reforms that undermined the position of the church and the nobility alike, and the *liberales* who had forced it through in the famous *cortes* of Cádiz (and from whom the term *liberal* originates) were therefore confronted by an opposition group who were given the scornful nickname of the *serviles* (literally, "the servile ones"). In reality, however, the feelings that motivated this latter group went back well before the Peninsular War. Thus, the enlightened absolutism of Charles III (r. 1759–1788) and Charles IV (r. 1788–1808) had seen the Spanish state make considerable advances at the expense of the church and the nobility, and the dissatisfaction of these two privileged corporations had been one of the chief factors underpinning the political turmoil that had produced the intervention of Napoleon I (r. 1804–1814/15) in Spain in 1808. It would, then, be a great mistake to think that the *serviles* simply wanted the restoration of absolute monarchy.

When the constitutional system was overthrown by a military coup in 1814—a coup, incidentally, that was led by *servil* generals, but based on widespread anger in the officer corps at the anti-militarism and mismanagement of the liberal administrations of 1808–1814—they were certainly pleased, but they made it very plain to Ferdinand VII (r. 1808–1833) that what they expected was a return to a semi-mythical golden age in which the privileged corporations would in effect be allowed to rule the roost under the aegis of a monarchy that would be a mere cipher. Weak, foolish, and unintelligent though he may have been, however, Ferdinand VII was having none of this. Content enough to repress the liberals, he therefore refused to abolish many of their reforms: the feudal system, for example, was never restored. From very early on, then, is evident the emergence of a deep split between traditionalists, who wished to roll back the frontiers of absolutism, and modernizers who had no interest in the Constitution of 1812, but at the same time wished to foment social, political, and economic modernization.

To see the conflicts of the nineteenth century as a clash between two Spains is therefore insufficient. Indeed, in the early stages of the long struggle, liberalism was something of a side issue. In 1820, certainly, renewed military dissatisfaction led to a further coup that forced Ferdinand VII to restore the Constitution of 1812. To the traditionalists, of course, this was anathema, and many of them rose in revolt: by 1822, indeed, many parts of the country were swarming with guerrilla bands organized by disaffected members of the elite. Given the fact that the *serviles*, or *apostólicos* as they were now known, were associated with the restoration of feudalism, their ability to secure the popular support that this suggests is rather surprising. However, the manner in which the liberals had implemented such policies as the sale of the common lands had left them with few friends among the rural populace, and the latter was therefore easy enough to manipulate, especially as economic misery made promises of pay and pillage very attractive.

Undermined by the guerrilla operations of the traditionalists, the liberals were finally overthrown by a French army in 1823. For a brief moment it seemed that *servilismo* might finally have triumphed: angry at the manner in which he had been betrayed by the army in 1820, Ferdinand VII allowed himself to be persuaded to abolish it in favor of a peasant militia based on the guerrilla bands of 1822–1823. With the power of the state subverted in this fashion, absolutism might finally have been vanquished, but it was not long before Ferdinand came to his senses and ordered the regular army to be restored. Sensing that their moment was slipping away, the *apostólicos* became increasingly disaffected. Indeed, in 1827 a group of them led a serious revolt in Catalonia known as *la guerra de los agraviados* (the war of the aggrieved). But for the time being, most of *servilismo* were content to place their hopes in the succession to the throne of Ferdinand VII's younger brother, Charles (1788–1855). This seemed assured, for the aging Ferdinand was childless. And at the same time, Charles was by no means as pragmatic as his brother. An extremely devout Catholic, he was inclined to accept the ultramontane pretensions of the *servil* elements of the clergy, while he also held what he saw as Ferdinand's constant tacking responsible for the survival of liberalism after 1814 and therefore believed that the cause of absolute monarchy depended on an alliance with the *apostólicos*.

Grumble though many *apostólicos* did, the outlook for their cause seemed bright enough. In 1830, however, the situation was suddenly transformed. Ferdinand had taken a new wife in the person of María Cristina of Naples (1806–1878), and in that year she produced a daughter named Isabella (later Isabella II, r. 1833–1868). As daughters could not inherit the Spanish throne, the *apostólicos* were initially not overly concerned, but then Ferdinand delivered a bombshell: his father Charles IV had, or so he claimed, secretly revoked the law that women could not inherit the Spanish throne, the result being, of course, that his baby daughter could take the place of Charles as his successor. Given that Ferdinand showed no signs of abandoning the bureaucratic absolutism to which the *apostólicos* so objected, from this moment full-scale civil war became inevitable.

THE CARLIST WARS, 1833–1836

Indeed, no sooner had Ferdinand expired in 1833 than revolt broke out in many parts of the country. Among the provinces most affected were Galicia, where the system of landowning prevalent in the province made the local elites particularly vulnerable to the land reforms espoused by liberals and enlightened absolutists alike; Navarre and the Basque provinces, where the elites were encouraged in supporting the self-styled Charles V by the threat that these same two forces posed to the system of privileges that gave the region the highly favored relationship it enjoyed with the Spanish throne; and Catalonia, where the experiences of both 1822 to 1823 and 1827 had given rise to bitter memories of repression in an area where large parts of the peasantry had already been radicalized by intense social and economic change.

In the struggle that resulted—the so-called first Carlist War—fighting raged for six years, but want of arms and supplies was a constant problem for the rebel forces, while they were unable to conquer any major city. Exhausted and heavily outnumbered by the loyalist forces, who were supported by both Britain and France, they were eventually forced to surrender in 1839. However, Carlism was not dead: the hatreds generated by the fighting, indeed, imbued it with a certain capacity for hereditary self-perpetuation. In the years 1848 to 1849 and 1873 to 1877 there were therefore two further conflicts, but in these, too, the Carlists were defeated, whereupon they drifted to the margins of Spanish politics, and were not to re-emerge until the crisis of the 1930s gave them a new validity and lease on life.

TOWARD THE SPANISH CIVIL WAR

It should be noted, however, that by the late nineteenth century Carlism was not the only standard bearer of extreme conservatism in Spain. On the contrary, returning to the followers of María Cristina and the infant Isabella II, it may be seen that they were themselves deeply split between unreconstructed absolutists and those who favored the introduction of some form of liberalism. The loyalist camp had therefore witnessed a series of coups and revolutions as the many differences between neo-absolutists and moderate and radical liberals worked themselves out, and by the 1840s a new and more modern brand of conservatism had emerged and succeeded in entrenching itself in the corridors of power. Known as *moderantismo*, this stood for a constitutional monarchy, but one in which political power would be monopolized by a narrow social elite, all moves in favor of democratization resisted, and the rights of property protected by a policy of

the most brutal repression: it is no coincidence that it was this period that gave Spain the notoriously ruthless paramilitary police force known as the Civil Guard. Though challenged by revolutions in 1854 and 1868 that were to a large extent the result of disputes within their own ranks over power and patronage, the forces that gave rise to this system managed to maintain their power more or less intact until the coming of the Second Republic in April 1931, an important part of the history of that republic being the manner in which it finally healed the schism in the Spanish Right that had caused so much bloodshed in the nineteenth century. Thus, after 1876 Carlism had retreated into its heartlands of the Basque province and Navarre, and gradually rebuilt itself as a political movement known as the Comunión Tradicionalista (Traditionalist Communion). Until 1931 this had remained a relatively unimportant force, but the perceived need to defend the social order brought the Carlists many supporters from the ranks of constitutionalist conservatism. In this fashion Carlism was incorporated into the mainstream of Spanish conservatism, and in 1937 the process was completed by merger with the Spanish Fascist movement known as the Falange and the formation of the single National Movement.

See also **Conservatism; Revolutions of 1820; Spain.**

BIBLIOGRAPHY

Aronson, Theo. *Royal Vendetta: The Crown of Spain, 1829–1965.* London, 1966.

Carr, Raymond. *Spain, 1808–1975.* Oxford, U.K., 1982.

Esdaile, Charles J. *Spain in the Liberal Age: From Constitution to Civil War, 1808–1939.* Oxford, U.K., 2000.

CHARLES J. ESDAILE

CARLSBAD DECREES. The Carlsbad Decrees were a series of measures adopted by the German Confederation in 1819 that established severe limitations on academic and press freedoms and set up a federal commission to investigate all signs of political unrest in the German states.

The Napoleonic Wars had spurred the growth of a small but influential nationalist movement in Germany, which garnered some of its most fervent supporters from among students and professors.

After the anti-Napoleonic campaigns of 1813–1815, student veterans returned to their universities and founded a series of nationalist fraternities or *Burschenschaften,* which were intended to promote the values of "Germanness, militancy, honor, and chastity." While the *Burschenschaften* were active throughout Germany's Protestant universities, the radical hub of the movement was Jena. There students and like-minded professors took advantage of the new press freedoms granted in Saxony-Weimar's 1816 constitution to promote liberal and nationalist positions and critique the slow pace of reform in Germany since the Congress of Vienna. Saxony-Weimar was also the site of the Wartburg Festival (October 1817), in which students gathered to sing nationalist hymns, issue vague demands for freedom and unity, and burn a list of books they deemed reactionary or anti-German. These developments were viewed with alarm by the Austrian chancellor Clemens von Metternich, who saw the student movement as a serious threat to the Restoration order established at Vienna. Metternich maintained that such radicalism was encouraged by an overly lenient attitude among government officials in Prussia and by the broader push toward constitutional government in Baden, Bavaria, Württemberg, and Saxony-Weimar.

Metternich was already seeking to clamp down on the *Burschenschaften* and their supporters when they provided him with a perfect pretext. On 23 March 1819 the student Karl Sand assassinated the conservative playwright August von Kotzebue in his apartment in Mannheim. Kotzebue had been a vociferous critic of the radical nationalist movement (one of his books was on the list burned at the Wartburg Festival); moreover, as a prolific and highly successful author of light comedies he was widely seen as the embodiment of Old Regime frivolity and lasciviousness. Recently it had become known that Kotzebue was sending reports on German cultural affairs to the Russian tsar. Sand, a student of theology at Jena and a member of the local *Burschenschaft,* resolved to take matters into his own hands, striking down this "traitor" to the German nation. With Kotzebue dead, Sand attempted to kill himself but was instead arrested, tried, and eventually executed. Meanwhile, a deranged student had made an attempt on the life of a district official in Nassau, adding to the sense of unrest and imminent revolution.

Sand's act represented a substantial reversal for the reform party in Prussia, as moderates like Karl August von Hardenberg and Karl von Altenstein lost influence with Frederick William III (r. 1797–1840) to more reactionary members of his cabinet. At a meeting in Teplitz on 1 August, Metternich and the Prussian king agreed that their states would take a common hardline policy against the "revolutionary party" in Germany. The outlines of that policy were hammered out two weeks later at a conference of ministers from ten leading German states, which took place in the resort locale of Carlsbad. The conference drafted a series of decrees, which were then approved unanimously at a meeting of the Federal Diet on 20 September 1819.

The Carlsbad Decrees consisted of four laws. The University Law established a state plenipotentiary for each university, who was responsible for maintaining proper discipline and morality. The state governments were obligated to remove any teacher who taught subversive doctrines or otherwise abused his authority and to enforce existing laws against secret student organizations (that is, the *Burschenschaften*). Professors fired by one university could not be hired by another, and students found guilty of involvement with the *Burschenschaften* were banned from future employment in public office. The Press Law required that all books and periodicals shorter than 320 pages be approved by a censorship board before they could be published. Periodicals that harmed the interests of a German state could be shut down and their editors banned from publishing for as long as five years. An Investigative Law set up a federal investigative body that was charged with examining and reporting on all evidence of political unrest in Germany (though prosecution of suspects was left to the individual states). Finally, the Provisional Execution Order granted the Confederation the authority to take action against states that failed to suppress revolutionary activities within their borders.

The immediate effect of the Carlsbad Decrees was a stifling of liberal political expression in Germany. The *Burschenschaften* were banned, liberal professors were fired, and students suspected of illegal activities found the path to government office blocked. Thus Prussia and Austria were able to impose an effective conservative hegemony within the Confederation, hampering efforts toward liberal or constitutional reform. Once the decrees attained permanent status in 1824, government spying and censorship became a way of life in Germany, often lamented in the writings of Heinrich Heine and Ludwig Börne. Yet the impact of the Carlsbad Decrees should not be overstated. Application of these laws was always uneven, and opposition figures became quite skillful in skirting the censors. Moreover, the Revolution of 1830 in France would unleash a new wave of political unrest in Germany, which led to new constitutions in Hannover and Saxony and liberal reforms in a number of other states. Still, it required another revolution (that of 1848) before the Carlsbad Decrees were finally repealed by the Federal Diet in April 1848.

See also **Frederick William III; Hardenberg, Karl August von; Metternich, Clemens von; Restoration.**

BIBLIOGRAPHY

Büssem, Eberhard. *Die Karlsbader Beschlüsse von 1819: Die endgültige Stabiliserung der restaurativen Politik im Deutschen Bund nach dem Wiener Kongress 1814/15.* Hildesheim, Germany, 1974.

Huber, Ernst Rudolf. *Deutsche Verfassungsgeschichte seit 1789.* Vol. 1: *Reform und Restauration 1789 bis 1830.* Stuttgart, Germany, 1957.

Sheehan, James J. *German History, 1770–1866.* Oxford, U.K., 1989.

Williamson, George S. "What Killed August von Kotzebue?: The Temptations of Virtue and the Political Theology of German Nationalism, 1789–1819." *Journal of Modern History* 72, no. 4 (2000): 890–943.

GEORGE S. WILLIAMSON

CARLYLE, THOMAS

CARLYLE, THOMAS (1795–1881), Scottish historian, biographer, translator, and social critic.

Born in Ecclefechan in the Annandale section of Dumfriesshire, Scotland, Thomas Carlyle was raised by stern Calvinists of low social stature. Carlyle enrolled at the University of Edinburgh in 1809 to prepare for the ministry but turned instead to mathematics. In his early twenties, Carlyle studied German literature and idealist philosophy. He came especially to admire the writing of Johann Wolfgang von Goethe and Friedrich Schiller. In 1821 he met the sharp-witted Jane Baillie Welsh, whom he married five years later, despite her family's higher social rank.

In August of 1822, Carlyle underwent a transformative religious experience on Leith Walk in Edinburgh. His personal vision convinced him that a transcendental, godly presence animated the universe and put him at odds with what he saw as the wicked materialism of the times and its adjutants: pride, secularism, agnosticism, liberalism, and democracy.

Carlyle came to regard poets and writers as the new prophets of the age. In 1824 he published an English translation of Goethe's *Wilhelm Meister's Apprenticeship,* and in 1825 he published his own *Life of Schiller.* In 1827 he published four volumes of translations from the work of prominent German writers, known together as *German Romance.*

In 1828 he and his wife, Jane, moved to the isolated outskirts of Craigenputtock in Scotland. From there Carlyle wrote and published *Sartor Resartus* (The tailor retailored) when *Fraser's Magazine* agreed to serialize it in 1833–1834. His prose immediately stood out. It was combative, emphatic, satirical, highly allusive, metaphorically recursive and often boldly paradoxical, embedded in a loose, elliptical sentence structure. His book called for a redressing of the imbalance between spiritual and material values in modern European society through personal, inward reformation. In 1834 he and wife, Jane, moved to Chelsea, London.

The publication of *The French Revolution* in 1837 transformed Carlyle into a public figure. No dependable history yet existed in English of the French Revolution. Carlyle penned it in a fiery, momentous style that made his narrative palpable to readers. Characteristically, he ranked personalities and circumstances ahead of abstract analysis, contending that history was driven by the irrational and often dark emotions of individuals. Its completion was unexpectedly delayed by two years. In the

Thomas Carlyle. Portrait by Michele Gordigiani. Scala/Art Resource, NY

winter of 1835, he loaned the manuscript to his friend John Stuart Mill and Mrs. Harriet Taylor, in whose possession it was mysteriously burned. For Carlyle, social instability and violence in France as elsewhere could only be checked by strong, heroic individuals, a subject he elaborated upon in *On Heroes, Hero Worship, and the Heroic in History* (1841).

After *The French Revolution*, Carlyle turned to social questions in the form of essays and biographies. His 1839 publication on Chartism and his 1843 book, *Past and Present*, sharply attacked the social misery generated in England by the Industrial Revolution, especially that of women and children working in factories and mines. *Past and Present* targeted the "idle dilettantes" of the agricultural aristocracy who, he argued, ruled without virtue or talent. He also inveighed against

the Corn Laws that kept the country elite enriched. He censured the unfeeling utilitarianism of the political economist Jeremy Bentham that championed a godless "profit and loss philosophy" and the laissez-faire policies that divided mankind into atomized cogs in vast profit-making machines. His social reformism was also motivated by fear of radical revolution from below. He derided democracy as mob rule.

Carlyle's later publications alternated between the biographical and the social, with *Oliver Cromwell's Letters and Speeches* (1845), *Latter-Day Pamphlets* (1850), and his six-volume *Frederick the Great* (1858–1865). He was elected Rector of Edinburgh University in 1865, the year of his wife's death. That same year, Governor Edward John Eyre of Jamaica suppressed a rebellion of plantation workers in Morant Bay, allowing at least 439 people to be killed retributively. Between 1866 and 1869 Carlyle headed a committee that defended Eyre in a fierce public debate that pitted him and his colleagues Charles Dickens, John Ruskin, and Alfred Tennyson against Charles Darwin, T. H. Huxley, and Herbert Spencer. In this same period, Carlyle renewed his attacks on popular representative government through debates on the Second Reform Bill of 1867. He died in 1881.

Carlyle influenced many later Victorians who first read him in the 1830s and 1840s. His impact is present in Benjamin Disraeli's *Sybil* (1845), John Ruskin's *Stones of Venice* (1851–1853), and in Charles Dickens's *Bleak House* (1852–1853) and *Hard Times* (1854), the latter being dedicated to Carlyle. Dickens's *A Tale of Two Cities* (1859) was based largely on Carlyle's *French Revolution*, which Dickens claimed to have read hundreds of times.

See also **Dickens, Charles; Disraeli, Benjamin; Ruskin, John; Tennyson, Alfred.**

BIBLIOGRAPHY

Ashton, Rosemary. *Thomas and Jane Carlyle: Portrait of a Marriage.* London, 2002.

Campbell, Ian. *Thomas Carlyle.* London, 1974.

Cumming, Mark, ed. *Carlyle Encyclopedia.* Madison, N.J., 2004.

Heffer, Simon. *Moral Desperado: A Life of Thomas Carlyle.* London, 1995.

Kaplan, Fred. *Thomas Carlyle: A Biography.* Ithaca, N.Y., 1983.

STEPHEN VELLA

CARPENTER, EDWARD (1844–1929),

English socialist and theorist of homosexual emancipation.

Although by the time of his death in 1929 Edward Carpenter was known as one of the great socialist visionaries of England and a champion of both women's and homosexuals' liberation, there is little in his early years to account for such a radical vision. The son of a former naval commander with a lucrative career as a barrister and investor, Carpenter's early life followed the course prescribed by his privileged station, and he was educated at Oxford and Cambridge, where in 1868 he began a career as a lecturer at Trinity Hall.

During his second year at Trinity, he was elected a clerical fellow and ordained a deacon. Carpenter's family had raised him in the relatively liberal doctrines of the Broad Church, and he soon found himself in conflict with the tenets of Anglicanism that he was expected to uphold. By 1871 this conflict had led to physical debilitation, and after a brief leave of absence, he resigned his church roles and functioned solely as a lecturer.

With church responsibilities behind him, Carpenter devoted himself to a relatively new program, the University Extension Program. The program was started by James Stuart (1843–1913) of Cambridge in response to pressures from women demanding access to education. Stuart saw it as a chance to forge an educational institution that would give equal access regardless of class or gender, and his democratic vision attracted Carpenter. By 1877 Carpenter was a key player within the extension program.

Following the death of his parents in 1880 and 1881, Carpenter resigned his teaching duties and devoted himself to full-time study at Millthorpe, a retreat he bought in the Sheffield countryside. He began what was to become a key part of his theoretical vision, a systematic study of eastern religions and particularly of the Bhagavad-Gita. He also completed his epic poem cycle, *Towards Democracy* (1883), which was strongly influenced by the American poet Walt Whitman (1819–1892).

Through his involvement with such groups as the Progressive Association, the Fellowship of the New Life, the Fabians, and the Social Democratic Federation (SDF), he met important political and social theorists such as William Morris, Havelock Ellis, and Olive Schreiner, one of the leading socialist feminists of the time.

In 1884 William Morris broke alliance with the SDF and formed the Socialist League, and Carpenter followed suit. The development was crucial for Carpenter, for the League viewed the task of socialism to be the creation of a new inner consciousness for all people. This mingling of politics and spirituality enabled Carpenter to synthesize his own religious past, his current embrace of eastern mysticism, and his strong allegiance to social reform into a unique vision that might be best termed *mystic socialism.*

Perhaps the most significant event in Carpenter's life happened in 1891, when returning from a journey to India, he met George Merrill, with whom he found an immediate and mutual attraction. Merrill had been raised in the slums of Sheffield and had no formal education. The attachment between the two men was undoubtedly one of real affection, but it also enabled Carpenter to achieve one of his long-standing goals in life: the realization of a bond between men that refused to be hindered by the rigid class divisions of English society—the type of bonding professed by Carpenter's poetic idol, Whitman.

The two men took up residence at Millthorpe, and Carpenter began the period of radical theorization that produced the works on which his reputation largely rests: *Love's Coming of Age* (1896), *The Intermediate Sex* (1908), and *Intermediate Types among Primitive Folks* (1914). The tracts extend Carpenter's mystic socialism into a discussion of female gender equality and same-sex desire, and argue that by ending the oppression of "the sex-love passion," society can instill a new type of individualism that will lead to liberation and democracy.

The Intermediate Sex, Carpenter's most famous tract, argues that through both social and natural evolution, sex has outgrown its simple biological purposes, and that increased instances of *uranism*—Carpenter's term for homosexuality—represent the evolution of a distinctive third sex designed to lead society into a new set of social relations.

Carpenter became a hero to the first generation of Labour politicians. During the short-lived Labour government in 1924, Carpenter's eightieth birthday was marked by a commemorative greeting signed by every member of the Cabinet. For unknown reasons, Carpenter and Merrill left Millthorpe in 1922 and moved to Guildford in Surrey. George Merrill died in 1928, and Carpenter a year later. They are buried together in a grave in the Mount Cemetery, Guildford.

See also **Ellis, Havelock; Fabians; Feminism; Homosexuality and Lesbianism; Morris, William; Socialism; Symonds, John Addington.**

BIBLIOGRAPHY

Primary Sources

A Bibliography of Edward Carpenter. Sheffield, U.K., 1949.

Carpenter, Edward. *Selected Writings.* Volume I: *Sex.* Edited by David Fernbach and Noel Greig. London, 1984.

———. *Towards Democracy.* London, 1985.

Secondary Sources

Jones, Gareth Stedman. *Outcast London: A Study in the Relationship between Classes in Victorian Society.* Oxford, U.K., 1971.

Pierson, Stanley. *Marxism and the Origins of British Socialism: The Struggle for a New Consciousness.* Ithaca, N.Y., 1973.

Rowbotham, Sheila, and Jeffrey Weeks. *Socialism and the New Life: The Personal and Sexual Politics of Edward Carpenter and Havelock Ellis.* London, 1977.

Weeks, Jeffrey. *Sex, Politics, and Society: The Regulation of Sexuality since 1800.* London, 1981.

GREGORY BREDBECK

CASTLEREAGH, VISCOUNT (ROBERT STEWART)

(1769–1822), influential Anglo-Irish statesman.

Robert Stewart, Viscount Castlereagh and Second Marquess of Londonderry's tenure as one of Britain's most influential foreign secretaries (1812–1822) coincided with a period of considerable tumult both at home and abroad. Born into an Anglo-Irish landed family and baptized a Presbyterian, Castlereagh had the requisite background for a smooth entry into Irish politics. Following the lead of his father, who sat in the Irish Parliament from 1771 to 1783, Castlereagh began his political career by winning a seat for County Down in 1790. He became chief secretary of Ireland in 1798, the same year the Irish Rebellion erupted. Prompted by the radical changes witnessed in the French Revolution and initially led by the anti-English and republican Society of United Irishmen (established 1791), the Rebellion and the small French invasion accompanying it were quickly and ruthlessly suppressed. To prevent further threats to stability, Castlereagh looked to union with Great Britain. He shouldered the difficult task of securing the Irish Parliament's approval of his plan for Irish representation in the British Parliament. Convincing Irish politicians to support the dissolution of their own representative institution has been described as a process of intense bullying and bribery, but it is also true that this aptly reflected an eighteenth-century politics of patronage. Despite fierce opposition from many Irish Protestants, Castlereagh pushed through the Act of Union, which took effect on 1 January 1801. For Castlereagh, the success of the union depended on addressing Irish grievances. He thus supported progressive measures like Catholic emancipation, the right of Catholics to hold seats in Parliament. When King George III (r. 1760–1820) refused to sanction this policy, Castlereagh joined the Tory prime minister, William Pitt (1759–1806), by resigning from office in 1801.

His principles failed to thwart his ambition. Castlereagh returned to office in July 1802 as president of the Board of Control for India. The government's primary concern throughout this period was the ongoing war against Napoleon I (r. 1804–1814/15). As secretary of war (1807–1809), Castlereagh expanded British regiments by offering a bounty to militiamen who transferred to the regular army. Later charged with corruption and military incompetence, and facing the likelihood of losing his War Office post, Castlereagh resigned. Having learned that the foreign secretary,

George Canning (1770–1827), had secretly maneuvered against him, Castlereagh challenged his rival to a duel and wounded him in the thigh.

Castlereagh's major contributions to British politics were still to come. Back in office in 1812 as foreign secretary in the Tory administration of Robert Banks Jenkinson (Lord Liverpool, 1770–1828), Castlereagh this time battled Napoleon through diplomacy. His first priority was reinvigorating a military alliance of Russia, Prussia, Austria, and Britain and thus preventing any one state from negotiating a separate peace with Napoleon. He achieved this needed unity with the Treaty of Chaumont (1814), which committed each allied power to fielding 150,000 troops. His next priority was shaping the peace settlement, which stands as his most striking legacy. Working closely with his Austrian counterpart, Clemens von Metternich (1773–1859), at the Congress of Vienna, Castlereagh promoted a "just equilibrium," in which a European balance of power was maintained by protecting the sovereignty of small states and preventing the aggression of large ones. No state would gain enough power to threaten European stability. Adhering to this principle during negotiations in Vienna and Paris, Castlereagh rejected a punitive peace against France but supported the formation of buffer states, an independent Kingdom of the Netherlands for example, to check future French aggression. The Quadruple Alliance (1815) incorporated another of Castlereagh's goals by establishing the Congress System, whereby Russia, Prussia, Austria, and Britain agreed to meet periodically to monitor the peace settlement and anticipate conflicts.

Castlereagh soon realized, however, that the other Great Powers sought to use the postwar framework in a way he never intended. Castlereagh rejected their assertion that the Congress powers could interfere with the internal affairs of other states, which in practice meant crushing liberal and nationalist movements. Castlereagh instead favored nonintervention and gradually detached Britain from the Allies' reactionary policies. This was not apparent to many at home, where he was criticized for hobnobbing with European autocrats. Moreover, the added burden of serving as the leader of the House of Commons exposed him to attacks on unpopular and often repressive policies at a time of acute domestic unrest. A mental breakdown and increasing paranoia preceded his suicide on 12 August 1822. His old rival Canning succeeded him at the Foreign Office, and although with a very different style, largely followed the general direction of British foreign policy already established by Castlereagh.

See also **Congress of Vienna; Great Britain.**

BIBLIOGRAPHY

Primary Sources

Castlereagh, Robert Stewart, Viscount. *Memoirs and correspondence of Viscount Castlereagh, second Marquess of Londonderry. . . .* Edited by Charles Vane. 12 vols. London, 1848–1853.

Secondary Sources

Bartlett, Christopher John. *Castlereagh.* London, 1966. A valuable summary but does not use unpublished sources.

Hinde, Wendy. *Castlereagh.* London, 1981.

Thorne, R. G. "Stewart, Hon. Robert." In *The House of Commons, 1790–1820,* edited by R. G. Thorne. London, 1986. A useful corrective to the emphasis on Castlereagh's career as foreign secretary.

ELISA R. MILKES

CATHERINE II (1729–1796; ruled 1762–1796), empress of Russia.

Catherine II (called Catherine the Great) was born Sophie Auguste Frederike, Princess of Anhalt-Zerbst, on 2 May (21 April, old style) 1729 in the Prussian town of Stettin (now Szczecin, Poland) on the Baltic Sea. Although her father was an obscure German princeling, Princess Sophie's mother had connections to the royal houses of Sweden, Denmark, and Russia. Most importantly for Sophie's future, her mother's cousin had been married to Peter the Great's daughter Anna, and her elder brother had been engaged, before his sudden death, to another of the tsar's daughters who went on to rule Russia as Empress Elizabeth (r. 1741–1762 [1761, O.S.]).

In January 1744 Empress Elizabeth invited young Princess Sophie to Russia to be the bride of Karl Peter Ulrich, Duke of Holstein-Gottorp, a grandson of Peter the Great and heir to the Russian throne. Princess Sophie arrived in Russia that winter, converted to Russian Orthodoxy (as Grand Duchess Yekaterina [Catherine] Alekseyevna), and then married Grand Duke Peter (Karl Peter's Russian christened name) the following year.

The two were a poor match, and their marriage proved an unqualified disaster. Catherine's charm, intelligence, and clear-eyed desire to please her new countrymen clashed with Peter's drunken antics, boorishness, and open disdain for all things Russian. The years spent as the grand duchess were the most difficult of Catherine's life. Her sole responsibility had been to bear an heir to the throne, but Grand Duke Peter proved incapable of fulfilling his part of the task. Empress Elizabeth eventually forced Catherine to take a lover, and in 1754, she finally gave birth to a son, Paul (ruled as Paul I, 1796–1801). The question of Paul's paternity remains a mystery, though most believe Catherine's lover, Sergei Saltykov, to have been the father.

Lonely, bored, and vulnerable to the deadly intrigues forever swirling at the Russian court, Catherine read extensively and began developing the innate political skills she used to such exceptional effectiveness throughout her life. Although she had no legal claim to the Russian throne, Catherine, driven by an irrepressible ambition, believed that she would one day rule Russia and began preparing herself for the role.

The grand duke succeeded Empress Elizabeth to the throne upon her death on 5 January 1762 (25 December 1761, O.S.). One of Tsar Peter III's first acts was to pull Russia out of the Seven Years' War (1756–1763) and conclude a peace treaty with Frederick II of Prussia. The move was poorly thought out and deeply unpopular with the Russian officers. When a series of erratic actions followed, opposition to the new ruler began to take shape. After it became apparent that Peter was considering locking up his wife in a convent, Catherine struck back with a coup of her own with the aid of Grigory Orlov, her lover at the time, and his brothers, backed by the capital's elite guards regiments. On 9 July (28 June, O.S.) 1762 Catherine was

Catherine II. Portrait by Alexander Roslin. Musée des Beaux-Arts, La Rochelle, France/Bridgeman Art Library

proclaimed empress of Russia. Peter III abdicated the throne and was murdered at his palace outside St. Petersburg several days later under murky circumstances.

CATHERINE IN POWER

During the first several years of her reign Catherine worked to consolidate her power and to set Russia's poor financial house in order. In December 1763 she reorganized the Senate in an attempt to reinvigorate the badly neglected central administration. That same year Catherine issued the second of two manifestoes to encourage foreigners to resettle in Russia and develop its open spaces. In 1764 Catherine secularized the property of the Russian Orthodox Church as part of her strategy to replenish the treasury's depleted coffers. In her dealings with the other European powers, Catherine sought above all to avoid conflict and maintain friendly relations.

Catherine's greatest effort at reform during this period came in 1767 with the convening of the Legislative Commission, whose purpose was to devise a new Russian legal code. To help guide the commission's work, Catherine, who had been drawn to the writings of the French philosophes for some time, drafted her famous *Nakaz* (Instruction), based largely on the works of such thinkers as Cesare Beccaria and the Baron de Montesquieu. Catherine's legislation expressed her recognition of the multiplicity of religions in the empire and in 1773 she issued a decree that indirectly acknowledged religious tolerance.

WAR, REBELLION, AND THE YEARS OF REFORM

In 1768 the Ottoman Empire attacked Russia, prompting Catherine to close the Legislative Commission and to focus all her energies on war preparations. At the height of the war, two crises shook Russia. First, a deadly plague broke out in Moscow in 1771 killing thousands and spreading panic. Two years later a peasant revolt led by the Cossack Emelian Pugachev erupted, sweeping across the countryside and threatening the foundations of Catherine's power. Catherine surmounted these crises with the help of the war hero Grigory Potemkin, her new favorite whom she most likely secretly married in 1774. Potemkin became her most trusted advisor, commander in chief of the armed forces, governor-general for southern Russia, and eventually a virtual coruler of the empire.

In 1774 the Treaty of Kuchuk Kainarji marking Russia's victory over the Turks was signed and the Pugachev rebellion put down. With peace at home and abroad, Catherine returned to her project of reforms, and the next thirteen years witnessed many of the major achievements of her reign. In 1775 she enacted the so-called Provincial Reform aimed at improving local government; in 1782 the Police Ordinance established more effective, rational control over the urban population; and in 1785 charters to the nobility and the towns stipulated the rights of these two social groups for the first time in Russian history. Catherine granted private persons the right to establish printing presses in 1783 and promoted the expansion of the educational system through a series of initiatives and reforms. Potemkin developed the expansive southern territories, and through his urging the Crimea was annexed in 1783.

WAR, REVOLUTION, AND CATHERINE'S FINAL YEARS

Seeking to avenge its earlier defeat, the Ottoman Empire declared war for a second time in 1787. The war did not begin well for Russia and took a drastic turn for the worse when Sweden attacked in 1788, thus opening a second front in the north. Russia's main ally, Austria, proved of only limited help, and Prussia, seeing Russian forces pinned down in the north and south, threatened to invade from the west. Effective diplomacy and a series of dramatic victories over the Turks began to turn the tide. In 1790 Sweden dropped out of the war, and a British threat in spring 1791 to send warships against St. Petersburg if Catherine did not immediately sue for peace with the Turks evaporated in the face of stiff domestic opposition. The Treaty of Jassy, concluded with the Turks in January 1792 (December 1791, O.S.), solidified Russia's possession over the Crimea and the northern Black Sea littoral. It was a great victory for Catherine, clouded only by the death of Potemkin in autumn 1791.

The outbreak of the French Revolution in 1789 did not initially worry Catherine much, both because France had long been a foe of Russia and unrest there would deprive Turkey of an important ally and because she, like most other European rulers at the time, could not yet perceive where events in France were heading. When Poland proclaimed a new constitution in 1791, however, Catherine feared Jacobinism had spread to Russia's borders and decided to act. After offering subsidies to Sweden, Prussia, and Austria to lead the fight against France, she set about imposing Russian control over Poland. Russian troops invaded in 1792, and through the partitions of 1793 and 1795 Poland was divided among Russia, Prussia, and Austria and disappeared from the map of Europe.

The Revolution also led Catherine to clamp down on perceived dissent at home. In 1790 she ordered the writer Alexander Radishchev arrested and exiled to Siberia. Two years later Nikolai Novikov, a leading Freemason and journalist, was arrested and imprisoned. Masonic lodges across Russia shut their doors soon thereafter. In September 1796 Catherine established strict censorship and closed the private presses. Special posts were established at key ports and border crossings to keep out revolutionary ideas. This proved to be one of Catherine's final acts: she died of a stroke on 17 November (6 November, O.S.) 1796.

ASSESSMENT

The wars against Turkey, Sweden, and Poland put an end to Catherine's reforms and placed a heavy burden on the state's finances. The partitioning of Poland and imposition of censorship at home cast an undeniable shadow over her final years. These developments, along with the continued plight of the peasantry—the vast majority of the Russian populace, whose condition changed little under her rule—represent the low points of her reign.

Nevertheless, Catherine the Great is justly considered one of imperial Russia's most enlightened rulers whose reign marked a period of rare social, political, economic, and cultural development. She was the only intellectual ever to sit on the Russian throne, a prolific writer and patron of the arts, imbued with boundless energy and optimism. The lurid tales of her private life that have made Catherine a legend were fabricated by her enemies, chiefly foreign, intent on destroying the reputation of a woman who wielded with such confidence power traditionally reserved for men. Internationally, Catherine led Russia to victory in several critical wars, added more territory to the empire than any other ruler since Ivan IV (r. 1553–1584), and solidified Russia's status as one of the great European powers.

See also **Paul I; Russia.**

BIBLIOGRAPHY

Primary Sources

Cruse, Markus, and Hilde Hoogenboom, eds. and trans. *The Memoirs of Catherine the Great.* New York, 2005.

Smith, Douglas, ed. and trans. *Love and Conquest: Personal Correspondence of Catherine the Great and Prince Grigory Potemkin.* DeKalb, Ill., 2004.

Secondary Sources

Alexander, John T. *Catherine the Great: Life and Legend.* New York, 1989.

Dixon, Simon. *Catherine the Great.* Harlow, U.K., 2001.

LeDonne, John P. *Ruling Russia: Politics and Administration in the Age of Absolutism, 1762–1796.* Princeton, N.J., 1984.

Madariaga, Isabel de. *Russia in the Age of Catherine the Great.* New Haven, Conn., 1981.

———. *Catherine the Great: A Short History.* 2nd ed. New Haven, Conn., 2002.

DOUGLAS SMITH

CATHOLICISM. The Catholic Church as an institution was at the center of many of the most intense and significant political debates in the long nineteenth century. The Catholic Church was a potent political force because it frequently combined forceful leadership and a clear agenda with a membership that made Catholicism the largest single religious denomination in Europe. Although not evenly distributed throughout the Continent, Catholics were a clear majority in southern and western Europe—Spain, Portugal, Italy, Austria-Hungary, France, and Belgium (after 1830)—and constituted substantial minorities in the Netherlands, Switzerland, and Germany.

Not everyone baptized as a Catholic, of course, took their religion to mean the same thing, and levels of religious practice and commitment to the institutional church varied, sometimes sharply, on the basis of region, gender, and social class. But even lukewarm Catholics would have been familiar with the general teachings of the church about salvation and how to obtain it. And a majority of Catholics remained committed to the sacramental system that celebrated and sanctified key transitional moments in their lives. It is impossible to be certain what such participation means, but when combined with evidence of devotional vitality at shrines such as Lourdes, it appears that Catholicism continued to provide a "sacred canopy" for vast numbers of European Catholics. Catholicism functioned, therefore, not only as an institutional church, but also as a cultural system of symbols and rituals that provided a sense of meaning and order for its adherents.

THE CULTURE OF CATHOLICISM

Catholicism in the nineteenth century inherited from the medieval era and from the reforms of the Council of Trent (1545–1563) a vision of a transcendent world beyond the here and now and a rich variety of rituals that allowed Catholics to communicate with that world. Heaven remained the goal for Catholics as a blissful realm where God and his saints resided for eternity. But if there was a heaven, there was also a hell, a place where those outside the church, and those within it who sinned and were not forgiven through the Catholic sacrament of penance, would suffer forever. Throughout the nineteenth century, preachers continued to resort at times to grisly descriptions of the horrific tortures awaiting the damned, as famously reported by James Joyce, whose fictional account of Father Arnall's sermon in *A Portrait of the Artist as a Young Man* (1916) mirrors many of those delivered in churches during the period. Such preaching might lead some to skepticism and fuel anticlericalism, but it could also provoke religious dread, which along with hope for salvation constituted essential elements of Catholic culture. For Catholics, as opposed to Protestants, the afterlife also included purgatory, a third place where those who deserved neither eternal reward nor punishment would suffer for a time before being welcomed into the community of saints.

Since the 1980s historians have observed how visions of the afterlife evolved over time, producing changes in the basic frameworks people used for interpreting their lives. In the nineteenth century, Catholicism, while never abandoning the threat of hellfire, tended to emphasize the possibility of redemption, at least for Catholics, and inflated the significance of purgatory. Indulgences granted by the church for prayers and devotional practices proliferated, offering believers a way to shorten not only their own time in purgatory, but also the period of suffering endured by departed loved ones. This shift can be seen as a response to complex changes, including concern about competition from secular ideologies, and enhanced attention to affective relations within families whose members could not tolerate the possibility of eternal separation. The increasing influence of the moral theology of the Italian priest Alphonsus of Liguori (1696–1787), who taught that confessors should take a paternal approach to their penitents and keep them from despair, provides another window onto a Catholic spiritual world that was softening in subtle but important ways its Tridentine patrimony.

Catholicism provided a map of the afterworld for its adherents, and through its rituals offered people a way of channeling the grace needed to gain heaven. Catholic culture was infused with a sense that Jesus and his saints, especially Mary, his mother, would respond to the prayers and supplications of believers. In particular, the sick and their families sought help and healing through the shrines that were ubiquitous in the Catholic world and through the devotions associated with them. Processions were common, especially in rural areas, to celebrate the feast day of a parish patron, to request divine help to stop a drought or an epidemic, or to seek protection from invading armies. Such practices, which had been regarded with suspicion by many clergy during the eighteenth century, were officially encouraged after the French Revolution, as the church sought to strengthen its ties with ordinary believers.

For the clergy and many of the laity, however, the Mass was at the center of Catholicism, and at the center of the Mass was the moment of consecration, when the officiating priest pronounced the Latin phrases "Hoc est enim corpus meum" (For this is my body) and "Hic est enim calix sanguinis mei" (For this is the cup of my blood), thus transforming the bread and wine into the body and blood of Christ. Catholics were obligated to attend mass each Sunday, and to confess their sins and receive Communion during the Easter season. These two practices have been used by sociologically minded historians, inspired by the work of Gabriel Le Bras in France, to measure levels of Catholic commitment. The French case has been the most thoroughly studied, but the reports of clergy from throughout Europe allow us to form a general picture of Catholic observance, which varied widely according to a number of factors.

Throughout Europe some regions were renowned for their devout populations. Brittany in western France maintained high levels of religious practice among both men and women throughout the century, while the clergy in Limousin, southwest of Paris, despaired over the low

Solemn Communion. Painting by Jules Octave Triquet celebrating the transcendence of the communion ritual. MUSÉE DES BEAUX-ARTS, ROUEN, FRANCE/BRIDGEMAN ART LIBRARY/LAUROS/ GIRAUDON

levels of practice among their flock. Father Ramòn Sarabia, who preached throughout Spain in the early twentieth century, was pleased with the piety he found in the north, in Castile, Aragon, and the Basque country, but was shocked by what he found in the southern provinces of Andalusia and Extremadura. In the city of Azuaga in 1913, for example, only ten men and two hundred women, out of a population of eighteen thousand, attended mass regularly. Ireland and the Polish-speaking territories were also sites of high levels of Catholic practice, which may even have increased in the course of the nineteenth century. In the Irish case, greater mass attendance in the wake of the potato famine of 1846 resulted in part from the organizational work of Paul Cullen, who was named archbishop of Armagh in 1850 and of Dublin in 1852. But in Ireland and Poland, Catholic practice was also an important means of expressing cultural

opposition and political dissent directed at foreign rulers.

Gender as well as region emerges as a crucial factor in studies of religious practice. Women tended to be more devout than men, a pattern that became stronger in the course of the century, to judge by the French case. In the middle years of the century, when slightly more than half of the French population received Easter communion, two women practiced for every man. When the percentage of Easter communicants dropped to around 25 percent in the early twentieth century, the ratio of females to males approached five to one. Finally, social class and urbanization were important factors in determining religious practice, with Catholic preachers throughout the century bewailing the alienation from the church of workers, who were being led astray by the seductive appeal of cities and the corrosive ideology of socialism.

There is a good deal of evidence to suggest that clerical laments about the problems posed to Catholicism in a modern age marked by materialism and unbelief were more than just groundless complaints. The positions of clerical hand-wringers and sociologically minded historians have converged to produce an argument that sees religion in general, and Catholicism in particular, as out of step with the modern world. According to this view, the secularization of Europe is an inevitable process that accompanies the rise of science and the progress of reason, the growth of the state as a provider of basic services, an urbanized society with a large working class, and ideologies that provide alternatives to traditional religion as the basis for moral codes and a sense of meaning. All of these developments had a negative impact on Catholicism, and declining levels of practice do suggest an attenuated attachment to the institutional church. However, historians have become increasingly attentive to the numerous exceptions that qualify a vision of Catholicism in decline. The high levels of orthodox practice in Poland and Ireland have already been noted as important indications that Catholicism could flourish when associated with national political movements. Similarly, the sustained loyalty of women works against models of decline that give privileged status to the behavior of men. The minority status of Catholicism in the newly unified Germany also led to higher levels of attachment to the church. Among the urban working class in Germany, Catholics were much more likely to practice their religion than were Protestants. Polish Catholic miners in Prussian-ruled Silesia went to Mass on Sunday and prayed to Saint Barbara as they descended into the coal pits.

Sunday Mass attendance and Easter communion are not the only ways to measure the attachment to Catholicism. Throughout Catholic Europe those who did not go to Mass on a regular basis still generally insisted on participating in the sacramental system, which established a series of rites of passage that marked their path through life and death. In Paris during the 1860s, only 14 percent of the population made their Easter duty, but over 90 percent of the children continued to be baptized. Anticlerical societies made an effort to promote civil alternatives to religious services in the last third of the century, but despite their efforts the vast majority continued to insist on Catholic baptism, first communion, and rituals for marriage and death. It would be excessive to conclude that all those who participated in these rites of passage were thoroughly familiar with and committed to the doctrines and beliefs that the church understood as the underlying principles. But the vast majority of Catholics would have heard either through an occasional sermon or a catechism class required for first communion, that baptism took away original sin and thus made eternal salvation possible. And when the clergy attempted to limit access to the sacraments, especially extreme unction, administered to the dying, or to deny the dead a Catholic burial, they faced angry congregations, a fact that made priests increasingly hesitant to adopt too rigorous a standard for admission to the sacraments. Count Cavour (Camillo Benso) and King Victor Emmanuel, under whose leadership Italy was united at the expense of the pope and his papal territories, and who were officially excommunicated by Pius IX (r. 1846–1878), asked for the sacrament of the dying, extreme unction, and were able to find accommodating clergy to minister to them on their death beds. The Catholic sacraments drew popular support because they provided individuals and communities traditionally sanctioned rituals appropriate to celebrate the most important moments as people moved through life. This need was channeled through rituals that also opened up the promise of salvation. Catholic culture in the nineteenth century thus operated on both a horizontal plane, where it sanctified birth, marriage, and death, and a vertical one, where it provided access to grace and salvation.

ULTRAMONTANE CATHOLICISM: GOVERNANCE AND IDEOLOGY

Catholicism was a cultural system constituted by beliefs and rituals, but these were maintained by a hierarchical church with an institutional and political agenda that was complex, contested both internally and externally, and in constant evolution. From the perspective of the institutional church, the most noteworthy change in the nineteenth century was the increasingly centralized and authoritarian governance by officials at Rome and particularly the pope. Papal authority grew

Cartoon satirizing Catholic emancipation, England, c. 1829. The Duke of Wellington, English prime minister, and Sir Robert Peel, sponsor of the 1829 Catholic Emancipation Act, are depicted as subservient to the pope, while Lord Eldon, one of the most outspoken opponents of the legislation, is shown as a lion in defeat. Passage of the act allowed English and Irish Catholics to sit in Parliament. ©HULTON-DEUTSCH COLLECTION/CORBIS

relative to national churches, a point evident in the series of concordats that Rome negotiated with state governments, starting with the treaty between Pius VII (r. 1800–1823) and Napoleon I in 1801 that resolved the decade-long battle between the revolutionary republic and the church in France. Throughout the rest of the century concordats were established with most of the states in Europe, including Protestant Prussia, that specified the rights of Catholics to practice their religion freely, to train their clergy, and to educate their young, frequently in state-funded institutions.

The centralization of church governance, or ultramontanism, was defended in theoretical terms

by writers such as Joseph-Marie de Maistre (1753–1821) and the vicomte Louis-Gabriel de Bonald (1754–1840), who saw Roman authority as the only alternative to the disorder of the revolutionary era. Devout Catholics in the nineteenth century never forgot the attacks on churches and the clergy that accompanied the radical phase of the Revolution between 1792 and 1794. The revolutionaries' association of Catholicism with fanaticism and counter-revolution was matched by the conviction among most French Catholics that republican institutions posed a mortal threat to their religion. The sacking of the episcopal palace in Paris in the wake of the French revolution of 1830 and the violent deaths of two archbishops in Paris during the June days of 1848 and the uprising of the Paris Commune in 1871 served as powerful reminders of the continuing threat revolution posed to the church. The memory and continuing fear of revolution, and the consequent desire for order, provided a powerful impetus for popes to form alliances with established governments, even those of non-Catholics. Thus, Pope Gregory XVI (r. 1831–1846) condemned the Polish insurrection of 1830–1831 and called on Polish Catholics to remain loyal to the Russian tsar, despite government policies that favored the Orthodox Church and discriminated against Catholics.

Revolutionary impulses were linked to liberalism, which was condemned in a series of papal pronouncements that fulminated against claims for the rights of individual conscience, freedom of the press, and the separation of church and state. Pope Gregory XVI set the tone for such statements in *Mirari Vos* of 1832, directed against the French priest Felicité de Lammenais, whose newspaper *L'avenir* (1830–1831) envisioned a liberal Catholicism allied to democracy and independent from state entanglement. Pope Pius IX's famous "Syllabus of Errors," which accompanied the encyclical *Quanta Cura* (1864), included the following among the propositions it condemned:

15. Every man is free to embrace and profess that religion which, guided by the light of reason, he shall consider true.

. . .

77. In the present day it is no longer expedient that the Catholic religion should be held as the only

religion of the State, to the exclusion of all other forms of worship.

. . .

80. The Roman Pontiff can, and ought to, reconcile himself, and come to terms with progress, liberalism, and modern civilization.

By bluntly opposing freedom of religious choice and the separation of church and state, and insisting on the incompatibility of Catholicism with "modern civilization," Pius IX identified the church with a reactionary posture, a connection that has since shaped the attitudes of many Europeans, both Catholics and non-Catholics.

Socialism, like liberalism, was defined by the Catholic Church as a modern ideology that needed to be contested and defeated under the leadership of the pope. Associated with a materialist philosophy and an assault on the family, property, and established religions, socialism was forcefully condemned in papal pronouncements in the second half of the nineteenth century. *Rerum Novarum* (1891), the important encyclical of Pope Leo XIII (r. 1878–1903) on the condition of the working class, vigorously defended private property, and asserted that "the main tenet of Socialism, community of goods, must be utterly rejected, since it only injures those whom it would seek to benefit, is directly contrary to the natural rights of mankind, and would introduce confusion and disorder into the commonweal." But *Rerum Novarum* included as well a critique of uncontrolled capitalism and its consequences for the working class, whose rights to organize and strike were defended. By the end of the century, Catholic leaders realized that jeremiads condemning the modern world were an insufficient response to the new social conditions. In practice as well as theory, Catholicism showed itself adaptable to modern conditions in ways that belie some of the more extreme rhetoric of Gregory XVI and Pius IX.

Nationalism was in some instances another powerful ideological enemy of ultramontane Catholicism. The unification of Italy under the leadership of the Piedmontese monarchy crushed the hopes expressed by writers such as Father Vincenzo Gioberti in the 1840s that the pope might assume the leadership of a federal Italian state. Instead, the popes consistently condemned the new state, and insisted that the papal territories be restored, a claim that was not settled until the Lateran Treaty with Mussolini in 1929. In Germany the unified nation-state that emerged after 1870 engaged in a decade-long Kulturkampf, a culture war fought by the chancellor, Otto von Bismarck, and his government against a church whose members were thought to owe their primary loyalty to the pope rather than to the German emperor. In a sense, the drive for creating a unitary nation-state in Europe parallels the impulse toward papal infallibility, as both nationalism and ultramontanism sought to clarify lines of authority, and to strengthen central authority at the expense of the provinces.

Ultramontanism was a defensive ideology directed against newly emerging competitors, but it was also a positive statement affirming the truths of Catholic doctrine and the power of the pope to define and defend them. Ultramontanism achieved its most dramatic victory with the declaration of papal infallibility at the Vatican Council that met in Rome in 1870. Although this decree was opposed by a minority of bishops, including the archbishops from Vienna and Paris, most of the dissidents eventually accepted the doctrine, which claimed that the pope could not err when he taught Christians on matters of faith and morals, and also called on all Christians to submit to Rome on questions of discipline and governance. This affirmation of papal authority was accompanied by an enhanced symbolic status for the person of the pope, who became an object of popular veneration, a representative figure for a Catholic identity that transcended national boundaries. Images of Pius IX, for example, were widely distributed among Catholic populations, providing Catholics with a symbol of unchanging truth, doctrinal certainty, and the defense of their communities from the threats posed by increasing state authority and rapid social change.

ULTRAMONTANE CATHOLICISM: POLITICS AND SOCIETY

Ultramontane Catholicism embraced papal authority and rejected modern ideologies it saw as immoral and destructive. It is easy to understand why so many liberals, nationalists, and socialists saw Catholicism as a reactionary force, a defender of authority and hierarchy that needed to be opposed and defeated for the sake of human dignity, freedom, and progress. Some historians have suggested, however, a more complicated version of Catholicism as it affected political and social development in the nineteenth century. The church rejected the right of individuals to make personal judgments about religion, but it also opposed the claims of the nation-state when it infringed on the freedom of Catholics to practice their religion, and educate their children. Catholics in Belgium formed an alliance with liberals that produced a constitution in 1830 that affirmed the principle of popular sovereignty and granted religious toleration. Margaret Anderson has argued that the Catholic Center Party in Germany, which represented a third of the electorate in the last third of the century, was an important instrument for training German Catholics about the democratic process. In Poland and Ireland, Catholicism ended up in an alliance with ethnic groups whose aspirations to throw off the tutelage of foreign rulers were combined with a powerful Catholic identity. In all of these instances, Catholicism can be seen as fueling movements in favor of liberty and democracy, thus challenging any easy generalization based only on papal encyclicals. But it is important to note as well that the successful efforts of Catholics to mobilize a mass constituency could be based at times on targeting religious enemies, roles played by Protestants, Freemasons, and Jews. The French newspaper *La croix*, published by the Assumptionists starting in the 1880s, was particularly effective in using anti-Semitic language and images to reach a mass audience and played an important role in provoking the controversy surrounding Jewish army officer Alfred Dreyfus's conviction of treason in 1894.

On social questions Catholics inspired by the traditional obligation to help the poor played an important role in providing relief in a period when state welfare systems were either nonexistent or in their infancy. Frédéric Ozanam's Society of St. Vincent de Paul, established in Paris in 1833, brought together middle- and upper-class Catholics who involved themselves directly with the needy. Ozanam's goals for both the givers and receivers of charity were spiritual as much as social, and the Society did not embrace a program of social reform, but by the middle of the century chapters had spread throughout Catholic Europe, and were offering help to thousands of the poor, answering their basic needs. In the Prussian Rhineland, Father

Adolph Kolping (1813–1865) founded an association that provided cheap housing and educational opportunities for young unmarried workers, an initiative comparable to the work of Father Don Bosco, who founded a religious congregation in Turin to work with the growing youth population in Italian cities. Toward the end of the century, in the wake of *Rerum Novarum*, Catholic labor unions were organized, providing support for workers ranging from miners in the Ruhr Valley to agricultural laborers in Sicily.

Catholic women practiced their religion more regularly than men, but the role of women in Catholicism was not limited to passive participation in rituals celebrated by a male clergy. Organizations provided an important outlet for female sociability, creating networks in which women assumed leadership roles, organizing charitable work and managing pilgrimages for the sick to Lourdes, for example. Female religious congregations were particularly important, growing throughout the century, from 11,000 to 40,000 in Spain between 1797 and 1904, from 12,000 to 135,000 in France from 1808 to 1878, and from 7,794 to almost 50,000 in Germany between 1866 and 1908. The schools and hospitals run by sisters provided crucial services, but they also gave women opportunities for leadership and power unavailable elsewhere in European society.

Catholic labor unions and religious congregations were part of an organizational network that expanded rapidly in the late nineteenth century, creating in many areas a subculture that encompassed schools, churches, a specialized press including daily newspapers and periodicals, and leisure activities. The People's Association for Catholic Germany (*Volksverein*) was a model of Catholic organizational success, enlisting over eight hundred thousand members by 1914, establishing itself as one of the largest voluntary associations in imperial Germany. Historians of the Netherlands, where Catholic schools and organizations were especially important, have used the concept of *pillarization*, to describe a process whereby Catholicism formed, alongside Protestantism and socialism, a comprehensive framework for the lives of its members. German Catholicism could be described in similar terms, providing its members with schools, churches, youth clubs, reading rooms,

A group of Carmelite nuns pray at their convent in France, 1904. The Discalced Carmelite nuns were established in France in 1604 and convents were soon established throughout the country. The order was suppressed during the French Revolution but reestablished in 1854. Discalced Carmelites are a contemplative order, committed to prayer and spiritual purification. ©HULTON-DEUTSCH COLLECTION/CORBIS

and adult education programs—a whole range of institutions that generated a sense of identity and empowerment, but that also marked Catholics as separate and insular.

Some of the most popular Catholic organizations had as their main goal the support of missionary activity, which experienced a major renewal in the nineteenth century. The Society for the Propagation of the Faith, founded in Lyon in 1822, published a magazine full of stories about heroic preachers spreading the gospel throughout the world; by 1860 there were over two hundred thousand subscribers for a journal that was translated into over ten languages. New congregations of priests and nuns, such as the Oblates of Mary Immaculate, and Sisters of Saint Joseph de Cluny, along with older ones such as the Jesuits (reestablished in 1814) provided European clergy for the missions, who staffed schools and hospitals as part

of their conversion efforts. Catholic missions contributed to the sense of religious revival that was common in the nineteenth century, and along with Protestant efforts helped define the "civilizing mission" that European states used to legitimize their expansion into the world.

DEVOTIONAL AND THEOLOGICAL DEVELOPMENTS

Ultramontane Catholicism, understood as an ideology, took a defensive and intransigent posture toward the modern world, as being assaulted by revolutions, new ideologies, and aggressive nation-states, forces opposed by a heroic and infallible leader. But the ultramontane program included as well a devotional and theological component that, while linked to the political and social agenda of the church, established new modes of thinking and feeling about God and the saints. Early in the nineteenth century the writings of Catholic Romantics such as Friedrich Schlegel, Joseph Görres, and François-René du Chateaubriand challenged the rationalist critique of religion represented most prominently by Voltaire (1694–1778). They argued instead that religion needed to be valued as an emotional and aesthetic experience, and they looked to the spiritual writings and religious architecture of the Middle Ages for inspiration. Catholicism, however, produced few intellectuals of great significance for most of the rest of the nineteenth century. Ignaz von Döllinger revived historical studies of the church from his position in Munich, but was marginalized as a result of his opposition to infallibility. John Henry Newman, whose conversion from Anglicanism to Catholicism drew attention throughout the Catholic world in 1845, argued for a developmental and historical approach to theological doctrine, but he was more an influence on the twentieth than the nineteenth century. Early in the twentieth century Pius X (r. 1903–1914) stifled Catholic intellectual life through his assault on "modernism," an attempt by scholars such as Alfred Loisy to interpret the Bible using the tools of modern historical criticism.

An intensified emotionalism characterized Catholic popular devotions, exemplified in the cults of the Sacred Heart and of Mary, which exploded in the nineteenth century, fueled by millions of rosary beads, holy cards, novenas, and confraternities. In 1858 Pius IX provided doctrinal support for Marian devotionalism when he defined the doctrine of the Immaculate Conception, which asserted that Mary, alone among humans, had been born free of original sin. The Immaculate Conception had been a subject of theological debate since the Middle Ages, and Pius IX's decree resolved the debate in a manner that elevated Mary, already the most important of Catholic saints, to an even more exalted position. Christological devotions remained important as well, however, as Thomas à Kempis's fourteenth-century spiritual classic, *The Imitation of Christ* remained immensely popular among Catholic readers. The devotion to Christ took more somber forms as well. The Stations of the Cross, based on contemplating the suffering of Jesus during his passion and death, continued to spread from its base in Italy, and a number of women became famous throughout the Catholic world for sharing the wounds of Christ and thus his redemptive work. Anna Katharina Emmerich (1774–1824), a Westphalian mystic who dictated widely read and detailed accounts of the life of Christ based on her visions, experienced the stigmata, as did Gemma Galgani (1878–1903), a young Italian woman from Lucca who became the first person who lived into the twentieth century to be canonized as a saint. In France, Thérèse Martin (1873–1897), who entered a Carmelite convent when only fifteen years old, authored a spiritual autobiography that became enormously popular among Catholic readers after its publication in 1898. Sister Thérèse (who became known as the "Little Flower") advocated a life of constant self-sacrifice, but rejected the spiritual tendency that emphasized pain and blood. Both of these models had broad appeal, especially among women, and along with the high levels of female religious practice and the prominence of female religious congregations suggest a "feminization" of Catholicism in the nineteenth century. This development needs to be understood, however, within the context of a church that still concentrated most of the power in the male clergy, and substantially increased the authority of the pope. Few generalizations bearing on the complex institutional and cultural system that made up Catholicism can be maintained without the need for such qualification. Catholicism in the long nineteenth century faced enormous political and social challenges, and even a sympathetic historian would acknowledge that it struggled at times in adapting to them. Even historians critical of Catholicism would acknowledge that in 1914 it had reinvented itself as a potent political, social, and cultural force, figuring centrally in the personal and collective lives of millions of Europeans.

See also **Anticlericalism; Catholicism, Political; Center Party; Concordat of 1801; Leo XIII; Manning, Henry; Newman, John Henry; Papacy; Pilgrimages; Pius IX; Separation of Church and State (France, 1905).**

BIBLIOGRAPHY

Anderson, Margaret Lavinia. "Voter, Junker, Landrat, Priest: The Old Authorities and the New Franchise in Imperial Germany." *American Historical Review* 98 (1993): 1448–1474.

———. "The Limits of Secularization: On the Problem of the Catholic Revival in Nineteenth-Century

Germany." *The Historical Journal* 38 (1995): 647–670. A valuable critique of secularization and an excellent starting point for German Catholicism.

Aston, Nigel. *Religion and Revolution in France, 1780–1804.* Washington, D.C., 2000. Synthesizes the enormous literature on this crucial topic.

Atkin, Nicholas, and Frank Tallett. *Priests, Prelates, and People: A History of European Catholicism since 1750.* New York, 2003. Brief and even-handed, with a good bibliography.

Broers, Michael. *The Politics of Religion in Napoleonic Italy: The War against God, 1801–1814.* New York, 2002.

Burton, Richard D. E. *Holy Tears, Holy Blood: Women, Catholicism, and the Culture of Suffering in France, 1840–1970.* Ithaca, N.Y., 2004. Examines an important set of devotional beliefs.

Callahan, William J. *Church, Politics, and Society in Spain, 1750–1874.* Cambridge, Mass., 1984.

———. *The Catholic Church in Spain, 1875–1998.* Washington, D.C., 2000.

Chadwick, Owen. *The Popes and European Revolution.* New York, 1981.

———. *A History of the Popes, 1830–1914.* New York, 1998. Chadwick's volumes on the papacy are rich in detail and generally sympathetic.

Christian, William, Jr. *Person and God in a Spanish Valley.* Princeton, N.J., 1989. Brilliant evocation of rural Catholicism.

Curtis, Sarah A. *Educating the Faithful: Religion, Schooling, and Society in Nineteenth-Century France.* DeKalb, Ill., 2000. Valuable study of how nuns were recruited and trained and the work they did.

Gadille, Jacques, and Jean-Marie Mayeur. *Histoire du christianisme des origines à nos jours.* Vol. 11: *Libéralisme, industrialisation, expansion européene (1830–1914).* Paris, 1995. Comprehensive, with chapters on individual states and developments in theology, practice, and missionary work.

Gibson, Ralph. *A Social History of French Catholicism, 1789–1914.* London, 1989. The single best overview of French Catholicism.

Grew, Raymond. "Liberty and the Catholic Church in Nineteenth-Century Europe." In *Freedom and Religion in the Nineteenth Century,* edited by Richard Helmstadter, 196–232. New York, 1997. Challenges conventional views on the subject.

Kertzer, David. *The Popes against the Jews: The Vatican's Role in the Rise of Modern Anti-Semitism.* New York, 2001.

Kselman, Thomas. *Death and the Afterlife in Modern France.* Princeton, N.J., 1993.

Larkin, Emmet. "The Devotional Revolution in Ireland, 1850–1875." *American Historical Review* 77 (1972): 625–652.

Smith, Bonnie G. *Ladies of the Leisure Class: The Bourgeoises of Northern France in the Nineteenth Century.* Princeton, N.J., 1981. Shows how middle-class women drew on Catholicism in shaping their separate sphere.

Sperber, Jonathan. *Popular Catholicism in Nineteenth-Century Germany.* Princeton, N.J., 1984.

Strikwerda, Carl. *A House Divided: Catholics, Socialists, and Flemish Nationalists in Nineteenth-Century Belgium.* Lanham, Md., 1997.

Wintle, Michael. *Pillars of Piety: Religion in the Netherlands in the Nineteenth Century.* Hull, U.K., 1987.

THOMAS KSELMAN

CATHOLICISM, POLITICAL.

Political Catholicism evolved hesitantly in the aftermath of the French Revolution, establishing a presence in the 1830s and 1840s and finally becoming a prominent feature in the life of several nations, most notably Germany, France, and Belgium, by the close of the century. Never a single movement, it comprised several different initiatives, as Catholics debated how best to promote their interests. Their concerns seemed threatened in the post-1789 world when states, whatever their religious background, were less indulgent toward organized religion. Social and economic problems associated with the Industrial Revolution also demanded a reply if secularization was not to overtake the popular classes. These trends prompted Catholics, particularly members of the lower clergy and laity, to experiment with modern forms of popular representation, for instance political parties, trade unions, youth movements, study circles, journals, and newspapers. It also entailed Catholics embracing a multitude of issues, not just religious matters, that straddled the political divide.

THE POLITICIZATION OF CATHOLICISM: 1789–1815

Under the old regime, the church routinely involved itself in political matters but felt no necessity to organize itself in a political manner. The French church was alone in having a single representative body, the Assembly of the Clergy, and even that did not speak for Catholics in the peripheral provinces of the kingdom. This lack of organization was largely because, in Catholic Europe, church and state enjoyed a mutually supportive relationship. Admittedly this was under strain. Driven by Enlightenment principles and a need to raise revenue, even the most pious governments interfered more and more in the internal affairs of the church. For the moment, however, it was left to high-ranking ecclesiastics to parry these demands. Even Catholics laboring under Protestant rule, for instance the Catholic majority in Ireland, were slow to mobilize politically, partly because discrimination was unevenly enforced and partly because they feared placing themselves outside the body politic. It is frequently said that accommodation, not opposition, was their aim.

It was the French Revolution of 1789 that forced Catholics into the political domain. This tumultuous event articulated notions of social organization and citizenship that ended the privileged position that the church had hitherto enjoyed. The revolutionaries' initial design, embraced in the Civil Constitution of the Clergy (1790), was to turn the church into a department of state, concerned above all with the promotion of social good rather than with popular piety. The French clergy was not altogether hostile to this ideal but was alienated by two things: first, by the introduction of clerical election, which implied that a secular rather than a divine authority was the source of their power; and second, by the leftward drift of the Revolution. Under the Terror (1793–1794), the revolutionaries supplanted Catholicism with new cults of reason and the Supreme Being, accompanied by a violent dechristianizing campaign. Though dechristianization and the revolutionary cults were not enthusiastically exported abroad, French conquests in the 1790s meant that most Catholics in conquered lands lost any residual sympathy they might have had with the Revolution and came to see hereditary monarchy as the best guarantee of stability. This ensured that political Catholicism, at this stage, was associated with an early-nineteenth-century conservatism, expressed most eloquently by such writers as François René Chateaubriand, Louis de Bonald, and Joseph de Maistre. Together, they rejected the rationalism of the eighteenth century in favor of a romanticized, corporatist, and hierarchical world

that would restore the pre-1789 standing of the church.

THE MOBILIZATION OF THE LAITY: 1815–1870

That recovery, at least in France, was assisted by Napoleon (r. 1804–1814/15) who, in 1801, inaugurated a concordat regularizing church-state relations. Though the government firmly held the upper hand, in the Restoration period (1814–1830) the papacy saw concordats as the best means of protecting clerical interests. Not only did these arrangements facilitate secular support in the rebuilding of the faith, guaranteeing income, and ensuring clerical freedoms, they also acknowledged the supranational authority of the papacy, whose temporal power had nearly been extinguished by Napoleon. Concordats were also a valuable means of halting the growing independence of the laity. In the face of revolutionary persecution, many Catholics, especially women, had continued to practice their religion but often in secret and not always with a priest present.

A flurry of concordats were signed after 1815, but not all Catholics were pleased. A small group of intellectuals welcomed the ways in which the Revolution had both intentionally and unintentionally empowered the laity who, it was argued, had much to offer church and society. One such was the French priest Félicité de Lamennais. An early supporter of papal infallibility, he reconsidered his position after the 1830 revolutions in Belgium and Poland where Catholic majorities had been badly treated by non-Catholic rulers. Whether a state was Catholic, Protestant, or Orthodox, in his mind it was vital to separate throne and altar so as to allow Catholicism to breathe. "A free church in a free state" pronounced his newspaper, *L'Avenir*, founded in 1830. Similar views were expressed by Charles de Montalembert, a French nobleman, and Henri Lacordaire, a Dominican priest, who were insistent that the laity should be more active in the day-to-day activities of the church, championing Catholic freedoms through petitions, newspapers, and elections. Additionally, they espoused a social Catholicism, which echoed that being formulated by such paternalist thinkers as the Count de La Tour du Pin and Frédéric Le Play, who were alarmed at how industrialization was undermining religious observance among the working classes.

Thereafter, political Catholicism was frequently interlarded with social Catholicism, making it difficult to tell them apart.

It was too much for the French episcopacy, as well as for Gregory XVI, who, in the encyclicals *Mirari Vos* (1832) and *Singulari Nos* (1834), condemned Lamennais' position. This injunction could not halt growing lay participation in politics. In the early 1840s, Catholics organized fledgling political parties in Belgium, Holland, and Prussia, and drew sustenance from the Catholic Association of Daniel O'Connor that, a decade earlier, had mobilized Catholic interests in Ireland. Paradoxically, liberal Catholicism was also given hope by the election in 1846 of Pius IX, a theological conservative mistakenly labeled "the liberal pope" because of his open manner, willingness to entertain radical thinkers, and dislike of Austrian rule in Italy.

Just as the 1848 revolutions revealed the strengths and weaknesses of liberalism and nationalism, so too did the disturbances unveil the contradictions within political Catholicism. Much to the dismay of Italian nationalists, Pius IX proved himself an arch conservative. Within France, Catholics such as Antoine-Frédéric Ozanam, Henri Lacordaire, and Lamennais put themselves up for election, but were alienated by the violence and social egalitarianism that accompanied the Revolution. Most Catholics sided with the reactionary Louis Veuillot, who welcomed Louis-Napoleon Bonaparte as a bulwark against a socialist republic. It was in the German lands that political Catholics were most sympathetic to revolution, believing this might offer the chance to slough off both Habsburg and Hohenzollern interference, and open the way to a united *Reichskirche* (state church) such as had existed under the Holy Roman Empire. To promote these ends, many Catholic associations and newspapers were established, but they proved a transitory phenomenon, as the old order was restored and a new conservative climate overcame Europe.

Part of that climate was shaped by a growing ultramontanism that asserted the primacy of the pope in a wide range of matters, not just theology. This was underpinned by a series of papal pronouncements, notably the *Syllabus of Errors* of 1864 that denounced liberalism and "recent civilization," specifically a reference to the unification process in Italy, and the proclamation of papal infallibility that accompanied the First Vatican Council in 1870. Few of the subtleties of Rome's position were understood at the time, and it seemed that Pius IX had placed the church firmly in the camp of reaction, much to the dismay of liberal Catholics who had assembled for an international conference at Mechelen (Belgium) in 1863.

THE ANTICLERICAL CHALLENGE: 1870–1914

While ultramontanes seemed all powerful, in the final third of the nineteenth century it was clear that the church needed to engineer a more supple engagement with the secular world if it was to protect its interests. In the newly united states of Italy and Germany, in the newly created French Third Republic, in neighboring Belgium, and even momentarily in Spain and Portugal, Catholicism came under assault. In each of these states, middle-class liberals and radicals were generally in charge. Driven by positivist, materialist, and scientific ideals, these secular men were set on the promotion of nationhood, citizenship, and social harmony, ideals that would additionally fend off the challenge of socialism, something that also alarmed Catholics of all persuasions.

In the face of this hostility, Catholics fought in the political domain. This process was most marked in Bismarck's Germany, where the laity possessed a tradition of organization dating back to the *Katholikentage* (Catholic congresses) that had met since 1848. It was here, too, that state persecution, known as the *Kulturkampf* (culture struggle), was fiercest. Polish Catholics, whose loyalty was disputed, were openly persecuted and the place of religion within public life was steadily eroded. The Catholic response was spearheaded by a variety of agencies: the clergy who adopted a position of passive defiance; a large Catholic press represented by such titles as the *Kölnische Volkszeitung;* and the Zentrum (Center Party), created in 1870 by Ludwig Windthorst. The latter became a skillful player in the coalition politics of the Reichstag and won particular support among the industrial classes, though by 1914 the party had lost ground to the Socialists. By this time, the Zentrum had also become part of the establishment, keen to boast its patriotism and resist the "red menace."

Left-leaning Catholics found a more welcoming home in the trade union organization Christliche Gewerkvereine Deutschlands, founded in 1899, whose membership in 1910 approached two hundred thousand.

Within Belgium, too, a tradition of organization helped withstand the anticlerical assault of the 1870s. In the period from 1884 to 1914, the Catholic Party, founded in the 1840s, secured a preponderance of seats, thanks to its ability to harness both middle and working-class support. In France, despite the heritage of Lamennais and the intensity of the anticlerical struggle of the 1880s, Catholics were slower to react. Only a minority, significantly the exmonarchists Albert de Mun and Jacques Piou, understood that the Third Republic had to be accommodated. This, too, was the position of Leo XIII, author of *Rerum Novarum* (1891), the encyclical defining social Catholicism. In the 1890s he urged a *ralliement* (reconciliation) between church and state. Emboldened by this support, in 1901 Piou established the Action Libérale Populaire, an embryonic Catholic party, but one that never broke out of the Catholic heartlands, despite a fresh round of anticlerical legislation resulting in the separation of church and state in 1905. Still, France could boast several popular movements addressing the "social question," most famously the Semaines Sociales and the Union Fraternelle du Commerce et de l'Industrie. While popular among workers, these movements were divided internally as to whether they should adopt a paternalistic approach to the social question or whether they should allow genuine worker participation. Favoring the latter course was Marc Sangnier's Sillon, which was banned by the papacy in 1910 as it came close to wholeheartedly embracing liberal values, a step too far for many Catholics in France and elsewhere. Two years later, Sangnier created a political party, Jeune République, though historians suggest it was perhaps the Rennes daily paper *Ouest-Eclair*, founded in 1899, that did most to promote Christian democracy.

Elsewhere, political Catholicism made less headway either because clerical interests were best represented by existing, nonconfessional parties (Austria), or because state hostility was short-lived (Spain and Portugal). Everywhere, initiatives depended on the support of local hierarchies.

When that was not forthcoming, as in the Netherlands, political Catholicism was constrained. In Italy, especially, the pope forbade Catholics from partaking in the liberal state and, in 1904, disbanded the Opera dei Congressi (Catholic lay social and charitable organizations) influenced by *Rerum Novarum*, reconstituting them into the broader Catholic Action movement. Only with the electoral growth of the Socialists did the papacy lift restrictions on political engagement, although a Catholic party, the Partito Populare Italiano, was not founded until 1919. Tellingly, Rome did not discourage members of the faithful from involving themselves in those far right political organizations springing up at the turn of the century, such as the Italian Nationalist Association and the Action Française of Charles Maurras. Intensely nationalistic and openly racist, these bodies valued religion primarily as a social cement and had particular allure for Catholics struggling to come to terms with a modern world. It is no wonder that such Catholics would later rally to authoritarian and fascist regimes. Only after 1945 did Christian democracy become the dominant force within political Catholicism.

During the nineteenth century, political Catholicism had been shaped primarily by the challenges confronting the church: the French Revolution; social and economic change; and growing state indifference and hostility toward organized religion. The answers to these challenges were inevitably diverse: the conservatism of de Maistre, the social paternalism of La Tour du Pin, the embryonic Christian democracy of Lamennais and Lacordaire, and the integralism of Charles Maurras. What politically active Catholics, both lay and clerical, had in common was a willingness to mobilize, albeit through many agencies. This troubled the papacy, which was eager to maintain clerical discipline. Before 1914, with the assistance of national episcopacies, that discipline was mostly upheld; in the twentieth century it proved difficult to preserve, creating tensions between Rome and the remainder of the church, not just in Europe, but in North America and the developing world.

See also **Catholicism; Center Party; French Revolution; Kulturkampf; Lueger, Karl; Secularization; Socialism, Christian; Windthorst, Ludwig.**

BIBLIOGRAPHY

Atkin, Nicholas, and Frank Tallett. *Priests, Prelates, and People: A History of European Catholicism since 1750.* New York, 2003.

Buchanan, Tom, and Martin Conway, eds. *Political Catholicism in Europe, 1918–1945.* Oxford, U.k., 1996.

Chadwick, Owen. *A History of the Popes, 1830–1914.* Oxford, U.K., 1998.

Fogarty, Michael. *Christian Democracy in Western Europe, 1820–1953.* London, 1957.

Irving, Ronald E. M. *The Christian Democratic Parties of Western Europe.* London, 1979.

Misner, Paul. *Social Catholicism: From the Onset of Industrialization to the First World War.* New York, 1991.

Rémond, René. *Religion and Society in Modern Europe.* Translated by Antonia Nevill. Malden, Mass., 1999.

NICHOLAS ATKIN

CAVOUR, COUNT (CAMILLO BENSO)

(1810–1861), first prime minister of Italy.

The future first prime minister of Italy and chief architect of its unification was born in Turin on 10 August 1810 to a family of the Piedmontese aristocracy. The second son of the marquis Michele Benso of Cavour and the Swiss Protestant Adèle de Sellon, he was always close to his maternal relatives, and Protestant influences are thought to have influenced his character development. Piedmont, the central region of the Kingdom of Sardinia, was a department of the Napoleonic Empire at the time of Camillo's birth. While the legitimate ruling House of Savoy was holding out against Napoleon on the island of Sardinia protected by the British navy, the Cavour family supported Napoleonic rule on the mainland. The young Cavour was held at baptism by Napoleon's sister, Pauline Bonaparte, and her husband, Prince Camillo Borghese, after whom the child was named. The family regained royal favor and was reinstated at the Savoyard court after the defeat of Napoleon. Rebellious, headstrong, and impulsive, the young Cavour manifested liberal tendencies that did not sit well with his conservative father and older brother Gustavo. With Gustavo first in line to inherit the family fortune and title, the family followed the custom of the Piedmontese nobility of destining the second-

born male for a career in the army. In military academy, which Camillo attended from age nine to sixteen, he showed his temperamental dislike for military discipline and was considered politically suspect because of his liberal views. Army routine bored him. A stint as court page to Carlo Alberto soured him permanently on the future king and on court life in general.

Cavour left the army in 1831 and for the next four years traveled extensively in England, France, and Switzerland; observed and developed an admiration for British liberal government; indulged his passion for gambling; played on the stock exchange; and was rescued from the verge of bankruptcy by his father after some unfortunate ventures in stocks. Cavour carried on several affairs and never married, but he did settle down to manage the family estates. In that role he found success and achieved financial independence. He was an attentive manager, put in long hours, demanded much of his workers, introduced new crops, and experimented successfully with the latest farming methods. Although partial to agriculture, Cavour also took an interest in industrial manufacturing and railroad construction. In an article published in 1846 in the French *Revue Nouvelle* he argued that railroad construction would create a single market in the Italian peninsula, link it to the rest of Europe, and revive the Italian economy. A national system of railroads would enable Italians to take advantage of opportunities offered by the building of the Suez Canal and restore Italy to its historical role as the commercial middleman of Europe. Cavour thus approached the question of Italian unification as an economist and businessman. At heart a laissez-faire liberal, he favored private initiative and free trade, but made exceptions for government protection and encouragement of developing industries.

POLITICS AND PUBLIC AFFAIRS

Politics and public affairs began to absorb Cavour's attention in the late 1840s, when he had attained financial independence. In 1847 in partnership with Count Cesare Balbo (1789–1853) and other Piedmontese aristocrats, he founded the journal *Il Risorgimento.* The journal gave Cavour an entry into politics and a name to the movement for Italian independence and unity. Cavour's views were those of a moderate liberal of his time: he was opposed to absolute monarchy and republicanism; was an admirer of the *juste milieu* (the middle course), constitutional monarchy, and British parliamentary government; and was a believer in voting rights limited to property owners and the educated. The constitution that Carlo Alberto granted in 1848 met with his approval, as did Piedmont's declaration of war against Austria in March of that same year, but Austria's decisive military victory a year later convinced him that Italians could not win their independence without outside help. Such help was to be obtained by diplomacy, by the traditional strategy of balancing Austrian and French ambitions in Italy to Piedmont's advantage. Italian independence under Piedmontese leadership would come with the defeat of Austria. The more difficult goal of Italian unity would be achieved later.

In 1849 Cavour entered parliament as a supporter of the moderate liberal government headed by Massimo d'Azeglio (1798–1866). He served d'Azeglio as minister of agriculture and commerce and minister of finance, and made his mark in parliament speaking in support of bills to curb clerical influence. His often caustic speeches made him enemies and earned him a reputation as a formidable and dangerous debater of high ambition destined to replace the more moderate and gentlemanly d'Azeglio, whom he did replace in November 1852. The infighting preceding his appointment showed Cavour at his best and worst. Faced by the prospect that conservatives inimical to constitutional government might gain power and clamp down on freedom of the press, Cavour reached out to democratic legislators. Critics denounced this turnaround as unprincipled political opportunism and an illegitimate union (*connubio*). Some historians see it as a precedent for political *trasformismo,* the practice whereby sordid party politics supposedly triumph over principles and drain moral content out of public life. For Cavour and his defenders the *connubio* was an act of statesmanship that brought together moderate democrats and moderate conservatives, formed a viable political center, preserved civil rights and parliamentary government, and reflected Cavour's uncanny talent for political improvisation.

Cavour held the post of prime minister from November 1852 until his death, with only one brief interruption. He worked with King Victor Emmanuel II (r. 1849–1861), who succeeded Carlo Alberto to the throne in 1849, with some friction and mutual dislike, in defense of constitutional government and parliamentary prerogatives, which the king was not always willing to respect. Cavour's energetic leadership transformed the Kingdom of Sardinia into the most economically and politically progressive Italian state, marginalized conservatives and radicals, made him the arbiter of Italian politics, and gave him international stature. Patriots and exiles from other Italian states were attracted to Piedmont by government subsidies and opportunities for employment in government and education. Cavour excelled at building bridges toward potential collaborators, ostracizing only the diehard republican followers of Giuseppe Mazzini, while winning over more moderate republicans like the respected Daniele Manin and the charismatic Giuseppe Garibaldi. Building bridges between monarchists and republicans, liberals and democrats, was the task of the Italian National Society founded in 1857 with Cavour's tacit support. Its slogan was "Italy and Victor Emmanuel" and its program was to fight for Italian independence and unity under Piedmontese leadership.

Republicans were probably right in charging that Cavour had no commitment to Italian unity. Italian identity was for him a cultural construct that he shared with many other educated Italians, but it was not in his character to use politics in pursuit of cultural ideals. He regarded politics as the art of the possible and believed in taking advantage of opportunities as they presented themselves one at a time. He followed Piedmont's traditional policy of using the ambitions of greater powers to state advantage. The Crimean War (1853–1856) gave him an opportunity to do so when Austria hesitated to join the anti-Russian coalition led by England and France. Cavour yielded to English and French pressures and sent a Piedmontese contingent of fifteen thousand troops to fight in the Crimean peninsula. The move isolated Austria, burnished Piedmont's image as a liberal state, and improved its relations with England and France. It was Cavour's ability to improvise that made the difference, for he decided to intervene when pressured to do so by the two powers whose support he knew he needed to challenge Austria.

France offered the most promising prospects because Napoleon III (r. 1852–1871) had a long-standing personal interest in Italian affairs, wanted France to replace Austria as the dominant Continental power, needed success abroad to live up to the Napoleonic image at home, and practiced personal diplomacy. Their interests and ambitions converged in the secret agreement of Plombières of July 1858: France was to provide two hundred thousand troops and Piedmont one hundred thousand for a war against Austria in northern Italy. Piedmont would gain the Austrian regions of Lombardy and Venetia, and the Po Valley provinces of the Papal States. Central Italy would become an autonomous kingdom ruled by a relative of the French emperor, the Kingdom of the Two Sicilies would remain unchanged territorially, but the governing Bourbons might be replaced by pro-French royalty. The pope would retain Rome and receive the honorary title of president of a symbolic Italian confederation, as a gesture of respect for his authority and a sop to the sentiment for national unity. In return, Piedmont would pay for the war and turn over to France the territories of Nice and Savoy.

The War of 1859 (Second War of National Independence) did not go as planned, for the French decided to pull out after fighting the two bloody battles of Magenta and Solferino. Their decision to seek an early armistice may have been motivated by fear of a Prussian attack from the Rhineland and by the knowledge that Cavour was plotting to annex Tuscany against the understanding of Plombières. The French and Austrians signed the armistice of Villafranca behind Cavour's back on 11 July 1859. Piedmont received Lombardy but not Venetia or the papal provinces. Chagrined beyond measure, Cavour insulted the king who was sensible enough to accept the armistice, resigned as prime minister, and threatened to go to America and expose everyone else's duplicity.

TOWARD UNIFICATION

None of what happened in the six months that Cavour was out of office was scripted in advance. Patriots in the central duchies of Tuscany, Modena, Parma, and the papal provinces staged uprisings, set up provisional governments, and demanded union with Piedmont. Cavour was called back into office in January 1860 to deal with these developments, gain international approval for these annexations, and organize the fusion of old and new territories. He won French approval for this territorial bonanza by agreeing to cede Nice and Savoy and assuring the other powers that Piedmont must step in to keep dangerous radicals out of power. But the dangerous radicals were not so easily foiled, for no sooner was the question of central Italy settled than emissaries of Giuseppe Mazzini stirred up an insurrection in Sicily and trouble began to brew in the entire South.

Garibaldi's legendary Expedition of the Thousand that sailed from Piedmontese territory in May 1860 in support of the Sicilian insurgents presented Cavour with the most serious challenge of his political career. He opposed the expedition, but did not dare prevent it for fear of offending patriotic sentiment, losing control of parliament, antagonizing the popular Garibaldi, and crossing Victor Emmanuel, whom Cavour suspected of secretly backing Garibaldi. The government therefore adopted an ambiguous policy that allowed volunteers to sail for Sicily and avoid interception at sea. Garibaldi's unexpected battlefield victories changed Cavour's mind: he allowed reinforcements to go to Sicily, but also tried, unsuccessfully, to wrest control of the island from Garibaldi to prevent him from invading the mainland. When his attempt failed and Garibaldi marched triumphantly into Naples, Cavour sent the Piedmontese army to finish the fight against the Neapolitans, and to disarm and disband Garibaldi's. The papal territory that the Piedmontese army occupied on its way to Naples was added to the rest of the booty and became part of the Kingdom of Italy that was formally proclaimed on 17 March 1861.

Cavour had a few months left to live in which to organize the affairs of the Kingdom of Italy, which did not yet include Rome and Venetia. Putting the state on a sound financial footing, regulating relations between church and state, and forming a unified whole out of disparate regions were pressing issues. The southern regions were of particular concern, for their customs, laws, and economy struck most northerners as antiquated and out of step with the rest of the country, and Cavour had not contemplated their quick acquisition. Fear that the fledgling Italian state might succumb to its enemies at home and abroad may have predisposed him to rush matters, adopt a centralized form of government, deny republican calls for a national assembly that would deliberate the terms of union, and extend the laws of Piedmont to the rest of the country. Relations of church and state were another troublesome issue, for the pope regarded unification as an act of robbery, urged Catholics to boycott the government, and excommunicated the leaders of the national movement, including Cavour. Cavour proposed financial compensation for the church and regular relations on the basis of "A Free Church in a Free State," but the Vatican rejected the formula as a secular aberration. Little time was left for Cavour to agonize over the future of Italy. In poor health since at least the fall of 1860, his condition worsened rapidly in spring 1861. He died of natural causes on 6 June 1861, after receiving the last sacraments of the Catholic Church administered by a clergyman in disregard of Cavour's excommunication, wanting it known that he died a good Catholic.

See also **Garibaldi, Giuseppe; Italy; Kingdom of the Two Sicilies; Mazzini, Giuseppe; Piedmont-Savoy; Revolutions of 1848.**

BIBLIOGRAPHY

Coppa, Frank J. *Camillo di Cavour.* New York, 1973.

Mack Smith, Denis. *Cavour.* New York, 1985.

Whyte, Arthur J. B. *The Early Life and Letters of Cavour, 1810–1848.* London, 1925.

———. *The Political Life and Letters of Cavour, 1848–1861.* London, 1930.

ROLAND SARTI

CENTER PARTY.

The Center Party, or Deutsche Zentrumspartei, in imperial Germany was the vehicle for political Catholicism in both the national Reichstag and in several state parliaments. Although the party traced its origins back to the short-lived Catholic caucuses in the Frankfurt National Assembly during the revolutions of 1848–1849 on the one hand and the Prussian parliaments of the 1850s on the other, it was only when Prussia defeated Austria in 1866 and established the German Empire in 1871 that the Center Party emerged as a coherent and long-term feature of Germany's political landscape. To safeguard their interests in this new Germany, where they formed a mistrusted minority, anxious Roman Catholics reorganized the Center Party as a broad-based movement cutting across class lines. Despite Catholic denials that the Center was a sectarian organization, the party's electoral base—in predominantly Catholic regions like the Rhineland, Westphalia, and Silesia in Prussia, or Bavaria and southwest Germany—together with its preoccupation with religious issues and Catholic civil rights, antagonized Germany's Protestant majority. This situation soon led to the Kulturkampf, a conflict between the state and the Roman Catholic Church that convulsed the country between 1871 and 1887.

Although traditional assumptions locate the renewal of Catholic political allegiance in this dispute, some scholars place the reemergence of political Catholicism in the period between 1866 and 1871 and explain that reappearance in terms of a remarkable religious revival within the Roman Church during the two decades or so after 1850. It was the mobilization of mass religious sentiment that reinforced Catholic political loyalties and led to important political victories in 1870 and again in 1871.

What the Kulturkampf did do, however, was to solidify or energize the electoral base, forging the Center into a formidable obstructionist bloc implacably opposed to Chancellor Otto von Bismarck's (1815–1898) ecclesiastical program. No politician better personified that resistance than Ludwig Windthorst (1812–1891). From the moment he emerged as the Center's undisputed leader in the early 1870s until his death in 1891, his followers idolized him for his consistent, effective, and single-minded dedication to their cause.

POLITICAL ORIENTATION

The end of the Kulturkampf in 1887 and Bismarck's dismissal from office three years later, gave the Center Party an opportunity to escape its isolation and to wield considerable influence in both domestic and foreign policy. With its 91 to 106 seats in the Reichstag, the Center Party occupied a key position among the empire's political forces that permitted unusual political flexibility and afforded it the opportunity to form coalitions with either Left or Right to pass or block legislation. Following Windthorst's death, and except for the brief interlude of the Bülow bloc (1907–1909, named for Bernhard Bülow), the party adopted a more nationalistic and pro-governmental stance. It not only provided key support for a new, national civil code in 1896 and the naval bills of 1898 and 1900, but also lent valuable assistance to the Conservative Party in the Prussian parliament over the issues of confessional schools and army expansion.

Center PartyThe Center's shift to the right during most of the Wilhelmine era, according to some historians, owed much to the backward economic conditions so characteristic of Catholic districts. Economic retardation meant that the peasantry and a *Mittelstand*, or middle class, composed chiefly of artisans and shopkeepers, were overrepresented among the party's rank and file. Pressured from below by this constituency, the Center's leadership espoused protectionist and other policies that divided the Center from parties to the left, impeding coherent, systematic reform.

Apart from the socioeconomic character of Germany's Catholic areas, historians also stress the inability of the Center's leadership in the era before 1914 to reconcile antagonistic interests within the party. The diversity of groupings and plurality of interests within its ranks meant that the Center found itself unable to agree for long about priorities and programs. Even when the party endorsed reforms or fought for the preservation of private and public freedom against exceptional legislation, its enemies, not without reason, called attention to the Center's political opportunism and its willingness to sacrifice principle for the satisfaction of its special interests.

REFORM POSSIBILITIES AND INTERNAL DISCORD

What is clear is that the harmonization of these contradictory interests and the mobilization of the party faithful required the party leadership to resort to what has been described as a demagogic political style. While this approach contributed to a superficial unity, it also led the Center to adopt slogans indistinguishable from those of the imperial government and the Conservative Party, forge closer ties with the Right, discredit Centrists among the political Left, and complicate the task of political reform in imperial Germany.

This demagogic style, moreover, rarely provided the extraordinary political cohesion enjoyed by the Center during the Kulturkampf because the end of that church-state dispute meant that political, social, and economic issues took precedence over confessional concerns. Whereas eighty-five percent of Catholic voters cast their ballots for the Center at the height of the Kulturkampf, that number fell to fifty-five percent by 1912. This loss was especially noticeable among the Catholic working classes who resented the predominant influence of agrarian interests and propertied groups within the party who espoused conservative tax and tariff policies.

Attempts to retain working-class loyalty and to break free from the constraints and limitations of minority-group politics through interconfessional trade unions and an appeal to non-Catholics, however, made little progress during the imperial era, generating instead long-running disputes, like the so-called *Zentrumsstreit* and *Gewerkschaftsstreit*, that divided the party between 1906 and the outbreak of war in 1914. The failure of these reforming efforts left intact Germany's traditional barriers of religion and class, confined Germany's Catholics to a subcultural isolation, and reinforced those narrow ideological constituencies that so handicapped cooperation among imperial Germany's political parties.

See also **Catholicism; Catholicism, Political; Germany; Kulturkampf; Leo XIII; Pius IX; Windthorst, Ludwig.**

BIBLIOGRAPHY

Anderson, Margaret Lavinia. *Windthorst: A Political Biography.* Oxford, U.K., 1981.

Bachem, Karl. *Vorgeschichte, Geschichte und Politik der Deutschen Zentrumspartei.* 9 vols. Cologne, 1927–1932.

Blackbourn, David. *Class, Religion and Local Politics in Wilhelmine Germany: The Centre Party in Württemberg before 1914.* New Haven, Conn., 1980.

Evans, Ellen L. *The German Center Party, 1870–1933: A Study in Political Catholicism.* Carbondale, Ill., 1981.

Loth, Wilfried. *Katholiken im Kaiserreich: Der politische Katholizismus in der Krise des wilhelminischen Deutschlands.* Düsseldorf, 1984.

Ross, Ronald J. *Beleaguered Tower: The Dilemma of Political Catholicism in Wilhelmine Germany.* Notre Dame, Ind., 1976.

Sperber, Jonathan. *Popular Catholicism in Nineteenth-Century Germany.* Princeton, N.J., 1984.

Zeender, John K. *The German Center Party, 1890–1906.* Philadelphia, 1976.

RONALD J. ROSS

CENTRAL ASIA. Long before geographers named the region "Central Asia," it had become known by the name of "Turkestan" (land of the Turks) among peoples in the surrounding region. Bordered on the north and east by the plains of southern Siberia and the deserts of western China, and on the west and south by the Caspian Sea and the Pamir mountain chain, this area had gradually become the domain largely of Turkic-speaking peoples. Their principalities (khanates) had thrived economically as long as the Silk Road commerce had carried precious goods through their region from China to the Middle East and Europe. Their Muslim religious schools had for a time in the Middle Ages been centers of learning as well as piety. But by the nineteenth century, little remained of those good times. Trade had dwindled, leaving only the farming in the oasis areas (mainly by Uzbeks) and livestock raising by pastoral nomads (principally Kazakh and Kirgiz) to sustain economic well-being. The small Turkic states fought sporadic wars among themselves, using the meager resources of their peoples to maintain their poorly equipped armies and to pay for the backing of allied nomadic tribes. Until the mid-nineteenth century, no Western empire threatened their independence.

THE RUSSIAN CONQUEST

That threat became a reality with the expansion of the Russian Empire. For centuries the empire had moved toward the east and south onto the European and Asian steppes (plains) in territories previously controlled by nomadic tribes. Its primary goal, similar to that of the United States in the nineteenth century on its western Great Plains, was to subjugate the unruly nomads beyond its control and to exploit the resources of the steppe.

Troops came first, and then came settlers to cultivate the fertile land. This process of Russian conquest encountered little effective opposition. By the 1860s, the border between the empire and Turkic peoples had reached the northern region of Central Asia. In the following decade, military leaders attacked the forces of the Turkic principalities. This move, which was initially the decision of frontier commanders, received the backing of the government when victory appeared certain. By 1875, Russian troops had defeated all the opposing armies. The largest area became the Russian governor-generalship of Turkestan, with its capital in the city of Tashkent. Two principalities (Bukhara and Khiva) became protectorates of the Russian Empire. Their rulers remained in power, but were under the control of Russian advisers.

Russian conquest of Central Asia provoked the opposition of the British Empire. Its diplomatic sphere extended beyond its Indian colony into Afghanistan and Persia, just south of Turkestan. Russian and British agents competed for influence among the tribes in these lands in secret operations baptized by observers as the "Great Game." This struggle for empire was finally settled in the early years of the twentieth century. The 1907 diplomatic agreement between the two empires delimited their spheres of influence, and confirmed the formal borders separating Turkestan from Persia and Afghanistan (now the southern borders of Turkmenistan, Uzbekistan, and Tajikistan).

Turkestan resembled in many ways an overseas colony of other Western empires. Until railroads reached its territory late in the nineteenth century, the deserts that separated it from European Russia made transportation and communication as difficult as though an ocean lay between these lands. The Russian army officers who became the first colonial officials there had as little knowledge of their subject peoples as European officials in newly conquered Asian and African colonies. They assumed the Muslim population to be deeply hostile toward the presence of "infidels," and believed as well that the way of life of the various peoples, settled as well as nomadic, was backward, even "barbaric," as measured by the standards of Western civilization.

In the opinion of some officials, colonial rule required stern policies of military occupation and close surveillance to prevent Muslim rebellion.

The Surprise Attack. Painting by Vasili Vereschagin, 1871. Russian Cossacks in Turkestan are beseiged by Kyrgyz nomads.
TRETYAKOV GALLERY, MOSCOW, RUSSIA/BRIDGEMAN ART LIBRARY

Others argued that the empire's primary obligation was to encourage these subject peoples to acquire the economic skills useful to a market (capitalist) economy and to accept their responsibilities and rights as citizens in a multiethnic, centralized empire. This divergence of views remained unresolved as long as the empire endured; the problems that it created contributed to the outbreak of the major uprising that occurred in Turkestan in 1916.

RUSSIAN COLONIAL REFORMS

Even the most ardent supporters of the progressive integration of Turkestan into the empire recognized that its peoples would remain ethnically and religiously unique. The Central Asian colony was inhabited by a population speaking Turkic dialects and deeply committed to the Muslim faith. The empire's laws made religious toleration a fundamental right of its peoples. Local Islamic authorities were stripped of the power to punish violators of religious laws, but the empire's laws required protection of every Muslim's right to worship. Pilgrimage to holy sites, including Mecca, was permissible; Muslim religious schools continued to flourish. Some of Russia's empire-builders there believed that Islam was no obstacle to peaceful rule.

In the long run, these reformers expected the benefits of their colonial rule to win the backing of the population. Their domination put an end to the local wars among the khanates, and stopped the periodic raids by nomads on the settled population. Agricultural production expanded rapidly. The most important crop became a new variety of cotton, imported by Russian agronomists from the southeastern United States and rapidly adopted by the local farmers. They sold their crop to the cotton mills of Russia, readily accessible after the turn of the twentieth century when rail lines finally crossed the desert to Turkestan. Turkestan's economy became heavily dependent on the sale of this commodity, and Russian authorities were convinced that the colony was finally becoming a profitable undertaking. One senior government official (borrowing from a British prime minister's description of India) called Turkestan the "jewel in the crown" of the Russian Empire. By then, education officials, in the hopes of encouraging the population to adapt to Russian culture, had established a small number of state-run bilingual schools offering elementary education in Russian and Uzbek (or Kazakh) languages.

Turkestan farming prospered, but so too did Muslim practices. The railroad took cotton north to Russia, but also opened the way for many thousands of pilgrims to travel rapidly and safely each year to the Arabian holy places. A few subjects collaborated with the Russian rulers and adopted a Western style of life. Most families kept the old traditions. In the late imperial period, the seclusion of Muslim women became even more pervasive and strict than in the past with the gradual spread, among townspeople and even villagers, of public use of the total body veil (the *paranji*).

THE REVOLT OF 1916

Russian military officers remained in charge of the region. They claimed that their presence was indispensable to the security of Russian rule, pointing to occasional unrest among their subjects as evidence that the Muslim population continued to be opposed to the empire. They called for mass colonization by Russian farmers of fertile areas, in the belief that only when a large number of Russian settlers had made Turkestan their home would real integration of Turkestan within the empire be possible. Some officials warned that the seizure of land by a massive influx of pioneers would provoke a major rebellion, especially among the nomadic tribes, but their advice was ignored. In 1900 Tsar Nicholas II himself authorized Russian colonization in Turkestan. By 1914, European-style farm villages had appeared wherever pioneers had moved in, taking legally or by force pastureland of the nomads.

In the summer of 1916, the Russian government called up the male population of Turkestan for labor service in the war against the German and Austrian empires. Its reckless action triggered protest demonstrations, attacks on Russian settlers, and finally a major uprising among the nomadic tribes. Before Russian troops and militia could repress the rebellion, thousands of Russians lost their lives. The authorities' brutal repression caused many more deaths among the Turkestan nomadic tribes. Ethnic hostility, already stirred up by the colonization campaign, became the cause for recurrent attacks by Russians on nomads, and by natives against Russians. Even before the 1917 Revolution brought down the Russian Empire, the consequences of Russia's failed colonial mission there had, in the words of one Russian official, "destroyed this jewel of the Russian state."

See also **Colonies; Imperialism; Russia.**

BIBLIOGRAPHY

Bacon, Elizabeth E. *Central Asia under Russian Rule: A Study in Cultural Change.* Ithaca, N.Y., 1966. An inquiry into the impact of Russian rule on the way of life of Turkestan peoples

Brower, Daniel. *Turkestan and the Fate of the Russian Empire.* London, 2003. Study of Russian colonial ideology and policies in Turkestan.

Khalid, Adeeb. *The Politics of Muslim Cultural Reform: Jadidism in Central Asia.* Berkeley and Los Angeles, 1998. A thoughtful inquiry into Muslim efforts to reform Turkestan's society.

Meyer, Karl E., and Shareen Blair Brysac. *Tournament of Shadows: The Great Game and the Race for Empire in Central Asia.* Washington, D.C., 1999. Dramatic story of Russian-British contest in Central Asia.

Pierce, Richard A. *Russian Central Asia, 1867–1917: A Study in Colonial Rule.* Berkeley and Los Angeles, 1960. A survey of imperial rule in Turkestan.

DANIEL R. BROWER

CÉZANNE, PAUL (1839–1906), French artist and forerunner of twentieth-century avant-garde artistic movements.

Paul Cézanne was born on 19 January 1839 at Aix-en-Provence, in the south of France. His father was a wealthy banker. From 1856 to 1858, Cézanne studied academic drawing in Aix. In 1859, despite his father's disapproval, he decided to dedicate himself to painting as a career.

At the urging of his childhood friend, Émile Zola (1840–1902), in 1861 Cézanne settled in Paris where he painted freely at the Académie Suisse and studied the old masters at the Louvre. But, having failed the entrance exams to the École des beaux-arts, he returned to Aix feeling that he had no artistic future. While working full time in his father's lucrative banking business, Cézanne still took art lessons. In late 1862, he returned to Paris but failed again to gain entrance to the École des beaux-arts. Back in the obscurity of Aix, Cézanne painted regularly but the Salons refused his works. This early Romantic period, which consisted of figure compositions and landscapes, is marked by vigorous light-dark contrasts (*The Abduction*, 1867). Angered at being denied entry to the École des beaux-arts for a third time, in 1866 Cézanne sent a letter of protest against the jury system to the director of the school, an act that inspired Zola to pen his novel *Mon Salon* in defense of modern painting.

From 1866 to 1869, Cézanne alternated his stays between Aix and Paris, where he socialized with those modern young painters who would come to be known as the impressionists. In 1869, he started a love affair with model Marie-Hortense Fiquet, who would bear him a son in 1872, and began living with her at L'Estaque on the Mediterranean coast. Over the years, Cézanne would paint thirty-three portraits of her, all entitled *Madame Cézanne.*

CÉZANNE'S MATURE STYLES

After 1870, like the impressionists, Cézanne began working outdoors and building form with color rather than with strong tonal contrasts. During this impressionist period that stretched from 1871 to 1877, he painted his first important landscapes, including *The House of the Hanged Man at Auvers* (1873) and *Landscape near Auvers* (1874). In 1874 and 1877, he participated in the first and third impressionist exhibitions. But Cézanne's association with the impressionist circle came to a gradual end as he attempted to develop his own independent style. He returned to Aix and for the next ten years, highly irritable and suffering from diabetes, he worked in almost complete isolation.

From 1878 to 1887, Cézanne created the paintings of his constructivist period as, looking for an ever-greater formal organization of the natural world, he strove to capture the exact relation between structure, organization, and color. Between 1883 and 1887, he painted some of his most celebrated landscapes, including many views of Mont Sainte-Victoire (*Mont Sainte-Victoire Seen from Gardanne,* 1885–1886), of L'Estaque (*Houses at L'Estaque,* 1883–1885; *Rock at L'Estaque,* 1882), and of the Bay of Marseille (*Bay of Marseille Seen from L'Estaque,* 1883–1885), as well as some noteworthy still lifes and figure compositions.

In 1886, he married Fiquet, and his father died, leaving him a small fortune. He broke with Zola after the publication of the latter's *L'oeuvre,* which features an unflattering character modeled on Cézanne's cantankerous personality.

From 1888 to 1898, he created the paintings of his synthetic period, in which he achieved a new geometric and expressive order. Anticipating cubist explorations of space, Cézanne translated houses,

Portrait of Louis-Auguste Cézanne, the Artist's Father. Painting by Paul Cézanne, 1866–1867. Cézanne the elder is reading *L'Evénement,* a newspaper that had recently published an article by Emile Zolá defending the impressionists. ©Archivo Iconografico, S.A./Corbis

landscapes, and other subjects into cones, cylinders, and spheres, as he sought to synthesize multiple planes of color and abstracted images. He painted masterpieces like *The Kitchen Table* (1888–1890), *The Card Players* (1890–1892), and *The Bathers* (1890–1891). His fame growing, in 1895 Cézanne had his first one-man show in Paris.

THE LATE CÉZANNE

In 1899, Cézanne left his wife and son and was distraught over the break-up for the rest of his life. The French avant-garde became aware of his importance. Post-impressionist painters traveled to Provence to seek his counsel. Annoyed at first, he finally seemed to welcome the attention.

From 1900 to 1906, Cézanne created the paintings and watercolors of his late period, his art becoming more and more abstract and geometric as forms were created from interlocking color surfaces and the disappearance of the background (*The Park of Château-Noir*, 1900; *Nudes in Landscape*, 1900–1905; *Large Bathers*, 1899–1906), and he began writing down his views about painting. These developments set the ground rules for the debates about painting in the early twentieth century. In 1902 the death of Zola affected him deeply. Two years later Cézanne was given a whole exhibition room at the Salon d'Automne, which established his European reputation. In 1906, caught in a storm while painting outdoors, he collapsed and died in Aix, on 22 October, of pneumonia.

See also **Avant-Garde; France; Impressionism; Zola, Émile.**

BIBLIOGRAPHY

Primary Sources

Bernard, Émile. *Souvenirs sur Paul Cézanne.* Paris, 1911. Letters focus on Cézanne's artistic theories and upon general aesthetic questions.

Doran, Michael, ed. *Conversations with Cézanne.* Translated by Julie Lawrence Cochran. Berkeley, Calif., 2001. Biographical and stylistic documents on Cézanne's last ten years, including interviews with the painter and correspondence with Émile Bernard.

Kendall, Richard, ed. *Cézanne by Himself.* London, 1988. Previously unpublished documents by Cézanne on his late paintings and works on paper.

Rewald, John, ed. *Paul Cézanne: Letters.* Translated by Marguerite Kay. Oxford, U.K., 1941. Reprint, New York, 1995. Cézanne's ideas on art are to be found in these numerous letters to friends, critics, and fellow painters, assembled and presented by the renowned British art historian John Rewald.

Secondary Sources

Athanassoglou-Kallmyer, Nina Maria. *Cézanne and Provence: The Painter in His Culture.* Chicago, 2003. Documents Cézanne's regional alliance, which deeply affected his stylistic innovations.

Baumann, Felix A., Walter Feilchenfeldt, and Hubertus Gassner, eds. *Cézanne and the Dawn of Modern Art.* Essen, Germany, and New York, 2005.

Becks-Malorny, Ulrike. *Cézanne.* London, 2001. Provides an excellent introduction to the artist's life, work, and stylistic periods.

Cachin, Isabelle, and Françoise Cachin, eds. *Cézanne.* Paris, 1996. Exemplary exhibition catalog published in conjunction with the major international retrospective organized on the centenary of Cézanne's first solo exhibition mounted in Paris.

Dorival, Bernard. *Cézanne.* Translated by H. H. A. Thackthwaite. New York, 1948. Most important introductory text to the life and art of Cézanne published before 1950.

Faure, Élie. *Paul Cézanne.* Translated by Walter Pacht. New York, 1913. Classic study of the poetic significance of Cézanne's subject matters by one of the best-known French art historians of the first half of the twentieth century.

Fry, Roger. *Cézanne: A Study of His Development.* London, 1927. First serious study of his artistic evolution.

Mack, Gerstle. *Paul Cézanne.* New York, 1935. First pre-World War II English-language biography that chronicled Cézanne's life and artistic evolution.

Rewald, John. *Paul Cézanne, A Biography.* New York, 1937. Reprint, New York, 1968. Still one of the best biographies of Cézanne by one of the world's leading authority on French impressionism.

———. *The Paintings of Paul Cézanne: A Catalogue Raisonné.* 2 vols. New York, 1996, Definitive research tool.

Rubin, William, ed. *Cézanne: The Late Work.* New York, 1977. Published on the occasion of the landmark 1977 retrospective exhibition held at the MOMA.

Schapiro, Meyer. *Paul Cézanne.* New York, 1952. Thorough introduction to the stylistic evolution of Cézanne by America's best-known twentieth century art historian.

Wechsler, Judith, ed. *Cézanne in Perspective.* Englewood Cliffs, N.J., 1975. Documented reference work for art historians and students alike that chronicles and contextualizes Cézanne's life and art.

MARIE CARANI

CHAADAYEV, PETER (1794–1856), Russian intellectual and writer.

The publication of the first of Peter Chaadayev's *Philosophical Letters* (1836) in *The Telescope* was a landmark event in the history of Russia. Its unfavorable comparison of Russian culture with the culture of the West and its questioning of the significance of

Russian history challenged the chauvinistic "Official Nationalism" of Nicholas I (r. 1825–1855) and infuriated the reading public. The regime responded by firing the censor who had permitted the letter's publication, shutting down *The Telescope* and exiling the journal's editor to a remote corner of the realm. The author was declared insane and placed under house arrest. Nonetheless, Chaadayev had a profound impact on the Slavophiles and Westernizers in the 1840s and continues to influence discussion of Russia's national identity in the early twenty-first century. Moreover, the story of his life as mystic, progressive, Freemason, martyr, and close friend of the Decembrists and of Alexander Pushkin inspired several generations of the intelligentsia. In 1915 the poet Osip Mandelstam wrote that "the trace of Chaadaev in the consciousness of Russian society remains so deep and so indelible that one cannot help but wonder, did he not write with diamond on glass?" (Burlaka, Ermichev, and Zlatopol'skaia, p. 401).

Born in Moscow on 7 June (27 May, old style) 1794, Chaadayev was descended from an old noble family. His maternal grandfather, Mikhail Shcherbatov (1733–1790), a statesman and historian, was a leader of the aristocratic opposition to Catherine II (the Great; r. 1762–1796). Chaadayev began his formal education at Moscow University in 1808 but left three years later to participate in the Napoleonic campaigns. He was decorated for his bravery and, after the war, appointed to posts close to the tsar. In 1821, disenchanted with life at court, he resigned his commission, abandoning the promise of a brilliant military career and slighting the monarch who had shown him favor. In 1823 he sold his serfs in order to finance travels to Europe that would last for three years. While abroad he acquainted himself with the work of several authors who would influence his *Philosophical Letters,* including the German idealist Friedrich Wilhelm Joseph von Schelling and the French Catholic writers François-Auguste-René de Chateaubriand, Joseph-Marie de Maistre, and Félicité Lamennais. Chaadayev's European travels also inadvertently protected him from arrest. Had he been in Russia in 1825, he would probably have been implicated in the ill-fated revolt of the Decembrists.

Chaadayev composed the eight *Philosophical Letters* in French during the years 1829 to 1831,

and he spent the next few years attempting to publish them. The work of a deeply Christian thinker, the *Philosophical Letters* attempt to give Russia a coherent philosophy of history. The first letter, the only one to appear in Russia in the nineteenth century, examines Russia's relationship to the West. Chaadayev was most impressed by the development in Catholic Europe of the Middle Ages of a unified Christian civilization and by the unfortunate impact of Russia's isolation from that civilization. A second factor in Russia's underdevelopment was its lack of a usable past. Chaadayev believed that successful civilizations build upon history but that Russia did not have a history on which to build. As a result, its culture and social life were formless.

> Look around you. Do we not all have one foot in the air? It looks as if we are traveling. There is no definite sphere of existence for anyone, no good habits, no rule for anything at all; not even a home; nothing which attracts or awakens our endearments or affections, nothing lasting, nothing enduring; everything departs, everything flows away, leaving no traces either without or within ourselves. (Chaadayev, 1969, p. 28)

While Chaadayev admired the west, he rejected its liberalism. The remaining *Philosophical Letters* are devoted primarily to a critique of the Enlightenment and the intellectual arrogance of reason untempered by faith.

Chaadayev was truly surprised by the strong reaction to his work. He claimed, somewhat disingenuously, that he had outgrown his views and that *The Telescope* had published them without his permission. Shortly thereafter, he wrote "Apology of a Madman" (1837) in which he defended himself from attacks on his patriotism and conceded that Russia might benefit from its shortcomings. Unencumbered by a national history of its own, it could learn from the mistakes of other nations and thereby assume a leading role in the spiritual life of Europe.

The diagnosis of insanity and the house arrest were lifted less than a month after they had been pronounced, but Chaadayev was banned from publishing for the rest of his life, while others were forbidden to mention his name in print. Nonetheless, he continued to exert influence on Russian letters through correspondence with younger writers, conversation at Moscow salons, and the publication of the *Philosophical Letters* abroad.

Chaadayev died in Moscow on 26 April (14 April, old style) 1856.

See also **Russia; Slavophiles; Westernizers.**

BIBLIOGRAPHY

Burlaka, D. K., A. A. Ermichev, and A. A. Zlatopol'skaia, eds. *P. Ia. Chaadaev—Pro et contra.* St. Petersburg, 1998.

Chaadayev, Peter. *The Major Works of Peter Chaadaev.* Edited and translated by Raymond T. McNally. Notre Dame, Ind., 1969.

———. *Philosophical Works of Peter Chaadaev.* Edited by Raymond T. McNally and Richard Tempest. Dordrecht, Netherlands, 1991.

Kline, George L. "Petr Iakovlevich Chaadaev." In *Russian Literature in the Age of Pushkin and Gogol: Prose,* edited by Christine A. Rydel, 101–109. Detroit, Mich., 1999.

McNally, Raymond T. *Chaadayev and His Friends: An Intellectual History of Peter Chaadayev and His Russian Contemporaries.* Tallahassee, Fla., 1971.

Peterson, Dale E. "Civilizing the Race: Chaadaev and the Paradox of Eurocentric Nationalism." *Russian Review* 56, no. 4 (1997): 550–563.

PETER C. POZEFSKY

CHADWICK, EDWIN (1800–1890), English reformer.

Born 24 January 1800, near Manchester, Edwin Chadwick was the son of a radical journalist. Although trained as a barrister, he never practiced law. After two years as secretary to Jeremy Bentham (1748–1832), he attempted to put the utilitarian sage's principles into practice as a government reformer. Chadwick's articles on current social problems and proposed administrative solutions brought him to the attention of political economists like Nassau William Senior and reform-minded Whig leaders like Henry Brougham. Through them he was brought in as an expert investigator on two new royal commissions in 1832—on the poor laws and on child labor in the factories. Chadwick proved quite willing to suppress evidence contrary to his opinions, and crafted his reforms partly in terms of the advancement of his own career. Ignoring the call of the followers of Thomas Malthus (1766–1834) to abolish the poor laws altogether, Chadwick insisted that a public relief system could be safely maintained if it was rigorously overhauled and infused with deterrent strategies.

REFORMS

The major recommendations of the report of the royal commission on the poor laws, written largely by Chadwick and issued in 1834, were the principle of less eligibility and the use of a workhouse test. The former embodied the concept that the condition of the pauper receiving public relief should be less eligible (less desirable) than that of the lowest paid independent laborer. The workhouse test was designed to put this into practice. The harsh regimen of the new workhouses would act as a test of destitution for the able bodied, since only the truly desperate would subject themselves to the discipline, hard work, and monotonous diet of the new workhouses. These recommendations were embodied in the New Poor Law of 1834. Chadwick had been simultaneously involved in a commission on factory children, and the resulting Factory Act of 1833 abolished all labor for children under nine and limited it to eight hours per day for those aged nine to thirteen.

Chadwick was passed over for one of the three poor law commissionerships under the 1834 act, accepting the lower position of secretary. In this post he was unable to prevent what he considered a gross maladministration of the new law, characterized by a fitful and very partial application of the workhouse test. Nonetheless, he carved out new areas of social inquiry and reform. The most important of these was a sanitary investigation, ostensibly conducted by the Poor Law Commission, but in fact carried out entirely by Chadwick. Published in 1842 as *The Report on the Sanitary Condition of the Labouring Population,* it is Chadwick's greatest work. Deploying a formidable array of statistics and expert medical testimony, he made a compelling case for the connection between illness and poverty. He also demonstrated that much, if not most, sickness was due to the appalling overcrowding and lack of sanitation in the towns. Chadwick called for dramatic government action to provide fresh water and create radically new sewer systems using small-bore earthenware pipes so that urban refuse could be efficiently removed before a deadly "miasma" (believed to be the predisposing cause of most illness) could form.

With the passage of the Public Health Act of 1848, Chadwick at last tasted real executive authority. While he considered the statute defective in its coercive powers over recalcitrant local authorities, he set to work vigorously with his colleague on the General Board of Health, Lord Shaftesbury (Anthony Ashley Cooper) to reform England's sanitary institutions. Using his limited coercive powers to the full, he compelled many reluctant municipalities to appoint local boards and begin the process of draining, sewering, and providing fresh water. He also made numerous enemies by his dictatorial and dogmatic manner. This proved to be the undoing of both Chadwick and the General Board of Health. In 1854 Chadwick was stripped of his post, and the general board was reorganized and placed under the control of one of his leading critics. It was his last paid government position.

REPUTATION

In spite of this repudiation by Parliament, Chadwick continued to be a dynamic force in administrative reform and the public health movements for the remaining thirty-six years of his life and was at last granted a knighthood a year before his death in 1890. While he is rightly viewed as an intrepid early pioneer in the making of the British Welfare State, he has come in for less favorable treatment by historians since the late twentieth century. Two hagiographic biographies of 1952, by R. A. Lewis and S. E. Finer, hail Chadwick as an indefatigable fighter to improve society and its institutions. A less flattering picture was presented in 1988 by Anthony Brundage, who details Chadwick's personal ambition, hostility toward rival reformers, and devious political strategies. A more sweeping indictment came in 1997 with Christopher Hamlin's study, in which Chadwick is depicted as having subverted an older, more humane tradition of public health reform, substituting impersonal bureaucratic structures and dubious engineering nostrums for real engagement in the lives of the poor.

See also **Great Britain; Malthus, Thomas Robert; Public Health; Statistics.**

BIBLIOGRAPHY

Primary Sources

Chadwick, Edwin. *Report on the Sanitary Condition of the Labouring Population of Great Britain* (1842). Reprinted with an introduction by M. W. Flinn. Edinburgh, 1965.

Secondary Sources

Brundage, Anthony. *England's "Prussian Minister": Edwin Chadwick and the Politics of Government Growth, 1832–1854.* University Park, Pa., 1988.

Finer, S. E. *The Life and Times of Sir Edwin Chadwick.* London, 1952.

Hamlin, Christopher. *Public Health and Social Justice in the Age of Chadwick: Britain, 1800–1854.* New York, 1997.

Lewis, R. A. *Edwin Chadwick and the Public Health Movement, 1832–1854.* London, 1952.

ANTHONY BRUNDAGE

CHAMBERLAIN, HOUSTON STEWART (1855–1927), Anglo-German writer, cultural critic, and race theorist.

At his death in 1927 Houston Stewart Chamberlain was famous as the "renegade" Englishman who repudiated his native land and championed German nationalism. A leading race publicist, he occupied a special place in the pantheon of the Third Reich (1933–1945) as one its most important ideological forerunners.

Chamberlain was born at Southsea, England, on 9 September 1855. His father became an admiral and several of his uncles had distinguished military careers. Soon after Chamberlain's birth, his mother died and along with two brothers he lived with relatives in France. Since his health was poor, he was mostly privately tutored and lived a peripatetic life on the Continent, quickly becoming more at home in the cultural traditions of France and Germany than in his native England. His older brother, Basil Hall Chamberlain (1850–1935), was also drawn to a foreign culture, Japan, where he lived for many years and achieved renown as a scholar of Japanese language and literature. In 1878 Houston married a Prussian girl and, after a brief ill-fated business venture on the Paris stock exchange, he completed a science degree at the University of Geneva and began a doctorate. A recurrence of bad health, probably a nervous breakdown, foreclosed his hopes for an academic career and for the rest of his life he lived as a private scholar, largely funded by family money, first in Dresden, later Vienna, and finally Bayreuth.

The chief intellectual influence on Chamberlain was the composer Richard Wagner (1813–1883) who at Bayreuth in Bavaria had established a festival for the performance of his music-dramas. Chamberlain attended the Bayreuth Festival in 1882 and soon after collaborated on the journal *La Revue Wagnerienne* whose aim was to publicize Wagner's music and ideas for French audiences. After the composer's death, Wagner's widow, Cosima, and an inner circle of advisors sought to establish control over the interpretation of Wagner and to promote Bayreuth as a shrine of German culture. By the 1890s, writing mostly in German, Chamberlain had completed two books and innumerable essays on Wagner and was a leading publicist of the growing cult. It was as a Wagnerite that he developed his views on politics, culture, and race; more than anyone he forged close links between the composer's legacy and the mainstream of German conservatism and racial nationalism. Under Bayreuth's spell Chamberlain became increasingly anti-Semitic and supportive of both an authoritarian political order and a German imperial mission.

International fame came to Chamberlain with the publication of *The Foundations of the Nineteenth Century* (1899). Over one thousand pages in length, the book was testimony to its author's encyclopedic knowledge and eclecticism. It tried to substantiate two major ideas: that racial struggle was the chief propelling force of human culture and that a superior Germanic or Teutonic race (also called the Aryan race, a term more in vogue decades before) was the major architect of modern European civilization. Chamberlain traced Germanic achievements from ancient Greece and Rome to the formation of nation-states and modern accomplishments in industry, science, and art. The two negative forces in his historical drama were first, the Semitic races, in particular the Jewish race, which was depicted as the historical adversary of the Germanic type, and second, miscegenation

between unrelated or dramatically different racial types. The fall of the Roman Empire was attributed to racial mixing and in the dark age that followed the Roman Catholic Church had corrupted Christianity. The Germanic race, Chamberlain argued, was the bearer of true Christianity and a long, involved chapter rejected the idea that Jesus was a Jew and asserted that his mortal heritage was Aryan. Chamberlain was claimed as a precursor by the Aryan or German Christian movement in the Nazi era. He was influenced by an acquaintance of Wagner's, the Frenchman Count Gobineau (*On the Inequality of Human Races*, 1853–1855). But whereas Gobineau saw racial decline as irreversible, *The Foundations* incorporated the dynamism of Darwinian struggle and eugenic theories of racial selection and improvement.

Endowing his book with an aura of science and scholarship, Chamberlain sustained the deepest prejudices of many of his readers: their pride in German culture and imperialism, anti-Semitism, anti-Catholicism, and their readiness to see manifestations of decline in liberalism and socialism. *The Foundations* received thousands of reviews, sparked heated debate, and won many admirers. It was political ideology thinly veiled as cultural analysis. By 1915 sales exceeded 100,000 copies and a popular edition in 1906 sold over 10,000 copies in ten days; translations appeared in French and English. Its most famous enthusiast was William II, the German emperor, who gave out copies to visitors and members of his entourage. Soon Chamberlain was invited to court and the two men corresponded regularly for over twenty years.

The attentions of the emperor convinced Chamberlain—as nothing else could—of his mission as a German prophet. Two major studies followed: *Immanuel Kant* (1905) and *Goethe* (1912). They challenged the recent revival of academic interest in these two thinkers around 1900 and sought to harness them to a racist and conservative viewpoint. Kant's philosophy was interpreted as safeguarding an inner realm of idealism, faith, and subjectivity while clearly demarcating the outer limits of reason. The philosopher was used to bolster Chamberlain's race theory and attack the excessive claims of scientific rationalism. In Goethe's case Chamberlain focused on his neglected scientific writings rather than literary works, seeing in them the model for an alternative methodology to scientific positivism. Neither book achieved the acclaim of *The Foundations*. Now the most renowned writer associated with the Wagner cult, Chamberlain's personal connections to Bayreuth became even stronger when, after a painful divorce, in December 1908 he married Eva, the youngest daughter of Richard and Cosima Wagner, spending the rest of his life in Bayreuth.

During World War I Chamberlain became one of the most prolific and extreme propagandists for Germany. Hundreds of thousands of copies of his war essays were distributed to German soldiers and civilians. Attacked as a "turncoat" in Britain, he was awarded an Iron Cross and became a German citizen in 1916. The war brought him into close relations with numerous ultranationalist and anti-Semitic organizations, including the Pan German League and the Fatherland Party, founded in 1917 to mobilize opposition against peace negotiations. Chamberlain was prominent among those who insisted that "internal enemies"—liberals, socialists, and Jews—were stabbing Germany in the back, undermining its war effort. Fearful that without complete victory, Germany would be convulsed in revolution, his politics became increasingly radical and his racial rhetoric more vehement and prescriptive. After Germany's defeat, Chamberlain and the Bayreuth circle endorsed counterrevolutionary movements that sought to overthrow the newly established Weimar Republic. His health had deteriorated (probably from multiple sclerosis) but he continued writing political essays, an autobiography, and *Man and God* (1921). Meeting Adolf Hitler in Bayreuth in October 1923, Chamberlain was captivated by the Nazi leader and publicly announced his support. He never lived to see the Bayreuth Festival turned into a kind of Nazi rite, but Chamberlain became a fixture of the regime's hagiography and much cited by its leading ideologue, Alfred Rosenberg (1893–1946). Chamberlain's funeral—attended by Hitler and a Hohenzollern prince representing the deposed emperor—symbolized the direction of German politics with World War I; his career poses the question of the relationship between earlier German racism and the policies of the Third Reich. Chamberlain cannot be held directly responsible, but he helped forge the climate in which Nazi crimes were possible.

See also **Anti-Semitism; Civilization, Concept of; Race and Racism; Wagner, Richard.**

BIBLIOGRAPHY

Field, Geoffrey G. *Evangelist of Race: The Germanic Vision of Houston Stewart Chamberlain.* New York, 1981.

Lindner, Erik. "Houston Stewart Chamberlain: The *Abwehrverein* and the 'Praeceptor Germaniae 1914–18'." In *Leo Baeck Institute Year Book* 37, edited by Arnold Paucker, 213–236. London, 1992.

Schüler, Winfried. *Der Bayreuther Kreis von seiner Enstehung bis zum Ausgang der Wilhelminischen Ära.* Munster, 1971.

Spotts, Frederic. *Bayreuth: A History of the Wagner Festival.* New Haven, Conn., 1994.

GEOFFREY G. FIELD

CHAMBERLAIN, JOSEPH (1836–1914), British politician.

Joseph Chamberlain was born into a striving middle-class Unitarian family in 1836. Trained in business practices by his father, Chamberlain learned more than economic lessons. Controlling outcomes, managing variable markets, and exerting power over potential business rivals helped construct an aggressive and competitive personality. He learned his lessons well: in 1854 he moved to Birmingham from his native London to begin work in a new family business. As a young man, he made important contacts among Birmingham's business elite and became known as a leading entrepreneur and civic booster. He was chairman of the school board, served on the town council, and was three times Birmingham's mayor (1873–1876). Redesigning the mayoralty from its traditional role as a ceremonial institution into a dynamic policy-making office, Chamberlain dominated Birmingham political life. He became a radical Liberal member of Parliament at a by-election in 1876. The following year, he established the National Liberal Foundation, the first and most famous "caucus." Designed to promote progressive causes, such as free nonsectarian education and an extension of the franchise, the NLF also served as an important vehicle for Chamberlain's ever expanding ambition.

When the general election of 1880 returned William Ewart Gladstone for his second administration, Chamberlain—with only four years' parliamentary experience—effectively stormed the cabinet. He threatened the Liberal leadership with the formation of an independent "pure left" party unless he was given office. Appointed president of the board of trade (1880–1885), Chamberlain had only a mixed record: his uncompromising attitude occasionally alienated important interests, especially shipowners. He enjoyed more success in cultivating opinion in the countryside. His personal "Unauthorized Programme" of 1885 advocated a more active government role in improving the life of the poor by, for example, making smallholdings and allotments available to agricultural workers. To his critics, leading Liberals among them, Chamberlain sounded suspiciously socialistic.

During Gladstone's brief third administration in 1886, Chamberlain broke with the Liberal Party over Home Rule for Ireland. Fearful that Home Rule would lead to Irish independence, Chamberlain revealed his emerging imperialist convictions. Leading a knot of like-minded Liberal Unionists in the House of Commons, he contributed to the defeat of Home Rule and the resignation of Gladstone. Although he was out of office for nearly a decade, his intensifying imperial ideas inclined Chamberlain and his followers to act on occasion with Salisbury's (Robert Arthur Talbot Gascoyne-Cecil, third marquis of Salisbury) Conservative government. After a brief Liberal interlude from 1892 to 1895, the Conservative and Unionist alliance was again returned to power at the general election of 1895. Chamberlain, weary of the political wilderness, eagerly accepted the position of secretary of the colonial office (1895–1903) as his reward for supporting Conservative initiatives. His primary aims during the new Salisbury administration were to develop the economic viability of the colonies, to protect British access to global markets, and to consolidate the British Empire. In pursuing these aims, he was one of the architects of the Boer War (1899–1902). By the war's end, Chamberlain had come to symbolize "both the will and the power" (as one admirer wrote) of British imperialism.

Capitalizing on his reputation as imperial spokesman, Chamberlain launched a new national campaign in 1903. It was the last great campaign of his life. He proposed an imperial union based on a system of reciprocal preferential tariffs by which England and its colonies would establish economic advantages over foreign imports, thus strengthening the empire through material ties of trade and commerce. As a sign that he had not forgotten his radical past, he promised that under such a system, domestic workers would have higher wages and the government greater revenues, sufficient to fund social legislation such as old-age pensions. Creating a Tariff Reform League to harness financial and political support and beating the drum for tariff reform at enthusiastic meetings throughout the country, Chamberlain seemed to carry all before him.

Alarmed at his early success, the Liberals—condemning tariff reform as a risky protectionist policy—fell back on their traditional support of free trade. It was not, however, the Liberals who defeated Chamberlain's policy, but Chamberlain himself. As the campaign progressed, it became increasingly clear that Chamberlain was determined to force Arthur James Balfour, the Conservative and Unionist prime minister (1902–1905), either to declare for tariff reform or to resign. It seemed to many suspicious Conservatives that the ungentlemanly Chamberlain wanted the party leadership for himself. Matters came to a head when Balfour retired from office in December 1905. The ensuing general election was disastrous for the Unionist alliance: the Liberals won in a landslide. Chamberlain had overreached himself. He had split the Conservative Party just as he had the Liberals two decades earlier. His health undermined by his constant political maneuvering, he suffered a stroke in July 1906. Partially paralyzed for the rest of his life, he died on 2 July 1914.

Although he never attained the highest political office and his imperial dreams did not withstand the test of time, Chamberlain nevertheless accomplished much. In Birmingham, he created a model for municipal reform. On a national scale he brought to an emerging and expanding electorate the most critical issues of the day in a clear and incisive manner. Most particularly, in emphasizing the importance of public education and national welfare, he strengthened the view that the modern state had fundamental responsibilities for all its citizens.

See also **Boer War; Conservatism; Great Britain; Tories; Trade and Economic Growth.**

BIBLIOGRAPHY

Garvin, J. L., and Julian Amery, eds. *Life of Joseph Chamberlain.* 6 vols. London, 1932–1969.

Jay, Richard. *Joseph Chamberlain: A Political Study.* Oxford, U.K., 1981.

Marsh, Peter T. *Joseph Chamberlain: Entrepreneur in Politics.* New Haven, Conn., 1994.

Porter, Andrew N. *The Origins of the South African War: Joseph Chamberlain and the Diplomacy of Imperialism, 1895–1899.* Manchester, U.K., 1980.

TRAVIS L. CROSBY

CHAMPOLLION, JEAN-FRANÇOIS

(1790–1832), French linguist and Egyptologist.

Jean-François Champollion, *le jeune* (the younger—to distinguish him from his older brother, Jacques-Joseph Champollion-Figeac), was born in southeastern France, near Grenoble, on 23 December 1790, and died forty-two years later in Paris on 4 March 1832. During his short life Champollion had achieved such an extraordinary feat—the decipherment of ancient Egyptian hieroglyphics—that he was called the most important man in France.

EDUCATION AND EARLY CAREER

Champollion, the second son of a bookseller wed to a merchant's daughter, was a linguistically precocious youngster who at the age of five had taught himself to read by matching passages he had already memorized to the words in his mother's missal and figuring out the phonetic system. He began his studies under his older brother, then attended the new lycée at Grenoble. There, in 1801, he met the illustrious mathematician Baron Jean-Baptiste-Joseph Fourier, who inspired his total dedication to the study of hieroglyphics.

Fourier had been one of about 170 scholars and scientists who had accompanied General Napoleon Bonaparte on the Egyptian campaign in 1798–1799. In fact, Fourier had recently composed the preface to the *Description de l'Égypte* (1808–1825; Description of Egypt), which elevated French enthusiasm for Egyptian history and culture. Fourier showed the youngster his copy of the inscriptions on the Rosetta Stone, a black basalt stele bearing the same inscription (from 193 B.C.E.) in Greek, hieroglyphics, and an ancient Egyptian cursive script called "demotic." French soldiers had stumbled onto the Rosetta Stone at al-Rachid in the western delta in July 1799 while digging for stones to use for building fortifications at Fort Julien. It was immediately recognized that this could be the key to unlocking the secrets of ancient Egyptian civilization. Therefore, Champollion studied all the ancient and Oriental languages needed to unlock the mystery of hieroglyphics—a project that led him to study sixteen languages and that took him twenty years.

In 1807 Champollion read a paper at the Academy of Grenoble about the Coptic geography of Egypt, which resulted in his admission to this body. He left Grenoble for Paris, where he spent the next two years (1807–1809) taking courses at the Collège de France and the École des Langues Orientales (School of Oriental Languages), laying the foundation for his own manuscripts—a grammar and a dictionary of the Coptic language. In 1809, still only nineteen, Champollion returned to Grenoble as adjunct professor of history of the Faculty of Letters and rose to professor in 1812. The geographical introduction to his *Égypte sous les Pharaons* (Egypt under the Pharaohs) was published in 1811, and the complete work in two volumes came in 1814.

Champollion's career was interrupted in 1815, when Napoleon returned from Elba. Bonaparte had founded the Institut d'Égypte (Institute of Egypt) and given Champollion an exemption from military conscription. In March 1815 Napoleon was received at Grenoble, and Champollion-Figeac became his secretary. When Champollion was presented to Napoleon, the latter inquired how his work was progressing and, learning that Champollion's Coptic grammar and dictionary had never been published, promised to see that it would be. Subsequently, the minister of interior sent a letter to the Third Class of History and Ancient Literature of the Institute National des Sciences et des Arts asking them to evaluate these two works and Champollion's system of translation. However, in the interval between when they started the review and when they reported back on 7 July, Napoleon was defeated at Waterloo. Consequently, the forthcoming negative evaluation dealt a crushing blow to any hope of publication by the current government. "The Jacobin of Grenoble," as his Bourbon enemies called him, also lost his university position.

DECYPHERING THE ROSETTA STONE

Unemployed, but undaunted by this change of fortune, Champollion continued his research. In 1821 he followed up with *De l'écriture hiératique des anciens Egyptiens* (Hieratic writing of the ancient Egyptians). Thereafter, he turned his attention to decipherment of the Rosetta Stone, and in 1822 published his *Lettre à M. Dacier relative à l'alphabet des hieroglyphes phonétiques employés par les Egyptiens pour écrire sur leurs monuments les titres, les noms, et les surnoms des souverains grecs et romains* (Letter to Mr. Dacier relative to the alphabet of phonetic hieroglyphics employed by the Egyptians in order to write on their monuments the titles, names, and surnames of the Greek and Roman sovereigns), whose fifty-two pages contained the complete hieroglyphic alphabet as well as his explanation of the whole system of ancient Egyptian writing, which he developed further in *Précis du système hiéroglyphique des anciens égyptiens* (1824; 2nd ed. in 2 vols., 1828).

By 1822 the brilliance of Champollion's pathbreaking discovery that hieroglyphics was both ideographic and phonetic overwhelmed his political foes, and his career resumed, although his discovery caused an international fracas among scholars. A Frenchman had deciphered the Rosetta Stone now in the British Museum as a spoil of war, and not only had the leading British linguistic scholar Dr. Thomas Young (1773–1829) been proven partially wrong but Champollion refused to share the credit. Only the posthumous publication of Champollion's grammar (1836–1841) and dictionary (1841–1844) finally removed all doubts about the correctness of his decipherment, which had been challenged by other German and French scholars as well.

With the support of the Royalist duc de Blacas, in 1826 Champollion obtained the Egyptian curatorship at the Louvre. With Ippolito Rosellini as his second-in-command, in 1828 he mounted a Franco-Tuscan expedition up the Nile, during which he collected artifacts for the Louvre and

copied ancient texts. This resulted in two great sets of plates: *Monuments de l'Égypte et de la Nubie* (4 vols., 1835–1847; Monuments of Egypt and Nubia) and *I monumenti dell'Egitto e della Nubia* (9 vols., plus 3 vols. of atlases, 1832–1844).

Upon returning to Paris on 5 March 1830, he was finally named to the Academy of Inscriptions. King Louis-Philippe (r. 1830–1848) created a chair of Egyptology for Champollion at the Collège de France, where Champollion taught until a fatal series of strokes hit him from 13 January to 4 March 1832, ending his brilliant career at a tragically young age.

See also **Egypt; France; French Revolutionary Wars and Napoleonic Wars; Imperialism; Napoleon; Napoleonic Empire.**

BIBLIOGRAPHY

Primary Sources

Hartleben, Hermien, ed. *Lettres de Champollion le jeune.* Paris, 1909.

Secondary Sources

Hartleben, Hermien. *Champollion, sein Leben und sein Werk.* 2 vols. Berlin, 1906.

Meyerson, Daniel. *The Linguist and the Emperor: Napoleon and Champollion's Quest to Decipher the Rosetta Stone.* New York, 2004. The role of Egypt in Napoleon's vision of establishing a French empire stretching from India to the Atlantic as motivation for encouraging Champollion's work.

Reid, Donald Malcolm. *Whose Pharaohs?: Archaeology, Museums, and Egyptian National Identity from Napoleon to World War I.* Berkeley, Calif., 2002. Places Egyptology within the context of Egyptian nationalism and international imperialistic rivalry.

Vercoutter, Jean. *The Search for Ancient Egypt.* New York, 1992. A visual feast—richly illustrated with many documents and quotations in sidebars as well as a documents section.

JUNE K. BURTON

CHARCOT, JEAN-MARTIN (1825–1893), French physician.

Jean-Martin Charcot was arguably the best-known physician in France during the early Third Republic. He was recognized for his brilliant accomplishments in three separate fields of clinical medicine: neurology, geriatrics, and internal medicine. He was also renowned for the circle of loyal and talented medical students he mentored and for his flamboyant stage demonstrations of pathological syndromes. Beyond his medical activities, Charcot hobnobbed with powerful politicians, strove to advance the legislative agenda of French republicanism, and gathered the elite of Parisian cultural society at his home for weekly salons.

CAREER COURSE

From humble artisanal origins, Charcot rose to the apex of the French professional elite. His medical elders recognized his abilities and industry early on, and as a result his medical and academic career advanced rapidly. He received his M.D. from the University of Paris in 1853 with a dissertation on arthritis. In 1860 he was named *professeur agrégé,* or associate professor, in medicine. Two years later, he was appointed *chef de clinique,* or head of a hospital clinical service, at the Salpêtrière, a historic hospital complex on the southeastern edge of Paris, where he would spend the rest of his career. During the same period, he began to deliver weekly bedside lessons to medical students, a pedagogical genre he eventually mastered. Across the 1860s, a decade of great productivity for him, Charcot published books on infectious illnesses, geriatrics (especially gout and rheumatism), and diseases of the lungs, heart, liver, and kidneys. He also founded or cofounded numerous medical journals. In 1872 he was brought onto the Paris Medical Faculty, the most prestigious body in French academic medicine, as professor of pathological anatomy.

During the 1870s, Charcot turned with great effect to the emerging field of neurology. In traditional accounts of medical history, he is often labeled "the father of neurology." Along with John Hughlings Jackson and William Gowers in Britain and Carl Wernicke in Germany, Charcot carved the clinical specialty of neurology out of general medicine. There followed an outpouring of publications in this new field, much of it taking the distinctive form of compilations of illustrative case histories. His finest work concerned multiple sclerosis, cerebral localization and lateralization, Parkinson's disease, aphasia, locomotor ataxia (tabes

dorsalis), Tourette's syndrome, and amyotrophic lateral sclerosis (Lou Gehrig's disease). In several instances, Charcot provided the initial clinical description of these classic pathological syndromes. "Charcot's joints" refers today to pain and swelling of the joints from advanced syphilitic infection, which was then rampant in European society.

DECADE OF FAME

Charcot achieved the height of his fame in the 1880s. For his labors, he was rewarded with the creation of the chair for the diseases of the nervous system, the first such professorial post in the world. The ministry of the interior also granted him the resources to establish a special ward for the treatment of the nervous and neurological infirmities. His voluminous publications were gathered up into a nine-volume set of collected works, and he was elected an honorary member of learned medical and scientific societies across the Western world. The wealthy, including aristocracy and royalty, sought his medical counsel.

Charcot's published medical work bears several distinctive stylistic and methodological features and was most influenced by the traditions of René Laennec and Claude Bernard. From the former physician and his followers he learned the technique of correlating bedside symptoms with postmortem tissue abnormalities. Like Bernard, the central figure in French medical positivism, Charcot believed that medical practice should integrate closely with laboratory chemistry and biology. He considered the pathology room, histology laboratory, and science lecture hall indispensable corollaries to the hospital ward. Charcot wrote in a crystalline, Cartesian style much admired by his contemporaries. He isolated a pathological syndrome by abstracting and then combining what he believed were its key symptomatological features into a kind of clinical ideal-type of the disease. By all accounts, he excelled at differential diagnosis. Many of his publications highlight Charcot the diagnostic virtuoso, discriminating precisely among the signs of complex cases that combined organic and psychogenic etiologies.

During the 1880s, Charcot took up the subject of hysteria. His work in this area attracted widespread attention, both inside and outside medicine, but ultimately it seriously compromised

A Lesson in Hysteria by Jean Martin Charcot. Nineteenth-century print after the painting by André Brouillet. ©Corbis

his scientific reputation. Late-nineteenth-century medical practices across Europe included large numbers of patients with shifting nervous complaints that mysteriously failed to reveal any known organic cause and that resisted all manner of treatment. Often, the manifestations of these disorders imitated neurological symptoms, such as twitches, spasms, paralyses of the extremities, and difficulties of sight, speech, and gait. Charcot interpreted these baffling cases as hysteria and sought to discover their nature, course, and cure.

Most of what had previously been written about this ancient disorder Charcot dismissed as errant nonsense. According to his "scientific" model of the disease, hysteria was caused by a hereditary predisposition combined with an environmental trigger, which usually consisted of a physical accident or psychological trauma. Its underlying pathology took the form of a lesion of the central nervous system, although the exact location of this structural defect

remained unknown to him. Pseudoneurological symptoms—or what he called "hysterical stigmata"—were central to its profile, and hysterical seizures consisted of certain stylized phases. Charcot played down the possible role of sexuality in the disorder and rejected the historic notion of hysteria as "the disease of the wandering womb." Illustrating this point, a third of Charcot's published case histories of hysteria feature male patients, most of whom were drawn from the working classes. Because Charcot traced the malady to bad heredity, he believed hysterical disorders were incurable in the present state of medicine. He sought, rather, to alleviate symptoms with the application of massage, medications, hydrotherapy, and electrotherapy. Charcot advanced his clinical observations and theoretical ideas in works such as the *Leçons sur les maladies du système nerveux* (Lectures on diseases of the nervous system) and *Leçons du mardi* (Tuesday lessons), which consist of scores of case reports.

During the 1870s and 1880s, Charcot attracted medical students from throughout Europe and North America. Playing on the French term *charcuterie* (pork butcher's shop), observers dubbed his circle *la charcoterie*. An 1887 painting by André Brouillet, titled *Une Leçon clinique à la Salpêtrière* (A clinical lesson at the Salpêtrière school), captures the scene of Charcot as the medical master discoursing to a rapt audience of followers. Nineteenth-century France witnessed the high point of the patronal system of medical training: aspiring physicians studied with a famous figure whose work they were expected to champion uncritically and who in turn promoted their careers. The most powerful of the early Third Republic patrons, Charcot trained a generation of young French neurologists and placed them in provincial medical faculties across France. His best-known students were Joseph Babinski and Pierre Marie, who continued his work in pure clinical neurology, and Pierre Janet and Sigmund Freud, who explored the psychological aspects of the hysterical disorders. On academic leave from the University of Vienna, Freud studied with Charcot for several months in 1885–1886 and later translated into German two of the Frenchman's books. Because of Freud's subsequent fame, Charcot has often been characterized as a figure in the prehistory of psychoanalysis.

CONTROVERSIES AND CHALLENGES

The last several years of Charcot's career, during the late 1880s and early 1890s, brought dramatic challenges to his intellectual and professional authority. His therapeutic pessimism was increasingly deemed unsatisfactory in an age when well-to-do nervous sufferers sought hope and solace. With the rise of the germ theory of disease, his degenerative hereditarian model became evermore old-fashioned. A major medical debate in late-nineteenth-century Europe centered on the nature of general paralysis of the insane, which Charcot argued was an independent pathological syndrome but which was increasingly discovered to be syphilis of the spine and brain. Some observers also asserted that Charcot was brusque and uncaring with his patients, regarding them as little more than "clinical material."

During this same period, Charcot's extravagant theories of hysteria came under attack. Critics charged that his patients had been secretly coached to perform the requisite symptoms. Similarly, the techniques of hypnosis Charcot employed in his demonstrations were discredited by sensationalistic street demonstrations. And Charcot-style hysteria appeared as a subject, image, and metaphor in plays, novels, journalism, and popular culture. (Tourists to Paris, it was said, wished to visit the Eiffel Tower, the Folies-Bergère dance hall, and Charcot's medical demonstrations!) What is more, Charcot's blatant nepotism in placing his students, and blocking the careers of others, aroused resentment; a campaign to topple "the Caesar of the medical faculty" gained momentum. Even some of his former students came to resent his stern, authoritarian manner. ("The Napoleon of the neuroses" was one of his nicknames.) Charcot's immediate posthumous years brought an eclipse of his reputation. During World War I, however, physicians returned to his medical writings on hysterical vision, mutism, amnesia, and paralysis, which seemed to presage the phenomenon of wartime shell shock and since around 1990, new editions of his writings and a major scientific biography have appeared.

POLITICS AND CULTURE

An additional source of Charcot's historical interest involves his activities outside the medical field. Charcot married into the wealthy Laurent family. He and his wife maintained a lavish home in the Saint-Germain neighborhood of Paris as well as a summerhouse in the affluent western suburb of Neuilly. They invited prominent writers, thinkers, poets, scientists, scholars, and politicians to their high society dinner parties. Charcot had passionate cultural interests. He traveled widely to view museums and architecture, and he illustrated his personal letters with sketches of places and people. His artistic interests were conservative, however, and he seems not to have appreciated the revolution in French painting (i.e., impressionism and neo-impressionism) occurring around him. He read some six languages and assembled one of the largest private medical libraries in Europe, the remnants of which are still on display at the Bibliothèque Charcot on the grounds of the Salpêtrière.

Politically, Charcot was an aggressive advocate of French secular republicanism, which came to power in France during the 1880s. The journal *Le Progrès Médical,* which his protégé D.M. Bourneville founded in 1873, led the charge to laicize French hospitals, which mandated that medically trained nurses replace Catholic personnel. Charcot embraced the tradition of Voltairean anticlericalism. He diagnosed many past Catholic saints as hysterics, although he was not beyond sending some of his patients to the Catholic healing shrine at Lourdes. During the Franco-Prussian War of 1870–1871, when Paris was shelled heavily, Charcot remained in the capital city to treat wounded civilians and soldiers. From that time onward, he refused to attend medical congresses in Otto von Bismarck's Germany. It was said at the time that the Franco-Russian Alliance of 1894 was brokered at the Charcot home. Charcot's son, who was married to the novelist Victor Hugo's granddaughter, became a celebrated Antarctic explorer whose ship, the *Pourquoi-Pas?,* was lost at sea. For such reasons, Charcot became a figure in the cultural and political, as well as medical, history of his time.

See also **Anticlericalism; Bernard, Claude; Eiffel Tower; Franco-Prussian War; Freud, Sigmund; Hugo, Victor; Impressionism; Laennec, René; Positivism; Psychology; Syphilis.**

BIBLIOGRAPHY

Primary Sources

Charcot, Jean-Martin. *Clinical Lectures on Diseases of the Nervous System.* London, 1878. Reprint, edited with an introduction by Ruth Harris, London, 1991. A reissue of a key medical text.

———. *Oeuvres complètes de J. M. Charcot.* 9 vols. Edited by D.-M. Bourneville et al. Paris, 1886–1890.

———. *Charcot the Clinician: The Tuesday Lessons.* Translated with commentary by Christopher G. Goetz. New York, 1987. Another valuable compilation in English translation.

Freud, Sigmund. "Charcot." In *The Standard Edition of the Complete Psychological Works of Sigmund Freud.* 24 vols. Translated by James Strachey et al. London, 1953–1974. Vol. 3: 9–23. A discerning commentary written upon Charcot's death during the summer of 1893.

Janet, Pierre. "Jean-Martin Charcot: Son oeuvre psychologique." *La revue philosophique* 39 (June 1895): 569–604. Along with Freud's obituary, this is the most perceptive posthumous assessment.

Munthe, Axel. *The Story of San Michele.* Translated from the French. London, 1929. Chaps. 4, 17–19, 23. The liveliest of the literary pastiches of Charcot.

Secondary Sources

Brais, Bernard. "The Making of a Famous Nineteenth Century Neurologist: Jean-Martin Charcot (1825–1893)." M.Phil. thesis, Wellcome Institute for the History of Medicine, University College London, 1990. A brilliant—but unfortunately unpublished—account of the world of Parisian medical politics during the Charcot era.

Didi-Huberman, Georges. *Invention of Hysteria: Charcot and the "Photographic Iconography of the Salpêtrière."* Translated by Alisa Hartz. Cambridge, Mass., 2003. An in-depth discussion of the more sensationalistic aspects of Charcot's work on hysteria.

Goetz, Christopher G., Michel Bonduelle, and Toby Gelfand. *Charcot: Constructing Neurology.* New York, 1995. A thorough, authoritative, and enormously informative biography of the man and his work, with special attention to the pioneering output in neurology.

Goldstein, Jan. "Hysteria, Anti-Clerical Politics and the View beyond the Asylum." In her *Console and Classify: The French Psychiatric Profession in the Nineteenth Century,* 322–377. Cambridge, U.K., 1987. Despite containing numerous errors of interpretation, Goldstein's chapter is an excellent study of the anticlerical theme in Charcot's career.

Harris, Ruth. "Women, Hysteria, and Hypnotism." In her *Murders and Madness: Medicine, Law, and Society in the Fin de Siècle,* 155–207. Oxford, U.K., 1989. Arguably the best analysis of Charcot from a feminist perspective.

Lellouch, Alain. *Jean-Martin Charcot et les origines de la geriatrie.* Paris, 1992. A detailed and intelligent study of a neglected but important topic.

Micale, Mark S. "Charcot and the Idea of Hysteria in the Male: Gender, Mental Science, and Medical Diagnosis in Late Nineteenth-Century France." *Medical History* 34, no. 4 (1990): 363–411. A specialized study placed in medical-historical context.

———. *Approaching Hysteria: Disease and Its Interpretations.* Princeton, N.J., 1995. Includes scattered ideas and information about Charcot.

MARK S. MICALE

CHARLES X (1757–1836; ruled 1824–1830), king of France.

The Comte d'Artois, the younger brother of Louis XVI of France (r. 1774–1792) and the future Charles X, was born in 1757. At age sixteen he entered into an arranged marriage with the daughter of King Victor Amadeus III of Sardinia

(r. 1773–1796). The diminutive Marie-Thérèse (d. 1805) was a year younger and then stood barely more than four feet tall. Irresponsible behavior, as well as the stubbornness that would always characterize him, marked the future king's adolescence and young adulthood. He also developed a lifelong love of playing cards and, above all, hunting (writing in 1825, "Bad weather has forced me to cancel hunting; therefore, I have decided to consider questions of the hour"). At the time of his spouse's death in 1805 Charles had not seen her in ten years.

Adamantly opposed to reform and strongly influenced by a coterie of reactionary advisors, he once proclaimed, "I would rather be a woodcutter than to reign in the fashion of the king of England." He remained an uncompromising advocate of unmitigated royal sovereignty. Following the Revolution, in July he became one of the first royals to leave France for exile. Now "king of the exiles," he helped organize various royalist conspiracies, but did not participate in the armies raised to invade France and attempt to restore the monarchy. With his brother, the Comte de Provence (the future King Louis XVIII [r. 1814–1824]), he encouraged the Brunswick Manifesto of 1792, in which Prussia and Austria warned that the French would be punished if any harm came to Louis XVI and his family. This helped inspire the popular insurrection that established a revolutionary Commune in Paris on 9 August, leading to massacres in the Tuileries Palace. On 21 January 1793 Louis XVI was guillotined.

At the time of the first Bourbon Restoration in 1814, Artois opposed the Charter that his brother, Louis XVIII, granted his subjects, which referred to "public liberties" and establishing a legislature that would be elected, albeit by extremely limited suffrage. Whereas Louis XVIII realized that the risks of trying to turn the clock back to the *ancien régime* included the strong possibility of civil war, Artois maintained close ties to the ultraroyalists, many of whom were angry émigrés who had "learned nothing and forgotten nothing," and who refused any accommodation with the Revolution. With the aged Louis XVIII gradually withdrawing from an active role in monarchical politics, the influence of Artois continued to rise. The assassination in 1820 of his son, the Duc de Berri

(1778–1820), the heir to the throne, by Louis-Pierre Louvel, whose goal was to extinguish the Bourbon line, only reaffirmed the intransigence of Artois.

Upon the death of Louis XVIII in 1824 Artois ascended the throne at age sixty-six as Charles X. His coronation in May 1825 was spectacularly controversial. Charles attempted to heal crippled people with the "healing touch" of a new monarch. The ceremony, one that came right out of the Middle Ages, drew derisive contempt from liberals. At the Papal Jubilee in 1826 the king prostrated himself before the archbishop of Paris during an expiation ceremony in remembrance of the execution of Louis XVI. Émigrés were compensated for losses of property during the sale of the *biens nationaux* (national property), while rumors circulated that such lands purchased during the Revolution would be returned to their original owners and that Charles X planned to allow the church to collect the tithe. The Chamber of Deputies passed a law making sacrilege—any crime committed in or against a church—a capital offense. Although no one was executed for sacrilege, the law generated great opposition from liberals, who railed against the alliance of altar and throne.

Charles remained seemingly oblivious to the possible consequences of the mounting organized opposition to his rule, reflected by the election of an increasing number of liberals to the Chamber of Deputies. In August 1829 he appointed as chief minister the reactionary prince Jules de Polignac (1780–1847), who had been one of two members of the Chamber of Deputies who had refused to take an oath of allegiance to the Charter in 1814. Charles delivered an aggressive address to the Deputies, insisting that the opposition had failed to "understand" the king's will. Two hundred twenty-one deputies called on the king to remove from power a government of which a majority in the Chamber did not approve, directly raising the issue of monarchical sovereignty. Charles dismissed the Chamber. However, new elections in July again brought a clear liberal majority. On 26 July 1830 Charles X promulgated the July Ordinances, which dissolved the newly elected Chamber of Deputies, disenfranchised almost three-quarters of those eligible to vote, and clamped down on the press.

In Paris, demonstrations turned into skirmishes with troops. Paris rose up in revolt during the "three glorious days." Seeing that there was no way of maintaining his power, on 31 July Charles X named as Lieutenant-General of the Realm Louis-Philippe, the duc d'Orléans, the junior branch of the Bourbon family, who had a reputation of being liberal and who had fought in the revolutionary armies. Charles then abdicated in favor of his grandson, the Duc de Bordeaux (1820–1883), on 2 August. The victorious liberals then offered the throne to the duc d'Orléans, who assumed the throne as Louis-Philippe I (r. 1830–1848). The tricolor of the Revolution replaced the white flag of the Bourbons, a transformation taken to represent the principle of national sovereignty, embodied in the change in royal title from "king of France" to "king of the French." The electoral franchise was lowered, doubling the number of eligible voters. Charles X, the last of the Bourbon monarchs of France, went into exile to Britain, and then to Prague, dying in Goritz on 6 November 1836.

See also **France; Louis XVI; Louis XVIII; Louis-Philippe; Marie-Antoinette; Restoration; Revolutions of 1830.**

BIBLIOGRAPHY

Alexander, Robert. *Re-Writing the French Revolutionary Tradition: Liberal Opposition and the Fall of the Bourbon Monarchy.* Cambridge, U.K., and New York, 2003.

Beach, Vincent W. *Charles X of France: His Life and Times.* Boulder, Colo., 1971.

de Bertier de Sauvigny, Guillaume. *The Bourbon Restoration.* Translated by Lynn M. Case. Philadelphia, 1966.

Bordonove, Georges. *Charles X: dernier roi de France et de Navarre.* Paris, 1990.

Griffon, Yves. *Charles X: roi méconnu.* Paris, 1999.

Merriman, John M., ed. *1830 in France.* New York, 1975.

Pinkney, David H. *The French Revolution of 1830.* Princeton, N.J., 1972.

JOHN MERRIMAN

CHARLES ALBERT (1798–1849), ruled as king of Sardinia-Piedmont from 1831 to 1849.

The future king of Sardinia, Charles Albert, was born on 2 October 1798 into the Savoia-Carignano branch of the ruling house of Savoy, the son of Carlo Emanuele, Prince of Carignano, and Princess Maria Cristina Albertina of Saxony-Courland. His parents were known sympathizers of the French Revolution, hence politically suspect in court circles. They chose to remain in Turin when the court retreated to the island of Sardinia in 1798 after the French annexation of Piedmont. They soon moved to Paris with their infant son and lived there until 1812 on a French stipend of 100,000 francs per year after their assets were confiscated. The father died in 1800; in 1812, mother and son moved to Geneva, Switzerland, where Charles Albert was educated by a Protestant pastor and developed the habits of hard work and self-discipline that made him an austere and aloof figure.

Charles Albert's brief stint as an officer in the army of Napoleon I (r. 1804–1814/15) began and ended in 1814 with Napoleon's defeat. He returned to Turin in May 1814 as heir presumptive to the throne because his distant relatives, King Victor Emmanuel I (r. 1802–1821) and King Charles Felix (r. 1821–1831), had no male descendants. Charles Albert married Maria Teresa, daughter of the grand duke of Tuscany, in 1817. Their firstborn son ruled as Victor Emmanuel II of Sardinia-Piedmont (r. 1849–1861) and as first king of the unified kingdom of Italy (r. 1861–1878).

Although Charles Albert was more at ease using the French language, after returning to Piedmont he openly favored the use of Italian at court and gravitated toward Italian literary figures, gestures that were interpreted as showing sympathy for the cause of Italian independence. During the Piedmontese uprising of 1821, while serving as regent after the abdication of Victor Emmanuel I and the temporary absence of Charles Felix, he acceded to the insurgents' demand for a constitution, but that decision was promptly revoked by Charles Felix. Charles Albert left Turin for a period of exile in Florence on his uncle's orders. To regain royal favor and the support of legitimists, Charles Albert volunteered to lead troops against liberal forces in Spain. His performance in Spain rehabilitated him in the eyes of conservatives, angered liberals, and gave rise to the image of Charles Albert as *Re tentenna* (King Waffle), the indecisive and untrustworthy figure that was the subject of political caricature. His equivocal conduct in 1821 can perhaps be interpreted charitably as an unsuccessful effort by an inexperienced young man to mediate between conservatives and liberals.

Charles Albert inherited the throne at the death of Charles Felix on 24 April 1831. In the first years of his reign, he went out of his way to allay lingering conservative suspicions and stay on Austria's good side. In the years 1833 and 1834, he cracked down hard on the Young Italy movement's network and disrupted its plans for revolution. But once the threat of revolution was past, he abolished feudal privileges in Sardinia, adopted uniform legal codes, introduced an advisory council of state, eliminated internals tolls, encouraged maritime trade, and negotiated commercial treaties with France and Great Britain.

A monarch jealous of his royal prerogatives and a devout Catholic, Charles Albert nevertheless gave secret encouragement to moderate liberals, hinting that he nurtured anti-Austrian feelings and favored Italian independence. When revolution broke out in Austrian-ruled Lombardy, Charles Albert granted a constitution and, on 23 March 1848, marched his army into Lombardy, thus starting Italy's first war of national independence. Desire for territorial aggrandizement played a role, but there were also other motives. Charles Albert was eager to lead the fight against Austria, champion the cause of Italian independence, and was determined to prevent Giuseppe Mazzini (1805–1872) and other republicans from gaining control of the national movement. Austria's victory over Sardinia-Piedmont and its Italian allies forced Charles Albert to abdicate in favor of his son Victor Emmanuel II on 23 March 1849. He went into exile in Portugal, where he died on 28 July 1849. His most important legacy was the *Statuto,* the only one of the constitutions granted by Italian monarchs in 1848 that survived the defeat of revolution. It served as the constitution of the Kingdom of Italy from 1861, when the country was unified, to 1946, when a popular vote abolished the monarchy and made Italy a republic.

See also **Cavour, Count (Camillo Benso); Italy; Mazzini, Giuseppe; Piedmont-Savoy; Revolutions of 1820; Revolutions of 1848.**

BIBLIOGRAPHY

Hearder, Harry. *Italy in the Age of the Risorgimento, 1790–1870.* London, 1983.

Roland Sarti

CHARTISM. Chartism, which flourished between 1838 and 1848, was a movement to secure a democratic system of government in Great Britain. It took its name from the People's Charter (1838), a draft parliamentary bill to transform the House of Commons into a democratic chamber responsive to the wishes and needs of the people as a whole and not just the propertied classes. The idea for such a bill emerged from discussions between a small group of radical members of Parliament (MPs) and leaders of earlier reform movements in London. Most of the latter had been members of the National Union of the Working Classes (NUWC), which had agitated for the Reform Bill in the years 1831 and 1832 and had taken part in the struggle to secure an unstamped press, partly successful when the stamp duty on newspapers was reduced to one penny in 1835. This campaign, with its combination of externally organized pressure coupled with parliamentary lobbying and support from inside the House of Commons provided the first model for what was to become Chartism. The NUWC was virtually reconstituted as the London Working Men's Association (LWMA) in June 1836 with William Lovett (1800–1877) as secretary.

In June 1837 a committee of six MPs and six working men, including Lovett, issued the Six Points, which became talismanic for the future movement: universal suffrage, which meant *manhood* suffrage; no property qualifications for MPs, so that any man might stand for the House of Commons; annual parliaments, so that MPs might become accountable to their constituents and that bribery might become ineffective; equal representation, so that the representation in Parliament might be proportionate to the people in the country (important for Ireland); payment of members, so men without private means might enter Parliament; and vote by ballot, so that illegitimate pressure could not be put on voters. The intention was thus not only to demand the central plank of manhood suffrage but also all those other measures necessary to make that a reality.

The draft bill itself was a lengthy and sophisticated document, going well beyond the Six Points, and it was to evolve over time to include important constitutional changes such as repeal of the Act of Union between Great Britain and Ireland (1800). Long-term, the Charter drew on a tradition that went back to the later eighteenth century, strengthened in the wake of the French Revolution by Thomas Paine's *Rights of Man,* published in 1791–1792. But what gave the People's Charter additional edge was the Reform Act of 1832, which had transformed the parliamentary franchise in the boroughs, rationalizing it and putting it on the basis of a £10 property qualification. In practice, the Act confused the system rather than simplifying it, especially with its complicated system for voter registration, and having removed the sanctity of age from the nature of the voting qualification it almost invited further amendment. This the People's Charter sought to do. The idea was not unreasonable but it was perhaps wishful thinking to believe that the Charter would be carried, given the radical transformation to the representative system that it entailed.

Parallel with these developments, a similar movement appeared in Birmingham, where the local MP, Thomas Attwood (1783–1856), was disillusioned with the Reform Act. He had been a leader from 1830 to 1832 of the Birmingham Political Union (BPU), which had done a great deal to organize public opinion in favor of reform. The BPU was revived in May 1837 with a National Petition for parliamentary reform in the belief that what was widely regarded as the BPU's success in 1832 could be repeated. The BPU adopted the People's Charter on 14 May 1838 to secure the greatest possible popular support, and the National Petition and the People's Charter were formally endorsed at mass public meetings in Glasgow and Birmingham on 21 May and 6 August 1838, respectively. Lecturers were simultaneously sent out to rouse public opinion in the country.

A third source of Chartism was dissatisfaction with the social and economic conditions created by rapid industrialization and urbanization, especially in centers of textile manufacture in the Midlands, north of England, and western Scotland. Reformers believed, unlike modern historians, that the Reform Act had been a victory for the middle classes, whose possession of property had enabled them to elect a House of Commons to carry legislation specifically in their narrow class interests. Such "class legislation" included measures against trade unions, a reluctance to restrict working hours in factories, and, above all, the Poor Law Amendment Act of 1834, which removed the traditional parochial support for the poor and threatened them with either starvation or the workhouse. The attempt to introduce this system from 1837, just as a major depression hit industrial Britain, produced widespread disturbances that fed into popular support for a thorough reform of the House of Commons. The strategy here was to reinforce the National Petition and the People's Charter with a delegate meeting in London, the National Convention, which looked like a rival People's Parliament to challenge the legitimacy of the real one. This strategy was based on the successful Irish campaign of the 1820s that had by mass mobilization and threats of revolution secured a major constitutional change in 1829 with the Catholic Emancipation Act. The acknowledged leader was a former Irish MP, Feargus Edward O'Connor (1796–1855), whose father and uncle had been members of the United Irishmen during the revolutionary 1790s. His instruments were his own powerful oratory, especially outdoors when addressing mass meetings, and the *Northern Star,* begun as an anti–Poor Law paper in Leeds in November 1837 but which under O'Connor's ownership rapidly became the main Chartist paper and the organ through which he came to dominate the movement.

THE CAMPAIGN TO SECURE THE CHARTER

The campaign to secure the Charter reached three peaks of activity, in 1839, 1842, and 1848, centered on the collection of signatures for the National Petition and the election of delegates to the Convention in London. On the first occasion there was a genuine mass movement as all sections of Chartism united at large public meetings where the Charter was proclaimed and delegates to the Convention elected by show of hands. The violent language used by some of the speakers at these meetings led to swift action by the local forces of law and order. Actual violence broke out sporadically, most notably in the mid-Wales textile district in April 1839. Troops were sent to control the Midlands and north of England. The situation was increasingly tense as 1,280,000 signatures were collected on the Petition and Convention delegates assembled in London to oversee the presentation of the Petition to Parliament. Strong language used in the debates about what to do if the Petition were rejected led to all but one of the BPU delegates resigning. Events were delayed by the collapse of the Whig government and the so-called Bedchamber Crisis, and the Convention moved to Birmingham. Here riots led to troops and the London police being called in, and William Lovett was arrested for his part in protesting against the violent conduct of the police. When the government crisis was over, the depleted Convention returned to London, the Petition was presented on 14 June, but in the ensuing debate was rejected by 235 votes to 46.

The problem was what to do next. The idea of a general strike failed in the midst of unemployment and trade-union skepticism. The strategy of mass action had made the word *Chartism* synonymous with violence, an image reinforced as some disillusioned delegates returned to their local areas to whip up further support. Frustration led to further violence, notably in the valleys of south Wales, where several thousand armed men marched on Newport on 4 November 1839. There were smaller attempted risings in the West Riding of Yorkshire and widespread arrests followed with both local and national leaders, including O'Connor, sent to jail, mostly for riot. There followed a lull in Chartist activity, but the movement was sustained, largely by the *Northern Star* and new local leaders who emerged to form in July 1840 the National Charter Association (NCA). Until 1848, Chartism as a movement was to be defined by the NCA and the *Northern Star* under the leadership of O'Connor, who emerged from jail on August 1841 with his reputation greatly enhanced by his "martyrdom."

The NCA began another Petition in the autumn of 1841. Other groups of Chartists who favored the alternative approaches of the defunct LWMA and BPU went their own ways. In April 1841, William Lovett set up the National Association to promote political education, but it made little headway. Birmingham reformers, led by the

NOT SO *VERY* UNREASONABLE!!! EH?

"Not so very unreasonable, eh?" A cartoon defending Chartism that appeared in *Punch* in 1848. GETTY IMAGES

Quaker philanthropist Joseph Sturge (1793–1859), formed the Complete Suffrage Union to unite middle- and working-class reformers in January 1842, but its petition was rejected in April 1842 by 226 votes to 67. The NCA in effect became Chartism. It arranged for a new Convention, which met in London in April 1842 and a new Petition, which was presented with 3,317,752 signatures on 2 May 1842—and rejected by 287 votes to 49. The mass strategy had again failed, despite better organization and the increased number of signatures which, if genuine, represented a majority of the adult working people of Britain (the movement never really caught on in Ireland) and certainly far outnumbered the official electorate of around one million in 1841. A summer of strikes and violence then spread throughout the industrial districts of the north of England, often led by local Chartists, although the motivation of the strikers was mainly economic. O'Connor made the mistake of associating the NCA leadership with the strikes just at the point when they were beginning to fail. Mass arrests and imprisonment again disrupted the movement, though this time O'Connor escaped jail on a technicality.

This marked the end of Chartism as a mass movement in many parts of the country. As economic conditions improved for the first time since late 1836, and as it became apparent that, far from Chartism being the key to unlock the door to social reform for the working classes, instead the way was open to piecemeal reform without the Charter: the Corn Law, which most Chartists wished to see abolished despite their suspicion of the motives of the factory masters who dominated the Anti–Corn Law League, was repealed in 1846, and the following year the Ten Hour Bill restricted hours of employment in factories. O'Connor turned his mind to another, more peaceful, strategy: a national lottery to raise money to settle the fortunate winners on the land, thus withdrawing surplus labor from the towns and improving conditions there while at the same time giving people the freedom and potential political power that came from holding a small piece of real estate. The Land Plan was an enormous success in maintaining Chartism and carrying it to parts of the country scarcely touched before, although it had little to do with the Charter and produced further divisions among the leadership. Ultimately the legal and financial problems of the Land Company took O'Connor's energies away from the needs of traditional Chartism and weakened his leadership at a critical point during the third and final Chartist crisis in 1848.

The third effort to call a Convention, raise a Petition, and secure the People's Charter began in 1847, when O'Connor was elected MP for Nottingham. This was followed by renewed industrial depression and then outbreaks of revolution in Europe. Serious rioting in Britain, notably in London in March 1848, were followed by a mass meeting on Kennington Common in south London on 10 April 1848, prior to a march on Parliament with the Petition, containing an alleged 5,700,000 signatures. Though both the meeting and the march were illegal, O'Connor negotiated permission to hold the meeting. When the giant Petition reached the House of Commons it was ridiculed, the number of signatures being reduced to "merely" 1,975,476—still twice the electorate—and it was rejected. Parliament was more concerned about the security situation in Ireland, which seemed to be following the Continental path to revolution. The Convention broke up in disagreement over what to do next. Some delegates reconvened in a provocatively named National Assembly; others went back to their local communities to hold mass meetings amid increasing threats of violence. The government struck hard throughout the summer, and mass arrests once more deprived Chartism of its effective leadership. This was the end of Chartism. The leaders emerged from jail into a world that was unwilling to rally to the old cause. The dominance of the NCA, the *Northern Star,* and Feargus O'Connor was broken, and what remained of the movement was fragmented, some seeking an accommodation with moderate reformers, some seeking piecemeal reform or joining single-issue campaigns for temperance or the final repeal of the newspaper stamp.

INFLUENCE OF CHARTISM

The reasons for the failure of Chartism are not hard to find. The initial strategy of the LWMA was unlikely to succeed but it was totally undermined by the mass campaign centered on O'Connor. The only chance for his alternative approach was if the government were genuinely cowed by the threat of numbers. It was not and had the means at its command to suppress what it could not dissuade. The strategy of so-called physical force was a gamble that failed and in failing it destroyed the alternative strategies. O'Connor was an inspiration to his followers but he could brook no rivals and so divided the leadership of the movement. Despite the NCA he was never able to turn mass mobilization from an agitation into an effective organization. Chartism was thus dependent on external factors, such as the state of the economy, and when that improved, and when piecemeal reforms began to be granted, it had no way of sustaining mass support in the face of repeated failure.

Yet the paradox is that Chartism was not a failure. It achieved none of its objectives and may have set some back by its identification of reform with violence, yet among its followers it created a popular political culture that over the next generation was to feed into the lowest levels of local government as democracy was extended—beginning with school boards after 1870. What was of long term significance was not the mass movement of the three peak years of petitioning, but the formation of local associations and "localities" of the NCA, where Chartist men and women lived out their democratic aspirations in the formation of what has been called a "Chartist culture." This often took its inspiration from Protestant nonconformity. None of the religious organizations endorsed Chartism, and the Chartists themselves came from many religious backgrounds—and none—but the traditions of the nonconformist chapel ran deep in many of the working-class communities where Chartism was strong. These traditions—of lay leadership, social meetings for mutual improvement, sermons that became lectures and Bible study that became reading, the *Northern Star*—helped Chartism become the means by which politics were embedded in community life.

Chartism has been claimed by many subsequent movements but it is hard to accept that specific later ideologies have an exclusive right to a Chartist pedigree. Chartism was a working-class movement in the sense that it appealed largely to working people. This is unsurprising given that over four-fifths of the population were wage earners and Chartism had widespread appeal, mainly to those below the top fifth. But Chartism was not the forerunner of *the* working-class movement later embodied in the twentieth-century Labor movement. The language of class was used, but as much by opponents who wished to belittle the Chartists as by the Chartists themselves. The latter more usually used the language of the people, by which they meant both the majority who lacked the vote and those in the voting classes who sympathized with them. Its strategy was to adopt a language that deliberately avoided class. Equally, Chartism was not a socialist movement. Some leaders— James O'Brien (1804–1864) and Ernest Charles Jones (1819–1869), for example—might sometimes use the language of socialist economics but not in a consistent or "modern" sense. Chartists were opposed to the exploitative capitalism of factory masters but they were not anticapitalist as such. The great majority of the factory "proletariat" at this time were women and children; many

workingmen Chartists were small producers still owning some of their own means of production or aspiring to do so. O'Connor's peasant ideal was still close to many hearts.

Chartism was also not the forerunner of anything resembling modern feminism. Although some of its leaders—including William Lovett— favored *universal* suffrage, the program of the Chartists was only for *manhood* suffrage, by which was meant the people as represented through adult males. The language of domesticity and separate spheres was dominant, as women sought through their families those social and economic benefits which it was believed would be brought by the suffrage. Women were part of the early mass movement and local Chartist activities, but they had little place in its formal structures. So long as men and women were equally deprived, the separate issue of individual female enfranchisement was rarely advanced within Chartism.

So Chartism was many of the things that a later century was to find important. It was an agitation that achieved remarkable maturity in its response to the Reform Act of 1832 through a campaign to secure for the ordinary working people of Britain the advantages of democracy against the perceived political influence of the emerging new urban elites of industrialists, merchants, and larger shopkeepers. Despite its failure, Chartism created a political culture that was to shape the semidemocratic dawn in Britain as the franchise was extended at local and then national levels between 1867 and 1918. Though former Chartists were to place themselves in both Liberal and Tory parties—and some were to live long enough to join various socialist or Labor parties—the democratic ethos of Chartism largely contributed to Liberal Britain. But the vitality of Chartist political culture was such that popular politics were never completely subsumed within "popular Liberalism." It maintained instead a watchful and troublesome democratic presence on the progressive fringe of British political life.

See also **Class and Social Relations; Corn Laws, Repeal of; Great Britain; Labor Movements; O'Connor, Feargus; Socialism.**

BIBLIOGRAPHY

Allen, J., and Ashton, O., eds. *Papers for the People: A Study of the Chartist Press*. Rendlesham, U.K., 2005. Essays on aspects of the Chartist press.

Ashton, Owen, Robert Fyson, and Stephen Roberts, eds. *The Chartist Legacy*. Woodbridge, U.K., 1999. Further thematic essays.

Briggs, Asa, ed. *Chartist Studies*. London, 1959. A collection of essays, mainly local studies that stress the economic background to Chartism.

Epstein, James. *The Lion of Freedom: Feargus O'Connor and the Chartist Movement, 1832–1842*. London, 1982. A major attempt to rehabilitate O'Connor as a positive figure in Chartism.

Epstein, James, and Dorothy Thompson, eds. *The Chartist Experience: Studies in Working-Class Radicalism and Culture, 1830–1860*. London, 1982. A collection of thematic and local essays that exemplify the political and cultural approach, in contrast to the Briggs collection, above.

Finn, Margot C. *After Chartism: Class and Nation in English Radical Politics, 1848–1874*. Cambridge, U.K., 1993. Includes an interpretation of later Chartism and the impact of international concerns.

Goodway, David. *London Chartism, 1838–1848*. Cambridge, U.K., 1982. A major study of the key area omitted from earlier regional studies.

Jones, David J. V. *Chartism and the Chartists*. London, 1975. A thematic interpretation that advanced the view of Chartism as a political and cultural movement.

———. *The Last Rising: The Newport Insurrection of 1839*. Oxford, U.K., 1985. A major reassessment.

Jones, Gareth Stedman. *Languages of Class: Studies in English Working Class History, 1832–1982*. Cambridge, U.K., 1983.

Pickering, Paul A. *Chartism and the Chartists in Manchester and Salford*. New York, 1995. An important study of Chartist activity and culture in a key provincial center.

Roberts, Stephen, ed. *The People's Charter: Democratic Agitation in Early Victorian Britain*. London, 2003. Reprints of eight of the more important recent articles on Chartism.

Royle, Edward. *Chartism*. New York, 1980. 3rd ed. 1997. A brief overview and thematic survey with illustrative sources.

Schoyen, Albert Robert. *The Chartist Challenge: A Portrait of George Julian Harney*. London, 1958. Contains a great deal about Chartism, especially its international aspects.

Schwartzkopf, Jutta. *Women in the Chartist Movement*. London, 1991. A feminist perspective.

Taylor, Miles. *Ernest Jones, Chartism, and the Romance of Politics, 1819–1869*. Oxford, U.K., 2003. Reinterprets the former socialist hero of Chartism.

Thompson, Dorothy. *The Chartists: Popular Politics in the Industrial Revolution*. London, 1984. Thematic chapters offering the fullest reinterpretation of Chartism along political and cultural lines.

Thompson, Dorothy, ed. *The Early Chartists*. London, 1971. A collection of sources to challenge the traditional interpretation.

Ward, John Towers. *Chartism*. London, 1973. A chronological survey history of a traditional kind.

EDWARD ROYLE

CHATEAUBRIAND, FRANÇOIS-RENÉ (1768–1848), French statesman and writer.

Soldier, diplomat, statesman, one of the foremost authors of nineteenth-century French literature, initiator of the nineteenth-century genre of travel literature to the Middle East, memorializer and translator of Milton's *Paradise Lost*, François-René Chateaubriand was intimately associated with an age of great upheaval and transformation and may be considered as representative of the currents of thoughts and sentiments of his time. The incidents of his life are all interwoven with politics and the tremendous changes brought about by the French Revolution and the First Empire. His statement reflects accurately his own plight and that of his generation: "I found myself between two centuries like at the meeting of two rivers; I dived in their troubled waters getting away with regrets from the old shore on which I was born and swimming with hope toward the unknown shore where the new generations were landing." ("Preface testamentaire," *Mémoires d'outre-tombe*, p. 1–6).

Chateaubriand was born in Saint-Malo on 4 September 1768, the youngest son of René Auguste de Chateaubriand, Count of Combourg, Brittany, and Pauline Suzanne de Bédée. He studied in the boarding school of Dol, later in the College of Dinars before returning to the family home. Before his father's death on 6 September 1786, René received a commission of Second Lieutenant in the Regiment of Navarre in Cambrai, in Northern France. During this period he spent time in Paris, witnessing the fall of the Bastille and the subsequent unrest as well as the formation of the National Assembly in Paris. He foresaw the fall of the monarchy. He supported some republican ideas, but disliked the mob violence. In January 1791 he prepared his departure for the United States. Chateaubriand left Saint-Malo on 8 April 1791 on the *Saint Pierre,* a ship chartered by the Saint-Sulpice Order to transport French seminarians to Baltimore, Maryland. The ship reached Baltimore on 19 July 1791.

Chateaubriand left immediately for Philadelphia, eager to meet President George Washington (1732–1799). He was impressed by Washington's simplicity and courtesy. Chateaubriand called the president "a citizen soldier, liberator of a world" (*Mémoire d'outre-tombe,* p. 280). From Philadelphia, Chateaubriand visited New York; Boston; Lexington, Massachusetts; Albany; and Niagara Falls. He claimed to have visited the Carolinas and Florida and to have followed the Mississippi as far as the Natchez country. The most important element of his journey was that he collected material for *Atala* (1801) and *Les Natchez* (1826).

After the arrest of King Louis XVI (r. 1774–1792) in his attempt to escape France, Chateaubriand decided to return to France in January 1792. Upon his return, he married his sister's friend, Céleste Buisson de la Vigne (1774–1847), joined the Émigrés' Army of the Princes, composed mainly of nobles, and participated in the brief campaign against the French revolutionary army. At the siege of Thionville he was wounded and contracted smallpox. Discharged from the Émigrés' Army, he crossed Belgium on foot, finally reaching the port of Ostende, where he was put aboard a ship. He arrived in Jersey Island, where his uncle's family nursed him back to health. Then he left for London. He joined the emigrant colony, surviving by doing translations and teaching French, and published his first work: *Essai historique, politique et moral sur les révolutions anciennes et modernes, considérées dans leurs rapports avec la révolution française (Historical, Political, and Moral Essay on Revolutions, Ancient and Modern)* in March 1797, began working on a translation of John Milton's (1608–1674) *Paradise Lost,* and finished *Les Natchez* and *Atala.*

Chateaubriand returned to France on 6 May 1801. *Le génie du Christianisme* (*The Genius of Christianity*) was published in 1802. Napoleon I (r. 1804–1814/15) saw the potential of Chateaubriand's book about Christianity as a tool for reconciling his government to Rome and for encourging the acceptance by the French people of the Concordat between Napoleon and Pope Pius VII (r. 1800–1823) on 8 April 1801. When Napoleon appointed Chateaubriand's uncle, Cardinal Fesch, ambassador in Rome, Chateaubriand became secretary of the embassy. However, he was not happy in this position and his rapport with the ambassador was tense. He wished also to return to Paris. Napoleon assuaged him by naming him consul to the Canton of Valais in Switzerland but Chateaubriand never assumed his new position. Horrified by the execution of the Duc d'Enghien (Louis-Antoine-Henri Condé, 1772–1804), the last of the Bourbon-Condé royal princes, on 21 March 1804, he resigned the next day and never served in Napoleon's regime again.

On the advice of his wife, Chateaubriand prepared his voyage to the Middle East. On 13 July 1806 he left Paris. The account of the voyage was published as *L'Itinéraire de Paris à Jérusalem* (1811; Itinerary from Paris to Jerusalem), which became the nineteenth-century model for nearly all the French travelers to the region.

After the restoration of the monarchy in 1815 Chateaubriand served Louis XVIII (r. 1814–1815, 1815–1824) as ambassador to Berlin (1821–1822) and as ambassador to Great Britain (1822), and then became a member of the French delegation to the Congress of Verona held in October 1822. Composed of delegates from Russia, Prussia, France, Austria, and Great Britain, the congress was concerned about the Spanish situation. Chateaubriand played an important role in deciding in favor of a French military intervention. The congress authorized France to send troops. In 1824 Ferdinand VII (r. 1808, 1814–1833) was restored to the throne of Spain until his death.

Chateaubriand was named minister of foreign affairs in January 1823; in spite of the success of the Spanish expedition he was dismissed in 1824. In 1827 the journal of his early travels in the New

World was published under the title *Voyage en Amérique* (*Travels in America*). In 1828 King Charles X (r. 1824–1830) appointed him ambassador to Rome, where after the death of Leo XII (r. 1760–1829), he began activities to promote the election of a pope favorable to French interests. Indeed, the new pope, Pius VIII (r. 1829–1830), was inclined toward France. In 1829, upon Chateaubriand's return to France, he expected to receive another cabinet position, but when Auguste-Jules-Armand-Marie Polignac (1780–1847), an antiliberal, became prime minister, Chateaubriand resigned his ambassadorship; after the abdication of Charles X in July 1830, he refused to swear allegiance to Louis-Philippe (r. 1830–1848) and resigned from the house of peers. He continued to work on his memoirs from 1833 to 1841. In 1836 he published his *Essai sur la littérature anglaise* (Essay on English literature) and a French translation of *Paradise Lost*. In 1844 he published, supposedly as a penance imposed by his confessor, *La Vie de Rancé* (Life of Rancé), a meditative biography of Armand-Jean Rancé (1626–1700) the founder of the Trappist Order. Chateaubriand had sold the rights to his memoirs to a corporation in exchange for a yearly pension, but in 1844 Émile de Girardin (1806–1881), director of the leading Parisian newspaper *La Presse*, bought the rights to publish the memoirs in his paper before their publication as a book.

Chateaubriand decided to rewrite certain portions of his memoirs, which he felt were too sensitive for publication in a newspaper serial; in 1847 his memoirs were published. His wife, Céleste, died on 22 February 1847. On 4 July 1848, Chateaubriand died in his apartment on the rue du Bac in Paris, having witnessed the overthrow of Louis-Philippe and the birth of the Second Republic. He is buried on a small island, the Grand Bé, in the bay of Saint-Malo.

In his memoirs Chateaubriand described himself as "a traveler, soldier, poet, publicist, it is among forests that I have sung the forest, aboard ships that I have depicted the sea, in camp that I have spoken of arms, in exile that I have learnt to know exile, in courts, in affairs of the state, in Parliament that I have studied princes, politics, law, and history." (Preface testamentaire, *Mémoires d'outre-tombe*, p. 4).

As a writer, Chateaubriand was the paramount example of the French Romantic school, the "great Sachem of Romanticism" as Théophile Gautier (1811–1872) put it. His novellas *Atala* and *René* embody the ethos and pathos of Romantic emphasis on the self, the emotions, and rapport with nature.

As a traveller, Chateaubriand was one of the foremost interpreters of America to the European public, as well as a forerunner of nineteenth-century Orientalism and the vogue of travel to the Middle East. His *Itinéraire de Paris à Jérusalem* awakened new ideas about the Middle East.

As a statesman and a man of letters, Chateaubriand best exemplified the committed writer actively engaged in politics. His pamphlet *De Buonaparte et des Bourbons et de la nécessité de se rallier à nos Princes légitimes pour le bonheur de la France et celui de l'Europe* (1814; Of Bonaparte, the Bourbons and the necessity of rallying round our legitimate princes for the happiness of France and of Europe) was "worth a hundred thousand men" in the words of Louis XVIII. Chateaubriand's *De la monarchie selon la charte* (1816; Monarchy according to the Charter) analyzes the nature of representative government and attempts to reconcile the Bourbon dynasty with constitutional government and the nation with the old dynasty. As a statesman and a writer, Chateaubriand saw his main task as effecting reconciliation between the past and the future, between monarchy and democracy, between France and the Bourbons. For him, the constitutional monarchy was the ideal form of government; his political creed was "King, Religion, Liberty." He felt strongly that opposition to governmental policies restricting freedom was not only legitimate but also necessary to a viable constitutional monarchy. In the house of peers, he denounced with eloquence the censorship of the press, believing the periodical press to be an immense force that cannot be stifled by violence and censorship.

It cannot be denied that there appears a certain incoherence in Chateaubriand's political attitude during the Restoration. Personal likes and dislikes had much to do with his conduct; nevertheless, he always strove in his public position for the greatness of France and its glory, even when doing so resulted in personal and financial losses. In his later years' writings, he announced the prevalence of democracy, the constant strife of the individual against the power of the state, foreseeing that progress is also crisis, that history is never finished. Chateaubriand merits his place as a major innovative writer and thinker in nineteenth-century French literature and history.

See also **France; Napoleon; Romanticism.**

BIBLIOGRAPHY

Primary Sources

Chateaubriand, François- René. *Atala/René.* Translated by Irvin Putter. Berkeley, Calif., 1952. Has an excellent introduction, a very readable text, and notes clarifying the text, but no bibliography.

———. *Chateaubriand's* Travels in America. Translated by Richard Switzer. Lexington, Ky., 1969. Introduction deals with the actual travel and the publication of the voyage in 1826.

———. *Genius of Christianity.* Translated by Charles I. White. Albuquerque, N.M., 1985.

———. *Memoirs of Chateaubriand.* Selected and translated by Robert Baldick. New York, 1961. An abridged version of Chateaubriand's masterpiece, *Mémoires d'outre-tombe*; the translation is of good quality and this book is an excellent starting point for a student.

Secondary Sources

Dubé, Pierre, and Ann Dubé. *Bibliographie de la critique sur François-René de Chateaubriand.* Paris, 1988. A bibliography of 5,000 entries dealing with Chateaubriand and his family, his correspondence, the literature and culture of his time, theses, and critical books and articles.

Evans, Joan. *Chateaubriand: A Biography.* 1939.

Lynes, Jr., Carlos. *Chateaubriand as a Critic of French Literature.* New York, 1973. A scholarly study of Chateaubriand's affinity for Classicism in French literature. Faithful to the age of Louis XIV.

Maurois, André. *Chateaubriand, Poet, Statesman, Lover.* Translated by Vera Fraser. New York and London, 1938. An enjoyable general biography by one of the best-known French biographers detailing Chateaubriand's achievement in literature, politics, and love.

Painter, George D. *Chateaubriand: A Biography.* Vol. 1: *The Longed-for Tempests.* New York, 1978. An outstanding work that presents Chateaubriand in his daily life, describing his private personality and lived experiences in detail.

Porter, Charles A. *Chateaubriand: Composition, Imagination, and Poetry.* Saratoga, Calif., 1978. Study of Cha-teaubriand's style, focusing on stylistic traits of contrast and parallelism with emphasis placed on images.

Sieburg, Friedrich. *Chateaubriand.* Translated by Violet M. MacDonald. New York, 1962. A lucid analysis of the politics of the Restoration; Chateaubriand's political career discussed with balance and keen judgment.

Switzer, Richard. *Chateaubriand.* New York, 1971. A very readable work presenting all aspects of Chateaubriand's life and works with a focus on Chateaubriand's America.

Switzer, Richard, ed. *Chateaubriand Today.* Madison, Wisc., 1970. A collection of essays in French and English by various critics on the many aspects of Chateaubriand's life and writings.

FRANS C. AMELINCKX

CHEKHOV, ANTON (1860–1904), Russian playwright and short story writer.

Anton Pavlovich Chekhov was born in Taganrog, Russia, on 29 January (17 January, old style) 1860, the grandson of an emancipated serf. His father failed as owner of a small shop; to escape his creditors, he fled to Moscow. Chekhov was left on his own to finish school. He did so brilliantly and won a scholarship to medical school. While still a student, he began publishing (under one or another of several pseudonyms) comic sketches for popular journals in Moscow and St. Petersburg. He did not at this early stage perceive his writing as "literature." As the major provider for his parents and siblings, he wrote simply to supplement his income as a doctor.

From 1880 on, Chekhov wrote numberless jokes, gossip pieces, parodies, and humorous anecdotes for such rags as *Dragonfly* and the weekly magazine *Fragments*. For the next five years his publications (with the exception of two rather unremarkable novel-length pieces) consisted of short, pointed vignettes, pithy and funny, but sometimes with a tinge of the melancholy that would become more apparent in his later work.

In 1885 (after finishing his medical degree) Chekhov visited St. Petersburg, where he was received with deep admiration by some of the most respected names in Russian literature. Chekhov was amazed and chastened by this turn, and he began to write longer and more carefully crafted stories. These were not suitable for the ephemeral publications where his previous work had appeared. But he became a friend of Alexei Suvorin, the powerful and wealthy publisher of the leading Russian daily newspaper, *New Times*. Chekhov's longer and more serious works became a staple of Suvorin's vast publishing empire, to the mutual advantage of both men.

Chekhov now began writing plays: *Ivanov,* a study of that archetypal creature, the Russian superfluous man, was successfully produced in 1887 and 1889. *The Wood Demon* had less success when staged in 1888 but was later reworked into one of Chekhov's late masterpieces, *Uncle Vanya* (1899). In this new phase of his career Chekhov also began publishing longer prose works, such as "The Steppe" (1888), which brought him attention in the more serious journals of the day. The stories of this period are marked by close attention to the natural landscape and detailed descriptions of people in crisis. In "Name-Day Party" (1888) he describes a woman undergoing a miscarriage, while in "A Dreary Story" (1889) a distinguished professor is brought low by old age as he approaches death. These stories reflect Chekhov's experience as a practicing physician and have the form of brilliant case histories.

By this time Chekhov defined himself as a writer, rather than a doctor, but not without some guilt. In the great tradition of Russian writers who felt they owed a debt to their society, Chekhov in 1890 made a journey across Siberia to the Pacific island of Sakhalin, where he applied his diagnostic eye and clinical descriptive skills to describing the community of native tribes and Russian convicts who inhabited the island (published as *The Island of Sakhalin* in 1893). He continued to treat peasants on his estate, and was active in famine relief. His high morals attracted him to Leo Tolstoy in the late 1880s, but by 1890 Chekhov became disillusioned with the religious aspect of Tolstoy's system. Chekhov, a believer in the Enlightenment and a much-traveled cosmopolitan, regarded Tolstoy's contempt for medical science as a sign of dangerous ignorance.

Chekhov's insistence on the clinical truth can be painful: Nikolai Stepanovich, the hero of "A Dreary Story," forces his beloved ward, an aspiring actress, to admit finally that she has no talent. And then, in a characteristic Chekhovian stroke, the old man says to Katya, "Let's go to lunch." The revelation of secret weaknesses—the human, all too human, aspect of Chekhov's best stories—results from his pitiless eye and his unsentimental recognition of the power of the quotidian.

In 1899 Chekhov prepared a complete edition of his works, entirely rewriting some of the earlier stories. But his last years were primarily occupied with his activity in the theater. The first performance of *The Seagull* in 1896 had been a failure. The cast and audience simply were not prepared for the novelty of Chekhov's revolutionary drama of indirect action, in which most of the action occurs offstage. But two years later Chekhov started his epochal collaboration with Konstantin Stanislavsky's Moscow Art Theater (MAT), and a new chapter in the history of European drama began. The 1898 MAT production of *The Seagull* was a huge success, as was the 1899 production of *Uncle Vanya,* destined to become a staple in theaters all over the world. *Three Sisters,* produced in 1901, once again illustrated Chekhov's ability to find tragedy and high drama in the subtlest psychological effects. Chekhov's last play, *The Cherry Orchard,* was first performed on his final birthday, 29 January 1904. A profound historical commentary on changes in Russian society, it is as well an exquisite, if muted, comedy.

During his last years, Chekhov battled with tuberculosis. He found some happiness, nevertheless, in his magnificent house overseeing Yalta harbor and in his marriage to the MAT actress Olga Knipper. He died at the spa in Badenweiler, Germany, on 15 July (2 July, old style) 1904. In a final irony (that he would have appreciated), his body was conveyed back to Russia in a special railroad car used to transport oysters.

See also **Dostoyevsky, Fyodor; Gogol, Nikolai; Ibsen, Henrik; Meyerhold, Vsevelod; Tolstoy, Leo; Turgenev, Ivan.**

BIBLIOGRAPHY

Bloom, Harold, ed. *Anton Chekhov.* Philadelphia, 2003.

Chudakov, A. P. *Chekhov's Poetics.* Translated by Edwina Jannie Cruise and Donald Dragt. Ann Arbor, Mich., 1983.

Finke, Michael C. *Seeing Chekhov: Life and Art.* Ithaca, N.Y., 2005.

Gilman, Richard. *Chekhov's Plays: An Opening into Eternity.* New Haven, Conn., 1995.

Gottlieb, Vera, and Paul Allain, eds. *The Cambridge Companion to Chekhov.* Cambridge, U.K., 2000.

Johnson, Ronald L. *Anton Chekhov: A Study of the Short Fiction.* New York, 1993.

Magarshack, David. *Chekhov, the Dramatist.* New York, 1960.

Malcolm, Janet. *Reading Chekhov: A Critical Journey.* New York, 2001.

Rayfield, Donald. *Chekhov: The Evolution of His Art.* New York, 1975.

Senelick, Laurence. *Anton Chekhov.* London, 1985.

MICHAEL HOLQUIST

CHEMISTRY.

CHEMISTRY. A mature discipline by the late eighteenth century, chemistry had thrown off the taint of both manual labor and alchemy; it featured a corps of practitioners, specialized journals, practical techniques and theoretical themes, and growing prestige; and it was thoroughly modernized by the revolutionary transformation that centered on the French chemist Antoine-Laurent Lavoisier (1743–1794). Led until the mid-nineteenth century by Jöns Jakob Berzelius (1779–1848) of Sweden, chemistry as a field of study and research increased in coherence and productivity. Chemical industry had engaged chemists throughout the century, but sustained and mutually reinforcing interactions of science and industry appeared only after midcentury. As World War I approached, reinterpretations issuing from physics as well as forces of fragmentation threatened the integrity of chemistry; but it resisted both reduction to physics and piecemeal assimilation to neighboring fields.

CONSOLIDATION OF A FIELD

The chemical revolution replaced the phlogiston theory—that combustion and the formation of metallic "calces" (oxides) were losses of phlogiston—with the oxygen theory—that they were additions of oxygen; perfected a new nomenclature that designated compounds by composition; systematized pneumatic chemistry (which had revealed that air is plural and that airs could enter into chemical combination); explained, with the caloric theory of heat, changes in states of aggregation; accommodated the study of neutral salts, which had been dominant in prior practice; and established the "balance sheet method"—vital for pneumatic chemistry—that followed chemicals gravimetrically through reactions. Lavoisier's textbook, *Traité élémentaire de chimie* (1789; Elements of chemistry), epitomized these innovations.

Berzelius enlarged this synthesis with two further novelties: the chemical atomic theory, first articulated in England by John Dalton (1766–1844) and developed further by Berzelius; and the chemical effects of the electrical battery, devised in 1800 by the Italian Alessandro Volta (1745–1827). The atomic theory enhanced emergent notions of "stoichiometry" (the laws of chemical combination, especially definite and multiple proportions) and suggested that the law of definite proportions distinguishes compounds from mixtures. Berzelius undertook a vast project of chemical analysis that met new standards of precision. His goal: to distinguish compounds from mixtures and analyze all natural and artificial compounds. Both Berzelius and Humphry Davy (1778–1829) of England showed that the battery could decompose substances into electrically opposing constituents (e.g., salts into acids and bases). Berzelius reconceived inorganic chemistry by (1) according bases—formerly seen as passive substrates for coagulation of acids—positive properties, opposite to those of acids; and (2) anticipating that any compound, saline or not, consisted of paired, electrically opposing components. He thus characterized all compounds both quantitatively and qualitatively (by determining the constituents stoichiometrically and characterizing them electrochemically). Berzelius revised Lavoisier's nomenclature to suit, replacing its French with Latin paradigms; and he devised the still-used symbols of composition (one- or two-letter abbreviations for the elements and superscripts—later changed to subscripts—for the numbers of atoms). The culmination of his work, comparable to Lavoisier's *Traité,* lay in his *Essai sur la théorie des proportions chimiques* (1819; Essay on the theory of chemical proportions) and his atomic weight tables of 1826.

This "electrochemical dualism" guided the next generation of chemists. Berzelius himself pursued it in mineralogy, a Swedish and German antecedent of academic chemistry, and in the nascent organic chemistry (of plant and animal substances). In mineralogy, Berzelius in 1814 showed that silica, traditionally thought a base, was an acid and that minerals were complex silicates; and his student Eilhard Mitscherlich (1794–1863) in 1818 discovered isomorphism, in which minerals preserve their crystal forms despite indefinite substitutions of some elements by chemically related ones. With minerals thus subjected to dualism, Berzelius boosted the subdiscipline of crystal chemistry. In organic chemistry, his work was informed by the claim of Lavoisier and his colleague Claude-Louis Berthollet (1748–1822) that organic compounds consist chiefly of carbon, hydrogen, oxygen, and nitrogen; by Lavoisier's belief that groupings of these elements (organic radicals) behaved like individual elements; and by Berzelius's own conclusion that organic matter occurred in mixtures of similar compounds. The task was therefore to separate distinct compounds from generic mixtures, analyze them, and interpret their composition dualistically. By 1814 Berzelius exemplified this approach, having performed among the first precise analyses of organic compounds. Thus conceived, organic chemistry dominated the discipline from the 1830s.

INSTITUTIONALIZATION: ACADEMICS AND INDUSTRY

From 1800, chemistry was increasingly institutionalized academically. In Sweden, posts in governmental laboratories and mining and metallurgical enterprises were complemented with professorial positions, the first Swedish chair in chemistry appearing at Uppsala University in 1750. Berzelius, a medical graduate, held a post at the Karolinska (medical) Institute in Stockholm. In Britain, academics grew dominant after midcentury. In France, professorial posts appeared in institutions of applied science (schools or faculties of medicine, pharmacy, agriculture, mining, and engineering), where the distinction between pure and applied science encouraged teaching of theoretical chemistry and enhanced its social

value. In Germany, institutionalization descended from pharmacy, especially the institute for chemical education and research-training founded in 1826, initially as a pharmacy school, by Justus von Liebig (1803–1873) at the University of Giessen and perpetuated by his students, notably August Wilhelm von Hofmann (1818–1892), in London and Berlin. It became the model for the proliferating German research institutes in natural sciences, the most prominent sites for chemical education and research-training in the nineteenth century. The laboratory and related resources commanded by German professors of chemistry fostered the growth and disciplinary identity of the field.

In the first half of the century, heavy chemical industry—especially production of "soda" (sodium carbonate) from sea salt by the Leblanc process, the lead-chamber process to produce sulfuric acid and its improvement by the Gay-Lussac tower, and the use of chlorine products in bleaching—involved inventors, entrepreneurs, and chemists, but no characteristic patterns dominated their relations.

CONTROVERSIES: ATOMISM AND ORGANIC COMPOSITION

Disagreements persisted about the atomic theory and organic composition. Though distinct, in their resolution these questions were linked. Most chemists, seeing atoms as hypothetical, insisted on empirical "equivalent weights," eschewed determining the supposed actual weights and formulas, and relied on conventions. The diversity of these conventions, however, hindered communication and obscured or distorted relationships among substances. In inorganic chemistry, theoretical commitments and experimental anomalies hindered the reform of atomic weights and formulas; but problems in organic chemistry fostered it. Dualism was undermined by the discovery of substitution—in which electronegative chlorine, for example, could replace electropositive hydrogen with little change in properties—and by other evidence that organic radicals were mutable. Berzelius insisted that inorganic chemistry remain the template for organic; younger chemists demanded the reverse. Charles-Frédéric Gerhardt (1816–1856) and Auguste Laurent (1807–1853) of France

Woodcut showing the laboratory of Justus von Liebig in Giessen, 1845. ©BETTMANN/CORBIS

portrayed the diverse reactions of organic compounds as substitutions of atoms by radicals in simple, inorganic types, and they founded this "type" theory on reforms of atomic weights and formulas. Their successors, especially Alexander Williamson (1824–1904) of Britain, Hofmann, and Friedrich August Kekule von Stradonitz (1829–1896) of Germany, proposed a new, structural theory of organic chemistry, relying on the reforms of Gerhardt and Laurent and exploiting the newly conceived property of valence to interpret chemical combination. To foster consensus on atomic weights, structural chemists called the first international chemical congress, at Karlsruhe, in 1860. The persuasive analysis of atomic weights presented there by the Italian Stanislao Cannizzaro (1826–1910) encouraged gradual agreement. Organic chemistry now flourished. Jacobus Henricus van't Hoff (1852–1911) of Holland and Joseph-Achille Le Bel (1847–1930) of France pioneered the analysis of the spatial arrangements of atoms in compounds, and others synthesized many new substances.

Chemistry also spawned additional subdisciplines. Biochemistry (initially, "physiological chemistry"), emerging from both chemistry and physiology, was lodged in German physiology institutes. Physical chemistry, emergent from disparate strands, focused on solutions, thermodynamics, electrochemistry, and spectroscopy. Two of its leaders, Wilhelm Ostwald (1853–1932) and van't Hoff, founded its first journal, *Zeitschrift für physikalische Chemie* (1887; Journal of physical chemistry). The field flourished in Germany and after 1900 in the United States. Inorganic chemistry, long overshadowed by organic, re-emerged following the creation (in 1869) by the Russian chemist Dmitri Mendeleyev (1834–1907) of the periodic table, itself resting on the post-Karlsruhe consensus; and coordination chemistry, created in the 1890s largely by Alfred Werner (1866–1919) of Germany.

From the 1850s, artificial dyestuffs and their control and synthesis by structural organic chemists transformed both chemical industry and academic chemistry. Firms proliferated in Britain and France, but from about 1870, German firms, benefiting from the expertise of academic chemists and new patterns of interaction with them, grew dominant. They created industrial research laboratories staffed by academically trained chemists; and they diversified into fine chemicals, pharmaceuticals, and agricultural chemicals. Their near monopolies often lasted until the end of World War II.

RELATIONS WITH PHYSICS AND OTHER FIELDS

Physics had long interacted episodically with chemistry, but the advent of physical chemistry announced increasing intrusions. The discovery of the electron in 1897 by the English physicist Joseph John Thomson (1856–1940) and the demonstration by the New Zealand-born British physicist Ernest Rutherford (1871–1937) that atomic mass is concentrated in the nucleus led to new theories of valence on the part of the American academic physical chemists Gilbert N. Lewis (1875–1946) and Irving Langmuir (1881–1957), who found in the electron pair the basis of the chemical bond. Physicists' studies of atomic structure now distinguished the elements by atomic number, representing the positive charge on the nucleus, rather than by atomic weight, and permitted the accommodation of isotopes into the periodic table. After World War I, quantum mechanics transformed interpretations of chemical bonds and molecular structure. So profound have been the influence of physics and of the proliferating chemical subdisciplines, interdisciplinary interactions, and practical applications of chemistry, that some analysts regard the field as having lost its core identity in the twentieth century; others hold that the theoretically driven questions and the persistent importance of laboratory techniques, departmental structures, and teaching commitments of the professoriate have preserved the integrity of the field.

See also Education; Science and Technology.

BIBLIOGRAPHY

Bensaude-Vincent, Bernadette, and Isabelle Stengers. *A History of Chemistry.* Translated by Deborah van Dam. Cambridge, Mass., and London, 1996.

Knight, David, and Helge Kragh. *The Making of the Chemist: The Social History of Chemistry in Europe, 1789–1914.* Cambridge, U.K., 1998.

Levere, Trevor H. *Transforming Matter: A History of Chemistry from Alchemy to the Buckyball.* Baltimore, Md., 2001.

Melhado, Evan M., and Tore Frängsmyr, eds. *Enlightenment Science in the Romantic Era: The Chemistry of Berzelius and Its Cultural Setting.* New York, 1992. Reprint, New York, 2003.

Travis, Anthony S. *The Rainbow Makers: The Origins of the Synthetic Dyestuffs Industry in Western Europe.* Bethlehem, Pa., 1993.

EVAN M. MELHADO

CHILDHOOD AND CHILDREN.

"Christopher Columbus only discovered America. I discovered the child!" proclaimed the French writer Victor Hugo (1802–1885). Hugo was hardly the first author to make such a "discovery," but he was certainly prominent among those Romantic poets who did much to arouse an interest in childhood during the nineteenth century. The period produced a torrent of paintings, poems, and novels featuring children; advice manuals on child rearing; childhood reminiscences by famous literary figures; scientific studies of human development; polemical works on child welfare; and literature specially written for the young. Meanwhile political elites in Europe came to realize that children embodied the future of their societies, and so took steps to improve their health, education, and moral welfare. All this attention was not an unmixed blessing for children: attitudes toward them remained ambivalent, and historians have talked of a "colonization" of childhood by adults through schools and other welfare institutions.

IDEAS ON CHILDHOOD

The vast majority of people in a traditional agrarian society, as much of Europe remained before 1914, had a relatively "short" childhood. They went through infancy, under the supervision of their mothers and other female caregivers, until somewhere between the ages of four and seven. After that, they gradually melted into the adult labor force as they worked around the house, on farms, and in workshops, according to their physical strength and stamina. This may help to explain why for centuries contemporary scholars found little to interest them

Fritz Pauk, born in 1888 in the German town of Lippe, describes life as a farm servant aged ten.

During the summer I had to get up at three-thirty in the morning. First there were twenty-five to thirty pigs to be fed, and afterwards fifty sheep to be taken care of. It was six o'clock by the time all that was done, and time for breakfast. Every morning there were coarse ground oats with milk and bread crumbs. You ate with a wooden spoon. School began at eight o'clock, but I had an hour-and-a-half's walk to get there. Still I was happy to go because it meant a relief from the heavy work at the farm. School was already over at ten o'clock. Everyone ran back home. If the farmer had something for me to do, I didn't go to school at all. If the teacher asked why you hadn't come, you only needed to say that the farmer had work for you. That took care of it. There wasn't really much to learn in the little village school. Most of the time was devoted to the catechism and innumerable Bible passages.

Source: Alfred Kelly, trans. and ed., *The German Worker: Working-Class Autobiographies from the Age of Industrialization* (Berkeley, Calif., 1987), 402.

in this stage of life. However, from the seventeenth century onward, there emerged in elite circles the idea that young people needed an extended period of "quarantine" from the corrupt and dangerous world of adults. For a minority of upper- and middle-class boys in particular, several years attending school brought a "long" childhood. Reactions to this varied: former English public schoolboys tended to look back with nostalgia to their time at school, as in the case of Thomas Hughes with his *Tom Brown's School Days* (1857), while their French counterparts often developed a fierce hatred for their *lycée*. Either way, the increasing numbers of young males delaying their entry into the labor force paved the way for the supposed "discovery" of adolescence around 1900. This invariably involved a "second birth" with puberty, and the idea, now commonplace in Western culture, that the period running from the age of fourteen to the mid-twenties is one of "storm and stress." It only remained for the child-study movement, particularly active in Germany, to attempt to discover the laws of normal

child development. Psychologists and physiologists began in the early twentieth century to divide infancy, childhood, and adolescence into increasingly fine phases.

Associated with a long and sheltered childhood was the notion of childhood innocence. The sociologist Chris Jenks has drawn attention to the contrasting images of the evil "Dionysian" child and the sunny, poetic "Apollonian" child in Western civilization. The eighteenth-century Enlightenment and the later Romantic movement gave the latter a huge boost. The Romantics asserted that the original innocence of childhood involves a sense of wonder, an intensity of experience, and a spiritual wisdom lacking in the adult. The English poet William Wordsworth's *Ode, Intimations of Immortality from Recollections of Early Childhood* (1807) reverberated down the nineteenth century. His line "Heaven lies about us in our infancy" was repeatedly quoted, plagiarized, and adapted by later writers. At the same period the German painter Philipp Otto Runge provided a compelling image of juvenile vitality with his *Hülsenbeck Children* (1805–1806). The logical corollary of this stance was some form of child-centered education, and measures to protect the young from the realities of the adult world, such as the need to earn a living or the experience of sexual relations. However, the alternative vision, of children tainted with original sin, was also of some influence, notably among devout Christians. The English evangelical writer Mrs. Sherwood (1775–1851) thundered, "All children are by nature evil, and while they have none but the natural evil principle to guide them, pious and prudent parents must check their naughty passions in any way they have in their power" (Darton, p. 169). The logical outcome of this conception was a strict regime of child rearing, and principles of authority and respect in education.

FROM WORK TO SCHOOL

A slow but inexorable change affecting most children in Europe during the nineteenth century was a shift from work on the land or in the workshops to formal education in the school system. Why this occurred remains a matter of some controversy among historians. The first historians to investigate child labor usually highlighted the role of factory

The Hulsenbeck Children, 1806. Painting by Philipp Otto Runge. Romantic painter Runge provides a compelling portrait of youthful vitality. HAMBURG KUNSTHALLE, HAMBURG, GERMANY/BRIDGEMAN ART LIBRARY

legislation, with heroic figures such as Anthony Ashley Cooper (1801–1885), known as Lord Ashley (later Lord Shaftesbury), in England or enlightened textile magnates from Alsace in France campaigning against "exploitation" in the factories. From this perspective, what counted was effective legislation, such as Althorp's Act of 1833 in England, and similar laws around 1840 in Prussia and France. However, other historians countered that it was technical progress and rising real wages during the latter half of the nineteenth century rather than state intervention that encouraged the

withdrawal of children from industrial employment. There is also the assertion that compulsory school attendance was the decisive influence on this withdrawal in the end, since it was easier to enforce than factory legislation.

Much of the work done by children was in fact casual and undemanding. Although they often started to help their parents around the age of six or seven, many jobs on the land and in the towns required more strength than a child could muster. On small, family farms, for example, both boys

The Children of the Factory. Engraving, France, 1842. Depictions of children working under harsh conditions helped spur movements for the curtailment of child labor during the nineteenth century. BIBLIOTHÈQUE DES ARTS DECORATIFS, PARIS, FRANCE/BRIDGEMAN ART LIBRARY/ARCHIVES CHARMET

and girls confined themselves to simple but time-consuming tasks such as looking after younger brothers and sisters, fetching water, picking stones, scaring birds, and "minding" a few cattle, pigs, or sheep. Such work in agriculture, the handicraft trades, and the service sector remained uncontroversial during the nineteenth century. Around the farms, the practice of finding little jobs for children before and after schooling continued unobtrusively throughout the nineteenth century.

As for the children who worked in the proto-industrial workshops of the countryside—the factories and the urban "sweatshops"—they were most in evidence in those countries that started early on the path to industrialization, notably Britain, Belgium, France, and the western parts of Prussia. Factory children were always a minority among

child workers, and were concentrated in a few industries, particularly textiles. In textiles, some started work as early as seven or eight years, but most waited until they were ten or twelve. This would be later if they were in a heavy industry like iron and steel. Most children acted as assistants to adult workers, for example, mending broken threads for mule-spinners, winding bobbins for weavers, and operating ventilation doors for miners. How grim their working conditions were is open to question. Nonetheless, children in industry did work more regularly through the year than their peers, endured longer hours, and labored more intensively.

Efforts to compel children to attend school gained momentum at the beginning of the nineteenth century. Stung by defeat at Jena in 1806, Karl Wilhelm von Humboldt (1767–1835) and his successors in the Prussian administration planned a system of primary, secondary, and higher education. By the 1830s as many as 80 percent of children aged six to fourteen were attending elementary schools in Prussia. Britain and France were slower to act, though in the 1880s both made primary education free and compulsory. Contrary to accusations made by contemporaries, parents and children in peasant and working-class households were not necessarily hostile to the schools and the literate culture they promoted. Basic literacy might help in a trade or in a bid to move up the social scale. However, there was a greater incentive to acquire it in an industrial and commercial society than in an agrarian one: in 1897 no less than 87 percent of females and 71 percent of males in the Russian Empire were illiterate. In addition, nineteenth-century education systems were riven with inequalities, according to social background, gender, and region. During the 1820s conservative Prussians like Ludolf von Beckedorff (1778–1858) called for schools to support orders or estates rather than "artificial equality." Elementary schools in the nineteenth century curbed the freedom of children to mix in their own society, taught the poor to "know their place," and all too often relied on rote learning, backed up with fierce corporal punishment.

HAPPY FAMILIES?

A number of historians have identified the eighteenth century as a turning point in parent-child relations. They contrast the indifference of parents, or more specifically mothers, to the development and happiness of their offspring in earlier periods, with the attention lavished on the health and education of the young during the nineteenth and twentieth centuries. They also identify the well-off middle classes as the innovators in this sphere, leaving an often dismal image of family life among the poor. A more plausible interpretation of the evidence suggests a strong element of continuity in the long term, with parents always trying to do their best for sons and daughters. On the surface, a number of child-rearing practices that drew the fire of reformers appeared to reveal widespread negligence among parents until the end of the nineteenth century. The large majority of mothers in the past breast-fed their own children, but those in aristocratic circles, and those involved in small businesses in countries such as France and

Italy, routinely sent their newborn infants out to a wet-nurse. This abruptly separated mother and child, but arguably it allowed those dependent on help from their wives, such as silk-weavers in Lyon and Milan, to remain solvent. Families in some countries also abandoned infants on a large scale: in St. Petersburg during the 1830s and 1840s the equivalent of between a third and a half of all babies born in the city ended up in a foundling hospital, in Milan somewhere between 30 and 40 percent. This seemingly heartless custom partly reflected the desperate situation of poor families, and partly the policy in the Catholic part of Europe of providing institutional care for foundlings. There was sometimes a hard edge to relations between parents and their children in peasant and working-class households. However, autobiographies suggest that children understood how a grinding work routine left little scope for physical warmth. Adelheid Popp, born near Vienna in 1869, felt deprived of motherly love during her childhood, but still recalled with fondness "a good, self-sacrificing mother."

In the nineteenth century, then, concerns over such issues as infant mortality, child abuse, and juvenile delinquency gradually encouraged philanthropic and state intervention at the expense of paternal authority. One can point to a range of institutions dedicated to child welfare that appeared in the nineteenth century, notably infant milk depots, health visitors, *crèches* (day nurseries), reformatories, industrial schools, societies for the prevention of cruelty to children, and laws to remove children from cruel or negligent parents. The philanthropic motives of reformers need not be doubted, nor the benefits of their schemes for the young, yet it is hard not to see the rise of what Michel Foucault (1926–1984) called a "disciplinary society" behind it all.

See also **Demography; Marriage and Family; Population, Control of.**

BIBLIOGRAPHY

Darton, F. J. Harvey. *Children's Books in England: Five Centuries of Social Life.* London and Newcastle, 1999.

Davin, Anna. *Growing Up Poor: Home, School, and Street in London, 1870–1914.* London, 1996. Exemplary case study of childhood in a big city.

Dickinson, Edward Ross. *The Politics of German Child Welfare from the Empire to the Federal Republic.* Cambridge, Mass., 1996. A "top-down" approach to childhood.

Heywood, Colin. *Childhood in Nineteenth-Century France: Work, Health, and Education among the Classes Populaires.* Cambridge, U.K., 1988. Focuses on the shift from work to school.

———. *A History of Childhood: Children and Childhood in the West from Medieval to Modern Times.* Cambridge, U.K., 2001. A long-run survey of the themes raised in this essay.

Hopkins, Eric. *Childhood Transformed: Working-Class Children in Nineteenth-Century England.* Manchester, U.K., 1994. Full synthesis of recent research in this area.

Jenks, Chris. *Childhood.* London, 1996. Useful insights from the social sciences.

Kertzer, David I. *Sacrificed for Honor: Italian Infant Abandonment and the Politics of Reproductive Control.* Boston, 1993.

Pollock, Linda A. *Forgotten Children: Parent-Child Relations from 1500 to 1900.* Cambridge, U.K., 1983. Forceful statement of the line that there were few changes in parental care at this period, based on British and American sources.

Ransel, David L. *Mothers of Misery: Child Abandonment in Russia.* Princeton, N.J., 1988. Excellent monograph on this aspect of children's experience.

Stargardt, Nicholas. "German Childhoods: The Making of a Historiography." *German History* 16 (1998): 1–15.

COLIN HEYWOOD

CHINA.

When the French Revolution took place in 1789, China's last dynasty (the Qing, 1644–1912) had been in power for nearly a century and a half and under Emperor Qianlong (r. 1735–1796) was at the height of its power economically, culturally, and perhaps even militarily. Chinese influence in Europe was strong, and European scholars from the Baron de Montesquieu to Voltaire all showed great interest in China. The French coined the word *chinoiserie* to express their enthusiasm about the country, the eighteenth-century English garden took on many of the characteristics attributed to Chinese gardens, and French rococo art was probably also influenced by Chinese styles. The enthusiasm for China and its culture even led European kings to copy the ritual plowing of the earth performed by the Chinese

"Our Celestial Empire possesses all things in prolific abundance and lacks no product within its own borders. There was therefore no need to import the manufactures of outside barbarians in exchange for our own produce."

Emperor Qianlong's mandate to George III, 1793. In *Imperial China,* edited by Frank Schurmann and Orville Schell (New York, 1967), pp. 108–109.

emperors every spring, after Voltaire praised the Chinese practice. China also benefited from its interaction with Europe, and European arts and sciences, especially Western astronomy, cartography, and mathematics, had a major impact on intellectual activity in China.

CLASH OF CIVILIZATIONS

After the turn of the nineteenth century, however, in the wake of the French Revolution and the Enlightenment, the cult of China quickly faded. The German philosopher Georg Wilhelm Friedrich Hegel argued in the early 1820s that China was a typical non-free country where only the emperor had free will. China's lack of interest in commerce and maritime explorations meant that it had fallen behind Europe and even came to be considered "outside the World's history." The increasing predominance of negative Western attitudes toward other cultures in the nineteenth century reflected the disdain felt by the Europeans when they compared their dynamic industrializing societies with the seemingly traditional and static China, and these assumptions profoundly affected relations between China and Europe.

The change of attitudes reflected both a clash of civilizations and the reversal of the fortunes of China and Europe. At a moment when Europe was becoming stronger and wanted to have economic and diplomatic relations on an equal footing with China, the Chinese still believed in the age-old dream that China was "all under heaven," and considered all others, including Europeans, as barbarians. The Europeans started to identify problems with China, among them the Chinese justice system. The Qing legal system was based on hierarchical social values, but the Europeans considered it arbitrary and unusually cruel. Another cause of conflict between the Chinese and Europeans was the Chinese attitude toward foreign trade and diplomacy. In the eighteenth century, the Qing state did not have a ministry of foreign affairs in a modern sense. Instead a number of organizations were responsible for foreign affairs. The Office of Border Affairs (*lifan yuan*) was responsible for Qing relations with its neighboring countries, including Russia, and for maintaining order in China's dangerous northwest area. The Board of Rites (*libu*) and the Imperial Household Office (*neiwufu*) also managed foreign affairs. Relations with countries bordering on the southern crescent of China's coastal and land frontiers were supervised by the former, while the latter was primarily in charge of European missionaries in China. Chinese foreign relations were determined not by diplomacy but by the tribute system, which was key to understanding China's interaction with Europeans. In the case of foreign trade, the Qing state did not want foreigners to have unlimited access to Chinese markets, and under the Guangzhou system that was established in the early eighteenth century foreign traders were allowed to conduct trade in only one port, Guangzhou, and only at a certain time of the year. They could deal only with the Qing court-licensed Chinese merchants, known as the hong merchants, whom Qing held responsible for the payment of all customs duties and for good conduct of foreigners. Under this system, the central government did not deal with European traders directly and kept them at arm's length.

THE MACARTNEY MISSION AND ITS IMPACT

While China tried to restrict foreign trade through the Guangzhou system, the British government was determined to expand its trade with China. In 1792 Lord George Macartney (1737–1806) was appointed "ambassador extraordinary and plenipotentiary from the king of Great Britain to the emperor of China." The purpose of his mission to China was to establish equal diplomatic and economic relations with the Qing state and in particular to end the Guangzhou system and negotiate a new set of commercial agreements. The British also wanted the Qing state to allow permanent foreign diplomatic residences in Beijing. To facilitate his

mission's success, Macartney brought a fine array of presents from King George III to Emperor Qianlong, including telescopes, terrestrial globes, a great lens, barometers, clocks, air guns, fine swords, and exact replicas of British warships.

The gifts were intended to show off British scientific and manufacturing skills and achievement, but the Chinese treated the Macartney mission as "tribute emissaries" who had come to celebrate Emperor Qianlong's birthday. They therefore allowed the British to go to Beijing. In his summer residence, Qianlong received the Macartney mission, along with emissaries from other countries, with considerable signs of favor. But when Qianlong was informed of the true purpose of the Macartney mission, he was not pleased. He rejected each and every request from the mission and issued edicts to George III explaining that China would not increase its foreign trade because China needed nothing from other countries. China also thought itself too great to consider itself equal to others, and therefore it was impossible to allow foreign countries to establish an equal relationship with the Chinese. His mission was a failure, but Macartney left China with firsthand observations of that country from which he concluded that China was not as strong as it pretended to be or looked. He described China as "an old, crazy, first rate man-of-war" that could be dashed to pieces on the shore, and this conclusion was crucial for explaining Britain's subsequent decision to use military means to impose its will on China.

The Macartney mission was the first official attempt by a European power to establish diplomatic and economic relations with China based on equality. This first official contact between China and Britain, however, was probably doomed from the outset because of the mutual misunderstandings and clash of civilizations, and it served to increase British prejudices against China. In 1816, immediately after Napoleon's defeat at Waterloo, the British sent a second diplomatic mission to China with the same purpose as the Macartney mission. This mission was led by Lord Amherst, but the Chinese soon expelled him from the country.

AGE OF IMPERIALISM

When diplomatic and peaceful efforts failed, the British waited for an opportunity to use other means to force China to accept its terms. That opportunity arose in 1839 when the Chinese decided to ban the opium trade. In response the British government immediately launched a war against China. From the first Opium War on, Britain and the other Great Powers repeatedly used gunboats to force China to join the international system and sign a series of unequal treaties. The unequal rights the Europeans and other powers imposed on China lasted until 1943, so that after the 1840s China gradually lost its national sovereignty. Foreigners, especially the British, controlled crucial Chinese resources such as the imperial Maritime Customs Bureau, which was for many years under the control of Robert Hart, a British subject. After being defeated by the Great Powers in 1842, 1860, 1895, and 1901, China was forced to pay indemnities. Hong Kong, Taiwan, and other large territories were ceded to foreigners so that many parts of China became foreign spheres of influences.

Foreign aggression and the larger access enjoyed by foreign traders and missionaries in the second half of the nineteenth century had a very negative impact on the Chinese economy and society. Disputes and clashes between Chinese and missionaries escalated, and the European powers used these disputes to further advance their invasion of China. In 1870 the clash between the local Tianjin population and French missionaries led to the death of sixteen French men and women. In 1875 local tribesmen in Yunnan murdered a British consul named Augustus Margary. On these occasions, the governments of France and Britain, respectively, forced the Qing state to open more ports, pay indemnities, and agree to additional unequal rights. Moreover, the Great Powers had their eyes on China's traditional tributary zones. France fought a war with China in 1884 and 1885 to win over Vietnam, an area that for many centuries had been under Chinese control. In 1886 the British followed suit by declaring Burma, another Chinese tributary zone, a protectorate. In 1894 the Japanese tried to take away Korea, a Chinese traditional tributary state, from China, and in the first Sino-Japanese War, China was defeated. The Treaty of Shimonoseki (April 1895) concluded the war. It proved to be disastrous for the Chinese. China had to recognize full Korean independence; pay 200 million taels (about US$ 264 million) to Japan; open four more treaty ports; cede Taiwan, the Pescadores, and the Liaodong Peninsula; and allow the Japanese to build factories and other industrial enterprises in the treaty ports.

The Treaty of Shimonoseki started a scramble for concessions in China, and three European powers, Russia, France, and Germany, now joined forces in the Triple Intervention. They collectively forced Japan to return the Liaodong Peninsula to China, in exchange for which Japan received an additional indemnity of 30 million taels (about US$42 million) from China. The true reason for the Triple Intervention was that Russia had its own ambitions on Liaodong. Because France had an alliance with Russia, it provided support. Germany wanted to keep Russia occupied in the Far East so as to lessen its presence in Europe, and so joined the intervention. Japan was humiliated by the Triple Intervention, which laid the seed for the Russo-Japanese War (1904–1905) and Japan's declaration of war on Germany in 1914.

NEIYOU WAIHUAN AND CHINA'S QUEST FOR A NEW IDENTITY

The rise of Europe and foreign imperialism in China coincided with the social, political, and economic crises of the Qing state, and the European invasions made the crises even worse. "Nei you wai huan" (troubles from within and threats from without) was the central theme in Chinese policy from 1789 to 1914. Between 1795 and 1840 there were at least fifteen major uprisings in China, which had important consequences for Qing's dealing with the European invaders. After the first Opium War, serious rebellions in China such as the Taiping Rebellion (1851–1864), the Nian Rebellion (1853–1868), and the rebellions of Chinese Muslims in the southwest and northwest (1855–1873) tied the Qing's hands to domestic affairs and brought China into a state of civil war that cost the Qing court crucial military and financial resources to put the rebellions down. In order to focus on the suppression of these domestic challenges, the Qing adopted a conciliatory policy toward the European and foreign powers and were willing to sacrifice national interest. The "nei you wai huan" phenomenon also comprised the background for the Qing court's several attempts at reform. Starting in 1861, after the joint Anglo-French forces entered Beijing, the Qing state

EN CHINE
Le gâteau des Rois et... des Empereurs

The Royal Cake; or, the Western Empires Sharing China Between Them. Color lithograph from the French publication *Le Petit Journal,* 16 January 1898. Queen Victoria, Kaiser William II, Tsar Nicholas II, Marianne (a symbol of the French republic), and Emperor Mutsuhito of Japan are shown carving up a cake representing China; Emperor Kuang-Hsu attempts to stop them. PRIVATE COLLECTION/BRIDGEMAN ART LIBRARY/ARCHIVES CHARMET

launched the so-called *yangwu yundong* (foreign affairs movement) and *ziqiang yundong* (self-strengthening movement). In the area of foreign affairs, it accepted the treaty system in order to appease the foreign powers. It established the Zongli Yamen, a temporary foreign ministry in 1861, and in 1876 China finally sent its first permanent diplomatic mission to London. In the domestic area, it put more non-Manchu Han Chinese in positions of real power in order to fight against the rebels. Although it still thought it was superior culturally and morally, the Qing did realize that it needed to learn from Western technology and military skills. It therefore set up arsenals to supply modern arms and built rail-

ways and a modern navy. A large number of European textbooks in technology and international law were also translated into Chinese.

Defeat at the hands of the Japanese in 1895, however, brought about the total collapse of the self-strengthening movement. Many Chinese realized their political system had serious problems and that to survive in the West-dominated new world order China needed to engage in serious political reforms. The reform movement of 1898 under the leadership of Kang Youwei, Liang Qichao, and others, with support from Emperor Guangxu, was a direct response to this new thinking. The reformers introduced a series of laws to make China a modern state with the establishment of modern education and modern ministries. Unfortunately the reform of 1898 lasted for only about three months before Empress Dowager Cixi put the emperor under house arrest and forced Kang and Liang into exile. After the disastrous Boxer Rebellion in 1900, even Cixi realized the Qing court could not survive without major reform. Therefore, three years after she killed the 1898 reforms, Cixi did exactly what the 1898 reformers wanted to accomplish. Under the name of "New Policies," the old civil service examination was abolished, a modern education system was introduced, and six ancient ministries were supplanted by a dozen modern departments of government, including the ministry of foreign affairs. For many Chinese, however, the New Policies were too late and too little. The Qing collapsed quickly following the outbreak of rebellion in central China on 10 October 1911. On 1 January 1912 the Republic of China was founded under the strong influence of the French and American political systems. When World War I broke out in 1914, this new China was ready to enter the new world order under its own initiatives.

See also **Boxer Rebellion; Imperialism; Opium Wars; Shimonoseki, Treaty of; Trade and Economic Growth.**

BIBLIOGRAPHY

Hsü, Immanuel C. Y. *Rise of Modern China.* 6th ed. New York, 2000.

Peyrefitte, Alain. *The Immobile Empire.* Translated by Jon Rothschild. New York, 1992.

Spence, Jonathan D. *The Search for Modern China.* 2nd ed. New York, 1999.

Waley-Cohen, Joanna. *The Sextants of Beijing: Global Current in Chinese History.* New York, 1999.

Xu Guoqi. *China and the Great War: China's Pursuit of a New National Identity and Internationalization.* New York, 2004.

XU GUOQI

CHOLERA. The traditional ecological cradle of cholera was Bengal. Because of the intensification of geographical mobility in India, as well as occurrences of colonization wars and more active merchant activities, the epidemic expanded first to the whole of India (1817–1818), and then to Ceylon (1819), to the eastern coasts of Africa and to Asia (1821–1822), and also to the northwest to Astrakhan (1823). This first pandemic ended, and in 1829 a second one began (lasting until 1837), the first to reach all the continents and affect all European countries as well as the United States. Cholera followed the merchants' routes and arrived in Europe via the Russian Empire, Poland, Germany, the Baltic Sea, Denmark, and England. In some months, several hundred thousand deaths occurred, with huge effects on the economy, social cohesion, and political regimes. During the nineteenth century, cholera was the first broad epidemic imported since the time of the last plague in the south of France in 1720 to 1722. Moreover, each generation experienced several pandemics: the third one spanned from 1840 to 1869, the fourth one followed from 1863 to 1875, and the fifth one lasted from 1881 to 1896. In France (out of a total population of 32 million) more than 100,000 people died because of cholera in 1832 and 150,000 in 1854, while in England (with a population of 17 million) 54,000 died over several months in 1849, which created a shock. Cholera's symptoms were spectacular: severe vomiting and diarrhea, cold sensation, trembling, and dehydration, sometimes leading to a blue-colored face; some victims died within a few hours or a couple of days, while others survived following a long convalescence.

Western European medical doctors assessed this new threat with confidence when the epidemic was still limited to eastern Europe. But very quickly a division manifested itself between those who tried to show that it was a contagious disease, like smallpox or plague, and those who thought, as neo-Hippocratism emphasized, that it was a noncontagious disease linked to specific climate changes, the growth of large cities, and "miasmatic" emanations (that is, that people were infected by bad air). As the traditional plague regulations enforced in Russia and eastern Europe led to social tensions, violent riots broke out. Because these regulations contradicted the new ideology of free exchange and trade, and because there was no medical consensus, governments decided to enact controls. Cholera occasioned a new "English" system. Instead of sanitary cordons and quarantines, medical controls were set up to monitor those arriving and to follow them at least during the succeeding weeks. Fever hospitals were established to shelter poor patients, while middle-class people were allowed to stay at home, another fact that heightened social tensions. But to make such a new system efficient, the western European countries placed considerable pressure on the Turkish and Egyptian governments to enact measures to keep cholera from entering the Mediterranean Sea. (After the opening of the Suez Canal in 1869, the danger was seen to be Muslim pilgrims going to Mecca.) The less-controlling system in western Europe was possible because of greater controls on the eastern frontiers of Europe.

CHOLERA CAUSES AND TREATMENTS

Different methods to try to cure patients followed contemporary medical theories. On one side, followers of the French physician François-Joseph-Victor Broussais (1772–1838) and his inflammation theory of the intestine believed that the body could be "calmed" with leeches and bleeding. In contrast, followers of the French physiologist François Magendie (1783–1855) argued that the body was really weak and thus had to be helped to fight against weakening with exciting drinks (including punch), blankets, and steam to keep it warmer. Others were aware of the necessity of giving lots of water to their patients (which was the right thing to do when confronted by dehydration symptoms). In London and Paris some doctors tried to give intravenous or anal injections of water and salt. Furthermore, some drugs (e.g., ipecacuaha, laudanum de Sydenham) were used to stop the symptoms.

Woodcut of travelers being disinfected, Paris, nineteenth century. Disinfectants are dispersed into the air of a Paris rail station in an attempt to slow the spread of cholera. ©BETTMANN/CORBIS

All over Europe, the "miasmatic" explanation for the cause of cholera remained paramount among officials and doctors until the 1860s. During the 1854 cholera epidemic, however, the English physician John Snow (1813–1858) noted particularly high mortality among users of a water pump on Broad Street in London's Soho district. He showed that the number of deaths from cholera among customers of the Southwark and Vauxhall Water Company was six times higher than among customers of the Lambeth Waterworks Company, and he emphasized that the latter was pumping water from the Thames far from sewage, and the former drew water at the most polluted place in the river. This evidence did not change the view of a select parliamentary committee, which continued to believe that cholera was carried in the air. Finally William Farr (1807–1883), an English epidemiologist, acknowledged the committee's error upon studying the last London epidemic in 1866. He

was impressed by the fact that the epidemic had been confined to a small area of Whitechapel. Farr demonstrated that the East London Waterworks Company's reservoirs had been contaminated. It was precisely this company that served the Whitechapel district.

Throughout the century, but particularly in the early decades, each cholera epidemic had been seen to pose an immense political threat to governments. The poor accused the rich of trying to poison them; doctors were suspected of carrying out experiments on poor people. The political opposition also tried to use the epidemic to criticize governmental policies; many newspaper caricatures linked political issues to the epidemic. The cholera epidemic reflected a destabilization of contemporary societies. Even if the official thesis remained that the epidemic was not contagious, the population at large believed the contrary and fled large cities, stores, workshops, and markets. Social and economic life ground to a halt for some weeks. In France, in 1832, Casimir Périer, the prime minister, died, as did the leader of the republican opposition, General Jean-Maximilien Lamarque. This led to riots in Paris because republicans suspected that the latter's death was not the result of cholera but of someone on the government's side having poisoned him. Cholera epidemics also brought to light tensions in Russia, Poland, Austria, the German states, and England, as well as in France. René Villermé (1782–1863), a pioneer of French public health, demonstrated that following the 1832 epidemic, the poorest districts of Paris were those most affected by the epidemic, and that the number of cholera deaths in these areas was higher than in the wealthier districts.

The wealthy and the doctors criticized the way in which the poor ate, drank, and generally behaved in daily life, suggesting that they were responsible for their own misfortune. Such views influenced the social representation of cholera. The first epidemics had even been used by authorities in an attempt to obtain greater conformity of behavior in the general population. The Catholic Church organized special relief efforts for families struck by cholera, attempting to recapture popular support.

In 1883 the German physician and bacteriologist Robert Koch (1843–1910) finally identified the *Vibrio cholerae* bacterium as the cause of cholera. Henceforth, it was no longer possible to argue that a cholera epidemic was not contagious. Yet in Hamburg in 1892, leading citizens of the municipality decided to adopt a thesis more compatible with their own commercial interests, ignoring Koch's discovery from the previous decade, which had led to restrictions on emigration from Hamburg, one of the major activities of the bustling harbor. Hamburg's most serious epidemic followed. A vaccine had even been available since 1885, purified by the Russian bacteriologist Waldemar Haffkine (1860–1930) at the Pasteur Institute in Paris in 1892. But medical progress was not sufficient to convince local politicians, nor did it prevent the spread of the disease. Nevertheless, Hamburg was an exception in Europe. Outbreaks of cholera declined in gravity after the 1860s. In most countries the last attack occurred in 1884 and 1885, with fewer deaths than during the previous epidemics.

As has been seen, relevant theories on the spread of cholera existed before the epidemics but were in some cases ignored. Despite this, accumulated knowledge led to better prevention and care. After each pandemic, improvements in both public sanitation, especially the improvement and the extension of sewage systems, and water supply systems accelerated. And because of political considerations, the cholera epidemics also tended to focus public health policies more on sanitation than on attempts to improve the lives of the poor.

See also **Disease; Koch, Robert; London; Paris; Public Health; Smallpox; Syphilis; Tuberculosis.**

BIBLIOGRAPHY

Aisenberg, Andrew R. *Contagion: Disease, Government, and the "Social Question" in Nineteenth-Century France.* Stanford, Calif., 1999.

Delaporte, François. *Disease and Civilization: The Cholera in Paris, 1832.* Translated by Arthur Goldhammer. Cambridge, Mass., 1986.

Durey, Michael. *Return of the Plague: British Society and the Cholera, 1831–1832.* Dublin, 1979.

Evans, Richard J. *Death in Hamburg: Society and Politics in the Cholera Years, 1830–1910.* Oxford, U.K., 1987.

Kudlick, Catherine J. *Cholera in Post-Revolutionary Paris: A Cultural History.* Berkeley, Calif., 1996.

McGrew, Roderick E. *Russia and the Cholera, 1823–1832.* Madison, Wis., 1965.

Morris, R. J. *Cholera, 1832: The Social Response to an Epidemic.* London, 1976.

Pelling, Margaret. *Cholera, Fever, and English Medicine, 1825–1865.* Oxford, U.K., 1978.

Snowden, Frank M. *Naples in the Time of Cholera, 1884–1911.* Cambridge, U.K., 1995.

PATRICE BOURDELAIS

CHOPIN, FRÉDÉRIC (in Polish, Fryderyk Franciszek Chopin; 1810–1849), Polish composer and piano virtuoso.

Fryderyk Franciszek Chopin was born in the Duchy of Warsaw—Napoleon's tiny puppet state created after Poland was partitioned among its neighbors. During the years following the Vienna

Congress (1814–1815), Warsaw, as the center of the Polish Kingdom (Congress Kingdom), enjoyed relative autonomy under Russian rule and experienced a cultural renaissance. These circumstances and Chopin's associations with Warsaw's intellectual, artistic, and political circles exposed the young composer to the newest intellectual trends, world-class musical events, and developed in him ardent patriotism aimed at the restoration of sovereign Poland. Chopin received his general education at the Warsaw Gymnasium (where his father was a teacher), and his musical training through private instruction and in the newly established Warsaw Conservatory. In 1830, he left Poland on a concert tour from which he never returned, presumably because of the November Uprising against Russian rule and its repressive political aftermath, but also to advance his career. Although for the rest of his life he made his home in Paris, he never shed the identity of a Polish expatriate. His intimate circle of friends included Parisian artists and intellectuals— the composer/pianist Franz Liszt, the painter Eugène Delacroix, the cellist August Franchomme, and the writer George Sand (pen name of Aurore Dudevant), who was Chopin's partner for almost a decade—as well as Polish émigrés who were particularly important to him in his last years.

Chopin started his career as a virtuoso pianist, but he quickly abandoned this path feeling that the virtuoso concert was too focused on frivolous display of instrumental skill for unsophisticated audiences. Instead, he supported himself in Paris by teaching, composition, and private performances in salons. As a result of social and economic changes taking place in the early nineteenth century, the piano became the preferred instrument for home entertainment. Piano education was a sign of social standing, for women in particular, and Chopin was a favorite piano teacher of Parisian bourgeois and aristocratic elite, in addition to teaching a handful of pupils who went on to become professionals. The same social and cultural forces produced an insatiable publishing market for small piano compositions. Chopin took up these salon piano miniatures and exercises—waltzes, mazurkas, polonaises, nocturnes, preludes, and etudes—and elevated them to the rank of masterpieces. He preferred the salon over the concert hall: in smaller acoustic spaces, his intimate

Frédéric Chopin. Portrait by Eugène Delacroix. Réunion des Musées Nationaux/Art Resource, NY

compositions and artful improvisations fared much better, and the subtleties of his pianistic style were more audible. Moreover, salons with artistic aspirations offered audiences of professional musicians, sophisticated music amateurs, and connoisseurs, who truly appreciated his art. At the end of his life, during his ill-fated trip to England and Scotland, he again played in public concerts, but by then he presented his audiences with compositions typically belonging in private spaces—nocturnes, waltzes, scherzos—instead of the genres expected by audiences of a virtuoso concert (concertos and variations, or fantasias on favorite themes).

Chopin's reputation as a composer was built, exceptionally, on works for a single instrumental medium: the piano (though he composed a handful of songs and chamber works, some of them masterpieces). New advances in fortepiano construction transformed it into a highly versatile and expressive instrument, permitting ever greater virtuosity. But Chopin's music achieved its lasting position in the canon of Western music not only by setting new standards of pianistic virtuosity in difficult bravura figurations (Etudes opp. 10 and 25). More remarkably, he made use of the new piano's potential for lyrical melodies (inspired by operatic *bel canto*) and employed a rich palette of sonorities through his imaginative use of the instrument's natural registers and pedals. Even his daring explorations of harmonic language at times caused an overlap in the functions of harmony and instrumental color (Prelude op. 45 and the Berceuse op. 57). Chopin's ingenious phrasing defied the confines of traditional metric and melodic patterns. His innovative approaches to musical form epitomized the Romantic fascination with the fragment (Preludes op. 28) or, in larger pieces, explored narrative processes loosely related to the traditional sonata form (ballades and scherzos). In these larger narrative works and in his late sonatas he mustered all these resources to create riveting musical dramas without words.

Chopin's harmonic language, attention to timbre, and experimentation with phrase and form had profound influence on contemporary and future composers, including Claude Debussy, Richard Wagner, and Alexander Scriabin. But the reception of Chopin's music was often troubled by his association with the salon and the national contexts of his music. His Polish biographers, in particular, emphasized the nationalism of his music, at times to the point of xenophobia, as in the repeated attempts to Polonize his father's French origins. Russian, French, and German critics sought to appropriate Chopin as exponent of their national traditions: the French, for instance, by building a national historical narrative leading from François Couperin and his contemporaries through Chopin to Debussy. In contrast, the Victorian English-speaking world saw Chopin's music as belonging in the drawing room, a view often associated with charges of effeminacy. Consequently, Chopin scholarship in English for a long time remained the domain of the musicological amateur. In the twenty-first century some of the most up-to-date Chopin scholarship is issued in English.

See also **Delacroix, Eugène; Liszt, Franz; Music; Romanticism; Sand, George.**

BIBLIOGRAPHY

Chopin, Frédéric. *Selected Correspondence of Frederick Chopin. Abridged from Fryderyk Chopin's Correspondence*. Collected and annotated by Bronisław Edward Sydow. Translated and edited by Arthur Hedley. New York, 1963.

Eigeldinger, Jean-Jacques. *Chopin: Pianist and Teacher as Seen by His Pupils*. Trans. by Naomi Shohet with Krysia Osostowicz and Roy Howat. 3rd ed. Cambridge, U.K., 1986.

Goldberg, Halina, ed. *The Age of Chopin: Interdisciplinary Inquiries*. Bloomington, Ind., 2004.

Kallberg, Jeffrey. *Chopin at the Boundaries: Sex, History and Musical Genre*. Cambridge, Mass., and London, 1996.

Rink, John, and Jim Samson, eds. *Chopin Studies*. Vol. 2. Cambridge, Mass., and London, 1994.

Samson, Jim. *Chopin*. Oxford, U.K., and New York, 1996.

HALINA GOLDBERG

CINEMA. From the early nineteenth century to the beginning of World War I the cinema emerged slowly, first as a new technology and then, after 1895, as a new industry to take its place among the various older forms of popular entertainment. As a technology, the cinema ultimately combined three distinct nineteenth-century lines of development. The first of these was the invention and refinement of photography, which had begun with the work of Joseph-Nicéphore Niépce (1765–1833) in France. Niépce probably had a camera and a working method of producing images as early as 1816, but it was Jacques-Louis-Mandé Daguerre (1789–1851) who finally refined the process and sold it, in 1839, to the French government for free public use. But this first viable system of photography was far from suitable for the cinema: the images were not reproducible and required very long exposure times. It would take most of the remainder of the century, and the work of many hands in Europe and the United States, before cameras could record reproducible images at exposures of less than a thirtieth of a second. The final ingredient necessary for cinema, flexible-roll celluloid, came only near the end of the century.

The second strand of technological development was the synthesis of motion from individual still images. Inspired by the research of the English scientists Peter Mark Roget (1779–1869) and

Michael Faraday (1791–1867), the Belgian Joseph Plateau (1801–1883) invented the *phénakistoscope,* a rotating disk with narrow radial slots and a series of drawings on one side. The viewer held the rotating disk in front of a mirror and looked through the slots at the reflected drawings; the slots functioned as a primitive movie shutter. If expertly drawn, the images appeared to be in motion. Plateau's device was quickly followed by variations and improvements, most notably the Zoetrope, which replaced the flat, vertical disc with a horizontal cylinder. This line of development was to culminate in 1892 with the first public exhibition in Paris of Emile Reynaud's (1844–1918) *Théâtre Optique,* in which extended sequences of moving images were projected onto a screen. But this was not yet the cinema, for the images were drawn and painted, rather than photographed.

The essential addition of photography came through the third stream of technology that fed into the cinema: the analysis of animal locomotion. The English photographer Eadweard Muybridge (1830–1904) first used a series of cameras to study the movement of horses in his work in California during the 1870s. In 1881 he toured Europe with his striking images, and in response the Parisian Étienne-Jules Marey (1830–1904) was moved to adopt photography to his own researches. By 1888 Marey had developed the first true movie camera; however, the French scientist had little interest in synthesizing the motion he had analyzed. He showed his device to Thomas Alva Edison (1847–1931), who was touring Europe in 1889, and it was the American who saw commercial potential in the apparatus. He added a series of perforations at the edges of the images and changed the film base from paper to celluloid, making Marey's "chronophotographs" viewable in apparent motion. In 1891 Edison unveiled his Kinetoscope; whether this was finally "the cinema" depends on how one defines the word, for Edison's machine was a peepshow device, incapable of projecting the images onto a screen. This final step was taken by many mechanics and tinkerers at roughly the same time, but the most striking commercial success came to Louis Lumière's (1864–1948) *Cinématographe,* which opened commercially in Paris in 1895 and quickly became the entertainment sensation of the century's end. Lumière had further improved on

Edison's adaptation of Marey's technology, perfecting an easily portable machine that served as camera, projector, and contact printer.

The Cinématographe entered a crowded field of European popular entertainments. Most enterprises were family-run and solidly entrenched in the lower fringes of the middle class. There were circuses, theater troupes, magicians, wonders-of-science exhibitions, and other attractions. In the large cities these could be in permanent locations, but in most of Europe, which was still largely rural, they were traveling affairs that went from town to town in well-established circuits. The cinema was largely to replace this whole economic sector, but it started its commercial development as one attraction among many.

The most important film producer was the Lumière company. Its operators quickly began to crisscross Europe and the world, showing half-hour selections of the company's films (and making more). Each film, or "view," lasted a little less than one minute, and showed one action or interesting environment: boats leaving a harbor, workers tearing down a wall, a busy city street, or the famous *Workers Leaving the Lumière Factory* (1895).

At first Lumière refused to sell its films and equipment to other exhibitors, but competing machines and production companies sprang up almost everywhere the company's operators took their traveling show. By far the most successful early competitor was the Frenchman Georges Méliès (1861–1938), proprietor of a magic theater in Paris. His *Trip to the Moon* (1902) was probably the most widely seen work of the cinema's first decade, and he all but single-handedly created the medium's second major genre (after the "view"), the "trick film," based on humorous, magical, and often grotesque transformations (of flowers into women, or moon people into puffs of smoke, and so on). At the same time in England, other producers began to elaborate these and other genres. The English dabbled extensively in film comedy, of which they were the first true masters, but they also pioneered the action melodrama, of which Cecil Hepworth's (1874–1953) *Rescued by Rover* (1905) is a remarkable early example. *Rover* and films like it were probably the high point of the contributions of the English entrepreneurs, who

A scene from the 1914 film *Cabiria*. KOBAL COLLECTION

were soon eclipsed by the medium's first large-scale capitalist enterprises.

This new stage of development had begun in France in the late 1890s, when two small businesses began to evolve into modern giants: Pathé Frères (1896) and the Gaumont company (1895). They became the first examples of the "studio system" that would dominate world film production until the middle of the twentieth century. Organizationally, they had three important characteristics: (1) they were vertically integrated, combining production, distribution, and exhibition; (2) they employed large numbers of specialized contract workers—directors, scriptwriters, and so on; and (3) they had access to capital through the financial markets (stocks and bonds). Soon the French "majors" were ready to act assertively in the marketplace. Pathé Frères, for example, cut the prices of its films by one-third in England in

1906, effectively "dumping" product onto that market and impeding further development of a domestic cinema industry.

By this time some of the early genres, such as the Lumière "views" and the "trick film," were in eclipse, but others were developing to replace them. The most important of these in France was the *film d'art*, or "art film," essentially filmed theater with famous actors—either direct adaptations of plays or play-like original scenarios such as *The Assassination of the Duc de Guise* (1908). These films were made with larger budgets and longer running times, and they appealed to socially upscale audiences. This represented a qualitatively new development, making obsolete virtually the entire fairground exhibition circuit; it arose in part because of competition from an unexpected source: Italian production companies such as Cines and Itala Films.

That Italy could develop the only European industry to provide serious competition to the French had several causes: (1) labor and capital costs were much lower there; (2) the Italian market had all but skipped the "fairground" stage of exhibition, with little popular or entrepreneurial interest in cinema before roughly 1906; and (3) beginning at that time, a wave of popular interest and entrepreneurial zeal sparked the greatest film exhibition boom in all of Europe. Unlike France, which remained dominated by its two "majors," Italy had a profusion of mid- to large-sized firms (one critic estimated eighty, in 1914); these were able to attract talent, technicians, and capital from France, England, and elsewhere. For this new industry, a new genre was the flagship product in the battle for the international film market: extravagantly produced historical spectacles, such as *The Last Days of Pompeii* (1908, directed by Luigi Maggi for Ambrosio Company). Largely from this generic line—and from its competition with the French *film d'art*—there emerged, by the early 1910s, the modern (though still silent) "feature film," telling a coherent, character-based story in more than an hour—sometimes much more, as in the remarkable *Cabiria* (1914, produced and directed by Giovanni Pastrone [1883–1959] with a text by Gabriele D'Annunzio [1863–1938]). Many of the earlier genres survived as "short subject" accompaniments to the features. Programs such as these were ill suited to traveling fairground shows, which by 1914 had been decimated by competition from movie theaters in cities and towns. The world power of the new medium was France, with Italy in close second place; other European countries had weak domestic industries with minority shares of their own markets—except for Russia, which had managed to develop a relatively healthy, although not export-oriented, cinema industry. All of this would change, of course, and change dramatically, with World War I.

See also **Lumière, Auguste and Louis; Méliès, Georges; Popular and Elite Culture.**

BIBLIOGRAPHY

Primary Sources

British Film Institute and Film Preservation Associates, eds. *The Movies Begin: A Treasury of Early Cinema, 1894–1913*. New York, 1994 (5 videocassettes) and 2002 (5 DVDs).

Pastrone, Giovanni. *Cabiria*. New York, 1990 (videocassette) and 2000 (DVD).

Secondary Sources

Abel, Richard. *The Ciné Goes to Town: French Cinema 1896–1914.* Updated and expanded edition, Berkeley, Calif., 1998.

Chanan, Michael. *The Dream that Kicks: The Prehistory and Early Years of Cinema in Britain*. London and Boston, 1980.

Leprohon, Pierre. *The Italian Cinema*. New York, 1972.

Leyda, Jay. *Kino: A History of the Russian and Soviet Film.* New York, 1973.

Pratt, George C. *Spellbound in Darkness: A History of the Silent Film*. Revised edition. Greenwich, Conn., 1973.

Williams, Alan. *Republic of Images: A History of French Filmmaking*. Cambridge, Mass., 1992.

ALAN WILLIAMS

CITIES AND TOWNS. During the nineteenth century Europe became a more urban civilization than the world had ever seen. London, Paris, and Berlin grew to be (along with New York) the most populous cities in human history, and as many smaller towns expanded even more rapidly, Europe's urban population increased sixfold in the course of the century. Britain's 1851 census revealed it to be a country with a majority of town-dwellers. Belgium, the Netherlands, and Germany crossed the same threshold half a century later, most other countries later still, so Europe still had a rural majority in 1914, but it was generally acknowledged that, for better or worse, the future belonged to the cities.

The accuracy of these numbers depends, of course, on the definition of a town. (Rarely does anyone make a firm distinction between larger "cities" and smaller "towns.") Often a minimum population size of two thousand has defined a town; sometimes the population must be five thousand or more. Towns near the bottom end of this category might have remained sleepy places, having little in common with faraway Moscow or Madrid, but most qualified as towns because they were not rural: that is, most residents did not

COKETOWN

It was a town of red brick, or of brick that would have been red if the smoke and ashes had allowed it; but as matters stood it was a town of unnatural red and black like the painted face of a savage. It was a town of machinery and tall chimneys, out of which interminable serpents of smoke trailed themselves for ever and ever, and never got uncoiled. It had a black canal in it, and a river that ran purple with ill-smelling dye, and vast piles of buildings full of windows where there was a rattling and a trembling all day long, and where the piston of the steam-engine worked monotonously up and down like the head of an elephant in a state of melancholy madness. It contained several large streets all very like one another, and many small streets still more like one another, inhabited by people equally like one another, who all went in and out at the same hours, with the same sound upon the same pavements, to do the same work, and to whom every day was the same as yesterday and tomorrow, and every year the counterpart of the last and the next.

Source: Charles Dickens, *Hard Times* (1854).

depend on agriculture for their livelihoods. In 1789 only a handful of capitals and ports could claim to be truly bustling and cosmopolitan. By 1914 the major cities had become many times as large and some of the smaller ones had been utterly transformed into factory towns as populous as the largest cities had been a century before. In 1800 Europe's twenty-one cities with populations exceeding one hundred thousand were home to less than 3 percent of the Continent's population. A century later, there were 147 such cities, and one European in ten lived in them.

Towns and cities also had to be delineated geographically. The administrative border that divided town from country was usually clearly drawn, and in 1789 it was often clearly visible as well. Many towns were still surrounded by walls and, in some cases, forts and free-fire zones that left a clear gap between the town and any suburbs. These walls were often centuries old and militarily obsolete, and most were demolished in the course of the nineteenth century, but the legal limits of many towns remained marked by gates where travelers and their merchandise were inspected, excise taxes were collected, and soldiers might be posted.

Meanwhile, beyond the city limits, suburbs grew haphazardly. Sometimes they were under the town's jurisdiction, sometimes not, but rarely did they display any of the visible order characteristic of the grandest central districts. Some suburbs developed as comfortable enclaves of well-to-do urban merchants, especially in England, but most suburbanites were poor, often recent migrants from the country who could not afford town dwellings or who practiced trades that were physically repulsive (such as tanning) or legally dubious.

As cities grew, physical and psychological lines between town and country faded. Urban housing and trades spilled over into the adjoining countryside, and cities annexed parts of it. Meanwhile, migrants from the countryside diluted local identities. In the overwhelmingly rural society of premodern times, town dwellers and their typical occupations—artisans and merchants—had been alien presences in a world of lords and peasants, and they were bound by different laws. Where, as most clearly in Germany before the Napoleonic reorganization, many towns remained largely independent of central state authority, their citizens cultivated a distinct urban identity to accompany their legal status. Even a poor backwater of a thousand souls stood proudly apart from the countryside, with its market streets lined with tall houses, its trades and guilds, and its charter as a free city. Although trade linked town and country, towns might have been said to dominate the countryside in only a few of the most urbanized corners of Europe, such as northern Italy, where city-states had long ruled their hinterlands, and the Netherlands. Legal distinctions between town and country remained important as long as peasants remained in serfdom, as was the case well into the nineteenth century in much of eastern Europe. As the territorial reorganization of central Europe in the decades after 1789 swept away most of these legal distinctions, however, urban identities gradually became subordinated to national ones. Local elites nevertheless cultivated civic pride as a means to unite their communities and to protect their authority.

A rough classification might identify four kinds of towns: administrative centers, especially capitals; merchant and port cities; mining and factory towns; and tourist and leisure towns at spas and seaside or mountain resorts. To a greater or lesser extent, however, all towns were a mixture of types. Most administrative centers developed large commercial sectors; and many merchant towns, in turn, became major industrial centers as well. Some old towns, bypassed by rail lines or dependent on obsolete industries, stagnated, but most grew. Although few of the burgeoning cities were completely new, some had begun the century as tiny market towns or even villages. This was most typical of mining towns or those that developed around a single booming industry. Multi-centered urban regions were most likely to develop where mining areas industrialized. Examples included Lancashire and Yorkshire in England, early in the century, followed by Belgium and, later, Upper Silesia and especially the Ruhr region of Germany.

Elsewhere, workshops and factories clustered in the older cities, which usually remained the economic centers for their hinterlands. Although many early factories were built outside of towns, to be near waterpower or coal mines or to be away from guild regulations, urban growth became increasingly inseparable from industry. Factory villages grew into cities, and later in the century factories usually sought out urban locations, where transportation and skilled workers were to be found. Even where factories were not the main source of urban growth, industry fueled it indirectly, as the expansion of trade transformed ports and merchant towns. Cities in less industrialized regions of southern Europe grew more slowly. Notable examples were Constantinople and Naples, two of Europe's four largest cities in 1800, but no longer among the top ten a century later.

SOCIETY AND CLASS
Aristocrats played a prominent role in the social and political affairs of some cities, but control typically lay in the hands of a middle-class elite of merchants, bankers, industrialists, and professionals—a group of families, often well acquainted with (if not necessarily well-disposed toward) one another,

who saw themselves as responsible for the town's reputation and well-being. These families' wealth ranged from great to modest, but in their villas or flats, which were well staffed with servants, they lived very differently from the poor majority. Men from these families usually took charge of urban affairs, either formally, through local government, or informally, through professional and civic organizations. Social events held at home, as well as many social service organizations, became the responsibility of their wives and sisters.

Even as the economic activities of merchant and industrialist families were reshaping the cities, so, too, were their efforts to bring order to urban space and to spread the moral and cultural principles they cherished. Their presence and their money helped create many urban institutions. For many middle-class men and women, high culture offered far more than pleasure: they saw it as an essential source of moral as well as aesthetic refinement for themselves and their children. They also held out hope that it might improve the degraded lives of the urban poor. They founded museums, theaters, and opera houses in every city, and these became prominent architectural monuments as well as favorite places for socializing. Composers, conductors, and museum and theater directors ranked among the leading citizens, mixing with professors, bankers, merchants, factory owners, physicians, clergymen, and government officials.

Neither aristocratic houses nor rude taverns and inns suited the middle-class elite, so its members patronized new urban institutions such as grand hotels and restaurants as well as their own private clubs. Their wealth also enabled the middle class to purchase goods that most people had to make for themselves or do without. In the most prestigious districts, new shops transformed the streetscape. Elegant shopping later moved indoors to more exclusive spaces, first in enclosed arcades built through the center of city blocks, then in the splendid new department stores that opened after midcentury, first in Paris and then in many other cities. This shift was partly intended to entice well-to-do female shoppers who might wish (or be expected) not to linger on the streets unaccompanied.

The allure of elegant shopping and entertainment districts persisted into the night, which was transformed by the gas street lamps installed in

TABLE 1

Most populous European cities	
1800	Population (in thousands)
London	948
Constantinople	570
Paris	550
Naples	430
Moscow	300
Vienna	247
Saint Petersburg	220
Amsterdam	217
Dublin	200
Lisbon	195
1913	
London	7300
Paris	4850
Berlin	4000
Saint Petersburg	2400
Vienna	2150
Moscow	1900
Manchester	1600
Birmingham	1500
Glasgow	1500
Hamburg	1500

SOURCES: Bairoch, "Une nouvelle distribution des populations: villes et campagnes," in Jean-Pierre Bardet and Jacques Dupaquier, eds., *Histoire des populations de l'Europe* (Paris, 1998), vol. 2, p. 227; Tertius Chandler, *Four Thousand Years of Urban Growth: An Historical Census*, 2nd ed. (Lewiston, N.Y., 1987), p. 540.

many cities by the 1820s, and even more by the brighter electric lights that came into use at the century's end. Nighttime in the city became a very different experience from night in the country, and the night no longer seemed as lawless as before. Even if night in the brightly lit city centers ceased to hold some of its terrors, however, the rapidly expanding cities frightened many thoughtful Europeans. Many rural aristocrats disdained the urban world of moneygrubbing merchants, but the objects of their scorn often shared their fears about the uprooting of the masses from the old rural order. Even a liberal such as the German social reformer Friedrich Naumann (1860–1919) warned that a new kind of darkness threatened to engulf all civilization in the modern "seas of houses, floods of stone, anthills of millions, where people perch next to one another and atop one another like birds in cages, ... where the individual is nothing, a forlorn grain of sand, chaff in the wind, where below a resplendent upper class there lies a dense, dark human mass that is

always pushed and pulled about" (quoted in Ladd, p. 243).

It was true that in nearly every city a poor majority far outnumbered a wealthy minority. However, it is important to remember that such impassioned descriptions of the faceless urban masses come from outsiders who saw the urban crowd as nothing but a teeming horde of uncultured and alienated paupers. More careful investigation of the urban masses reveals a society that was diverse and often well ordered, if rapidly changing, with as many minute social gradations as the well-to-do knew in their own social circles.

Artisans and small shopkeepers formed the core of the preindustrial urban population, and they remained important in the economy and society of industrial towns. Artisans' places in town economies and, often, government were still protected by guild regulations in much of central and eastern Europe in the early part of the nineteenth century. These regulations, which had been largely abolished in France and Britain before 1800, controlled prices, the quality of goods, training, and entry into a trade, and offered a social safety net to widows, orphans, and the disabled, but they could not guarantee the well-being of weavers or cobblers or bakers in a rapidly changing European economy. During the course of the century, some trades lost out in competition with cheap factory goods, while others thrived. In the face of change, many trades maintained their commercial and fraternal organizations and their traditional neighborhoods, and they continued to play visible roles in town affairs. Sooner or later, however, the guild organization of urban working classes was overwhelmed—by free-trade laws, by the growth of factories, and by poor immigrants, some with usable skills, most without. Many of the immigrants found work in new factories, while others remained dependent on casual labor. Factory towns became home to a burgeoning proletariat, in Karl Marx's sense: a large body of wage laborers who did not own tools or machines.

Much of the urban population growth was due to the natural increase that came with falling death rates, but a great deal was fueled by migration. Most migrants were young, single adults from the surrounding countryside. They usually came in search of work, and they found a whole new world.

No doubt many city dwellers prized their new-found freedom, while others despaired of it, but the extent of urban anomie has been exaggerated. Most migrants formed new social networks or re-formed old ones in the cities, often moving into neighborhoods filled with others from their home regions. Most rejoined or formed nuclear families, if they stayed in the city. Many kept their rural ties, returning seasonally or perhaps permanently. In fact, statistics on net migration into the cities, impressive as they are, understate the degree of mobility, since they do not include the many migrants who returned to the country, temporarily or permanently, or the many others who moved within and between cities.

Loyalty to a home region, sometimes reinforced by a distinctive spoken dialect, was one allegiance that helped workers find their place in the city. Religion was another source of identity that set groups apart in some places. Some towns had long been religiously diverse; more became so with immigration. Ethnic and national identities, usually defined and reinforced by language, and sometimes by religion, also created social barriers within cities. In most west European cities, foreign ethnic groups remained distinct if significant minorities, such as the Italians in Marseille, Poles in the cities of the Ruhr, or the Irish in many English towns. Ethnically diverse cities were more typical of eastern Europe, where the gulf between city and country was often all the greater because most city dwellers spoke a different language than did nearby peasants. Thus there were many predominantly German towns in Czech and Polish regions, Polish- and Yiddish-speaking city dwellers surrounded by Lithuanian or Ukrainian peasants, and, farther south, Italian or Turkish towns in Slavic areas. In these regions immigration had long made most cities ethnically diverse. Constantinople was the most diverse of all, a Muslim capital with a Christian majority for much of the nineteenth century, thanks to migrants from the Ottoman Empire's European and Asian territories as well as from western Europe.

In some places, ethnic, class, and even religious identities were largely coterminous. The most maligned minority, the Jews, present the clearest case of a group concentrated in particular trades and, often, particular parts of town. Urban Jews were a minority defined by their religion and, in the case of most east European Jews, by their Yiddish language as well. Cities were also, however, places to change language or identity. Marriages across religious or ethnic lines were not rare, and social mobility was often aided by linguistic assimilation, as when Ukrainians in Kiev or Yiddish-speaking Odessa Jews learned Russian, or Warsaw Jews began to speak Polish. Immigration and rapid growth changed ethnic balances in many cities. For example, an 1867 census showed the population of Riga to be 24 percent Latvian, 43 percent German, 25 percent Russian, and 5 percent Jewish. Until then, the city had no Latvian upper or middle class, so successful ethnic Latvians assimilated into German society. By 1913 a population that had grown from one hundred thousand to four hundred eighty thousand was 39 percent Latvian and only 16 percent German, with Polish and Lithuanian minorities alongside the Russians and Jews. Although Germans still dominated politics and the economy, there was now a Latvian middle class, which made Riga the intellectual center of Latvian nationalism. Similarly, Prague became a Czech city and Budapest became a Hungarian one, whereas Kiev became a hotbed of Ukrainian nationalism even though the proportion of Ukrainian speakers in the city's population fell relative to Russians, Jews, and Poles. Indeed, ethnic diversity did not prevent cities from becoming the centers of national resistance to Russian or Austrian rule.

STREET LIFE

For most city dwellers, life was organized around long hours of manual labor in factories, shops, docks, rail yards, or warehouses. Many women, especially, worked in others' homes as servants, or in their own, for example as seamstresses. For nearly everyone, wages were low and employment insecure. The workplace was usually not far from home, with the immediate neighborhood offering all the amenities workers had access to. Numerous dwellings might be interspersed with shops and businesses within the confines of a single alley or court, or even a single building. The writer Isaac Bashevis Singer (1904–1991) later recalled the excitement of his family's move into "a new house with gas lights and toilets" in Warsaw in 1914. Number 12 Krochmalna Street was

Harbor at Genoa, Italy, 1868. The port city of Genoa, long an important trading center, became vital to the economy of the nascent Italian state during the nineteenth century. ©HULTON-DEUTSCH COLLECTION/CORBIS

like a city. It had three enormous courtyards. The dark entrance always smelled of freshly baked bread, rolls and bagels, caraway seed and smoke. Koppel the baker's yeasty breads were always outside, rising on boards. In No. 12 there were also two Hasidic study houses, the Radzymin and Minsk, as well as a synagogue for those who opposed Hasidism. There was also a stall where cows were kept chained to the wall all year round. In some cellars, fruit had been stored by dealers from Mirowski Place; in others, eggs were preserved in lime. Wagons arrived there from the provinces. No. 12 swarmed with Torah, prayer, commerce, and toil. (Singer, pp. 226–227)

Many churches and synagogues remained important neighborhood institutions but, especially in the larger cities, they usually did not become the centers of community life that they typically were in the country. Statistics on church attendance bear

out the contemporary belief that city dwellers often drifted away from organized religion. More than the church, the corner tavern or café became the typical gathering place for working-class men. The streets and courtyards themselves were the places where children played, women exchanged news, and peddlers and street entertainers made their rounds. Larger entertainment venues—for sporting events, music, stage shows, and later the cinema—drew crowds from farther afield. As literacy became widespread, mass-circulation newspapers emerged as the new media that linked city dwellers in a common discourse of sports, gossip, sensation, and politics.

Control of the streets was nearly always contested. Everywhere in Europe, the wealthier classes regarded the crowded neighborhoods with suspicion and fear. The events of Paris in 1789 and 1830 and of many cities in 1848 were enough to convince the authorities that the seething discontent of the urban crowd was a threat to the established order. However, the authorities often failed to distinguish between the visible disorder represented by transients, petty criminals, beggars, and the homeless on the one hand and the more respectable but potentially better-organized working classes on the other. Crime was indeed a problem in the cities, but statistics suggest that, contrary to popular belief at the time, it was generally no worse in cities than in the country. Threats to the political order were another matter.

The poor, in turn, often mistrusted the police, the most visible representatives of higher authority. They expected that their very poverty—clearly visible in their clothes, perhaps also in their demeanor and poor nutrition—would make them targets of harassment by policemen pursuing the routine vices of the city: gambling, drinking, prostitution, and rowdy entertainment, including traditional festivals. Violence was a normal part of popular culture, whether in the organized collective fistfights of Russia or the cockfights and dogfights of England, and it often threatened to get out of hand. In the teeming streets, a minor altercation would quickly draw a crowd and could easily turn into a major crisis. Conversely, protests against high rents or food prices might escalate into violence. Mob violence might be directed against representatives of authority, against shops, or against minority groups. Toward 1900 Russian cities saw an upsurge of murderous mob attacks on Jews.

The police were also charged with enforcing whatever regulations restricted political meetings, mass demonstrations, and labor-union activities. Sometimes these assemblies were explicitly illegal, especially in eastern Europe; in other circumstances, general laws on public order and the flow of traffic might be applied against them. Even in times and places where most political activity was legal, such as in Britain and France in the latter part of the nineteenth century, an undercurrent of fear and suspicion accompanied working-class organizational life in all its forms. With the industrialization of the cities, labor unions and other workers' organizations increasingly loomed as the most serious challenge to the economic and political order. Often they were rooted in the social networks of the working-class neighborhoods as well as in the workshops and factories. The earlier workers' organizations, most visible in Paris, grew out of the city's many small shops. The later growth of large labor unions and socialist parties was more characteristic of newly industrialized centers dominated by large factories, notably in German cities and, later, in Russia. By 1900 St. Petersburg embodied social change at its most rapid and disruptive: enormous new factories, massive migration, divided families, grinding poverty, and atrocious housing conditions. Out of this lethal brew arose the radical Russian socialist movement and the 1905 and 1917 Russian revolutions.

MUNICIPAL GOVERNMENT AND SOCIAL REFORM

The nineteenth century saw the consolidation of national governments at the expense of smaller units, including formerly self-governing towns. At the same time, however, urban elites across Europe sought and gained greater powers of self-government. Urban government reforms created far more elected mayors and city councils by the end of the century than at the beginning. Most were elected by a limited franchise. There was, in fact, less variation across Europe in local than in national voting rights. Whereas Germany had universal suffrage in national elections after 1871, for example, most municipal elections remained limited to property owners or taxpayers; while in Russia, cities acquired a similar, if more restrictive, franchise in 1870 long before there were any national elections at all. Elsewhere the widening of the municipal franchise largely paralleled the expansion of national voting rights.

The extent of local government powers was a matter of endless dispute, with central governments especially keen to maintain control over urban police forces. Fear of the cities was, however, often accompanied by practical efforts to improve conditions in them. Although municipal governments could and often did serve the interests of the wealthy few to the detriment of the disenfranchised majority, they also provided a forum for the middle class to demonstrate its commitment to the civic community. In some countries, notably Germany, cities offered middle-class liberals political authority that they could not attain at the national level. Some social reforms were initiated by national governments, but many municipalities became more active laboratories of social reform in the decades before World War I. Paternalist concern, pressures from the poor majority, and fear of the crowd all contributed to the expansion of municipal government services. A particularly open appeal to taxpayers' self-interest is apparent in a Russian call for municipal action in 1896: "Hundreds of thousands become corrupted by begging, commit crimes, threaten public safety, and ultimately land in prison and cost several times more than the most expensive cases of relief" (quoted in Brower, pp. 137–138).

Poor relief was typically guided by a belief that the middle class could offer moral instruction that would help the destitute improve their lot. This kind of charitable work had once been left to the churches, but increasingly the municipal governments mobilized volunteers, often middle-class women, to administer relief. Sooner or later, the scope of urban woes also galvanized new factions of urban reformist liberals committed to government social programs, even those that required intervention in the workings of the free market. In cities where at least some workers could vote, their representatives—often socialists—supported some of the same reforms. Activist mayors came to power in many cities and the scope of municipal government grew rapidly. The quadrupling of Budapest's municipal budget between 1892 and 1912 was not unusual. Birmingham, England, was a city that acquired a reputation for innovative programs under its mayor in the 1870s, Joseph Chamberlain (1836–1914), before he moved on to national politics. In the following decades, German cities were widely admired for their civic ethos, professional management, and innovative provision of services.

Among the largest municipal budget items were schools, hospitals, and poor relief. The construction of grand new streets, squares, and public buildings also put a visible stamp on the cities, but public works and sanitation projects more fundamentally altered the way the cities functioned. These included the lighting, paving, and cleaning of streets, trash collection, the construction of municipal slaughterhouses, the creation of parks, and, most important, the construction of sewers and waterworks.

Clean drinking water was a rare commodity in the growing mid-nineteenth-century cities, with piped water available in few places and wells increasingly contaminated. Although some older cities had sewer pipes in 1800, the pipes drained only small parts of town and were quickly overwhelmed by growth. In most cities, for much of the century, human waste was stored in cesspools and disposed of in buckets or in open sewers, often running down streets and into rivers. The stench was inescapable. But it was the fear of disease that brought about change. The most frightening scourge of the century was cholera, unknown in Europe until it arrived in 1830. New epidemics returned every few years throughout the century, each time sweeping through the cities and killing thousands, rich and poor alike. Year after year, however, even more people died from endemic diseases such as typhoid (spread, like cholera, by contaminated water) and tuberculosis. Theories tracing disease to contaminated air, water, and soil were widely accepted even before scientists identified the cholera and tuberculosis bacilli late in the century.

Public-health reformers such as Edwin Chadwick (1800–1890) in England argued that the most urgent projects were the construction of water and sewer systems. Despite the immense cost, most cities built them after midcentury. Clean water was the higher priority, with the sewer system typically coming soon after, since the introduction of abundant piped water encouraged the installation of flush toilets, which overwhelmed the old drainage gutters. (Even the combination of water and sewers often transferred the problem only as far as a nearby river, since little sewage was treated before the twentieth century. One early product of London's new drainage system was the "Great Stink" of 1858, when the dry Thames was overwhelmed by effluent.) Some early water systems supplied unfiltered water, as was apparent in the dirt and occasional small fish that came out of the tap, but filtering soon became the norm, especially after it became clear that filtered water did not spread cholera. The last European cholera epidemics, just before and after 1900, struck only cities with unfiltered water, notably Hamburg, Naples, and Russian towns.

A market square in Antwerp, Belgium, late nineteenth century. The central market square is perhaps the oldest and most distinguishing feature of European towns and cities. ©HULTON-DEUTSCH COLLECTION/CORBIS

In most places, rapid urban growth first led to increases in death rates. Later the construction of water and sewer systems, along with other public health measures, led to a marked drop in urban disease and mortality rates. Many cities became, statistically speaking, healthier places than the countryside.

THE REORGANIZATION OF URBAN SPACE

City streets were a feast for the senses: the lights and signs; the ceaseless motion and murmuring of the crowd; the shouts of the hawkers and the clatter of horses and wagons; the aromas of food for sale and the less pleasant stench of garbage and sewage. Some people reveled in the cacophony, while others, disturbed by it, sought to bring some order to the cities. The dramatic effects of sanitary reforms might have been apparent to the nose, but not necessarily to the eye. More visible projects included new streets, grand public buildings, and comprehensive plans for urban expansion.

As cities grew and urban land became more valuable, old buildings were replaced with taller ones, new wings filled former courtyards and gardens, and structures encroached on the street when the authorities turned a blind eye. Paris in 1850 was an extreme but hardly unique case of the relentless density of European cities. Few streets were more than fifteen feet wide, and few ran in a straight line or for very far. With more people, commerce, goods, and wagons, streets became all but impassable for much of the day. Only infrequently did cities amass the necessary powers to cut new thoroughfares through the labyrinth. Much admired examples from early in the century were Regent Street in London and Napoleon I's (r. 1804–1814/15) creation of the Rue de Rivoli in Paris.

At midcentury, the more systematic work of Napoleon III (1808–1873) and his prefect of Paris, Georges-Eugène Haussmann (1809–1891), set a model for the rest of France and beyond. It was easy to see the virtues of the wide, straight streets they tore through the old city. By providing space for the circulation of people, vehicles, and fresh air, the new boulevards eased acute problems of traffic and sanitation, opened the city center to redevelopment, and enhanced the authorities' ability to oversee and control the densely populated neighborhoods. However, the cost and disruption caused by these projects made them controversial and hard to imitate elsewhere. Cities that began the century smaller than Paris or London were more likely to bypass the tangled old quarters and lay out new extensions with wide streets. The grandest plans were possible where fortifications were removed. Two influential examples from the 1850s were Vienna and Barcelona, where the freed-up land beyond the old town walls was transformed into showcase districts with grand apartment buildings and boulevards for shopping and entertainment.

In general, East looked to West for urban models. Germans and Austrians often admired Paris (in the eighteenth century they had frequently imitated Versailles); Russians looked to Germany, if not beyond; and Vienna was the model for Balkan towns. Opinion on the Continent was divided about the virtues of England's more sprawling, low-rise urban development, but few considered it a viable model for their own towns.

Even the grandest plans barely kept up with growth. The imposition of order in the city center, as in Paris, often merely pushed the visible disorder to corners of the city that mattered less to civic leaders. A planned royal capital such as St. Petersburg might retain its elegant center, but smoking factory chimneys, visible from almost everywhere in the city, were an inescapable reminder of the capitalist mayhem of more remote districts.

Even as growth brought increased density of buildings and populations, then, it also led to the reorganization and segregation of urban space. In 1789 only a fortunate few could afford taxis or private carriages. Everyone else got around cities on foot, assuring that they would live, work, and play in close proximity to everyone else. Merchants and professionals lived and worked in their town-houses, and even factory owners often built their villas next to their mills. The poor majority lived near at hand, on upper floors or in adjoining courts and alleys.

Factories and railroads were the agents of change, with the placement of rail lines and stations often dictating the direction of later growth. The first stations at midcentury were typically built at a city's edge. New commercial quarters sprang up around them, often drawing banks, offices, hotels, and theaters out of the old town center. Factories lined up along rivers, canals, and rail lines, and they in turn attracted residential construction nearby. The presence of a labor force might then attract even more factories and workshops, since few workers could afford public transit before the end of the nineteenth century.

For most of the century public transport within the cities was limited to horse-drawn buses and streetcars, which were used mainly by the middle class. A dramatic increase in mobility came in the 1890s with the rapid spread of electric streetcars, which could carry far more passengers and do so more quickly and cheaply. They, along with the rapid-rail lines built above and below ground in a few of the largest cities, helped make cities much more bustling places. The increased mobility enabled those who could afford the transport services (at first a small minority) to live farther from work. As a result, purely residential districts could develop, while at the same time the resident population of city centers dropped as homes were displaced by offices and workshops. By the end of the century, the rich and the poor were also less likely to live next to each other, although often they still did. Workers still usually lived near factories, while much of the middle class, able to afford transportation, moved to quiet suburbs or to spacious flats or townhouses in exclusive residential neighborhoods, such as those created by reconstruction projects in Paris and Vienna. Thus areas of both the city center and the urban fringe became increasingly segregated by class and by use. The separation of home from work was most pronounced for the suburbanizing middle class of England, and it most affected women, who were subsequently less likely to be around and involved with shops and other family businesses.

THE HOUSING QUESTION

With larger, more segregated cities came the idea of slums, frightening no-go zones where respectable people rarely ventured. These might be found in the tangled lanes of the old town centers after the middle class had moved out, or in newly built tenement districts. The relatively few prosperous visitors to working-class districts recoiled at the filth and misery in which the urban poor were living. In 1843, for example, a magazine article lamented the conditions in the Old Town of Edinburgh, where

> the houses are often so close together, that persons may step from the window of one house to that of the house opposite—so high, piled story after story with the view of saving room, that the light can scarcely penetrate to the court beneath. In this part of the town there are neither sewers nor any private conveniences whatever belonging to the dwellings; and hence the excrementitious and other refuse of at least 50,000 persons is, during the night, thrown into the gutters, causing (in spite of the scavengers' daily labors) an amount of solid filth and fetid exhalation disgusting to both sight and smell, as well as exceedingly prejudicial to health. (quoted in Engels, 1958, p. 43)

The writer's conclusion was typical: "Can it be wondered that, in such localities, health, morals, and common decency should be at once neglected?" (p. 43). The living conditions of the urban working classes became a focal point for middle-class reformers worried about disease; about the immorality that they thought was breeding in the dark, damp, crowded conditions; about the violence that seemed endemic to the slums; and about the revolutionary potential of these concentrations of poverty, misery, and vice.

The rapidly growing cities faced chronic housing shortages. Housing construction was a major industry, with construction crews and half-built houses the typical sights at the city's edge. The lifting of many feudal regulations on the sale and ownership of land helped create a speculative housing market. Enterprising builders did a remarkable job of tapping sources of cheap capital, acquiring plots of land and covering them with as many new dwellings as the law permitted. Even as city populations doubled and tripled within a few years, most British and German cities (among others) largely kept up with the demand for housing. Not

so in Russia, where self-built shantytowns dominated the urban fringe.

Real-estate developers adapted local architectural traditions and building materials to their own needs and those of renters. In England, the Low Countries, and a few parts of northern France and northwestern Germany, builders continued to produce variations on the attached row house. These usually had only two stories, but when they were packed around narrow alleys and courts, living conditions could be stiflingly dense. In large cities farther south and east, but also in Scotland, five- and six-story apartment buildings became typical. Many middle-class reformers could not conceive of a decent existence in a building with a hundred or more residents, as became typical in major cities from Berlin and Vienna eastward.

Even when they found housing, the poor usually could afford little space for themselves. After spending (typically) half their incomes on food, families pinched pennies on rent, their second-largest household expenditure. An inability to pay the rent was the main reason why families moved very frequently within the cities. Most working-class housing was extraordinarily crowded. A population of several people per room was all too common across Europe; in St. Petersburg, it was the norm. Even when a family had its own one- or two-room apartment, it might take in lodgers, young men who often paid only for use of a bed. Middle-class observers found their presence in the home particularly distressing, fraught as it was with (as they saw it) danger to the sexual purity of women and children.

The sanitary problems endemic to overcrowded apartments were exacerbated by the lack of sunlight reaching many courtyard and alley dwellings. Worst of all, and cheapest, were damp cellar apartments, numerous in many towns. In addition, many residents long had to face the dangers and indignities of courtyard wells and privies. Even where water and sewer connections were in place, few apartments had bathrooms, while toilets were often located outside apartments and shared with other tenants.

At the dawn of the industrial age most building codes put only the most limited restrictions on the size and density of housing, although fire

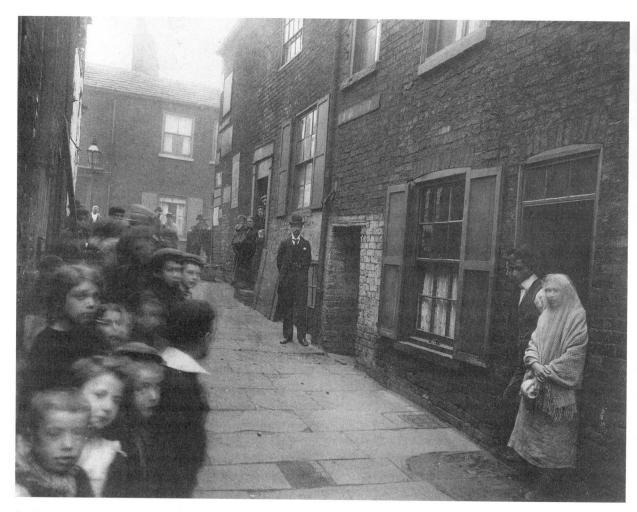

Sanitary inspector, Leeds, England, 1899. Residents watch as a sanitary inspector examines housing in an impoverished area of Leeds. A center of industrial expansion during the nineteenth century, the city also experienced the corollary problems associated with overcrowding. LEEDS LIBRARY AND INFORMATION SERVICES, LEEDS, UK/BRIDGEMAN ART LIBRARY

regulations contributed to brick and local stone largely supplanting wood as an urban construction material, except in Scandinavia and Russia. Late in the century reformers pushed through revised codes requiring better access to light and air, and cellar dwellings were prohibited in some places. Efforts to reduce crowding made little headway, however, in the face of high rents and housing shortages, despite the efforts of many civic activists engaged with the "housing question." A few employers built model housing for their workers, but that was rare in cities. More important were nonprofit housing societies and cooperatives that sprang up to build model tenements. Some reformers proposed government-sponsored housing, but most cities built little or none before World War I.

THE PROMISE AND DANGER OF CITY LIFE

An industrial boomtown like Manchester in 1840 inspired awe. The hulking factories and warehouses, the smoke and clamor, the crowds of workers streaming in and out—visitors had seen nothing remotely like it. The magnificent cotton exchange and the splendid villas hinted at the extent of the fortunes being made by the families molding this new urban world, while the slums and their inhabitants bore witness to the unequal distribution of the new wealth. Alexis de Tocqueville (1805–1859) declared, "Here humanity attains its most complete development and its most brutish. Here civilization works its miracles and civilized man is turned back almost into a savage." "Rightly understood," wrote the novelist and politician Benjamin Disraeli (1804–1881), "Manchester is as great a human exploit as Athens." After tramping its back streets, the young German socialist Friedrich Engels (1820–1895) came away with a darker view of a town sharply divided between factory owners and their armies of workers: "Once I walked with one of these middle-class men into Manchester. I spoke to him about the shabby, unhealthy construction and the disgraceful condition of the workers' districts. I declared that I had never seen such a badly built town. He listened patiently and, at the corner of the street at which he left me, he remarked: 'And yet there is a great deal of money made here. Good morning, Sir.'" (Engels, 1844, p. 489).

Cities laid bare the dangers of a turbulent and materialistic age. The evils Charles Dickens (1812–1870) displayed in his fictional Coketown only began with its repellent ugliness and filth. The inescapable poverty of the slums seemed all the worse in light of the deadening monotony of life and the dissolution of old social bonds, apparent in the reduction of the relation between master and men to a mere "cash nexus," as well as in the presence of so many beggars, prostitutes, and criminals. (As a percentage of the population, they were probably not much more numerous than in the countryside, but their visibility made them seem so.) Dickens was one of many people who became convinced that something had to be done about the seething urban cauldrons—to transform them or somehow get rid of them—before they exploded in a revolution that would destroy everything modern Europe had achieved.

At the same time cities embodied the hopes of a dynamic new world. Out of the factories, banks, and exchanges poured hitherto unfathomable riches. The heady excitement of urban life and the great achievements of the talents collected in the cities added to the ever-growing allure of the great capitals—Paris, London, Vienna, Berlin—but were also ever more apparent in the Manchesters and Düsseldorfs. Sooner or later even these provincial towns could boast stately new buildings, grand boulevards, and elegant crowds utterly unlike anything they had known before. Arguing against the prevailing Romantic ideal of pastoral beauty, which saw the cities as crimes against nature, some commentators insisted on the grandeur of the metropolis. Cities might dissolve old social bonds, but, as pioneer sociologists argued, the resulting freedom gave men and women the chance to build a new society that honored individual achievement. Even fierce critics of capitalist splendor such as Engels and his colleague, Karl Marx (1818–1883), looked to the cities to fulfill their hopes for a successful revolution that would enable everyone to share the bounties of industry, while more moderate reformers continued to believe that industrial Europe had only begun to realize the promise of city life.

See also **Athens; Barcelona; Berlin; Class and Social Relations; Crime; Disease; Factories; Housing; Industrial Revolution, First; Industrial Revolution, Second; Paris; Professions; Prostitution; Public Health; Race and Racism; St. Petersburg; Vienna.**

BIBLIOGRAPHY

Briggs, Asa. *Victorian Cities.* London, 1963.

Brower, Daniel R. *The Russian City between Tradition and Modernity, 1850–1900.* Berkeley, Calif., 1990.

Clark, Peter, ed. *The Cambridge Urban History of Britain.* 3 vols. Cambridge, U.K., and New York, 2000.

Daunton, M. J., ed. *Housing the Workers, 1850–1914: A Comparative Perspective.* London and New York, 1990.

Duby, Georges, ed. *Histoire de la France urbaine,* vol. 4: *La ville de l'âge industriel.* Paris, 1983.

Engels, Friedrich. *The Condition of the Working Class in England.* Translated and edited by W. O. Henderson and W. H. Chaloner. Oxford, U.K., 1958.

———. *Die Lage der arbeitenden Klassen in England.* 1844. In Vol. 2 of *Werke* by Karl Marx and Friedrich Engels. East Berlin, 1972.

Evans, Richard J. *Death in Hamburg: Society and Politics in the Cholera Years, 1830–1910.* Oxford, U.K., and New York, 1987.

Gavrilova, Raina. *Bulgarian Urban Culture in the Eighteenth and Nineteenth Centuries.* Cranbury, N.J., 1999.

Hamm, Michael F., ed. *The City in Late Imperial Russia.* Bloomington, Ind., 1986.

Hohenberg, Paul M., and Lynn Hollen Lees. *The Making of Urban Europe, 1000–1994.* Cambridge, Mass., 1995.

Hurd, Madeleine. *Public Spheres, Public Mores, and Democracy: Hamburg and Stockholm, 1870–1914.* Ann Arbor, Mich., 2000.

Jackson, James H., Jr. *Migration and Urbanization in the Ruhr Valley, 1821–1914*. Atlantic Highlands, N.J., 1997.

Ladd, Brian. *Urban Planning and Civic Order in Germany, 1860–1914*. Cambridge, Mass., 1990.

Lees, Andrew. *Cities Perceived: Urban Society in European and American Thought, 1820–1940*. New York, 1985.

Lenger, Friedrich, ed. *Towards an Urban Nation: Germany since 1780*. Oxford, U.K., and New York, 2002.

McKay, John P. *Tramways and Trolleys: The Rise of Urban Mass Transport in Europe*. Princeton, N.J., 1976.

Merriman, John M. *The Margins of City Life: Explorations on the French Urban Frontier, 1815–1851*. New York, 1991.

Olsen, Donald J. *The City as a Work of Art: London, Paris, Vienna*. New Haven, Conn., 1986.

Pinol, Jean-Luc, and François Walter. "La ville contemporaine jusqu'à la Second Guerre mondiale. " In *Histoire de l'Europe Urbaine*, Vol. 2: *De L'Ancien Regime à nous jours*, edited by Jean-Luc Pinol, 11–275. Paris, 2003.

Roberts, Robert. *The Classic Slum: Salford Life in the First Quarter of the Century*. Manchester, U.K., 1971.

Schlör, Joachim. *Nights in the Big City: Paris, Berlin, London 1840–1930*. Translated by Pierre Gottfried Imhof and Dafydd Rees Roberts. London, 1998.

Singer, Issac Bashevis. *In My Father's Court*. New York, 1966.

Walker, Mack. *German Home Towns: Community, State, and General Estate, 1648–1871*. Ithaca, N.Y., 1971.

Waller, P. J. *Town, City, and Nation: England, 1850–1914*. Oxford, U.K., and New York, 1983.

BRIAN LADD

CITIZENSHIP. The concept of citizenship claims a venerable intellectual tradition. The lived history of modern citizenship, however, was born in conflict and revolution. In June 1789, when the French Estates-General reseated itself—not as the three estates of the land but as the National Assembly—and proclaimed that it would not disband until it had written a constitution for the French nation, the delegates in Versailles had declared themselves citizens. Their right to form a new government, a new covenant between themselves, stemmed from universalist principles of natural law and freedoms inherent in their humanity.

In making revolution, Abbé Emmanuel Sieyès explained, the people reclaimed their sovereignty from absolutist monarchy and set forth to remake state power in their own image. By placing popular sovereignty at the center of the exercise of power, this profound transformation of political personae from subjects of royal power to self-actualized citizenry stirred hopes and fears that shaped politics and state boundaries for the next century.

DEFINITION OF CITIZENSHIP

The French Revolution of 1789 may have fused popular sovereignty and nationhood as powerful philosophical abstractions, but what did it mean when men and women addressed each other as *citoyens* and *citoyennes*? Scholars have helpfully distinguished between seventeenth-century natural law arguments, which that established the discourse of rights protecting individual liberties from state incursions, from the older tradition drawn from Athenian civic republicanism that emphasized individual virtue along with the duties and obligations of belonging. While analytically important in understanding political discourse, most working models of participatory government mix the two, balancing the negative expressions of rights (the delimitations of state power) with positive assertions of membership (also conceived of as rights) that name the entitlements and responsibilities of inclusion.

In the juncture of events during the French Revolution, however, the process of limiting royal power also exposed unbridgeable disputes over the purposes of good government and the nature of representation, particularly as they addressed popular participation and the welfare of the people. Thus when Louis XVI withdrew his grudging support of constitutional monarchy and appealed ineffectively to royalists within and outside French borders, the pressures of maintaining the Revolution through internal dissension and external war turned principled disagreements into factional struggles that toppled and led to the convening of many forms of government. Between 1791 and 1815, there were a total of four constitutions, each of which radically restructured the relationship between executive and legislative power and redefined the practical meaning of participation and self-governance.

THE ROLE OF REVOLUTION

Although the Revolution gathered many critics, it also enjoyed avid defenders. From the constitutional monarchy of 1789 to the Jacobin republic of 1792, to emergency wartime rule by the Committee of Public Safety, to the oligarchy of the Directory, and finally to the charismatic authoritarian plebiscite democracy of Napoleon I—each phase of revolutionary development reached across state boundaries to inspire different groups of sympathizers in neighboring territories and across the Channel. Thus when the concert of old European monarchical empires aligned to defeat the French Republic in 1792 and later in 1815 to restore the balance of power among themselves, they quickly realized that the threat to their social and political order was internal as well as external. Although the Congress of Vienna (1814–1815) was supposed to have reestablished autocratic power, in fact, Europe's absolutist rulers mostly understood that old regimes could not be restored without some concessions to participatory government. Balancing their fear of revolution against their anxieties over power sharing, entrenched aristocratic elites made selective accommodations to the upper echelons of non-noble property owners. Hence even in the symbolically freighted restoration of the Bourbons to the French crown, Louis XVIII governed with a charter (the Charter of 1814) that placed constitutional limits on his power and provided an elected chamber, albeit with a highly restrictive franchise that excluded 90 percent of the adult population.

In Great Britain after 1820, the ascendancy of moderate Tories and Whigs pushed through electoral changes resulting in the Reform Act of 1832, which doubled the number of voters among householders and modified the dominance of the landed gentry. Constitutional movements in the southern German states met with equally positive responses. By the early 1820s, the duchies of Nassau and Saxe-Weimar-Eisenach and the kingdoms of Bavaria, Baden, and Württemberg had given themselves written constitutions based on compromises between the old aristocratic order, the crown, and new principles of bourgeois society. Reforms within Prussia had begun before 1815, and even though the constitutional movements associated with Heinrich Friedrich vom Stein and Karl August von Hardenberg failed, reformers succeeded in bringing the bureaucratic state under the rule of law and instituted some safeguards for civil liberties.

Could these autocratic states and limited monarchies have met the participatory desires of its haute bourgeoisie and middle classes without conceding the primacy of their power base and monarchical principles? Each locality, of course, offered its own story, but pragmatic compromises were often eclipsed by the recent memory of revolution. By their example, revolutionaries in France had forever cast aside any belief that patient supplication to sovereign rulers was the only route for attaining political change. Moreover the intellectual culture of the Revolution had drawn conceptual links between various liberal demands, creating a coherent program for change. Hence when liberals thought of themselves as citizens in the post-Revolutionary era, the systemic incompatibility between theories of popular sovereignty and theories of monarchical authority (particularly those of absolutist hereditary rule) reminded them that they lived at odds with the basic political tenets of their society. In such a context, annoyances moved easily to principled opposition.

LIBERALISM

This revolutionary potential built into liberal aspirations was enhanced by the possibilities of radical alliances. In Paris during the summer of 1830, for example, the more strident agitation of craftsmen, journeymen, university students, and journalists joined with the protest of liberal elites against press censorship and royal usurpations of the Charter of 1814. Their collective power was demonstrated at the barricades when, after only a few days of bloodshed, Charles X abdicated. In the German states, the French Revolution of 1830 reactivated liberal movements that had turned in solace to romantic quests for a pan-German community through spiritual reform and self-improvement (in such associations such as the Turn-Vereins and Burschenshaften). In Munich, Göttingen, Hanover, and Frankfurt, as in Paris, bourgeois and middle-class militants combined with artisans, workers, students, and journalists to organize festivals and political banquets. In the spirit of civil disobedience, they offered toasts, made incendiary speeches, and sang the "Marseillaise."

In the 1830s, state authorities everywhere in central Europe crushed the flowering of rebelliousness before the new popular alliance could be tested. Despite the evident potentials of their combined forces, bourgeois liberalism and radical democracy were fundamentally not alike. They appealed to different conceptions of society and politics. And although they both held that the citizen was sovereign, they differed on who could be a citizen. Within a liberal worldview, only those individuals who were legally free to enter into contracts as self-possessing agents could participate in public life. Conceiving the civic realm as growing out of associational life, self-government among equals meant the setting of common rules as part of the broader protection of individual freedoms. By contrast, radicals often invoked an almost literal understanding of the common body as the basis of collective life, leading to very different descriptions of the bonds between citizens, of mutual obligation, and of equality. Against the barriers established by property qualifications, artisans and the laboring poor claimed that their skills or their labor constituted property. In so doing, they joined other groups who also challenged the liberal definition of the autonomous individual handed down from seventeenth-century theorists, which conceived of personhood not only as inseparable from landed and productive wealth but also in terms of proprietary rights in others: wives, children, servants, and slaves. Thus not surprisingly, the discourses of slave emancipation and feminism shared a common appeal to self-possession as the natural precondition for self-determination and civic participation as equals.

INEQUALITY AND CITIZENSHIP

In other respects, however, the deeper challenge faced by these disenfranchised groups against persisting distinctions between "active" and "passive" citizens first introduced in the French Constitution of 1791 centered on the difficult task of redefining "civic virtue." Here the "disqualifications" represented by race and sex take different forms. During the French Revolution and throughout much of the nineteenth century, the exclusion of women from active citizenship as creatures inherently incapable of justice or dispassionate reason was part of the process of defining the public realm as an

expression of bourgeois masculinity. Hence, the "impairments" of femaleness named were multiple and contradictory—setting the vindication of feminine capacity and moral rectitude in the following century in often opposing directions. Through the century, feminists maintained their critique of liberal individualism, although the women mobilizing for change demanded both special laws and services that addressed their specific conditions and contributions as women and argued for the irrelevance of bodily distinctions in sharing the rights and entitlements granted to men. Ironically, the long-awaited recognition of women's "worthiness" for citizenship finally came in the twentieth century as the liberal model of citizenry underwent radical transformation at the initiative of state authority.

Contrary to expectations, given the inability to fully integrate citizens of non-European descent in the Europe of the early twenty-first century, racial equality in citizenship was not an empty promise in the French Revolution. The National Assembly recognized and defended the claims of the few colonial mulatto and free black men who fully qualified for the franchise. The more consequential issue came with abolition. In both French and British colonies, the claims and entitlements of former slaves exposed the contradictions of the liberal legacy. Although the course of emancipation took very different routes in the two empires (slavery was abolished in French colonies in 1794, reinstated in 1802, and abolished again in 1848; British abolition was accomplished in 1833), both the French and British colonial administrations framed the question of citizenship for freedmen and -women fully within the problem of managing a potentially disorderly labor force. For abolitionists, the central questions of inclusion and belonging stalled around questions of "worthiness." Discussions of freedom were thus redirected to the questions of tutelage. There, the long probation of blacks became inextricably entwined with congenital interpretations of bodily differences in European science and politics. What might have begun as the prejudices of class centered on the impossibility of those who must labor to claim civic virtue became the indelible disqualifications of phenotype.

These enduring problems of sexism and racism have recast assessments of radical movements for direct democracy in the first half of the nineteenth century. Scholars have mostly interpreted these political programs in light of the social discontents behind protest (poverty, subsistence crises, unemployment), but as the masses mobilized by the People's Charter (1838) in Britain demonstrated, their radical democratic vision did not come primarily from workplace or marketplace struggles (despite the many close connections to Owenite socialism). Rather, the Chartists formulated a populist theory of justice as part of the broader agitation led by the middle classes against the Corn Laws and for extending the franchise. Out of a shared political arena, the Chartists articulated a vision of citizenship distinct from their liberal counterparts. On the Continent, although radical artisans, journeymen, and the laboring poor were influenced by various schools of socialist thought (Saint-Simonians, Fourierists, Louis Blanc, and later Karl Marx, Ferdinand Lassalle, and Pierre-Joseph Proudhon), in France and the German-speaking states where guild traditions were strong, models for participatory democracy often spoke the language of the corporatist tradition mixed with the universalist language of freedom and rights from the French Revolution. Nonetheless, the solidarities of working men typically demanded honor and recognition *as men*—despite the fact that working women also fought for universal suffrage (before upper-class women mobilized for the equal franchise), salaried elected representatives, and collective responsibility for the livelihood of the poor. Working women readily mounted to the barricades to demand price maximums on subsistence goods and national workshops to redress unemployment in female-dominated trades. Similarly, although socialist rhetoric was internationalist, working men organized within national political boundaries and conceived of politics from within national traditions. Support for abolition (especially among the Chartists) and fleeting expressions of solidarity aside, few nineteenth-century radicals thought systemically about the possible connections and commonalities between colonial subjects and the European poor. Yet from the perspective of political economy, the theory of wage labor as free labor was conceived at the point at which colonial and metropolitan economies joined.

CITIZENRY AND STATE AUTHORITY

Despite the limits of masculinist and nationalist blinders, class-based analysis and alliances remain significant in comprehending the revolutions that swept across the continent again in 1848. The near victories but ultimate defeats of liberalism and republicanism brought out the familiar refrain that the bourgeoisie had preferred to compromise with autocratic power rather than to risk threats from below. Whether one believed that the temporary triumph of antidemocratic forces was the result of betrayal or cowardice, certainly the arrest and deportation of radicals marked a dramatic setback for all populist causes. At midcentury, European politics was dominated by the territorial conquests and limited wars of German and Italian unification. But looking beyond the changing European balance of power to the domestic policies of empire/nation building, one sees that revolution and popular sovereignty still preoccupied the politics of reaction. For example, the new constitution for the German Empire granted universal male suffrage but negated the power of the vote by denying any real decision-making power to the federal representative body. While the Reichstag nominally held the purse strings, the crown retained its independence because the military and the foreign office remained constitutionally under the control of the emperor and his chancellor. But even such structural guarantees were not enough. The preservation of the old landed and military elites ultimately depended on Otto von Bismarck's ability to manage the new sources of social power emerging from a rapidly industrializing empire. Here, the German chancellor's innovations both transformed the nature of autocracy and remade civil society. While the empire prohibited the independent self-organization of industrialists, middle-class professionals, workers, peasants, Catholics, and others, Bismarck wooed each group with specially targeted benefits. The results were often unexpected. For example, the much more politically conservative German Empire was far ahead of Britain and France in providing state-sponsored insurance and old-age pensions for the working classes. But, at the same time, the German Social Democratic Party, the largest socialist party in Europe, was outlawed.

By recognizing that citizens had claims on the state, modern autocratic states further shifted the power relations between state and citizenry in favor of state authority—not only through repression or usurpations but also by ascribing new responsibilities to itself and cultivating new clients. While such expansions of state power may seem unremarkable within an existing autocratic structure, parallel patterns—those emerging in late Victorian Britain and the French Third Republic as parliamentary politics stabilized through the disciplining practices of new political parties—are noteworthy. By the early twentieth century, the prevailing wisdom in the competitive system of European nation-states was that their very modernity rested on an effective compromise between enlightened statecraft from above and populist nationalism from below. To the degree that bureaucratic organizations needed popular mandates to effectively harness the nation's productive and reproductive power, to build military might, and to garner international respect, citizens as entitled subjects of state power also gained many benefits through public resources. As the sociologist T. H. Marshall would later theorize in the middle of the twentieth century, but that European states had already begun to put into practice decades earlier, a comprehensive population policy covering health, education, housing, and old age attached to the entitlements of citizenship promoted new understandings of social progress and equality. But such policies also empowered bureaucracies as the guarantors of rights and entitlements. While the rules therein were open to legislative and procedural change, the expansion of state power was unmistakable. Even in moments of popular protest and discontent, the state remained the object of petition and the source of recognition.

CONCLUSION

Taking the century-long view then, one is tempted to ask: Is the history of citizenship between 1789 and 1914 the story of its containment and management? Ideologically, "the people" have become indispensable. But once their consent has been mobilized, they become marginal to the everyday tasks of governing. Could the much-touted final triumph of liberalism in the parliamentary democracies of western Europe at the end of the century be said to be the result of the conscious demobilization of citizenry through the routinization of politics? While popular sovereignty may be both the victim as well as the spark that ignited the anguished transformation of political power from

absolutist monarchies to modern nation-states, the evocative power of citizenship even as abstract principle has continued to mobilize hope. In the twentieth century when centralized power has collapsed in wartime and other severe political crises, such as between 1917 through the mid-1920s and immediately after 1945, citizens in neighborhoods, union halls, and even soldiers' barracks have readily claimed collective self-rule. In the early twenty-first century, as new groups bring their aspirations for inclusion and belonging, the utopian appeal of the concept of citizenship invites mobilizations fueled by desires that are difficult to extinguish. There thus remains an "unruly" promise in the vision of citizenship first announced in eighteenth-century revolutions that seems always to exceed the limits of received politics.

See also **Minorities; Nationalism.**

BIBLIOGRAPHY

Arendt, Hannah. *On Revolution.* New York, 1963. Reprint, Westport, Conn., 1982.

Brubaker, Rogers. *Citizenship and Nationhood in France and Germany.* Cambridge, Mass., 1992.

Dubois, Laurent. *A Colony of Citizens: Revolution and Slave Emancipation in the French Caribbean, 1787–1804.* Chapel Hill, N.C., 2004.

Heater, Derek. *A Brief History of Citizenship.* New York, 2004.

Hobsbawm, Eric J. *The Age of Revolution: Europe, 1789–1848.* London, 1962.

———. *Nations and Nationalism since 1780: Programme, Myth, Reality.* Cambridge, U.K., 1990.

Holt, Thomas C. *The Problem of Freedom: Race, Labor, and Politics in Jamaica and Britain, 1832–1938.* Baltimore, Md., 1992.

Marshall, T. H. *Citizenship and Social Class, and Other Essays.* Cambridge, U.K., 1950.

Nipperdey, Thomas. *Germany from Napoleon to Bismarck, 1800–1866.* Translated by Daniel Nolan. Princeton, N.J., 1996.

Riesenberg, Peter. *Citizenship in the Western Tradition: Plato to Rousseau.* Chapel Hill, N.C., 1992.

Scott, Joan Wallach. *Only Paradoxes to Offer: French Feminists and the Rights of Man.* Cambridge, Mass., 1996.

Sewell, William H., Jr. *Work and Revolution in France: The Language of Labor from the Old Regime to 1848.* Cambridge, U.K., 1980.

———. *The Rhetoric of Bourgeois Revolution: Abbé Sieyès and "What Is the Third Estate?"* Durham, N.C., 1994.

Thompson, Dorothy. *The Chartists: Popular Politics in the Industrial Revolution.* New York, 1984.

TESSIE P. LIU

CIVILIZATION, CONCEPT OF.

According to the historian Lucien Febvre, the French word *civilisation* was first coined in the middle of the eighteenth century, and denoted the state of being conditioned into civility or polite society (often associated with a state, *civitas*). The same concept was expressed in English by the word *refinement* (before the advent of the word *civilization*) and in German by *Kultur* (even after the invention of *Zivilisation*). Eventually, "civilization" would accumulate additional meanings: the process of acquiring culture or refinement, the sum total of cultural assets at a certain level of development, and the identity of a group sharing these assets. Although the last definition gave rise to a looser usage—seemingly interchangeable with designations such as "people," "culture," or "race"—"civilization" in the nineteenth century was usually applied to what were considered "advanced" groups, often appearing as the last of a developmental triad with "savagery" and "barbarism."

Writers have never agreed on the precise form of development denoted by civilization, but generally the concept was understood to include some or all of the following: written language, the dominance of intellect over passion and superstition, dissemination of knowledge by education, religious monotheism, political organization, technological mastery over the natural environment, and the progress of economic subsistence through modern agriculture, urban commerce, and manufacturing.

For the Enlightenment philosophers, who saw civilization outside of Europe as well as within it, the concept implied a unitary standard of human values. Civilization rested on a universalistic, democratic optimism that all human societies were united by the capacity for progress along the same path, either on their own or through the tutelage of others. At the same time, the concept implied (rather undemocratically) a hierarchy of peoples according to where they stood presently on the continuum between primitive or savage and civilized. In the middle of the nineteenth century, these core beliefs became the foundation of what is known in the history of anthropological thought as classical evolutionism (lucidly explicated by George Stocking). In spite of the etymological association of civilization with Enlightenment ideas, nevertheless, it is clear that many nineteenth-century Europeans understood civilizations and cultures through a lens of Romantic pluralism: different civilizations were *essentially* different, might have had different origins, and might be subject not only to progress but also to degeneration or disappearance. Some peoples, according to this worldview, might even be incapable of reaching some of the milestones of civilization (and therefore could be disregarded or even sacrificed to European expansion).

Whatever its philosophical underpinnings or exact definition, civilization, in the words of Norbert Elias, became essentially "the self-consciousness of the West." Europeans' confidence that their civilization was of a level unprecedented by any other in human history was further solidified by the political and especially (as Michael Adas argues) industrial-technological transformations of the late eighteenth and early nineteenth centuries.

Europeans' generalized identity as civilized, however, never entirely overshadowed the divisiveness of national identities. Many thinkers invented nationalistic variants of civilization and claimed that theirs was the most advanced.

CIVILIZING MISSION

Civilization's putative universality made it transferable beyond Europe and thus seemed to give new purpose and justification to European expansion. Indeed, the term *civilizing mission* has traditionally been associated with European activities in Asia and Africa. But only since the late twentieth century has its role *within* Europe taken a prominent place in the work of historians. Arguably, one of the first civilizing missions was the spread of the French Revolution—that great crusade for progress—throughout Europe by Napoleonic France. Afterward, European states and elites undertook the extension of civilization downward on the social scale and outward from capitals to the rural world.

As Eugen Weber has described it, the process of making "peasants into Frenchmen"—rooting out linguistic and intellectual parochialism and instilling what were considered proper manners, mores, and mentalities through nationalizing institutions such as schools—was essentially a civilizing mission. According to Weber, the completion of this process came relatively late (between 1870 and 1914), but many historians have described such civilizing activities earlier in the nineteenth century.

While such campaigns seemed natural to those with a nationalistic worldview, Europeans' efforts to conquer, exploit, and dominate peoples on other continents stood in greater need of a justifying slogan. And because of the starker cultural differences between Europeans and their overseas subjects, such a slogan had to surmount doubts about those subjects' capability of being improved. Few historians argue that the civilizing mission was the core motivation or origin of European imperialism. To the contrary, many describe it as humanitarian window dressing to excuse the sins of imperialists in the eyes of both metropolitan audiences and the colonized themselves. It included projects such as schooling; conversion to Christianity; the development of commerce; administrative, legal, and judicial reform; scientific research on local cultures and natural resources; public-health efforts; and campaigns to instill new norms of domesticity. Each of these spheres gave rise to its own discourse of civility and civilization. Many of these activities, although packaged as the fulfillment of humanitarian obligation, were at least in part matters of expediency and self-interest, undertaken to enhance European states' control and domination of colonized peoples. Most historians would agree, nonetheless, that the concept of civilizing mission—by constraining rhetorical strategies, setting moral standards (even if these were not always followed in practice), and expressing European vanity—did help to shape imperial policies.

CONTROVERSIES AND VARIANTS

Civilizing missions rarely treated the non-European milieu as a tabula rasa for the simple replication of European standards. Usually the civilizers pursued their goals using a combination of indigenous and European elements, engendering controversies over when to supplant native customs, when to modify them, when to leave them alone, and how

much agency to give subjects in their own improvement. The outcome of such debates depended upon both pragmatism and views of subjects' civilizational status and capacity for progress. The imposition of European ways was most aggressive when local practices seemed to conflict sharply with "civilized" mores, as in campaigns against cannibalism, sati (ritual widow-burning in India), slavery, brigandage, child marriage, brutal punishments, and tyranny. Even in these initiatives, attempts were sometimes made to present changes less as interventions from outside than attempts to make practice conform to native traditions (e.g., in the case of sati, to satisfy the principles of Hinduism).

Historians have shown that European descriptions of colonized peoples were often fashioned around the assumptions of the civilizing mission; subjects were rhetorically "savaged" (sometimes against available evidence) to demonstrate their need for European tutelage. This was even done to peoples who by some definitions were considered civilized—in particular adherents of Islam and Judaism. Muslims (who were present in all of the major empires) and Jews (considered imperial subjects only in Russia) were, in spite of possessing many attributes of civilization, often subject to the most aggressive cultural manipulation. (In the blood libel, which survived from medieval times, Jews were falsely accused of the most primitive of behaviors—human sacrifice and cannibalism.) In effect, non-European variants of civilization were as objectionable as lack of civilization. But the imperial powers were not always glad to see their efforts succeed; they were wary and spiteful toward the subjects who became most Europeanized, such as Bengali *babus* in British India and Muslim *jadids* in the Russian Empire.

The chief proponents of a civilizing mission outside of Europe were the British, French, and Russian empires. Britain tended to preserve native institutions and hierarchies, in effect presenting its civilizing mission as an attempt to recapture subject peoples' own degraded civilizations. The model for this indirect rule was established in India and then exported to other British colonies in Africa and Asia. The French approach was traditionally labeled assimilation (being strongly influenced by Republican egalitarianism), giving colonial subjects many of the same political-social structures as those

N° 697 — 19ᵉ Année   PRIX DU NUMÉRO : 40 CENTIMES   26 Novembre 1898

La Caricature

JOURNAL HEBDOMADAIRE   JOURNAL HEBDOMADAIRE

Abonnements : France, 1 an : 20 francs. — 6 mois : 11 francs. — Union postale, 1 an : 26 francs. — 6 mois, 13 francs. — Bureaux : 79, boulevard Saint-Michel.

LES PIONNIERS DE LA CIVILISATION. — par LION

JOHN BELL. — Heureusement que nous sommes là, nous, les bons Anglais, pour pacifier et civiliser le Monde.

Pioneers of Civilization: John Bull Bringing Peace and Civilization to the World. The cover illustration of the French journal *La Caricature,* 26 November 1898, lampoons the harshness of British colonial policies. BIBLIOTHÈQUE DES ARTS DECORATIFS, PARIS, FRANCE/BRIDGEMAN ART LIBRARY/ARCHIVES CHARMET

of France proper (although not always viewing them as potential French citizens) and concerned with the process (*mise en valeur*) of making subjects useful for France. Russia's approach was the most direct and genuinely assimilatory: administrators talked of the organic integration of Asian peoples into the Russian nation, and while many native structures continued to exist they were absorbed into Russian polity and society. And although the British and French attempted to put distance between metropolitans and colonials, Russia's idea of civilizing mission was also distinguished by encouragement of miscegenation between the "core" Russians and colonized peoples on the frontier.

Many Russians acknowledged the civilizing mission's unique compensatory aspect for their country: the mentorship of supposedly lesser peoples could counterbalance the image of Russia as backward itself. This required that the improvement of dominated peoples not be pursued along generic European lines (which was possible since the Russian aristocracy was traditionally steeped in French and German culture) but be approached as tantamount to Russification. In the context of rivalry with Britain, tsarist statesmen also claimed that Russia was a more just and more humane carrier of civilization to Asia because its peasant masses on the frontiers were closer in mentality to Asians and more tolerant of cultural differences than were Europeans settling in overseas colonies. Indeed, Russian imperialism was bound to appear more egalitarian because the Russian people themselves had few political rights.

But civilizing missions were not only the work of imperial states wielding power through laws and institutions. They also involved autonomous efforts on the part of European society in both metropole and colony: church missions and missionary societies; capitalists marketing their products to subjugated peoples; belles lettres and journalism as tools of colonial muckraking; women's organizations advocating improved conditions for their gender in the colonies. Many of these activities were in effect forms of middle-class self-expression, and therefore it is not surprising that of the imperial powers they were least evident in Russia, whose bourgeoisie was least developed.

All the empires shared concerns about relations in colonial settings between metropolitans and natives and expressed anxiety about whether the former were truly capable of representing a higher civilization to the latter. The seamier sides of European life—vagrancy, prostitution, violence, drunkenness, insanity—were often on display for colonial subjects to see. These problems challenged the validity of nineteenth-century Europe's transformation of civilization as an attribute of class or status groups into the property of larger national and racial collectivities. European societies were aware of having failed to achieve their internal civilizing missions, although the language of empire often assumed success. Indeed much recent research on nineteenth-century imperialism has shown the simultaneity and interdependency of the two processes.

METAMORPHOSIS

By the late nineteenth and early twentieth centuries, a number of trends led to the decreased appeal of the concepts of civilization and civilizing mission as they had been known. The increasing hybridity of societies in the European overseas colonies (and Russian imperial borderlands) made the concepts' ambiguities harder to deny, traditional dichotomies harder to defend, and the empires themselves harder to maintain without a change of approach. The increasing secularization of European culture weakened the Manichean frame of mind that had separated peoples into the civilized and uncivilized. The rise of an industrial, self-reliant Japan, and its defeat of imperial Russia, challenged the assumption of the inherent superiority of Europe over Asia. And the cultures of many Eastern and "primitive" peoples found positive appreciation in European anthropology and in artistic and philosophical movements.

By most accounts, however, it was the cataclysm of World War I that decisively jolted Europeans and their non-European subjects alike out of old ways of thinking. Britain, France, and Russia described their struggle (for which they mobilized their colonized peoples as well as their Continental populations) as the very defense of civilization—yet the foe was within Europe, not outside it. The carnage produced by a continent focusing all its ingenuity on perfecting methods of killing and destruction made European authorities and elites look rather like the savages they had been dedicated to transforming both at home and abroad. If Europe's achievements could still be considered civilization, that word's meaning had to be reassessed to account for the accompanying dislocations and "discontents" Sigmund Freud (1856–1939) would later describe.

A new understanding of civilization emerged—more pluralistic and inclusive, and stripped of much of the nineteenth-century ethnocentrism and arrogance. This shift challenged imperial powers to justify their actions in new ways, leading to some new approaches (in France, associationism, which preserved more elements of subjects' native cultures, and in Russia, indigenization, invented by the Bolsheviks to undo the effects of tsarist chauvinism), and eventually to decolonization.

See also **Citizenship; Colonialism; Eurasianism; Imperialism; Manners and Formality; Minorities; Race and Racism; Slavophiles; Westernizers.**

BIBLIOGRAPHY

Adas, Michael. *Machines as the Measure of Men: Science, Technology, and Ideologies of Western Dominance.* Ithaca, N.Y., 1989.

Bullard, Alice. *Exile to Paradise: Savagery and Civilization in Paris and the South Pacific, 1790–1900.* Stanford, Calif., 2000.

Burton, Antoinette. *Burdens of History: British Feminists, Indian Women, and Imperial Culture, 1865–1915.* Chapel Hill, N.C., 1994.

Conklin, Alice L. *A Mission to Civilize: The Republican Idea of Empire in France and West Africa, 1895–1930.* Stanford, Calif., 1997.

Cooper, Frederick, and Ann Laura Stoler, eds. *Tensions of Empire: Colonial Cultures in a Bourgeois World.* Berkeley, Calif., 1997.

Elias, Norbert. *The Civilizing Process.* Vol. 1: *The History of Manners.* Translated by Edmund Jephcott. New York, 1978.

Febvre, Lucien. "Civilisation: Evolution of a Word and a Group of Ideas." In *A New Kind of History: From the Writings of Febvre,* edited by Peter Burke. Translated by K. Folca. New York, 1973.

Geraci, Robert P. *Window on the East: National and Imperial Identities in Late Tsarist Russia.* Ithaca, N.Y., 2001.

Mani, Lata. *Contentious Traditions: The Debate on Sati in Colonial India.* Berkeley, Calif., 1998.

McClintock, Anne. *Imperial Leather: Race, Gender, and Sexuality in the Colonial Contest.* New York, 1995.

Metcalf, Thomas R. *Ideologies of the Raj.* Cambridge, U.K., and New York, 1995.

Slezkine, Yuri. *Arctic Mirrors: Russia and the Small Peoples of the North.* Ithaca, N.Y., 1994.

Stocking, George W., Jr. *Victorian Anthropology.* New York, 1987.

Williams, Raymond. "Culture and Civilization." In *The Encyclopedia of Philosophy,* edited by Paul Edwards. New York, 1967.

Weber, Eugen. *Peasants into Frenchmen: The Modernization of Rural France, 1870–1914.* Stanford, Calif., 1976.

ROBERT P. GERACI

CIVIL SOCIETY. The term *civil society* is an elusive and often contradictory abstraction that has been used by various philosophical traditions, and different types of civil societies have existed under a variety of regimes. *Civil society* may be briefly defined as a web of self-organized voluntary arrangements outside the direct control of the state that structure individual and collective action. A particularly important component of civil society is the public sphere—the domain of civil society that emerged during the Enlightenment, separate from and often antagonistic to the state, where public opinion can be formed. To many twentieth-century theorists, associations constitute the institutional core of the public sphere of civil society. Civil society is understood to be a construct of the educated and propertied classes, or bourgeoisie (*bürgerliche Gesellschaft*). The public sphere is also usually understood to be bourgeois but, if lacking a basis in private property, it may also be plebeian. Civil society is frequently tied to certain assumptions about individual autonomy that are Western or "liberal." Neo-Tocquevilleans regard civil society as the locus of individual liberty, initiative, and non-state sources of community. The concept is also attractive to the post-Marxist Left as a non–class based locus of grassroots political activity, more welcome than the socialist movement to the participation of marginalized groups, that seeks to influence state policy and democratize the social and political order.

CIVIL SOCIETY IN EUROPEAN THOUGHT

Philosophers have imagined civil society as that which something else is not. To ancient political thinkers such as Aristotle (384–322 B.C.E.) and Marcus Tullius Cicero (106–43 B.C.E.), civil society was coterminous with the political community (*polis, civitas*); it was not the family and household. In early modern political thought, civil society was gradually separated from the political community, or state. Thomas Hobbes (1588–1679) and John Locke (1632–1704) theorized a civil society that protected certain prepolitical natural rights such as equality, freedom, and property. Thus, civil society was not the state of nature. Philosophers of the Scottish Enlightenment such as Adam Ferguson (1723–1816), David Hume (1711–1776), and Adam Smith (1723–1790), as well as Georg Wilhelm Friedrich Hegel (1770–1831), theorized a sphere of human relationships, institutions, and associations of autonomous individuals that satisfied needs and pursued (Enlightened) self-interest through the work and exchange of commercial society. Civil society meant "civilized" society, in contrast to barbarism or "rude" society. Philoso-

phers of the Continental Enlightenment such as Charles-Louis de Secondat, baron de Montesquieu (1689–1755) regarded the intermediary bodies of civil society as a bulwark against despotism and the abuses of political power and privilege. Civil society also signified a society of civility and religious toleration.

According to Hegel, civil society mediated between the family and the state. For the past two centuries this has been the dominant model. However, Hegel believed that for regulation and ethical guidance, civil society was dependent on the state. Like the Scots before him, Hegel saw a darker side of civil society—a possessive individualism and atomized relationships based on property. This was civil society as understood by Karl Marx (1818–1883)—egoism, individual isolation, disorder, and corruption, a "battlefield" where private interests struggled against each other. Marx reduced civil society to a product of the bourgeoisie and to the market relations of property, labor, and exchange. Marx's revolutionary project was to abolish capitalistic relations and to fuse state and society into one under socialism.

By the mid-nineteenth century, *society* largely replaced *civil society* as a concept, an indication that in western Europe propertied and educated men were secure in civil society. In the twentieth century the Marxist Antonio Gramsci (1891–1937) restored civil society as a conceptual framework. Gramsci detached civil society from the capitalist economy and made the former a contested arena of identity formation and cultural reproduction that mediated between the latter and the state and transmitted a bourgeois ideology, thereby permitting the bourgeoisie to achieve "hegemony."

The model of the public sphere of Jürgen Habermas (b. 1929) is very close to the civil society of Gramsci and has influenced many historians. Habermas defines the public sphere (*Öffentlichkeit*) of civil society as that space where private people, freed of duties and obligations to the ruler, come together voluntarily as a public to deliberate matters of common concern, voice opinions, and represent interests. It emerged under royal absolutism in the network for communicating information—the institutions and practices of market capitalism, a lively print culture, and new structured urban spaces where propertied men sought sociability, among them the salons, cafés, Masonic lodges, stages, and academies of London and Paris. Yet in the same way that it subjects the state to pressure, the public sphere is used as a vehicle of empowerment by groups, such as women and the propertyless, excluded from participation in civil society.

The usages of the term contain many contradictions. It is frequently unclear what is a condition, or prerequisite, for the existence of civil society, and what is a consequence of its development. It is often used to describe an existing state of affairs, but it may equally describe an ideal. When contrasted with the state, civil society signifies elements of the private world; when contrasted with the family, it signifies the public realm. It can signify an individualistic, amoral, neutral space; yet it is also seen as the site for the formation of civic virtues and community. It may be regarded as the site of property and market relations or as the noncommercial sphere. Civil society and the state may be in relations of harmony or conflict, or both over time within the same polity.

Despite the paradoxes of civil society, historians from a variety of national fields of nineteenth-century Europe use the concept, along with the public sphere, to examine the relationship between society and the state, and in particular society's gradual emancipation from state authority and the prospects for liberal democracy; class, gender and the construction of citizenship; sociability; the pursuit of science and learning; and movements for improvement and reform. The concept of civil society offers a way to study the capacity for individual initiative and the methods by which talent was mobilized for public purposes, civic cooperation, and interest group articulation and representation.

CIVIL SOCIETY AND THE STATE

The relationship between civil society and the state, especially on the Continent, was ambivalent throughout the nineteenth century. Civil society in most of Europe evolved from a state-enabled and often state-guided entity to one dominated by private initiative. Civil society was more likely to grow in scope when it avoided political activities that directly challenged authoritarian states.

In France, different regimes were suspicious of any spontaneous public initiative that might con-

tradict state goals and repressed the intrusion of seemingly harmless associations of private persons into realms, such as religion and politics, considered to be the domain of the state or the established church. From 1810 to 1848 French civil society was highly regulated and, after a brief moment of freedom in 1848, again regulated under the Second Empire. Labor and industrial organizations, benefit societies, and scientific, literary, and artistic associations sprang up anyway in the Third Republic; though not officially authorized, some associations were tolerated and existed in a legal limbo. As the authoritarian state retreated during the second half of the century, the institutions of civil society were able to operate despite government restrictions and scrutiny, although it was not until the law of 1901 (*contrat d'associations*) that an association could be formed freely without prior authorization. Thus, France provides the example of a statist political culture underlying several regimes—monarchy, empire, republic—that combined tolerance with a high degree of regulation and supervision of civil society.

A similar pattern prevailed among the paternalistic authoritarian states of central Europe. German liberals sought a harmonious collaboration between civil society and the state in many enterprises, such as the provision of charity and the dissemination of new farming techniques. Prussia lacked freedom of association until 1849, and even then the authorities carefully scrutinized civil society; freedom of association was not granted until 1908. Because the German states prevented organized society from participating in political matters, seemingly innocuous activities acquired political implications; what began as collaboration and deference by the 1840s increasingly became confrontation and rebellion against authoritarian rule.

By creating and framing public opinion, exposing abuses of power and privilege, and making accountable the actions of officials, emerging European civil societies became breeding grounds for democratization. Clubs, reading societies, and cultural and patriotic groups along with universities and the press were basic building blocks of liberal political culture. But the institutional guarantors of civil society canonized in Western political thought—freedom from personal dependence and arbitrary domination, inviolability of person and

EUROPE 1789 TO 1914

domicile, the rule of law, civil rights, and a parliament or assembly of the estates—were present in only a few polities of western Europe and North America. States everywhere put up resistance to democratization, and the capacity of civil society to democratize the political order and state institutions varied greatly. This capacity was greatest in Great Britain, where civil society was strong, monarchical power was limited, and political society—that is, political movements and parties, parliamentary institutions, and elections (highly contested terrain between civil society and the state)—had already successfully claimed to represent the nation.

In southern, central, and eastern Europe, civil society offered a substitute for a highly controlled or denied popular representation. The public sphere of an emerging civil society was the site of individual and group assertion of rights against authoritarian regimes unwilling to recognize institutional limitations to their power. But the effort to create civil society was coterminous with the struggle for representation in political society, making the strength of the former and the democratization of the latter problematic. In many parts of Europe, civil society failed to create or secure democracy because of state resistance; fragile, fragmented, and polarized political institutions; and the character and dynamics of civil society itself. Low levels of urbanization and literacy, ruling oligarchies, the power of local notables and patronage networks, and low participation in public affairs were reasons for unsuccessful democratization, especially in southern Europe. In central and eastern Europe, institutions of civil society were divided along class and confessional lines and could not work toward consensus building. Although civic activism intensified throughout Europe, so too did political polarization.

CIVIL SOCIETY, CLASS, AND GENDER

Historians and social theorists of both liberal and Marxist persuasions have long postulated a link between the institutions of civil society and the middle class. In a venerable liberal sociological narrative, market capitalism and the bourgeoisie are the preconditions for civil society, the public sphere, and successful liberal democratic states. In the Marxist narrative the bourgeoisie carries out its historical mission by wresting economic and political power away from the landed aristocracy, thus effecting the "bourgeois" revolution. In much late-twentieth-century work, inspired by Gramsci, culture trumps capital, identities trump income, and values trump vocation. From this perspective, the hierarchies of value in civil society, commonly attributed to the bourgeoisie, were articulated through voluntary associations by a wide spectrum of liberal landowners, professionals, and government officials; the key markers are not class but education, urbanization, and sensibility.

Gender was also a factor in the formation of civil society and the public sphere. Reason, civil rights, property ownership, and the ability to judge and represent others in civil society corresponded discursively to the capacities of men, while the private sphere of nature, passion, and dependence corresponded to the capacities of women. Nineteenth-century civil societies were considered to be associations of free men, and insofar as most women—and many men, as well—were not legally free in their person, property, or labor, they were not considered fit for membership and were relegated to the private world of the household economy and family. Gender analysis provides an insight into the way in which the disenfranchised could and did enter the public realm despite exclusionary laws or practices. Especially in Great Britain, but also later in France and Germany and even Russia, women could join philanthropic, moral, and reform societies.

SCIENCE AND SOCIABILITY

Inspired by Habermas, many historians have noted the significance of new forms of sociability that mushroomed in the eighteenth and nineteenth centuries. A variety of new settings, including literary clubs and societies of science and philosophy, nurtured new forms of sociability that stressed reciprocal and egalitarian Communication. Beginning in the eighteenth century Continental monarchs enabled, if not created, the institutions of civil society to encourage and patronize scientific, charitable, and cultural activities that could further national progress and demonstrate their "enlightened" reigns. In the nineteenth century, associations as well as other components of civil society aspired to assist and advise states in the collection of knowledge and in the improvement of the natural and human world for the public benefit. Despite the fact that on the European continent associations required government permission, tens of thousands of associations existed by the end of the nineteenth century. By providing new models of moral and cultural authority, science enlarged the space of a secular climate of opinion. Such institutions offered new forms of sociability, self-definition, and private initiative. In this way, scientific and learned societies enabled men to display distinction and gain recognition from others in civil society for their experience, talent, expertise, self-mastery, cultural stewardship, and civic leadership.

Civil society was the locus of movements of individual and social reform, especially efforts to provide education, to promote self-improvement and rational leisure as well as a thirst for positive knowledge, and to mobilize a public for reform causes. In this way, the poor, for example, could be removed from the state of nature in which they were commonly regarded as living and enter civil society. Private initiative founded associations to promote technological development and economic growth; to improve public health; to found public libraries and museums; to organize national congresses, public lectures, and scientific demonstrations; and to pursue sport and recreation. Major cities were the sites of an unofficial art public, a network of private persons outside state art academies that cooperated to patronize, produce, distribute, evaluate, and consume works and performances of art. Physicians, teachers, engineers, and lawyers, among others, developed in civil society a professional consciousness and fashioned a new ideal of public service. In this process, while men of science undoubtedly acted for personal and professional interests, they also claimed to represent the public or the nation.

CONCLUSIONS

Theories of civil society rarely provide a perfect fit to the historical experience. Most theories of civil society presuppose the existence of civil rights guaranteed by a state based on law; likewise, the public sphere requires a certain degree of publicity regarding affairs of state and of access to the public arena. By these criteria, only a few polities of western Europe have spawned robust civil societies.

Elsewhere, notably in southern, central, and eastern Europe, the development of civil society was more contested.

The growth of civil society presumes the autonomy of the self-directed individual—the propertied nineteenth-century man. But civil society was also the site of internal conflict, as marginalized groups struggled for their own autonomy. The institutional core of civil society constituted by voluntary associations frequently preceded constitutions and representative bodies. The growth of civil society challenged the habit of authorities to demarcate "separate spheres," to borrow a term from gender history, of the state and of private life. By compelling the state to legitimate itself before public opinion, a voluntarily constituted, self-organized civil society acted as a counterweight to authority based on tradition, force, and ritual.

See also **Associations, Voluntary.**

BIBLIOGRAPHY

Arato, Andrew, and Jean Cohen. *Civil Society and Political Theory.* Cambridge, Mass., 1992.

Bermeo, Nancy, and Philip Nord, eds. *Civil Society before Democracy: Lessons from Nineteenth-Century Europe.* Lanham, Md., 2000.

Blackbourn, David, and Geoff Eley. *The Peculiarities of German History: Bourgeois Society and Politics in Nineteenth-Century Germany.* Oxford, U.K., 1984.

Bradley, Joseph. "Subjects into Citizens: Societies, Civil Society, and Autocracy in Tsarist Russia." *The American Historical Review* 107, no. 4 (October 2002): 1094–1123.

Calhoun, Craig, ed. *Habermas and the Public Sphere.* Cambridge, Mass., 1992.

Clowes, Edith W., Samuel Kassow, and James West, eds. *Between Tsar and People: Educated Society and the Quest for Public Identity in Late Imperial Russia.* Princeton, N.J., 1991.

Habermas, Jürgen. *The Structural Transformation of the Public Sphere: An Inquiry into a Category of Bourgeois Society.* Translated by Thomas Burger. Cambridge, Mass., 1989.

Hall, John A., ed. *Civil Society: Theory, History, Comparison.* Cambridge, U.K., 1995.

Harrison, Carol. *The Bourgeois Citizen in Nineteenth-Century France: Gender, Sociability, and the Uses of Emulation.* Oxford, U.K., 1999.

Keane, John, ed. *Civil Society and the State: New European Perspectives.* London, 1988.

Kocka, Jürgen, and Allan Mitchell, eds. *Bourgeois Society in Nineteenth-Century Europe.* New York, 1993.

Nord, Phillip. *The Republican Moment: Struggles for Democracy in Nineteenth-Century France.* Cambridge, Mass., 1995.

Seligman, Adam B. *The Idea of Civil Society.* Princeton, N.J., 1992.

Taylor, Charles. "Modes of Civil Society." *Public Culture* 3, no. 1 (fall 1990): 95–118.

Tester, Keith. *Civil Society.* London and New York, 1992.

Trentmann, Frank, ed. *Paradoxes of Civil Society: New Perspectives on Modern German and British History.* New York and Oxford, U.K., 2000.

JOSEPH BRADLEY

CLASS AND SOCIAL RELATIONS.

Class is a relationship between producers and those who extract a surplus from their labor. A variety of social classes existed in Europe between 1789 and 1914, and the relations among these disparate classes raise some of the most interesting problems of nineteenth-century European history. Class transformations were characteristic features of nineteenth-century Europe, and relationships among classes changed significantly over time. But class transformations and class relationships followed no inexorable logic. They were profoundly shaped by historical conjunctures and by cultural and political forces as well as by economic forces.

ARISTOCRACY

During the course of the century class relationships changed at every level of society. At the very top, aristocrats managed to retain considerable power, but they had to renegotiate their relationships with both rulers and bourgeoisie.

In general, the character of aristocratic economic power changed over time. In Great Britain the least change occurred because, although membership in the House of Lords still conferred considerable power, in most areas the aristocracy had lost almost all legal prerogatives before 1789. But they retained their economic power: at century's end seven thousand individuals owned 80 percent of all privately owned land in the United Kingdom, and most of these great landowners were aristocrats.

Even late-nineteenth-century Liberal leaders such as Henry Campbell-Bannerman ended their careers with a knighthood.

In most of Europe, however, a hereditary aristocracy secured by legal privilege essentially evolved toward landlordism. Despite the loss of feudal obligations, noble families such as the Stolberg-Wernigerodes and the Von Ratibors in the German empire and the Schwarzenbergs and Liechtensteins in Austria-Hungary owned huge expanses of national territory. In Russia aristocratic power was greatest and least constrained.

Everywhere great landowning aristocrats were also cultural pacesetters. Custom and often law required that aristocrats lead an "honorable lifestyle" that included fighting, dueling, sports, gambling, religion, and government. The aristocratic gentleman might have intellectual interests, but he must be a dilettante, interested in art, poetry, and literature in an amateur capacity only.

The aristocratic lady also had her prerogatives. While it was important that a woman bear legitimate male children to carry on the family line, once she had carried out this obligation there was leeway. Aristocratic women often possessed some control over the dowry or were able to draw on family financial resources and so enjoyed a measure of independence. The elegant salons of the late eighteenth and early nineteenth century gave aristocratic women a setting in which they could exert independent power. While the double standard was the rule of European society, like so many rules, it was not always enforced as rigorously among the aristocracy. Many an aristocratic couple, considered successfully married, had separate bedrooms, with separate access, in different wings of their townhouse.

As consolidated states expanded their power, aristocrats found it necessary to adapt. Before 1789 many aristocrats saw themselves as part of a French-speaking international ruling class whose self-identity was defined by honor, race, and lifestyle but certainly not by national loyalty. They felt free to offer their services wherever they might receive the most recognition. In the stormy 1650s, the great general, the Prince de Condé, fell out with Cardinal Jules Mazarin and transferred his loyalties from the king of France to the king of Spain.

The Bellelli Family. Painting by Edgar Degas, 1858–1867. Degas, born into a wealthy family and originally trained as a lawyer, here portrays his aunt, her husband, and her two daughters. The material prosperity and propriety of the family is offset by the composition of the painting, which clearly reveals tensions between the members. MUSÉE D'ORSAY, PARIS, FRANCE/BRIDGEMAN ART LIBRARY

No contemporary thought that his actions were in any way dishonorable.

As the century went on, aristocrats increasingly reconciled themselves to a new statist Europe that required national loyalty; in return, they continued to lead the armies and staff the diplomatic services of all the powers. British radical John Bright even referred to the diplomatic services as "a gigantic system of outdoor relief for the aristocracy." In many cases, aristocrats needed such aid because declining agricultural revenues over the long nineteenth century often left them indebted, and the aristocracy always included a mass of smaller aristocrats unable to

pursue ignoble occupations while unable to afford aristocratic lifestyles.

BOURGEOISIE

The aristocracy's chief rival for power in the nineteenth century was a bourgeoisie consisting of property owners who made their living in commerce, banking, or industry. Throughout the eighteenth century the bourgeoisie had accumulated its grievances against the aristocracy even while it was thrilled to associate with aristocrats in Masonic fraternities, scientific societies, and the theater. But the grievances generated in such potentially awkward situations were sometime deeply felt. In 1769 Antoine Barnave, a future revolutionary, happened to be at the theater of Grenoble with his mother when the governor of the Dauphiné arrived and declared that he wanted the mother's seat for his friends. Barnave's mother refused to leave, and the governor called in troops to drive her out.

The most powerful element of the bourgeoisie was the haute bourgeoisie, a small minority of bourgeois men and women who owned factories, banks, and large trading establishments. In the first half of the nineteenth century a new bourgeois aristocracy had emerged whose names would resound through the century: in Britain and Ireland, Cadbury, Courtauld, and Guinness; in France, Schneider and Wendel; and in Germany, Stinnes, Thyssen, and Krupp.

In the years between the onset of the French Revolution and the revolutions of 1848–1851 capitalist elites and the solid middle classes often looked upon aristocrats as rivals and opponents. In England middle-class radicals scorned the leisured life of the aristocracy, mocked their lack of a work ethic, and deplored the decadence of both their art and their personal lives. Throughout Europe the French Revolution had inspired fear among the aristocracy, while the liquidation of aristocratic land and the provisioning of revolutionary and then of Napoleonic armies made many mercantile fortunes. After 1815 in France the restored Bourbons sought to reestablish aristocratic power and could not forgive bourgeois leaders, some of whom had voted for the death of King Louis XVI and many of whom had rallied behind Napoleon I in his ill-fated attempt at a comeback during the "Hundred Days." As late as 1830 bourgeois leaders felt comfortable in helping launch a popular revolution against Bourbon rule.

The revolutions of 1848 changed all that. In Paris, and to a lesser extent in Berlin and Vienna, revolutionary-minded bourgeois discovered that popular insurrections could threaten bourgeois order. Young middle-class sons who had played a leading role in early-nineteenth-century secret societies increasingly confined their interest to Masonry. By the end of the century, the bourgeoisie and aristocracy had largely reconciled their differences. Faced with their fear of popular revolu-

Interior, Woman at the Window. Painting by Gustave Caillebotte, 1880. Caillebotte portrays the comfort and leisure enjoyed by middle-class Parisians. PRIVATE COLLECTION/BRIDGEMAN ART LIBRARY

tion from below, the aristocracy, the haute bourgeoisie, and the solid middle classes discovered interests in common. In the second half of the century, the effects of this reconciliation were particularly striking in the Austro-Hungarian (after 1867), German, and Russian empires where monarchs possessed considerable autonomous power and where aristocrats dominated the upper administration, the army, and important portions of the countryside. Here Marxist exhortations to bourgeois elites to make a bourgeois revolution were greeted with profound skepticism and deep suspicion. In turn, the weak opposition of liberal bourgeois politicians to monarchical and aristocratic power contributed to the evolution of independent working-class parties.

The power of bourgeois elites increased greatly after 1848 but as it did, they frequently adopted aristocratic lifestyles, and eagerly accepted titles, becoming aristocrats themselves.

In great cities such as London, Paris, and Berlin, centers of aristocratic society, such amalgamations proceeded more swiftly than in great commercial and manufacturing towns such as Birmingham and Hamburg where the middle-class population was large and the aristocratic population almost non-existent. Successful businessmen nearly always purchased landed property and added a country home to their urban townhouse. They or their sons and daughters interested themselves in literature and the arts as they sought to enter an aristo-cratic-dominated high society and to intermarry with the aristocracy. Père Goriot, the protagonist of Honoré de Balzac's great novel of the same name (published in 1834), was a bourgeois who had made his fortune by subverting the grain controls of the Terror, but his money and both his daughters eventually ended up in aristocratic hands. A key element to bourgeois entry into the aristocratic world was the dowry. Many an indebted aristocrat was able to continue his lifestyle only by marrying bourgeois wealth.

Below the haute bourgeoisie was the solid middle class of society doctors, famous lawyers, top civil servants, small manufacturers, and whole-sale merchants. Economically secure, they could not live off accumulated wealth. Already by the beginning of the nineteenth century, ideals of domesticity flourished among the solid middle classes. Here wives were expected to stay at home, to provide a peaceful refuge for a husband involved in the competitive business world and to rear and educate children. Educating children was an important function because the solid mid-dle-class male child would need an education to succeed and the female would need an education to fulfill her maternal role. Despite the ideology of domesticity, solid middle-class women played an indispensable role in sustaining the family's economic position. The wife's dowry was often an important element in the family's membership in the solid middle class. The social ties that she maintained with other middle-class women were important in creating networks of ties that gave solid middle-class society its coherence and also facilitated her husband's business connections. In an age of partnerships in which family fortunes depended on the integrity of partners, family ties enabled businessmen to bind partners more

closely to themselves and also provided intimate surveillance of their character.

LOWER MIDDLE CLASSES

Below the solid middle classes were the great mass of the middle classes, the so-called petite bourgeoisie, consisting largely of shopkeepers, lesser state officials, and most lawyers and doctors. The lower middle classes possessed small amounts of capital and were required to work for a living; indeed many were often on the brink of proletarianization. Many a petit bourgeois dreamed of a financial coup or a string of successes that might lift him and his family into the solid middle classes while envying the skilled worker who earned as much as he did without having to worry about fussy customers or the responsibilities of management.

Most shopkeepers either owned or rented their own shops and lived in a few rooms adjoin-ing the shop. The private world of the middle-class family only partially extended to this world and then only to the wealthiest members. Most shopkeepers' wives and children worked with their husbands and fathers in the shop. The success or failure of a shopkeeper depended not only on the size of a wife's dowry but also on her business ability. Perhaps the family was saving to send a talented son to an elite secondary school, but more likely, children were expected to learn the business on the job. The shopkeepers' children would have to find their way largely on their own, depending mostly on their education or on the training they picked up in the shop. Their parents did not possess sufficient money to retire and hand the shop over to them, and so they would have to establish themselves largely by their own skill and talent, although perhaps with a loan from their parents.

By the very nature of their business, the estab-lishments of the lower middle classes were scattered all over town. In the more prosperous areas, shopkeepers and doctors tended to be wealthier and better off than in the poorer areas where they were continually opening and shutting down. Shopkeepers were recruited partly from the sons and daughters of shopkeepers. In Paris, most shopkeepers were recruited from provincial shopkeepers. But more typically they were from the working classes. In working-class areas, middle-class shopkeepers and the working classes lived side by side. Because they frequently extended credit to workers, these shopkeepers' fates were bound up with that of the working classes. The precarious financial position of many shopkeepers in working-class areas also gave them a stake in the vicissitudes of popular life. During much of the nineteenth century, the lower middle classes, particularly those located in working-class districts, rallied to popular causes. A great part of the power of the revolutions of 1848 stemmed from the successful union of the lower middle classes and the working classes.

The lower middle classes had played a leading role in the revolutionary struggles up to 1848 and continued to serve as revolutionary fuel into the 1870s. Yet in the second half of the long nineteenth century the alliance between the lower middle classes and the working classes became more problematic where it did not collapse altogether. The growth of class-conscious socialist and trade union movements undermined the petite bourgeoisie's sense of belonging to an encompassing popular class, a feeling that had provided cross-class unity in 1848. Grocery chains and catalog shopping were deadly threats to the lower middle classes, yet their working-class neighbors became prime customers of these retail innovations. Consumer cooperatives, a popular tool of the socialist movement, particularly alienated the lower middle classes as did the spread of trade unionism, which threatened to raise the wages of the helpers who gave the lower middle-class family a little extra time to take care of family needs.

WHITE-COLLAR PROFESSIONALS AND SERVICE WORKERS

Meanwhile a new social stratum of formally educated professional men and women was emerging. Despite the rhetoric of laissez-faire, governmental services increased greatly during the period. Between 1850 and 1914, railways expanded along with the railway workforce, and postal services increased rapidly as did the number of postal workers. Everywhere the number of teachers grew apace and secretaries, administrators, and accountants all were in high demand. The number of

those employed in banking, health, entertainment, and insurance also grew.

Were these service workers and urban professionals a new middle class or a white-collar working class? Unlike the working classes, both artisans and factory workers, these workers did not work with their hands and were far more likely to be women. While many artisans earned more than clericals, the white-collar workers were required to dress for work and they possessed more formal education than the most skilled workers. At a time when industrial labor was becoming more masculine, white-collar work was feminizing. Emerging from technical training schools, women were hired as secretaries and typists and female lay teachers often replaced nuns in teaching young women in a still largely sex-segregated educational system in which they routinely received lower wages than their male counterparts.

White-collar identities varied according to political or social circumstances. In some countries such as France, teachers, civil service workers, and other groups formed unions and mobilized their constituents into popular movements. In Germany though, they were more likely to remain separate from the working classes and to identify themselves with a broadly construed middle group, the *Mittelstand*.

WORKERS

Even putting service workers and professionals aside, the working classes themselves were a diverse group that included skilled artisans, factory workers, domestic servants, and sweatshop tenement labor. Over the course of the century the number of factory workers increased considerably, the number of artisans and domestic servants declined, while sweatshop labor first expanded and then declined.

In manufacturing, preindustrial forms of labor slowly gave way to factory and millwork. Preindustrial work had its own distinctive characteristics. It was dispersed over town and country and was organized along family lines. Preindustrial workers controlled the pace and rhythm of their own work and often possessed a monopoly of knowledge about their job. They often had their own internal job hierarchy and their own distinctive occupational identity. Oftentimes, preindustrial workers lived close together to fellows who performed the same job. Skilled artisans, such as puddlers (makers of wrought iron) or glassblowers, tended to live in their own communities within the city or village; they often had a shared leisure life based on common work and residence patterns. Glassworkers retained their own sense of identity when thrown together with other groups of workers. These workers were capable of considerable solidarity, but waves of innovation, such as the mechanization that swept the glass industry in the 1890s, were capable of reducing them to relative penury.

In early-nineteenth-century cities, the largest groups of workers were usually domestic servants who catered to the needs of upper- and middle-class families. Whether they resided with a wealthy family or performed cleaning services for a middle-class family, servants were under the close scrutiny of their employers, and this limited their ability to act independently, either personally or collectively. Personal contact might result in lifelong friendships between older servants and the wealthy children they had raised. But it was also a great source of personal pettiness. One English domestic servant recounted how all the silverware used in her servants' quarter was engraved with the message "Stolen from the household of" followed by the family crest. Despite its relative security, higher wages, and contact with the upper classes, indeed perhaps because of its interclass contact, first men and later women fled domestic service for factory and secretarial work as it became available, and the proportion of the population in domestic service slowly declined.

The world of the newly emerging industrial workers was quite different from that of domestic service. They inhabited an urban world. The factory or mill was almost always sex segregated and, as the century wore on, males increasingly dominated the workplace; sons might expect to find work in the same factory as their father, but they seldom were trained by their parents. Industrial workers were supervised outside the traditional job hierarchies, and formally educated supervisors or engineers increasingly controlled their labor. Industrial workers who labored in the same factories did not tend to live together

in the city but lived in new working-class sections of the city or the suburbs where they lived next to other workers but not necessarily workmates. In this environment it became increasingly easy for workers to identify themselves less with a specific occupation and more with the general working class.

The nineteenth century also witnessed the growth of homework and sweatshop labor, a growth disproportionately concentrated in great cities. Erratic and low-paid male labor, such as dock labor, forced wives and children to accept the miserable conditions, long hours, and low wages that characterized many portions of the garment trades, particularly those engaged in homework or in small shops. The spread of piecework and putting out extended many of the most scandalous characteristics of the early Industrial Revolution into the second half of the nineteenth century. Toward the end of the century, however, waves of political reform imposed new restrictions on poorly paid laborers, and the size of this labor force declined.

The spread of socialism and trade unions among male workers—artisanal, highly skilled, and factory workers—was one of the most powerful nineteenth-century political trends. Although many of the largest factories remained peripheral to the labor movement until the interwar years, class-consciousness created a powerful sense of identity among proletarians. While middle-class intellectuals such as Karl Marx and Friedrich Engels had elaborated key doctrines of the labor movement, workers rallied behind banners that featured bare-chested manual laborers; read newspapers that announced their proletarian allegiance; joined cooperatives and lyceums that explicitly appealed to workers; and, particularly in the Scandinavian and Germanic worlds, formed bicycling societies, temperance societies, and chess clubs open only to workers. The old camaraderie between proletarians and the petite bourgeoisie faltered when faced with such exclusion. Many male teachers and salesmen avoided clubs controlled by blue-collar workers who mocked their clothes and envied their education.

The spread of explicitly proletarian political and social organizations did not make workers more revolutionary, but it did isolate them from

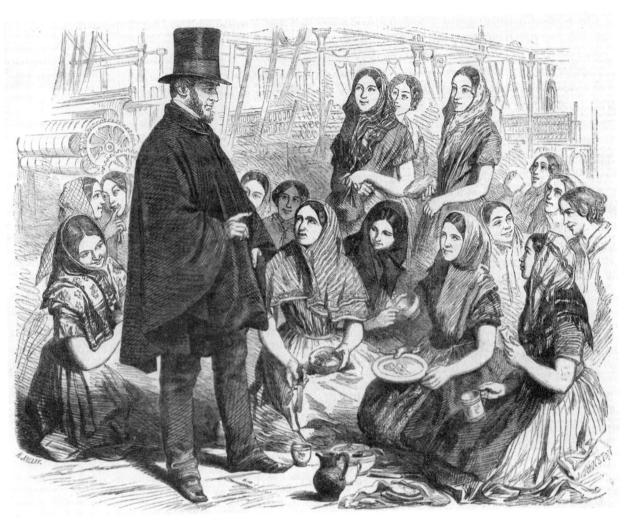

Dr. Baker and Factory Girls. Engraving from a photograph in *British Workman*, 1856. A Victorian doctor lectures working women on the importance of saving money. During this period, wealth and a standing in the upper classes were equated with moral superiority. MARY EVANS PICTURE LIBRARY

other class groups. As socialist parties and trade unions grew more successful, they often became more preoccupied with immediate tasks than with their proclaimed goal of proletarian revolution. To many the democratization of the German Empire and the defeat of French militarism seemed far more immediate concerns than proletarian revolution. Everywhere labor movements, including not only socialist reformists but also anarchosyndicalists, gave more consideration to immediate reforms. Yet socialist organizations often found it difficult to reach out to those middle-class and agricultural constituencies who shared their democratic and antimilitaristic goals. Despite Continental labors' growing moderation, most peasants and solid middle-class and petit

bourgeois Europeans thought only of revolution when they saw the red flag.

PEASANTRY

In spite of the presence of the sickle alongside the hammer on the red flag, labor movements seldom paid careful attention to agriculture or to the peasantry. Marx and Engels had predicted that economic trends would undermine the peasantry, forcing them into the ranks of revolution. While Marxist economic analysis was not wrong, the decline of the peasantry would take decades, and the failure to accommodate peasants in the here and now was a crucial socialist failure in the years before 1914.

Although the rural world in many parts of Europe was rapidly changing, peasants still played an important role. In 1789 as in 1914 the majority of Europeans were agriculturalists and a majority of these were peasants. Peasants are members of a household whose major activity is farming. They produce a major portion of the goods and services they consume. They exercise substantial control over the land that they farm, and they supply the major portion of the labor requirements within their own households. While peasant agriculture predominated in Europe it did not extend everywhere. In Spain and southern Italy, peasant agriculture gave way to large estates or ranches on which large landowners used overseers who directed huge gangs of landless laborers. In England, medium-sized farmers rented from aristocratic landlords and hired landless laborers.

Between the emancipation of the peasants of Savoy in 1771 and that of the Romanian peasantry in 1864, a host of legally enforceable obligations embodied in monopolies, tithes, personal obligations, labor services, and arbitrary financial exactions were either abolished or converted into rents. An unfree peasantry, resentful of aristocratic rule and suspicious of bourgeois commercialization, had represented a powder keg in European society. The prospect of an alliance between the working classes and a rebellious peasantry chilled many an elitist heart. Yet the possibilities of such coalitions declined after 1848 and the wave of emancipations that accompanied and followed it.

One result of emancipation was the weakening of the village community that was a distinctive feature of European peasant life and a center of agricultural rebellion. The village community had been based on common decisions about planting, harvesting, and sewing or on common control over woodlands or other resources: emancipation often involved the loss of common control or at the very least its weakening. The village community was based on the parish and on the willingness of the priesthood to represent its interests as well as on the strength of formal and informal organizations employing coercive means, such as so-called rough music, shivarees, and *Katzenmusik,* to enforce discipline on community members. The weakening of agricultural controls over communal resources and the evolution of the rural

clergy toward the political right undercut the strength of this independent peasant society. The migration of many unmarried youths to urban work also diminished the village institutions that had been the tools of village society for enforcing its codes.

Emancipation created new political opportunities in the countryside, but its results were different than many had expected. While political radicals and workers and agriculturalists were able to form alliances in portions of France, western Germany, and Italy, the advent of protectionism in the latter part of the nineteenth century enabled large landlords to rally peasants and to reknit relationships between aristocrat and peasant sundered in the first portion of the century. The rapid spread of agricultural protectionism throughout Europe in the 1880s and 1890s rallied many peasants behind conservative forces and brought them into conflict with labor movements that generally supported free trade. In Europe, before 1914, the grand coalition between unfree, impoverished peasants and hard-pressed workers that seemed imminent in 1848 never really took shape.

Over the course of the long nineteenth century, the aristocracy and haute bourgeoisie reconciled their differences without a clear victory for either side. The petite bourgeoisie became a less and less reliable member of a grand coalition of the popular classes. A new white-collar labor force emerged, but its class identification varied across states. A powerful socialist movement emerged but found itself politically isolated. Emancipation brought internal divisions to the village community, and in some regions aristocratic landlords recovered their leadership of the rural community by leading a battle for agricultural protectionism. Class was an important force in nineteenth-century Europe, but class relationships were historically contingent and class behavior could not be predicted from a logic inherent within class categories.

See also **Aristocracy; Bourgeoisie; Capitalism; Cities and Towns; Labor Movements; Peasants; Popular and Elite Culture; Socialism.**

BIBLIOGRAPHY

Primary Sources

An Old Servant. *Domestic Service.* Boston, 1917.

Secondary Sources

Berg, Maxine, Pat Hudson, and Michael Sonenscher, eds. *Manufacture in Town and Country before the Factory.* Cambridge, U.K., 1983.

Berlanstein, Lenard R. *The Working People of Paris, 1871–1914.* Baltimore, Md., 1984.

Blackbourn, David, and Geoff Eley. *The Peculiarities of German History: Bourgeois Society and Politics in Nineteenth-Century Germany.* Oxford, U.K., 1984.

Blum, Jerome. *The End of the Old Order in Rural Europe.* Princeton, N.J., 1978.

Breuilly, John. *Labour and Liberalism in Nineteenth-Century Europe: Essays in Comparative History.* Manchester, U.K., 1992.

Coffin, Judith G. *The Politics of Women's Work: The Paris Garment Trades, 1750–1915.* Princeton, N.J., 1996.

Crossick, Geoffrey, and Heinz-Gerhard Haupt, eds. *Shopkeepers and Master Artisans in Nineteenth-Century Europe.* London, 1984.

Daumard, Adeline. *Les Bourgeois de Paris au XIXe siècle.* Paris, 1970.

Davidoff, Leonore, and Catherine Hall. *Family Fortunes: Men and Women of the English Middle Class, 1780–1850.* Rev. ed. London, 2002.

Kern, Stephen. *The Culture of Time and Space, 1880–1918.* Cambridge, Mass., 1983.

Kocka, Jürgen, and Allan Mitchell. *Bourgeois Society in Nineteenth-Century Europe.* Oxford, U.K., 1993.

Mayer, Arno J. *The Persistence of the Old Regime: Europe to the Great War.* New York, 1981.

Mommsen, Wolfgang J., and Hans-Gerhard Husung, eds. *The Development of Trade Unionism in Great Britain and Germany, 1880–1914.* London, 1985.

Nord, Philip G. *Paris Shopkeepers and the Politics of Resentment.* Princeton, N.J., 1986.

Smith, Bonnie G. *Ladies of the Leisure Class: The Bourgeoises of Northern France in the Nineteenth Century.* Princeton, N.J., 1981.

Wishnia, Judith. *The Proletarianizing of the Fonctionnaires: Civil Service Workers and the Labor Movement under the Third Republic.* Baton Rouge, La., 1990.

MICHAEL HANAGAN

CLASSICAL ECONOMISTS. *See* Economists, Classical.

CLAUSEWITZ, CARL VON (1780–1831), Prussian general and theorist of war. Clausewitz's *On War* (1832) is the most celebrated study of its subject yet produced.

Carl von Clausewitz was born in Prussia in 1780 and entered the army at the age of twelve, on the eve of what would prove to be almost a quarter-century of conflict between the conservative monarchies of Europe and Revolutionary France. He first saw combat as an officer-cadet in the Rhineland campaign of 1793, an indecisive exercise in political maneuver typical of warfare under the Old Regime. He was also present thirteen years later, in October 1806, when Napoleon I (r. 1804–1814/15) crushed the Prussian army at the twin battles of Jena and Auerstädt, a defeat that exemplified the contrast between the cautious principles of the past and the new military dynamism the French Revolution had unleashed. Prussia's subsequent decision to align itself with its conqueror left Clausewitz embittered, and in 1812 he resigned his commission to serve in Russia. There he witnessed at firsthand the epic struggle by which Napoleon's grip on Europe was broken. As war moved back into Germany, Clausewitz helped organize irregular forces against the French. The Waterloo campaign (1815) found him once again in a Prussian uniform, as chief of staff to a corps.

Clausewitz's work as a historian and theorist of war rested upon these experiences, without being limited by them. Most interpreters of Napoleonic warfare were inclined to see it as the epitome of the military art, in which principles and practices dimly anticipated in earlier times had at last been fully realized. Clausewitz, on the other hand, recognized that Napoleon's achievements were historically contingent, arising from social and technological circumstances that were bound to change. It was thus wrong to imagine that any temporarily ascendant set of military methods could possess permanent validity. For Clausewitz, the goal of theory was not to codify the best practices of a given moment, but to grasp the essence of war as a whole. It is for this reason that his ideas have continued to afford insight, long after the historical conditions that inspired them have faded into the past.

Clausewitz's work stands at some distance from the mainstream of military thought in the early nineteenth century, which was overwhelmingly concerned with the spatial and temporal relationships of armies as they maneuvered against each other. Clausewitz recognized that such relationships might be highly significant. But he was equally concerned with other, less tangible factors that also shaped the outcome whenever such forces actually met. Foremost among these were the political goals that brought the combatants within weapons' range of each other in the first place. Armed forces were the creatures of political communities. War was therefore a political instrument, which could never be understood exclusively in its own terms. Political interests defined military objectives, and often set limits on the scale of violence that a belligerent was prepared to employ to achieve its ends. At the same time, the emotions violence incited might challenge and even alter the aims of policy, setting in motion an escalatory spiral that knew no natural limit. Thus politics calls forth the violence of war, shapes its character, and determines its scope; but it may also become subject to war's passion and destructiveness, bending in turn to accommodate its unique demands.

Few students of war have ever been as sensitive to its psychological dimensions. The political purposes of belligerent communities, the raw contest of wills that motivates violent struggle, the talent and insight of commanders, the morale of troops, the loyalty of the citizen—these are the essential building blocks from which Clausewitz's vision of war was constructed. Regardless of the form it might take, war was always an environment dominated by chance, and made unique cognitive and moral demands on those caught up in it. For Clausewitz, the fear and confusion that pervade war were not exogenous variables, but fundamental realities that underlay that most universal of military experiences: the tendency of things to go terribly wrong, which he characterized as "friction." Friction in turn found its natural complement in the concept of "genius," by which Clausewitz meant those ineluctable qualities of character and intellect that made a successful commander. It was the will and intelligence of the commander that drove the machinery of war for-

ward—but always at the risk of wearing it out completely.

Clausewitz was intensely interested in these sorts of complex, ambiguous interactions. He habitually analyzed important concepts in terms of creative tension, by which opposing ideas or countervailing forces are seen to define each other. Risk and reward, attack and defense, friction and genius, strategy and politics, reason and chance, victory and defeat—these and other mutually dependent concepts weave their way recursively throughout his work, and provide its distinctive texture. *On War* lacks the categorical judgments and didactic purpose that are characteristic of modern strategic theory. Its aim was not to teach people how to fight, but rather to show them how to think about war. It has always been regarded as a formidable text, and its initial public reception, while respectful, was decidedly limited: the first edition of fifteen hundred copies appeared posthumously following Clausewitz's death from cholera in 1831, and it was still in print twenty years later.

His ascendancy as the preeminent theorist of modern war dates from the latter decades of the nineteenth century, when, in the wake of Prussia's victories over Austria and France (1866–1871), the military architect of those triumphs, Count Helmuth Karl Bernhard von Moltke (1800–1891), drew attention to Clausewitz's work. One must be cautious about assigning direct influence to any work of scholarship. Many of the ideas that future generations would come to consider "Clausewitzian"—an emphasis upon decisive battle, concentration of effort, tactical agility, and the overriding importance of moral forces—were commonplaces among intelligent soldiers of post-Napoleonic Europe, to which Clausewitz's work may, at most, have lent some additional intellectual authority. In general, the appeal of Clausewitz for professional soldiers has resided primarily in his emphasis upon the central virtues of initiative, aggressiveness, mental flexibility, and self-reliance at all levels of command. These ideas comported well with the decentralized command systems that would be required to wage war in the industrial era. At the same time, the mechanization of war strengthened the technocratic and managerial ethos of military officers, and with it their natural resistance of Clausewitz's most distinctive claim: that war is permeated by politics not just in its origins and outcome, but at every level of its conduct. Even among soldiers who accept their subordination to civilian authority as a constitutional principle, the introduction of political considerations into the conduct of military operations is still widely regarded as interference in an activity best left to professional experts.

See also **Armies; French Revolutionary Wars and Napoleonic Wars; Military Tactics; Napoleon.**

BIBLIOGRAPHY

Aron, Raymond. *Clausewitz: Philosopher of War*. London, 1983.

Clausewitz, Carl von. *On War*. Edited and translated by Michael Howard and Peter Paret. Princeton, N.J., 1976.

————. *Historical and Political Writings*. Edited and translated by Peter Paret and Daniel Moran. Princeton, N.J., 1992.

Paret, Peter. *Clausewitz and the State*. Oxford, U.K., 1976.

DANIEL MORAN

CLEMENCEAU, GEORGES (1841–1929), French republican parliamentarian.

Georges Clemenceau helped shape the political culture of republican France. As an uncompromising republican he promoted egalitarianism, anticlericalism, positivism, individualism, and nationalism. Following his father's profession, Clemenceau studied medicine in Nantes and Paris; there he was briefly arrested in 1862 for opposition to the Second Empire. By 1870, after an extended trip to the United States, Clemenceau was again in Paris and active in Radical politics. During the Franco-Prussian War armistice (1871) he was elected deputy for the department of the Seine. He quickly resigned to protest the peace settlement. Clemenceau had also been appointed mayor of the Paris neighborhood of Montmartre and in 1871 was in the midst of the Parisian uprising against the peace treaty and the conservative National Assembly. Clemenceau sympathized with the patriotism and republicanism of the Communards, but rejected their socialism and their willingness to secede from the new republic. With like-minded republicans Clemenceau attempted to negotiate between the Communards and the National Assembly. Conciliation failed. After the brutal repression of the Commune, Clemenceau blamed the leaders of the National Assembly as responsible for the bloodshed and at the end of the decade he led the movement seeking amnesty for the Communards, which was achieved in 1880.

Having largely abandoned medicine, Clemenceau strengthened his political career through electoral victories: member of the Paris Municipal Council, 1875; deputy for the eighteenth Paris *arrondissement* (which included Montmartre) in 1876, reelected in 1881; elected deputy for the southern department of the Var in 1885. He also acquired a circle of friends who shared his Radical republican views and his political ambitions. These fashionable men-about-town also had interests in impressionist painting, theater, opera, and the young actresses behind the stage doors. Clemenceau gained a reputation as a formidable duelist eager to settle personal and political affronts.

By the 1880s Clemenceau was the recognized leader of a growing group of Radical republican deputies who sat on the far left of the Chamber of Deputies. He established a newspaper *La Justice* to promote their politics, backing anticlerical legislation and championing the legalization of divorce. They were sympathetic to workers' demands and criticized the use of the army to repress strikes. Their first legislative priority was to reform the constitution and the electoral system in order to safeguard popular sovereignty. In 1886 this agenda led the now powerful Clemenceau to force the moderate republican government to accept his choice for minister of war, General Georges Boulanger. Boulanger then launched a disparate movement that attracted all those dissatisfied with parliamentary government. Soon many feared that the dashing Boulanger was plotting a coup. Clemenceau had been Boulanger's patron; the Boulangist movement appropriated the Radical demand of constitutional reform; key members of the Radical group became leading Boulangists. Only when convinced that Boulanger posed a threat to the republic did Clemenceau join with moderates in a successful effort to contain the movement in 1889.

These complex associations with and his repudiation of the Boulangist movement diminished Clemenceau's political authority and the ranks of his followers. In addition, the Boulangists, vowing revenge, charged Clemenceau with corruption. During the 1893 legislative elections an antirepublican coalition launched a bitter campaign against Clemenceau, who was defeated. Two years later he resigned from *La Justice*. He pursued a career as a freelance journalist. In 1897 he joined the staff of a new paper, *L'Aurore*. He sponsored the publication of Émile Zola's scathing indictment of the army for its condemnation of an innocent officer, Alfred Dreyfus. Thus began the public and political phase of the Dreyfus affair, in which Clemenceau played a key role. The campaign for Dreyfus's acquittal again placed Clemenceau at the center of politics. However, his restored prominence did not diminish his distance from former Radical associates. Although Radicals gained the most from the Dreyfus affair, they had been neither early nor ardent Dreyfusards. Clemenceau remained aloof from the organization of a formal Radical Party in 1901. In 1902 after a nine-year absence he returned to parliament as the Radical senator from the Var, a position he held until 1920.

Following the legislative elections of 1902 and 1906 Radicals dominated the Chamber of Deputies. Clemenceau had no active role in the Radical government of 1902–1905, although he supported its militant anticlerical legislation and its foreign policy—alliance with Britain. In 1906 Clemenceau became minister of the interior in a new Radical government. Eight months later Clemenceau was called on to serve as premier.

Everyone expected his Radical government to be energetic and productive. Ministerial posts went to Radicals and independent socialists. A ministry of labor was created, promising renewed interest in labor reform. The Radical finance minister was committed to the progressive income tax. However, this reformist agenda was overwhelmed by an ever-intensifying conflict between the state and syndicalist unions. Clemenceau's intransigent republicanism necessarily led him to abhor working-class anarchism and antimilitarism. He completely opposed efforts to unionize civil servants and used force against what he considered illegal strikes, as well as against small winegrowers demonstrating for government aid during the *révolte du Midi* (1907). To his opponents Clemenceau became the "chief cop of France." The officers of the executive committee of the Radical Party condemned the premier's repressive actions. However, the Chamber of Deputies' majority endorsed these same actions, and most Radicals voted with this majority.

In 1909 the Clemenceau government fell. Clemenceau returned to the senate, having loosened all ties to the Radical Party. Preoccupied with foreign affairs, he was convinced that war with Germany was inevitable. He fought for the extension of French military service to three years and promoted the Entente with Britain. In the desperate wartime crisis of 1917, Clemenceau was appointed premier for a second time.

See also **Anticlericalism; Boulanger Affair; Dreyfus Affair; France; Radicalism; Republicanism; Separation of Church and State (France, 1905).**

BIBLIOGRAPHY

Duroselle, Jean-Baptiste. *Clemenceau.* Paris, 1988.

Geffroy, Gustave. *Georges Clemenceau, sa vie, son oeuvre.* Paris, 1919.

Watson, David Robin. *Georges Clemenceau: A Political Biography.* London, 1974.

JUDITH F. STONE

CLOTHING, DRESS, AND FASHION.

During the nineteenth century, fashion (that is the design, manufacture, promotion, retailing, and consumption of clothing created according to the dictates of cyclical trends) became one of the defining cultural products of European civilization. The production and circulation of fashionable dress drove the expansion of industrial and commercial empires and formed a focus around which urban societies structured complex hierarchies based upon the expression of class position and the exercising of taste. Beyond the elite, whose engagement with fashion had long symbolized high social status, access to fashionable sartorial products was opened up to a broader constituency than ever before as new systems of manufacture and a revolution in communications brought modish goods within the reach of middle and working-class consumers with unprecedented speed.

This is not to suggest that fashion was a new concept in itself. Since the fourteenth century at least, court societies in the Italian and German states, France, Spain, England, and the Low Countries had developed magnificent systems of corporeal display, drawing on trade in rich textiles, innovative cutting techniques, and regularly changing silhouettes. By the end of the seventeenth century, the political and competitive power of fashion had been harnessed by the court of Louis XIV (r. 1643–1715), whose chief minister Jean-Baptiste Colbert (1619–1683) famously observed that "fashion is to France what the gold mines of Peru are to Spain." With Paris swiftly recognized as the European center for the creation of luxury goods and the source of fashionable knowledge, by the following century other nations began to challenge assumptions that all fashion originated in the French capital. In Britain, for example, the mass production of cotton clothing, utilizing raw-materials and "exotic" designs originating from the British Empire together with the harnessing of local technological and entrepreneurial expertise, formed the basis of interlinked industrial and consumer revolutions that set the context for an increasing democratization of fashion. London was also widely recognized as the prime location for male tailoring from the 1780s onwards.

PARIS AND THE BIRTH OF THE FASHION DESIGNER
Yet it is fair to claim that Paris never lost its reputation as international capital of high fashion, and from the 1790s its *marchandes de modes* (forerunners of the modern couturier or fashion designer), were well placed both to benefit from traditions that had been in place for a hundred years and to institute new directions in the origination and control of

fashionable dress. The French Revolution failed to completely eradicate the deeply hierarchical and conservative organization of the Parisian clothing trades, and the international renown of its most revered practitioners ensured that the city's close association with luxury and chic endured into the 1800s and beyond. Dressmakers to the new nobilities of the Directoire and the empire could continue to purvey a distinctively elegant product to clients with sufficient money or social connections in the same manner that their well-known predecessor Rose Bertin (1714–1813) had ministered to Bourbon circles (most famously Marie-Antoinette [1755–1793]) until 1789. Louis Hippolyte Leroy—skilled at structuring the subtle lines of the new neoclassical styles of dress—enjoyed the patronage of the Empress Josephine (1763–1814), Queen Hortense (r. 1806–1810) and the Duchess of Wellington. The elaborate work of Mesdames Palmyre, Victorine, and Vignon was similarly prized by the leading socialites of the July Monarchy.

By the 1840s the rarefied rue Saint Honoré, which had housed the showrooms of these elite establishments, had been joined by the rue Richelieu and the rue de la Paix, forming the heart of an aristocratic fashion district. The neighboring Palais Royal, together with the rue Saint Denis, reflected changing times in their provision of ready-made fashion goods for the rising middle classes and for tourists eager for the latest "look." What all these areas held in common was the strong belief of their inhabitants and customers in the global supremacy of Parisian fashion. This was the local business context that fostered the emergence of grand couture from the 1850s and eased the birth of the modern fashion system with the designer at its apex.

CHARLES FREDERICK WORTH AND FASHION DESIGN
Widely credited as the first autonomous fashion designer (creating and dictating trends rather than merely responding to the demands of clients) and an undoubted giant of the nineteenth-century fashion scene, the Englishman Charles Frederick Worth (1825–1895) founded his empire in the rue de la Paix in 1858. Prior to this, Worth had trained as an apprentice at the draper's Swan and Edgar in London's Piccadilly Circus (followed by a short period at Lewis and Allenby, silk mercers

Women in the Garden. Painting by Claude Monet, 1867. Monet often copied clothing styles from fashion magazines in his work. MUSÉE D'ORSAY, PARIS, FRANCE/BRIDGEMAN ART LIBRARY/GIRAUDON

of Regent Street), and then from 1845 he had worked as an assistant and then as chief cutter at Gagelin-Opigez in the rue de Richelieu. In this manner, Worth accumulated valuable experience in the selection and presentation of a broad range of textiles and an understanding of the power of new selling techniques which co-opted the drama of display as a means of encouraging consumer desire. His later success was credited to a unique ability to choose and manipulate fabrics to suit a client's appearance and mood, and an almost theatrical skill in styling ensembles to create atmosphere and impact. These skills were clearly honed in the innovative retail sectors of London and Paris, rather than via the more usual workshop training available to aspiring dressmakers, but their influence was felt most directly in the aristocratic scenario of state balls, court receptions, military parades, and gala performances that formed the center stage for the development of a fashion sensibility in the mid-nineteenth century. The rue de la Paix venture, entered into in

partnership with the Swedish businessman Otto Bobergh, brought Worth's work to the attention of the Princess Pauline Metternich (1836–1921) and via her to the Empress Eugénie (1826–1920), who by 1864 relied on Worth for the supply of all her official and evening wardrobes.

With the seal of royal approval firmly set, and concerned to ensure that his products were not reduced to the level of mere commodities, Worth was able to raise his prices and refine his public image. Part of the value of his work lay in the fact that his designs were associated with the aesthetic ideals and tastes of one man alone, and with this in mind Worth spent much effort promoting himself in the manner of an artist rather than a tradesman, as a self-conscious arbiter of style. Published portraits depicted him in the velvet bonnet and fur-lined cape of Rembrandt, and his huge country villa at Suresnes outside Paris became the focus for the ostentatious display of Worth's collections of paintings, furniture, and ceramics and the setting for extravagant shows of hospitality. At the rue de la Paix, Worth conducted his professional affairs with a similar imperious flourish. Regardless of her status, the personal client had to keep to an appointment system, submit to the couturier's vision, and select her garment from his current range, to be made up to her precise measurements.

The salon closed temporarily on the collapse of the Second Empire in 1870. But from its reopening in 1871 to Worth's death in 1895, the company enjoyed a turnover and international reach of extraordinary proportions. In 1871 Worth employed 1,200 draftsmen, cutters, seamstresses, hand and machine embroiderers, clerks, vendeuses, models, and traveling salesmen. His business ran from the bespoke dressing of an individual client to the syndication of a model for reproduction across the globe (rich Americans formed an important market for his aspirational goods) via the medium of the new fashion and society magazines. From decade to decade, Worth's output dictated the look of middle- and upper-class women in Europe and beyond. His sketchbooks record the introduction of the flat-fronted crinoline and gored skirts in the mid 1860s, the mermaid-like "princess line" of the 1870s, and the revival of gigot sleeves in the 1890s. Whether or not his intensive promotion of such styles constituted a form of invention is beside the point. What was significant was the bracketing of Worth's reputation with such glamorous novelty. The prominence of his name undoubtedly benefited from his distinctive artistic vision and his ability to encourage the consumer to believe in the spectacular uniqueness of what was essentially a serial, industrialized product. This trick of perception set a distinctive template for the enduring myth of modern high fashion, marking out a path for the careers of such celebrated designers as Jacques Doucet (1853–1929) and Paul Poiret (1879–1944) in the 1890s and 1910s and situating Paris at the heart of a reinvigorated couture culture.

FASHION PRODUCTION AND DISTRIBUTION BEYOND COUTURE

Paradoxically, the myth of sartorial individualism promoted by Worth that so encouraged the symbolic predominance of couture also influenced the increasing provision of mass-produced, readymade and wholesale fashion clothing to an ever broadening market from the 1850s onwards. So much so that sometimes the boundaries between bespoke garments—tailored on the premises to the measurements of the individual customer—and those that were ready-made—constructed to a range of sizes in bulk or to order, either in a factory or by a network of outworkers, and sourced directly through a wholesaler—were very blurred. It may then be most useful to view the production of fashionable dress in the period as a complex and interlinked chain, its sections informed by cross-cutting considerations of the supply of raw materials and labor, and the application of skill, technology, distribution, and marketing know-how that traverse national boundaries and reveal the nineteenth-century fashion system to have been a truly global phenomenon.

Beyond couture, other methods of production provided bespoke garments to a middle-class and provincial market that could not stretch to Paris prices, but may well have been inspired to acquire approximations of the latest Worth-endorsed trends by their reading of fashion plates and paper patterns included in the fashion magazines published in London, Berlin, and Paris. Skilled professional tailors and dressmakers were widespread in all European towns and cities and were well able to coordinate the cutting-out of intricate shapes, the manipulation of seams and the insertion of bones,

pads, and trimmings that went toward the creation of fashionable dress. Much of this work was completed by a team of workroom employees, but certain elements might also be sent out to piece-workers or "sweaters" who worked from home for low wages, paid according to the volume of items finished rather than the time spent in employ. Sweating was a form of employment associated particularly with immigrant (especially Jewish) workers, whose presence played an increasingly significant role in the development of urban life in most major European cities.

When the services of a professional were not available, the respectable woman could rely on her own creativity and perhaps the assistance of a maid to provide a proportion of her wardrobe herself. The acquisition of sewing skills was viewed as a prerequisite in the education of working- and middle-class girls, who could be expected to produce simple underwear, children's clothes, and men's shirts as part of their domestic duties. From the 1860s, with a range of new household publications to guide her, the ambitious home-sewer could also attempt more complicated patterns on the sewing machine, including mantles, washable day dresses, and some formal wear. Though machines were first patented in the United States (in 1846), their introduction made a gradual and significant impact on the production of garments in the commercial and domestic spheres across the globe. Undoubtedly the complex construction of nineteenth-century women's clothing and a residual suspicion of the social worth of cheap ready-made clothes meant that full mechanization was embraced more quickly by menswear producers. However, the circulation of half a million sewing machines worldwide in 1871 (from just over 2,000 in 1853) contributed toward a rapid fall in the price of clothing and a huge increase in the scale of operations in the garment trades.

The economic (as opposed to the cultural or aesthetic) supremacy of the nineteenth-century department store probably has been overstated. Smaller and longer-established high-street competitors accounted for a much higher proportion of custom than is often realized, and in Britain alone department stores probably only accounted for about 10 percent of clothing sales around 1900.

Consumers thus directed much of their custom to independent dressmakers, drapers, haberdashers, and milliners. For men, a complex network of tailors, outfitters, and hosiers provided the essential elements of the dandy's wardrobe. Small independent stores thus used display and marketing techniques that were as radical as any proposed by Aristide Boucicault (1810–1877, the proprietor of the innovative Paris department store Le Bon Marché, founded in 1852). This is not to suggest that the impact of the department store on the tenor of fashionable life was inconsequential. As built edifices dominating the street with their plate glass and architectural whimsy, and as dreamlike spaces informing the psychology of shoppers, their effects were considerable. By the 1860s the act of shopping at such establishments had become part of the fashionable round, their goods and displays offering the consumer a guide for living according to capitalist principles.

LIVING THE FASHIONABLE LIFE

The proliferation of fashionable styles promoted by an expanding fashion industry also ensured that the social signals given out by dress became increasingly complex during the nineteenth century. Following the relative freedom offered by neoclassical dress in the late eighteenth century, by the 1830s the respectable woman's wardrobe echoed a much narrower conception of idealized femininity. Close fitting bonnets, sleeves, and corseted bodices, heavy skirts and enveloping shawls bespoke the gentle submission of the "angel in the home"—that domestic paragon to which most genteel European women aspired. By the 1860s the opportunities afforded by new technologies had introduced bright synthetic dyes and the extraordinary support of the wire crinoline to the middle-class wardrobe. In this manner the expanding horizons offered by consumer culture dictated a more assertive display of fashionable products. The fashionable woman had to learn to use the decoration of her body as a sign of her family's prosperity and good standing. Individual elements of the wardrobe came to be associated with the rituals of life-patterns, so that a woman with pretensions to Society might be expected to change several times a day. This effect found its most concentrated form in the intensified clothing

Servant, nineteenth century, probably English. Among wealthy Europeans, the clothing and appearance of servants were important to the family's social status. © Hulton-Deutsch Collection/Corbis

regulations applied to christenings, coming-of-age and court presentations, weddings, and deaths in the family.

If a tightening of the rules of etiquette was necessary to ensure that an engagement with fashionable display was properly "moral," then their loosening could also be a sign of the heightened sensibility of the fashion consumer. The emergence of "countercultural" modes of dressing from the 1870s onward, especially in Britain, Belgium, Austria, Spain (Barcelona), Scandinavia, and Germany, played an important role in the modernization of clothing habits for many ordinary European men and women that was in full progress by 1900. Aesthetic, Artistic, and Rational dress was partly a means of self-identification for those members of metropolitan circles who associated themselves with bohemian pursuits and with progressive political sensitivities, and partly a response to the unhealthiness and perceived ugliness of contemporary fashionable style. But it reintroduced a real notion of freedom and common sense with its incorporation of "natural" colors, "tasteful" historicist, folkloric, and non-Western inspiration, and unrestrictive cut. Prominent proponents of the style included the German dress reformer Gustave Jaeger, the London retailer Arthur Liberty (1843–1917), and the Belgian architect Henry Clemens van de Velde (1863–1957).

Masculine clothing had benefited from a more rational design since the 1770s in a process that later fashion writers were to identify as the "Great Masculine Renunciation." Yet despite the apparent simplicity and uniformity that the respectable male wardrobe seemed to offer, the acquisition and use of its content were just as complex as its female counterpart. With different styles of coat for a variety of professional and leisure contexts and a whole range of accessories, from sticks and gloves, to shirts and hats, shopping for men's fashion was a serious business. Underlying the wearing of such clothing was a theory of "gentlemanliness" that bound the "correct" usage of the male wardrobe to a celebration of moral rectitude, physical prowess, and aesthetic "good form." In its more adventurous forms—for example, when the dapper evening suit was taken up as a badge of belonging for London dandies and Parisian "boulevardiers" in the 1890s, or when the relaxed lounge suit began to break down the stuffiness implied by the frock coat in the same decade—male fashion offered a universal template for modern dressing. Women rapidly took up its adaptable components, like the washable shirt and the tailored suit, to form a wardrobe more suitable to the expanded lifestyle of the New Woman in the early twentieth century. Like other aspects of European fashion, the man's suit proved to be a flexible barometer of cultural change. Its development illustrated how accomplished fashionable consumers were at reconciling the material plenitude of contemporary life with their social and emotional needs.

See also **Body; Industrial Revolution, First; Industrial Revolution, Second.**

BIBLIOGRAPHY

Abler, Thomas S. *Hinterland Warriors and Military Dress.* Oxford, U.K., 1999.

Breward, Christopher. *The Hidden Consumer: Masculinities, Fashion, and City Life 1860–1914.* Manchester, U.K., 1999.

———. *Fashion.* Oxford, U.K., 2003.

Coleman, Elizabeth Ann. *The Opulent Era: Fashions of Worth, Doucet, and Pingat.* London, 1989.

Cunningham, Patricia A. *Reforming Women's Fashion 1850–1920: Politics, Health, and Art.* Kent, Ohio, 2003.

Perrot, Philippe. *Fashioning the Bourgeoisie: A History of Clothing in the Nineteenth Century.* Princeton, N.J., 1994.

Steele, Valerie. *Fashion and Eroticism: Ideals of Beauty from the Victorian Era to the Jazz Age.* New York, 1985.

CHRISTOPHER BREWARD

COAL MINING. From the late Middle Ages to the end of the eighteenth century, coal had been occasionally used as a fuel mainly for house heating in various places in Great Britain, the Low Countries, France, and Germany. Starting in the sixteenth century, coal mined around Newcastle and Durham was shipped to London and other towns. Beginning in the mid-eighteenth century the First Industrial Revolution opened new markets for coal: the iron and steel industry using coke in blast furnaces, and steam engines associated with the development of textile and manufacturing industries. The Industrial Revolution provoked a spectacular development of coal mining not only in Great Britain but also in Belgium, Upper Silesia, and Rineland, Germany. According to E. A. Wrigley, the Industrial Revolution was a revolution in energy supply. Between 1770 and 1830 the European economy gradually shifted from an advanced organic economy based on natural, renewable energy resources (wind and water power) into an economy mainly based on mineral, nonrenewable energy resources—coal. For the first time in history, James Watt's steam engine managed to transform thermal power (steam produced by coal) into mechanical power. Coal rapidly became "the bread of industry." In the 1870s and 1880s the improvement in steel production (via the Bessemer, Siemens-Martin, and Thomas-Gilchrist converters) and the invention of the dynamo for producing electricity (1869) paved the way for the Second

TABLE 1

Estimated consumption of U.K. coal by uses, 1816–1913 (percent)

	1816	1840	1869	1887	1913
Export	1.0	5.0	9.5	14.0	25.5
Iron and steel	11.0	21.0	26.5	17.0	13.0
Manufacturing	28.0	29.0	26.0	28.5	23.5
Domestic	53.0	34.0	18.0	17.0	12.0
Railways	–	1.0	3.0	4.0	5.0
Steamships	–	2.0	3.0	5.5	6.0
Gas and electricity	–	3.0	6.0	6.0	8.0
Collieries and others	7.0	5.0	8.0	8.0	7.0
	100.0	100.0	100.0	100.0	100.0

SOURCE: Mitchell, p. 12.

Industrial Revolution, associated with a boom in coal output. The new electrical sector constituted a new market alongside the market of gas power stations. Increasing urbanization from 1870 to 1914 was also associated with improvements in domestic coal-based heating systems. Cheap coal stoves made coal heating affordable for even modest households.

For most of the nineteenth century Great Britain was the major coal producer in the world. According to B. R. Mitchell, British output skyrocketed from 13 million tons per year in the period from 1801 to 1805 to 67 million tons in 1856 to 287 million tons in 1913. Most of the British coal fueled domestic heating in London and other cities in 1800, but in the following decades, it was mainly used in manufacturing, iron and steel plants, and stationary and locomotive steam engines. Coal was not only used for British industries and transports (railways, steamers) but also shipped worldwide (see table 1). In 1910, two-thirds of the coal exported on the world market was mined in Britain. Coal production and export were stimulated by the development of railway networks and steamships in Europe from 1840 onward. The famous smokeless steam coal of South Wales—suitable for new steamers—gave birth to an important overseas market after 1840. Cardiff became the world harbor for steam coal trade.

During the late nineteenth century, Germany and the United States seriously challenged Britain's coal production supremacy (see table 2). By 1900 U.S. production had surpassed that of Britain.

Until the 1960s, coal mining remained a labor-intensive industry. Most of the underground work was performed by men using picks and shovels at the coal face. Therefore, coal miners constituted a key element of the working class. In 1908 Europe counted more than 1.8 million coal miners (966,000 in Britain, 591,000 in the German Empire, 191,000 in France, and 145,000 in Belgium).

One of the major problems of coal trade was the prohibitively high cost of inland transportation. This is why the first coalfields mined were situated alongside the seashore—in northeastern England—or rivers. Since the eighteenth century, ship canals made British coal relatively cheaper and more abundant. The challenge of coal transportation also gave birth to railways, which were primarily used to carry coal to harbors (starting with the Stockton & Darlington Railway, which began operating in 1825). Because of the high cost of haulage, industrial coal consumers, including iron and steel companies, manufacturers, and glassmakers, moved to the coalfields. A truly new landscape emerged in the first half of the nineteenth century: the industrial districts that were coalfields too.

"King Coal" was not present everywhere in continental Europe, however. Six major coalfields formed a "coal arc" between northern France and the eastern Ruhr. The oldest exploited fields were those alongside the Haine, Sambre, and Meuse Rivers in Wallonia (Belgium). The French Valenciennes basin extended from this so-called Belgian Borinage and has been mined since as early as the 1750s. Because of prohibitive transportation costs, however, Valenciennes coal was consumed locally until 1845 when it could be shipped by canal to Paris. From that time onward, new coal mines were opened in the Nord and Pas-de-Calais departments, as well as in Lorraine. There were other coalfields in central France that have been associated with regional industrialization, including Le Creusot, Saint-Étienne, Decazeville, and Carmaux. Compared to Britain and Germany, France was disadvantaged not only in terms of coal location and quantities but above all in terms of coal quality. France lacked coal suitable for coke and had to import it from Britain and from the Ruhr. In the German Empire the main coalfields were located in the Saar district, the Ruhr, and Upper Silesia (now in Poland), the huge basins in the latter two

TABLE 2

Coal production (thousands of tons)

Country	1850	1880	1900	1909
United Kingdom	40,000	146,969	225,181	263,774
France	4,434	19,508	32,325	37,840
Belgium	5,820	16,866	23,463	23,518
German Empire	–	49,978	109,290	148,900
Austria (Bohemia, Galicia)	–	5,889	10,992	13,713
Hungary	–	(1882) 799	(1902) 1,002	1,397
Netherlands	–	–	320	1,121
Donets Basin (Russian Empire)	(1855) 70	(1885) 1,900	11,300	(1907) 17,380
Poland (Russian Empire)	(1855) 70	(1885) 1,800	4,190	(1907) 5,490
United States (*)	–	71,482	269,684	(1908) 415,843

(*) in short tons of 907 kilograms

SOURCE: Gruner and Bousquet, p. 6.

regions ruled by the Prussian government. The Ruhr was the most impressive industrial basin in nineteenth-century Europe. Industrialization started after 1815 when the Ruhr took advantage of the Prussian kingdom's industrial support and the establishment of the Zollverein monetary union. The high quality of coal seams and the discovery of a perfect coking coal near Essen dictated the location of the German iron and steel industry. In fact one of the main characteristics of industry in the Ruhr was the early integration of collieries and ironworks in single large firms during the second half of the nineteenth century. The Ruhr was also characterized by the formation of cartels such as the Rheinisch-westfälisches Kohlensyndikat (Rhineland-Westphalia Coal Syndicate), a coal-trading cartel created in 1893.

Productivity in coal mining mainly depended on geological factors. In the period from 1874 to 1878, for instance, the annual output in metric tons per worker varied from 135 tons in Belgium, to 154 in France, 209 in Germany, and 270 in the United Kingdom; Upper Silesia, meanwhile, enjoyed the highest productivity in Europe. If technological improvements contributed to increase output and productivity from the late eighteenth century onward, coal mining remained a labor-intensive sector. In order to improve productivity, new technologies were introduced. The "long-wall method" of laying out coal replaced the older pillar-and-stall techniques in the early nineteenth century. Coal shafts received special attention from engineers. New methods of sinking and consolidating

shafts were introduced, while cages progressively replaced baskets for coal raising and for ferrying workers. Shafts usually reached 800 to 1,000 meters (2,600 to 3,280 feet) deep in the mid-nineteenth century. To reach such depths, increasingly powerful steam engines were introduced for pumping water from the bottom of the shaft, for ventilating underground galleries, and for haulage. Good ventilation of underground galleries and coal faces was necessary not only for the activity of workers and horses, but also for preventing the accumulation of gas and firedamp explosions. It was for this reason that safety lamps replaced candlesticks from the 1820s onward. The first safety lamp, invented by Sir Humphry Davy in 1815, was quickly adopted in British collieries as well as those in Belgium. Davy's safety lamp received major improvements by Mathieu Mueseler in Belgium and Jean-Baptiste Marsaut in France. As far as mechanical ventilating was concerned, various types of mechanical ventilator fans were introduced between the 1830s and 1850s, but the ventilator invented by the Belgian engineer Armand Guibal was largely adopted in Europe by the mid-nineteenth century. Horses progressively replaced pit boys (and girls) for underground haulage from the 1820s onward. Pneumatic boring machines were introduced in the late 1850s, and a new rock drill (the Dubois-François rock drill) debuted in the 1870s. Some attempts were also made in the 1860s to introduce coal-cutting machinery, but these efforts were not successful until the introduction of electricity in underground galleries. Electricity, the

"NAKED TO THEIR WAIST; AN IRON CHAIN FASTENED TO A BELT OF LEATHER RUNS BETWEEN THEIR LEGS": A GIRL "HURRIER" IN A HALIFAX COAL-PIT OF THE 'FORTIES.

A female coal worker. This engraving, which appeared in the *Illustrated London News,* depicts the deplorable conditions under which miners labored in the nineteenth century. THE ILLUSTRATED LONDON NEWS PICTURE LIBRARY, LONDON, UK/BRIDGEMAN ART LIBRARY

last major technical improvement of the nineteenth century, was introduced in the 1880s for lighting, pumping, and underground haulage.

All these improvements and the development of coal mining itself were stimulated by public authorities. On the Continent, the French Revolution had abolished the *ancien régime* mining legislation. A law enacted on 28 July 1791 declared coal and ore mines to be at the disposal of the nation. Only the state could give a mining concession. The Conseil des mines de la République (Council of mines of the Republic) was placed in charge of inspecting and encouraging the adoption of new technologies. On April 1810 new legislation reinforced the fundamental principles of the previous one and became the model for mining legislation in Belgium, part of Germany, Italy, and Spain. The French legislation continues to be in force in the early twenty-first century.

See also **Industrial Revolution, First; Industrial Revolution, Second.**

BIBLIOGRAPHY

Debeir, Jean-Claude, Jean-Paul Deléage, and Daniel Hémery. *In the Servitude of Power: Energy and Civilisation through the Ages.* Translated by John Barzman. London, 1991.

Gruner, É., and G. Bousquet. *Atlas général des houillères.* Vol. 2: *Texte.* Paris, 1911.

Hempel, Gustav. *Die deutsche Montanindustrie.* 2nd ed. Essen, West Germany, 1969.

Leboutte, René. *Vie et mort des bassins industriels en Europe, 1750–2000.* Paris, 1997.

Milward, Alan S., and S. B. Saul. *The Economic Development of Continental Europe, 1780–1870.* London, 1973.

Mitchell, B. R. *Economic Development of the British Coal Industry, 1800–1914.* Cambridge, U.K., 1984.

Wrigley, E. A. *Continuity, Chance, and Change: The Character of the Industrial Revolution in England.* Cambridge, U.K., 1988.

RENÉ LEBOUTTE

COBBETT, WILLIAM (1763–1835),

English journalist and essayist known as the "poor man's friend."

William Cobbett, a plowboy turned self-taught writer, achieved enduring fame and transient fortune through the power of his brilliant and vitriolic pen, publishing some thirty million words over the course of forty years. Having come to notice for his vigorous defense of the British establishment under the pen name Peter Porcupine, Cobbett changed his politics but not his unbuttoned style and converted to radicalism in horror at the scandals and incompetence revealed during the Napoleonic Wars. In 1802 he established the weekly *Political Register* to expose the workings of "the Thing," the war-inflated rentier culture of political corruption and financial plunder that imposed an intolerable tax burden on the poor. The first periodical to introduce a leading article as a regular feature, the *Register* was to run for eighty-nine volumes, or some 402,000 pages, until his death. Cobbett also undertook other major publishing ventures linked to his commitment to open access to public information, which he saw as the necessary first stage in political education toward the panacea of parliamentary reform: these included the publication of a complete collection of state trials and the collecting and printing of parliamentary debates, a project he was soon forced to sell to the printer T. C. Hansard, who was to gain eponymous credit for this enduring and indispensable public service. No less important were Cobbett's efforts to broaden the audience by a number of innovations and exercises (including self-help spelling and grammar guides) in cheap publication. Here the agenda extended no further than the political basics: no space was allowed for the theoretical stuff and nonsense of those he termed (with characteristic prejudice) "Scottish feelosofers." The self-proclaimed "poor man's friend," Cobbett brought out a special cheap broadsheet edition in 1816 of his weekly *Register,* promptly dubbed by opponents "two-penny trash," a title he was delighted to appropriate. This was to prove a vital contribution to what historians have called the politicization of discontent: throughout the land, impoverished workers, thrown into dire distress by the transition to peace without plenty after Waterloo, took heed of Cobbett's advice not to riot but to agitate instead for parliamentary reform, their only guarantee of economic amelioration.

When the government shortly afterward introduced special legislation to curb the exponential growth of the radical movement, Cobbett left for the United States, a controversial course of action that allowed him to continue publishing but provoked censure from other radical leaders who remained to contest (and endure) repression. Cobbett returned in late 1819, bearing with him the bones of the republican revolutionary Tom Paine, hallowed testimony, as it were, of his radical credentials. But his reputation remained in question until his wholehearted support (and speechwriting) for Queen Caroline in the unseemly divorce proceedings instigated by George IV on his accession to the throne. When public interest in the affair waned, Cobbett, having established himself as a successful experimental farmer, turned his attention to the depressed state of English agriculture. Relishing the opportunity to escape London, "the Great Wen," he toured his beloved southern England, raising the standard of parliamentary reform at county meetings and conversing on diverse topics with rural laborers, or "chopsticks," the "very best and most virtuous of all mankind." Published in 1830 as evocative travel literature, these *Rural Rides,* with their occasional detours into the alien North and beyond, have retained a powerful appeal to those whose imagined sense of Englishness centers on an idyllic, preindustrial, anti-urban, southern pastoral. The image was to be complemented by Cobbett's portrayal of social Catholicism, a nostalgic reconstruction (subsequently echoed by late Victorian socialists) of inclusive welfare and care in preindustrial merrie England—a damning benchmark by which to expose and condemn the harsh utilitarianism of the Whig and Benthamite reforms of the 1830s.

Ironically, when Cobbett was able to fulfill his long-held ambition to enter Parliament after the Reform Act of 1832, his constituency, Oldham, was located in the industrial North. By no means the high point of his lengthy public career, his spell in the Commons was also a time of difficulty on his farm in Surrey, which he was compelled to leave to his wife and seven children as a bankrupt estate. This unfortunate ending notwithstanding, Cobbett's reputation has remained high among succeeding generations. The personification of the English yeoman, Cobbett the radical reformer embodied the English sense of fair play, old-time hospitality, and manly sports, hence his continuing appeal across the political spectrum.

See also **Corn Laws, Repeal of; Great Britain; Press and Newspapers; Trade and Economic Growth.**

BIBLIOGRAPHY

Dyck, Ian. *William Cobbett and Rural Popular Culture.* Cambridge, U.K., 1992.

Spater, George. *William Cobbett: The Poor Man's Friend.* 2 vols. Cambridge, U.K., 1982.

JOHN BELCHEM

COBDEN, RICHARD (1804–1865), British political and economic reformer.

Richard Cobden was the leading spokesman in mid-nineteenth-century Britain for free trade, laissez-faire, and internationalism. He was the very personification of the "Manchester school" of political and economic reform—opposed equally to the corn laws and to trade unions as restricting the free movement of goods and persons. Cobden came from a rural southern background (he was born in Heyshott, Sussex) and often styled himself the friend of the farmer. Underlying his various campaigns for free trade, retrenchment in defense spending, and nonintervention in European affairs was a consistent commitment to land reform. His vision of a future of social stability, prosperity, and peace throughout Britain and Europe was premised on the redistribution of land ownership: the demise of large "feudal" landowners with a concomitant increase in individual "freehold" proprietorship of the soil. However, his work in the freehold land movement and for land reform generally has not featured prominently in most biographical accounts.

Cobden is remembered as the manufacturer turned consummate political agitator who secured the repeal of the Corn Laws in 1846, the smooth operator who complemented the more emotive approach of his famous political partner, John Bright (1811–1889). Cobden certainly contributed much to the success of the Anti–Corn Law League, the most famous example of "pressure from without" in Victorian politics. Having moved north in 1832 to be close to his calico-printing business interests, Cobden was soon involved in the campaign to gain incorporation for Manchester, acquiring in the process an expertise in organization, lecturing, and election tactics, which he was later to impart with dramatic effect to the League.

Following fierce Chartist opposition to its initial efforts to maximize extraparliamentary support, the League, steered by Cobden, quickly took steps to avoid unwelcome intervention. The unruly crowd was excluded by ticketing, direct mailing, door to door canvassing, registration of voters, and other mechanisms of the "politics of electoral pressure": the mobilization of electoral pressure to persuade candidates and political parties to commit themselves to promote particular legislation. In Cobden's unashamed words, the League became rather "a middle-class set of agitators," concentrating its efforts on existing and "respectable" voters, to whose numbers provident free-trade supporters were to be appended by purchase of forty-shilling freeholds.

Cobden also provided ideological inspiration, transforming the level of economic argument in League propaganda, showing how the Corn Laws were not only a check on consumption but also an obstacle to the balanced economic progress of both manufacturing and agriculture. Free admission of foreign corn would increase overseas demand for British manufactures while the lifting of protection would encourage domestic agriculture into more modern and competitive processes with improved drainage, crop rotation, and enhanced investment. Much influenced by the economist Adam Smith (1723–1790), Cobden viewed freedom in utilitarian terms as the absence of all restraint (except in education, where as a leading supporter of the National Public Schools Association he contended that "government interference is as necessary for *education* as its non-interference is essential to *trade*"). Repeal of the Corn Laws in 1846 raised Cobden to iconic status, but despite such celebrity his political influence diminished: a great symbolic victory, the defeat of agricultural protection did not presage a middle-class "Manchester" revolution. Ranged across a number of issues, including various schemes (forerunners of today's building societies) to create freehold votes in large county electorates surrounding the towns, Cobden's subsequent campaigns lacked emotive focus and proved no match for Lord Palmerston's (Henry John Temple; 1784–1865) unashamed patriotism.

As the critic of Palmerston's aggressive foreign policy, Cobden has been lauded as an anti-imperialist, but his noninterventionist stance rested on what has itself been called the "imperialism of free trade": expensive gunboat diplomacy was not required when Britain's dominance of world trade was assured by virtue of its manufacturing and commercial supremacy. Although he was to fall from public favor, reaching a nadir during the Crimean War (1854–1856) and his defeat at the 1857 election, Cobden was not without some success in his later political life, most notably the Cobden-Chevalier Treaty of 1860. A symbol of international harmony between Britain and France, this was the first of eight "most favored nation" treaties that Britain negotiated in the 1860s, and the model that other European countries followed until the revival of protectionism in the 1880s. Cobden was in poor health thereafter but continued when possible to attend to his parliamentary duties as MP for Rochdale where he was elected in 1859, having previously served as MP for Stockport (1841–1847) and the West Riding (1847–1857).

See also **Chartism; Cobden-Chevalier Treaty; Commercial Policy; Corn Laws, Repeal of; Liberalism; Protectionism; Trade and Economic Growth.**

BIBLIOGRAPHY

Hinde, Wendy. *Richard Cobden: Victorian Outsider.* New Haven, Conn., 1983.

Morley, John. *The Life of Richard Cobden.* 2 vols. London, 1881.

Taylor, Miles. "Richard Cobden." *Oxford Dictionary of National Biography.* Oxford, U.K., 2004.

JOHN BELCHEM

COBDEN-CHEVALIER TREATY.

The Cobden-Chevalier Treaty of 1860 lowered or eliminated duties levied on goods traded between Britain and France, and signaled a victory for liberal economic policies. Named for its two primary negotiators, British Richard Cobden (1804–1865) and French Michel Chevalier (1806–1879), the treaty inaugurated a period of relatively free trade among many European nations that lasted until the early 1890s. The treaty continued Britain's move toward lowered tariffs that had begun in the 1820s, notably through the 1846 repeal of the Corn Laws. In France, the treaty marked a clear departure from protectionism, shaped industrialization, and sharpened political opposition to Napoleon III, emperor of France.

Well before 1860, both Cobden and Chevalier had acquired reputations as advocates for free trade and held influential positions within their respective governments. Cobden, a member of Parliament (MP) who made his fortune in Manchester textiles, won international acclaim as a radical campaigner for free trade through his success with the Anti–Corn Law Association in the 1840s. As a young man, Chevalier adopted the Saint-Simonian principles that the state's economic policies should promote the material and moral elevation of the masses. Chevalier taught in the Collège de France before his appointment to the Council of State as an economic advisor to Napoleon III in 1852.

During the 1850s, Napoleon III worked to create political stability through prosperity. He and Chevalier agreed that the state should encourage industrial modernization and improved transportation in order to increase productivity and make more goods and services accessible to more people. They believed that free trade would further these goals. Businessmen in wine, railroads, ports, and steamships favored lower duties. However, French textile manufacturers, cereal growers, and mining companies supported protectionism, and the Legislative Corps repeatedly blocked attempts to lower tariffs. Chevalier awaited an opportunity to use a treaty to accomplish his goals, because the empire did not require the Legislative Corps to approve treaties.

The right moment arose in July 1859, when tensions between Britain and France increased due to France's interventions in Italy. The British MP John Bright called on Britain to lower its tariffs in order to improve its relationship with France. Chevalier took this opportunity to contact Cobden in the hope of coming to a free trade agreement. Beginning in October 1859, the two nations, led by Cobden and Chevalier, entered into negotiations. The treaty stating the principle of lowered tariffs and setting maximum values at 30 percent was signed on 23 January 1860. The British Parliament approved the treaty in March, in large part due to the support of Chancellor of the Exchequer William Gladstone.

Conventions signed in the fall of 1860 through negotiations between French Minister of Commerce Eugène Rouher and Cobden set the new tariffs. Britain eliminated most duties on *articles de Paris* (toys, haberdashery, imitation jewelry), silk, wine, and spirits. The French could maintain a maximum of 30 percent duties on some goods, but many were taxed as low as 10 percent. Any tariff decreases that France or Britain offered to a third nation would be extended to each other. Treaties lowering trade barriers among most major European nations, excluding Russia, soon followed.

Cobden and Chevalier viewed the treaty not as an end to itself, but as the first step in improved Franco-British relations. However, some British politicians believed the French used the treaty as a distraction from their Italian policies, and that the treaty would leave the British handicapped in case of war. The two nations soon became involved in a naval arms race.

The treaty's influence on French industrial modernization is difficult to measure amid other factors, including the development of domestic markets and the cotton shortage during the U.S. Civil War (1861–1865), but most scholars agree that the treaty speeded technological and structural change in France. French users of charcoal forges, forest owners, and textile manufacturers suffered from the influx of British coal and textiles, but some modernized using low-interest loans offered by the government. The treaty did not significantly affect British industry.

In France, the political consequences proved significant. Protectionists, led by politician Adolphe Thiers, felt that Napoleon III had betrayed their interests and their trust by secretly negotiating a treaty that might cripple their industries. They pressured the emperor to make liberal political concessions.

The tariff remained in effect until 1882, when Britain and France could agree only to mutually maintain most-favored-nation status. Once France's treaties with other nations lapsed in 1892, protectionists led by Jules Méline raised duties, although never to the prohibitive level in effect before the Cobden-Chevalier Treaty.

See also **Cobden, Richard; Corn Laws, Repeal of; Liberalism; Trade and Economic Growth.**

BIBLIOGRAPHY

Dunham, Arthur Louis. *The Anglo-French Treaty of Commerce of 1860 and the Progress of the Industrial Revolution in France.* Reprint, New York, 1971.

Edsall, Nicholas C. *Richard Cobden: Independent Radical.* Cambridge, Mass., 1986.

Price, Roger. *The French Second Empire: An Anatomy of Political Power.* New York, 2001.

RACHEL CHRASTIL

COCKERILL, JOHN (1790–1840), English entrepreneur.

John Cockerill was one of the pioneering entrepreneurs of the Belgian iron and mechanical engineering industries. He was the third son of William Cockerill (1759–1832), a peripatetic English inventor who had a gift for constructing models of industrial machines and who worked in Russia and Sweden before moving to the Low Countries in 1799. John spent most of his childhood with relatives in Lancashire until joining his father in Verviers in 1802. William was then working with Simonis et Biolley, the most important woolen producers in the Low Countries, and building machinery for woolen textile manufacturing. Louis Ternaux (1763–1833), a major French woolens producer, established a further mill at Ensival, near Verviers, equipping it with Cockerill spinning machinery. John was apprenticed to his father and, with his brothers William II and Charles, moved to Liège in 1807, where their father established a number of his own workshops to produce machinery for spinning and weaving wool. John was a manager in the family business by 1807 and, with his brother Charles, took it over on their father's retirement in 1812. During that year, the Cockerills produced twenty-six hundred machines, primarily for woolen spinning. Also at this time, the Cockerills obtained a steam engine from England, but it would appear that they did not produce their own for a further six years.

Following the collapse of Napoleonic Europe in 1814–1815 and the consequent decline of the Verviers woolen industry, John and Charles opened a Berlin workshop for producing wool-spinning machinery through the patronage of Peter Beuth, responsible for the Department of Trade and Industry within the Prussian Ministry of Finance. However, the venture only lasted about two years, as John decided to return to the Low Countries, opening an ironworks at Seraing in the former bishop's palace. This was to be the final step in the family's shift from initially producing textile machinery to building steam engines with their enterprise's own iron, a developmental path followed by a number of other continental European mechanical engineering plants—Koechlin, Schlumberger, Sulzer, and Wyss—during the first half of the nineteenth century. The first Cockerill steam engine was built at Seraing in 1818, and by 1830 the works had turned out a further 201.

John worked in partnership with his brother Charles and the Seraing enterprise began production on 25 January 1817. Initially, it had the backing of William I (r. 1815–1840), the king of the Netherlands, who personally invested £100,000 (4 million francs) as a silent partner in the venture—the Etablissements John Cockerill—a stake that was part of state support for industrializing his newly established kingdom. This royal patronage also led to the Société Générale (Algemmeene Nederlandsche Maatschappij ter begunstiging ven de Volks-slijt) providing Cockerill with a fifty-thousand-florin credit during the late 1820s to finance a cotton mill.

In 1821 Cockerill attempted to use English coal-based technology at Seraing for smelting iron, but these efforts were not to be completely successful until eight more years had passed. Nonetheless, the Cockerill works had become the "industrial wonder of Europe" by the mid-1820s. It employed two thousand workers at an integrated production site that smelted iron and transformed the metal into not only girders and rods but also complex machinery including steamboats. The product range included cotton textile machinery from 1825 (power looms from 1827), mechanical presses from 1828, glass-polishing devices from 1834, and railway locomotives from 1836. These were exported throughout Europe. In developing his business, Cockerill quickly obtained copies of new industrial machines from England, which were used at Seraing as models to be copied and emulated for his widening range of European customers. Cockerill's advantage over English mechanical engineers lay in lower Belgian labor costs.

The creation of Belgium in 1830 led to the cessation of Dutch royal financial backing, and Cockerill became the sole owner of the Seraing works in 1835. By then he also owned cotton and wool mills at Liège and a paper works at Andenne, all operated on the same large scale as his Seraing ironworks. Without state backing, Cockerill was forced after 1830 to rely on short-term credits from the Banque de Belgique to sustain his Seraing enterprise, but he overcame severe financial difficulties during 1839, when an economic depression forced his firm into liquidation.

In acting as a disseminator of the new industrial technology pioneered in Britain, Cockerill's life mirrored that of his father. He continued to play this role until the end. In 1839–1840 Cockerill went to Saint Petersburg to present plans to Nicholas I (r. 1825–1855) for building railways within the Russian Empire (although this may also have been an attempt to obtain financing for his ailing Belgian company). However, when returning to Seraing he caught typhus in Warsaw and died on 19 June 1840. The Seraing works then comprised four coal mines and two blast furnaces together with associated rolling mills, forges, and machine shops. His creditors continued the enterprise by converting it into a joint-stock company—Société Anonyme des Établissements John Cockerill.

See also **Coal Mining; Engineers; Industrial Revolution, First.**

BIBLIOGRAPHY

Briavoine, M. N. Extract from *De l'industrie en Belgique*, vol. 1, pp. 302–305. Brussels, 1839. Reprinted in *Documents of European Economic History*, edited by Sidney Pollard and Colin Holmes, vol. 1: *The Process of Industrialization, 1750–1870*, 322–323. New York, 1968.

Hodges, Theodore B. "The Iron King of Liège: John Cockerill." Ph. D. diss., Columbia University, 1960.

Milward, Alan S., and S. B. Saul. *The Economic Development of Continental Europe, 1780–1870*. London, 1973.

Mokyr, Joel. *Industrialization in the Low Countries, 1795–1850*. New Haven, Conn., 1976.

Pasleau, Suzy. *John Cockerill: Itinéraire d'un géant industriel*. Alleur-Liège, France, 1992.

Westebbe, Richard M. "State Entrepreneurship: King Willem I, John Cockerill, and the Seraing Engineering Works, 1815–1840." *Explorations in Entrepreneurial History* (April 1956).

PHILIP COTTRELL

COFFEE, TEA, CHOCOLATE.

Coffee, tea, and chocolate were all increasingly widely consumed in nineteenth-century Europe. They had numerous apparent benefits: they offered appealing taste and stimulating effect (from the caffeine), yet they were not alcoholic. They were prepared with boiled water (which people understood made water safe), and were thought to have medicinal benefits. In contrast, the water in many cities was polluted and unfit to drink, which had led to high consumption of light beer or light wine. Londoners in the early nineteenth century had particularly bad water, which led to several outbreaks of waterborne illness and prompted London hospitals to serve only alcoholic beverages to their patients. Factory owners encouraged the drinking of tea or coffee rather than beer or wine because of the dangers associated with running machinery while intoxicated and perhaps because stimulants increased productivity. On the downside, coffee and tea replaced beverages that provided more nutrition. Chocolate, tea, and coffee were also associated with the increasing demand for sugar in Europe, because sugar lessened their bitterness. And as with any popular commodity, all were targeted for taxation by governments.

COFFEE

Originally from Ethiopia, coffee was introduced to Europe by Italian traders in 1600. In the seventeenth century, coffee houses became important literary and political places, and they retained this character through the nineteenth century. The Spanish, having been chocolate drinkers since they introduced it from the Americas, were late to embrace coffee, and it was not until the nineteenth century that coffee houses began to prosper in Spain.

However, in France coffee was an essential beverage. Coffee was deemed so essential that in 1806, when Napoleon I (r. 1804–1814/1815) decided to make France self-sufficient (to cut Britain off from its European trade customers), he sought a substitute for coffee. Since coffee cannot grow in Europe, the French substituted the herb chicory during this period. When foreign policy changed, the French went back to true coffee, although sometimes mixed with chicory.

The medical qualities of coffee had been investigated since its entry into Europe. This inquiry continued in the 1800s, with some researchers praising its energizing effects and others deploring the stimulating aspects as upsetting the body's natural balance. Caffeine was isolated in the 1820s, although not all critics of coffee's healthfulness understood that caffeine was the active substance. By the late 1800s, it was clear that excessive consumption of coffee created a recognizable syndrome.

By the early 1900s, afternoon coffee became a customary occasion in Germany. The derogatory term *Kaffeeklatsch* was coined to describe women's gossip at these affairs (although now the term simply refers to relaxed conversation).

Coffee became an international commodity, and one of Europe's major sources was Brazil, where the coffee plant was tended by slaves. With the abolition of the slave trade in Brazil in 1850, the coffee industry, and the culture of Brazil, was slowly forced to change as the existing slaves aged and died. Other changes in the coffee trade were due to technical developments such as steam pressure espresso, vacuum tins to package roast coffee (which hurt the market for local roasting shops), soluble instant coffee, the filter-drip coffee process, and the process for decaffeinating coffee beans.

Coffeehouse in the Clerkenwell district of London. Undated engraving. In many parts of Europe, cafés were an important locus of sociability. PRIVATE COLLECTION/BRIGDEMAN ART LIBRARY

TEA

Europe was introduced to tea in the mid seventeenth century; in Spain, Italy, and France, it was a drink for the upper classes. In England and the Netherlands, tea was drunk by all.

The well-known British preference for tea was well established by the nineteenth century, partly because it was easier to brew than was coffee, partly because the British East India Company advertised profusely, and partly because smugglers offered tea at cheaper prices than did legal sellers, who had to pay high taxes. Especially in Britain, "tea" was not simply a drink but a social event. By the 1880s, afternoon tea had become an important daily event. Also by the 1880s, the price of tea—or what was sold as tea—had dropped enough so that working-class folk could afford a steady supply.

Because until the nineteenth century tea only came from China, it was often expensive. This led many tea sellers, both Chinese and European, to supplement the tea leaves with additives. Sometimes the adulteration was harmless, as in the case of adding orange or lemon leaves. Some adulterants were harmful, such as the dye added to green teas: a mix of Prussian Blue and gypsum, which added both plaster and cyanide to the tea. The British parliament did not pass a "tea act" to check the quality of tea until the end of the nineteenth century.

Tea was so important to the British that the East India Company engaged in a complex trade by which the British traded opium to Chinese merchants for tea. The Chinese emperor had forbidden opium importation and requested that the British stop the opium trade, but the British refused. This tension led to the First Opium War of 1839–1842, which the British won. Ironically, by about 1840, the British actually had another source of tea, India.

CHOCOLATE

The Spanish introduced chocolate to Europe in the early sixteenth century, and consumption was well established by the late eighteenth century. Chocolate was taken as a beverage, and, because of the high cost, chiefly drunk by aristocrats. Less austere Catholic clergy welcomed chocolate as a drink allowed on fast days. This association with the upper classes and the clergy conflicted with the ideals of the French Revolution and turned French opinion against chocolate in the late eighteenth century. In Britain, cocoa was popularized by the navy; hot, nutritious, and nonalcoholic, it was considered the perfect drink for sailors on watch duty.

Chocolate underwent several processing improvements in the nineteenth century. In 1828, Dutch chemist C. J. van Houten discovered how to remove most of the bitter fat; the "Dutch process" of alkalization neutralized acids and made chocolate more soluble in water. Van Houten's work led to the production of the first chocolate bars in 1847, although milk chocolate was not developed until 1875.

As with other expensive and exotic products, chocolate was subject to adulteration. In the mid-nineteenth century, a British study found that 90 percent of the fifty brands of commercial cacao were adulterated with starch fillers or brick dust and toxic red lead pigment.

See also **Alcohol and Temperance; Diet and Nutrition; Wine.**

BIBLIOGRAPHY

Coe, Sophie, and Michael D. Coe. *The True History of Chocolate.* New York, 1996.

Hobhouse, Henry. *Seeds of Change: Five Plants That Transformed Mankind.* New York, 1986.

Pendergrast, Mark. *Uncommon Grounds: The History of Coffee and How It Transformed Our World.* New York, 1999.

Pettigrew, Jane. *A Social History of Tea.* London, 2001.

Weinberg, Bennett Alan, and Bonnie K. Bealer. *The World of Caffeine: The Science and Culture of the World's Most Popular Drug.* New York, 2001.

KATHRYN A. WALTERSCHEID

COLERIDGE, SAMUEL TAYLOR

(1772–1834), English poet and critic.

Born in the market town of Ottery St. Mary, Devonshire, England, but largely educated at a charity school in London and then at Cambridge University, Samuel Taylor Coleridge soon made himself a poet. He is best known for "The Rime of the Ancient Mariner" (1798), a ballad about a sailor who kills an albatross during a nightmarish voyage from England to the equatorial Pacific; and "Kubla Khan" (1797 or 1798), a visionary "fragment" about a medieval Mongol emperor. Coleridge drew inspiration from many sources, both literary and natural, and particularly from William Wordsworth (1770–1850). After meeting Wordsworth in the mid-1790s, he collaborated with him on *Lyrical Ballads*, first published in 1798, which began with "The Rime" and became a landmark of the English Romantic movement. But most of Coleridge's poetry appeared in volumes entirely his own, beginning with *Poems on Various Subjects* (1796), and he wrote virtually all of his best poems by the time he was thirty. Their style and subject matter range from the supernaturalism of "The Rime" and the rhapsodic tone of "Kubla Khan" to the natural, familiar, conversational style of poems such as "The Nightingale" (1798) and the poignancy of "Dejection: An Ode" (1802), an agonized lament for the poet's incapacity to create that is paradoxically couched in a language of exquisite lyricism.

Coleridge was himself a paradox. In 1800, convinced that he "never had the essentials of poetic Genius" even after plainly demonstrating them, he roundly declared, "I abandon Poetry altogether," leaving Wordsworth to write "the higher & deeper Kinds" and himself to explain them. Though Coleridge actually did write some poetry after 1800, though he saw many editions of his poetry appear throughout his life, and though he revised one of his early plays (*Osorio*, later called *Remorse*) for a successful run at the Drury Lane in 1813, he chiefly devoted the ensuing years to prose on an astonishing variety of topics, ranging from politics and religion to philosophy and literary criticism. Indeed, given his bouts of suicidal depression and his long-term addiction to opium (beginning in the late 1790s),

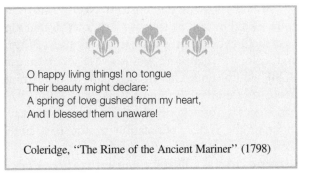

> O happy living things! no tongue
> Their beauty might declare:
> A spring of love gushed from my heart,
> And I blessed them unaware!

Coleridge, "The Rime of the Ancient Mariner" (1798)

it is amazing that he managed to produce so much.

His writing on politics began with the radical political lectures that he delivered in Bristol in 1795, when the sparks of reform spread by the French Revolution still fired his hopes. After the bloodthirsty aggressiveness of the Revolution made him a Tory, his political theory became at once more philosophical and more religious, as exemplified by *The Statesman's Manual* (1816) and *On the Constitution of the Church and State* (1830). His philosophical writings—such as *Aids to Reflection* (1825)—reflect the influence of German transcendentalism, which he first imbibed during a sojourn at the University of Göttingen in the late 1790s.

Coleridge's most influential work in prose, however, is his literary criticism. In 1811–1812 he delivered three series of lectures on William Shakespeare, John Milton, and drama. In 1817 he published *Biographia Literaria,* a book that weaves literary criticism and literary theory into the story of his life. Because several of its chapters draw without acknowledgement on the work of German philosophers, especially Friedrich Schelling and Immanuel Kant, Coleridge has been often accused of plagiarism. But whatever it owes to others, *Biographia* remains a singularly original expression of Coleridge's life and mind as well as a fascinating reply to Wordsworth's poetic autobiography, *The Prelude,* which Coleridge heard the poet read aloud in January 1807, soon after Wordsworth finished the first full-length draft of it. Besides telling the story of his own early life, just as Wordsworth had done, Coleridge recalls his first exciting discovery of Wordsworth's poetry and their intimate collaboration on *Lyrical Ballads.* Most remarkably, he

offers Wordsworth a bouquet of roses bristling with thorns. Even while extolling the beauty and power of his old friend's poetry, Coleridge attacks his theory of poetic diction, particularly his dictum—in the preface to the second edition of *Lyrical Ballads* (1800)—that poetry should speak "the real language of men."

Along with Wordsworth, Coleridge revolutionized English poetry and launched the movement now known as Romanticism. Equally adept at explaining the plays of Shakespeare, the poetry of Milton, and the originality of Wordsworth, he takes his place in the line of great English critics stretching from Samuel Johnson (1709–1784) through I. A. Richards (1893–1979). And in the history of conservative political thought, he remains a formidable successor to Edmund Burke.

See also **Conservatism; Romanticism; Wordsworth, William.**

BIBLIOGRAPHY

Primary Sources

Coleridge, Samuel Taylor. *Biographia Literaria; or, Biographical Sketches of My Literary Life and Opinions.* Edited by James Engell and W. Jackson Bate. Princeton, N.J., 1983.

Halmi, Nicholas, Paul Magnuson, and Raimonda Modiano, eds. *Coleridge's Poetry and Prose: Authoritative Texts, Criticism.* New York, 2004.

Secondary Sources

Bate, W. Jackson. *Coleridge.* 1968. Reprint, Cambridge, Mass., 1987.

Holmes, Richard. *Coleridge: Early Visions.* London, 1989.

Magnuson, Paul. *Coleridge and Wordsworth: A Lyrical Dialogue.* Princeton, N.J., 1988.

JAMES A. W. HEFFERNAN

COLONIALISM. Now that colonial empires are gone, historians may be tempted to put colonies at the margins of French, British, German, Belgian, Dutch, Spanish, or Portuguese history as excisable aberrations that can be set aside when writing histories from a national perspective. But the opposite approach can be dangerous too: Studies that portray colonialism as the "dark side of modernity," weave it so deeply into the fabric of European life that the tensions and debates over colonization also disappear. The peculiar quality of much colonial history stems from the questionable notion that old empires turned into nation-states and then set out to take colonies in the name of the nation. A more supple conception of state, empire, nation-state, and colony might give a more dynamic view of the place of colonization in European history.

POLITICS AND MORALITY IN THE SPACE OF EMPIRE

The extension of European rule over distant people was fiercely debated in the late eighteenth century. Some theorists of the rights of the "people"—in Britain as well as France—posited a cultural minimum that had to be met for full participation in a polity, an idea which justified the subordination of people considered uncivilized, not to mention women. Others, like l'Abbé Grégoire (1750–1831), were sharply critical of colonial oppression and enslavement and had a universalistic vision of humanity, holding up a Christian, European social model to everyone. Still others, notably Denis Diderot (1713–1784), not only asserted European states' unworthiness to rule others but also saw cultural difference as part of humanity and opposed a European model masquerading as universality.

The question was more than theoretical. During the French Revolution, plantation owners, property owners of mixed origins, and finally slaves from the crucial colony of Saint-Domingue each claimed that the ideals of the Declaration of the Rights of Man and of the Citizen applied to them, and in 1793 the revolutionary government freed slaves, hoping that black citizens would join in the defense of the Republic against royalists and rival empires. The Saint-Domingue revolution (1791–1804), Napoleon I's (r. 1804–1814/15) reinstatement of slavery in the French Empire (1802), and his failure to regain control over Saint-Domingue set precedents that would echo for the ensuing century and a half: A struggle for liberty *within* an empire, whose failure resulted on the one hand in secession (giving rise to Haiti) and on the other in reinforcement of distinction and discrimination in the remaining colonies.

Britain's loss of the thirteen North American colonies led its leaders to make a sharper distinction than before between a core that was truly British and colonies that were less so. Yet even in the 1780s ethical questions crossed lines of distinction within the empire. Edmund Burke's (1729–1797) parliamentary attack on the exploitative mistreatment of the Indian population by the East India Company—a private entity under royal charter—suggested that as a British company had been drawn into governing, the British government should acknowledge that its name and sense of itself were implicated in the way the empire's people were treated. By century's end, the antislavery movement was raising even deeper questions about the moral and political meaning of what went on in colonies under the British flag.

Mobilization over colonization and slavery did not end exploitation, discrimination, or political exclusion in old or new colonies, but it did make such issues subject to debate until the very end of colonial rule. The taking of colonies in the nineteenth century was part of the broader strategies of European states to exercise power at a distance in the economic interest of the empire, what Ronald Robinson and John Gallagher famously called the "imperialism of free trade." Especially after the fall of Napoleon, Britain was in a good position to use pressure and the occasional gunboat to grease the wheels of commerce in Latin America, Asia, and Africa. Formal colonization could occur when informal mechanisms broke down, when rivalries heated up, or when ambitious military officers took strong initiatives. The extension of British rule in South Asia—notably in Burma in the 1820s—and France's conquest of Algeria in 1830 were part of the process.

In India during the early and middle nineteenth century company rule was becoming more colonial. An orientalist conception of India as a once-glorious empire now quaintly backward but retaining its own cultural integrity was giving way among British elites to a harsher view of Indian society as crying out to be remade. France began in Algeria a bloody process of subduing Berber and Arab populations in the countryside more thoroughly than the Ottomans had attempted and encouraging settlers—mostly from non-French areas around the Mediterranean—to build a new sort of colony, divided between an immigrant minority moving toward French citizenship and an indigenous, Muslim majority defined as subjects distinct from citizens. Spain, meanwhile, lost most of its colonial possessions in the Americas as part of a crisis of empire precipitated by Napoleon's conquest of European Spain and disputes between American and European Spaniards over how to run the empire. Some scholars argue that the rise of national sentiments among American Spaniards was more consequence than cause of the crisis of empire. At the same time colonial rule deepened in the Spanish island of Cuba as planters enjoyed a sugar boom, retaining slavery until 1886 even as Britain abolished slavery in its colonies in 1834 and France in 1848. Portugal retained an empire of enclaves along the African and Indian Ocean coasts—at risk of incursions from other empires—with the very large exception of Brazil, where offshoots of the royal family constituted the Brazilian Empire, whose vast internal expansion and lively trade with Africa seemed to overshadow its European ancestor.

A NEW IMPERIALISM?

Although historians have debated whether the last part of the nineteenth century witnessed a "new imperialism," some writers at the time were convinced that "modern colonialism"—the work of engineers, merchants, teachers, and doctors, and not of conquistadors—would produce a rational system of economic complementarities that would serve the imperial center while helping to civilize colonized populations. In Great Britain missionaries and other humanitarians increasingly moved from criticism of British colonizers to calls to save indigenous societies from slave traders and tyrannical kings in Africa, to end the mistreatment of women in India, and to remove the impediments posed by backwardness to the extension of Christianity, orderly commerce, and civilization. The Indian Mutiny of 1857 fostered efforts to make rule more thorough and transformative, but pointed up the need to be careful about upsetting Indian social structure; its most concrete effect was to eliminate the East India Company and put India under crown rule. In France after 1871 political leaders began to advocate an explicitly republican form of colonialism, serving the national interest while extending French civilization to Africa and

Southeast Asia, holding out to some unspecified future the possibility that colonial subjects could become citizens. It is not clear how much of the public in either Britain or France was fully convinced of the colonial project, and colonization proceeded in ad hoc ways, keeping costs down, relying on recruitment of indigenous troops or local allies to do much of the conquering. Colonial rule would be rule on the cheap.

Creeping colonization became a scramble in the 1870s and 1880s, especially in Africa, as each Great Power feared that others might preempt current trading interests and future possibilities. German and Belgian entrance into the imperial game added to uncertainty in a European world with a small number of actors, each with supranational resources of unknown potential. Europe's industrialization not only gave the powers more cost-effective means to intervene overseas—the machine gun, the steamship, and the telegraph—but also more need for predictable supplies of minerals, vegetable oils, cotton, and other tropical products, and hence the temptation to secure such supplies from European rivals and unpredictable indigenous producers.

For a time, European leaders sought to avoid violent conflict with each other over colonial territory and to define rules of the game. Conferences at Berlin in 1884–1885 and Brussels in 1890–1891 produced agreements that power should be claimed by effective occupation of territory, meanwhile committing colonizers to abolish trade in slaves, arms, and liquor. The agreements posited a Europe of civilization and tutelage and an Africa of backwardness and subordination. That differences among people were by the late nineteenth century increasingly seen in racial terms is sometimes attributed to the influence of scientific racism in European thought, but colonial racism must also be understood on the ground. That Africans or their descendants—in the West Indies as well as Africa itself—did not always play by the rules of wage-labor production and property relations led to an increasing tendency of European administrators and traders to portray their interlocutors as racial exceptions to the universal laws of economy. Conquest had contradictory effects: Colonizers relied on the authority of indigenous intermediaries in order to govern but often excluded

The Colonials. Lithograph from the French satirical journal *L'Assiette au Buerre,* August 1902. A European officer is shown nonchalantly preparing to shoot an African. The caption reads, "while waiting for reinforcements, we work a little ourselves." CENTRAL SAINT MARTINS COLLEGE OF ART AND DESIGN, LONDON, UK/BRIDGEMAN ART LIBRARY

Africans educated through an older mission presence from any role in government and colonial society. In colonies with large and well-established white settlements—South Africa and Algeria to an extreme, as well as Kenya, the Rhodesias, Côte d'Ivoire, Vietnam, and others—racial lines were the sharpest.

COLONIAL POWER AND ITS LIMITATIONS

Much literature contrasts—with reason—the moralizing claims European conquerors made with a sordid history of bloody conquest, oppressive rule, and meager spending on education and health. Recent scholars add an emphasis on both the limits and the unintended consequences of colonial rule. Ruling colonies was much more difficult than conquering them. Conquest proceeded rapidly thanks to differences in military technology and communications, the concentration of force,

the terrorizing of villages, and the ability to reward allies among already colonized populations. Setting up routine administration—capable of maintaining order, collecting taxes, encouraging peasant production, and recruiting labor—was another matter. Having worked to define African kings, chiefs, and elders as backward tyrants, colonial administrators had to redefine them as representatives of traditional authority in order to have the intermediaries that empires, as in the past, needed to make good the chain of command. In Asia as well as Africa, indigenous elites sometimes gained recognition of their authority reified as "customary" law, enhanced patriarchal power, and further access to wealth and status.

Economic projects of colonizers ranged from attempts at systematic, imposed change—efforts at turning slaves and peasants into wage laborers on mines, plantations, and transportation networks—to ad hoc efforts to pillage resources and live off African commercial networks. Charter companies in the Belgian Congo and French Equatorial Africa relied on coercion and terror to make people collect wild rubber and other natural resources, while in other parts of Africa and Asia indigenous producers used family, tenant, or hired labor for exportable crops, sometimes leading to modest peasant prosperity, occasionally to wealthy propertied classes. The worst abuses—particularly those of second-tier European powers like King Leopold II (r. 1865–1905) of Belgium or the Portuguese—gave rise to international movements at the beginning of the twentieth century that turned antislavery ideology against European practitioners of coerced labor. Great Britain and France had their forced-labor scandals too.

Missionaries did not necessarily colonize the minds of those they educated or converted, but unintentionally or otherwise provided them with material they could use selectively to get around the constraints of patriarchal authority within their own communities, to find alternatives to the cash-crop production or wage labor colonial officials wanted to see, and to challenge the white missionaries themselves. The publications and petitions of African activist organizations such as the African National Congress in South Africa

(1912) evoked Europe's rationalizing, civilizing assertions against the daily brutality and denigration that so many experienced.

On the eve of World War I the unevenness of the colonial presence stands out. British India was tied together by a civil service, railway network, and census system, but the vital need for imperial intermediaries reinforced the power of Indian elites, led to increasingly reified notions of "caste" and other cultural institutions, and meant compromises on the extent to which agrarian relations could be remade in a British image. It was also in India that the opposition to imperial rule went furthest both in turning British idioms against the government—developing a liberal critique of imperial repression and stagnation—and in developing alternative conceptions of political order based on idioms asserted to be Indian. With the organization of the Indian National Congress in 1885 a crucial step was taken toward articulating a national alternative to colonial domination. But the importance of acting within imperial structures and on the basis of imperial ideology remained, as Mohandas Gandhi's (1869–1948) encouragement of Indians to join the war effort against Germany in 1914 made clear. Britain's perceived failure to keep its side of the imperial bargain and expand internal self-rule marked a breaking point in the politics of imperialism and nationalism.

In Africa divisions were enhanced by colonial strategies of rule and by economic fragmentation. Africans often "straddled" rural farms and urban jobs, jobs and small-scale marketing—in many cases both entering and holding at arm's length the colonial order. Opposition took many forms—movements to enhance or restore chiefly power, revolts against colonial intrusions within culturally specific milieus, efforts by Africans to take over churches from white missionaries or invent their own versions of Christian or Islamic community, and insurrectionary movements that crossed ethnic lines or followed networks established by religious figures and trade routes. As early as 1900 Caribbean and African American activists pioneered pan-African conferences and connections, attempting to bring together people of African descent across the world to challenge the racial ideologies and the structures of power on imperialism's global scale. While colonial policies

had long been subject to critique in Europe, the violence of conquest, the brutalities of coerced labor at the turn of the century, and tensions over the Anglo-Boer war of 1898–1902 led to movements in Europe—linking up unevenly with Africa-based mobilizations—that attached the "ism" to colonial and made the overall project an object of questioning and mobilization.

By 1914 the civilizing and missionizing impulse that was part of the colonial story had become more conservative as European powers realized the limits of their own power; their reluctance to invest in economic, political, or social infrastructure; and the danger—following from their own naturalization of indigenous cultures—of people pulled out of "their" milieu. The use France and Britain made of African and Indian troops and porters during the world war led first to claims by colonial subjects that paying the "blood tax" should give them the rights of citizens, then to efforts by officials in the postwar decade to insist that it was tradition, not imperial citizenship, to which colonial subjects should aspire. France and Britain both considered "development" plans to make the exploitation of colonial resources more systematic, but both decided that they neither wanted to spend metropolitan funds on such an effort nor upset "traditional" authority too much. By the early twentieth century, European states had extended rule over nearly half of the world's surface but had yet to satisfy themselves that they had found ways to exploit those regions in systematic fashion, let alone mold that world in their own image. The assertions and counterassertions that followed a war that was never simply European echoed possibilities raised 125 years earlier in the Franco-Haitian revolution: That colonies were part of a supra-European, supranational polity whose people would demand their due, inside or outside the bounds of colonial empire.

See also **Africa; Civilization, Concept of; Colonies; Imperialism; India; Race and Racism; Slavery.**

BIBLIOGRAPHY

Bayly, C. A. *Imperial Meridian: The British Empire and the World, 1780–1830.* London and New York, 1989.

Conklin, Alice L. *A Mission to Civilize: The Republican Idea of Empire in France and West Africa, 1895–1930.* Stanford, Calif., 1998.

Cooper, Frederick. *Colonialism in Question: Theory, Knowledge, History.* Berkeley, Calif., 2005.

Dubois, Laurent. *A Colony of Citizens: Revolution and Slave Emancipation in the French Caribbean, 1787–1804.* Chapel Hill, N.C., 2004.

Goswami, Manu. *Producing India: From Colonial Economy to National Space.* Chicago and London, 2004.

Holt, Thomas C. *The Problem of Freedom: Race, Labor, and Politics in Jamaica and Britain, 1832–1938.* Baltimore, Md., 1992.

Muthu, Sankar. *Enlightenment against Empire.* Princeton, N.J., 2003.

Robinson, Ronald, and John Gallagher. "The Imperialism of Free Trade." *Economic History Review,* 2nd series, 6 (1953): 1–15.

Stoler, Ann Laura. *Carnal Knowledge and Imperial Power: Race and the Intimate in Colonial Rule.* Berkeley, Calif., 2002.

FREDERICK COOPER

For Reference

Not to be taken from this room

ICELAND

Norwegian Sea

Faroe Islands
(Denmark)

Shetland
Islands

NORWA

Christiania

Orkney
Islands

*North
Sea*

DENMA

Copenha

Firth of Forth
•Edinburgh

Trent

Shannon

Dublin•

Isle of
Man

UNITED
KINGDOM

Amsterdam•
NETHERLANDS

Cologne•
Rhine

Elbe

GERM

ATLANTIC
OCEAN

•Bristol
London•

Thames
Severn

BELGIUM
Brussels•

Seine
Aisne

LUXEMBOURG

Frankfurt•

Main

Wesen

Neckar

Danube

Paris•

FRANCE

Loire

SWITZERLAND

A
L
P
S

Munich•

Lyon•

Rhône

Milan•

Venice•

Po

Turin•

PORTUGAL

Douro

Tagus

Madrid•

SPAIN

Garonne

Pyrenees

Ebro

ANDORRA

Genoa•

Marseille•

A
P
P
E

Arno

Tiber

ITALY

Corsica
(France)

Barcelona•

Rome•

Lisbon•

Balearic Islands (Spain)

Minorca

Majorca

Iviza

Sardinia
(Italy)

Seville•

Mediterranean Sea

Spanish
Morocco

ALGERIA

TUNISIA

MOROCCO